Autobiography *of an* Unknown Indian

Part II

Thy Hand, Great Anarch!

* * *

India 1921-1952

Autobiography
of an
Unknown Indian

Part II

Thy Hand, Great Anarch!

* * *

India 1921-1952

Nirad C. Chaudhuri

JAICO PUBLISHING HOUSE

Ahmedabad Bangalore Chennai
Delhi Hyderabad Kolkata Mumbai

Published by Jaico Publishing House
A-2 Jash Chambers, 7-A Sir Phirozshah Mehta Road
Fort, Mumbai - 400 001
jaicopub@jaicobooks.com
www.jaicobooks.com

AUTOBIOGRAPHY OF
AN UNKNOWN INDIAN: PART II
ISBN 978-81-7992-830-1

First Jaico Impression: 2008
Fourth Jaico Impression: 2013

Printed by
Repro India Limited, Mumbai

This book has three morals for
three kinds of men,
to wit:

FOR RULERS

Nous courons sans souci dans le précipice,
après que nous avons mis quelque chose
devant nous pour nous empêcher de le voir.

Pascal

FOR INDIVIDUALS

II arrive quelquefois des accidents dans la
vie d'où il faut être un peu fou pour se
bien tirer.

La Rochefoucauld

[*Not sometimes. But always for me.*]

FOR WRITERS

Quand on voit le style naturel, on est tout
étonné et ravi, car on s'attendait de voir
un auteur, et on trouve un homme.

Pascal

Contents

Explanation about Indian names

An explanation on this score is called for because I have adopted a manner which may give rise to confusion. That is about Bengali names only. These are exactly like European names, i.e. one or two personal names followed by the surname, which is hereditary. But colloquially the Bengalis do not employ the surname. Instead, they use the personal name, with or without an honorific suffix. For instance, equals or elders would address or mention me only as 'Nirad', but where a respectful manner is expected I would be both referred to and spoken to as 'Nirad Babu'. So, I have referred to those Bengali public figures whom I knew as so and so Babu, e.g. Subhas Babu or Sarat Babu. In the index all Bengali names are cross- referenced, both under the surname and personal name.

The manner over the rest of India has in recent times become chaotic, although strictness was the rule traditionally. Therefore in mentioning non-Bengali Indians I have used the form either used by the holders or by the public generally. With some figures, it is simply the popular honorific title, e.g. Mahatmaji for Gandhi.

In case of doubt the reader should turn to the index where everyone mentioned by me is formally identified.

Acknowledgements

Acknowledgements I have to make for this book have to be on the same lines as for my life as lived to this day: neither would have been possible without generous help voluntarily given by those who saw something in me. Here I mention only those who helped me to write the book, and of course those who enabled me to survive equally stand behind it. My very first obligation is to Professor Edward Shils of Chicago and Cambridge, who had so much confidence in me and such eagerness to see the continuation of my autobiography, that he gave me a large sum of money from his own resources either as a loan or as a gift, so that I could stay in England to write the book. I regard this as a loan, but it still remains a gift.

After him I have to mention Christopher MacLehose who, when with the British publishers Chatto & Windus, of his own initiative, offered to enter into a contract and give an advance for the book. That was in 1979, and it enabled me to begin the book. After Mac Lehose, Hugo Brunner took over at Chatto and helped and encouraged me in every way possible. Apart from what help he himself gave, he approached others for me, and as a result I got grants from the Arts Council as well as from the Royal Literary Fund. I also got a grant from the Leverhulme Trust. For these, I would record my deep sense of gratitude to these patrons of literature, and more especially in this connection I would thank Mr John Gross and Mr Victor Bonham-Carter. Hugo Brunner found to his dismay that instead of giving short measure for the money received, I gave overweight, which in these days of publication is worse than defaulting. But the present management of Chatto faced even this task, which showed not only courage, but also literary idealism.

I have to thank Mrs Elsie Summers for preparing the final typescript of the book from pure friendship; Century Hutchinson Ltd for permission to quote from Rufus Isaacs by the Marquis of Reading, Eyre Methuen Ltd for permission to quote from *The Life of F. E. Smith* by the Earl of Birkenhead and the Rt Hon. Viscount Norwich for permission to quote from his father's memoirs on Independence for India.

NIRAD C. CHAUDHURI

INTRODUCTION
Apologia pro Biographia sua

This book continues the story of my life and thoughts from the point of time at which it was left in *The Autobiography of an Unknown Indian*, published in 1951. That was my first book, and in it I gave an account of my childhood and student days which came to an end in 1921, when I was twenty-three years old. How I began to write an autobiography in the middle of 1947, when I was short by six months of being fifty, I shall relate in the last part of this book, which deals with that stage of my life. Here I shall only say that even then it was my intention to bring down the story to 1947, the year of the British withdrawal from India, so that I might conclude it with a decisive historical event and be enabled to give a complete account of the decline and fall of the Indian Empire of Britain. But the narrative of my early life alone had become so long that there could be no question of including what I did and what happened in India after 1921 in the same book.

The contemplated but unwritten part of the story is now offered. But as things turned out, I could not begin it till the spring of 1979, when I was eighty-one, and I have taken more than six years to complete the work. I am formally dating the completion on 23 November 1986, when I have also completed eighty-nine years of my life. I dare not ask even myself what marks age is imprinting on the book. I leave that to be judged by the reader. For myself I shall plead that I have tried as best as I can to forget the lapse of time, and to write the book on the same lines and in the same spirit as its predecessor.

However, even now I have not been able to give the book the end one would expect it to have. Of course, autobiographies cannot have the same logical end as biographies always have. But they are generally brought down to the time when they are written. This book falls short of even that by thirty-two years, for it only covers my 'working life', which began in 1921 and came to a close at the end of 1952. Since then I have been 'independent' and have lived by my writings. Although this period of my life, too, has had its vicissitudes and has ended by bringing a man who travelled on elephants in his boyhood to England in a jumbo jet to spend his last days there, that part of the story will in all probability never be written.

I shall now explain in what way this book is a sequel to *The Autobiography of an Unknown Indian*. In spite of its tide, that book was not truly an autobiography. It was a picture of the society in which I was born and grew up. In its preface I set down the purpose I had in mind in writing it. 'The story I want to tell,' I wrote,

'is the story of the struggle of a civilization with a hostile environment, in which the destiny of the British Empire in India became necessarily involved. My intention is thus historical, and since I have written the account with the utmost honesty and accuracy of which I am capable, the intention in my mind has become mingled with the hope that the book might be regarded as a contribution to contemporary history.'

Both in point of intention and of execution, the present book seeks to do the same thing. In actual fact, in it the struggle of a civilization with its environment reaches its climax and the British Empire in India disappears. So, I have avoided calling the book an autobiography.

Nevertheless, there is more autobiography in it than there was in the previous book, the *soi-disant* autobiography of mine. The reasons for this will be given at the end of this introduction. Actually, this book has three elements in it: first, my personal life which I have made the framework of whatever history I wish to offer; second, my thoughts and feelings about the public and historical events through which I have passed; and third, an account of what happened in India in the political and cultural spheres in the period from 1921 to 1952, free from the current myths.

About the political element in the book, I would say that there was a stronger compulsion to give it the place it occupies in it than there was in the first instalment of the autobiography. The period from 1921 to 1947 was one of intense political excitement and activity in India, and it ended with a climax which was significant for world history as well. As it happened, in the very year I took up employment, i.e. 1921there also began a wholly new phase of the Indian nationalist movement under the leadership of Mahatma Gandhi, which, with its ups and downs, ran its course until in 1947 it came to its end with the result it had sought to bring about, that is to say, the disappearance of British rule in India.

Thus, the first twenty-six of my thirty-one years of working life ran *paripassu* with the spectacle of the decline and fall of the British Empire in

India, and if the working life continued for five more years that had little political significance, for the real post-independence India did not begin to emerge until the Fifties were well on. The five years from 1947 to 1952 were the twilight of the Empire after its sun had set. But the sunset was not in India alone. After the abandonment of India there was no possibility of the survival of British rule over non-European peoples anywhere in the world; and not only that, the rule of other European countries, too, was doomed at the same time. Decline of the political power of Europe began in India. Thus, so far as this book is history, it is the first chapter of the very much larger history of the end of European rule over non-European peoples.

This political history had also a cultural complement within India, about which nothing has been written and therefore nothing is known. That was the decline of the modern Indian culture which was created by Indians during the British rule under the impact of European civilization. It was mainly the creation of Bengalis who had received their education in English.

In this book I come forward as a witness of this double decline. Furthermore, as a Bengali, I have to record a decline which has a poignant relevance to me. During the same period of political and cultural decline in India I had also to observe the eclipse of Bengal as a force in Indian politics and culture. From the beginning of British rule down to 1920 the Bengali people dominated the political and cultural life of India. How positive their domination in politics was will be realized if I recall the curious idea which the British administrators in India held about the extension of self- government to Indians. This, they said with anger and contempt, would be handing over India to the Bengali Babu, whom even in 1911 Kipling called Caliban. But from 1921 onwards the influence of Bengal in Indian politics began to decline. In the cultural field the same decline became perceptible to me, and I myself took some part in what might be called the Bengali *Kulturkampf*. With independence, the eclipse of Bengal was completed.

As years passed after I had begun adult life in 1921, the spectacle of an all-embracing decline in India pressed so heavily on my mind that I set down my forebodings in a passage of *The Autobiography of an Unknown Indian*, written just before India became independent on 15 August 1947. This was what I wrote:

'If there is to be any vanished or vanishing Atlantis to speak of in this book, it should be and would be all our life lived till yesterday. All that we have learnt, all that we have acquired, and all that we have prized is threatened with extinction. We do not know how this end will come, whether through a cataclysmic holocaust or slow putrid decay. But regarding the eventual extinction there does not seem to be any uncertainty.'

That was written in 1947, and now the scene has become clearer. I can see that it is going to be putrid decay and not the clean blaze. The three initial decades of this tragic process is covered in this book.

The very conception of the work was bound to make it a kind of political and cultural history. But even if I had intended to write only an autobiography I could not have excluded the public and collective themes because they were part and parcel of the personal lives of all Indians of that age. Above all, politics was the main preoccupation of the mental life of all of us, the vortex of all our thoughts and emotions. Even more than in contemporary Europe, we in Bengal were *politique d'abord, politique partout, politique toujours, politique uniquement*. It impinged even on our workaday life. In my case, my personal career would not have been what it became except for the political developments described in the book. Moreover, those developments were interwoven with the very strong sense of vocation I had from a very early age. I wanted to be a writer, and one who was to be involved with public affairs. I always thought that a writer was a man of action in his way, and since I could not take part in real action I conceived of my role as an observer with a practical purpose, that of being a Cassandra giving warnings of calamities to come. I began to utter them from the very beginning of my career as a writer, and many of them will be included in this book. Therefore, the events that provoked them could not be excluded from it.

But there are also more matter of fact reasons for making it some sort of a historical narrative. I have now come to the conclusion that no true history of the disappearance of the British Empire in India will ever be written. For one thing, none of those who are now writing full or partial histories of this epoch have any personal experience to be able to appraise the events correctly, far less to be able to recreate the spirit and atmosphere. All of them were too young, and many not even born when the events were happening. This objection would at first sight seem to be wholly pointless because most historians write about events they have not seen, and even those which are far removed from them in time. But these historians have the means by which they can reconstruct the past, both factually and imaginatively, in adequate source material, to interpret which they can bring to bear on them some analogous experience. Both are absent in the case of recent Indian history, in spite of its recentness.

To deal with the question of sympathetic reconstruction. The Indian nationalist movement had such a peculiar character and atmosphere that nobody who has not lived through it can have a true idea of what it was like, and nothing like that has been seen in India after it had gained its object, or elsewhere at any time. The inadequacy of the sources is a more serious handicap. Due to this, the historians cannot come upon all the facts, some of which have never been recorded, some forgotten, and some even deliberately suppressed.

The historians of today have to depend almost exclusively on the official papers written during British rule and preserved in the record office of the Government of India and in the library of the India Office in London. My opinion of them will be found set down with some bluntness in the book. Here I shall only say that as records of events they are incomplete, and as their interpretation very misleading. If the British officials in India could understand what was happening in the country the Empire would not have disappeared so soon or would have been abandoned honourably. Moreover, it has to be pointed out that many of the records in which the frankest opinions were to be found were destroyed.

The insufficiency of the official papers, it might be argued, can be made up from the newspapers, most of which voiced nationalist opinions. Even so, they are not frank records of real opinions, and often they could not even publish facts. This was due to the existence of severe laws of sedition which compelled both the editors and reporters to beat about the bush. The gaps of information thus left cannot be filled up from private papers of the Indian leaders in the form of letters or diaries written at the time of the events. Indians are not in the habit of keeping diaries, or even of writing frank letters. In the last days of British rule there were also considerable risks in sending letters through the post. Letters from or to anyone who was connected with politics were intercepted. Even some of my quite innocuous letters to Jawaharlal Nehru were kept back by the police and I have been told that some of them are among the records. I never got some of the letters an Indian nationalist in the United States wrote to me, and he also did not get my letters.

One more point about the inadequacy of the records, printed or in manuscripts, must be made. The proceedings of the numerous conferences and formal discussions never gave any idea of the real motives and thoughts of the participants. They were all concerned to present a case, attempting at best only plausible advocacy. Let me give one example, that of the voluminous records of the discussions on the partition of India. No one will find in them any evidence as to the real forces at work to bring about the catastrophic event, nor of the motives which made the parties concerned accept it.

Given all these insufficiencies in the source material, it is not surprising that most of the historical works which profess to give a scholarly view of the events of this period are arid, shallow, uninspired, totally devoid of atmosphere, and at times even false. The only accounts which have colour are the Indian nationalist myths, but even their luridness is made dull by the crudity of style of the writers. As if that was not enough, this period of Indian history has become the lush pasture of the intellectual fops who want to air their cleverness or earn money by selling historical tinsel to an ignorant, Western Indophile readership. The pictorial presentation, whether in films or TV features, is the most spurious of this merchandise. When looking on them no one ever says: *Caveat emptor*.

Besides, there are emotional compulsons on both British and Indian historians to falsify history. It is of one kind among the British writers, and of another in the Indians. A majority of the British writers cannot deal with the period without focusing their minds on the exit from India and justifying it. Many even glorify it. But there are also others who write with romantic nostalgia about the last days of the Empire, reconciling themselves to its disappearance with the words of King Arthur:

> The old order changeth, yielding place to new,
> And God fulfils himself in many ways,
> Lest one good custom should corrupt the world.
> Comfort thyself.

The Indians, on their part, do not need comfort, they congratulate themselves as the legatees of the British, and they cannot be critical about the demise of their political father, even if his death was due to political delirium tremens and political tertiary syphilis. But in some Indians there is another compulsion. Most of the young historians who are writing about the period are the sons of officials who served the British Government in India 'loyally', and when they are not, they are in any case sons of the 'loyal Indian gentlemen' who remained on the safe side. They have all to make up a great deal of arrears of loyalty to the nationalist movement, more especially, to the Congress.

They, therefore, show a partisanship in regard to both which is all on the surface and often extremely unpleasant. Some of them indulge in taunts and sneers at the British in a manner which in British days not even the more uneducated Indian journalist of extremist persuasion aired. Their writings do not shed any dignity on the nationalist movement or its leaders. They reduce both to their own mental level. Some of the greatest of modern Indians have been pitiable victims of their shallow biographers.

In reality, the Indian nationalist movement was too stark and elemental a movement to be understood by mediocre minds. Whether quiescent or in eruption, it had an evil grandeur, redeemed only by an apocalyptic faith in the advent of political independence for India. The spectacle which the hatred and faith presented in combination was like that of a volcano against the light of dawn, the red of the foreground burning more lurid against the white background. I have tried to describe the living as well as livid scene as I saw it. Its smell, too, when not sulphurous, was fetid.

This will account for certain omissions in my account which will be noted by those who will read it as history. While I have not sacrificed historical truth anywhere in the book, I have not tried to write a formal history. My view of the events and circumstances as presented in it is for the most part that which I formed as I was passing through the events, when I had no knowledge of all the facts, especially in respect of the motives, intentions, and calculations of the actors. I have since then learnt a good deal of these, but I have not taken account of them in my presentation of history. I judge policies and actions by their results, and not by the intentions of the participants. I learned very early in life that the path to hell was paved with good intentions. The most extraordinary fact about the recent history of India is that none of those who, whether Indian or British, were in reality Agents of Evil, had any suspicion that they were that and not Children of Light. I have therefore quoted extensively from my contemporaneous writings, and I present the views expressed in them to be judged in the light of the ultimate historical result. A true student of history knows that history does not forgive. In India she has not.

I have yet one more explanation to give in connection with the historical scope of the book. That is about the importance assigned to Bengal, Bengali life, and Bengali culture in it. Of course, that would be considered perfectly natural in a Bengali who is writing an autobiography. But I would have done the same thing if I had been a non-Bengali writing about British rule in India as a whole. A British historian concerned with the permanent results of that rule would and should give as much importance to Bengal, and so would and should a sociologist or historian dealing with cultural interactions.

The reason for doing so should have been obvious, but it is curious that British historians have not even been conscious of it, in which they have been victims of the prejudices of their countrymen in India. Even in the political sphere the Bengalis were the pioneers of the modern nationalism of all Indians. However, this in itself was so disliked by the British administrators that they removed their capital from Calcutta in order to get away from it. Bengal was still more important in another sphere not less significant, which was the cultural.

So far as British rule had a psychological aspect and a civilizing mission in India, its greatest achievement was seen in Bengal. That was the renovation of the culture and mental life of a people who had become almost fossilized culturally. British rule, by bringing European cultural influences to bear on Indian life, created what was virtually a new culture. Its cradle and centre of diffusion was Bengal. Its quality, too, was very fine, in spite of its limitations and weaknesses.

But it was created and preached by the Bengalis, and not by the British administrators or the British community. With the exception of a very small number of very wise British administrators, and the missionaries generally, this new culture and its creators, i.e. the Bengalis, were hated by the local British. They did not like the adoption of their culture by the Indians, and displayed throughout British rule an unmeasured rancour against the activity.

In this lay the greatest failure of British imperialism in India, for no empire can last without practising cultural proselytization. The British in India rejected this role. Their attitude presented a total contrast to that of the Romans, who were true imperialists. They felt proud to have given peace to the Mediterranean world, but were not ashamed to confess that the conquered Greeks conquered them culturally. The British were not required to adopt Indian culture, and were expected only to spread their own culture. Even this inspired them with horror, and their abuse of the Bengalis and other Indians who were assimilating European culture was not only unrestrained but indecent and aggressive. This behaviour is unparalleled in the history of all civilized peoples in ancient or modern times, and even for the study of this perverse phenomenon, Bengal is the most suitable region in the world. I think I have now produced enough justification for the historical aspect of this book.

But in this book I have also put a good deal of myself, that is, about my personal life and fortunes. At the beginning of this introduction I said that I shall explain why I have done so. The first reason is that the reader has the right to know what kind of man is this writer who seems to claim a prophetic role for himself. As no fruit can be better than the tree, I am presenting myself quite frankly.

Besides, whatever might be my qualifications to pose as a judge of contemporary events, in my personal life I may be an example to others, because my life is a striking instance of the survival of the unfittest. Even when I was thirty-four years old as well as married, my father used to say: 'I have no anxiety for my other sons, but Nirad is utterly unfit to go through the world.' Yet of his six sons, it is this son who, in the ultimate resort, has done best even in the worldly way.

This certainly should have a moral, and the moral will be underlined if I explain why my father held his opinion about me. He was fully aware of all the physical and mental limitations I had. I shall give some idea of them.

First, as to my physical unfitness, I was a seven-months' child of an ailing mother, who became worse after my birth, and could not feed me after my third month. I had to be fed on cow's milk, which was always contaminated. So, from that time to almost my sixtieth year, I suffered from stomach troubles which weakened my heart. I never really enjoyed passably good health until I came to England in 1970, and that was at best making a derelict cottage fit to live in for the time being.

Furthermore, from my fourteenth year I had to live away from home for my education, and never got the food I needed. So I suffered from malnutrition, and never grew into a healthy and strong young man. Thus, born plain, I became even worse, scraggy and pinched in my limbs and features. I remained just over five feet tall, and only six stone in weight until over seventy. There was no question at any time of my life of my being physically impressive.

My mental handicaps were not less formidable. I was timid and shy till I was almost forty, and could not mix easily with men. I was indolent by disposition, in addition to being forced to be so by my physical weakness. Furthermore, although very obstinate in pursuing ends which lured me, I was weak in respect of rational exercise of the will. To add to that, I had a pride and sensitiveness which made me incapable of asking for anything from others, and I had also an unconquerable dislike for pushing myself forward, which I considered very vulgar.

Yet I have survived with some achievement: proportionate to my abilities of course; but neither more nor less. Even in the best of worlds, by all normal expectations, a man like me would have remained obscure. But in the world in which I was born and had to make a living my bodily survival alone should be regarded as a biological freak, and to have had some achievement as a psychological miracle. This should encourage those who from lack of courage throw in the sponge, and from weak despair commit suicide or do worse - become Communists. Communism is a strange political and social doctrine: in individuals, it arises from egotism denatured beyond reason by envy and hatred, and in its collective application it destroys individual liberty.

How was my survival possible? So far as that was due to anything within me, I owe it to an obstinate will to live and to a capacity for self-assertion through writing, for neither of which I can claim any moral credit because I was born with them.

But I was also helped by others, for which they can take credit. This outside help came to me unsolicited, given freely to me by some of my countrymen but mostly by individual Englishmen, all of whom perhaps saw something in me which was worth supporting. I can only hope that this aid of theirs was not as unwise as the immense amount of money given by the nations of European origins to the so-called Third World. But the mere fact that I was helped to survive shows how little point there is in thinking ill of mankind and complaining about injustice. Whenever I had the energy to do something my work was recognized.

Without in any way intending to take away from the generosity of these benefactors, I would add that in helping me they obeyed a power above themselves in whose existence I believe. I think there is a great mercy immanent in the universe which takes care precisely of those who are least fit to take care of themselves. This belief of mine has nothing to do with rational inference, and is justified only by faith. I arrived at a new faith for myself after having lost faith very early in life in all established religions. Belief in the mercy is part of that faith.

But I also think that my personal life has a relevance to the general human situation today which has been created by history. I shall make no mystery about it and shall set it down in plain words without beating about the bush. The problem which I had to face in my personal life was how to pass through an age of decadence without being touched by it. At the end of my life I have come to the conclusion that civilized human existence all over the world is completing the latest cycle of its history by descending into its natural Avernus. I think our times are comparable to the fifth century of the Christian era when St Augustine saw the Graeco-Roman world crumbling- all around him. The present situation of humanity is different from that only in this, that the scale is larger and the decadence universal. It embraces even the Americans who are in fact a young nation in point of age, and are placed in the van of human progress.

To develop the point further. The civilized world we have known and lived in, and whose evolution through fifteen hundred years has been described in detail by historians, will certainly come to an end soon enough as time is judged by the historical scale. But it will not do so through the hypothetical catastrophe over which there is so much lamentation and even gnashing of teeth and tearing of hair by many and above all by young people, that is to say, a nuclear war. This eschatological fear is exactly like the fear of the Day of Last Judgement which haunted the minds of those who Hved in the first centuries of the rise of European civilization. Just as that did not come to pass, today's expected end also will not. Civilized human existence will perish through internal decay as the Graeco-Roman world did. I have been a life-long spectator of this decay, and the experience has made me feel like a heretic being burnt at the stake, but without release from the torture by death.*

I shall not say that thoughtful men are not conscious of the decadence and of the working of powerful destructive forces. But no one seems to accept its inevitability and its sweep, and regulate their thinking on the

* The connection between the social and cultural decadence with technological progress, both features of our age, will be discussed in the Epilogue.

present situation of humanity in the light of this sentence of death. I attribute this insensibility or reluctance to a strange limitation of the collective human mind. Nobody travels along a road without knowing where it leads to. No captain of a ship sets out on a voyage without his charts and, while sailing, without taking his position every day. But nations travel through time without orienting themselves in it. Even if they perceive weaknesses and ailments in their condition they attribute it to passing disorders amenable to treatment, and cannot recognise that these may belong to the end of a life cycle. The really dangerous aspect of decadence in human communities is the insensibility to it which it always creates.

As it happened, my experience made me look at the changes through which I was passing in a different way. I began to feel alienated from the society in which I was living even from the time I entered the world in 1921, when I was in my early twenties. As I wrote in the first instalment of my autobiography:

'I distinctly felt that the world around me had changed in the meantime [i.e. during the previous five years when I was engaged in my studies]. The changes were negative as well as positive. Certain things and qualities, dominant in the old order in which I was born and brought up, had disappeared or were disappearing. Certain other things, previously absent, were entering or holding the field. There was no aspect of our existence in which the voids and the intrusions were not crying aloud for notice.'

I noticed them, and being irritated instinctively by them, resolved to resist them even without realizing their true character. Gradually, I came to see that these were the emerging symptoms of the decay of that Bengali way of life which had been created by modern Bengalis under the influence of European culture during British rule. By the nineteen-thirties I had fully realized that there was no future for the Bengali people and their culture.

This made me think of leaving Bengal and migrating to northern India, because I assumed that the Hindi-speaking people of that region had more vitality and therefore promise. It seemed to me that they were more simple. After my marriage my wife always wanted me to do so. But it was not possible to act on this conviction because I was then tied down to Calcutta by the compulsion of earning a livelihood. But when an opportunity came to leave Bengal without losing the means of living, I gladly took advantage of it. I went to Delhi, where I lived from 1942 to 1970. However, even before that long sojourn was over - in fact, by the time independence came to India in 1947 - I discovered that the speakers of Hindi were in no better predicament than we Bengalis. I even found that they were sunk deeper in decadence, for they were fossilized while we in Bengal were decomposing. Theirs was certainly a simpler state of human existence, but it did not have the simplicity on which I had reckoned.

More anticipation of decadence was to follow. Even before independence came to India, I had begun to think of migrating to England to escape from the Indian decadence, and on this too my wife was insistent. But that was not practically possible. Nevertheless, even without first-hand experience of English life I developed very strong misgivings about the future of the English people just after the war. My confidence about it was thoroughly shaken, and I shall narrate in the book what I did when that happened.

The subsequent thirty years have fully confirmed my fears. It is a fatality with me that wherever I go the spectre of decadence treads at my heels like the Foul Fiend. It has, even to the shores of the Pacific at Vancouver, and to Texas in the United States, which is supposed to breed the modern savage. It is certainly the base of the gigantic power which sends spacecraft to travel beyond Jupiter, but those projectiles rise from a moral swamp in which human beings are being sucked in as were dinosaurs of old.

It has taken me sixty years to have this revelation. The experience is now decisive to convince me, although certainly not in its full unfolding. But a man who was born in the year of the Diamond Jubilee of Queen Victoria and has lived to this day could not have asked for a more thorough and lengthy demonstration. If anyone thinks that one lifetime, however long, could not have seen both the high noon and the falling dusk of European civilization, the greatest known so far in history, I would only tell him that my life lived so far is slightly longer than the period of ancient history from the reign of Constantine the Great - from the year of the Nicene Council to be precise - to the year of the capture of Rome by Alaric the Visigoth. St Augustine's life was shorter and he never lived under a great emperor. Yet his experiences were decisive enough for him to make him give up all hope for the City of Man, fix them on the City of God, and formulate his terrible doctrine of theological predestination. I think my experience of more catastrophic events during a longer life entitles me to put forward my doctrine of historical predestination.

It may be thought that I am speaking too dogmatically, too absolutely like Machiavelli, but I am not afraid of being a believer in absolutes: I have not only written but also acted all my life in the light: of values which I have regarded as absolute. Indeed, could anything be more ridiculous than the idea of the relativity of values in a world in which every individual, however uneducated, claims an absolute right to live according to his whims, however tawdry? Ever since the beginnings of civilized existence for man the same things have been believed to be true, right, and beautiful and accepted as such by all peoples in all ages with a unanimity which makes them valid. The ideas of what is true, right, and beautiful are relative only in their achieved amplitude and variety. They can never be relative in their essential quality. Because of this belief in absolutes I have never been *carried away* by the currents of history, I have *navigated* through them.

However, I have not been able to tell the whole story of this navigation in this book. It deals only with the first thirty years of the voyage, during which my resistance to the currents was confined to my immediate environment in Bengal and India. The book as a fully worked out picture of a process of decadence is thus an inset in a very large canvas which has already been painted by history but cannot be by me. When I was passing through the events I have described, I had no perception of their universal affiliations. But writing about them after intervals ranging from thirty to sixty years, I could not remain unaware of these affiliations. And I would ask the reader too not to forget that.

I do so in the first place because what the book contains is only the first chapter of the long but still unfinished history of the Decline of the West, of which Spengler spoke. My second reason is that the restricted experience of decadence which I had gave me the opportunity and time to devise a pattern of behaviour which has served me throughout life and enabled me to pass unscathed through the more extensive and intimidating decadence I had to witness afterwards. This might help others if they adopted it. I would, however, assure the reader that I have not allowed my knowledge of after events to colour my account. There are in the book historical verdicts made in retrospect. But I have kept them distinct from my description of what I saw, and from the recording of my opinions, forebodings and malaise as they were, retaining their immediate intensity.

But whatever there might have been of imprecision or uncertainty in my diagnosis of the historical situation in which I was placed there was none whatever in my prescription for the disease. I seemed to have acted on the advice of Machiavelli who wrote: 'Physicians say of consumption, that in the early stages of this disease it is easy to cure but difficult to diagnose: whereas later on, if it has not been recognised and treated at the beginning, it becomes easy to diagnose and difficult to cure. The same thing happens in affairs of state.' Thereby I have been able to save myself, as in any case I was determined to do, although in regard to others I could only give warnings without being heeded. I have succeeded in living my life according to my lights, and the prescription for it is very simple.

Its first ingredient is the capacity to shake off the fetters of the present. No one who is in bondage to it can have any true view of life. So I would not accept an opinion simply because it was a product of the times. Fashion, the tyrant of humanity taken in the mass, had no hold on me. Moreover, it has never been in my character to form opinions or formulate even historical conclusions with no apparent practical application, without seeing their relevance to my personal life and acting on them. Doing that all my life, I took risks which were incalculable in advance, but from which I have profited in retrospect.

This has led me to a ceaseless conflict with the world in which I have had to live. For this reason at one time I thought of giving the title *One Man against his People* to this book. But that would have given quite a false idea of my life. I was against historical trends, not any people. I have had no personal maladjustments, far less quarrels of my own seeking, with the society in which I have lived, due either to injustice or frustration. I was born and brought up in a class of Bengali society which had been dominant through the ages, and became even more dominant during British rule. Again, the class which dominates India today is some sort of an extension of the Bengali class to which I belonged. Thus, if I speak of alienation from a world, that does not mean social or personal alienation. Tocqueville once said that when he talked to a *gentilhomme* he felt that he belonged to the same family, although he shared none of his opinions, wishes, or thoughts, whereas a bourgeois was always a stranger. It has been the same with me. Although I have rejected the whole ideology of the dominant order in India, I am socially at home only among them. I could have shared their position and prosperity if I had wanted that, and if I have not, that has been my free choice. Therefore, I have never been under the compulsion to go on that wild goose chase which in these days is called 'discovering one's identity'. I never lost mine, and never had any doubts about if.

Finally, just as my opinions have been a part of the act of living for me, so have been my writings. In fact, the increasing commercialization of authorship often creates in me an unconquerable revulsion from calling myself an author, and the fear of being included among the manufacturers of books gives me recurrent fits of nausea. Writing has never been for me a means to a career. Through my books and articles I have tried in the first instance to understand the world in which I have lived for myself, and next to warn others about the dangers in it. They were my reactions to the events I saw and the situations I had to face. Never in my life, even under the pressure of dire necessity, have I written to earn money by supplying an *existing* demand. On the contrary, most often I have chosen subjects in which there was no interest. For example, I could easily have made my first book a biography of Nehru. Instead, I made it the autobiography of an unknown Indian. I can guess what a biography of Nehru by me, published in 1951, could have done for me, and the reader of this book will find what my actual choice brought on me in India.

Yet writing as I have done, I have been able to create an interest in my books and earn a livelihood which has been adequate for living a basically civilized life. If on account of that I can be included among the small number of men who have lived by imposing their terms on the world, it does not speak less for the world. It cannot be as tyrannical as many people think it to be. That has induced me to allow for the play of free will within its limits in my very deterministic view of human life. That combination, I would call: *libertas in imperio.*

BOOK I

LIVELIHOOD AND POLITICS

1921-1922

Prefatory Note

This book deals with my working life, which began in July 1921 and ended in November 1952. I am using the phrase 'working life' in its current acceptation, i.e. as the description of that period of a man's life in which he maintains himself by working for another party, called the employer, and receives in return the money which this employer chooses to give him. Normally, he does not do what he wants to do, but what the same employer wants him to perform. This way of making a living is now called employment, and this is regarded as the birthright of every man or woman, so much so indeed that the task of meeting this birthright is considered to be the first duty of every State.

In reality, the modern employment is the ancient slavery supported by the State, and mitigated only by the contemporary slave's power to blackmail his master. So, in all modern societies, there is an unceasing cold Servile War. What I call working life is a different thing. It is that period of a man's life in which he has the capacity as well as the disposition to do what he wants to do from a sense of vocation and considers himself justified in claiming from society some remuneration for the products of his industry or his services to the extent they are of use to it. This relationship between human labour and its monetary reward is now to be seen only in exceptional cases. What is more significant is the fact that the free man's old aversion to becoming a hireling has also virtually disappeared. It is even regarded as unnatural and illogical, so that a man who maintains himself by doing what he likes to do is called a self-employed man, i.e. a man who is a slave to a master created by a legal fiction which splits his personality.

My working life, as covered in this book, was indeed in form a hireling's life. But except for the first five years, two important reservations as to its character have to be made. First, for nearly six years out of the thirty-one years and odd covered in this book, I was unemployed in the current sense, but without any unemployment benefit. Next, over the rest of the period, I never accepted a salaried post under any employer, even the Government of India, unless the work in it harmonized either in itself or collaterally with what I regarded as my vocation. What was not less significant, never in my life did I apply for a job, although for the two posts under the Government of India I had to submit a formal application after it had been decided that I should have them.

My first salaried employment was what I have called slavery. I was compelled to accept it; in fact, I welcomed it, because my working life began with a defeat – the only one which I have accepted in my life. That was my failure to secure the MA degree in 1920. This has been described at some length in *The Autobiography of an Unknown Indian* (American edition, 1951, pp. 351–53). It put academic employment out of my reach, because in India no one could become a university teacher without the MA degree. So, to redeem my failure, I took up the only employment which came in my way. Without it, I should have been demoralized.

CHAPTER I
Employment

After I had decided not to try for the M A degree a second time, there was no point in my staying with my parents at Kishorganj, where I was born and they lived. I had to look for employment, and Calcutta was the only place where I could do that. So I went there early in the summer of 1921. I parted from my father in deep distress. After hearing about my decision he had taken up an attitude of detachment in regard to me which was not natural in him. He had also become very cold to me. Both hurt me deeply, and I saw no softening of his severity when I started for Calcutta. There was also no hope to counteract my depression. I was prepared indeed to take up any kind of employment that might come in my way without being fastidious about the work or the salary. But I also knew how difficult it was for young Bengalis with even the highest academic qualifications to find any job whatever, without reference to his wishes or expectations, and my qualifications were only a second best.

To make matters worse, the journey to Calcutta was the most unpleasant I have had in my life. There was a strike on the new railway line which served Kishorganj, and so I had to go to the old railway station which was seventeen miles away. Since the opening of the new line in 1917 communications on that side had become very casual. The boat in which I took the last lap of the journey arrived at the station just in time to let me hear the whistle and puffing of the starting engine. There was no other till the next morning.

So I had to spend the night in the bazaar, in what in such places was called a hotel. I was given an abominable meal of very hot stuff which I had to swallow from hunger, although it burnt my tongue. I was then shown to a large bed covered with a dirty sheet on which a dozen persons were expected to sleep. The joke about these hotels was that if you slept on your back the charge was double. The pillows had no cases, and they were enamelled with grease and grime, besides smelling of rancid oil from the hair of the sleepers. Even so, a man refused to give me a pillow which he said was his, and there was not another for me. I tried to sleep without a pillow, but the man pressed me with his sweating sticky back. In disgust I got down from the bed and slept curled up like a dog on my trunk which was lying on the mud floor. Arriving in Calcutta, I found that the rains had started, and so the atmosphere was dull and misty and the streets were wet and muddy. All this was no good augury for me.

As soon as I arrived I went and saw a cousin of mine who was middle-aged and held a senior post in the Military Accounts Department of the Government of India. I asked him if he could secure a job for me in his office, which kept the accounts of the ordnance factories of the Indian army. He promised to do all he could. In the meanwhile, I resumed my old habit of going to the Imperial Library to read. The distance from our house was over four miles, and I, of course, walked because I had no money to pay the tram fare. I did not like to ask my brother for pocket money. Fortunately, in our society board and lodging were always provided for unemployed relatives. That was our unemployment benefit. But in the library too, I read books which were not cheering. I do not know how at that very time I came upon the Rougon-Macquart series of Zola, and read, of all books, the novel *La Terre*. The effect was thoroughly depressing.

I Become a Clerk

However, within a few weeks the psychological weather broke for me. One afternoon my cousin called, and after the usual inquiries he asked me if I was still willing to take up a job in his office. When I readily consented he was pleased, for he had already done something for me. Actually, he had got a post reserved. I was to go to his office the next day with an application for the sake of form, so that my appointment might be recorded on it. He had also secured for me a starting salary which was double the normal one for a clerk. In the way of money I could not have done better if I had taken a first-class MA degree and succeeded in getting the post of tutor or junior lecturer in Calcutta University, as had been my original ambition. Of course, the salary was only about £100 a year but at the time it was a good start in life for any Indian who was not exceptionally fortunate.

The next day, when I arrived at his office, my cousin took me to the colleague of his who was in charge of appointments. That official looked at me in astonishment and exclaimed: 'Why, he is only a boy!' When after that I was taken to the section in which I was to work, the clerks there were equally surprised. Probably the news of my higher starting salary, which was higher than that of many of them although they had been in service for many years, had got about, and nothing in my appearance seemed to justify it. Many of them wore a coat also (without a tie of course). I was wearing only the Bengali cotton tunic on my dhoti, for I had given up the coat, that ill-matched adjunct to the Bengali costume of my young days.

Afterwards I learned the story of my appointment. It would be regarded as jobbery or nepotism. I would say that I got the post in the manner in which in old days the sons of the English gentry got into the army or the civil service, i.e. through what was called 'interest'. However, the British heads of offices were fully aware how posts under them were being filled. As Mr. E. Harvey, OBE., the head of our office, told my cousin: 'Do I not know that a Banerji brings in a Chatterji, and a Chatterji a Mukherji? But what can we do about it? We cannot recruit our staff ourselves.' In fact, the man who was the Assistant Superintendent of my section was a Chatterji who had come in through the influence of his father-in-law, a Banerji.

I should explain how I got the post. There were two vacancies in the office, and to one of them a colleague of my cousin had got a young relative appointed, and also secured for him the same higher salary as mine, because he was a MA. That official was from West Bengal. So, my cousin and a friend of his in the same rank as his, who was also from East Bengal, suggested my name for the second vacancy, and on the higher salary. They were not so crude as to demand a quid pro quo for agreeing to the other candidate, but fully understood, and East and West Bengal came to an agreement.

The Office

The office in which I was to work was under a Deputy Controller of War Accounts (afterwards called Controller of Factory Accounts). It paid the bills and audited the accounts of the eight ordnance factories and two clothing factories of the Indian army. The section in which I worked paid the salaries and wages of the personnel of these establishments.

It was housed in a very impressive building along with some other military offices. The aspect was also very fine. The building stood on the Esplanade, and from its front verandah we could see the Victoria Memorial, gleaming in white marble across the Maidan. It had been originally built as the office of Lord Kitchener, when he was Commander-in-Chief in India. It had some architectural pretension, probably due to him. It had a high central block which from the front looked like a gate-house, and this block had a pediment resting on tall columns of the Etruscan order. The entrance to this building was through a high arch under the central block, which was flanked by two smaller arches. So that this part of the building looked like the arch of Constantine in Rome. The central block had two wings with towers at the corners. The whole facade was faced with greyish cream stone, and the frieze which ran along the top of the wings was adorned with medallions, on which the heads of Mars and Venus were alternately carved.

The inside was also impressive. The floors were of marble, and the staircase of polished wood with very wide and low steps. Clearly, the building was not meant for mere clerks and their supervisors, and we did nothing to maintain the original dignity of the rooms. They were all cluttered up with shabby and scruffed tables and chairs, and on the former were piled up shabbier files and audit registers. One of my new colleagues, who was also a BA like me, said to me in English when I looked at his table-top and betrayed some surprise: 'My work is multifarious and so my table is always surcharged with papers.' He afterwards organized our trade union. Incidentally, four years later I spoke at its inauguration, and ended with the peroration: 'If our enterprise is called egoistic I would say with Baron Sonnino, *c'est égoïsme sacré*,' and brought my fist thumping on the table. I had read a good deal about the Versailles Conference by that time. If all of it was absurd, it was also part of my quest for a vocation.

The Work

The work I had to do was very formal and dull, but at first I performed it conscientiously. At this time I did not seriously consider whether the routine work to which I would be tied down if I remained in the Military Accounts Department would not become uncongenial or even intolerable to me. For one thing, I was immensely relieved at being rescued out of the dismal state known as 'educated unemployment' among us. The salary I was getting was more than what I would have got in an academic post. Furthermore, I was pleased with the encouragement that I was getting from my superiors. They said that they would soon allow me to appear at the departmental examination for the next higher grade. They also added that if I showed capacity in that grade they would recommend me for the highest cadre in the Finance Department of the Government of India. My cousin had taken the precaution of not taking me under him, probably from the fear of being accused of partiality. But his friend, under whom I worked, was not less kind. I think he once thought of having me as his son-in-law. I was, however, to betray the faith of my well-wishers in the office. But otherwise I would have betrayed myself.

Another reason for my not taking the bit of clerical work in the teeth at this stage was that I was prone to curious illusions about any employment I could secure. I have often been unemployed and gone through long periods, not only of want and anxiety, but also of humiliations, and so I was not only glad whenever any job came my way, but also began to imagine that I would reach the highest post in that line. I had confidence in my ability, and thus as soon as I got the post of clerk I began to imagine that one day I would become at least a Deputy Military Accountant General.

This was not so very stupid. Actually, as I was told soon after I had taken up my work, the supreme head of our side of the accounts of the Indian army was a Bengali and he had started on a salary which was lower than mine. Eventually, he became even a Member of the Viceroy's Executive Council and was knighted. In fact, after I left the Department the man who had entered with me on the same salary did eventually become either a Deputy or Assistant Military Accountant General. Also, a relative of mine who had entered the department soon after me on a salary which was not even half of mine, rose to a post carrying a salary which even in my most prosperous days I did not have with any employer.

As it happened, to foster my illusions I soon got a promotion. I wrote a note on a claim by a soldier which very much pleased our English chief, and he sent for me. I went, and he asked me a number of questions. I was told afterwards that he did not think that I spoke as well as I had written. But he set that down to shyness. Thus it happened that when our Assistant Superintendent proposed to go on leave I was appointed to act for him.

That was over the heads of many of my colleagues senior to me. They could not have been pleased, but they did not show any feeling to me. But the Assistant Superintendent who was a MA and in whose place I was to act, showed it in a different way. He was apparently piqued at the chiefs praise of me, and wanted to show that he could do better. A ruling had come from the Adjutant General of the Indian army in connection with the claim of an officer. He got ready to dispute that claim in a note. He gathered all the books of rules and regulations around himself, turned them over and peered into them with extreme concentration and even tenseness. His pen spluttered over the note-sheets. I watched him closely, with suppressed amusement, but his enjoyment of his own work was even greater. He stopped from time to time and read over what he had written, as a painter steps back to see what he has painted. He smiled and resumed writing, and when he had finished asked all the rest of us who worked with him whether we would listen to what he had written. Of course, we showed great curiosity, and he read out his refutation of the Adjutant-General, and concluded with this flourish: 'The Adjutant-General's ruling must be taken with a grain of salt.' He was an MA in English and perhaps did not know where the phrase had come from. Otherwise, he would certainly have written: '*Cum grano salis*'.

CHAPTER 2

The Course of the Non-Co-operation Movement

The main reason behind my not feeling the tedium of office work and not considering whether I should be able to stick to it, was that during its first months my mind was wholly occupied with the Non-Co-operation Movement led by Mahatma Gandhi. The movement got that name because its main aim was to induce the Indian people to withdraw and withhold all forms of co-operation with the British administration in India and thereby paralyse it. Mahatma Gandhi said that if his prescription was followed implicitly, the British would be forced to leave India in less than a year, which was, of course, perfectly true, but the condition set for it saved British rule for the time being at least. The programme had been adopted by the Congress at the end of 1920, and it was put into effect in January, 1921, with a boycott of the elections held under the Government of India Act of 1919.

I was then at Kishorganj with my parents. At that time I had left behind the violent hatred of British rule which had been roused in me by the repression of 1919, more especially by its brutal exhibition at Amritsar, and reverted to my historical view of that rule. I felt repelled by all the features of the new movement. But I showed moderation about the rejection of the Montagu-Chelmsford reforms. I said that in spite of their inadequacies they should have been worked, if for nothing else than to gain administrative experience. But, of course, neither Mahatma Gandhi nor the Congress cared for practical matters.

For the Gandhian specialities, however, I felt only disdain, and did not mince my words. I said that if we must spin in order to be self-reliant in respect of clothing, we should also plough in order to eat; or, if we were sure to get political independence in six months or a year by not going to schools and colleges, giving up our professions, and resigning from Government service en masse, we would get it even sooner by committing mass suicide. My father would not say anything to all this airing of intellectual superiority, but my mother would get irritated and tell me curdy to be less flippant and more reverential.

One day, an elderly uncle of mine, who had come to visit us, joined in the argument. He lived in an out-of-the-way village to which we could go only on elephants or horseback or by palanquin, there being no roads to it. But even there he kept in touch with world affairs. Thus he lectured me not only on Gandhi, but passing on to Egypt even on Zaghlul Pasha. After that he took out a piece of paper from his pocket and said that he would sing to us a song he had written and set to music. Besides being the village squire, he was also a poet and composer. He sang his song about Gandhi with great expression and emphatic gestures. Those who have seen a popular picture of Rouget de Lisle composing La Marseillaise, and his daughter taking it down with an ecstatic countenance, will be able to form an exact idea of my uncle's performance. I give the first three lines of the song:

> Ké phukichhé singa,
> Kon tunga sringé,
> Emana marma bhediyé?

'Who is it that is blowing his horn, and from which high peak, to pierce the heart in this manner?' The message of Gandhi had reached even the backwaters of East Bengal. But everyone was accepting him in his own way. At the bathing ghat an old Brahmin priest told me with flashing eyes: 'He has come to re-establish Hindu Dharma.'

In the middle of the year I left Kishorganj for Calcutta, where I found the movement to be in full swing. I could also see its proper magnitude and feel its real power better in a great city than in my Sleepy Hollow of Kishorganj. It was not possible any more to air cleverness about it. I felt its intensity. I had started work in my new office, and, going home by tram in the afternoon, I heard and saw what might be described as the son et lumière of the movement. In every square huge crowds stood in serried ranks, listening with excited gestures and shouts, to the harangues of the leaders. There could be no mistaking the enthusiasm. If in all its phases the nationalist movement gave an exhibition of the hatred of British rule made visual by mass hysteria, it also provided mass amusement for the people.

In Indian life of those days every one of these movements of agitation created a psychological atmosphere comparable to our monsoons with their storms. There was no possibility of remaining unaware of the disturbed psychological ambiance and it was not necessary to collect statistics to discover that something was on. The excitement could be felt in the air, so to speak, and was in any case visible in the movements, stances, and expressions of even those who pursued business as usual with the utmost stolidity of behaviour and expression.

The general appearance of inertness and impassivity vanished. Animation could be seen on all faces, and quite ordinary people were lifted out of the tedium and stuffiness of their day-to-day existence. Their looks became keen, gestures lively, movements brisk, speaking more voluble, and they showed an interest in what was happening around them which was not normal with them. In the everyday life of the Indian people only the religious festivals brought one kind of enjoyment. The nationalist movement also brought another, and of a different kind. It was equally real. The relief from the crushing load of boredom which it gave was one of the sources of strength of the nationalist movement.

The excited mood was sustained to a pitch of tenseness by the nationalist press, both in English and the Indian languages. All Indian journalists were themselves extremists, and in any case no newspaper proprietor could afford to be less than extremist if he wanted to sell his paper to Indians. Those who could not or would not join the agitation actively, saved their conscience by participating in it emotionally by reading the newspapers. So, the circulation of the papers always went up during the active phases of agitation. To read the reports and gloat on the brutality of the police and heroism of the nationalist volunteers was like the daily devotions of religious Hindus, combined with the vicarious emotion roused by the films. A poet friend of mine described very wittily and truly the patriotic elation produced by reading the papers. He wrote that every clerk rose from the perusal of his morning paper - he actually mentioned the most fiery among them - in holy wrath and rushed at his wife, yelling 'You slut!'

People also spilled out in the streets after office hours on weekdays or on Sundays to see the fun, and it was this even more than the meetings which gave rise to trouble. The Government could not afford to make itself invisible and allow the crowds to have the run of the streets. So, they stationed pickets of soldiers at street crossings.* The crowds on their part, whenever they saw the police or the soldiers, stood at a distance and stared. This, in turn, provoked the latter to charge.

In one sense, this was almost an animal reaction in the British soldiers,

* The troops assigned to internal order were always British. Of the forty-four battalions of British infantry normally stationed in India, twenty-seven were allotted to 'internal security' from 1921 onwards.

who could never bear Indians looking at them with a mocking, frightened, or even curious expression, and invariably charged. But this was also enjoined on them by the code of practice of the Government. The police and the soldiers were not to allow large crowds to stand in the streets, lest excited by the mere consciousness of numbers they should begin some sort of mischief. Unless the outbursts were checked at once they could give rise to serious trouble. In one of his stories Kipling described the practice in the best days of British rule. He wrote: 'The science of defence lay solely in keeping the mob on the move. If they had a breathing space they would halt and fire a house, and then the work of restoring order would be more difficult, to say the least of it. Flames have the same effect on a crowd as blood has on a wild beast.' And he described the execution of the principle in these words: 'I heard the shouts of the British infantry crying cheerily: "Hutt [move on]. Ye beggars! Hutt ye devils! Get along! Go forward there!" Then followed the ringing of rifle-butts and shrieks of pain.'

So long as the work of keeping peace in India remained one of maintaining it between Indian and Indian, there was in this task a combination of two feelings in the British soldiery: resigned submission to an unpleasant duty and the exuberance of going out on a spree. So, on the one hand, Kipling made his Deputy-Commissioner say when he saw on the pavement a man lying with a battered skull: 'It is expedient that one man should die for the people. These brutes were beginning to show their teeth too much.' On the other, he made the soldiers who were going out in the aid of civil power say:' "No ball cartridges - what a beastly shame! Hope I shall meet my money-lender there. I owe him more than I can afford."' And when they had gone through all that, which they regarded as being all in the day's work, they went back to the barracks singing: 'Two lovely black eyes!'

With the coming of the nationalist movement this detachment came to an end. The British officials, officers, and men became partisans and acquired the ferocity of partisans. A friend of mine who saw an English sergeant coming at him with a raised stick, and was afterwards hit, said to me: 'I could never have imagined that a human face could look so brutal.'

On the other hand, those who were trying to put an end to British rule non-violently and without hating the British, following Gandhi's admonition, blamed the police and the soldiers for the breaches of peace. They always said that the processions were peaceful and would have remained peaceful but for the presence of the police or the soldiers, who always gave a provocation. This argument I heard in India for twenty-five years, and I am now hearing it in England. I am not surprised because it is bound to be heard whenever there is an attempt to put an end to an established order.

The Government was put in a dilemma by the nature of the movement. It was perfectly aware of the danger latent in it, in spite of the profession of non-violence. At the same time, it did not want to be too drastic and give a recapitulation of the repression of 1919, which was regarded as a mistake. Therefore this time the police or the soldiers employed only the minimum force. There were nonetheless one or two regrettable incidents which I shall describe later. But even if these had not happened and only the minimum of force had been applied, there would still have been accusations of police and military brutality. In the last days of British rule the guardians of law and order were always represented in the Indian press as hooligans or terrorists. This is also being recapitulated in Britain.

Moreover, the Indian public actually felt disappointed if there was no governmental violence. Their hatred of British rule, with its accompaniment of a feeling of helplessness against it, made all nationalist Indians who could not join the agitation, enjoy the stories of brutality in order to amplify their sense of grievance. Thus the use of force against the Non-Co-operarion Movement, on the whole moderate as it was compared with the serious nature of the defiance of the Government, was magnified out of all proportion.

Lord Reading and the Movement

Such was the general character of the Non-Co-operation Movement as I saw it. I shall next relate a few particular incidents over which I showed strong feeling. The first of these was a speech by Lord Reading at a dinner given to him at the Chelmsford Club of Simla on 30 May 1921. In it he gave an explanation of his meetings with Mahatma Gandhi. The first of these took place on 15 May at Simla. It was followed by five more meetings, and the discussions between Lord Reading and Gandhi were spread over a total period of twelve hours and forty-five minutes. At first nothing was disclosed about the purpose and subject of the discussions, and so there was a good deal of suspicious speculation in British as well as Indian circles about them, as if there was something underhand in them. I had not paid much attention to the meetings or the rumours, but Lord Reading's speech made an unpleasant impression on me. The following was its explanatory part:

'Unless it be thought that there was any concealment about it, I will tell you what happened. Mr Malaviya came to me and we had several interviews to my profit and I hope also to his [laughter], because I think two men cannot exchange ideas and discuss problems without deriving benefit to either side. He left me with the impression that he would like me to see Mr Gandhi. Well, it did occur to me that my address was not altogether unknown [prolonged laughter]. But I informed Mr Malaviya that if Mr Gandhi applied to me for an interview I would readily grant it and I should like to hear his views. The consequence was that in due course Mr Gandhi did apply, and there was not only one interview but several interviews between us.'

I thought that this was an arrogant assertion of his own position by Lord Reading, as if he was wanting to inflict his Canossa on Gandhi by making him come to the Viceregal Lodge at Simla as a suppliant. And the airing of his wit in doing that seemed to me to be in very bad taste. The remark stuck so firmly in my memory that even though I forgot all about it in the succeeding years it came back to me when I was thinking about the topics of this chapter, and, on checking up the speech in the periodicals of the time, I have found my recollection of the words exact.

However, Lord Reading was driven to it by his awareness that the Indian nationalists on the one hand and the British community in India on the other were bound to take diametrically opposed views of any conciliatory move by him. Yet he wanted to take such a move. When in England at the time of his appointment as viceroy, he had not taken the Non-Co-operation Movement seriously. But after his arrival in India at the end of April 1921, he changed his opinion and reported to the Secretary of State, Edwin Montagu, that the situation was much more dangerous than he had thought. So, when, soon after. Pandit Madan Mohan Malaviya, the veteran nationalist leader, suggested that he should meet Gandhi, he agreed, but on one condition - that the request for an interview must come from Gandhi in due form. In a letter to his son written at that time, Reading explained why he had insisted on this procedure. 'I have,' he wrote, 'taken a firm stand against sending for him until he takes the first step, since otherwise my action would be grossly misinterpreted amongst the Indian people by unscrupulous propagandists and the people would never really understand what happened.'

But this was not known to the public, and the British community raised the clamour that the Viceroy had truckled to the nationalists. As they were fiercely opposed to any concession to Indian nationalist demands, they received Lord Reading's explanation and the witty sally in it with immense glee.

From his point of view Lord Reading was right in insisting on an application from Gandhi, but I think he might have spared his listeners and the readers of his speech the pleasantry. It could have been a sally on the spur of the moment due to two reasons: first, to his desire to placate the local British, who with their attachment to vested interests and their racial arrogance (about which I shall have a good deal to say) were angry with Lord Reading for meeting Gandhi; and, secondly, to his cleverness, which he was tempted to show, being a very clever man. He gave a more felicitous exhibition of his wit when speaking about the legal profession. He said that it was no bed of roses, it was either all bed or all roses. This delighted the members of the legal profession in India. I hope I have given the epigram correctly, for I am quoting it from memory after nearly sixty years.

Naturally, the explanation had the opposite effect on Indians, who showed a disposition to criticize Gandhi for seeking the interview and thus humiliating his country and people. Mr Ramananda Chatterji, the noted Bengali publicist, who was not directly involved in the movement and was even critical of some of its aspects, commented severely on the episode. In a note in his influential magazine. The Modem Review, he made the point that in spite of Lord Reading's official position Mahatma Gandhi was a far greater man, and there could have been no loss of prestige if the Viceroy's Secretary had invited him in his master's name. As regards Gandhi, Ramananda Babu wrote that in his humility he might have seen nothing wrong in applying for the interview, but he had no right to compromise the honour of his country and people. As he put it: 'Mr Gandhi, the greatest political leader of his countrymen, who had set at naught the satanic bureaucratic government and raised their self-respect to the highest pitch, had no right to act in a way which was calculated to produce a secret sense of humiliation and wounded self-respect in the minds of his countrymen.'

One should have thought that in so serious a matter as arriving at an understanding between the British Government and the Indian nationalists such questions of form and precedence were trivial and even irrelevant. But it was not so. By that time any overture by one party to the

Other had become a matter of loss of face for one or other of them. When that point is reached in political life it may be assumed that a particular dispute has passed beyond the stage at which a statesmanlike solution can be found for it. In India this stage was reached by 1921. It had become a question of who would get the better of the other.

In his dealings with Gandhi and his movement Lord Reading was not only astute, but also sober. He was not rattled and was resolved not to be panicked into any kind of action which could be regarded as unjustifiable severity. Both he and his government regarded the Muslim counterpart of the Non-Co-operation Movement to be the more mischievous of the two. It was called the Khilafat Movement, because it was a protest against the treatment of Turkey by the Allies and in favour of the Caliphate, the old Islamic institution which was both political and religious. In fact, it was an outburst of the new pan-Islamic feeling, which I very much disliked. This added to my dislike for the Non-Co-operation Movement. One of the reasons which had prompted Lord Reading to meet Gandhi was to persuade him to curb the activities of two fanatical Muslim leaders, Shaukat Ali and Mohamed Ali.

17 November 1921: Calcutta and Bombay

I shall now tell the story of my only brush with the movement. It had been decided before Lord Reading came to India that the Prince of Wales (the future Edward VIII) would visit the country as a gesture of reconciliation. But the Non-Co-operation Movement had begun, and Gandhi and other leaders declared that all Indians should boycott every ceremony connected with the visit. This caused great embarrassment to the Indian Government, as well as the Home Government, for they could not cancel the visit without serious loss of face. On the other hand, trouble was equally certain. The Prince was to land in Bombay on 17 November 1921, and Mahatma Gandhi called for a general *hartal* (strike) for the day in order to give a demonstration of India's hostility, not so much to the Prince as to British rule, and forbade all participation in the celebrations. We knew that the call was going to be obeyed in a spectacular manner. Yet the Government offices could not be closed. So, I decided to go to my office on foot, because the trams were not running. Others were also doing the same thing, playing for safety on both sides. I saw them walking in a continuous file when I came out of our lane into the main street, which was Cornwallis Street at the Shyambazar end. But I also saw Congress and Khilafat volunteers strutting up and down the street, asking people who were going in cars or on cycles to get down or go back. It was the sight of the Khilafat volunteers which roused my anger. They were recruited from the lowest Muslim riffraff of Calcutta and looked more repulsive still in their shabby uniforms of a military type. They were particularly aggressive and were brandishing their whips at people. This at once put my back up, and I decided to go home, get my cycle, and ride on it to the office, four miles away. All my life I have resented and defied any attempt at coercing me.

Of course, they ordered me to get down. But I went along at great speed without heeding them. When I had gone about a mile I saw a crowd of young men and boys standing across the street shoulder to shoulder and three deep, barring the way. Certainly, I could not make them let me pass. However, looking back, I saw a car coming at full speed, and I resolved to spin close behind it and take advantage of the gap made by it. I did, but when the crowd saw me they shouted: 'Beat the sala [bastard or son of a bitch]!' But I was beyond their reach.

But the sprint had made me breathless, and I was compelled to go slowly. So, when I had gone only about half-a-mile further, a tall Hindustani darted from the pavement, pulled me down from the cycle, dragged me to the pavement, and said: 'Now, go on foot!' As I walked along, dragging the cycle with me, I heard the elderly clerks who were going to the office saying loudly: 'Was there any sense in being so rash as to try to go on a bicycle?' But after walking another mile, I reached the comer of Wellington Street and Dhurrumtollah Street, where I found the police patrolling the street because it was the boundary between the Indian and the European quarters of the city. So I got on the cycle and reached my office without any further incident.

I was naturally very angry and began to abuse the mob to my colleagues. To my astonishment they all declared against me and for the hartal, although they had taken care to arrive at the office long before the usual time. I was harangued, and our Assistant Superintendent aired his English by telling me that the will of the masses was more binding than the interest of the classes. I had to swallow this mortification as well.

After office I decided not to go back on my cycle. I took it to the house of my cousin who lived not very far from the Esplanade, left it there, and began to walk back home. It was getting dark, but immense crowds were on the streets. People had come out to see the fun. It was a typical November evening in Calcutta. The normal mixture of smoke and fog had descended on the city, making the street lamps look a ghastly yellow.

When I reached the corner of Wellington Street and Dhurrumtollah, where in the morning I had again got on the cycle, I saw a piquet of English soldiers in their battledress. They had steel helmets on, and stood at attention with their sword bayonets fixed to their short Lee Enfield rifles. The yellow light fell on the knifelike blades, which gleamed as if they were made of brushed silver. I looked with admiration at their bearing. It was certainly curious that at that moment those alien soldiers, belonging to the army of our foreign rulers, seemed to me, who had always resented political subjection, to be the sole defenders of civilization.

In fact, on that day all normal life had been paralysed in Calcutta, and the next morning the British newspapers of Calcutta furiously denounced the goonda raj (gangster rule) of the previous day. These papers voiced the feelings of the powerful British community of the city. The result was that the Congress and Khilafat volunteer organizations were declared illegal and dissolved. Lord Ronaldshay, the Governor of Bengal, made a strong speech in which he said that his Government would not tolerate any interference with the normal life of the city and freedom of its inhabitants. After this there were no attempts at disrupting the normal life of Calcutta, although processions, demonstrations, meetings and occasional strikes continued.

But in Bombay where the Prince of Wales had landed there were serious clashes between the Parsis and Eurasians of the city and the followers of the Congress and Khilafat organization. These developed into widespread riots which lasted three days. The first day had begun peacefully. Near the wharf and in the streets along which the Prince was taken in procession, large crowds stood on both sides and cheered. The Times correspondent who was on the spot saw them, and estimated the spectators at half a million. He reported that he could not pass through the ranks of the spectators. He even added that this was proving the call for boycott of the Prince to be ridiculous.

But in the Indian quarters of the city Hindu and Muslim crowds began to collect and they assaulted the Parsis who had gone to welcome the Prince. These attacks provoked retaliation by the Parsis and the Eurasians, and fierce street fighting soon developed. It went on for three days and in its course many persons lost their life. The Government put the number of dead at 36, of whom two were Europeans, 3 Parsi, 14 Hindu, and 17 Muslim. This indicated that the deaths were due to counter-attacks by the Parsis and Eurasians for the most part. The nationalists put the figures much higher, as usual.

Mahatma Gandhi was horrified, and more shocked to learn that his 'Parsi sisters' had been molested and insulted to the point of being stripped of their clothes. He said that he had got proof of such outrages and no one denied that these had taken place. He at once undertook a fast by way of penance, and for the time being tried personally to prevent the fighting by intervening between the rioters.

Two Deplorable Incidents

After these violent outbreaks there was a temporary lull. But immediately afterwards we heard of a horrible tragedy. It was not connected with the Non-Co-operation Movement, but arose out of a Muslim insurrection known as the Moplah rebellion. It was the most serious rising against British rule in India since the Mutiny. The Moplahs or Mapillas were Muslims of Arab origins, and were notorious for their fanaticism and truculence. Inflamed by the preachings of the Khilafat Movement, they rose in revolt in the late summer of 1921, and perpetrated murders, arson, and looting over a wide area. Their violence was directed as much against the Hindus as the Government, which had to deploy a very large military force to quell the uprising. This took months, and the casualties in death among the Moplahs was put at four to five thousand. This did not rouse any indignation in India, but an unfortunate incident due to carelessness did. On 19 November one hundred Moplah prisoners were sent by train to the jail of a town at some distance. They were packed into wagons which had no ventilation. So, when the doors were opened after a five hours' journey, the prisoners were found to be in a state of collapse, with horrible wounds inflicted by bites and blows on one another by the struggling men. In all eighty-two men died. A Commission appointed by the Government laid the blame on the railway company and also held a sergeant guilty of negligence.

It was a windfall for the nationalists. In the light of the Hindu-Muslim killings both before and after independence, which numbered hundreds of thousands and were extenuated by both sides, it can hardly be assumed that the sorrow of the Hindus at the death of some eighty Moplah Muslims was deep or even sincere. But the deaths were attributable to the British, and that made an essential difference. The Indian press denounced the inhumanity, and the Congress passed a resolution declaring that it was 'an act of inhumanity unheard of in modern times and unworthy of a Government that called itself civilized'. It deprived the British of the right to dwell on the Black Hole tragedy of 1756. My own feeling was a sense of horror at the deaths, and of anger at the carelessness.

The second incident was not so serious, but it created a very strong feeling in Calcutta, and also provided a significant illustration of the British attitude. In December 1921 a party of British soldiers was chasing a crowd at the junction of College Street and Harrison Road and bringing down their rifle butts on the backs of those they could overtake. As it happened, just at that time Principal Heramba Chandra Maitra was passing that way. He was one of the oldest and most venerated academics of Calcutta, a Brahmo puritan who was a figure like Dr Pusey and besides a noted exponent of Carlyle and Emerson. He felt angry at the behaviour of the soldiers, and asked one of them: 'What offence have these men committed that you are beating them?' The man referred him to his officer across the street, and when he came over Principal Maitra put the same question to him. He did not at first reply, but when the Principal repeated his question he was given a push by the officer and fell down. He was put on his feet by two passersby.

The manhandling of so aged and eminent a man naturally caused an outcry in the press, and even the Governor of Bengal, Lord Ronaldshay, expressed his regret privately. The incident was also raised in the Bengal Legislative Council, and Sir Henry Wheeler, the member of the Governor's Council in charge of law and order, had to give an explanation and express his regret. But he also committed a faux pas. He could not resist the temptation to improve on the occasion by adding that what Principal Maitra had done with the best of motives would have been interpreted in London as obstructing the military in the discharge of their duty. This was a fling at the habitual invocation of English liberties by us. Of course, the nationalist papers at once commented that soldiers were not employed in England to deal with political demonstrations. I might add incidentally that we were far better posted in regard to British history and politics than the local British, however highly placed. I thought this airing of superiority in very bad taste, in spite of my dislike for the Movement. But I was actually angered by the attempt of The Statesman of Calcutta, the mouthpiece of the British community, to sharpen its wit on Principal Maitra. He had employed the word, so far as I remember, 'shove' in describing what was done to him. The Statesman gleefully asked whether it was a shove or a push. The malice was mean, but it was typical of the British community in India, which always tried to hold up our use of English to contempt and ridicule.

The British Attitude to Gandhi in 1921

This would give an indication of the British attitude towards Indian nationalists, but at this point I would give an account of the attitude to Gandhi, although not as full as it might have been made. It hardly needs to be said that the attitude was not what it is today. At that time with hardly any exception British opinion was hostile, and even contemptuous of him. There was no disposition to admit even Gandhi's personal greatness. Some of that has to be put on record.

There were various shades of British opinion about Mahatma Gandhi, and the most honourable was that of the avowed enemies, e.g. Winston Churchill. He regarded Gandhi as the enemy of the British Empire and therefore with undisguised hatred. He did not try to be merely loftily disdainful. Two months before Reading's appointment to the Viceroyalty was announced, Churchill ragged Edwin Montagu, the Secretary of State for India, at a dinner, and said that Gandhi 'ought to be laid, bound hand and foot, at the gates of Delhi and then trampled on by an enormous elephant with the new Viceroy seated on its back'. Churchill was then the Secretary of State for War in the British Government. He later described Gandhi, in a phrase which became famous, as a half-naked Fakir. Some absurdities were also uttered seriously and publicly. Colonel Yates, who with Sir William Joynson-Hicks was a stem and uncompromising defender of British interests in India, suggested to the Secretary of State for India in the House of Commons that Gandhi should be deported as a Soviet agent because he had declared that he preferred Bolshevist rule to British rule. Here one kind of prejudice, that of Gandhi, was pitted against prejudice of another kind, that of the British ruling class. Edwin Montagu could not even be ironical about the suggestion. He gravely replied that he was leaving that to the judgement of the local authority, i.e. the Viceroy.

At all events, there was no airing of superiority in these outbursts. That

Olympian prerogative has always belonged to The Times. Its correspondent wrote after the events of 17 November 1921: 'One must realize that Gandhi has long realized his waning influence and the hopelessness of his cause. There was a time when, in the full bloom of sainthood, he might have gone to the mountains, to return at some moment with serious, very serious results. He has missed the market. Not only has his sainthood been tarnished, both by his failures and the disreputable character of some of his followers, influential associates like Patel and Barucha, but even his reputation as a successful politician has been badly impaired.'

The Times itself commented: 'Perhaps too much stress has been laid in the past upon the loftiness and purity of his motives. In practice he is revealed as a mistaken and mischievous crank with a talent for fomenting trouble.'

The British community in India showed even greater irreverence. A police officer who had seen Gandhi during the riots in Bombay reported that when there was danger for him, he ran with an agility remarkable in a man of his age. The whole of the British press in India was facetious about it. The British press even questioned his statement that he had served in the Boer War as an orderly in the military ambulance.

The aversion to him persisted. It became sharper with the Civil Disobedience Movement of 1930. For instance, on 28 June of that year Archbishop Cosmo Lang wrote to Lord Irwin that Gandhi was 'a perverse and dangerous mixture of the mystic, the fanatic, and the anarchist'. The Archbishop was not prepared to credit Gandhi even with political sense, for he wrote about C. F. Andrews: 'He seemed to me as much in the clouds and as little possessed of political sense as his master', meaning, of course, Mahatma Gandhi. To put Gandhi and C. F. Andrews on the same footing in respect of political sense showed a complete incapacity for making distinctions.

But the strangest part of the matter was that it was possible to hold these unfavourable opinions on Gandhi quite honestly and plausibly. If I were asked to choose between the English admirers and the English detractors of Gandhi I should certainly prefer the detractors. They were more natural and, psychologically, healthy Englishmen. The present-day adulation of Gandhi in England and elsewhere in the West differs only in degree and not in kind from the other and more unpleasant and harmful forms of Hinduizing by Occidentals.

Lord Reading, who had to deal with Gandhi, would not be committed to a one-sided view. He remained balanced. He had not found the Indian leader physically impressive, and was also exasperated and bewildered by him at times. He was baffled by Gandhi's disinclination to be concrete and his proneness to generalities. He also found his application of religion to politics difficult to understand. In the end he thought that there was a contradiction between Gandhi's political conduct and his religious and ethical side. This was also the impression formed by other Viceroys after Reading. If, however, these British dignitaries had known anything about Hindu religious life, they would not have been surprised by the apparent dichotomy.

But Reading was quite appreciative of Gandhi's genuinely religious nature, which he had discovered even after one meeting. Besides, as his son records in his biography of his father, till the end of his life Reading never spoke of Gandhi in any terms but those of sympathy and regard. All this was quite rational. The British became sub-rational about Gandhi only after abandoning India.

Suspension of the Movement

The Moplah tragedy and the assault on Principal Maitra added to the excitement in Calcutta. The agitation continued. Coming home one evening I even saw at a street corner a lorry full of British soldiers with a Lewis machinegun in a firing position. All this added to the vicarious enjoyment of the onlookers and hearers of news, who form the most numerous class of nationalists in India. From the second-floor verandah of our house in north Calcutta I could hear the maidservants discussing the day's events while scrubbing the utensils and dishes under the running tap in the courtyard below. One day I heard the excited voices in a shriller treble above the patter of the tap water. They were discussing the arrest of the wife of the great nationalist leader, C. R. Das, and her companions. One maidservant said: 'As soon as the lady was arrested, all the others cried out in English: "My dears, we will also go with her to jail", and they went.' Even the rolling Bengali drunkard joined in. We were going to Kishorganj for the Christmas holidays, and when the train was on the point of getting into motion, four coolies pushed in two tottering young men who were crying or rather drawling, but at the top of their voices: '*Bolo, Bande Mataram*' (Say, Vande Mataram), and then in their English: 'Swaraj will be come soon!' The coolies also repeated the cry of *Vande Mataram*.

However, at the beginning of January 1922, I began to sense a slackening of the excitement, although in the UP peasant discontent was being whipped up to keep the agitation going. The suppression of the peasant demonstrations, in some cases by shooting, was increasing the anger of the common people. Elsewhere, perhaps even Mahatma Gandhi felt that boosting was needed and he issued an ultimatum that he would launch the next stage of agitation, i.e. civil disobedience or defiance of law unless the Government released all prisoners who had been convicted or were under trial, and bound itself not to interfere with any form of non-violent political activity, aimed at putting an end to British rule in India.

This was on 4 February. On the same day, however, a terrible outrage was committed by a mob of peasants and Congress volunteers at a police station in the UP. This was the Chauri Chaura incident. In it twenty-one policemen (all Indians) were murdered with extreme brutality. Mahatma Gandhi was so shocked by this that he declared that he had committed a Himalayan blunder, undertook a fast for five days as expiation and eventually suspended the movement. With this the Non-Co-operation Movement collapsed all over India.

But this did not prevent the Government from arresting Gandhi on 13 March 1922. He was tried for sedition and sentenced to two years' imprisonment. No outbreak of violence followed, and this surprised the British authorities. Thus Lord Rawlinson, the Commander-in-Chief of the Indian army at the time, wrote in his diary:

'India is certainly no easy country to govern nowadays. One never knows how she will take things. We arrested the Congress volunteers, most of whom were wild men or hot-headed youths, expecting that a demonstration of firmness would rally the moderates to us. Instead, our action inflamed them to passion and made things worse than ever. Now we have arrested Gandhi and looked for no end of trouble, and, lo! the arrest has caused no trouble at all.'

The sentence of imprisonment, too, produced no excitement. It was received with complete apathy. However strange all this might seem to outsiders, those who knew the psychology of the Indian masses and their pattern of behaviour, would not have been surprised, although they might not have been able to predict any particular reaction, because one of the constants of the behaviour was its unpredictability.

CHAPTER 3

Character of the Indian Nationalist Movement Under Gandhi's Leadership

In the account of the Non-Co-operation Movement which I have just given I confined myself to setting down what I saw and felt as I went through it, and did not offer any interpretation. I could not, because I did not arrive at any general conclusions about the movement then, but was only irritated by certain features in it which offended my political and moral susceptibilities as they were at the time. It was only twelve years later, and after going through the second Gandhian agitation of 1930-32, that I understood the real nature of the Indian nationalist movement as led by Mahatma Gandhi. Then I also saw that the features which had repelled me in 1921 were integral to the movement as a whole. I shall therefore bring forward my final assessment and set it down here. As Mahatma Gandhi never changed his ideas or methods after 1920, there will be no anachronism in my doing so.

However, I shall be frank and say this about my final assessment that I could never take any view of the nationalist movement that was independent of my attitude to things English. This had three aspects. There was, first, my historical view of British rule in India, which I regarded as the best political regime which had ever been seen in India, in spite of its shortcomings and positive evils. Next, I had to reckon with my loyalty to English life and civilization and through that to the larger phenomenon of European culture, by both of which my own personality was formed. Last of all, there was my identification with British greatness, which was the natural result of the two previous factors. Thus, unless alienated by some special exhibition of nastiness by the British in India, I remained ambivalent between a nationalist (Indian) and an imperialistic (British) view of Indian history. However, this has not made me overlook the shortcomings of British rule or of the Indian nationalist movement either. So, I shall offer my interpretation of the nationalist movement with complete confidence in my objectivity.

Nihilism of the Nationalist Movement

What made me hostile to the campaign of non-cooperation launched by

Mahatma Gandhi in the first instance was its wholly negative character. He urged the boycott, not only of all kinds of service under the British administration, but also of all the professions connected with it as well as the schools and colleges run by the existing educational system. In respect of British textiles he went beyond boycott, and insisted on their being burnt if possessed by Indians. The boycott of education was disapproved of by Sir Ashutosh Mookherji, who had made the University of Calcutta what it was then. The poet Tagore, who was a Nobel laureate, condemned the ritual holocaust of British cloth which was going on all over India as senseless. This made him very unpopular, because those who burnt their cloth felt differently. British cloth had become so closely associated with the hated British rule that they felt that they were literally cleansing their bodies from physical pollution by burning their cloth of British manufacture. Indian women felt this all the more strongly.

To me all these demands of Mahatma Gandhi seemed not only extreme, but even crude and irrational. It appeared to me that his entire ideology was driven by a resolve to abandon civilized life and revert to a primitive existence. I thought that he was preaching the rejection not only of European civilization, but of Hindu civilization as well. I could see that he had not the slightest understanding of the higher features of Hindu culture, and of its complexity.

One of his economic recommendations, i.e. advocacy of hand-spinning, had something positive in it. Even so, I did not like his insistence on it as an obligatory accompaniment of agriculture. And I positively disliked the religious and ethical rigmarole he brought into his advocacy of hand-spinning, representing it as a means of moral and spiritual improvement. Tagore was openly ironical about it although he was not less religious than Gandhi. In an article entitled 'The Call of Truth', published in *The Modem Review* for October 1921, he drew attention to the paradox of Gandhi's rejection of European machines and his fervent championship of the primitive machine. 'But if a man is stunted by the big machines,' he wrote,

'the danger of his being stunted by small machines must not be lost sight of The Charka [spinning wheel] in its proper place can do no harm, but will rather do good. But where, by reason of failure to acknowledge differences in man's temperament, it is in the wrong place, then the thread can only be spun at the cost of a great deal of the mind itself. The mind is no less valuable than cotton thread.'

It was not possible for Mahatma Gandhi to ignore Tagore and he replied in his journal, *Young India*. But the article contained nothing beyond the familiar catchwords we could always expect from him.

What I did not perceive at the time was that the negative features which repelled me arose out of the very nature of the nationalist movement as it was between 1921 and 1947. It was only after going through the Civil Disobedience Movement of 1930-32 that I discovered that by 1921 Indian nationalism had lost all its positive content. Henceforth it had only one passion to drive it, namely, a crude hatred of British rule. It had also one aim - ending this rule as soon as possible and, if that could not be done, to oppose and embarrass it in every way in order to keep the hatred alive by feeding it continuously. That was why the nationalist leaders were so unwilling to make use of the reforms introduced by the British Government for the sake of gaining political experience. That would have made them suspect to the people, and they themselves feared that even limited cooperation might weaken their hatred and their desire to put an end to the British connection.

No one showed greater *a priori* hatred of British rule and therefore of any kind of practical cooperation with the British administration than the two emerging young leaders of the nationalist movement, Jawaharlal Nehru and Subhas Chandra Bose. Both were by nature extremists. Nehru refused even such limited association with the administrative system as he would have had if he practised his profession as a barrister for which he had been educated at Harrow, Cambridge, and London at considerable expense by his father. Bose did something more spectacular. He had been selected for the Indian Civil Service, a career which was regarded by middle-class Indians as the most prestigious worldly prize open to them, and refused to join it. Both these men disobeyed their fathers, but they exulted as patriots.

But the curious fact was that although the new nationalist leaders sought to lead the masses of India and were also accepted by them, they had no knowledge or understanding of the common people of India, nor any fellow-feeling for them, being all upper-class men. They were the products of the most ancient and rigid class system that was surviving into the present-day world, and were besides members of the new professional class created by British rule. They were also overwhelmingly urban, and in the normal way they would not have had anything to do with the common people except, when possible, living on them as professionals. By becoming political leaders they only gave up economic exploitation for the more satisfying business of exploiting the hatreds and grievances of the common people. Even Mahatma Gandhi shared only the simple moral and religious outlook of the Hindu masses and beyond that he was interested only in curing them of their moral ills. Neither he nor the other leaders knew the common people of India well.

Even more curious was the fact that as long as British rule lasted in India it was the British administrators who were more closely in contact with the Indian masses and had the most thorough knowledge of their good as well as bad points, and, besides, the greatest practical sympathy for them. This made them think that if an appeal was made to the common people of India over the heads of the nationalist leaders they would declare for British rule. Thus Lord Sydenham, one time Governor of Bombay and one of the British 'Ultras' most opposed to the extension of self-government to Indians, pointed out that the parliamentary Select Committee which examined the Government of India Bill of 1919 had called as witnesses only those who could speak English, and therefore the rural and working classes, the landholders, and the fighting races were not heard. He implied that had they been, they would have declared their preference for British rule.

In one sense. Lord Sydenham was not wrong. The common people of India did have a genuine respect for British rule and British administrators, and also confidence in their fairness when dealing between Indian and Indian. But all British administrators who held views like Lord Sydenham's overlooked the dichotomy in the outlook of the Indian masses. The side which they saw was like the visible side of the moon, on which shone the personal likes of the masses, which were wholly sincere. But the invisible other side had on it the predispositions created by history, in which xenophobia in general and hatred of the British in particular were inbuilt and sub-rational. These deep-seated predispositions had greater power over their behaviour when their collective passions were roused. The nationalist leaders knew how to appeal to that, but they did so more through their shared hatred than by working on the mind of the masses as a matter of policy.

But they could not pursue their negative aims without becoming negative themselves and sacrificing the positive content of Indian nationalism. The leadership of Mahatma Gandhi completed the negation. Before him no Indian political leader had seen the aim of ending British rule apart from the greater task of rebuilding the entire fabric of Indian life, which they considered as the main duty before them. The triumph of negation made it inevitable that if the political change the new leaders were trying to bring about ever took place, it would be radically different from all the great revolutions of the past. I have read about three of them, viz. the American, the French, and the Meiji in Japan. I have also passed through and read about all the revolutions of our age, viz. the Young Turk, the Chinese, the Russian, and the new Turkish led by Kemal. In every case, those who carried out these revolutions knew what they were going to put in the place of the regimes they were going to destroy. There were full-fledged ideologies as well as partly worked-out programmes. In the Indian nationalist movement there was not only a total absence of positive and constructive ideas, but even of thinking. These shortcomings were to have their disastrous consequence in 1947.

From my student days, tired of the anti-British talk and dismayed by the negative obsession of my nationalist friends, I used to criticise their attitude. But I always got one miserable cliché as answer: 'Destruction must precede construction.' The intellectual poverty of the nationalist movement gradually became intellectual bankruptcy, but nobody perceived that because the hatred for British rule left no room for rational ideas. Even I was caught in its stream and carried away by it for a short while.

No other leaders showed this negation more than the three who really had a hold on the mind of the Indian people, namely, Gandhi, Nehru, and Subhas Bose. Over the whole period with which I am dealing none of them put forward a single idea about what was to follow British rule. Perhaps objection will be raised to so sweeping an assertion in respect of Mahatma Gandhi, but his political ideas so far as they were positive belonged to the myths of Hindu political life, which had created the ideal of a Rama-rajya, that is to say, the imperium of Rama, the hero of the epic Ramayana, under whose rule everyone enjoyed peace, prosperity, and justice. But this myth had no relevance to present times, and it was not the creation of Gandhi. It had been held by the common people of India through the ages, and was revived in the nineteenth century by the preachers of the new Hindu nationalism.

What was even more astonishing, none of these leaders were qualified to put forward any positive idea because none of them had any worthwhile knowledge of Indian history, life, and culture. I shall indicate later in what way Gandhi lacked this knowledge. Here I take only Nehru and Bose.

Nehru was completely out of touch with Indian life even of his time, except with the life of the self-segregating Anglicized set of upper India who lived in the so-called Civil Lines. He was educated at home by English tutors, and from the age of sixteen to the age of twenty-three he was in England, i.e. away from all Indian influences in the most formative period of his life. He did not know Sanskrit at all, and not even Hindi well, when without some knowledge of the first and a good deal of knowledge of one or other modern Indian language it was impossible to acquire any insight into Indian life, culture, and character, or feeling for them. All that Nehru knew was derived from his very narrow personal experience and from English books written by Englishmen. Most serious of all, he had no knowlege, direct or secondhand, of Hinduism, and besides was not sympathetic to it. Thus he had no direct access to the Indian mind and, as I had opportunities to observe, he had a strong antipathy to traditional Hindu ideas and habits. The love he professed for India was in no way different from an Indophile Englishman's.

As to Subhas Chandra Bose, he belonged to the Bengali Hindu gentry and before he went to Cambridge was educated like any Bengali of the upper class. The culture of this class was created in the nineteenth century as a combination of what was regarded as the best in the West and in the East. But there were two schools of this culture, the liberal and the conservative. The latter was strongly Hindu in character, and Subhas Bose imbibed this Hinduism as part of his political outlook. When he emerged as a leader, the neo-Hindu culture of his young days was already obsolescent, and what the younger generations were doing was to adopt both Communist and Fascist ideas of contemporary Europe. The link between Subhas Bose and the younger generations in Bengal was through his pronounced Fascist leanings. I did not see in Subhas Bose any disposition to understand Hinduism from its original sources. But he did not seem to be wholly immune to Hindu superstitions which had a strong hold on the neo-Hindus of Bengal.

Again, none of these leaders, nor the nationalist intelligentsia as a whole, showed that positive love for the concrete features of India or Indian civilization, e.g. landscape, literature, art, or music, which was always present in the pre-Gandhian nationalism, although at times as mere adjuncts of nationalist feeling. The indifference to music was particularly significant, for in the previous epoch, in Bengal at all events, music was as much 'food of patriotism' as it was 'the food of love'. This indifference, which all the nationalist leaders showed with a rather weak exception in Nehru, was the result of the decline of modern Indian culture created in the nineteenth century. From 1921 onwards the nationalist movement was carried on in a growing cultural void. The civilization of ancient India became only a subject of chauvinistic bragging. Even Hinduism, which was certainly the most stable, deep-rooted, and authentic cultural force among a great majority of Indians, became in the Westernized Indian a nationalistic myth.

After losing its positive cultural moorings, the nationalist movement began more and more to coalesce with the old Hindu xenophobia which had appeared before the Muslim conquest and become hardened under Muslim rule. It did not die out with the end of that rule, and was transformed or rather broadened from hatred of the Muslims to the hatred of the British. This atavistic feeling emerged with the very establishment of British rule in the eighteenth century, and remained fierce even at the end of the nineteenth century when to all appearance British rule appeared to be indestructible. It simmered underground and at times erupted in open defiance of British domination.

But the new nationalism created by educated Indians in the nineteenth century under the influence of European political ideas was able to keep it confined to its underworld. This ended with the Gandhian movement. The negative hatred reasserted itself and completely swamped the old nationalist movement, driving out all its positive elements. From 1920 onwards this trend was helped by Mahatma Gandhi's efforts to bring the masses of India into the nationalist movement, because they could be worked upon only by an appeal to the old xenophobia, which was the sole form of opposition to foreign rule they understood.

This had its effect on the social and personal life of Indians as well, because the decline of positive idealism in the nationalist movement was bound to produce a corresponding tendency in the non-political sphere as well. Mere negation can exist in political feeling as hatred of a particular set of foreign rulers whose yoke cannot be shaken off. It cannot exist in private and personal life. So the vacuum created by the decline of positive idealism was filled up there by a positive passion of a very low order, viz. love of money in its most sordid form. It gained ground until, when political independence was achieved, nothing but the desire to make money as quickly and easily as possible remained as the only practical driving force in private life.

But while British rule lasted the growing love of money did not divert the mind of modern Indians, especially those who were the most able and ambitious, from the hatred, because the greatest obstacle in the way of satisfying that love were the British in the country, who monopolized all the higher opportunites of gaining wealth. The hatred was thus reinforced and refurbished and did not disappear even with the end of British rule. Actually, it survived and gave definite direction to the internal and foreign policies of the new Indian government. It had become so indispensable as a means of emotional satisfaction that it just could not be given up. Besides, the inclination to hate is like acquiring a drug habit. Once adopted it cannot be shaken off.

Nationalism as a Mass Movement

The second thing which roused my hostility to the Non-Co-operation Movement while it was on, also became its basic feature during the whole period from 1921 to 1947. That was its transformation into a mass movement. I could air intellectual disdain for its ideology, but its method filled me with disquiet and anger. I regarded Mahatma Gandhi's incitement of the masses by the kind of appeals he made to them as very dangerous. I always had a profound distrust of indisciplined mass movements. It was strengthened in me when Gandhi made his deliberate attempt to draw the masses into his movement by playing on their xenophobia. I felt angry and disgusted, for I did not believe that his insistence on non-violence would make any difference to the long-established pattern of social behaviour of the Indian masses. It is true that the masses of India, both Hindu and Muslim, had a simple morality and piety. Mahatma Gandhi shared it, but he did not realize that this was their regenerate side, and that they had an unregenerate side always prone to violent action.

Having been brought up in East Bengal I knew a good deal of this, especially of the violence among the Muslim peasantry. Mahatma Gandhi's efforts to make the masses join his movement, I feared, would rouse the aggressive side of the common people of India. Their individual behaviour and collective behaviour were quite different. Mahatma Gandhi thought that his admonitions about non-violence would be listened to. Of course, they were not and could not be. Eventually, he had to admit that he had committed a Himalayan blunder. Mahatma Gandhi had an extraordinary command of such verbal flourishes and he employed them to hypnotize his people into complete forgetfulness of his mistakes and miscalculations.

In 1921 nobody saw the potentiality for violence from the masses more clearly than the Viceroy Lord Reading, and his officials. They did not take Gandhi's preaching of non-violence seriously, and in the light of their historical experience they were quite right.

Even in the most tranquil days of British rule and indisputable power, when there was no challenge to it to make the administration nervous, those at its head never overlooked the possibility of a sudden eruption of violence among the Indian masses. They knew that beneath the peaceable and law- abiding behaviour of the common people of India there always lurked an irrational and desperate rebelliousness. This they attributed to ignorance and religious superstition. Thus, Sir John Strachey, one of the greatest of British administrators, wrote at the end of the nineteenth century:

'It is hardly less true now than it was in 1857 that we are liable at all times to such dangers as this. Nothing is too foolish or too extravagant for general acceptance. This ought never to be forgotten. Ominous signs from time to time appear which ought to remind us how easily in India a terrible conflagration may be lighted up. There is no limit to the liability of such a population to be influenced by the assurances and suggestions of religious fanatics or political agitators, or to be disturbed by interference with its prejudices and beliefs.'

Sir James Fitzjames Stephen, who was at one time Law Member of the Viceroy's Council, also wrote:

'Should the British Government abdicate its function, it would soon turn order into chaos. No country in the world is more orderly, more quiet, and more peaceful than British India as it is; but if the vigour of the Government should be relaxed, if it should lose its essential unity of purpose, and fall into hands either weak or unfaithful, chaos would come again like a flood.'

Nothing had been seen in India since then which disproved the truth of these observations. I had not read these opinions then, but my distrust of popular movements was very strong. This was due in the first instance to my temperament, and next to my study of military history which made me feel that the only way in which an established government could be overthrown was by organized insurrection. However, the curious thing was that until I actually saw mob violence from 1919 onwards I shared the opinion of all middle-class Indians that the only way to make the British let go their hold on India was to bring the masses into the nationalist movement and resort to passive resistance. By 1932 I had shed this view completely.

I was even more opposed to rousing the masses in Bengal, or rather East Bengal. It was bound to lead to Hindu-Muslim riots and even massacres, which did take place later. I have now learnt that Mahatma Gandhi was warned about this by a friend. In one of his articles in *Young India* he quoted this friend's letter, which ran as follows:

'I desire to tell you, that if civil disobedience is begun in East Bengal, the consequences will be much more serious. The Musselmans there number more than 70 per cent of the total population. The majority of them are turbulent. As soon as the passions of these men are aroused, they will fall upon the Hindus and commit terrible outrages and terrorize the Hindu landlords and creditors. The saner and the more respectable section of the community will fail to control the turbulent. Hindu-Muslim unity will vanish at the first touch.'

This happened in 1930 as soon as the Civil Disobedience movement was launched by Mahatma Gandhi. The writer added with justified confidence that he knew the conditions in Bengal, while Mahatma Gandhi did not. The latter mentioned in his article that this was not the only warning he had got. Yet he persisted in his incitement of the common people, who followed him in their own way.

Emergence of the Hindu-Muslim Conflict

Another and a far stronger reason for my antipathy to the Non-Co-operation Movement was the alliance between the Congress and the Muslim Khilafat movement. In 1920 the Muslims of India were as disaffected against the British government in India as were the Hindus.

The immediate reason for this was the treatment of Turkey by the Allies, as finally seen in the Treaty of Sevres. Its territorial provisions envisaged a substantial dismemberment of Turkey, and this was resented by the Indian Muslims. They did not regard it as an attack on Turkey alone but on the entire Muslim world, because the Sultan of Turkey was also the titular head of that world as the Caliph. So the Indian Muslims made common cause with Turkey and gave a demonstration of the solidarity of Islam.

As all Muslims constituted an extra-territorial human community united by a common religion, which was also a complete way of life making no distinction between its secular and religious aspects, the Muslims of India were bound to sympathize with Turkey in her sad predicament. But the *casus federis* which the Indian Muslims made with Turkey went far beyond this, and was the result of the very much more powerful sentiment of Islamic solidarity created by the Pan-Islamic Movement of the late nineteenth and early twentieth century and fostered for his own purpose by Sultan Abdul Hamid II. It had secured a strong hold on the minds of the Indian Muslims by the beginning of this century, and even Czar Nicholas II had warned Britain about its danger through the British ambassador at St Petersburg.

As it happened, I had acquired an antipathy to the Pan-Islamic movement from my boyhood. I regarded it as a danger to Indian unity and to our nationalist movement. On account of this very strong feeling even as a schoolboy I was delighted by the Italian attack on Tripoli in 1911, although even my father called it downright robbery, which indeed it was. I also rejoiced over the victories of Serbia, Bulgaria, and the other Balkan countries in the two Balkan wars, when almost the whole of India was pro-Turk. And when at the end of 1914 Turkey joined the German side I thought that the Muslims would be taught a lesson. I felt the British defeats in the Dardanelles and Mesopotamia as strongly as any Englishman could. And unfair as the Treaty of Sèvres was I was not very much shocked by it.

I shall give some illustrations of the kind of local experience which strengthened my suspicions of the Pan-Islamic feeling in India. When Britain declared war against Turkey in November 1914, a mullah hoisted the Turkish flag in a field near Kishorganj and proclaimed it as the Caliph's territory. He was, of course, promptly arrested. In 1915 I had a trivial but significant experience which would illustrate how insidious the influence of Pan-Islamism was becoming in East Bengal. I was at Kishorganj for a vacation, and by chance I met a Muslim young man. I brought him to our house and had a talk with him. In its course I asked him what fruit he liked best. Without any hesitation he replied: 'Dates from Iraq.' I was not amused by this preference in a Muslim who had certainly not stepped outside even our district, but furiously angry that he should have declared this preference, because I knew where it came from. The remark had its significance, which was not lost on me.

With all these indications of the extra-Indian loyalties of the Indian Muslims I could not but have anything but disapproval for the alliance which the Congress under the leadership of Gandhi had struck up with the Khilafat movement. I regarded it as thoroughly opportunistic, and in the light of what happened afterwards it is impossible to hold any other view of it historically.

I could plainly see that both Gandhi and the Congress had brought about this alliance in order to have the Muslims working with them. It was impossible to assume that they felt very strongly about the unfair treatment of Turkey, and in any case Gandhi knew that the Muslims were no practitioners of non-violence. I also knew that all Hindu political leaders were profoundly suspicious of Pan-Islamism and its influence on Indian Muslims. What made them support the Khilafat movement was their knowledge that at that moment the most active and virulent opposition to the British Government in India came from the Muslims who were in that movement. They wanted to have its power behind themselves. The only thing which was sincere in this Hindu-Muslim entente was the hatred of British rule, shared equally by both the communities. Its effervescence at the time made them overlook the far older and stronger hatred of the Hindu for the Muslim, and of the Muslim for the Hindu, and the danger of confirming the Indian Muslims in their Islamic group-consciousness.

The Muslims of India on their part were induced to co-operate with the Indian National Congress by their temporary hostility to the British. From the very beginnings of the Congress in 1885 they had held aloof from it for fear of losing their Islamic identity. In Bengal they had shown themselves hostile to the anti-partition agitation from 1905 onwards. It was only with the Italian attack on Turkey and the unwillingness of the British Government at home to condemn Italy that they began to be alienated from the British Government in India. This alienation was completed by the Treaty of Sèvres, and the Indian Muslims resented the pro-Greek attitude of Lloyd George. So, two opportunistic policies brought about the collaboration between the Congress and the Khilafat movement in 1921.

This came to an end soon enough with the victories of Mustafa Kemal in 1922 and the Treaty of Lausanne of 1923. By deposing the Sultan and abolishing the Caliphate Kemal destroyed the Pan-Islamic movement, and cut the ground from under the feet of the Indian champions of that Islamic institution. This was to have a profound effect on Muslim politics in India. Deprived of the support, psychological rather than practical, which they had found in the ecumenical order created by Islam, they became anxious about their position in India, felt isolated and therefore weak in relation to the Hindus who formed the majority of the population of India and who considered India as their country and nobody else's. Of couse, the Hindus regarded their group-consciousness as Indian nationalism, and the sense of Islamic identity as disloyalty to that nationalism. But that was not likely to have the slightest effect on the Muslim collective attitude. The Indian Muslims became increasingly convinced that they would not be able to maintain their Muslim identity unless they had some territory of their own; that is to say, after considering themselves to be the members of an extraterritorial society, they wanted to have a territorial base for their life. The immediate effect of the Treaty of Lausanne was a recrudescence of Hindu-Muslim conflicts, in the form of murderous rioting. Some of the worst were seen in 1924.

The cynicism of the temporary alliance between the Hindus and the Muslims was thoroughly and disastrously exposed by the entire history of Hindu-Muslim relations between 1923, when the opportunistic alliance was dissolved, and 1947 when India was divided. By allying itself with the Khilafat movement the Congress had encouraged the most retrograde form of Islamic group-consciousness. Yet from 1923 onwards it disapproved of the very sense of Islamic identity, calling it the 'two-nation theory'. The Congress refused to make any concession to it, when if anything was self-evident in India, that was the separateness of the Hindu and the Muslim societies. No historical argument was too false or too foolish to be trotted out by the Hindus to contest the demand of the Indian Muslims to have their own way of life.

The Hindus and the Muslims drifted further and further apart, and not even Mahatma Gandhi or Jawaharlal Nehru, who were not unsympathetic to the Muslims, could persuade the Congress or the Hindus in general to concede even the legitimate demands of the more moderate Muslims, which would have allayed their fear of being submerged in the Hindu majority. This finally led to the partition of India, the most retrograde and harmful event in the country's long history. Yet the Hindu-Muslim conflict has not been ended by the partition. It is pursuing its baleful course in two forms, one in the domestic sphere and the other in external relations.

In this book I shall describe such Hindu-Muslim conflicts as I saw them at first hand, and also set down the view I took of the whole question at different stages. As is always seen in the case of intractable human conflicts, which from the mere despair created by its real nature, make men unwilling to see it for what it is, there was an immense amount of well-intentioned talking about Hindu-Muslim reconciliation and unity. The obvious truth was trotted out that this would be for the good of both the communities, and, like most obvious truths pitted against passions, it went unheeded. As I listened to the endless lectures I felt sceptical at first, then irritated by the failures, and last of all contemptuous. I came to the conclusion that the more well-intentioned people were, the more prone did they become to utter drivel.

Mahatma Gandhi's Ideas and Methods

Having dealt with the three features of the Non-Co-operation Movement which repelled me originally and whose real significance I discovered later, I shall now offer a general appraisement of his ideas and methods. But I shall first take up a side issue: the Western admiration for Gandhi. This I find to be very strange, not only because it runs against every predisposition of the European mind, but also because it is untenable both intellectually and morally. The European conception of Gandhi is certainly not based on anything Gandhi himself wrote or did. Nothing is more baffling than an attempt to form a precise, coherent, or even intelligible idea of what he really meant, if one goes to his writings. Anything more vague, inconsistent, elusive, or evasive than his own exposition of his ideas cannot be conceived of. The very copiousness of his written and printed output is more a hindrance than help. If his ideas are to be presented as a system, at every point the expositor will have to supply the connecting links, introduce glosses of his own, and perform a feat like putting together a jigsaw puzzle to make a coherent pattern which never existed, and which would really be the picture in the mind of the man who was playing the game. As to his actions and behaviour they puzzled even his followers, so far as they could be rational. And finally, he had no practical achievement, as I shall show when I deal with his death. What is attributed to him politically is pure myth.

The Indians who contribute to this myth have at all events rational motives. It enables them to keep their political hold on a people given to man-worship. He is their holy mascot. But the European and American admirers of Gandhi have no such practical urges: their compulsion is emotional, arising out of all that is weak and passive in the European moral tradition. To be specific, the gospel and apologetics of Gandhism current in the West is the handiwork of the pacifists. For them Gandhi is the last support for the discredited and ineffectual doctrine of pacifism. Pacifistic ideas, so influential in the inter-war years, not only failed to prevent the second World War, but even helped to bring it about by giving moral validity to the cowardly fear of war among the British and the French people which permitted Germany to launch her war of revenge. After being proved to be dangerous ideologues by that war, the pacifists have now fallen back on Gandhi as their last prop, and are arguing that by liberating India from foreign rule by his non-violent methods he has proved that nonviolent methods and ideas are sound. Unfortunately, the British abandonment of India before Gandhi's death has given a spurious and specious plausibility to what is in reality only a coincidence without causal relationship. The pacifists refuse to see that fear of war is the most insidious breeder of wars.

The failure of pacifism is no less blatantly seen in the postwar era. It has been estimated that since 1945 there have been more than forty minor wars fought with what are called conventional weapons, which have resulted in more than a million deaths, and Gandhi's own country has fought a few of them without any political gain but with an egregious exhibition of militarism. Furthermore, almost every country in the world is engaged in war preparations, incurring military expenditure on a scale never before seen in human history. What is even more horrifying, these preparations are for inventing and manufacturing means of destruction and slaughter which no military leader of the past ever recognized to be part of war operations or justified. To give the example of India again: an egregious but senseless militarism has taken possession of the minds of the ruling class in India who are prospering politically on Gandhi. The only achievement of pacifism in our times has been to incite feeble-minded persons to march wildly through city streets or create insanitary conditions in rural areas.

But even more disingenuous than their reliance on Gandhi is the invocation of Christianity by the pacifists. If Christianity could be appealed to in support of pacifism, the Old Testament would not have been regarded as the Word of God by Christians, nor would there have been the Crusades or the Inquisition. I am perfectly aware of the Christian affiliations, such as they are, of pacifism. There is only one scriptural injunction which supports it, and that is: 'Resist not evil. Whoever shall smite thee on the right cheek, turn to him the other also.' No Christian has ever obeyed it, and in any case it is a command to refrain totally from resisting evil and not merely to be non-violent in doing so. It even enjoins going the extra mile. If Gandhi, out of his profession of Christian nonviolence, had acted consistently in South Africa, he should have surrendered without protest to apartheid, and even built ghettoes for his fellow-Indians. And in India he should have submitted to British rule, remembering the saying that 'Blessed are the meek for they shall inherit the earth.' His countrymen have indeed come into that inheritance but without being poor in spirit.

The dominant Christian doctrine about wars was propounded by St Augustine and St Thomas Aquinas. An illusionist pacifism has been advocated only by certain dissident and eccentric sects, and in Britain, above all, by the Quakers. These harmless and well-meaning Sectarians have shown themselves to be, so far as India is concerned, mischief-makers on the one hand, and victims of Indian political sharpers on the other. The pacifists do not say that they would not resist evil, they say that they would not resort to violence in doing so. But they do not say how else evil can be resisted. No pacifist has indicated how assertive evil can be fought except by assertive righteousness. Their stock phrase 'passive resistance' is a contradiction in terms, because all resistance is active. I have come to the conclusion that the doctrine of non-violence, i.e. preaching the abjuration of violence, stands for nothing else than merely *not killing*, with its corollary - not to be killed themselves. That sort of doctrine can only be described as the moral refuge of cowards who want to take credit for resisting evil without taking the consequent risks. But Mahatma Gandhi's non-violence never excluded social and psychological violence whose object was moral coercion.

This was seen even in the so-called Non-Co-operation Movement. To have given that name to the movement was an attempt to hide its real intention and character. As a simple 'non-co-operation movement' it was launched with the object of making those who *co-operated* with the British administration in India refrain from doing so. This, however, would not have made it a mass movement in any way, because those who co-operated with the British did not constitute even one per cent of the population of India. Yet Mahatma Gandhi had every intention to make it a mass movement, that is to say, to rouse the Indian people to revolt against British rule, which, in whatever light he saw it, was bound to be what the French word *émeute* implies, and that on an all-India scale. But the strangest thing was that Mahatma Gandhi would never admit that he intended such an uprising, and in this he was certainly sincere. He never seemed to have understood the implications of his method. I have to point out that even in South Africa his movement of 'passive resistance' led to riots. On 18 November 1913 The Times reported serious riots in Natal. At Ladysmith more than one thousand Indians created serious disturbances, in spite of Gandhi's admonition to be nonviolent, and besides 5000 Indians struck work at Durban. In India the upper classes did not become violent, but neither did they take his preaching of non-violence seriously. They set it down to opportunism, in which they were, of course, grossly unfair. The masses of India became practically violent in executing his non-violent policy.

But in the pursuit of his *idées fixes* Gandhi showed such a disregard of the plainest facts of life that people would rather attribute cunning to him than naiveté of that order. I always heard most Bengalis of my class saying that all of Mahatma Gandhi's non-violence was political ruse, and they rather admired him for the duplicity they attributed to him. Some others explained his unrealistic attitudes to what they described as his 'one-track mind', which was a favourite catchword with all pro-Gandhi intellectuals, the anti- intellectual mind of whose Guru had an exceptional capacity to ignore what he could not accept morally. In reality, Mahatma Gandhi's political ideas and methods were created by his family antecedents, education, and upbringing, and it is these which I have now to describe in brief

He was born and brought up in a backward princely state of India, one of one hundred and ninety-three princely states in Kathiawar, a fractional area of India. His father intended him to follow in his footsteps and become the Diwan or Chief Minister of the State, and sought to give him an education to fit him for the post. It was with this object that he was sent first to Bombay, and then to England at the age of eighteen, already a married man of six years and a father. There he was expected to qualify himself to become a barrister, and he did.

Like the career envisaged for Gandhi, his moral and religious development was also very traditional. The Hinduism in which he was brought up, and quite naturally brought up as a member of the Bania or trading caste, was the popular Hinduism created and preached by the popular prophets of the fifteenth and sixteenth centuries, especially by those of the Vaishnava persuasion, without any affiliation to the higher forms of Hinduism. The religious life of those who belonged to these sects was very simple - it was quietist and, above all, passive in its attitudes. There was nothing in it of the sophistication, complexity, and power of the higher Brahmanic Hinduism. In spite of all that has been said about Gandhi's reverence for the Upanishads or the *Gita*, there was nothing in his religious sentiment which could be traced to those ancient texts. If he had known much of them he could not have made the crude *Ram Dhun*, the intoning of a hymn to Rama, his prayer. The particular form of Hinduism which was Gandhi's could have made him a Puran Bhagat at the end of his life if it had run the course intended for him. But that could never have made him what he became - a Hindu holy man concerned with political and moral evils of a colossal magnitude.

No Hindu religious or moral teaching embodied in any of its scriptures asks a Hindu to fight temporal evils like injustice and oppression. Even the idea of social justice in the European sense is totally absent in Hinduism. This is due in the first instance to the organization of Hindu society in a rigid system of castes, and, secondly, to the doctrine of Karma, which makes the Hindu accept the condition in which he was born. Of course, there was also behind Hindu political thinking, so far as it was developed, the notion of a war of righteousness against unrighteousness, described as Dharma Yuddha. But that was an attempt to make Hindu militarism moral, and no people were more militaristic than the high-caste Hindus. Moreover, war too was fought by the powerful against enemies who also had power but never by the powerless against those who had power. The powerless were not expected to resist anything or anybody at all.

Gandhi's non-violence was conceived in London from Tolstoy's interpretation of the New Testament. Of course, he already had Vaishnava non-violence in him, but that was transformed into a new attitude during his three years' stay in England. At the next stage it acquired its political character in South Africa, where he went to plead a case as a barrister in 1893. There he saw the inhumanity of racial arrogance and racial consciousness made into a political doctrine and erected into a system of apartheid or segregation. Unless he had seen what a White minority was doing to an Indian minority in South Africa he would never have given the Indian nationalist movement the particular character he gave to it. He would not perhaps have begun his campaign against untouchability in Hindu society as well. Brought up as he was in India, he would have ignored that social distinction, because Hindu society was based on the same concept of racial superiority and practised the same apartheid as the South African Whites. It should be pointed out that Gandhi's mother, deeply religious as she was, would not allow him to come in contact with untouchables.

But he got a different view of class segregation and apartheid in South Africa, which was a reversed image of that in Hindu India, because it was applied to Hindus by Europeans. On the one hand, this strengthened the effect of Vaishnava teaching on him, and the teaching was that the Vaishnava God knew neither caste nor caste distinctions. On the other, so far as Gandhi shared the Brahmanic Hindu feeling that the Hindu was superior to all other human beings, he must have thought it obscene that White Europeans, i.e. the despised Mlechchhas or unclean foreigners, should apply to Hindus what only a Hindu had the right to practise against non-Hindus.

It was his South African experience which made Gandhi the kind of political leader and social reformer that he became as soon as he came back to his country in 1914. To begin with, he became a social reformer, with a campaign against untouchability, and then he went to the help of the peasants of Bihar who were being exploited by the White indigo planters. But these beginnings had still a humanitarian complexion, and it was only at the next step in his moral thinking that he sought to extend it to the political sphere in order to fight British rule in India. He looked upon that, too, as a moral campaign because he saw in that rule a replica of the White rule he had seen in South Africa. So he was also led to make his new campaign a replica of what he had done there.

He regarded British rule in India as no less of a moral evil than White rule in South Africa. In this he was mistaken, but he made the mistake through ignorance. He knew very little, if anything at all, about British rule in British India, and its history not probably at all. His first-hand knowledge of British India began really after 1914, when British administration was not what it had been in its best days and the true historical view of the British Empire in India was becoming blurred even among those Indians who were not only living under British rule but were leading a life which was shaped solely by that rule.

Also, Mahatma Gandhi never lived in any of the big cities of India, such as Calcutta, Bombay, or Madras, which were the cradles and centres of modern Indian culture and where alone the cultural results of British rule could be seen and appreciated. He was not interested in modem Indian culture created by the impact of the West, and was even hostile to it. He was wholly ignorant of the views of the greatest modem Indians, Hindu or Muslim, on British rule, who saw that judging British rule was not simply a matter of pronouncing on foreign rule, but one of understanding very complex cultural and social developments, which would not have come about without British rule.

Politically, he saw in India a replica of the South African situation, i.e., a White minority ruling a vast majority of coloured people. He also saw economic exploitation, denial of political rights, as also racial discrimination of the kind he had seen in South Africa. And the discrimination was made worse by the fact that it was enforced against a civilized people and not against primitives. The local British who practised the discrimination blatantly, with utter disregard even of humanity, not of good manners alone, did not have the justification which the Whites in South Africa could put forward with some plausibility - that it was for them a matter of survival with their White identity. And the Whites in South Africa had become as much natives as the Blacks were. They were no more foreign colonists in fact than were the Americans in the United States who had virtually exterminated the original inhabitants. In India the local British were only sojourners, and as such extremely privileged. Yet they abused that privileged position. If therefore it was natural for Mahatma Gandhi to see British rule in India in the light of his experiences in South Africa, he was wrong in completely ignoring its good and regenerating side. But since he did that, it was natural for him to describe British rule as Satanic.

But Gandhi was as mistaken in his prescription and treatment of the disease in India as he was in its diagnosis. There was no similarity between the situations in the two countries, nor could there be any in the methods applied to them. It is strange that he could even think that he could apply the same method to both and it would seem that he was not conscious of the difference at all. Yet even to him that should have been obvious.

In South Africa Gandhi was not objecting to White rule, nor was he asserting the right of native Africans to be masters in their country. He was only protesting against the treatment of an imported minority, whose position in South Africa was as anomalous morally as was that of the Whites, perhaps, subconsciously, he even resented that the Indians in South Africa should be put on the same footing as the African Blacks. He sought to remove a limited injustice, a set of specific rules. He never wanted to do away with European rule. In India he raised that fundamental issue, and there was no question of limiting his activites to resisting particular laws: he wanted to destroy a foreign system of government. The method of passive resistance he had applied to the African situation could not be applied in India without transforming it into a comprehensive rebellion against British rule. And if that was attempted, the whole power of the State in India was bound to be brought into action to resist it. This was done, and the British administration in India suppressed his movements with political power alone and, what was more significant, with the help of Indians on a large scale.

But there was more to it, and that was not less significant. Mahatma Gandhi did not regard his role as political in the true sense. Therefore political logic did not embarrass him. He was incapable of playing a political role unless he thought it was at bottom moral and religious. On this score, there is a general misconception. It is thought that he brought religion into politics in order to raise it to a higher plane. On the contrary, the truth was that Mahatma Gandhi took politics into religion in order to become a new kind of religious prophet. He felt at home only in religion, and throughout his life showed no interest in politics *qua* politics, i.e. when it presented only secular political problems.

It was only when a political situation raised moral issues and faced him with a moral task that he would involve himself in it. Even then it had to present something more than a straightforward moral problem for which a solution could be suggested. It had to face him with a moral evil with such overwhelming temporal power behind it that for all practical purposes it was irremoveable by any kind of rational action, and could be met only by means of passive moral defiance and nothing more. As soon as even a moral evil became amenable to remedies, he lost interest in it. As to problems of government or even good government, no one could be more indifferent. So, after independence, and even from the moment it became a possibility in which he could believe, he took no further interest in Indo-British relations and turned himself to the ineradicable evil that the Hindu-Muslim hatred was, only to become a martyr to his cause.

Thus even in his political role Mahatma Gandhi could only be a man of religion, and since he was a devout Hindu - of a certain kind of course - he became a Hindu holy man, a Sadhu or a Guru with a political cloak. In the homeland of Hinduism he could play a religious role only by becoming a Hindu Sadhu in his manner of living. Thus he founded an *ashram* near Ahmedabad soon after his return to India. However, at that time he showed more concern with the social and moral evils in Indian life, especially untouchability, than with politics. He also imposed the Hindu Sadhu's rule of life on himself and his followers. He had already collected *chelas* or disciples round himself in the Hindu manner.

This in its turn was bound to strengthen in him a trait which he must have developed in South Africa as the leader of a political movement, namely love of power. Politicians are actuated mainly by that. As it happens, this is also one of the strongest traits in the personality of a Hindu Sadhu. It must not be forgotten that the Hindu Sadhu is as much a seeker and lover of power as is a politician, in spite of being a devotee and an ascetic. The devotee's or the quietist's side of Gandhi was derived from Vaishnavism, but his love of power came from the more assertive Brahmanic side of Hinduism. In my book on Hinduism I have explained that Hindu spirituality is a quest for power. Both in his religious life and in his political life Gandhi showed himself to be relentless in seeking power. There was no contradiction between the two aspects of his personality.

This was what successive Viceroys of India failed to perceive. They thought that in many of his political moves Gandhi was going against the moral and religious principles he professed to follow. They attributed the egoistic urge in him to his political side and created an unnecessary dichotomy. For instance. Lord Reading wrote: 'I have always admired him as a social reformer and as an ethical teacher. I have always believed in his sincerity and devotion to high ideals, but I have always doubted the wisdom of his political leadership and felt that personal vanity still played far too important a part in his mental equipment.'

If Lord Reading had come in contact with Hindu holy men he would have seen that what he attributed to Gandhi's worldly or human side belonged equally to his moral and religious side, being only the reverse side of the personality of the Hindu holy man, who was above everything else a lover and seeker of power.

Gandhi was a typical Hindu Sadhu in his entire behaviour: in his ostentatious airing of humility combined with overweaning moral arrogance; in his vagueness and tortuousness; in his skill in weaving a spider's web of unctuous words of platitudinous moralizing; in his readiness to take money as an exercise of spiritual privilege; in his tyrannical urging of an unnatural asceticism on perfectly normal men; and not less in his attitudinizing and theatricality as a means of self-advertisement. All these were comprised within the privileges of a Hindu Sadhu: he could be unworldly without sacrificing egoism. Yet Gandhi's saintliness, in all that the word stands for, was also real. He was a holy man, but of the special Hindu type.

Over and above, he added to the assertive loquacity of the Hindu Sadhu an astonishing facility in writing, which was a European and not Hindu habit. The Hindus are extremely unwilling to commit themselves in writing. They have a saying: *Satam vada, ma likha* - say a hundred things, but never write. But Mahatma Gandhi did not subscribe to that dictum. The articles which he poured out in an unceasing stream in *Young India* and *Harijan* were an exercise in edifying with a figurative bludgeon. They illuminated nothing, not even that verbal obsession of his - Truth. He probably wrote more than a million words on that alone, but after reading all that no one could discover what exactly he meant by Truth. But he himself was never aware of any dishonesty or prevarication.

Finally, there were two sides to his leadership. The first of them created by what he himself was and wanted to do, the second sprang from the way in which his people were ready to accept him as leader. By way of summing up, I might say that Mahatma Gandhi offered himself to the nationalist movement on his own terms, while his people accepted him on theirs. There was no similarity between the two, yet they intermingled throughout from 1920 to 1947. The basic antithesis revealed itself only after independence and destroyed him.

Goal of the Nationalist Movement

I shall now consider the other features of the nationalist movement in India which too emerged at this stage. The goal of the movement was already fixed in the minds of the Indian people and of their leaders, although it was not proclaimed at the time. It was dictated by passion and not rational analysis. In 1923 three spectral hatreds were skulking on the Indian political stage: the hatred of all Hindus for British rule; the same hatred on the part of the Muslims; and the mutual hatred of the Hindus and the Muslims, which was ineradicable.

The Muslim hatred for British rule needs a word of explanation. It was not perceived, or rather it was kept very cleverly suppressed in respect of action from 1923 onwards. The Muslim hatred for the British was very real and venomous, because it was they who had been supplanted in the enjoyment of political power by the British, and the deprivation was also recent. But the Muslim leaders knew that their fight against the British would be carried on by the Hindus, and there was no necessity for them to sacrifice the immediate advantages they could gain by showing apparent friendliness to the British Government and siding with it against the nationalist movement. There was a strong motive for acting as they did. They were thoroughly frightened by the likelihood of an end to British rule, because that was bound to hand over India to the Hindus. So, what they wanted to secure was British support for their claims when they decided to hand over power. The Muslim leaders played this game of *Realpolitik*, which hid their real attitude, with Machiavellian finesse, and got what they wanted.

I could not gauge the real strength of all these hatreds in 1923, nor anticipate what these could do. But I was throughout both dismayed and irritated by the exhibition of the hatreds. It was only in 1947 that I realized what the true position was in 1921.1 saw that it was identical with that in 1947, so far as British rule was concerned. That is, even in 1921 Indian nationalists were not going to be satisfied with anything short of complete political independence, or accept any compromise which in principle allowed a continuation of British rule.

That was why Lord Reading found Gandhi so vague and evasive about the nationalist demand, and unwilling to give a precise definition of Swaraj. Gandhi knew very well what he and his countrymen wanted, but he knew equally well that for him to be explicit about it would put an end at once to all discussion with anybody representing Britain, because any demand for independence was bound to be rejected out of hand. Even the possibility of fixing a definite date for ending British rule in India in any foreseeable future could not be entertained by any British Government or the British people. Thus, in all their political discussions die two sides were at cross-purposes.

However, this situation did not imply that either Gandhi or any other nationalist leader, or for that matter Indian nationalists as a body, thought that they could put an end to British rule and gain independence by their own efforts then or at any calculable time. The strength of Indian nationalism lay in its apocalyptic character, and nothing that prevailed here and now made any difference to the belief that British rule would disappear. This gave the Indian people such comfort that no nationalist leader could disregard it. In 1921 they knew for certain that the time was long past when their people could be emotionally reconciled to a continuance of British rule, whatever they might do for the sake of worldly interests. The leaders not only respected the emotion, they also shared it. On that depended their own position and influence as well as the continuance of the nationalist movement. Of course, they also knew that the British Government in India had the power to suppress any agitation they could mount. Still, they could only say to that Government: *Franges non ftectes* - You will break but never bend us.

Watershed of Indo-British Relations

The emotional impulse to be hostile to British rule was transformed into compulsion by a distrust in the promises of the British Governments, complete loss of faith in the goodwill of the British people, and even greater suspicion of the British bureaucracy in India. By 1920 all these had become ineradicable.

It was the bureaucracy which the Indian people looked upon as their particular enemy. All this distrust and suspicion was shared by the leaders. On this score Mahatma Gandhi did not show any evasiveness, and was very frank. As Lord Reading wrote to his son at the time: 'I asked the question pointblank: what is it in the actions of the Government that makes you pursue the policy of non-cooperation.' The reply, repeated more than once during our interviews, was that he was filled with distrust of the Government, and that all their actions, even though apparently good, made him suspect their motive.'

It was a suspicion which had a long history behind it. It had begun with the Ilbert Bill in Lord Ripon's time, and had been deepened by the conduct of the British civil service in the decades following, especially by the obstinacy of the British officials over the Rowlatt Bill. It was the hatred generated by this conduct which made all Indians resent the speech of Lloyd George in 1922 in which he described the Services as the steel frame of the whole structure of British administration in India. Even the Indian Legislative Assembly censured the speech formally, to the scandalization of Lord Peel, the then Secretary of State for India.

The year 1918 saw the beginning of the final breach between the Indian Civil Service and the Indian people. In that year the Indian nationalists got the impression that the British Government was backing out of the promise to give self-government to Indians made in the Declaration of 1917 (which with the Balfour Declaration of the same year, was one of the two notorious trouble-makers for Britain), because the proposals in the Montagu-Chelmsford Report fell far short of Indian expectations.

To make matters worse, the Rowlatt Report on the revolutionary activities recommended a continuation of the emergency measures for detention without trial in a permanent form, and a bill to that effect was introduced and passed against determined opposition in the Indian Legislature on the part of the nationalist members. The obstinacy showed by the officials over this measure was unjustified by the political conditions, and the spirit shown by the British section of the Indian Press was worse. I remember reading in *The Statesman* of Calcutta the very superior comment that 'the Pandit talked the leg off a donkey', apropos of a very measured speech made by the elder Indian nationalist politician. Pandit Madan Mohan Malaviya (who brought about the meeting between Lord Reading and Mahatma Gandhi).

This led Mahatma Gandhi to launch a campaign of resistance to the measure, and the disproportionate severity with which it was suppressed brought about the final alienation of Indian nationalists from the British administration. The Amritsar episode, in which General Dyer shot down a defenceless and flying crowd and afterwards inflicted humiliations of a barbaric order on the population of the city, must be regarded as the watershed of Indo-British relations. Followed by that stupid soldier's bragging about not only his brutality but what he described as his mercy, by the condonation of his actions by the British House of Lords, and by the gift to the General of a large sum of money raised by the *Morning Post*, convinced all Indians that the whole British people stood behind the inhumanity of Dyer and no fair treatment of India could be expected from them.

That was why Mahatma Gandhi demanded the stopping of the pensions given to Sir Michael O'Dwyer and General Dyer, and why he called British rule Satanic. The whole of India agreed with him. Even I felt like the rest of my countrymen over this episode. And I have never changed my opinion that the Dyer affair was the worst exhibition of the spurious and arrogant imperial sentiment which was created in Britain at the end of the nineteenth century.

The stories which circulated among us Indians about the attitude of the local British heightened the impression of British callousness. They regarded the cashiering of Dyer by the Army Council, which was approved of by the British Government of the day, including two of its members who were better imperialists than the British crowd in India, namely Churchill and F. E. Smith, as a cowardly appeasement of the Indian extremists. I also read contemporary accounts which reported that after the shooting at Amritsar some British officers had said that they heartily enjoyed the shooting down of the sweating niggers. In addition, I read in the reminiscences of Sir Almeric Fitzroy that during the debate on the cashiering of Dyer in the House of Lords, in the course of which Lord Sinha, the Bengali Under-Secretary of State for India, made a very moderate and sensible speech, an obscure peer was heard to say: 'If they are all like him the more they massacre the better.' These sequels to Amritsar did nothing to wipe out its memory. Yet the local British were so stupid that they reassured one another by saying that Indians were forgetting all about the episode and were ready to let bygones be bygones.

On the contrary, the whole Amritsar episode left such memories behind that they coloured even our literary responses. Anatole France was very popular in India even before he got the Nobel Prize in 1921, and after that he became more so. But Amritsar made it impossible to make educated Bengali readers understand one of his most famous stories, namely, the *Procurator of Judaea*. I could not make my friends, who were always very keen on remaining abreast of the latest literary trends in Europe and began to read even Mauriac from 1922, grasp the point of that story. They thought it was a satirization of imperial pride and arrogance in the person of a colonial governor like Sir Michael O'Dwyer, who was the Lieutenant-

Governor of the Punjab at the time of the Amritsar shooting. 'Dyers and O'Dwyers' became a symbolic, anti-imperialistic phrase.

Nothing could make any Indian forget or forgive Amritsar, because it was not clean killing, as the slaughter during the Mutiny, horrible as that had been, was. The intemperate words that were uttered by the peer were not worse in substance than the considered judgement of a majority of the House of Lords, who disapproved of the cashiering of Dyer and declared that his action had saved British rule in the Punjab. Their idea of the danger and their assessment of Dyer's achievement were equally imaginery. Those who in Britain supported this stupid soldier did not realize that their expression of loyalty to a countryman on the principle of my family right or wrong, was disloyalty to the British Empire in India.

In addition, there was a greater handicap. Anything said in the Government's favour, even if it could be put before the Indian people, would not have been believed. The time was long past when they would take even a fair view of British rule in India in its historical aspect. Even down to the beginning of the twentieth century educated Indians could rise above their sense of humiliation at political subjection to admit that British rule had given them what no previous political regime had. Apart from peace and protection from blatant oppression, which it had brought, it had also emancipated their minds, so that they could turn to social and religious reform and cultural creation. They were so changed in outlook that addressing the Bengali graduates of Calcutta University at a convocation in 1864 Sir Henry Maine, the Vice-Chancellor, could say: 'There is not one in this room to whom the life of a hundred years since would not be acute suffering if it could be lived over again.' But by 1920 all this was completely forgotten.

I saw the growth of the incapacity to take an historical view from boyhood. The teachers at schools and colleges taught from the approved text-books. The students took down all that, and reproduced it in their examination papers. But neither side believed one word of what they taught or wrote, and had their private convictions. Even now it is not possible to make Indians believe that good came out of British rule. In 1976 I was giving a lecture at an American University on the significance of British rule in India. After it was over an Indian came up and told me: 'You have not said the most important thing: that India was the wealthiest country in the world before the British came, and was left the poorest by them.'

Hatred had destroyed the capacity of all Indians to see any historical situation for what it really was. In 1921 I did not know that the motive power behind all democratic politics was and could only be hatred. I saw the power of hatred all the time, but was awakened to its mischief gradually.

CHAPTER 4
British Resistance to the Nationalist Movement

But the hatred could make no impression on the edifice of British rule in India so long as it remained structurally sound. Thus it happened that from 1921 the opposition between Indian nationalism and British rule was seen in a long-drawn-out *impasse*, which neither side could break. The nationalist movement, although incapable of rousing the Indian people against British rule except in mere demonstrations, and that too at long intervals, kept up the underground fire. British rule, on the other hand, remained morally weak, although retaining all initiative in respect of action and also remaining capable of suppressing the nationalist agitation.

The British Weakness

The simple truth was that neither the British people nor their political leaders believed in the continuation of their rule in India, and hardly even in its moral validity. The deathwatch beetle was always ticking in its roof Even Warren Hastings assumed that it was bound to disappear, and he did so within twenty years of its commencement. In recommending an English translation of the *Gita* to the East India Company in London he wrote: 'These will survive when the British dominions in India shall have long ceased to exist and when the sources it once yielded of wealth and power are lost to remembrance.'

This assumption found expression even in the casual conversation of practical politicians like Lord Salisbury, who never created political problems in advance, and he was Secretary of State for India twice. In 1901, when he was still Prime Minister, he said to Lady Curzon in regard to her husband's work in India: 'George is having a very great career in India. His frontier policy will keep us in India fifty years longer than we should have kept it otherwise.' He certainly did not realize that the extension of fifty years he spoke of was already in operation.

It was again Baldwin's recognition of the inevitability of having to hand over India to Indians which caused a breach between him and Churchill. By 1930 there was a general agreement among all the English political parties that there should be self-government for Indians, and Baldwin approved of Labour's policy. This made Churchill leave the shadow cabinet, to remain in the wilderness for nine years. Commenting on this Alfred Duff-Cooper wrote in his reminiscences:

'I hated the decision to abandon India [in 1947], but I believe that the decision was wise and could not have been long postponed. It was not the Indian people nor Indian sentiment that made it impossible for the British to remain in India. It was the British people and British sentiment, strongly supported by the sentiment based largely on ignorance, of their American cousins. The idea of an island in Europe governing against their will an Asiatic population ten times more numerous than themselves is not acceptable to the modern mind.'

Furthermore, apart from a small minority which held strong views on this question, largely from threatened self-interest, there was no interest in India among the British people. And such interest as was displayed by simple-minded Britons before Indians was not likely to help the perpetuation of British rule in India. A young relative of mine who was returning to India through London after completing his education in Boston (M I T), was having his shoes blacked near St Paul's. Suddenly, the man looked up and asked him: 'Sir, what do you think of *our* rule in your country?' Poor innocent! He did not know that over the question of Indo-British relations we Indians had no sense of humour. Therefore the young man told me after his arrival in Calcutta, believing me to be some sort of an Anglophile: 'Even their *muchis* [cobblers] think that they are our masters.' Lord Reading noted the apathy after his return from India and wrote: 'People only ask you about India to make conversation. They don't want to be told.' So he kept his knowledge to himself and remained silent about his experiences, with sadness and bitter feeling.

Post-mutiny Failures

Lack of conviction in the perpetuation of British rule resulted, as I see the matter, in two failures on the part of the British administrators. The first of them was the incapacity to create a new social and economic justification for British rule; and the second, reliance on the desperate attachment to material interests which the Indian people always showed with total disregard of patriotism and even morality. Each of these has to be considered.

I have always held the view that after Pax Britannica had lost its appeal by becoming a routine matter, the only way by which the British people could have saved their rule in India was to have made their agents there carry out a drastic revolution - a social and economic revolution, in favour of the Indian masses. This would not only have rallied these masses behind them, but done more - brought about the social and economic eclipse, if not downfall, of the middle-class created by British rule. Since this class was the real support behind the nationalist movement, it would have lost both its credit and its power.

However, both temperamentally and for reasons of policy the British could never do that. For one thing, in India they became even more conservative than at home, because they saw the Liberal principles could only be a dissolvent of British rule. Next, they sincerely thought that by interfering with the social and economic institutions of the Indian people they would jeopardise their empire. The Mutiny had driven that lesson into their minds even more forcefully than before. So, Queen Victoria in her famous proclamation promised that there would be no interference with the religious practises and ancient usages of the Indian people. But to say that was to block for ever the possibility of a social and economic revolution in India under British auspices, although that was more needed than a political revolution.

Sir Walter Lawrence, who served in the Indian Civil Service and was also Private Secretary to Lord Curzon, summed up the position very aptly. He wrote: 'I can understand and appreciate the great men in India [meaning the great British administrators] of the last century who decided that the best policy was the policy of "better not".' But he added: 'If they deliberately decided to regard Religion and Custom as inviolable, it was strange that they should admit the solvent of English education.' This was very true, and it has been my opinion for the last forty years that Queen Victoria's proclamation was the beginning of the end of Britain's imperial role in India.

Apart from that, the British authorities in India always thought that they had to support those who had vested interests or, as they put it, those who had a 'stake' in the country, as against the nationalists, who, they maintained, had none. It was the final argument against the nationalists from 1885 to 1920 to say that they represented nobody in India but themselves and were irresponsible agitators. The British authorities had an absurd regard for an Indian with property or money. I can illustrate this by a story told to me by a friend of mine in the Thirties. He had been summoned as a witness in a case, and naturally his reliability had to be examined. So, the English judge asked him pointblank: 'What are you worth?' My friend replied with a counter-question: 'On the credit or debit side. Sir?' Disregarding this facetious sally, the judge only repeated his question, to which my friend replied: 'All that I can say is that there's a decree for seventy-five thousand rupees or so of the High Court against me, although I have not as yet admitted it.' After that no question was raised about my friend's credibility as a witness.

But in this, the British administrators were not as mistaken as might be thought at first sight. Only, they were keeping their eye on one side of the Indian personality, which alone the Indians who served them showed to them. This was clearly perceived by Alexis de Tocqueville who at one time thought of writing a book on British rule in India. But he gave up the project and left only notes. In one of them was a very true observation about the habit the Indian people had to submit to foreign rule. He wrote: 'L'Inde s'est toujours montrée le pays le mieux preparé pour la conquete et la servitude,' because 'le principal effet de leur civilisation avait été de *les attacher à leur bien-être plus qu'à leur independance.*' Certainly, the British administrators also thought so, and, so far as they could see, rightly. But in regard to that, I shall repeat what I have already said about the British belief in the attachment of the Indian masses to British rule: that they were ignorant about the other side of personality, which was possessed by an unappeasable hatred of foreigners. Even in regard to those Indians who were most ready to succumb to the lure of material interests, this was true. As a matter of fact, these men were more cunning. They did not join the nationalist movement for reasons of worldly interest. They knew that it would be served equally well if the nationalists could drive out the British without there being any need for them to sacrifice their ease and prosperity by joining the movement. Therefore these men, too, put their emotional support behind it, and in the upshot lost nothing by taking care of their prosperity as long as the British remained their rulers.

British Evasion

It was all this which makes an extraordinary and baffling paradox of the fact that no one dared to say a word about leaving India. Every British politician knew this, and so far from making an announcement did not even like to face the question. I give a story, again from Sir Walter Lawrence's reminiscences.

An Indian, whom Lawrence described as a great Indian publicist, used to visit him in Calcutta when he was private secretary to Lord Curzon, although he did so secretly knowing that if the report got about that he went to Government House that would be an end to his influence over his countrymen. He admired Curzon, and one day asked Lawrence to induce the Viceroy to make an announcement that at some date the right of self-government would be given to Indians. He said: 'We do not ask for Home Rule now, nor in ten years, nor in twenty; but all we ask is that he will not shut the door of hope on us. Ask him to say that perhaps in fifty years India may be self-governing.'

Lawrence was so impressed by the man's sincerity and eloquence that he went to Curzon who was in the next room, and told him about this. Curzon thought well of this journalist, and pondered for a long time. Then he said: 'No, I'll say nothing, for it might embarrass my successor if I raised hopes or expressed any opinion as to when self-government will come.' Lawrence remonstrated that since it was bound to come some day, it seemed cruel to close the door of hope. Curzon replied: 'It will not come in my time, and I cannot say what may happen in the future.' Yet the end came in less than fifty years from the date of this conversation, although not during Curzon's lifetime. Sir Walter Lawrence did not give the name of the publicist. But it seems he was Moti Lai Ghose, the famous editor of the *Amrita Bazar Patrika*, with whom he was well acquainted.

The British Community in India

The attitude of the British community in India has to be taken into account as a very important factor in the political relations between India and Britain. Formally, they called themselves 'Europeans', and not the British. For instance, their political organization in Calcutta was called the 'European Association', while the first political organization of Indians in that city was called the British Indian Association. The name showed that the British in India looked upon themselves as a special ethnic group of White men.

Theirs was always an evil influence on Indo-British political and social relations. What I am going to write about them will be unfair to many individuals, and more especially to those who were responsible for governing India at the highest level, who often had to fight the influence of the British residents, and were also attacked by them. The residents once contemplated the kidnapping of one viceroy, and misrepresented others whenever they thought concessions of any kind were going to be made to Indians. Their conduct to all classes of Indians was arrogant to the point of being indecent, and this exhibition came from every section of the British community: officials, soldiers, clergymen, journalists, merchants, industrialists, planters, and, above all, from the womenfolk of all these classes of men, who showed themselves collectively to be vixens. With an infatuated belief in their power, in every case of confrontation with Indians they argued like the wolf in Aesop's fable. They aired their contempt for all classes of Indians blatantly.

From the very beginning they opposed all political concessions to Indians, and this they maintained till the end of British rule. By so doing they could drive all reasonable Indians to despair, but could not intimidate those who were driven by hatred. The local British showed the same incapacity to gauge the power of Indian hatred as their people at home showed later to the power of hatred incarnate in Hitler.

They took up this attitude primarily for their vested interests. But these interests were not the stakes of colonists, that is, of settlers who had adopted India as their country as the British and the Dutch were in South Africa or the French in Algeria. The British in India with very rare exceptions were only sojourners. They were not numerous in the professions. They were numerically strong in the services, both civil and military, in trade and in industry. But strong as was their attachment to material interests, their arrogance and obstinacy did not come primarily from that. These were products of race pride. They demonstrated the truth of Julien Benda's saying that in politics the satisfaction of a pride is more important than the satisfaction of an interest. And this pride they paraded with total disregard of justice and humanity.

In cases of material injury Indians could at times secure justice against the British in law courts, but in the case of murder never. In the first place the white murderers were screened and the evidence suppressed. The general British attitude in this matter was known to Lord Curzon and he refused to submit to it. As he wrote to the Secretary of State for India; 'I will not be a party...to the theory that a white man may kick or batter a black man to death with impunity because he is only "a d-d nigger".' But it was Lord Curzon who was humiliated for his attitude by a British rabble at the Delhi durbar of 1902.

So at the next stage, when cases of murder went to the courts, the British jury always aquitted their countrymen on the ground of insufficient evidence. In my young days an English planter was tried for the murder of the husband of a coolie woman, whom he was trying to seduce. My brother was present during the trial in Calcutta. The entire British press in Calcutta took up the cause of this man as a victim of racial persecution! The man was acquitted.

What they regarded as the principle behind their conduct was the trite dictum of pseudo-morality: My family right or wrong, and in being loyal to their countrymen in India they never considered how disloyal they were being to their country. To make no bones about it, in their general behaviour the British community in India taken as a whole showed moral and intellectual bankruptcy equally. They practised a racial discrimination against us which makes their current denunciation of apartheid in South Africa a bizarre exhibition of hypocrisy.

The Whites in India lived in quarters in the big cities to which it was very difficult for Indians to gain admittance. For all practical purposes there was complete racial segregation. The clubs and other social institutions were reserved for the Whites. The railway carriages were marked 'Europeans' in the lower classes, and if Indians entered first-class carriages they were either not allowed to go in by the White passengers or thrown out. Even the most eminent Indians were. The public conveniences were marked 'European', and 'Natives' (afterwards 'Indians'). I have also heard that Indian Christians were not allowed to sit in the coolest places under the fans in the Anglican churches.

I never tried to go to any place from where we were excluded, even for the sake of protest. I knew that instead of being acclaimed as a hero like Gandhi in South Africa, I would simply be insulted and manhandled. South African apartheid at least gave us the glory of becoming martyrs, the apartheid practised by the British in India only allowed us to nurse the grievance of being kicked in our own country. Even so, twice in my life I had to find what the British apartheid in India was like.

The first occasion was in 1925 - that is, after the beginning of the Gandhian phase of the nationalist movement, which had made those who were running the British administration in India despair about its future, but had made no difference to the attitude of the British community to us. In that year I went to the famous seaside resort of Puri on the Bay of Bengal, which was also a famous place of pilgrimage for all Hindus. At one end of the town, away from the Indian side, there was a hotel run by the Bengal Nagpur Railway, reserved for Whites. It was situated on high ground about three hundred yards from the beach.

One afternoon I was walking along that part of the beach, at a distance of about fifty feet from die edge of the water. About a hundred feet farther out a dozen White women were bathing in the surf. It should be kept in mind that in those days swimming costumes were not what they are today. Nonetheless, a policeman was standing there to protect the modesty of these White women from our gaze. This man came up to me and said that when Mem Sahibs were bathing no Indian was allowed to walk on the beaches and be within observable distance. So I must go up to the road above. Of course, I had to.

Nowadays, living in England, I relate this story with immense glee to the champions of racial equality and denouncers of South Africa, and rub in the moral by saying: 'What parts of an Englishwoman's body can I not see today without spending even five pence?' In actual fact, being a Victorian, I have often to shut my eyes out of modesty when looking out of a window.

The second incident took place in Calcutta itself in 1928. From 1909, when I first came to live in Calcutta, to about 1930, after which I ceased to go to the Eden Gardens there, I always saw the big lawn before the bandstand divided into two halves by ropes tied to the lamp-posts. We Indians had to sit on the side away from the bandstand, and only Whites would sit on the other side. Policemen stood at intervals to enforce the segregation. But my discomfiture did not arise from any attempt to defy this apartheid. It came from a situation which even at that time would have been considered impossible.

In the afternoon, when there was not a soul in the Eden Gardens, I was walking from the High Court side towards Outram Ghat along the pavement of Strand Road which skirted the Gardens, being separated from the lawn of the bandstand by a low balustraded wall. When I was almost opposite the bandstand on the pavement, an Indian policeman came up and ordered me to go over to the pavement on the other side, because, as he told me, no *desi admi* (native man) could walk on that pavement. I thought the man was officious, and seeing a British sergeant with a revolver hanging from his belt nearby, I went up and asked him if there was actually any such order. He replied that there was. And the end of the British Empire in India was not even twenty years away!

When I tell these stories in England today and anti-racialists reply 'We are not the same people,' I answer 'Of course, you are not. You have not got die power to be different. But if you had, would you be different?' When listening to such protestations I cannot but recall the maxim of La Rochefoucauld which I read when I was young: 'When vices leave us, we flatter ourselves that we have left them.' I may add that I have never believed in the chastity of impotent men.

The BBC's Record

I shall show that even when the end of the Indian Empire was near there was no disposition in the organization which is most vociferously anti-racialist in Britain today, to show even decency to us. It was the B B C, which in these days brings in coloured persons in its TV features even when there is no obvious reason to do so.

I am speaking of incidents in Broadcasting House, New Delhi, which is the headquarters of AIR, the broadcasting organization of the Government of India. I was then on its news broadcasting staff, and the date was either the end of 1944 or beginning of 1945, I am not sure. Some units of the B B C were housed in the same building, and their personnel was constituted by a crowd of British men and women, in educational or journalistic occupations in the Far East, who had run like hares before the Japanese and taken refuge in New Delhi. But, when there, they were trying to show us that the British spirit was as high as ever.

As a senior member of the AIR staff, I had my room in the main building, but my colleagues who broadcast news in the Indian languages and for whom I wrote commentaries on the war, worked in the hutments behind. As it happened, one BBC unit was also there. For more than two weeks I heard grumblings among my colleagues about the BBC, and one day I asked what it was about. They said that these men had scribbled a very insulting inscription in their lavatory, and I had better go and see it. I went and read it. It was as follows:

'Indians cannot use such lavatories. They roost like hens, and they should go to the peons' lavatory.'

I at once wrote a note to the Administrative Officer to have that inscription erased, or, I threatened, I would report the matter to the highest authorities. It was, and I told my colleagues that there was no virtue in nursing or enjoying grievances.

At about the same time my unit, which had to write the commentaries, was transferred from its old room to the circular gallery in one of the towers. As their furniture was being moved, one of my juniors came running to me to say that the Englishman of the B B C who was in charge of the German unit which worked in the same room, had told him that if he and the other Indians were to be in that gallery at all they should be out of his sight beyond the curve. Actually, when I went up I found that one of the tables had been removed to that end. I asked the Englishman, who was at least six feet tall and I a mere five-foot pigmy: 'Did you say?' -I repeated what I had heard. He replied: 'Supposing I did.' I rejoined: 'Then I would say that we are here in our own right, and not by your leave. If anybody has to be out of sight it will have to be you.' He then said: 'I was only joking.' I replied: 'Yes, that's exactly like you Englishmen. When you find that somebody can stand up to you, you try to back out by saying you were joking.' Perhaps I shouted rather loudly. An anti-Nazi German who was working in that B B C unit at once got up and brought back the table. Henceforth the man said 'Good Morning' to me whenever he met me in the corridors.

Self-respecting Indians: Tagore and Others

When the collective inter-racial situation was such, it could not be expected that there would be satisfactory personal relations between Indians and the British residents. Nonetheless, a large number of Indians taken individually tried to hobnob with the local British, either for the sake of worldly interest or merely from the habit of servility. When a British individual was particularly decent he would respond to such advances with frigid politeness, and unless the Indian presumed too much would not be rude. But the more common practice was to put the Indian in his place, and that not too gently.

Therefore all Indians with any personal or national self-respect never tried to cultivate Englishmen. And the man who had an unconquerable revulsion from it was the great Indian poet and writer Tagore, who won the Nobel Prize for literature by writing in English. I shall quote from one of his letters written in 1893. It should be mentioned that besides being one of the leading Bengali writers Tagore was also the son of one of the wealthiest landowners of Calcutta, and the father was a noted religious leader. Tagore was also the younger brother of the first Indian to get into the Indian Civil Service, S. N. Tagore. Furthermore, his grandfather, when in Paris, had entertained King Louis-Philippe with his Queen at his hotel. Tagore was at Cuttak in Orissa, visiting a relative, who had invited the local British notabilities to dinner. In a letter to his niece (dated 10 February 1893) Tagore wrote:

'It is the lamenter who stumbles into a ditch. As it is, I cannot stand Anglo-Indians [in the old sense of "British residents"], and so it happened that at a dinner last night there was a particularly striking exhibition of their churlish nature. The principal of the college here [it was the Government College, Cuttak, and the principals of all government colleges at the time were always Englishmen from Oxford or Cambridge and in the Indian Educational Service] is an egregious Englishman - clean-shaved, with an enormous nose, cunning eyes, a yard-long chin, deep voice, r-less drawled articulation - altogether a full-blown John Bull. He had a lusty go at our people ... The fellow gratuitously raised the topic [of trial by jury] and went on arguing with Mr B—, saying that the moral standard of the people of this country was low, they have not got sufficient faith in the sacredness of life to be fit to be jurors. I cannot tell you how I felt.. .Just imagine! With what eyes do they see us when they can speak like this after being invited to dinner at the house of a Bengali and in the company of Bengalis."

But Tagore's greatest anger was directed against those Indians who wanted to curry favour with Englishmen. He expressed his contempt for them in the Same letter. He wrote:

'The Sahibs openly spurn us, they kick us a thousand times. Yet these pertinacious flunkeys will never detach their feet from English thresholds. When they are not allowed to go into any place with their shoes on [this was enforced on Indians in certain public places and there was a notorious case in which a great Bengali scholar and social reformer who was also welcomed as a visitor in the house of the Lieutenant-Governor of Bengal, was asked to put off his shoes when he went to see the Indian Museum and came away] they take them off; when they are not allowed to go in holding their head high they go in salaaming; they enter the railway coaches our countrymen are forbidden to enter under the disguise of Europeans. They [the British] do not want us to go into their company, join their amusements, meddle in their affairs, and yet we make every effort, create any pretext, resort to any flattery, agree with any vilification of our countrymen, and swallow every insult to our country, so that we might, by any means obtain salvation by coming into a grazing contact with them. I do not want to pose as such an exception - if you have no respect for my people, I will not seek to be your protege with an affectation of being cultured.' (Translated from the Bengali)

There was much more in that vein but what I have quoted should be enough to illustrate the attitude of Indians with any sense of self-respect towards having personal relations with Englishmen in India. We were not ready to give the benefit of the doubt to an individual Englishman because we could never be sure in advance what his conduct would be.

That, however, was not the height or depth of the indecency of the British behaviour in India. They had to be more unpleasant, and showed that by developing a peculiar kind of cowardice on account of their bad conscience. They tried to justify their conduct by developing a myth that the Indian people would rise in a mass and slaughter them to a man. This was instilled in them after the Mutiny, and even in the unchallenged days of British rule they trotted out this fear and frightened their children with it. And when the nationalist movement created some risk for them, they squealed. I shall have something to say about this also later.

Such was the conduct of the local British towards us. But my opinion about them has never made any difference to my historical judgement on British rule, and, as I shall also relate, I had to pay a heavy price for setting that down.

Epilogue to British Indian History

The British personages who between 1921 and 1947 were responsible for the Indian Empire at the highest level were thus caught between two extremes: one presented by the Indian nationalists, and the other by the local British community.

Indian nationalism could not bring down British rule in India, nor did it perform that feat in 1947, but it created an apocalyptic faith in its ultimate victory, and this fanatical confidence made Indian nationalists unappeasable, and therefore unwilling to accept any halfway compromise, all the more so because the British authorities whether at home or in India could not reject die demand for political independence in principle.

On the other hand, the British opponents of Indian nationalism had behind them not only a majority of the members of the civil and military services, but also very powerful supporters in some politicians in Britain, who could always rouse the passions of an ignorant public. No government in Britain was ready to face that clamour.

So, what every government in Britain did was to put off the final solution as long as possible, only giving what could not be withheld, and that too they conceded too late. This tergiversation was accompanied by a continuous flow of arguments, some of which were valid then and remained valid even in 1947, and others specious, against not only the nationalist demands but even the nationalist movement. Indian nationalist leaders on their part could not agree to a compromise even when they did not share the extremism of their people.

Thus the last twenty-five years of British rule in India were a period of stalemate in substance, although broken by two superficial activities. The first of these was the nationalist agitation revived cyclically, and the second was a bout of talking recurring cyclically in the same manner This latter activity was seen in the summoning of conferences, creation of commissions, and sending of missions, whose purpose was to arrive at an agreed solution, but which achieved nothing. The strangest part of this activity was that the failure of each of these sessions of 'dialogue', as they would be called today, only inspired more desire for the same kind of 'dialogue', just as miscarriages produce immediate pregnancies. At last the British will to keep India collapsed, and what was bound to happen happened.

It was after independence that I became fully aware of the futility of all the political moves between 1921 and 1947, and since then I have firmly held the view that the best date for transferring power to Indians, as was done in 1947, was 1921. If that could not be done outright, even the fixing of a final date then and adoption of a plan of concessions in stages would have spared India the calamities which followed the inevitable transfer in 1947.1 would add that a good opportunity came in 1935. If in that year a decisive step had been taken, instead of passing the Government of India Act of 1935, which demoralized the British administration in India without satisfying the nationalists, that would have been a second-best. That opportunity was missed.

I know what the answer to this contention of mine would be - that to do in 1921 or 1935 what was done in 1947 was impossible in view of British public opinion. That I would not dispute, but that would only justify the moral which I wish to draw in this book that neither human intelligence nor human free will matters in shaping the movements of history. If a political cataclysm that the abandonment of India by Britain was, could not be foreseen and provided for even twenty-five years in advance, it is utter vanity to speak about these two faculties in man. The same public opinion not only accepted what was done in 1947, but also applauded that as an act of statesmanship.

That is why ever since I have become capable of thinking I have despised public opinion. I have realized that it follows events and cannot influence them, and, besides, shifts with a blind fickleness which is terrifying to watch. By showing fear of this kind of public opinion the Conservatives of Great Britain brought about the second world war as well as the abandonment of India. They are the real destroyers of the greatness of Britain.

But these years which the locusts ate up, have been spared by white ants. All the futile discussions between 1921 and 1947 have left behind them an immense accumulation of papers, which are worthless in themselves but are serving a humanitarian purpose. They are enabling academics or aspirants after academic preferment to produce theses, articles, and even books in order to provide themselves with jobs. The papers constitute the foundations on which the academic factories known as Centres of South Asian History in Britain and America stand. The activity certainly has a long future before it, for one generation of researchers do not destroy the papers they live on as do white ants. They will remain useful to successive generations of them. Otherwise, this colossal pile of papers would only have been a monument of human stupidity made of paper-pulp.

No commitment regarding the date of ending British rule was made before 1942, when largely due to pressure from President Roosevelt, Sir Stafford Cripps went to India to declare that India would get Dominion Status after the war. He was not believed. Even in 1946, when everything showed that British rule in India was going to be wound up, the people of India were not sure. And when it ended the next year, Indian nationalists thought that their exertions had brought that about and, so far as they gave any credit to their British rulers, it was only for surrendering in time instead of deciding to die in the last ditch. Hindus do not kill their enemies, they prefer to inflict moral degradation. They have succeeded in inflicting enough of that on their former rulers.

The unwillingness of the British authorities, whether at home or in India, to announce even a provisional date for transferring power to Indians was due in part to doubts about the capacity of Indians to govern their country and to a residual loyalty to the imperial ideal of protecting the Indian people from anarchy. Both the doubt and the sense of duty were sincere. And in the light of what has happened since India became independent, it cannot be said that the scruples were unjustified.

'I myself lost all faith in our political leaders even before the Act of 1935. But the doubts had become irrelevant by 1921, because no British Government was prepared to continue British rule in India indefinitely and take the drastic measures necessary to enforce that policy. Therefore the British authorities should have disinterested themselves about the consequences that would follow from a withdrawal from India. After all, their well-founded scruples did not prevent the capitulation of 1947.

I feel that the doubts would not by themselves have prevented a specific declaration. What really stood in the way was the pride of possession, racial arrogance, and vested interests of the British community in India and their spokesmen in England, who could always raise a clamour and rouse popular opposition. No British politician was willing to face that.

BOOK II

TOWARDS A VOCATION

1922-1925

Prefatory Note

The suspension of the Non-Co-operation Movement put an end to the tension in my mind which had lasted a whole year. I thought I would now have repose of mind. I did not know then to what extent the recovery of tranquillity of mind was to make me aware of the dullness of my work in the Military Accounts Department, and how that awareness was to lead me to take the decision to leave the Department as soon as possible. I finally left it, and with that I left behind for the rest of my life not only affluence and ease but also the minimum degree of worldly security.

In the chapters which follow I shall relate the first part of this personal story, which I am describing as groping towards a vocation. The groping was not due to any weakness or doubt in my sense of vocation, but to my weakness of will in trying to realize my vocation. The result was that, instead of marching towards the vocation, I only toddled towards it. The decision was both intellectually and morally right, but I did not execute it with the required energy. Thus it was only by drifting that I at last landed on my vocation. The story will not reflect any credit on me.

CHAPTER I

Ennui, Renovation, Ennui

I have now to begin the story. At the beginning of 1922 my prospects were bright. By the time the Non-Co-operation Movement ceased suddenly, and made me capable of considering my future critically, I was given the opportunity to improve the position in the Department by being recommended for an examination for promotion to the next higher cadre, after passing which I could double my salary. I was too young and inexperienced and too junior to attempt the examination and certainly if I had considered the matter carefully I would not have agreed to take that examination at that stage. But my cousin and my superior, his friend, had confidence in me and wanted to push me forward. I did not like to disappoint them and I felt that I owed it to their kindness to do my best to justify that. So, my immediate preoccupation was to prepare for that examination by mastering the regulations which bore on the work of the Department. These were just ad hoc and arid. Only the Army Regulations, both British and Indian, had some intrinsic interest because they were concerned with military organization. The examination was to be in July, and it was March. In the meanwhile, a new domestic situation had arisen for me.

Meeting the Scholar Gipsy

From the end of 1919 we had been living in a house in northern Calcutta, and since taking up work I was living with my brother, the advocate, his wife, also a sister of mine, and the brother next to me, who was a medical student, constituting five in all. My sister-in-law had appeared at the Matriculation examination, and the long vacations for my sister and student brother were approaching. So it was decided that they would go to Kishorganj, and my elder brother, the advocate, was also to follow. He was not making any progress in his practice in the High Court, and it was contemplated that he would go and practise at the district court at Mymensingh. Thus the establishment was wound up, and all of them went away. I went to live in a commercial boarding house.

I was quite used to living in hostels or boarding houses. But the boarding house to which I went was of a different kind. The lodgers were all low-paid office workers, of different social origins and affiliations, and altogether a very mixed lot. I did not even get a room to myself, but had to share it with another man. Those who lived in the same room - and at times even four people did so - were called 'room-mates' in English. During the first fortnight I did not see my room-mate at all, and considered myself very fortunate. My good fortune was due to the fact that the man, as I learned afterwards, was a very debauched person and spent his nights in various brothels. But those who stayed put were no better, as I could judge from conversations at night between the room-mates who lived in the next room. Actually, that room was part of the same room, divided from mine by a wooden partition.

I went to bed early, but was awakened one night by their giggles, and repeated exclamations: 'Hush, hush, speak low - the man in the next room is a bachelor.' I did not catch their words, but I could form an idea of their conversation from what I was often forced to overhear in the office among the clerks. One thing which distinguished virtuous 'white-collar' workers from the frankly and unashamedly licentious was their habit of dwelling on the physical details of their relations with their wives. The rakes had enough variety of experience to be free from the compulsion of rescuing their sexual life from insipidity by evoking crude sensations and images. The party in the next room was clearly discussing the experiences they had with their absent wives. One evening I felt so provoked that I took a very unusual but effectual sort of revenge. I opened one of the volumes of the history of contemporary France edited by Lavisse which I had just bought, and began to read out the French text loudly. At once the hum of conversation stopped, and one voice asked: 'What is that language." I replied, 'French', and there was an awed silence, in the course of which I fell asleep.

But very soon I was driven out of the boarding house by the rake who was my room-mate. The night was very hot, and I was sleeping on a mat near the open door to get a little breeze. All of a sudden I was awakened by feeling a man treading on me. He was the absent room-mate who had come to his room at last, but in a very drunken state. When he found what he had done, he was profusely apologetic. Drunkards on the borderline are always polite. After that he went to his bed and slept. I resolved to leave the boarding house the next day.

I did, and went to stay in the house of my uncle, who with his family had gone away for the summer to his village, leaving the house in our charge. There were no arrangements for meals in that house. But I took them in a hotel, and afterwards made arrangements in the next house as a paying guest for meals only.

From the beginning of May I was given leave for two months to prepare for my examination. But instead of reading the Regulations and manuals of book-keeping, I read literature, and had my 'enlightenment' or 'conversion'. I do not know how it happened that although I had read a good deal of Matthew Arnold's prose, including even *Culture and Anarchy*, I had never read any of his poems. I read these then, and, above all, I read 'The Scholar Gipsy'. The poem clinched the matter for me.

As I Read

> Thou hast not lived, why should'st thou perish so?
> Thou hadst *one* aim, *one* business, *one* desire;
> Else wert thou long since number'd with the dead!
> Else hadst thou spent, like other men, thy fire!

I realized in a flash that I was giving up, not only my vocation, but even my life. One futility from which my mind has always recoiled is to sacrifice life for livelihood. I read on:

> For early didst thou leave the world, with powers
> Fresh, undiverted to the world without,
> Firm to their mark, not spent on other things;
> Free from the sick fatigue, the languid doubt,
> Which much to have tried, in much been baffled, brings.

I felt I should be condemned to a living death if I remained in the Military Accounts Department for the sake of worldly security. I always felt the urge within me to write and project myself. That could not be satisfied by doing one thing for livelihood, and doing something else by way of vocation. To me living and the means to live had to be fused to form one whole. At that time the life I had in mind was one dedicated to pure scholarship. So I decided at once to leave the Military Accounts as soon as my younger brother, the medical student who was living with me, would have completed his education, which was to be in 1926.

In the meanwhile, I gave up the idea of appearing at the departmental examination. The immediate compulsion was not so much the larger idea as the unpreparedness for the examination. I did not like to risk a failure in such an examination. But I also thought that if I passed it and got my promotion to the higher grade my family would not allow me to leave the Department, and also feared that I myself might get attached to the immediate money and future prospects and be tempted to sacrifice the higher aims of life I cherished. So I did not sit for the examination, which very much disappointed my well-wishers in the office, and angered my father.

Anyway, the decision to leave the Military Accounts was irrevocable, and I had no intention whatever of trying again for the examination. In July 1922 I took up residence in what was called a 'mess' amongst us, which was a hostel run co-operatively by the boarders. The house was at 41 Mirzapore Street, to be made memorable by a great Bengali writer, whom I brought there. We were about thirty in number, and some of the inmates I had known since my college days. One or two were even literary men, although not professionals. My brother lived with me, and we had one room to ourselves. According to our standards I was comfortable in this hostel, and lived in it for nearly two years.

New Interests

In the first part of my autobiography, which covered my life only to the end of my student days, I gave what might be regarded as a peep in a crystal ball into my later life, summing up its character as a series of moultings in which I shed the feathers that were becoming worn and shabby and grew a new set of them. But the earlier of these moultings gave me only immature plumage, and I do not think that I began to acquire my adult plumage until after the publication of the autobiography in 1951, when I was nearly fifty- four and had only one year of working life before me. Thus, at the end of this book, which will carry the story to 1952, the reader will find me still in a sorry state of brown eclipse, as they say of ducks. At this point I am going to describe my first moulting after entering the world. I might add that I entered it in very low spirits.

The slight revival of spirit which had been brought about by securing employment was coming to an end with disillusionment, and I should certainly have fallen completely into the same dejection as I had after my academic failure if I had not begun to take some mental tonics even before the appearance of my dissatisfaction with the Military Accounts Department. These were provided by my recreational reading at this period.

I have already mentioned what effect 'The Scholar Gipsy' produced on me. It stirred me to take a decision which from the worldly point of view proved to be very troublesome. But the vision it gave me of the pursuit of an ideal filled me with an inextinguishable longing not devoid of resolution, although that was fitful. I also read other things which had a nostalgically disturbing effect on me, but these also left behind a mood of happy sadness. One of these experiences came from reading the address on *Recreation* which Lord Grey of Fallodon delivered at Harvard, and which I bought in its pamphlet form before it was incorporated in his *Fallodon Papers*. It gave the same kind of peace of mind as I had found in reading White's *Selborne*, to which Lord Grey too referred in his essay. The account it gave of his duck ponds and of his excursion with President Theodore Roosevelt in the New Forest in order to satisfy the President's desire to hear English bird songs, showed to me that I had no reason to lament what politics had made of man by making him depart from Nature's Holy Plan.

Lord Grey remarked that it was certainly not without significance that a British Foreign Secretary (dealing with the growing Anglo-German antagonism) and a President of the United States (occupied with not less serious matters) could go in quest of bird song and be lost to the world for a day or two, and even meet adventure by having to wade through a stream quite unexpectedly in spate. The stream's behaviour Lord Grey regarded as its response to the spirit of adventure in the President. Moreover, Lord Grey's idea of what was not a very large space delighted me. He said that it was really not necessary to have very large spaces to keep wild ducks. His three duck ponds did not cover more than seven acres in all. I certainly thought that this was quite the minimum *Lebensraum* needed not only by ducks but by any civilized individual.

A wholly different kind of illumination came to me at the same time from a wholly different kind of book. It was Margot Asquith's autobiography, which I borrowed from the Imperial Library. I read it sitting on the lawn of the Curzon Park in front of our office, of course playing the truant from it like a schoolboy. I have read that Mrs Asquith was regarded as a madcap, and her husband's colleagues thought that she would ruin his career. But as I was hardly less mad, although in a different way, I immensely enjoyed the book. It described life as a romp. What I got from it was an idea of the sophistication of high life, which had a great fascination for me. In this case, the sophistication might be called 'manneristic' or 'rococo' in the psychological order, and Mrs Asquith might be regarded as its Caravaggio. Yet this woman at the end of her life had to recall Dante's words: *Nessun maggior dolore...*

A counterpoise to the reading of this book was provided by Vallery-Radot's life of Louis Pasteur. I had just before read an essay by Lord Haldane entitled 'The Dedicated Life', and here was the perfect dedicated life. Suddenly, a cloud of sadness descended on my mind at the thought that I had lost my chance of leading that kind of life, but it also freed me from my small discontents.

However, at this stage my mental recovery came very largely from the intellectual enterprise of my elder brother, the advocate. From as long as I could remember we had been living a common life. We were, so to speak, mental twins. Whatever he did I took up, following his lead in everything. For instance, as soon as he began learning French I also did. Trying in this manner to keep up with him, I was always two years in advance of my mental age when I was a boy. For this I was set down as a forward child in the bad sense by our conventional elders, but there were others who had more insight and spoiled me. I often startled them with my precocity.

There was, however, a significant difference between my brother and me. He never persisted in anything that he took up, except in always reading everything unconnected with his profession, sitting under an electric fan. If I were to liken him to a character of fiction I would say that he resembled Mr Bennett of *Pride and Prejudice*. He has always shown the same placid wisdom about life, tinctured with irony which has always been free from malice, and he has always enjoyed the exhibitions of foolishness given by fellow men.

I, in contrast, never lost sight of any prey I wanted to hunt down. I often showed an indolence which was worse than my brother's, but it came from physical weakness, and was not natural laziness. If an impulse took hold of me I was capable of feats of exertion like the sprints of a cheetah. It is this, and never any steady application, which has brought me as far as I have come.

My brother's influence began to work on me as soon as he came back to Calcutta in November 1922. The idea of going to Mymensingh to practise was given up, and he came back to Calcutta and resumed his attendance at the High Court. In the meanwhile, there had been a calamity in our family.

My mother had a serious stroke, and was paralysed in half of her body. She must have had very high blood pressure, but it was not detected. My brother was present at Kishorganj when the attack took place. When I went to see her in October, my brother told me about it and of how shocked he was by the convulsions he had to see. I was very much horrified, and equally distressed when I found that she could not even sit up in her bed nor speak distinctly. She remained bedridden for the rest of her life, which was only a year and a half.

When it seemed that her condition would neither improve nor worsen my brother came away to Calcutta leaving his wife at Kishorganj to look after our mother. He went to the High Court daily, but his interests were different. He took two rooms in my uncle's house and boarded with his family. Free from the bother of housekeeping, he began to attend what are called cultural events. To begin with; he took me to the exhibition of paintings of the new Bengali school headed by Abanindra Nath Tagore in the galleries of the Society of Oriental Art. I had never before seen original works of this school, and what I saw in that year's exhibition made a tremendous impression on me.

One incident was both comical and significant, and it happened when my brother wanted to buy some of the prints which were on sale. Modem Indian painters and their salesmen have a curious weakness, which persists till today. They cringe to any White customer or patron, but show an outrageous snobbery to fellow-Indians. So, as soon as my brother asked for the prints, the salesman looked haughtily at him and said: 'They are five rupees [about 7/6] each.' He obviously expected us to decamp, but was absolutely struck of a heap when my brother replied 'That's all right', and selecting fourteen prints paid down seventy rupees in cash. The salesman must have told the story to others, and whenever afterwards we went to the gallery the artists looked at us with curiosity, and we were always treated with the greatest courtesy. After that my brother bought two rather expensive books on two modem Bengali painters, which further improved our status.

At this stage I was very unenterprising in my intellectual quests, and could not take any initiative to strike out in a new line. Soon my brother helped me in one of these. He told me that he had seen two very fine books on Chinese and Japanese painting in the Imperial Library, and they were in a series with the tide *Ars Asiatica*, published by Van Ooest. I at once went and had a look at the books, and was entranced by the plates which illustrated flower pieces of the Sung period. This was the beginning of my interest in Far Eastern painting. We bought the book on Far Eastern painting by Lawrence Binyon, and my brother showed an even greater enterprise by subscribing to the famous Japanese art magazine *Kokka*. Beginning with the rather easily accessible schools I was able to go back-to the Tang age, and even bought reproductions of the roll of Kukaichi.

But our real intellectual adventure at this time was Westward. My brother paid a subscription to a Calcutta newsagent for the *Nation and Athenaeum*, then edited by Massingham, and he followed it by subscribing to the *Times Literary Supplement*. These opened up new intellectual horizons for me. I already knew a good deal of European thought at the higher and more rarefied levels, but was more or less ignorant of contemporary trends. For the first time I could follow both political events and literary activity in England from week to week.

Now, when I am a very old man, the mere turning of a page of the *New Statesman* produces anaesthesia in me, although I have recently contributed reviews to it. But at that time both the *Nation and Athenaeum* and the *T.L.S.* gave us thrills. The discussions I read and the ideas I found in these journals produced an effect on me which could be compared to re-potting an aetiolated house plant or the oxygenation of anaemic goldfish in a small tank. I was stirred to a new mental life.

I can give a good reason for all this excitement. The intense mental activity which had been produced in Bengal by the first impact of European culture on us and had given rise to wholly new currents of thought on politics, social life, religion, and culture, had reached its point of exhaustion, and whatever ideas were still being discussed were only a rechauffé of the old ones. In contrast, in those years even in war-ravaged Europe there was a revival of mental life, following the check given by the war. The stunned state of mind produced by trench warfare by itself led those who could think and feel to re-examine and re-assess life, and I do not think that the talk about a Brave New World was a mere pose or fashion. I would say that men did feel that European life and culture had to be rebuilt like the cathedral of Rheims. The later disillusionment about this should not lead one to undervalue its initial fervour. Even the tedium of trench warfare was not presented as a state of stupor or squalor, but was transfigured in a book like C. E. Montague's *Disenchantment*, which I read with great admiration.

The *Nation* soon after changed hands and passed to the Bloomsbury Group. I had still a long way to go before I lost my respect for the men who formed it. I admired the cleverness of all these writers, because I had within myself something of the spirit of the Bloomsbury men. But neither my brother nor I gave up the writers we read in *Nation* at first. I had become an admirer of Middleton Murry after reading his *Problem of Style,* and my brother at once subscribed to his new magazine *Adelphi.* He also bought Katherine Mansfield's *Garden Party* as soon as it was published, and soon after he also got her *Bliss.* I was very familiar with Chekhov, but I must say I was puzzled by Katherine Mansfield.

The *T.L.S.* on its part opened up even wider vistas, with its reviews and long articles. Just to give one example, in 1923 it published a long article on Renan on the occasion of the centenary of his birth. It created such an interest in him in me that I at once bought the only book about him that I could get in Calcutta. It was his correspondence with his sister Henriette. Soon after I read the reminiscences of his youth. Apart from the attraction his life as a scholar had for me, I was enthralled by his evocation of the City of Is, because, even though far short of middle age (I was twenty-five then) I had already begun to hear within me 'les bruits lointains d'une Atlantide disparue et sonner les cloches de la ville d'Is,' which were coming from the East Bengal I had lost.

The *T.L.S.* also gave an unusual direction to my literary interests. From it I renewed my initiation into fine printing, typography, and book illustration which I had received from the magazine *Library* in my student days. I read not only the text, but also the advertisements. Those by the Nonesuch Press, which had just begun issuing its books, fixed my attention at once. I liked the very typography of the advertisements. Afterwards I bought some books published by it. When decades afterwards I met Sir Francis Meynell - I knew about Alice Meynell - and told him about my interest in the Nonesuch Press, he asked me how I had come to know about it in Calcutta. The *T.L.S.* was the explanation. What I did with this knowledge I shall describe in the next chapter but one.

Life as Lived

These interests kept me in a state of happy excitement, and to some extent prevented my getting drowned in the boredom generated by my work for a livelihood. But they could not cancel my life as lived, which was not, and could not be, living in the clouds. With all our intellectual 'high falutin' we had to reckon with a different sort of daily life. I know something of the contrast between the philosophy of Abelard and the life that his epoch imposed on him, and also of the contrast between Villon's poetry and his life. The contrast between the life I lived in the mind and that which was dragged on in the world was not less stark, but it neither got nor deserved notice. My everyday and workaday life did not have the distinction of being even picaresque: it was drab and mean. In their parallel existence the two lives were like a dusty road by a garden. We knew beforehand what every weekday would bring, and what kind of change the weekend offer. Some of my fellow-boarders washed their dirty dhoties on Sundays and called it recreation.* They would tell me with a shy smile that since they did not have to work in the office on that day they thought they would wash their dhoties, which they did squatting in the open courtyard of the house under the running tap, raising the recreation to a higher level only by using Sunlight soap.

In fact, my official superiors considered the Sunday in Calcutta to be the day of dissipation, instead of being the Sabbath according to their lights. As my immediate superior in the office told me: 'At Ranchi [a provincial capital] we always went to the office because there was nowhere else to go. We could meet our friends there, and we could also make up any arrears of work left over from the past week. In Calcutta they never come to the office on Sundays - there are so many distractions.'

Although I never went to my office on Sundays to make up the arrears, those accumulating on my desk during the week made my Sundays a day of mental torture for me. My revulsion from work was growing at such a rate that I never dealt with any bill unless there was a compulsion to pay it at once. That existed only for the monthly salary bills which had to be audited and passed for payment before the first of every following month. They began to come in from the 25th of every month, and the days before the end of the month from that date were the only ones on which I went home without a sense of guilt, and with the contentment that comes from performing the day's task honestly. While, when leaving the office during the rest of the month, I could always feel that my face was drawn and rough, on these days I found the cheeks and forehead to be smooth. Yet on the

* Of course, D I Y and the servantless life have brought about the same kind of transformation of recreation in England: going to a laundrette and lying under a car are actually enjoyed

Other days I never touched a paper unless it was going to be reported as outstanding for the third time. The Superintendent took this roll call of papers every Wednesday. The strange thing was that I could have disposed of all the arrears by working hard for only a week. But what I did was to put that off and look forward to Saturday as the day of rejoicing. I usually did make the Saturday evening one at least of forgetfulness. But from the morning of Sunday the anticipations of Monday began to prey on my mind, and the evening of Sunday brought in a depth of misery which was like the *Weltschmerz* of the Romantics (I knew the word very well), and the entrance to my office with its Roman arch appeared before my eyes with the inscription on the entablature: 'Lasciate ogni speranza voi ch'entrate ...' 'Abandon all hope, ye who enter here.' Of course, I knew this line in the original as well.

I realized the folly of it, but did not have the will-power to put an end to it. Yet I would seek, not absolution, but a little understanding, by giving only one example of the loyalty to red tape which I was expected to show. The papers dealt with in one section of our office had to be sent to another section for the next stage of disposal (as it was called) through a book called the 'Peon Book', because the clerks were not expected to carry even two sheets of paper to a colleague in another room. All papers going out of a room had to be carried by the peons. The filing clerk entered them in the book, and after that the peon took it to the destination. One day I had to send a large bundle of papers to another section and I myself entered them, but as they made a thick bundle which could have broken the binding of the peon book I tied them up with the closed book with a string. When I took the parcel to the Superintendent for his countersignature, he was horrified at my unorthodoxy. Although he was a Bengali and normally spoke to me in Bengali, this time he spoke in English. 'All papers,' he said, 'must go *through* the peon book, and not *outside* it.' Then he himself put the bundle between the two covers and tied up the whole with the string I had provided.

In the boarding house there was no way of escaping from another kind of routine even through ignoble shirking, for I would have had to starve if I wanted to do that. We had the same menu in the same order, with the same fishes and the same vegetables. Since only those in season were bought for one whole quarter, we ate exactly the same things every day for three months. For me that destroyed the pleasure which I should have felt when the fishes and vegetables for the next quarter began to appear in the markets. But as I ate the new things I only felt the taste they would have after three months of continuous eating. Nobody else seemed to mind the monotony. In fact, monotony was what appealed to them: it satisfied their yearning for security and stability.

Yet strange to relate, unhappy as I was, I was nevertheless regarded by my fellow-boarders as the happiest man of them all. One fellow-boarder told me one day with a smile: 'You are a very happy man.' When I asked him how, he replied that he often saw me coming back from the office with a book or something new in my hand, while they, he said, came back in the lowest of spirits. This was felt even more strongly by them when one day they saw me coming back with Lytton Strachey's *Queen Viaoria*, and their envy increased when they learned that I had paid the equivalent of a guinea for it. They also saw books and periodicals coming to me from Thacker Spink & Co., the English booksellers of Calcutta, into whose shop they dared not enter. They were particularly struck by the glossy parts of the *Outline of Literature and Art* edited by Drinkwater and Orpen and published by Newnes, which were delivered by a peon. I did not lessen the idea they had of my felicity by getting bread and rolls delivered in my room by the British bakery in Calcutta. There were also pots of jam there, because the breakfast was personal. All these means of happiness were attributed to my 'Government Service'.

CHAPTER 2

Stumbling on a Friend: Bibhuti Banerji

Whatever the trials of my life as a clerk, I secured great personal happiness at that time by forming a friendship Which lasted as long as that friend lived,' and was shared by my wife after I married This friend was in every Way a remarkable man, and his name was Bibhuti Bhushan Bandyopadhyaya (anglicized, Banerji). The friendship began by sheer chance.

'Soon after I had settled down at 41 Mirzapore Street I saw a young man coming down the stairs as I was going up. He looked down at me closely and cried out, 'Nirad!' At first I could not make out who it was that Was addressing me' so familiarly; 'but in a moment I recognized the face: it was that of a fellow-student at Ripon College during the years 1914 to 11916. There he had the reputation of being very well-read and well-informed, although just Out of school. But I was not very intimate with him, and was inclined to think that he was rather over-assertive with his opinions on all conceivable subjects, a trait or foible common in young Bengalis with an intellectual turn. But I had forgotten that impression and was very glad to meet ah old acquaintance again. He asked me where I lived, and when I told him that I lived in that very house he said he would come and see me, adding that he himself lived next door.

He came the very evening, and was very pleased to see my books. He told me that it was not the first time. Two or three years earlier he had seen me reading in the Imperial Library, with a huge pile of books before me – as he put it – and was very glad to find that an old fellow-student was still pursuing his intellectual interests. He said that he had also asked me questions. But I had no recollection of the incident.

After that he told me about himself He had to give up his studies when he was in the MA class for want of means, and was now a teacher in a village school about twenty miles south of Calcutta, to which he went every day by train. I learned later that he was three years my senior in age, but none of us felt the difference. He was obviously a bachelor, but he informed me that he was actually a widower. He had married while still at college, and had lost his young wife in the great influenza epidemic of 1918, after only a year of married life.

We soon became very intimate, and I may add that he was one of only three or four persons outside my family with whom I became at all so in personal relations. He told me the very first evening that he had already published a story in the foremost Bengali monthly magazine *Prabasi*. As soon as he mentioned its tide I recalled it, for I had read it, and although I did not remember the name of the writer I had thought that it showed great originality and a delicate sensibility. I might mention here that in less than ten years he became one of the leading Bengali writers of fiction. His first novel, published in 1928, at once established his position, and the book has now become known all over the world in its film version by Satyajit Ray. It is *Pother Panchali*. In 1924, as soon as he had written the first few pages, he read them out to me. I felt so confident about it that I prodded him for three years to finish it. After its publication as a serial in 19281 was able to secure a publisher for the novel in book form.

With, his intellectual interests he wanted somebody to talk to. He was very lonely and needed companionship. So, he would come almost every evening and spend some time with me. The account he gave of his student days and of his working life since his wife's death distressed me very much. When I was at college with him I knew nothing of the poverty in spite of which he was carrying on his studies. What he told me was afterwards embodied by him in his novel *Aparajita (The Undefeated)*. This story has also been filmed in two parts by Ray, and those who have seen the films will understand what Bibhuti Babu went through. Certainly, it was he who was undefeated. I, of course, had never to experience anything like that, and had no idea of the hardships of such a life.

Although by caste he belonged to one of the highest clans of Bengali Brahmins, socially his family was of the humblest rank of the Bengali gentry, His father was a *Kathak* or expositor of Hindu mythology, and these men stood very low in the priestly hierarchy. This man was poor, and in addition a Bohemian given to wandering. But he was also a character, and wrote verse besides keeping a diary, which has survived to be used by Bibhuti Babu's biographer. I learned all this piecemeal, for he was extremely unwilling to speak about his father and family antecedents. He even indulged in some amount of mystification about them. I was often puzzled by this, for I came from a class in which talking about ancestors and parading genealogy was habitual.

My intimacy with him developed in shared mental life. I might explain that in Bengali society what is understood as social life in the West does not as a rule extend beyond family and marriage relationships. What attracted young Bengalis to one another were mental affinity, intellectual interests, and tastes. Money or social position never stood in the way of such associations.

I acquired a great respect for his mind, which had a wide range of interests. But I certainly did not expect a young Bengali of his class and education to show interest in astrophysics and human palaeontology, which he did. He would talk to me of E. P. Hubble, the astronomer at Mount Wilson Observatory, and his theories, although he had never been a student either of mathematics or physics. I had heard about Jeans and Eddington, and had also read a little by or about them. I had Einstein's book on Relativity as well. But I had not heard of Hubble. Bibhuti Babu also showed me Sir Arthur Keith's *Antiquity of Man,* which in spite of his want of means he had bought. At that time I had only a smattering of human palaeontology and prehistory, but he created such an absorbing interest in them in me that I soon went far beyond him, and not only read Boule's *Les Hommes Fossiles* and other standard works, but also bought the massive monographs on palaeolithic art by Piette, Carailhac, Breuil and others, ordering them from Paris. What I did immediately was to make Bibhuti Babu buy Burckit's *Prehistory*, when it was published in 1923, of course to read it myself.

It did not take me long to discover that his interest in these subjects was not strictly scientific. He was an out and out romantic, and was drawn to them by that. Even if he himself and his family had belonged to the well-to-do section of Bengali society instead of to the poorest, he would have been a romantic, because the commonplace and staid ease of that class would have irked him and driven him to break out of it, in spirit at least. But his poverty-stricken and drab life made romanticism a condition of mental survival for him. As he told me, even during his hard student days he would not confine himself to his text-books, to do which was necessary for examinations, but would read anything that came in his way. He did not do well in them; nonetheless he became a writer.

With the death of his wife and adoption of the profession of teaching the necessity became greater. As things stood, teachers in Bengal were very poorly paid – when they entered the profession they could never hope to have more than three pounds a month. So, they had to live very bare lives.

What was worse was that as a class they made their mental life equally bare. In Calcutta those who were inclined that way could enliven their existence by going into literary or political circles as hangers-on of the established figures. But in the villages in which Bibhuti Babu worked there was no question of such relief, for village life was hidebound and trivial and so withered even in its traditionalism that it could be regarded only as the fossilized survival of civilized Hindu society. The village, at some distance north of Calcutta, in which he first worked seemed to have been worse than the normal run of such places. He could not talk to anybody and lived in a bazaar near the railway station.

To all this was added the desolation of his bereavement. He told me how he sat in the evenings in his miserable hovel in the light of the flickering oil lamp and thought of his loss until the whistle of the late train from Calcutta reminded him that it was time to go to bed. The memories of his wife kept him from marrying again for twenty-three years. I always noticed a packet of papers in his breast pocket, and an embroidered hand-made fan by his pillow. He never referred to them, nor did I ask. But I could easily guess that the packet contained the few letters his wife had written to him, and that the fan was made by her. I and other friends of his tried persistently to get him married again and settled properly. They as well as I at times even brought proposals. His curiosity would make him go and have a look at the prospective brides. Once or twice matters went even farther. But in the end he always managed to give the slip. I joined in three bridal inspections.

His wife's death led him to an interest which I could not share. It was spiritualism. He had already read Myers, Lodge, and Conan Doyle. He tried to convince me of the reality of the ghostly world by throwing his authorities in my teeth. His dependence on one writer provoked me sorely. He was the German Schrenk-Notzing, whose book on ectoplasmic emanations disgusted me. But just as he could not convince me, I too could not shake his faith in the survival of the human personality. At last we tacitly agreed not to discuss this subject, although we talked incessantly on many others. I continued to hear, however, that to others he preached his faith eloquently, and in later life he wrote two novels with supernatural themes. I would add, however, that he showed the stronger side of his preoccupation with death by buying the little book which Dean Inge wrote on his daughter who died in childhood. I borrowed it from him and was deeply touched by it.

I could easily see why he had become a spiritualist, but did not wish to hurt his feelings by making use of the *argumentum ad hominem.* I also saw a gradual shift in his motivation. If at first he wanted to believe in,life after death for the sake of his wife, in his later days he clung to the same faith from his own love of life. So, belief in after-life became in him not only a dogma but even a superstition. Yet I could see that he was not religious. All that he wanted was to be assured of his personal continuity. I suspected that his interest in scientific cosmology and prehistory was the product of his effort and yearning to find a cosmic location for his world of the dead. Even when approaching death he repeated his credo. He died at the relatively early age of fifty-six in 1950.

However, it must not be imagined from all this that he was always mooning about the supernatural. On the contrary, he could be very matter of fact and concrete. Indeed, in his novels he showed an astonishing capacity for detailed observation of both nature ,and human character, combined with great humour and tenderness in describing what his observation discovered. His hard life had not embittered him, nor made him a cynic. His sympathy for ordinary people was unlimited, and he was not repelled even by the squalor in which such people had to live in our society. Somehow, he could always make them rise above their surroundings; I would even say- far above the limitations of their world.

But as he actually lived, he never, even when he had the means to do so, rose above the shabby ways of the Bengali lower middle class. In fact, he was quite insensitive to the external amenities of life, and in spite of being very sensitive, at times too self-consciously so, to beauty in nature, he did not have any perception of man-made beauty, differing radically from me in this. His room was never well-furnished, not even tidy. I had often to put it in some sort of order. He never dressed well, and had no idea of good living.

Many years later, after my marriage, he became very friendly with my wife, and would come and talk with her for preference. But instead of remaining in the sitting-room, he would go straight to her bedroom, and sit cross-legged on the embroidered bedspread, placidly smoking his *biri*, the stinking lower middle-class smoke. My wife would make him throw it away, and ask the servant to get a packet of respectable cigarettes for him. As I never smoked, no supply was kept at home.

But the strong side of his loyalty to the shabby life was that, on the one hand, he was never intimidated by wealth to become servile to rich people, sand, on the other, he never became envious of them. He worked for some time as a tutor in one of the wealthiest families of Calcutta. The drawing-room of that house was a faithful replica of a room in an English country house. In fact, these Bengali houses used to be furnished by British decorators, -and often with furniture imported from England. Once he showed me the drawing-room, but he seemed to be wholly unaware of what lit contained and what it lacked like. He was equally indifferent to his employer's car – an enormous Cadillac. On the other hand, he could describe both the owner of the house and his ways with mischievous but never malicious humour. I have seen very few men who like him were totally resistant to external pretensions and unawed by it.

Bibhuti Babu will come again and again into the story of my life. At this point, however, I shall only relate how within a few months I got him settled at 41 Mirzapore Street, in a room above mine. In this room, with temporary absences, he lived for nearly twenty years till his second marriage.

One afternoon, a few weeks after I had first met him, he suddenly made his appearance in my room very proudly with a garland of marigolds round his neck. He explained that he had come from the farewell meeting at the school, where he had resigned. This surprised me very much, because he added that he was not going to a new and better job but had become unemployed. I did not press him about the reason, nor did he tell me how he carried on during the period of unemployment. Within a few weeks he got a very odd job, and it was then that I learned that he had at times to go without regular meals before he got it. Sometimes he ate a few pice worth of gram, at others a shopkeeper gave him a full meal on credit. I scolded him severely, and told him that he should have become my guest. He only replied that he did not want to bother me.

The job he had secured was queer enough. It was to lecture against the slaughter of cows on behalf of the Cow Protection Society of Calcutta patronized by the Marwari millionaire Keshoram Poddar. He described the durbar of the great man with humour to me, particularly how he was always sitting with half-a-dozen telephone sets around him, which brought him news of the stock market. So, off he went to the southern part of Chittagong district, to save cows in that predominantly Muslim area of Bengal. He said a good deal about the opportunity this lecture tour gave him to learn public speaking. Afterwards he often addressed literary meetings and conferences. Soon he gave up this job and became private secretary to a well-known landowner in Calcutta. I asked him to come over to the boarding house I was in, and got him the room I have spoken about, which he shared at first with another literary man, also known to me.

It was then that I learned the story of his resignation. It had a romantic history behind it.* When working in the school south of Calcutta he had first taken up lodgings with a Brahmin family of the village. There was a young girl in it, who found that he was utterly incapable of looking after himself and so when he was at school she came into his room, tidied it up, and made everything comfortable. She took a fancy to him, which certainly could be called love, and after some time she began to leave letters for him. I have read these, about ten in all so far as my recollection goes. There was not one explicit word of love in them, but no one could make any mistake about their spirit. I have never read anything more simple, sincere, and pure: they gave expression to an intense yearning to serve him, as if she was saying: Behold your handmaiden! But the girl did not belong to his subcaste of Brahmins, and so in those days there could be no question of his marrying her. To prevent awkwardness, he first came away to Calcutta, and then resigned from the school.

This was not, however, the only one of his affairs of the heart, which were always begun and carried on by the girls and not by him. Somehow he attracted girls, and in his later years his literary standing helped him. In those days Bengali girls who were taking to higher education developed a tendency to fall in love with the writers they admired (of course, novelists and poets, and never writers like me) without ever seeing them, and afterwards tried to get personally acquainted, with the sole *avowed* object of hero worship. In his own response to these opportunities, Bibhuti Babu did not adhere to the strict principle he had followed in the affair just mentioned, but seemed to enjoy the game without getting entangled himself. He also seemed really to believe that the girls too would not suffer. If I had read Trollope then, I would have compared him to Johnny Eames.

Until I married he would come and tell me about these affairs, and I always scolded him. He never took that seriously, and either thought that I

* I would make it clear at this point that whatever I am writing about Bibhuti Babu is being given from my own first-hand knowledge or from accounts given by him immediately after the events I have completely ignored other accounts, because I have found that his recollection was not always exact after some time had passed, and others gave differing accounts.

was a puritan and prig, or merely the tail-less fox. After my marriage he transferred his confidences to my wife who showed a good deal of amused tolerance of his affairs even to the point of looking on with enjoyment when one day he brought a little girl of about twelve and about four feet tall to our house and sat on my wife's bed with her little hands clasped in his very big ones.

But one affair made her angry. As it happened, a highly educated modem Bengali girl fell in love with him and out of that feeling went on repulsing a most devoted lover of hers. This girl was very well known to my wife, and a friend of hers who knew the ill-treated young man came to her and complained about the dog in the manger. My wife, of course, gave a long lecture to Bibhuti Babu, without producing the slightest effect on him. He would even take a long and uncomfortable journey of three hundred miles to see the girl when he did not have the slightest serious intention.

In the end Bibhuti Babu played the game once too well, and was caught in matrimony, and that at the age of forty-seven. But he did not feel punished at all, and lived happily ever afterwards. He continued his visits to my wife, and told her of his married happiness, how his wife would tie the end of her sari to the end of his dhoti and prevent his getting out of bed too early in the morning. Now, this is a very effective means of keeping a Bengali when you do not want to part with him. Bibhuti Babu himself applied the same method to me without going to its extreme length. When I went to see him and rose to take my departure he would seize the flounce of my dhoti and keep it firmly in his closed fist. In that situation, given the manner in which we wore the dhoti, nobody could get away without leaving it behind.

His curiosity about women, even when he was not involved in a love affair, was uncontrollable, and it would lead him to situations which were farcical at his expense.

Here I give some examples. When he was a little boy of about five or six his father brought him to Calcutta and took lodgings in a slum in a rather disreputable quarter of the city. Next to their house was a better house, and a kept woman lived there. She would invite little Bibhuti to talk or to play with her. Of course, had his father been a normal parent such a thing could never have happened. He was not, and so Bibhuti became very fond of the woman. However, towards the evenings she would say: 'Now, child, go home, for my Babu [protector] will come.' That must have been before 1900.

And one day in 1925 or so he came to the house where I was living with my brothers after leaving Mirzapore Street, in a state of utter panic and seemed to be ready to say as Wellington said of Waterloo: 'It was a damned nice thing – the nearest run thing you ever saw in your life.' The story was this. He quite remembered the house and its location, and, out of an overwhelming desire to see the woman, had gone to it. By that time it had become a regular brothel, and when the young women saw my friend with all his embonpoint they all fell on him, and each one tried to drag him to her room. Bibhuti Babu told me that he loudly protested his innocence, and was treated to hilarious and pitiless laughter. At first I also roared with laughter. But afterwards I gave him a lecture on common sense.

At about the same time he came again and told me that he was going to see the girl for whose sake he had resigned his job, because he had heard she was now married and he wanted to find out if she was happy. I was horrified and tried to dissuade him. But, of course, he would not listen. The next day he came again, and from his face I could guess how the visit had gone. He said that he had just come from the station and related his story. When he arrived he was received very politely, but before he could inquire about the girl he heard piercing screams coming from the inner house, and he was told apologetically that their niece was having her confinement. Bibhuti Babu added that he did not wait to hear another word, and ran as if for dear life. I only said that he had got what he deserved.

On another occasion, when he was over forty, a very mischievous writer friend of mine played him a cruel practical joke, and he came to complain about it to me in furious anger. He said that the wicked man had promised to show him an Anglo-Indian (Eurasian) prostitute if he would go and wait in Wellington Square at nine in the evening. He had gone and sat in the cold on that November night for two hours and neither the friend nor the prostitute had come. 'Could you imagine anything more treacherous?' Bibhuti Babu asked me. The reason for his curiosity was that at that time Eurasian prostitutes were, regarded by Bengali young men as quite the *de luxe* things in that line, and so he wanted to find out if their reputation was justified. Yet I know if the woman had come Bibhuti Babu would have taken to flight, as he actually did on another occasion. This time I was in no mood to be amused. I told him that I thought he still had some self-respect left not to be led away by curiosity of that order, especially when he knew as well as I did what the character of our writer friend was.

Probably at the bottom of all this weakness was the fact that Bibhuti Babu rather piqued himself on his looks. He was a stout man of middle height, and physically not unimpressive. He also had a very intelligent and pleasant expression. But nobody would have called him a handsome man. But he never took that view and he would often twit me on the smallness of my eyes. He would say that they were like little snails while his were long and large.

He also had a great fascination with himself, and would ponder over his personality. He was very fond of Tolstoy's *War and Peace*, as I also was, and he would tell me that he was like Peter Bezukhov. I, who had no less fascination with myself, at once replied that I would rather be Prince Andrew Bolkonsky. Then he suddenly asked me: 'And who do you think is Boris Drubetskoi?' And he took my breath away by saying: 'Don't you think it is X?', mentioning the name of a friend of mine whom he knew only by report. That friend, in spite of his great qualities, was something of a climber, and had in fact pushed his way into the highest circles in Calcutta. I did not expect Bibhuti Babu would be able to detect such a character.

These almost childish weaknesses made him more lovable. But there was one trait in his character which after two decades of familiarity with him caused me both puzzlement and dismay. This was a sort of hardness, which lay at the core of his outwardly soft nature and made him incapable of strong personal affection for anybody. His stories revealed a deep compassion and tenderness for the joys and sorrows of humble people taken in the mass and typicalized as individuals. But personally I saw often that he could be totally indifferent even to those very near him. It may have come from his intensely egocentric nature or from the first sorrow of his life which made him grow a protective callousness. I heard that he doted on the son of his old age, who was very young when he died. But that sort of love in an old man is often a form of self-love.

Nonetheless, his egocentric nature showed a good side as well, for he never felt any envy or jealousy over the success or good fortune of fellow- writers. The writer class is not distinguished by this virtue, and in Bengal it is still less so. Bibhuti Babu was, however, immune to this meanness. Once, when to my thinking he was being lazy over the completion of his first novel, I wrote to him that he must hurry up, because some others – I gave names –

were already becoming well-established without having his ability. He replied that it did not matter, he did not grudge anybody's success, nor did he feel upset by his slowness. He would do what he wanted to do in his time, and he did.

CHAPTER 3
Some Incidents and Bereavement

My life continued in the manner I have described, and this phase ended with a great bereavement, which was the death of my mother. I shall first describe some of the incidents of this period.

Official Incidents

In the spring of 1923 I ran into trouble over this very Government Service. Many of us in the office were holding our appointments temporarily (s.p.t. ffi *substantive pro tempore*), for the duration of the war, and the war period was declared officially at an end then. So, in order to remain in service we had to be confirmed, and the first requirement was that we should be found physically fit. We were asked to go to the Medical College, Calcutta, whose chief physician, an English colonel of the Indian Medical Service (known in India as the I M S), was to certify us finally. I came through that, but as I wore glasses I was sent to the Ophthalmic Department, under another English colonel. Both my brother and I became a little worried because we had learnt that minus 2.5 glasses for myopia was the limit for acceptable eyesight, and my power was minus 4.5. Therefore, as a matter of precaution, my brother asked his brother-in-law, who was a retired captain of the I M S and a house surgeon in the Medical College hospital, to speak to his Bengali oculist colleagues, who would first examine me and only have what they wrote signed by their chief, the English colonel. I went with him to them, and they were extremely reassuring.

But they played me a trick when actually examining me. They wrote that I had an organic defect in my eyes which was known as corioiditis and put the report before the colonel, who took up an instrument, just looked into my eyes for a second or so, and signed the report. On seeing this, the physician colonel disqualified me provisionally and asked me to come again if only the other colonel reconsidered his opinion. My brother and I understood the affair perfectly. The treacherous Bengalis had expected gratification and not being offered it had played their hand.

We were not the men to cringe to underlings. So, I told my brother that it would not do to beg for reconsideration because those in authority did not like to stultify themselves, but that I Would go to the private clinic of the oculist colonel ,and for his opinion as if I was,another man, and I knew that I could never be disqualified for that particular defect. In fact, my own oculist, when told of it, was surprised, because one of the reasons for corioiditis was syphilis. There was of course, the risk that the oculist colonel would recognize me, and if he did he could not only turn me out but also get me into trouble for trying to deceive him. Nonetheless, I said I would take the chance. I dressed myself like a Bengali bridegroom instead of the Bengali clerk he had seen, and went straight to his private clinic. My brother waited outside. I said to the colonel that I was a candidate for employment in the Finance Department of the Government of India and since I was doubtful about my eyesight I should like to have his opinion whether that could disqualify me . He examined me Very carefully and wrote down oh his own stationery that except for the rather high power I had ho defect in my eyes and also,that in his opinion that should not disqualify me for the kind of work I was to do; But he added to me after he had handed me the certificate-that he had seen a man somewhat like me at the College who did have organic defects in his eyes. I thanked him, and, of course, gave him his full fee. With his certificate I went in triumph to the other colonel's house and asked for an interview.

I was called in, and, as soon as he saw me, he began to scold me: 'Why have you come here?' I replied simply that I wished to show him a certificate from his colleague the other colonel. He took the paper, and whatever his private feeling said very calmly: 'Come with this tomorrow to the College.' I offered him the usual fee, but he refused. I explained that I had come to him professionally and I should pay. He replied that he could have refused to see me on learning my business and name, and so it was his doing. I went to the College the next day and since the colonel had not come in I showed my certificate to his Curious Bengali assistants. They grinned and remarked: 'It's wholly the opposite kind of opinion.' The colonel came in, and without shoeing the slightest sign of recognizing me, asked me my business; I handed him my certificate.He looked at it, asked- his assistants to give him the file, took out the previous certificates tore them up, and gave me a clean bill My brother, who was very angry, said that he would call in the Bengali doctor who had disqualified me to our house, ask him to treat me for Corioiditis, and if he could not- which was bound to be the case – give him a thrashing But when the temporary excitement had subsided we did not pursue our vindictive intension. This, how ever, gave me the hang of handling medical authorities, and I made use of my experience later.

My personal Life

But my confirmation in the Military Accounts did nothing to reconcile me to my work in it, nor did my life in the 'mess' become more tolerably,. But among the conventional inmates I was at least the Robin Good fellow or Puck, and in Bibhuti Babu, living above me, I found a good associate Although he lived very shabbily, he could bring his imagination to play,on his behaviour. That first happened immediately after-the Tokyo earthquakes in September 1923. One early morning we had a sharp shock. I had experience of earthquakes and just rushed from the verandah where I was sleeping into our room to drag my sleeping brother out, By that time the shock was over, but the conchshells were blowing in all the houses, their sound being regarded as an antidote to earthquake by all Hindus.

I went up to see what Bibhuti Babu was doing, but did not find him in his room nor in the house. Naturally, I was anxious. After about half an hour he walked into my room, and when I asked him where he had been, he replied: 'O Nirad, what a fright I have had! I was awakened by the blowing of the conchshells, and I at once knew that it was an earthquake. Crashing and burning Tokyo rose before my eyes, and I jumped down from my bed. I remember nothing after that, but when I got back my consciousness, I found that I was lying on my back on the football field of the Eastern Bengal Railway club, and the vast blue sky was before my eyes.' It was reminiscent of the scene in his favourite *War and peace,* in which Prince Andrew, wounded at Austerlitz, woke up from his swoon to look at the sky above him. In order to reach that football field Bibhuti Babu had actually run a quarter of a mile and climbed oven a six-foot brick wall. He himself wondered how he had done that.

A few days later he involved me in a very unpleasant row with the police. The meals in the mess were managed by the members themselves, one of them becoming the 'manager' he was called, for the month. Bibbuti Babu was that month's manager, but he could not get himself obeyed by the cook and the servants. There was a clamour among the others against him , all the more loud because he was the only West Bengal white crow among the rest of us who were normal black crows from East Bengal. Both the sides came to me, the members to complain against 'your friend.', and

Bibhuti Babu to ask for protection. One day I said I would order the meals, and gave my orders both to the cook and the shopping servant. I ate my dinner without noticing anything, and retired to my room.

Soon I heard a noise and going down I found those who were eating in very bad temper about the absence of some dish. As I had ordered it, I asked for an explanation from the cook who said that the servant had not bought the ingredients. I then went to that fellow, and asked him why he had not. The man replied very insolently and I gave him a mild hiding. All of us did that sort of thing off and on, and I went back to my room without any fear of the consequences. About half an hour later some of the younger boarders came and told me that a police Head Constable had come to inquire and was asking for me. This was so unexpected that I lost my presence of mind, and only went on muttering, 'It's absurd.' In the meanwhile, my followers pushed out the Head Constable and shut the door in his face.

In another half an hour a whole squad of some fifteen policemen armed with staves arrived, and there was also the Head Constable and a Sub- inspector with a revolver. They came in, caught hold of anybody they found in the corridors, and at last came to my room. One policeman dragged out my brother from his bed, and another came to arrest me. As I resisted, two of them just lifted me up in their arms, with me kicking like a child. They took me into the street, all the time abusing me in filthy language. About eight of us were arrested and marched off to the Bowbazar police station. Many of us, including myself, were barebodied and barefooted, and we were shut up for the night in a cage which was exactly like the cages for tigers in the Calcutta zoo. I learned then that some of the boarders out of spite against me had instigated the servant to go to the police, and, as we sat in the cage chaffing and joking, one source of comfort for me was that among us was one whom we suspected to be one of the instigators. He was wailing loudly about his innocence and the injustice done to him.

In the morning the full complement of clothing was brought to us, and soon some bigwigs with influence over the police came to intercede for us. After ten we were taken to the police headquarters at Lal Bazar, and produced before the Deputy Commissioner, who was to decide whether to commit us. Lawyers had been engaged and they got us off on the payment of a contribution to the police charity fund. But the charge was serious – obstructing the police and assaulting them in the discharge of their duties.

I could have gone badly at least for me, and a convicted Government servant was dismissed from service.

I came back to the boarding house in great rage, and, first of all, went about with a whip to give a few lashes to those who, I heard, had gloated over our arrest. But everybody kept their doors shut. Then I inquired about the cook and the servant. But they had fled, and never came back even for their wages. They certainly feared that the customary Bengali gentleman's vengeance would be meted out to them, and that was getting those who insulted us murdered by hired roughs. I cannot say that while in the cage I had not nursed that design. But as the offenders had run away I was not called upon to take a decision. As nobody else contributed towards the expenses I was seriously inconvenienced about money for some time.

It was, however, reserved for Bibhuti Babu, the real begetter of this row, to provide light relief to the episode. When I met him after my return from the police headquarters, he told me what he had done when the police arrived: 'O Nirad,' he said, 'I was so frightened! I thought they would come for me also. So I picked up a bottle of medicine from one comer, put that and a glass on the table, covered myself with a quilt, and lay groaning, so that if they came I could tell them I had fever and knew nothing about anything.' With anybody else I would certainly have been angry and contemptuous after such an avowal, but with Bibhuti Babu I only laughed. Not only its frankness but its complete naturalness amused me. After all, it is only genius which can arise from any rank of society, but behaviour and outlook are moulded by the tradition of a class, and we belonged to two traditions. Besides, it was his imagination which had inflated his fears, and it was the same imagination which made him capable of making his hero Apu rise above all the squalor of his actual life.

A Literary Lion

The next few months passed quietly, marked for me only by meetings with a great literary figure in Bengal. My brother's father-in-law, a landowner and lawyer of Dacca, who had also been involved in a case of revolutionary crime in his young days, was very fond of the novels of the great Bengali novelist Sarat Chandra Chatterji, and from time to time he went to see his literary hero. At that time he had for the first time become well acquainted with me, and had formed such a good opinion of me that he wrote to my father that it was a great mistake to have put a son who was so talented in the

Military Accounts Department. Of course, this was not my father's doing. In any case, he thought he would introduce me to men whom I would admire and respect. So he took me to Sarat Chatterji.

He lived on the west bank of the Hooghly river, in a southern suburb of Howrah. His house was of the old type, very large and rambling. As we entered through the front gate, an elderly man, wholly barebodied and barefooted, came towards us across the wide front courtyard, and recognizing my elderly relative he asked us to come in. He was Sarat Babu. We were taken to a small room about twelve feet by twelve feet, which had no furniture except three small and low whatnots with his books. The whitewashed walls were bare, and on the floor was a mat, on which we sat down. This was the great man's study and writing room. I had not yet become familiar with the stripped material existence of Bengali writers, and was surprised to come upon such bareness in the house of a man who was known to be earning a good deal of money from his books. I knew Sarat Babu was unconventional in his personal life and had heard that he lived with a thistress in that house. But the material setting of his unconventional personal life was very conventional lower middle-class Bengali. My family had a wholly different style of living, even though not at all wealthy.

I visited him twice in the company of my brother's father-in-law, and I shall combine here what I heard on both occasions. Sarat Babu had a great reputation for being a witty and anecdotal conversationalist. But to us he only held forth. The reason may have been that both of us were from East Bengal and one of us was a very young man. We were regarded as humourless, priggish people, and indeed we were as a general rule. So perhaps Sarat Babu measured his conversation to our assumed receptivity.

Though a great admirer of his novels, I was at that time also critical about his pretension to be a great thinker and something of a prophet in Bengal. Now I have even greater respect for his literary genius, but an even poorer opinion of his intellectual pretensions. Here, however, I shall relate what I heard and felt then. In his conversation he showed nothing of the writer side of him – he was a born writer and in his style alone he was great. Apart from that he showed a marvellous devotion to truth infused with compassion in dealing with Bengali life even at its humblest level, and he also put before his readers idealized young men and women of fiction who actually inspired young men and women in real life to try to become something like them. He showed nothing of this to us, and aired his intellectual eminence. He pointed to his shelves and said to me: 'I am not one of those uneducated writers of these days. I have read all those books.' I was amused, because even then I had read at least three thousand books in four languages, and my own collection of books was larger than his by far.

Then he scandalized me by exhibiting an arrogant contempt towards Bankim Chandra Chatterji, the creator of Bengali fiction and to my thinking still the greatest of Bengali novelists. Sarat Babu severely criticized one of the most famous novels of Chatterji on the ground that he had not shown sufficient understanding of the character of a beautiful woman who had enticed away a husband from his loving young wife, and eloped with him. Sarat Babu observed that Bankim Chandra was so crude that even a schoolboy could no longer read his stories. Then he added: 'I owe nothing to him.' Whatever the merits of his predecessor, I did not expect a writer who had come after him could be so indecorously impious in his comments.

Then Sarat Babu turned to politics. He was a typical Bengali middle- class nationalist, and had nothing but disdain for the Punjabis. He remarked that they were supposed to be martial, but had run like poltroons before a few bullets. The unfeeling reference was apparently to Jallianwallah Bagh. Then he wound up the argument by saying: 'The rest of India will do nothing. Our freedom will be won by a few Bengali young men.' He had obviously in mind the Bengali revolutionaries. And he wrote a half-baked book about them, which the Bengal Government had the stupidity to proscribe.

He was equally crude about British rule in India. He said that there were no greater enemies of human worth and dignity {*manushyatver satru*) than the English people – the Bengali word being an exact equivalent of the Latin word *virtus*. I was horrified, although I knew how beastly the British in India could be personally. In fact, the political police in Bengal entered in their black book as politically suspect any Bengali who was philanthropic, athletic, or public spirited, and even if studious. But they were not the 'English people'. An essential distinction had to be made.

One day I was present at a search in a Bengali house, and discovered how the mind of the Indian police officers, as instructed by their great anti-terrorist chief. Sir Charles Teggart, worked. The inspectors had only laid by a number of books belonging to the young men in that house, and were making an inventory, when their chief, the Deputy Superintendent in the

Intelligence Branch, entered. He sat down, asked a few questions, when his eyes suddenly fell on the books. He noticed one and taking it up said: 'Are you taking this away?' When the subordinates showed some puzzlement, he explained: 'You should note what books the young men read, because that shows the character of their mind and the direction of their thoughts. This does.' The book was a life of Pilsudski, and the D S P said: 'It shows a military bent. You should have noticed that.' That sort of thing, of course, perfectly entitled us to regard British rule in India as Satanic.

But British rule as it was impersonally and historically was a wholly different thing, and Sarat Babu showed neither any knowledge nor any understanding of that. On the contrary, Bankim Chandra Chatterji, in spite of being the creator of modern Bengali nationalism, did. Even about Warren Hastings, who still remains the subject of silly historical controversies, Bankim Chandra could write:

'Warren Hastings has been represented as an oppressor in history. Able men are often compelled by their duties to resort to repression. The men who bear the burden of defending a State might be merciful and just personally, nonetheless they might be compelled to be oppressive in the interest of the State. They think that when the repression of a few would be to the good of the whole body-politic that sort of repression is a duty. In fact, it is never possible that men who like Warren Hastings were capable of founding empires would not be merciful and just. A great achievement like that cannot be brought about by men who have neither mercy nor justice in their nature – because that sort of men bear no exalted character but are small men, and small men do not do such things.' (Translated from Bengali)

Sarat Chatterji had no inkling of all this. He fully shared the negative hatred which had become the driving force of Indian nationalism by his time, and being a writer he took it to a greater emotional intensity.

What struck me in Sarat Chatterji was the presence of the hatred, and it dismayed me by confirming my diagnosis of Indian nationalism as nihilistic. If a man like him, who showed such compassion for human beings at the personal level could be so negative in his historical views, I thought that could have no corrective. At that time I again and again thought of writing an article on the prevalence of hatred in India and of the wholly negative character of Indian nationalism, and of sending it to some journal in England. I did not have the energy to do that, and I regret it still.

My Mother's Death

In April 1924, I decided to ask for a transfer and leave Calcutta. The reason was half the very unsatisfactory situation in the office, and half personal – a quarrel with my brother in which I insulted him. I do not remember the exact character of the incident, but it rankled so much in my mind, mostly as shame for myself, that I thought I would turn a new leaf in my life by going away to some distant place. I asked the office and was transferred to Poona, to the accounts section of the Ammunition Factory of the Indian army at Kirkee. I liked the idea, because Poona was famous in Indian history and in the hills and forts around it had associations with the great Maratha and Hindu hero Sivaji. I began to prepare for my journey. I informed my father, and learned later that my mother was very much grieved over the news, fearing that in her state of health she would never see me again. She did not, because she died before I started for Poona.

I had seen her last early in 1923, when the family was at Banagram, our village, waiting for a new house to be built at Kishorganj. I went there on leave, and while I was there she had a second stroke. I was sitting by her bed when she had it. My father was away at Kishorganj, supervising the building, and I was terribly frightened. I kept my fingers on her pulse, and since I did not feel anything thought that either she was dead or would soon die. But the doctor arrived and pronounced that she was in no immediate danger. My father came back and took over from me, and as my leave was coming to an end I returned to Calcutta. I never saw her again.

One afternoon, a few days before my intended journey to Poona, my brother came to 41 Mirzapore Street, and told me that he had got a telegram asking us to go at once to Kishorganj because there was very little chance that our mother would recover from her latest stroke. I at once wrote to the office asking them to cancel the transfer and grant me leave, and all of us started for Kishorganj.

Whatever might be my pessimism about the world and life in general, I was an incurable optimist regarding personal life, and I never really believed that any serious harm would come to me or my family. So, however grave the telegram, I expected to see my mother. The train started at half past eight from Calcutta, and I soon fell asleep from tiredness. Then I had a dream. I saw a pyre burning fiercely, with its red and yellow flames leaping up, and I felt convinced in my dream that it was my mother's funeral pyre. I woke up with a start. There was nothing to be surprised at such a dream in such a situation – my fears could have brought it about. But the strange thing was that at that very time my mother was being cremated on the grounds of our house at Kishorganj. And not less strange was the fact that I had no fear about my mother, in spite of the dream, during the following day as we continued the journey. We reached Kishorganj late in the evening, and asked the servant who had come for us how my mother was. He said quietly that she was well, and I felt very much reassured. But as we were entering the inner courtyard of our house my father came forward saying in a broken voice: 'Your mother has left us.' I was absolutely stunned by this unexpected news and sat down on the ground, only exclaiming: 'How could that happen?'

The next day I learned the details from my sisters and the brothers who were present at her death. Actually, before that last attack she was in better spirits and relatively better in health, because two months before that my youngest sister had been married into a very wealthy family, related to us. That had made her happy. When my sister came to visit her after her marriage my brothers with their friends staged a play, as we used to do before. It was one by Tagore, and in its last scene a disillusioned worshipper threw down an image which my youngest brother, who acted the part, had got specially made for the occasion. My mother was watching the performance with many other women, but just after it was over she had her stroke, and never regained consciousness. The neighbours as well as the town regarded it as the punishment inflicted by Kali for our sacrilege. The Hindus could always be devilishly cruel without any sense of guilt from their besotted superstition as the people of the West can now be from their degraded sensuality.

We went through the funeral ceremonies without showing much grief externally. But on me my mother's death had a profound effect. I showed nothing externally, yet for months I could not get rid of the feeling that my mother was crying out to me. Especially if it was a rainy or stormy night, I seemed to hear her imploring me to take her into the house. I recalled that during the last seven years of her life I had quarrelled with her, and had not always treated her kindly. All of it filled me with bitter remorse. My sense of guilt was heightened by the fact that just after my mother's death I bought and read Mauriac's *Génitrix*. I felt somewhat like Cazenave. My grief played sharp notes of gnawing pain against the dull continuo played by my boredom with my office work.

What was worse was the fact that the dejection arising out of this first bereavement in my life did not remain personal, and spilled out to my general outlook on life, and made me more pessimistic than ever before about life and the world in general. In spite of my twenty-six years only, and in spite of the new intellectual interests I was developing, I was becoming more disgusted with myself and life, and was pressed down with a feeling of heavy sadness.

CHAPTER 4

Written in Despair

When I was in that state of persistent dissatisfaction with myself, with my work for a living, and with the world in general, one day I heard a story in the office. In another office, I was told, an old clerk had died suddenly at his desk, and as his family was not in town his colleagues had cremated him. But there were reports that they had got drunk in the burning yard and behaved disgracefully. I was given some squalid details.

This brought back to my mind some experiences of cremation I had had in the famous Nimtollah burning ghat of Calcutta. As it happened, I was never present at the death of my nearest relatives – father, mother, the brothers and sisters or my father-in-law and mother-in-law, and I had not seen their cremation. Therefore I was never subjected to the shock which people get when they see the bodies of those they have loved consumed by fire before their eyes. But I had seen my grandmother (on my mother's side) cremated at Nimtollah when I was seventeen and that being the first cremation I saw it left an impression which never lost its vividness. Later, I also saw other relatives cremated, and those scenes renovated the first shock. However, in all those cremations there was no sense of deep bereavement, for all the relatives were old. What I found harrowing was the ghastliness of the end of the human body on a Hindu funeral pyre.

It has to be pointed out that burial and cremation (which in India takes place on open pyres) produce quite different mental reactions. In the case of burial, it is possible to imagine a suspended prolongation of bodily life and an ultimate resurrection of the body, with which our love is entangled. Not so in cremation, however. He who sees his loved one being devoured by the flames feels as if his own flesh is being seared and reduced to ashes. This gives such a shock to our love of life that it cannot be counteracted by anything but defiance of the kind which the old cremating Achaeans or Vikings threw out. Hindus, too, probably had that spirit in ancient times. But among modern Hindus protection is sought only in callousness. Thus in Bengali society it was customary for a near relative to suggest an immediate second marriage to a man who was cremating his wife. But if a man retains his natural sensibilities nothing is more impossible for him than to acquire a quietist's attitude to death after seeing a cremation.

The spectacles I had seen had induced a generalized emotion in me, and when I heard the story of the clerks that emotion was roused to activity, and my despairing mood began to crystallize around the thread furnished by the incident. After some time the idea of writing a story with the theme came into my mind, and I worked on it for more than two years from 1924. I wrote the piece in English, and began, not with the death, but with the arrival of the party at the ghat, because I was in a hurry to describe the central episode.

I neither completed the story by adding the beginning, nor published it. In fact, in 1926 I threw it aside because I thought my English was not good enough for fiction. However, the manuscript has survived, and upon going through it recently I found that the writing was not so very bad. What was more important, I found that the story reflected my state of mind very faithfully, and would be revealing as an autobiographical document. So, I am reproducing it as it was written without considering its merits or demerits as fiction. As my doubts were mostly on the score of the dialogues because of my unfamiliarity with English as spoken outside novels, I might give an explanation. In those days Bengali clerks in their excited moments spoke English of a very high-flown type. This I employed when I made them speak in English. As to their dialogues in Bengali I put that into as good colloquial English as I then knew. But every detail of the descriptions is authentic, and some of the incidents are from real life. Here then is the story without further apologies.

A FUNERAL MARCH

[Being a story written by the author in 1924–5]

They clattered over the flagged path through the gate into the yard, and with a last, exhausted *Bolo Hari, Hari Bol,** laid down the charpoy on the ground. The tired bearers stretched themselves, rubbed their shoulders, and growled, shooting angry glances at the corpse all the while. Only Grandfather* kept his temper.

* This is the cry with which the bodies of the dead are carried to the cremation ground by the Bengalis. It means 'Take the name of Hari (i.e. Vishnu)'.

* In Hindu society colleagues and friends are often addressed as relations, i.e. as uncles, elder brothers, or when very elderly as grandfathers. The leader of the party was the Head Clerk or Bara Babu, the Grandfather of the Office.

'I can now understand,' he murmured in his beautiful soft voice, which only had an added ring of conviction in it, 'why his young wife would never come and live with him. It was putting too great a burden on the poor girl's shoulders.'

This at once restored the good humour of the men. Their peevishness melted away in a general grin, and they turned round to contemplate the immense bulk of the dead man, who was lying like a huge bale of cotton in his trappings of rope and white sheets.

'What shall we do now?' asked Sudhir.*

'In the same great hurry as ever, Brother,' gently remonstrated Grandfather. A faint smile mingled with indulgence and reproach hovered about his lips.

'I tell you,' he added with decision, 'it's absolutely no use. You cannot hustle death. Learn patience, my boy. Perhaps you will, this very day.' But the next moment he relented and said, 'Well, since you are so anxious to have done with it, I'll see what I can do. Look here, Kamini, run down to the death registration office – it's on the side farthest away from the gate through which we came – and see if you can speed up things a little.'

Kamini ran out as directed. 'It's no use, though,' muttered Grandfather as he followed the man with his eyes. 'It's absoluely no use,' he said again when Kamini had finally disappeared through the inner gate. He gave a vigorous shrug to his broad shoulders and sank exhausted on the ground.

Sudhir did not remain with them. He wanted to have a look round the place. It was shut in on all sides by high plastered walls, once perhaps of a dazzling white, but now dirty yellow with streaks of black from the smoke of its perpetual fires. They had probably not been whitewashed since the yard was built. Nets of soot hung from the electric wires which ran along the top, and these trembled in the hot air rising from the pyres below. Four of these were burning in the yard in four magnificent blazes. The red flames roared and whistled. The yellow tongues leaped. Their glow was caught and reflected on the bronzed foreheads of the men who were standing at attention near each pyre with long bamboo poles in their hands. And the flames set on fire the burnished gold ornaments which loaded the shapely arms, wrists, necks and hips of the curious women who hung about in clusters near the pyres to watch the bodies turning into ashes.

The curiosity of these women never abated. As one group moved off

* The character in the story through whose eyes the incidentes are see.

another came in. All day long the procession streamed in and out. They rustled over the courtyard littered with cinders, dry twigs, and charred bones. They stood whispering before the pyres in their slumbrous grace, hardly seeming to look out of their tired and drooping eyes. They went out jingling their bangles, anklets, and chains. Heavy clouds of fragrance rose behind them, and floated about in the air for a while, to be sucked in at last by little whirlwinds of heated air charged with ashes, smoke, dust, and the stifling smell of burnt flesh and hair.

The men stood gravely at their posts, and did not even glance at the men and women around them. They threw logs into the fire when it flagged, and poked the corpses with a careless, defiant air. They had got their bearing from long familiarity with death. At the other end of the yard, on a bed drawn close to the door of his room, which opened on the burning yard, sat a fat old gentleman comfortably propped up by snow-white bolsters, placidly smoking his hookah, and keeping an eye on the proceedings below.

At one pyre a man was looking closely to see whether the body was burning evenly. He noticed that the skull was resisting the fire. The hair, the skin, and the flesh on the head and face had been burnt up, but the skull itself was glowing like white-hot metal, without burning or bursting. The man raised his pole, and with one blow shattered it, so that splinters of bone flew off and some pieces struck Sudhir's feet. The brain slid out, fell on the glowing bed of charcoals below, and burnt away with a crackling and spluttering sound.*

No one at any of the pyres cried, except one old man in a comer. The wretch was rolling in the dust and giving out the wail – 'Where are you gone, O Master!' When Sudhir passed him he raised his haggard, furrowed face to him, and uttered the cry. It sent Sudhir's blood ice-cold to his heart. He stopped and, seeing the stubs of beard bristling on the man's unshaven cheeks, felt like shrieking out – 'Why have you not shaved?' No one else noticed the man or his cries. The Doms, a fine manly set of men who attended the place, went about twirling their arrogant moustaches.

Another pyre to which Sudhir walked up suddenly went out. Three weeping women who were sitting close by, rose from the ground with their pitchers. They came back in a little while with water from the Ganges, and poured it on the red, hissing embers, believing they were cooling thereby the quenchless spirit of the dead. Sudhir watched them attentively and

* This incident and the two which follow, I saw with my own eyes.

thought. He was wondering whether the earth on which they were leaving their men, women, boys, and girls was hospitable enough. Suddenly, he went down on his knees, and began to dig a hole in the ground with his nails. They broke. It was hard and cruel – this red, charcoal-strewn earth.

'What are you doing there?' someone shouted. Sudhir jumped up in confusion. It was Grandfather calling. He went back slowly to his companions and found them all in a bad temper. The man at the office had told them that nothing could be done until they had got the death certificate from the medical officer. And they blamed Sudhir for it, because he had hurried the departure from the office.

'You seem to enjoy the confounded place quite, Brother,' said Grandfather, 'I saw you digging a hole in the ground like a child. But we can't be so happy. What shall we do? It gives me the creeps to look at these pyres.'

'Why Grandfather, you're old enough to be left here for good,' was somebody's ill-timed attempt at a joke. Grandfather growled with inarticulate ferocity at the speaker.

Sudhir learned that it would be some time before the certificate was likely to come from the office, and thought he would go out of the enclosure and sit on the steps of the ghat on the river. As he went through the gate on that side, he heard Grandfather ordering somebody to bring one or two bottles to make the waiting less boring. He walked along a paved path to the river, went down the steps and took his seat on a parapet.

It was late in the day. The broad river glistened in the sun from the west. There still were a large number of bathers in its water. He could not count the heads, which kept shifting. In the women's ghat close by, the cropped heads were those of religious old widows. The young women who were there came mostly from the houses for which the neighbourhood was well-known and frequented. They came to the Ganges every day to wash away the sins of the nights in her holy water.

There they stood, bust deep in water, rubbing their bodies with towels or praying with folded hands. The serried rows of naked breasts splashed by the ripples of the ochre-coloured stream seemed to belong to a legion of damned women, struggling, jostling, imploring in the eddying pools of hell. When coming to the burning ghat Sudhir had noticed many of them in the streets, returning to their homes after their bathe. They stopped at every wayside shrine, and devoutly handed in their offerings. Their foreheads and cheeks were dotted with sandal paste in fanciful leaf-like patterns, and their faces shone with angelic radiance after their cooling bath.

Sudhir had not been looking long at the river when he heard people coming down the path behind him. It was his companions bringing down the corpse to be washed in the holy Ganges before being cremated. They were breathing very hard. The load was heavy and the legs of the men were unsteady. As they tottered down the steps, one of them slipped. Sudhir jumped up and caught one of the legs of the charpoy. However, the shock sent all of them headlong into the water. The men yelled with delight, and began to splash water on the body and on one another. Sudhir went back to his place and sat down again in his wet clothes.

The wild cries of the men had attracted the attention of some girls who had come to bathe in the Ganges and were standing at the edge of the main stream at some distance. They looked in the direction of the burning ghat. One of them pointed that way, and spoke to her companions. Thereupon four of them began to advance. They clutched their saris with one hand, and daintily picked their steps over the ugly bank of mud laid bare by the ebbtide. They came quite close and stood staring at the big, stark-naked body in open-eyed and open-mouthed curiosity. One of them was in white, and the rest were in blue. How much fresher and younger they looked, Sudhir thought, than the women he knew. The girl in white, especially, was a very winsome creature. She was a brunette with long eyelashes and a budlike mouth. Every line of her faultless figure could be guessed through her half-transparent muslin sari. She stood a little apart, gazing at the dead man with wide wondering eyes, bending forward in her perplexity. She looked, so it seemed to all who saw her there, like a phantom of the spirit of life.

Sudhir's companions ogled at the girls from their mud puddle. Grandfather asked in a honeyed voice: 'What can we do for you, my little ones?' The girls looked at him with immeasurable contempt, which said plainer than words: 'We are not for the like of you.' They walked off, looking over their shoulders to see whether the young gentleman sitting so quietly on the parapet had seen them and understood.

The men stood motionless, looking after the girls till they reached their bathing ghat and waded into the water. They then heaved heavy sighs, rose from the water with their burden, and slowly went back to the burning yard. Sudhir neither stirred nor looked at them. He gazed at the river before him.

A battered and derelict cargo boat lay moored off the far bank before the workshop of a firm of ship-repairers. Some men were hanging by her side in baskets, re-painting the hull in red and black. The river was not crowded at all. Only two or three country-boats laden with straw were going north. A slow tug with a barge full of coolies in tow passed them by leisurely. The boats and the tug were overtaken by a swift steamer of the Port Commissioners' ferry service. The strawladen boats rose and fell in its wake. Tinkle, tinkle – sound of silvery bells came floating across the water and the steamer came to a standstill in midstream.

Sudhir could easily read the name on a board fastened to the rails of the bridge, *Amina. Amina?* The name was familiar, and the smell too was. As a child he had always associated the smell with the lake of burning brimstone in hell, for his earliest notion of that place had come from the stoke-holes of the steamers in which he used to travel so much. He had never put the slightest faith in what his father had told him about those shadowy figures down there: that they were the men who put coal in the furnaces which made the steam in the boilers. He knew more than that about demons and hell. And he was indignant that his father was trying to deceive him.

The steamer in midstream was in motion again and steered itself to its station a little distance away. Sudhir forgot all about it, and thought of what he used to do in the river in his village. He would wade into it, casting fearful eyes at the herd of buffaloes wallowing in the reed beds. On the green bank opposite, cows grazed and stared, and near the end of the meadow stood a jackal, which slunk away among the tall sugar-canes.

The jackal was elusive in daytime. But at night he was not. His weird howls mingled with the dark stillness and with the terror of a little boy falling down, down through endless regions of shivering cold and emptiness. Bump, bump, the fall comes to an end. You wake up with a smothered shriek, and look about you with bewilderment. Where is the windswept rock strewn with bones? You are only in the familiar bed with Suro on one side and Mini on the other digging cruelly into your ribs with their knees. You kick them away. 'Sudhir', comes in a soft whisper from the big bed. 'Mamma', one tries to reply. But one cannot find one's voice, and makes only a senseless, hoarse, and gurgling noise.

You lie on your back and contemplate the pattern on the canopy of the mosquito net. Ages pass. The howls begin again. Out there the mother jackal is playing with her little ones. You could not see her, but you could people the inky chaos around you with countless brown, sharp-muzzled creatures, seeing into your very soul with their piercing oblique eyes. It would have been nice to go out and play with them. But they looked so clever and always so ready to laugh at you. Yes, they looked at you in that queer way whenever you went into the neighbour's orchard to steal mangoes.

One creeps to the window. One presses one's temples against the hard, cold, iron bars. The room changes into a boat gliding ever so slowly down a dark stream. Everything about you moves and floats. Only the sky above broods motionless. Through innumerable holes in it a soft light filters through and dribbles down upon you from the refulgent lands where the dead people go. Sudhir woke up. How the ceaseless rattle of a crane working in a jetty nearby grated in his ears.

Hearing footsteps, he turned round and saw two of his companions, who began to tug at his clothes.

'Have you left anything behind?' he asked them.

'Yes,' they replied, 'we have left you. Do you think we shall let you sit here like a Nabob while we are slaving there?'

Sudhir did not answer, and turned his back on them.

'The Captain's orders,' they shouted angrily, 'are you coming or not?' Sudhir paid no attention.

'Let's take him by force. Come, Bipin, take hold of his legs and I'll hold at the shoulders.'

Sudhir now turned round, scanned them calmly from head to foot, and then said with a low laugh: 'Will you go and sit in that water for half an hour and get sober?'

'The fellow calls us drunkards. He thinks we are drunk. Lets show him what drunken men are worth,' and they both fell on him. The attack was so sudden that in sheer self-defence Sudhir was compelled to push away the first comer. The man fell down on the steps with a yelp of 'Help'. 'He's murdering me,' he shouted.

Sudhir stood aghast. He could hear footsteps of men coming down the path. He quickly kneeled by the side of the prostrate figure, rubbed his bruised face, and whispered, 'Hush, hush, don't scream so. It's nothing. Let's go in.'

'Nothing indeed,' whined the other.

'Don't,' implored Sudhir, and helped him on to his feet.

'What's happened?' asked one of die men who had arrived. 'Nothing serious,' said Sudhir. 'It's my companion. He has had a fall and hurt himself.'

'Is it very bad?'

'Oh no, only a slight cut here,' replied Sudhir, pointing to a cheekbone. They went back to the yard.

*

A very strange sight met Sudhir's eyes. The Doms were going about as usual. The men who had come in later with other bodies were bowed down with grief, or gravely watchful. But his companions were marching round a huge pile of faggots on which they had placed the body of their dead colleague. Each of them held a torch of dry jute stems in his hand, and flourished it over the head. The march grew more and more rhythmic till it developed into a dance. Men and women looked on with amazement. The dance went on for about two minutes, and then broke up.

Grandfather threw away his torch, and asked in a stentorian voice: 'Have you arrested the deserter?' He was panting after his great effort, and his round belly quivered from shortness of breath.

'No,' replied the men who had gone to fetch Sudhir, 'he refused to come and beat us.'

Grandfather turned furiously on Sudhir. 'How dare you?' he cried, 'I proclaim martial law in this place.'

Sudhir prepared to leave. But Grandfather was too quick for him. He darted forward and caught hold of Sudhir by his shoulders, shook him ferociously, and muttering between his teeth:

'Trying to run away, eh? The arm of the law is long. You don't know what martial law means. I sentence you to ten years' imprisonment. No, I sentence you to death. Kamini, give me the knife. I'll cut his throat. No, no, no, no, I'll throw him into the pyre with Old Brother.'

All the rest caught up the cry: 'Throw him into the pyre, throw him.' Then they began to drag him towards it. He resisted as best as he could. The onlookers stood as if spellbound, and were paralysed by the sheer incredibility of what they saw. Four of the Doms rushed up and tried to separate the men. Grandfather threw some coins on the ground, and they went off to pick them up. One of the spectators ran out to fetch the Inspector. The Doms saw this and went up to the still struggling group, entreating them to stop. 'They have gone to fetch the Inspector Babu. Stop, for Heaven's sake.'

'Give them more money,' shouted Grandfather, and he himself began to drag Sudhir, who was completely exhausted.

Suddenly someone came up from behind and asked sternly: 'What's this? Jhamru,' he called to one of the Doms, 'call die other men and turn these fellows out of the yard.'

It was the Inspector. Grandfather became sober in a moment, and the others too. Two or three who had become quite naked in the tussle picked up their dhotis. Grandfather calmly faced the official.

'What are you saying, Inspector Babu,' he cried, 'Do you really think we were creating a row in this holy place.' Are we not Hindus?' And he struck his breast.

'This young man,' he continued pointing to Sudhir, 'is the dead man's son. He was trying to jump into the pyre from grief We were only holding him back.'

The Inspector looked at him incredulously. Grandfather saw that, and added, stretching his arm towards the Doms: 'Ask them.' The Doms had already made some profit out of the affair, and hoped to make more. So they loudly corroborated Grandfather's story. The Inspector still looked undecided. He looked at Grandfather, and at the Doms, and then went away. When passing Sudhir he cast a glance of compassion on him and told Grandfather, who was seeing him safely out of the yard, to console the young man and tell him that such exhibitions of grief did no good, but on the contrary were very painful. Grandfather assured him that he would do his best, but the young man had taken it so bad.

When he came back all the rest looked at him with immense pride and admiration. What would have happened had he not been there.' The Inspector had frightened them terribly. Even the Doms approached him with respect. They grinned and scratched their heads, and intimated their expectation of some more bakshish.

'Listen, my sons,' replied Grandfather, 'I do not wish to disappoint honest fellows like you. But if you think that you can blackmail me for the most insignificant scrape in my life, you are greatly mistaken. Here's something, however, for you to buy pan with."

The Doms protested that nothing could be further from their thoughts

* The Bengali equivalent of pourboire.

than the idea of blackmailing the honourable Babus. They were humble folks who lived on the bounty of the great, and called down on the heads of their benefactors the blessings of the gods.

When they were gone Grandfather sat down to have some rest. He was still in a temper with Sudhir. He began to give him a dressing down. 'You think too much of being a BA,' he said, 'but you will stink like any of us when you bum. Your letters B and A won't help you. You will stink just the same even if you had the whole alphabet from A to Z tagged to your name. But frankly,' he went on, 'I do not bear him any malice, though he did put me in a very awkward fix today. Come, brother, don't look so glum. Cheer up and come over to us..

'I say Grandfather,' shouted one of the men, who had gone up to the pyre. 'If he bums at this rate we won't go home till tomorrow morning.'

'Pshaw!' ejaculated Grandfather, 'he is the same tiresome fellow as ever. Give me the pole, Abani.' With it he walked up to the pyre. 'There,' he observed, 'I thought so. These Doms are no good. And what were all of you here for? You've put too many logs under him, and there is no air. Come up, four of you, and help me.'

With a good deal of pushing, pulling and poking they succeeded in drawing out some of the logs from the bottom of the pyre. It blazed up at once. But its neatness was all gone. Grandfather tried to smooth his ruffled temper by giving some blows to the body and saying: 'Lie flat, lie flat, my friend.' He thrust the pole under the body and used it as a lever to raise it.

'Oh don't, don't,' cried a soft-hearted young man, rushing forward with outstretched hands.

'Don't be sloppy,' Grandfather retorted angrily, 'if I were to die tomorrow you'd do exactly the same to me. Besides, who cares for the discarded clothes that this body is. I do not think you have ever read the *Gita*, the godless young dog that you are. Hear then what our Lord says:

Vasamsi jirnani yatha vihaya
Navani grihnati naro 'parani
tatha sarirani vihaya jirnany –
anyani samyati navani dehi.

'What does that mean? You don't understand, of course. I'll translate it for you: "Just as, casting aside tattered clothes, a man puts on new ones, in the same way the soul leaves behind the worn out body and goes into a new one." That's it.'

'That's true, that's true,' said one of them. 'It's no use sorrowing. We shall all die. But our Old Brother was such a good man. We shall never forget him.'

'That he was,' said all the others. But one of them ventured to observe, 'But it was not good of him to marry again at that age ...'

'You know nothing of men,' replied Grandfather. 'Old men are like that. They would have a hundred wives if they could. Dasaratha, you know, had ten thousand. But we live in hard times.'

'How many have you?' inquired one of the young men.

'He has only one wife,' replied Kamini for Grandfather, 'but he knows all of them hereabouts. Surely, Grandfather,' he continued, struck by an idea, 'you must know the girls who came to the ghat. Can you tell me where they live?'

'Don't be indecent,' replied Grandfather with an appearance of severity. But he wore a gratified smile.

'How's Old Brother's wife to look at?' he inquired of Kamini in a whisper.

'Ask Haren,' replied that person, 'he is a neighbour of her father's, and ... was ... er er sweet on her.'

'The young rascal!' growled Grandfather, shooting angry glances at Haren, a puny and shrinking young man who was sitting opposite him.

'It was before her marriage,' the poor fellow stammered.

'Let's hear all about it,' they all cried in one voice. Haren would not speak at first. The request awakened many memories. Since all his hopes had vanished in thin air, where was the fitness, he sorrowfully mused, of raising their ghost at this late hour of the day? And he remained softly silent, lost in a sad reminiscent wandering into the past.

The sympathetic voices of his friends insisting on hearing his story roused him from the chasm of reverie. They had noticed his abstracted air and knew something of the great chagrin of life. Their first impulse was to press him no further. But on second thoughts they considered it best to make him speak, for, as one of them explained in a whispered aside, nothing lightened our heart so much as speaking of our sorrows to our real friends. Pressed by them, Haren began in a low voice, with his eyes fixed on the ground.

'Her father and mine were neighbours, and I used to see her almost every day ever since she was quite a little girl. However, when she was about eleven and old enough to be married, her mother would not allow her to come out of the zenana. They began to look for a bridegroom for her. But, you know, they had no money, and they could not find one. Two or three years passed. Everybody said that she had grown very pretty. I wanted to see her ever so much. But her mother was very watchful. I did not, however, lose all hope, and hung about their house in the hope of having a glimpse. At last, I met her one day by the side of a bamboo clump when she was going back to the house with a pitcher of water from the back-ghat.'

'A regular love affair!' they all cried out, greatly touched. 'We thought it was only a one-sided affair. But go on!'

'After that I saw her almost every day beside that bamboo grove ... till ... till Old Brother came and snatched her away.'

'But do tell us what you two did there, what you said, and how at last you parted from her in tears.'

Haren gave them an imploring look, and murmured, 'Ask me no more.' 'Certainly not, if you would have us rather not.' But one of them could not resist the temptation to ask: 'Did you not want to commit suicide when she was married."

'Why should he?' remarked another. 'He who fights and runs away, may live to fight another day. Now that Old Brother is gone, if he chooses he can marry her.'

'Widow re-marriage?' cried out Grandfather, shocked and scandalized.

'Why not.' The law allows that,' replied the man who had made the suggestion.

'But whose law?' asked Grandfather quickly, turning on the speaker. 'The law which the English have made, is it not.' The English and chastity? Oh, Oh! Marriage of widows is adultery.'

'Then they might turn Brahmo. Brahmos are nice people. I go to the Brahmo Samaj meetings every Sunday. Brahmo ladies ...'

He was interrupted by Kamini who had been busy throwing logs into the pyre, and had caught only the last words.

'Brahmo ladies?' he said, 'who is talking of Brahmo ladies? Ladies indeed! Brahmo wenches ... Brahmo prost... better still. I know them. At our college we had a Brahmo girl reading with us. Her name was

Kamala. We used to run out before her after the lectures, and write on the walls: 'How I should like to have Kamala on her back... and such things.'

'Ha, ha, ha, how funny,' laughed the others.

'I'll tell you,' went on Kamini greatly encouraged, 'how only the other day I snubbed a Brahmo woman and put her in her place.

'You remember the day we had a party in honour of the Managing Director. After it I was going home in a tram-car. A Brahmo woman was next to me. I was telling a Madrassi on the other side – he was quite a jolly fellow – how I had made off with a bottle of sherry from the Sahibs' table. It was sherry you know. You have never tasted such wine in your life. I asked the Madrassi if he had. He said he hadn't, but would like to. I stood up and asked the other passengers: "Have any of you ever drunk Sherry? Those of you who have, please raise your hands." People smiled. But a white- bearded old fogey had the impertinence to ask me to sit down and stop this talk. There were ladies in the car, he said.

'I sat down, but also muttered: "Ladies, yes. But neither fair, nor young." I looked sideways at the woman to see whether she had heard. She had, for she was white with anger. It was such fun. I again muttered: "Neither fair, nor young." This time she rose to go away. When she passed by me I touched her skirt with my knee. It was very soft, but did not feel like muscles. She was a lean school-mistress. I think she had put on three petticoats to swell herself out. "Neither fair, nor young", I again cried after her. She rang the bell and got down. Ha, ha, ha, what do you think of that?'

The champion of the Brahmo Samaj had been listening to him in boiling rage. He cried out, 'Don't boast as if we did not know the whole story. Rajani of the Sales Department saw everything from the second-class car. Didn't two gentlemen take you by the collar, drag you down from the car, made you apologize to her on your knees, and then kick you away?' He counted off the stages of the punishment on his fingers.

Kamani was at first too astounded to speak. However, in a moment he recovered himself and cried out in a terrible voice: 'Repeat those lies if you dare.'

'I will, and they are not lies,' thundered the other: 'Two gentlemen made you apologize to her on your knees and then kicked you away. There, are you satisfied?' He snapped his fingers in the face of Kamini.

'You lying blackguard ...' roared Kamini, and in the inkling of an eye he picked up a log and flew at his detractor.

Grandfather rushed forward to intervene. The blow came down before he could place himself between the belligerents. He got it full on his outstretched knuckles. Disregarding the pain he gallantly threw himself between the young men, and pushed them away from each other. The others also came up and dragged away the combatants.

'He who steals my purse steals trash; 'tis something nothing; but he that filches my good name makes me poor indeed,' snorted the man of frustrated vengeance. 'My good name ... makes me poor indeed ... my good name ... makes me poor indeed,' Kamini went on repeating between violent pants.

Grandfather sternly came forward, and taking both the culprits by their arms made them sit to his right and left. Then he delivered a severe lecture, giving them each of his bruised hands to massage, which they meekly did until the pain was gone.

*

A little after sunset the last of the blazing logs went out, leaving behind a handful of red cinders glowing in the middle of a grey bed of ashes. It was finished.

The men jumped up, and rushed to the Ganges. They quickly came back with pitchers laden with water. They poured it on the glowing bed of charcoal. The water gurgled out and the dying embers hissed and sent up little snakelike curls of vapour, which rose and faded in the air. After the last man had emptied out his pitcher they carefully went round the pyre to see if any live charcoals were left. There were none. The place was quite drenched, and the whole bed was a mass of shiny black. There was a pause of silence. Then the conversation broke out in a bubbling murmur. They went down to the river again to have their bathe, talking and chaffing.

On their way out they passed through the yard again. Sudhir stopped to have a last look at the place where the pyre had been. It was dark. The lamps were not lighted yet. Only two or three flickering pyres were shedding their uncertain light all around. The curious women had all hurried home to prepare their lengthy toilets. Looking on the vague dark spot where they had burnt the old man, Sudhir's eyes suddenly filled with tears, and he burst out into an uncontrollable fit of sobbing. The electric lights flashed out. He wiped his tears and hurried out of the place.

He felt no desire to rejoin his companions. But they were waiting for him at the crossing. Seeing him Grandfather came forward with outstretched arms and said: 'Brother, we're very sorry for what we did to you. Forgive us and forget all that has happened today.'

At first Sudhir did not understand. But when recollection came back to him he felt as if it taxed all his power of self-control just to stand still and keep quiet, instead of screaming and doing some mad and rash thing. With a terrific effort he overcame his wild impulse, but he could not speak. Distressed beyond measure by his silence. Grandfather took both his hands in his own and said in a voice quivering with emotion:

'See, we've reconciled the other two. Their quarrel was far more serious and bitter. But see how friendly they are now. Will you allow the sun to go down on your anger.' You do not speak.'

Sudhir looked into his eyes. They were brimming with tears. Slowly, two pearly drops rolled down his bloated cheeks and fell on the flagstones at their feet. He had told the truth. The champion of the Brahmo Samaj and Kamini were fully reconciled. They stood on the pavement with their arms round each other, one in his dripping dhoti and other in his wet trousers. A passerby turned his head to observe the group, which apparently had come from the nearby yard. A troubled look came over his face and he quickly turned away as if unwilling to face a dreaded fact. Sudhir tried to draw away his hands from Grandfather's clasp. But they were in the grip of a vice. Grandfather murmured: 'An old man implores you. Forgive and forget.'

'Yes, yes,' Sudhir replied hoarsely. 'Thank you, thank you,' said Grandfather stepping away from him with alacrity, 'a great load is off my mind. Thank you again.'

They walked along side by side. After a while Grandfather said in a more matter of fact voice: 'By the way, come to the office half an hour earlier tomorrow. We shall have to make up the bill, you know.'

They parted ways at another crossing half a mile further on. One by one his companions took Sudhir by the hand, pressed it tenderly, and said goodbye. Sudhir stood motionless for a few minutes looking at the figures disappearing down the dimly lit street, and then resumed his walk. They have not yet got the liquor off their head, he said to himself. But his thoughts did not linger over his companions. He went home in a strange exultation of despair.

How many years was it since the day on which his little brother had run into the class-room where he was repeating his history lesson before the wrinkled and spectacled Mr Ganguly, the third master, and told him between convulsive sobs that Papa was dead? How many wealthy relatives had his mother begged to help the poor fatherless boys? After eighteen years he was independent again. What more did he want? What more could he want? He was contented.

But on that cold winter evening, as he walked along the street, shivering and chattering in his teeth in his wet clothes, a terrifying desire took possession of him. He wanted a woman's love, a love which would give a sharp edge of agony to his petrified suffering. In a wild vision he saw death and love enlaced together in an eternal embrace. He could feel their arms about him, their warm breath was on his face. When he looked into their eyes, he recognized the countenance of the girl he had seen at the ghat. Could he not take shelter in that bosom, lose himself in that soft flesh, and find there a delicious aching annihilation for his starved body and senses?

A loud abuse in Hindustani reached his ears, and someone gripped him by the arm. He woke up and saw that he had overturned the tray of a hawker of sweets. The man was holding him and abusing him in filthy language. He murmured some apology, freed himself, and walked on. But the man was not appeased. He ran up behind him and gave him a slap on the back of his head. Sudhir tottered forward but did not fall. He did not turn back upon the man. He did not care.

*

The clock on the landing struck half past nine when Sudhir entered the hall in which he worked. He found his companions of the previous day assembled round Grandfather's table in a full conclave. The leader motioned him to a chair, and resumed the discussion.

He was dictating the bill to Kamini. In his right hand he was holding a small bit of paper on which he had noted down the actual expenses. From time to time he stopped and contemplated the paper with knitted brows. His task was not an easy one. The funeral of a Hindu costs a trifling sum, but there were extras which had swelled the bill suspiciously. Besides, he could not put all the items in the bill, and the problem of distributing them over the normal and respectable items of funeral expenditure was proving more difficult than he had anticipated in his usual confident mood. The whole company was watching him anxiously. Grandfather resolved to be bold. The accountant was a Eurasian and had not the slightest idea of what a Hindu funeral cost. It was upon this that Grandfather reckoned. His audacity might take in the accountant or it might not. They really had no alternative. They had already spent money out of their own pockets and they had to make the Company pay it back. But if the accountant made independent inquiries? They half repented having volunteered to bum Old Brother.

Grandfather at last hemmed, cleared his throat, and said briskly: 'It's really not worthwhile wasting so much time over such a small matter. The actual price of fuel and other things is seven rupees and nine annas, and we have spent eight rupees to keep up our spirits. Therefore the bill must be at least for fifteen rupees and nine annas. Take down, Kamini, and don't nibble the end of your pen. Firewood – eight rupees ten annas, new cloth – two rupees, four annas and a half, the priest – three rupees eight annas, earthen pitchers – ten annas, ghee – six annas, and er... er... er... flowers – ten pice. Add them up.'

'They come to fifteen rupees and nine annas.'

'That's all right. Give me that paper,' said Grandfather, and when he had got it he scored off the items one by one with the nail of his forefinger. After he had added them up again, a doubt struck him.

'But there is one more difficulty still,' he observed. 'The accountant is sure to cut something. I think it would be safer to leave a margin for retrenchments. What do you say?'

'We agree,' all of them replied.

'Make it twenty then,' suggested someone.

'Now, now,' remarked Grandfather, 'I should like to say something to that. You have entrusted this to me, and I am sure I could not be more sensible of the honour done to me than I am. But since you have left it to me, wait to see what I do and be so good as not to meddle until I have failed. Here's a suggestion to make the bill for twenty rupees. A little reflection would have convinced the speaker that there was no surer way to make the bill look suspicious. Can actual expenses ever be round sums?'

'Why do you pay heed to every idle remark? We leave it entirely to you,' observed the others.

'Let's go on,' said Grandfather mollified. 'I propose to add five rupees one anna to the bill, and make it for twenty rupees and ten annas. But in that case I must ask you to take into account this fact too. If the accountant passes the bill in full, and as he is an ass he is likely to, the nine of us would have five rupees one anna to share among us, which means nine annas for each. That is rather an awkward sum for a gentleman to accept. I want to add a few more rupees to that bill.'

'For shame!' cried out Kamini, throwing the pen on the table, from where it rattled down to the floor. 'Shall we make money out of the last rites of a comrade?'

'Kamini, Kamini,' said Grandfather. He had not expected this from his favourite colleague. His protégé might have stabbed him in the back.

'Did you hear that?' he observed to the others. 'Did I want to make money out of a comrade's death? Or did I want only to be on the safe side, in case the accountant cut something, for the sake of our wives and children? We have spent money of ours to cremate our brother. We could lend our shoulders to him. We could give the strength of our bodies. We could sacrifice comfort. But can we sacrifice our substance? We have our families to think of If we had a duty towards our brother, we also have an equal duty to our dependents. I don't pretend to be a martyr. Kamini can. He paid nothing yesterday.'

'Are you taunting me with my poverty." asked Kamini with emotion.

'No, I am not,' retorted Grandfather, 'But I know how easy it is to be virtuous when one has nothing to lose.'

'Don't forget. Grandfather, that you get one hundred and forty rupees, and I get only forty,' rejoined Kamini.

'I forget nothing. But enough of this sordid squabble. Gentlemen, one of us objects to my proposals. I leave the decision to you.'

'You are most unjust,' protested Kamini. 'I never had any idea of making a formal objection. Why do you put my hasty remark before my brethren?'

'I don't understand you,' replied Grandfather severely, 'why do you open your mouth if you do not mean what you say?'

'I am so sorry. But you should not have taken me seriously. Grandfather. It frightens me so.' He began to wipe his eyes.

'All right, all right, don't speak like that in future. I suppose everybody is then agreeable to what I say.'

'Yes, yes,' they all assented. Grandfather took a pen and quickly drafted a new bill.

By this time the other clerks had begun to come in one by one. When they saw the committee in earnest discussion they eagerly came forward.

'What, have you left Old Brother to rest for ever on the banks of the Ganges?'

'Yes,' replied Grandfather rising solemnly and dissolving the meeting with a sweeping gesture. 'Yes,' he went on, 'we have lost a comrade for ever. It was a good deal of trouble. But who could refuse to lend a shoulder to do the last duty by a brother? Death spares nobody, ever so high or low.'

He bowed down his head in acquiescence to man's inevitable destiny, and after a moment's pause remarked with a mournful smile, 'One of these days you will have to carry *me* there.'

Some of the younger clerks protested that their Grandfather would be spared them for many a long day to come, but they could not reassure him with full conviction. They could easily understand that the death of an old colleague who had worked and aged with him at the same desk had brought the idea of death very near to the old man and their hearts went out to him in sympathy for his resigned waiting. Outwardly, however, they made light of his anticipation, pressing round him until they heard the energetic footsteps of the Sahibs on the wooden stairs.

In some way or other, at about midday the true story leaked out. The clerks whispered to one another with smiles and jests of cynical flippancy. But at the back of their minds was a sharp aching sense of injury. They could not keep out the thought that while they had been at their perennial slavery, some of their colleagues had seized the occasion, such an occasion as rarely came in anybody's way, to enjoy a day of joyous freedom.

The accountant passed the bill without asking any question. The surplus was divided among the eight of them, for Sudhir did not take his share. So these eight got a little more than they had allowed for.

*

This story reflected the state of my mind in those years very faithfully. It will be seen, however, that it contained reactions to two distinct things: the first, the brutal and often squalid end of the human body in the burning grounds of Calcutta, and the second, the conduct and behaviour of a set of Bengali clerks. If the first reaction showed only a heightened state of my mood of despair, the second could be regarded as a savage exhibition of antipathy towards men who might have been my colleagues. Perhaps my attitude will be described as one of overdone cynicism. I would not, however, admit the presence of cynicism in my mental constitution. When I was young I did at times affect cynicism. But that was never very sincere, it was only a weak form of exhibiting anger. I could never reconcile myself to a low view of human nature, and when I saw lowness I got too angry to be cynical, for cynicism calls for coldness of temperament, which I never had. I would now say that cynicism tries to compensate for the absence of moral courage by airing malice.

More justifiably, I could be accused of arrogance towards ordinary humanity. But I have never believed in the innocence or innocuousness of the so-called common man, who has been created in the image of individuals of the urban lower middle class. The peasant is far too elemental to be classed with these men. The commonness of the common man is not less dangerous than the uncommonness of the criminal, because it injures insidiously. As soon as I entered the world, I began to catch glimpses of a clammy vileness in a certain class of my fellow-Bengalis who seemed outwardly to be wholly colourless. If a man has any moral perception he soon discovers that a weak, diluted, and seemingly impotent corruption permeates the subsoil of lower middle-class existence. In fact, the difference between the active viciousness of criminals and the passive proneness to vice which this class has, is that which exists between carbon monoxide and carbon dioxide, with the added stench of sulphureted hydrogen.

All this is perhaps truer of Hindu society as it has been in recent times than of any other society. It has a shallow top soil of dry-as-dust prudery, but one can easily hear the squelching of the soggy layer of weak vice underneath. The moral weather of Hindu society is regulated by the high and low pressure of the winds of opinion.prevailing in it, and not by absolute moral judgements. No one can become tolerant of this kind of commonness without becoming deadened in moral sensibility.

I must add that I was not provoked to write about clerks in this way by the conduct of my immediate colleagues. They were always polite to me, and never made me share their private conversation or life. All that I felt was an unconquerable revulsion from their life and outlook. In the story this came out with some exaggeration, which could be set down to impatience at being compelled to work as a clerk against the grain.

However, I did not persist in writing fiction, although even after this piece I wrote a few sketches both in English and Bengali. So far as writing was a safety valve for me, it took another line, although I did not persist even in that. I was very fond of reading aphorisms, especially those of La Rochefoucauld and Pascal, and I thought I might imitate them by trying to embody my view of life (such as it was) in maxims. I wrote down a number of them. As in the story, in these too, will be found my intolerance of commonplaceness. I reproduce some of the aphorisms I wrote in 1925 and 1926, because they also are relevant to my autobiography.

Some Maxims

1. Detractors of humanity are wrong. Idealists are equally so. The average man is neither so good nor so bad as we take him to be. But this mediocrity is so terribly hard to endure.

2. The strength of mediocre people lies in the fact that they are so sublimely unconscious of their own shortcomings.

3. Nowadays anthropologists are almost unanimous that all the existing races of men belong to the same species-*Homo sapiens*.

Yet there is a greater gulf between an Einstein and an honest clerk than there is between an honest clerk and a chimpanzee.

4. The bourgeoisie are always ready to believe any gossip about the higher set, and they are overjoyed when the law-courts let loose a really first-class scandal. Conscious of their inferiority in worldly goods, education, culture, manners, they must soothe their wounded self-love by an assumption of superiority in morals. But this is done in perfect good faith and sincerity.

5. Anatomists tell us that at the age of twenty-five or so, our bones harden and we cease to grow in body. Though there are no bones in our brain, I should think something similar happens to our mind at the same time. Only a few fortunate ones stand as oases in the forbidding desert of middle-aged stupidity.

6. I have seen the gradual petrification of a mind. I have also seen something infinitely worse – the shadow of mental inertness creep upon the face, robbing the eyes of their brightness, thickening the skin, and marking the low forehead with deep horizontal wrinkles.

7. In nine cases out of ten the movements, and the looks of a dog betray intelligence.

In nine cases out of ten a man's do not.

Control over the facial muscles has made man look more stupid than he really is.

8. When you are so blind as to see nothing but the groove in which you are turning your neighbours will call you a practical man.
9. It is only foolish young men who are prepared to die and to live for an ideal. Heaven or money, people above the age of forty will not barter their souls for less.
10. The distinction between a misanthrope and a moralist: A misanthrope despairs of himself as well as of his fellowmen; a moralist despairs of his fellowmen only.
11. Crown of sorrow: We give our respect to one whom melancholy has marked for her own. But a man who has allowed his leg to be caught in a sentimental trap and is limping through life for the benefit of his fellowmen, is a ludicrous sight, and most of the sorrow of this world is of this brand.
12. Unquestioning complacency: facile pessimism; chastened hope and unrebelliousness; a stem, almost exultant despair – these are the four stages in a man's maturing outlook on life.

Just as I do not know which of the last two is more deserving of admiration, I do not know which of the first two I despise more.

To that, at the end of life I would add only this – that there is no greater misfortune for a man than to die with a sense of bitterness; he should die, not simply with reconciliation even, but with a sense of triumph, whatever his worldly lot has been. When I say triumph, I mean triumph over the worldly world. No one can have it on one's side unless he has the strength to kick it, or the weakness to prostitute himself to it.

CHAPTER 5
Literary Apprenticeship

Although I was always writing in bits and scraps whenever the mood came on me, and also, without a doubt, cherished literary ambition, still I do not think that by myself I would have sent anything to any editor. As has been seen, I was always trying to improve what I had written, and this alone was such a strain that I could not finish anything. Besides, my physical and mental energy was not enough to enable me to see anything through. So, I should probably have dawdled on without publishing anything. Nevertheless, by the end of 1925 I did appear in print. This was due to an accident, a chance meeting with my old teacher of English at school. He was Mohitlal Majumdar, about whom I have written a few lines in *The Autobiography of an Unknown Indian*. I also said there that 'he made a writer of me almost by main force.'

My Teacher and Guide

One afternoon towards the end of February 1925, I was walking home from my office, as I usually did for the sake of exercise. It was a distance of just over three miles. I was in a cheerful mood, for on the previous day I had got from Paris through a Calcutta bookseller a very beautifully printed limited edition of *Sur La Pierre Blanche* by Anatole France, published by La Connaissance. It contained the famous story of *Gallion*, with the theme of St Paul's appearance before Gallio, Proconsul of Achaia. It was illustrated with woodcuts by a modem French artist, and there was a duplicate loose set of the pictures at the end of the book. The title-page was in two tones, and it faced a beautiful figure of Aphrodite. The initials were in red and black. I had taken the book to my office, just to be able to feel it as a material object, and although I had shown it to my colleagues they did not take any interest in it. But holding it in one hand I walked back with light and brisk steps.

When I was near the prayer-hall of the Sadharan Brahmo Samaj on Cornwallis Street, I saw Mohit Babu coming towards me. He was now a teacher in the Metropolitan Institution founded by the great Bengali scholar and reformer, Iswar Chandra Vidyasagar. We had not met since I left school early in 1914, but my brother had met him occasionally, and I knew that besides being a teacher he was now one of the leading young poets of Bengal. I also knew that for some years he had been in die Government's service in a minor administrative post (on a higher salary, nonetheless, than that of a teacher in a school), and had worked in the districts of northern Bengal.

Although I was now twenty-seven and he about thirty-seven, we had no difficulty in recognizing each other. Both of us had kept our youthful looks. He asked me what I was doing, and when I told him that I was working in the Military Accounts Department he seemed to be pleased to learn that in those days of 'educated unemployment' I was in a secure Government job. He told me that he had come back to Calcutta and was now in the Metropolitan Institution, which was nearby. I replied that I also knew that he was a poet. But I did not know much about what he had written recently, and referred to some of his early poems. He smiled and informed me that he had written many things besides, and had also published a volume of his poems.

Then he noticed the book in my hand, and asked to see it. When I handed it to him, he saw what it was and asked me if I knew French. He was very pleased to find an old pupil reading French literature in French. Of course, he knew about Anatole France, but he himself could not read French. He looked at the book with interest and observed that it was a very well-printed book. Then he asked: 'How much did you pay for it?' – for he could easily see that it was not quite an ordinary edition, although it was, like all French books, without a binding. When I replied that I had paid the equivalent of two guineas for it, he again asked: 'For the whole set of Anatole France?' When I replied that it was only for that small volume, he blurted out: 'Are you mad?' It was my turn to smile, and to explain to him the esoteric merits of the book. I told him that this was a very special limited edition, and turning to the usual incantation at the end of such books, I rattled it off in French: 'Il a été tiré de cet ouvrage ...' etc., and showed him the number. Then I translated what I had read. He was entranced, because he did not know anything about the 'cult' of limited editions although he cared about good printing and, so far as it was seen in Bengali books, he was familiar with the standards. He again took the book in his hand to look at it more attentively. At that moment a friend of his was passing by. He was a lecturer in English literature in Calcutta University. He called to him to come back and see my book. Then he asked me to read out the publisher's note again and translate it. Then he said to his friend: 'Is that not very creditable for an old pupil of mine?' He took my address, and told me that he would come to see us. We then parted.

He kept his promise and called in the afternoon of the very next Sunday. He had a small book in his hand. It was the only collection of his poems printed till then. Its tide was *Svapan Pashari, Pedlar of Dreams.* He gave it to us. When I took him upstairs to our sitting-room where my brother was, he looked at the large book-case against one of the walls, with its rows of bright books neatly arranged, and remarked: 'It's not enough to buy books. They have to be properly kept and displayed.' In fact, the cases were made in England, and they were of the type which could be taken down in pieces. My father had bought them for us at a secondhand furniture shop.

Mohit Babu went up to the shelves and looked at the books. I took down a few which were of some typographical merit, and explained their points. I showed him a book designed by Bruce Rogers and printed in Caslon type. It also had a number. I told him all about types, starting with Jenson and Aldus Manutius and coming down to Bodoni and Firmin-Didot, with Caslon, Baskerville, etc., in between. He was quite bowled over, because he did care about good printing although he did not know much. I also told him about the layouts, and more particularly about the desirable width of the margins. When I told him that if the inner margin was one inch, the top had to be one and a quarter, the outer one and a half, and the bottom two inches, his eyes were ready to burst out of their sockets. He observed emphatically: 'Yes, it has to be so,' and opening a limited edition of *Atalanta in Calydon* published by the Medici Society he checked up the ratio of the margins. I might add that the book was printed on deckle-edged handmade paper, and had very generous margins on all sides. He was not familiar with deckle-edges and felt them. So far as the Bengali presses in Calcutta could do anything, he was a stickler about printing, and I found that for a Bengali book his was printed better than most. But he now realized the immensity of the subject.

Then I sprung more surprises on him, and they were about book illustrations. In the next few weeks I told him about the revival of true book-illustration since the end of the nineteenth century, and showed a book which the *Studio* had published about French book illustrations from about 1890 to 1923. He did not admire the pictures very much, but at all events he was immensely interested in the processes. I had to tell him about the difference between photographic reproduction of pictures and true engravings. He listened with rapt attention on the one hand to my explanations about half-tone, photogravure, and collotype, and on the other to my lectures on woodcuts, line engraving, etching, dry-point, aquatint, mezzotint, etc. I even showed him reproductions of the copperplate engravings of Dürer issued by the British Museum. Altogether between us, we had a bout of high and happy excitement, for I had not been able to make even my brothers interested in engraving and typography.

On that very first visit he also read one or two of his poems from his book, and, of course, we listened with pleasure, for we loved poetry and he recited it very well. I must also add that poetry is not something which can be read silently if one likes poetry. Mohit Babu's own poems were very striking in rhythm and sound, and although he employed a wide range of metres and diction, from the light and tripping to the grave and stately, he was always effective.

On later occasions, too, he would read something to us, and during the next two or three years whenever he wrote a new poem he would come and read it out in manuscript to us. We considered it a privilege. On one occasion I recited a few lines from one of his long poems in the course of a discussion. He seemed to be surprised, and remarked: 'You have a good ear.' When he read his poems in our ground-floor sitting-room, the windows of which always stood open during the day and in the evenings, people waited outside on the pavement and listened. One of the poems which he wrote and recited in 1925 was an ode to Schopenhauer. It can be regarded as one of his best.

He was apparently telling stories about me to all his friends, literary or not. At times he would take me out to meet them. From the way they looked at me I guessed that my one-time teacher had been exaggerating my learning. They showed great but surprised curiosity, because most probably they had not expected the reported learning in so small and insignificant a young man. But they were compelled by Mohit Babu to be very respectful of my learning, because quite casually he would raise extremely varied topics to make me go through my paces. On most occasions he would come back satisfied with my performances, but at times he also observed after one or other of them: 'You did not seem today to have produced the impression you usually do.' I could only reply with an awkward laugh: 'My dear master, one cannot always be thinking of the impression one produces.' It was embarrassing to be exhibited like a performing animal. But I had sufficient detachment in regard to myself to be amused as well, and I could say this for myself that I performed without self-consciousness. I talked quite naturally, because the things we talked about were always in my mind, and I was continuously and deeply interested in many things. The vocation which was absolutely natural for me was that of a preacher. So I never had to get up my conversational sessions.

It was obvious to me that Mohit Babu was taking an immense and affectionate pride in me, and was to all appearance determined to push me forward. His generosity in this respect was unbounded. This, however, was a general characteristic of most established Bengali authors of my young days. They were always ready to advance the prospects of any young man of promise, of those in whom they discovered potential talent. Nearly all of them had a bunch of proteges, whom they would introduce to editors and publishers, and also to literary society. In regard to this a very undesirable change has come over the character of Bengali writers today. They show fear of new talent.

My First Appearance in Print

I have now to tell the story of my first appearance in print, in which my dear master certainly acted as impresario, but so discreetly that I could feel that the piece was published solely on its merits. It was an exercise in literary criticism, or rather a very personal essay, on an old Bengali poet of the eighteenth century, whose name was Bharat-Chandra Ray(a). It appeared in the leading Indian magazine in English, *The Modern Review*, edited by Ramananda Chatterji, who was one of the most respected and influential journalists of the country. This was the beginning of my career as a writer in English, and to secure publication in that magazine was in itself a great honour for a young and unknown writer. The article was published in the November 1925 issue of the review. I might add that I began my career as a writer in the English language, and did not begin to publish in Bengali till 1927.

My failing as a writer was that I could never finish anything I undertook, but I wrote off that piece in an exceptional burst of energy in the autumn of 1925, and I did so without any thought of publication. This became a habit with me. I wrote on impulses provided by some incident or situation, and tried to secure publication later. Therefore I always clearly remember what made me write an article or even a book. But in the case of this very first published piece of writing by me, I do not remember the antecedents. The subject itself, an old Bengali poet, was not topical in 1925.

But I had become very fond of Bharat-Chandra by that time, and to be interested in him then would never have been set down to any creditable motive. His name was certainly famous. That, however, was as the author of the most frankly erotic poem in Bengali literature, the story of a secret love affair between a princess and a prince in disguise, which gave circumstantial details about their sexual intercourse, so circumstantial that they are not paralleled even in the Arabian Nights. Therefore the book was regarded as obscene by educated Bengalis, who were at the time under the sway of the moral teaching of the Brahmo Samaj and therefore very prudish and puritanical. Thus even the tide of the story, *Vidya-Sundar*, would not be uttered except in a furtive whisper. A highly respected elderly relative of mine who was shocked by Anatole France's *Red Lily*, said to me: 'It's almost as bad as *Vidya-Sundar*.' However, in the decade preceding, Bharat-Chandra was taken up by a radical and influential Bengali critic, Pramatha Chaudhuri, who was a barrister besides being married to Tagore's niece. He tried to rehabilitate the old poet, but only for his art and mastery of the Bengali language, not for his treatment of the subject of love. This inadequacy might have given me the idea of writing about Bharat-Chandra, whom I admired both for his art and for his mind.

All the available editions of his poems were execrably printed on execrable paper. Even so I had got one of these bound in white parchment, with gold-tooling. I showed this to Mohit Babu, who admired the binding, and was more interested when as a contrast in the same genre I showed him my set of Casanova in French, bound in black calf and black-and-white marbled paper to match, as I told him, the dark beauty of the writing. My Bharat-Chandra was borrowed from me by a literary friend, who, of course, never returned it. Mohit Babu was not familiar with Bharat-Chandra, and so when I recited some felicitous passages to him he would burst out in exclamations expressing his admiration of the sheer virtuosity. But he rather shrank from some of the sensual passages (not the most frank ones) which I read out to him.

When, however, I showed him my essay he was very enthusiastic. He was, apparently, quite overwhelmed by its cleverness. I should explain that in spite of my very correct and chaste training in matters literary, I was then passing through a phase of cleverness, amounting to what might be called literary dandyism. I had fallen under the influence of some of the younger prose writers of the day, e.g. Lytton Strachey, of course; but also Aldous Huxley, Percy Lubbock, C. E. Montague, Middleton Murry, and so on. The long first articles in the *T.L.S.* also cast their anonymous spell on me. To these writers, I added Lionel Johnson from the previous epoch. Furthermore, although in regard to French prose, I was wholly dominated by La Rochefoucauld, Pascal, La Bruyère, and among the contemporaries by Anatole France, when it was a question of ideology I fell under the influence of many fashionable French writers. One of them was Rémy de Gourmont, whose essay on the association and dissociation of ideas had impressed me very much. I certainly wanted to imitate some of their *jeux d'esprit*. I must have thought that Bharat-Chandra with his eroticism would enable me to pull off some crackers. I wanted to have a go both at the puritanical rejection and the consciously unconventional rehabilitation.

Thus it happened that the article exuded all the cleverness I had acquired by that time. I was certainly proud of it in the months following its publication. But very soon I developed such an antipathy to it that I never read it again till I had to write this chapter, except that in 1928 I quoted a passage from it in a Bengali article dealing with eroticism in literature. I felt very much embarrassed by this debutante of mine, whom I considered over-dressed, over-made-up, and over-perfumed. Now I would pronounce it only as a mixed performance. Perhaps I might give an idea of the queerness of the mixture.

Anyone reading the article and taking note of the airs and graces in it, would not-only think that I seemed to be determined to lose no advantage, but was also insufferably affected. However, just as I did not talk selfconsciously, I also did not write self-consciously. On the other hand, I was not also natural in the sense of being just myself I was neither more nor less sincere than an actor who identifies himself with the part he had taken. I had conceived a psychological portrait of the old Bengali poet after a certain European type, and tried to present the creation of my imagination by means of a style of writing conforming to the type.

I had noticed that Lionel Johnson practised inversion of the syntactical order in some of his sentences. So my article opened with this sentence: 'Bharat-Chandra, it has become the fashion, of late, in advanced literary circles to praise.' There were allusions to the French Parnassians, Baudelaire, Anatole France, Maurice Barrès, not to speak of Voltaire, Diderot, Choderlos de Laclos, etc., who were associated with Bharat-Chandra by me as fellow-writers of the eighteenth century. In speaking of his mastery of form, the following quotation from Gautier was inevitable:

> Oui, l'oeuvre sort plus belle
> D'une forme au travail
> Rebelle,
> Vers, marbre, onyx, émail.

Regretting the absence of a well-printed edition of the poet (which even now is not available), I wrote: 'If a publisher is enterprising enough to take up the venture, I, for one, shall be ready to subscribe to a sumptuous edition of Bharat-Chandra, printed on deckle-edged handmade paper, as crisp as his verse, and decorated with copper-plate engravings in the style of Boucher.'

About Vidya, the princess, who was the famous heroine of Bharat-Chandra, and who was regarded almost as a bitch in the puritanical circles of Bengal to which I belonged, I wrote:

> Beautiful Vidya! Where art thou? O unstable!
> Livest only in the land of fable,
> Only in the poet's fairy strain?
> As a dream or half-forgotten story ...

This hymn was the English version of Schiller's 'Ode to the Gods of Greece', set to music by Schubert – *Schöne Welt, wo bist du?...*

In order to enjoy or appreciate such airs the readers ought to have been aware of their sources. That question did not trouble my mind. I gave even more recondite airs, and thus wrote:

'To be a fanatic in Gaul or indulge in irony and dilettantism with Nero? When the question posed itself, Bharat-Chandra decided for Nero and irony and dilettantism, though thereby he put himself in a blind alley.'

Would anyone in India have guessed that this was from Maurice Barrès? In his *Jardin de Bérénice* he had put these observations in an imaginary letter from Seneca, the philosopher and mentor of Nero, to Lazarus who had risen from the dead:

'Il vous faut peser si ce vous sera un mode de vie plus abondant en voluptés de partir avec Mesdemoiselles vos soeurs pour être fanatique, en Gaule, ou de demeurer à faire de l'ironie et du dilettantisme avec Néron ...

'Néron, mon cher Lazare, excusez-moi d'y insister, est un esprit infiniment plus large que vos deux excellentes soeurs, mais il est dans son genre le bout du monde; en lui les idées entrent dans un cul-de-sac; Marthe et Marie sont deux portes sur l'avenir.'

It can also be asked how many people would have grasped the point made in this apostrophising. Again, siding with Vidya whom our moralists consigned to hell-fire, I wrote:

'I give all discerning men the choice between living in hell and being in a fool's paradise. As for myself [actually a puny but ferocious puritan, who lived the life of a puritan], what have I to do in paradise? But to hell will I go. For to hell go the fine clerk and the fine knight; the brave soldier and the free-born man, and the goodly poet and spirited *conteurs*.'

This was from the medieval French story of Aucassin and Nicolette. Lest anyone should get the impression from all this that in my very first literary venture I was showing myself as a dancing monkey, I would add a few other citations, just to indicate that I was also capable of sensible judgements. For example, I said that Bharat-Chandra 'ought to be above the condescension of half-insincere critics as he is above the contumely of solemn puritans, for he is in the purest and highest classical tradition of the literature of Bengal.' I also wrote: 'An ironical philosophy has this merit at least that it enables us to laugh at fools and rogues, whom but for it, we might be so weak as to hate.' However right in itself, the observation was an insincere literary pose in me, for I hated both fools and rogues, and did not consider myself weak. This was Anatole-Francing on my part. Another remark of mine was this: 'Some of the most passionately erotic poets have been the most self-contained of men.' But perhaps I showed my good sense more clearly in the following passage dealing with the erotic descriptions in Bharat-Chandra: 'Bharat-Chandra,' I wrote,

'treats the charming, bizarre, repelling, pitiful, overpowering facts of sex-life with wit, flippancy, and, as many would consider, indecency. On this question, a war of arguments is likely to be waged between the upholders of the romantic conception of love and the advocates of what, in the absence of a better adjective, has been termed its realistic conception. No controversy should be more irrelevant and less fruitful. Love is too deep- seated, complex and protean a passion to be contained in either of these two simple entities: sensuality and sentiment. The poet or the novelist's idea of love, whether as something ethereal and disembodied or something frankly carnal, is not the outcome of a scientific investigation like that of Mr. Havelock Ellis. It is purely ideal (in the artistic sense) and is the result of the process of simplification and selection which is unconsciously and ceaselessly going on in the artist's mind and which endows his visions with a beauty and harmony of effect unattainable in real life.'

This may seem commonplace today, but was not in 1925, especially for modem Indians. Coming from me, it was remarkable because I was a firm votary of romantic love, and set down this view of erotic writing with an exercise of the will.

Mohit Babu, on his part, was charmed by the piece and not repelled by its affectations. He read the article, which I had got typed without any definite idea of offering it to an editor, and thought of me more than before as a father regards a son who appears to be a prodigy. It must be kept in mind, however, that this kind of showing off was very common in our critical writing, especially if we wrote in English. The weakness continues.

Anyhow, Mohit Babu took me to some of his friends and made me read out the piece to them. It seems curious now how tolerant the Bengalis were of this kind of infliction. Actually, they did not think of listening to the reading of newly-written pieces by their literary friends as an infliction at all. My master even brought his friend. Professor S. K. De, to our house – to make him hear the piece, but Dr (of London) De chose to read it silently himself, and observed with a smile: 'It is very new in manner.'

Soon after, Mohit Babu asked me to go out for a visit and take the article with me. He wanted to introduce me to Ashoke Chatterji, son of the famous editor, who was in charge of the production of *The Modern Review*. He was a Cambridge man, a good boxer, one-time trooper in the Calcutta Light Horse, a volunteer regiment of the Indian Army, altogether one of the *jeunesse dorée* of Calcutta. We went to his house, not to the office, and found Ashoke Babu seated at his desk.

He looked me over, and certainly did not think that I belonged to his class in looks or clothes. But in good Bengali society of those days a reputation for learning and literary gifts could always compensate for other deficiencies. Thus Ashoke Babu was very polite and treated me almost as an equal, although he had acquired the reputation of being a snob. I am sure he had been briefed by Mohit Babu beforehand. So, when I finished reading out the article he simply stretched out his hand and said: 'Give it to me.' I did so and he put it away in a drawer without saying another word about it. We talked about other things. Afterwards I was told by Mohit Babu that it was going to be published in the next issue of *The Modern Review*. He also brought the proofs, showed me how to read them, and when it was published he brought me the payment for it. I was launched to his satisfaction.

But that did not mean he had given up his old role of teacher, for he scolded me for the manner in which I had read the piece to Ashoke Babu. It was very bad, he said, and implied that I had disgraced myself by such poor reading of English before a Cambridge man.

He particularly objected to my pronouncing the 'g' hard in words of Greek derivation, e.g. in panegyric, hegemony or gyroscope. Over pronunciation he was very touchy. One day, when talking with Dr De I pronounced 'bibliophile' in the French way, whereas soon after Dr De did so in the English manner (bibliophile). Afterwards Mohit Babu referred bitterly to this lapse of mine, and when I told him that many words in English were pronounced differently by different people, he was not placated. He said excitedly that if anyone pronounced a word in a different way after he had pronounced it in his way, he felt as if he had been given a slap in the face. I could not help laughing out at that. When everyone of us was speaking English very badly it seemed absurd to me to be so very sensitive. But every educated Indian thought that he spoke and wrote English best. This weakness, too, persists.

First Incursion into Public Debate

As a writer I remain till today one of the *engagés*, involving myself in every aspect of political, social, and cultural life, almost all over the world. And this side of my vocation as writer made its appearance simultaneously with the writing of the article with which I have just dealt, and in which I showed myself to be as much of a believer in art for art's sake as it was possible for me to be. Almost at the same time I wrote another piece, which dealt with an aspect of the cultural situation in India which was being discussed at the time on account of the publication in April 1925, of a book entitled *The Heart of Aryavarta* by Lord Ronaldshay (the future Marquis of Zetland).

Lord Ronaldshay was Governor of Bengal from 1917 to 1921. Although it was a period of political ferment and agitation in India, he also showed a lively interest in the cultural situation, especially as it was in Bengal. I was told that he read *The Modern Review* regularly and kept the issues on his study table. His book took a view of the cultural situation in India which was justified by the trends it showed from the beginning of the century to 1920. It was a period of domination of conservative Hindu thought, which was particularly noticeable in the political field. Modern Indian nationalism, which was derived wholly from Europe, showed its foreign affiliations in social and cultural thinking as well. But towards the end of the nineteenth century a movement of Hindu revivalism arose, and in spite of the fact that its historical basis was furnished by the researches of Western Orientalists, it became very strongly Hindu, according to its own interpretation of Hinduism. The first movement of nationalist agitation, which was known as the Swadeshi Movement, had the thinking of this school as its ideological basis. Certainly, the revivalist thinking retained its influence till the end of Lord Ronaldshay's period of Governorship, and in his book he extended the idea to cultural life in order to explain the nationalist movement. It embodied the thesis that culturally India would remain loyal to Hindu ideas and emotions. The last word of his title,*Aryavarta*, summed it up. It meant 'Land of the Aryas or Aryans.' The ancient Hindus never called themselves 'Hindu', but only Arya. The neo-Hindus revived this term and always boasted about being Aryans.

I had become convinced otherwise. It was perfectly true that taking note of the opinions prevailing when he was Governor, Lord Ronaldshay could come to his conclusion. But taking a closer view of the realities of our mental and cultural life I thought that the revivalist talk was both superficial and artificial, although not consciously insincere. In any case, in respect of cultural activities and even social behaviour I held without any hesitation that a very large degree of derivative, diluted, and secondhand westernization, was inescapable. That was the view I wanted to set against Lord Ronaldshay's.

It was certainly bold for a young Bengali to pit himself against him. His book was being widely discussed in India, and had also commended itself to the nationalists, because, whatever they did in practice, in their thinking and precepts they could not become free from their retrograde and negative nationalism. I scoffed at their talk.

It may also seem curious that I should be able to write two pieces so different in their subject and treatment almost at the same time. But the impact of Western life and civilization on us in India, and the interaction between the two cultures of which I was a product like thousands of others were a matter of serious intellectual concern for educated Bengalis. I also was one of them, and the subject has retained its interest for me all through my life. In fact, all my writings are in one way or other commentaries on this very large theme.

Finally if I was bold in challenging Lord Ronaldshay, I was perhaps even more so, given my lack of enterprise and diffidence at the time, in seeking publication for the article. Without telling anybody, not even Mohit Babu, I took it to the office of *The Statesman of* Calcutta, one of the leading newspapers in English in India, generally regarded as the mouthpiece of the local British, and certainly both owned and edited by Englishmen. In those days it hardly published anything by an Indian, however distinguished, except in very special circumstances. But one afternoon I walked into the old office of the paper at the head of Chowringhee Road, as into a lion's den, and left the article in a tray pointed to me by a sub-editor who hardly looked at me. Since I was in Government service then I did not want my name to be published, but asked them to print it as from a correspondent.

I did not read this newspaper then, nor did I make any inquiry. I thought they would write, and since they did not I assumed that the article had been rejected. One day, however, towards the end of January 1926, a young student, who was formerly Mohit Babu's pupil but at the time in Calcutta University, called on me with a clipping from *The Statesman*, and asked me if I could make a guess as to the writer of a brilliant and trenchant article. I at once saw that it was mine. He was surprised, for he had attributed it to Bepin Chandra Pal, a famous Bengali writer and nationalist leader, who was old then. Mohit Babu came in by chance, and was very pleased. He knew nothing about this article of mine. He read it carefully, and was very complimentary to me. He could not have liked my airy dismissal of the conservative position, for in his social and cultural thinking he belonged to the revivalist school. But he admired the writing. I might add that the student who brought the article to my notice later entered the Indian Civil Service and rose to the highest rank in it.

As it happens, this clipping (without date and even the name of the paper) is the only record I have of this bold enterprise of mine. The date of publication I got from *The Statesman* office very much later.

The article was published in *The Statesman* on 15 January 1926. I summed up Lord Ronaldshay's view of the nationalist movement by saying that he was representing it as the by-product of a clash of cultures and I commented:

'The theory of an eternal conflict, secular and spiritual, between the two antithetical civilizations – so it is said – of the East and the West is, of course, not new. It has been accepted as a working hypothesis by most historians and political thinkers for the last fifty years, in their ruminations over the relations of Europe and Asia, and under its influence the intermittent warfare between the peoples living on the borders of the continents have been welded into a unified drama whose first act was played out on the plains of Marathon and the last act is yet to come. Lord Ronaldshay has affiliated the Indian nationalist movement with this tremendous historical phenomenon.'

I added rather maliciously that this view was not only philosophically satisfying but had the additional merit of being acceptable to the Indian nationalists because Lord Ronaldshay was attributing to them a role in history whose want they must have felt keenly in their newly awakened national self-respect.

But I asked: 'Is this picture of India as a battlefield of rival civilizations true?' The object of the rhetorical question was, of course, to say politely that it was not. I said that our real cultural role was much less ambitious, to wit: 'It is to assimilate, by slow degrees, the ways of Europe, till at last civilization in India becomes the provincial edition of the civilization of Europe, palely reflecting like the moon its borrowed light from the sun beyond.'

I went on to say that such a view might seem to be very fanciful in view of the clamorous proclamation of nationalist views concerning every aspect of life in India. As I put it: 'There is on the surface, loud and insistent, so much gloating over the failure and bankruptcy of European civilization, so much profession of faith in the ideals of ancient India, so much wearing of khaddar and so much apostrophising of Englishmen to go back with their good and bad alike to their far-away homes across the "Seven Seas",' so that, I added, 'no one who is in touch with facts can deny that an elaborate anti-European philosophy of life and emotional predisposition has come into being.'

But all of it, I declared, had no substance. The revolt against Western influences was only in words. After that I analysed the cultural activities in which the loyalty to Indian or rather Hindu traditions was supposed to be very assertive, and I tried to show that the 'Orientalism' was only on the surface when not a pose. More particularly, I denied the existence of nationalist thinking. I said:

'The nationalism of Indian thought is a composite product possessing unity from this point of view alone that it is aimed at the system of authority which the British have established in India. Provided a system of thought or an institution is likely to prove an intellectual dissolvent of British power, the nationalist thinkers are eclectic enough not to worry whether it comes from the Gita or the Bible, Fascist Italy or Communistic Moscow. The conflict of civilizations in India, so far as it exists, instead of being the cause of the political discontent is in reality its effect. Had the political power of the British in India vanished today, the Indian would have cared as little about the national shibboleths as the Turk cared about the Caliphate or the Fez. As things are, the paradoxical obstacle in the way of a complete Europeanization of India today, is the British power in India.'

It was bound to be so because, as I observed in the article, 'natural forces are stronger than artificial checks.' I also said that 'the process of Europeanization is going on at a rate which is as remarkable as it is imperceptible.' I concluded by saying that 'there is no reason to hope that the political struggle will abate with the gradual progress of Europeanization. Only it will be transformed into a sort of civil war in which the disciples of Europe will be ranged against her sons.'

All this was written by a young man of twenty-seven, and recalling it at the age of eighty-four I cannot say that I did not have some inkling into the future. As to the issue of Westernization of Indian life, the article certainly gave evidence of my capacity to see through appearances and perceive the reality behind them. When I wrote the article, rejection of Western influences was being preached by the Gandhian school of nationalism in one way and by the Bengali neo-Hindu school in another. Lord Ronaldshay, looking at the cultural scene as an outsider, was bound to take their preaching seriously. It was not easy for an Indian, Hindu or Muslim, to do otherwise. Yet I had the realism to perceive the latent power of Western influences. But what I could not foresee then was the transformation that was to come over the nature of the Westernization – that it was to concern the mind less than behaviour and externals. The disintegration of a genuine modern Indian culture by the 'democratic' or 'Pop' culture of the West has become the great sorrow of my life.

I am glad that I was led by Lord Ronaldshay's book to turn away from literature in the strict sense to deal with ideas and cultural questions. Literature would have made a wholly different sort of writer of me, for although literature has been a part of my life as lived and a good influence on it, as an exclusive subject of literary activity on my part it would have held out temptations to that side of my character which pulled me very strongly towards becoming a dilettante, amateur, or aesthete in the good as well as bad senses of the words. Fortunately, I was able to suppress the dandy side of myself without losing my sense of humour, and also to shed priggishness without sacrificing seriousness. This was brought about partly by the awfully tragic character of the public events all over the world since the first World War. Otherwise, I should perhaps have been quite happy to say before dying: *Qualis artifex pereo!*

CHAPTER 6

The Literary Situation in Bengal

However, in spite of this politico-cultural foray, I did not continue to write on public questions, and resumed that only in 1929. In the meanwhile, I was led into a literary controversy by my teacher Mohit Babu, and I emerged as a writer in Bengali in the field of literary criticism. At this point I shall describe the initiation and background of that phase of my life.

Incubation of a Literary Controversy

Within two years I became deeply involved in Bengali literary life, established myself as a literary critic, and became the editor of a magazine of literary polemics. In fact, that was the real beginning of my career as a writer. My English articles were only exploratory forays, and in any case they could give me only a journalistic standing, and could not establish me as a writer. But this literary involvement of mine was not so much in literature as such, as in literature as the expression of the cultural and mental life of a people. It was also involvement in a quarrel which I might describe as our version of the French *querelle des anciens et des modernes* of the seventeenth century, but with a deeper cultural significance. We who began the quarrel thought that certain new trends which were appearing in Bengali writing threatened not only literature, but also the Bengali mind and Bengali culture as a whole. More of this later.

Here I am concerned with its incubation and describe the literary situation which made me inclined to become a crusader. My final attitude was very largely influenced by Mohit Babu, who knew more about the contemporary situation and felt more strongly about it than I did. I knew Bengali literature up to 1920 very well, but had ceased to keep myself abreast of the latest writings because, on the one hand, I had developed other interests and, on the other, had a feeling that the Bengali literary effort was reaching the point of exhaustion. Tagore and Sarat Chandra Chatterji dominated the Bengali literary scene, but to me it seemed even they had touched the limits of their creative achievement. And so far as I read anything by younger writers, they seemed to be both crude and shallow as a rule. I became deeply suspicious of their manner as well as matter.

But I did not feel any deep concern. That was roused in me by Mohit Babu, who in spite of being one of the young writers, with his most mature work still before him, showed a violent dislike for any kind of writing which was not affiliated with the established tradition. His own individuality was only an extension of that. The tradition, itself the creation of fifty years of effort and innovation, had by 1920 reached a state of fixity which allowed only variations to be played on it, as on the main theme of a musical composition. Mohit Babu felt very strongly in literary matters, for Bengali literature was his life. Apart from that, he was also a Bengali Hindu conservative of the school of Bankim Chandra Chatterji and Swami Vivekananda.

I myself had my susceptibilities. Even before meeting Mohit Babu I had developed an antipathy to a young Bengali poet, whom, I found later, he disliked even more strongly. He was a Muslim named Kazi Nazrul Islam, who had served in the 49th Bengali Regiment in Mesopotamia in the first World War. This regiment was not a success and was disbanded after the war, but Nazrul Islam had reached the rank of Havildar in it, which was equivalent to being a sergeant. This made him inclined to make use of some cheap military claptrap in his poems, which were accepted then as the expression of a new revolutionary spirit. Through all that he became something of a rage. But in spite of having a good deal of untaught skill in the use of language and metre, to me he seemed very superficial, indisciplined, and frothy. As if that was not enough to prejudice me against him, I was repelled by his references to torpedoes and mines as symbols of the revolutionary spirit. I had outgrown even the real Bengali revolutionary spirit of the early days of the nationalist movement, and was not likely to be impressed by the exhibition of it in a weak and spurious form.

I cannot describe the contempt I felt when I saw a procession of Muslims marching under my windows at 41 Mirzapore Street, chanting one of Nazrul's poems on the victory of Mustafa Kemal in 1922. It was a long rigmarole, which certainly Kemal, if he ever came to read it, would have trampled under foot, and it had the refrain: 'Hurro, ho, hurro, ho, tu-ne kamal kia, Bhai!' (Hurrah, hurrah, thou hast pulled it off splendidly, O brother!) This was not Bengali but Urdu – and this was consistent with the Bengali habit of employing English or Urdu and Hindi when in a passion. In the poem the use of the word *Kamal* (which meant perfection or something splendid) was a pun on Kemal's name.

My dislike for Nazrul Islam grew, and soon after the publication of the article on Lord Ronaldshay's book I sent a sarcastic article on Nazrul to *The Statesman*. But in those days the newspaper was not interested in Bengali literary movements, and it returned the article. However, my first incursion into Bengali journalism was made with a severe review of a new collection of poems by Nazrul. It was published in the foremost Bengali magazine, *Prabasi*.

That was after I had met Mohit Babu. But with all his dislike for certain aspects of Nazrul's poetry, Mohit Babu admired his virtuosity as a versifier, and often recited his poems in our house, and put as much gusto into the reading as he did in his own poems. Incidentally, I might mention that the feud between the two is continuing posthumously.

But it was not simply this or that writer individually who was creating my aversion to the writing which was attempting to be new. I disapproved of the general trend, in which I found decline of taste, sensibility, and sincerity, as well as decline of purely technical competence. It seemed to me that in all that was appearing in print from the younger writers there was an indication of the decline of the whole cultural life of Bengal. I thought that the Bengali literary effort, which was the most successful cultural enterprise of the Bengali people, was running into a channel which led only into a desert or a morass, in which it would lose itself.

Modem Bengali Literature

To make this feeling of mine intelligible, which led to my involvement later in a literary campaign, I shall have to give an account of the rise of modern Bengali literature. By 1900 the literature whose language could be recognized as modem Bengali was already some five hundred years old, that is, as old as English literature properly so-called. But it was severely limited in its forms and subject matter. There was no prose literature at all. All of the literature was in verse, some of which could be regarded as poetry, some only as story-telling in verse form. The subjects were old Hindu myths and legends retold in a simple manner. There was a small quantity of lyrical poetry which was of high quality, but with mythological themes. Within these confined limits Bengali literature achieved a good deal of fullness and sophistication by the end of the eighteenth century.

Then came a comprehensive revolution, which created what was a new literature with new genres and new themes, as well as new sentiments and ideas. This was brought about by the knowledge of English literature which came with British rule. In the immense extension of manner and matter which followed, the most important creation was prose literature, and in it the most successful genres were novels and short stories. In poetry there was a complete break with tradition, and adoption from English of forms and metres which had never before been seen in Bengali poetry, fairly old as it was. In spirit it was an acclimitization of both European classicism and romanticism. At the turn of the century anyone familiar with European poetry of the period could even sniff a little of Swinburne or Mallarmé in Bengali poetry of the times, although there certainly was no conscious imitation.

This literature, taken with English literature in the original, virtually remodelled the Bengali mind with new ideas, feelings, and sensations. The forms were also wholly new. So the conservatives called the literary innovators mere imitators, and held them up to ridicule as mere apes. Their writings were criticized as being artificial and insincere. When the charge was repeated by one of the most eminent Bengalis of the day, who himself was a religious reformer, the challenge was taken up by Bankim Chandra Chatterji, the greatest of the innovators, who was the creator of Bengali fiction and remains according to my view the greatest novelist in the Bengali language, although we have some very fine novelists who could stand comparison with any European novelist.

He did not offer apologies for whatever imitation there was in the new Bengali literature, but explained why its creators had to be sedulous apes with their eyes open. He declared boldly that imitation was the first stage in the creation of any new civilization or of a new literature within it. He set down his view of cultural imitation in an article in Bengali in 1876. He said in it that only the earliest civilizations had arisen by themselves by what might be called spontaneous generation without borrowing from any outside source, and among these early civilizations he mentioned the Egyptian. But since then, he went on to say, all new cultures had begun their life by following an external example set by an older civilization. He gave as the first example of this the creation by the Romans of their own culture by following the Greeks. As he put it: 'The result of that imitation was the elocution of Cicero, the histories of Tacitus, the epic of Virgil, the drama of Plautus and Terence, the lyrics of Horace and Ovid,' and so on. Continuing, he said that modern European literature, whether by the

Italians or the French, was an imitation of the Attic drama, and he declared this also the case in the fine arts. Then to give force to his argument he asked a very pointed question, which was likely to go home because it was the Englishman in India who were most loud in calling us apes: 'What will those who get angry at our eating or clothing ourselves in the English manner say to the English people's adoption of French fashions in clothes and French cuisine.' At all events, we imitate our political masters, whom do the English people imitate?'

He set down a view about the cultural result of British rule in India which will surprise those who in these days have noted the extreme chauvinism of Indians who cannot even speak their own languages correctly and come to Oxford or Cambridge to make themselves respectable. Chatterji said that when two different types of life, one superior and the other inferior, come in contact, it is natural for the inferior life to imitate the superior life. With greater pointedness he wrote: 'The Bengali sees that an Englishman is superior to him in everything, in culture, in education, in strength, wealth, and happiness. Then, why should he not try to be like an Englishman. The question, however, is: How to do that? The Bengali thinks that if he does as the Englishman does, he would be as educated, prosperous, and *happy* as the Englishman. Any people, whichever they might be, would have done the same in similar circumstances.'

I shall explain the significance of Chatterji's reference to greater happiness in the life of Englishmen, which might seem curious in a cultural argument. Here let me conclude the summing up of Chatterji's defence of imitation. At the end of the article he set down a number of cut-and-dried propositions regarding the process of cultural interaction. He actually numbered them. Here they are:

1. In human societies civilization originates in two ways: certain societies become civilized independently, by themselves; others learn from elsewhere. Acquisition of civilization in the first-mentioned way takes a long time; it is quicker in the second manner.

2. When a relatively uncultured people come in contact with a people of higher culture, it is through the second method that culture begins to flow in quickly. In such a situation social evolution takes the form of a wholesale imitation by the uncivilized society of the ways of the civilized society. This is the law of nature.

3. So, the obvious imitativeness of Bengali society is neither unnatural nor due to any defect in the Bengali character.

4. Imitation is not harmful in itself. On the other hand, very beneficial results may come out of it. The first stage of imitation is followed by the later stage of independence. If one takes note of the state of Bengali society it cannot be asserted with dogmatism that the inclination to imitate is bad. Rather, there is much to be hoped for from it.

5. Nonetheless, serious evil may come out of imitation. If the imitative tendency remains strong after the proper time for it is passed, or if even during that period it is indiscriminate and uncontrolled, disaster will follow. [from Bengali]

I do not think that any historian of civilization or an anthropologist dealing with what is called 'acculturation' could have pronounced on cultural interaction more sanely and soundly. I shall translate only one other sentence of Chatterji's to show how free from commonplace nationalist prejudices he was. He wrote epigrammatically: 'It is, indeed, a matter of hope for die Bengali people that they are imitating the English.' Yet Chatterji was the creator of the Hindu nationalism of our times. What he wholly condemned and regarded as despicable was imitation by those who were devoid of talent. But he was detached enough to say that the majority of the Bengali imitators were of that undesirable type. He went even further and said that no other people were such adepts in imitating all the worst features of a foreign culture, and of neglecting the best.

However, imitation in literature in Bengal was not mere copying even at the beginning. Any genre or any literary form taken over from European literature was wholly recast in the Bengali mould and completely naturalized, so that die new had no strangeness, and created only vital feelings of delight which comes from growth and awareness of growth. Within forty years of the beginning of the new Bengali literature around 1855, all the poetic and prose genres and forms borrowed from English were naturalized.

To give an example from the field of metre, blank verse was completely foreign to the Bengali poetic tradition, although Sanskrit poetry had no rhymes. In contrast, traditional Bengali poetry was jingling and singsong, and often became mere doggerel. So at first, Bengalis had extreme difficulty in reading blank verse and had to be taught carefully, as I also was as a boy. There is a story that one day Michael Madhusudan Dutt, the creator of Bengali blank verse, was walking along a street and he heard a grocer chanting his epic poem, which was based on an episode of the Ramayana, as if he was reciting his Bengali Ramayana. Dutt at once stepped in, and showed the grocer how to read his verse. But towards the end of the century blank verse had become such a part of literary culture that on the wedding night when it was customary for the sisters-in-law to put the bridegroom through his paces and rag him if he failed, they would ask him to recite a passage from Dutt's epic. Only if the bridegroom could do that well was he considered to be a fit husband for their sister. The sonnet, too, was acclimatized in the same manner. And the structure in Bengali was both Spenserian and Petrarcan.

The new prose was at first only a toddler, and for some decades it remained heavy and gawky, as if it had not yet found its natural movement. But by 1900 Bengali prose at its best was as smooth and limpid as the prose of Anatole France. Even with the prose works of either of the two great Bengali writers, i.e. Bankim Chandra Chatterji or Rabindranath Tagore, a history of Bengali prose style can be written.

The foreign literary genres were also acclimatized by being made natural in their subjects and themes. None of the innovators tried to introduce exotic subjects, in addition to exotic forms. At first the subjects were taken from ancient Hindu myths and legends or history, and after that from contemporary Bengali life as lived. In short, there was a complete integration of Bengali literature and Bengali life. Of course, the Bengali life as described in the literature was the Bengali life which was transforming itself under Western ideas and examples. Thus there was no clash between life and literature. These evolved *pari passu* and finally mingled in one historical stream.

But this thoroughgoing assimilation and naturalization of foreign literary influences did not mean that educated Bengalis ceased to read or take interest in the English and European writers of their times. Actually, their reading became wider. For one thing, literature of every kind was a great enjoyment for them, and after that they were extremely curious about new ideas. So they went on reading both English authors and such European authors as were available in English. At the popular or relaxed level they read Rider Haggard, Marie Corelli, Hall Caine and went forward to Charles Garvice, Edgar Wallace, and Wodehouse. On the higher and more prestigious level they read Wells, Yeats, Shaw, or even Synge, and talked about the Abbey Theatre and the Neo-Celtic Movement as if they were Irishmen. I myself read Syñge's *Playboy of the Western World* as a young student and could not understand at all what the fuss was about.

Among the Europeans the literary Bengalis read Ibsen, Bjornson, Strindberg; three great Russians; Romain Rolland and Anatole France, and even Paul Bourget; Gerhart Hauptman and Hermann Sudermann, to mention the more notable names. Anatole France somehow had acquired a reputation for immorality, and when I was a student at the Presidency College, Calcutta, between 1918 and 1920, his books could not be issued to the students from the library, although I could see in it very coarsely obscene annotations on the margins of Boccaccio and Rabelais in English translations.

To be up to date about literary fashions was a greater craze among us than to be up to date in clothes is with society women, and this desire became keener with the introduction of the Nobel Prize for literature. Not to be able to show at least one book by a Nobel Laureate was regarded almost as being illiterate. So I read Sienkievicz {*Quo Vadis*, of course) as a schoolboy, and saw even Mistral in the hands of very fashionable young Bengalis, and not to have read Maeterlinck was inconceivable. On the strength of the Nobel Prize Rudolph Eucken was placed on the same plane of philosophical eminence as Bergson, who did not get the prize until 1927 but was recognized to have intrinsic greatness. In their race for modernity the Bengalis came at the stage of which I am going to speak, to Knut Hamsun and Gorky.

But all this new reading and discussion made no inpact on Bengali literature, nor on the Bengali personality. The habitual reading of foreign authors created an outer ring of the literary life of the Bengalis. Its atmosphere was not only rarefied but also artificial, so that the educated Bengali read these books with something like a psychological gas-mask on. He breathed naturally in the world of Bengali literature, so that there existed in his literary life a duality, which was also seen in his putting on of European clothes and eating European food. But reading foreign literature was on a far greater scale than the wearing of foreign clothing or the eating of European food.

Literature and Life in Bengal

Bengali literature and its enjoyment in combination provided a self-contained and self-sufficient mental world. It has to be pointed out that in die latter half of the nineteenth century Bengali life and Bengali literature had become very closely connected, and literature was bringing into the life of educated Bengalis something which they could not get from any other source. Whether in the cities and towns or in the villages, where the Bengali gentry still had the permanent base of their life, it was the mainstay of their life of feeling, sentiment, and passion. Both emotional capacity and idealism were sustained by it.

It was through literature again that they sought to bring happiness into their life. Traditional Bengali life had for a long time been singularly drab, narrow, and harsh, except when it was softened by religion. Life in the world was sordid, and often rapacious. The awareness that happiness had a claim on human beings came to the Bengalis at first from their reading of English literature and observation of English life, and, after that, the actual business of bringing happiness into life was taken over by Bengali literature. That was what Chatterji meant when he spoke of the Bengali's perception of greater happiness in the life of Englishmen. Thus it was that through the interaction of life and literature the Bengalis for the first time arrived at that fullness of human existence which can be given to it only by a free and abundant play of emotion, feeling, and imagination.

The practical consequence of this combination of life and literature was that even in remote villages one could come upon a good collection of Bengali books. In 1914 I went to visit relatives in a village near Kishorganj. The village could be reached only by riding a horse, elephant, or latterly cycle, as there were no roads to the place. Women went in palanquins. But when after arriving I opened a side door of the main room, I came upon another whose walls were lined with book-cases, and all the Bengali classics and bound volumes of the foremost literary magazines were on their shelves. I spent some happy days in that room.

The inspiration to form libraries, at first awakened by the desire to affect the manners of the English gentleman, was sustained by Bengali fiction. Many of the heroes were young men of leisure given to reading and building up libraries. The young heroines, too, were in the habit of buying all the new novels, and on a more exalted level the heroines formed libraries for their undeclared lovers and as altars of their own undeclared love. In actual life, too, books meant a good deal. For instance, when my sister was married in 1916, a college friend of mine presented her with fifteen of the latest novels by the foremost writers, and my sister certainly did not prize them less than her far more costly clothes and jewellery. In fact, sales of fiction and poetry as wedding presents were a sure standby for their publishers. So, to make them wear a wedding-present look the books were bound in coloured silk and, besides, given padded and bevelled sides.

The compass of that mental life was not wide, nor was its perimeter large. But in its integration of life and literature it was coherent, authentic, and sincere. Perhaps I could not give a better idea of what it stood for than by translating a passage from a story by Tagore. Its hero is one of those who belonged to the type called Young Bengal, an MA, BL by education and a lawyer by nominal profession, but whose real vocation was reading, extended somewhat by teaching a little girl, the daughter of one of his neighbours, and trying to initiate her into the joys of literature.

He had the misfortune to be jailed for an offence which though formally criminal was really political. On his release after five years in prison, he had nowhere to go but was surprised to find a landau and pair waiting for him at the gate of the jail. He was taken in it to a strange house, and shown into a room which had large book-cases all around, on whose shelves were ranged beautifully bound books shining in their colours and gold-tooling. Bending over the table at which he was sitting he saw a cracked slate on whose frame a name was written in large black letters in his own hand. He at once understood where he had come, that it was the house of the little girl, but he had not heard that she was now a young widow. He fell into a reverie of his old days:

'That happy life of the past had nothing which was uncommon or excessive. In it the days followed days without awareness of their passing in trifling occupations and small happinesses, and teaching a little girl pupil could not be regarded as anything but a negligible activity against the pursuit of his own studies. But the passing of those solitary days among the village fields, the confined peace, the exiguous happiness, and the small face of the little girl – all that began to gleam as if they were independent of time and place like heaven, and had forms which could not be grasped, so that they existed only among the shadows evoked by imagination in the realm of aspirations.'

All that, instead of being high falutin, was very concrete. We who grew up in that world knew how real it was. Bengali life as lived in the everyday Bengali world made us fall back on a sanctified escapism.

What I began to feel with growing misgiving as the Twenties progressed was that this world in which we had reached manhood was going to be destroyed by forces which were not only unfamiliar and unknown, but also malign and irresistible. The purely literary situation was only part of a larger, disquieting phenomenon – total decadence of modern Bengali life and culture. But it was in the literary arena that I first felt the onset of decay. A new type of writing was appearing which neither emerged out of the established tradition, nor had any connection with real Bengali life. It was proceeding from an indiscriminate imitation of certain trends in postwar Europe, and seemed to be destructive. They were taking the consolidated front of Bengali literature in the rear and breaking it up.

Since the Bengali mind had been very largely shaped by literature the new literature had wider implications than those which were merely literary, although these, too, were undesirable in themselves. This meant that, so far as Bengali mental life was concerned, the new trends were going to change it, and as I thought change it for the worse.

This was due to the crucial role played by young people in maintaining Bengali mental life, its vitality, and its forward movement. Among us Bengalis the active functions of the mind, e.g. sensitiveness to ideas, capacity for passion, idealism, and yearning for intellectual adventure were virtually confined wholly to the young, to persons between the ages of sixteen and thirty, or even twenty-five. Beyond that was a mental desert, for as soon as a Bengali crossed that age line, he became increasingly dead to ideas and emotions, and wholly incapable of any kind of innovation.

Elderly Bengalis, and generally it would be true of all Hindus over the whole of India, divided themselves into two types: the worldly and the pious. Those who formed the first type became more and more sordid as they grew older, with only one unworldly weakness, which was superstition. But that, too, was often for securing worldly advantages, because even in his worldliness a Hindu is not as a rule manly and self-reliant. The second group of Bengalis did not lose their moral sensibilities, but took a typically Hindu line with them. They retired into a pious quietism of the traditional Hindu type. And the really significant aspect of this retirement was that those who took refuge in it were those who as young men had been most radical in Westernization. The inclination to abandon Westernization came to them as the inclination to leave the world comes to religious men.

The reason for this was that the Westernization, and even the new

Bengali culture which was created by a fusion of Hindu and European influences, were felt as a burden. Not to speak of developing it, even to carry it was a strain. It could be borne only as long as physical strength and vitality remained unimpaired. All conservative and traditional Hindus knew this and based their hopes of victory on it. They would say to a young Bengali radical with a very realistic estimate of his radicalism: 'Let the hot blood of youth cool, and we shall see.' This used to be said to me also. So, the relapse could be described as the inevitable anticlimax to the pursuit of Westernization which had created the modern Bengali culture. Incapable of bearing the burden of their own creation elderly Bengalis took refuge in traditional Hindu morality and spirituality. That is, having risen from the Hindu dust, they went back to the Hindu dust.

This irresistible drift into staticity gave to the young people of Bengal a cultural and creative role which was far more important and exclusive than what was assigned to the youth of the West. Virtually all movement and progress depended on young Bengalis. And I felt in the Twenties that the young were beginning to transform their own function from creation to destruction. In short, youth was corrupting youth. So, one could say to them: 'Ye are the salt of the earth: but if the salt has lost his savour wherewith shall it be salted.' It is thenceforth good for nothing, but to be cast out and to be trodden under foot of men.'

I will not say that I perceived all this with the clarity with which I am now describing it here. My perception then was indeed real but it was also very vague. I only felt that I was being rubbed the wrong way, and had a growing feeling of maladjustment with the world in which I was born and brought up. But such vagueness in itself has very little significance if anyone wishes to fight trends which are harmful. When political, social, and cultural evils are clearly diagnosed as such they are always past the stage at which they can be removed. Soundness and quality in life cannot be maintained without the capacity to have presages of coming evils. In the practical management of human affairs premonition is everything. It is akin to the wild animal's sense of danger, or the insect's sensitiveness. But in human beings this capacity is naturally weak, and when a society approaches decadence even that degree of capacity is atrophied. One trait specially developed by man is the capacity to become inured to the worst possible conditions of existence without perceiving that anything is wrong.

I arrived at a clearer conception of our future within a few years, and wrote a number of articles on the decadence of Bengali life and culture. But they fell flat. So far as I tried to perform a public function through my writings, I have failed completely. But at least I have saved my life. That is the only gain I have had out of my natural inclination to become a Don Quixote.

BOOK III

THE SCHOLAR GIPSY

1926–1928

Prefatory Note

The year 1925 was decisive in my life. The first significant event in it was the accidental meeting with Mohit Babu, which I have already described. The next event was my appearance in print, which, too, I have related. I have now to continue the story of my personal life from where I left it in chapter three of Book II. I had another year of discreditable dawdling in the Military Accounts Department, and made my inglorious exit from it in the middle of 1926. This was followed by a period of unemployment till the end of 1928. That, of course, meant being without money and therefore becoming a dependent on my family,, and yet I did not look for a job – a quest from which I have shrunk all my life. The first stage of this period of unemployment was particularly humiliating, and it could be regarded as my punishment for choosing to become the new Scholar Gipsy.- It had also some frivolous and farcical elements in it, so that the life I led could be compared to that of a scholar and a gipsy towards the end of the Middle Ages. I was rescued from the last stage of it by my father who came down from Kishorganj and took me back with him from Calcutta at the end of September 1927, when I was two months short of being thirty. Thus at that point I could say like Villon:

> 'En I'an de mon trentiesme aage,
> Que toutes mes hontes j'eus beues,
> Ne du tout fol, ne du tout sage,
> Non obstant maintes peines eues,
> Lesquelles j'ai toutes receues
> Soubz la main ...'

... I cannot say like Villon – from the hands of a vindictive bishop. It was my doing. On the other hand, I did not also disappear from the world like Villon after that, and am writing this account in my eighties.

CHAPTER I

I Become the Scholar Gipsy

I became the Scholar Gipsy by giving up my post in the Military Accounts Department. But my entry into vagabondage had a very happy prelude, which was my first sight of the sea and of great Hindu temples.

This I obtained by going to Puri, the seat of Juggernaut (Jagannath – Lord of the Universe), and also to Bhubaneswar, famous for its temples; both places of pilgrimage for Hindus. I went to them in July 1925. My sister was there. My brother-in-law had taken her there for a change of-scene after she had lost her only child. I decided that I would go and stay with them, and so I took leave from my office and boarded the train for Puri one evening.

The Sea and Temples

When I woke up early next morning the train was approaching Cuttack, the chief town of Orissa, and passing over the long bridge of the Mahanadi or the 'Great River', as its name was in Sanskrit. It was indeed a great and gorgeous river, especially at that time when it was swollen by the monsoon rains. The next place which the train passed by on its way to Puri was Bhubaneswar. The country had become hilly, and to the right I could see the long line of hills of northern Orissa. To the left was the plain on which stood the temples of this ancient centre of Hinduism. I could see a whole cluster of spires or rather towers, and rising above all of them was the tower of the great Lingaraja temple, dedicated to Siva. Near it were two other temples in a good state of preservation. Their colour was rusty and they had elaborate decorations on their sides, which I could clearly see. At their top were magnificent finials, looking like intricately carved lids of the enormous jars that the towers were, and rampant lions were protruding from the sides of these towers. There also were a number of temples which were literally dilapidated, but the loose stones resting on one another preserved in a skeletal form the shapes of the temples as they originally were. To my right I saw two hills, and on one a white temple. They were the famous hills of Khandagiri and Udayagiri, which had some of the oldest cave sanctuaries in India.

From the next station, Khurda Road, the train turned left and moved into very low and level country in order to reach Puri on the coast. Soon it was passing through what seemed to be endless swamps and marshes, and the railway embankment was the only strip of land, a narrow ribbon of it, which rose above wide stretches of dirty brown water. Across them I suddenly caught sight of the great pagoda of Jagannath. The sun was shining on its cream-coloured plastered sides. After that the train passed through sand dunes.

Finding nobody waiting for me at the station, I took a hackney carriage, asking the cabman to take me to the hotel where my sister was staying. When I had gone halfway, I saw her and her husband walking towards the station, and took them in. The hotel was right on the beach jiardly fifty yards from the edge of the water, and as the carriage took a sudden turn the sea came into view. I was, so to speak, transfixed. I had never seen anything like that. As the day was sunny the sea was of an intense blue.

I had, of course, seen hundreds of pictures of the sea, and used always to be fascinated by them, whether they showed only seascapes or battles like Trafalgar and Jutland. I also often dreamed of seas. But to one who has not seen a natural scene of a particular type with his eyes, what comes in dreams is always a reproduction of the pictures he has seen. Of all the pictures of the sea I had seen, two had made the deepest impression on me in my boyhood by virtue of their realism. The first of them was a representation of a scene from the Ramayana in which Rama was shown standing with his bow drawn to punish the Sea God for obstructing the building of his bridge to Lanka. It was by Raja Ravi Varma, a prince of the house of Travancore, who painted in the academic style of the late nineteenth century and was very competent technically. Nothing could be more close to the reality than his picture, which showed a sea of dazzling blue crested with white foam, rushing upon a rocky foreshore, creating an illusion of motion. The other picture was the popular painting entitled 'Off Valparaiso' by an English painter whose name I have forgotten. It had made an overwhelming impression on me. And at Puri I was seeing the same scenes, but now made tumultuously living. I could never imagine that our solid and firm Mother Earth could so change her appearance, and by throwing her immobility to the winds become the *perpetuum mobile*.

I did not wait for a breakfast to be given to me by my sister and went down to the beach to get my feet wetted by the creeping surf. After breakfast I sat for some time on a boulder before the hotel, and after that sat in an easy chair in the verandah of the hotel to look on the tossing sea. From the horizon* to about a quarter of a mile from the sandy shore the sea came on in huge rollers, one behind the other, but at that line it suddenly broke with a boom to form a ridge of white surf from the far right to the far left. Then it came on again in smaller rollers to break again quite close to the shore, and after that to creep on the yellow sands. When I went down the next morning I saw what the surf had left on the foreshore during the night: shells, jellyfish, baby squids, small ray fish, all dead, and even one or two dead yellow sea-snakes with their backs broken.

What struck me even more were the four daily cycles of the ebbs and tides. The Hooghly in Calcutta was tidal, but there we saw the tides as only high or low water, and very rarely as bores. Here at Puri I could see the pull of the moon on the sea, as if it was dragging the waters to itself and then relaxing its hold. At the ebbtide, the sea at times became as glassy as a lagoon, and one day at that time I swam to the line where the rollers broke in the middle distance. There my feet suddenly touched ground, and I found it rising to a crest as if I had come upon something like a line of reef. So it was, and I was told that on account of it ships or even smaller sailing sloops never tried to come inshore at Puri.

The sea in perpetual motion provided that constant accompaniment of motion – sound, and what a sound it was! The boom was rising from it day and night, with its varying pitch but regular rhythm. On land I had heard nothing like that, and its plangency was like music. At first I was deafened by it, and could hardly hear conversation, but it soon became such a background that even whispers were not lost on my ears.

Every morning the beach offered a busy spectacle – the fisher-folk, known locally as the Noolias, going out to the sea to fish in their catamarans.† They put together the pieces, tied them to convert them into unsinkable rafts, and launched themselves with their nets and gear into the surf They rode the surf and went over the two lines at which the waves broke gloriously. Beyond that line, to the far horizon, I could see the boats like small black specks rising and falling in the sea. They came back either at midday or early afternoon with their catch, and we ran to the boats to buy

* There was no shore to the south nearer than Antarctica.

† The primitive form of a raft or crude boat made up of two or more logs tied together. The word is derived from Tamil.

fish. There were usually mackerel and prawns, both grey and pink, and also young sharks and ray fish. The hammerheaded sharks particularly interested me.

I went down to bathe in the sea every day, and often twice a day. Although I was a good swimmer and was quite used to the rivers of East Bengal, the sea at first was too much for me, and I took a Noolia with me as a precaution. My sister would be anxious, because a few days before her arrival a young Bengali had been washed out to sea and found the next day dead on the beach. But very soon I became confident and dispensed with the escort, although to protect my head I wore the Noolia's bamboo cap. I never came to any harm, but one day I failed to plunge into the foot of a huge wave in time, was caught in its roll, and sent spinning on to the beach.

A quarter of a mile to the west a different kind of bathing was on exhibition for our edification. It was the religious dip in the sea of the pilgrims, both men and women. The men did not bathe gracefully, but at least they came through it, the women never. They could not balance themselves even in knee-deep water, and came tumbling on the shore with their saris above their waists, making even their priestly escorts laugh. Just by the side of that spot for religious bathing was the burning yard of Puri, where the pyres blazed and sent up the same stench which I had inhaled at the Nimtollah Ghat in Calcutta. One day I had to accompany a cremation there too. The whole bathing and burning ensemble was called *Svarga- Dvara* – Gateway to Heaven. It provided a spectacle of barbaric confusion.

Yet these scenes were cleaner than those provided half a mile to the north by the White women who came down from their hotel for 'Whites Alone' to bathe in the sea. It was on this occasion and at that spot that I was made to leave the beach by an Indian policeman in the interest of the modesty of these women. Among them there certainly were women who by their commonplace adultery were bringing disgrace upon the great European tradition of adultery established by all the historic adulteresses from Cleopatra to Madame de Stael. The British had to come to India to vulgarize even their vices and make them despicable.

Of course, the sea did not make me neglect either the temples or the religious life of Puri. On the morning of my second day at Puri my sister took me to see the great temple. It was about a mile inland. That too was a great experience. Used as I was to religious ceremonies and festivals at home, I found that I had yet to form a correct idea of the power of

Hinduism on the people of India taken in the mass. Here at Puri were men and women from every part of India, distinguishable by their appearance and costumes, but unified in spirit. I saw at once the pan-Indian and the timeless aspects of Hinduism. Men and women in their thousands came to the temple, filed into the dark sanctuary of Jagannath to go round his image and those of his brother and sister, which were of wood and of the crudest in execution, unmindful of the caning they got as they went in. They were equally unmindful of the extortion from the Pandas or priests, who had their clients from all over India. Every family of priests kept a register of the families of its clients, and if the pilgrim looked respectable the chaperoning priest asked his name and the name of his village, and could at once trace both in his register. My family as well as that of my brother-in-law were on their register, and woe to a priest who tried to entice away from his proper priest any member of the family of his clients. My brother-in-law duly performed the routine rites and submitted to the exactions of his hereditary priest.

Externally, the whole temple complex with its main and minor temples, pavilions, courtyards, and high enclosing walls, was very impressive. The great temple was not architecturally beautiful, and it was spoilt by having plaster on its outer surface and crude colours on its statuary, but it was high and massive. Besides, it had its full complement of three pavilions placed *en echelon*: the Jagamohan or vestibule, Nat Mandir or dancing hall, and Chhatra Bhoga Mandapa or the hall of feasts. The notorious erotic sculpture of the temple was very crude and totally devoid of artistic merit, in which it differed from that at Khajuraho. Only some friezes in black diorite brought from Konarak and placed on the basement of the front pavilion had some beauty, and they were maliciously satirical of religious hypocrisy. But I never noticed any pilgrim paying attention to the sculpture.

In front of the main eastern gate stood a column, and from that point a wide avenue ran towards a villa with a temple, which was supposed to be the house of the aunt of Krishna, and to which the Car of Juggernaut was drawn. The car festival was over when I went to Puri, but I saw the high car parked by the roadside. This avenue could be called the Champs Elysées of Puri. The town behind the temple was the usual maze. In front of certain houses I saw young girls in yellow saris. They were the well-known Deva Dasis, the Maidens of the God, who danced in the temple in the evenings. I never went to see their dance, although it might have been formally interesting. For all other purposes, they were just common prostitutes, and the prettier of them were reserved by the priestly families for themselves. These were very wealthy.

Before leaving Puri all of us went for an excursion to Bhubaneswar. We stayed there for two days, taking two rooms in the free hostelry provided for all pilgrims by wealthy merchants, and eating the food, 'pleasure of the gods' as it was called, cooked in the temple. We had to pay for that, however.

The hostel was on the large artificial lake called Bindu Sarobar, and the fine temple of Ananta Vasudeva was by its side. There are few views of Hindu temples which are more beautiful than the cluster seen across the lake. I had seen a picture of it in childhood, and it had haunted me always. Now I had the good fortune to see it with my eyes. On the southern side, above some smaller temples, rose the great Lingaraja temple, dedicated to Siva. It also had all its front pavilions. This temple was far more beautiful than that at Puri, both in its outlines and sculpture. Its colour was a mellow russet. It was surrounded by high walls and nobody but a Hindu could pass through its gates. I was shown a high scaffolding with a platform just outside the northern wall, which, I was told, had been built to enable Lord Curzon to see the courtyard of the temple. Of course, Hinduism could say 'No' even to the British Viceroy of India.

I wandered about by myself and went into all the temples, even those which were abandoned and overgrown with weeds, at the risk of meeting cobras. The group to which I went more than once were those around two tanks built to hold the hot water coming out of the springs below. They were like the tank at Bath, though smaller and without a roof I saw people bathing in them to be cured of ailments of various kinds, but I also saw so much skin disease that I did not go into the water. But the temples around it were very beautiful, although small, and that of Mukteswar with its gateway was particularly so. I also paid particular attention to a temple with a different form which was the oldest at Bhubaneswar and was called Parasurameswar. It dated from the eighth century.

But the place I liked best was the courtyard of the Lingaraja, with the great temple rising in the middle and small temples scattered all round it. Although this was the only temple at Bhubaneswar where the full routine of worship was kept up, it was less crowded than the temple of Puri, and in the evenings, as the shadows fell, there was ineffable peace inside. I noticed a strange effect: that the courtyard itself seemed to become like a great roofed-in hall. The Hindus never learned architecture properly, that is, the art and skill of enclosing space. Thus their temples had small and dark sanctuaries inside, and on the outside seemed to be gigantic pieces of carved forms. All of it was stone carving and not architecture. Nonetheless, the courtyard supplied the missing enclosed space. There was the same interplay of light and shade in it as within a great Gothic cathedral or a basilica, and as within a great mosque. The spacious quadrangle appeared to have a roof, and the temple at the centre seemed to have been carved out of solid rock, as if it was like the great rock-cut temple at Ellora. This time I did not see the Rajarani temple, which was the finest architecturally and had the finest sculpture.

We also went to Khandagiri and Udayagiri to see the old cave monasteries and shrines. We went there in a bullock cart. I had never before travelled in one. But at Bhubaneswar at that time, and even in 1939 when I went again, there was no other conveyance available. But that was consistent with the historic antiquity of the place and the leisureliness of life in it. We passed through a very wide plain, with the bushes of *nux vomica.* The cows which were grazing on the meadows never touched the poisonous plant, we were told. We saw the caves on Udayagiri, with their old friezes, and also the famous inscription of King Kharavela, the conquistador. The other hill, across the road, was higher, and it had on its top a Jaina temple. From there we could see spread out below the delta of the Mahanadi and the expanse of waters through which we had come. The plain of Bhubaneswar through which we had passed has now been built on, because it was selected as the site for the new capital of the province of Orissa. An ugly assemblage of brick and concrete now occupies it. The proximity of this new town is a blot on Bhubaneswar. What time and even the Muslim invaders had spared, the new rulers of India have desecrated. What reigns at Bhubaneswar today is the vulgarity which only these rulers can create. Midas transformed into heartless gold everything he touched. The Hindu politicians turn everything into leaden vulgarity.

When we were leaving Bhubaneswar a scene which is regarded as a token of the under-developed state of India was enacted behind our bullock cart. A crowd of about fifty beggars, both men and women, followed us. These were, of course, the inhabitants of Bhubaneswar, turned into beggars for our benefit. Unable to prevent their following us to the railway station my brother-in-law took a large handful of coppers and threw them among the beggars. At once they went on all fours to pick up the coins. In the meanwhile, the cart-driver raced the bullocks and got rid of the pursuers. I had never before seen bullocks galloping and pulling a cart at the pace of a horse-drawn carriage.

I Leave the Military Accounts

I came back from Puri after spending one month there, and for something like a fortnight after that I had the sea before my eyes and its sound in my ears. As I walked along the shabby unending streets of Calcutta, I expected every moment to turn a comer and come upon its glorious blue and the open spaces. Mohit Babu came to hear about my holiday and was fascinated by what I told him. He had just then written a magnificent ode on a Muslim iconoclast, who was really a Hindu convert and therefore all the more intolerant of idol worship. The man's name was Kalapahar or Black Mountain, and he carried out a foray into Orissa. I saw some of the destruction of statuary carried out by him, as well as evidence of the more extensive vandalism of later Muslim rulers. But Mohit Babu represented him as the Avenger of God for all the wrongdoings of the Hindus and injustices in the Hindu order. Having seen Puri, I could appreciate the sonorous Bengali Alexandrines in which he described how at the mere roll of his drums the idol cracked of itself, the bolts of the great doors of the temple flew apart, and the priests rushed out to fall prostrate on the flagstones of the court. I told him of the grandeur of the temples, and even of the voluptuous beauty of Orissan sculpture.

But the interlude at Puri only made my work in the Military Accounts Department more unendurable than before. I could perhaps be patient, for there was only one more year to go for the date to arrive at which I had decided to leave the Department, and my brother who was the medical student would appear at his final examination in April 1926. But for me it was like a hungry man's waiting only an hour before dinner was served. I neglected my work more recklessly and brought discredit on myself, and sorrow to my cousin and well-wishers.

I pronounced judgement on myself for this at the end of the first part of my autobiography, and the passage was written in 1948, that is, thirty-three years ago. It was severe, and today I feel shame to read even that. Yet the decision to leave the Department was *absolutely* right. What was utterly wrong was the method of executing it. I would request those who are reading this to refer to the judgement as a whole (pp. 454-55, *The Autobiography of an Unknown Indian*, American edition, 1951). Here I quote a few sentences:

'I went on neglecting my work and not only losing the good reputation I had earned for myself in the first few months, but also putting my friends in the office in a very awkward position. No one could have gone on like this without having to pay for it, and if I was not made to do so by being turned out of my job, I had to make up in mental distress. It was of two kinds: first, the distress arising out of the aversion I felt for my work, and, secondly, the distress caused by my consciousness of my neglect of duty. Only one of two things could put an end to it – either conscientious work in my post or its immediate relinquishment. But as I did not possess the strength to have recourse to any one of these two remedies, the only result was that double- edged suffering turned inward and corroded me. There never was a time in my life when I was so passively and weakly pessimistic.'

I shall give an example. One day a friendly colleague of mine said to me very seriously: 'You ought to have some ambition.' I replied sadly: 'If I had any, would I have come to this Department.-" The original mistake was to have accepted this job at all, which I should have known would never agree either with my temperament or the sense of vocation which I possessed to an obsessive degree.

However, let me relate the story in factual terms. After working for a few months I decided to take leave. At first it was for a short period, and as I wanted it on medical grounds, I furnished a certificate from a general practitioner. When this period expired I applied for longer leave, this time on half pay. I knew the office would think I was malingering – which in a sense was true – and perhaps send me to the highest medical authority for the Government, the Civil Surgeon of the district, who was an English colonel of the IMS. I decided to forestall this and get a certificate from the colonel. Having once managed the colonels successfully I was not afraid. I even joked with my brother, the medical student, about the ease with which certificates could be obtained from even the highest of his tribe. He explained the medical ethics on this point. He said that a medical officer examining a man who said that he could not go on working from physical exhaustion, could not refuse him a certificate, especially if he did look ill.

Of that there could be no doubt in my case: I looked weedy, besides being naturally small and very slight. So, I went to the colonel's house. Incidentally, they were allowed to have private practice.

However, I was not ready to look more unpresentable than I was naturally – that is, without clothes. Thus I again dressed myself like a Bengali bridegroom: with silk tunic and silk scarf, all complete. Over and above, more by instinct than by design, I did something else. On my way to the Colonel's house, I went to the English booksellers of Calcutta, and bought two volumes of reproductions of etchings by James McBey and D. Y. Cameron, and took them with me. I knew that personal relations could not be established on a footing of equality unless the two parties felt that they belonged to the same 'psychological species'. This is somewhat like two dogs sniffing each other's posterior before becoming friendly.

I told the colonel that I was feeling very poorly and very unfit to work, because I was suffering from stomach ailments (this was chronic in me), and that I wanted to rest for a while. Even before he had examined me he said that I looked very weak, and examining me he gave me both a prescription and a certificate, recommending rest for three months. I gave him his fee, and he came out with me into the waiting-room, where the books of etchings caught his eyes. He took up the volume on McBey, and turning a page found a picture showing a town in Palestine. He was surprised and pleased at the same time, and turning to me he said, pointing to the picture: 'I was here when I was in Palestine in the war, with Allenby's army.' We had hit it off.

I heard later that at first my superior ordered me to be sent up to the Civil Surgeon, but when the 'dealing clerk' pointed out to him that the certificate was from that dignitary, he had no alternative but to grant me the leave asked for and recommended. When I rejoined after this period of leave my old section would not have the black sheep. Therefore I was sent to another section where I was expected to check up the cost of every shell in metal and TNT, of every piece of harness and saddlery, of every wheel of the gun- carriages, and of every hundredweight of cordite. It was more boring than my other work, and so I decided to send in my resignation. My brother had appeared at his final medical examination, and there was no doubt that he would pass out brilliantly. Apart from that, I could not bear to be looked at in the office as a pariah. Even so, I do not think I would have taken the final step if I had not got a handsome cheque for my article in the *Statesman.*

This made me think that I might be able to scrape a living from freelance writing. I did not inform my family, not even my father, before I resigned.

In the office there was both sorrow and jubilation, the first among my friends and the second among the jealous and unfriendly. The latter triumphed because they had got a demonstration that being a BA did not make a good clerk like themselves. But both sides were agreed that I must have been mad. This I learned a few months later. One day I met a college friend after many years in Chowringhee. After the usual greetings I saw him looking at me with a curious smile. I asked him why he was smiling. At first he hesitated, and then said with the same kind of smile: 'I have heard that your "brain has become cracked".' This is a collocation in English often employed by the Bengalis. I did not mind that at all, although as this acquaintance was a very conscientious student and produced his tutorial essays beautifully, I expected him to understand me. Many years later I learned from a colleague who was his uncle that soon after leaving college he himself had become wholly insane.

This report about me he had got from an elderly Bengali who was a Superintendent in our office and his relative. This man continued to tell stories about my folly even after I had secured employment in the *Modern Review* office. He told all his acquaintance that there had once come to his office a young graduate who had the madness to give up 'government service' and was now somehow dragging out his existence on a salary of Rs. 25 a month in a private office.

I left five jobs in my life, and one extraordinary result of that in each case was that my former colleagues always remembered the bad reputation I left behind or my folly in giving up employment. But they never anticipated my future, and so when it turned out that by giving up each job I only stepped into a better career, both financially and in status, they did not feel happy and their pity or contempt for me turned into jealousy. Even knowledge of the great distress through which I passed in each intermezzo of unemployment, about which they kept themselves well informed, did not make them forgive my subsequent successes. Yet when I left their company they could truly say that they were not only more fortunate than I was, but also superior to me in the particular skills I shared with them.

However inglorious my career in the Military Accounts Department might have been, I did not at least stain it by the sort of dishonourable conduct which, to my astonishment, is nowadays praised by a large section of the British people. Not to make a mystery of it, I did not become untrue to the salt I was eating and did not claim credit for moral courage by doing so. Yet I was an Indian and my employers were British, to whom I owed no duty to be true except what was implicit in my choosing to serve the foreign rulers of my country for livelihood.

In the East it has always been preached as a moral duty to be faithful to the party which was providing bread to live on for us. The Hindus said: 'He who gives food is even as is the father.' The Muslims, on their part, looked upon betrayal of faith to someone whose salt has been eaten as one of the worst of sins.

But in England today class hatred has developed to such an extent that the betrayal of the employer on the pretence of conscientious scruples is even praised as moral courage. Anyone with a straight moral sense would have said: 'I do not work for any employer whose actions I consider immoral for the sake of money.' And these persons have so much moral courage that they practise their treachery in secret so that they might go on getting their money. Once in my career in the Military Accounts Department an opportunity came to me to show moral courage in this new English manner. But I did not. This is its story.

One day in 1924 or 1925 a document came to me which was marked "Secret". It was on the deployment of artillery in the Indian Army. Neither I nor even my office had anything to do with it. It had come into my hands obviously through the mistake of a clerk in the Army Headquarters. So, I had no duty to respect the secrecy. Yet I did. The document showed to my surprise and even horror that batteries of medium artillery, whose pieces in those days in India were 6-inch howitzers and 60-pounder guns, were assigned to internal security duties. This meant that such weapons of destruction could be used to suppress the nationalist movement in cities or densely populated villages, into which the infantry could not go safely. I simply filed the document, and did not even bring it away with me when I resigned in 1926. I took it as a matter of course that I could not be untrue to any employer of mine even if I was leaving his service. Later, in 1930, I got the paper abstracted through another person, but I did not give it to the press. I only had a question put in the legislature in an indirect manner. At that time the batteries had been withdrawn from this particular duty. But it should be mentioned that artillery was used in 1930 to shell Pathan villages on the frontier.

Hindu-Muslim Riots and More About Bibhuti Babu

At the time I left the Military Accounts serious Hindu-Muslim rioting had begun in Calcutta and it went on for some time. It started with the familiar '*music-brfore-mosque*'* in the Burrabazar area, and was carried on by the Hindustani Hindus and Hindustani Muslims of the city. Bengali Hindus and Bengali Muslims were not drawn into it. Even so, it was not safe to go about in the disturbed areas. There were killings, and they followed the usual pattern – murder of Hindus in dominantly Muslim areas and of Muslims in the dominantly Hindu areas. I did not feel any anxiety for myself and went even into notoriously dangerous areas if I had business. Once I went to inquire about the delay in getting my monographs on palaeolithic painting from Paris to my Muslim bookseller, whose house was in such an area. He actually scolded me for this, and sent me out with an escort of his own men. I learned after my marriage that my wife, who was at school in Calcutta at the time, had to go back to Shillong because the school was in a disturbed locality and the authorities closed it.

Our house was in a respectable Hindu locality and we saw nothing. But an industrial area where the workmen were both Hindu and Muslim and all Hindustanis, was not very far. At night we could hear their challenging yells, and the cry of *Allah ho akbar* was the louder. That prevented peaceful sleeping, for me specially because I slept on the roof, but caused no anxiety.

I was, however, anxious about Bibhuti Babu, because 41 Mirzapore Street was in a predominantly Muslim area, and Bibhuti Babu's imagination knew no limits. Therefore one day I went to see him, and found all my anticipations well-founded. He was in a state of utter panic. He told me piteously that he had not been able to sleep since the troubles started, and every yell of *Allah ho akbar* almost stopped his heart from beating. He added that he had decided to leave that 'City of Evil *(Pap Puri)*', and he asked me to help him to get away. I did. But before telling that story, I have to describe some of Bibhuti Babu's further adventures in acquiring experience of the world, whether he meant to draw on it or not for his novels. His curiosity was mostly disinterested.

He had already informed me that he was defending me against the

* Hindu religious processions were always accompanied by musicians, and if these passed before mosques when the Muslims were praying there always trouble. Nearly all Hindu-Muslim clashes began with such an incident.

allegation of being mad, and had, indeed, quarrelled with some of his fellow-boarders over that question. Then he tried to draw me into one of his psychological explorations. Bibhuti Babu never introduced sexual life in the narrow and more lurid sense of the phrase into his novels and stories. He made his hero Apu mutter to himself in English when he first saw his bride: 'They breed goddesses at Slocum Magna.' (I really do not know where he got that line of poetry from.) But, as I have shown, his curiosity about the other side of the shield was irrepressible.

So, one day he came to me and said: 'Nirad, do you remember X—, who was with us at Ripon College? He has become a great scholar, reads French, and goes to [he mentioned one of the leading literary figures], and do you know what he has done.' He was a teacher in the village of his father-in-law and lived in his house with his young wife. Latterly, the whole village began to talk about his relations with his mother-in-law. It became a great scandal, and now he has actually run away with her, and is living with her in [he mentioned a street near 41 Mirzapore]. I have seen them. Why don't you come with me and see the fun?'

Now, such affairs were not uncommon in upper class Bengali society, because very often the mothers-in-law and sons-in-law were very near to each other in age,* while her daughter was very young and immature and not a patch on the mother for attraction and experience. Therefore in the old days, those of my father for example, the mothers-in-law if they were strict hardly ever appeared before their sons-in-law, and in any case they kept their veils down. Around Calcutta the possibility of mischief was heightened by the fact that the men always worked in Calcutta and left early in the morning by train and did not return till late in the evening. Thus the resident son-in-law was exposed to the gravitational pull of the mother-in- law if she had die special disposition. This had happened with Bibhuti Babu's X—.

He also told me that the mother-in-law was very fine, and X— seemed to be very happy. Nonetheless, I refused to visit the mother-in-law mistress and son-in-law lover. Bibhuti Babu kept it up, and he came next with the news that X— had managed to abduct his young wife from her father's house, and now the mother and daughter were both living with him. 'Come

* My mother-in-law and her first son-in-law were almost of the same age. As for myself, I was almost midway between my wife and my mother-in-law and so could be ambivalent, if so inclined.

and see them,' he expostulated. I again refused. He came twice after that to bring further news: on the first occasion to tell me that the wily father-in- law had come and taken away his wife, depriving X— of his mistress *pro tempore*; on the second occasion, that the father-in-law had also taken away his daughter, leaving X—to lead a bachelor's or lone jackal's life. Bibhuti Babu's excitement over this denouement was something to see.

But the Hindu-Muslim riots furnished a different story. Bibhuti Babu dressed up and asked me to take him to the nearest tram stop, so that he could go to Howrah station to take the train to Serampore where he had a relative. I took him to the crossing of Mirzapore Street and Harrison Road, and waited at the tramcar stop. Suddenly, I heard a great noise further up, on Harrison Road. Looking that way, I saw a Muslim running for his life before a number of Hindustanis with clubs, who were chasing him. They were coming in our direction. One thing about me is that I am extremely timid in anticipation of danger, but when a danger actually arrives I lose all capacity for emotion, and become a mere instrument for registering sense impressions and reacting to them. Thus I at once began to run towards the flying Muslim in the hope of saving him, and I heard Bibhuti Babu crying after me: 'Nirad, what are you doing? Come back. They will kill you, or the police will come and open fire.' Nonetheless, I ran on.

But before I had gone half way the man was overtaken at the crossing of Harrison Road and Amherst Street, and brought down with a blow. Then to my horror, I saw the man who had given the blow kneel down and plunge a dagger into the man's back. When I reached the wounded man the attackers were gone. The Muslim moaned: 'Give me water.' A Hindustani stepped down from the pavement and cried: '*Salako garam pani do*' ('Give the bastard boiling water'). Another Bengali who had also come up went to a sweet shop and brought some water. Just then a police lorry came up, and the policemen took away the wounded man.

I retraced my way and, not seeing Bibhuti Babu anywhere, wondered what had become of him. As I approached the tram stop, I heard a wail: 'Nirad, Nirad, I am here.' I saw him emerging from behind the sacks and boxes of a grocer's shop. He came out and implored me not to leave him, but to put him in the very next tramcar which came. It soon came, and Bibhuti Babu jumped into it, leaving me on the pavement. By that time a huge Muslim crowd had assembled at the opposite comer and were shouting in fury. Although they were Bengali Muslims of the area, I did not like to face them. Therefore I went to a boarding house nearby where a friend of mine lived and asked him to give me a stick or a weapon so that I could defend myself if they attacked me. He said he would come with me, and we went together down Mirzapore Street to the house of a cousin of mine, which was near. As we walked in the middle of the street the Muslims shouted: 'Kill the fellows.' But beyond that they did nothing to us. I went back home after the tumult had ceased.

Soon after that Bibhuti Babu took up a better post at Bhagalpur in Bihar, and but for occasional trips to Calcutta on business was away from Calcutta. I saw him when he came down, and for the rest wrote letters. He had already shown me the first pages of *pather Panchali*, which I thought very fine, and urged him to complete the story. I have already mentioned how I prodded him, and in what terms he replied. He did not come back to Calcutta permanently till late in 1927 or early in 1928.

CHAPTER 2

Punishment for the Scholar Gipsy

The sense of relief created for me by my exit from the Military Accounts Department did not last long. Within months I began to undergo punishment for becoming the Scholar Gipsy. But this too was preceded by a second happy experience, a visit to Benares, the Eternal City of the Hindus, and I shall first describe that. I spent only four days in the city, but the impression it made on me was overwhelming, and that has never faded from my memory. At Benares the power of Hinduism was revealed to me with even greater force than at Puri.

In August 1926, I was asked to escort an old lady who was a widow and my brother's grandmother-in-law, to Benares where she lived. She had come down to Bengal to see her family and was going back, and no one else was available to escort her. I gladly agreed. I had already seen Puri, and I thought Benares would not be a lesser experience.

We travelled by a train which went through Benares, and so no change was called for at the junction of Mogalserai. I knew we would cross the Ganges before reaching Benares, and therefore I should be able to see one of the most famous views in India – that of the river front of Benares. I eagerly looked out, and just as the train was coming on the Dufferin Bridge (the one whose building Kipling described in his story of *The Bridge-builders*), the splendid crescent came into view. It justified its reputation. The palaces and steps, all in stone and built by Rajput and Maratha princes in the eighteenth century, rose from the river and presented an unbroken facade of more than a mile. The Ganges here takes a bend and flows almost north, and the curve seemed to make the river a terrace for the buildings. The highest structure in this frontage of architecture was Aurangzeb's mosque with its two slender and very tall minars. The Great Mogul had built it on a temple of Siva, so that the Faithful might trample on the heathen god's head. We Hindus, however, never called the mosque a mosque, but 'the Standard of Veni-Madhava'. At the end of the eighteenth century Thomas and William Daniell made watercolour drawings of the river front, and afterwards many aquatints from them. I have one of the finest – a view of Dasaswamedh Ghat with Raja Man Singh's palace.

The train soon moved into the main station of Benares, and we took a tonga, a horsedrawn trap, to go to the old lady's house. But instead of stopping at the door of a house, the conveyance stopped at a street crossing, where there were scores of these vehicles. Arrived at her city, the old lady took over command, settled the cabby after a good deal of haggling, asked a porter to carry her luggage, and marched on foot. She was to go to her house in the Bengali quarter of the city. I did not know the topography of Benares, and therefore was ignorant that except at two ends and in the middle, the city was not pierced by roads, and the residential areas were mazes into which one could go only along narrow lanes, hardly more than eight feet wide. So, no wheeled vehicles could go to any house unless it was on the two or three main roads, and in order to go to a house in that quarter everybody had to walk.

The old lady and the porter who were walking before me suddenly disappeared into a side alley, and I followed them into what seemed to me to be a maze – an impression not lessened by our having to turn right or left almost every hundred yards. What surprised me in the lanes was the endless files of human beings going in and out like two processions of ants, and the human ants walked with the same jerky motions and nods of mutual communication. At last we came to a door at an angle of two lanes, and the lady took me upstairs into a court which had rooms opening into it. A large number of people lived in the house, which was large, and the old lady had two rooms in it.

I do not know how I managed it, but after two or three outings, in the course of which I took wrong turnings, I always succeeded in emerging out of the maze into Dasaswamedh Ghat Road and returning to the house. At one point there was a recognizable landmark, a very large house with a gate which always stood open, through which people were always going in or coming out. A strong smell of boiling rice came out of it, for it was an *anna satra* or free kitchen which supplied meals to all who came to it. This charity was established by a well-known woman landowner of my district, Mymensingh. I could see people squatting and eating in the courtyard and corridors. Of course, this place was always crowded.

All the lanes, even at this spot, were incredibly filthy, reeking either of urine, both human and bovine (the famous sacred bulls obstructed these lanes), or of faeces and dung from the same sources. Nobody seemed to mind the stench or the deposits, and all, including women, showed a marvellous nimbleness in jumping over each pile. I at first resented that, and the day after my arrival I asked the old lady: 'Grandmamma, what do people become if they die in Vyasa Kasi?' She was scandalized at being questioned on a point of Hindu legends to which even a child knew the correct answer. Vyasa Kasi was a minor place of pilgrimage very near Benares, which was supposed to have been the hermitage or ashram of the great sage Vyasa. It was cursed on account of an unintentional affront by the sage to the Mother Goddess, who said that everybody who died there would become an ass in his future birth. The lady condescended to say so, but she did not anticipate the next question: 'And what do people become if they die in Kasi [Benares proper]?' She replied: 'Of course, they go to heaven.' I retorted: 'No, they become swine.' However, she only shrugged her shoulders at my irreverence. The power of Hinduism could cancel material discomforts.

It also could do that for human vice, and Benares was notorious for it. It had an extensive underworld, and the police of Benares flourished on it. Furthermore, its floating population of pilgrims and permanent population of vagrants made vice and crime widespread. There were the Pandas or priests, far more rapacious than those at Puri and more violent. Over and above, there were widows young and old. From Bengal it was not only the devoted women who came to Benares, but also women who had taken a false step in life, and wanted to live quietly instead of drifting into brothels. Nonetheless, 'harlots of Benares' was a byword.

As it happened, even during my short stay I met a lady of my class who had a history. In fact, she was the mother of a young colleague of mine in the Military Accounts. She was a striking woman of middle age, with thick eyebrows joined together and burning black eyes. She dressed like a widow. One day she surprised me by remarking, after asking me about her son, that he loved and respected her very much. The remark seemed so gratuitous that I became curious, and on my return to Calcutta spoke about her to my cousin of the Military Accounts Department, who knew the family well. He only curled his lips and told me not to talk about her. Becoming even more curious, I went to his wife and asked. She explained that the lady's husband had surprised her with a lover, killed him, and got a life sentence for murder. Whether he was still living or not I do not remember. The Bengali quarter of Benares was a sheltered port for all the derelict barques of Bengal.

But the behind-the-scenes of that city were taken for granted, and they made no difference either to the veneration for it or its attraction. That was obvious everywhere, in the lanes, in the few broad streets, in the temples, and on the bathing steps. Dasaswamedh Ghat Road to which I have referred was the only road which at the centre of the city led down to the river, and at its end was the sacred steps where according to legend Brahma had sacrificed ten horses: hence the name. The spot was very holy, and I saw hundreds of men and women always bathing in it.

As it was the monsoon season the water was very high, and some of the fallen temples and towers only showed their red upper surfaces. The fine palace of Raja Man Singh was next to the Ghat, but I could not go to it from the side of the river. Benares in spite of its magnificent water front had no strand, and only in the dry season could people skirt along the exposed bank to reach other ghats and the palaces. Now the floods were high.

So, in order to have a view of the whole of the river front I went to Dufferin Bridge again and walked along the pedestrian's path on it to the middle. My first impression of the view was confirmed by it. Then I went down the steps at Raj Ghat and took a boat. Boats were as numerous in Benares as gondolas were in Venice. The boatman took me upstream from one end of the city to the other, pointing out and naming every ghat and every palace. I saw that at Ghusla Ghat the water had gone into the courtyard of the Raja of Nagpur's palace through the wide gate. There was one ghat which did not require any pointing out. It was the famous Manikarnika Ghat, the main burning ghat of Benares, the Ghat of Perpetual Fires. I saw a number of blazing pyres. I could not anticipate then that my father would be cremated there in eight years' time.

But the spectacle which was of the greatest human interest in Benares was the bathing in the river. They were standing in deep or breast deep water in their hundreds, scrubbing themselves, or dipping under water, or praying. This impressive sight has been filmed by everybody who has concerned himself with Benares by way of artistic representation. In one of my books I have said that the bathing came first and the gods next, to take advantage of a pre-existing holiness conferred by the river.

I also saw the temples, and above all the most important in Benares – that of Viswanath, the Lord of the Universe. The present temple was not the original one, but it was only the latest one, because from the tenth century onwards the temples of Benares had been periodically destroyed by the

Muslims and rebuilt by the Hindus. Not far from the present temple stood the ruins of a mosque which had been built on the penultimate temple by Aurangzeb. But important as the temple was no one could tell where it was from the main road, unless one noticed one narrow lane down whose mouth a larger number of people were going than into the others, and also the flower stalls. The temple was not impressive architecturally. It had many features of Islamic architecture, for it was built only in the late eighteenth century by a Maratha princess. But there always was a crush of men in it, and the great bell always rang. Nearby there was another temple, in whose hall young priests learned the chanting of the Vedas, moving their right hand horizontally or vertically to mark the correct rhythms.

One could go further down the lane and come upon the river, and go down the steps. Through another lane I went into the palace of Man Singh, saw the famous observatory on its roof, and, of course, the monkeys: they were as numerous on the roofs and cornices as the bulls were in the lanes. It was the experience of exploring Benares and finding my way in that city which later enabled me to wander about in Renaissance Rome between the Corso and the Tiber, and find the Palazzo Farnese, the Piazza Navona, or the Pantheon without asking anyone for directions.

But just as I saw in Benares the continuing power of Hinduism, I saw at a place not far from it the remains of another religion which had originated in India, but had disappeared from there, because its end was not power, but peace. Eight miles from Benares was Sarnath, which was known in ancient times as the Mriga Dava (Deer Forest), and then as Dharma Chakra Pravartana Ksetra, because Buddha had first preached his religion or turned the Wheel of Dharma (Law) there. I was bound to go there, and I did. On the first day I went by tonga, i.e. horse-drawn trap. It was a festival day, and I saw horse-drawn chariots racing along the road to Sarnath. A fair was held on the site, and the place was crowded and cheerfully noisy. Hawkers sat by the roadside or under the trees with their cheap and tawdry merchandise. But what transcended that was the gladness of ordinary folk, men and women who had come to the fair and were walking about and chattering incessantly. They disturbed me somewhat, but I saw the remains, and more especially the Dhameka or Dharma Rajika Stupa, which was at least two thousand years old. I also saw the truncated Asoka column, which had the famous lion capital. I went into the ruins of the monasteries and crept through the tunnels. I saw some sculpture, but the best specimens, with the lion capital among them, were in the museum, which was closed on that day. I could not leave Benares without seeing them, and so I decided to come again.

However, I settled that for the second visit I would walk to Sarnath. I recalled that pilgrims had come from far-off China on foot to visit the place of origin of their religion, and I thought it would be sacrilegious softness if I went to Sarnath in a horse-drawn carriage. So I started to walk, although it was very hot and the sun was high in the sky. I was dressed at my Calcutta best, in silk tunic and pumps, with the half-inch wide black moire ribbon of my rimless pince-nez dangling down my chest.

First of all, I went into the museum and looked at the lion capital. There could be no question that it justified its reputation as a fine work of sculpture. I had read *ad nauseam* the controversies in the learned journals whether it was Persian or Indian, but remembered nothing. The beauty of its carving engrossed me. I also saw the equally famous Buddha of Sarnath, and ail the other Buddhas as well as the Bodhisattvas. I was deeply touched by the beauty of the human figures in stone, whether male or female. I had already formed the opinion that Indian sculpture reached its first phase of full achievement at Sarnath. The serene beauty of the faces sank into my mind. When after returning to Calcutta I told Mohit Babu what a contrast in their chaste beauty the figures of Sarnath presented to the voluptuous beauty of Orissan sculpture, he was very much moved. After seeing both Sarnath and Orissan sculpture I was able to make the discovery, confirmed by my study of other regional sculptures, that the figures in every case were idealized representations of the local human types. I found the Sarnath faces reflecting the faces I was seeing in Benares, as I had also found Orissan sculpture reflecting the Orissan faces.

On my way back I went up to the mound of Chaukhandi, which was the remains of a high stupa, with a well inside. At its top was a stone kiosk built by Akbar, the Mogul Emperor, to commemorate the fact that his father Humayun had taken refuge in this mined stupa in his flight towards Delhi after being defeated by an Afghan rebel. From the top of Chaukhandi I saw the plain of Samath and the mango groves below me, and also in the far distance the two minars of Aurangzeb's mosque in Benares. The setting sun was glistening on them.

I resolved to be more adventurous on my return journey to Benares, and so, instead of following the high road by which I had come, I began to walk along the railway line, hoping to reach Benares by a shorter route. I had not gone a mile when I was overtaken by a peasant or rather farmer. He looked at me in surprise, then at my clothes, and asked: 'Where are you going, Babuji [Sir] ?' I replied that I was going to Benares and I thought this would be a short cut. He said that it would be more difficult and I would not be able to cross the river Varuna. When I looked puzzled, he offered to take me with him to Benares by a better route. He was an elderly, tall, and strong man, like the men from Oude who once were soldiers in the East India Company's northern army. He had a long bamboo staff in his hand. He could easily have robbed me, or even killed me in the scrub of tall pampas grass and reed into which he was taking me. But I felt no fear, and soon we came to the river, which we crossed by a ferry. After walking some more distance we came upon a broad road. It was dark, but the road had lamps. He pointed towards its end and said: 'I have now to go another way. Please follow this road straight without turning, and you will be right on Dasaswamedh Ghat.' I did so and came home very late. I found the old lady and others of the house very much worried about me. When I related what I had done I was scolded very severely.

I left Benares soon after, staying rather longer than I had intended. There was a strange aftermath to the visit. It was partly a result of the impact made on my senses by Sarnath sculpture, and perhaps partly of an emotional vacuum in my mind. As I sat in the patio of the house I observed a young Hindustani girl often coming out to the verandah of the house opposite the old lady's. She was about fifteen or sixteen, and had a very good figure and the regular features of Sarnath sculpture. She was as typical of the region as were the sculptures. I watched her with fascination, and the more I saw her the more I forgot which was the girl and which was the sculpture.

But I did not feel any emotional disturbance at all, the impact, though powerful, was on die senses. But it was felt to be different when the train started from the Raj Ghat Station of Benares. As it thundered on to the Dufferin bridge which was close to it, and the river front began to recede away, I felt something snapping in my heart and a violent fit of grief seizing me, as if I was leaving a beloved person for ever. The emotion was so strong that I lay down on the bench of the compartment, in which there was no other passenger, and cried off and on like a child until the train reached Patna three hours later. There a Bengali gentleman bound for Calcutta entered the compartment, and I sat up and talked with him.

Surely, at my age – I was over twenty-eight – such behaviour could be regarded as idiotic, perhaps foolish even in an adolescent. Nonetheless, I somehow feel that in exhibiting this idiotic infatuation I showed more manliness than if I had been an habitue of all the brothels of Calcutta in their hierarchy of graded fees. The gracious memory of that experience has always haunted me, but I did not recognize it for what it really was until in old age I read Chateaubriand's account of his *fantôme d'amour*. Like him I had created my Sylphide. I could say like him that with my Sylphide 'nous descendions les fleuves saints dont les vagues épandues entourent les pagodes aux boules d'or; nous dormions aux rives du Gange, tandis que le bengali, perché sur le mât d'une nacelle de bambou, chantait sa barcarolle indienne.' I remained susceptible to such fits of passion until I married.

Of course, nobody had any inkling of this secret life of mine. Those who saw me, especially my colleagues and acquaintances or even friends like Bibhuti Babu, never thought that I was capable of passion. They set me down as a dry-as-dust scholar or even pedant (according as they liked or disliked me), and on external grounds they were not wrong. I was scraggy in body, pinched in the face, and had deep wrinkles between my brows. I thought I looked pensive, but many thought I was peevish. That was a misjudgement.

But it was a misjudgement arising out of an attitude to the sexual aspect of the man-woman relationship which was traditional and fixed in our society. The attitude was crudely extrovert. A man was not regarded as capable of love unless upon seeing any attractive woman he got into a state of mind, which without putting too fine a point on it could be called plain rut. I saw this attitude in Bengal, and still more clearly when I moved to Delhi. A Punjabi father would not give his daughter to a young man who had a refined expression, instead of looking like a stud bull or stallion. 'Not in good health', would be the judgement. And a man who was habitually thoughtful and introspective would be laughed at everywhere if he pretended to be capable of love. They would say that no woman would look at him.

I had become familiar with the attitude, and laughed to myself, all the more because I could see that in their pride of virility they had considerable pity for me. Nobody perceived my internal storms, because they were like magnetic storms and were not wind storms.

I should certainly have been able to disregard the pitying looks at me even without external support. But very soon I found it. In 1928 or 1929 I read Julien Benda's *Lettres à Mélisande*, in which I read the following lines: 'Ainsi s'expliquerait que les hommes capable de l'amour le plus aigu sont ceux qui savent le mieux prendre conscience des idées qui accompagnent leurs émois ou que, sebn le mot d'un maître et contrairement à l'opinion courante, le vrai érotique soit l'analyste et non l'impulsif, l'appolinien et non le dionysiaque.' I never threw this saying in anybody's teeth, for nobody was explicitly contemptuous of me. But for their unuttered disdain I had my unuttered defiance.

Unorthodox Dependency

I intended to describe the life I led and the troubles I went through after resigning from the Military Accounts in some detail, so that what I shall have to say about the effect that life had on me might be fully understood. But I find that, however clear and exact my recollections, I cannot set them down without reviving, even after fifty-five years, the pain, despair, and resentment I then felt. I would again have the sensation of being steeped in the old humiliation. Besides, to give my side of the story would be grossly unfair to my brothers with whom I was then living. I tried them sorely, and if they felt provoked I cannot now blame them. Actually, they treated me less harshly and contemptuously than was common in the joint families of those times, in which the earning members and more especially their wives thought no insult too undeserved for the unearning members and their wives. My sister-in-law, the only female member of the family, never had anything but affection for me.

My acute sense of humiliation and even degradation was due to the fact that my dependence was unorthodox. In landed families, for which the joint family was a very natural social unit, there was no question of dependence or independence, because the income of the family was joint. It was when the members of such families became professional men or salaried employees that this unequal relationship developed. Even then a wealthy lawyer or doctor and a well-paid official did not mind supporting an unemployed brother or close relative, although the inequality would be felt as well as shown. The dependents submitted to being treated as inferiors, there being no unemployment insurance or benefit.

But I was not a normal dependent. I had myself given up a salaried and permanent job, and a government job at that. If that made me a n'er-do-well in the eyes of my brothers, in the eyes of my more distant relatives I became a scapegrace, if not a rascal. I also felt the descent from having been the only earning member of the family to becoming a dependent myself. Next, instead of becoming meek and all-suffering, I became defiant, and went berserk in my fits of extravagance. So, I gave provocations and my brothers could feel exasperated.

On the other hand, during this period, my father forgot his old anger against me which he had felt at the neglect of my prospects in the Military Accounts, and he helped me whenever I put myself in a distressing situation. I shall give one example only of his concern for me from the last months of my unemployed life. I was then living with my elder brother, who had some income of his own. My doctor brother, who was rising in practice had his own house, a much larger one. My father had come down to Calcutta and was staying with him. My sister who was expecting was also there with her husband. I slept on the roof for most of the year, and used by my free choice only a mat and a pillow. As there were no stairs to the roof of the house I lived in, I went up by a rickety bamboo ladder which only a very light person could climb. It was late spring and I had gone to bed early. Suddenly, waking up, I saw a man stooping over me, and was very much surprised to find that it was my father, barebodied and barefooted. I asked him: 'What is it, father?' 'Nothing,' he replied, and without giving any explanation he went down from the roof and then out of the house.

I went the next morning to my doctor brother's house and meeting my brother-in-law told him about the incident. He said that he was responsible for it. My sister and he were sitting together and talking with my father, when without any thought he remarked that I was in such straits that I did not even have a bed to lie on and had to sleep on the bare floor. He added that my father at once got up, though it was after nine o'clock, and without dressing went out of the house. So he had walked more than a mile undressed, and had climbed up that risky ladder, to find out if that was the case. Yet the same father took me aside at that very time and said: 'Nirad, I wish to tell you one thing. There is nothing more dishonourable than for a man [he employed a Bengali word which was the exact equivalent of *vir* in Latin] than to be without an income. Try to earn whatever you can by writing or any other means, and give that to your brothers.'

My brothers never made any insulting remarks to me. But I could see how they disapproved of me. I also saw, rightly or wrongly, looks of cold contempt when they met me. What distressed me most then was the alienation from my elder brother, who had led me into jaunts of buying books and pictures. Even late in 1924 we had come triumphantly home with a porter behind us carrying many volumes of the Arden edition of Shakespeare, and though he himself did not read French he had abetted me in buying a very pretty edition of Molière in eight volumes which had once belonged to Sir John Lubbock (Lord Avebury). But he had become not only wholly unco-operative but also hostile, so much so that after buying a Medici print of the Mona Lisa in 1926 I hid the print for some weeks to avoid giving offence to his eyes.

More distant relatives were vocally abusive. Although they were not supporting me, they were making very insulting remarks, even going to the length of saying that I should be whipped. And these remarks were always brought to me by those to whom they were made. What exasperated them was in the first place my giving up a Government post. That was bad enough, but not satisfied with that offence I went just then on a wild spree of spending on books and pictures. I might say I went berserk. This was not the kind of extravagance which they could disapprove silently. If in my desperation I had begun to visit brothels or taken to drugs or drink, nobody would have said a word, for in our society it was not decorous to be open about such failings. But what I did was not so clearly immoral as to become unmentionable, but was offensive enough as behaviour to be condemned.

I ordered expensive monographs on palaeolithic paintings from Paris, Pascal's complete works in fourteen volumes in the series Grands Ecrivains de la France, the Julian edition of Shelley in ten volumes at five guineas each, the Nonesuch Dante, a magnificent edition of Anatole France to be illustrated by some of the greatest book-illustrators of France and to be completed in twenty-six volumes. I also ordered a set of woodcuts by a modern French artist which illustrated a modem ballad by a contemporary French poet in an edition of which only thirty-five copies were printed. All of these came. The book of woodcuts had the number 11. And all of them awaited payment. Driven to extremes, I borrowed a sum of money from a distant relative, whom I could not repay in time and who therefore not only wrote importunate letters to me, but probably also to my brother, who in his turn wrote to my father, who in his turn duly paid the debt. My father also paid the booksellers when I could not.

The relatives did not matter much, but even in my family, owing to my oversensitiveness, things came to such a pass that in my desperation I often lost my temper and made scenes which resembled the worst in joint families. I have written about them in my *Continent of Circe* in the following words:

'In the course of the quarrels all reticence and reserve is thrown to the winds, and grossest abuse and even blows are exchanged. The weak are beaten, equals hurt one another, until other members of the family and at times even neighbours separate the parties. Otherwise kind, decent, honourable, and educated men do things which remain in the mind like unwashable stains of shame, and are felt as unhealed festering sores. All men as well as women, show a perverse genius in discovering words which will wound most.'

I wrote this with my behaviour in mind as well as that of others. What I at times did then has remained like 'unwashable stains of shame' in my mind, and to recall them would be like re-opening the sores that festered once. I shall not write about them. What made things worse was that I did not have the faculty of forgetting such incidents and going on living placidly in the joint family. This capacity for tolerance was generated by the very abnormality of life in these families. As I also wrote: 'Somehow an alkali is always present with the acid of Hindu life: it is a marvellous and boundless tolerance of bad language and blows, which is some sort of a conditioned reflex of forgiveness. The Hindus possess a faculty of callous charity.' I never acquired that, and therefore I suffered more than typical or orthodox Hindu dependents.

I would offer an explanation at this point for the main article of my offending, which was reckless and non-traditional or rather *anti-traditional* extravagance. I do so because in a less extreme and irresponsible form it has persisted throughout my life. I spent on things on which by the time of which I am speaking upper-class Bengalis had ceased to spend. But my habit was partly inherited, partly an extension of that legacy by me. If I had a good income I would have spent a substantial part of it in acquiring furniture, books, pictures, and other objects of personal use with an aesthetic appeal. Even before the British came this was natural in the landed gentry of Bengal in a simple form. For instance, the mat walls of our thatched huts in Banagram were made with extreme care for their appearance. I have myself seen beautiful panels of fine mat and bamboo cane inset with bits of mica in our ancestral house, and I was told that such a panel – not more than nine feet by three feet – took six months to make. My grandfather would send for his gardener and ask him to put in its place a twig of the jasmine bush which he saw dangling out of line with the cascade.

With the coming of European household objects, this habit took a European line and was developed to a considerable point of elaboration. I have written in my autobiography that our Banagram house, in spite of consisting of such simple huts, had lustre chandeliers and sconces made in England. Even at Kishorganj we had table lamps burning paraffin with glass pedestals and shades, and candlesticks with springs inside them and glass globes. Most houses had pictures, although these might be mere oleographs. I was only trying to take that to a higher point from my knowledge of European interior decoration. I was already buying the Studio Yearbooks of Decorative Art, and I have written about my hobby of book-collecting. This inclination was strengthened in me by what I had read about the personal life of great European writers. I had seen pictures of the rooms in which Anatole France or D'Annunzio lived and worked. My father, who had these tastes, had also indulged us by buying good furniture for us from the antique shops. In the house in which we lived we had marble-topped console tables with carved legs, and a set of Regency dining chairs with velvet seats, made in England.

But by the time I was cultivating these tastes, or trying to, a great change in regard to material adjuncts of life had come over Bengali society. The lower middle class, of course, never had any standard of living at any time, and lived as shabbily as possible. As it happened then, the upper middle class was also falling in line with the lower middle class. And the East Bengal gentry who were coming to Calcutta for the sake of earning money, took to these lower middle class ways very quickly. They never considered Calcutta as their home, and regarded it only as a place to earn money, so that in old age they could go back to their villages to live like gentlemen. So, they saw no point in spending money in living well or decorating their houses. Thus I was born out of my time.

Apart from that, my want of means and want of employment made living according to my usual standards a matter of self-respect. I thought I had descended low enough by having no money, and if I after that adopted the shabby way of living of the lower middle-class I would feel degraded, and probably get reconciled to that life. I always took particular care about my clothes and manner of living when I was unemployed, although I did not mind wearing a torn shirt when people knew I was earning money. All that does not excuse the irresponsibility I showed, but that is the explanation.

Besides, books were to me mental nourishment, as much as they were material adjuncts of mental life at a civilized level. Therefore I did not think I could give up buying books and artistic objects simply because I had no money or very little money. In any case, though I bought things on credit I finally paid for them with my own money or at its worst with my father's. But, of course, in our society as it had become even spending one's own money on such things was not approved of. An elderly relative of mine said to me one day: 'I do not ask you to give up buying books, but at present you should lay by something, and when you have enough buy books.' I could not tell him to his face that he might as well have told me to put off eating until I had enough in the bank. I might add here that even at the end of my life, I have not gone back on my conviction that our beautiful material possessions are only the outward signs of an inward grace, or in plain words material symbols of a full and active mental life. I have always held the saying 'Plain living and high thinking' in contempt. Plain living (which is not simple living) results in very poor thinking.

Bohème sans Mimi

I shall bring to a close this account of my unemployed days by relating what I did in the last months of this first phase of my unemployed life. I can give the details, for I alone was responsible for what I suffered. At the end of 1926 I told my father that I would study for the MA degree and appear again the next year, and in order to do so I would rent a house of my own and study there instead of continuing to live with my brother, if he would help me partly. He saw its desirability and agreed. So in January 1927 I took two rooms or rather a flat in a house in one of the backward suburbs of Calcutta, because that was cheap. It was beyond the Maratha Ditch. The locality had no sewerage, and in it all the drains and latrines were open. The houses were rather big, and the residents were all old inhabitants of the district. My rooms were on the first floor. There was a shed for a kitchen on the large terrace which separated my block from the main house. I engaged a maidservant to cook for me, and got all my things removed from my brother's house.

The district was primitive, i.e., very orthodox and traditional in its way of living. Here I saw religious practices and social customs which had disappeared long ago even from the villages of East Bengal. But they were preserved like visible archaeological remains in this corner of Calcutta. I saw the worship not only of the goddesses of small-pox and cholera, but also of skin diseases. Small boys came for subscriptions to her worship and like Christmas carollers sang their special songs. They wound up with assurances to the ladies in very vivid and alluring language: 'Those who give in loaded plates will get golden bracelets, and those who give in stone vases will have bloated carcases.' I was immensely amused.

The residents on their part at first showed great curiosity about the unfamiliar bird of passage which had come among them. They were astonished at the sight of my books when they were unloaded on the front verandah of the house. They had never seen such big and magnificent books. One old gentleman who was passing by remarked: 'Why, a very funeral banquet of books seems to be going on here.' Those who have seen the splendour of Hindu funeral banquets will understand this remark.,

One very young man, however, stopped, stepped forward and bending his neck read some of the tides. Then he took out some of the books one by one and examined them. Of course, he did so without asking me, for he was paying a compliment to my status by doing so. The books he looked into were Bernard Berenson's *Three Essays in Method,* Roger Fry's Transformations, and Lawrence Binyon's Painting of the Far East. He was obviously impressed and asked me very respectfully: 'Are these books yours and are you coming to live up there?' When I said that I was, he introduced himself as a student, and added that if I would permit him he would like to come and visit me. I found him to be very intelligent and full of intellectual curiosity. Over and above, he had taken music lessons and was a very good singer, especially of Tagore songs. He became very friendly with my two youngest brothers who were of his age and who often came and stayed with me. We kept it up very gaily, and had no problems about eating as the four Bohemians of the opera had. It goes without saying that I did not study for the examination and made use of the money given by my father for the examination fee for our living expenses. I also had a little myself.

We often stood on the front verandah watching life in the locality. In traditional Calcutta this was always suspect in young men, for it was assumed that the object could only be to spy on the girls. To disarm their suspicions and establish my respectability I from time to time brought my sister-in-law and sister to spend a day with us. They created a sensation as they walked uncovered down the lane after leaving the carriage, in their resplendent saris, crêpe de chine blouses, velvet sandals, holding long-handled and gorgeously coloured Burmese parasols over their heads. The ladies of the house I lived in came and talked with them, but they went back scandalized to see that my sister-in-law, who cooked special dishes for us, had her shoes on while she manipulated the ladle.

I created a further sensation by going out one day to shoot ducks in the marshes east of Calcutta with a cousin of mine, who had a repeating Winchester shotgun. We got no duck, but killed some unfortunate gulls, which we could not eat.

The quarter was very staid, and had its unvarying routine. That which sounded most romantic to me, because it recalled my young days at Kishorganj, was the loud chanting of the school lessons by the boys. It was almost like regular hymn singing in churches. Very near my rooms a young boy took seven days to memorize: 'The boy stood on the burning deck, whence all but he had fled,' accompanying his chanting with the repetition of an atrocious Bengali translation of the poem. Then his father would take up the grammar lesson, and teach gender at the top of his voice. One day I heard him teaching the *ess* feminines. He did not confine himself to words like *lioness* or *tigress*, but gave to his son such unusual terms (which no Indian boy was ever likely to employ) as *songstress, seamstress.* Suddenly he boomed out to the ten-year-old boy: 'Say, *adulterer* – *Vyabhichari* [the Bengali or rather Sanskrit equivalent], and *adulteress* – *Vyabhicharini*.' In learning the plural of *madam* the poor boy was always made to say *mesdames* just as it was spelt.

We soon ran into trouble with our sociological curiosity. As if our standing on the verandah was not bad enough, one day my two youngest brothers brought a rather good Kodak camera (without film) and tried its focus from the verandah. I was in the room, and suddenly I heard shouting from it as well as from the roof opposite. The house belonged to an old woman who was a widow and a fairly well-to-do washerwoman. It was one-storied, but its wide roof was used as their drying yard. It was one of the sons of the washerwoman who was shouting at my brothers.

What had happened was that the young man's sister-in-law was putting up the washing on the lines when my brothers began to try the camera, and they were assumed to be taking her photograph. She ran down and told the family, and her mother-in-law and brother-in-law came up. She was standing at a distance and watching with extreme curiosity through her veil: the young washerman who was hardly ten feet away, was abusing my brothers. They explained and even showed that the camera had no film, but nothing appeased the young washerman. He continued. My youngest brother, who was the fighter of the family, cried: 'Come on then,' and went down into the lane. I, of course, followed him.

The young washerman confronted us. Never able to forget my knowledge of European art, I rushed at him crying: 'Is your sister-in-law the Venus de Milo that we would photograph her?' Looking up, I saw my other brother in the balcony trying his best to suppress a grin. I shouted to him: 'Bring down my gun, I would shoot this fellow.' This was, of course, sheer bluster, but they had seen the dead gulls, and so the washerwoman shouted from the roof: 'Just look at the cheek of the man, lives in rented rooms, and threatens to shoot us.' My brother and the washerman closed in, but half-a-dozen old gentlemen of the locality separated them. By that time I had recovered my common sense and showed the gentlemen that we had nothing in the camera and were only trying to focus. They were convinced of our innocence.

I had, however, to dress up at once for a very important cultural gathering. There was a body in Calcutta called the Society for Indo-French Friendship, which had been set up by some distinguished Bengali intellectuals who were doctors of the University of Paris: the leading figure among them being my old teacher. Professor Kalidas Nag. They were all invited by the Governor of the French colony at Chandernagore for a meeting and a reception, and I was to be among the guests. There was also my distinguished friend, Dr S. K. Chatterji, the philologist, and Mr Pramatha Chaudhuri, the foremost Bengali literary critic of the day.

At the meeting in the Hotel de Ville of Chandernagore three distinguished Bengali Sorbonnistes spoke in impeccable French and the Bengali Mayor of the city in very bad French. After that we went to the Governor's house for the reception. I had taken with me the newly published book on Victor Hugo's drawings to prove my affiliation to French culture. The Frenchmen were very interested because it was a new and very expensive book, and they had not yet seen it. The drawings were very fine, of the highest merit, but they had never been reproduced before because Hugo thought that the processes of reproduction of his times were not adequate.

Now they were brought out in all their beauty, in colour as well as in monochrome, as I could judge later when I saw the originals in his house in the Place des Vosges. After the reception there was a sumptuous feast in the Bengali style in the Bengali Mayor's house. I returned home late at night to be reminded of the ludicrous incident of the morning.

Depth of Degradation and a Ray of Hope

But the comedy or farce which I carried on was going to end in squalor. The reckoning was approaching. I soon came to the end of my resources, and after not appearing at the MA examination I could not ask my father to continue his support. The rent and the maidservant's wages were falling in arrears. The parties in the rooms ceased, and I could not even buy enough food. For some time I took only one meal a day to economize, but I found that I could not afford even that. I was becoming weak, and the landlord and the maid were pressing for their dues.

Even so, the worst problem was not to satisfy them, but to pay the booksellers for their big bills. They were impatient, and their collectors had tracked me down in that suburb. To escape the creditors, I at first went out immediately after breakfast and came back late in the evening. But after some time I found that I could not walk any more. So I remained in my rooms, padlocking them from inside with a spring lock on the rings outside. I could do that from the inside. After that I lay down in a comer where I could not be seen even if anybody pressed the double-door, and looked through the chink. Even so, I could hear my creditors talking outside and my landlord replying that I was not in and the room was locked. It was in this ignoble inaccessibility that I had some rest at that time.

But even this became impossible and I at last decided to sell some of the books. It was heartbreaking for me, but I called in a secondhand book dealer. He did not offer me even a quarter of what he was likely to get, but I was compelled to accept his prices. I parted even with Aurel Stein's portfolio of the paintings from the Thousand Caves of Tun Huang in agony. With the money I settled some of the creditors, but could not pay the landlord, nor could I buy food, and so, leaving everything locked up, I went to my brother's house with a small bundle of clothes, and told the servant – neither my brother nor my sister-in-law – that I would stay and have my meals there. Nobody asked any question, and I took shelter in a groundfloor room.

One very unpleasant incident took place soon after. I shall not describe it, but another which followed I cannot avoid mentioning. The landlord to whom two months' rent was due went to my doctor brother, when he found that his tenant had absconded. But he did not break into my room to seize my goods. My brother not only paid him, but got my things removed to where I was staying. My worst humiliation came out of this.

My sister and her husband were staying in Calcutta and they had taken rooms in a hotel. One afternoon I went to visit them. Soon after, my doctor brother who had paid the rent came in, and seeing me said something very insulting. He was an impulsive and, though generous, a very hot-tempered and ruthless man. Unable to bear that, I gave him a blow. Infuriated, he turned on me to give me a beating. I should certainly have been severely injured if my brother-in-law had not rushed forward and encircling my brother round the body with his arms kept him from moving. But my brother began giving blows on his back with his free fists. My sister and I stood stockstill by their side. As soon as my brother ceased after becoming exhausted, I left the room without a word.

I did not know where to go. I could not show my face anywhere after such an incident. So, I wandered about in the streets until it was late in the evening. Then having no other place to go to, I went to the waiting hall of Sealdah railway station and sat on a bench. I could not even sit up, and when it was about eleven I lay down on it. I fell asleep, but a man from the station came to me, and told me that no one was allowed to stay in the hall at night. I came out, and having no other place to go to and finding the platform gates open, I went in and took shelter in a standing train. I lay down on a bench and tried to sleep. I dozed off, but my sleep was disturbed by the workmen who walked along the track, examining the coaches and their wheels. I feared they would look in and discovering me take me to the police. So, as soon as I heard voices approaching, I went under the benches and lay down for some time. In this way some hours passed. Then the train suddenly got into motion. I knew it was going to a siding, and it did. This siding was about a mile away, and very near my old rooms. I remained in the coach for some time, and then got down and began to walk along the railway track although it was very dark. I had walked there in the early mornings from my rooms, and gone even as far as Dum Dum station, four miles away. But on that day I was tired. I had not taken any food for nearly twenty hours.

Therefore when I had tottered over the bridge which crossed the new cut canal and was over the road which led into the city I stepped down from the railway embankment to reach the road. But the bank was twenty feet high and steep, and so from its middle height I slipped and fell down. I struck a steel strut of one of the telegraph poles and got a severe blow. I lay at its foot panting and half-unconscious and then getting up on my feet walked to my brother's house. They had surely heard of the incident and looked for me, but nobody asked me any question. I had fever and was delirious and in the course of my deliriums uttered imprecations against the world. Within a few days my father came down from Kishorganj. My brother must have written to him. But he also asked me nothing, and only told me that I had better go with him to Kishorganj for change and rest.

I was miserable, for by that time I had lost all my defiant spirit and even self-respect. However, a ray of hope fell on me. One day Mohit Babu came and asked me if I would write for a new magazine that he, Ashoke Babu, and two other literary friends were bringing out. It was not a new magazine, but a revived old one. It had originally been published as a weekly journal during the Non-Co-operation Movement to satirize it, and its name was *Sanibarer Chithi {Saturday Letters)*. But after the end of that movement it had ceased publication. Now Ashoke Babu, who was its proprietor, and Mohit Babu with two other friends were proposing to revive it as a monthly journal of literary polemics to attack the new trends and writers which and whom I have described in the last chapter. I readily agreed, and gave them a piece.

Now, there is one thing about my writing habits, and that is this: whatever my circumstances and the state of mind produced by them, no trace of my mental suffering has ever appeared in the articles or books I have produced during those periods. I could always write with gusto and be high-spirited. I was very much so in the article I wrote then, and indeed airily ironical. In fact, its opening was an exact translation of the first lines of Pascal's first Provincial Letter. I thought my friends would be pleased with it. For some days, however, I heard nothing and felt discouraged. But on the day before that on which I was to leave for Kishorganj, I met the editor and another friend in the street, and the former came forward to clasp me to his breast with profuse congratulations. He said that the article was wonderful, and it would be 'intellectual whipping of a very high order'. I felt, not only relieved, but even elated. At all events, I was not so worthless as I had thought. The next day I started for Kishorganj in a more hopeful frame of mind than I had had for months.

CHAPTER 3

Lost Rivers and Lost Happiness

I Leave Kishorganj For Ever

On 27 November 1927, I left Kishorganj to go back to Calcutta. I had no definite purpose in mind in doing so, and no plans or expectations about the future, which was as uncertain and unsatisfactory as it had become when I quitted the Military Accounts Department. Actually, the uncertainty was worse than in 1921, when I had gone to Calcutta with the intention at least of looking for employment. This time I had no hope of getting a job, and no intention either to look for any. I only knew that nothing but a literary career was open to me and for that I had to live in Calcutta. But whether that would keep me I did not know. I did not even consider the question. The course of my life as it has been in respect of livelihood till today – which was no course at all but merely drifting on the off-chance of being rescued and provided with some means of bodily survival – was becoming fixed.

However, there were two immediate gains. First, the stay at Kishorganj with my father, short as it was, had restored the normal poise of my mind, which had been lost in the previous months of humiliation. None the less, those experiences were more traumatic than I consciously knew them to have been. For some time hallucinations which were oppressive like nightmares would come over me in sleep, or in illness, and I would then have a conviction that the period of my humiliations had been much longer, probably by a year or two, and that I had suffered a lapse of memory in respect of it from the sheer inability to endure the strain. No such hangover was left in my mind by the much longer periods of want and anxiety I went through afterwards.

But as will be seen at the end of the story, or even from the high spirits with which I am relating it, I was not damaged in character or warped in my outlook on life by poverty, nor even by insults and humiliations. I certainly was born with a natural resilience against adverse conditions like those plants and animals which are very lowly in the biological scale, e.g., scrub, grass, or mice. Even the proverbial church mouse does not acquire pessimism or Marxism, which on human analogy it should. Of course, that depends, if one is like a plant, on how firm the roots are and how pliant the upper growth; and, if one is an animal, on how irrepressible the will to live.

A man is an animal for the most part, and what human part they have, they fritter it away by worrying about what they will eat and what they will put on. The cowardly talk one hears incessantly in these days about *stress* is due to the fact that men have forgotten how to behave like animals, which means that they have lost the animal's capacity to submit to the conditions of survival imposed by Nature. I had not. Yet I was born with a morbid sensitiveness to slights and abuse. I used to bum under them as if sprinkled with acid, and wince as if I was being branded with a red-hot iron. It is only after being scurrilously, ceaselessly, and of course stupidly attacked and abused as a writer for decades in my country that I have at last grown a protective shell like a tortoise.

To come back to my immediate situation. I was going back to Calcutta with no definite purpose indeed, but still with a sense of success. My article had come out in *Sanibarer Chithi*,. and was sent to me. My friends at Kishorganj were delighted that one of them was becoming a writer. My life was again in motion. Besides, by writing in that magazine I was entering a literary coterie as well as a literary movement, and therefore I had the feeling that I had the support of a group behind me. Without that there is very little prospect of success in a literary career.

But before giving an account of the literary campaign in which I took part, I have to speak about what I was leaving behind. When the train moved out of Kishorganj station on that November morning and passed through the tranquil landscape which was so familiar to me from many journeys, I had no idea that I was never again to see East Bengal. What that signified I did not fully realize even during the long period of fifteen years that I spent in Calcutta after leaving Kishorganj, because I was always overworked for livelihood and had no time to brood over the deprivation. It was indeed true that I could sustain my mental life only in Calcutta, but as the material base of my life it almost destroyed me. I was saved from early death only by moving to Delhi in 1942.

But with that I also became an expatriate, which I have remained since then. After coming away from Calcutta once, I did not revisit it for twenty-six years, and my subsequent visits, added up, have not covered a longer period than six weeks. It was through that absence from Bengal that I became fully aware of the significance of the geographical setting of my early life, and it was this realization that gave those overtones of fervour which are to be found in the descriptions of East Bengal scenes and life in my autobiography. But I also wrote in that book that to be once uprooted was to be for ever on the road.

My ancestry and early life have made me incapable of being a contented city-dweller, although I have had to live in big cities ever afterwards. Thus I have remained a countryman, unchanged and unchangeable in my habits and outlook. Moreover, it is by drawing on the memories of boyhood in East Bengal that I have been able to resist that atrophy of sensibilities which city life brings about inexorably.

Town and Country in Bengali Life

But not only atrophy, something worse – fossilization, has come over the mind of Hindu Bengalis on account of the separation of their life from its natural environment, which was brought about by the partition of 1947. For present-day Bengalis, Bengal is nothing but Calcutta as it is now, and such a city cannot support either happiness or creativity. The most serious loss is the severance of contact with the waters of Bengal, and more especially with the three great rivers which have made Bengal what she is geographically. These are the Padma (the main channel to the sea of the Ganges at the present time), the Brahmaputra (locally known as the Jamuna or Jabuna), and the Meghna. All three are now in the new state known as Bangla Desh.

Of course, Calcutta still stands on a river, and that is a branch of the Ganges. Although known in English as the Hooghly river, its Sanskrit name is Bhagirathi, and the Bengalis have always called it simply Ganga (the Ganges). In the past this branch was the main outlet to the sea of the waters of the Ganges. In the early part of the nineteenth century it discharged so much water into the Bay of Bengal that Bishop Reginald Heber, when coming to Calcutta in a sailing ship in October 1823, found that even at a distance of one hundred miles from the mouth of the Hooghly his ship was struggling against the current of that river. As he wrote: 'The mighty Ganges ran like a mill- stream at a fathom or two underneath, against which nothing but a very powerful gale could contend.' Even near Diamond Harbour, about forty miles below Calcutta, the river, Heber wrote: 'was still of vast width and rapidity.' The pilot informed him that the tides in it ran at a rate of 10 to 11 knots.

Moreover, in its lower reaches up to the sea the Ganges retained its sacred status only in this branch. The Padma had none. What was even more important, it was on the two banks of this branch of the Ganges, known locally as the Bhagirathi, that the culture which could be regarded as the distinctly Bengali form of Hindu culture, arose and flourished. Thus the traditional Bengali culture was a riparian culture. It had even a religious sanction behind it. For all Bengalis, to die in the waters of the Ganges was like receiving the extreme unction of the Roman Church, and therefore dying men and women were carried to the river even over distances of forty miles on the shoulders of their relatives. So it happened that the strip of territory of this width to the east and west of the river delimited the homeland of Bengali culture laterally, and all Bengalis tried to remain in touch with it socially, and culturally as well. The rest of Bengal lost cultural and social standing to a lesser or greater extent according as the areas receded farther and farther from these two lines.

But the cultural importance of the Bhagirathi has become a thing of the past. The river began to shrink and silt up even before the end of the nineteenth century, and has been kept navigable for ships in its lower reaches by continuous dredging. With the growth of Calcutta, it lost its cultural status and became only a channel of commerce, except for traditional Bengali Hindus who went to bathe in it as a religious duty. The modern Bengali culture which was created in Calcutta had no association with the river on which the city stood. Both the physical and cultural decline of the river is symbolic.

Fortunately, I did not have to live in Calcutta after the partition of Bengal in 1947, and so I have not been exposed personally to the general decadence of Bengali life. But even before the fatal partition, life in Calcutta was felt to be stifling by all sensitive Bengalis, because, in spite of being the centre of all intellectual activity among Bengalis, it eroded sensibility and feeling. This was felt, above all, by Rabindranath Tagore, the great poet and the greatest Bengali that has lived.

But Tagore had the means to live away from Calcutta. For Bengali writers of ordinary means there could be no escape from the crushing weight of its drabness. They had to live in it in order to carry on their writing, earn their livelihood, and yet deal with the ever-present problem of saving what they wrote from the city's polluted, corroding, and asphyxiating atmosphere. As a rule, when they wrote poetry or fiction, the only strong and lasting products of the Bengali literary effort, they drew on their experiences in the villages. But they could not raise their own life as lived above the material squalor imposed by the city and their very inadequate means of living. No one visiting their houses and observing their way of living could ever have imagined that they could be capable of such flights of imagination and feeling as they often displayed in their works. I know their life, and I myself have lived it, although I have never acquiesced in the material squalor of that life. But that rebellion, in its turn, has alienated me even from Bengalis of my class.

Bengali Hindus and Nature

But the curious thing was that the Bengalis taken collectively showed no awareness of their natural environment, not even of their great rivers. I shall give two examples of their indifference to it from my own experience, and the first will be from the very last journey from Kishorganj.

Between Mymensingh town and Jagannathganj Ghat there was a stretch of the railway line which ran very close to the old channel of the Brahmaputra, which flows diagonally through Mymensingh district. The view here was a favourite with me, and whenever I passed that way I tried to have a good look at it. This time too I wanted to see it, and so when the train came near it I got up from my seat and leaned out of the door at one end of the coach. I did not know that I was looking at it for the last time.

It was the beginning of the cold season, and the river had shrunk to a narrow channel of gleaming but almost still water, and the rest of its bed had become continuous banks of silver-grey sand on either side. Beyond the bare fields on the far side, the villages hidden by bamboo clumps formed an azure border to the light blue sky, on which the Garo Hills were etched in steel-grey. This vast scene in spite of its openness created an atmosphere of deep seclusion, and the only place inhabited by human beings seemed to be the train.

After the train had moved out of this section of its track I came back to my seat. An elderly person who was sitting opposite to me had apparently Watched me and been very much puzzled by what seemed to him total absence of purpose in my movement, for he had not seen me going into the toilet at the end of the coach. He asked me why I had gone to the door, and when I replied that I wanted to have a look at the river he remarked: 'What is there to see in it." Rather annoyed, I replied tartly, 'You won't understand.' But he did not take offence, instead, seemed to feel an interest in me. So, when we got into the steamer at Jagannathganj, he came up to me and asked me who and what I was. I learned that he was a police inspector.

But certainly his interest in me was not professional. Perhaps he thought that I was an original.

But in the other incident, which had happened six years earlier, I did not evoke even this kind of interest. I was then coming from Calcutta and got on the steamer at Sirajganj Ghat. The river was the great Brahmaputra, and a fresh wind of early morning was blowing. I always like to feel the wind against my face. So, leaning on the railing, I contemplated the broad river. The waves were showing crests of foam. For some time I remained there. This time, too, I became an object of observation, for when I came back an elderly Bengali put a question to me which showed that not only had he taken note of my behaviour, but also drawn his conclusion from it. Skipping all leading remarks, he simply said: 'A BA or MA, I suppose." When I nodded, he snapped, 'Nobody in these days thinks anything of B As and M As.' He obviously thought that by looking at the river in that way I was giving superior airs on the strength of a university degree. So he wanted to put me in my place.

This sort of indifference to the geographical environment of their life was part of the traditional attitudes of all Bengalis. Before they had become conscious of the beauties of nature by reading English poetry they did not show any awareness even of the Himalayas, although they had some of the peaks just north of Bengal, e.g. Everest, Kanchenjunga, Chomo Lhari or Kulha Kangri. Sir George Burrard, in his book on the Himalayas, noted with surprise that these peaks had no Bengali or Sanskritic names, although the people of north Bengal must have seen them every day. In contrast, all the Himalayan peaks north of the U.P. have Sanskritic names. Furthermore, there were no places of pilgrimage in the section of the great mountains, north of Bengal.

This was significant in a way, but not surprising, because the natural environment of Bengali life was the alluvial plain between the Himalayas and the sea. That makes another insensibility all the more strange. Traditional Bengalis showed no awareness of what must be regarded as the grandest feature of the landscape of Bengal, namely, its waters in forms of a bewildering variety, and, above all, the great rivers. Yet through the ages they had carried out a thorough adaptation of their manner of living with these waters, and for a part of the year they lived almost like amphibians. In those parts of Bengal which were subject to monsoon floods people went from one homestead to another, and even from one hut to another in the same homestead, in rafts in the rainy season. My mother told me that once, when she went to her mother's village which was in the eastern part of Mymensingh, the floor of the hut in which she slept was always Under knee-deep water, and from her bed she could see fish and snakes swimming in it.

The traditional Bengali attitude to water, when not religious, was wholly utilitarian. The rivers in their secular presence were only means of communication and transport, and most widely used as such because travelling by land was both expensive and arduous. Before horse-drawn carriages were introduced, and many parts of Bengal never had them at any time, it had to be done on horseback, on elephants, in palanquins and doolies, or bullock carts. Transport of merchandise was virtually confined to boats. Routine visiting of relatives was done in boats, and in the rainy season. Even havocs created by floods, bores, or cyclones were considered normal. In those days no Bengali complained about them, and the houses were built in such a way that they could be set up again within weeks if not days if they came down.

But the Bengali insensibility to nature and its beauties was part of a very much wider insensibility shown by all modem Hindus all over India. Whatever the reason, they had lost the acute sensibility to nature of the ancient Hindu. Sanskrit literature contains descriptions of every kind of natural beauty, whether in the mountains and hills, by the sea, or in the forests. Let me give only one example from a play by the Sanskrit poet Bhavabhuti, who is assigned to the eighth century. He is describing the Vindhya region: 'Here are the Prasravana hills, with their soft azure made softer still by the ever-drizzling clouds, their caverns echoing the babbling Godavari, their woods a solid mass of green, made up of tangled foliage.'

A whole anthology of such passages can be compiled from novels, poems, and plays in Sanskrit. Some of this sensibility survived to give to Vaishnava poetry in Bengali its idyllic quality, but even these passages were not noted until the sensibility to nature was revived among the Bengalis by English poetry.

The Revived Interest

The character of the revival was very peculiar. Generally speaking, when modern Bengalis acquired a feeling for the beauties of nature they showed it by a vicarious enjoyment of those described in the source of their new feeling, namely, English literature. Thus English and Scottish landscapes in their imaginative evocation became the staple of the enjoyment. For instance, as a boy I recited not only 'Call for the robin redbreast and the wren' and other poems by English poets, but also 'My heart's in the Highlands, my heart is not here,' or 'Ye banks and braes o' bonnie Doon,' or 'O Caledonia, stem and wild, meet nurse for a poetic child,' by Scottish poets, with a gusto which annoyed our unpoetic elders.

One day I was called to order over this habit of mine by a typical elderly Bengali. I was about thirteen then, and used to go to my school in Calcutta from a rural suburb as a daily passenger (called commuters in these days). On one return journey, when I should have forgotten my books, I suddenly opened my poetry book and began to recite loudly, 'My heart's in the Highlands ...' A Bengali, an elderly clerk in one of the English mercantile houses, cherishing no love for his masters and dead tired from the daylong quill-driving, could not stand my enthusiasm, and shouted at me: 'Stop that, I say. Don't show so much keenness, you will die before your time.' This last observation emanated from the superstition that precocious children die early. He thought that I was trying to show off my cleverness.

To admire the beauties of nature in terms of the English landscape was a general habit. My wife even now tells me about the impression made on her by the *Ode to Autumn* of Keats:

> Seasons of mists and mellow fruitfulness,
> Close bosom-friend of the maturing sun ...

I have not been able to forget the romance of the Malvern Hills or of Windermere imbibed from pictures. What is not less significant is that when modem Bengalis recognized beauty in nature in India, they never placed it in Bengal, but in the Himalayas, by the seaside, in Kashmir, or in the Vindhyas. The Bengali scene never seemed to catch their eye, except in certain very special ways which will be particularized presently. However, before accusing Bengalis of ignoring the beauty of appearance of their country, it is necessary to ask and answer one question: 'Does Bengal possess any beauty of landscape to speak of?' Certainly, the British saw none, and most Bengalis as a matter of consciously held theory also did not. My own feeling for the Bengali landscape was two-sided in my early years. Consciously, I never credited Bengal with beautiful landscapes. Yet when I passed through one or other of the most commonly seen aspects of the

Bengali landscape, for instance, a great river (and I have journeyed in boat or steamer on all the big three), the rice fields either in their green or in their gold stretching to the horizon and billowing under strong winds, the bamboo clumps or the great banian tree, there was not one occasion when I did not lose my sense of being a viewer only and become one with these scenes like Wordsworth's boy.

I shall never forget one such occasion. It was on 14 April 1913,that I was going from Goalundo Ghat to Narayanganj in the river steamer *Condor*. The journey was over one hundred miles. The Padma, though very wide in this region, is a comparatively shallow river with many sandbanks. It being early summer, these had already risen above the water and made the river a maze of serpentine streams, like the background of Mona Lisa, of course with this difference that there were no rocks. Nonetheless, the sandbanks presented a strong contrast to the grey water, because that year the sands were golden instead of being only silvery. Never before had I seen sandbanks of this colour in the Padma, and I did not see anything like them again when I journeyed afterwards. The light on the river was like moonlight, but on the sandbanks it was that of sunset. How that happened I cannot tell.

There were very few passengers on the steamer that day, and I had the run of the deck. But to have a better view I went up to the bridge and looked round. I had just read about Turner's paintings in a book. In fact, the book was lying on my box on the deck below. The glow of his paintings, visualized by imagination, seemed to lie on the wide landscape all around me.

At that point there was at that time an immense sandbank – many miles long – which stretched away from east of Tarpasha to almost Chandpur, and the steamer had to make an immense detour in order to enter the Meghna, up which it had to go in order to reach Narayanganj. When near the meeting of the rivers, I saw the long and sharp line which marked off the ochre-coloured water of the Padma from the grey-green water of the Meghna. The steamer crossed this line, the steering wheel spun in the hands of the helmsman, and making a turn of 24 points to port, it went ahead past the great pagoda of Rajabari, with the engines thudding and the paddles chunking. What I saw registered itself on my mind as if it was only a photographic plate or film. I never became aware of any feeling.

But when I grew up I began to put this question to myself: does the Bengali landscape have any beauty, as beauty of landscape is commonly understood? I could not be sure. I could feel that it was imbued with a limitless peace and stillness, so that when I went to my ancestral village I never consulted a watch or clock because there time seemed to have stopped in its flow and become a lagoon. A lagoon may lull you to sleep, but it cannot rouse you to rapture.

But one day I had an experience which I can regard as 'conversion' in the religious sense. That was in 1927 during that very last stay at Kishorganj. I was always in the habit of taking long walks, and on that day I was strolling along the railway embankment northwards from Kishorganj. After I had gone about three miles I suddenly noticed a homestead with half-a-dozen huts to my left, which was silhouetted against the sunset. There was a long pool of water by the side of the railway line, and the homestead was across it. There was also the usual pond before it. The blue sky and the red and pink clouds were reflected in the water of both. The glow of the sunset could be seen through the bamboo clumps behind the homestead. The whole scene was like one of Constable's landscapes, and I can confirm the impression after seeing the Constable country. It came to me in a flash that the Bengali scene too had a particular beauty of its own, very quiet and intimate, but not less moving for that. It was like suddenly waking up to the beauty of a girl in the family, after looking for it only among film stars. I do not know whether other Bengalis have felt like me, but for me it was like enlightenment bestowed in a blessed moment.

I have just said that the Bengalis gave expression to their awareness of the beauty of nature in India in special ways. One of these was wholly political. To boast about the beauty of the Indian landscape was a part of their nationalism. One Bengali playwright dealing with the invasion of Alexander the Great made him deliver a long harangue about the beauty of India. Of course, nobody could quarrel with these Bengalis if they threw the Himalayas at the head of the rest of the world, but they themselves did not become aware of the Himalayas until Englishmen taught them to brag about them. Nowadays the Bengalis say that it was a Bengali who discovered Everest. His name was Radhanath Sikdar, and he was a mathematician who did the calculations for the Survey of India, under its chief, Sir George Everest, after whom the peak was named. After going through the observational data gathered by the field workers he told Sir George: 'Sir, I have found the highest peak in the world,' or some such thing. The Bengalis had also the right to be proud of their rivers, but the scorn which they put into any mention of the Thames as a river was not justified by any knowledge they had of their own rivers. A Bengali poet of some standing wrote in my young days that in Bengal storks and crows nurse their young with more than maternal care. Reviewing the poem, a Bengali editor who always brought in strong whiffs of common sense in his criticism, wrote: And, of course, in other countries they peck them to death. But this sort of common sense was very rare among the Bengalis, and even when present evaporated quickly when their patriotic feeling was roused.

However, it must not be imagined that the Bengali feeling for Bengal's landscape was always so factitious. It was deep and sincere when not consciously stirred up. That feeling was most clearly perceived both in Bengali poetry and fiction, and in a very remarkable way in fiction, which gave expression to the notion of romantic love acquired from European literature. Now, this kind of love can never be separated from the beauties of nature, and when Bengali novelists began to write stories of love they had to put them in a convincing geographical setting; that is, love had to be correlated to the Bengali scene. This correlation was carried out with complete success, but by means of intuition rather than any conscious process of reasoning.

A cue was, however, taken from the old Bengali poetry of pre-British times. Old Bengali Vaishnava poetry (mostly from the sixteenth century) was interwoven with water in Bengal. One of these poets, Vidyapati, describes in one of his most famous lyrics the heartache of a woman who is separated from her husband or lover in the rainy season. She contrasts the void in her home with the fullness of the rains in the month of Bhadra (August-September). Another Vaishnava poet describes a girl sleeping in her disarrayed sari, but in unconscious happiness because of the rumble of rain. Even in the most erotic poem in the Bengali language, in which love is depicted at its most carnal, it was not deprived of the romance which Bengal's waters could bring into it. So the princess says to her husband: 'We shall go a-boating up and down the river, and at night, clasped in each other's arms, listen to the murmur of the rain and rustle of the wind.'

In modern Bengali fiction the correlation was taken a step further: even the themes and incidents became interwoven with the different forms of water according to their character. Happy love was placed in the ambiance of a full, flowing river, hopeless love in a destructive form of water, and guilty love in a scene of desolation. It is in Tagore's stories that this interweaving is seen at its closest. I shall give only three examples.

In one story a young man had rejected a proposal of marriage with a girl with whom he used to play as a boy. In the latter part of the nineteenth century and even down to my young days, Bengali youths faced themselves with an unnecessary choice between patriotism and love, as many Christian youths did between religion and love. Their first decision was to serve the country and never marry. In most cases, they married. In doing so, they obeyed as sons, but did not have to sigh as lovers. But some dedicated young men chose the country. The young man of the story had done that, but for livelihood he had to be a schoolmaster in a small town in East Bengal.

There he found that the elderly lawyer who lived next door to him had married the rejected girl. When he went to visit the lawyer, he could feel her presence behind a partition, got the scent of her hair-oil, heard the tinkle of her jewellery and the rustling of her sari, and almost looked into the large black eyes he knew so well. A sudden pang shot through him, and this became a fixed pain. The more he tried to persuade himself that the girl was nothing to him, the more did his heart reply that she could have been everything. There could, of course, be no question in those days of meeting her in person.

However, one night when the lawyer was away on a case, he heard the roar of the cyclone and the rush of the great bore of the estuary of the Meghna. He took refuge on the high bank of a reservoir, and then saw another person coming up to it from the other side. It was his lost love. Soon everything all around was engulfed in a raging mass of water. They stood there side by side under a sky which did not have even one star in it, with their eyes fixed on the mad torrent of death. They did not exchange one word even, not one greeting. When the water went down each went back home. But he felt that, although he had become neither a Mazzini nor a Garibaldi, but was only a poorly paid second master in a ricketty school, he had nevertheless tasted eternal bliss that night. The waters which had dealt out death to others had left to his life an imperishable gift of fulfilment.

Another story shows a different kind of correlation. A wealthy landlord had fallen in love with the daughter of the doctor who was treating his invalid wife, the most devoted wife one could have. She saw it, and in order to make him happy, and not out of jealousy, took poison. With her last breath she entreated him to marry the girl and not grieve for her, because she was dying happy in the certainty that he would be happy with the girl. He did marry her, but happiness was not for him. The girl herself remained frozen as if there had been some sacrilege in her marriage. He on his part was pursued by a sense of guilt, which made him hear in every kind of sound at night, whether that of a flight of migratory birds or the ticking of the timepiece, a question from his dead wife: 'Who is she, dear."

To escape this terrible visitation he took his young wife on a boat journey on the Padma. At first it seemed that she was waking up to her married life in that spacious setting. It was not to be, though. One evening when they were walking on a sandbank, blanched by moonlight, the red shawl slipped from the wife's head. He saw the beautiful face uplifted like a lily, and kissed her lips. But that kiss was petrified by a loud cry from nearby: 'Who is she, dear! Who is she?' It was only the cry of a startled aquatic bird. But those who have seen the sands of our big rivers at night and heard such cries will understand both the beauty and the terror of the scene.

Even nearness of death after being wrecked in a storm was raised from terror to beauty by these rivers. A young man named Ramesh had been married against his wishes by his father, and was coming back with his bride to his village on the Padma in a boat from the village of his father-in-law, where the wedding had taken place. In the evening, as is usual in early summer, a Nor'wester struck the boat and it sank. At dead of night, Ramesh found himself stretched on a sandbank lit up by the moon. He got up in order to find out if anybody else had been saved. I translate the Bengali passage in the novel:

Between two arms of the branching Padma, the white islet of sand lay on its back like a naked child. Ramesh walked along the edge of one of the branches to the end of the sandbank and turned round to explore the other side, when at a short distance he glimpsed something like a piece of red cloth. Quickly going forward, he saw his bride in her red silk sari lying as if lifeless.

He knew how to restore the drowned and began the movements.

In a little while the girl began to breathe gently. Ramesh was so exhausted himself that he sat still, unable to control his own breathing so as to put a question to the girl, who had not as yet regained full consciousness. He examined her and found her breathing unobstructed. Then, on that spot between land and water, and at that moment between life and death, he waited with his eyes fixed on the face of the girl in the pale moonlight. The virginal face was small, but in its tender beauty it was blooming in all its glory as the only thing worth looking at under that vast sky and that immense expanse of moonlight.*

But in real life these cyclonic storms created more horrors than beauty, although even there scenes of tragic beauty were not absent. I give one example of the scenes created by a great cyclone in East Bengal at the end of October 1876, from the autobiography of a well-known Bengali poet, who was a magistrate and present with his Commissioner (an Englishman) at the scene of devastation on the banks of the Karnaphuli river near the town of Chittagong. The storm lasted about six hours, beginning at midnight and ceasing at dawn. In the morning he went down with his superior and saw the dead, and he recorded what he saw in these words:

Oh God! Is all that I saw verily Your handiwork? Here lay a mother with her dead child clasped in her arms, there a father with a son and a daughter strapped to his body with his dhoti. At another spot I saw something which no human heart could endure: a husband had tied his wife to his body, and both were lying with their arms round each other – as if the two were sleeping in the enchantment of a dream of love. The woman's long tresses were trailing in the mud. The beauty of the couple was lighting up the bank of mud. As far as one could see, the same heart-rending scene: corpses and more corpses, and yet more corpses beyond, mingled with the carcases of beasts and birds.†

I myself saw the aftermath of a great cyclone in 1919, fortunately to look only on material devastation. It included one scene which I would not have believed to be possible unless I had seen it with my own eyes: a goods train blown off the track into a rice-field about fifty yards away.

Recalled in Later Life

I have not seen these scenes for more than fifty years, and it is not likely that I shall see them again. But I can say like Wordsworth:

* Tagore: *Nauka-Dubi.* My translation. The irony of the story lay in the fact that the girl was not Ramesh's bride, but another man's, whose boat had also been wrecked.

†Nabin *Sen: Amar Jiban.* My translation from the Bengali.

These beauteous forms
Through a long absence, have not been to me
As is a landscape to a blind man's eye;
But oft, in lonely rooms, and 'mid the din
Of Towns and Cities, I have owed to them
In hours of weariness, sensations sweet,
Felt in the blood, and felt along the heart...

Living in Delhi, I could see scenes like those in East Bengal when the Jumna rose in flood in the rainy season. There were the same rushing waters splashing the banks, the blue borders of the villages beyond the far bank, the pampas grass waving its plumes along it, and the fleecy clouds above.

But it was in two far distant countries outside India that the rivers of East Bengal came back to me with the revived force of a direct meeting. The first occasion was in 1967 in Israel by the Sea of Galilee, and the second in 1976 at Kingston in Canada by the waters of St Lawrence where it issues out of Lake Ontario.

I was staying at the hotel of Kibbutz Ginosar which stood on the edge of the biblical plain of Gennesaret close by the lake. In the opposite direction I could see the double crests of the Horns of Hatti where Saladin defeated the last of the Prankish Crusaders. The Sea of Galilee looked like the Meghna. It was breaking into ripples, and I asked my Israeli friend: 'The lake looks so tranquil, how could a storm like the one Jesus stilled rise in it?' He replied that at times it could become very turbulent. I found that the next morning.

I was awakened by the roar of waters, and looking out of the window I saw below it foaming waves rushing through the reeds growing in a small inlet. I dressed hurriedly and went out to a rocky promontory to find out what was happening. I could see no trace of wind in the tall eucalypti, although the lake itself was tossing wildly. I learned later that a storm was blowing from the south along the narrow and low valley of the Jordan. At nine I was at Capernaum. The Sea of Galilee was looking ink-black then, with the waves crested with white foam. I had seen exactly such a scene on the Meghna in 1907, near Bhairav Bazar.

At the end of 1976 I went to Canada to be reminded again of the waters of Bengal. I saw the St Lawrence both at Montreal and Ogdensburg. At those places the river did not seem to be anything but what I had thought it would be, having formed my idea from pictures of Quebec. But at Kingston, when I went out of the Faculty Club of Queen's University and stood by the extreme end of Lake Ontario, I could fancy that I was on the banks of the Meghna again. The expanse of water before me was not the St Lawrence proper, but the wide channel which separated the mainland from Wolf Island. However, it looked exactly like the Meghna. Somehow, if there is wooded country on the other side of a very big river, the trees look like grey-green curtains hanging on the water, and the faint blue of the sky can be seen through the shadowy trees, or at all events a mirage-like illusion is created. I had seen this sort of scene on the Meghna and saw them again at the lower end of Lake Ontario. It was almost seventy years since I had seen the Meghna, but standing by the waters of the St Lawrence I could murmur-*Super flumina Babylonis...*

CHAPTER 4
A Literary Campaign

I went to see my friends of the *Sanibarer Chithi* as soon as I arrived in Calcutta. The magazine had no office of its own, and not even a business organization. Financially, there was no problem because none of us wanted to make money out of it and those who contributed neither demanded nor expected remuneration for their articles. As to production, since Ashoke Babu was the formal owner of the paper we could get it printed at the Prabasi Press, and pay the Press from our sales. As the magazine sold well from the very beginning and went on adding to its circulation, there was no difficulty in bringing it out regularly. Afterwards, it even became moderately profitable.

Ashoke Babu solved the problem of accommodation as well. He allowed us to sit in the editorial rooms of the *Prabasi* after office hours. We regularly met there in the evenings and talked. This was as essential for us as the writing and the printing. We were fighters, and an *esprit de corps* had to be created. This was done very effectually in the course of the evening sessions. We discussed the plans for the forthcoming issues, reviewed the impact of each issue when published, and held a sort of soiree on the day of publication, at which all the contributors read their pieces before colleagues and friends. Ashoke Babu paid for the hot snacks.

My friends were very glad to see me again, and congratulated me on my article. We were profuse in mutual admiration, and it was sincere. Without it the zest of the undertaking could not have been maintained. I was asked to go on writing for the paper. I was not as yet quite of the group, but was admitted to it forthwith. I got into the spirit of the crusade, and contributed a regular feature every month. Mohit Babu gave it the name: 'Pronounced Topically', and in it I continued my judgements or rather onslaughts on the new writers, covering both their matter and manner. It became an expected feature of the magazine. Although formally there was an editor, ours was really a collective venture, and there was a sort of collective responsibility. We were crusaders, not entrepreneurs, and each of us brought to the magazine his special knowledge, judgement, taste, and temperament. On account of this I have to describe the personalities, before giving an account of our activities.

The Personalities

The regular writers, who might be called 'contributors on the staff were five: Jogananda Das, who was the editor; Sajani Das; Ashoke Chatterji; Mohit Majumdar; and myself. Jogananda had been the magazine's editor in its political incarnation, and he retained his formal position when it was revived. He had a subtle, ironical style of writing, but he was rather mild, and did not feel at ease with the rest of us, all of whom were aggressive, each in his own way. He did not also feel very strongly about literature. So, within two months he resigned, and I took over his formal position.

Our literary theorist was Mohit Babu, and as he was the oldest member of the group we looked upon him as our leader. He stood for the Bengali conservative tradition in literature and culture, and conferred both weight and respectability on our cause. But to succeed in our campaign, we needed liveliness and exuberance as much as we did seriousness. Above all, we wanted humour to be our main weapon. But in his prose writings Mohit Babu showed no humour. For that we depended principally on Sajani Das, although he was the youngest among us. He spread the mainsail for our ship and became our mainstay for appealing to the largest element of our readers, because he had to an exceptional degree the aptitude for satire which was one of the oldest and strongest strains in the Bengali literary genius. Its humour was basically malicious. But if it lacked innocence this was largely counterbalanced by its extravagance and burlesque. That made people laugh and overlook the ill-will. Sajani had this Bengali gift for extravagance in more than full measure. So, it was really he who created the popularity of the paper.

He was in every way a remarkable character. I was introduced to him by Mohit Babu in 1925, and becàme intimate with him before I joined the group. In his university days he had been a student of science, but had given that up and taken to literature, which was his real bent. When I met him first he was on the editorial staff of *Prabasi*. But that extremely grave magazine did not offer openings to Sajani's special genius in the literary way, and that was one of the reasons why he took the initiative to revive *Sanibarer Chithi*.

I was told about his capacity for farcical extravagance soon after being introduced to him. He was living in a boarding-house, and one day he quite characteristically offered a bet of five rupees by challenging anybody to take some human excreta from the toilet and eat it. He did it, and won his five rupees. By doing so he even acquired for the time being a reputation for holiness or saintliness in the Hindu manner, for it was one of the marks, indeed one of the requirements, of becoming and being recognized as a Hindu holy man that the aspirant should make no distinction between sandalwood paste and human faeces, and regard them as the same thing. This was called *chitta-suddhi*, i.e. purification of the mind. Thus it was quite natural that after Sajani had performed his feat, another young man should fall at his feet, crying in a broken voice: 'You are a Sadhu, you are a Mahatma. With your blessing, I shall also do the same.' So, he took a pinch of excreta from the toilet and tried to eat it. But he betrayed his inferior spiritual potential by vomiting it out. The others set him down as a presumptuous fool. This sort of catholicity in respect of means to an end was retained by Sajani all through his worldly career.

He also had a striking physical appearance, although he was more ugly than handsome in his features taken in themselves. He was thickset and burly, and had a chubby face with a small up-turned nose. But he had very bright black eyes, and thick black eyebrows. His smile was deceptively winning, and it showed no trace of the malice which was always lurking within him. As he was generally in a humorous mood that gave him an attractive expression. One day I suddenly realized that he was very much like Balzac to look at, and told him so, and at the same time I showed him a reproduction of Nadar's daguerrotype. Sajani looked at the picture intently for a minute or two, and then exclaimed: 'True indeed! How marvellously observant you are!'

It was after seeing him that I wrote to my sister that Bengali writers were a set of madmen, and it was Sajani who finally made me write down the aphorism: 'The vanity of a peacock and the malice of a monkey when combined with the divine gift of expression, make a literary man of the purest breed.' With more self-discipline he would certainly have left behind him a substantial body of writing which would have assured for him a permanent place in Bengali literature as a satirist, and also as a humorist, because when jealousy did not drive him to exhibit malice, he could be as innocent in his humour as Lear. He was also capable of genuine moral indignation, which made some of his satire another illustration to the old saying: '*Facit indignatio versum.*' But he chose to forsake his vocation, lured by tawdry worldly ambitions, and died before age could make him realize his mistake. In this, too, Sajani Das was a typical Bengali genius, all of whom possess with their genius a perverse readiness to become a traitor to it.

Ashoke Babu was the pure humorist of the group. His style was light, and I might describe his contributions as the foresails of our ship. He once diagnosed the ailments of our new writers as Ibsenitis, Whitmania, and Leninosis. His humour and irony was of the Bengali liberal school. He felt so sure of his motives that he was not afraid of parodying a very solemn poem by Mohit Babu and, strange to say, our leader, so touchy in everything, did not mind it at all. Ashoke Babu ran a number of papers at various times. In one of them he published a caricature of myself I was very short and given to pulling my very scant and straggling moustaches. I also quoted La Rochefoucauld in every possible context. So I was shown standing on a stool before the oval mirror of the dressing table of my sister-in-law, trimming my moustaches with a gigantic pair of scissors, and spouting: 'La Rochefoucauld says!' Ashoke Babu was not wholly without malice, but he never allowed it to appear in his writings, which only displayed his gift for the pure comic. He, too, forsook literature for business.

In this group I stood for a wholly different standpoint. I was not in the first place a Bengali literary traditionalist like Mohit Babu or a conservative who opposed change because it was change. I was always for change, but I was a traditionalist in this sense that I believed that novelty could only grow as a new shoot out of a tradition. I had already realized that change by itself meant nothing unless we could diagnose its character, for it led both to progress and to decay, and it could be good as well as bad. This enabled me to brush aside the argument of the new writers that we were no better than the conservatives who condemned the great writers who had created modem Bengali literature. I tried to expose the mischief inherent in the newness they were practising.

Next, I tried to base our criticism on standards which were less parochial than those adopted in current Bengali literary criticism. My aim was to make our criticism and condemnation of the new trends as broadly and firmly based as possible by adopting a standard of reference which would place these against the highest excellence achieved in literature in all ages and among all peoples. I had already come to disbelieve in progress in art and literature, and on the contrary held that great literature and art of all ages and all peoples had the same level of excellence, although not the same kind of excellence. However, I was ready to admit, and indeed formulated for myself the historical view of literature, that within its expression in a certain language and among a particular people literature evolved like anything organic; that is to say, any particular national literature had birth as well as death, with childhood, youth, maturity, age, and senility in between. The corollary to this theory was that new trends in both literature and art could stand for decay and disease as well as for growth.

Thus I was never afraid of referring to distant precedents, whether they were to be found in Indian or European literature, in a bygone age or in our times. Among Bengali writers this kind of critical writing was not common. Actually, literary criticism was the weakest side of Bengali literature. When I was young only Pramatha Chaudhuri, who was of our parental generation and was the leading literary critic in Bengal, had introduced the fashion of referring to European literary movements in connection with literary problems which were purely Bengali. He had adopted the forms of spoken Bengali in writing his prose articles, and justified that by comparing the 'naturalization' he was recommending with what the French Romantics did in the face of opposition from the Classicists. This was a false analogy, but he certainly broadened our approach to literary questions. I tried to go one better, and I even quoted the manifestos of Ronsard and Du Bellay.

Actually, in my discussion of Bengali literature I was trying to be something like a European, and more especially a French, critic. Circumstances so shaped my literary career that I became and have remained a controversialist. If, however, Bengali literature had remained in the stable condition it had reached by the turn of the century and had not begun to show what I considered symptoms of disease and decay, I should certainly have become a literary critic of the type of Sainte-Beuve, or at least like Jules Lemaître and Anatole France. They all wrote their criticism in a form which, by adapting a well-known phrase, I would call *critique-feuilleton.* But I got involved in an irreconcilable quarrel between the established traditions of Bengali literature and what I regarded as wholly disruptive trends.

In fighting them I certainly gave very highbrow airs, and paced the decks with all my orders worn on the breast like Nelson, which made it easy for our enemies to shoot at me with particular malice. This was made easier by the fact that I wrote in wholly intelligible language, so that those whom I criticized understood what I was saying and got all the more angry. This was also the result of a particular view of writing I had. I regarded it as an instrument of action, and not merely as a game of words. By themselves, my contributions would not have kept our ship going, nevertheless they were certainly the top sails.

But in spite of my desire to hit hard, I never mentioned any particular writer by name. I treated the writers whom I criticised as a team or rather a pack, which certainly as a group they were. I also took particular care to be always urbane in manner, however severe I might be in substance. I followed the motto: *suaviter in modo, fortiter in re*. But that only made our enemies bolder in attacking me. Their smutty wit was especially directed at me, for Sajani could reply so devastatingly in kind that they only snarled at him, without trying to sharpen their wit on him, although it was he who among us employed the most homely personal language against them.

Mohit Babu called my manner my 'French sophistication', and would at times tell me that I had not quite maintained it. My father, who always read my articles, wanted and expected me to be uniformly courteous in my polemics, and he would not pass over anything which he regarded as a lapse. I give one example of his criticism of me. In one of my articles I had written quite airily that I did indeed wish to remain unaware of the existence of the new writers, but asked: 'How could one forget the shoe-nails which were always pricking one's feet?' My father told me gently that such remarks were not good manners. In fact, he did not like at all that I should be a polemicist. He wished that I would leave others alone, and say what I myself had to say.

In addition to those of us who made up the inner circle, we had many occasional contributors. This was a great satisfaction for me as editor, for what a magazine like ours needed was variety in ideas, manner, and style, albeit within our united front against the new trends. This variety our outside contributors brought with their special knowledge, particular sensibility, and also, I should add, their individual grievances, personal or ideological. All of them were, and indeed had to be, brilliant. That, even our enemies could not deny. But they aired their defiance by calling us the 'Saturday Gang.'

Crescendo of the Campaign

In this book I shall speak only of my contribution to the campaign. My first articles dealt with questions of style and diction, and these brought me a compliment from Pramatha Chaudhuri. Although I did not write in the new diction he had introduced and to which he had converted even Tagore, who was his uncle-in-law, he was very generous to me. One day, at a literary party, he came up to me when a friend of mine had pointed me out to him and said: 'Sir, you write very well.' I naturally felt very much elated.

What I disliked in the new writers was their monotonous posturing and showing off. Conscious trying for effect, I would have condemned in any writer, and this was the most conspicuous weakness of those whom we were criticizing. To make matters worse, what they showed off was very immature and even crude. Their affectations could not even be classed as euphuism, because they were almost illiterate. Some of them were still students, and they tried to put into their writings whatever they were reading in their textbooks. One young writer made a Bengali girl read *Hydriotaphia* sitting on the bank of a village pond in Dacca district. Another writer brought in Vittoria Colonna. I described them as Pierrots and Harlequins, using these very two words in my Bengali articles. I also disliked their affectation in another direction, which was to drag in old Bengali folk rituals and speak about them with false sentimentality. I had seen these in my boyhood when they were performed with genuine faith, but these young writers had not, and being sons of urban professional people or officials, knew nothing of them at first hand. I regarded their attempts to garnish their weak effusions with archaistic allusions almost as sacrilege.

But, above all, these writers based their claims to be revolutionaries in literature on the erotic descriptions and suggestions which they put into their stories or poems in order to heighten their appeal. As ladled out by them, these were very diluted stuff, neither as burning as the erotic writings of the past, nor as coarse and corrosive as that of today. But as seen against the established tradition in modem Bengali literature, which was extremely puritanical – so that kissing even within wedlock had at times to be apologized for – the very childish or rustic indecencies appeared to be outrageous. This sort of writing, all published in the new magazines run by these writers themselves because no established ones would accept such stuff, both scandalized and titillated the reading public in Bengal, which neither read nor knew much about Sanskrit and old Bengali literature, in both of which very frank erotic descriptions were quite common. The scandalisation was more perceptible in the vocal reaction, but, in the private, perhaps the titillation was uppermost. This I disliked more and considered to be more significant.

For the Bengali reading public what was permissible and not permissible in literature as well as art was decided by moral principles taken over from Victorian England. Actually, not only erotic descriptions but even such suggestions were called 'obscene' by us, the English word being more commonly employed than its Bengali equivalent. These were regarded not only as offences against good taste, but against the criminal law as embodied in the Indian Penal Code, first drafted by Macaulay and finally enacted in 1860. It had a number of sections defining obscenity and prescribing punishment for it. The interpretation of these sections was generally both wide and strict. As I was very precocious I read the sections and the annotations on them even as a schoolboy in my father's copy of the Code, which with its edges coloured bright red, green, and yellow in addition to white, exercised a great fascination on me. The editor discussed whether the Judgement of Paris by Rubens, reproduced as a print from the original in the National Gallery, and the statement 'without consenting consented' in Byron's *Don Juan* came within the mischief of the law.

The antics of our young writers made even Tagore write just at that time that he was dismayed to find that the pen had discarded its veil, which made us think that we could count on him as a supporter of our campaign. The swaggering puppies, of course, yapped at him for this for some time. I myself could not assume the conventional puritanical posture, for I had already justified eroticism in literature. So, what I attacked was the crudity and feebleness of the erotic writing of these young men. It was these which made their bragging about it ridiculous and even absurd. They were really like adolescents in love, who think that they are the first in the world to have felt the passion. In their strident apologia some of them even drew our attention to Shakespeare, and one young writer threw Sir Toby Belch in our teeth. He quoted Sir Toby's apostrophising of Malvolio: 'Dost thou think, because thou art virtuous, there shall be no more cakes and ale?'

Having both eaten and drunk erotic fare which was far stronger than mere cakes and ale, I refused to be equated with Malvolio. I had already read the great classics of erotic writing, not only in Sanskrit, Bengali, and English, but also in French (in the original), as also in Greek, Latin, and Arabic (in translations). In French I had read not only Casanova but even de Brantome. Thus, instead of being scandalised by the display of obscenity by these writers I felt more inclined to jeer at them as in one of Kipling's stories the old Adjutant Bird scoffed at the young Jackal's bragging about his experience:

Ho! ho! ho!
In August was the Jackal born;
The Rains fell in September;
'Now such a fearful flood as this,'
Says he, 'I can't remember!'

I had given thought to the question of literary treatment of sexual life and set down my view on the question. So I thought I would have a go at their boasting, and in the spring of 1928 wrote a long article on the subject in my magazine. In it I tried to show that their 'calf-eroticism' was more laughable than calf-love, and also to demolish their claim to be revolutionaries, when in actual fact they were only indulging in juvenile exhibitionism.

I leaped into the arena in my war paint and with whoops, and began by saying that according to our young writers and their patrons 'obscenity' had made its first triumphal entry into literature in the Bengali year 1334 (1927) and in die cities of Calcutta and Dacca. But, in actual fact, its expression in human society was as immovable and unshakeable as the pyramids, but far older in time than even them. According to Eduard Meyer's chronology, I went on to say, the pyramids at their oldest went back to about 3000 BC, but 'obscenity' in art was so ancient that compared with it the pyramids seemed to be only of yesterday, for it dated from the Aurignacian phase of the palaeolithic age at the end of the Quarternary age. And, strange as it might seem to these young people, I said, in order to emerge, it did not have to wait for them or for the steam engine and the aeroplane. I rounded off that assertion by saying that obscenity had no connection with Communism or with middle-class unemployment in Bengal.

My sabre-rattling was continued as follows:

'It was an age when the animal which we regard as man (*Homo sapiens*) had just appeared in western Europe. Central Europe was still under the white sheet of ice of the fourth or Würmian glaciation. The elephant (*Elephas antiquus*), mammoth (*Elephas primigenius*), woolly rhinoceros (*Rhinoceros tichorhinus*), reindeer (*Rangifer tarandus*), bison (Bos priscus), cave bear (*Ursus spelaeus*), and others were roaming among the hills and forests of

France. And in that distant past our savage ancestors were cultivating "obscenity" by making nude female figures, e.g. Venus de Brassempouy, Venus de Willendorf, statuette of Mentone, Venus de Laussel, and many more.' (Translated from the Bengali)

This will give some idea of the gusto with which I was writing. I might add that I had got up my prehistory so thoroughly after taking it over from Bibhuti Babu that I did not have to refer to my books in order to roll off these names. I had them by heart. And I did not leave it at that. I went on to say that even though the nude in art might have gone back to the palaeolithic age, I thought that the representation of actual sexual intercourse in art might be the achievement of civilized man. But I had discovered that he had no tide even to that. Here too the Cromagnon man was his predecessor, as I had found from a recent issue of *Nature*. It had published a note about the discovery of a plaque with a relief on it, which was at first believed to be the representation of a burial, but which Professor Verneau of the Institute of Human Palaeontology of Paris had identified as a picture of coitus after a careful analysis of the muscles and postures.

Our enemies were at first struck all of a heap by this display of recondite learning. But they soon rallied and refused to be intimidated by it. I shall presently relate how they did that, only remarking at this point that there is no arrogance more self-confident than the arrogance of the dunce. But I also got some appreciation. That was given in the Bengali intellectual's typical manner. As somebody said to me: 'Your pieces are splendid. But who would understand them?' I perfectly understood that he had one exception in mind. As every intellectually inclined Bengali regarded himself as the foremost intellectual of his age, I was bound to accept the remark as a great compliment to me. I might add that at that time there was no inclination in Bengali literary circles to banish learning or even the pose of learning to academic zoos, instead of accepting it as a normal feature of civilized life in its literary expression. Only jealousy would at times make one author stigmatize the presence of learning in another man's writing as pedantic. That sort of deprecation was also my lot to receive at times. But all of us of the Saturday Group tried to wear our learning easily.

It must not be imagined from all this that in my criticism I was only indulging in Rabelaisian extravaganza. There was some Rabelaiserie in me of course, but that was roused in me by the combined childishness and pretentiousness of the erotic exhibitions of these young writers. I could not understand how after reading what was to be found in the Sanskrit classics known to every college student, anyone could brag about eroticism on the strength of the weak stuff which at its best was the product of naive adolescent sensuality. So I asked: 'What has happened to the old Hindu drunkard who did not allow even the neat brandy of *Amaru-Sataka* or *Sringara-Sataka* to go to his head that he should call this watery stuff a drink?' And I answered by saying: 'The old drunkard is dead, and the poseurs we are seeking are urchins who have taken a stolen puff at their father's hookah, and fallen to the floor in a fit of dizziness.'

In the serious part of the article I tried to show that both eroticism in writing and its condemnation as obscene had more complex origins than was commonly assumed when people presented it as an issue between art and morality, which to my thinking was a barren quarrel. I said that both reticence and loquacity in respect of sexual activities were natural, although in quite different ways.

I developed the argument in this manner. I said that there was in all animals, and not in man alone, an inclination to secrecy about the primary as well as secondary features connected with the sexual act. Even savage tribes never did it openly except by way of ritual. That was due, I said, to the fact that bare sexual exhibition was unaesthetic and could not by itself sustain even the impulse to procreate. Therefore even birds and beasts stood in need of aesthetic extensions of the activity. A veil of mystery had to be thrown on it, and exposure offended against the very instinct of survival.

Thus, I said, the notions of decorum and indecency arose out of that necessity, and were in their origin biological, indecency and immorality not being identical. Murder, theft, or adultery hurts our moral sense, but does not appear as obscene, whereas open exhibition of the sexual activity offends against decorum and not our morality. I added that the notion of indecency or obscenity, being biological, was older than the idea of immorality, which had social origins.

On the other hand, curiosity about forbidden things was the stimulus behind writing and speaking about the sexual act, and another compulsion behind the vicarious dwelling on it was the need for perpetual excitement, so that it would not sink into dullness. Even so the natural shame about it made writing about sexual activities facetious. Though this was not at all pleasant, the solemn and even lachrymose eroticism of the young writers was even more unpleasant.

There was a good deal more in my article, but its most important theme was the futility of trying to understand sexual life with the help of the intellect. That, I affirmed, was suicidal, because it struck at the very roots of life. Nobody could retain faith in life by making it subject to the intellect, which could lead only to disillusionment and sorrow. I had just then read a statement by Freud that the longer he lived the more firmly was he becoming convinced that life offered only sorrow, and so he was experiencing a profound revulsion from life. That, I wrote, was the punishment for the scientist's sacrilege against life. Actaeon, I said, was torn to pieces by his hounds because in spite of being innocent he had by accident come upon bathing Artemis. The scientist had fallen under the curse of the Artemis that Life was.

I am repeating the argument of that early essay of mine because in spite of its incompleteness it has an application to the erotic writing which has become a common trade today. Its products are coarse and crude and should never be confused with the erotic literature of the past. Men and women of our age have become so reduced in vitality that they cannot continue a biological activity without swallowing large doses of coarse aphrodisiac provided by the scribbling quacks. What makes the trade despicable is that instead of admitting that they are carrying on a trade, the writers put forward a pompous scientific or artistic apologia which makes their trade even more despicable. How much more decently did ancient writers offer their compositions in this line.

A Debate Before Tagore

Soon after the publication of this article we heard that Tagore had expressed a wish to call a meeting of both the sides at his house and hear our arguments. We were invited to go. At first both Mohit Babu and I were somewhat hesitant. We thought that it might be a trap or even an ambush. But finally we revised our opinion, thinking that if we did not go we would be condemned by default.

We did, headed by Mohit Babu. It was decided, however, that I should put our case. We found ourselves part of a large gathering of young and old writers assembled in the large hall which was on the first floor of an annexe to the big ancestral house of Tagore. It was meant for such gatherings, musical soirées, private theatricals, and ceremonials, and was called Vichitra Bhavan – the House of Variety. Tagore came in later, and took his seat among his intimates at the far end of the room. Among the latter were Pramatha Chaudhuri and one or two distinguished writers, as well as a young lecturer in English literature in Calcutta University, whom at that time we regarded as the court jester of Tagore.

He had been at Oxford for many years, but had not lived only an undergraduate life. He went into literary circles, met Robert Bridges, Logan Pearsall Smith (whom he familiarly referred to as Logan), and even Henry James. He had written some musical criticism for Peter Warlock as his understudy. He used to appear in his classes in Calcutta in the striped jacket of his Oxford college, but that evening he was in the full flowing Bengali costume. During the discussion, he often indulged in exclamations of wonder and giggles, which were duly noted by a contributor of ours and dwelt on in his report of the meeting.

After some others had spoken I took up the debate. But I do not think I spoke well at all. I was not then used to public speaking or debate, however cavalier-like I might have been with my pen. The only advantage on our side was that our enemies spoke even worse. Their main spokesman was a young writer from Dacca, who spoke with the strong accent of his city. Tagore did not say anything, but only listened with an impassive face.

On the whole, we came back satisfied. But some days later we heard that Pramatha Chaudhuri had called both the sides callow. Mohit Babu told this to me not without a motive, which was to pique me to a display of my naughtiness against Pramatha Babu. I took the bait, because having the conceit of sophistication above every other form of *amour propre*, I did feel nettled. I thought I would show how callow at least I was. So the very opening shot in the article which I wrote was a quotation from Maurice Barrès.

Within a few days I came to my friends with the piece on Pramatha Chaudhuri, which was topical because Pramatha Babu had just celebrated the silver jubilee of his literary career. I called it a 'Pencil Sketch' – perhaps a better description for that kind of thing than the word 'profile', which has now become current. I read it out, and all the listeners grinned from ear to ear, and most gleefully of all, Mohit Babu. In point of composition alone it was very finished, and did not have the slightest stridency. But the irony, respectful in form as it was, was at the same time sharp. I singled out more particularly Pramatha Babu's francophile attitudes, ventilated in such sayings as that the Germans manufactured only the gas of scholarship while the French set it alight in a brilliant cluster of lamps, or that Kipling was as unreadable as Anatole France was readable. He was the titular head of the Indo-French Socieiy to which I have referred before. In addition, all his admirers regarded him as the most cultured man in Bengal. One day, when Mohit Babu reported this opinion of him as coming from one of our most learned professors, I demurred and remarked: 'No, I would not admit that. Pramatha Babu is too weak to be cultured.' Mohit Babu was surprised by my comment, because we were accustomed to regard a cultured man as some sort of a hothouse plant, but he at once replied that I was right.

In my article I mainly dwelt on this, describing him as a dilettante and not very deep in any of his views and judgements. As it happened, he had provided me with a good illustration of that. When the first World War broke out, in his magazine *Savuj Patra (Les Cahiers Verts)* he took the line of the Allied intellectual propaganda that Germany had for a long time been drifting away from the real moorings of European culture. I had even in 1915 read a series of articles by L. T. Hobhouse in which the same argument was put forward. Pramatha Babu did not simply say the same thing, but for the benefit of Bengali readers set down the main principles underlying European civilization in the words of Charles Seignobos, the French historian, taken from one of his popular books. Even when at college I had not only read these volumes but also the solid history of Europe from 1815 by him as well as his book on the methodology of history. In 1922 I had bought the whole set of the history of contemporary France edited by Lavisse, to which Seignobos had contributed three volumes (6, 7, 8). So, I thought I might patronize Pramatha Babu a little, and wrote that he did not feel embarrassed to collect information about European civilization from a school textbook.

The sequel to this performance was an outcry which resembled the clamour raised by a pack of hounds in full cry. Boldness was generally expected from us, but nobody thought that young people like us could be so irreverently audacious. Yet my observations could not be dismissed as a child's naughtiness. I was attacked equally from the right and the left of the Bengali literary world. The most comical aspect of the outbursts was that the revolutionary young writers became the champions of Pramatha Babu and of traditionalism in Bengali literature.

One critic said that I must be very foolish if I thought that I could perform the conjuring charlatan's vanishing trick with such a block of granite as Pramatha Babu was. Another writer, who had probably seen me wandering in the streets of Calcutta the previous year or in any case heard of it, wrote that Pramatha must be nothing in my eyes because he was not a fellow vagabond on Calcutta streets. Yet my learning remained to be dealt with, and one critic wrote ironically: 'May the respected editor of the *Sanibarer Chithi* procure catalogues of books from Thacker Spink & Co., and make his emaciated body even more emaciated by memorizing the tides of the books. He might not have any capacity to think, but nobody can deny his capacity to cram.' Now, this was the typical observation from any college student who was jealous of another student's academic success. The rivals always attributed it to cramming and never to brains.

Pramatha Babu himself felt very much mortified, and said that I had hinted that he was not even an educated man. But in spite of the attack he never lost his interest in me nor his cordiality, amounting to almost affection. When I went into something of an eclipse afterwards he inquired about me.

This din continued for some months. I only published a skit on the defenders of Pramatha Babu, but Sajani took over the main attack on him. He published some very malicious and unfair pieces of which I could not approve. But I had by that time left die *Sanibarer Chithi*. That had quite a number of reasons.

Disappointment and Disillusionment with the Campaign

In spite of the immediate excitement and exhilaration produced by the success of our magazine, a feeling of disillusionment was coming over me. There was no doubt about its success. It had increased its circulation and had become even financially profitable. But I was not satisfied with the quality of the response. I was perceptive and realistic enough to see through our popularity. We were regarded, by and large, as providers of amusement – as suppliers of a literary version of cockfights. Scurrilous disputations, mostly personal, between poets jealous of one another were a traditional feature of Bengali literary life. We were supposed only to continue that in a new form. Very superior persons even affirmed that in so many words. What I saw was that there was no interest whatever in the arguments and ideas we produced, nor any awareness that we were defending a cause.

Most people thought that we were jealous of the stir that the new writers were making, and were trying to represent our explosion of jealousy as a disinterested crusade. They only found us amusing as brawlers.

Unfortunately, the suspicion was not wholly untrue. Although I could say that in our criticism we always kept the ideas under fire and would not make barefaced personal attacks, I also perceived that some of us had private grudges. For instance, if fellow students at Calcutta University or Oxford and Cambridge were seen to have got the start of any of us in the way of gaining public attention and coming under the limelight, some of us were piqued, and that would lend an edge to our criticism of their political activities or literary performances. Sajani made matters worse by going among the writers whom we were not only criticizing but representing as cultural vermin. He had no sense of embarrassment in meeting those whom he cruelly lampooned, and, what was more marvellous, while with them he had the extraordinary faculty of hypnotising them into friendliness. But after gathering information in this way, he would make use of that for his satire. This I extremely disliked and disapproved of I myself never met any of those whom I criticized, and this aloofness I maintained in later life as well. So, I tried to dissuade Sajani from his insinuating forays. But I did not succeed. All this gave room for assuming personal malice or ill will in us.

But I do not think that even with all these doubts coming over my mind I would have given up the connection with the magazine and abandoned the campaign as quickly as I did, except for a grotesquely ridiculous consequence of our eagerness to fight obscenity in literature.

One day, in late May or early June 1928, so far as I remember, I as the editor of the magazine got a letter from the police headquarters of Calcutta in Lal Bazar to go and see a Bengali Inspector of the Criminal Investigation Department (CID), whose duty it was to keep an eye on all Bengali publications in respect of sedition. We had heard of him, and he was by report a pleasant man in his manners, whatever might be his work. So I went to see him without any misgivings. He also received me very politely, and explained that an official matter had compelled him to ask me to come to his office. Then he took up a file from his table, and said: 'Will you come with me? The Deputy Commissioner wants to see you.' I was very much surprised, for the Deputy Commissioner was an Englishman, by name Bartlett, so far as I remember, and I could not make even a remote guess as to the reason for his wishing to see me. He was sitting in his chair, and the Inspector put the file before him. I took a chair in front of him. He turned to a page, and asked me if I was the editor of the *Sanibarer Chithi*. When I replied that I was, he very deliberately read from a sheet of paper before him: 'I give you notice to cease from publishing the obscene material you have been publishing in your magazine, and if you go on doing so you will be prosecuted.' I was too astounded to reply coherently and only said, or rather mumbled: 'But we are fighting obscenity.' He would not listen, and wrote on the paper 'The editor has been warned.' The Inspector made a sign to me to follow him out of the room, and when we came out, he said with the same blandness as he had shown before: 'That was all!'

I came back in a fury and told the whole story to Ashoke Babu and others, all of whom only grinned. The explanation that I got made the charge even more ridiculous and absurd to me. What had happened was that from the time we had begun the campaign we had been publishing a feature which gave extracts from the writings of the new writers with the object of exposing them. Sajani, who was in charge of it, of course selected those he thought particularly naughty, and it was these which had made me guilty of publishing obscene matter. There was no question of prosecuting those who had written the passages or the papers which had published them. I came to know later that the step was prompted from very high quarters, and this particular method to intimidate us and make us cease the attacks had been adopted after serious legal consideration. I naturally felt very bitter.

Even so, I would not have given up my editorship if Sajani had not gone on a wholly unnecessary spree of his own, which could involve us in a case for libel. It was against a Guru and the goings-on in his Ashram. This kind of religious charlatanry and the disgusting indulgence in sensuality which resulted from it were far too common in Hindu society for us to interest ourselves in them. Besides, this Guru was a particularly low specimen of his order. I had seen him some years before and knew a good deal about his Ashram. I saw no need to put our hand in this muck. But Sajani was led to it by an Indian Christian who had become a Hindu and was introduced to us by one of our most respected friends.

This man had been in the Ashram, and his wife was having an affair with one of the followers of the Guru. Of that there could be no doubt. We were shown quite compromising and disgusting letters. We were one day taken to the house of this Christian and saw his wife, who looked the character and had all the appearance of a brazen and defiant hussy. It was none of our business, but Sajani got into a pose of holy wrath and began to write exuberantly satiric pieces on the Ashram, with a good many salacious hints. I told him that unless he discontinued the series I would resign my editorship and would write no more for the paper. He said that he would not and I could do as I pleased. I at once resigned and did not write again for the magazine for many years.

Something even more absurd was to follow. Soon after I left, Sajani was prosecuted for obscenity, and his trial went on for some weeks. I was present at some of the sessions and thought of the proceedings as ridiculous. Even the trying magistrate was bored and would mildly deprecate the highflown eloquence of our advocate. Sajani was found guilty and fined. This prosecution, too, was inspired from influential quarters, so I was told.

I must set down at this point that, as things turned out, our campaign was a total failure. Instead of checking the new trends, we established them by the publicity we gave them. We also made the reputation of some of the young writers, who without us would not have gained the position they finally had. The moral of it is that nobody can resist historical trends. Bengal was destined to pass out of Indian history, and to try to resist it was kicking against the pricks. I lost all interest henceforth in Bengali literature, except so far as Bibhuti Babu was in it.

By that time I had not only realized that our campaign was futile but also come to the conclusion that Bengali literature itself had no future. I also remained critical of Sajani Babu's way of running the paper. But at that time when I had deliberately turned my back on the literary status which my connection with the magazine had conferred on me and had no worldly status whatever, it would have been useless if not ridiculous for me to air such views. However, after I had secured employment towards the end of 1928 and gained a different kind of literary status – as I shall relate presently – I wrote to Mohit Babu, who was then at Dacca, giving him a review of our campaign as a failure, with some sharp criticism of Sajani Babu.

Mohit Babu was furious and he replied in a thundering letter. He said that it was during those brief months of the campaign that he had seen me as a living man, with vitality as well as talent gushing out of me as from a spring; and that I had since then died and become a ghost – a gliding shade.

Apropos of some flippant remarks of mine he remarked that he had never suspected that with all my learning I had become such a monkey, and he threatened that he would write to my father. I was very much amused by this last assertion. I replied that he was my teacher, and I was ready even then to take a birching from his hands, but certainly I thought I had outgrown the age at which a pupil could be reported against to his father. He was too angry to reply, and for some years professed some disdain for my views on Bengali life and culture, more especially for my prognostications about the future. But at the end of his life he had to revise his opinion and admit that he was mistaken and I was right. I shall have to describe his disillusionment, which broke his heart and hastened his death.

CHAPTER 5
Rescued at Last

My withdrawal from the literary campaign had its immediate result in a period of unemployment without justification and therefore of great distress and humiliation. Mohit Babu was right in regarding me as a gliding shade for the time being, because for me the result of the withdrawal from the magazine was an intellectual and emotional vacuum. I fell into a state of listlessness, from which I tried to rescue myself by writing about the Kellogg Pact and other political topics. This was not very effectual. But I found some emotional satisfaction in an exercise of historical imagination. For some years it had become my scholarly ambition to write a history of modem Indian culture, and since that had to begin with a description of our life and culture on the eve of British rule, I had studied some of the sources illustrating the conditions in the eighteenth century. These revealed a state of culture which was altogether different from what we thought it was.

Phantom of the Past and of Love

The current view, which had been developed during the nineteenth century and still held the field, was that we were heirs to the ancient Hindu culture and were continuing it with some additions from the civilization of the West. This view was the prop of our self-respect against the uniformly contemptuous opinions about us and our culture held and proclaimed by the local British and also by some British writers who were not Orientalists. Our answer to them was that we were a civilized people when the British were leaping from tree to tree. That was, of course, an exploitation of Darwin's view of the descent of man in our interest.

I had found a wholly different picture in the sources I had so far studied. I discovered that when the establishment of British rule began to bring European cultural influences to bear on our life, we could hardly be regarded as a people with a high and sophisticated life and civilization. What we had was culture only in the anthropologist's meaning of the word, that is, a distinct and stable pattern of life. This I found to be very simple, and I felt I could describe it only as a folk culture. I came to the conclusion that there was a complete break between ancient Hindu culture and our life and culture as they had been in the eighteenth century, and that what we had was a reduction, to their simplest and most basic, of the elements of the very highly sophisticated culture of the ancient Hindus. I even called this reduction 're-barbarization', but without any pejorative implication. On the contrary, I had even a feeling of tenderness for it, as one has for childhood. I thought that by lying culturally fallow for some centuries, we had become fertile soil again, and as soon as European cultural influences began to play on us we also began to put forth green shoots. It was this view which made me accept with sympathy Bibhuti Babu's picture of humble Bengali life in *Pather Panchali*. Without my new view of our cultural evolution, I should have been repelled by the denudation of life which the novel exhibited.

The combination of this historical view and the listlessness produced by lack of occupation in my personal life created a very wistful mood in me. My personal position with its dependence on my family was very humiliating, but I was sustained by the romantic evocation of the past of my country, and to this was added a personal romance which, emotionally, was wholly inward. I became haunted by a phantom of love and this haunted state lasted longer than the mood produced by the fleeting apparition of the girl at Benares.

In May 1928, my elder brother and I moved into a fairly large house which had been taken by my doctor brother on a very important and busy street of Calcutta. I had my room on the second floor, fairly high up, and across the street was another big house in which lived a Bengali family, seemingly very well-to-do. Its wide terrace-roof was at the level of the floor on which I lived just across the street, and its front verandah was below me. On both I could see two young girls, who were between fifteen and seventeen. I also saw them in one of the front rooms, studying. They were certainly schoolgirls.

They were also clearly sisters, but I could not make out which was the elder and which the younger. The girl who was slightly taller, I assumed to be the younger sister. She was slim and straight, and quite comely, but not in any way striking. The other girl, though not fair by Bengali standards, was very handsome in the face and beautiful in her figure. Nonetheless, it was not simply these but the vibrancy of her body and face, of every line in them, which overwhelmed me. The curves of her eyes, eyebrows, cheeks, lips, and chin were like little bows drawn taut and ready to let fly arrows any moment. If she moved her face from side to side or raised it with a slight jerk to look at the sky, it seemed to flash beams in all directions.

And her body was of a piece with her face. It had just that swelling in its curves which made its lines rhythmic and prevented any impression of staticity which even a slightly greater slenderness or *embonpoint* would have produced. When she walked her body vibrated within a very narrow range of frequency, and that seemed to create ripples in the air around her. I am sure that there is a critical limit to the flatness and the amplitude in the curves of a woman's body which alone is capable of producing such an effect. What I saw in her body was like the vibrato in playing the violin or soft-pedalling on the piano. Her sister's body was moulded to play plain, but hers was full of resonances.

I fell head over heels in love with that vision. I am now convinced that a man's love for a woman is basically a matter of form, and therefore in its essence very abstract. However that might be, I made no attempt to be introduced to the family. I never came to know who she was. I worshipped her with my eyes, without ever giving the impression of staring or even watching. And only once or twice did I see her fixing her eyes on me as if she was conscious of my absorption in her. Soon after, we left that house and I never tried to see her again by coming to that street. But her apparition haunted me for something like a year, and I remained in love with her. And I also took her out of that commonplace Calcutta house and placed her in the ruined palace of an old Bengali chief, whose site was not very far from Calcutta. I thought I would go and meet my sleeping princess there even at the risk of being crushed by a python in those cold lairs. And she, coming in on her swift feet, would just see my living face before I died. All this foolish dreaming was my emotional food at the age of thirty!

As a consequence, the first and the only lines I wrote of my projected history of modem Indian culture were its dedication to her. But the strangest part of the matter was that, although I could not write French, the words of the dedication came out in one spurt in that language. I cannot still say whether this was passable French or not, but I reproduce it just as it was written:

À

L'Inconnue

dont la figure belle mais d'une tristesse infinie

me rappelant la face douloureuse et dejà obscurcie
de notre passé
suggera les pages qui suivent et les hante comme
une ombre gracieuse.

The phantom faded away gradually after a very strange evocation. One day, early in the summer of 1929, Bibhuti Babu came to ask me if I would join in an excursion to an old Nilkuthi or indigo-planter's lodge a few miles north of his village Barrackpore, near the small town of Bongaon on the river Ichhamati. The place, he said, was on the river, very wild, and very picturesque. A friend of his had bought a car and had offered to take him and his friends there one Saturday afternoon. I gladly agreed, for I had never seen Bibhuti Babu's part of Bengal, whose descriptions by him I admired so much.

Thus, the next Saturday afternoon seven of us (including the chauffeur) packed ourselves in the medium-sized car and sped along Jessore road. At about five we arrived at the town of Bongaon, which was about forty miles from Calcutta, and got down by the side of the river. The plan was to go to the indigo-planter's lodge by boat, picnic there, and come back by the car which would be driven there by the chauffeur over a narrow lane with thorn bushes on both sides, with the help of a local guide. The river journey would be about seven miles up-stream.

I liked the journey very much, for it reminded me of the boat journeys I had in my boyhood. We duly landed below the lodge, and climbed up the bank to it. The place was very wild, and all around were only scrub and small trees. When it was dark Bibhuti Babu took me into the scrub to get a fuller view of the place and he pointed to the ruins of the indigo-planter's big house. He was quite oblivious of the cobras and kraits. In the evening the car arrived, scratched by the thorny bushes, which very much annoyed the owner.

It was nearly eleven when we again packed ourselves in the car and started on our way back to Calcutta. The owner and the guide went on foot, making the car go at their pace, and they pushed back the hedges where the lane was too narrow and it was so almost all the way. After about an hour or so we reached Bibhuti Babu's village, which looked miserable enough, confirming the veracity of his description of it. He did not care to take us to his house, but made us get down before the house of one of the better-off villagers. It was a large brick-built house of the old type, but it had all the dinginess and mouldy smell I associated with such houses. Then we got on to the main road, and drove towards Calcutta at the rather high speed of about twenty miles an hour on the roads of Bengal.

The road was good enough for our part, but it had a peculiar feature. On account of the trees planted on its sides it was not simply an avenue but almost a Gothic nave of trees, because the branches of the trees touched across the road, though it was wide, to form a vault overhead. These were the exotic rain tree, which were spreading and had a dense foliage which provided deep shade. The trunks had the appearance of being the columns of the nave. I was sitting on the front seat and looking at the tree trunks lighted up by the headlamps of the car, and what surprised and almost startled me were very bright spots of green or red light suddenly flashing from the sides of the boles. I soon discovered that these were the eyes of the jackals which caught the light of the lamps, and the jackals themselves stood half-hidden by the trunks watching the passing car.

When we were about halfway to Calcutta, the car went down into the dry bed of a river and came up on the opposite side, and I remembered that the ruined palace of the old chief was some miles to the east. Then I lost consciousness of the journey and dreamt of my princess. I found myself, exactly as I had expected, in a room in the ruins, from one comer of which a huge python rose like a column to knock me down, and then entwined itself round me. The princess came running in just in time to find me able to cast a look at her before being crushed. We reached Calcutta and I was dropped at the door of our house. I went up to the roof to sleep on my usual mat, but I could only doze and feel the girl's presence near me. It soon became light, and when I awoke fully it seemed very prosaic. The image gradually faded away in the next few months. Nonetheless, during those months of renewed dependence and dejection her vision had given me enough ecstasy to make me remember her gratefully at the end of my life. Without that, those months would certainly have been a repetition of my experiences of 1927.

I Find journalistic Employment

My want of an income was, nonetheless, a very stark fact, and although accepted by my family as something arising out of my inherent nature I felt it very keenly as a very undesirable condition. Yet I would not look for a job for which I had an unconquerable dislike. Thus all that I did was to go on writing whatever came into my head, and polish and re-polish it, I hoped something would come out of it. But my elder brother did not put much faith in my literary marquetry, and living with him and my other brothers I could not overlook their writing me off as a bad debt of the family.

I have already said that we had moved to a new house from that in which we were living with our doctor brother. That was due to his decision to give up his practice in Calcutta and leave India to go eventually to some European country for advanced medical studies. He had always had that in mind, being talented, energetic and ambitious. Actually, he had tried to do so immediately after taking his medical degree in 1926. But he could not get a passport. At that time no Indian and, more especially, no Bengali could get one unless he was regarded as politically safe by the political police of the British administration. The policy was never to allow any Indian to go abroad if he had any political association in India, lest he should speak or write against British rule there. What good that policy did to that rule has been seen. But the British administration in those days had a whole complex of imaginary fears while ignoring the real one. The ineffectual caution was there as a fact of our life, and my brother did not merely have a political association, he was on the black list of the police as a revolutionary, because as a schoolboy he had joined a secret society. To make things worse, his name was confused with another young man's, who was suspected to have taken part in a political robbery. My brother could easily prove that he was not that man, but the police always gave the benefit of the doubt to themselves. Thus after passing out from the Medical College, Calcutta, my brother remained there, and tried to make a career for himself

He was doing very well as a general practitioner. But in September 1928 he suddenly found an opportunity to realize his ambition and give the slip to the police. A boat of the City Line had lost its doctor, and wanted to recruit one in Calcutta. My brother at once applied and was accepted. No passport was needed merely to board a ship, and so my brother sailed away. The step was imprudent, and he suffered for it. But he did get himself trained in Vienna and Tübingen and became, after he returned, the foremost pediatrician in Calcutta. As to a passport, he went to the office of a British Consul at one of the ports of call, probably New York, and got a valid passport without any questions being asked.

We had to give up the big house which we could not keep, and moved to another quite near the old one where I had lived previously with my brothers. It was not very small, and we had enough room for all the brothers. But my position was very difficult. The external symbols of my self-respect were also becoming worn. My clothes and shoes were becoming shabby, and what was more I had broken both the pairs of glasses, on which a good deal of the physical impression I made depended. One of them was of real tortoiseshell, used for reading, and the other the rimless pince-nez with the half-inch moire ribbon. Practically, too, I was very much handicapped in reading and moving in busy Calcutta streets. I could not buy new glasses for want of money, and did not even know when I should have a pair again.

Another source of low spirits was that Mohit Babu went away from Calcutta and I lost his encouraging company. He got a very much better post as a lecturer in Bengali literature in Dacca University, which was a great advance on his old position as a school teacher. For his sake I was particularly glad. In fact, it was I who drafted his application for the post. Though he had taught me English at school, at that time he had more reliance on my English than on his own. He told me afterwards that the style of his application was noticed by the English Vice-Chancellor of the University. But for me it was a great loss. He never referred to my position, but I could easily see that he tried to keep up my self-confidence.

But relief came to me suddenly and quite unexpectedly through him. He had come down to Calcutta in the autumn vacation. Just before he left again, and that was, so far as I remember, towards the end of October 1928, he came to see me. After talking about various other things he said: 'I have been to the *Prabasi* office to see Ashoke Chatterji, and I found that two of their assistant editors had left and they were looking for new men. Since you are doing nothing I suggested your name. I thought you might as well take up this work, which would be in your line. Ashoke Chatterji at once agreed, and they are ready to give you the same salary as you had in the Military Accounts.' Without any hesitation I at once accepted. I went the next day to the *Prabasi* office, and saw Ashoke Babu. He repeated what Mohit Babu had already told me, and showed by his manner that he was gratified to have me on the staff of their magazines. So I was at once installed, and I remained with them till the end of 1933.

Now, the scribbling *canaille* who had always been saying that we were the henchmen of Ashoke Chatterji and had become his hacks for the sake of what money he could give to us, took this opportunity to have a go at me. The world of writers in Calcutta was noted for gossip, and the news of my joining *The Modern Review* and *Prabasi* soon spread. So, in less than a month, a lampoon appeared in which it was said: 'Poor Nirad has now got his job, and the fellow was so *needy*.' In the Bengali doggerel the word *needy* was in English. I could not wholly ignore the jibe because despite my lofty pose of never caring for a job or looking for it, I had got one when I was *very needy* indeed.

Ramananda Chatterji

My chief was Ramananda Chatterji, Ashoke Chatterji's father. He was one of the greatest figures in Indian journalism, although he was not a newspaper man. He edited and published two magazines, one in Bengali, the *Prabasi*, which was the older, and the other in English, *The Modern Review*. Both were important in their different ways. The *Prabasi* stood for both nationalism and liberalism, and it was the magazine to which Tagore gave most of his new work. It also had the pick of the best work in fiction and poetry in the Bengali language. It was a great honour for any new writer to appear in it, and Bibhuti Babu had. The editorials of the *Prabasi*, all from the pen of the editor himself, were a force in shaping public opinion. *The Modern Review* in English had an all-India circulation and was more weighty politically. It was read with interest and respect even by the British Governors. Ramananda Babu, himself an ardent nationalist, could be included among the most radical of them known as the 'Extremists', and his views were a great support for the nationalists.

The popular view of Ramananda Babu's effectiveness as a publicist was embodied in one of the stereotyped formulas in English current among us. People said that he gave 'facts and figures' and did not write mere sentimental stuff. This reputation for concreteness was based on Ramananda Babu's extensive use of the volumes of statistics published by the Government of India, and he used them in a manner which made me repeat the well-known jibe at statistics that they were the greatest liar. He always drew on information in the spirit of a partisan, and yet never thought that he was only a lawyer for the prosecution. He could never be detached about British rule in India, and he considered it his mission as a journalist to deprive it of all moral justification. He showed the ability of an acute lawyer in doing this, and also showed the naive side of his nationalism by publishing any drivel by Americans on British rule in India.

The British administration in India showed equal naiveté by proscribing one of these books published by his concern, when with the right kind of confidence in their imperialistic mission they should have ignored it. It was a particularly low expression of the American rancour against the British Empire by an American Unitarian Minister, Dr Jabez Sunderland, called *India in Bondage*. Even *The Times* devoted a long article by Edward Thompson to refute it. The Bengal Government prosecuted Sajani Das as its formal publisher for sedition, and he was convicted for the offence and fined. Thus, in addition to being convicted for obscenity, Sajani was promoted to the highest rank of convicts, and earned the right to call himself a 'freedom fighter.' His portrait was published in *The Modern Review*.

While this was going on I got a warning that my house might be searched for the book. So I burnt it, although I could have sold my copy at three or four times its price on account of the proscription. I often regretted Ramananda Babu's total incapacity for detachment, but I also recognized that at that time in India neither the British rulers nor their Indian subjects could practise that virtue.

He was sixty-three years old when I joined his staff in 1928, but to my eyes he looked much older. He had the typical venerable bearded appearance of a Brahmo of the late nineteenth century, who, it might be added, looked in their Bengali dress very much like St Peter as represented in Renaissance painting. Thus he was once mistaken for Tagore when he was watching a session of the General Assembly of the League of Nations in Geneva.

He had come from a very poor Brahmin family in westernmost Bengal, and had made his way in the world through sheer intellectual ability. He had become, at a comparatively young age, the principal of a college at Allahabad, and left the educational field to become a journalist. At first he edited magazines published by others, and then published his own magazine *Prabasi* in Bengali. It was a hard struggle to get it established, and he once told me that towards the end of every year he thought he would give it up, but when the time for that arrived he revised the decision, saying to himself that since he had carried on so long he might as well continue for another year just on the off chance. It took him nearly ten years to make his

Bengali paper viable financially. Even before that he had started his English magazine.

His success was due to his strength of will. But on account of his social origins he could never overcome his natural shyness, which in so widely known and respected a man surprised me. People who came to meet him went back with the impression that he was an awkward and unsocial man. But to those with whom he was familiar he showed a keen sense of humour. He also never got over the social inhibitions of traditional Bengali society.

I give one example. Even in the most liberal and radical Bengali society sons never smoked before their fathers. Now, one day when I was working in the *Prabasi* office, Ramananda Babu's eldest son, Kedar Babu, who was over forty besides being a BSC of London University, as also a medical orderly in the BEF in France in 1914, was smoking in his room. Ramananda Babu suddenly came into it, and seeing his father Kedar Babu thrust the lighted cigarette into the lower side pocket of his tunic and got up from his chair. Within a minute or so the tunic began to smoulder, with smoke coming out. Ramananda Babu saw that, though Kedar Babu had become too nervous to notice anything. But a father could no more take cognizance of a son smoking than a son could smoke before the father. So, Ramananda got red in the face and yet could not warn his son. However, the manager of the office, who was Kedar Babu's uncle, came to the rescue. He dragged Kedar Babu out of the room, saying that he had something rather private to tell him, and while leading him away crushed the pocket and the cigarette end in it to put out the fire. Ramananda Babu would be equally embarrassed if he had to complain against us. He would never say a word, but after going home wrote a short and cold note, and after that would not look us in the face for some days, as if he himself had been the offender.

Till his death he remained a liberal of the Bengali school, although his brand of liberalism had become already out of date in Bengal by the late Twenties. His two magazines supported every movement of social and religious reform, and also literary and artistic novelties, of course those he understood. He was a steady champion of Tagore when the latter was being abused by chauvinistic Bengalis. In his magazines he published reproductions of the paintings of the modem Bengali school when its work was ridiculed everywhere. Above all, he was an unwavering advocate of women's education and also liberation in his sense. In fact, in regard to women his fixed dogma was that woman could do no wrong. To give one example, when the Civil Disobedience of Mahatma Gandhi was on (1930-31), there was also a revival of terroristic outrages in Bengal, and two Bengali girls shot dead the English District Magistrate of Comilla. Ramananda Babu would not believe them to be capable of murdering anybody even for political reasons. If he had ever heard the saying that the female of the species was more dangerous than the male, he would not have given any credence to it. So, he told me that he had heard a different story – that the girls had gone to see the magistrate on personal business and had been forced to defend themselves when the District Magistrate made improper overtures to them. The story was ridiculous of course, but with his faith in women Ramananda Babu believed in it.

The cult of woman to which he subscribed made him publish the educational or professional achievements of all Indian women in his two magazines, with photographs of the heroines. I was in charge of the sections in both the Bengali and the English magazine, and it was a sore trial for me because most of the women, young or elderly, were plain and at times even ugly. I used to describe this fad of Ramanada Babu as his 'sublimated debauchery'.

On one occasion this landed me in a very uncomfortable situation. I once received the photograph of a Bengali young woman who was very ugly to my thinking and who had made matters worse by overdressing and wearing very ornate jewellery. Her achievement was that she had become enrolled as a lawyer in a district court. I thought we had reached the limit of publishing feminine unloveliness, and yet I knew that Ramanada Babu was sure to publish that photograph. So I decided to suppress this young lady and threw her photograph into my wastepaper basket. After a few days a second copy of the same photograph arrived, and I consigned that as well to the same receptacle. However, soon after, Ramananda Babu came to me with a very worried expression and said that he had been expecting the photograph of a Bengali woman – he mentioned the name of the same girl – and as he had not got the photograph he had sent a telegram; yet he still had not received the photograph. Actually, both the copies were lying near my legs, but of course I could not pick them up and give them to Ramananda Babu. Thus I simply said that I vaguely remembered having seen a photograph bearing that name, and I would look among my papers. I picked up the photographs from the wastepaper basket as soon as Ramananda Babu went out of the room, but in order to keep up the pretence of forgetfulness took it to him after a decent interval. He looked at the name and was delighted. I kept the second copy for myself and showed it to my wife when I married in 1932. She at once recognized the lady, and told me that she knew both her and the family.

These traits made us more and not less loyal to Ramananda Babu. I never ceased to respect him and admire him for his courage and integrity, although I found many of his attitudes and opinions narrow and barred by time. He, on his part, was invariably loyal to those whom he admired, as for instance, Tagore and Gandhi. He had become an admirer and supporter of Gandhi from his South African days, and went on supporting him even when he could not wholly approve of his political views and methods. He was particularly critical of Gandhi's advocacy of Hindi as the national language of India, and showed himself capable of being ironical about Gandhi's use of that language.

Ramananda Babu's dislike for Hindi sprang from a loyalty which he placed higher than even his loyalty to India, and that was his loyalty to Bengal. He was a staunch Bengali above everything else, and, as I often thought, blind in his love. Ramananda Babu died on 30 September 1943.

BOOK IV

THE GANDHIAN REBELLION

1927-1932

Prefatory Note

In this part of the book I shall give an account of the second mass movement against British rule in India, which Mahatma Gandhi launched early in 1930. With a period of suspension, which was like a special truce in a war, the agitation lasted nearly two years, and then died of its own inanition. My reaction to it was in total contrast to all my previous ones in respect of the other active phases of the nationalist movement. Instead of remaining critical, I became wholly involved in it emotionally, and a partisan. For the first and last time I became a Gandhian. However, I recovered my historical detachment by 1934. The appraisement of the Gandhian movements to which that led, will also be included in my account.

It has, however, to be preceded by a narration of the antecedents of the movement, which appeared in 1927. The years 1928 and 1929 were like the time required by a locomotive to raise its steam. Why such a prolonged overture was needed will be explained fully in the chapter which opens this part.

CHAPTER I
The Rising Typhoon

During the years 1927 and 1928 my personal troubles were too acute for me to be able to take continuous notice of political developments in India. Moreover, there were other things to keep my mind away from politics. For some months at least I was fully absorbed in the literary campaign I have described. It gave me the exhilaration which came from the conviction of serving a cause. Finally, I was elated by the success of my first literary efforts. But in the India of those days it was not possible to ignore politics. Even if a man wanted to do so it would not leave him alone.

So, by the middle of 1927 nationalistic politics forced itself on my attention, although at that time my troubles were at their highest. That happened through the publication of a book in England and America. It was entitled *Mother India* and was written by an American woman, Katherine Mayo, who on the face of it had neither the qualification nor any business to write on India. But through that adventure of hers this miserable American woman will occupy a permanent place in the history of Great Britain and India as the busybody who sounded the crack of doom for the British Empire in India. It is curious to find that this solitary instance of the defence of British rule in India by an eccentric American did more harm to it than the persistent American disapproval ever did.

Five months later there was another furore, and that over the appointment of a parliamentary commission on constitutional advance in India, which was to be presided over by Sir John Simon, the eminent English lawyer and politician. Political India decided to boycott it, and when the Commission arrived in India in February 1928, there were demonstrations all over India. In spite of the fact that our literary campaign was then at its peak I went out to see the fun. Around College Square I saw people running helter skelter, chased by the Indian police and British sergeants, who were laying about with their sticks and batons on whomsoever they could overtake. A friend of mine who was reporting the tumult for his paper, asked me to leave the place which he said was not safe for me. However, I did not, and walked on quietly. As I did not show either excited curiosity or nervousness, the sergeants simply looked at me and did not strike.

This scene reminded me of what I had seen in 1921. Clearly, India was on the eve of another outbreak of political agitation. It came early in 1930, taking nearly two years to raise full steam or rather to form the depression which was needed to bring in a cyclone. The meteorological metaphor is more apt than that from mechanics, for the rhythm of the Indian nationalist movement was never regulated by rational political calculations, but was controlled wholly by the presence or absence of passion in the political atmosphere.

Cyclical Character of the Nationalist Movement

That passion came and went cyclically, which meant that the Indian nationalist movement had its 'periodic law'. I did not discover its existence till some years later. But in 1930 I could see that I was going through the third active phase. I had already seen two: that which began in 1905 with the partition of Bengal by Lord Curzon; and the second which really began in 1919 as a protest against the passing of the Rowlatt Act and continued, with a break in the middle, till the beginning of 1922. It was after passing through the third active phase of 1930-32 that I became fully aware that the nationalist movement had its alternating periods of activity and dormancy. This phenomenon of periodicity is so important for understanding the true nature and course of the nationalist movement that I set down my conclusions about it at this point, although I formulated it in an article only in 1935.

The reason for the cyclical character was that the nationalist movement was driven wholly by passion, and from 1920 by one single passion, which was wholly negative, viz. pure and simple hatred of British rule. The hatred itself was continuous, but it could not sustain uninterrupted agitation for a number of reasons, of which it is necessary to take note.

First, in order to erupt in action the hatred had to be boiling enough to counteract the immense weight of the inertia created by the power and stability of the British administration. This inertia was wholly in Indian life, because all the worldly interests of Indians were inseparable from the existence of British rule. This was particularly true of the middle-classes, the very class in which the nationalist feeling was most deep-seated and intense. This class looked upon 'government service' as the highest worldly prize as well as the surest guarantee of worldly security. In those days my joke was that the biological urge for the survival of the species was operating in favour of British rule. For instance, if the father of a girl could get a 'government servant' as son-in-law he would never consider anybody else. In fact, after I left 'government service' offers of marriage for me ceased dramatically. The shopkeepers also would not give credit to anybody except 'government servants'. Finally, in the big cities the landlords were very unwilling to let their houses to persons who were not in the employment of the Government.

This in itself would have called for an immense accumulation and intensification of die normally existent hatred before any active agitation could be mounted. Given human nature, such a degree of intensity could not be maintained for a long time. Thus the maximum period over which the active phases of the movement could be kept going was never more than three years, and at times less. For example, the 1905 agitation, which was the first active phase, lost its momentum by 1908; the second phase began in 1919 and was exhausted by 1922; and the third phase of 1930 was spent by 1933.

Secondly, even when the hatred had its greatest intensity, the attachment to worldly interests was such that no phase of agitation could draw more than one hundred thousand young men as active participants, and this in hundreds of millions in whom the hatred was present. This majority never had any sense of guilt for keeping cautiously aloof from the agitation. In fact, they very much resented any charge of being unpatriotic, because they felt that their sympathy for the movement was one form of participation. This dichotomy of attitude was seen at its most bizarre during the second World War.

Even this was not all. There was a third reason for the periodicity. Even before the natural slackening of the force of an agitation could be seen the British administration, down to 1942, always succeeded in breaking it. This was done with the help and co-operation of Indians, and did not require the employment of British personnel. Very high-placed Indian officials who were zealously carrying out the repression would say loftily when privately remonstrated with by their friends and relatives: 'A Government has to govern.'

Thus it happened that at the end of each phase of active agitation the participants could not see any tangible result of their efforts and sacrifices. If anything was achieved at all, that was a partial concession made by the British Government on its own initiative and in its own time, and the concessions when they came fell short of what even the most moderate nationalists in India wanted and would be satisfied with.

This produced very widespread disillusionment among those who took an active part in the movements and went to jail. They went back to private life, remained tied down to the difficult task of gaining a livelihood, and never again joined any movement. A permanent nucleus of agitators remained only among those who had burnt their boats and incurably injured their worldly prospects. So they felt that they had to remain lifelong nationalist workers. These men finally formed the regimental officer and NCO cadres of the nationalist movement. The privates had to be recruited from the growing generation untouched by the previous movement. As they joined the nationalist movement between the ages of sixteen and twenty, it needed a period of anything from eight to ten years for a new batch of recruits to reach the enlisting age. Thus the active phases of the Indian nationalist movement had the same intervals, unless slightly hastened or delayed by special circumstances. This cyclical recurrence was seen from 1905 to 1942.

First Provocation: 'Mother India'

Even so every one of these phases needed a fresh provocation before it could begin, just as an internal combustion engine needs ignition by an electric spark. And the required provocation was duly provided on each occasion by the British side. There seemed to be a fatality in this British behaviour. At every juncture the provocation seemed to be avoidable, yet it came inevitably. Both Hindus and Muslims had the same fatalistic formula for such a process: 'It was written'.

The first provocation for the 1930 movement was given in 1927, and as I have just mentioned by the publication of Katherine Mayo's *Mother India* in July. Her explanation for writing the book was that she had come to India with an open mind to observe the social life of the Indian people but was so shocked by what she saw and learned that she felt it to be her duty to write a book which would make them aware of the social and moral evils from which they suffered, so that they might be roused to get rid of them. To the end she maintained that she was a friend of the Indian people and more especially of Indian women. She even declared that her book was not a mere book but the service of a cause. She took up a posture of martyrdom when fiercely attacked in India.

Even now it is impossible to say whether it was an infinite capacity for self- deception or brazen hypocrisy which made her maintain that position. One had only to glance through the book to find that its manner and contents were wholly inconsistent with the benevolent intention the writer professed. Marks of the cloven hoof were imprinted on every page. Even the tide gave her away. No one with the object of liberating the Indian people from the social and moral evils which were eating into their lives would have chosen the phrase *Mother India* as the tide of a book which described these evils with a gusto rivalling the zeal of a prosecuting counsel who is not only producing every bit of evidence he thinks would be incriminating, but is also suggesting that the guilt of the person on trial is already established, for by so doing that writer would be identifying the evils he is describing with the country itself. Katherine Mayo showed India as an aged whore keeping a brothel. The reviewer of the London *Times* got that impression and Wrote: 'From reading the earlier chapters of the book one gets the impression – probably not intended, for Miss Mayo is only driving home her point – that all India must be peopled by over-sexed, degenerate folk which only the survival of the least unfit has prevented from disappearing.' It is difficult to understand why *The Times* gave her the benefit of the doubt in regard to her intentions.

The whole book not only rang untrue, but appeared palpably dishonest in its motivation and execution. It was unbalanced and described aberrations of behaviour on the fringes which had very little social significance. It was full of wrong or false statements, and of falsification and distortion of statements made to her or in their writings by Indians whom she met or read. The two men to complain publicly about this were the most distinguished Indians of that time – Tagore and Gandhi.

What made Katherine Mayo's plea of good intention wholly unconvincing was her persistent political moralizing when describing the moral shortcomings of Indians. At every turn it was suggested that on account of their low morals, especially in sexual life, Indians were not fit for self-government. The moral was eagerly grasped in England. For example, the *Saturday Review* wrote: 'The basic fact is that India is not socially fit for self- government. And the social evils are found in their worst form among precisely those who would be given political power.' The suggestion that sexual obsession and sexual indulgence make a people unfit for political independence will sound grotesquely absurd in today's West, but in those days it was bound to rouse prejudice among the British people.

As to myself, in spite of the clamour all over India I did not read the book till a year or two later, and then what struck me most was its shallowness and crudity. I said to myself and also to others that if I were so disposed I could build up a case against giving political independence to India which would be ten times stronger, and in respect of social evils, too, I could get at those which were deep-seated and widespread and which had real significance. Katherine Mayo had ladled out nothing but some exceptional details, which were both unsavoury and titillating.

At the highest level Indians took a remarkably cool view of the book. Mrs Sarojini Naidu even said that many things Miss Mayo had described were true. Mahatma Gandhi in writing about it in *Young India* (1 September 1927) gave the book a label which would have put Miss Mayo in her place if it had not contained a *suggestio falsi*. He called it the 'Drain Inspector's Report'. He obviously implied that since all drains contained filth, Katherine Mayo's reportage did not matter. But the woman was describing the presence of filth, not in Indian drains, but in Indian bedrooms and sitting-rooms, and so Gandhi's analogy did not hold. It was, however, not a fallacy on his part, but one of his *many casuistries*. With its help he saved his own conscience in respect of what truth there was in the book, and at the same time reassured those fellow-Indians who had a conscience that the truth in it did not matter much.

But generally speaking the Indian intelligentsia was furious. Its anger against the book was poured out in the press and also in books. For all that excitement there was explanation in the existing mood. Traditionally, the Hindus were contemptuous of judgements of non-Hindus on themselves. Till about the middle of the nineteenth century they could say about any detractor: 'Let the Mleccha [unclean foreigner] say what he pleases, he bites on granite.' But after getting a Western type of education in English they became conscious of the evils in their way of life and at the same time extremely sensitive to any foreigner's, especially any White man's, remarks and preaching about them. The same Western education had also made them aware of the greatness of the ancient Hindu civilization, and refurbished their old megalomania by providing an historical basis for it. So, they resented all Western criticism of the Hindu way of life as combined insult and injury.

I shall give only one precedent to the fury against *Mother India*. Only ten years before, i.e., in 1917, when I was a student, William Archer, the

English dramatic critic, had published a book on India – which was not at all in his line – in which he held up Hindu life and culture, and more especially Hindu religion, to contempt. He virtually said that India was not a civilized country. At once a noisy protest arose all over India, and the question: Is India civilized was discussed with ridiculous solemnity. Many distinguished Indians joined in this unnecessary controversy.

As it happened, its memory was revived in 1927, and by no less a person than George Bernard Shaw, who had become almost an idol of educated Indians. He republished some of the essays of Archer with his own endorsement of the criticism of Hindu culture and life by his friend. His Indian admirers were driven to cry in agony: *Et tu, Brute*! *Mother India* followed in its wake.

There was an additional reason for the sensitiveness in 1927. At that time the question of a further constitutional advance in India was under discussion between the British Government at home and that in India, and all over India there was an expectation of substantial concessions. The publication of Katherine Mayo's book just at this juncture both in Britain and the United States created the impression that it was a propaganda move designed to create public opinion against Indian political aspirations and demands.

Furthermore, all Indians assumed that the book had been inspired, if not actually commissioned, by the British officials in India, who were, as I have already said, the most determined opponents of giving political power to Indians. They thought that the officials had not only helped this American woman, but actually got her to write the book to prejudice public opinion in Britain and the United States against their claims. Even Mahatma Gandhi discreetly referred to this possibility. He wrote: 'Unsubsidized she may be, uncommitted and unattached she certainly fails herself to show herself on any page. We in India are accustomed to interested publication patronized-"patronized" is accepted as an elegant synonym for "subsidized" – by the Government... I hope Miss Mayo will not take offence if she comes under the shadow of such suspicion.'

I always wished that some research student would clear up the secret history of the book, and now an Indian scholar has written a book on it. My friend Neville Maxwell told me about it and then lent it to me. The book is not well-written, but it does give enough documentary proof to show that the British authorities in India from the highest to the lowest ranks were very ready to welcome and help Katherine Mayo. Two officials, more especially, seem to have supplied much of the scandalous details, and one of them, John Coatman, an Oxonian, held the important position of Director of Public Information to the Government of India. The author of the book summarizes one of his opinions from a document he saw among the papers left by Mayo to the University of Yale. I quote the passage: 'He [Coatman] proceeded to tell Mayo that the practice of sodomy was common and general among the Hindus. He averred that people practised it even upon their own sons, and that there was no shame attached to it. There was no public opinion against the practice. The clue to India's decadence, according to Coatman, lay in the prevalence of sodomy and of immature motherhood, of sexual excess and exhaustion.'*

I offer no comment beyond saying that it is opinions like this, aired during their days of power (although tottering even then), which make me unwilling to believe British authors and journalists when after the loss of India they praise India and Indians. If slander can be interested and dishonest, so can be praise. If malice is base, ineffectual malice is contemptible, and all British malice against us has proved to be ineffectual. Even before I read Jha's book, I, going on presumption, had very little doubt about it. No one, unless he had lived for a long time in India and had had access to the very specialized reports of crimes and social evils prepared for the Government, could have got at the facts with which she illustrated or rather garnished her arguments; she must have been helped by persons who were very much in the know. The best that can be said for her is that the officials, finding her simple-minded, put such facts before her as were likely to rouse her moral fury. But throughout the book she was seen to be so specious that even this seems improbable.

She revealed the official inspiration of her book by including in it two of the silliest arguments trotted out by the British bureaucracy and their spokesmen in the Press against political independence for India. One of these was that if the British withdrew their protection the fierce Muslims of the Northwest would descend upon the plains of northern India and slaughter the unwarlike inhabitants. And the other argument was that the Indian princes would never tolerate the rule of Bengali Babus. Katherine Mayo not only swallowed the arguments but even represented an Indian

*See Manoranjan Jha: *Katherine Mayo* and India, published in 1971 by the People's Publishing House, New Delhi, p. 43.

prince as saying to her that he would never submit to the Bengali Babu. Mahatma Gandhi did not believe this to be a true statement. But I have already shown that, under promptings from the British officials, the princes and indeed even 'loyal' Indians in British India were capable of these stupid utterances. Miss Mayo, if not an accomplice of these officials, was certainly their dupe.

The view, universally held in India, that the book was part of a conspiracy against political concessions to India on the part of the British bureaucracy and the British press, was strengthened by the refusal of *The Times* to publish a letter of protest against the book which a number of very distinguished Indians had sent to it. Altogether, the publication of *Mother India* will remain as one of the most stupid and unpleasant episodes in the last decades of British rule in India, when the British officials in the country did more to discredit it than any Indian nationalist could.

At one point I was almost drawn into the campaign against the book. Lala Lajpat Rai, the well-known nationalist leader from the Punjab, was writing a rejoinder to it, and it came out later under the tide *Unhappy India*. My friend, Pandit Benarsidas Chaturvedi, told me that the Lalaji was looking for someone who might help him as a literary assistant, and asked me if I might be willing. I did not show much eagerness and the proposal came to nothing.

The Second Provocation: the Simon Commission

The second provocation came in November 1927. It was given as I have related, by the appointment of an all-British Commission to report on the question of further constitutional advance in India. This review was promised formally in the so-called Montagu-Chelmsford Act of 1919, which had conceded responsible government only in a few restricted spheres of provincial administration and left all real power in British hands. The chairman of the Statutory Commission was to be Sir John Simon. The announcement was made on 8 November 1927, in the House of Commons, but the composition of the Commission without even one Indian on it was leaked out in India. So, before the British public came to know about the setting up of the Commission and its personnel, they learned that Indian politicans of all parties and shades of opinion had decided to boycott it. I was at Kishorganj when the announcement came and did not notice it. But as soon as I came to Calcutta three weeks later I found that there was a furore. It gained intensity, and excited demonstrations which began on 3 February 1928, on the day the Commission landed at Bombay, and continued throughout the tours of the body in India.

Sir John Simon and his colleagues paid two visits to India: the first from 3 February to 31 March 1928, and the second from 11 October 1928 to 13 April 1929. The opposition to the Commission was so manifest and violent that Sir John Simon, self-possessed and astute politician that he was, felt very much discouraged. During the second visit a very deplorable incident happened. When the Commission arrived at Lahore, on 30 October 1928, the demonstration against it – a black-flag procession shouting 'Go back Simon' – was led by the veteran Indian nationalist leader Lala Lajpat Rai. The police charged the procession and broke it up. Lajpat Rai, a man of sixty-three then, received some blows and died of his injuries on 17 November. An English police officer, I. P. Saunders, was believed to have beaten him, and he was shot dead on 16 December by a young revolutionary. The alienation between the Commission and political India was completed by these miserable and unnecessary incidents. The demonstrations against it became more widespread and overwrought, and in one of them Jawaharlal Nehru, too, received some blows.

I might add here that my wife, who was a university student in Calcutta at the time, was once drawn into one of the black flag demonstrations. Two well known women nationalist workers went to her hostel and got the Superintendent to allow a number of girls to go with them in order to swell the attendance at a protest meeting, as they told her. The presence of women, especially of fashionable girl students, added fervour to the speeches. So, my future wife and a number of other girls were taken to the house of the well known Bengali Congress leader, Dr B. C. Ray, and asked to wait. They noticed a stack of black flags and guessed the real purpose for which they had been brought. One of them phoned to the Superintendent, who came and took back with her the girls who did not want to go. This would show that it was very difficult to keep out of politics in those days in India.

Yet all this trouble could have been averted for two years. The Commission was appointed under the provisions of the Act of 1919, which laid down that there would be a review of the constitutional position with a view to further extension of self-government at the end of ten years from the passing of the Act. As the date of that was October 1919, the whole matter might have been kept in abeyance for a long time. But the British politician who brought it forward was that formidable Conservative, F. E. Smith, who as the Earl of Birkenhead became the Secretary of State for India in the Government which Baldwin formed at the end of 1924. He did that out of a political calculation which turned out to be a miscalculation.

However, when he took office he did not think that necessary. On 4 December 1924 he wrote to Lord Reading, who was still Viceroy, that he thought the Government should adhere rigidly to the date proposed in the Act of 1919. He went further and wrote that unless conditions greatly changed in the meanwhile it was very unlikely that the review would suggest the slightest extension of self-government. He was no believer in Dominion Status for India, and he added in the same letter that he found it inconceivable that India would ever become fit for Dominion self-government.

Although not so forthright in his public utterances, he expressed virtually the same opinion in a speech before the Lords in May 1925. He said:

'I am not able, in any foreseeable future, to discern a moment when we may safely, either to ourselves or to India, abandon our trust. There is, my Lords, no 'lost Dominion'* and there will be no 'lost Dominion' until that moment, if ever it came, when the whole British Empire, with all that it means for civilization, is splintered in doom ...'

These were brave words backed by a brave will. Nevertheless, in spite of the fact that it had a meaning for civilized human life as its disappearance is showing all over Asia and Africa today, the British Empire in India has disappeared. What has made Lord Birkenhead a false prophet is the fulfilment of the premise which he could not either accept or even envisage. A. L. Carthill was in his way right. Morally, already in 1924, India was a lost British dominion.

However, at the end of a year Birkenhead himself changed his mind, and made a volte face. He decided to advance the date of the review, and gave his reason in a letter to Lord Reading, who was still Viceroy, written on 10 December 1925. He wrote:

* An allusion to a book published in 1924, which created a sensation: *The Lost Dominion* by A. L. Carthill, the pseudonym of an English official of the I.C.S.

'When I made my speech in the House of Lords suggesting that it might be possible to accelerate the Commission of 1928 [a slip for 1929], if some measure of co-operation was forthcoming in India, I always had it plainly in mind that we could not afford to run the slightest risk that the Commission of 1928 [1929] should be in the hands of our successors. You can easily imagine what kind of a Commission in its personnel would have been appointed by Colonel Wedgwood and his friends.'

A general election was due in 1929, and if Labour came to power then, as it did, handling of the Indian question would pass into their hands. Birkenhead dreaded that, and as he informed Lord Reading, he thought he would play for safety by setting up the Commission in the middle of 1927. He also thought that Baldwin agreed with him.

But he had reckoned without his hosts. Certainly, neither he nor Lord Irwin, who had succeeded Reading as Viceroy in 1926, anticipated the fierce Indian opposition to an all-British Commission. It must also be admitted that formally there was no ground for opposition to such a Commission on the part of Indian politicians.

The Act of 1919 which promised a review of the constitutional position at the end of ten years, also made any extension of self-government subject to the discretion of the British parliament. Therefore it was only natural that the Commission would be composed of members of parliament. There was no legal obligation either to have Indians on the Commission. Thus India was claiming a right which had not been formally conceded. There was no breach of promise.

Nonetheless, both Birkenhead and Irwin did contemplate having Indians and gave the matter very careful thought. They knew that whatever might be the legal position, the recommendations of a commission would have far less weight in India if it came from an exclusively British Commission than they would have if the body had also Indians on it. But to their thinking, and they were right here, the practical obstacles to including Indians were insurmountable. There were so many communities and interests in India that the presence of two or three Indians was bound to be called unrepresentative, while by representing even the major interests the Commission would become too large for effective discussion and decisions. So, as a compromise, they contemplated a procedure for taking Indian opinion into consideration after the Commission had reported. This was to subject the recommendations to discussion by the Indian legislatures or at a round table conference.

In retrospect, it must be said that the Commission would have been a failure even if Indians were represented on it. The difference of opinion between the British and the Indian members would have been too great to permit a unanimous report. Furthermore, the British and the Indian members would never have worked happily together. Not to speak of political views, the differences in character, temperament, and manners would have been too wide for that. There would have been neither mutual respect nor friendliness.

Such as it was, even the casual contacts which Sir John Simon had with the foremost Indian leaders like Motilal Nehru, Srinivasa lyenger, Lajput Rai, and Jinnah, as also others less eminent, made him resentful of their attitude and contemptuous of their ability. Even in England Sir John would regard few of his fellow politicians as his equal. Simon's mother upset even Birkenhead by telling him that it was a good fortune for him to have been with John at Wadham College, Oxford. As Birkenhead wrote to Irwin:

'His [Simon's] opinion of the Swarajyists is, I think, at least as unfavourable as yours or mine, and his day to day association with his native colleagues is unlikely to endear them in any marked degree. I cannot imagine any more terrible fate in the world in the present situation in India than to try to hack out a new constitution with such talkative and incompetent colleagues. But perhaps your nomination may obtain better and more reticent men than I can hope for.'

He might well say so. Talking, or what is called 'dialogue' in current political jargon, was carried on between British and Indian politicians for over twenty years. No reticence was ever seen in them, nor any result. In the end what was decreed to happen by fate or history, happened.

The talking Indian leaders exasperated all the Viceroys from Lord Reading to Lord Wavell, and even the mild Lord Irwin observed to Birkenhead that 'to the Indian more than to most human beings there is apt to be a very wide gulf between words and thought.'

This was true generally. All Indians are in the habit of spreading the snare of words without ever being caught in their own nets. In regard to Indo-British relations, the words were bound to be even more meaningless because there was an irreconcilable difference of approach. As to the

Simon Commission, the Indians questioned the British assumption that the British parliament had the sole right to decide what measure of self-government should be given to India. They wanted full self-government, and regarded discussions between the two sides as a means of deciding the procedure for establishing this kind of government. To them, it was a question of negotiations across the table between two parties on an equal footing, and not one of an *ex parte* decision on an application from the Indian side.

Even so, the opposition to the Simon Commission on the ground that it was all British would not have been so general and fanatical if it had not been for the temper of the moment – if after the exhaustion of the 1920 movement in 1922 political excitement had not begun to rise. This was happening in obedience to the cyclical law of the nationalist movement, which I have already analysed. The ebb tide which had set in five years before was over, and the flood-tide was coming. To vary the metaphor, the boiler had generated enough steam to drive the engine of nationalist agitation, and what was seen in the boycott of the Simon Commission was the roaring escape of the bursting steam through the safety-valve, which preceded the engine's getting into motion.

A Hymn of Hate

The anger against the Simon Commission and Katherine Mayo's book was confined to the politically conscious middle class. Although this was enough to put an agitation into motion, the nationalist leaders and the press never missed any opportunity to bring into play the deeper and more irrational prejudices against British rule which existed among the Indian masses. As it happened, just when the excitement against the Simon Commission was at its height an incident happened which did offer a chance to exploit such a prejudice. This particular prejudice was embodied in a very popular legend about what was done by the British railway companies in India after a collision or derailment of trains.

The figures of death officially given out were never believed in, and it was always asserted that they were reduced substantially to avoid paying damages. The assumption never considered how the figures of the railways would affect damages when the relatives of the dead would be there to claim them. So, if the deaths were given in tens they would be inflated to hundreds. The standard account of how the suppression was carried out consisted in saying that the dead bodies were packed into waggons and taken to a distant place to be disposed of in a clandestine way.

I heard many such stories myself, and I would relate one. In December 1918, there was a minor collision at a junction less than two miles from central Calcutta and close to a populous suburb. Two or three days later I was travelling on the same line, and a fellow-passenger treated me to the story that waggons loaded with dead bodies were taken to Goalundo Ghat, a terminus by the river Padma one hundred and fifty miles away to which we were going, and then all the waggons were pushed into the river from the sidings, after removing the buffers at their ends. All these details were given to me as if the narrator had been present at the scene. It was futile to contradict him.

Now, on 8 July 1928, at 10.43 pm., there was an accident due to the derailment of a passenger train about seven miles from Howrah station, the Calcutta terminal of the East Indian Railway. It was quite serious, and the Company gave the figures of the dead at about twenty. There was furious criticism of the EIR in the nationalist newspapers, and the accident was attributed to negligence in not keeping the track in proper condition. The possibility of sabotage by strikers was put forward by the Company, and it was dismissed as a canard by the most fiery and popular of the nationalist newspapers of the day – *Forward*, which was controlled by the well-known Congress leader Sarat Chandra Bose. It said that the false plea was put forward to avoid paying damages.

Not satisfied with that. *Forward* published three letters on 13 July purporting to come from eye-witnesses of the disaster under the following heading: 'Railway Smash at Belur – Sufferer's Story – Killed and Wounded How Many?' The first of these was from a man who said that he was injured severely, saw other injured persons being killed by the railway men by bludgeoning, he himself escaped only by crawling into a bush. He signed himself as 'A Real Horrified Spectator', but gave his name and address as well. I quote the letter in full just as it was printed, without retouching the English:

'Dear Sir,

Although I am still lying on my deathbed as the results of train crash at Belur, I venture forward to give the real agonies that I saw so that my mind and heart may be relieved of the horrors that I saw on the ill-fated night. I request you, sir, to publish this, so that the public may know, what was actually done by the 'relief train' in that night.

'I was a passenger by that train and the train had already passed Lilloah station. We were nine in the inter class and some of the passengers were sleeping and I and a friend of mine (now dead) were discussing about the speed of the train. Both of us were of the opinion that the train was going above 40 miles an hour and I am dead sure of that. Suddenly there was a crash, a terrible sound and as I looked out, I was parted from my companion for ever. I was thrown at about 10 feet away from the line and (Bhagawan be blessed) I am still alive to tell the real facts. I lay there in that wood, crying with pain for about a long long time and after that the 'relief train' arrived. Lights began to flash, some complete dead bodies and the wounded from the rear part of the train (most of them in a serious condition) were placed on the line towards Howrah and taken away.

In the Dark Night

'But what was going on towards the front side of the crash? God bless me, silently during the dark night, some people were running hither and thither. The dead were being thrown into the covered wagons one after the other and as quick as possible. I could plainly hear weeping and cries of pain and agony. Accompanied with them I could hear heavy thuds and blows being delivered and the cries were diminishing at quick intervals. I could hear the voice of a European, 'Jaldi karo, maro usko' [Be quick, kill that man]. Somebody on my left at a distance of 15 feet cried: 'Hai, jal, hai marta, Babu jal, pani' [Alas, water, alas I am dying, sir, water]. A man came, there was a heavy blow and the dying man spoke no more. All was over with him and water had been supplied to him for ever. No more did that Indian voice cry. He had been hushed for ever and carried away and thrown over the heap in the waggon.

'I crawled into the tall grass and watched the tragic drama. I was at such a position that I could see what was going on from the engine to the guards van. Oh, Brothers! Oh, Indians! What a horrible sight it was! My eyes fail to describe it, searchlights were flashing in every direction. The wounded were being searched and 'killed', mind you 'killed', not saved. Where a cry arose, a Sahib came with a light, somebody delivered a heavy blow and the Royal Indian spoke no more. Oh, Brothers, Indian blood has been lavishly spilt, all the wounded and dying were killed and heaped into the waggons.

The waggons were locked before my eyes and I can recognize the man who did it. Oh, Brothers! I have been saved and I shall live to tell the horrible tale that actually happened. I shall tell the public how horrible murders were done. But where did the waggons go? No, not to Howrah. I can swear it. I can 'prove' it, where they have been dumped, where they have been thrown? into river? into sea? I call upon the 'noble Indian' public to bravely come forward and ask the Govt. what has become of the waggon – loads of dead bodies silently carried away before dawn. Why were they killed, for the crash the passengers were not responsible, then why were they killed, who cried for water, for aid, where have the waggons been secretly removed, was it to show less death? I challenge the relief train party to deny that no wounded were killed. Can they swear that only 30, say even 80 only have been killed? I am ready to prove to the public that 'more' than 300 are 'dead' and 50 p.c. could have been saved if the 'relief train' had not arrived and killed the dying with iron rods etc.

Coaches Full

'By chance before entering the train at Howrah I walked towards the engine for fresh air and I saw with my own eyes that all the III classes were full – nearly double than the carrying capacity and this 'will' be corroborated by plainly asking any crewman on duty, taken at random, or if I cannot be trusted, it can be verified by the booking-clerk, by asking how many III class and inter class tickets were issued for stations where the train was to halt? As regards proof, I dare say that I can identify 10 men of the relief party. However cleverly too they may be disguised, and even if you shut my eyes, I can recognize the European's voice (his gruff voice is still reinging in my ears). Indians! 300 innocent dead bodies (half of them were alive and cried for aid) have brutally been taken to God knows where and it is up to the Indian public to trace the clue, and I shall give the evidence and to which side the waggons went. I earnestly call upon all Indians, Barristers, leaders, public men to whatever political party, religion or caste they may belong to come forward and demand a public answer to where those over 300 dead bodies of those innocent, those poor, those royal Indians been despatched? Why were the wounded killed? If the authorities deny all these I shall go out to tell the world for the cause of departed souls. Oh! Indian, if you have any Indian blood in you, if you have any self-respect, sympathy, arise then now and come forward now, for your brothers have been treated worse than dogs. I hope all the national papers over and outside the country 'will' copy this report.'

I am,
A REAL HORRIFIED SPECTATOR,
Howrah

I was shocked and scandalized when I read this letter, and wondered how a newspaper could publish it. I must add that the story is even more extraordinary. Some years later I inquired about it of a relative of mine, who at the time was a sub-editor on *Forward*. He told me that he was asked by the editor to go to the address given and check the authenticity of the letter, and that he found no person bearing the name given. He also told me that after his report there was a consultation between the editor (a man whom I came to know well afterwards) and Mr Sarat Chandra Bose (whose private secretary I became in 1937) and the letter was published deliberately. I never dared to ask them about it.

The East Indian Railway at once sued the paper for libel and damages, and in May 1929, Calcutta High Court awarded heavy damages on the ground that the letter was a fake. But the board of the paper stopped its publication, and sent the holding company into liquidation. As the press -was only leased by the paper and not owned by it, the railway company had no assets to recover the damages from.

This case, extraordinary as it would seem to all normal persons, was as characteristic of Indian nationalism as Katherine Mayo's was of British propaganda against Indian nationalism. In fact, this letter and Katherine Mayo's book are only the obverse and reverse of the same spurious coin. Of course, the book was written in better English than the letter. But in politics crudity always wins. *Mother India* did not save British rule in India as its British promoters thought it would. On the contrary, the spirit of the letter injured the British Empire in India.

Dominion Status

There was a lull for some months. The Simon Commission left India after its second visit on 13 April 1929, and the excitement subsided. My work on *The Modem Review* and *Pabasi* was not very interesting. So I felt very much bored, and as was my habit when I got tired of doing something, or, to be more accurate, felt the tedium of earning a livelihood, I took up a new hobby or recreation. This time it was the study of Italian painting. I bought books on the subject and subscribed to *Apollo*, and although I could not see any originals in India I saw as many good reproductions as possible. I myself had, as I have said, some reproductions by the Medici Society. In the Imperial Library I consulted the more expensive books. That made and kept me very happy for some months.

But politics very soon forced its entry, and within a short time got me in its hold. The calamity which Lord Birkenhead had feared had come about. As a result of the general election of May 1929, Labour came into power, and the Indian question was in its hands. Birkenhead's move to foreclose it ended in failure. Although the Simon Commission was still drafting its report, Indian opposition to it had convinced the Labour Government that some other means of placating India must be found. The Commission's report was published in May 1930. By that time the so-called Civil Disobedience Movement led by Mahatma Gandhi had already begun. Its recommendations were stillborn, and were never acted upon. So, all the ill-feeling that its appointment had given rise to was seen to have been wholly unnecessary.

Even before that the Labour Government had decided to reassure Indian nationalist opinion, and so with authorization by both MacDonald and Benn, Lord Irwin made a statement at the end of October 1929 that Dominion Status was the final goal of the political concessions the British Government contemplated. Simon was not consulted about this, and he was critical of the offer of Dominion Status and of the propriety of making it before his Commission had reported. It was clearly by-passed.

Both Birkenhead and Reading were upset by this pronouncement. Birkenhead had resigned in October 1928, and had no official responsibility for India. But as long as he was in office he had insisted that the Commission's recommendations should be the basis of all further concessions. But the Commission was virtually being disavowed even before it had submitted its report. This made him very angry.

Apart from this, both Birkenhead and Reading deplored the offer, however eventual or contingent, of Dominion Status. This, they thought, was not a general term for self-government, but had acquired very definite constitutional and legal implications, and these they thought were inapplicable to India. Birkenhead was fully aware that there was a very strong and influential body of opinion in India in favour of total separation from Britain. He also knew that if an offer of Dominion Status was made the Indian leaders were bound to ask about the date of its fulfilment, and since it would be impossible to fix a date he thought the Indians would not weaken their demand for full independence. Anxious as well as angry, he asked the Conservative shadow cabinet to consider the matter. But to his dismay he found that Baldwin was in agreement with Labour over the offer.

My chief, Ramananda Babu, commented on it on lines expected from him in *The Modern Review*. I was utterly unconvinced that the offer was sincere. I knew enough about the history of the Commonwealth and Dominion Status to think that the status would be conceded to India in any foreseeable time. I had read the White Paper of 1926, and had a copy myself. It had defined Dominion Status in words drafted by Balfour which had evoked comparison with the Christian Athanasian Creed. I had nothing but intellectual disdain for the formula, which I knew was only a cover for a practical reality of a different order. That reality was not only the result of a long evolution but also in some cases of wars against rebellious constituents of the British Empire. The virtual independence that was conferred on the White Dominions by such a status was counterbalanced by the presence in each of these Dominions of a large British community which could counteract the separatist aspirations of the non-British elements. No Dominion was given the sort of sovereignty which Dominion Status embodied in historical or geographical circumstances which would allow it to treat Great Britain and other Powers on equal terms. At least in 1926 that was the position. And finally, self-government of the type introduced by Dominion Status was never extended to any part of the Empire where self-governing traditions, aptitudes, and institutions were not present. None of these prerequisites for the Status existed in the case of India.

So I thought that Lord Irwin's offer was only a diplomatic move, and that too not very subtle. He again dwelt on the superiority of Dominion Status to independence in a speech made on 7 February 1930, and said that the British Empire was a Commonwealth 'where the diverse gifts of each constituent part may be linked for the common betterment of the whole society and of the human race.' He also represented the British Commonwealth as a smaller League of Nations compared with the one at Geneva. This was too much for me and I decided to have a go at him in *The Modern*

Review. First of all, I pointed out that the real sanction behind the bond which the Commonwealth had created was the ethnic and cultural unity which existed between the British people and the inhabitants of the White Dominions, and which was not present in the case of India. Then I wrote: 'It is the sort of eloquent commonplace which since the promulgation of the report of the inter-imperial committee of 1926, it has become the proper thing to say about the British Empire in after-dinner speeches.'

Then I took up his analogy between the British Commonwealth and the League of Nations, and wrote:

'The League of Nations is founded upon positive ideals, however weak at the present moment in their hold over the thoughts of the present generation [I still had faith in that body and did not lose it until I saw its impotence at the time of the Japanese aggression in Manchuria in 1931]; the evolution of Dominion Status is a negative phenomenon, a progressive surrender to the self-assertiveness of Dominion nationalism, a loosening of central authority which once was effective, the dissolution of a super-state, a recognition in fact of the impotence of Great Britain which no amount of lip-service to the ideals of international co-operation will hide from the eye of the world.'

In conclusion I made a guess as to the circumstances in which Dominion Status might be conceded to India. I wrote: 'It seems to us that Great Britain may agree to concede Dominion Status to India only if and when she finds that there is a probability of Indians winning independence in spite of Great Britain.'

These remarks were published in *The Modern Review* for March 1930, and I do not think they contained a bad guess. The only modification to that forecast which I would make now is that the Status was given when the British people had lost the will to keep India, and was not forced by us. I shall explain that later.

Return of Mahatma Gandhi

It was curious that the change of political attitude in me should have come about when the temper of the Indian people was also rising. But this was only a coincidence. The causal relationship between the popular excitement and its harnessing to action was seen in the return of Mahatma Gandhi to active politics. From 1922 to 1929 he was virtually in eclipse. No one should assume from this that he was less venerated. Only, he could not be effectual in action. That was due to the cyclical law of the Indian nationalist movement, which I have explained earlier in this chapter. No leader could do anything if there was an ebb-tide of political passion in the people. Even Gandhi could not be above the workings of this law. That was why there was no outbreak of violence when he was arrested in 1922, and also why he could not regain his power to incite the people when he was released from prison in 1924. The emotional climate had changed so completely that he could not carry with him the two most influential of his colleagues, namely, Motilal Nehru and C. R. Das. They could even resist him successfully when he tried to make the Congress reject their policy of working in the Central Indian Legislature. This decline of Gandhi's influence was perceived by Lord Reading correctly even in 1922, and was noted quite emphatically in 1925. For instance, he wrote on 1 January 1925:

'Gandhi is now attached to the tail of Das and Nehru, although they try their utmost to make him and his supporters think that he is one of the heads, if not *the* head. It is pathetic to observe the rapid decline in the power of Gandhi and the frantic attempts he is now making to cling to his position as leader at the expense of every principle he has hitherto advocated.'

As a diagnosis of the symptoms this was correct, but neither Lord Reading, nor perhaps Gandhi himself, understood where the true cause lay. The simple fact was that the people of India were not in the mood for a mass agitation and for the time being were quite content to have their hatred of British rule vicariously satisfied by the fillibustering of the Swarajyist leaders in the Legislative Assembly. But Gandhi regained his power at one stroke in 1930 when the collective hatred had become active again. The volcano of Indian nationalism never lost its subterranean fire, but it could erupt only periodically.

These alternations in the exertion of Gandhi's power also illustrate in what way the people of India accepted his leadership. He was followed and could be effectual only when he voiced the hatred of his people for British rule and organized it for such action as was possible. For everything else he was not only ineffectual, but positively rejected. It seems he was aware of this, and so gave up the formal leadership of the Congress from a growing conviction that it was not accepting his moral principles wholly or sincerely.

I have also heard that he became very fond of a song by Tagore and would have it sung to him, although he did not know Bengali. This was the song:

> If nobody would come when you call,
>   March alone,
> If nobody looks back, and all turn their faces away,
> If all show fear,
> Set alight a rib from your breast,
>   And march alone ...

This was, of course, more or less true of all the nationalist leaders. As soon as they ceased to speak for the hatred and showed any interest in government, they were pushed out of the nationalist movement. This was all the truer for Gandhi. But this affected only his capacity to mount an agitation. At no time did the Indian people cease to respect him. His position as the greatest man in India was never questioned. But that was maintained by his religiosity, with its accompaniment of asceticism and renunciation paraded with every kind of theatricality. This exalted his practical political activity by throwing a veil over its real motive force, namely, the hatred of British rule, and by infusing into it a moral and spiritual value which it never had, although as I have already explained, to Mahatma Gandhi religion and nationalism were inseparable.

CHAPTER 2

India Under the Lathi

The years 1930 and 1931, more especially the former, were a period of tumultuous political agitation in India. I, who had clear recollections of all the previous phases of agitation, got the impression that it was the most spontaneous, widespread, and intense of all, and I do not think my involvement in it emotionally coloured my assessment. In offering my account of the upheaval, which will be purely personal, I have chosen as the heading to this chapter the title of a book by the eminent Labour politician, Fenner Brockway, afterwards Lord Brockway. He came to India to watch the movement of Civil Disobedience launched by Mahatma Gandhi, saw how it was being dealt with by the British administration, which was simply to beat the people with the long bamboo stave known as the *lathi*, and so chose his title.

This stick was always used by the peasantry in India for their fights. The police adopted it for night patrolling in peaceful times, but charged with it whenever there were widespread riots. In 1930 the Government of India and the provincial governments took care not to shoot unless there, was military risk or arson and murder by large bodies of rioters. Mere demonstrations were scattered by *lathi* charges. These generally kept the agitators within the bounds of non-violence enjoined by Mahatma Gandhi. Even so, precautions were there: 'Just in case'. One day, even towards the beginning of the movement, I was surprised to see at a street comer in north Calcutta a piquet of armed civilian police with the .303 Lee-Enfield rifle, instead of the old Martini-Henry, with which they were formerly armed. I was somewhat alarmed, but soon noticed that the magazines had been removed, and a steel plate closed the aperture. So I was relieved to think that there would be only one shot at a time.

The Gandhian Movement

By the time I had published my note on Dominion Status, from which I have just quoted, India was on the eve of one of the cyclical resumptions of active agitation. The Congress, in its session at Lahore at the end of 1929 which was presided over by Jawaharlal Nehru, had authorized civil disobedience, that is, defiance of the laws of British India, but it left the time and the method of defiance wholly to the discretion of Mahatma Gandhi. It was to be started if independence was not conceded.

On 26 January, however, India proclaimed psychological independence, thus departing from the American precedent. The American colonies resorted to war first and declared independence in the next year. The Hindus of India, who could not think that they would be independent in any foreseeable time, were keen to have the psychological satisfaction of declaring themselves free from British rule. From that date every year the day was celebrated with the hoisting of the national flag. The formula was: 'Up, up with the National Flag; down, down with the Union Jack.' The day is now being celebrated as Republic Day; and inevitably as an Indian, but very un-Gandhian, imitation of the parade in Red Square.

On 4 March 1930, Mahatma Gandhi sent a letter to the Viceroy, Lord Irwin, which was a sort of ultimatum. Characteristically, it was carried to the Viceroy by a personal messenger who was a young English Quaker named Reginald Reynolds. Even on that day the wild response that followed Gandhi's appeal could not be foreseen. There was only an air of intense expectation and the stillness in the air which is seen before the coming of a cyclone. On 12 March Gandhi began his march to the sea to break the Salt Laws. This was, so to speak, the formal opening, like Sarastro saying: '*Die Stunde* schlägt... Dich ruft dein Wort, die Stunde schlägt... wir sehn uns wieder' (The hour has struck ... Thy honour calls ... the hour has struck... we shall meet again). I must say that the call was not from nationalism alone, but as if from religion and morality, carried to mystical fervour. The people of India felt as if they had been asked to go through fire and water as their ordeal and emerge purified as well as triumphant. It was a message which was exactly like that pronounced by the Men in Armour: 'Fire, water, air, and earth will not defile you, you will have conquered the fear of death, and you will rise to heaven.' The people of India did not triumph, but they suffered their ordeal in exultant faith.

I cannot even now clearly explain how and why I, with all my detachment in regard to the nationalist movement, became attuned to this appeal. It was a very sudden conversion. When the independence day was proclaimed on 26 January I was very sarcastic, and said: 'We have got our independence without effort.' But that ironic pose had disappeared. Of course, my rather contemptuous attitude towards the declaration of independence sprang from my dislike for consoling ourselves with illusions and unrealities, but in respect of civil disobedience there was no unreality. All of us knew that the British Government was here and it would not be easy to shake it. I do not think that those who joined the movement either actively or in spirit ever thought that it would result in the expulsion of the British. All that they felt was that it was their duty to do something to gain political independence, and it was open to everybody to rise in rebellion and pay the price. That was not taking refuge in any unreality. Apart from that, the idea of doing our duty by our country, and also the idea of sacrificing our interest for our love of freedom, pushed the hatred of British rule more or less into the background at this juncture. Initially, at least, Mahatma Gandhi's message that we should fight British rule without hatred was accepted.

As for myself, I had, as a result of my thinking on Indo-British relations during the previous months, become very sceptical about the sincerity of the British side. I was particularly ironical about Lord Irwin and thoroughly disliked his unctuous special pleading. I never developed any kind of admiration for him, and came particularly to dislike his later record in the home politics of Britain as Marquis of Halifax. As for India, he fell between two stools. He did not bring any added prestige to the name of Halifax, which makes one expect brilliance, even though accompanied by the capacity to trim. But, considered deeply, my conversion to nationalism of the Gandhian type in 1930 was irrational, and may have been sub-rational. I am inclined to think that acquiring political passion is like falling in love, which for good or evil is always blind.

Let me now revert to the movement itself. Mahatma Gandhi began his defiance of the law by making salt illegally at Dandi on the seaside. His example was followed everywhere. There was defiance of the Salt Laws on the coast of the Bay of Bengal near Contai in Midnapore district, and also on the outskirts of Calcutta. To the east of the city there were extensive marshes of saline water, which were known as the Salt Lakes. I knew them very well, for I had not only taken long walks through them on the causeways, but also shot the gulls in them, about which I have written. Boiling this water could yield salt of a kind.

So, Satis Chandra Das-Gupta, a Bengali follower of Gandhi who was known among us as Gandhi Minor, established a camp on a mud-flat and began to make salt. I walked to the spot, and saw water being boiled in big cauldrons. I made a small donation and took a packet of salt. But I never tasted it, perhaps considering it too sacred for consumption. Das-Gupta was left alone for the time being, but people on the sea coast were treated to the *lathi* on a large scale.

Mahatma Gandhi was not arrested immediately, but the leaders who were considered more dangerous for their capacity to incite violence, were arrested. Among them was Jawaharlal Nehru, who gloried in his imprisonment. I began to collect photographs of the movement, including pictures of police charges and of wounded people, because I wanted to produce a picture supplement to *The Modern Review*. Many drawings by well-known Indian painters also came to us, and among them was a drawing in colour by the leading Bengali painter, Nanda Lal Bose, showing Gandhi marching to the sea with his long staff It was reproduced in colour in *The Modern Review*. A large number of photographs, together with a number of drawings, were published in the May issue of the magazine as a picture supplement of sixteen pages. Its preparation gave my mind great relief, because I felt that I was doing something for the movement. I was excited enough to wish to join it actively and to go to jail, but I thought with my responsibilities for the family I should not and could not. Except for this little contribution I should have felt very guilty. But the price for it had to be paid, not by me, but by *The Modern Review*. The issue was proscribed and the copies remaining after despatch to the subscribers were confiscated. I could, however, see my handiwork in the Bodleian, where the files of *The Modern Review* are preserved.

My elder brother, as the cool lawyer that he was, laughed in his sleeves at my infatuation. He said to others that he could never imagine that Nirad at the age of thirty-two could be so childish. To him my fit of nationalism seemed like the calf-love of adolescents, or even like the slavery of a foolish and doddering old man to a saucy little minx. But my brother's ironical attitude did not make me ashamed. Somehow my mind had got pitched to a very high key, and I felt an exaltation of the spirit like that I had felt at the beginning of our literary campaign. One thought which recurred to me during those weeks was that in spite of the troubles that I brought on myself by resigning from Government service in 1926, I had acted wisely, for I felt that I should not have been able to serve the British Government now, and yet if I resigned I should have had greater troubles. I should probably have been married, instead of being single. As my mind felt happy only when it was full of something, I was happy during the first months of the movement.

It was not long before Mahatma Ghandhi was arrested. On 5 May a party of policemen headed by a British official came to take him into custody and he was sent to prison. I felt very sad and more committed to the movement than before. For the June number of his magazine Ramananda Babu wrote a note which I reproduce below. The editorials opened with it.

'It is said, in the Gospel according to St. Matthew XXI, 46, of those who seized Jesus before his trial that "when they sought to lay hands on him, they feared the multitude, because they took him for a prophet." Perhaps for a similar reason those who wanted to arrest Gandhi went stealthily to his camp forty-five minutes after midnight and, though he is meek and nonviolent and physically weak and his companions unarmed and pledged to non-violence, the party of arresters consisted of the District Magistrate of Surat, two Indian police officers armed with pistols, and some thirty policemen armed with rifles.

'In Matthew XXVI, 55, Jesus is recorded as having said: "Are ye come out as against a thief with swords and staves to take me? I sat daily in the temple, and ye laid no hold on me."

'Gandhi might have said: "Are ye come out as against a robber with pistols and rifles to seize me.' I wrote to the Viceroy what ye held seditious and I taught the same daily in the villages and made salt and ye took me not.'

[*The Modern Review*, June 1930, p. 776 ff.]

If Ramananda Babu, a very sober and even prosaic commentator on public affairs, could write in this vein, the mood of the participants in the movement could be easily guessed. As I read the proofs, although I was no participant, tears came into my eyes. By that time all the others were also in jail. But neither Gandhi's arrest nor theirs made any difference to the intensity of the agitation. The people themselves took it over. If anything, it became more widespread and intense, with the passion supplied by the rank and file, not the leaders. Even when one could not see the country- wide agitation one could feel it, and hear its rumble and say in the words of Victor Hugo in his 'Une nuit qu'on entendait la mer sans la voir':

Quels sont ces bruits sourds?
Écoutez vers l'onde
Cette voix profonde,

Qui pleure toujours,
Et qui toujours gronde.

But even in Calcutta I could see typical exhibitions, as I did in 1921. But this time I did not feel any irritation, although I had not lost my sense of humour so far as not to be amused by certain things I saw. The crowds in the streets showed their usual eagerness in running towards a point where they thought something was happening, but also their quickness in running away in the opposite direction if they saw charges by the police. The news of risk travelled at the speed of light, because as soon as one group behind saw another group in front running back, it also began to run, putting other groups behind it in motion as soon as the flights could be seen by the eye.

I saw this one day, and it made me laugh heartily even in my nationalistic mood. I was standing near the Shambazar end of Cornwallis Street which, under different names, is the extension of one very long street running from south to north in a straight line more or less for about three miles from the comer of Wellington Square. Suddenly, people began to run away all around me, and looking southwards I saw more people running northwards, that is, towards me. But I saw no signs of any police force. However, about ten minutes later two armoured cars with their crew standing in the open turrets behind the machine gun came slowly towards me, and passed on. What had happened was that as soon as the cars had turned into Wellington Street from Dhurrumtollah, people had begun to run and communicated their motion to others by sight, which, of course, meant by the speed of light.

When the colleges re-opened in July after their long vacation, they were picketed by the striking students. Those who did not strike passed the line and attended the classes, although not without embarrassment and sometimes difficulty. One day, walking along Cornwallis Street, north of the Square with the same name, I saw a picket at the gate of Bethune College, the Government college for girls. There were girls among the picketers. The police who stood by left them alone, but if a crowd collected to watch they scattered it by charging with their *lathis*. I saw a few charges, taking care to walk to and fro, instead of standing.

Though the scene was interesting, it was surpassed for excitement by what was happening before the Scottish Church College on the other side of the square. The striking students there did not simply stand in a line to draw a cordon, but lay on the ground to obstruct those who wanted to go in.

It was a co-educational college, and my future wife was in it. Some girls, including her, wanted to join the classes. Some of them threaded their way through the gaps left in the human mine-field. Dr Urquhart, the Principal, himself came to the gate to reassure and welcome them. He extended his arms as each girl went forward, and said smiling: 'Come along, my dear.' He was the most amiable and level-headed man one could meet anywhere. Even so, the calumny was spread that he had trodden on one of the lying strikers in order to make a way for the girls. In later years I met the young man who said that he had been trampled on, and I heard that he had deliberately stretched his leg to brush against Dr Urquhart's.

One girl, however, got through without having to tread on any of the young men through the gallantry of another young man who had already got through. This girl was rather plump, and was very well known to my wife. She bravely advanced towards the gate, but after getting close to it she found that she could go no further without putting her feet on a young man lying on his back, or at all events without taking a jump over him. But the young man who had got through came to her help. He said: 'Please come along, step on my hands and I'll bring you over.' Then he knelt down, stretching his arms, and spreading out his palms. To the astonishment of all, the plump girl quickly placed her feet on the palms one after another, and landed nimbly on the other side. It was a feat worthy of a ballerina and her man partner. I am sure every spectator was amused. But the other girls, including my wife to be, took her to task and called shame on her for her immodesty. It was only the immodesty of stepping on to the hands of a young man, and not of bestriding, however momentarily, the supine young man at her feet.

My wife and some other girls of her hostel adopted another method of getting through. As the hostel was very near, they arrived early and went in before the picketers had taken their position. In this way they went in twice. But on the third occasion, after entering they could not come out. However, the lady superintendent of the hostel heard about it, and in order to give the girls their lunch arrived herself with the maids carrying the meals. She bullied the boys and got in. But all of them had to remain under siege in the college until the picketers departed in the evening. After that my wife gave up her attempts to join her classes until the row was over.

But it was not everywhere that such light relief was offered. All over India ugly scenes were enacted, and many bones were broken. Yet the agitation went on, for nothing could check it until its self-generated motive power was exhausted. Nevertheless, towards the end of 1930 and the beginning of 1931, a number of moderate Indian politicians who were known as Liberals and included among them some of the most eminent men of India, initiated moves to resolve the crisis by bringing about an understanding between the Congress and the Government. They saw both Gandhi and Nehru in prison. But so far as Nehru was concerned, they got nowhere. Mahatma Gandhi, however, showed a conciliatory spirit. He was ready to discuss the situation with the Viceroy, Lord Irwin, and if concessions were made, to suspend the movement.

He would not, however, go to the Viceregal Lodge in New Delhi, and repeat his mistake of 1921. Therefore the mountain in the person of Lord Irwin had to go to Mahomet in the person of Gandhi. They met in a house in the Daryaganj quarter of Old Delhi, belonging to Dr Ansari, an eminent Muslim doctor and a Congressman. I have seen the room and the shabby sofa on which they sat. Certainly no Viceregal, still less a future Marquis's, bottom had ever rested on a sofa like that. But an understanding was arrived at, and it was the famous Gandhi-Irwin Pact. Mahatma Gandhi agreed to join the second session of the Round Table Conference in London, which had already held its first session without the Congress, and therefore to no purpose. At the second session in September, Gandhi was to be the sole representative of the Congress. In the meanwhile, the civil disobedience movement was to be suspended.

It was, without delay. Many felt relieved. But others were critical, and Jawaharlal Nehru was angry. The critics said that Mahatma Gandhi had been wheedled by the wily British. But nobody could go against Gandhi publicly. As a result of the agreement, all the leading figures who were in jail were released. The agreement was called the Gandhi-Irwin Pact, after two well-known precedents: the Lucknow Pact between the Congress and Muslim League and the Kellogg Pact. Of course, all of them led to abortions. Let me describe the latest of them.

The Round Table Conferences and the End of the Movement

The abortion was very early, for it came in the execution of the very first proposal of the Pact; the holding of a Round Table Conference in London. Interest in it was confined almost wholly to the well-intentioned busybodies who were always trying to reconcile irreconcilables. It is now known that Mahatma Gandhi hesitated to go till almost the last moment. But in the end he went and arrived in London at the beginning of September 1931. My mind at that time was given to the revolutionary movement in Bengal, and I virtually ignored the Round Table Conference. But I read the reports, and could see that all the cranks who could be reckoned on to muster around Gandhi in London did so. There were the Dissenters, including Quakers. There was also as Gandhi's Chief of Staff, an ex- Anglican, who had contrived to make himself hated by the Establishment. He was C. F. Andrews, who can be regarded as the most feeble-minded of all well-intentioned men ever created by Nature or God. He had become something like a rope entangled round the legs of a horse or cow in respect of both Gandhi and Tagore. Gandhi's hostess in London was Miss Muriel Lester, a Quakeress, who ran a Community Centre in Bow, a suitably plebeian district. She provided the goat which was to supply milk to Gandhi. I wondered what sort of goat it was, and afterwards saw its photograph in India.

What amused me most in connection with Gandhi's visit to London was the popular print in gorgeous colours which I saw hanging in every grocer's shop. It depicted his entertainment by King George V and Queen Mary in Buckingham Palace. He was shown in a dining-room hung with gilt- framed pictures of the type found in wealthy merchant homes in India, and on the dining table a gold fruitstand on which there stood a pyramid of all kinds of Indian fruit. There were plates of gold, on one of which the Queen was offering fruit to a smiling Gandhi, in his familiar clothes. Both the King and the Queen were in their full regalia, wearing their crowns. I now regret that I did not buy and keep a copy of the picture. But, though not so intoxicated with my new nationalistic sentiment as to lose my sense of humour, I was at that time too reverential to Gandhi not to think that to keep such a picture would be rather cynical.

The Round Table Conference came to nothing, as all but those who thought that they could square the circle knew beforehand, and Gandhi returned to India even before the second session of the Conference formally came to an end on 2 December 1931. But the three sessions of the Round Table Conference left behind volumes of reports which stand in an impressive array on the shelves of the libraries specializing in Indian history, and specialists on British Indian history study them with the same reverence as students of theology show towards the Patristic texts. I have already set down my view of the immense accumulation of papers left behind by the dying British Empire in India and shall not repeat my expression of disdain for it. But what I find difficult to understand is that the historians of the last days of the Empire should include all these discussions among the historical events which should have a place in any history of the period. That to my mind suggests the little girl who was always saying 'We are seven', although two of the children were buried in the churchyard. Or rather, the inclusion of these feeble bouts of talking brings to my mind the fancy of a Bengali lady known to me by report in counting her children. She had many miscarriages but would never allow the foetuses to be taken away; she kept them in spirit in jars to include them among her living children by showing them to visitors. The academics include the various conferences and commissions, etc., among the events of Indian history exactly in the same way, for properly speaking all of them were miscarriages. I wish to emphasize here that *not one* move or initiative from the British side from 1919 to 1946 to solve the Indian problem – namely, the. Government of India Act of 1919, the Simon Commission, the Round Table Conferences, the Government of India act of 1935, the Cripps Mission of 1942, and the Cabinet Mission of 1946, to mention only the outstanding ones – succeeded in doing anything.

Mahatma Gandhi returned to India with the intention of resuming the Civil Disobedience Movement. Jawaharlal Nehru, who had bitterly resented the suspension, wanted to do so even before Gandhi's return so as to face him with a *fait accompli*. He wanted to exploit the agrarian grievances of the U.P. That showed how little understanding he had of the peasants or of the nationalist movement. Some foolish young historians of that epoch in India have presented statistics of agrarian discontent to show what a revolt Nehru could have brought about if he had not been arrested at the end of December 1931. They have never considered that in an agricultural country like India agrarian discontent has been perpetual, but it has never produced any peasant uprising. Only race hatred has. In any case, even if the peasants had their grievances they did nothing after the arrests of Nehru and of Gandhi and his lieutenants. It was a repetition of the course of events in 1922.

Actually, the suspension earlier in the year in accordance with the Gandhi-Irwin Pact, had taken the wind out of the movement. People had gone back to their usual passivity. Thus there were only some feeble demonstrations after the arrests, and then the whole movement petered out. As it happened, two of my younger brothers, the fifth and the sixth, decided to join these demonstrations as the last duty towards nationalism. I myself was feeling very guilty that I had not joined the movement actively. Therefore I approved of their decision, in order to do my duty by proxy.

On 26 January my brothers went and joined the Independence Day demonstrations, which were very feeble, and were arrested. I saw my fifth brother being taken by the police to the Amherst Street police station, uttering *Vande Mataram* in a low voice, as if he was saying his prayers. I did not see my youngest brother arrested. But the next day I went to the court and saw both of them sentenced to six months' imprisonment for only shouting *Vande Mataram* at two street comers. My elder brother, the lawyer, was also present and he saw to it that our brothers were classified as second-class prisoners, so as not to be placed with the lowest convicts. But as all the political prisoners were put in a special jail at Dum Dum this meant very little in practice. I heard that my brothers refused to have special treatment away from their fellow-prisoners.

Within the next few weeks political peace was established all over India, and there was no resumption of agitation till 1942. The complete absence of response during that long period to all attempts to rouse them, which the general population exhibited, baffled some of the leaders, and they closely scrutinized the rise and fall of prices in India to find out if they could exploit economic discontent. This futile interest in statistics amused me in the case of a very well-known Bengali leader.

This again demonstrated the nature of the forces driving the nationalist movement, which the young Indian historians who are writing about it do not seem to understand. They try to represent it as a planned and continuous movement for national independence, and glorify the active phases as acts of rebellion brought about by the volition of the leaders. The nationalist movement was no such thing. It was like those destructive natural phenomena which can never be predicted, such as volcanic eruptions, earthquakes, and cyclones. All that is certain is that the possibility of a revolt is always there, and nothing more.

Only one thing never slept, and that was the all-pervading hatred of British rule. But that too never rumbled, never gave voice to itself It was continuous like the beating of the waves of the sea on a rocky or sandy shore, but without the plangency. I was always aware of its existence, as if

I was laying my ears on the ground to hear its sound. But that did not bring the eternal note of sadness into my mind, because it suggested to me nothing more than

> ... the turbid ebb and flow
> of human misery.

The British writers on this period of history are also making their own mistakes. They are giving their minds to a perfectly pointless discussion of the abilities of the Viceroys who held office during this period; whether Irwin was better than Willingdon, and so on. I have read that Hailey did not think much of Willingdon and that Geoffrey Dawson, the editor of *The Times*, expressed his contempt for Willingdon, comparing him with his predecessor. Of course, it has now been seen as a truth of history that anything that *The Times* under Dawson recommended could only harm Great Britain. But it may also be asked in what way was Willingdon inferior to Irwin? By that time only two courses were open to the supreme representative of Britain in India: first, to crush every nationalist agitation, or to quit India. Since the second course was not even entertained for a moment as a possibility, Willingdon did the only thing possible. Or perhaps it would be more correct to say that he held firm until the nationalist movement lost its momentum. What was wrong with British policy was that it had nothing positive to offer. Thus, finally, what was bound to happen, that which was not even imagined to be possible, happened in 1947. The man who submitted to that necessity has been represented as a great statesman. If generalship was judged by the same criterion Napoleon's greatest achievement should be his ordering the retreat from Moscow. But those who are under no compulsion to seek consolation for national failure in myths and retain some common sense, would use much plainer English to describe the withdrawal in 1947. It was *ratting*, nothing more, nothing less.

CHAPTER 3

The Bengali Revolutionary Movement

In order to give an unbroken account of the Gandhian civil disobedience of 1930-32 in the last chapter, I disregarded chronology and said nothing about a parallel explosion of nationalist passion, which occurred even before the Gandhian movement reached its peak. That came from the Bengali revolutionary movement. I was wholly absorbed in the day-to-day unfolding of the Gandhian agitation and also practically engaged in producing the pictorial supplement for *The Modern Review* when, opening my newspaper *The Statesman* on the morning of 19 April, I came upon a sensational item of news. I read that in the previous night a large band of Bengali revolutionaries had raided the armoury of the Auxiliary Force (the British wing of the Territorial Army in India) at Chittagong, a large town in southeast Bengal, killed a British sergeant, and made off with a large quantity of small arms. Furthermore it was reported that the news of the raid was received in Calcutta by wireless from a ship which was in the harbour almost at the same time that the raid had begun and that at once a contingent of the Eastern Frontier Rifles, a paramilitary force of Gurkhas trained exactly like the regular infantry, had been ordered to Chittagong. It was also stated that the force had left Calcutta by an early train and was likely to reach Chittagong early in the morning of the 20th. In addition, I read that the Surma Valley Light Horse, a cavalry regiment of the Auxiliary Force, had been ordered to move into the Tipperah Hill Tract to intercept the raiders should they try to escape into that hilly and wooded region.

Never before had a revolutionary attack of this magnitude been mounted by the Bengali revolutionaries. Naturally, it created an immense sensation. It made a profound impact on the British community in Calcutta and also on the Bengali middle class. But in spite of my emotional involvement in the nationalist agitation I was not elated by the news. I was horrified and felt very anxious. I knew too much about military matters to think that any armed insurrection could be carried out by Bengalis, or to ignore what the armed forces could do against any such attempt. I shall presently relate what I thought of any such attempt before this event and also what opinion I formed of the attack at Chittagong. That morning my mind only dwelt on what was likely to happen to the Hindu inhabitants of Chittagong when the Gurkhas arrived, and it was full of the worst misgivings. As I became acquainted with the details in the next few days, I became more and more convinced that the attack was an act of mad folly. But before I say anything more about this particular incident and the other revolutionary outrages which followed I would give a resumé of the movement.

Antecedents

I do not think there is any other Bengali living today except myself who has seen the entire Bengali revolutionary movement from its beginnings in 1907, has followed its course at first hand, clearly remembers all the important events, and is capable of giving a balanced historical view of it. I have described the spirit of the earlier phases of the movement in the first instalment of my autobiography. Here I shall set down the story of its revival.

All those who were in prison, detention, or internment before 1919 had been released when the Montagu-Chelmsford reforms were being introduced, and among them were some relatives, friends and acquaintances of mine. After that no revolutionary activity was seen from 1919 to the end of 1923. But there was a sensational revival on 12 January 1924, when an Englishman named Day was shot dead on Chowringhee Road. The assailant was a young Bengali named Gopinath Saha. He was trying to kill the Commissioner of Police of Calcutta, Charles Tegart, and had mistaken Day for him. Day was only an employee of a mercantile firm, and had no connection with the Government. Saha was caught, tried, and hanged on I March 1924. It was quick work on the part of the British administration.

I was shocked by the outrage and thought it was both senseless and morally wrong. But there was a strange political sequel to it. Political assassination and the open nationalist agitation had been parallel phenomena since 1897, in which year a British civil servant and a British military officer were murdered at Poona. But never did the Congress or any other open political organization approve of or praise such deeds. On the contrary, their invariable practice was to condemn all murders in very strong language. Whatever the degree of sympathy for those who resorted to violence, there never was any publicly expressed sympathy for them when they were punished.

This time the Bengal Congress declared itself formally on the side of Gopinath Saha. At the provincial conference held at Sirajganj a resolution was adopted on 1 June 1924, which as a matter of form disassociated the

Congress from all violence and reasserted the principle of non-violence as enjoined by Mahatma Gandhi, but which also put on record that the Conference 'appreciates Gopinath Saha's ideal of self-sacrifice, misguided though it was in respect of the country's interests, and expresses its respect for his great self-sacrifice.' The man who led the discussion to adopt this resolution was C. R. Das, the foremost Bengali nationalist leader who had become an adherent of the Gandhian doctrine of non-violence in 1920.

There was at once a loud outcry among the British community that the Congress was a supporter of political assassination. Mahatma Gandhi was scandalized, and himself spoke for a new resolution before the All India Congress Committee, when it met on 29 June 1924. It regretted the death of Mr Day, offered condolences to his family, and unequivocally condemned political murders. But C. R. Das moved an amendment, by which the expression of sympathy for Gopinath Saha as embodied in the Bengal resolution was to form part of the Congress resolution. In the voting Das's amendment was lost. But the voting was significant. Seventy members of the All India Congress Committee voted for him and seventy-eight against. Unconditional non-violence won only by eight votes.

Not less significant were certain words used by C. R. Das. He said that if the Congress had any sympathy for the sentiment of Bengal they should all vote unanimously for his amendment. In plain words, he commited Bengal to political violence in its lowest form, political murder. In this Das and the Bengalis had the support of the delegation from Maharashtra, where political murder had begun. Dr Paranjyape, a veteran leader and one of the first Indian Senior Wranglers from Cambridge, said sarcastically that Mahatma Gandhi was indeed one of the many saints of India, but he was trying to ram his saintliness down the throats of his less saintly countrymen.

Mahatma Gandhi took his victory by only eight votes as a defeat, and wrote strongly about his feeling. He said that those who spoke in favour of Das's amendment had room for political murder in their philosophy and had argued that the philosophy which accepted violence was the common philosophy of all civilized nations. He declared that it was a false philosophy and had failed everywhere. He talked even of leaving the Congress.

From this date began the alienation of Bengal from the Gandhian nationalism, which finally inflicted irreparable harm on Bengal, and from which the Bengali people are still suffering. The anti-Bengali feeling in Mahatma Gandhi increased with the years, and made him indifferent even to the real injustice inflicted on Bengal from 1932 onwards. Yet the irony of the situation was that the Bengalis could neither accept Gandhi nor resist him. They fell between two stools. I shall have to tell that miserable story.

At this point I shall explain their infatuation with violence. It had very deep origins, and these lay in the first instance in religion. The Bengali Hindus belonged to two schools of Hinduism, the Saktas, or those who worshipped power in the Mother Goddess, and the Vaishnavas, or those who were followers of Krishna, and practised non-violence. Now, the higher castes of Bengalis who were the social element behind nationalism, were overwhelmingly Sakta and therefore no believers in non-violence. They even despised Vaishnava non-violence, and all the more so because the Vaishnavas of Bengal were overwhelmingly traders. Even those upper-caste Bengalis who had lost their Hindu beliefs retained the psychological predisposition. The followers of Gandhi in Bengal were mostly Vaishnavas, to whom his doctrines would naturally appeal.

With that predisposition there was combined a later psychological acquisition: the militaristic outlook the Bengalis of upper castes acquired from their reading of European history. Even Frenchmen were not greater worshippers of Napoleon. I also imbibed that militarism. But while my militarism made me a serious student of war and of military history, and finally made me not only condemn but even despise political murder as a degradation of the military spirit, the Bengali gentlefolk in their half-baked militarism identified it with political terrorism, which they began to glorify. Their basic fallacy was to equate killing in war with killing by stealth, because they had never been truly warlike. The soldier kills as a matter of duty, and equally accepts the risk of being killed. The political murderer does not. This made a fundamental difference between a soldier's moral position and the terrorist's.

I had never confused the latter with the former, and this view of militarism was confirmed in me by what a Dogra, who had been in the 41st Dogra Regiment of the Indian Army and had fought in Mesopotamia, told me one day in 1929. He showed me a wound on his hand which he had received when crawling out from his trench to save his British officer. I said: 'You might have lost your life.' He replied with perfect simplicity, which was without any trace of self-consciousness: 'Sahib, those who die find release, and it is those who live that suffer.' I at once understood what Hindu militarism was, and recognized that I was speaking to a warrior and not a murderer. I had also never admitted die specious Bengali doctrine that the end justified the means. My disapproval of violence in politics was also due to the knowledge that Bengali violence would be invariably feeble and ineffectual. I was not ready to admit that a set of feckless young men would become effectual simply because they had become hysterical. I have not been proved mistaken by the entire history of the Bengali revolutionary movement.

But even the callow militarism of the Bengali did not support the movement for long, although it had begun with the idea that terrorism was only a preliminary to a general military rebellion. Within a decade from its beginning in 1907 Bengali violence in politics was integrated with the Bengali violence in social life. The Bengali gentry were given to a sort of blood feud resembling the vendetta of the Corsicans. They did not indeed kill themselves, but they got the relatives against whom they had any grievance murdered by hired assassins, and the sense of grievance was most often a passion carried to boiling point by long brooding. The vendetta was between families as well as individuals.

In the late Twenties my brother-in-law (my sister's husband), who was a wealthy landowner, told me that he never rode back to his village when he came to the subdivisional town on business, mostly legal, if it became dark before he could re-start, although the distance was only seven miles. When I asked him the reason, he replied that there was a vendetta on (he used the Bengali equivalent of the word), and there were very convenient marshes by the roadside. I had ridden on that road and had seen the marshes. But the strange thing was that the man to whom he attributed the murderous intention was an elderly and very wealthy relative, whom I had met, talked to, and found to be a most amiable Bengali gentleman. But the feuds were wholly irrational in their cruelty, fears, and persistence.

Young men of the higher class when insulted by men of lower classes often felt maddened and became murderers themselves. The brother-in- law of a first cousin of mine was one day insulted by a man who may have been his tenant. He nursed his grievance and when a month or so later he heard that the same man had come to a feast in another house in the village, he went there and killed the offender with a spear as the man was eating. As long as the fit is on them the Bengalis with a sense of grievance remained possessed as if with an evil spirit. The young man was sentenced to transportation for life.

The young Bengali terrorists only carried this social tradition into the political sphere, and as long as they remained revolutionaries they also were like possessed men. They developed the grievance against their British rulers from the age of fourteen or so and remained, so far as the British were concerned, in a state of insane vengefulness. It was only necessary to put a pistol or a bomb in their hands to make them set out to murder an Englishman. By the Thirties another sinister development had taken place. Bengali girls began to come into the movement, and they became even more hysterical in their hatred.

These young men and women never suspected their real mental condition, and never realized what an ineffectual political method terrorism was. Their minds were indoctrinated by European theories of political assassination. The Bengalis had read about the Carbonari, Nihilists, and Anarchists in Europe, and in the Twenties they had become fanatical admirers of the Irish terrorists, whom they almost worshipped. The success of the Irish in securing independence for their country by this method made them think that they too would succeed. They never could imagine that the Irish terrorist was a mad dog which could bite, while they went mad only to be killed. I have now come to the conclusion that terrorism is really a mental disease arising out of nationalism. It can with perfect truth be described as political rabies, and nothing is easier to contract if highly strung people acquire a political grievance. But the Bengali revolutionary's proneness to the disease was not accompanied by any capacity for action as above all in the Irish. I once wrote that the Bengali revolutionary spouting his ferocity was as grotesque as a bloodthirsty sheep.

To this proneness to violence, the Bengalis added another penchant, worship of authoritarianism in government. All my life I have been hearing the exclamation from them: 'We want a dictator.' Thus as soon as Mussolini emerged in 1922, Bengali intellectuals showed themselves as his great admirers and as equal admirers of Fascism. I heard Bengalis educated at Oxford, Cambridge and London speak with enthusiasm of the march on Rome. In the early Thirties a great Bengali scholar, and one of my most respected friends, told me how uplifted above the commonplace he had felt when he heard Italians on their way to Eritrea in a ship which was passing his near the Suez Canal, shouting: 'Il Duce, il Duce.' What a contrast that was, he said, to the womanizing Frenchmen on the streets of Paris. I, on the contrary, almost despised Fascism, and regarded Mussolini from the very first as a poseur and a fraud. I have reason to think that some Bengali intellectuals were paid by the Fascists.

The admiration and enthusiasm for Mussohni and his Fascists was only transferred to Hitler and his Nazis, but in a more exalted form. Even in 1929 or 1930 I published a story in Bengali in *Prabasi*, which was entitled '*Hitlerite*', and written by a Bengali who had a German doctorate. It was written in a very crudely theatrical style. The enthusiasm for Hider grew, and at that time we did not know what Hider's opinion of British rule in India was, because we had only the bowdlerized translation into English of *Mein Kampf*. But my doctor brother who returned from Germany at the end of 1931 had the German edition with him, and he told me about that. I got the passages translated by him, and published them in *The Modern Review*.

I was very unhappy at what I saw of the resurgence of the revolutionary movement in Bengal and even angry, and what I heard by the middle of 1929 made me very anxious. The information was given to me by a friend. He was one of the contributors to the *Sanibarer Chithi*, with whom I had become quite intimate. His name was Gopal Haldar. He was a contemporary of Sajani Das, who had introduced him to me. He was a student of philology, had come to Calcutta to become a writer and perhaps also with political ambition after giving up his lecturership in Feni College. At that time he was completing a thesis on a dialect of the Bengali language, and was also looking after a monthly magazine edited by Ashoke Babu. For our magazine he had written some witty articles, and I found him to be a very quiet and level-headed young man. But he was already involved in some way with the revolutionary movement. Later, he was detained without trial. Finally, he became a Communist, and after independence a member of the Bengal legislature. He published some books, and was respected as a writer in Bengal.

One day he came to me and told me of a plan that was afoot to bring about a concerted uprising in the districts all over Bengal, and also that arms had been collected for this purpose. He did not tell me when this was to be. But I felt so alarmed that I spoke to Ramananda Babu about this and requested him to write a warning editorial on the folly of attempting any such thing. I remember that he did write an editorial note in *Prabasi*. The Chittagong raid was obviously part execution of the plan, but there were no other uprisings. I have now to tell the story of the failure at Chittagong and all that it brought in the way of suffering for the Hindus of that town.

The Chittagong Raid

The raid has been described even by some British writers, who were present in India at the time, as a neatly executed affair. But it was neither efficiently planned, nor neatly executed except for the initial surprise. It is on record, however, that the Government of India was not very much upset, and they were certainly right. I should think that the British administration would have liked die whole nationalist movement to take an insurrectionary form, because that would have enabled them to suppress it easily and to justify the suppression. It was Gandhian non-violence, which really was the wolf in sheep's clothing, that presented a difficult moral problem.

There were much more serious disturbances on the north-west frontier. The Pathans even gained temporary control of Peshawar. But the situation was brought quickly under control by the army. In contrast, in Chittagong, after a one-sided shooting by the Gurkhas at long range, the police alone were able to deal quite effectively with the revolutionary activity. Actually, there were no further attacks at Chittagong except one murder, and the Hindus were subjected to collective fines, imposition of punitive police, and strict surveillance.

But it is not easy to give a true account of the affair. The Chittagong raid has been made into a Bengali myth both by word of mouth as well as in writing. This is quite characteristic. From 1920 onwards the Bengali lead in Indian nationalist politics had been declining, and by 1930 it had disappeared altogether except for terrorism. Therefore, glorification of that, however ineffectual and harmful it might have been, had to come and its legend as well as the apologia for Bengali failure. No other set of people in India are able to console themselves more easily with illusions. Thus the Chittagong raid has naturally taken its place in the apology. With a number of other failures it supplies emotional compensation to the Bengalis.

Even at the time I came to the opinion that as a military insurrection, which it was intended to be, nothing could be more mismanaged. First and foremost, the plan was not kept secret. As it happened, by the evening of the 19th, when no further details had come to Calcutta, I came to know who were involved in it, including the name of the leader, who was Ananta Singh, as well as the fact that his Baby Austin was there. All this information I got from a brother of one of the raiders, who was a fellow- student with one of my brothers at Jadabpur Engineering College. He lived in the hostel, but fearing that he might be arrested that night – in fact the police went for him – he asked for shelter in our house in north Calcutta. My elder brother, the advocate, was at Dacca, and so I as the master of the house agreed. He gave me the details, and since I got them even in Calcutta the police could well have possessed them at Chittagong.

I asked him how the raiders could be so foolish as to attempt such a thing when a ship was in the port, for it was bound to send the news to Calcutta by wireless, even though the telegraph lines had been cut. He gave me the extraordinary reply that the plot had become known to the police, and in a day or two all the prominent conspirators would have been arrested, and so the attack had to be brought forward. But to what end.' - I wondered.

What followed showed that there was no clear conception of what was to be done after the initial raid. The authorities and, more especially, the British community of course said that the idea was to occupy the town and massacre all the Europeans. But nothing like that was attempted. The revolutionaries scattered and moved out of the town in their attempt to escape. The District Magistrate of Chittagong behaved with great courage and presence of mind. Faced with an insurrection of as yet undisclosed magnitude, he arrived at once on the scene, after having ordered all British women and children to the ship, and found none of the raiders. He manned the Lewis gun which had not been taken away. In fact, not even rifles and rifle ammunition had been taken. The revolutionaries took away only the .450 Webley-Scott service revolvers, which was quite consistent with their terroristic ideas. They probably thought that they would be able to lie low with their weapons and carry on their secret activities.

I could not have imagined that an insurrection could be so incoherently planned. Knowing a good deal about Pathan raids on the frontier, I compared this raid with them, and more especially with the raid on the military post at Tut Narai in Waziristan, which was carried out with masterly efficiency and spectacular success. The young men of Chittagong had not even made arrangements for provisions in case they had to remain hidden in the jungles. A *seer* (just over two pounds) of pressed rice and a lump of molasses would have kept each of them alive for many days, and that could be carried in a small bag. So, they had to send for food in the town. Two young men came to a Muslim bakery and ordered about fifty loaves. The baker at once became suspicious. He asked the young men to wait and sent for the police. When the latter arrived, they ran for cover into a drain, where they were shot like mad dogs. One of the young men was the younger brother of the student to whom I was giving shelter. I kept the news from him.

Since there was no resistance in the town there were no killings and reprisals at Chittagong as I had feared. But something hardly less tragic happened. A large party of the revolutionaries were found on a hill near Hat Hazari, north of Chittagong, and the Gurkhas picked them off from another hill. The raiders had no long-range weapons to reply. They did not have the good sense even to take cover on the other side of the hill, which anyone with any military experience would have done. The dead bodies were all photographed for identifications, and copies of the photographs were privately supplied by the photographer to Bengali families, and I myself saw a large bundle, which was brought to the *Prabasi* office. It was a most painful experience to look on the dead faces, and since the heads had been shaved some silly fools even told the story that these were photographs of the Gurkhas who had been killed by the revolutionaries. I could easily see that they were of Bengali young men.

Now, ever since the revolutionary movement had started, we had got into the habit of acquiring photographs of those who were hanged or killed and of keeping them as mementos. So, sets of the Chittagong photographs were in circulation in Calcutta. For the sake of safety they were put in charge of girls, and my future wife, who was at college then, was asked to keep a set in her trunk because she had no political associations. The girl who asked her was in the movement. But my wife refused. I learned all that after my marriage in 1932.

The conduct of the young man to whom I had given shelter was very irresponsible. He compromised us by writing letters in secret to the revolutionaries who were in Calcutta. One day, suddenly, three girls arrived at our house and asked to see the young man. One of the girls was the one who had asked my future wife to keep the photographs. She looked a dour and fanatical little doll. When I asked her if she knew of the death of the brother of the young man, she said quite calmly that she did. I asked her not to mention it, but I think she did, for she was not the sort of person to regret such a death. Another girl was the daughter of one of the leading advocates of Calcutta High Court, who was also a popular novelist. From the giggles I heard behind closed doors I wondered how much of the discussion was revolutionary and how much flirtatious. The European combination of love and terrorism was being taken over, but fortunately it has not survived.

After seeing such absence of consideration for those who were giving him shelter, I thought I could not allow the young man to stay on in our house without serious risk at least for my brother, who was his friend. So, I told him that I would take him away to a house which he would not know. Afterwards I learned that the police had traced him to our house, but were leaving him at large to be able to trace other revolutionaries through his letters and movements. Finally he was arrested.

I spoke to a relative of mine who was an employee of the Government of India in one of its offices in Calcutta, and he agreed to keep the young man. After that one evening I sent for a hackney carriage, put him into it, put up the shutters, and took him to that house. There too he behaved in exactly the same way, and jeopardized my relative. He was sent away. Nonetheless, the political police called my relative and asked him why he had given shelter to a revolutionary. He pleaded complete ignorance of that, and said that he thought the young man was temporarily without accommodation. The police only warned him to leave Calcutta unless he wanted to court trouble. He got himself transferred to upper India and did not return to Bengal for nearly twenty years.

The search for the Chittagong revolutionaries continued, and all of those who survived were finally caught. The absconders could not remain in the Chittagong region or even in East Bengal, where they were likely to be reported to the police by the Muslims. Therefore they tried to come to Calcutta. Two young men were almost caught at Noakhali railway station and escaped capture by firing from their pistols. Four succeeded in reaching the town of Chandernagore, which was French colonial territory, by taking a devious route through Sylhet and Shillong. They stayed in a villa for some time and were supplied with money by the revolutionary party in Calcutta as well as some front rank political leaders.

But the police in Calcutta came to know of their refuge, and one night in September the Commissioner of Police of Calcutta, Sir Charles Tegart himself, violated French territory to capture them. The refugees were surrounded, and one of them was shot dead when he jumped into a pond. Of those captured, one was a fourteen-year-old boy. He was finally sentenced to life transportation, was released from the Andamans in 1940 and kept interned till 1946. He now lives in London with his wife, who is the first cousin of my eldest daughter-in-law. There was no place for him and his wife in India after independence. But Britain gave him employment. When there was some virtuous indignation in England after the Israeli raid in Beirut I wrote a letter to the British press on the British raid into French territory. But the letter was not published.

The greatest sensation of the pursuit of the Chittagong revolutionaries was that their leader, Ananta Singh, himself went to the headquarters of the political police in Calcutta and surrendered. I heard from police sources that when his name was taken in there was consternation, and the police officers came armed. Ananta was sentenced to life transportation, but was released at the time of independence.

I asked Gopal Haldar why instead of going underground and continuing his activities, Ananta had done that. His reply was equivalent to saying that there was no underground to go into. The Chittagong raiders at large were being hunted like beasts of prey which had strayed into human habitation. The Muslims gave information about all suspicious-looking strangers. Not even Hindus would give them shelter for fear of becoming politically suspect and harming their worldly prospects. The strain of even getting food for the day was unbearable. Thus they preferred surrendering to the British.

I might set down here what happened in our family. My elder brother on his return from Dacca was seriously annoyed when he learned what had happened in his absence. He did not say anything to me, but severely scolded the brother who had brought in the young man. When coming back from work I found him standing at a street corner near our house and in tears. He said that my elder brother had turned him out of the house. I, of course, took him back and no questions were asked. This sort of thing happened with all the revolutionaries as long as British rule lasted. People who were not already compromised politically would have nothing to do with political suspects. They were, of course, all in sympathy with the terrorists, but from a safe distance. This was the great difference between the Irish and the Bengalis who thought that they were the Sinn Fein of India. Their eagerness to identify themselves with the terrorists after independence ceemed even more disgraceful to me.

There was, however, one incident which redeemed the miserable Chittagong raid, so far as such a fiasco could be redeemed. One young girl being pursued had taken shelter in a house near Chittagong with a young man. They were surprised there and surrounded by the police. In normal circumstances Bengali terrorists surrendered even with revolvers in their hand. But the girl tried to fight her way out and was shot dead with her companion. Her name was Priti Ohdedar.

In all thirty-two young men were put up for trial, and after a prolonged trial eleven of them were transported for life to the Andaman Islands. Among them was the fourteen-year old boy captured at Chandernagore. One got a light sentence, another boy was sent to Borstal. The rest were acquitted but detained under special laws.

In this case die British administration did not act in any inhuman or vindictive manner. Only an elderly revolutionary who had planned the raid was arrested in a different connection and after a trial was hanged. His name was Surya Sen. But this did not end the story of Chittagong. Collectively, the Hindus of the town became politically suspect and had to suffer more, for which they remained bitterly anti-British till the end of British rule. But independence only made their fate worse. Chittagong became part of the new Muslim state created by the partition of India in 1947, and most of the Hindus of that region migrated to West Bengal to become expatriates.

More Revolutionary Outrages

The Chittagong raid was followed by many more revolutionary outrages, some quite sensational. On 25 August 1930 two young men tried to kill Sir Charles Tegart, the Commissioner of Police of Calcutta, by throwing a bomb at his car on the south side of Dalhousie Square. Tegart was unhurt, but one of the assailants was found to be fatally wounded and he died when being taken to hospital. The other was caught by a Sikh taxi-driver, who though unarmed went after the terrorists. This man was tried and sentenced to life transportation. Four days later, on the 29th to be precise, Lowman, who was the chief of the Bengal political police, was shot at Dacca, where he had gone on a tour of inspection. He was brought to Calcutta, but died. Another police officer named Hodson, who as a young man had been at Kishorganj, my native town, was also shot at the same time but recovered. The assailant was not caught, but a young revolutionary who was supposed to have shot Lowman died miserably in Calcutta later in the year in an incident which is next on my list.

This was a sensational murder on 8 December 1930, and in Writers'

Building itself, the headquarters of the Government of Bengal. Three revolutionaries got into the building and killed the Inspector-General of Prisons in Bengal, Colonel N. F. Simpson, of the Indian Medical Service. His offence was only that he was in charge of the prisons. I was very much distressed by this murder because only a few days before this incident I had spoken to him over the telephone about a political prisoner.

This I did impersonating Satyendra Chandra Mitra, a member of the Central Legislative Assembly and a prominent Congress man of Bengal, according to his direction. It was my friend Gopal Haldar who involved me in this. He had established a mixed relationship with an egregious and absurd political woman of Bengal, named Bimal Prativa Devi. She belonged to a wealthy family, was the wife of a doctor, and in ail her photographs published in the press was shown as a young woman with some pretension to looks and wearing a diamond tiara. But I heard all sorts of reports about her revolutionary as well as amatory propensity, and myself once saw a demonstration. I met her in her house more than once, and she seemed to be very high-strung, although always smiling. Gopal Babu, who took me to meet her somehow developed a sort of infatuation for her, which made me grumble that I saw no merit in becoming Jude the Obscure. Her extremely neurotic temperament helped her in getting released from prison, for detention invariably made her ill and she showed clear symptoms of tuberculosis by vomiting blood. These disappeared as soon as she became free. The letters which she was allowed to send from prisons to her young friends provided considerable amusement to the police officers who had to censor them, by their frankness. Some were addressed to Gopal Babu and I heard some very explicit passages quoted.

Now she was in prison and had become very ill as usual. Gopal Babu on hearing it got frightened and asked Mr Satyen Mitra whom he knew very well to speak to Colonel Simpson to consider her case. Mr Mitra in his turn asked me to speak to the Colonel on the telephone, as if it was he who spoke. I did, and Colonel Simpson was very courteous and sympathetic and said that he would do whatever he could. Therefore I was very much grieved to hear of his death in that manner.

The whole incident was grotesquely tragic. Three young men had gone into Writers' Building, and asked for an interview with Simpson. Getting in, they shot him dead. There was panic in the whole Building, and most people ran for shelter. There were no armed guards, and word was sent to

Lal Bazar police headquarters. The police contingent took some time to arrive, and in the meanwhile the terrorists might have escaped and if necessary fought their way out with their revolvers. Actually, however, they chose to take potassium cyanide. When the police arrived, they crawled along the walls of the corridor, with their pistols cocked. But they found the three young men lying unconscious. Two were already dead, and one of them was a young man named Binoy Bose, who was supposed to have shot Lowman. The third was living, and he was taken to a hospital to be treated. His name was Dinesh Gupta. He recovered, was tried for murder, and hanged on 7 July 1931. The prisoner of hatred whom potassium cyanide had spared was overtaken by the rope. When under trial he sent a story which was a satire on the police and an adaptation of a story by Tolstoy to the *Prabasi*, which I published. The police themselves had passed it. The episode was as much a joke on the part of the police as of Dinesh Gupta.

On 14 December 1930 the District Magistrate of Comilla, whose name was Stevens, was murdered by two young girls. They were students, two sisters, and their names were Santi and Suniti. They were given life transportation. Soon after, our house was searched by the police. Arriving home after five in the afternoon, I found a policeman standing at the door, allowing people to go in but not to come out. Going in, I found a police inspector with more policemen conducting a search. It was for Gopal Babu, and was due to an indiscretion of his. Some months before, his father with his family had become our sub-tenant. The house was large, and the rent rather high. So, we had sub-let it. Now, Gopal Babu himself was suspect, but he had given his address with a sketch map of its location and of our house to a revolutionary on the list of the police, who was a young friend of Bimal Prativa Devi. This young man's rooms had been searched that morning. He was arrested with the revolver which was under his pillow, and there was the sketch map.

The police did not wait for the next morning, but came straight to our house in the afternoon to search Gopal Babu's rooms. They were also likely to search ours, and my anxiety was about some confidential military books which were on my shelves. I went into my room, which was also my library, and at first thought of hiding the books behind the other books. But I knew that the police always put their hand behind rows of books. So, when they were busy in the other rooms I scratched out the printed word 'secret' with a safety razor blade, and since there was no lettering on their backs I put them back in the front row with the other books. The Inspector duly passed his hand behind the rows of books, but did not notice anything special about these books. Gopal was taken away for interrogation and came back only the next day, very much shaken. He wanted to send an urgent message to Bimal Prativa, but did not think it advisable to go himself. I had to go instead and see her. She had been released, and seemed to be as smilingly revolutionary as ever.

On 7 April 1931, Pedie, the District Magistrate of Midnapore, was murdered, and the assailant could not be caught or even traced. On 7 July, as I have said, Dinesh Gupta was hanged, and there was a terrible reprisal. Garlick, the District Judge who had sentenced him, was shot dead in the court on the 29th. This caused a loud outcry among the British in Calcutta.

They had been breathing fire and slaughter for many months, and now let themselves go in full cry. The exhibition was, to my mind, as cowardly as it was ferocious. The chronic obsession which the British community had with the prospect of being murdered wholesale by the Natives, and which (as I have said) was a cover for their atrocious racial arrogance, now became activated into a real fear for their skins. This combination of cowardice and ferocity is always exhibited by people who live in a situation of danger without being exposed themselves to any personal risk; as for example-, by civilians during a war. The British community in India, and more especially its trading element, showed this self-generated pseudo-bellicosity.

I have no doubt that on all occasions of real danger the British officials in India would have shown themselves cool and courageous, as did the Magistrate at Chittagong. But when nothing happened even they seemed to find enjoyment in nursing their fears, although except in special cases, which could not be prevented during such a time of widespread political excitement, the police, who were Indian, could quite effectually ensure their safety. Compared with what is happening in Ireland today, the outrages in Bengal were really few in number.

But it was in Calcutta where most of the British in Bengal lived and were engaged in commerce or industry, that the noise was loudest. They barked, yapped, and snarled like frightened street dogs. They even spread the story that handkerchiefs contaminated with secretions of venereal diseases were being left on the benches of the tramcars on which the less well-paid British traders and their womenfolk travelled. If for nothing else, the report was absurd for the simple reason that no revolutionary was likely to have any access to the infecting liquid. They were all too puritanical for that. As for their love affairs to which I have alluded, though not based on sight alone like my infatuations, they were as unfleshly. The clever Bengalis on their part, especially those who were educated in England, were too cynical even to believe that the British people stood in need of Bengali revolutionaries to contract venereal disease. I have heard them repeat what must have been a stale joke in England: 'I gave it to the maid, the maid gave it to father, father gave it to mother, and mother gave it to the parson.' In any case, there were the bazaar prostitutes in India to spread venereal disease among the British in India, who did not stand in need of contaminated handkerchiefs from Bengali revolutionaries to contract it.

It was the British section of the Indian press in Calcutta which voiced this fury, and it was *The Statesman* which became the combined bass and soprano soloists of the chorus. It reminded the Bengalis of Calcutta that there were in their city ten thousand Englishmen and Scots who had seen service in the last war. At their head was a triple blue from Oxford. After the murder of Pedie at Midnapore the paper wrote that it was with difficulty that the British staff of the railway works at Kharagpur were restrained from burning down the town.

Even before that last blast of the avenging trumpet, there had been two attempts on the editor of *The Statesman*, who was Alfred Watson. He was knighted for the risk he was undergoing. But the attempts were unsuccessful and Watson lived to be ninety-one. He was, however, not the actual writer of the editorials which gave offence to the revolutionaries. The offender was a member of the editorial staff named Arthur Moore, who before he went to Calcutta was on *The Times*, and I believe had also served in the war and been educated at Oxford. He became editor after Alfred Watson, and a friend of mine who was a well-known Bengali journalist in Calcutta told me that Moore always kept a loaded revolver in his right-hand drawer. But he took the matter rather lightly, and said that it was all in the day's work. The precautions against Bengali visitors to *The Statesman* office were very strict. Another friend who at times contributed to the paper told me that when he had gone to see one of the assistant editors two Gurkha guards stood so close to him on two sides that he could hardly move his arms. These Gurkhas were always ex-servicemen. *The Statesman's* outbursts against Bengali terrorists took a line in September 1931, which made me play a role which was a slight departure from that of an outside observer. I shall now tell that story.

Intervention on Behalf of an Englishman: 1931

By the time Mr Garlick was murdered, the Government of Bengal had almost brought the campaign of terrorism under control. But there was another sensational murder on 30 August 1931 at Chittagong. A Muslim Inspector of Police named Ashanullah was shot dead. At once the Muslims of the town rose in a body and began to attack Hindu houses and loot Hindu shops. This was allowed to go on by the administration, and when the Hindus went to the Magistrate and asked for protection they were jeeringly asked to go to the Congress. It was clearly a case of reprisals by the British at secondhand, that is, by proxy. The already existing bitterness among the Hindus of Chittagong rose to a higher pitch. The Congress appointed an unofficial inquiry committee which reported severely against the district officials. The feeling against the British officials was shared by all Bengali Hindus.

Then on 14 September there followed a very deplorable incident of firing on the *détenus* at the Hijli camp near Midnapore. The Hindustani armed police who guarded the camp had been provoked by the *détenus* in many ways, as is always done by political and war prisoners. It was stated that the *détenus* had attempted to rush a gate and overpower the sentries. But after repelling the attempt the armed police got out of hand and fired among the *détenus* in the main barrack. I heard that the Hindustani police shouted in Hindi: '*Ramji mauka mila diya*' which meant that Rama, the incarnation of Vishnu who was worshipped as God, particularly as the warrior God, by the Hindustanis, had at last provided them with an opportunity. Two of the *détenus* were killed and one was a newly married man whose wife was expecting her first child. All over Bengal there was great indignation, and a Government inquiry found the policemen guilty. The bodies of the dead young men were brought to Calcutta and carried in an immense procession to the burning ghat.

A very regrettable part of the matter was that no news of the looting at Chittagong and of the shooting at Hijli was published in England, and both the incidents were played down in the British section of the Indian press. On 24 September a friend of mine sent a full report of what had happened in the Hijli camp to the *Daily Herald, the Manchester Guardian,* and some other newspapers, and also to the British news agencies. The account given in this report was substantially the same as it was in the later judicial report.

But nothing was published in England. The same thing was seen in the case of Chittagong.

Then a young Englishman took the matter in hand. His name was Christopher Ackroyd. He was a lecturer in history in St Paul's College in Calcutta, an institution run by missionaries of the Anglican Church. He came from a well-to-do family in Yorkshire, and his home was Harden Hall in the village of Harden in the Brontë country. I had met him a few months earlier, and became very friendly with him, although he was many years younger. In Calcutta he always wore the Bengali dress in handspun and loom-made khaddar. He wrote a pamphlet on the attacks on the Hindus by the Muslims at Chittagong and presented it to the members of the Calcutta Missionary Conference. There arose at once a shrill outcry from the British in Calcutta voiced by *The Statesman*. With an air of injured innocence the paper dwelt on the misdeeds and evil intentions of the Bengali terrorists and accused Ackroyd of suppressing these and singling out only the attacks of the Muslims. Actually, in so many words the newspaper and the British community in Calcutta hinted that Ackroyd was in sympathy with the terrorists. There was a fulminating editorial on the pamphlet in *The Statesman* of lo October 1931, although Ackroyd had not sent it to the paper. The paper's tone was like the usual squeals after the terroristic outrages.

A member of *The Statesman* staff, who was the local correspondent of the Observer of London, sent a report to his paper and it was pubhslied in it on 11 October 1931 under the heading 'A Missionary College and Polities'.

In it not only was Ackroyd's pamphlet referred to, but even Dr Bridge, the Principal of the College, was mentioned as a sort of accomplice of the terrorists. The report said that among a number of persons, including Bimal Prativa Devi, arrested while trying to escape after an armed raid on a shop in a car, was 'a student of St Paul's College, a Church Missionary Society institution, the head of which has been reported to the Government on a charge of interfering with the police in the execution of their duty.'

I thought I would expose all these manoeuvres in the nationalist press and sent a long letter to the *Amrita Bazar Patrika* on 4 November. It was published on the 6th under the heading 'The British Press and Indian News Suppression and Distortion of Facts'. I referred to the suppression of news about Hijli and Chittagong and to the attempt to get Ackroyd removed from his post. I wrote: 'I have good reason for believing in the strong rumour in Calcutta that besides individual Europeans, the European Association has been taking official note of Mr Ackroyd's pamphlet, and is trying to use its all-powerful influence with the Government of Bengal to get disciplinary action taken against the Professor of History in St Paul's College.' I, of course, had more than rumour to go on in saying this, as I shall explain presently. In the same letter I took up the charge against Dr Bridge in some detail and set out the real facts. I am quoting the whole passage in my letter dealing with Dr Bridge:

'On Saturday 3 October, a party of policemen under the charge of an Indian officer came into the compound of St Paul's College in order to search the rooms of Narahari Sen-Gupta, a student of the College, who was arrested on the previous night in connection with an alleged political robbery. On seeing the policemen, Dr Bridge, the Principal of St Paul's, came out and asked them what they wanted. They said that they had come to make an inventory of the belongings of Narahari Sen-Gupta. Upon this, Dr Bridge suggested if it was only to be an inventory, he would prefer, if the police officer did not object, to have the belongings of Narahari brought into his own room and make a list. On the police officer agreeing, Narahari's things were brought from the hostel to Dr Bridge's room, and the search took place in the presence of half a dozen ladies and gentlemen, both Indian and European. While the making of the inventory was proceeding, a policeman with something in his hand made repeated attempts to come near Narahari's belongings. On being asked as to what he was doing, he replied that he had brought a piece of cloth to compare it with the dhobi-mark on Narahari's clothes. The piece of cloth had blood stains on it. Dr Bridge then insisted on writing on the cloth that it had not been found with Narahari's possessions.

'No more was said on the occasion. But on Monday 5 October the Chief Commissioner of Police wrote informing Dr Bridge that he had a report before him stating that Dr Bridge had hindered the police when they came to the College to search Narahari's room. The police on Saturday emphatically stated that they had come to make an inventory and not to conduct a search. The Commissioner informed Dr Bridge that this was a breach of a section of the Indian Penal Code, and that unless he had an explanation from the latter before 11 a.m. on Tuesday 6 October, he would forward the papers to the Government. Dr Bridge replied asserting his innocence and asking for details of the charges against him, so that he could answer them. The reply of the Chief Commissioner was that the file had been forwarded to the Government of Bengal with the recommendation that the case against Dr Bridge should be allowed to take its course. Dr Bridge was not informed of the specific details of the charges against him, and these remain known only to the Chief Commissioner and possibly the Government of Bengal, from both of which nothing has been heard.'

I got all these details from the College, and I give them here in order to show what sort of a 'police state' the British rule was in its last days, when it was to all appearance being wound up. The police were not afraid to persecute even an Anglican clergyman and the principal of a well-known college.

Nothing, of course, happened to Dr Bridge, but the British community was still bent on getting Christopher Ackroyd expelled from the College. Their animus against him was unappeasable. So, I thought I would expose their moves. I had actually seen a letter written by the Provincial Branch of the European Association of India to Dr Bridge calling for action against Christopher Ackroyd. It was shown to me in confidence, and therefore I could neither copy it nor ask for a copy. But I resolved to copy it myself by burgling the rooms of the person with whom it was likely to be. I knew that this person was to dine out on a certain evening and I planned to steal into his rooms. It was a risky step, but the rooms were an adjunct to the hostel, and I thought my presence near them would not be noticed. But if I were caught it could be a police matter, or in any case be a situation extremely embarrassing both for me and the custodian of the letter. But I decided to court the risk.

It was the evening either of 4 or 5 November, and it was cold and rainy. I passed through the gates of the College and into the hostel unobserved. I also succeeded in getting into the suite of rooms without being seen. I knew that the missionaries did not normally lock their rooms. I had brought a candle and a match-box with me, because I could not light the electric lamps. I went straight to the desk in which I knew the letter would be, took it out of the drawer, lay on the floor, and copied it in the flickering light of the candle. I might say that sweat was running down my cheeks even on that cold evening. I finished the copying, listening to footsteps all the time. I succeeded in stealing out, passed through the gate where a door-keeper always sat, but suddenly discovered that I had left my fountain-pen on the floor. I had to go back, taking the same risk, but my luck held. On the 6th, after the publication of my long letter, I went with another letter to the office of the *Amrita Bazar Patrika,* and it was published the next day, i.e. the 7th. In it the letter of the European Association was reproduced in full. I give the letter with the heading which the *Patrika* gave to it:

AN AMAZING LETTER: ANOTHER FEATHER IN THE CAP OF THE EUROPEAN ASSOCIATION

To the editor,

Sir, I have to thank you for publishing my letter of 4 November. I am sending you today another example of the pretensions of the European Association. The following letter was addressed by it to the Principal of St Paul's College, Calcutta, on the subject of Mr Ackroyd's pamphlet:

'European Association,
17 Stephen Court,
Park Street,
Calcutta,
October 28, 1931

'From the Secretary,
Bengal Provincial Committee
European Association
'To
The Rev. P. G. Bridge, D. D.,
Principal, St Paul's College,
Calcutta

'Dear Sir,

'I am directed by my Committee to address you on the subject of a pamphlet entitled "Chittagong Riots" over the signature of Christopher Ackroyd, Professor of History, St Paul's College, Calcutta, and dated October 1, 1931.

'My Committee views very seriously the publication of such a pamphlet, the subject of which was, at the time of publication, a matter of official inquiry and is even now *sub judice*. Apart from this aspect, in the opinion of my Committee, Mr Ackroyd's pamphlet is both prejudiced and unfair since it is based on the findings of a self-constituted committee (some of the members of which were and are hostile to the British connection) which did not call upon any European residents or Government or Police officials to give evidence before the inquiry in order that they might have the opportunity of refuting the charges levelled against them.

'My Committee views even more seriously that Mr Ackroyd must in his capacity as Professor of History and Warden of a hostel have under his care a number of immature youths or young men who are likely to be influenced by subversive and more particularly anti-European and anti-Government teaching as is contained in the pamphlet, when it is expounded by one who is, my Committee is informed, himself of British origin.

'I am directed by my Committee to ask you to be so good as to inform my Committee whether you as Principal of St Paul's College or the Governing body have taken cognizance or propose to take action in regard to this matter.

'Yours faithfully,
'(Sd.) H. L. Walker
for Secretary
Bengal Provincial Committee

"This is an amazing letter, as amazing in its mendacity in stating that the unofficial inquiry committee on the Chittagong riots did not call upon Government and Police officials to give evidence before it, as in its attempt on the part of a "self-constituted" association of foreigners, to interfere with the freedom of opinion and speech of a private individual and the internal administration of a college. Your readers will also note that this letter is in marked agreement in sentiment with the telegram sent by Mr Villiers* to the *Daily Express* that the schools and colleges of Bengal are centres of seditious and subversive teaching, and is an attempt to dictate the educational policy of the country. In any other country, this impertinence would surely have been brushed aside without ceremony. But it is perhaps no exaggeration to say that the Government of Bengal is only a subcommittee of the European Association. I have it on reliable authority that the Director of Public Instruction, Bengal, has, apparently at the dictation of the European Association, called upon the Principal of St Paul's College to summon a meeting of the Governing Body to consider Mr Ackroyd's

* He was the President of the European Association, and there was an attempt on his life as well.

pamphlet. The purpose of this preliminary move is to make the authorities of St Paul's College either throw over Mr Ackroyd or commit themselves to this action, and thus enable the Government to take disciplinary action against the College.'

120/2 Upper Circular Road	Assistant Editor, *The Modern*
Calcutta NIRAD C. CHAUDHURI	*Review*

I have to add that Christopher Ackroyd knew nothing of my intention to write the letters, and I never consulted him about my plans. But after the publication of the last letter he said to me that he appreciated my cleverness. The European Association only inquired of Dr Bridge whether he had shown the letter or given it to any Indian. He could with perfect truth say that he had not. For he did not show it to me in the first instance, and Ackroyd certainly did not inform him about my knowledge. Nobody but myself knew how I had obtained a copy of it.

But Christopher Ackroyd was not going to be let off so mildly. The Bengal Government and the Europeans pursued the matter, and the College found it expedient to send Ackroyd to England on home leave for some months. He went away after some days, and left his gramophone and three boxes of records with me, and with them I pursued my new hobby of European music.

Before the decision to send him off was taken he was also summoned by the Metropolitan of India and the Bishop of Calcutta who bore the honoured name of Westcott, and was the head of the Anglican Church in India. I asked Ackroyd what happened at the interview. He smiled and said he had got a lecture on his unwisdom, which I understood to be a dressing down. I was not surprised at all, for it was in line with the code of conduct of the Anglican Church, which at home and even more so in India was a worshipper of power. Of course, the Roman Church was also that, but at all events it worshipped its own power; the Anglican Church was and remains subservient to temporal power in the form of king or state.

It is strange that I should write in this manner of the Anglican Church, for it is the only form of English Christianity which I admire, and I am wholly repelled by the Non-conformists and Dissenters. But I can explain my mixed attitude. The admiration is for the Catholic inheritance of the

Anglican Church and the contempt for its Protestant accretion, which is responsible for its moral turpitude and even wrong-headedness. Its members squealed against terrorism in Bengal. I saw a letter from an Anglican clergyman in Chittagong to Ackroyd which was full of bitter recriminations against his pamphlet, and also of this parson's expressions of terror at being in Chittagong and having to sleep with his revolver under his pillow. Now the same Church sends money to terrorists, because they seem to have temporal power behind them. I should add that the hostility of the Anglican Church also extended to Mahatma Gandhi at that time. In 1930 it was very critical of him. For instance. Archbishop Lang (of Canterbury) wrote to Lord Irwin on 28 June 1930 that Gandhi was a 'perverse and dangerous mixture of the mystic, the fanatic, and the anarchist'. If the pejorative suggestions were taken out of this remark, it would be wholly true, but the Archbishop intended to denounce and not to define. It was exactly like a Czarist dignitary's opinion of Tolstoy.

Suppression of the Revolutionary Movement

In Bengal the most exciting feature of these two years of political turmoil were these revolutionary outrages, and they kept all of us on tiptoe, although the Civil Disobedience of Gandhi and the Hindu-Muslim riots also claimed and got their share of attention. The excitement began to subside by the beginning of 1932. There was, however, at that time a last display of revolutionary fireworks, which dazzled but in its effect was a damp squib. Sir Stanley Jackson, the Governor of Bengal, was shot at as he was presiding over the convocation of Calcutta university as its Chancellor, on 7 February. The assailant was a young girl graduate named Bina Das, who was the daughter of a headmaster. She missed him and was caught by the Vice-Chancellor, a Muslim, who was immediately knighted. She was sentenced to nine years of imprisonment.

Sir John Anderson, who had experience of government in Ireland in the years before the treaty which made Ireland independent, succeeded Sir Stanley Jackson soon after. The Bengali middle class recalled this and feared a Black and Tan regime. But Anderson most emphatically pronounced against any policy of reprisals, which would have pleased the British community. Reassured by this the clever Bengalis, especially the barristers who had been called to the Bar from the Inns of Court, began to be facetious and called the new Governor either 'Johnny Anderson' or 'John Anderson, my Jo, John'.

But there was not much left to be done to suppress the revolutionary movement completely. This was almost completed by rounding up all suspected young men and their older leaders, and keeping them under detention without trial. The police had adopted the medical principle of prevention is better than cure. They depended on a new system of tracing the revolutionaries they had developed, which was to establish the personal connections of all known revolutionaries and arrest the whole network of terrorism. They threw their net fairly wide. But on the whole very few persons unconnected with the revolutionary movement were deprived of their freedom. The police had plenty of informers from the same class as the revolutionaries, and one could hardly be sure who might not be an informer. The police noted their reports without naming them, only recording what Deponent No. X stated. The arrests were made on the strength of concurrent reports. The revolutionaries, too, by their indiscreet correspondence implicated many.

The numbers placed under detention were many hundreds, and probably a few thousands. Those classed as the brains of the movement were sent as far as a hill fort in Rajputana. Among those detained were not only some well known figures of the open movement, but two of the highest political figures in Bengal, Sarat Chandra Bose and his younger brother, Subhas Chandra Bose. Subhas was the idol of the Bengali nationalists and had no occupation except nationalist politics, with close associations with the revolutionaries. Sarat Bose was an eminent barrister of the Calcutta High Court, but as the brother of Subhas and also his supporter, he too was very much in the know of what was going on secretly. Both of them were arrested. Sarat Bose was interned at Kurseong, a hill station near Darjeeling, and he retaliated by calling the Tibetan dog he acquired there 'Coulson', after the English police officer who became the Commissioner of Police, Calcutta, when Sir Charles Tegart retired. He was kept interned for four years, and after he had rejoined the bar and politics with his release in 1936, I became his secretary.

The detained young men were generally well-treated, although the tradition they followed of giving as much trouble as possible to the authorities at times led to deplorable consequences. These, however, were few compared with the numbers involved. The *détenus* got ample allowance for food and personal expenses, and at times the relatives who depended on them were also helped.

Although the situation was brought fully under control by the middle of 1932, when even the open agitation was exhausted, the Government of India and the Bengal Government thought it necessary to make a show of military power behind British rule by ordering one battalion of British infantry, six of Indian infantry, all Gurkhas, and two brigade headquarters to Bengal. The troops were stationed in the more disturbed districts, and paraded there in route marches to impress the villagers. I saw trains full of Gurkhas at a station in northern Bengal when returning to Calcutta from Shillong in November 1932. Some of the expenditure on the troops was saddled on Bengal, and I wrote an article against that in *The Modern Review*. The years which followed were singularly quiet politically.

To close this account of the Bengali revolutionary movement I would offer a few general remarks on its nature and long-term results. As to its causes, a very shallow theory was current from the very first that the revolutionary movement was due to unemployment in the Bengali middle class. 'Educated unemployment' or 'Bhadralok unemployment' – i.e. unemployment of the gentry, became clichés, which are trotted out even now. It is necessary to show the falsity of the theory, all the more so because all British and American historians of today who are writing on this period of Indian history and on this subject, have nothing else to go upon except the mistakes of the British epigoni and myth-making of the Indian nationalists. But the theory also chimes in with the economic superstitions of our days.

For one thing, unemployment could have nothing to do with the revolutionary movement in Bengal for the simple reason that the young people began to join it by the time they were about fourteen and hardly ever entered it after they were eighteen. So there could be no problem of livelihood for them. Next, ail of them came from fairly well-to-do homes, some even from the wealthy. Most of them were sons of professional men like lawyers, doctors, teachers, government servants, or even police officers, as was a young man who was rated as a most dangerous revolutionary, and after being in detention for five years before 1937, was again arrested in my house in Calcutta in 1940, where he was staying with me, and was detained till 1946. So was another young man whom I employed as the tutor of my sons. Those who had problems of livelihood had no time for revolutionary activities.

Besides that, one must say that the economic theories of political violence and terrorism are total nonsense. I would set down most emphatically that nowhere in the world has terrorism been, or is, a product of economic distress. It springs solely from racial or class hatred. This is seen more clearly than ever before in our age, which is *par excellence* the age of political hatreds and violence all over the world.

But the Bengali terrorists of 1930-31, even though driven by racial hatred, did not try to spite the British Government by dying of hunger in prisons. There was, however, a sensational and most prestigious example to induce them to adopt that course. In 1929 a Bengali revolutionary named Jatin Das, who was sentenced to imprisonment and kept in Lahore jail, undertook a fast to better the treatment of political prisoners. The British authorities would not give in, and he died after a fast of 64 days on 13 September 1929. His body arrived in Calcutta on the 16th, and there was a procession from Howrah Station to the burning ghat at Kalighat whose length was longer than that which had followed the bier of C. R. Das in 1925.

This Bengali sacrificed his life in imitation of the Irishman, Terence MacSwiney, Mayor of Cork, whose death took place on 25 October 1920. MacSwiney was almost worshipped by politically conscious Bengalis, who had obviously forgotten their old traditions and never realized that the Irish extremism in fasting was a perversion of the time-honoured Hindu practice of applying moral coercion by undertaking fasts. To carry that to death deprived fasting both of its logic and effectiveness as an instrument of policy, by making it unworthwhile. The Hindus undertook to fast in order to impose their terms, with perfect awareness of its possibilities and limitations, in personal relations, family relations, social relations, and business relations. It was a contest of wills, and the party whose will was stronger always won before any tragic results followed. There was no dishonour in yielding either way before fasting became a means of dying. It was not 'cricket' in Hindu society to mock at the side which gave in.

I myself tried the method to coerce my mother when a small boy, and one evening refused food. My mother, who was of the reforming school, sent met to bed and ate herself in the most un-Hindu way for a mother. The next morning I was so famished that I could not rise from the bed when a hurried, special breakfast was prepared for me and had to be carried to it. Nobody said anything, but I was cured so far as my mother was concerned.

After my marriage, however, I tried the method at times on my wife, for even if a Hindu mother could eat when her son was going without food, that sort of heartlessness was inconceivable in a Hindu wife, who was not less ready to starve to death with her husband as she was to bum herself with him. But my wife acted exactly as my mother, and cured me finally by calling my bluff. This for her was quite in character, for as a student in Calcutta she had refused to join the funeral procession of jatin Das when asked by the other girls of her hostel, and for this she was dubbed by them in English as 'an unfeeling girl.'

The Hindus also applied this method of psychological coercion against the East India Company's government soon after the establishment of British rule. An account of a collective fasting in protest against the imposition of a tax in Benares will be found in Bishop Heber's Journals.* The Government of Calcutta could not of course yield in form, but after the fast was abandoned it removed the tax. As it happened, Mahatma Gandhi went on his fasts in pursuance of the Hindu tradition, and never forgot that it was only a means to an end. If it did not coerce the British administration, it immensely increased his power over his countrymen. He always refused to go to the Irish extreme, being as great a practitioner of non-violence against himself as he was in regard to other men. The non- Gandhian Bengali revolutionaries, in spite of their apotheosis of jatin Das, did not try the method at all from 1930 to 1937.

What surprises me today is the naïveté shown in regard to this method of psychological coercion, which is both cowardly and immoral. With the Hindus it was nothing more than a particular application of their general strategy of going successfully through their worldly existence by exploiting the decencies of other people. Thus it was cunning, but never fanatical. To admire a method which has lost even its cunning by becoming fanatical, is only possible in a world afflicted as much by a degeneration of compassion as it is by unappeasable hatreds. In former ages Europeans could be humorous over the Hindu method, about which they were well-informed even in France.

For instance, Merimée knew enough about it to make it a joke in his novel *Colomba.* In it Orso Antonio della Rebbia hints at this method of coercion when the beautiful Miss Lydia Nevil expresses a doubt whether she would be able to visit Orso in his village. Thus Orso says: 'Vous

* *Narrative of a Journey through the Upper Provinces of India* (1828) Vol. 1, pp. 432–36

rappelez-vous ce que nous contait l'autre jour monsieur votre père de ces Indiens qui menacent les gouverneurs de la Compagnie de se laisser mourir de faim s'ils ne font droit à leurs requêtes?' Lydia Nevil replies: 'C'est-à-dire que vous vous laisseriez mourir de faim? J'en doute. Vous resteriez un jour sans manger et puis Mlle Colomba vous apporterait un *bruccio* si appetisant que vous renonceriez à votre projet.'

In their days of power the nations of the West considered us to be very stupid. I now think that the situation has been reversed. Today we Hindus can outwit them. Their compassion has become so unintelligent that it has ceased to be compassion and become *bêtise*. We can now live on the Western nations without even threatening to fast to death.

I shall now close this summing up of the revolutionary movement of 1930-31 by saying a few words about its ultimate results for Bengal and the Bengalis. As an active movement it came to an end, and there was no revival till the end of British rule, in which terrorism played no part. One thing which was clearly demonstrated by the last years of its history in Bengal is that any government with the will to do so can suppress terrorism by an intelligent employment of its police force alone. Anything more ridiculous and more libellous to real military action cannot be thought of than calling terrorists urban guerillas. There still are weedy and wispy little Bengalis who pretend to be that, but they would all be knocked down by the recoil of their rifles if they had any, and power will be seen to lie in the butt of a gun, and not in its barrel.

But the obsession with weak violence has harmed Bengal and Hindu Bengalis permanently. A province and a people who had led in the nationalist movement have lost their place in Indian politics, and their contribution to Indian independence has been so neglected in the histories of the nationalist movement written after independence that it has become a political grievance of the Bengalis. This process of political exclusion began long before independence, and was the final outcome of a progressive alienation from Gandhi and the all-India Congress.

That made its first appearance at the session of the Congress in Calcutta in December 1928. In it Subhas Bose gave a theatrical exhibition of militarism. He organized a volunteer corps, put the volunteers in military uniform, and even provided steel-chain epaulettes for the men of the simulated cavalry of the volunteers. His own uniform was made by a firm of British tailors, Harmans, with English material. He called himself its GOC, and a telegram addressed to him as such was sent to the General commanding the Presidency and Assam District of the Indian Army in Fort William. It was redirected to the proper addressee from there, and naturally that caused great amusement among the British in Calcutta. The volunteer corps had its women's contingent, in which my future wife also served, but the girls were not put in any kind of uniform. Sajani Das published caricatures of both Subhas Bose as GOC and of the girls, which I disliked although I was not a very ardent nationalist then. All this was an expression of the vicarious military inclinations of the Bengali middle class, which Subhas Bose shared. I saw an infantry training manual of the British army annotated in his own hand. Mahatma Gandhi called all this show Bertram Mills' circus, and gave great offence to Bengalis.

But even this shallow and theatrical militarism was better than the infatuation with weak violence showed by the Bengali middle class in 1930. The events of those years were too tragic to be subjects of satire. I felt deep sorrow all the time. Yet all educated Bengalis were in sympathy with the revolutionaries. Some middle-rank nationalist leaders were in the movement, and the two foremost leaders, Subhas Chandra Bose and his brother Sarat Chandra Bose, were all through in the know, as I have said.

The alienation from the main Indian nationalist movement which this partiality for violence brought about grew into a split in the Congress in 1939. The full story of this split and its consequences for Bengal will be told in a later chapter of this book. I shall only sum up here with the observation that Bengal was thereby isolated from the main stream of the Indian nationalist movement.

The Bengali revolutionaries closed the door to the future, and they found no place in the new ruling order of India after independence. This was a result which had never been seen in any country in which there had been a political revolution. After such revolutions the revolutionaries invariably formed governments. Only in India and Bengal was there an exception to this. As a class, the Bengali revolutionaries played no political role. Some, like two of my friends, Gopal Haldar and Tridib Chaudhuri, became Communists and went into the Opposition, but in India after independence the Oppositions in the legislatures were oppositions only in form with no chance of holding office. After remaining under the Congress faction for many years the Bengalis have indeed tried to maintain their separatism by electing Marxists to the legislature and thus creating Marxist governments for themselves. But this Marxism in effect has been no more Marxist than Mrs Indira Gandhi with her alignment with the Soviet Union was Communist.

CHAPTER 4

Emergence as a Publicist

My emotional involvement in the Civil Disobedience Movement had a very vitalizing impact on my intellectual life. I was always thinking of political and cultural issues, but never had the energy necessary to put down my thoughts in writing. Lacking bodily strength, and the will power that comes from it, I needed an added take-off, so to speak; that is, a prompting from passion. It was the emotional excitement produced in me by the personality and crusading spirit of Mohit Babu which had made me write with such verve in the *Sanibarer Chithi*, and the disillusionment with the campaign would certainly have led me to literary sterility if a new emotional impetus had not been provided by the Gandhian movement. It made me emerge as a writer on public affairs, and, to begin with, I wrote on military affairs. After that I took up the question of Indian unity as raised both by the local nationalism of the provinces and the Hindu-Muslim discord. In this chapter I shall relate my entire contribution to these questions.

Writer on Military Affairs

I knew a good deal about the organization of the Indian army, but had not written anything on it. I began in 1930, and that established me as a journalist of the type called 'publicist.' This was as well, because on account of my character and temperament I could never have succeeded in journalism by becoming a reporter. I had not the minimum of social aplomb - cheek, to put it bluntly - needed by a reporter, and I had too great intellectual conceit not to feel contempt for those I would have had to interview. As a journalist, I could only be a leader writer or a freelance writer with special knowledge of some subject connected with politics. I had that sort of knowledge about war and the Indian Army, and through it I did make a reputation quickly, and in later life that enabled me to earn a respectable livelihood as a commentator on the Second World War.

But I did not acquire the knowledge, nor did I make use of it, for the sake of a career. For more than a decade I had been a close student of the science of war and of military history. It was wholly disinterested, and when I devoted myself to those subjects I had no idea whatever that I would ever write on them. It was a hobby to which the Bengali militarism of which I have written led me, instead of making me a terrorist. Bibhuti Babu used to laugh at me for this as I did for his interest in Spiritualism, and asked me if I had it in mind to become the Minister of War in free India. I did not become that, but I would nevertheless say that anything done disinterestedly provides tangible rewards, besides giving a satisfaction in itself

The provocation to write on military matters was given by, of all things, the report of the Statutory Commission on Indian constitutional advancement, presided over by Sir John Simon. The first volume of the Commission's report was published on lo June 1930. The Press office of the Bengal Government sent intimation that copies would be handed out to the press in the evening. On behalf of *The Modern Review*, I went to Writers' Building to collect our copy, and gave it to Ramananda Babu.

Although by that time the Labour Government of Britain had initiated new moves for dealing with the demand for self-government by Indians and had already bypassed the Commission - which angered Lord Birkenhead - we did not realize this in India, and thought that its proposals would form the basis of the discussions which were going to be held at the Round Table Conference in London later in the year. Therefore we looked forward to the Report and its recommendations with great eagerness. The Report consisted of two parts: the first, entitled 'Survey' and devoted to an examination of the conditions of political life in India, which would necessarily determine the recommendations for further constitutional advance; and the second, containing the actual recommendations. The first part was released on 10 June, and the second two weeks later.

The reception of the first volume in India was unfavourable. Ramananda Babu commented in the July issue of his paper that 'the first volume has been written in such a way as to lend to it a deceptive air of impartiality.' I, on my part, found it to be an exercise in *deception* rather than merely *deceptive*. I got very angry, and could guess what the recommendations would be. It was a specious presentation of the arguments made familiar to us over decades about the political incapacity of Indians. Its only originality lay in the air of lofty intellectual integrity and detachment with which the *rechauffé* was served.

The consciousness of superiority to those who were to profit by the recommendations of the Commission, combined with the urbanity and equipoise of its style, made the report a supremely Simonian performance.

It was as if the wolf, when presenting his argument to the lamb for eating it was assuming that he was speaking only to a fellow-wolf, his equal, and at the same time taking it for granted that if the lamb was not persuaded it must be a very unreasonable animal. This sort of attitude infuriated me more than the ill-mannered and violent abuse of the local British.

Of course, Sir John Simon could not have written the report himself, but he had as his associates and on his team others who were imbued with the same spirit, for it was shared by the whole British ruling order in its topmost ranks. They employed a chicanery which was as elegant and clever on the one hand as on the other it was shortsighted. Put at the service of immediate and sordid self-interest, it finally contributed not only to the destruction of the Empire in India but also to the Second World War, which destroyed Britain's greatness. Even Attlee, who finally scuttled the Indian Empire, showed himself endowed with the same qualities, for he signed the report as one of the members of the Statutory Commission, and it contained the following very bland dismissal of the parliamentary capacity of Indians: 'British parliamentarism in India is a translation, and even in the best translations the essential meaning is apt to be lost. We have ourselves in attending the debates in the Assembly and provincial Councils been more impressed with their difference than their resemblance to the Parliament we know' (all the members of the Commission were members of Parliament).

Yet at that time the debating capacity of Indians in legislatures was perhaps shown at its best by men like Motilal Nehru, Srinivasa Iyenger, Satyamurthi, and others like them. However, as an absolute judgement on the aptitude of Indians for running a parliamentary democracy, the hint was not incorrect, and it remains true still today. But in the circumstances of those times, when there was no determination to keep India permanently under British rule, but on the other hand its final abandonment was contemplated, as also in the light of the stupid opportunism shown by the British press after independence in proclaiming India as the biggest democracy in the world, the Olympian judgement would appear as the height of intellectual dishonesty and moral trickery. I have never changed my opinion that the Simon Commission's report was a dishonest document.

What made me particularly angry was the argument put forward against handing over the responsibility for defending India to Indians, because military ability was not evenly distributed in the entire Indian population, and even the capacity to fight was confined to the martial races. In the recommendations, therefore, it was proposed that the task of defence should be 'leased out' to Britain.

To justify this the report trotted out the familiar theory of the martial races of India. It was asserted and held by the British military authorities in India after the Mutiny and proclaimed as an axiom not requiring any proof. It rested basically on the undeniable fact that owing to the specialization of social functions created by the caste system, fighting was the business of certain classes of the population, and there was no such thing as enlistment of soldiers from the entire population or a national army. But, as developed in previous history, this specialization was seen all over India, so that each region had its martial and non-martial classes. What the British practice put into effect after the Mutiny did was to confine recruitment predominantly to the Punjab, representing the Punjabis as the main or even the only fighting people of India. In short, what was in fact a Punjabization of the Indian Army from policy was represented as the effect of an old social evolution. The Simon Commission triumphantly produced the statistics that out of the 158,200 combatants of the Indian Army, 91,600 came from the Punjab and the North-West Frontier Province, the rest of India made relatively small contributions to the strength of the Army, and Bengal, Assam, and Orissa did not send a single man.

I decided to expose the speciousness of the Commission over this. So far, no Indian had challenged the theory of the martial races. I thought I would. As the report came into my hands only after 10 June, and I published the first instalment of my article in *The Modern Review* on 1 July 1930, it was quick work. No statistics were public and even any kind of information was available only in very specialized publications as also in a number of official reports which were not easy to get at, some being even on the confidential list and therefore not on the general catalogue of the Imperial Library in Calcutta. I had, however, read many of diem, and knew of others. But unless I had studied the subject before, I would not have understood the significance of the facts which were in the official publications, nor could I have produced my articles quickly.

These were entitled *The Martial Races of India*, and were published in four instalments in the July and September issues of 1930 and January and February issues of 1931 of *The Modern Review*. I had to prepare my statistics myself and with their help I tried to show that British practice had changed the old pattern of distribution of military ability and activity in India, and worsened the old specialization which was due either to the caste system or special demographic evolution. One striking change was the shifting of the recruitment, even when based on the theory of martial races, from the Gangetic basin to the Punjab. Before the Mutiny the northern Indian army was indeed recruited from the so-called martial classes, but these classes belonged to the Gangetic plain and were comprised of the fighting Brahmins and Ksatriyas of that region, whereas after the Mutiny, as a result of deliberate policy, recruiting was predominantly in the Punjab and the so-called martial races were assumed to exist more or less exclusively in that province. I gave the entire history of this revolutionary change, which did great injustice to the other parts of India. I further showed that even between 1900 and 1930 there were shifts of predominance between class and class in the Punjab itself For instance, in 1900 the Sikhs of the Punjab were the most numerous element in the Indian Army, but in 1930 they had fallen to third place, while the Punjabi Mussulman had risen to first place, with a proportion of 27 per cent of the infantry. I analysed the composition of 82 active and 18 training battalions of the Indian infantry and of 21 cavalry regiments. This I could do only because I had studied the Army Lists, and had copies myself

The articles were nothing but pioneer and tentative work. I never pretended that they were anything more. But such as they were, they got a good deal of attention and recognition. Sir P. S. Sivaswamy Aiyar, an eminent Indian politician who had given special attention to the Indian Army, wrote congratulating me even before the series was completed. One day Ramananda Babu came in to give me a report of the Foreign Policy Association of New York in which my articles were quoted and referred to. This very much pleased me, and I was more pleased to find two years ago from a paper sent to me by an American friend that in 1976 an American scholar, DeWitt C. Ellinwood by name, who submitted a thesis on the ethnic changes in the Indian Army in World War II to the State University of New York in Albany, had opened it with a reference to my pioneer work. He had written:

'In 1930-31, Nirad Chaudhuri, then a relatively unknown Bengali journalist, wrote a series of articles on "The Martial Races" for *The Modern Review,* an important Indian journal. Indian nationalists were generally not very interested in military matters, but Chaudhuri was an exception ...

Chaudhuri based his articles on an extensive study of British government documents and other British writings, and his study of "ethnicity" in the Indian Army remains worthy of examination. In the 1970s we have available more documents and also sophisticated analyses of ethnicity made by anthropologists, sociologists, and political scientists. Nonetheless, we still seek historical perspectives on ethnicity in the Indian Army, a goal which Chaudhuri set for himself forty-six years ago.'

This is very generous praise, and I feel very gratified to be recalled in this way after nearly half a century from the date of my work. But I also exerted some immediate influence. Early in 1931 it was announced that the Government of India was setting up a committee to prepare the scheme for establishing a college in India to train the Indians who would be admitted to the Indian Army as officers. The composition of the Committee, known as the Indian Military College Committee, was also announced. There were to be on it, besides the Commander-in-Chief of the Army in India, Sir Philip Chetwode, other senior British officers as well as a number of distinguished Indian politicians. Among the latter. Sir Sivaswamy Aiyer was, of course, included. On the strength of his letter to me, I at once entered into a lengthy correspondence with him about the work of the Committee. I was very suspicious of its British members and, as things turned out, my distrust was not unfounded.

The question of giving Indians commissions in the Indian Army had a long history behind it, having arisen even in the Eighties of the last century. But until 1917 no Indians were given commissioned ranks, and after that only a very small number was taken every year. All of them were sent to Sandhurst to be trained. From the Indian side there was a continuous demand that the pace of Indianization should be quickened and also that there should be a military college in India. It became so insistent that at the first session of the Round Table Conference in London held from 12 November 1930 to 19 January 1931, a resolution for establishing a college was formally adopted (Res. No.2 (C) of Sub-Committee No. VII concerned with defence). The Committee I am dealing with was set up in obedience to this resolution, and it concluded its work on 15 July 1931, by signing a report with many dissenting minutes.*

Even before the Committee had its first sitting on 25 May, I had written

* Report of the Indian Military College Committee, 1931. HMSO No.70256.

my first letter to Sir Sivaswamy. I shall quote one or two passages from the correspondence. I knew that the British military authorities in India were opposed to extensive Indianization, as well as to the establishment of a military college in India. Their hesitation was most serious over the question of pace because of their knowledge of what the retired officers of the Indian Army were saying - that they would not send their sons to serve under natives. To avoid this in all forms, the Indians already holding commissioned ranks were assigned to eight units of Indian infantry and cavalry selected for complete Indianization, and no British officers were posted in those regiments if they had to be under Indians. Thus there was segregation. Secondly, the army authorities did not think that a college in India would turn out officers who would be up to the mark. Field-Marshal Sir William Birdwood, the C.-in-C. before Chetwode and himself an officer of the Indian Army, was wholly opposed to the idea. I also read in one of the Indian newspapers, owned by British proprietors, the report of its military correspondent that 'the normal service opinion in the matter has generally remained constant, that a college in Indian environment will not produce the quality nor attract enough of the type of officers who come successfully through Sandhurst.'

Being fully aware how typical and widespread such attitudes were, I thought it necessary to warn Sir Sivaswamy. In my first letter, which was dated 30 April, I laid down what to my thinking should be the basic principles of any attempt at fully Indianizing the army. These were: (1) the cadets should be recruited from all over India without any regard for the theory of the martial races; (2) the education should be fairly inexpensive; (3) the trained officers should be posted to all the regiments and not only to the segregated ones; (4) the curriculum of education should not denationalize them by tearing them up from their social environment; and (5) there should be preparatory training in schools and colleges on the lines of the OTC in Britain. I singled out the question of education and wrote:

'It is particularly important to insist on a suitable kind of education. The officials here, both civilian and military, will do their best to confine recruiting to the most wealthy classes and convert the cadets into imitation polo-playing English subalterns, weaned away from their habits and traditions, which will make them as ineffective or offensive as the majority of the Indian members of the services. What is more, the ideal of an imitation Englishman will never attract the best manhood of India. There will be plenty of people, of course, who will join the army for the sake of money or prestige. But from the military point of view they will hardly be the candidates who are most desirable.'

I felt so strongly about the possibility of social and cultural uprooting that I again wrote to Sir Sivaswamy on 15 May:

'I believe the most controversial questions will be (1) the consideration of efficiency; and (2) the lack of candidates of "suitable" type. A part of the objections on these lines is mere camouflage for political suspicion and racial arrogance, but part of it is genuine. The English have their own notions of efficiency, derived from their national and public school ideals. They comprise some really good and valuable traits and some purely external ideas of good form, and the English set as much store by the external paraphernalia as they do by the intrinsic qualities. Now, you can have, or at least develop, some of the valuable English traits in Indian boys, but you cannot make them swallow the code of good form without making them snobs.'

It will be seen that I had already developed a distrust of the' anglicized Indian class, which was to become very much strengthened later. But, of course, what I wanted to be prevented was the very thing which was imposed, and even today the Indian Army has not got over the defects introduced into it by the system of education imposed on its officers by the British authorities in 1931. Nonetheless, the selecting authorities went on complaining till 1939 about the unsuitability of the majority of the candidates and lamented: 'Where are the natural leaders of the Indian people?' One result of uprooting the cadets was soon evident. They all came back from their vacations with stomach ailments, because after getting only European food at the College they ate so much Indian food as relief in their homes that they got indigestion.* This complaint was officially put down in the reports.

But personally I had one satisfaction. Sir Sivaswamy in his dissenting note referred with appreciation to my articles, and quoted from them, and another Indian member of the Committee, General Rajwade of the Gwalior Army,

* The Army authorities in India held very strongly that military ability could not be developed on Indian food and cuisine, just as I hold that good English cannot be written on the same diet.

signed it along with him. The C.-in-C. at first objected to this as irrelevant, but as the two members said that they would not sign the report unless these references were included he withdrew his objection. This objection was also made about the other dissenting minutes, and in allowing them Sir Philip wrote very loftily: 'The greater part of the dissenting minutes consists either of criticism of the terms of reference of the Committee, as laid down by the Government of India under instructions from His Majesty's Government, or of dissertations upon matters which have nothing to do with the details of the establishment of a military college.'

I examined the report in an article published in *The Modern Review* for October 1931, and called this an ungenerous and unintelligent sneer. I pointed out that the difference between the points of view of the Indian and the British members of the Committee was fundamental. The Indians were preoccupied with the problem of creating a national army, while the British members would have nothing more than a partial concession to Indian opinion in the matter of giving Indians a few jobs in the army. Therefore the Indian members had to define their basic position in order to justify their objections to the details about a college. My final observations on the report were put in blunt language. I wrote:

'The military authorities in India have secured through it [i.e. the Report] what they wanted; the restriction of the number of Indians to be admitted to their co-fraternity to a negligible fraction of the total number of commissioned officers in the army and the careful sterilization of the men to be taken in ... to a degree of innocuousness which will never become a danger to the "spirit" and the "tradition" of the army.'

This ended my writing about the Indianization of the Indian Army for some time, but I continued to write on related subjects. One article on the employment of the Indian Army for operations outside India in British international interests was published in April 1931. I do not know how it found its way into the police dossier on me, as I was informed afterwards. I corresponded with Jawaharlal Nehru on this subject, and this correspondence was intercepted by the police. I have been informed that my letters to him are preserved in a file in the National Archives of the Government of India.

There is only one other story that I shall relate in connection with my military interests at that time. I had given a good deal of thought to the so-called Frontier Question, and had come to the conclusion that the boundary between India and Afghanistan, which was known as the Durand Line, was an offensive frontier and not a defensive one. It was imposed on the Amir and was bitterly resented by him. This frontier divided the Afghan nation, all of which spoke the same language, i.e. Pushtu, and was homogeneous in religion and culture. This I thought was at the root of the Frontier problem because it had on the one hand created Pathan discontent and on the other a task of redemption for the Afghan ruler. I thought that this trouble from Pukhtu irredentism could be avoided by ceding all Pathan territory to Afghanistan.

I said this to Jawaharlal Nehru in November 1931 in Calcutta. He was then free under the terms of the Gandhi-Irwin Pact, and I was seeing him for the first time. A Hindustani friend of mine, Pandit Benarsidas Chaturvedi, about whom I shall have something to say presently, took me to Nehru. I was very much surprised by his air. He seemed to be totally preoccupied with something else when being spoken to by other people, and hardly seemed to be hearing what was being said to him. I observed this and thought he was not giving any attention to what I was saying about the Pathans. But I was wrong. As soon as I had finished, he said very clearly and emphatically: 'Perhaps this could be done by a strong Indian Government in the future. But it is not to be thought of now.' Of course, now that the same Pathans are in Pakistan the present Government of India has become a supporter of their demand for a Pukh- tunistan.

Unity of India

At this time the question of maintaining the unity of India was very much in my mind. For one thing, my interest in military questions was bound to lead me from the problem of defence to the problem of unity. Next, the difference between the Gandhian agitation and the Bengali revolutionary movement was a strong reminder of something I had been feeling for some years, viz. die alienation of Bengal from the rest of India in almost all things. Lastly, there was in Bengal a new form of the Hindu-Muslim conflict which made me aware of the most crucial aspect of Indian unity, which was presented by Hindu-Muslim relations. But it was not simply the pursuit of an intellectual problem for me. I was full of disquiet, and over this matter there was a feeling of urgency.

Let me deal with the new aspect of the Hindu-Muslim conflict first. In the late summer of 1930 the Muslim peasants of the western part of Kishorganj subdivision of the district of Mymensingh, which was my subdivision as well as district, rose in a body, attacked Hindu houses and property owned by Hindu landlords and money-lenders, killed people, and massacred one family known to us, to the last man. This was the first conflict in recent years, i.e. in just less than a century, of any such thing between Bengali Hindus and Bengali Muslims, with the exception of two minor incidents in 1906 and 1907. I had seen with my own eyes three Hindu-Muslim riots in Calcutta - in 1910, 1918, and 1926 (they seemed to come in cycles of eight years) - but they were between the Hindustani Muslims and Hindustani Hindus of Calcutta. As I have related, we Bengalis were not involved in them. The attacks of 1930 were by the Bengali Muslims on Bengali Hindus.

The murdered family was that of the son-in-law of a friend of my father, a fellow-lawyer at Kishorganj and our close neighbour. The old man had gone to visit his daughter, and was killed with all of her family. In my boyhood I often saw this lady as an unmarried young girl, who was certainly the prettiest in Kishorganj. Her brother was a friend of my brother. So, the murders were brought home to us very vividly. The rioting continued for some days, for, as the authorities said, the rioting bands ran into the tall jute plants of the fields as soon as the armed police arrived and could not be reached. This was true, for the behaviour of the Muslim peasants of our district was controlled by the growth of the jute plants, which were the main cash crop of the district. When the jute plants were young, i.e. between April and June, the peasants were too busy attending to them, thinning them out, and weeding the fields to think of anything else. But when from July onwards the plants grew to a height of even six feet, they used the shelter these gave for seduction, abduction, rape, and rioting, and when after October these yielded the jute for sale they used the money for litigation.

All this rioting proved the truth of the warning which a Bengali friend of Mahatma Gandhi had given him in 1921, that as soon as a civil disobedience movement was started in East Bengal the Muslims would rise and loot the houses of the Hindu landlords, as well as murder them. The economic argument was, of course, trotted out after these riots were over.

But there were landlords and money-lenders among the Muslims as well and they were in no way less extortionate than the Hindus. But in these riots their properties were never touched. There were attacks on Hindu houses in the city of Dacca, where there could be no agrarian discontent. In one house two girls fought back the Muslims with lathis. We praised them as heroines, which they were. This was better than adding a girls' corps to the terrorist movement.

This was the beginning of a conflict between the Hindus and Muslims of Bengal which grew with the years and broke out from time to time to reach its climax in the great killings of 1946 in Calcutta. These finally induced the Bengali Hindus to demand and bring about a partition of Bengal which has permanently harmed both the Hindus and Muslims of the region.

But I saw this outbreak of 1930 as the culmination of a general trend in East Bengal, and even from the mid-Twenties that was not only causing me anxiety, but also suggesting to my mind the drastic idea of a wholesale migration of the Hindus of East Bengal to West Bengal, which, of course, took place after 1947.

Our family was not concerned, because we had disposed of all our properties and come away from East Bengal. But my sisters were both married to wealthy landowners, and my anxiety was for all those who were placed like them. It was not that I was opposed to the Muslims getting a dominant position in East Bengal. They had the right to have it because they were a majority. What repelled me was the idea of living under Muslim social and cultural domination. I knew that they would re-shape even the Bengali language.

On account of the Pan-Islamic ideas of the Muslims of India I was, as I have related, strongly anti-Muslim in 1920. But after the disappearance of Pan-Islamism that feeling disappeared, and as yet I had not taken the demand for a Muslim state in India so seriously as to become anti-Muslim again. On the other hand, I was ready to admit, which even the topmost Hindu political leaders were not, that the Muslims of India constituted a society of their own with a distinctive culture, and would never be absorbed in a unified nation which could be called Indian. I was very much in favour of the understanding which C. R. Das had arrived at with the Muslims, which would certainly have gone a long way to remove their economic grievances. But C. R. Das died in 1925, and afterwards the Hindu nationalist leaders of Bengal did not honour the agreement. By the middle-Thirties I was fully convinced that the Muslims had genuine grievances and were justified in trying to retain their Muslim identity. I wrote some articles on the question both in English and Bengali. But by 1939, when my last article on this subject was published, I had lost all hope of Hindu-Muslim reconciliation, and actually wrote that, short of a miracle, the question had passed beyond the possibility of a rational solution.

My next source of anxiety was the maladjustment between Bengal and the rest of India, and more especially the antithesis between Gandhi's method and the Bengali revolutionary method. But the disagreement was deeper and older. It arose out of the very lead which the Bengalis had obtained over the rest of India, and particularly over the Hindi-speaking north Indians, in education, culture, and political leadership. This was summed up in a sort of rule of three that what the Englishman was to the Bengali, the Bengali was to the Hindustani. The consciousness of Bengali superiority, which in itself was a fact, had made them absurdly arrogant. They applied all sorts of contemptuous and even abusive epithets to the Hindustanis. This Bengali pride, which was the creation of British rule, was carried back historically to the ancient period. The Bengalis quite seriously proclaimed that Kalidasa, the greatest poet of ancient India, was a Bengali, that the Ajanta frescoes had been painted by them, that it was they who had carried Hindu civilization to Indonesia and Indo-China, that they had colonized Ceylon, and that they had taken Buddhism to China.

I felt sick of all this bragging. I thought that this Bengali arrogance was not only out of date, but had become indecorous and injurious in the utterly changed circumstances of the day. So I thought I would have a go at it, and wrote a long article. To begin with, I read it at a meeting of our literary club, which was called the Sunday Club. Usually, its meetings were held in turns in the house of a member. But this promised to be an important meeting and a hall was taken in a hotel. The attendance was very good, and, besides, the most notable literary figures of Bengal headed by Pramatha Chaudhuri came by invitation. Pramatha Babu was not the man to bear a grudge because I had attacked him, and he listened very attentively to me.

The quality he had above everything else was urbane generosity to all young writers. His objection to my paper on Bengali provincial feeling was on one point of interpretation. I had become aware that to a greater or lesser degree all the ethnic groups of India, speaking one fully developed language each, had a consciousness of their separateness or identity whatever it might be called, and that all over the country they were entering into a sort of sub-national rivalry, which could be called the true national rivalries of India. So, in dealing with the highly developed Bengali provincial patriotism I could not overlook its pan-Indian setting. This, I saw as an illustration of the organization of political passion in the modem world about which Julien Benda had written in his famous book *La Trahison des Clercs*, which I had bought and read. I was even more impressed by the little book in which he gave an exposition of his political philosophy, viz. *Mon Premier Testament*, which also I had. Pramatha Babu, who had of course read Benda, objected that Benda had spoken of hatred between the nations and the organization of this hatred, and he asked me where did I find hatred in the Bengali provincial sentiment. There indeed was, but I had not made that explicit in the article. Atul Gupta, another intellectual elder of Bengal and a friend of Pramatha Babu, regretted my petulance in criticizing Bengali provincial sentiment and said that if I considered the matter dispassionately I would realize that the development of provincial feeling was something like nationalism, and it was both unavoidable and natural. My paper was published in the *Prabasi*, but after publishing the first part Ramananda Babu, the militant Bengali that he was, refused to publish the second part of my argument in which I would have pleaded for an understanding with the speakers of Hindi. I was, of course, severely criticized by other Bengali writers, who saw no point in my complaint against the Bengalis. Ramananda Babu's comment was that no one should too harshly criticize his own people.

There was, behind this spirited attack on Bengali provincialism by me, an undisclosed assumption, which if known would have made my critics more indignant. It was the faith in the political role of the speakers of Hindi, the largest group of Indians speaking the same language. By that time I had come to the conclusion that in the absence of British power the only people who could maintain the unity of India against the natural centrifugal forces of all kinds present in India, were the speakers of Hindi or, as I called them, the Hindi-speaking block, which virtually occupied the whole of northern India between the Himalayas and the Vindhyas. This was a deduction from the observed facts of national unity in other countries, which showed that in any country with a heterogeneous population the largest and strongest group with a developed sense of identity either brought about or sustained the unity of the whole country, as for example, the Prussians, the Muscovites, the speakers of langue d'oïl, and, I would add, the West Saxons. So, I even wished that the speakers of Hindi would become assertive or aggressive and create a Hindustani imperialism.

But that precisely was the bugbear and fear of the Bengalis. Ramananda Babu gave expression to the dislike for the Hindustanis in cool and at times ironic language. But my master Mohit Babu used to foam at the mouth at the mere mention of them. He asked me to consider solely the 'beauty' of the Hindi surnames, e.g. Tandon. The general mass of the Bengalis shared his emotional repugnance.

There was a personal reason behind my new liking for the speakers of Hindi. Only since 1928 had I been coming in contact with educated Hindustanis, and that was due to a new business enterprise of Ramananda Babu. He brought out another monthly magazine which was in Hindi, and chose as its editor one of the most respected journalists and writers in Hindi, Benarsidas Chaturvedi. In the office we always called him only Panditji. He also had as his assistants two or three very competent young men. The magazine was called *Vishal Bharat, or India Magna*.

I have met few men in my life whom I have respected or liked more. His manliness was combined with a very great simplicity, one aspect of which was his imperturbable equanimity. For an Indian nationalist of the Gandhian school, the last attribute was the last thing to expect. He was also a controversialist, but without a trace of acerbity or malice. He was a Brahmin of the highest order from the U.P. His name meant 'an expounder of the four Vedas', but the Chaturvedis in Calcutta were known to be astute stockbrokers and money-makers. Pandit Benarsidas had, however, chosen poverty and simplicity. He came to the office only in a *dhoti*, but without any Gandhian affectation of being scantily clad. He spoke and wrote English with elegance, and was something of a specialist on Indians living in the British colonies abroad. With all his devotion to Gandhi, he was quite capable of taking an objective view of his apostle. One day I told him how at times I felt disposed to call Tagore an actor. He smiled and said that Tagore could never approach Gandhiji in this role.

In his office I also met other Hindi writers, and formed a very favourable idea of their character. So far as I learned to read a little Hindi, I also felt that their language reflected their character. Bengali had by that time become horribly affected, due to self-conscious attempts at achieving style. Hindi, to my mind, had the lucidity and sincerity of expression which our language was losing. One writer whom I often saw in Panditji's rooms specially struck me by his manliness. He was a Brahmin, but of the peasant- soldier sub-caste. He wrote about shikar and also hunted big game, at all events leopards, and had his rifle. When the Simon Commission was in India he took one of its members. Major Milner, to his house, gave him only rice-pudding to eat, and made the gallant M.P. sleep on a charpoy in the open courtyard. His name was Sriram Sharma.

But in later life, when I had moved to Delhi and had greater opportunities for meeting the speakers of Hindi, I discovered that I was wholly wrong in my assessment of their potentiality. The simplicity which I saw in them was not the simplicity of the green shoots in cornfields, but that of the hard and brown stubble. I saw that they were the most retrograde, fanatical, and least Westernized of all Hindus, that they were more possessed by the sterile hatred of the British than even us Bengalis. Our hatred was hysterical, and therefore partly subject to respites. The Hindustani anti-British hatred was fossilized, dour, and incurable. Even Sriram Sharma one day told me a story which would prove this. It was when the Civil Disobedience movement and the so-called agrarian discontent in the U.P. were at their height. He related that from a distance of about a quarter of a mile he saw Sir Malcolm Hailey, the formidable Governor of the U.P., angling in one of the ravines of the Jumna, and he bitterly regretted that he did not have his rifle with him. I became more familiar with this retrograde hatred in 1942 and again in 1946. When in 1947 independence came, to the masses of the U.P. it was nothing but *la revanche* for the ruthless slaughter of their ancestors by the British during the Mutiny.

The manifold aspects of Indian disunity were making me very anxious, but the approach to them by our politicians and publicists evoked nothing but contempt in me. There was unceasing palaver from a crowd of well- intentioned people bent on proving that there was no disunity in India and it was all a question of the birds and beasts in the Garden of Eden living together. It was not only an absurdly large number of Indians who maintained that flow of talk, but they had as their fellows British and American busybodies convinced of the same truth, and ready to help their Indian clients to achieve the unity.

Their talking was creating a flood which was obliterating all the well-known landmarks of political life in India, e.g. that there were Hindus and Muslims in India, that there were the untouchables and the high castes, that there were Bengalis, Tamils, Marathas, Gujaratis, and so on. One after another, conferences of all the political parties, all the religious communities, all the different elements of the population of India were being held, and they were producing reports, which left nothing to be done except implementing them. Even for resolving the conflict between India and Britain, a collection of well-intentioned people was formed in London under the name of the India Conciliation Group. I cannot explain how every contact between the Indian nationalists and that otherwise admirable religious sect, the Quakers, invariably produced the greatest amount of ethical imbecility that could be conceived of among good men. Compelled to watch all this activity, repeated at the time of the second Round Table Conference in London, I lost patience and wrote an article entitled 'Unity Conferences' and got it published in *The Modern Review*. I served Truth, but should not have waited even so long to realize that well-intentioned people, or those who are called 'do-gooders' in these days, were the worst mischief-makers in human society.

My article has some relevance even today in view of the internal hatreds which threaten the life of most nations in the world. Those who might feel interest in it could read it whole in *The Modern Review* for February 1933, pp. 221-225. It was terse but thorough. I shall only quote some passages from it. I wrote:

'The fundamental weakness of these conferences should be plain to everybody. They begin by admitting the right of every one of the communities which take part in them to retain a separate group personality and then go on to strive for a measure of agreement among them by means of bargaining. In other words, what our leaders and politicians are trying, unconsciously perhaps, to do in these conferences is to give the final touches to the process of parcelling out the Indian population into a number of highly self-conscious communities, each determined to be a separate and self-contained entity, politically, culturally, and socially, and each determined to be the sole judge and guardian of its own interests, and then, as if as an afterthought, to establish a federation of these autonomous groups on an agreed basis of sharing the economic resources of India. One need not really be a political philosopher or politician to see that this will never lead to the unification of India.'

I continued:

'One more futility will be added to these already strewing the pages of history if Indian leaders do not wake up in time to the peril of taking the same nerveless course to the same chaotic goal.

'One result of the determination of our politicians to tread the path paved only with illusory hopes is already manifest. Every unity conference leaves the communities which participate in them more and more self- conscious and strident about their separate aspirations. But supposing for a moment that a marvel has come to pass and the conferences have brought us an agreed document, would that give us the thing we wish for? One would emphatically say - No. The utmost that these pacts and agreements can give us is what I shall call a contractual or legal unity which will not function in the absence of an external and disinterested coercive authority.'

I added that this was what was happening, and wrote:

'Every one of these pacts which are born after an incredibly painful travail, if they are not also always stillborn, is sent up to the British authorities to be ratified and acted upon. If the British were not here to guarantee and enforce these agreements, it can hardly be hoped that the peace they would bring would last longer than the time taken in haggling them into existence.'

Finally, I defined the character of true national unity: 'True unity,' I said, 'is more inward. The laws of all civilized countries confer certain rights and duties to husbands and wives, parents and children. But if men and women were to take their stand on these laws to make their domestic life a success, most homes would be as sordid a place as a divorce court.'

Of course, my writings did not exert the slightest influence on opinion. But I do not feel ashamed for that. I know the definition of a prophet: 'When a prophet speaketh in the name of the Lord, if the thing follow not, nor come to pass, that *is* the thing which the Lord hath not spoken, *but* the prophet hath spoken it presumptuously: thou shalt not be afraid of him.' Even now my countrymen have not learnt to be afraid of me, and pay no heed to what I write. That is because their minds are so constituted that if they ever acquire an idea, whatever its value, they become impervious to a second idea, as if they were ova which once they are fertilized by a racing spermatozoon, will at once grow a hard coat to prevent the entry of another.

But, at all events, one distinguished Indian politician of that time complimented me on the article. After its publication Benarsidas Chaturvedi took me to see Pandit Govinda Ballabh Pant, one of the leading Congressmen of the U.P., who had come for a visit to Calcutta. He said that he had read my piece and remarked: 'It was like a breath of fresh air in a close room. But we politicians do not have the freedom to remain in the open.' What a terrible confession was that to make!

BOOK V

INTO MARRIED LIFE

1932-1937

Prefatory Note

In this part of the book I shall give an account of my marriage and of the first quinquennium of my married life. It would read like a madman's tale. But since I have pulled off that bout of madness and succeeded in keeping my wife fifty-four years, it will perhaps be conceded that prudence has very little to do with happiness and unhappiness in the married state. Of course, it might be said that my wife had no freedom to leave me because until recently there was no divorce for the Hindus. But there were *de facto* separations even in very traditional Hindu families. These were due to physical repulsion, incompatibility of temperament, or too wide a disparity in worldly circumstances. In such cases the wife could leave the husband and go back to her parental home just as the husband too could lead his own life in any way he pleased. My wife, who was the daughter of a well-to-do father and had money of her own and was also highly educated, could easily have sought that sort of escape from a husband who by normal worldly standards was as impossible as I showed myself to be. But she did not. I cannot say whether that was due to her acceptance of the Hindu doctrine that marriage was a sacrament. But with me my marriage has certainly been something like that. It conferred regeneracy on me, and gave me a sense of purpose to live for. If, however, prudence was no part of my regenerate state I had no qualms about its absence, for I regarded prudence as an attribute of the unregenerate state.

But instead of theorizing I had better set down the facts. At this point I have to explain that early in 1931, i.e. about a year before my marriage, I separated from my brothers and lived independently in rooms taken in a house in the northern suburb of Bagbazar in Calcutta.

CHAPTER I

Sacrament of Hindu marriage

Arranged Marriage

I was married on 21 April 1932, at the age of thirty-four years and five months. My bride was nearly twelve years younger. That was very late for a young man of my social class in Bengal. My elder brother was married at the age of twenty-five in 1920, and since I was only two years younger I should have been married in 1922. In the worldly way nothing stood in its way. I could not indeed be a brilliant match for a girl of our class, but as 'educated spinsterhood' was as rife in it as was 'educated unemployment' I' was quite an acceptable son-in-law, because I was in 'permanent government service', and had prospects. Yet my marriage was delayed by ten years.

That was due to myself. I put forward the objection, which I did in obedience to a new trend: that I did not have a sufficient income. My brother had married without any income whatever, I had some at least. But in those days Bengali young men at college or just out of it had begun to resist their fathers' wishes and were objecting to marriage on the plea of no income. The fathers promptly brushed it aside, seeing through it as a face or modesty saving plea. At Kishorganj a friend of my brother, the son of the leading lawyer of the town, raised the objection, and the lawyer sent for my brother to deliver his ultimatum through an intermediary. 'Tell your friend,' he said, 'that if he waits to marry until he can keep his wife on his own income he will become so old that no father will give his daughter to him. I will disinherit him unless he obeys me.' This threat worked.

But my objection was sincere. I was living with my brother and his wife, and his income from his profession - he was an advocate in the Calcutta High Court - was still negligible. So, I did not want to take on an additional burden. Probably my father saw that and did not press me. After my resignation from the Military Accounts Department there could be no question of my marrying. Even when I became employed again I did not want to marry, and remained a bachelor for three years after that.

In the meanwhile, I had acquired a dislike for arranged marriages, and thought quite unrealistically that I might manage to get married through love. Of course, there was not the ghost of a chance of my succeeding in that line. Yet I persisted in my dream, and, as I have indicated, suffered to lead a single life. My father was very distressed at the mere social aspect of it. He had been obliged, wholly contrary to custom, to marry his fourth son before the second and third, and now that his third son, the doctor, had also returned from Europe and was receiving very eligible proposals it seemed he would have to skip me again. This would have been a great sorrow for him. Thus it was a great relief to him when in November 1931 I went up to him and told him that I was ready to marry, and he could look for a bride for me. He was then staying with my brother in Calcutta.

From the wholly worldly point of view it was a wild and irresponsible step on my part. If I showed practical good sense in giving up my dream of marrying through love, I completely went back on such wisdom as I had shown ten years before in refusing to marry on the salary I had in the Military Accounts Department. I had now the same salary but without any prospects. I had better mention what the salary was: about eight pounds a month. Yet the final result was good, in spite of the troubles my wife and I had in the first five years of our married life. Had I not married my life would certainly have been lost like a river in a desert. Marriage made the river cut through rock and push through shoals to reach the sea. Even for my wife, I would say, it has been worthwhile, although I could, without unfairness, be accused of showing no consideration for the inevitable trials I was going to inflict on a young girl who had been brought up in affluence. But she is now the wife of Nirad Chaudhuri, instead of being the nameless wife of a nameless official or professional, rotting in the low prosperity of a suburban house near Calcutta. But the real gain was that both of us have arrived at an understanding of life and of its value which never comes unless one has passed through misery. Our misery was worse than that of the men and women whom Hugo depicted as typical *les miserables*. Their misery has evoked compassion, our misery was drab and drew on us only indifference and contempt. But in the end he laughs best who laughs last.

In our society fathers and sons do not discuss marriage face to face. But I had no such inhibition. I told my father that I was giving him a *carte blanche* without any mental reservations. I might as well add that I have always been a wholehogger. So, in respect of marriage, after having first thought that in my marriage preliminaries there will be no *father*, I now decided that there will be no *son.* I told my father that he had only to tell me when and where I should have to go, and I would go and marry the girl he chose. My brother who was present during this conference at once objected. He said that Nirad was quite grown up and it would be unwise and even absurd for him to marry without seeing whom he was going to marry. I curtly replied that if that was insisted on, I would relieve them of the task, and shift for myself as best as I could. What I considered brutal and utterly without justification was for a young man to go and look at a girl for the purpose of marriage, and then choose or reject her for her looks. What should I feel, I asked, if a girl came to have a look at me in the same way and refused to marry me for not being handsome enough? I would feel compelled to marry the first girl I saw. So it did not matter if I saw anyone or did not.

My father at once agreed with me, and said that he would do his best and if things went wrong he would take the responsibility. I replied: 'I am giving you complete freedom to choose a wife for me with the confidence that you will choose the most suitable one for me. If after doing so, I find even on the wedding night that I shall not be happy with the girl, do you think one word will come out of my mouth, not to speak of blaming you?'

My father was very pleased and said that he felt relieved. But he asked me: 'Tell me if you want anything special, and I shall look for that so far as possible.' I replied: 'I have nothing special myself, and I have no right to demand anything special in my wife. See that she comes from our class, and is of a type which would fall in with our ways.' Still, not fully convinced, and perhaps thinking that I was showing false modesty, he asked again: 'Of the intellectual type?' This he did in English. I also replied in English. I tapped my forehead and said: 'Enough for two.' The truth was that I disliked nothing more than pretence, and of all pretences that of being intellectual was the most insufferable. I knew that if the girl I married did not have real intellectual ability but had its conceit I would make her life miserable. My father understood, and set about the business. However, nothing happened for about two months. Only at the end of January or beginning of February 1932 did I hear that something was on.

That happened through my married younger sister who had come from her country home to the family's town house in Calcutta. She became friendly with a lady in the next house, and asked her if she knew of a suitable girl for her brother. 'Why?' the lady replied, 'there is a very nice girl next door to you now.' Her brother, a doctor and a retired captain of the Indian

Medical Service (IMS) was married to die daughter of a gentleman of Shillong, and this gentleman, who visited Calcutta with his family every cold season, was staying with his son-in-law. It was his unmarried third daughter who was in question. The match was made up very quickly after that.

My future bride had been at school in one of the most fashionable girl's schools in Calcutta, and had taken her first university diploma from my own college, Scottish Church College, in Calcutta, which had become coëducational. The family was liberal and modern. My future father-in-law was supposed to be wealthy. But there was no question of money or presents discussed between my father and my future father-in-law. When the latter pointedly asked if we had any demands in money or in kind my father replied: 'You will give your daughter what you can, and I can have nothing to say.' But my father-in-law gave a hint that my bride, like her sisters, had some money set apart for herself, and his own property, since he had no son, was to come to his daughters.

My father must have been pleased about this, being unable to foresee easy circumstances at any time for me in respect of money. I learned all this after my marriage, and before that I showed no curiosity whatever not only about the family, not even about the bride. In actual fact, I did not get any precise information about the family even when my future father-in-law came to our house to make the engagement formal. As to the bride, I learned something about her only a week or so before the wedding from a girl who knew her at school. So, it was in every sense an arranged marriage or a leap in the dark.

But the other party was not so casual. As I learned afterwards, before the engagement was made final my future brother-in-law, the captain in the IMS, had 'inspected' me without my knowledge in the *Modern Review* office. This was done through Kedar Babu, whom he knew. Kedar Babu had given me a character, and had also been apologetic about the salary the magazine was giving me, saying that it was not equal to my merits. But he could not make me physically impressive. When I was told about this visit of inspection after my marriage by my wife I recalled vaguely that one day Kedar Babu had sent for me to his office without any apparent reason and that a stranger was in the room. I was also told that the captain's report was unfavourable as to looks and stature. This was natural because he was tall even for an Englishman, and was heavily built in addition. My clothes were also very shabby. I was in an old woollen khaki shirt, with the sleeves rolled up to the elbows, which showed two forearms like pea sticks. But both my father-in-law and mother-in-law were of the old reformed Bengali type, and they set greater store by 'education' than by stature. So, they overlooked the reported physical insignificance. Immediately after the wedding my wife, who could not improve me basically, at least made me give up that shirt.

Another well-wisher of her family warned my father-in-law about my financial standing. He said that the daughter of so well-to-do a gentleman should not be given in marriage to a man who had so low a salary. He even reduced my salary by twenty rupees, and reported it as Rs.80 a month, instead of Rs. 100, as it was. On this score, too, my father-in-law showed his previous indifference. He said, as all reformed Bengali gentlemen said in those days, that he was considering only the young man, and not his money. That attitude has unfortunately disappeared, and nowadays all fathers boast about marrying their daughters to salaries, and not to men.

My bride who heard this did not take at all kindly to her well-wisher, and told me the story, so far as I remember, on the third night after the wedding. This resulted in my being very rude to another young man, a friend of the family, whom I took to be the meddler. Actually, this young man had given a very important report, which was to tell them that I had taken a flat and was not going to live with my brothers in a joint family. I made up to him later. Thus the arranged marriage without sufficient income took place.

The Preliminaries

I was in the most serious mood in the weeks preceding the event. Years of waiting for my marriage had given me time to reflect on every aspect of married life except the monetary, and even if I had not already been living separately from my brothers I would have set up on my own after marriage. I knew I could not bring my bride to my rooms in Bhavanath Sen Street, because there was neither kitchen nor bath with them. I would not also have begun married life with only two rooms to live in. So, I took a flat in a block which was being built and would be ready by the time I was married. It had four rooms, kitchen, bath and all that, and was very modem and smart for Bengalis of the middle class. The rent was to be half my monthly salary. I did not bother about it, and paid one month's rent in advance. The flat was on the second floor, and had a sunny and airy aspect.

The next problem was to provide myself with wedding clothes. In our class a bridegroom had to be very respectably dressed, and if he had any taste very elegantly as well. I had taste, but not the money, especially after paying the rent in advance. Therefore I went to Ashoke Babu and asked him to advance me the next month's salary. He smiled and at once had the payment made, because he understood. He was himself one of the best- dressed young men in Calcutta. My wife, who was a student at the college where he taught economics as an honorary lecturer and had attended his lectures, told me afterwards that he used to come to the class in such resplendent clothes that the girls called him the 'bridegroom'. I took the advance in great glee, without reflecting on its consequences, which were to be very humiliating, as I shall relate presently.

I provided myself with silk and cotton tunics, very fine loom-made dhotis, and also a pair of white Indian shoes worked with gold thread. Shoes of the European type did not go well with the Bengali dress or with a wedding. The cotton tunics at first created a problem. Formerly, I had mine made with the finest poplin or calico, but in my new nationalistic mood I could not reconcile myself to cloth made in England or even in Indian mills. But the workaday khadi was rather coarse, and I could not bear the idea that a young girl would rest her head against that sort of cloth. Fortunately, very fine hand-woven khaddar made from very fine hand- spun yam was available. It was elegant but expensive. Nevertheless I had a few made.

Toiletries were also a problem. Before my conversion to Gandhism I used Yardley's things. These I would not buy now. So I bought the best that were made in India, including the Mysore sandal soap. On the wedding night this created what I might call a dissonant chord in scent between my bride and me. She was not affected by nationalism in this respect, and used the German No. 4711 toiletries, and so I smelt rather crude by her side.

Ashoke Babu also had the most gorgeous invitation cards printed for me. I took note of my resources and ordered a few simple white cards to be printed at the *Modern Review* press. But when I went to take delivery of them I was given large-sized envelopes and cards in yellow handmade paper, printed in colours and gold, with decorations in the most elegant Indian style. In fact, the blocks used for the card and envelope had been made for the wedding cards of an Indian princess. Ashoke Babu also promised to take me to marry in his very large Citroën limousine, which was to be decorated elaborately with flowers, with a large butterfly, the symbol of marriage, on the radiator. I was not, however, destined to ride to my wedding in that style.

There was another aspect of my presentation as a bridgroom to be attended to. I had begun to lose my teeth from the age of twenty-seven. My teeth were bad, and two front ones were false. By 1932 I had lost two more, and the gaps showed if I smiled. Yet I had no money to pay for new teeth. However, a friend of mine, a former college fellow, who had become a dentist after taking his training in America, offered to do everything for me on credit. My natural teeth were cleaned and the new false teeth provided. But I could not pay him, and he never pressed for it. He lent his car for the procession.

While these practical questions were being attended to, my mind was preoccupied with the moral problems presented to me. What was it going to be like to have a wife and be living with a young girl all the time? I think I have given indication enough that in spite of being a portentous commentator on public affairs, very highbrow in respect of aesthetic tastes, as well as a writer on military affairs who was taken seriously enough to have his views cited in an official bluebook, I was like a callow adolescent in regard to women. The more I brooded on the different aspects of marriage the more did I feel the need of purity, so that by the time the wedding day arrived I was like the esquire keeping his vigil in a chapel for his initiation into knighthood.

Both the bride and the bridegroom have to fast the whole day before their wedding at night, and I was resolved that for me it would be a real fast. The immediate onset of hunger made me feel as if I was Sir Galahad pursuing the Holy Grail - such a sense of decarnalization it brought about - and that made me capable of going on foot to invite some of my friends personally without feeling tired. However, I had decided that I should rest in my own rooms in Bhavanath Sen Street alone and not spend the day in my brother's house from where I was to go to the bride's house. I was terribly afraid that unless I rested and had some sleep during the day I would look more pinched and cadaverous in the face than I was. Before lying down to rest I even put a lot of cold cream on my face.

But I could not sleep. For one thing, there was the excitement, and after that the perpetual monetary worry. It had been found the previous day that we might fall short of money for the wedding feast in our house, and so I wrote to Bibhuti Babu to lend me two hundred rupees, and sent the letter by the hand of a nephew. I had not got a reply and was worried. But my nephew came and told me that Bibhuti Babu had given a cheque in my father's name. I could not repay him immediately, and my wife had to settle the debt for her own marriage in instalments. That gave her the opportunity to become friends with Bibhuti Babu.

I am forgetting to mention another worry of a moral kind which I had all through those weeks, and that was about my newly developed liking for European music. It had become almost like religious meditation to me, but I feared I might have to give it up. I knew what dislike we Indians generally had for European music, especially the vocal. My brother who was so devoted to Indian music, would not allow me even to bring my records of European music into his house. I could not anticipate what attitude my future wife would take up. But one thing I had allowed for. If she disliked it I would give it up, whatever the sacrifice. Nonetheless, that did not put an end to my suspense and nervousness.

The Wedding

Anyway, in the afternoon I presented myself in my brother's house in all my splendour or rather elegance, and waited for my friends, who were to form the bridgroom's party. I think they were to be about thirty, Bibhuti Babu being one of them. He arrived and had a good look at me, and expressed his admiration for my clothes. But he did not even wink at me to reassure me about the loan.

The evening approached, and the cars, lent or hired, were ready. But Ashoke Babu with his decorated car had not arrived. Message after message came from the *Modern Review* office which was nearby, to inform us that he was delayed at the florist's and he asked us to wait until he arrived. I was unwilling to go before he came and sacrifice so much grandeur. But my father got very impatient, because the wedding time fixed by the priests astrologically was rather early. I do not know how for once I lost my will and did not resist when I was shuffled into the car lent by my dentist friend. Off we went, to my dismay.

But when my car, in which my nephew accompanied me, was going along Wellington Street I saw Ashoke Babu's decorated limousine going along in the opposite direction. I looked at my nephew, pointed in that direction, making an unintelligible sign to follow the car, so that I could change over and get into the other car. But my nephew did not understand, and I could not be articulate. We sped on and I got down at the bride's house in high dudgeon. I looked very peevish, not knowing that the womenfolk of the house were peeping at me from a vantage point. When my father came I told him that I had seen the car and he should apologize properly to Ashoke Babu. He arrived later, and after the banquet took some of my friends on a jaunt in the decorated car. The next day he took me and my bride home in the same car, but it was not decorated.

For the time being, I lost touch with my family and friends, being taken over by the bride's family. Only a servant who was accompanying me as valet remained behind to give change of clothes, bathing and shaving things, etc. The ceremony was gone through with great *éclat*, my friends shouting all the time when my bride was going round me seven times. I must confess that after the ceremony was over, I was more pleased with the goods and chattels I had got than with my wife. In the way of furniture I got a complete bedroom suite in solid teak (no veneer), mahogany finished, as I learned later, according to the bride's wishes. For myself I got a desk, chair, and revolving bookshelf. I was given silk clothes, including even silken underwear, and a pair of claret-coloured patent leather pumps. All this was supplemented by 22 carat gold cufflinks and studs, a ring, and an 18 carat gold wrist watch. I felt very happy and soothed. My wife, I should add, came with over one kilogramme of solid 22 carat gold.

It was near midnight when, after breaking my fast, I was taken to the room where the bedroom suite had been placed. At first I was alone, and looked at the bed. I had never slept in a bed like that. There were obviously two mattresses on which was spread a very fine bedsheet.* There were two big and deep pillows with fringed pillowcases for each of us. I also noticed a bedspread of linen embroidered in silk thread folded nearby. The room was fragrant with bunches of tuberose and garlands of jasmine. The mild fragrance of the creeper *Quisqualis indica* was coming up through a window, which was open to brilliant moonlight.

I was terribly uneasy at the prospect of meeting as wife a girl who was a complete stranger to me, and when she was brought in by my eldest sister-in-law and left standing before me I had nothing to say. I saw only a very shy smile on her face, and timidly she came and sat by my side on the edge of

*It was the beginning of the hot season, and there could be no quilt or blanket. There is hardly another phrase coarser than 'under the sheets' for married couples.

the bed. I do not remember how after that both of us drifted to the pillows, to lie down side by side.** Then the first words were exchanged. She took up one of my arms, felt it and said: 'You are so thin. I shall take good care of you.' I did not thank her, and I do not remember that beyond noting the words I even felt touched. The horrible suspense about European music had reawakened in my mind, and I decided to make a clean breast of it at once and look the sacrifice, if it was called for, straight in the face, and begin romance on such terms as were offered to me. I asked her timidly after a while: 'Have you listened to any European music?' She shook her head to say 'No.' Nonetheless, I took another chance and this time asked: 'Have you heard the name of a man called Beethoven?' She nodded and signified 'Yes.' I was reassured, but not wholly satisfied. So I asked yet again: 'Can you spell the name." She said slowly: 'B, E, E, T, H, O, V, E, N.' I felt very encouraged. After that we talked about other things aimlessly and dozed off.

But the extraordinary thing was that my wife took to European music as soon as she heard the first records that I played to her. The two pieces which are interwoven with our first wedded days are: the first movement in allegro of Mozart's symphony in E flat major (No.39) and the slow movement in larghetto of Beethoven's second symphony. We did not begin badly. My wife got to like them so much that she reacted to the melodies even about fifty years later. We were at Oxford, I was eighty, and she nearly seventy, when the allegro movement of Mozart came on BBC's Radio 3. She came into the sitting-room, placed her hands on my shoulders, and said: 'Reminds me of home.'

Yet what a home had I brought her to - only to five years of poverty, anxiety, privations, and humiliations? But the memory of all that was washed off by Mozart. That prompts me to say that if one does not allow oneself to be beaten and sullied by the world, the misery inflicted by it does not lodge in the memory, and only the happiness that could be wrung out of that misery remains.

I shall never pretend that I did not provoke the world to do its worst to me and inflict its punishment on so intractable a subject. But that does not extenuate the world in which I lived. The Christian faith puts a believer to a

** Of course, fully dressed. We Hindus (at least as long as we remain Hindu) consider both the extremes — fully clad and fiilly nude - to be modest, and everything in-between as grossly immodest. No decent man wants his wife to be an *allumeuse.*

severe test. A leper in the last stage of decomposition appears to the penitent sinner and says:

' "Ah! je vais mourir!... Rapproche-toi, réchauffe-moi! Pas avec les mains! non! toute ta personne."

'Julien s'étala dessus complètement, bouche contre bouche, poitrine sur poitrine.

'Alors le Lépreux l'étreignit; et ses yeux tout à coup prirent une clarte d'étoiles; ses cheveux s'allongèrent comme les rais du soleil; le souffle de ses narines avait la douceur des roses; un nuage d'encens s'éleva du foyer, les flots chantaient.. .Julien monta vers les espaces bleus, face à face avec Notre Seigneur Jésus ...'

The society I had to live in also showed itself to my eyes as a leper, but not of this kind. It was like the leper in Kipling's story of 'The Mark of the Beast', and it went round and round me for years mewing and trying to put the mark of the beast on me. In the story the victim was saved when Strickland branded the leper with red-hot irons. I could not brand the leper who was attacking me, but I branded myself with red-hot irons and kept myself clean, in spite of all the filth he was throwing at me.

However, that phase of our married life was still to come. During the first few days I walked on air. I was married on a Thursday. The banquet at our house, for which supplementary money had to be borrowed from Bibhuti Babu, was given on the next Sunday. It went off very well. All my friends, including Bibhuti Babu and Ashoke Babu, came. I presented myself to them in all my glory, dressing myself this time with the clothes and jewellery given to me from the bride's side. I went up to Ashoke Babu and asked: 'How do I look." He examined me from head to foot and said in his usual truthful manner: 'Like chewing gum** wrapped up in gold leaf.' On that occasion he and my other colleagues presented my wife with a pair of gold earrings or rather ear pendants and a fine sari, all packed in a box covered with Indian handwoven silk, and with a greeting card which had a large design in colours taken from one of the painted ceilings of the Ajanta caves.

The Aftermath

When I came to England in 1955 for the first time, one evening my friends in the BBC entertained me at the Elizabethan restaurant in Kensington.

* The word in Bengali was not chewing gum, but a form of candy, equally plebeian.

After we had dined on peacock and syllabub to the melody of a lute my principal host drawled out - the result of drinking too much mead - 'And now for the reckoning!' *L'addition* I had to face was much worse.

Externally, nothing was amiss. The flat was ample for the two of us. I had brought in what I had, arranged my books, of which any collector of my age could be proud, hung up my Medici prints and Mogul pictures, and besides put all the new acquisitions from my father-in-law in their proper place. I had engaged a man servant who was also to be cook. I might say incidentally that in our class the wives did not cook, unless it were some exceptional dish on an exceptional occasion. And poor as I was, I did not even dream of making my wife cook for me. The servant washed and polished up everything, and remarked: 'Now the house is looking as if it were a palace. But the problem would be to keep it up.' He had in mind the problem of daily cleaning and spit and polish - Ronuk and Min furniture polish had been bought. But the remark had a more ominous application to me. And I am now going to write about that.

My wife came over to the flat ten days or so after the wedding. During those days I had some money in my pocket, because I had got what in Bengali is called *pranami,* crudely translated as 'fee for doing obeisance' to the elders. Every bridegroom has to touch the feet of his elderly in-laws, both male and female, and he is given some money, always in silver coins and at times in gold as well - in sovereigns or old Muslim *mohurs.* This is also called 'blessing money'. The same thing is done for the bride. So both of us got some money. I was keeping up appearances in the two weeks following the wedding with my share. But by the beginning of May it had run out, and nothing had come in as salary on account of the advance. I was in mortal fear of my new wife coming to me for housekeeping expenses, because after a mistress had come to the house the servants would not come to me but go to her, and she would have to ask me. But she did not. Yet I ate well and did not dare to make inquiries. I learned afterwards that, feeling shy, she was spending her 'blessing money'.

Before the middle of the month, however, a particular crisis developed. The previous October, when there was no idea of my marrying or agreeing to marry, I had bought some shawls and other warm dress material from my old Kashmiri shawl dealer for myself and to give to my brothers and some others. Like my self-indulgence, my generosity too was based on credit. These dealers gave what we wanted and waited till April or May for payment, if we did not pay before that by instalments. The beginning of May was the very latest time limit for payment, because after that the Kashmiris went back to Kashmir. My man had come once or twice, and was now insistent. I had failed to keep my word, and he was nervous. I gave him a date, and when it arrived I had no money. So I went out in the morning in the vain hope of borrowing money from somewhere. I could not, and came back home in very low spirits.

As it happened, on that day my sister-in-law, that is, my brother's wife, and other relatives had come for lunch, and the house was full of guests. As I entered, the nephew of mine who was with me in the Military Accounts and still there, opened the door. I asked him if the shawl merchant had come. He replied that he had, and that 'auntie' had settled the bill. When I looked up in curiosity, he explained that my wife had given him some of her gold coins to sell and he had brought her the money. There was no alternative but to go in and meet my wife. I found her sitting alone on a chair in the dining room. The conversation between me and my nephew had taken place at the door and she must have heard it. As I entered, she looked up, and I fell on my knees at her feet, and, hiding my shamed face in her lap, said: 'Forgive me.' She only passed her hand through my hair.

My sister-in-law who was passing by saw me in that posture, and said afterwards that she had no notion that I could be so romantic or maudlin. She could not guess what it really was - my unavailing contrition towards a wife not yet a month old. Nearly fifty years have passed by since I was married. We have discussed our past troubles and trials many times. But never could I refer to this incident: so far as I remember, this is the only thing over which we have been reserved with each other.

I do not remember now how I managed for the rest of the month. But June arrived and with it some relief But externally nobody could perceive that anything was wrong. I fitted brass curtain rods to the windows, which no Bengali did; I also hung curtains, which, too, no Bengali did. On account of my nationalistic mood the curtains were of green khaddar; later I changed them to silk and net. We also had silk or glass shades to the electric bulbs, another non-Bengali feature. I might add that I had a spotted deer skin on the floor below the divan, and an otter skin on it.

What effect my style of living after my marriage produced on those who had no knowledge of the behind the scenes I shall illustrate by telling a story. I had a visit from a distant relative who was younger than me soon after my marriage, when my wife was away on a two-day visit to her sister in Calcutta. He was very uneducated and also rustic, living in his village. But at times he came down to Calcutta, paying his fare by reading the palms of the ticket inspectors by claiming to be an astrologer. He was very dark even for us, and also very deaf So, he always used an ear-trumpet and brought it close to the mouth of those to whom he was speaking. He was at first struck of a heap to see my rooms, and, more especially, the electric bell at the door, which was very rare in Bengali houses then. He had rung it many times for the sheer fun of it, as also did some of my neighbours.

He was given to speaking in English when excited, and on the whole spoke it grammatically. He asked me in that language: 'Dada, [which means 'elder brother' and not 'father'] you are a poor-salaried man [the common description for a Bengali whose salary was below Rs.200 a month], but how can you have set up like this?' I only smiled instead of replying. Then he went into the bedroom, and was even more struck with wonder. Suddenly, his eyes fell on the bed, and he cried out, this time in Bengali, 'Ho, ho, I've understood. You have married.' I replied 'No,' but he at once retorted, pointing to the two sets of pillows and in English: 'Then, why two pillows?' Next, he put a significant question: 'Was the bell, too, given by your father-in-law?'

By the end of June my wife began to feel unwell and had nausea. It became so bad that she had to lie in bed like a seasick person. I was terribly frightened, for the newly married wife of a friend had died recently of such symptoms. But when I went and told my sister-in-law she laughed and did not sympathise. My doctor brother was consulted and he brought a gynaecologist, who reassured me. In the meanwhile, my father-in-law had gone back to Shillong with his family, but when he was informed he at once arranged to take his daughter there, so that she might be looked after, and also be comfortable in the cool of the hills to which she was used. She went at the beginning of August, and was to come back at the end of November with her parents, when they were to make their annual visit to Calcutta. The child was expected in February. I was to go to Shillong in October.

Shillong

The thought of seeing Shillong kept me even more excited than the expectation of being with my wife. I had indeed gone to Shillong, but that was as a baby. The last time I was taken there was in 1900, when I was two and a half years old. So I remembered nothing. But, as I have related in my autobiography, my mother was always telling us stories of Shillong with its hills, gorges, springs, falls, pines, oranges and pears, as well as English babies and Gurkha soldiers, and hearing them I had made Shillong the unseen fourth environment of my early life, in addition to my birthplace, ancestral village, and mother's village. Thus I began to prepare myself to meet the reality. I bought a large-scale map of the Shillong area (six inches to the mile), and particularly studied the contours because I wanted to know beforehand what sort of climbing of steep hill faces I should have to undertake. I began to prepare myself as if I was going mountaineering.

But I wrote some of my most solid articles on public affairs as well, to keep myself occupied. Two of them were published in the October issue of *The Modern Review*, one under my name and the other under a pseudonym. The first was on British policy towards Afghanistan after the second Afghan War and the second was on the control of the Indian Press in the interest of policy. As holiday reading for Shillong I took a new biography of Ludendorff and Heinrich Wölfflin's book on styles of painting, and if I read a few pages of Ludendorff on the train, I did not open any of the books at Shillong. I had other things to do. I should add that I had to borrow money to go to Shillong - no departure from the norm.

The month I spent in Shillong was one of the happiest in my life, and not simply because I did not for once have to think about money every day. I had never before been at a hilly place. I had indeed seen low hills in Orissa, but Shillong was at an altitude of 5,000 feet. The town was situated on a wide ledge at the foot of a plateau, which rose sheer for one thousand feet to upper Shillong, on which was the Shillong Peak, 6,400 feet high. Before the British had chosen the place as the capital of Assam, the hills were bare, but afterwards they were planted with pine. There was a beautiful lake and park at the centre of the city. I did not, however, join the crowd in the bazaar of the town, but went out early in the morning for long excursions in the hills and woods within a radius of four miles, sometimes walking even ten miles. On occasions, I climbed up to the plateau, on others went down gorges 800 feet deep, at times going on all fours on gradients which were 1:3. At first, I did not know how to walk on hills, either to climb or to descend, and I lost breath by trying to maintain the usual walking pace I had in Calcutta. However, I observed the Khasis going up and down even with huge loads, and soon adopted their measured steps. Actually, I found going down a slope more arduous than going up.

My father-in-law was worried about me. One of the wooded hills where I often went was believed to have wild animals, and a new son-in-law of another family had slipped from a cliff and was found dangling from a pine which had caught his fall. He did not want to lose his son-in-law in that fashion. But I was not, in spite of my frail body, a Bengali with no control over his limbs or so stupid as to ignore elementary precautions. Thus before I chose the morning's walk I studied the contours very carefully and followed the easiest slopes. In the afternoons I took out my wife, who was now fully recovered and could go about like a normal person, for walks in the park among the pines. The curious thing was that in those morning walks I never met any Bengali or even an Englishman, but only Khasis, who looked curiously at so abnormal a Bengali.

My preference was for the highest places I could climb up to, so that, perched there, I could gaze down on the inhabited world below. Brought up in East Bengal, I felt at home only when I saw rice fields stretching away to the horizon or was on water all around me. At Shillong I enjoyed the openness in another form. If I was not like Cortez on a peak in Darien, I was on the top of Shillong Peak, sitting on a grassy mound at 6,400 feet. And this was what I saw:

'There was before and below me the road to Cherapoonji and, branching off from it, the road to Mawphlang. There was the Laidyngkot bridlepath. There was also the place which I thought would be Nongkhrem, famous for its Khasi dance, and the place further to the right where I placed Mawphlang, with the beautiful gorge and rapids of the Bogapani. Turning round, I could see the bare ridge of Lum Dingei, the green and grassy Bhoi country, the dome-headed Sopet Bneng in the middle distance, and farther away the blue hills of Nongkhlaw.'

This is from my autobiography. Incidentally, I could talk about what I saw in Shillong only with my father-in-law, who alone knew the topography of Shillong well, and not my wife's 'boy friends' (truly so-called) who were studying science or economics in Calcutta.

But I also wanted to go down to Plutonic depths in my exploration of the courses of the rivers in Shillong. The town had two streams which mingled at its northwest comer, and, becoming the Umiam, flowed finally into the great Brahmaputra. These streams were called respectively Um Shirpi and Um Khra. My mother's people used to live just above the Um Khra, and she often spoke about it. But she invariably applied to it a word in Bengali which was the equivalent of the English word 'rill'. Coming from the plains she would not call a hill stream even a stream.

I followed both the streams and tracked down the Um Khra to its descent of some three hundred feet at one leap at the Beadon Falls to join the Um Shirpi. But at first I found the Um Shirpi lost among the woods and down into a gorge. I was determined to go down to this gorge, and so one day I climbed down eight hundred feet to the stream's bed between two high walls of almost perpendicular cliff face. The stream was not more than ten or twelve feet wide and it was flowing over boulders. On each bank there was a level ledge about six feet wide, overgrown with lantana, leading towards an opening in the rock, through which I could see the sky. I placed the famous Bishop Falls (about 450 feet) there and wanted to see the head of the fall. I walked to a distance of about ten feet from the far end, and then sensed danger. The water was running fast but like a solid block. I came back, and it was fortunate that I did, for I always became giddy if I looked down from a height. If I had gone there and seen the water falling over I should have lost my balance and gone over.

But I was not ready to give up. So I climbed up the gorge again and took a path which led towards the Beadon Falls. Seeing a track going down I took it, and suddenly I found myself on a very narrow ledge with the Bishop Falls right in front of me across the gorge. Half of its plunge was above me and the other half below, and I hung in the middle. There was a tremendous roar, and spray was rising from the pool at the bottom, with a magnificent rainbow in it. I decided to go further down, walk along the river, and reach the power house at the Beadon Falls. I did, but not without some risk. I lost my way among the lantana, and pressing them got their mintlike smell on myself Suddenly, I saw the river two hundred feet below me and the edge of the cliff was just at my feet. I swung myself back holding the branch of a tree, and managed to find the track to the power house. After reaching it I climbed up another cliff about three hundred feet high and found myself on the motor road from Gauhati. When I told my father-in-law of these climbs he did not like it, but he told me how once he had been made to climb the cliff at Beadon Falls by the Lieutenant-Governor, Sir Bamfylde Fuller. The Lieutenant-Governor decided to climb the cliff instead of going up by the path, and wanted to test his Bengali subordinate. For the honour of Bengal my father-in-law followed him, but he had to remain in bed for three days owing to the pain he had at the joints. I as his son-in-law had no pain and got no aching joints.

I came back to Calcutta at the beginning of November, and my father-in-law came down with his family at the end of that month for his annual stay in Calcutta. I took away my wife to our house from the railway station, but on the way stopped to pay a visit to my brother. My sister-in-law noticed the fat cheeks of my wife and attributed the fatness to the fruits of the Khasi hills, and she also noticed the bloom due to the cool. Khasi girls always had the red of apples on their cheeks and had what the English called the gipsy complexion. Bengali girls who lived in Shillong, too, had the same bloom, but lost it in Calcutta, to recover it when they went back to die hills.

My Illness and Our Firstborn

My wife was not the woman to lose her command of the house because she was expecting. I found that she was even more energetic than before in running the house properly. It was still about three months before her time. But both of us were very impatient to have our child, and wished human pregnancy were shorter. Then something regrettable happened. One day, early in December, I was going to visit my father in my brother's house when returning from work, and suddenly I felt very dizzy and was on the point of falling down in the lane. I somehow maintained my balance and tottered to the house. But I could not go in, and finding a bench outside lay down on it. My father and others came out in great alarm and at once sent for my brother, the doctor. He came and after examining me said that there was nothing serious in my condition, but that I was very weak and must have complete rest for some time. I was taken home in his car. My wife when she saw me brought in supported by others, came up gravely, and saw me put in bed. Beyond her serious and watchful expression I noticed no sign of fear on her face. I smiled to reassure her. When all the others were gone she sat by me, attending tenderly. The next day my brother brought a leading cardiologist to examine me. He, too, found nothing basically wrong, but asked me not to work for some time and keep to bed. It was about a month before I went to the office again. My wife continued to show her self- possession, but she told me afterwards that very often she felt very depressed and pondered what would happen to her if she were left alone with a child. She was twenty-three then. My weak condition, accompanied by symptoms of functional heart trouble, continued for nearly two years. All of it was due to overstraining myself by hill climbing, when I had no experience of it.

In the meanwhile, her time was approaching. I had decided that our child would be born in our house, and as I put it *under my auspices*. At that time it was inconceivable for Bengali women of our class to go to a hospital for their lying in, but there was an almost immemorial custom for a young wife to go to her father's house for the birth of her first child. I had not seen any departure from this even in our family. And, of course, all the expenses were also borne by the father. The custom had grown up because in those days of early marriage young married girls lost all freedom of movement in the house of her father-in-law, and was likely to be embarrassed to tell about her condition and discomforts. So, she went to her mother. But by our time the custom had been transformed into something like the guarantee for a watch or a car and of free servicing for at least a year.

I was resolved to have nothing to do with the custom, and although my wife's parents were in Calcutta I had made arrangements to have the confinement in my flat. It was, of course, understood that my mother-in-law would come over and stay with her until she was able to go about. But the management of the affair was to be in my hands, and also the entire expense was to be mine. I said flippantly: 'If I had gone off on the jaunt of having a child, its consequences ought to be borne by me. Folly or pleasure, the responsibility was mine.'

The doctors were not likely to cost me anything. My brother, with his friend the gynaecologist, was to be in attendance. But I engaged a midwife and a nurse. Very few persons with a monthly income of eight pounds had their first child born attended by an obstetrician trained in Munich, a paediatrician trained in Vienna and Tubingen, and by a midwife and also a nurse. Even without any fee for the doctors the affair cost me almost three months' salary, but I had this satisfaction at least that when I looked at my child I did not have to admit that my son, like our bedroom furniture, was also a gift from my father-in-law.

The doctors had anticipated the date to be 21 February. From the 19th my wife began to feel uncomfortable. The doctors came on the next day, and so did my mother-in-law. There was, however, no immediate likelihood of anything happening. So that they went away, to come again in the evening. They did, and finding my wife in very great pain, decided to sit up by her the whole night. I went to the sitting-room, and tried to sleep on the divan. But no sleep came. I was feeling like Levine for Kitty in *Anna Karenina*. My brother-in-law (sister's husband) was in the house, and sitting by me was ragging me. He said that so uxorious a husband was bound to have a daughter and not a son. He forgot that my sister had been twining him round her little finger for sixteen years and he had had no son so far.

I could hear the groans of my wife throughout the night. At about four o'clock in the morning of 21st February, the nurse came and told me that my wife wanted me to go to her. Even apart from the fact that husbands are not present anywhere at the confinement of their wives, it was inconceivable in Hindu society. When I entered, my mother-in-law, who felt very embarrassed, made a sign to me and told me to go back. But I advanced to the bedside. My wife looked up, took one of my hands in two of hers, and with tears running down her cheeks said: 'I am in great pain.' I stood silent, but she seemed to quieten down. The doctors and the others were all standing in an alert posture. The obstetrician said: 'It's more than twenty- four hours. I do not think we can wait any longer,' and he asked my brother to apply the anaesthetic, which he did. The child was brought out with the instrument, and put in a basin. As it did not cry I thought it was stillborn. I knew nothing about this, of course. The doctors attended to my wife, while the nurse knelt down to the baby - it was a boy. Suddenly it cried, and I saw that it was living. It was washed and dressed and put in a cradle or something. But my wife was without consciousness. I went back to the sitting-room. My brother-in-law had heard that it was a son, so he did not revert to his joke. I was too moved to talk.

We all thought that my wife would recover quickly, for she was strong and robust. But there was some infection, and from the third day she began to have a temperature. The doctors had everything examined and analysed, and found that it was a bacillary infection. Therefore my mother-in-law remained with us for about a month, until my wife was fully recovered. The child was very fat, and so besides giving it a formal name, I also gave it a pet name, which was something like the Bengali equivalent of the English 'snubby', with a suggestion that the mind was also of the same order. My father was scandalized that his first grandson should be so named. But it was a common and traditional name in West Bengal, given to avert the Evil Eye, and I stuck to it. The boy, now grown to middle age, is still called by that name in the family, although his only child, a daughter, bears the very adventurous, exotic, and smart name of Papagena.

I had a very happy time with the child. Although by Bengali standards I was almost an old bachelor by the time I married, I had always been very fond of babies, and very successful in keeping them happy in my arms. My sisters' babies would not go to them from me. My wife, on the contrary, could not handle very young babies and feel comfortable. So she took over our children only when they ceased to be mere lumps of flesh. Even at night I got up and changed them if they cried.

The baby gave no trouble whatever, and that was due to the very simple but strict rules that my paediatrician brother laid down for us. The baby was to be breastfed, and indeed all my three children were so fed till their seventh month, after which they were gradually weaned. That not only gave the children a strong constitution, but also saved me a lot of expense on artificial baby food - in Calcutta Cow and Gate and other things made in England were given. Secondly, the baby was to be left alone, except for feeding very regularly and changing. No lights were to be kept on when he slept, and, above all, visitors were not allowed to gossip in the bedroom where the baby slept. And the last rule, very surprising in a paediatrician trained in Europe: the baby was to sleep snuggling against the mother like a puppy. That has prevented my children from sucking their thumbs, which I always see children in England doing even to the age of seven or more. All this was also very un-Bengali. But I had done so many un-Bengali things in my life that nobody minded that in me. The child grew to be very fond of me, and would cry if after coming back from the office I did not take him in my arms.

But the picture had another side, very vexatious and even humiliating. My salary was totally insufficient, and I was falling in arrears in respect of rent and all other dues. The dunning was not pleasant. Fortunately, at that time my wife observed the purdah, and none of the creditors could speak to her. But their clamour at the door must have upset her. To make things worse, I went out in the morning to avoid the dunning, and the creditors showed more impatience.

To escape all that I accepted an offer of a better job at the end of 1933, and left *The Modern Review*. The outcome was to be a situation which was far worse than the period of unemployment I had from 1926 to 1928. It lasted for nearly three and a half years. Thus, if during the first two years of my marriage my marrying looked like an act of madness, in the light of what happened in the next three years it could be described as a criminal's doing. I am going to relate that experience in the next chapter, but I would anticipate it with the declaration that all that was worth going through.

CHAPTER 2

Blessed are the Poor with Spirit

Within three months of my leaving *The Modern Review*, the hopes with which I had done that vanished, and, as I have just said, I was thrown into a renewed state of poverty, which for most of the time was acute distress. From April 1934 to March 1937 I was wholly without regular employment and income, and this time I had a wife and children to support. Besides, my father, on whom I could fall back if the worst came to the worst, died suddenly in April 1934, at the not very old age of sixty-seven. The only redeeming feature in my worldly situation was that I did not become dependent on anyone, and thus had no sense of moral degradation added to my poverty. What I had to endure was solely the strain of providing daily bread in the literal sense for my family, without any hope of relief from any quarter.

Both my wife and I went through that without thinking or speaking about what we were having to do, because we knew that to brood or to talk would only be adding to our misery. I might add that throughout our married life we have never discussed our financial position when it has been bad, although very often it has been so. We gave our special interpretation to the proverb that words break no bones. But now I recall the experience with dread, and get rid of the fear with which I am seized by saying to myself that nothing like that could happen to us again.

It was like being on a raft after being shipwrecked, and drifting on the off-chance of being picked up by a ship. As it happened, the ship eventually arrived, but it took a long time to do so. All this was perfectly consistent, however, with the law that has governed my worldly existence - or should I call it *kismet*? - that I have never been able to ensure bodily survival for myself and my family by taking thought, that is, by planning or willing, and that it has always been accomplished for me by sheer chance. What the Fate watching over me demanded from me as the barest discharge of my duty by her was to keep up my spirits. I did what I could, and at all events I did not tempt her by consulting astrologers then or at any other time of my life. If I have been a fatalist in worldly matters, I have at least exercised freewill by totally refusing to join the band of those fatalists, numbering hundreds of millions in India, who never attribute a man's successes to his ability but always set them down to luck, who are nevertheless engaged day in day out in trying to surprise Fate in her secrets.

I simply waited for something to turn up. A little did from time to time during those three years, and I got casual or temporary employment. Sometimes I got literary commissions as a hack. Besides that, I got a contribution of Rs.1 a day from my youngest brother who lived with me and would not forsake me in my distress. That also was his entire income, and he handed it over to his sister-in-law. The money earned in the periods of temporary employment went mostly towards settling old bills, and what remained was just enough to buy food for a few days. Thus, except for a total of some thirty days over those three years, I went to bed every night without a penny in my pocket, a handful of rice to boil or a piece of coal to bum. Yet, I had to feed ourselves, and especially two babies, and that could not wait beyond the next morning. Yet the miracle was that I mas able to do that - how, I shall presently relate.

That story is worth telling to the economists, sociologists, and politicians of today, who declare that unemployment leads to Communism, to race riots, or to vandalism, besides making fathers batter their children and mothers abandon or kill their babies. What would a mouse say to these theorists? Perhaps only this: that human beings scream about human rights and squeal as even mice have never squealed. When I have told the whole story it will perhaps be conceded that nobody had a greater right to become a Communist and snarl like them than my wife and I. But, instead of doing that, we behaved like natural animals, who either find food to eat or drop dead. Above all, living in Calcutta, we did not behave like the Bengalis in that city today, who will work for any capitalist on any salary and save their Communist souls by voting Marxist.

Yet I was under no illusion about the spirit and temper of the age in which I was living. I could face both without accepting the eschatology offered by Dialectical Materialism. It was in 1929, to the best of my recollection, that I bought and read *L'Avenir de l'intelligence* by Charles Maurras. In it I came upon a passage which shocked me into the full realization of a truth which before that I had only vaguely perceived. I find that the remarks have been omitted from the version of the book in the new collected edition of the works of Maurras, which is condensed. Here it is, though, from the original edition of 1904. As there was no English translation of the book I translated the passage myself in order to quote it in a Bengali article of mine, published in 1937.

'The reign of gold, the master of iron, and now become the arbiter of all secular thought, will continue unless ..wrote Maurras.

'An aristocracy in externals of life but a barbarism truly democratic in things of the mind: such is the lot which the future holds for us. In that coming order, the dreamer and the thinker will have to maintain himself at the cost either of his dignity or of his wellbeing, and position, success and fame will reward the suppleness of the mountebank. More than ever, in a measure unthought of in the age of iron, the hero and the saint will expiate for their pride in poverty and loneliness. They will either starve with folded arms over the banquet spread before them or, in order to get a bone to gnaw, cringe and sink to the level of dogs.'

However, I never applied this to myself, and even now I do not think that the choice is so stark. But my case is perhaps exceptional, and I have no right to contradict Maurras. Furthermore, I did not even quote the passage to support any general argument of mine, as I did in 1937, until I had come through my troubles, lest it should be thought that I was pleading my case by proxy. The cause of compassion is a very noble one. But I hold the opinion, and held it more strongly in the days of my distress, that as long as a man remains in a position which makes him an object of compassion in the eyes of the world, he has no right to demand it even for others. There must be no suspicion of self-pity or self-justification in any advocacy of compassion. My friend, Bibhuti Babu, whose novels and stories are a long plea for compassion, never quite realized this. With all his gift for evoking it, he seemed to be incapable of asking for it on behalf of anybody who was not a sort of projection of himself.

Misfortune Never Comes Alone

However that may be, let me tell my own story. The troubles which I brought on myself by leaving *The Modern Review* had their origin in my acceptance of an offer to become the editor of a new newspaper to be started in Calcutta. This was going to be an extension of the journalistic enterprise of a man named Sadananda from Madras, who had already established himself as a newspaper proprietor in Bombay. I believe he had modest middle-class antecedents, but had risen in the world wholly through his energy and ambition. He had begun with a news agency in London and Bombay, which he called the Free Press of India. He justified the name by providing news with a strong nationalist emphasis, which was free from suspicion of being under the influence of the Government of India, as the two established news agencies, Reuter and the Associated Press of India, were believed to be. Naturally, his service was welcome to the nationalist press, which had to be extremist and hostile to the Government. The success of this venture made Sadananda start a newspaper in Bombay, which was called *The Free Press Journal*. His undertakings prospered to the point of making him recognized as a 'somebody' in the world of Indian politics and business. Growing more ambitious, he wanted to have a chain of newspapers all over India, and more especially in Calcutta and Madras.

He put the organization of the Calcutta paper in the hands of a young Bengali who was the brother-in-law of a friend of mine from boyhood. They thought of me, and one day called at the *Modern Review* office to ask me if I would be interested in its editorship. The financial inefficiency of *The Modern Review* had made me very impatient, and I agreed to take up the job without giving much thought to the nature of the work. The salary proposed was not very high, nonetheless it was double of what I was getting. So, from I January 1934I began to work for the new paper, which was to be called *Free India*.

For the time being there was joy in two families, mine and that of my wife. Both thought that their son and daughter were at last coming out of their hand-to-mouth existence. To add to the mood of elation, there was a very happy event in our family - the marriage of my doctor brother. He was going to be married to the daughter of a very wealthy man, who, besides, was a judge in Calcutta. The pourparlers had been going on for some time, for my brother was very eligible as a son-in-law, at all events potentially. I did everything to promote the match from prudential considerations. The curious thing in my attitude was that, "however imprudent I might be in respect of myself I always showed myself as an advocate of prudence for others. My brother stood in need of it. He was very ambitious and was running into heavy debts in order to establish himself as a private practitioner. I thought that it would be very difficult for him to do so if he had to find the means of carrying on from day to day while trying to build up a practice. Apart from that, a certain person was advancing him money as a loan with the idea of making him marry his daughter. I wanted to check this as well as provide him with capital, which could come only from a wife with money. However, we did not have to sacrifice other things for it. The girl was desirable in herself During the negotiations my brother took the bit in his mouth and jibbed. One day he had an argument with our father, and declared that he would never become the lackey of a wealthy father-in-law and of a wife with money. But I managed the affair with great tact, and he was brought round. The wedding took place with great pomp. The marriage was my brother's making. Eventually, he became a very wealthy man. My young sister-in-law was very quiet outwardly. But she seemed to have an inborn flair for breaking wild horses without shouting.

I did not join in the revels of the wedding. After having seen through the marriage negotiations, I turned to the work of organizing the new office and supervising the setting up of the linotype machines and the rotary press. I did not go to the bride's house for the wedding, nor was I present at the banquet in my brother's house. But before the wedding I had an experience which was memorable. I was in the office watching the work on the press with the young manager by my side, when suddenly the whole building began to tilt to and fro and the floor rolled from side to side under our feet. I, of course, understood that it was a severe earthquake. All the staff and workmen ran out, but the young man and I remained where we were. We smiled mechanically and the tremors seemed to be going on for minutes. I was glad to see a brave young man. It was the famous Bihar earthquake of January 1934, in which about 40,000 people lost their lives. It was only less tragic than the great Quetta earthquake of the next year.

As soon as the tremors were over, I thought of my house as well as that of my brother. I was not very anxious about my house. It was a building on steel frames and my wife, having been brought up in Shillong, was very familiar with earthquakes. But I was really anxious about my brother's house. It was a detached old brick building of a very large size, and could come down like our house at Kishorganj in 1918. My father was there, as well as my sister with her very young baby. So, I first ran to their house, to find all safe. My father told me that my brother's car had been sent to fetch my wife and the baby. I waited, and soon saw them coming in.

My wife told her story. Far from being in any kind of shocked state, she was not even upset, although she was expecting her second baby and was not well. She had, she said, sent up our servant to the loft and was giving him directions from the passage below. Suddenly, the servant cried out, 'Mother what is it? The loft is moving.' Of course, she knew what it could be. So, after asking the servant to come down at once, she ran to the bedroom to fetch the baby and went out to stand on the narrow landing, which she thought would be much safer than the courtyard two floors below, where masonry, if any fell at all, would hit people. But looking over the railing, she saw a crowd there, raising a hubbub. The wife of a friend of mine who lived in one of the lower floor flats, an elderly lady, was also there. She had great affection for both my wife and the child, and she shouted: 'You miserable girl, what are you doing there.' Come down at once unless you want to die with your child. What, you are grinning.?' However, the earthquake stopped.

After the excitement of the wedding was over, I busied myself about the paper more seriously than before, and even spent the nights there instead of coming home. We brought out the paper, but it did not make any impact. The times were very bad for starting a new paper, because there was no political excitement whatever in the country, on which alone papers could thrive, what was worse, the money needed for a new enterprise was not forthcoming. The salaries of the editorial staff and the wages of the printers were not paid. They waited for some weeks and at the end of March they struck. I was more inclined to be on their side than on that of the proprietor. Nothing further was done to redstart the paper, and the Calcutta project was given up altogether. But the proprietor had better luck with the Madras paper. However, like all too ambitious upstarts, he had overshot the mark. He disappeared from the journalistic scene, and his enterprises were taken over by a financial magnate.

I should really not have accepted that job, for I had no experience of newspapers. But I prided myself on my ideas, and also thought that so far as routine work was concerned I would have the assistance of experienced sub-editors and leader-writers, which I had. I do not like to recall this episode. It was a very shabby affair, but I cannot blame myself for the failure, which was due to want of money.

The immediate consequence of the failure was unemployment for me, followed by all the distress I have generally indicated. Yet, the strangest part of the matter was that if I had not been thoughtless in undertaking this work and remained on *The Modern Review*, I should have remained stuck there and not made the progress in the world which I eventually made. My inertia in respect of world advancement has always been so great that so long as I could carry on somehow, I showed no inclination whatever to better my financial position. I could never drive the coach of worldly existence, but would only put my shoulder to the wheel when actually stuck in the mud of want. Thus my first act after the crash of *Free India* was to take the path of least resistance. I went to Kedar Babu and asked him if I could go back to my old work. He was very much embarrassed, but had no alternative but to tell me that I could not, for he had taken on a new man. After that interview I came home with a sinking feeling in my heart. Yet my wife tells me even today that unless that had happened, I should have remained where I was in Calcutta. Therefore I can perhaps say: 'Out of this nettle danger, we pluck safety.'

It is all very well to say that in retrospect. But while the nettle was in the hand it kept at bay all idea of safety. However, although I had no money in my pocket I was not hopeless immediately. I expected to have some to last a month or so from one source. It was to come from a security deposit of a very special kind. In those days in India, nobody could publish any periodical without a declaration from the editor and the printer before a senior magistrate, and his permission. This permission was given freely only when the editor had a good political record with the police. But when a reference about me was made to the Calcutta police by the magistrate they reported me as a political suspect, and so the magistrate ordered that I should have to put in a security of Rs. 500 with the court. This was done by the management. I could take the sum as my salary, because it was paid in my name and would be refunded by the court only to me.

The police report against me was the most fantastic thing imaginable in its mixture of truth and falsehood. My connection with the Chittagong student was on the file. So also was my connection with a Communist organization called Labour Research Bureau, into which I was drawn by a friend. But the police also reported that I was in the entourage of Subhas Chandra Bose, the well-known nationalist leader, with involvement in the revolutionary movement, whereas actually I had not even seen him till then. But the report at all events ensured some compensation for me for the loss of the job. However, it took a long time to get the deposit refunded.

In the meanwhile, there was a grievous death in our family - that of my father. It was very sudden. After the wedding he had gone back to Benares, where he lived then, all by himself. He was happy both on my account and my brother's, and his health seemed even to have improved. On being unemployed again, I was bound to inform him, although I knew that in his circumstances he could not help me, nor did I suggest any such thing. I was expecting his reply, when suddenly a telegram from him came to my doctor brother asking him to go to Benares because my father was not feeling well. He at once went. I was not very anxious, but the very next day another telegram came from a doctor friend of my father who was also at Benares, which informed us that he was dead. After receiving it my elder and youngest brothers started for Benares for the funeral ceremonies. When my brothers came back I heard the whole story.

For some days he had been anxious about himself, and fearing some sudden worsening had telegraphed to my doctor brother. But he felt very much better, and told his friend that he regretted that he had sent that telegram which might unduly alarm us. He had come to visit that friend, and suddenly said that he was not feeling well at all. At the same time he fell down from his chair, pressing his heart, and collapsed. Nothing could be done for him. He was cremated at once by friends and neighbours. But when my brothers arrived they found that everything in his rooms, including a large sum of money which was known to be with him, had been stolen. It was useless to complain to the police, because in Benares they were known to be in league with all the crooks and gangsters for which the city was notorious.

The day I heard of his death I also got a postcard from him, which was a reply to my letter. It was written just before his death, and in it he informed me that he was very sorry to hear about my unemployment and would soon come down to Calcutta to see what he could do for me. That assurance was the last communication I had from a father who always overlooked my faults because he had confidence in my talents. But he died only with the knowledge of a fresh failure, and never lived to see even my moderate successes. He died exactly ten years after my mother.

I was thirty-six then. Still, I felt as if I had been deprived of the only source of protection I had, and had become an orphan. The feeling did not come from expectation of monetary help from him, for I knew that he could not do much. It was die loss of the moral support which I felt was at my back, that made me consider myself totally helpless. I was faced with the fact that henceforth I should have to fight my battles alone. Even then I did not realize what a support my wife would be to me. My father, however, had complete confidence in her, and thought I was safe in her hands.

Unemployed

By the end of June the money I got from the deposit was spent, and unless I chose to starve I had to find some source of income. Knowing that it might be years before I would have spare money to spend on such things and also that my son was just old enough to need such toys soon, I made it the first charge on the money I got to buy a number of educational toys for him. Among these was a box of Lett's building bricks. These were all of British make, for in those days such toys were not made in India. Such extravagance was to bring disrepute on me.

Equally characteristic was my negative behaviour. This must have brought greater disrepute, but that never reached my ears. Far from looking for a new job, I did not even think of finding one. My wife also showed herself to be an exceptional wife by falling in with my view. Not to speak of wives, no relatives left an unemployed man in peace if he did not go out every day in search of a job. The nagging was so continuous and sharp that just to avoid that all unemployed young men went out of their houses after breakfast and trudged the streets of Calcutta day after day, to come back in the afternoons to report failure every day, which made the next day's nagging worse. What was more surprising, the unemployed themselves also thought that jobs could be secured by simply trudging.

In later life I had to interview literally scores of young men about employment, and all of them told me that they had worn out their shoes and made their feet sore by walking from office to office, and yet found no work. This extraordinary persistence surprised me until I discovered that it was a throw-back to the nomadic stage of human existence. All pastoral people remain on the move. If grass dries up at one place they think they will come upon fresh pastures simply by moving on. Curiously enough, this nomadic behaviour extended to urban employment satisfied the relatives.

I refused to follow the tradition. I knew that employment in India came along certain channels, and could not be obtained by merely looking for it. To go and ask for a job because one needed it or had the qualification for it, was to court not only refusal, but humiliation. So, I kept quiet, knowing that unless employment came to me out of an interested demand from someone who was an employer it would never come because I wanted it. My wife saw like me, and never asked me to look for a job.

Waiting, however, was not pleasant. It became more so because I was not disposed to take advantage of the only kind of unemployment benefit we had in our society. This was to live on relatives. Although they often insulted the dependents they never refused to keep them. But a more popular custom was to send the wife and children to the house of the father-in-law and make him support them until the young man found employment. No father in our society would refuse to keep a daughter in such circumstances. Besides, if a son-in-law was brazen enough, he would himself go and live in the house of his father-in-law and expect to be treated as he was on the day he first went there as a bridegroom, even grumble if he was not.

I did not fall back on this assistance, although my father-in-law was then living in Calcutta in a house of his own. I did not send my wife there, nor would she go. During those days of distress she would not go even for a few days to get relief from the strain and anxiety. She only went to visit them occasionally just as she would have done in normal circumstances. She did not ask her father for loans, nor even for her own money which was deposited with him. In later years, but not then - there was no occasion to explain at the time because I never asked her to get money in that way - she stated her view of the situation to me. She said that her father had chosen me as his son-in-law knowing all the circumstances and she could not make him feel sorry for his decision, nor bring discredit on me, by asking him for help. I have also to add that neither my father-in-law nor my mother-in-law questioned me or their daughter about our circumstances, although they must have felt both anxiety and distress. They respected our independence, and I must say that I have not seen any father-in-law or mother-in- law in our society taking that line. Normally, the mother-in-law talked and interfered, creating bad blood between husband and wife.

My mother-in-law was exceptional in other ways too. A close relative of mine, a lady, reported my extravagance about providing toys for my son, which she resented, to her, and when my mother-in-law came to see us after that, she wanted to see the toy which was so expensive. It was the box of building bricks at about *7s.6d.* She asked me very gently whether in the existing circumstances I should have spent money on such a thing. I replied very quietly but firmly: 'I know if I smoked or drank or for that matter even went to a house of ill-fame, you would have kept silent and never even referred to such things, but you are objecting because I have bought a toy for my son.' I should explain that in our society parents or elders would not take notice of the bad habits and even depravities of young men for fear of appearing to be lacking in decorum. However, seeing my mother-in-law very much confused, I went on: 'I shall explain why I bought that toy even in my present circumstances.'

I went into a long and elaborate, if not decidedly pedantic, explanation about the connection of handwork and motor activity with the development of the brain, knowing that I was appealing to her most susceptible side.. Bengali ladies of the class and kind to which my mother and mother-in-law- belonged were worshippers of education, which, of course, they understood in the widest sense, and the most contemptuous word which they could utter about a young man was that he was 'uneducated'. My mother-in-law listened to me with great interest and attention, and then observed: 'My son, then it is a matter of education. I had no idea of that. Your - (mentioning my close relative who had carried the tale to her) - put it in such a way that I misunderstood it, and thought you should not have spent money in this manner. Do not remain offended with me;' I was too touched by that even to reassure her. At least, she learned just before she died that I had got a very good post under the Government of India and her daughter was not likely to live in want any more. She died before her time at about the age of fifty. Had she lived only ten years longer, she would have seen her son-in-law greeted as an author in London and New York. With her veneration for letters, she would have rejoiced in that.

The problem of finding money for our day to day existence continued, and the only thing I could or would do was to write articles. Editors always welcomed them, and the fees, though not high, were something. I wrote specially for a new magazine whose editorship Sajani Das had taken up. But there was one extra contingency for which I had to provide. That was my wife's second confinement, which was expected at the end of September. Our first son was not yet even eighteen months old and he could not walk, because he had a very large and heavy head. My mother-in-law naturally felt worried. In spite of the custom in our society which permitted and even required that the first children of a young wife would be born in her father's house, I was determined to follow the precedent I had established with my first son. There could be no difficulty about doctors. My brother would see to that, and there was no difficulty about a nurse; that too was fixed up. And I thought that by the time the child was due according to the doctors, I would collect the money for my articles.

But on 8 September 1934, my wife woke me up early in the morning and said that she was feeling pain. I was taken aback, and tried to reassure myself by thinking that it might be only a false pain. I asked her, but she shook her head. Still, I waited for more than half an hour. Then I arranged the room, hearing her groans all the time. I sent word to my brother and to my father-in-law. The doctors and my mother-in-law were expected at nine o'clock. I had not as yet bought the medical supplies, and had only a few annas (about one shilling) with me. Of course, if I could not buy these either my brother or my mother-in-law would at once have got them. But the discovery by them of such a state of affairs was the humiliation I dreaded. I kept walking in the narrow passage, with cold sweat running down from my forehead. Yet I could not think of any way out before they all came. But at about quarter to nine, the door bell rang, and opening it I saw Sajani Das standing on the landing. He said: 'I have come to give you the money owing to you for your article. I was going to the office and thought I might as well call and give you the money myself He did not know that I was expecting an addition to the family. He lived very near me, and so came in casually. I at once called my brother, gave him the money and the list of medical supplies. I was arranging them on the table in my wife's room when the doctors arrived, and in a few minutes my mother-in-law also came in, accompanied by her eldest daughter, who also lived in Calcutta.

At quarter to eleven the child was born. It was an easy confinement this time, and my sister-in-law came to tell me that it also was a boy and very pretty, although relatively small. I felt so relieved that I went out at once and wandered over Calcutta visiting my literary friends. I had eaten nothing, and did not eat during the whole day. I came home at about four without feeling hungry. There is a French proverb that he who sleeps dines. I suppose he who is relieved from humiliation also does that.

This son of mine, born in such distress, is now a distinguished academic in the highest position in London, and his latest books have been received as epoch-making contributions to his subject by those who can judge. Without in any way envisaging the future, I named him after my great-great-grandfather, Kirti Narayan Chaudhuri, who had made the fortune of the Chaudhuris of the New House of Banagram and established us as a county family, so to speak. Naming after an ancestor was not customary with us, but it was justified.

CHAPTER 3
Calcutta Corporation

About two months after the birth of this son I got employment for a month as the acting editor of the official journal of the Calcutta Corporation, which was a great civic body and the only one then completely in Indian hands. The Congress controlled it. For me even this short respite from anxiety was a windfall. I got the job through its editor, Amal Home,* who was a great friend of mine, and about four or five years older than I was. He was very sorry for me after the debâcle of *Free India* and wanted to help me in my unemployed state. He did not tell me about it beforehand, but wishing to take a holiday got me to officiate for him. I must say a few words about him, for he was a remarkable man *manqué*.

His official position as the editor of the *Calcutta Municipal Gazette* was neither very important nor influential. His salary too was not such as to inspire awe in the Bengali intelligentsia, although it was higher than what most comfortably placed middle-class Bengalis got. If he had been only the smooth round peg of the proper size for the round hole in which he was in the worldly way, he would have led an easy, untroubled, and unmaligned life. But that was precisely what he was not. Even from his student days he was a talked-about character as a leader in the student politics of Calcutta University, which was centred in the Calcutta University Institute, the local equivalent of the Oxford Union. This, however, was not balanced by his academic achievement. In fact, he had none. He was too smart to take even his degree. So, he went into journalism.

That aggravated the dichotomy of his status. He came to know and be on familiar terms with eminent men all over India, beginning with the great nationalist leader, C. R. Das, as well as the great poet Tagore, and continuing his high connections with Jawaharlal Nehru, whom he always addressed as Jawahar, because he had worked with Nehru when the latter brought out his newspaper *Independent* in Allhabad.

Socially too, he belonged to the highest circle of Bengalis in Calcutta.

* He was a Bengali of course. We have that surname, which should properly be spelt without the 'e'. Once Amal Home got a reply to a letter of his from London, in which he was addressed as the Amalgamated Home.

His family was Brahmo. In those days there were a number of young men from that community of monotheistic Bengalis who could be called the *avant garde* in intellectual activities, and Amal Home was one of them. Furthermore, he was tall, well-built, and handsome, and did not cancel these advantages by being ill-dressed. Actually, he was somewhat of a dandy. Whether he appeared in Bengali, Muslim, or European costume, he was always smart, in clothes of the best make. He also affected exotic splendour by putting on the Tibetan gown known as *Bakku*, as well as the Tibetan cap. Besides, instead of appearing bareheaded like the general run of Bengalis, he most often had an Astrakhan cap on.

All this created a prejudice against him, to which one day my touchy maestro, Mohit Babu, gave vent. For his wedding Amal Babu had printed a resplendent invitation card in the form of an old Bengali manuscript, with two sheets and two covers. The latter had very beautiful designs, and in the prototype prepared by the artist they were of bevelled hard boards. I saw them. Mohit Babu was, of course, invited by Amal Babu, and he came to our house to show me the card, which he admired. In sheer spirit of mischief I said: 'Why? It hasn't got the bevelled covers. Your card is not the *de luxe* edition, but the ordinary edition.' Mohit Babu burst out in his fury: 'What, does Amal Home think he can slight me by sending the ordinary edition of his wedding invitation to me because he wears an Astrakhan cap? I am not going to his wedding feast.' Somehow I appeased him, and he did go.

Besides being a dandy he was also a snob in the good as well as bad senses of the word. His ways leaned to the grand side, and so Sajani Das wrote a limerick on him in which he said that although Amal Home went about in tramcars he sat in them as if he was in a Rolls-Royce. His manners were impeccable to the point of being finicky in some eyes, to people of his class, but to ordinary people he was not only cold but very stand-offish. This, in a sense, was quite out of character, because naturally he was a very kind and affectionate man. Nonetheless, as things stood, he was unpopular. It is not that in India people had a natural resistance to snobbery. Ordinarily, they were servile to the worst arrogance. But that was when a cad had power or money. They never forgave airs in a man who had neither. So, generally, Amal Babu was regarded as an adventurer and a fake. There was no heavy and leaden ballast to bear his tall superstructure.

Even this would not have affected him if he had opportunities to show the ability he possessed to an exceptional degree. He was very efficient in everything he undertook, and a great organizer. His real vocation was that of a showman, an impresario. He could certainly have been a Diaghilev in lines other than ballet. But all impresarios require performers and employers matched to themselves. There were none such among us. Thus he did what he could, but needed an extraordinarily large amount of money for whatever he did, like many architects of genius. This was criticized and was a point against him. It was, however, of a piece with his personal conduct. He was very extravagant, even more so than I was or could be, and was most often in debt.

I knew him from his university days in my own school days. His father came from our district, Mymensingh, and he was very well known to my father. From others, too, I heard about his precocious brilliance with some jealous feeling. But I became intimate with him only after joining the Saturday group in 1927. Some years later, taking advantage of his friendly sentiments towards me, I asked him a question which had often arisen in my mind after hearing him misrepresented and even vilified almost everywhere: 'Amal Babu, how have you contrived to make so many enemies?' He winced as if he had been branded, and did not answer me. Perhaps he had some awareness of something wanting in himself, which made him a man who was always considered to be arriving but never did. His end was very sad. Even after the age of sixty he had to work very hard, and had a stroke from overwork. He never recovered from that, and remained bed-ridden for more than ten years, supported by a devoted younger brother. He died after I came to England in 1970. Thinking of him, as also of others, I wonder why in so many cases I have to utter a very melancholy formula. Nearly all of them were not only outstripping me in early life, but also showed greater promise for the future. Yet, after their deaths, I have to say: 'One more unfortunate!'

Two years before his loss of movement and speech, he wrote a letter to me in Bengali, in which the following sentence was in English: 'Your friendship has enriched my life as hardly any other friendship has. And I shall ever cherish it, Nirad.' He was then half-blind from cataract and yet wrote with his own hand. I would only add that I did not prize his friendship less, in spite all that I heard against him.

Let me, however, tell the story of my experience of the Calcutta Corporation. When I went to officiate for Amal Babu I was seeing its working for the first time. By that time its first decade under Indian self- government had been completed. It was the first important public body to pass from British to Indian control in India, and its revenue was more than that of many minor Indian provinces. The new dispensation had begun with very high hopes for us natives in 1924, when C. R. Das became its first Mayor, and Subhas Chandra Bose its first Executive Officer. We thought at last we should have the same amenities as the European quarters, and we did. Within a year asphaltum began to be put on the streets of Bengali Calcutta, and we did not have to splatter our clothes with mud during the rainy season.

But C. R. Das, the only man who could make the self-governing Calcutta Corporation serve the public interest as part of an enlightened policy of promoting private interest, died in 1925, and young Subhas Bose, who as its Chief Executive Officer had shown energy in putting through some reforms, was put in jail for his association with the revolutionary movement. After that there was no one to check its steady descent into inefficiency and graft. The last had reached such proportions when I went to work for it that the popular name for the Calcutta Corporation was the 'Calcutta Corruption'.

Amal Babu told me a story before I joined which would show that in the estimation of the citizens of Calcutta even the Corporation building had become as greedy as the Councillors who reigned in it. He said that one day, as he was going up one of the staircases to his rooms, he saw an old Bengali gentleman stooping on them and looking this way and that. At the same time he was muttering: 'O Corporation stairs, my children, are you as rapacious as your masters." Amal Babu asked him: 'Have you lost anything, sir? May I help you?' He replied: 'No, it's nothing. Only a two-anna piece slipped from my hand, and seems to have rolled off somewhere.' Then he hurried down. As an official of the Corporation Amal Babu was very much amused to come across so realistic an estimate of his masters. According to the old man, they had corrupted even the stairs so far by their example that these would not bear the weight of those who used them without a bribe.

I had before that heard any number of stories with which the exasperated citizens of Calcutta consoled themselves for its inefficiency and corruption. I shall repeat one of them to show that the tradition of graft went back even to the days of C. R. Das. Not only all kinds of profiteers but even the nationalist workers began to regard the Corporation as the mine from which they could get reparations for their sacrifices in the worldly way. Thus one day a well known second-rank leader went to C. R. Das and said to him: 'Sir, we have lost everything for the country. Now that you are master of this place, may we not expect some recompense? After all, we have to live.' Das got him a contract for supplying boots to the inspectors of the dustmen of Calcutta, who formed a very large labour force and had to be supervised in their work by hundreds of minor officials. The Congress leader turned a contractor of boots, however, discovered something which he had not anticipated. The Corporation was always very miserly and accepted only those tenders whose quotations were lowest. Thus the price fixed for each pair of boots was such that not even the cost price could be recovered. Panic-stricken, he went again to C. R. Das and related his woes. He said that he had not foreseen that he would become a bankrupt through that favour. Das laughed and replied that it was not his job, he had better hand it over to a sub-contractor and take a commission.

So, the Congress leader went to the old contractor, who had been deprived in his favour. He was a Muslim and a seasoned veteran. When he heard the story he was ready to split with laughter. He said: 'You Babus know nothing about these matters. Did you think you could make a profit out of that contract by supplying a pair of boots to each inspector.? We did that only by supplying one boot a year to one man.' Totally baffled by this remark, the Congress man asked for an explanation, which was given.

The Muslim contractor said that he had a list of all the inspectors and their addresses. He went to each of them, gave him two rupees, and requested him to wear his boots for two years, but to give him a receipt every year that he had received his pair. All this was arranged through the stores department of the Corporation, and so, each year, the Muslim contractor supplied boots only to half the number of inspectors, which meant one boot a man a year. The Congress leader gladly agreed to hand over his contract for a commission.

Now, I could not say whether the story was true or apocryphal. But when reporting the Corporation proceedings as the acting editor of its journal I one day heard a Councillor make an amazing statement, which could prove the story of the boots to be true. This Councillor was a zealot for purity of administration, and when he spoke on any subject his eyes flashed fire. His charge was a terrible one, and, if true, a matter of such shame as should have its place in a Guinness Book of Records for corruption. It was that a contract for supplying goods of a certain character had not been fulfilled at all and yet the money for it amounting to hundreds of thousands of rupees had been paid.

The contract was for the gravel needed for the streets of Calcutta, which were asphalted on a bed of gravel about ten to twelve inches deep. As Bengal was an alluvial plain, this material came from quarries in a place in Bihar. The Councillor declared that one or two trains-full had not arrived at all, but the documents were in perfect order - there were signed payrolls of the workmen in the quarries, the bills of lading from the railway company, the receipts for delivery from the Corporation officials. The proofs were complete. I watched the Mayor and the Councillors from the reporters' benches. They were impassive, even bored, as if thinking: 'What a fuss about a trifle known to everybody!' Even the iconoclastic Councillor forgot his indignation, and grinned sardonically.

While attending the meetings, I saw that the contracts were regarded as the most important business the Councillors had to see through. Although the sewage clearing system of Calcutta was in shambles, and the stench coming from the silted up discharge channel, which was a river to the east of Calcutta, could be inhaled in the eastern suburbs of the city, as I did when living in one of them in 1927, and although the Chief Engineer was putting his scheme to replace the old system before the Corporation every year, nothing was done. But I saw Councillor after Councillor rising from his seat to speak in favour of the contractor he favoured. The eloquence of their advocacy was overpowering. At first puzzled by this - the greenhorn that I was - I asked the reason from the cognoscenti of Corporation affairs and got a perfectly satisfying explanation: 'Why, did you not notice the visitors' gallery.' All the contractors were there to watch if they were getting value for their bribes.'

Three years later I became the private secretary of the leader of the Congress in Bengal and chairman of the Congress Municipal Association of Calcutta, and gained a deeper inside knowledge of the affairs of the Calcutta Corporation. I shall give an account of my horrible enlightenment when I deal with that period of my life. Here I shall relate one amusing conversation I heard with my own ears. Some Councillors and members of the Bengal legislature were sitting before Mr Sarat Bose, and a very light topic of discussion was raised - whether the Hindu or the Muslim councillors were more corrupt. A cynical young councillor - a Hindu belonging to the old gentry of Calcutta - said without a moment's hesitation that although both were equally corrupt, the Muslims were more honestly so. That paradox needed an explanation and the Councillor provided it. He said that the Muslims took bribes from one party to work for him, but we Hindus took them from all sides and worked for none sincerely. I heard and saw more in later years of their disconcerting honesty in being corrupt.

I also noticed a feature which surprised me as I studied the agenda of the meetings before going to them. I saw that one contractor, a Bengali firm, had tenders for every kind of service or goods: e.g. straw, coal, machinery, building material, even electrical goods. I asked of somebody how one firm could be so versatile. I got the reply that it was a firm of contractors owned by a former revolutionary, who claimed them by virtue of that status. He got them and handed them out to proper contractors, who now became subcontractors under him. It was the story of the boots on a grander scale.

I could, of course, explain why the Calcutta Corporation had reached that state after it had passed into Bengali hands in 1924. I knew the social history of Calcutta very well. Under British administration all the lower echelons of power in Calcutta were constituted by the Calcutta gentry, who had dug themselves in administrative, civic, and mercantile positions and created enormous vested interests. As soon as they saw that with the Indianization of the Corporation by the new Muncipal Act of 1923, it was bound to pass under the control of the Congress, owing to that body's popularity with the electors, they rushed to become zealous Congressmen overnight. The Congress, too, welcomed them owing to their old position and money, and thereby had its crude nationalism swamped by the sophisticated worldliness of the Calcutta gentry. The whole class was hardened by more than a hundred years of successful self-seeking under British rule. It was his observation of this class that made Macaulay write his notorious character sketch of Bengalis in 1841. 'What the horns are to the buffalo,' he said,

'what the sting is to the bee, what beauty according to the Greek song is to woman, deceit is to the Bengalee. Large promises, smooth excuses, elaborate tissues of circumstantial falsehood, chicanery, perjury, forgery are the weapons, offensive and defensive of the people of the Lower Ganges. All those millions do not furnish one sepoy to the armies of the Company. But as usurers, as money-changers, as sharp legal practitioners, no class of human beings can bear comparison with them.'

We the general mass of the Bengali gentry showed an unnecessary susceptibility by taking offence at this description, although Macaulay did represent a part as the whole. We should have seen that he was describing the class of which he had experience. I saw enough of the same class to agree with him. It was this class which had taken over the Calcutta Corporation. Even if they had to share some of the gains with the nationalists who became the nominal rulers of Calcutta, they could transform the spirit of nationalism.

I had two more opportunities to see the workings of the Calcutta Corporation the next year and in 1936, and, as I have said, I gained full knowledge of its backstairs, backshops, and kitchens as secretary to the Congress leader. But even before I gained that extended knowledge, the experience of 1934 alone made a profound and permanent impact on my political opinions and outlook. I anticipated that transfer of political power to Indians would make the Indian people victims of an insidious exploitation unparalleled even in the long history of their sufferings. I became opposed to the idea, and said to myself in the words of the cliché that India in that event would become Calcutta Corporation writ large.

I saw that happening in Bengal and in all the other provinces of India in 1937 with the introduction of provincial autonomy by the British Act of 1935, and after 1947 I saw that phenomenon in the Central Government. All the nationalist beggars who filed into the enormous buildings bequeathed to them by the fleeing British, realized what treasures were there to be looted by them, and they must have thought that their sacrifices were at last rewarded. Although none of them were educated enough to know what Blücher was reported to have said when he saw Paris the first time, they must have exclaimed in the same words out of their own heads: 'What places to plunder!'

CHAPTER 4

More Ordeals

Even in that space of one month in the Calcutta Corporation I had gained valuable knowledge and experience which helped me in my role of an observer of the Indian political scene. But the money I gained did not last long. Before the year 1935 was one month old, my situation became desperate. I could, of course, write articles from time to time, but this freelance work could not bring in enough even to pay the rent for the flat regularly. There were other expenses, and, especially, the babies to feed. Very fortunately I was spared anxiety on the score of the latest arrival. My wife was able to feed all her babies till their seventh month, without giving them a drop of external food. That pleased my pediatrician brother, who though trained in Vienna and Tübingen, always insisted on natural feeding. But my wife was herself underfed, and in order to give to others she deprived herself to an extent of which I had no idea, because in our society husbands and wives did not eat together at the same time, and she never told me till long afterwards. What I could see was that the feeding of the weaned elder child was going to be a problem. He needed enough milk.

Tackling the anticipated difficulty at once, I called the milkman who supplied us. He was a Hindustani of the peasant class, who kept a number of cows in a shed and made a living in Calcutta, selling their milk. There were hundreds of such milkmen in Calcutta, most of whom supplied a mixture of half milk half water. I told him frankly that I had no employment and no regular income, so would not be able to pay him regularly; if in such circumstances he wanted to stop supplying milk to me he could. He replied at once and very simply, as if his answer was the only natural one, without any air of making a concession: 'It cannot be that children will go without their milk. I shall continue the supply. You may pay me when you can.' He did that for more than two years. Once or twice he did indeed loose patience and said rather sharp words. That was not unjustifiable, for he too was a poor man and had to live. But the dues to him were allowed to become so large that it took me nearly a year after I got employment to clear the arrears. I shall never cease to remain grateful to him.

I might as well set down here what I always did for my children with the whole-hearted agreement of my wife even in our worst days. First, whatever the cost, I would not deprive them of the food they needed to grow into strong and robust children. I remembered my under-nourishment due to ignorance. Next, I would not deprive them of clothes because children's self-respect always depends on them. I even bought their clothes from the best English shops in Calcutta whenever I could afford that. Lastly, I never deprived them of toys and playthings, knowing that deprivation of these created a sense of frustration. I always said in defence of these expenses, regarded as culpable extravagance in our society, that the times for certain things wanted by human children were strictly limited to certain ages, and it was no use giving these to them later. If the needs could not be met when they were felt, a father should be reconciled to their faulty growth to manhood.

I am afraid I cannot recall my benefactors in my class with the same gratitude as I feel for the milkman. I had at times to borrow what were large sums of money for me from wealthy men who were moneylenders, some of whom ran loan offices. I always had to pay usurious interest to them, and on one occasion the usury was atrocious. My wife, intending to relieve my distress and worry, pawned some of her gold in order to get a loan of Rs.100. I released her ornaments by paying about three hundred rupees in interest in less than six months. These men always ended as Congressmen.

I also borrowed small sums, hardly ever exceeding two rupees at a time, from my friends. When I went to do so I talked aimlessly for about an hour as if I had come to pay them a social visit, certainly not deceiving them, and at the last moment blurted out the request. They always gave and I repaid them scrupulously, although only to borrow again and again. They must have looked upon me as a nuisance, and would never give a large sum of money, such as twenty-five rupees (about £2.00).

With the birth of a second child before the first could even walk, another expense was forced on me. I had to keep a servant to look after the first child. I engaged a maid at first, and as she was not satisfactory got a boy servant. He came early in 1935, and remained with us till 1984. I could depend on him as I can on my sons. He still writes to us in England and says that his only regret is that he will not see *Babuji*, his one-time master, again. He calls my sons his brothers. What is more, his loyalty to me and love for my sons are more than that of close relatives. He shared all our difficulties, and now has the joy of seeing my achievements. I procured good employment for him in the Government of India, and he could have left me. But he did not, and also served me on a nominal salary while working in his office.

Let me continue the story of my trials. I saw no prospect of getting employment, and felt increasingly anxious. My wife one day suggested that as educated women could get employment more easily than men as teachers in the schools for children she might try to get one of these jobs. I only said to her that it was my duty to keep her and not hers to keep me. So, both of us shared equal want. In those days I never slept in the same bed with my wife, and have not done so even in the same room whenever I have been able to afford separate bedrooms for us. Now I think that there is hardly anything more unintelligent and even vulgar than for husband and wife to sleep together. I believe in functionalism in personal life, and also in the independence of both husband and wife.

At that time in the cold season I slept in a separate bed in the same room, and in the hot season on the verandah. But my sleep was not peaceful or uninterrupted. I never quailed before troubles during the day. But at dead of night it was wholly different. As I always went to bed very early, by nine o'clock as a rule, in times of distress I always woke up at about one o'clock, and remained awake until, three or four hours later, I again fell asleep from sheer exhaustion. These hours were like those assigned in popular legend to sinners who cannot rest in their unquiet graves and come forth to wander about the haunts of their living days. I also walked in the small verandah, and saw my wife sleeping in the bed with her two babies. I often felt a craving to go to her for comfort, but checked myself, thinking that I should not disturb her rest as well. I saw her sleeping in tranquility. But when we had come out of our distress she told me that she too could not sleep and saw me on the verandah. But she would not come to me lest both of us should break down and that would help neither of us.

Just after that an offer of employment came to me. That was through Kedar Babu, who must have felt very sorry to turn me away when I went to him after the *Free India* episode. He wanted to make up for his inability to help me then, and exercised his influence with the owner of a very big firm of printers in Calcutta to procure a good job for me. They were bringing out a new illustrated weekly of a very popular kind and wanted an editor. Kedar Babu persuaded the proprietor to appoint me. He told me to go and see him in his house and fix up the matter formally.

I was to see the eldest of three brothers, who were the joint owners. He was the chief, and one evening I went to his flat, which was above the press. I dressed myself as carefully as I could, but my shoes were worn out and the big toe of my right foot could be seen peeping out through a hole. I let down the flounce of my dhoti to hide it, but I think my host noticed it, or I thought he did, for men in my situation were likely to be over-conscious of their deficiencies. He was a very gentlemanly and affable man, and he assured me that everything was final, and I could begin work.

From the next day I began to go to the press and plan the paper. To be frank, I was no more qualified to be the editor of such a paper than I was to be that of a daily newspaper. But I thought I owed it to my family to try to do my best, and even more to Kedar Babu not to let him down. As I prepared the plans, I felt more and more that to publish pictures of cinema actors and actresses and of football players was not my vocation. Even so, carrying on for about ten days, I went one day to the actual manager of the press to ask him some questions. He was the second of the brothers, and a typical upstart. He was supervising the setting up of a machine, and when I spoke to him he said very curtly that he was not to be disturbed when he was busy otherwise. I got very angry, and left the office, not to go back to it again. I had not got any money, nor did I expect any. So, I did not think it necessary even to give notice. They must have been surprised, and appointed another man. Kedar Babu was also a little offended for I had in the end let him down. But I could not give the reason for leaving to him or to the elder brother, because for me to have to say that I was insulted by a man like the younger brother would have been a greater humiliation than to have been ill-treated. I have always held that insult should be felt and resented only among equals. Supposing a street dog bit me. I would not call that an insult.

I carried on somehow after the loss of this opportunity. Some of my writer friends who wanted to avoid labour or did not have the style, asked me to write articles or even books for them, of course giving me the material. I did that for them, and they gave me some money. Although I was very grateful to these friends, my wife did not like this sort of work at all. She told me that others were becoming well-known writers through my labours, which, published in my name, would have established me. I explained to her that this sort of work was not what I would do to gain the status of a writer, and my books when written would be quite different. She had to be satisfied with this assurance, which I could not prove to be true until fifteen years later.

Then by a lucky coincidence I again got employment for two months in the Calcutta Corporation. The year 1935 was that of the Silver Jubilee of the ascent to throne of George V, and Amal Babu persuaded the nationalist Calcutta Corporation to bring out a special Silver Jubilee issue of his paper, the *Calcutta Municipal Gazette*. I was to help him both in designing it and writing some of the articles. Amal Babu proposed to make that issue a magnificent souvenir and proceeded in his grandest manner, wholly misleading the authorities about the expense. He got hundreds of photographs to select his illustrations from the foremost photographic agencies in England, and even got the frontispiece, which was to be a portrait of the King-Emperor, printed in England, because there was no press in India which could reproduce paintings in colour photogravure. I also for once got my chance, and worked wholeheartedly for Amal Babu. The work took longer than two months, and since he could not get my term of employment extended I worked for him without pay for another month. I did so for the sake of the work too, for I was proud of it. I planned the dummy, and there was no departure even by a page from it, and no pictures had to be shifted. I added to the text when it fell short, and cut out when it was too long for the space. The special issue, when it came out, was more a book than a magazine. There was, of course, the expected row over the expenditure, but even the barbarians that the councillors were, could not say that it was not a fine production. There was another gain for me besides the money. It was while writing the chapter on the history of India during the reign of George V that I arrived at the idea of the cyclical character of the Indian nationalist movement, and it was first set forth by me in print in that chapter.

But my satisfaction over the souvenir could not keep away the problem of subsistence when the money was spent, and it was quickly. When that happened it was the holiday season in Bengal, the autumn, the time of the great festival of the worship of Durga. But as I had given up Hindu religious observance long since, I did not miss the exhilaration of the festival. But I did miss the joy which the coming of autumn always brought to me. It was perhaps the most beautiful season in Bengal, with its clear blue sky flecked with snow-white fleecy clouds, its flowers, and its shining waters. In Calcutta none of these could be seen, and since 1932 I had not been able to leave Calcutta for any holiday. I had no money. For my wife, too, it was a trial, for she was used to her beautiful Shillong hills in that season. At that time all Bengalis who could afford it left Calcutta to go to the famous places of pilgrimage in northern India or to spend their holiday in the Himalayas. My brother went. But we had to stay on in our flat on a very noisy main street of Calcutta. It was not that at any time we neglected to keep it tidy and clean. But our first pride in it was gone. It seemed very much the worse for wear. Even in Calcutta the autumn light of Bengal was golden, but the dust which rose from the street and made even the blue of the sky dirty, floated in the air in our rooms and in the afternoons, as the golden light poured into them, we saw only grey particles dancing in their myriads.

To add to all our anxieties, two wholly unexpected, and as we thought quite unnecessary, troubles overtook us. In that year there was a great outbreak of epidemic dropsy in Calcutta, due to adulteration of the cooking oil which all Bengalis used with a poisonous substitute. Almost everybody had it, including my wife. However, I escaped somehow. It lasted in her, accompanied by weakness of the heart, for about a year, and what was worse she developed glaucoma in one of her eyes. I was terribly frightened. Fortunately, my brother took her to one of the foremost oculists of the city, and she was completely cured. But she was half-blind for some time, although the worst I feared did not come about.

Then, one of my brothers who was holding a highly paid job in a factory in South India, lost it in a redundancy, and there was no compensation for that in India. Besides, he had been as extravagant as I was, and had no resources to fall back upon. There was nowhere else he could go to. So, I felt it my duty to keep him and his family. After some months he probably felt that it was putting too great a burden on me and went away to live by himself But during the period of unemployment he suffered even more grieviously than I did, for, being an engineer, he was wholly dependent on getting a job.

However, at the end of 1935 a new hope came to me. Sajani Das was doing very well as a publisher and printer, and a wealthy friend of his, who had literary tastes, suggested to him that he should bring out a weekly journal, which he would finance. Sajani Babu at once fell in with the idea, and offered the editorship to me. I accepted it with great enthusiasm, for I did not think that I was unqualified to run a journal of that kind. There were a number of weekly journals in Calcutta. Some of them were merely mouthpieces of coteries without any revenue, and one or two which were profitable were printed on brown newsprint in greyish ink, which made the lettering almost illegible. That was not so great a disadvantage as might be thought, because the text was generally unreadable to an educated Bengali.

I thought that in this line at least I would do better than others. I wanted to make my paper a 'glossy', as such journals are called nowadays, and I did not do at all badly. I got the whole journal printed on art paper, and put very good illustrations in it. But it ran only for five issues. The scale of expense I adopted did not suit the financier, and he refused to support the journal. Here was another fiasco for me. Sajani Babu made my extravagance responsible for it, and high words passed between us. Although he forgot his grievance in the years that followed, he remembered it in his later days when I made a name as a writer in English, and taunted me in his memoirs. So did the scribbling *canaille*, who probably had resented the quality of the journal and resenting my literary standing in the English-speaking world wanted to remind me how unqualified I was to run a Bengali journal. Their taunts did not show any anger, but just their intolerance of any kind of superiority.

But I too should have realized that I was not born to be an entrepreneur or manager. I could be only a producer. If I had any capacity as a manager, financial insufficiency by itself would not have stopped that paper. Sajani Babu, too, had no capital, but he was never lacking in it whenever he wanted money. He could always persuade capitalists. I was only a primadonna in the literary way, and stood in need of impresarios of the proper sort. Unfortunately, there were no such in Calcutta. If the Bengali publishers were in the musical line they would not have discovered anything even in Maria Callas before she arrived. My real literary successes, unprompted by a coterie, I owe only to English publishers in London, and after that, of course, the Bengali publishers have taken me up.

But at all events this failure made me take a sensible decision - i.e. not to wait for jobs to come to me, nor to take up an enterprise, but to take my stand only on writing, and do what I could by freelance journalism. I resumed writing for the *Sanibarer Chithi*, which was now being edited under Sajani Babu's proprietorship by another Bengali writer, Parimal Goswami, for whom I acquired very great respect. These articles brought me a little money, but I did something more through them. I set down my views of Bengali life and culture which I had developed, and I stopped writing in Bengali in 1937, when I came to lose faith in the future of die Bengali people.

I also got a literary commission. An Indian prince, the Maharajkumar (or heir apparent) of the State of Sitamau had written a considerable work of historical research on the rise of the Maratha principalities in Central India or Malwa in the eighteenth century. He had got a doctorate for it, and wanted to publish it as a book. When he wanted editorial help, Sir Jadunath Sarkar, our most eminent historian who knew me well, suggested my name. So I got some money out of this commission as well. I found'the prince to be altogether a different kind of character from the Bengali upstart who had shown rudeness to me. These princes could get people murdered out of anger, but they could not be rude. This prince proved die truth of the old saying that courtesy is the grace of princes and the other saying that the greater the man, the greater is the courtesy. Of course, I have read the saying of Chamfort: 'Amitié de cour, foi de renard et Société de loup.' But when a people are particularly rich in the population of human foxes and wolves, one does not find even counterfeit courtesy unpleasant. This prince, moreover, had more intellectual capacity than I would normally have expected in an Indian prince of our times. He had done his research himself, and wrote good English.

I must say that my last desperate resolve to depend only on my wits paid, or rather began to pay, even from that year. I was in my fortieth year in 1936. Before that my income was never more than a thousand rupees a year. But in the last four months of that year I earned Rs. 1000, and after that I made it a point, quite uncharacteristically, to increase my income by at least one thousand rupees every year. This I did, without looking for jobs, although I also got them.

CHAPTER 5
Remaining Homo Sapiens

The Abbé Sieyès lay low during the Terror and reappeared only after Thermidor. He was then asked what he had been doing. He replied tersely: 'J'ai vécu,' I remained alive. After I had emerged alive at the end of these three years out of a different kind of terror, I could claim to have done better by saying: I not only kept alive but remained throughout *Homo sapiens*. I never lost my capacity to think even under the worst of conditions. In fact, it was during this period that I arrived at the ideas about our life, history and civilization which have remained the basis of my interpretation of these things. When I did not formulate them then, I developed those which were only inchoate before. To reap that harvest out of such distress was not simply like getting crops by putting smelly manure in the fields, but also to get them from severe drought.

This must have been due primarily to the necessity of having some compensation. I had no other refuge from my anxieties and difficulties than keeping my mind engaged in deep study or searching thinking. Some of my hardest work in that line I did during this period. But my persistence in thinking and reading was also due to my deep-seated respect for thought, by which I understood not only intellection but also the exercise of intuition. Even at that time I had a vague awareness of a truth which I perceived fully only very much later in life - that to man alone among all living creatures has been given the power to produce from his mind something which would extend and supplement what the cosmic process had created, namely, matter and life. As this truth has been the first article of my faith in life, I shall fully explain what I mean in the Epilogue. Here I shall only set down that, subscribing to this truth, I have always wanted to be a participant, to the extent of any power I have been born with, in that process of specifically human creation, that is, mental creation. In an article intended for *Sanibarer Chithi* in 1928, which I never completed, I uttered a prayer like Renan on the Acropolis, but its content was different. I implored God to release me from the ignoble strife of getting on in the world by giving me a minimal body like that of a protozoic creature, amoeba or radiolarian, but allowing me to retain the human brain, so that without being hampered by the need to keep my metazoic body going I could think perpetually, and could also enjoy my sense perceptions, realizing that without enjoying there was no meaning in perceiving. Mohit Babu liked the paragraph.

That innate inclination towards a life of thought was strengthened in me by all my reading, and more especially of Pascal. I had not yet come out of college when in my very first readings in French I came upon his famous aphorism: Man is a reed, the feeblest reed in nature, but he is a thinking reed. When I bought his complete works I, of course, read the following:

'Man is visibly made to think; in that lies all his dignity and all his vocation; and it is his duty to think correctly. Now, the proper order for thinking for a man is to begin with the self and go on to his creator and to his end. But what does the world think about' Never about these - only about dancing, playing the lute, singing, composing verse, tilting at the ring, etc., in fighting, and in making oneself king, without caring to think what it is to be a king and to be a man.'

I cannot describe fully the impact such passages made on me. I was raised to a plane of despair, triumphant and defiant at the same time, by reading Pascal's declaration that man was superior to the universe because he knew that it could kill him with a whiff of vapour or drop of liquid without drawing on even a fraction of its enormous power, whereas the universe had no awareness of that at all. But I would add that the desire to lead a life of contemplation never made me think of subscribing to a closed system of thought, far less of creating one, because I felt that all such systems led one away from real perceptions.

But let me return to my ideas. Those developed during this period covered all aspects of Indian life, and within that framework, Bengali life as well: e.g. the nature of ancient and modern Indian culture; Bengali life and culture; the future of the Bengali people; Hindu-Muslim relations in India; nature of Indian nationalism; and finally, Indo-British relations. On none of these subjects did I have to abandon later any of the ideas I then formulated, although I have developed all of them.

Unfortunately, during those years I did not possess the physical strength, which also creates mental effervescence, to enable me to put down all my conclusions in writing. So all of them remained like shadowy photographic negatives. It was under the dire compulsion of subsistence that I embodied them in a few articles during 1934 and 1935. But even then and more especially when I began to write with an exercise of the will in 1936, I showed no flagging of spirit. This has always been seen in me. There are times I cannot write *at all,* but if I do so at all I always *exhibit high spirits.*

This I showed in one of the very first articles I wrote in that period of distress. No one would or could have expected that kind of writing from me if he knew my circumstances or my state of mind. The piece was a full-blooded denunciation of the Bengali habit of taking the line of least resistance in everything, avoiding every difficulty. I gave to the article, which was published in the *Sanibarer Chithi,* the title 'The Easy Path.' Stranger still, in a spirit of philosophical analogy I brought into it Himalayan geography, of which I made a thorough study then. I especially noted the hydrography of the entire region, and was astonished to discover that none of the great rivers of India had risen on the southern slopes of the great mountains, but from the other side, and cut their way through the Great Himalayan Range. The only exception was the Jumna, but that, too, comformed to a second feature, which is that these rivers not only pierce the Great Himalayan Range, but do so under the highest peaks.

The correlation between these peaks and the deep chasms through which they pass in order to flow down to the plains, is quite impressive: the Indus does so near the great peak Nanga Parbat; the Sutlej near Riu Phirgyal; the watery braids which join to form the Ganges skirt a cluster of peaks - Kedamath, Badrinath, Kamet, Trisul, Nanda Devi; the bed of the Gandak lies below Dhawalgiri; the Kosi passes by Kinchin Jangha; the Brahmaputra flows between the twin peaks of Gyala Peri and Namcha Barwa, and even the Jumna does so between Srikanta and Bandar Punch. Why has that happened? It seems to prove the falsity of the idea that water always follows the line of least resistance. On the contrary, it seems to choose the most difficult. So it should be in human life, individual or collective. The recovery and conquest of Bengal by Clive in 1757 was like the breaking out of a river through the highest section of a mountain range near its source, whereas in the period with which I am dealing in this book the river of the British Empire in India split itself into narrow and sluggish channels in a flat delta to be silted up wholly or to grope its way out in mangrove swamps.

There was my moral: nothing.that is strong, creative or fertilizing condescends to take an easy path. That, however, was the Bengali way, and the explanation for the Bengali's incapacity to sustain effort. I asked fellow

Bengalis to give that up and face the challenges. I wonder why at that precise time, when my preference for the hard way was inflicting so much trouble on me and my family, I wrote that article. Did I do that to justify my obstinate refusal to play safe, for which all my relatives and acquaintances were blaming me?

But this was my single attempt at general moralizing. In my other articles I dealt with concrete issues and set down my conclusions. I shall describe what they were later. In this chapter I shall refer to one subject only, on which I did *not* write, although I was very much excited over it and had actually planned to write, not merely articles, but a whole book. That subject was Indo-British relations or, to be more precise, the future of British rule in India. The provocation for that came from a move by the British Government at home, the presentation of a new Government of India Bill to parliament by Sir Samuel Hoare, as Secretary of State for India, with the full support of the Conservative Prime Minister, Stanley Baldwin. It infuriated me, because by that time I had wholly rejected the idea of a transfer of power to Indian hands by Britain as a possible solution of the Indian problem. On the contrary, I thought that power in Indian hands would be a calamity for the Indian people.

I had come to the conclusion that India stood in need of a revolution, covering all the aspects of human life - political, economic, social - which had to be more far-reaching and radical than the French Revolution, the Meiji Revolution, the Russian Revolution, the Chinese Revolution, and the two Turkish Revolutions. Without that no new life was to arise in India. Yet I saw that it was not likely to come from an application of the policy of transfer of power to Indian hands. That was why I rejected all the ideas and policies which were on the tapis.

Even the superficial experience I had of the Calcutta Corporation had made me disbelieve the administrative efficiency and honesty of Indians in power. Behind this was a deeper disbelief - distrust of my own class, i.e. the anglicized upper middle class. I had found its members weak in character, mediocre in intellectual ability, and totally lacking in idealism and public spirit. Their sole preoccupation was promotion of their individual and class interest, and I saw that in the event of British rule coming to an end in India these men would be the real heirs of the British.

This distrust made me feel so strongly about the new India Bill by which it was proposed to create full provincial autonomy, that is, self-government by Indians in the provinces, that I thought of preparing an exhaustive memorandum, fully documented from my knowledge of Indian self-government in the Calcutta Corporation and elsewhere, and send it to Churchill, who was opposing the measure. I thought he was right and after seeing the result of the Act of 1935 I was confirmed in my opinion that he was. He was correct in his idea that it would fatally injure the British Empire in India. It did, by demoralizing the British administration and yet failing to satisfy Indians. The weakness and blunders of that administration in India from 1937, when the Act became operative, to 1947, when India had to be given up, would make a sorry, if not shameful, tale. What Churchill did not see was the harm that even this limited extension of power to Indians would inflict on the Indian masses. As I shall deal with all that when I tell the story of that period of my life, I shall not say anything more about it here.

But I did not prepare or send the memorandum to Churchill. In the first place, I did not have the physical strength to write so serious a document. But a moral scruple also held me back. I thought I should do nothing to promote doubt on Indians so long as even a small chance remained of their proving their capacity. My disapproval of the methods of British rule in India as they were then, made me reluctant to be on its side.

But although I gave up the idea of sending a document to Churchill, I did not abandon the idea of a theoretical opposition to the idea of a transfer of power. This I thought I would present in a full-length book to be entitled *The Real Indian Revolution.* In it I would first set down what consequences a transfer of power *per se* was likely to have, then plead the case for a revolution, and finally argue that it could not come from any group of Indians, because of their moral and intellectual shortcomings, to which I have already referred. The needed Indian revolution could come only from a collaboration between those Indians who had still some idealism left in them and elements in Britain who would be enlightened enough to see the need for a revolution in India and offer their experience and ability in the political field to us. I assumed the existence of such an element in Britain. But this project, too, I did not execute, the reasons being the same as those which had kept me back from sending the memorandum.*

* I was delighted as well as surprised to find from the seventh volume of Martin Galibert's biography (p. 351) that Churchill's thoughts on future Indo-British relations ran along lines similar to mine. In a secret and personal telegram to the Viceroy, Lord Wavell, dated 27 May

I regret that now, but not from any idea that I could have produced any practical effect by it. I would only have felt easier in conscience by registering my protest, and I could have proved now that I had the capacity to anticipate the results of self-government in India. In the practical sphere not everything can be done in every age, and even the most judicious course which sound reasoning would seem to recommend, and which would be proved right by the events, can be rejected out of hand when it should be adopted. That happens because any dominant public opinion is shaped by the historical trend, and no opinion opposed to it has any chance of being accepted and acted upon.

Now, the dominant public opinion in Britain was set against all forms of British greatness, and working in favour of British decline. The Government of India Act of 1935 did not stand as an isolated expression of British policy. It was of a piece with all other aspects of it, and foreign policy above all. I now include the Act in the fatal series which finally led to the eclipse of Great Britain as a great power: namely, complaisance to Japan in 1931, fear of Italy in 1935, and appeasement of Germany from 1934 to 1938. Sir Samuel Hoare's Act was not only the precursor of his pact with Laval, but also of Chamberlain's Munich, a Munich unredeemed by a revision of policy.

The historical trend, which had created the policies, had also created its executors: the official Conservative Party and its leader, Stanley Baldwin. I have now come to regard that man, and not Hitler, as the real architect of British ruin. His use of political power has demonstrated that in human affairs mediocrity when accompanied by self-seeking cunning, is more dangerous than even the most diabolical evil, such as Hider was. Baldwin was that because he raised mediocrity to the level of genius.

Of course, he could not have accomplished what I am attributing to him without the official Conservative Party, which had adopted him as its leader. The two were perfectly matched, and between them they made

---

1944 and confined in its circulation to the King and Sir Edward Bridges alone, he said that Gandhi was 'largely in the hands of native vested interests', and then he added: 'I look forward to a day in which it may be possible to come to an understanding with the real forces that control India and which, at any political settlement, will be allied with a marked improvement in the well being of the masses, whom the reformers often forget, but who constitute for us a sacred duty.' That day never came, because the British administration in India was blindly attached to the backward looking vested interests in India.

their virtually continuous run of power from 1922 to 1939 a calamity for the British people. No Bolshevist, Russian or British, no Fascist or Nazi, no British leftist, nor the Labour Party destroyed British greatness: that was done by the Conservatives. Every act of theirs during that period roused anger in me.

However that may be, I created a vacuum in my mind by not writing that book, and to fill it up I applied myself to a study of history in a large way. It was in 1935 and 1936 that I read the first three volumes of Arnold J. Toynbee's *Study of History*. I am not one of those students of history who refuse to see the wood by restricting themselves to counting the trees. Thus I read Toynbee with great admiration. It was more the sweep of his work than his particular conclusions which excited my admiration. I wrote to him to say so. He replied to me in his own hand. He told me how the idea of writing the book had flashed into his mind as he was travelling on the Orient Express, and how he had jotted it down on a single sheet of paper. As I had written that the pattern of history he had discovered was helping me to arrange and clarify my own ideas about Indian history, he replied that his ideas were mainly derived from his study of Greek and Roman history and that such ideas did not do any harm unless one became a slave to them. I showed that I was not enslaved by rejecting his interpretation of Indian history and sending him a number of notes on it. The correspondence with him was a great comfort to me at that time, and I waited eagerly for his replies.

In the meanwhile, I went on writing my articles on Bengal in Bengali, and at the beginning of 1937 there came to me an opportunity to present my interpretation of modem Indian culture and of its decline in a clearcut manner in a formal address. That was done in an address which I delivered as the president of a literary conference at Patna at the end of January.

CHAPTER 6

The Siege is Raised

The year 1937 opened in comparative peace of mind for me. The money I had earned by writing was not exhausted, and at the end of the year 1936 I again officiated for Amal Babu for another month. This, however, did not come to me without a typical display of the spirit of the Calcutta Corporation. Amal Babu had planned to go on leave earlier in the year, and had proposed me as usual as his locum tenens to the Services Committee. But feeling secure, he had not spoken to its members in my favour (the procedure was something like the visits of a candidate for a seat in the French Academy to the sitting Immortals), and so a Bengali minor official of the Corporation put a spoke in my wheel. He represented that he (an MA) was ready to work in Amal Babu's place for only Rs.80 in addition to his salary, which would be a saving of Rs.120 for the Corporation. The councillors being fiends of economy for everybody who was not one of their relatives or protégés, that man got the post. Amal Babu was furious and refused to go on leave, saying that he had no confidence in the substitute appointed. Taking time to allow this to be forgotten, he pulled the wires and got me appointed.

By the middle of 1937 I got a new job which was fairly well-paid by our standards and which I could regard as reasonably secure, at least for some years. In March, before that came to me, my friends had secured a part time job for me. I shall relate how I got them and what they were. At this point I shall say to those of my readers who after going through all that I have written so far, have felt more sorrow than anger for me, that I shall not have to inflict more harrowing details on them in this book.

But even before I had any idea that the siege under which I was living was coming to an end in six months, I had a joyous feeling at the prospect of going to the conference at Patna. Such gatherings were a typical cultural recreation of the Bengalis working and settled outside Bengal, the expatriate Bengalis as they were called: the Bengali Diaspora, who never forgot their Zion in Calcutta. Thus in every important city or town in northern India there was a cultural club to keep alive the traditions of Calcutta life. Patna was a big city, the capital of the province of Bihar and

Orissa, and it also had a large Bengali population, among whom many were very highly placed. There was one of these Bengali literary clubs in Bankipore - the new extension of Patna, which E. M. Forster said was the model of his Chandrapore. It could not have been, for life in Patoa, whether official, professional, academic, or merely social, British, Muslim, Hindustani or Bengali, was not of the kind shown in Chandrapore. Pataa had officially a Governor and his Council, a High Court, colleges, newspapers, and a club like the one which invited me. It also had the finest library of Islamic manuscripts in India.

I was to preside over the annual anniversary of the club for 1937. On such occasions these clubs always brought over lions from Calcutta, and gave them a lionization which they never could get in their city. This year the club in question had selected our coterie for lionization. Besides me, Sajani Das, Parimal Goswami, who was the new editor of the *Sanibarer Chithi*, and Brajen Banerji, a notable historian of modem Bengal, were invited.

On the morning of the day we were to start for Patna Bibhuti Babu came to visit us. I asked him if he would care to go with us. 'Why not?' he replied, 'if you will take me.' I at once went with him to Sajani Babu and put the matter to him. He, too, was pleased. We decided that all of us would travel third-class and pay Bibhuti Babu's fare from our saving. I came back with him to my house, and my wife asked him whether he had enough warm clothing, for Patna was likely to be very cold in January. Although Bibhuti Babu had lived for nearly four years in Bihar and talked poetically of its cold winter winds, by that time he had no warm clothes of any kind left. When he confessed that, my wife called my younger brother and asked him to lend his chesterfield overcoat and other warm things to Bibhuti Babu. As soon as these were brought in, Bibhuti Babu tried them on and looked at himself in the large mirror of my wife's wardrobe, with exclamations of wonder and admiration at his appearance. 'Am I not looking smart?' he asked. I, for my part, had my own warm things which were quite adequate, and over and above was lent additional robes of grandeur by Amal Babu, which were his Tibetan gown and cap, as also a quilted and padded shawl in satin, which was purple on one side and green on the other.

In the afternoon, as my wife was packing my things in a holdall with the help of a servant, Bibhuti Babu came in with his luggage, which was nothing but a little bundle of cloth, containing a half-dirty dhoti and a red towel of the flimsiest texture. My wife at once threw them away and gave Bibhuti Babu some of our clean things. His spirits rose even higher than mine.

We went into a third-class carriage in the train, and Sajani Babu made me sit on one whole bench in the Tibetan robe, with the cap on my head. He would not sit himself with me, nor allow any of our companions to do so. They sat huddled together on the opposite bench. This was like being the Lama in *Kim*, but Sajani Babu knew what he was doing. The crowds looking for room in the third-class carriages did not enter ours when they saw me, for they would not cause discomfort to a holy man, and those who were forced to come into our coach at last sat tightly packed on the far bench. Sajani Babu would not address me in any other way than as 'Mr President', and compelled the others of our party to adopt the same mode of address. We travelled very comfortably. At all events, I did. We were received with great ceremony by our hosts and taken to the houses of those who were to put us up.

I was very happy, and so were the others. It was a welcome break in the monotony and routine of our life in Calcutta, and I had not been able to get away from that for four years. I was also very proud of the printed address of twenty-two crown octavo pages with a colour cover, of which five hundred copies were taken with us for distribution at the conference. We were not only lionized but almost killed by the hospitality shown to us. We were invited to lunches, teas, and dinners at the houses of the Bengali élite of Patna until all of us except Sajani felt sick at the sight of food.

I was very pleased to see one recreation of the elderly Bengali gentlemen, which was growing the latest and the most fashionable roses. Even the H.Ts. were regarded as out of date, and the craze was for the new variety then known as the Pemetians and also for the polyanthas, the forerunner of the floribundas. The gentlemen were seen in the mornings, secateurs in hand. An exceptional sort of entertainment was provided for me, because it was known that I liked European music. A young lecturer in English literature in a Patna college had visited me in Calcutta and seen me listening to my records. He also was a lover of European music. So, he took us all to his rooms, which were in an independent wing of his father the judge's big bungalow. He played Mozart's G-minor quintet, which I had not heard before, and kept my friends deaf and dumb for the duration.

The sessions of the conference were very well attended, actually in hundreds. In India lectures always attract very large audiences, however abstruse the subjects. To our surprise, the audience in Patna consisted as much of women as men. I thought that all the fashionable Bengali young women of Patna came to hear us. Bibhuti Babu persisted in saying that a very pretty girl in the front row was making eyes at him, which was, of course, the very last thing they would think of doing.

The guest writers read either from their works or spoke on literary questions, as Bibhuti Babu did. On the first day he read one of his stories, and on the second discussed literary creation. But the real sensation in the way of lectures was provided by Brajen Banerji, although as a ponderous research worker he wrote in the most ponderous style. But this time his thorough research produced the opposite effect, and that was partly due to me. In order to relieve the awful solemnity of my address, I asked him to write on a light topic on which I too had done some research along with him. The subject was a revolution in the costume of Bengali women in the nineteenth century. I helped him to write his paper with great gusto.

It was indeed a revolution, but the men who preached it did that in the name of morality not of beauty. Traditionally, Bengali women wore only one sari, and nothing else with it. Besides, the higher the position of the woman the thinner was the sari. Thus, a charming Englishwoman who came to India in search of the picturesque in the thirties of the last century and was invited to the best homes in Calcutta, wrote in her journal when she saw Bengali women of the highest class: she now understood why none but their husbands or brothers were allowed to go into the zenana. To the reformers, who were all puritans of the most fanatical English type, this was abomination of desolation sitting where it ought not. From 1830 they began to denounce the scanty dress of the Bengali women, strengthening their argument by giving lurid descriptions of their semi-nudity. Brajen Babu, who had done as thorough a research on this subject as on all his other specialities, quoted these descriptions in his paper, which he read in the most monotonous style.

As he quoted one example after another, I thought at least these would bring some smiles, especially on the faces of the ladies. Instead, I was dismayed to watch a progressive hardening of the features, and realized that the modern girls in the audience retained all the puritanism of the reformers, although they no longer needed that. Sajani and others also noticed that. I gently pulled the tail of Brajen Babu's tunic and looked at him. He did not pay any heed to that. Sajani from the other side gave a violent pull. Brajen Babu seemed to wake up to the realization that something was wrong. He looked at me, and then at Sajani, and after that, instead of skipping the examples and bringing his address to a natural close, he stopped at the end of this quotation: 'Thanks to the muslin dhotis and saris from Dacca and Santipur, the males and females of Bengal are becoming lechers and lecheresses. When they put on these abominable things what remains to be unseen?' Then he sat down with a thud on his chair. He was a very bulky man. There had to be some formal applause, but it was very faint. The audience, and more especially the feminine part of it, looked as if they said: 'We are not amused.' However, the feasts of the evening covered up our dismay, and the next day we returned to Calcutta, very much refreshed in spite of the shortness of the break.

The problem of securing a steady and regular income remained with me. But it was not left to me, and a part solution came in March through the initiative of others. Some of my friends who thought it a shame that a man like me should have so much trouble over mere livelihood, got together and obtained part time employment for me as literary assistant to a notability of Calcutta. He was a member of the wealthiest Bengali family of the city, the Laws (Lahas in Bengali), and head of one of its cadet branches. His name was Satya Churn Law. Besides being wealthy, he was very highly educated; in fact, an author and a doctor of Calcutta University. His subject was ornithology. Furthermore, he was a councillor of the Calcutta Corporation, and had that year been appointed as Sheriff of Calcutta. For all this varied work he wanted some assistance. Although competent to do all that he wanted to do or was expected from him in his position, he, like his other literary kinsmen, was easygoing and preferred to have all the spadework done for him. He was also somewhat undecided, and could not make up his mind on any subject quickly. So, I had to read up for him, guess what he would like to say, and present the product to him. But he got frightened if I put something strong in his mouth and would make me beat about the bush. This rather tried my temper at times. In his manners, however, he was extremely gentlemanly. He would never treat me as his employee, but only as his friend. After I had worked for him for a year or two, he hardly ever asked me to write anything. I remained as the paid talker, and after we had exchanged formal greetings, he would say: 'Now, Nirad Babu, talk.'

After the war began in 1939, I had to talk about the war with him. I worked for him for five years from March 1937 to March 1942.

He had found the energy needed to write his ornithological thesis in an effort to forget the death of his wife. After that he wrote papers on ornithological subjects from time to time, but devoted most of his energy to collecting birds and building huge aviaries for them in his villa near Calcutta. They were larger than those in the Calcutta zoo, and he had more aviaries on his estate at Darjeeling, the Himalayan hill station. The man in charge there had to telephone every day to report the health of the birds.

The middle class in Calcutta never believed that villas were maintained by the wealthy for birds or for any innocent purpose. So people told me that Dr Law kept a Jewish mistress there. Both my wife and I had gone through the whole house, including even the bedrooms, and would laugh at these reports. But we could not convince the gossip mongers. They told me that when we went the mistress must have been removed to some other place. Obviously, they knew nothing about the character of the mistresses of the great.

My wife always enjoyed these visits, and Dr Law also welcomed her when she went to the villa. They could talk to each other because my wife too was interested in birds and plants, and the garden of the house was very fine. It had even the *amherstia nobilis*, which was a legend in India among flowering trees. She was also extremely amused to see Dr Law's concern for his birds. Besides the rare birds, he also keptpigeons of many breeds and of the highest pedigree, and would go as far as Delhi to buy them. Now, one day he told my wife that one of the pigeons had a bad cough, and he was very worried over it. Then he invited her to accompany him to see the administration of medicine. A servant followed us with a box full of homoeopathic medicines. In one cage, among scores of pigeons he spotted the sick one, and had it brought to him. A servant held it up before him. Dr Law inclined his head to listen and told my wife: 'There, don't you hear the coughing.' She could just catch the sound of wheezing. A globule was administered to the bird. Openly, my wife showed her edification, but privately she was hugely amused, although I did not think she had any right, for she herself showed as great interest in caterpillars. Dr Law also kept dogs, and especially Pekinese and Airdales. One day when we went to the villa, we found him sitting speechless and grief-stricken. His secretary whispered that his favourite Airdale had been bitten by a cobra which it had chased and had died almost instantaneously.

What I gained from my association with Dr Law was a scientific knowledge of Indian birds. I learned to identify them, and also acquired a good deal of book knowledge, for he had a good library in ornithology. There I read not only the standard works, but even such esoteric books as Meinerzhagen's *Palaearctic Birds*, Stuart Baker's *Nidification of Indian Birds*, and Ticehurst on the *timalidae.* Yet for most of the time Dr Law was a bored man. Except when in the company of his birds, he felt very much alone.

At the same time I found another opening, and that in broadcasting, which in the end led to the highest salary I had in regular employment. It had, however, a very humble beginning the previous year, i.e. 1936, in a neighbour's sympathy for my plight. A Bengali writer who was also a singer of comic songs, had taken the flat below ours. His name was Nalini Kanta Sarkar. I knew him slightly before that, but now we became friends. His wife became even a closer friend of my wife. She felt very strongly for both of us and often told my wife that she was always telling her husband, who was an employee of All India Radio, the Government broadcasting organization, to do something for me in that institution, because she thought it was a shame that so learned a man as I was should be in such trouble for mere livelihood. She also added that her husband, too, spoke to the Programme Executive of the Calcutta Station, but not to any purpose. Then Nalini Babu decided to get me in through the backdoor under his control. He was the editor of the Bengali fortnightly of the Station, and he asked me to contribute a regular feature to it. He could give me only five rupees for each contribution or ten rupees a month. As even that was a welcome addition to my earnings, I accepted the offer at once. For me it turned out to be like the camel's thrusting of its nose into the Bedouin's tent. In 1937 I was taken on as a regular commentator on international affairs in Bengali, which brought me a larger amount of money. Finally, I went to Delhi to take up a regular job in All India Radio, which reached a salary of more than one thousand rupees a month by the time I retired fifteen years later. That meant an increase of one hundred times on the starting money from All India Radio. We have never ceased to be grateful to Nalini Babu and his wife for their sympathy. Nalini Babu died in 1984, his wife had died before him.

When I was assured in this manner of a minimal regular income I took stock of my debts, and made plans to pay them gradually. I was not given time, however. In less than a month from getting Dr Law's job, two humiliations came upon me. The bank with which I had mortgaged my wife's gold threatened to foreclose unless I paid off the arrears of interest at once, and they were heavy. I paid that with my first month's salary. Next, my landlord, a Bengali millionaire who kept ten Dalmatians, which always barked at me whenever I went to his office to plead for time, perhaps speaking for their master, sued me for arrears of rent, which also were heavy. I explained to the manager that I had at last secured employment and would clear off the arrears, besides paying the monthly rent regularly. Even the bill-collector of the landlord, who was a Hindustani, pleaded for me. He said that a gentleman who kept two servants for two sons could never cheat anybody. But the manager would not listen. Fortunately, I had a lawyer friend who saved me the trouble of going to the court, and got instalments for me. I paid them every month on the stipulated date into the court, which was the procedure ordered by the judge. When five instalments were paid in this manner the landlord's lawyer said to my lawyer friend: 'Your client or friend seems to be very unintelligently honest.' They had expected that, following the normal behaviour of defaulting tenants in Calcutta, I would pay one or two instalments, and after that disappear without leaving my address. Even after getting their decree the landlord's manager was expecting to lose die arrears of rent. Why then did they sue me?

I had worked for Dr Law for about four months when another opening came for me. One day, after coming home from work, I found that Suresh Majumdar, owner of a very large newspaper group, had called and left a note. My wife gave it to me and I read: 'Nirad Babu, I have secured a very good job for you. Come and see me in Ae office in the afternoon.' We wondered what it could be. Upon going and meeting him, I was told that he had persuaded Sarat Chandra Bose, the great nationalist leader who wanted a Secretary, to have me. I had very great distrust of politicians, including the nationalist leaders, and so I was at first unwilling to take up the post. Suresh Babu scolded me and asked me not to be foolish. He said that he would take me to Sarat Bose in the evening, and he did.

I perfectly understood why Suresh Babu had gone to this trouble. He had read my articles and liked them, and was particularly impressed by die piece which I had written on the unfairness of foisting a part of the expenses of keeping troops in Bengal. As he told me, he said to his editors: 'why could you not write that, instead of leaving it to be done by Nirad

Chaudhuri?' The newspapermen in Calcutta were not prepared to give me any credit for knowledge or intellectual ability, being even more unwilling on this score than the academics of the city. So, they replied to Suresh Babu: 'In what way was that particularly meritorious? Nirad Chaudhuri goes to the Imperial Library and makes up his articles out of what he lifts from the books he finds.' Suresh Babu told me what rejoinder he then made: 'Have I forbidden you with an oath on my head [*mathar dibbi* - the most awful oath in Bengal] to go to the Library and lift from its books?'

Perhaps he would have liked to take me on his editorial staff. But even a proprietor cannot go against the editorial department easily. Then, with a view to helping me, he asked me to write regularly for the weekly journal he published, which had a very large circulation. As to remuneration, he said that the editorial department would settle that. When I asked what it would be, I was told that I would be paid Rs.5 per article. I asked for Rs.10 and was refused. I did not write, although the twenty rupees a month offered would have covered the expense on daily supplies over the whole of it. However, as it happened, five years later I was paid Rs. 150 for one article in Suresh Babu's English newspaper. He himself ordered that.

Failing in his own office, Suresh Babu looked elsewhere, and when Sarat Bose asked him if he could recommend a man as his private secretary he at once mentioned me. Sarat Babu was a leading barrister of Calcutta and, in addition, a front-rank nationalist leader. For some years he was a member of the Central Indian Legislature as a Swarajyist. He was also the elder brother and financial supporter of Subhas Chandra Bose; he and Jawaharlal Nehru were the *Dioskuroi* of Indian nationalism. Sarat Babu was, as I have written, arrested in 1932, and kept in detention without trial for association with revolutionary activities. But he had been released in 1936, and had rejoined both the bar and politics. With the introduction of provincial autonomy under the 1935 Act in April 1937, he became leader of the opposition in the Bengal legislature. He was also a member of the Working Committee of the Congress, its supreme executive body. He was sacrificing a substantial part of his practice for the sake of politics, but could not cope with all the routine work himself. That was why he had asked Suresh Babu for a secretary.

Sarat Babu was forty-eight then, and I was nearly forty. The actual difference of age was not great, but he looked ten years older than his age and I perhaps ten younger. Besides, he was tall, heavily built, and portly, and in the face both chubby and florid. In contrast, I was short to the point of being puny, very thin, and pinched in the face, besides having two deep wrinkles between my eyebrows. By that time I had lost two more teeth, and had not been able to get false teeth. So, two gaps showed when I spoke. There were other peculiarities of appearance. First, I do not know why at that time I wore Hitlerian moustaches which never projected beyond the edges of my nostrils. Secondly, at that time I had a closely cropped head. I naturally had very thick and plentiful hair, but I cut it only twice in the year, and with unvaried exactitude on 15 May and 15 November of every year. When I went to Sarat Babu the hair had not grown and my head was round. I was thus a complete contrast to him.

After I had worked for him for about a year I perpetrated my joke on this. Our typist, too, was very thin, and he had a very peevish expression. To add to his household, Sarat Babu suddenly wanted to have a dog, and asked a barrister friend, who had dogs and among them a magnificent alsatian, to give him one. This false friend, not wishing to have a superior in respect of canine ownership as he had in legal practice, gave Sarat Babu a miserable little mongrel, scraggy, short-haired, and with one ear pricked and the other drooping. The great man knew nothing about dogs, and had, when I asked him to have a pedigree dog from the kennels of the Maharaja of Jhind, told me that his establishment was fit only for homely dogs. So he welcomed the wretched mongrel, and spoke to it in English. When it was brought in I could not help making the remark: 'Sarat Babu will have a well-matched staff in the trio - the Secretary, the Typist, and the Dog.' This was carried to him, and he spoke to me about it with great amusement.

However, when I went to him for the first time he must have thought differently, and favourably. To see a priggish little man, with the moustaches and expression of Hitler but a face which was like Voltaire's in its features, must have impressed him. Later he told me what he thought about me. People did not rate him as a good judge of men, but he rather prided himself on that. He said that he had at once detected that I was a puritan, and besides, if not a Brahmo, at least an atheist. I was at once taken on.

The fact was that on account of the factional rivalries and intrigues which rent the Bengal Congress, Sarat Babu was extremely suspicious not only of anyone connected with it, but even of those who had political associations. His political files had been stolen a short time before, and he wanted a man who would be non-political and honest. I seemed to him to meet his requirement. I began to work for him from the middle of July 1937. The reader, if he has been able to develop any compassion for me in spite of my follies, will be glad to learn that with the combined salaries from him and from Dr Law my monthly income, without taking into account what I earned by writing, became at once three times as much as I got even in my employed days up to the age of forty. For the first time since 1921, when I began my working life, I was able to balance my domestic budget.

The years of distress bequeathed to me a stock of ideas which were to serve me throughout my life as a writer. I shall summarize the more abstruse of them in the epilogue to this book. Here I shall single out for mention the moral consequences. First, in spite of all our distress and the hardship I inflicted on my wife, we never quarrelled during these years over money. As to different kinds of quarrels, when a husband and wife are so placid as not to quarrel at times they do not deserve to have married life. Secondly, going through all that want, I did not, during the period, lose even one ounce of over two pounds of solid 22-carat gold with which my wife had come as bride.

Both of us felt that we had won a great victory over the world. But there was one loss which I shall regret all my life. I have not had the courage to ask my wife what she feels. The horrible poverty was like frost-bite on the love of our early married life. The buds could never open. When I came home from work I saw that she expected me to take her in my arms. I did not, and she had to. With what face could I utter empty words of love and make empty gestures.' I knew she did not want anything of this world. But I could not forget that, and felt ashamed.

There has, however, been a great gain. I have learnt the significance of suffering without understanding why it should be the lot of human beings to have it inflicted on them. It does not regard innocence, nor wrongdoing, but comes upon all impartially. It seems to be some natural, inescapable phenomenon like storms, floods, earthquakes, or volcanic eruptions. Looking upon it in this light, I have come to feel that there is nothing more foolish than to hope to be exempt from it and nothing more cowardly than to nurse a grievance for it. Above all, I have come to hold that it is frivolity of the worst kind to air cheap compassion over it. There are only two victories over suffering offered to man: either to rise above it or to submit to it without complaining. That is being *Homo sapiens* in the first instance.

BOOK VI

EXPERIENCE OF POLITICS

1937-1939

Prefatory Note

I worked for Sarat Chandra Bose from the middle of 1937 to the end of 1941, i.e. for three years and a half. The experience was not only wholly new to me, but was also fruitful in other ways. First of all, I became acquainted with the reality of nationalist politics. I was enabled to see its live working behind the public image created by the newspapers. It was like seeing the interior of a great house after having looked only at its facade. I was already alienated from its ideology. Now I acquired a strong dislike for its personal aspect.

Next, my work with Sarat Bose made me a different man by changing my behaviour, although it did not affect my character. On that score, it was like the breaking out of a moth from its pupa. I am very much amused to note how like an insect I have been in the development of my personality. Working for Sarat Bose, I became extrovert so far as I could do so. No one who sees me in my old age would believe that until the age of forty I was, as I have already said briefly in the introduction, a shy, awkward, timid, and retiring man; taciturn among all but intimate friends and as incapable of being at ease with strangers as I was of making them feel at ease with me. Inescapable and continuous meetings with strangers and all classes of men made a social animal of me. As the secretary of a public figure, I was compelled to suffer fools and tolerate adventurers. If I did not do that gladly or charitably at heart, at all events I did it in a polite manner outwardly. My rough edges were rubbed off.

My work for Sarat Babu ended in December, 1941, for political reasons. After that I was offered new employment in Delhi in the broadcasting organization of the Government of India. Accepting that, I left Bengal permanently.

CHAPTER I

Joys and Trials of a Secretary's Life

The combined salary from Sarat Bose and Dr Law not only put an end to my poverty and want, but, with the added income from my writings and broadcasts, even made me affluent by Bengali standards. But the physical strain of doing all the work was at first crushing. I had not done any regular work for over three years, and so the prospect of being pinned down all the time to a desk would have been irksome. But my burden was far heavier. I had to work for nearly all my waking hours. I had not a day off, and, in fact, attendance on Saturdays and Sundays at Sarat Babu's house had to be longer, because on those days he did not go to court, but attended to politics from seven in the morning till noon, and again from about four in the afternoon till ten o'clock at night. I had to be present all that time.

On the working days my routine was like this. After getting up at about half-past five I started for Sarat Babu's house at six, without breakfast or even tea - for I drank neither tea nor coffee at that time - and travelling by tram reached there just before seven. The distance from my house to his was about five miles. I remained with him till about half-past ten, when he rose to go to the High Court. On my way home I visited Dr Law, and remained an hour or so with him, getting back home at about one. I lunched and had an hour's sleep, and after that started again for Sarat Babu's house, to remain there till about a quarter to ten in the evening.

During the first weeks of this routine, I felt every day that I could not bear it. But I knew I had to go through with it. I had inflicted enough want on my wife and thought I had no further right to shirk any work that came to me. Knowing that I had not sacrificed my pride in order to obtain employment, I could in no way add to that kind of selfishness by sparing my body. Therefore I bore my burden with an exercise of the will.

Nonetheless, I know that if this routine of work had not been ended by the wholly unforeseen circumstance which Sarat Babu's arrest created, I should have been dead by the time I was fifty. But my face showed the strain. I looked older and more emaciated at that time than I did even at the age of seventy. Young men in the tramcar at times addressed me as the 'Old Man!', and yet I was only forty.

Sarat Babu's House

He lived as a Bengali gentleman of his position and income was expected to, or rather, even above it. Being in politics, he had to sacrifice a part of his possible professional income. Still, he lived as if he had the full income, and it was not his habit to save money. The house was large and with its three storeys quite high. It was placed back from the street, and was separated from it by a largish lawn, with flowering shrubs on the far side, and low beds of English annuals by the house. There was an iron gate, which had by its side a small lodge for the gate-man. From the very early morning, and as long as Sarat Babu remained in the house, it was crowded with clients, solicitors, junior barristers, politicians, councillors, job and charity seekers, i.e. all the sorts of persons who are called *Ummidwars* (expectants) in India. A similar crowd began to re-appear from about six in the afternoon. When not crowded, the interior gave an impression of space, peace, and repose, even heightened by the passing of a quiet footman, the chimes of a grandfather clock on the quarter, half-hour, and hour, the faint but pervasive smell of incense sticks burning in the study, and the sheen of the black and white marble floors.

The entrance hall was furnished with ornate tables and chairs. My room opened on to the hall at one end. At the other end was the broad marble staircase, under which the wide door of the dining room could be seen. The staircase was hung with large photographs instead of with pictures, and one of the photographs showed Sarat Babu in impeccably tailored morning dress complete with top hat. When Mahatma Gandhi came to stay in the house a few months later the photograph amused him very much.

All the rooms were high, fairly large, and of good proportions. In the middle was a very large waiting hall, with a large table and chairs in the Queen Anne style all around, and the table top, not less than twelve by five feet, was covered by a single sheet of plate glass. On one side of this hall was Sarat Babu's study, with shelves of books on all sides, and a large writing table in the middle. Chairs around it were in the Chippendale style. Sarat Babu's own chair was a swivel one.

But except for formal meetings he never sat in the study. With visitors of ail kinds he sat in the south verandah, because it was open and cool. Even in the cold season he would sit there, with the large bamboo screens let down. On the side opposite the study, there was a spare bedroom on the ground-floor for political friends, and whenever Jawaharlal Nehru visited Sarat Babu he was given that room. All the rooms were provided with lavatories and some even with bathrooms, fitted with basins, toilets, etc., in gleaming porcelain and chromium plate, all imported from England.

One speciality of the household was the attention and care bestowed on maintenance. Even the wealthiest Indian houses were notoriously careless about this. But neither Sarat Babu nor his wife tolerated that. An architect's firm regularly sent inspectors to examine the house for damp and deposits of saltpetre as also for any loosening of the marble slabs. The leading Indian firm of sanitary engineers in Calcutta sent plumbers every week to see to the taps, cisterns, and baths. Sarat Babu had clocks in every room, and in those days they needed winding. So, a man came every Saturday to wind and regulate them.

The furniture was of the best quality, and was supplied by the leading Bengali cabinet makers of Calcutta, the Chatterjees. All the pieces were of solid teak, and were very well finished. Once a carved seat for a bow window, with buttoned upholstery, was brought in by at least twenty porters. The owner of the firm, finding me knowledgeable about furniture, which Sarat Babu was not, talked to me when he came to the house, and told me that he had mahogany which had been seasoned over fifty years. Of course, it goes without saying that the house was kept scrupulously clean throughout. Mrs Bose herself would come down during the day and see that the cleaning was properly done.

The kitchen and servants' quarters were in a separate building adjacent to the main house. After a year another house, a smaller one, was built to accommodate my office and a flat for a son. Sarat Babu's old nurse lived in the kitchen annexe, as also did a cockatoo, which screamed all day.

There was a large staff of servants, maids, cooks, gardeners, sweepers, along with one chauffeur and one lodgekeeper. I got on very well with all of them. They appreciated the notice I took of their working efficiency. On this score, the servants had a grievance. They complained that no member of the family ever took any notice of their work. Indeed, the extremely efficient head servant, who had to attend to the large number of visitors, many of them unreasonable, and succeeded in avoiding giving offence to anyone, said to me: 'Secretary Babu, [that was how I was addressed by the domestic staff], In this house, an elephant has the same standing as an ant and the ant the same as the elephant.' The gardeners liked me because I spoke to them about their flower borders, and the sweepers even told me when the bitch kept by Sarat Babu was in heat, and how many matings it had on each occasion.

During the first three years of my work at Woodburn Park I had three of my four daily meals in Sarat Babu's house. He had made that arrangement, in view of the very unusual hours of attendance, and told me about it as soon as I took up the post. That was most considerate of him. However, before giving an account of my response to his offer, I shall describe what the business of eating was like in Sarat Babu's house.

Now, in the households of professional Bengalis of Sarat Babu's standing, who were not only wealthy but also 'England-returned', as they were called, eating had two forms, one European or at all events Anglo-Indian, and the other traditional Bengali. Therefore two "separate kitchens and cooking establishments were maintained. Before *c.* 1910 all Bengalis who went to England lost caste, and could marry only into 'England- returned' families, in which the women also had an anglicized style of living and eating. But by 1920 this rigidity had disappeared, and many Bengalis who had received professional or technical education in Britain were accepted for marriage by traditional and even very orthodox families. It was with this development that the dichotomy in eating in the households came about. Sarat Babu had married into one of the best-known traditional families of Calcutta, and his wife did not follow the anglicized style of living.

That was the reason why his house also had two eating styles and establishments. The European kitchen, run on gas, was in the main house, under a *Bawarchi*, i.e. Muslim cook who knew European cuisine, a *Khansama* or waiter who was also called 'boy'*irrespective of his age, and a kitchen boy. Food cooked in this kitchen was taken in the dining-room in the European manner. The Bengali kitchen, run on coal, occupied a separate building under the *Thakur* or Brahmin cook and a number of maids.

Sarat Babu divided himself equally between the two styles. In the morning he would have a fairly large English breakfast, with a very swollen

* An Anglo-Indian usage. Although a translation of *garcon,* the word was applied to native servants of all kinds. 'England-returned' Indians adopted the workaday vocabulary of the local British.

omelette. He would take it at his desk, while attending to his solicitors or whoever was with him in the south verandah, and it was brought to him at about eight. Before going to High Court, he would have the usual Bengali midday meal of about five courses. His lunch was purely English, and it was taken to the bar library by the 'boy'. On returning home he would, at about half-past five, take the usual Bengali refreshments for afternoon, which were mostly sweets. At night he took the full English dinner of at least four courses, with a very liberal helping of pudding. He did not drink wine, nor, I should add, did he smoke. But in spite of his anglicism, he chewed betel or *pan* all the time he was at home, an ample supply of which was kept in a silver casket by his side. Nobody could sustain such eating over decades, and most got diabetes or some such chronic ailment after ten years. As it happened, Sarat Babu also developed serious complaints within three years of my joining his service. After that he was put on a very lean diet.

Let me now pass on to my adaptation to this routine of eating. My breakfast, in the English style, but not so heavy as Sarat Babu's, was brought to my room, and so was the equivalent of my afternoon tea (sweets). As to my dinner, I was at first asked to take it with Sarat Babu and go through the elaborate meal that was his. But after a few days I found that I could not keep up with such a routine, being used to the normal Bengali dinner, i.e. rice, lentils, fish, etc. So I excused myself and was handed over to the *Thakur* or Brahmin cook.

Sarat Babu's Children were given a choice between the two styles. In the afternoon they would be asked: 'Dinner or Thakur?' Most often they chose the latter. Sarat Babu never dined with his wife, who dined in the Bengali manner by herself, or with the children. As a rule, he dined in solitary English splendour in the dining-room. The table could seat twelve, and the dinner service was made for him specially in Japan, with his monogram. I must say that I enjoyed all this and thought it was great fun, although the work was very arduous.

Sarat Babu The Man

As a politician and nationalist leader, he was overshadowed by his younger brother, Subhas Bose, who was eight years younger. In both roles his abilities were underrated, because they were not of the kind which were needed or appreciated in the agitational or, as I prefer to regard it, the purely negative, nationalist movement of the day. In fact, even to this day, he has not received what was due to him. At best, he is mentioned as the financial supporter of his brother, and also, quite wrongly as I think, as an aider and abetter of his actions. He was not what his brother was - a demagogue. He was a good speaker, but his style was that of an effectual advocate. He preferred to make his points and hardly indulged in diatribe, the main armament in verbal warfare of the popular nationalist leader.

His strong point was his capacity for mastering any case, however complicated, thoroughly and yet quickly. Of course, he would not have been the successful barrister he was without that. But psychological insight, as an ability to understand complex and, more particularly, dubious human motives and behaviour, was not a faculty of his mind. So he, as a rule, did not take up criminal cases. His own emotions were simple and straightforward.

Such a mental constitution would have made him a good and even great administrator. I found evidence of that in the way he handled his personal correspondence and affairs. His private papers were always at hand, and when needed he could produce even an old letter from his drawer in a minute. In this I was a sad contrast to him, for whatever other abilities I might have possessed, the ones I did not were those associated with a model secretary. I have to confess that at times I tried his patience by my failure to produce a letter quickly.

Had he become a minister, his department would have been run to some purpose, and he would never have been the mere Censor to put *nihil obstat* to the papers placed before him by his officials and clerks. But he was never given such an opportunity except only once, when he became a member of the so-called Interim Government of Nehru in August 1946. That, too, was for three months only and he was dismissed. Even after independence he was not given office either at the Centre or in Bengal. His political weakness came in the way. A born administrator like him could function only like a Colbert or Turgot, with the political support of a king behind him, or at least of a royal mistress. Nehru was not Louis XIV, and certainly even less of a Louis XV.

In his ready acceptance of social responsibility Sarat Babu was more than just liberal, he was generous. I did not deal with his private charity, but I knew something of its extent. I saw his business clerk fill in money-order forms for needy relatives or dependents. I noted his liberality in political matters, because I had to manage a fund he had raised to help poor and needy political workers, especially those who had been kept in detention by the British administration.

One day a young man came to see him and related a long tale of political persecution and present penury. He even said he had contracted tuberculosis and his sole desire was to take advantage of an offer a friend had made to put him up in his house in a more healthy place than Calcutta and to die there in peace. While saying all this slowly in a feeble voice he panted. Sarat Babu looked at me and asked me to give him some money. I had it, but had grown somewhat suspicious and thought I would make some inquiries. So I gave the false excuse that I did not have the cash in hand and would have to get it from the bank. At once Sarat Babu took out his own purse and gave the young man all that he had in it. It was twenty rupees.

A week or so later he received a very repentant letter from the young man, informing him that he was neither a political sufferer nor ill, but had come to Sarat Babu because he was at the end of his resources. He felt most sorry for the deception he had practised. Sarat Babu gave me his direction for a reply on the top of the letter: 'Please write in appreciation of his honesty.'

The next qualities he had were urbanity and kindliness, both of which were unfailing. In him these were not merely a manner, but deep-seated in character and feeling, as indeed the politeness of any real gentleman always is. As his secretary, I was able to observe the manner in which he reacted, not only to the routine sycophancy a man of his position always receives, but also the impertinence he is obliged to bear daily. One has to live in India to discover that a beggar snarls as well as whines. But he never lost his temper in social intercourse, although he was prone to do so in certain matters. He was always very patient with me in my shortcomings as a secretary, but his consideration went further. He would never allow me to be treated as a mere secretary by others.

One morning a well-known barrister, an elderly man, had come to him for consultation. Sitting down in front of Sarat Babu, the barrister picked up a weekly law report, which was uncut. Seeing me standing at Sarat Babu's side, he held out the book in one hand, and, without a word, made signs with the other hand to tell me he wanted the pages cut. Sarat Babu noticed this and said: 'What is it you want? Give me that.' Perhaps only assuming that he wanted to see the report, the barrister unsuspectingly handed it over. Sarat Babu took it, picked up a paper-cutter, and, having cut every page himself, returned it to the man. I did not observe that he even felt embarrassed. But I was almost moved to tears. The man later became Vice-Chancellor of Calcutta University.

Another incident was lighter, and amusing. I had a reputation in Calcutta of being a good writer of English. Many of Sarat Babu's courtiers, political and legal, did not feel quite happy about this. Thus on one occasion they looked pleased to see something happening. I had brought the draft of a long political statement to be sent to the press by Sarat Babu, and he was going through it, making rather frequent cuts and changes. The expression on the faces of those sitting before him was telltale. Perhaps Sarat Babu too noticed it for he raised his eyes to me and said: 'Are you upset? Don't be. You are too idiomatic, and this would not go down with our people.' At that, the others turned away their eyes which, until then, they had kept directed at me.

In spite of all this, Sarat Babu had acquired a reputation, which was widely current, of being an arrogant man. I could easily account for that undeserved reputation. I saw that the impression was created by two pronounced traits of his personality, which were part of the nature he was born with, re-enforced by upbringing.

In the first place, he was very efficient himself and could not tolerate inefficiency in those on whom he had to depend to get things done. One significant feature of his love of efficiency was that he was even more intolerant of inefficiency in small things than in big things. He did not subscribe to the tenets of the ambitious but weak Bengali gentry that a man might be deserving of very high office and discharge its duties with credit to himself even when he was incapable of doing a very small thing, like fitting an electric bulb to its holder. Sarat Babu was not disposed to entrust big tasks to associates who could not do small things.

I once heard of an exhibition of this attitude. The occasion was a meeting of the Congress members of the Bengal legislature to be held in his chambers near the High Court and not, as was usual, in his house. When he arrived for the meeting a little late after finishing his work in the courts, he was surprised to find that no tea and refreshments had been provided for the assembled members. When he asked the reason he was told by the man next in authority, the Secretary of the Party and a fellow barrister, that there was no appliance in the rooms for boiling water. 'Is that so?' he asked, and, calling his clerk, told him to get hot water from a restaurant close by. This was done, tea was served, and the meeting proceeded. He told me the story himself, and he was not the man to forget the incident. Whenever the Secretary would not come up to his expectations in party matters, he would say to him: 'You could not even get hot water for tea.' After he had done so more than once the worm turned and said defiantly: 'Why are you bringing up that utterly trumpery thing every day?' Such ways were not likely to make anyone popular anywhere, least of all in Calcutta.

But there was also a more subtle reason why people got the impression that he was stand-offish, if not snobbish. That was due to his unconscious class-consciousness, which was a combination of attitudes that all men who belong to a social class groomed to a certain pattern of behaviour by old traditions and aristocratic *mores* always exhibit. They would never fail in politeness, but after meeting them those who did not belong to that class would feel that the man they were talking to had a strong sense of who were 'We' and who were 'They'. That is the awareness from which the word 'peer', used by the European aristocracy, has come into general currency.

I noticed that Sarat Babu had wholly different attitudes to his political associates according as they came from a certain group or did not. The members of the Congress Party in Bengal fell into two distinct groups. In the first were politicians who were also first-rank professionals in Calcutta or members of old Bengali landed families, and in the second the district lawyers, etc. turned politicians, and also Congress agitators who had no profession other than that of the elected representatives of the people. They were all clearly distinguishable from the men of the first group in looks, clothes, air, and their English and even Bengali accent. Sarat Babu did not pay the same attention to the second group as he did to the first, and his political confidants were all from the first group. This attitude had nothing to do with money, but was created by a bias of the mind. Certainly, Sarat Babu had a certain exclusiveness, but it was not of the kind which F. E. Smith displayed in England. He never had to assert his superiority because it was never questioned.

Sarat Babu's innate magnanimity was shown to me in another way. He knew that I did not share his political opinions and, in one respect, that could create difficulties. In regard to Indian politics, I could never be as anti-British as he was, and I was even pro-British in international politics. At that time I was broadcasting regularly for All-India Radio from its Calcutta station on international questions. If my talks had had any bias, that would have been in favour of Britain, although never for the Chamberlain ministry. I asked Sarat Babu if I could continue my broadcasts. He said: 'Certainly'. After the outbreak of the war in 1939, my pro-British attitude gave offence to the Bengali nationalists, but he would never ask me to give up my talks. However, he gave the appearance of sanctioning them on monetary considerations rather than with any avowed intention of allowing me to act according to my convictions. But at times he would also mildly disapprove of my spreading myself too widely by saying: 'Nirad Babu, you have too many irons in the fire.'

I had no doubt that he allowed me to go on with my broadcasts out of respect for my convictions. He himself was as anti-British in international politics as he was in Indian politics. He did not give Britain credit for disinterested motives even when in 1939 she went to war with Germany. He delivered a long and decidedly anti-British speech in the legislature. As it contained many historical references, people thought that I had written it for him. Actually, I was not even aware that he was preparing such a speech by himself, and had been doing so much background reading. He would never ask me to prepare any statement for him on subjects on which he knew I would have conscientious objections to give verbal form to his ideas. That saved me from situations which might have compelled me to leave his service.

In small matters he would even defer to me. He had somehow formed the impression that I was choosy in respect of food, and especially sweets. So if a supply of the famous Bengali sweet *Sandesh* came to his house, he would say to me: 'Taste one of these and tell me what you think of it. I have seen that you have a very fastidious palate as regards sweets.' One day he saw a tin of biscuits in my hand, with which he was not familiar. It was that of ginger-nuts by Romary of Tunbridge Wells. When I told him that these were the best of their kind, he observed: 'You are a Sahib', that is, an Englishman.

Finally, he taught me a moral lesson which I needed and which helped me in developing a retarded part of my character. I was weak in facing immediate obstacles and rather prone to give in. It was not indeed that I ever lost sight of any goal I had set for myself or that I would not pursue it, but I was discouraged by any frontal resistance and would take a roundabout way to get past it. I might say that I was like a small river making its way to die sea by winding in hairpin bends which were almost loops.

Sarat Babu's example encouraged me to try to overcome the obstacles with energy and courage, and to make me less ready to dodge. I was surprised to see how he would not accept checkmates or be deterred by opposition. Of course, he had none to encounter in his career as a lawyer. But as a politician he had to face many trials. He was kept in detention without trial, and at every stage he had to overcome resistance. Yet at no time did I see him discouraged and resigned to defeat. In small everyday matters, too, he would not yield because of seemingly insurmountable difficulties. All this made me reflect on my own weakness. If, in regard to stupendous obstacles, I had learnt from the rivers of India, that was on a very rarefied moral plane. The lesson that Sarat Babu gave me was personal and concrete.

Men like him who belonged to the true aristocracy of character in Bengal have disappeared for ever. Bengali society at large is no longer producing them, nor is the order to which he belonged transmitting its old qualities to its children. A Frenchman, J. A. Barbey d'Aurevilly, wrote that the hands of a Stuart, even when he was in poverty-stricken exile, could be distinguished through his torn gloves and that adversity 'n'efface pas l'aristocratie puisée aux mamelles de sa mère et les traditions de son berceau.' This has not been proved to be true in the case of the progeny of the old Bengali gentry.

Suppliant- Claimants

The heaviest, that is to say, both mentally and physically the most strenuous, exertion I had to go through as Sarat Bose's secretary was to attend to those who called on him. These persons were numerous, for, as an object of visiting, Sarat Babu might be described as a trinity. He was the barrister with a large practice; the political and nationalist leader; and a notability of the established type in the Bengali society of Calcutta.

The clients of a barrister in Calcutta as a rule came for consultations to his house both morning and evening with their solicitors, and on his side Sarat Babu would have the juniors who devilled for him. Next, not only had a political leader to remain in personal touch with his followers; these latter, too, would come to him whenever they wished, in the pursuit of their interests. Lastly, all the notable personages in Calcutta were visited by two kinds of regular private callers. The first kind was composed of their friends, who were really their gentlemen-in-waiting or *Mosahebs*, as they were called in Bengali, who listened to his remarks, smiled and exchanged glances of appreciation and admiration with the others of their kind, and contributed to the sense of importance of the great man. The others were frank seekers of charity, some humble and sincere, some real scroungers. Even if Sarat Babu had been only one kind of VIP in Calcutta he would have had a fair number of visitors. His triple greatness more than tripled the number of his visitors.

Fortunately, I had to deal with only one class of them. I had nothing to do with his professional callers, nor could I regulate his political visitors. The clients always came by appointment, and they were in the hands of his legal clerk. The political visitors had the right of free access to him without any appointment, and would at times even interrupt a professional consultation. To impose restraint on them would have meant political extinction. My task was only to receive those who came for personal help, in the form of recommendations for employment or money.

Their numbers were not small. I knew from my study of the social history of Calcutta and Bengal that all wealthy men had to face demands for charity, which was more social assistance than charity. Although the normal seekers of help were humble in manner, they were not apologetic in doctrine. The poor in India acted on the assumption that it was Fate and not personal merit or demerit which had made the rich rich and the poor poor; therefore it was the right of the poor to demand money from the wealthy and the duty of the rich to help the poor. In this way, the opposite caprices of Fortune were to be cancelled out. Therefore, traditionally, where the obligation to spend money was social, as for instance in the marrying of daughters, the seeker of charity would apply to the rich for it without any shamefacedness. On the whole, the suppliants always behaved like claimants.

It is this doctrine of the relationship of the wealthy to the poor which has now been extended to India's economic relations with the West. The strident lectures read by the Government of India to the IMF, the World Bank, and generally to all wealthy Western countries, that it is their duty to give money to the poor countries of the world like India, is the international form of an established social demand, whose application to Sarat Babu I was to experience.

This doctrine, however, had been very much strengthened by the nationalist agitation. To join in such agitation always harmed worldly prospects. Till about the middle of the Twenties, most of these political sufferers were reconciled to their sacrifices, and somehow tried to make the best of their worldly disadvantages. But when the control of the Calcutta Corporation came into the hands of the Congress, jobs in it were demanded as compensation for political sacrifices. This trend went on increasing and those who had suffered politically expected to be compensated in all the institutions over which the Congress gained control.

The political character of the demand for social charity was revealed in an almost Winding glare in 1937, because the demand for it rose to a level which was self-defeating. That was due to the introduction of provincial autonomy under the Act of 1935. Thousands of young Bengalis had been arrested for their association with the revolutionary movement from 1930 to 1932, and detained without trial in various camps. There was a general amnesty for them in 1937, and they were being released in their hundreds. They wanted to be established in life and sought employment. As their claim was political, they came to the political leader for help. I had to take them to Sarat Babu in batches and afterwards give them letters of recommendation. That confirmed my dislike for the Act of 1935.

It was a wholly novel experience for me to meet so many strangers every day, and it was also exasperating, because almost all of them were unreasonable, passively or actively. But I felt the sadness of it most. The released *détenus* were all young, around twenty or so, and had been isolated from the real world for five years or more. They had been drawn into the revolutionary movement by their impulsive patriotism, and were having to pay the price. Unemployment for the educated youth of Bengal was bad enough at its normal level, and the needs of these young men made it worse. I had to see hundreds of them in the course of my first year with Sarat Babu, and what I heard from them gave me a chastening idea of the reality of the nationalist and revolutionary sentiment as it existed in the Bengali middle class.

Some of the young men told me bitterly that they could not even get a private tutor's job on five or ten rupees a month, which was the last desperate standby for unemployed young men, on account of their political record. As soon as the parents or the guardians heard that they had been *détenus*, they would not employ them for their children. But their expectation that Sarat Babu could help them in their predicament was not less saddening.

He was not in office, but only in the Opposition. So he had no patronage at his disposal. The only thing he could do was to give them letters of recommendation to all and sundry in business or industries, recommending the cases on grounds of compassion. I had to prepare these in their hundreds, and the ones I thought most useless were those addressed to Sir George White, head of the shipping concern in Calcutta which managed the P & O and BISN lines, whom Sarat Babu knew because Sir George was a member of the Bengal legislature. Yet the young men had implicit faith in these scraps of paper, and would not pay any attention to my advice not to seek them.

With these, they would trudge from office to office and some of them came to me afterwards to tell me of their failure. But their naïveté was pathetic. None of them had any vocational qualification, and yet when I asked them what sort of job they wanted, they would invariably reply: 'Any job.' I would then ask: 'An electrician's, accountant's, typist's, shorthand writer's, etc.?' and the reply would be - 'No, No, No.' Then I would testily remark: 'Then why did you say "any job"? You want a clerk's job.' They would agree.

However, not all were so passive. Some would come with ideas of openings, and actually it was these young men who were the most unrealistic. One day three of them marched into my room carrying three very heavy sacks, and wanted Sarat Babu's help with more assurance than the other job-seeking *détenus* showed. They produced three or four large blocks of reddish stone from one of the sacks and said: 'See, we have discovered gold ore in a place near Ranchi, and if Sarat Babu would recommend us to a capitalist [in spite of their communist leanings they used this word for a financier with great respect] we could start working the mine.' I could only ask them to put the bags in one corner of my room and assure them that I would discuss the matter with Sarat Babu. I shall presently relate what I did with the blocks supposed to be gold ore.

Another case was not less remarkable. Two young men came and said they wanted to start a steamer line for carrying the raw materials of Assam, and they had indeed secured a capitalist. But that man of money wanted one requirement fulfilled. The young men must first secure a monopoly of carrying all goods from the Assam Government, which was then under the control of the Congress. So, the young men said, if Sarat Babu would only ask Gopinath Bardoloi, the Congress Chief Minister, to give them the monopoly, they would at once start the business. I professed great interest in the enterprise and asked them what sort of steamers they had in mind - screw-steamers with turbines or paddle-steamers with reciprocating engines. They did not feel offended, and replied that they could not buy the steamers until they had secured the monopoly. The most pathetic thing about their enterprising spirit was that they did not even notice how rude I was and how absurd they were.

Yet I found that of all the visitors I had to deal with, these utter illusionists were the best. Contrasting them with the realistic cadgers I came to the conclusion that the only good Bengalis were those clinging to their illusions. The calculators sickened me. But the experience also made me somewhat cynical. In the end I said that of any group of hundred visitors of various descriptions that Sarat Babu had to receive, perhaps only one was disinterested. But I would add this: for this cynicism I could put forward La Rochefoucauld's plea: 'The author of these reflections has only considered men in their deplorable condition in which their nature has been corrupted by Sin, and does not concern those whom God has saved by his special grace.' I would include the *détenus* in the latter class in spite of all their foolishness.

I also learned a good deal from them. They told me how well they were treated by their British jailers. They were treated like prisoners of war and not like convicts. They were given allowances for food and personal expenses with which they ate better than they had ever done in their own homes. One *détenu* told me that all of them had their weight taken when they came to the camp and when they left, and in every case they gained from detention. I also noticed that they were more plump and smooth-faced than the normal run of unemployed youth of Bengal. I was also told that all of them left with portable gramophones, Parker fountain pens and things like these. Above all, they were allowed to continue their studies, and the University of Calcutta held special examinations in the camps for them. Many of the men obtained degrees while detained, and two with whom I became very friendly afterwards, even received MA degrees with distinction.

I had the pleasure of making the acquaintance of one of them in the second year of my work. He had already been appointed office secretary of the Congress Party in the legislature on the strength of his educational record and intelligence. As he told me later, he had avoided me because of reports from the other *détenus* who had met me and who had told him that I was like a block of ice. At our first meeting he himself also looked ice. But there was something on the table which changed his attitude. It was a copy of *The Wind in the Willows,* which - of all people - belonged to Subhas Bose. It had been presented to him by an Englishman, who must have mistaken his personality. But I had enjoyed it immensely, and kept it lying on the table as a sort of touchstone for those whom I had to see. So far, no one had taken notice of the book. But Tridib Chaudhuri - such was the name of the visitor - took it up, and, looking at the first two pages or so, broke into a smile and said: 'What a wonderful passage!' And he read: 'Never in his life had he seen a river before - this sleek, sinuous, full-bodied animal, chasing and chuckling, gripping things with a gurgle and leaving them with a laugh ...' etc.

From that moment we became friends. I have written about him in my previous autobiography and shall do so in this book as well. To meet such men in that crowd of innocents as well as crooks was both instructive and reassuring.

It was, however, such a topsy-turvy world that, on one occasion, my over-cautiousness in dealing with the revolutionary *ci-devants* landed me into a very great absurdity. Indeed, I was made a fool of. In spite of the fact that the game went against me I take great pleasure in recalling it. One morning a young girl called on me and explained that she had a younger brother who had been a *détenu* and she had come for a letter of recommendation from Sarat Babu. I at once took down the name and asked her to come at six o'clock the next day. I had, of course, meant the afternoon, but upon arriving at Sarat Babu's house at about seven the next morning I found the girl waiting for me. She said that, according to my word, she had come at six and been waiting for me. I said very apologetically that I had told her to come in the afternoon. She seemed to take offence at that and replied: 'Say that you did not get the letter ready, and are making an excuse.' I said quietly: 'I could have given you the letter in fifteen minutes. But since you are taking this line, you will have to return in the afternoon.' She jumped up from her chair and went away seemingly in a huff.

I got the letter ready before I went home. But I became anxious. From 1930 our girls had begun to join the revolutionary movement, and they were not only excitable themselves but also had lovers who could and would avenge any insults to them. I feared that she might come with three or four of her 'followers'* and insult or even assault me. Such incidents had happened and in such assaults slippers had been used. One principle I have always followed has been never to be taken by surprise by unpleasant situations and I was also resolved never to tolerate anybody's hand on my body. So, when returning to Sarat Babu's house in the afternoon, I took some weapons with me. I had two full-sized real Gurkha kukris, and a sword-stick. I wore the kukris hanging from a belt under my tunic. The sword-stick I carried in my hand. On reaching my office I first of all bolted the backdoor to the room in order to prevent an assault from behind. (I had read so much about the danger of having to fight on two fronts.) Then I took out a number of blocks of the gold ore, none weighing less than five pounds, and put them in the drawers of my desk, in order that I might be able to use them as missiles against a second wave of attack. After taking all these precautions, and putting the letter in front of me, I waited rather restlessly fidgeting with the weapons. Exactly at six, with marvellous punctuality, instead of the girl, a very feeble young man entered the room, and said: 'You told my *Didi* [elder sister] that you would have a letter for me in the afternoon. I have come for it.' I handed the letter to him, and he left most respectfully. I had never felt more foolish in my life, and indeed I have not till this day.

But the suppliant-claimants of the traditional type whom I had to deal with put all my stoicism to the test. I shall give only two examples, which were perfectly true to type in our society. The first is that of a young man who wrote that he wanted to take a course of technical education and had secured admission to the well-known technical college at Jadavpur near Calcutta. But, he wrote, he did not have the means to go through the four years' course. He therefore asked Sarat Babu whether he would support him in this plan. Sarat Babu with his usual generosity agreed and wrote to him that he would give him an allowance of Rs.25 a month (equal to about £2) which would cover all his normal expenses, as long as he himself continued his legal practice. The young man replied to him, taking offence at his conditional promise: 'You have said that you will give me the allowance as long as you continue your practice. But you are a nationalist leader, and any moment you might decide on a patriotic impulse to give it up and devote yourself to the service of the country. What would happen to me if you did so before my course was completed? If you want me to accept

*See Cranford for the word

your offer, you must give an absolute promise.' Believe it or not, this is an exact reproduction of his letter. Sarat Babu capitulated and gave the absolute promise. Here was the formula 'no strings to foreign aid' in its seminal form.

However, this was not enough. One morning I got a telegram from the young man. I handed it to Sarat Babu. He was informed that the student was arriving in Calcutta in two days and would stay at his house until the college hostel opened a week later. In panic Sarat Babu called his manager, and asked him to make arrangements for the student at a boarding house at his expense. On the day of arrival the manager went with Sarat Babu's car to receive the young man and take him to the boarding house. Regularly thereafter, I saw the student call on the first of every month for his allowance.

The second request for charity was exceptional even by our very submissive Hindu standards. It came from a young man in a village in north Bengal. He wrote that he had decided to do something which would be a revolutionary act of social reform, for which he felt justified in asking Sarat Babu to help him. It was to marry a girl who was not only outside his caste, but of a very low caste. He declared that he had every qualification for marriage except money. So he asked Sarat Babu to give him an allowance of Rs.50 a month until he had a sufficient income, and in addition, to give him a lump sum of Rs.3000 in order to build a house so that he might lead a proper married life, after being turned out of the parental house for disregarding caste. This, too, is an absolutely truthful reproduction of the young man's letter. At Sarat Babu's bidding I replied to him saying that for personal reasons he could not give the help asked for. The reply to this came directly to Sarat Babu and not to me. The young man wrote: 'A person named Nirad Chaudhuri, calling himself your private secretary, has replied that you are unable to help me. I am sure that the letter has been withheld from you and the man has taken it upon himself to deny me the help. I am equally certain that if you had heard of such a case as mine you would never have refused to support it with your money. Please reply quickly, because the girl is both uneducated and rustic, and there is no knowing what she might not take into her head to do.' This time Sarat Babu signed the letter that went in reply.

I could not have worked for Sarat Babu without the relief that I derived from such experiences. Such relief was also provided by another class of visitors, cranks and even mad people. Somehow, all my life I have attracted abnormal persons, and my readiness to talk with them has been a serious annoyance for my wife. I give only one example of madness I had to face when working for Sarat Babu. One day a man who looked perfectly normal came in. He spoke quite rationally about a grievance he had against a well-known industrialist of Calcutta, who, he said, had cheated him of a large sum of money. He wanted Sarat Babu's help to recover the money. All this was both normal and very common. But as he pressed his case I became suspicious. At first he said that he was not a mere nobody, because an ancestor of his had been the Commander-in-Chief of Siraj-ud-daula's armies at the battle of Plassey. After that he spoke about his own achievements and informed me that he was a greater mathematical physicist than Einstein. I asked him with due modesty what was his contribution. He at once said angrily: 'What do you know of mathematical physics that you would understand if I told you.' I at once apologised and placated him by saying that I would speak to Sarat Babu.

I had also my trials in another way, but perhaps that is the lot of all private secretaries. The great men want these poor creatures to bear the burden of their dislikes and discourtesies. If they do not wish to see anyone who is a *persona non grata*, they want to be protected by their secretaries. One day this happened to me in a striking way. A lady, very well known in social and political circles in Bengal, and connected with a famous family of Calcutta, came to see Sarat Babu. She had always been somewhat notorious. When I announced her, Sarat Babu said quite decisively that he would not see the lady, for whom he had no respect. I was asked to get rid of her. I could not dismiss so well known a person, and therefore told her that Sarat Babu would come out presently and talk to her. I knew he was rising for the morning to go to the High Court and would have to pass through the hall to reach the stairs. Then he would be compelled to talk to her and be held responsible for whatever incivility he wanted to show. I was standing by the lady when Sarat Babu did come out, but on seeing her, he stepped forward with eagerness, as if he were meeting a long lost love, as pure as a lily washed by the morning dew. The lady cast a glance at me whose scorn I could understand. I consoled myself by looking at her elderly figure, dressed in the fashion of the young girls of her own youth (c. 1900). For a secretary, all this is part of the day's work.

The ordinary callers whom Sarat Babu would not or could not see, I could somehow turn away. But even one or two among them took the offensive, without providing any comic relief to me. One day a young man called and was very insistent for an interview with Sarat Babu. Even so I remained firm. As he was going away he remarked: 'I know how busy he is. If I grease the Secretary's palm he will at once become less so.' He was standing at the head of the stairs. I leaped on him and gave him a kick which took him to the next landing. I followed him there and gave another kick, which sent him to the ground floor. Not satisfied with that I took him by the scruff of the neck and dragged him to the front gate. The servants and the lodgekeeper looked on with amazement. Sarat Babu heard about this and said to me: 'Nirad Babu, you lose your temper very easily. Don't you see what I have to bear with, not only impertinence but even insolence?' Of course, I could not be his equal in forbearance on account of the difference in our positions.

These varied experiences with all sorts of people - more of which will be related in the chapters to follow - succeeded in rubbing off most of my rough edges. Nonetheless, I was being worn down by the abrasiveness of the process. Even after three months of this kind of work I felt I could not go on, but was delighted to learn from Sarat Babu that he was going to a hill-station in the Western Ghats during the long vacation of the High Court. I also decided to have a change, which I had not had after 1932. My wife had an uncle at Ranchi, who invited us. I went with the whole family, that is my wife and the two children we then had. It was a very pleasant holiday, and I felt refreshed, almost rejuvenated. But at the end of three weeks I got a letter from Sarat Babu asking me to return to Calcutta as soon as possible. There was going to be a meeting of the Working Committee of the Congress in his house, and Mahatma Gandhi himself was going to stay with him. So I returned to Calcutta.

CHAPTER 2

The Gandhian Congress

When I got Sarat Babu's letter asking me to come back to Calcutta as early as possible, I was rather annoyed at being compelled to cut short my holiday at Ranchi, the first I had had in five years. However, when the whole affair was over I was glad of the experience. This gave me my first direct visual contact with the Congress leaders and from it I also gained a knowledge of their ways, which I could never have had otherwise. It transformed what was so far only a public image, an abstraction, into a thing of flesh and blood. I was enabled to see the practical human aspect of the activities of the Congress, because for the first time in my life I saw all the important Congress leaders with my own eyes, and, above all, Gandhi. Of these, I had seen only Nehru for a short time. On this occasion I was able to observe him for a longer time. Furthermore, I got a peep into the work-room of the Congress, and could form a correct idea of its method of carrying on the nationalist movement. I would not say that as a result of that knowledge I came to underrate the power and importance, as well as the effectiveness, of the Congress on its impersonal, public plane. But I discovered that its leadership existed on another plane: that the Congress edifice had also a basement. Or, varying the metaphor, I would say that I saw something of the greenroom behind the lighted stage, and the actors without the makeup as well as with its application. That is what I shall describe in this chapter.

Let me, for ease of understanding my account, particularize the occasion. What was going to take place was, first, a meeting of the All-India Congress Committee, which might be likened to a shareholders' meeting of a great company. Secondly, there was to be a meeting of the Working Committee of the Congress, consisting of twelve members and the President, which was like a directors' meeting. The discussions at the former were always public, and in the latter always private. The All-India Congress Committee was to meet under a marquee in Wellington Square, while the meetings of the Working Committee were to be held in Sarat Babu's house. For the Boses therefore it was to be a great occasion, made greater still by the condescension of Gandhi, who agreed to be the guest of Sarat Babu and Mrs Bose during the meetings of the Committee.

Gandhi and His Staff

After my return from Ranchi I found that already the preparations for receiving the Working Committee and the august leader were in full swing. Mahatma Gandhi was to have one of the principal bedrooms on the first floor, which was made Gandhian, that is, as bare as possible. The meetings of the Working Committee were to be held in the drawing-room on the same floor in order to spare Gandhi the strain of having to climb stairs. His crowded prayer meetings, twice daily like matins and evensong, were to be on the terrace of the second floor, but, as these were of a religious nature, Mahatma Gandhi would undergo the strain of going upstairs as part of his ascetic routine.

Putting up Gandhi did not present a difficult problem; feeding him did. Mahatma Gandhi's dietary prescriptions were not only rigid and numerous, but also odd. Since they were not identical with the well known Hindu dietary rules but somewhat esoteric, Sarat Babu asked an orthodox disciple of Gandhi in Calcutta to let him have a list of the vegetables Gandhi ate. The list I saw was formidably long and representative of the ecology of Bengal. Of course, he did not eat the full range of vegetables at one meal or even on one single day, but he or his secretary in charge might demand one or other of them on a particular day or for a particular meal in order to test the resources and loyalty of his host. Also, the secretary would not specify the herb or vegetable for that day before ten in the morning, and Mahatma Gandhi wanted his meal at about midday. Therefore, no time would be available to buy a particular vegetable if demanded, and all had to be ready in the kitchen, so that the particular one called for would be at hand. To fail in supplying and cooking the vegetable was likely to be regarded as a shame on the Bose household. However, they were able to solve this problem quite successfully. Mrs Bose had a young nephew who was the superintendent of one of the markets of the Calcutta Corporation, and therefore could rouse the greengrocers to great effort, were this necessary. I knew him very well. He had no political pretensions but was a very energetic and enterprising person. He wanted to rise to the occasion, and if he had failed to procure all the vegetables regularly, I am sure he would have killed himself like Vatel, the major domo of the Great Condé, who threw himself on his sword because, when M. le Prince was receiving Louis XIV at Chantilly, he found that only two carts of sea fish had arrived instead of the forty he had ordered.

The supply of milk for Mahatma Gandhi presented no less difficult a problem, for he took only goat's milk and would not touch cow's milk because he felt that it excited concupiscence. But, before being permitted to serve Gandhi, the she-goats had to be screened by his principal private secretary, Mahadev Desai, and therefore no goat's milk could be bought or stored in advance. Thus the she-goat had to be brought to Sarat Babu's house and milked there. I never learned how Mahatma Gandhi got his milk at Sarat Babu's house on the first day, but on the morning of the second, when I arrived at about seven, I found a row of up to fifteen she-goats in the outer courtyard munching leaves and bleating away for all they were worth. Behind them, the goatherds were standing to attention as though on parade.

I was quite at home with goats, for as a boy I used to tend the large number of he-goats which were sacrificed in our house to the goddess Durga. But the contact with goats on this occasion, although equally religious, was different. These were volatile she-goats whose nature was totally unknown to me, because we Hindus never kept she-goats; in Bengal this being looked upon as a Muslim practice. The sacrificial he-goats I attended to were all bathed and garlanded before they were sacrificed. I wondered whether before being milked for Mahatmaji these she-goats, too, would be sanctified in the same manner. But what they got was only secular and hygienic inspection, but over and above that might have been moral as well. I was told that Mahadev Desai himself would come down to examine the she-goats, and choose the one which was to have the privilege of serving Gandhi as foster-mother. I felt so very curious about the preliminary that I joined the crowd of spectators in the courtyard. For the first time I saw the formidable Mahadev Desai. His reputation for efficiency was known all over India, but I had not known he was so very impressive physically. He was also very grave-looking. He slowly walked from the left end of the row of she-goats to the right end, and stopped before each to examine it carefully. I could not find out what he actually was looking for, but I saw that he looked severely into the eyes of the animals, and at last selected one. So I went about telling everybody frivolously that he was trying to find out which she-goat was the chastest among the lot and selected that one which stared back equally hard at him, instead of lowering her eyes from consciousness of guilt.

This gave me a foretaste of what I was to witness throughout the meeting. I naturally became curious about the cost to Sarat Babu of having Gandhi in his house and after a fortnight I got some information on this from his clerk.

It was well known that Gandhi with his vow of poverty would only allow three annas (about old three pence) a day to be spent on his food. But Sarat Bose's clerk told me four weeks later that already about three thousand rupees had been spent, which was six hundred times the amount allowed by Gandhi himself. This expense, however, covered the whole party.

I took particular care that I should not miss any part of the spectacle, which I knew would be a unique experience for me. Thus, on the day of the arrival of Gandhi, I hung about the hall. Of course, even if I had remained in my room there could be no missing of such an event. From the very early morning, in the street outside Sarat Babu's house, immense crowds had been gathering, from which arose a deafening wave of sound. This came in the form of shouts of *Vande Mataram*, accompanied by a great hubbub, and I knew that Gandhi's car had stopped before the main gate. But at first I saw a rush of strangers into the hall, and after that a pattering, swaying, and panting party, with Gandhi in the forefront. Although he was walking with staff in hand, he was nevertheless supported by men on both sides and even from behind. Among them I saw the energetic nephew who had supplied the eatables. With outstretched arms he was making way for Gandhi, keeping close to him all the time. Such a heaving procession of men I had seen only in my young days when the image of the goddess Durga was being carried" to our big tank for the ceremonial immersion in water. Gandhi was almost lifted from the group and taken upstairs to his room.

For the first time in my life I was seeing Gandhi face to face, and the impression was quite unlike anything I had expected. I had seen numberless pictures of him, and was quite prepared to see a man of insignificant frame and plain looks. All that, of course, was there, but unnoticed by me. What struck me was the expression on his face, which diverted all attention away from his features or figure. It was one of extraordinary innocence and benignity, with two soft beams streaming out of his eyes.

On the animal plane - and after all plain men can only hope to look as attractive as a plain animal - Gandhi suggested the primitive primate tarsier to me. But a beatific unworldly look suffused what was basically mere animal innocence. There was not a trace on his face of the repulsive arrogance which disfigures the face of every Hindu holy man. I must say that I looked on spellbound in spite of my dislike for Gandhi's ideas.

Over the many weeks that Gandhi stayed in the house there was no getting away from the noise, the bustle, and the comings and goings in that house. There were the leaders themselves and their aids, there were the journalists, there were the ever-importunate visitors, and, above all, the crowds on the streets, which stood from morning to evening in thronging relays to have, as they said, Mahatmaji's *darshan*, that is, sight of him as he appeared on the balcony. And whether he appeared or not, from time to time the shouts of *Vande Mataram* would ring out like the chimes of Big Ben, not so plangently, however. There was a block of flats just opposite Sarat Babu's house, which was occupied by Anglo-Indians, i.e. Eurasian families. I saw men and women of that community looking out of the windows with clearly discernible expressions of disgust and anger. The Anglo-Indians had not yet acquired the ambition to act the part of Gandhi by way of attaining celebrity, nor even courtesy for him as a living man. Of course, their peace was sorely disturbed, and once I got an abusive letter from that house, which was both natural and honest, because its inmates were bound to be intolerant of Indian noises and Indian crowds, and even more of Indian nationalism. In the letter, after receiving some choice abuse, the crowds were asked to go to the devil with their 'bandicoot mataram', which was how these demi-British of India transposed the cry of *Vande Mataram.* The Bengali Congressmen to whom I showed the letter were not well up in the English nomenclature of Indian rats, so I had to tell them what a bandicoot was.

For the first days the crowds were allowed to shout in order to summon Gandhi to the balcony, or just to show their solidarity with the Congress. But after the meeting of the Working Committee was over and Gandhi was due to leave, he suddenly had a heart attack. The doctors advised him to stay in bed, and not to leave the house. Thus he had to stay with the Boses for some weeks.

The crowds, not seeing him, began to shout even more insistently and loudly, which disturbed Gandhi. They were implored to go away after being told of his condition. Often they would not at the request of unimportant persons. Therefore Subhas Bose himself would appear on the balcony and try to persuade them to disperse. He would say that if they would not, Mahatmaji would be compelled to endure the 'insistence' and that would be harmful to him. He would close his admonition by uttering the word which was quite natural for him to use in the situation, but an absurd affectation in T. S. Eliot, viz. *Shanti, Shanti, Shanti!*(Peace! Peace! Peace!)

I have now to describe Gandhi's staff. During the stay at Sarat Babu's house three of his senior officers were in attendance. They were his indispensable personal assistants. I had heard about them of course. Now I saw them for the first time, and what I saw gave me a more or less adequate notion of what the Gandhian milieu was like. These men made up more than fully for what Gandhi lacked in the way of arrogance in looks and behaviour. I had never before seen such impassive hardness of countenance, nor such cold hauteur on the faces of men. They did not speak spontaneously to anyone who did not belong to the order of worldly power and position. If they were compelled to listen to ordinary persons, they did not look them in the face, but kept their eyes either turned away or lowered, and then answered in grave and slow speech. I never saw them smile or even look relaxed.

I suppose proximity to power engenders that sort of attitude and behaviour, and in any case those who graft themselves on personalities with primary power and wish to acquire derivative, secondary power, are bound to give this kind of exhibition. Their strength lies in being indispensable to the men of power. They are able men in service, but not less so in clinging to the men whom they serve. They climb upwards by entwining themselves round the tree of power as I have seen the Russian Vine (*polygonum baldschuanum* or Mile-a-Minute) doing on the trees they can get to. There is a necessary correlation between the tree-men and the creeper-men, because the trees need the creepers as much as the creepers need the trees.

The women followers of Gandhi, I had heard, were even more remarkable. Of course, in India holy men or gurus have attracted women even more strongly than men, and in this Gandhi was no exception. But his women were different in that they were not all young *dévotes*. Some of them were elderly and some young. Like the two mistresses of George I one could have been called Maypole and the other Elephant and Castle. They were, however, all feline, although some were catty and others pussyish. The only one I saw on that occasion was of the second kind, and she was more like a Persian cat than a Siamese. She corresponded to the type of female votaries of saints, being voluptuous and prudish at the same time. The severity was like a coat of rime, but the sensuality oozed through it like melting frost. She was short, but full, exhibiting a continuous throbbing of person in all her movements. She looked strong, but never walked firmly, and seemed always to be half-toddling. The end of the sari which rests on the shoulder of an unmarried Hindu girl was always slipping off a shapely slope. She used to take her morning walk in Woodburn Park on which Sarat Bose's house stood and which was always blazing with bougainvillias. But she would not go through the wicket gate which was about twenty feet from Sarat Babu's front door. She would use the front gate of the Park which was on the main road, about a hundred yards away, and to take her there the Birlas would always send one of their limousines. The vision of this single *ancilla domini* of Gandhi's gave me a better idea of the absurdity of his sexual attitudes and rules than all the prurient gossip I heard in Calcutta.

These were the persons who dealt with what nowadays are called public relations of Gandhi. The demands made on his time and energy were numerous and continuous. However, at the level at which they were attended to, these were made in gracious whispers rather than shouts, which came from the pavements. One insistent demand was wholly Western, and that was for autographs. Mahatma Gandhi never refused them, but gave them on one condition - that they must be paid for. The standard fee was five rupees a signature.

The autograph seekers would leave their albums with a five rupee note on the blank page with me, and I gave the pile in the evening to Mahadev Desai. He returned the albums the next morning with Gandhi's signatures. I did not like this method of collecting money, and looked upon it as a sort of keeping a shop. Those to whom I said so dissented vehemently and replied that Gandhi was not asking money for himself I, on my part, never admitted that justification, and said that taking money for one's fads was in no way different, or more praiseworthy, than asking for it in order to live. Even then I had a vague realization, which has become clear now, that humanitarianism could be a feeble form of egoism.

Gandhi's demands for money were made in the unabashed manner of all Hindu holy men. He would never be shamefaced about this. The day after his arrival the young women of the Birla family came to do their obeisance to him. But they had come solely with reverence, not money. So Gandhi said to them: '*Betiañ* - girls - you have not brought anything for me!' In the afternoon they called again with five hundred rupees each. They could not even think of putting the notes in his hands, but laid them at his feet. In order to get money, Gandhi would never hold out the beggar's bowl or the hat; his feet sanctified the money, which lost its pejorative description as filthy lucre when touched by them.

There were endless requests from busybodies and social climbers to meet him, and these requests were most numerous for his prayer meetings in the evening. All the *mondaines* of Calcutta had become *dévotes* for the occasion, and they would phone from their houses: 'May we come and join the prayers?' Mahadev Desai would invariably reply: 'Yes, of course!'

But that response was never for ordinary persons, even if they were young women. One afternoon I saw a young Bengali woman sitting with bowed head and dejected expression in the hall. I went up to her and asked her: 'Is anything the matter with you." She raised her face to me and said in a weak voice: 'I wish to see Mahatma Gandhi. I have been coming here these three days, but they would not let me go up. I have not taken any food these days, and I shall not till I have seen him!' I was aghast and said to her: 'I shall take you up and you will see him.' I had never gone upstairs even to have a peep at Gandhi, but this time I did. I left the woman at the open door and came down. At that time Gandhi was sleeping and no one was about. After a little while the woman came down and when I asked her if she was satisfied she replied sadly: 'Yes in a way, for I have seen him. But I have not seen his eyes. Nonetheless, since I can get nothing more, I shall make that do.'

Men and women of fashion went up as they pleased without even asking for an appointment. One day I saw Leela Desai, the famous film actress, going up with a male star of Bengali society. No one barred the approach of such persons. After seeing all that I realized that social classes, class consciousness, and class affinities are not created solely by birth, tradition, or money, but also by newspaper publicity. All those who were publicized by the Press formed a brotherhood, club, or class. Otherwise, I could not explain the failure of Gandhi to say to this film star: 'Woman! What is there between thee and me?'

But one day the populace took their revenge for this snobbishness. They had been driven to anger by their exclusion. When I arrived one morning at Sarat Babu's house, I found the collapsible grill to the doors broken and the doors damaged. When I asked the servants about these they told me that the crowds had seen selected people being admitted to the early morning prayer meeting and they themselves shut out, and in their anger they rushed the doors and forced their way to the roof. They declared that they were not going to tolerate their exclusion in favour of *Bara Log* - great people - any more.

What repelled me even more was what I saw and heard of the intrigues to take away Gandhi from Sarat Babu's house and restore him to the monopoly of the great Marwari financial house of the Birlas. Except for this visit, Gandhi invariably stayed with them. The concession made to Sarat Bose on this occasion had, as I have said, caused much heartburning in the Bengali Congress faction opposed to the Boses, whose chief at this time was Dr Bidhan Chandra Roy, about whom and whose opposition to them I shall have to write more in the next chapter. But the Birlas were even more chagrined. So they set on foot an intrigue to remove Gandhi from Sarat Bose's house on one plea or another. One day, after Gandhi's midday meal, Sarat Babu came down and told me: 'I had no idea that Ghanashyamdas Birla was such a cad. Do you know, he pointed at the dishes my wife was serving Gandhiji and asked: "Are the vegetables fresh?" '

The Birlas had Gandhi's son, Devadas Gandhi, working for them. He would suggest from time to time a removal ofhis father from the house. But Jawaharlal Nehru, who was also staying with Sarat Bose and who disliked Devadas, threw his weight on the side of the Boses, and as between Nehru and Devadas Gandhi the influence was greater for the former. Fortunately Gandhi had his heart attack. After that there could be no talk of taking him away. Even though Bidhan Roy was not pleased with the stay, his physician's conscience would not allow a removal. Over and above, a brother of Sarat Bose was the leading cardiologist in Calcutta. Even Bidhan Roy could not pit his medical opinion, in this case, against Bose's brother. Thus, for the time being, the bedridden Gandhi was left in the possession of the Boses to their gratification.

If all this irritated me, there was one further experience which caused distress. That was a visit of the aged and ailing Tagore to Gandhi at Sarat Bose's house, which he had never before visited. I saw him entering the house, and was shocked to see how bent he was. He was seventy-six then, and normally should not have been so broken. But, as I saw him, the upper part of his body from the waist was almost at right angles to the lower part, and he panted as he walked along. I had seen his tall and majestic figure before and could never imagine that it would be reduced to this state. What was worse, his eyes had a weary look, and his face was wan.

It irked me that Tagore was obliged to call on Gandhi, the far less disabled man, instead of Gandhi going to call on an elder and not a less celebrated man, because the protocol of the nationalist movement required that the merely literary man should acknowledge his lower status to the political man. And the ironical aspect of this formal keeping up of appearances between the two greatest men of modem India was that there was not even a tenuous moral or intellectual bond between them. Tagore had always disliked and disapproved of Gandhi's political ideas, and given expression to that publicly. He was denounced even by Bengalis for that. Yet that opportunistic form of fellowship, based on worldly recognition, had to be kept up in this cruel manner, without any protest on the part of Gandhi, who had no capacity to understand or appreciate the achievement, personality and views of Tagore, all of which were as complex as Gandhi's were stark and simple. Yet he aired a formal veneration, and always mentioned Tagore as *Gurudeva*, i.e. the Godly Master. This form of address for Tagore was an absurdly affected archaism in Tagore's school and university at Santiniketan. In recent centuries no Hindu had ever addressed a holy man except as Maharaj, Great King, and teachers were always addressed as 'Pandit' if they did not know English, and simply as 'sir' if they did. Nonetheless, this artificiality, originally introduced by Tagore himself for his school, became general, especially among non-Bengali politicians. Even apart from the mode of address adopted by Gandhi, his relationship with Tagore was an unpleasant exhibition of *amitié de convenance*.

If this was the passive assertion of the superiority of the holy man to the poet, I also saw the positive assertion of the superiority of holiness to science. One day, after his daily visit to Gandhi, Sarat Babu told me: 'Mahatmaji has just told me: "Sarat, there is more humbug in your science than in religion." ' I soon found that he was really disposed to treat as humbug one invention of science about whose existence and power there could be no doubt. At that time I was closely connected with the Calcutta station of All-India Radio, the broadcasting organization under the Government of India. The station's programme staff asked me if I could get Gandhi to broadcast a message through AIR, for which they were prepared to pay a fee. I told Mahadev Desai about this. He gave the reply, which I believe had Gandhi's approval, that Bapuji did not believe in that sort of thing. I could not help saying to myself: 'What does he not believe in?

he believes in telegraph, in telephone, in the railways, but why does he make an exception of the wireless?' I found that he believed in a more humble and utilitarian invention of science: the mud he smeared every day on his stomach and head had to be stored in Mrs Bose's refrigerator to keep it cool, to the exclusion even of the vegetables he ate. But perhaps the objection was political and not religious. Yet the station would have broadcast any religious message he wanted to give.

Oberste Heeresleitung des Kongresses

I have next to describe the Congress Working Committee and its members. They were twelve in number, whether in imitation of the Apostles or not - I am unable to say. But they were the leading members of the Congress Party. Congressmen had got into the habit of describing themselves in very grandiloquent political terminology. For instance, even Mahatma Gandhi, in writing to a President of the Congress, would call the Working Committee his 'Cabinet'. The public and the Press called it the 'Congress High Command', adopting a military and not civil terminology. This revealed the subconscious militarism of the Hindu mind, as also its admiration for the Germans and their military genius. The name Congress High Command was only a translation of the German *Oberste Heeresleitung*, although that might not have been consciously done.

Since the meetings of the Working Committee were held in Sarat Babu's house I had a very good opportunity for observing the appearance and expression of all the front-rank Congressmen. Mahatma Gandhi was never a member of the Working Committee. But he hovered above it like the Holy Spirit, and sometimes even descended in the form of the dove of peace. As these important men arrived I took note of them, and compared my firsthand impressions with the idea of their features and faces which I had been piecing together from pictures.

The first impression of the Congress leaders that I received from my visual experience was one of physical unattractiveness. With the exception of one or two, none of them could be described as handsome or even physically imposing. In this the leaders of the Gandhian era were the opposite of those of the pre-Gandhian period. From 1885 to even 1918 they were as a rule, handsome men, with expressions which were both intelligent and urbane. The new leaders showed none of these features. But what was strange was that in their physical insignificance they were not merely Gandhian. I have said that nobody upon seeing Gandhi noticed his features. In his followers, people would notice nothing else. The faces of all of them had a hard, worldly look, yet without the outward enamel which one could see on the faces of the high-ranking Indian officials, who were even more worldly.

Yet this unattractiveness was the least unattractive quality of the outward appearance of the Congress leaders. They repelled, instead of merely failing to attract. What struck a beholder most forcibly in them was an overweaning expression of arrogance, which coated their faces and seemed to he like make-up on cheeks and foreheads. They possessed the same haughty air as the Hindu holy men or the Gurus, but without any smooth outward unctuousness.

Over and above, their manners, in dealing with other fellow-Indians, unless they had worldly importance, were always peremptory. They seemed to be bursting with self-importance and awareness of their power, and were always standing on their dignity. I give one or two examples of what I saw. One morning I was making a telephone call, and a very important Congressman (a member of the Working Committee), was sitting with a friend nearby. My contact at the other end was speaking in very fast Hindi which I had difficulty in following. So I asked the important person if he would speak to the man and tell me what he was saying. Not even looking at me he said curdy that he would not. We Bengalis have a story to illustrate the difference between a man who is a gentleman and one who is not. It runs like this. One man asked another to do some little thing for him and got the reply: 'Am I your servant?' The other simply answered: 'Oh no, only I thought you were a gentleman.' Perhaps the Congress leader thought that I was ordering him as if he were my servant.

Another incident in which I was involved was more revealing, because it was created by a Congressman of a much lower rank. At the same time as the meetings of the Working Committee were being held upstairs, downstairs, in Sarat Bose's library, the Speakers of the Legislative Assemblies and Councils of the provinces in which Congress was holding power, had their conference. They met to have a concerted policy of giving as much trouble to the British administration as possible without giving a blatant exhibition of partisanship in conducting the proceedings. The Speaker of the Madras Assembly was a dark, hairy, and obese Tamil Brahmin, who was a strict Gandhian. Even when attending such formal meetings he would wear only a short loincloth reaching down to his knees, and for the rest would be barebodied. In addition, he wore the cast marks of a Brahmin.

One day at about lunch time he came out of the conference room and asked me to get a car to take him to the house where he was staying. I looked for Sarat Babu's cars and found that they were out, and said apologetically: 'I am sorry, all our cars are out.' There were, of course, many more cars in the forecourt. He pointed to them and replied: 'Ask any of the owners of those cars, and he would be proud to put his at the disposal of the Speaker of the Madras Assembly.' I could not do that, but to put an end to my dilemma, Tulsi Goswami was coming out, and I asked him if he could lend his car. 'Yes, of course,' he replied, 'but I'll just go home and send it back. It would not take five minutes.' He lived quite near. But the Speaker at once addressed Tulsi Babu directly: 'I must have it first, my business is more urgent.' Before Tulsi Babu could recover from his surprise, Kumar Debendralal Khan, son of the Raja of Narajol, said with his habitual politeness: 'Tulsi Babu, you may go home. My car will take Mr Speaker home. I am in no hurry. I will sit here and have more gossip.' So the Speaker went away in a much bigger car than Sarat Babu's or Tulsi Babu's.

Of all the Congress members, only Babu Rajendra Prasad, who was a member of the Congress Working Committee and after independence became the first President of the Republic of India, had impeccable manners and unaffected courtesy towards all. He would raise two folded hands to his forehead even before the other party who had caught his eyes had time for it. But Rajendra Babu had been in Calcutta with the gilded youth of that city, and besides had innate affability.

I also caught glimpses of the foremost lieutenant of Gandhi, whose opinions influenced Gandhi's on all practical questions. He was called the Sardar (Sirdar in the popular English spelling). The word was Persian and meant a chief, and primarily a military chief. For instance, when in Egypt, Kitchener was called the Sirdar. In the Gandhian age all the leading nationalists, dead or alive, had honorific tides. Since the people of India had given the title 'Mahatma' to Gandhi himself, he, in turn, bestowed appropriate tides to the others. For instance, Tilak was called Lokamanya, C. R. Das Deshabandhu, J. M. Sen-Gupta Deshapriya, and so on. Thus Patel was the Sirdar, and Kripalani the Acharya. In the Gandhian age these men were no more mentioned except under these titles than during

Napoleon's reign Berthier was addressed under any other name than Prince de Wagram, or Lannes except as Duc de Montebello, or even Junot except as Due d'Abrantès. Thus even Patel's daughter never referred to her father except as the Sirdar when she, as his principal aide-de-camp, had to convey his directions to others.

He had a wrinkled face, and looked crafty. In any case, he was cunning. He was also practical and, although he hated British rule, I am not convinced how much of that was truly emotional and how much politic. His role in the higher direction of the Congress, as distinct from his role as an agitator, was to check Nehru's extremism and idealism and employ both to further what I might describe as the temporal interests of the Congress leaders.

Subhas Bose, in a letter to Nehru himself, described the relationship between the two leaders quite correcdy but maliciously. He wrote that Patel allowed Nehru to talk as long as he wanted, and when he was exhausted asked him to draft Patel's resolution and not his own, which, being fond of writing, Nehru did enthusiastically. The relationship between the two can be described in a more objective manner by comparing it to that which exists between the engine which provides power in a factory and the machine-tool which employs this power for a practical end. To sum up, Patel's role within the widest ambit of Congress policy was one in which he succeeded marvellously: it consisted in harnessing the hatred against British rule and drawing hard on the reins early enough before that hatred could harm any personal interest of the Congress leaders, but not before it had inflicted irreparable harm on India. After independence, I heard even Englishmen praising the wisdom of Patel. It lay in nothing else but that. There could be no doubt that Patel's was the decisive voice in the formulation of the practical policies of the Congress, not only because of that particular kind of discernment but also because he was the strongest personal influence on Gandhi in practical matters, or rather, those which Patel himself regarded as practical. The second-rank Congress leaders followed him in this. They were as afraid, as were the British administrators of the era, of Nehru's extremism.

The strong point of the elders of the Congress was their loquacity. They loved to talk, and felt that they were denied openings for their talents unless allowed to do so. Sarat Bose as a barrister had to exercise effectual talking, and did so very successfully, so that he had a first-class professional income, so he felt sick of the endless talking at the sessions of the Committee. He would come down, after he had had enough, to have a break. Once he told me that the other members of the Working Committee talked for two hours about a question which could be decided in ten minutes.

The discussions of the Working Committee went on for three or four days. During this time the newspaper men sat in my room, waiting eagerly for any communication that might be brought to them about the decisions of the Committee. This was done in scraps and bits, and they would at once telephone to the editorial desks. I do not remember now what the discussions at this session were about, nor indeed was I interested in them at the time. What I was seeing was much more absorbing than the bits of paper which were being read out.

But there was also a deeper reason for my indifference. Even then I had some realization that the personal leadership which the Congress was offering was not a decisive influence on the nationalist movement. Indeed, what these men did or said did not give shape to the nationalist movement. It ran on its own power, and its course was like that of a river flowing down to the sea, either cutting its way at some places or winding round the obstacles in the bends. What the leaders did was to ride on this current.

During the entire period of the Gandhian phase of the nationalist movement I heard people talking about the organizing capacity of the leaders. Even the British administration seemed to have been overawed by the notion. They did not understand the source of the effectiveness of the movement. They saw a whole people acting in unison, seemingly at the behest of the leaders, and never perceived that the behests came from the people, only to be put in words by the leaders. These men gave what might be called the passwords for the situations. All the supposed organizing capacity of the Congress was among the people, who acted uniformly all over India from the shared passion of the moment. Of Congress propaganda it might be said that it was exactly like the propaganda of the French Revolution as described by Albert Sorel, who wrote:

'It surged up from the soil. No dams kept it back, no embankments controlled it, it spread on all sides at the same time. Nonetheless, however impetuous in its rush, it was forced to flow down old slopes. It could flood those valleys alone which had already been carved out by the waters, and cross the frontiers only through the gaps opened up long since.'

It was the age-old xenophobia of the Hindus which, after moulding a uniform pattern of behaviour, also became the real organizer of the Indian nationalist movement. The leaders lived from hand to mouth both in respect of policy and action, until they could take advantage of the eruptions in the collective behaviour.

Along with the men who ran the Congress, I also saw their women counterparts. The most eminent among them was Mrs Sarojini Naidu. She was fifty-eight at that time, being exactly midway in age between Gandhi and Nehru. She was deeply respected and valued as the prima donna of the nationalist movement. Balzac has written of a particular kind of respect which was like a young man's for a dowager. Mrs Naidu would not have been gratified by that kind of homage. She was spoilt since her youth for her lively mind and literary talent and, though never a beauty, for her extraordinary personal attraction, on which all reports were agreed. She was a Bengali, and though brought up in Hyderabad possessed to the full the particular charm which their mental constitution gave to Bengali girls. She had acquired the reputation of being a *femme galante* and had outlived it. But she had also lost her outward attractiveness, due to an operation, the cruelty of which she must have felt deeply.

Nonetheless, Mrs Naidu retained her youthful coquetish spirit as even I found. One day I was passing through the large waiting hall of Sarat Babu's house and was checked by a sudden pull at the tail of my tunic. Turning round I saw to my utter surprise Mrs Naidu holding it and feeling the material. 'Bhagalpur silk?' she asked most graciously. With a low bow I replied: 'Yes, madam.' I was not worth looking at for the figure or features I was born with, but the silk tunic had gained her notice for me.

She believed in the saying: 'Apparel oft proclaims the man', emending 'oft' to 'always'. Men of far greater worth than I was, and already established in the world, were avoided by her simply on the score of being plainly dressed, even if they had natural handsomeness. This happened to my esteemed friend Pandit Benarsidas Chaturvedi, of whom even Gandhi spoke well. He was an authority on the Indian settlers in Africa, and was nominated to be an adviser to Mrs Naidu when she was going on behalf of the Congress to Kenya to investigate their condition. But unfortunately he wore nothing but a simple dhoti with only a scarf around his neck. So Mrs Naidu would not have him.

Her whole life had fostered in her a far stronger notion of what was due to her than what was due from her, and that sort of egoism broke out in small as well as big things. One day, wishing to write a note, she borrowed a Parker pen, a very expensive model, from Sarat Babu's business manager, but did not return it. When asked very humbly about it, she said very curtly that she had left it on the table at which she had been sitting, which, of course, she should never have done. The pen was never recovered. This recalled to my mind the story I had read about her in 1930. She was lending her presence to the demonstration staged by Congress volunteers against the salt depot of Dharsana, and asked one of them: 'Could you imagine that a lady who stays at the Taj Mahal Hotel would spend a night at a place like this.-" That hotel was the Indian equivalent of Claridge's in London. But the volunteer replied: 'This place is much better than the Taj Mahal Hotel.'

I had not read much of her poetry, but what I had made me think that it was very luscious and Swinburnian at one remove. In her prose she was very eloquent, and that eloquence was employed to promote the ideas of the Bengali renaissance. One of its tenets was that the Hindu mind was all for 'synthesis' and would not cut up life into compartments. I was, of course, initiated into that even as a boy, and had reverted to it in writing an appreciation of the life and work of the great Bengali scientist Jagadis Chandra Bose, who died on 23 November 1937. This was for Sarat Babu who sent it to the press. After reading it Mrs Naidu came to him and said: 'Sarat, I liked your piece very much.' I was standing by, and Sarat Babu looked sideways at me with a sly smile. It did not seem to me that Mrs Naidu was very much interested in the talking upstairs, but would lounge through the house saying a word or two to anybody she found interesting.

I also saw another Congress woman of the opposite kind, who possessed nothing of the engaging flamboyance of Mrs Naidu. That personage was not a Congress woman in her own right, but only through her father. She was the widowed daughter of Vallabh Bhai Patel, and looked after him. She was his combined secretary and aide-de-camp. I often saw her bringing the commands of the Sirdar to others, and delivering them very peremptorily. She was still young, but looked like an old maid. I came in contact with her but once.

I was sitting at my table in my room, with a number of newspaper correspondents in front of me, one of whom was using the telephone to send a message to his office. He suddenly made a sign to me to look behind me and, turning round, I saw Mani Ben Patel standing very close to me. In response to my 'Yes?' she only pointed to the telephone without saying anything. I replied: 'Oh, yes, in a moment as soon as this gentleman has finished.' I did not observe her after that but the newspaper man did. As soon as she had finished her call and gone out, he said to me: 'You did not see what she was doing when you said you would give her the phone after I had finished.' When I said I had not, he told me: 'She was making faces at me all the time.' From what I had seen of her looks, I felt sure that they were more *des vilaines* than *petites moues*. All the satellites of the Congress leaders aired this exaggerated self-importance.

Jawaharlal Nehru

I also saw Jawaharlal Nehru often, because he was staying with the Boses, and had been given the bedroom on the ground floor - self-contained, with a bathroom and so on. After getting ready in the morning and taking his breakfast in the adjoining dining room, he would come out and go first to Sarat Babu and then proceed upstairs to the meeting.

He would always be dressed in dhoti and kurta, both in white khaddar, i.e. homespun cotton. Nobody noticed his dress because, except for very exceptional occasions, he was always seen in the same clothes after he had entered the nationalist movement. Yet it had a profound significance and was the visible material evidence of the sacrifice of convictions and habits he had made for the sake of Gandhi. Neither his father nor he in his young days ever wore anything but the Islamic sherwani and pajama as neglige, and the European dress as formal wear. Both as Kashmiris and as Islamized Hindus of the up they were not expected to do otherwise. But no one could be a Gandhian, i.e. a Hindu nationalist, without going into the dhoti, the supreme material symbol of loyalty to Hinduism. Although Nehru was both ignorant of Hindu traditions and even hostile to them, he had to adopt the dhoti. This was not opportunism, but a sacrifice, and in regard to apparel a repetition of the sacrifice of his convictions, from his intellectual conclusion that Gandhi was indispensable for the nationalist movement. I shall have to say a good deal about that sacrifice later. But as soon as independence was obtained for India he reverted to his normal clothes and to his personal opinions. No one saw him in a dhoti after be became Prime Minister of India, nor heard him professing Gandhism.

The abstracted expression which I had seen on his face in 1931 was still there; in fact, it was very much deepened, certainly because of the death of his wife. He had always felt alone, and throughout his life never got rid of the sense of being alone, being only by himself There was also an ineradicable sadness in all his expression.

Whenever people saw him or met him they raised two folded hands and said: '*Panditji, namasté*.' Nowadays even Englishmen, meeting an Indian, not only in India but even in England, say *namasté*. They do not know that the greeting is pure Sanskrit and not Hindi, and that it is not employed by anybody except the speakers of Hindi. The compound is *namah* (obeisance) plus *té*, the dative of the Sanskrit word for 'you'. I never used it, nor indeed did I so greet Nehru as a matter of form. He also did not greet me if he met me in Sarat Babu's house when passing through the rooms. I had corresponded with him and he knew me as a writer on military affairs, but I do not think he connected my name with me as secretary to Sarat Babu.

But when I had to talk to him on business I always addressed him as 'Mr Nehru'. He regarded this as natural and would always be perfectly courteous. He would speak in a very English manner. He disliked anyone fawning on him as well as the usual Hindu reverent manner. But there was also a linguistic factor which had an influence on his manners. His unaffected English gentleman's manner was adopted only when one spoke to him in an English which approached his in its accent. Towards anyone who had the Hindi or Bengali accent in his English he would almost behave like an Englishman to a 'native'. He seemed to have acquired the English sense of 'U' and 'non-U'.

This abruptness increased if there was in addition to the native accent the native importunity in begging anything from him. I saw and heard him actually scolding some Bengali students who had come to invite him to speak at one of their political meetings. 'Why do you come and disturb a very busy man in this way?' - he flung at them. And when he found that he had been too brusque he explained gently: 'This would not simply fit in with what I am having to do and think about now.' I wondered how he endured the English of normal Congressmen.

On another occasion even I was scolded at secondhand. He had just gone in to lunch when a young Communist leader from Bombay came to see him. This man had very close personal relations with Nehru and that was known to me. So when he asked me to inform Nehru of his arrival I told him that I would send word as soon as Nehru had finished lunch. But the

Communist said: 'Even so, please let him know that I have come.' I went into the dining room, but, instead of speaking to Nehru, I informed his secretary Upadhyaya, who relayed the message. Nehru at once exploded and said angrily: 'Am I never to be allowed even to eat." However, soon afterwards he came out to greet his friend in a manner which confirmed my previous opinion: that great men want their secretaries to be the receivers and purveyors of their rudeness.

Neither would Nehru tolerate intrusions on his privacy even if they were meant innocently as homage *à la Hindoue*. I did not witness this incident but was told about it. One morning he was writing in his room, when a man in the entrance hall became curious about him. Nehru's room opened into the hall, and the door was open because in India doors even of bedrooms are never kept closed. Only curtains hang there. The man drew them aside and peeped in. Nehru jumped up from his chair, caught hold of the intruder by the scruff of the neck, and did not let go until he had marched him to the garden gate. An ordinary Congressman's career would have been ruined by such conduct. But nobody really minded the residual anglicism in him. They knew what a sacrifice he had made of it in order to become a disciple of Gandhi, and made allowance for any unavoidable escapes into his anglicism through such safety-valves.

The Situation for the Congress

I shall close this chapter by giving a summary description of the political situation in India in 1937. At that particular juncture Indian politics had overtaken nationalism. The nationalist movement *qua* agitation was very much in the dumps. There was now no excited nationalist feeling in the country, nor could any be roused by the Congress. Thus, in its primary function of directing the movement towards political independence, the Congress could only maintain its routine pace. Like a deciduous northern tree it was having its rest period. A slightly less routine step was taken when it was informally decided during this session of the Working Committee that Subhas Bose would succeed Nehru as the next President of the Congress. He had just returned after a long exile in Europe, and at first much was expected from his elevation. But it had quite the opposite result as I shall relate in a later chapter.

In the meanwhile, it was not the nationalist agitation but politics in the narrow sense of the term which was ascendant. That was due to the introduction of the new system of provincial autonomy from April 1937, as provided for by the Government of India Act of 1935. Under its provisions, the elections held earlier in the year had given an overwhelming majority to the Congress Party in all Indian provinces except three. But the Congress leaders at first were not prepared to take office, and so in these provinces ministries were created which could be regarded as dummies. As the Congress had totally rejected the federal part of the Act, the central government remained what it was.

But within three months the Congress revised its decision and decided to accept office in every province in which it had a majority. This was due to practical calculations. By the new constitution, considerable, indeed almost full, powers were given to the provincial governments which were to be run by the majority parties. There could be no doubt that if the Congress so chose, it could exercise very great power in the provinces, and that could be employed not only to confer greater benefits on the people but also to embarrass the central government. Such prospects did not convince Nehru, who opposed the acceptance of office. But the more practically minded members of the Congress Working Committee thought that it would be a great mistake not to do so. They had their way, and I think they succeeded because they held out the threat of forming a new party within the Congress like the Swarajyists. So, office acceptance was approved of in order to maintain the unity of the Congress.

Thus Congress ministries were formed in eleven major provinces in the middle of 1937. At first sight this seemed to be a justification of the Act of 1935, which had roused such antipathy in me. The Congress had been won over to practical politics and weaned from its habit of barren opposition. But by its long-term results it fully demonstrated the correctness of my judgement. I have already said that the introduction of provincial autonomy under the Act demoralized the British administration in India without satisfying the nationalists. This was seen within months.

A fuddling gas seemed to have paralysed the capacity of the minds of the British officials to foresee any new situations. Their first miscalculation was over the results of the elections. Even the very high-placed among them believed that a majority of the seats would be won by the propertied and privileged classes, which supported British rule, on the strength of the peasant vote which they expected to be on the side of the

British. How after sixteen years of experience of the Gandhian Congress they could do so passes my understanding.

After miscalculating this fundamental fact, the British could not also be clear in their mind about how to meet the situation created by it. They could not accept the Congress ministries fully, but neither were they prepared to resist them. Thus the whole body of officials fell between two stools, creating a wholly defeatist attitude. Some of their decisions were indiscreet, and provided windfalls to the Congress to inflict humiliations on the British administration. One such incident happened in the province of Orissa. There was a Congress ministry in it, and when a new British Governor was to be appointed, the Government of India selected the British official of the ICS who was the Chief Secretary of the Congress administration in that province. The ministry at once objected that a man who was their subordinate could not be raised to a position in which he would have the constitutional power of overruling their decisions. Therefore, as directed by the Congress Working Committee, they declared that they would resign if the appointment was given effect. The Government of India had to cancel the appointment and to humiliate a man who had done nothing to deserve such treatment. Its own defeat, however, was not less blatant. The Congress was able to show that in accepting office it had not been weakened by its fleshpots. There was another such incident in the UP which was also able to inflict more humiliation on the British administration.

But if the Congress had not been weakened by its acceptance of office vis-à-vis the British authorities, it had been harmed internally. That turned out to be a worse result from the introduction of the Act of 1935 than the demoralization of the British officials: it was a disaster for the Indian people as well as for the Congress. For the latter, it signalled 'Paradise Lost'. It was as if the Congress organization as Adam had been coaxed by the practical leaders as a Congress Eve formed out of the ribs of Gandhi, to eat the forbidden fruit. Considering that aspect of the matter, one could conclude that the British Satan indeed had gained a victory. Let me explain that in matter-of-fact language. The acceptance of office, although only for an interlude of two years and three months, germinated the seeds of corruption both in the Congress organization itself and among the Congressmen, and the weeds have taken root permanently in the government of India.

I have already said how the experience of the Calcutta Corporation made me fear that if governing power in the country were handed over to Indians we should see the Calcutta Corporation writ large over the whole of it. The process actually began in 1937. The ministries had an immense patronage in every form at their disposal, and so a scramble at once started up between factions and individuals for their share. At the lower level, this was for jobs; at the higher, for careers as politicians.

The openings for personal gain were not simply for those who were in the nationalist movement. All the privileged persons and vested interests which existed in the country now came forward to seize the Congress, and they did so in the manner in which the Calcutta gentry had seized the Calcutta Corporation. The personal composition of the Congress became- diluted with unscrupulous seekers of wealth and position. And at first that was seen in a phenomenal increase in the membership of the Congress. It went up by leaps and bounds.

That was not, however, the end of the matter. The most harmful aspect was what Mahatma Gandhi called the 'bogus membership' of the Congress. This meant block memberships created by political adventurers with their own money in order to have fictitious votes in their favour for selection as candidates in the elections. It was a repeat of the bogus electoral list of the Calcutta Corporation on an all-India scale. Mahatma Gandhi continued in his denunciation of this evil, without achieving the slightest success.

While this was happening on the groundfloor of political life, on the upper floors there was vicious competition for office and other profits. The time of ministers and more especially of Chief Ministers was monopolized by the careerists who were also the supporters they dared not alienate. I have described how, even as the Leader of the Opposition, Sarat Babu was pestered by such men. Ministers in office could expect no respite. They were so exhausted by the dog's life they were being compelled to live, that in 1939 Jawaharlal Nehru wrote of them: 'I know personally that far personal reasons if no others, a good number of our Ministers would like the Ministry to go so that they might have some rest from the burden they have been carrying. They are worn out in mind and body and the troubles from all directions tend to increase. I would hate to have their job.' He was also disgusted by the personal and factional rivalries that existed among the Congress politicians, and kept aloof from them.

The immediate reason why political power was seen by all Indians as a means of personal aggrandisement lay in the fact that for two centuries they had had no political responsibilities. When these were laid on them, they naturally acted along the pattern of their private behaviour, which was to get on in the world. There was behind that, in addition, an old tradition which was perhaps only latent then, but was to come to the surface after independence. That was about the employment of political power in pre- British India. Those Europeans who were in India in the eighteenth century and had to deal with the indigenous rulers became fully aware of it. As the famous French soldier in India, Marquis de Bussy, who was an associate of Dupleix, wrote to the latter even in 1753:

'A patriot and servant of the nation - all these names so sacred among all peoples, are nothing to the Moors when they have to be earned at the price of self-interest and hopes of personal advantages. So also are all those grand ideas of honour of the nation, of public interest, which bind all the members of a state to their sovereign and fortify them for the common cause. These are chimeras in this country, in which each individual thinks only about himself and only seeks to turn to his advantage the troubles and the revolutions which make their appearance.'

Although written about the Muslim rulers of India only, such a judgement remains true of all Indians entrusted or endowed with political power to this day. Even after only a few months of the working of the provincial autonomy under the Government of India Act of 1935, I was convinced of the truth of La Rochefoucauld's maxim: 'It needs far greater virtues to bear good fortune than ill fortune.'

CHAPTER 3

Politics in Bengal: Governmental and Civic

In this chapter I shall describe the political situation and political life in Bengal as I saw them in the first two years of my work with Sarat Bose. They had two distinct spheres - the governmental and the civic. My account of govermental politics will show the demoralization of the Hindus of Bengal by deprivation of power, and that of the civic politics, their corruption by its enjoyment.

That would also be an appraisement of Sarat Babu's handling of the situation both as Leader of the Opposition in the Bengal legislature and as Chairman of the Congress Municipal Association. In his first capacity, he could only talk and do nothing because he had no executive power nor even any expectation that his turn for it would come at some time as it did to all leaders of opposition in a parliamentary system of government. He was condemned by statute to perpetual opposition. If that was odd, not less so was the fact that even in his second capacity, he could not be more effective, although the Congress Party, of which he was the leader, had full control over the Calcutta Corporation. In regard to both spheres, my account will be a story of failure.

Disenfranchisement of the Bengali Hindu

Let me begin with the political situation in the strict sense. The starkly obvious feature in it was that, under the provincial constitution imposed on Bengal by the Government of India Act of 1935, Bengali Hindus were *permanently debarred* from exercising any political power in their province, and, for that matter, even from having that amount of political influence to which they were entitled by virtue of their numerical strength, except through the charity of the Muslims, which was not likely to be bestowed. In plain words, they were reduced to a permanent statutory minority, disenfranchised as to power, although given the franchise to elect members to the legislature.

The system was as absurd intellectually as it was both inequitable and iniquitous morally. I shall describe the electoral part of the constitution in order to justify this opinion, even though I know that it will be unintelligible to anyone whose idea of a democratic electorate has been formed from British or American practice. But this very unintelligibility will give the measure of its iniquity.

That was seen most blatantly in the composition of the Bengal Legislative Assembly, a majority in which was the prerequisite for any claim to form a ministry in the province. It was to be composed, not of a general body of members elected by one general electorate as is the case in all true parliamentary systems, but of different groups of members elected by twelve separate franchises. The apportionment of its 250 seats was as follows:

1) Forty-eight seats for any resident of Bengal elected as member by a general franchise. 2) Thirty for persons belonging to certain castes of Bengali Hindus regarded as 'depressed' and enumerated in a Schedule to the Act, elected by the same general franchise. 3) One hundred and seventeen seats reserved exclusively for the Muslims of Bengal who were to be elected by a Muslim electorate. 4) Eleven seats for the Europeans, i.e. persons of British origin temporarily resident in Bengal elected by their own electorate. 5) Three for Anglo-Indians, i.e. persons of mixed European and Indian birth, chosen by their electorate. 6) Two for Indian Christians chosen by their electorate. 7) Nineteen for the representatives of the industries, commerce, etc. by their special electorate. 8) Eight for Labour chosen by a Labour electorate. 9) Five for the landowners of Bengal who had their special electorate. 10) Two for the Universities. 11) Two for women in general. 12) Two for Muslim women only, and 13) one seat for one Anglo-Indian woman.

This was a distribution of the seats among the various communities and interests in Bengal which was considered fair by the framers of the Act. If that was to be regarded as proportionate representation, one must say that it was the reduction of a rational system to an irrational one. But its real character was obvious. It was the application of the very old policy of *divide et impera*.

Therefore the distribution was bound to be as unjust as it actually was. To single out the more serious counts of unfairness:

1. The Hindus of Bengal were eligible for only 117 seats out of the 250, and in no circumstances could they offer themselves for more. Even this was split up between high-caste Bengali Hindus and certain low-caste Bengali Hindus, for whom thirty seats were to be reserved. The Muslims

in contrast could contest 203 seats. The weightage given to Muslim representation was justified on the ground that the Muslims formed a majority of the population of Bengal. Certainly, in 1937 they did so, but not in such numbers as to warrant the heavy weightage. The true extent of the Muslim superiority in numbers at that time is very difficult to ascertain. The accepted majority was based on the census of 1931, and some guesswork. But Muslims had begun to inflate their numbers in any case from 1921 in order to establish a claim for higher representation. The establishment of communal electorates had given them every inducement to do so. Besides, the census in India was never very accurate. Thus the accepted majority could hardly be anything better than an estimate which was likely to be influenced by political motives. I am inclined to think that the proportion between the Muslims and the Hindus in 1937 could not be more disparate than 54 per cent to 46 per cent but actually it may not have been wider than 52 per cent to 48 per cent. That did not justify the preponderance conceded in the Act. Besides, no attention was paid to the fact that the Hindus were the dominant element in the population of Bengal in wealth, education, culture and political as well as administrative experience. Perhaps that very fact was regarded as their handicap by the Muslims and therefore it was sought to be cancelled by the weightage given to them in the legislature.

11. The reservation of thirty seats for the members of the Hindu castes included in a schedule of the Act of 1935,* was based on what was only a notional assumption regarding their 'backward' or 'depressed' condition in respect of money, worldly opportunities, education, and social status. In reality, their position was neither invariably low nor invariably fixed. All these castes were really hereditary occupational groups engaged in trade, manufacture, social and personal service, and agriculture. Each caste was so highly specialized that gold merchants were distinguished as one from wine merchants and spice merchants, and goldsmiths from ironsmiths and brassworkers. Even sellers of betel-leaves were a caste. The distinction between the Bengalis of high castes and Bengalis of these castes was, if one disregarded the hereditary principle, exactly like that which existed in England between the gentry on the one side, and, on the other, that part of the middle class which was engaged in trade and the so-called 'lower classes'.

*For this reason these castes began to be called the 'Scheduled Castes', an absurd appellation.

But the hereditary functions of these castes, though generally accepted, did not prevent their acquiring a higher worldly position in any manner they desired, and, in fact, it was normally acquired by many. As regards money, if the peasantry was excluded, the incidence of poverty in these castes was no higher than in any of the high castes. Actually, some of these castes were more wealthy as a whole class than any of the high castes. Some families of these castes were among the wealthiest in Bengal. As to education, men of these castes did not, generally speaking, go in for higher education simply because they did not need it for their livelihood. But those who wanted always could and did, and when talented they reached the highest ranks in their fields. The most eminent physicist in Bengal in 1937, Meghnad Saha (elected FRS in 1927, and given a biographical entry in the *Encyclopaedia Britannica* - 1972 edition, Vol. 19, p. 878) came from a caste which was not only in the Schedule, but was also regarded by Hindu custom as 'untouchable'. The greatest linguist produced by Bengal, who held the post of Librarian of the Imperial Library established by Lord Curzon, was also of one of these castes. As regards social status, if any member of these castes adopted the style of living and professions of the Bengali gentry, no distinction whatever was made between him and any member of the higher castes, except that the orthodox among the latter would not take water to drink from his hands. What is called 'untouchability' in the caste system was a very restricted conception in Bengal. It had no suggestion of inferiority unless that was seen in the worldly position or function. Lastly, the inclusion of any of these castes in the Schedule was optional as well as arbitrary. Many groups which were economically backward had no place in it, and many which were very wealthy were included.

I give some examples from my personal experience to illustrate the absurdity of the Schedule. Dr S. C. Law who employed me and whose manner of living I have described, came from the wealthiest family in Calcutta, but his caste was 'untouchable' by Hindu religious injunction and custom. It should, however, be mentioned, to the honour of the members of this caste, that they did not want to be included in the Schedule to get special political and economic privileges. However, this was done by the caste to which the second highest landowning family in Bengal belonged. Its head had held the hereditary tide of Maharaja since the time of Warren Hastings and its last head to hold die tide was with me at college, but it was in the Schedule as a 'depressed' caste. Another member of one of these castes, in this case potters, was also with me at college, and joined the Indian Civil Service. To give only one more example, the most eminent leader of the caste which was normally composed of peasants and labourers and regarded as the lowest and most depressed in Bengal, who hated Gandhi and higher castes with equal intensity, and who pressed the claims of *his* caste most stridently from 1931 onwards, was a front-rank advocate in Calcutta High Court and a very wealthy man. On formal occasions he even wore the full English morning dress. One of *his* nephews (still Scheduled) is married to one of *my* nieces (still un-Scheduled). QED.

It cannot be denied that according to Hindu traditions many of these castes were low and inferior. But the notion of inferiority due to the simple fact of birth in one of these castes was disappearing, being condemned most strongly by the reformers of die high castes. But a historic sense of grievance still remained. Nonetheless, to make that a ground for conferring special privileges was, not to remove the grievance, but to perpetuate it. It is a social fact seen in every country that when unprivileged classes are given special privileges they do everything to become not only like the old privileged classes, but also a new privileged class nursing their old rancour and using it to blackmail society. In creating a privileged electoral class of the so-called Scheduled castes, the framers of the 1935 Act disregarded the spontaneous evolution of Hindu society towards equality, and sought to perpetuate class hatred in order to serve the interests of British rule.

III The Europeans, i.e. the British community of Bengal, were given a number of seats which was above 4 per cent of the total strength of the Assembly. Its numerical strength in die population was not above 4 per cent. All the other allocations were declared to be called for by the proportion in the population.

IV It was equally absurd to have given separate representation to industrial and commercial interests. Those who had such interests were important enough both in wealth and social position to be able to pull their weight in a general body of electors and in a general body of members.

What has been described above is the injustice in the constitutional provisions as laid down by statute. But in actual fact the position of the Hindus was worse, even if the members from the Scheduled castes were included in their strength. They could not win all the 117 seats for which they were eligible, nor did they. Besides, of those who won seats, some, both from the high castes and Scheduled castes, joined with the Muslims against the general Hindu group. Among them was one of the foremost figures of the Congress in Bengal from 1925 to 1937. He was made Finance Minister in the Muslim ministry for his defection.*

The nationalist Hindus in the Assembly remained a powerless minority in spite of being not very negligible in numbers. The Muslims could ignore their opposition because they knew it could never threaten their tenure of office. They could, besides, reckon on being consistently supported by the European group.

What was done in Bengal through the Act of 1935 was done deliberately, and I know the reason why. The disenfranchisement of the Bengali Hindus was the punishment meted out to them by that Act on behalf of the British community in India, which desired it. Of all the communities in India, it was the educated and high caste Bengali Hindus whom the British sojourners hated most. The first reason for the hatred was that the nationalist movement was created by these Bengali Hindus. The hatred due to that, however, was obvious and in some ways natural, although also unintelligent. But there was also another reason for this hatred which worked subconsciously for the political victimization of the Bengali Hindu, which was perverse. That was reserved for the upper-class Hindu Bengalis who devoted themselves most sincerely and with considerable success to the task of remodelling their character and outlooks in the image of an ideal Englishman. Their love of English literature and the English language was the most noticeable indication of this aspiration. But to the Englishman in India all that was psychological miscegenation. So they rejected the Bengalis, who wished to bring about this transformation, with even greater determination than they showed in making an outcaste of any Englishwoman who had married an Indian.

Neither the political calculation nor the hatred which inspired it succeeded in saving the British Empire in India. But both succeeded in their negative aim: they ruined Bengal and the Bengali people irreparably. The unjust provisions of the Government of India Act of 1935, which made of the Bengali Hindus a permanent minority without any prospect of

* He was from my district, and knew me very well from my young days. He was a very able man, but an out and out adventurer. Later, he even became a member of the Viceroy's Executive Council. The two other Hindu ministers in this Muslim ministry were the Maharaja, supposed to be low-caste, who was at college with me, and the leader of the Bengali untouchables whose nephew is married to my niece. What strange coincidences!

political power, turned their thoughts to the shortsighted remedy, that of re-gaining power by getting rid of the Muslim majority by means of a partition of Bengal. This has benefited neither the Hindus nor the Muslims of Bengal.

The rancour which the British community in India showed towards the Bengali Hindus presents a paradox which baffles understanding. It would have been logical if there had been present either in them or the British government at home the determination to preserve British rule in India at all costs. On this score, there was complete defeatism. No such determination was present. But what was perverse was the degree of immediate resistance to what was accepted ultimately as inevitable. This contradiction created the worst form of hubris that can paralyse the intelligence and moral sensibility of any people: it is seen in arrogantly gloating over temporary victories while in enjoyment of nothing but temporary power. The British rulers of India succeded at last in freeing themselves from their own hubris by transferring it to those to whom they had to surrender their power, namely, the new Indian ruling class formed in the degenerate image of the last three decades of British rule.

A Fleeting Opportunity Lost

This was the blind alley in which Sarat Babu found himself when as the head of the Congress Party he had to perform the constitutional function of Leader of the Opposition in the Legislative Assembly of Bengal. His predicament was worse than that of a hero of fiction in a similar situation. In Hugo's *Les Misérables* Jean Valjean was trapped by Javert in a lane and found that he could not escape and save Cosette except by climbing up one or other of two perpendicular walls at its sides. Due to the prodigious strength of his arms and legs, he was able to do that. Not so Sarat Babu. All his political efforts from 1937 to 1939 were directed only towards finding a ladder, which never came.

Yet just before the Muslim ministry was set up in Bengal there had come to the Congress and Hindus of Bengal an opportunity for exercising political power by sharing it with the Muslims. This possibility arose out of the existence of two Muslim political parties and not one in the province. The most assertive Muslim party was the Muslim League, but it was an all-India Party, and, besides, in Bengal it was the party of upper-class Muslims. Therefore, those Muslim leaders who stood for the poor Muslim masses had formed another party and gone to the electorate as members of this party. Its leader was Fazl-ul-Huq, and the party was called the Krishak-Praja Party or the party of the peasants and tenants. Its leader declared that he would form what he described as *Dal-Bhat* or 'Rice and Lentil Soup' ministry, that is to say, a ministry which would devote itself to the welfare of the masses and provide both the basic food and essential necessities of life for them. It had gained a majority of the seats reserved for the Muslims, but that was not sufficient for forming a ministry by itself On account of the electoral system, a ministry in Bengal could be formed only by a coalition. Many members of the party were nationalistic, and therefore inclined towards the Congress. So, at first, Fazl-ul-Huq showed a readiness to combine with the Bengal Congress and create a broadbased ministry of all Bengalis. This overture was not accepted owing to the decision of the all-India Congress not to accept office even in the provinces where it had obtained absolute majorities. It was also unwilling to let the Congress Parties in such provinces where they had no majority co-operate with any other party. It would not make an exception for the Congress Party in Bengal, even though an opportunity to enjoy power in so important a province was not likely to come again. Thus it happened that Fazl-ul-Huq turned to the other Muslim party and formed a Coalition Ministry, as it was called, with it.

The refusal to make a special case of Bengal was a serious mistake. Not to accept office in the provinces in which the Congress had a majority in the legislatures could not do any permanent harm, for if the Congress revised its attitude it could at once assume power in all of them. And only three months later that happened. But the lost opportunity did not come again to Bengal. Yet in regard to Assam the Congress did make an exception. It allowed the Congress there to join with other parties.

I am unable to say whether the treatment of Bengal by the Congress was deliberate. But there can be no doubt that there was indifference to Bengal in the Congress, if not some real antipathy, which, in spite of being only latent, influenced policies. I can attribute that to the character of Bengali nationalism, which was wholly un-Gandhian in its historic form, and that character persisted in spite of the fact that Gandhi had won over a large section of the Bengali Hindus to his way of thinking and feeling. Later, however, I had opportunities for discovering or at all events suspecting rather dubious motives behind the treatment of Bengal by the Congress.

About that more will be set down at its proper place. Here I have only to add that at that early stage even Sarat Bose showed lack of foresight by being opposed to office acceptance. That can be attributed only to the feckless extremism of all Bengalis. They had set their heart on the expulsion of the British from India, and thought nothing was worth having in the meanwhile. In 1917 Mustafa Kemal, as one of the Turkish commanders in Palestine under Falkenhayn, urged Enver to seek peace, because, as he put it, even on the assumption that Germany would win the war, that would not be of much use to Turkey if in the meanwhile the Turkish nation perished. Kemal was dismissed for that by Enver, but it was Kemal and not Enver who saved the Turkish people. There was nobody in Bengal, and not even in India, with the clear vision of Kemal.

Hindu-Muslim Relations in Bengal

The most important, and if not dealt with in time the most harmful, element in the politics of Bengal in 1937 was the unsatisfactory state of Hindu-Muslim relations. There was a menacing assertiveness on the part of the Muslims, and resentment without any will to fight among the Hindus. The latter did not even diagnose the gravity of the malady, although there was widespread suspicion of Muslim intentions. There was no perception of the crisis which had been created for the Bengali Hindus.

On the contrary, among the Calcutta Hindus at any rate there was the kind of hubris I have just criticized in the British community. They were fatuously gloating over their present power in the Calcutta Corporation and through that institution in Calcutta generally. I saw a disgraceful exhibition of that when I was acting as editor of the Corporation's official journal at the end of 1935. At one of the meetings of the Corporation, Khan Bahadur Abdul Momin, one of the most respected leaders of the Bengali Muslims, was shouted down with insults as he was pleading for greater opportunities for the Muslims in Calcutta. He left the council chamber to the accompaniment of jeers from some of the younger Hindu councillors. Some time after that the Muslims completely boycotted the meetings of the Corporation, and the Hindus of Calcutta voiced great satisfaction that the Muslim *salas* (literally brothers-in-law, but in its connotation the equivalent of the English word 'bastard' as an abusive epithet) had left. Even the *Amrita Bazar Patrika,* the mouthpiece of the Calcutta Hindus, politely commented on the same lines.

At that time I was bringing out the shortlived Bengali weekly I have written about. I at once wrote an article in it pointing out the folly of this attitude. I said that the Muslims had not quitted the Corporation in a fit of tantrums, but deliberately as a matter of tactics. I explained that soon the Muslims were going to have political power in Bengal, and one of their first moves would be to amend the old Calcutta Municipal Act to give greater powers to the Muslims of the city. Their councillors, I said, had come out only to inflame Muslim opinion to make use of the coming opportunity.

I have already said that at that time I wrote some articles in order to give expression to my growing disquiet about the Hindu-Muslim question and my own diagnosis of the ailment. The very first of these was published in September, 1936, in *Sanibarer Chithi*, the monthly magazine which I once edited. What I regretted in it was the general Bengali Hindu attitude, not confined to Calcutta only, towards the basic aim of the Muslims in India, which was to maintain their identity as Muslims in a society parallel to that of the Hindus, who were not ready even to consider it as legitimate. I, on the contrary, pleaded for the acceptance of this aim, and the doyen of the Muslim journalists of Bengal reproduced the article in his monthly magazine. It made fellow-Hindus angry, but I shall quote its final paragraphs. I wrote:

'Today, as a result of the Communal Award of 1932, there is going to be a dominance by the Muslims, as against the Hindus, over the governance of Bengal. What this is going to do for the Hindus is to put them in exactly the same position in 1937 as the Muslims were in 1907. They are apprehensive that as soon as the Muslims get political power they would, in education as in literature, undermine that very culture based on ancient Indian ideals which was the pride of the Bengali Hindu. This fear is neither baseless, nor unjustified. On the other hand, if the Muslims try to recast the official educational system in a Muslim mould that, too, would not be wrong from the Muslim point of view. Aristode has said that for every polity it is essential that there should be an educational system suited to it. All over the world every state is following this principle and trying its best to preserve its particularity through the educational system. There is no place for any other doctrine in the educational system of Russia except the communistic; in Italy no education is imparted which is not Fascistic; in Germany as well the Nazis are re-writing their histories according to their ideals. Upon getting political power the Muslims are also likely to do the same thing. And it cannot be said that the Hindus would not have done that. The notion of a 'totalitarian state*' is spreading over the contemporary world in such a manner that this trend is bound to become more and more established every day. It is not possible either for the Hindus or the Muslims to remain immune to it. Therefore it is wholly irrelevant to discuss who has more right or wrong on his side.' *Translated from Bengali*

Therefore, to conclude, I drew attention to the fundamental issue. I had begun the article by setting it down and I repeated that in the conclusion. I said: 'What is needed is an admission that Bengal has become "bi-centric". The Hindus and Muslims might be brothers, but after having reached man's estate both have discovered that they have their identities, and are therefore resolved to take their own ways.'

It was, however, this basic demand of the Muslims which the Hindus totally and uncompromisingly rejected. They declared that it was 'anti- national'. It was this which made their opposition to the Muslim demands in detail pointless. There could be no agreement in respect of them without a concession in the essential.

Yet the paradoxical thing was that the Hindus of Bengal were not prepared to fight even for their legitimate rights. In 1932 they had tamely accepted die Communal Award, while the Sikhs in die Punjab made it clear that if they did not get what they were entitled to, they would create trouble, and they got what they wanted even though in their province they were a smaller minority than the Bengali Hindus were in their province. The latter knew they had been reduced to a statutory minority, were aggrieved by it, but would make no serious effort to put an end to it by extra-constitutional agitation if that was needed.

In these circumstances the only thing the Congress leaders could do in Bengal was to try to get in touch with the Bengali Muslim masses over the head of their own political leaders. The name given to this attempt was 'Mass Contact Movement'. But to rub shoulders with any kind of masses was not in Sarat Babu's line. So, this was taken in hand by his brother, Subhas Bose, who might employ his demagogic aptitude to establish some sort of rapport with the Muslims. The distant prompting for this movement had come from Jawaharlal Nehru, but ui Bengal it was Subhas Bose who

* By 'totalitarian' here I meant functional totalitarianism, which is extreme etatisme.

had to do it. There was, however, a basic difference between the position of Nehru in the u p and Subhas Bose in Bengal *vts-à-vis* the masses of the two provinces. In spite of his Anglicism, Nehru had succeeded in making himself the champion of the peasantry in his province. Subhas did not have the same position even with the Hindu peasantry of West Bengal. Both the Bose brothers were brought up in Orissa, and belonged to the professional class. Subhas Bose in all his outlooks and aptitudes was an urban political agitator.

Thus his 'Mass Contact Movement' came to nothing. The idea behind it was to get at the Muslim masses through their traditional religious leaders, the Ulema, or the theologians, the very set of men who were the most active promoters of Muslim group-consciousness. Subhas Babu invited a whole host of them to meet him in Sarat Babu's house. Whether their travelling expenses were paid by the Congress or not, they came. One day I saw a procession of Muslim divines trooping into Sarat Babu's house. I was quite familiar with the modem Muslim dress, but had no idea that these learned Muslims wore different clothes. They did, for they had green gowns on and big turbans on their heads. Even the most Westernized people around Mohammed Riza Shah Pahlavi were aware of the Ayatollahs. We, the educated and urban Bengali Hindus, with not a fraction of their Westernization in our manner of living, did not even imagine that such persons existed in Bengal. I with my knowledge of Islamic painting could only assume when I saw them that they were crude incarnations of the Muslim divines I had seen portrayed in Persian or Mughal miniatures. Not to speak of Calcutta, even at Kishorganj in my young days I had never seen such figures.

Their faces were grave, and even stem. One face struck me very forcibly. It was pinched and peevish, but of an incredible ferocity. The eyes were large, black, and burning, and in that emaciated face they looked even blacker and larger. His parrot-green gown, too, was more resplendent than those of the others, but being of very cheap satin looked garish. He looked like an ill-dressed Robespierre, the sea-green Incorruptible. Sarat Babu's house was not only crowded for the occasion with these survivals of Islam, but even reeked of them.

The green Maulana came to me and asked me if he could be shown to a toilet. I at once ran to mine, and finding it occupied, came back to tell him that I would let him know when he could use it. I was made anxious by his expression. The Muslims are different in such matters from the Hindus. The latter are not abashed by calls of nature, but, on the contrary, proclaim them as the expression of their body's sponuneous impulse to remain clean. The Muslim's code of manners forbids even any mention of such matters. So, my divine must have waited to ask me, a total stranger, until *in extremis.* I saw the pain on his face, and to restrain himself he kept walking up and down in the hall, and, with every step, becoming bent backwards like a bow being stringed, though not drawn. I did not know what to do, but somehow word had been carried to Subhas Babu. I saw him coming with very quick steps towards us. He came close, and, putting one arm most tenderly round the divine, said to him: 'Come with me, Maulana Sahib.' He took the miserable sufferer to Sarat Babu's own lavatory, of which I do not know why I had not thought.

Sarat Babu in the meanwhile could only carry on the Opposition in the Assembly, giving effect literally to the dictum: 'The duty of the Opposition is to oppose.' He and his party opposed the measures which the Muslim ministry at once introduced to modify the Calcutta Municipal Act and to change the educational system in order to give more scope to the perpetuation of Bengali Muslim culture. The ministry also proposed changes in the law of land tenure, through which the Hindu landlords still maintained some of their old privileges. The Congress, claiming to stand for democracy, could not oppose the changes proposed by the Muslims in principle. But it was hampered in formulating a clear policy because the supporters of the Congress in Bengal were the Hindu gentry, most of whom were landowners in die districts. I, however, noticed a peculiar indifference in Sarat Babu towards the agrarian question in Bengal. He did not possess landed property, and did not have much knowledge of the land laws. The great majority of the Congress members of the legislature were, however, lawyers or landowners. But they were the very men, to whom, as I have already described, Sarat Babu did not feel very much attracted personally. Certainly, the political interests of the Bengali Hindus suffered from this indifference to the land question, which in its turn prevented a clear formulation of policy in regard to tenure on the part of the Bengal Congress. But that seemed-to be unavoidable.

Subhas Chandra Base

At this point I shall offer an appraisement of Subhas Bose's position and personality as I saw it in 1937 and 1938 after I had come to know him personally. I had, of course, followed his career closely from 1922 onwards, but it was one thing to read about him in the newspapers and quite another to see him actually at work. The year 1937 was a landmark in his career as well. In that year he came back from his long exile in Europe, and much was expected from him. The opportunity also came to him to show his full capability with his elevation to the office of President of the Indian National Congress.

But the situation was not favourable. So far as the basic aim of the Indian nationalist movement was concerned, there was no means of forcing the issue of putting an end to British rule. The British side seemed to have won in the latest round of the game with the passing and application of the Government of India Act of 1935. But to those who had eyes to see and brains behind them to understand the reality behind the appearance, it was only a stalemate in the contest of will between British imperialism and Indian nationalism, a temporary 'still' in a tense position in the exhibition of a movie. A friend of mine, Prafulla Lahiri, who had turned cartoonist after having been a lecturer in English literature and published under the name of Piciel (PCI), gave a cartoon on this subject to the editor of *Sanibarer Chithi*, who printed it in the number in which my article on Hindu Muslim relations was also published (September, 1936). I reproduce it on the next page.

Sajani Das composed a stanza as its caption, in which he too showed great percipience. He said that the spirited game between John Bull and the Congress Goat was going on, but we in Bengal had run away from the field of battle. This was the position Subhas Bose was expected to deal with.

And in that task he failed dismally and tragically. I shall have to tell that story in some detail, and it fills me with infinite sadness. He was my contemporary, only ten months older. In 1922, when I was only an obscure clerk in a government department, he had become an all-India figure. After completing his education in England and returning to India towards the end of 1921, in six months he took his seat on the Front Bench of the nationalist movement. With Jawaharlal Nehru, he seemed to assert the right of the youth of India to direct the movement, and, as between him and Nehru, he could say that he was their truer representative, for he was only twenty-five while Nehru was thirty'-two. I could

RESOLUTION AND DEFIANCE

John Bull and the Congress Goat
(A Cartoon by Piciel)
1936

The bellow: 'Dieu et mon droit,
Honi soit qui mal y pense.'
The bleat: 'Quit India, Quit India, Quit India!'

paraphrase Burke and say of him in 1938: it is sixteen years since I saw Subhas Bose just above the horizon, decorating and cheering the elevated sphere he just began to move in, glittering like the morning star, full of life, splendour, and joy. Little did I dream even in 1938 that in seven years I should have to see irredeemable disaster overtaking him. Yet that came. What then went wrong?

I would quote Burke again in trying to answer that question. 'All men that are ruined are ruined on the side of their natural propensities.' Subhas Bose was killed by himself. Up to 1937 it could be said that his relative lack of achievement till then could be set down to British persecution: long periods of imprisonment and exile imposed on him. But from that year he could exercise free will and he exercised it in a manner which made his failure inevitable. No other figure in the Indian nationalist movement presents the stark contrast he does between promise and legend on the one side and performance and historic career on the other.

His promise began to show from his adolescence. He passed out of school at the age of sixteen with brilliant results, and continued that record until he was selected for the ICS and took his degree at Cambridge. This secured for him the good opinion of the Indian intelligentsia in advance, for there is no set of people than its members who set greater store by examination results. He increased that appeal by giving up the career in the ICS, which all middle class Indians regarded as the highest worldly prize. Thereby he gained the status which in India is never accorded to anybody who cannot produce renunciation and sacrifice as his tides.

He was also physically impressive, being both tall, well-built and handsome. Perhaps his face was too chubby for Western taste, but in India where embonpoint is as much a masculine as a feminine grace, his *putto*-like face added to his attraction. Besides, he was very fair, and without a fair complexion nobody is regarded as handsome in India. Except for certain dour traits in his character, he could be likened to Bonnie Prince Charlie. But he was less like the feckless Stuart than another dazzling Scot, Claverhouse, Bonnie Dundee.

Next, there was no doubt about his patriotism, and it was of the very type which evoked the greatest response in India, which means it was of the uncompromising extremist type, and wholly negative. That extremism was not softened by any positive idea as to the future, when India would be free of British rule.

This negation gave him an advantage which was decisive with the Indian intelligentsia. He did not frighten that order by being too far above or in advance of them in his ideas. Yet he could give new force, plausibility and animation to widely held ideas. He had the popular political leader's supreme qualification, as pointed out by Tocqueville with incisive clarity, of being able to mingle with his followers and adversaries, to rise and fall to the level of all intelligences, to discuss and argue without repose, to say the same things in different forms, and to get animated without end in the face of the same object. Nonetheless, the commonness of it all was raised by the mere fanaticism with which he preached it to the level of revolutionary originality. To be an embodiment of all the thoughts, emotions and aspirations of the Indian middle class and yet to seem to be far above its level, indeed to appear to be different in kind when only differing in degree, was his forte, as indeed it is the essential endowment of any popular hero. But the true hero, though he is that, also adds something of his own which is novel, and wheedles his followers into following him by seeming to be all their own. 'Think not that I am come to destroy the law, or the prophets: I am not come to destroy but to fulfil', said Jesus. Subhas Bose could never rise to that level of leadership. But, at all events, he should have been able to lead his followers to some purpose as Hitler did the Germans.

If he could not do that, there must have been serious shortcomings in himself, as indeed there were. These were behind his failure, of which, too, there can be no doubt. The first of these shortcomings was his closed mind, which made him incapable of seeing any situation for what it was. But in this, too, he was a typical Bengali intellectual. Traditionally, Bengali intellectuals have been extremely sensitive to abstract concepts and equally skilful in spinning webs of words around them. This propensity of the Bengali mind was very much strengthened when the Bengalis came in contact with a welter of new ideas from Europe. But such was their enthusiasm on the one hand and the abundance of the supply on the other that they began to fall in calf-love with ideas, and the special, if not self-defeating, characteristic of this ideological calf-love was its constancy or rather tyranny. Thus, once he had accepted an idea, the Bengali intellectual closed his mind to all else, and employed all his mental ingenuity to confirm his slavery to it. Their minds compelled Bengali intellectuals to live in their ideological Procrustean beds, even if that made them cut off all their growing mental limbs. Subhas Bose was a supreme Bengali in this sort of unreceptivity.

This was seen in his incapacity to perceive that with the emergence of Gandhism his brand of nationalism had no chance. I shall have to say more about this in the next chapter. Here I shall only add that his unadaptability was also seen in his association with the Bengali revolutionary movement, which had become totally obsolete.

If his ideas were not broad enough, he did not also have much efficiency in acting. No man could be more unmethodical in conducting business. In this, he was a strange contrast to his brother, Sarat Bose. I shall give an amusing example of this. Often he would write his letters too late for the normal clearance. Then, wishing to send them to the GPO for late clearance, he would discover that he did not have the postage. He would send for the stamps to his brother who always kept a spare sheet in his drawer. But at times Subhas Bose would write a large number of letters, or Sarat Bose would not be available. This happened once when he had to send out a circular letter. He was going to send the copies to the GPO where stamps were sold from a special all-night counter. Then he found that he did not have the money. But his hypnotism as a nationalist leader was such that the clerk gave his emissary all the stamps needed on credit, only diffidently requesting that the money might be sent to him before ten the next day so that he could make up his account. This power, all the nationalist leaders of the front rank in India always had, and they made full use of it.

What was even more injurious was that Subhas Bose as party leader failed totally to create a party of devoted followers to support him. Even Hider could not have come to power without the Nazi Party, however strong his emotional appeal. Since Subhas Bose was challenging what might be called the nationalist Establishment in India, he needed a party all the more. Yet he never had one. His following was always floating, shifting from year to year to different factions. Even his close associates did not fully trust him, and therefore were not invariably loyal. The lower ranks of the Congress nationalists gave or withheld their loyalty to him according to their estimate of his power to serve or harm their interests, and showed the proverbial valet's disinclination to hero-worship. Thus he was never able to knock his enemies on the head, of whose illwill he was certain. On the other hand, he was paralysed all along by the factional quarrels of the 'professional' nationalists, into which he got himself enmeshed. Thus in the end his enemies succeeded in ousting him even from the leadership of the Bengal Congress.

This inability to evoke steady loyalty may have been due partly to his own character. He was very suspicious of the motives of all who came to him, be they high or low. He was also very prone to listen to talebearers, a weakness common to all great men in India. But if he always suspected disloyalty in others, they too got an impression that he was not to be wholly trusted. Whatever this might have been due to, perhaps above all to his conspiratorial approach to politics, his ways were tortuous. As to this, before I came to know both the brothers I shared the common notion that it was Sarat Bose, the *avocat*, who gave the serpent's counsel to Subhas Bose, the tribune of the people. I soon discovered that the interaction was of an opposite character, and that Sarat Bose was the straight man, while Subhas Bose was not.

The persistent inability that Subhas Bose showed was part of a larger turbulence in his personality. He was rocklike in his opposition to British rule, and unshakeable in his apocalyptic belief in its end. But when passing through here and now, he could not be so unintelligent as to overlook the stark fact that British rule showed no signs of a crack. He could not have helped the feeling that he was up against a wall. I believe that kept him in fits of rage like a caged beast of prey, and made him emotionally tense and unstable beneath a cold mask.

However, an intimate friend of his, who was also at college with me, seemed to attribute that to sexual repression. One day he said to me: 'The madcap is becoming more and more mad every day. Is there no frenzied, beautiful hussy in Calcutta who could shut herself up with him in a room and rape him, so that he would feel in honour bound to marry her? Then the madcap would become normal.'

I could not agree with him. I knew the type too well, being half of that type myself. Of course, I knew there was sexual repression. But in his case, as in similar cases in Bengal, I did not take a Freudian view of it. It could be explained by the psychological situation in Bengal from the end of the nineteenth century to my young days in the twentieth. I shall explain this in the next chapter. What I observed was Subhas Bose's indifference to women. I knew why at this age he would avoid being in any kind of intimate or confidential relationship with young women, and would rather seek female companionship among matrons, who could quizz him about becoming an old bachelor. This was quite common in our social life on the part of matronly acquaintances. But he would keep aloof from young women because with his delicate sense of honour he would feel that with his looks and position he would have an overwhelming advantage over any young woman, and would never be able to meet her even half-way.

In fact, after seeing both the brothers, I used to express the very decided opinion, certainly doing great injustice to others, that of all the men I had seen around the two Boses, they were the only ones I would trust with money or a woman. But Sarat Babu was in a strong *de facto* position to deserve this opinion. He was wealthy and he was very happily married. Even after the birth of eight children he remained a loving husband. His love for his wife created in him what seemed to be like a telepathic awareness of any danger to her. One day, as he was with his clients and I was standing by, he suddenly got up and went upstairs. I could not understand why, but afterwards he told me that he had a sudden feeling that his wife was in danger. 'I get this feeling,' he added. His wife for some years had been suffering from an intestinal obstruction. When he got upstairs he found that an attack had come on. In such circumstances, Sarat Babu could be indifferent to any other man's money or wife. But not so Subhas Bose a *priori*. But I felt he was. I knew that he was exercising an unceasing self-control, and with success. In any case, he was protected from temptation by the sheer absence of solitude which the monks regarded as an unavoidable promoter of concupiscence.

But this very thing also prevented him from considering his policies and courses of action deeply, and partly contributed to his failure. Like all men in India who had power, which also meant some sort of patronage, he had visitors coming to see him at all hours of the day, insisting on seeing him, and doing so. Thus it happened that he took many of his decisions late at night when he was tired, and, as I shall relate, one such decision brought about very serious consequences.

In his desperation he tried to protect himself from intrusion by making a pathetic appeal to the visitors. One morning, going to his house, I saw a large board hung up near the front door. On it, painted in large white letters on a black background, was a notice couched in the most persuasive and gentle terms. In it he said to his visitors that whether they saw him or not, he was always engaged in their service, but trying to see him at all hours simply came in the way of that service; so would they consider that they had more to lose than gain by disturbing him, and kindly leave him alone so far as they could?

Coming back, I found the same friend who had prescribed marriage for him in my room, and asked him if he had seen the notice. When he said that he had, I asked him: is it not like the notice in the zoo: "Do not feed the chimpanzee"?' He roared with laughter and said: 'That's it, that's it.' The visitors were such a plague to all the nationalist leaders that they really had peace only when sent to prison by the kind British authorities. Forced imprisonment was for them what self-imposed retreats were for devout Christians.

Attempts to Break the Muslim Ministry

After continuing in powerless opposition for about a year, Sarat Bose tried in the late summer of 1938 to bring down the Muslim ministry by moving a motion of no confidence. He hoped to persuade some dissatisfied Muslims and also the Scheduled caste Hindus, who were supporting the ministry, to vote with him. There was a good deal of canvassing, and on the eve of the voting it seemed as if the motion had a chance of going through by a narrow margin. But it did not. Fazl-ul-Huq, the Chief Minister, brought to bear all his influence on the Muslims and all his eloquence to prevent defections. There were massive Muslim demonstrations just outside the Assembly House for the Ministry while the debate was going on. Fazl-ul-Huq announced his victory from the steps of the Town Hall to resounding cheers from the Muslims. I was waiting in Sarat Babu's house to hear about the result. He himself told me about it in very simple words as soon as he reached home: 'We have lost.'

The next move of the Boses was to try to break up the ministry by inducing the most influential Hindu minister in it to resign. He was Nalini Ranjan Sarkar, the Finance Minister, who, if he resigned, could carry some Hindus with him and force Huq to resign. For this move the Boses needed Gandhi's support and intervention. Both Sarat Bose and Subhas Bose discussed the question with Gandhi many times, and came away with the impression that Gandhi supported the move. But immediately after Subhas Bose had had his last talk with Gandhi in December, 1938, he got a letter from him which showed that, so far from being in favour of bringing down the Huq Ministry, Gandhi was quite decidedly against it. This shocked Subhas Bose and a correspondence followed, which was bitter on the part of Bose and very bland on the part of Gandhi. I saw the whole correspondence, and I must set down my opinion, formed then and held afterwards, that in it Gandhi surpassed even his own record of casuistry. I, however, perfecdy understood where Gandhi's opposition was coming from.*

What happened was this. Shortly after Subhas Bose had his last talk with Gandhi, Nalini Ranjan Sarkar, who had got wind of the scheme of the Boses, went to see Gandhi at his Ashram in Maganwadi, Wardha, with two others, Ghanashyamadasa Birla, the great Marwari financial magnate whose influence over Gandhi as his unstinted provider of money was decisive, and Maulana Abul Kalam Azad whose opinion on any question concerning Muslims was also decisive. Thus Nalini Sarkar showed very great astuteness in engaging his *advocates* with Gandhi, who wrote to Subhas Bose about what happened at the meeting. The letter was sent by the hand of Birla and was not dated, but Subhas Bose replied to it on 21 December, 1938.1 quote the relevant passage of the letter:

'My dear Subhas Babu, [This was very formal which he never did in the ordinary way]

'I must dictate this letter as I am wilfully blind. Whilst I am dictating this, Maulana Sahib, Nalini Babu, and Ghanshyamdas† are listening. We had an exhaustive discussion over the Bengal Ministry. I am more than ever convinced that we should not aim at ousting, the Ministry. We shall gain nothing by a reshuffle; and, probably, we shall lose much-by including Congressmen in the Ministry. I feel, therefore, that the best way of securing comparative purity of administration and a continuation of a settled programme and policy would be to aim at having all the reforms we desire, carried out by the present Ministry. Nalini Babu should come out, as he says he would, on a real issue being raised and the decision being taken by the Ministry against the interests of the country.

* An American scholar, Leonard A. Gordon, has given a short account of this episode in his book: *Bengal: The Nationalis! Movemtnl, 1876-1940* (Columbia University Press, 1974), pp. 283-8 5, on the strength of an interview with me in 1964 and some documents shown to him by me. I have to give mine at first hand, and at greater length.

† The personal name of Birla was spelt here according to the popular pronunciation.

His retirement from the Ministry would then be dignified and wholly justified. I understand that so far as the amendment of Municipal Law is concerned, separate electorate for the Scheduled Class is given up. There is still insistence on separate electorate for Mussulmans. I don't know whether opposition should be taken to the breaking point. If the Mussulman opinion is solid in favour of separation, I think it would be wisdom to satisfy them. I would not like them to carry the point in the teeth of the Congress opposition. It would then be a point against the Congress.'

After referring to a side issue, Mahatma Gandhi concluded his letter by adding: 'Maulana Sahib is in entire agreement with this opinion and so are Nalini Babu and Ghanshyamdas.'

One should have thought that they would as a matter of course. All three were interested in maintaining the status quo: Maulana Abul Kalam Azad as a Muslim would not disapprove of Muslim domination in Bengal, Nalini Sarkar would like to keep his office, and Birla had his motive of which I shall say something later. As to the Ministry, it was an evasion of the issue to say that the changes that the Congress desired in Bengal could be brought about by working with the Muslim Ministry. Gandhi did not explain why it would follow Congress policy. But the most extraordinary statement in the letter was that if the Muslims wanted a separate communal electorate for Calcutta they should be allowed to have it. Whatever the British Government might have done, the Congress was on principle opposed to communal electorates for the Muslims on the ground that it would be accepting the theory of two nations in India. Gandhi made matters worse by sending his letter by the hand of Birla.

Subhas Bose was naturally very much upset by this letter and he replied in fairly strong language on 21 December 1938.

'My dear Mahatmaji,

'The letter which Sjt. G. D. Birla brought from Wardha came as a profound shock to me. I remember to have discussed the Bengal situation with you time and again. The other day at Wardha it was discussed between us once again. My brother Sarat also discussed the matter with you. Both of us have the clear impression that you have always agreed with the idea of a Coalition Ministry in Bengal. [He meant a coalition between the Congress and the Muslims.] I do not know what has happened since I left Wardha to make you alter your view so completely that you now write - "I am more than ever convinced that we should not aim at ousting the Ministry, etc." The papers say that after I left Wardha Sjt. N. R. Sarkar, Sjt. G. D. Birla, and Maulana Azad Sahib have seen you. Evidently, you have altered your view after talking to them. The position, therefore, is that you attach more value and importance to the views of those three gentlemen than to the views of those who are responsible for running the Congress organization in Bengal.'

Continuing Bose wrote:

'You are not in the habit of writing anything lightheartedly - hence I, shall be justified in attaching the fullest weight to what is your considered opinion. Your letter has given rise to a crisis in which it is necessary for me to speak very frankly and I crave your pardon at the outset for doing so.'

This was virtually a challenge to Gandhi, and the first question Subhas Rose dealt with was whether the Congress should or should not co-operate with the Muslims in those provinces in which they were in power or in a dominant position. These provinces were Bengal, Assam, and Sindh. In Assam, however, there was already a coalition between the Muslims and the Congress, and in Sindh, too, the Congress was supporting a Muslim ministry. Thus the only province for which the question remained open was Bengal, the most important non-Congress province in respect of governmental power and certainly not less important than any other province in respect of nationalist politics. Bose explained that over this, question there was a fundamental difference between him and Maulana Abul Kalam Azad, who he said, seemed to be holding the view that 'in the Muslim majority provinces like Bengal, communal Muslim ministries should be allowed to continue in office.'

'I', wrote Bose, 'hold, on the contrary, that it is imperative in the national interest that we should pull down the Huq Ministry as early as possible. The longer this reactionary Ministry remains in office the more communal will the atmosphere of Bengal become and the weaker will the Congress grow vis-à-vis the Muslim League. The same argument applies to the Sikandar Hyat Ministry also.' That was in the Punjab.

Then Bose dealt with the question of Nalini Ranjan Sarkar's resignation. He wrote:

'At long last, early in November, Sjt. Nalini Sarkar had been convinced that he should resign from the Huq Ministry. He assured me for the first time on the 9th December, before I left Calcutta for Wardha, that he would resign his office before the next Budget Session. What made him renege from the position within one week, I do not know. Your influence is going to be used not to get Nalini Babu to resign but to get him to stick to office at a time when even his closest friends want him to get out of the Huq Ministry. It has astonished me that you did not feel it necessary even to consult me before you arrived at a decision on such a serious matter.'

That Subhas Bose should have based all his calculations to create a coalition of Hindus and Muslims for the good of Bengal on the good will of so notorious an adventurer as Nalini Sarkar showed his utter incapacity to approach any political question with realism, all the more so because neither really trusted the other. Even more lacking in realism was the motive he avowed to himself and to others for this change. I cannot believe that, in trying to put an end to the Huq Ministry as it was, he did not want to recover for the Hindus of Bengal a position in the government proportionate to their number and social and economic position. But in trying to persuade Gandhi that the aim was right he made no allusion to it. On the contrary, he harped on the idea of forcing the British Government to make concessions to Indians by making them face a common front of both communities. In his letter he proceeded to make out his case for the change:

'It is necessary for me to explain why I attach such value to a Coalition Ministry in a province like Bengal. You may remember that I spoke to you at Shegaon on this subject, but now I shall repeat what I have to say. The position today is such that a Coalition Ministry in Sindh, Bengal and Punjab is within the domain of practical politics. If this change could be brought about (and in my humble opinion it can be) the Congress will be in a position to speak to the British Government on behalf of eleven provincial governments. This will mean that even without a Hindu-Muslim settlement, the Congress will be able officially to represent the people of British India, while dealing with the British Government, and we shall not be seriously handicapped because there has been no settlement with the Muslim League.'

After explaining further how this could be done, he reverted to his principal motive:

'If we carry out the above programme before the next Congress meets at Tripuri, we shall be in a position to put our national demand for Puma Swaraj* before the British Government and ask for a definite reply within a specified period. With a background of acute international tension, it will not be possible for the British Government to reject our demand lightly. And if they reject it or give us an unsatisfactory reply, we should start our Satyagraha campaign after giving due notice. As far as one can judge, the present international tension will continue for another 12 or 18 months. In such a critical situation the British Government cannot permit a major struggle to go on in India. They will have to make peace with India if they are to avoid weakening themselves in Europe. Consequently, a Satyagraha campaign on a big scale in 1939 will inevitably lead to a Peace Conference between the Congress and the British Government as a stepping stone to our victory.'

The idea to which Subhas Bose clung was that, frightened by Hitler and Mussolini, the British Government would concede political independence to India. Only Subhas Bose was capable of such an illusion. Gandhi paid no attention to the argument, for he never expected any international situation to promote India's independence. Even Nehru, who gave more attention to international politics, deprecated this idea of an ultimatum. Gandhi replied to Bose's letter in his bland style. Just as Subhas Bose's letter was a striking example of the hold which his *idées fixes* had over him, Gandhi's was an equally striking example of his invariable habit of never disclosing his real mind. His letter was dated 22 December 1938, and in it he first disposed of Bose's suggestion that he was going back on his previous opinion about the Bengal Ministry and was showing himself to be inconsistent. He wrote: 'My dear Subhas [he reverted to informality in the superscription], I can't understand why you were shocked over my letter. I have nothing to alter in what I said to Sarat. I still hold the opinion that if we can form a coalition ministry with honour and dignity we shall unhesitatingly do so.'

* Full self-government' in English.

That is to say, for him it was only a question of timing the move. He went on to explain why the time had not come: 'But from what I heard from Maulana Sahib and Nalini Babu and even Ghanshyamdas, I felt, as I do even now, that my first instinct, which I discussed at Calcutta often enough with you, is right. But if you think that my instinct and my data are at fault, then the coalition ministry idea stands. My letter is surely a warning too that you may be cautious on the issue I mentioned in my letter.'

Then he dealt with the charge that he was more inclined to be led by the Trinity of Maulana, Sarkar, and Birla than by the two Boses. He wrote 'Your complaint that I attach more value to the views of the three friends is not justified, for it is not their views which have affected me; it is the evidence they gave. Sarat had told me that Nalini Babu was coming, that I should try to influence him to resign, and I did. And he has agreed to resign on the issue I mentioned in my letter.'

One wonders whether Mahatma Gandhi was so unworldly as to beHeve that advocates and respondents produce any evidence which goes against their case. Anyhow, Gandhi proceeded to mollify Subhas Bose: 'You', he wrote,

'are unnecessarily alarmed by my letter. You know that with you I don't need to argue every point. There are so many things I take for granted and simply pass on my opinion which has got to be taken in conjunction with the past and the future. My position is fundamentally that of a helper where my help is sought or where I can offer help unsought. Therefore my opinion sent to you has no mandatory value and has only as much value as your reason approves of and no more. That letter can't be produced in order to thwart your plans because it is meant only for you and for those whom you want to take into confidence.'

Why did Gandhi then dictate the letter in the presence of those who wanted such a letter to be written, and even speak about their approval? But I would go on with the citation: 'Even in the course of our conversation', Gandhi wrote, 'I told you that I did not share your optimism. I share it still less now in view of what Maulana Sahib and the other two friends told me. When we discussed things, I had not had their evidence. If you had been at Wardha, you would have been present at the talks. They were not in confidence from you.

'One more thing', [he continued] 'when Maulana Sahib gives an opinion on matters regarding Muslims, we have given him an overruling authority. Has it not been the policy to yield to his opinion when we have not carried his with ours? What is the meaning of ousting the Huq Ministry? You will never oust Huq and several other members. Therefore, generally speaking, it can be said that a coalition ministry means some Congressmen in the Ministry with no undertaking that the Congress programme will be carried out. In such a case, I personally would prefer to keep the Congress out of the Ministry and endeavour to carry out the Congress programme through whichever Ministry there is an office.'

But how could Mahatma Gandhi expect that the Congress could make ministries execute its programmes by remaining outside them when he thought that it could not by having its members as ministers? After saying all this Gandhi issued a more decisive challenge to Bose than Bose had thrown out to him. I shall quote that part of the letter in the next chapter in which I shall deal with the major quarrel between Gandhi and Bose. The question of a coalition ministry in Bengal got submerged in that dispute.

Nonetheless, the passages I have cited here will give some idea of Gandhi's method of conducting a political debate. In this letter he again showed that side of his personality which puzzled every British Viceroy in India who had to deal with him. But to those of us in India who had no interest in suppressing truth and fostering myths, it was obvious that Gandhi was revealing himself both as the typical Hindu holy man and as the Hindu man of power. There was nothing but evasion in his letter. He never disclosed his real motives in opposing Subhas Bose or anybody else. The simple truth was that he had been confirmed in his dislike for Bose by his conduct as President of the Congress, and was resolved to get him out of Congress politics, unless he could make him an obedient follower. As this antagonism will be dealt with fully in the next chapter, I shall say nothing more about Gandhi's attitude. But the part that Birla played in this tortuous game has to be explained. If Gandhi was not ready to play Bose's game, he was always ready to oblige the Birlas by serving their interest.

Nalini Ranjan Sarkar had shown astuteness in taking Birla with him. He was associated with the anti-Bose and pro-Gandhi faction of the Bengal Congress, and, besides, was a fellow financial magnate of Birla, although not as great a plutocrat. And Sarkar could have guessed that Birla would have as great an interest in the Muslim Ministry of Bengal without any Congress Hindu in it as he himself had for the sake of his career. This interest I always suspected, and I shall now set down my hypothesis for what it is worth.

So intelligent a man as G. D. Birla could not have been unaware of the bearing governmental power in Bengal had on the interests of the community, the Marwaris, in the province.* These were very large. So long as British rule lasted, the Marwaris could do nothing to prevent the British trading and industrial interests being supreme and theirs being in second place. But theirs, too, was a close second, and some British companies took Marwaris as partners. But the more ambitious Marwaris wanted to supplant the British, not co-operate with them. Therefore they generally supported the Gandhian movement. Gandhi was given to understand by G. D. Birla that as regards money he could always depend on the house of Birla. But he would also want to see that the British withdrawal from India did not harm Marwari interests in India and, in particular, in Bengal. As regards India, he could depend on Gandhi and the Congress to support all Marwari interests. But the Bengali intelligentsia, which resented the overshadowing Marwari presence in Calcutta, might try to get rid of it. Birla also knew that the middle class Bengalis were inefficient in business and would not by themselves be able to harm Marwari vested interests. But the Bengali Hindus could become dangerous if they combined with the Muslims. Whether they did any good to themselves or not, the Hindus and Muslims between them could injure the Marwaris. So Birla's prime concern would be to prevent a combination of the Hindus and Muslims of Bengal. I have no doubt that in appearing to support the Muslim Ministry in Bengal, he had in mind the prevention of Hindu-Muslim co-operation. It was the British game which was adopted by the Marwaris.

There is no doubt that it succeeded. The Bengali Hindus were defeated or suffered by default on all fronts. The British wanted to take revenge on them by depriving them of political power through their Government of India Act; Gandhi had an innate dislike for the peculiar brand of

* The Marwaris were a merchant community from Rajputana; extremely enterprising, they carried on their financial and commercial activities all over India, and were dominant in Bengal. The house of Birla was the most eminant Marwari family in the last decade of British rule.

nationalism that was Bengal's and, in any case, he was repelled by any kind of intellectual pretension and would all the more dislike the Bengali's overweaning pride in his intellectual capacity. So, he too would not be disposed to help Bengali Hindus. Lastly, Subhas Bose was so obsessed with the aim of ending British rule in India that he had no time to consider whether, when the British were gone, there would be Bengalis of his own order left who could take the place of the British. And the Bengali Hindus by themselves would not fight for their position or even for their minimum rights. They preferred to fail and have the luxury of self-pity. That luxury, they have in abundance at present.

Civic Power in Calcutta

But the question still remains whether the Bengali Hindus would have acted to any purpose to provide an efficient and honest administration in Bengal. Their conduct in the civic sphere had already made it certain that they were incapable of that kind of achievement. I have written about the bad reputation which the Calcutta Corporation acquired when it had passed from British to Bengali control. When I was working for Sarat Bose the Corporation was still completely under the control of the Calcutta gentry, and the Muslims were only trying to poach in the Corporation's preserves. For four and a half years I saw the operation of Congress power in it, and that was the same as the power of the Calcutta gentry, against which all the public spirit that Sarat Bose and Subhas Bose displayed in words could avail nothing. The Congress Municipal Association was an evil organization in Calcutta. During all the time I was with Sarat Bose I never saw it acting for anything but the private interests of the class which had seized the Corporation. The main question was always what money could be got out of it, and never its proper civic functions. One could write a book to illustrate that. But that being impossible I shall give a few typical examples.

I have already described how cynical the Councillors of the Calcutta Corporation could be over corruption. They were not a whit less so about the methods they adopted to perpetuate their hold on the Corporation. I have also mentioned how at that time Mahatma Gandhi was denouncing bogus electoral rolls. The Congress Councillors of the Calcutta Corporation only felt amused by this naïveté, and one day I heard a characteristic comment on it. Sarat Babu was sitting at his desk, with some Councillors before him. I was by his side. A young and very smart Councillor exclaimed: 'What is this virtuous rampage over false electoral rolls? All of us have them. I have them. We would not be elected without them.' There was no display of virtuous indignation at this speech. Even Frederick the Great denounced Machiavellism. Sarat Babu, who was never qualified to be any kind of a Machiavellian, took the Machiavellism of his followers without any surprise, far less protest.

I came to know very soon how the false electoral rolls were dressed up, and, in addition, witnessed a performance of the trick. I must, however, explain first how the electoral rolls for the Calcutta Corporation were prepared. They were not under the authority of the Corporation, but of the political suzerain of the Corporation, namely, the Bengal Government. The Election Department with its staff worked in the Corporation building, and was under an Election Officer, all under the Minister for Local Self-Government. But with an utter disregard of common sense, the Chief Executive Officer of the Corporation was appointed the Election Officer as well. In the former capacity he was a servant of the Corporation and therefore of the Councillors, and in his capacity as Election Officer a servant of the Bengal Government, and quite independent of the Councillors. And he made full use of his dual position. The Councillors had to keep themselves in his good books, because unless he appointed the persons whom the Councillors wanted for making fictitious electoral rolls as clerks in the Election Department, the Councillors could not have their false rolls. On the other hand, the chief Executive Officer, too, wanted some Councillors to be serving his interest *qua* Chief Executive Officer. Thus there was sufficient inducement for complaisance on both sides. However, one day I saw how the scales were tilted in favour of the Chief Executive Office *cum* Electoral Officer.

Sarat Babu had sent me with a letter to the Chief Executive Officer, who most courteously asked me to take a chair and wait a little, until he had dealt with the paper in hand. I had seen him before, but this was the first opportunity I had to observe him more closely. He had been a barrister before he took up this very important appointment, and he was elderly, certainly above fifty at that time. He was immaculately dressed in an English suit, and had a pince-nez on his nose. He was well-groomed but had a very blase look, the reason for which I shall give presently.

As I waited, I was very much surprised to see a well-known and rather fiery young Councillor standing by his table in the posture of a suppliant. I could not understand why one of the masters of the CEO would not even take a chair but behave as an underling. But the cat came out of the bag very soon. When the CEO had done with his paper, he looked at the Councillor before looking at me and asked him gruffly: 'What is it that you want?' Now, as the difference does not exist in English, I must add that in addressing the Councillor the CEO employed the Bengali equivalent of the French *tu*, instead of that for *vous*. The Councillor replied very submissively: 'Sir, it's about the clerk's appointment in the Election Department.' Wishing to get rid of the Councillor, the CEO said: 'Find the application and give it to me.' The Councillor rummaged among the files on a what-not by the side of the table, took out one of them, and, opening it, said: 'Please sign here.' The CEO signed the application under the typed word 'Appointed', and the Councillor left, smiling. I felt rather astonished.

The Councillors could obtain money for themselves from bribes, large or small, according to their influence. But in India mere self-aggrandisement is not enough; it must be supplemented by nepotism, very widely interpreted. Thus, for any one person, the perquisites of his own power make up only one half, while the other half is made up of jobs for relatives, flatterers, and, of course, agents for dirty work of all kinds. So the scramble for jobs in the Calcutta Corporation was fierce and incessant. But here, too, an explanation is needed in order to understand the method of patronage in all its amplitude.. Appointments up to Rs. 200 a month were in the hands of the Chief Executive Officer, although he had to use his official power without displeasing his official masters. The higher appointments were made by the Services Committee of the Corporation, and competition for its membership was severe.

There was much more prolonged manoeuvring, and even fighting, for the higher posts. Therefore appointments to them were sometimes delayed for years until the members of the Services Committee could come to an agreement about the apportionment of jobs to each of them in all the vacancies likely to occur in the next five years. It took a very long time to arrive at a distribution satisfactory for all.

I shall give a typical example from my direct knowledge. The post of Superintendent of the most important engineering workshop of the Corporation was vacant. One of the applicants was a Bengali engineer who had not only high American qualifications, but had even worked in the USA on a fairly high salary. He prepared a dossier of his qualifications in the American manner, very beautifully typed and bound, and provided with his photograph and testimonials, one even from the Governor of the State in which he worked. The poor man did not know the difference between America and his own country, and would come to me and say in a tone of almost outrage: 'How they treat me, who had often been a guest of Governor L.' After one year of waiting, he told me that he had spent all his savings and was now going to raise money for another year of waiting by mortgaging his properties in his village. I do not think he got the job, for after that he never came to see me again.

The posts within the jurisdiction of the Chief Executive Officer were not subject to such delays, but the contests were sharper. Of this, too, I shall give an example, which will show that even the formidable Chief Executive Officer could not always have his way. A young Bengali, an electrical engineer, who had been employed by the Calcutta Electric Supply Corporation (a British concern) on a good salary and after that in Singapore by a British firm on a higher salary, was arrested as a political suspect when on a visit to Bengal. He was released in 1937, and as no British firm would employ him any more, he sought employment in the Calcutta Corporation, and the post of an electrical engineer on Rs. 200 (about 6) a month being vacant, he applied for it. As he was a political sufferer and, besides, had very good qualifications, both Sarat Babu and Subhas Babu took up his case, and recommended him to the Chief Engineer of the Corporation, whose decision in respect of such appointments could be regarded as morally binding on the CEO. The young man was recommended by the Chief Engineer, and came to tell me that his file was to be taken to the CEO the next day for formal appointment. He added that he was going tomorrow to see that everything passed off smoothly. He knew that there was some risk, for there was another candidate for whom a very influential Councillor, one of the devoted followers of Subhas Babu (at least in professions), was up and doing.

The next day the young man came and told me that he had failed to get the job, and he told me how and why. As the clerk in the Chief Engineer's office was taking his file to the Chief Executive Officer's office, which was on another floor, he followed him at a discreet distance. The corridor was very long and they had to pass the doors of the Councillors' lounge. The young man saw from a distance that the other candidate with his Councillor was Standing at one of the doors. When the clerk had reached it, the Councillor said in a most cheery manner: 'Hallo, where are you going?' The clerk replied: 'To the Chiefs room with this file.' The Councillor said very blandly: 'Give me the file. I shall take it to the Chief myself.' The clerk showed hesitation and replied: 'How can I, Sir? The Chief Engineer has asked me to place the file in the hands of the CEO.' 'Care for your own job?' asked the Councillor. 'You are the master. Sir,' replied the clerk and handed the file to the Councillor, who took it to the CEO, and got his candidate appointed. Our candidate was so struck by the utter absurdity of die whole thing that he smiled as he told me the story and forgot even to show himself injured. For such deeds we in Bengal have a collocation, which is: 'This is robbery in broad daylight.' So it was. But when I reported it to Sarat Babu he was not even surprised, far less angry. He took it as if it was all in the day's work. In such quarrels we Bengalis followed the old proverb: 'He who fights and runs away may live to fight another day.' So, we do not waste our energy in desperate contests. We wait for our turn to injure out enemy.

Competitions for such small jobs were mere skirmishes, and were brought to a head soon, even though with complete disregard for decencies. When, however, the stakes were the highest jobs in the Corporation, the publicity that their filling up got in the press, made it necessary for appearances to be saved, and no jobbery was permitted at that level except under the pretext of efficiency and purity of administration. Therefore, the intrigues were set on foot considerably in advance of the likely vacancies and were as elaborate as the arrangements for providing ready tigers to be shot by the Viceroy of India.

Usually, there was a sure sign by which one could recognise that a tussle for a big job was in the offing. This was like the detection of a low pressure coming from a distant zone, and it was to be seen whenever there was a sudden cry about revising the service rules in order to close the loopholes in it through which inefficiency could creep in. Actually, the revision was always meant to smooth the path for a desired appointment.

Thus, whenever a proposal for revising the service rule came up, cynical observers of Corporation affairs paraphrased a well-known French saying declaring: '*Cherchez l'homme.*' I give one instance. Before I became Sarat Babu's secretary and was working at times in the Corporation, a sudden cry was raised that too many old men were holding the highest posts in it, barring the promotion of younger and deserving men. An amendment was at once proposed that the retiring age should be lowered, and it was. In reality this general reform was aimed at getting rid of one man, the non- Bengali Secretary to the Corporation, the official who helped the Mayor to conduct the debates, and who was a man of exemplary efficiency. But he had the misfortune of having as his next in rank a young Bengali connected with some of the foremost political figures in Bengal. The post of Assistant Secretary was not suited to his social position. So he had to become the Secretary.

An absolute rule, however, could create an awkward situation when a favoured official of the Councillors was due to be superannuated. So a rider was always added to the amending rule that in very deserving cases the Services Committee could grant any extension it thought fit. It was granted to all who were favourites. I saw a very high official grovelling at the feet of the Councillors for an extension.

As it happened, I became involved in a proposal for a wide revision of the service rules of the Corporation. One day Sarat Babu received a letter from Dr B. C. Roy, who was the leader of the Congress faction in Bengal opposed to the Boses and a very ambitious man - indeed by remaining loyal to the Gandhian Congress he became the Chief Minister of Bengal after independence - that the service rules were very imprecise and casual and had to be made more comprehensive as well as clear. He enclosed a draft of the revisions he proposed. Sarat Babu asked me to look through it and tell him what it was like. I found the new rules to be even less precise than the old ones, and besides full of linguistic faults which would make interpretation very difficult. When I told this to Sarat Babu he asked me to draft a new set of rules, and informed Dr Roy that as soon as he had his proposals ready he would call a meeting of the Congress Municipal Association to consider them.

I drafted a wholly new set of rules, covering all the points Dr Roy had dealt with and going further. I took particular care that the phrasing should be unambiguous. Besides, I inserted a provision with a view to removing a glaring injustice to the employees of the Corporation already in service. It was notorious that when vacancies occurred in a higher grade these were filled by the protégés of the Councillors and very often extremely efficient men employed in a lower grade did not get a chance. This was causing great dissatisfaction and reducing efficiency. Therefore, I included a rule that in filling posts in the higher grades, a departmental candidate, provided he was equally efficient, would get preference over an outsider. I also inserted another provision to remove competition from over-qualified men for posts carrying low salaries. Owing to the pressure of unemployment among the middle class, young men with BA and MA degrees were applying for posts with salaries as low as £3 month, although anybody with a good school record could do the work. I therefore drafted a rule that for clerical posts no candidate with high degrees would be considered and a Matriculation or Intermediate certificate would be enough as regards educational qualification.

When I had completed the new rules, Sarat Babu had a visit from some of the young Councillors of his faction. They said: 'Sir, we have heard that you have made a new set of service rules. May we have a look at them?' Obviously, they mnted to make sure that no threat to their interests should be in the rules. Sarat Babu took out the long draft and put it before them. They begaa to go through it with heads put together. Suddenly the most cheeky one among them, the same pian who had been so frank about faked electoral rolls, cried out: 'What is this. Sir?' 'What is what?' inquired Sarat Babu. 'This rule about departmental candidates getting preference over outsiders.' Sarat Babu observed: 'That is only fair. Why should those already in the service of the Corporation work efficiently unless they were given prospects of rising?' 'That may be true,' replied the Councillor, 'but it is also true that there will always be qualified departmental candidates, and our relatives and friends will never get any job in the Corporation. This rule must go.' And it was taken out.

This question of departmental *vs.* outside candidates became much more controversial when the posts were very highly paid. There was already a rule that the highest technical posts in the Corporation like that of the Chief Engineer, Chief Medical Officer, or Educational Officer, would be filled, not by mere seniority, but by technical competence of the highest order available. Of course, this patronage was on the highest level, and in the existing rules only three or four posts were specifically mentioned as being in this category. But the young Councillors adopted what they regarded as an equally valid principle. With the help of that they wanted to enlarge the list of such posts. This was the new principle: 'Please include that post, Sir, it is liquid assets.' Another suggested another post on the same ground. Thus from less than half a dozen, the list of posts which would be filled by-outsiders, was enlarged to about two dozen. 'Liquid assets' meant any highly paid post in the Corporation likely to fall vacant within two years.

The formal meeting of the Congress Municipal Association was called soon after, and the Councillors sat round the big table in Sarat Babu's study. I stood by him. Dr B. C. Roy came in with his usual air of authority and took his seat by Sarat Babu's side. 'May I have a look at your draft?' he said to Sarat Babu and was given it. He turned over the pages purposively, apparently looking for something in which he was specially interested. He seemed to have found it, for he cried out: 'What is this list of posts to which outsiders can be appointed? It has all the posts which matter. Most of these must be taken out.' Taking up a red pencil he began to score through the list. I could hear his pencil scratching because he very angry and showed that by the vigour of his strokes. The young Councillors, who had extended the list, looked on in suppressed rage, but knowing Dr Roy dared not object. But the cheeky young one was not easily intimidated. He cried out to Dr Roy from the opposite end of the table: 'Sir, we know very well from where this tenderness for the departmental candidate comes.' Dr Roy cast a look of utter contempt at him and shouted back: 'S—, do not shout. I also know a few things.' Everybody knew what a tongue and, besides, what information about the motives of the Councillors he had, and even the cheeky little Councillor had to accept the scoring through.

Then Dr Roy took up the rule about overqualified candidates and said: 'This too must go. If I can get M AS on forty rupees, why should we not take them?' This rule also went down the drain. I had no *locus standi* there and could not say that we should not do that for three good reasons: the overqualified candidates would not stick to their stop-gap jobs and never give value for money; fathers would be put to the expense of four years of additional university education for jobs which would not be a good return on the investment; and the degrees of Calcutta University, already depreciated, would be further degraded. But since Sarat Babu would not mention this, Dr Roy had his way.

I came to know afterwards what the row about the question of departmental *vs.* outside candidates was due to. It was connected with an imminent vacancy in a very lucrative post. Sir Stuart Hogg Market, off the Chowringhee, was the most important and profitable municipal market in Calcutta, for it served the local British community and also Bengalis of the highest stations. Besides provisions of the best sort, it had shops for luxury goods of every kind from England. Its superintendent had enormous perquisites and received the best meat, vegetables, and fruit free every day, and could order any finery he or his womenfolk wanted, and get them as presents.

This most profitable post was falling vacant on the retirement of the incumbent. Dr Roy wanted a Bengali who was already Superintendent of the Cornwallis Street Market, the second market in importance, but confined to Bengali customers, to be raised to the higher post. This was well-known, but it was at this that the cheeky Councillor hinted when he taunted Dr Roy for his championship of departmental candidates. There were many other aspirants for this golden fleece.

But in fairness to the Councillors I must add that they were not sinning deliberately or knowingly in practising favouritism and nepotism. They did not believe that there were superior or inferior abilities. I argued the point with them and others many times. They simply told me: 'What is this rigmarole about aptitudes, special skills or experience? Put any man on the chair of a particular functionary, and the chair by itself will make him do what is wanted.' Another maxim of theirs was: 'Even a wooden cat catches mice.' So they argued that their live kittens or kittens-in-law would do better than dummy cats. All Hindus, and indeed all Orientals, believe in hereditary right, and regard kinship as the best tide to preferment.

But besides nepotism, I also heard of bribery in securing jobs in the Corporation. At times the bribers did not get the jobs nor refunds. I have to relate a very pathetic case of this. One day, when I had come home, my wife told me that the young wife of an official of the Corporation had called on her, because she felt too ashamed to see me or Sarat Babu herself She wanted my wife to tell me about her case, and make me secure redress for a grievious wrong. Her story was that her husband had been promised promotion in consideration of a large contribution to a party fund, which he had paid to a well-known leader. She mentioned the sum as three thousand rupees. They had raised the money by mortgaging her gold ornaments, but the husband had not got the job. She said that at least the money should be refunded. She had stretched out her arms to my wife saying: 'Look, I have nothing on my wrists except these conchshell bangles, and nothing round my neck. Make your husband do something for me for pity's sake.' I was aghast, but quite helpless. The circumstances were such that a refund was impossible, and I could not even substantiate the case so as to represent it to Sarat Babu.

Corruption in the Calcutta Corporation, so tragic in certain cases, became such a low farce in certain others that one could not work up indignation over it even by trying, and had to laugh out with unpardonable flippancy. As it happened, I had to hear of such a case in my official capacity as secretary to Sarat Bose, and of all persons in connexion with an old acquaintance of mine for whom I had great respect. He was a Muslim of Pathan descent, educated from childhood in England. His father was a very wealthy businessman, but he did nothing but live on his father although he was,middle-aged, and had made matters worse in the worldly way by becoming a Gandhian, wearing the Muslim costume in Khadi. His name was Badruddin Khan.

After becoming Sarat Boss's secretary I lost touch with him, but one day, in 1939 to the best of my recollection, I saw him walking into my office in Woodbum Park, and saying to me: 'Brother Nirad, can you recognize me?' That was how he addressed me even in English. I, of course, welcomed him, and asked him about himself He said that his father was dead, and so he had to do something for a living, not wanting to live on his brothers. I asked him what he was doing, and he replied: 'I am going to tell you, and I am in trouble over that.' 'What is it.?' I asked. 'You know what "assessment" is?' Of course, I knew and said that it was the assessment of the rates of the Calcutta Corporation to be paid by a house-owner. 'That's what it is. And when a houseowner is dissatisfied with his assessment, he wants it reduced, and he comes to me, for I came to have close relations with Congressmen, politicians and Councillors when I was in the Congress. I speak to them, and normally succeed in getting the rates considerably reduced. All of them then give me the amount of one year's reduction, of which I keep half, and give the other half to the Councillor or Councillors. That gives me a fair income.' 'What a marvellous way of having an income,' I observed without malice, because it was the cleverness of it which overwhelmed me. 'But', he went on, 'for once I was foolish, and am in trouble for it. I very foolishly introduced one houseowner to the Councillor, and the Councillor himself took all the money, and would not give me my half-share. Do you think you can speak to Sarat Bose about this, so that as President of the Congress Municipal Association he could make the fellow give me my proper dues?' I smiled blandly and replied: 'I do not really think it would be right for Mr

Bose to mediate in such a matter.' 'You think so?' he replied, 'then I'll not bother you.' And he went away. I had come to admire him for his unworldliness, but I could not anticipate that the Congress could also make such a man acquire its special worldliness, and that in so naive a way.

But I heard about far worse practises. Not to make a mystery of them, they were demands for sexual favours from the wives or daughters of the officials in order to grant promotions. In the light of what has become common in the West in such matters, I do not think that what I shall relate will seem very shocking. But India at that time was not the West. Our society was a very puritanical one and also very secretive about lapses which undoubtedly occurred. So what I heard did impress me. It seemed that no story, however extravagant, appeared incredible to the good bourgeoisie of Calcutta. The following story may have been apocryphal, but the mere fact that it was circulating would show what the ratepayers of Calcutta were ready to believe about their Councillors.

The story was this. A clever official of the Corporation had discovered the weakness of the Councillors for the wives of their employees, and was resolved to exploit it. Thus he persuaded a respectable-looking courtesan of Calcutta to act as his wife in a house specially rented for her, and gave that as his address to the Corporation. He himself lived very virtuously with his wedded wife in another house, and when a Councillor wanted the favours of his wife, he sent him to his *ad hoc* wife to be delighted by a perfect acting of shocked candour.

However, it was the Chief Executive Officer himself who had the worst reputation in this respect, and his blasé looks seemed to lend colour to it. Like many elderly rakes, he was said to have outgrown professional women and adulterous mature wives, but sought young unmarried and unsophisticated girls or young wives, who, in spite of being married, had remained in what he regarded as a state of novitiate. They were recruited from the poor middle class, and it was said that there were procurers for him who were given sinecures. I knew at least one of the men to whom this role was attributed. He *did* hold a substantial sinecure in the Corporation. I do not think the old roué died *in flagrante delicto* in one of his bouts like a French President, but hearing about him I thought he deserved only that sort of death in his bed.

One case provided, not by him, but by the Councillors I am forced to believe because it was reported to me by the husband himself, who refused to oblige and suffered for it. He was a Bengali engineer, an expert in a very specialized field of engineering, with no one who knew the work better than himself in India. He had held a very highly paid post in a very advanced Western country, and was married to a European woman. Unfortunately, in his student days he had been a revolutionary, and so when he came back to India for a visit, thinking it was safe, his passport was forfeited by the wretched British administration. Stranded, he had been compelled to accept a post on only Rs. 100 a month in the Corporation and that, too, was temporary and had to be renewed every six months. He often came to see me about the extension of his service. He told me a shocking story of his plight. He said that the Chief Engineer had offered him a permanent job on Rs. 500 a month, provided he either gave him his plans or certified that the present machines and methods were the best and most economical. It was well known that the Chief Engineer was paid large sums as retainers by the British dealers in coal, plants and machinery. The expert refused to do either, and so had to come every six months to be retained in his miserable job.

Then he added a still more shocking sequel to his story. Despairing of the Chief Engineer, he tried to get some Councillors interested, and they were ready to offer help on condition. They had heard of his White wife, and wanted a concession on that score. This also he refused. I left Calcutta after that and never learned what happened to him in the end.

I also came to know that a new field for *menus plaisirs* of that kind had been found by the Councillors among the large number of young women who were employed as teachers in the newly opened primary schools of the Calcutta Corporation. These women came from poor but educated middle class families, which were compelled to supplement their income by sending out their wives or daughters to work. They had a new kind of elegance which titillated the Calcutta gently, who were traditionally given to womanizing among the buxom professionals of the city. A majority of the teachers were honest, but there were black sheep, and I myself heard of some. They made the others vulnerable, and such harassment may have been more common than was publicized. I came to know of one case which shocked me.

One morning, when I was sitting in my office, a young woman rushed into the room with wild eyes, foaming at the mouth, and scarcely able to stand. Her hair was dishevelled, clothes disturbed, and the front of her blouse was torn. She told me in hardly intelligible words that she had gone to a nearby house to see a Congressman about her job in a school, and the man had shut her up in a room and tried to violate her. Somehow she had freed herself after a struggle, and, she added, had come running to Sarat Babu's house. 'Look at my condition,' she cried, pointing to her clothes. I was aghast. But I did not know what to think. I knew the man she accused, and could hardly believe it of him. But there was no doubt that she had gone through some terrifying experience, and there could be no question of play-acting. Her manner made that supposition impossible, and in any case there was no motive. She did not pursue the affair, and had obviously confided in me from extreme fear and shock. I implored her to be calm and told her not to expose herself in such a manner in future. She seemed to be recalled to herself after that and left quietly, never to come again.

I could go on relating more of my experiences, unusual or characteristic, according to how I or others look at them. But I think I have set down enough to show why I came to regard 'government of the people, by the people, and for the people' in India as the greater, and British rule as the lesser, evil of the two.

The knowledge of Indians in power that the Councillors of Calcutta Corporation and other men in public life gave me was one gain from my work with Sarat Bose in addition to those I have already mentioned. But I do not think they realised they were providing me with anti-democratic data. They had so much confidence in their own cleverness, were so intoxicated with power, that they never suspected that I had within me a closed-circuit TV equipment recording their sayings and doings. Or, to fall back on an earlier image, they never had sufficient intelligence to say to me:

> Either I mistake your shape and making quite.
> Or else you are that shrewd and knavish sprite
> Call'd Robin Goodfellow ...'

But, taking note of their attitudes to me, I could say even then that they –

> 'Sometime for threefoot stool mistake me;
> Then slip I from their bum, down topple they.'

CHAPTER 4
Gandhi-Bose Feud

Subhas Bose was accepted by Mahatma Gandhi as the prospective President of the Indian National Congress for 1938 in the autumn of 1937, and was formally installed in his office in the following spring at Haripura. As between the Boses and Gandhi, these months presented a situation which was often seen in English social life. A formidable nobleman, who had firmly refused to consider a young man outside his caste as the lover and future husband of his daughter, suddenly gives in and consents to the marriage, and he does this with a grandiloquent gesture which makes his surrender look like benevolence. The young man on his part overflows with gratitude and all proper feelings. Two instances of such compliance come readily to my mind - one from fiction and the other from real life. In Trollope's *The Duke's Children*, the Duke of Omnium (Plantagenet Palliser) consents to a marriage between his daughter Lady Mary and the commoner Frank Tregear, and in life the Duke of Rudand allows his daughter Lady Diana to marry the commoner Alfred Duff Cooper. Such was Gandhi's endorsement of Subhas Bose's presidentship of the Congress.

For Subhas Bose and his brother Sarat Bose these months were a period of fervid pre-marital honeymoon. They showed something like tender filial piety towards Gandhi. I watched the display with some amusement, remembering the longstanding and notorious antipathy between the sides. The joy of the Boses was not lessened by the chagrin they saw in the Bengali faction opposed to them.*

The marriage did take place in due time, but not to result in living happily ever afterwards. The repulsion which existed between Gandhi and Subhas Bose reasserted itself even as early as the middle of 1938 and soured the tenure of presidentship for Bose. This mutual antipathy, known to everybody, had a long history. On Bose's side it had made its appearance after his very first meeting with Gandhi, when in 1921 he decided to join the nationalist movement instead of taking up the post in the highest cadre

* In Bengali society success gives very littie satisfaction unless it causes mortification to enemies and rivals.

of the British Indian bureaucracy for which he was selected in England. He was then openly contemptuous of Gandhi. But after the death of C. R. Das in 1925, when he came to be regarded as the foremost representative of Bengal in the nationalist movement, he could not air the same lofty disdain, and had at least to keep up appearances. But no real intimacy and cooperation between him and Gandhi ever developed, as was the case between Gandhi and the still more anglicized Nehru. For over sixteen years Subhas Bose presented himself as an alternative and foil to Gandhi and they remained side by side in the nationalist movement like the tiger and the elephant in the jungle, for just as Bose could not overlook Gandhi's national and international stature, Gandhi too could not disregard the status of Bengal in the nationalist movement and that of her representative. This kind of symbiosis, achieved only through leaving each other well alone, seemed to be coming to an end with Gandhi's support for Bose. At last Bose was to be drawn into the main stream of the movement led by Gandhi. He was, for a short spell; but the two fell out very soon.

This was inevitable, because the collaboration was basically unnatural. Even from the middle of 1938 Mahatma Gandhi began to disapprove of Bose's management of Congress affairs, and his close associates gave expression to his dissatisfaction. The suspended antipathy between the two reasserted itself, and became both active and embittered with its renewal. This led to an open clash at the end of 1938, when the question of a new President for the Congress in 1939 came up. That finally resulted in a defeat for Bose, and he had to leave the Congress permanently. The break was fatal for Bose, and very injurious to Bengal. It led to his miserable death in 1945, brought about a greater estrangement between Bengal and India, and finally completed the eclipse of Bengal in Indian politics.

Yet the story of this significant quarrel has not been told fully, especially in its personal aspect which was the most revealing. Nor has its historical importance been brought out. One or two of the participants have given their versions, largely as apologia, and some of the correspondence has been published. Yet a good deal remains unknown; and, besides, the approach to the dispute has been partisan and not historical. As it happens, I can write .about it from first-hand knowledge. I had exceptional opportunities to watch the development, course, and consequences of the quarrel, and can describe what happened on the strength of documentary evidence as well as my recollections, because at the time I was secretary to

Sarat Bose, and not only saw all the correspondence between the parties concerned but also drafted some of it on behalf on Sarat Bose. In view of the importance of the incident and its deplorable consequences I shall set down what I know in this chapter.

To begin with, I shall give the general background of the relations between Subhas Bose and Gandhi, from which it will be seen that the final outcome was almost predestined. No two men could be more unlike in social affiliation, upbringing, character, temperament, opinions, and behaviour. As Gandhi's are well known I shall not particularize them, but only describe what Subhas Bose's traits were. In the first place, he was a Bengali gentleman and had that gentleman's class-consciousness, and with that a low opinion of the trading class to which Gandhi belonged; over and above, he had the Bengali gentleman's contempt for the proletarian which Gandhi had become by choice.* Next, Bose not only had the Westernized Indian's impatience with an attitude of mind which was anti-intellectual, and naive even in its ethics; he also had the modern highly educated Bengali's intellectual arrogance, which in every case became hypertrophied by an Oxford or Cambridge education. Thirdly, Bose was not only a nationalist of the Bengali stamp, but a Bengali revolutionary as well. This revolutionary type was nurtured on Italian, Russian and Irish doctrines and methods of revolution, and was prone to think in terms of militaristic as well as terroristic violence. Lastly, there was a definite Hindu streak in Bose's dislike for Gandhi, although he was in no sense a bigoted or even orthodox Hindu. But he had grown up in the first two decades of the twentieth century in Bengal, where, owing to the influence of Bankim Chandra Chatterji and Swami Vivekananda, there was a fusion of religion and nationalism, so that the nationalist feeling had a pronounced Hindu complexion and Hinduism a pronounced political character. Thus the neo-Hinduism of that era, being a part of Bengali nationalism, influenced Bose.

It not only made even highly educated Bengalis subject to old Hindu superstitions, but also gave them a sectarian prejudice derived from a traditional dichotomy in Bengali religious and social life. In their sectarian

* The Bengali gentleman's appellation for common people was *bajé lok* - i.e. useless, worthless, dispensable people. This was particularly used when he had to feed his tenants and others at weddings and festivals. His guests were classified into *bhadralok* and *bajé lok*, i.e. gentlefolk and insignificant folk.

affiliation, Bengali Hindus were divided between two cults, namely, that of Vishnu in the form of Krishna, which professed non-violence; and that of the Mother Goddess Durga, which extolled power and was militaristic. The adherents of Krishna were called Vaishnavas and the worshippers of the Mother Goddess, Saktas, which by itself means votaries of power. The worshippers of the Mother Goddess therefore always looked down upon the adherents of the non-violent sect as cowards. As this sectarian division very largely corresponded to the class division between the gentry and the tradesmen, the Vaishnavites got a double amount of contempt from the gentry, who were mostly Sakta - the tradesmen being Vaishnava.

As Gandhi was both a tradesman by caste and class, and a Vaishnava in addition, he would naturally be identified as regards his personality with a Bengali Vaishnava tradesman.* Subhas Bose could not perhaps have taken this view of Gandhi consciously, but the prejudice was so old and deep-seated that it was bound to be present subconsciously. I have heard typical Bengali nationalists call Gandhi *napumsaka*, a word which has no exact English equivalent, but means, literally, a man who is born without virility, and, figuratively, a feeble and ineffectual person, a dud in fact. Even more outrageously abusive language was used by the Bengalis about him.

As if these contrasts in personality and outlook were not enough to create the personal repulsion between Gandhi and Bose, equally strong ones were provided by the historical evolution of the Indian nationalist movement. The two men stood for wholly different forms of the nationalist movement, and the great paradox was that the younger man, even when only in his twenties, stood for a form which was already obsolescent, and the other man, nearly thirty years his senior, was the leader of the form which was of the present and future. Bose represented the European nationalism which had appeared in India at the end of the nineteenth century, and as a nationalist he was its product. He had even gone forward to adopt its most extreme revolutionary form, as I have indicated. It also had a special social affiliation in India. This nationalism was that of the new middle class created in India by British rule and Western education, and geographically it was the nationalism of the peripheral provinces of India, e.g. Bengal, Madras, and Bombay, with a partial extension in the Punjab. Mahatma

*Study of philosophy at Cambridge may also have made a European contribution to Bose's contempt for the Christianized Vaishnavism of Gandhi. I saw the works of Nietzsche in English translation on his shelves.

Gandhi's nationalism was the new version of the xenophobia of the Hindu masses moralized by Vaishnavism and Christianity. It appealed to these masses, and, above all, to the Hindu-speaking masses of the Gangetic plain. After this nationalism had emerged there could be no room for the nationalism of the Western type, although historically the form of Gandhi's nationalism was retrogressive. Nevertheless, Bose's influence remained strong among the intelligentsia.

In Bengal he had a retrospective glamour. He was the leader Bengal needed in 1905 during the Swadeshi Movement, and did not find in the aged Surendranath Banaerjea, nor in the younger Aurobindo Ghose. In 1921 he was the political Vivekananda born too late. If at that time India had been anything like Italy or Germany Subhas Bose would have been the Indian counterpart of Mussolini or Hitler. In his way, he had the making of both in him, and, curiously, Mussolini's traits were as marked in him as those of Hitler. But he was not born among their people nor did he have their opportunity. As it was, if Bose wanted to play a prominent part in the nationalist movement he had to secure the backing and patronage of Gandhi.

The only powerful nationalist leader who could have helped Bose in his clash with Gandhi was Jawaharlal Nehru. Both were young and Westernized. Both were educated at Cambridge. They also belonged to the same social class, i.e. the professional. Bose's father was a successful lawyer as was Nehru's.* They emerged as political figures almost at the same time, and could be regarded as the Dioscuri of the nationalist movement, working together within the same kind of nationalism. There was indeed a difference: Nehru was Socialistic and Bose Fascistic. But that did not have the same significance in India as it had in Europe. So long as opposition to British rule was offered with equal ferocity, the Indian people did not care what European complexion it had. It must not be forgotten that in the Thirties the Indian intelligentsia was as pro-Soviet as it was pro-Nazi or pro-Fascist, without feeling inconsistent.

But the two were not destined to work together. Gandhi came between them, and so a man divided those whom history should have united. Nehru had deliberately suppressed his opinions and preferences to become a follower of Gandhi, because he was convinced that the Indian nationalist

* It might be added that in regard to wealth both the fathers were self-made men, having started poor.

movement could not do without Gandhi if it had to get rid of British rule, and that was the supreme task of the moment. His socialistic ideas could keep, as indeed they did, of course until they were wholly *madérisé*.

Nonetheless, the relationship between Gandhi and Nehru was the strangest, as well as a dubious, paradox in the nationalist movement. The same antithesis of character, outlook, and behaviour, which prevented any collaboration between Gandhi and Bose should have operated between him and the even more anglicized Nehru. That it did not was due on Nehru's part to a suppression of his personal views, which was wholly sincere. But Gandhi's support for Nehru was not. Its very fulsomeness made it suspect to all intelligent observers. The collaboration seemed and was, in fact, wholly opportunistic, so far as Gandhi was concerned. It was due to calculation. But at the same time Gandhi's simplicity of character, which made him even more tortuous than the worst crook, made him only as wily a calculator as is an amoral wild animal.

Gandhi felt rather than knew that his own power of command and his appeal were limited to a certain section of the Indian people, the largest indeed but not such as could make him indifferent to the support of the section to which he could not by himself appeal. Even among those on whom his power was complete and unrivalled, that is, the Indian masses, his hold had its incompleteness. He commanded their veneration by means of his reputation as a holy man, but he could not rouse them to action except through their xenophobia. Yet the non-violence and abjuration of hatred on which he insisted as a holy man partially lessened his power as their xenophobic avatar. To make up for that attenuation of his own power he needed supporters whose hatred would not be so qualified. Both Nehru and Bose could supply that hatred of British rule. But Bose would not be pliant and became even some sort of a rival. So, for supplying the positive hatred called for by the masses, Gandhi needed Nehru. He needed him even more to work on the intelligentsia, who could not be roused or activated without political hatred of the Western type. Gandhi did not have it himself, and so he adopted Nehru, who rested on his Master's bosom like the Beloved Disciple.

However, so long as Bose did not openly revolt against Gandhi, the latter could not treat him ungraciously. It was already felt that in spite of Bose's sacrifices and sufferings the highest formal honour in the nationalist movement, i.e. the presidentship of the Congress, had been too long withheld from him. This had become even glaring when in 1937 Bose came back to India after his long exile, and when Nehru had been president for two successive terms. Thus the honour was conferred on Bose.

But it was more a gesture than a reality. Very soon friction made its appearance. Mahatma Gandhi did not indeed allow his basic aversion to Bose to appear, but it was always behind the complaints about the details of Bose's management of Congress affairs in which the maladjustment manifested itself publicly. Political co-operation and married life are on a par: from an unbrushed hat Sherlock Holmes deduced that the wearer's wife did not love him.

These complaints were many. The first complaint was that Bose neglected all-India politics for those of Bengal, and more especially that he remained too immersed in the affairs of the Calcutta Corporation, whose reputation for honesty and loyalty to the Congress was of the worst. Yet Bose would not give up his obsession, because it arose out of his very conception of revolutionary politics. His knowledge of the French and Russian Revolutions had made him regard a big city and its proletariat and student population as the most effective instrument of a revolution. Calcutta was the first corporate body in British India to pass under complete Indian control, and in point of wealth and population was almost like a small Indian province. In giving more attention to the Calcutta Corporation than to Congress affairs, Bose was in theory preferring practical power to agitational scope.

But the Calcutta Corporation itself had nothing revolutionary about it, and, as I have shown, it was not even an efficient or honest civic body. This justified the complaints of Gandhi and his followers. But Bose, as long as he remained in India, allowed this Old Man of the Sea with all his abominations to sit on his shoulders. Even at the height of his quarrel with Gandhi, when he was also gravely ill, he could not forget the Corporation, and he wrote about two of its Councillors (between whom I saw nothing to choose) from his sick bed to Sarat Bose on 4 April 1939: 'I have been thinking of the Corporation affairs. I am afraid Indu [Bhushan Beed] has been playing false - doublecrossing one of us at a time. Sudhir [Roy Chaudhuri] is more straight and sincere, I am glad to say.' All this, when the most urgent business for him was to come to an understanding with Mahatma Gandhi. No infatuation could be worse.

Furthermore, the Gandhians complained of Bose's inefficient business methods, and of the laxness in the offices of the Bengal Congress. This, too, was perfectly justified. Bose had no method in anything, while Gandhi's business acumen and efficiency were almost legendary. In spite of being a Hindu holy man, or rather because he was one, he saw no merit in being unbusinesslike. He also remained the methodical Gujarati Bania that he was by birth. Besides, Gandhi's trusted followers in the central Congress organization were very efficient. They began to spread the idea that Bose was no practical man.

Over and above, Gandhi's disapproval extended beyond Bose's methods to his principles and policies, over which, throughout 1938, they aired their differences. I have already described the disagreement in regard to the Bengal Ministry which reached an acrimonious level by the end of 1938. No less acrimonious was their disagreement over the general principles and policies to be followed by the Congress. Gandhi did not mince his words about them, and in his last letter on the Bengal situation he also referred to the wider disagreements. It was written on 22 December 1938 and in it Gandhi said:

'Since this letter is by way of caution, let me utter one more caution which is really overdue. I do not like your constant threats about Federation and ultimatum. You have said, quite forcefully, that so far as the Congress is concerned, Federation is dead. The idea of ultimatum is in my opinion premature. But here again it is the voice of a dying man that speaks and therefore it need not have any value if your innermost being says that the fight to a finish is coming much sooner than most people expect.'

Then came a flourish which everybody inside or outside the Congress would have recognized, had they seen the passage, as Mahatma Gandhi's familiar means of coercion and ultimate weapon against all those who opposed him. Bose had hinted that Gandhi was trying to impose his own views dictatorially, and written: 'I shall beg you to permit me to relieve myself of my present responsibilities at an early date for I cannot be a party to a policy which I believe to be harmful to the national interest.' Gandhi rebuked Bose for this petulant outburst and wrote: 'Your concluding sentence should have had no place in your letter. Nothing that I may say can possibly be allowed to deflect you from the course that you think is best in the interest of the country.' Then he explained the spirit in which he gave his advice:

'Let me give you this assurance that whenever you feel that my speech or my writing is an unwarranted interference you have but to say the word and you will find that there will be neither speech nor pen with reference to such matters as you may think should be tabooed. For responsibility is not mine but yours for shaping the national destiny. Therefore, when I cannot help, I must at least refrain from hindering you.'

From Gandhi this kind of language was like a threat of excommunication from a Pope like Innocent III. All this would show that the issue of the Presidentship was only the peg on which the basic opposition between the two men hung.

Nehru was placed in a very difficult and invidious situation by this clash. He had no alternative but to go with Gandhi, but he also knew that, if he did, his motives were bound to be misunderstood and attributed to jealousy or rivalry. Actually, this was done even.by Bose. When the quarrel was at its height (28 March 1939) he wrote to Nehru: 'I find that for some time past you have developed a tremendous dislike for me. I say this because I find that you take up enthusiastically every point against me; what could be said in my favour, you ignore.'

This was very unfair. But Nehru was so sure of himself that he remained unruffled by all such accusations and dealt with them in the most dignified manner. After the defeat of Bose there was a correspondence full of recriminations between the parties. In one letter to Sarat Bose written on 7 April 1939 Nehru fully explained his attitude and his actions. He felt called upon to do so not only because Sarat Bose had written to him about what happened at Tripuri, but also because Subhas Bose had directly accused him of being the principal agent of his persecution. As Nehru wrote: 'Subhas in a recent letter to me stated that it was his impression that I was at the back of all the agitation against him before, during, and after Tripuri.' He was shocked by that, but he would not keep the discussion on the personal plane. He knew what was really at the bottom of the clash and wrote: 'It matters little where I come in the picture. We have to consider bigger problems of vast import and there can be no doubt that behind the seemingly personal controversy there are impersonal conflicts.' So he dealt with them.

He said that during the two years of his Presidentship, and one of Bose's, i.e. over three years in all, he had suffered much agony of spirit, because during this period he had to come to certain decisions which amounted to suppressing himself, which he said was not a pleasant process for him. This became more acute with the clash over the Presidentship. He had been in Europe before that and on his return was compelled to face it. After considering it in the perspective of the three previous years, he came to the conclusion that Subhas Bose's election would unleash certain tendencies and conflicts which would injure the country. This, he said, was 'an impersonal conclusion taken in view of the then existing situation.'

He explained further that he was not for unity at any price, but, at that particular moment, he felt that disunity in the Congress would be dangerous. He found that it was not possible for Subhas Bose to function as President for another year with the co-operation of Mahatma Gandhi. Even for him, he said frankly, working with Gandhi was difficult, in spite of his long and close contact with him. For Subhas Bose, he pointed out, there were no such intimate contacts and understanding of each other. In fact, he frankly declared, there was a good deal of suspicion and distrust of each other. But, this he emphasized, had nothing to do with the merits or demerits of individuals. What Nehru did *not* say was that he was sacrificing himself and suppressing his own opinions for the sake of Gandhi, which Bose would not do. After this explanation, no person with detachment could fail to recognize the personal disinterestedness of Nehru.

Whatever might be the position of Nehru, Subhas Bose had made up his mind. He was not prepared to suppress himself for Gandhi, and he resolved to contest the election in spite of Gandhi's disapproval. And he won. Gandhi frankly declared that the defeat was his and not of his candidate only. The majority of votes by which Bose secured his victory was not large: he won 1,580 votes to his rival's 1,375. But the mere fact that anybody could win in a matter which concerned die Congress against die opposition of Gandhi was the achievement of Bose. At that time no body could even imagine such a thing.

But many accidentals had disturbed the tonality of the Congress. For one thing, in any election, whether for government, municipal affairs or Congress, the Indian electorates would vote to satisfy their emotions and not to endorse any practical course, and Bose was serving the hotter curry. Secondly, there always were a number of doctrinaire Leftist and splinter groups in the nationalist movement. These were generally ranged against Gandhi, and would combine in any negative gesture of disapproval. There was, besides, the appeal of Bose to the intelligentsia of the peripheral provinces.

But Bose had reckoned without his host. His strength lay in his emotional personal appeal, and his weakness in the institutional and organizational sphere. The establishment of the Congress was under and with Gandhi, and whatever Gandhi might say publicly, his followers were all experienced and resolute men, and they were determined that Bose would not get away with his election victory.

As it was, Subhas Bose was never very skilful in party management. Over and above, he provided a handy weapon to his enemies by an indiscretion of his. Before his election he tried to score a point against the Gandhians by suggesting that they were less anti-British than he was. This he did in a press statement in which he hinted that the so-called Rightists in the Congress had entered into a secret understanding with the British administration to accept and work the Federal provisions of the Government of India Act of 1935, which had been totally rejected by the Congress. This statement was issued in the characteristic Subhas Bose manner, that is, hurriedly and impulsively, and without consultation with his brother Sarat Bose, who learned about it only the next morning from his newspaper. He at once told me that Subhas had committed a mistake. He did indeed add that what Subhas had said was true, but there was no proof. Sarat Babu was very worried about the consequences of the statement.

His forebodings proved to be well-founded. The old leaders who formed the Working Committee of the Congress at once raised a clamour that a most serious aspersion had been cast upon them. They called for its withdrawal and expected an apology. Their attitude was one of scandalization that such an absurd charge could be brought against them. Perhaps there-was more calculation than sincerity in this exhibition of moral indignation, for the Gandhians could hardly have wished for a stronger weapon to attack Bose. It became clear that a collision between Bose and the members of the Working Committee was inevitable.

Nehru was again faced with a very difficult and unpleasant situation. This he sensed, especially in its personal aspect, as soon as the result of the election was announced. Two or three days later he had a meeting with Bose, and begged him to clear up the situation. Again, on 4 February 1939, he wrote a long letter to Subhas Bose in which for the second time he asked Bose to do so. He felt that so far as Subhas Bose was concerned political issues were involved in the dispute. There was, he said, too much vague talk of Left and Right, which threw no light on the situation. Above all, Nehru dwelt on the personal aspect. He wrote:

'Public affairs involve principles and policies. They also involve an understanding of each other and faith in the bona fides of colleagues. If this understanding and faith are lacking, it is very difficult to co-operate with advantage. As I have grown in years I have come to attach more and more importance to this faith and understanding between colleagues. What am I to do with the finest principles if I do not have confidence in the person concerned? The party rivalries in many provinces illustrate this and we find extreme bitterness and often an utter lack of scruple among people who are ordinarily honourable and straight. I cannot stomach this kind of politics and I have kept absolutely aloof from them for these many years. I function individually without any group or any second person to support me, although I am happy enough to possess the confidence of many. I feel that this provincial deterioration is now being transferred or extended to the all-India plane. This is a matter of the most serious concern to me.

'So we come to this: behind political problems, there are psychological problems,and these are always more difficult to handle. The only way to do so is perfect frankness with each other and I hope therefore that all of us will be perfectly frank.'

Unfortunately, Nehru found that just at dial juncture Subhas Bose had neither the time nor the inclination to clarify the political and personal issues. Even so, Nehru did not desist from giving his advice. Soon after, when Bose was going to Wardha to see Mahatma Gandhi, Nehru begged him again to deal with the personal aspect as die allegations he had made in his statements were a serious matter and could not be left where they were. Bose's subsequent explanations, Nehru thought, had not improved matters at all. Bose promised to Nehru that he would discuss the differences with Gandhi: But Nehru learned afterwards that Bose did not even mention die subject to Gandhi.

Thus the dispute took its inexorable course towards an open conflict between the two sides at the forthcoming general session of the Congress to be held at Tripuri (a fancy name for a rustic site near Jubbalpur in the

Central Provinces of India) at the beginning of March 1939. As it happened, Subhas Bose fell seriously ill before that, and was strongly advised by his physicians not to undergo the strain of the session. The older Congress leaders were ready to put off the session until Bose had recovered and was fit to attend. But Bose would not agree, and he went. The result was that he became even more seriously ill and could attend the session only on the first day, being carried there on a stretcher. For the rest of the session he remained confined to bed, and the respected Muslim member of the Working Committee, Maulana Abul Kalam Azad, conducted the proceedings.

That did not mean that Bose could escape all that was unpleasant in that session. His followers carried tales to him of the intrigues against him, and repeated to him what, they said, they had heard being said against him, This made him even more ill.

Subhas Bose had behind him a long record of illness. Even from his early twenties he had been delicate. More than once he fell ill in jail, and was at last released by the British administration on the understanding that ha would leave India and remain in Europe for treatment. It was only in 1937 that he came back.

The reason behind his illnesses was as much psychological as physiological. Although he had contracted tuberculosis, he did not look delicate or hectic. Looking at him, nobody could suspect any physical disability. Instead of having a heightened glow, his face, and his eyes more especially, were tranquil and steady, and he always had a pleasant smile on his face in ordinary social intercourse. In short, he looked neither like a fanatical revolutionary nor like a youth predestined to die young because God loved him. But since he often fell ill and had to undergo prolonged medical, treatment, he drew to himself all the tenderness which physical frailness earns for young men.

His inherent constitutional fragility always broke to the surface when he had to remain inactive, or was in any way thwarted and frustrated. With any compulsory restraint on his freedom of action, he showed consumptive symptoms. Such a baffling situation had developed even within days of his victory in the election. Its exhilaration began to evaporate. He found that he could not run the Congress in his way because he did not have behind him a united, loyal, and efficient body of followers. Those who had supported him were themselves divided, and, what was more, they all began to demand their price for having made common cause with him. It was useless to expect that he could build a non-Gandhian Congress with them.

On the other hand, he had every reason to fear non-co-operation, if not active hostility, from the experienced Gandhian leaders. In this dilemma he turned to Gandhi, who, even though defeated by him, had deprecated vindictiveness against him and even conceded patriotism to him, making a generous concession in a public statement: 'After all,' he said, 'Subhas Babu is not an enemy of his country.' It seems Bose was encouraged by this and made a public statement in which among other things he declared: 'It will be always my aim and object to try and win his [Mahatma Gandhi's] confidence for the simple reason that it will be a tragedy for me if I succeeded in winning the confidence of other people but failed to win the confidence of India's greatest man.' He met Gandhi after this and even came away with the impression that he would have the co-operation of Gandhi.

Nonetheless, whatever tacit or explicit assurance he might have got from Gandhi, the Gandhians were resolved not to have anything to do with Subhas Bose. In fact, they seemed bent on persecuting him for his aspersions on them. They demanded a retraction and an apology not only for Bose's offence against them, but also for the disrespectful remarks he had made about Gandhi in his book *The Indian Struggle*, published in England in 1935. (It was proscribed in India by the British administration and was not seen in India before 1938.*) As neither was offered by Bose, the Gandhians resigned as a body from the Working Committee on 22 February. It was understood that they would never work with or under Bose. Bose was cornered, and must have realized even then that he was at bay, and this must have brought on his illness.

Thus, when the Congress session opened at Tripuri, what was bound to happen happened. Both Sarat Bose and Subhas Bose went to Tripuri with a large band of followers. I did not go with them and did not see what I happened myself. But I heard enough from those who did, and, above all, I saw all the recriminatory correspondence which followed the defeat of Subhas Bose, in which the Bose brothers poured out their grievances with extreme bitterness. From all that I could form a very vivid impression of the scenes at the session.

* I, however, have a vague recollection of having seen the book before 1938. Possibly, I saw it In Sarat Babu's house. He must have received a copy.

The main item before the assembly was an elaborate resolution which was in effect a censure on Subhas Bose and an injunction on him to work as President only with die agreement of Gandhi. In its wording the resolution was colourless. Even so it gave rise to acrimonious debates. But mat was the least unpleasant part of what happened at Tripuri. The most nauseating feature was the gossip, often slanderous and always mischievous, which busy tongues emitted in the camp. This was due to the distrust and suspicion between the rival parties, which everyone noticed and afterwards admitted. Some of the followers of the Boses made themselves intelligence agents and carried tales to their leaders about what was being said about them by the Gandhians. A good deal of that must have been invention, but even when true the stories lost nothing in telling. What was more important, the Boses believed them implicitly. The accounts I heard gave me the impression that the tract of the Central Indian jungle which for the time being had been converted into the Congress camp, buzzed like a meat market with bluebottles descending in swarms on putrescent carcases. The stench could be inhaled even in the correspondence.

Mahatma Gandhi himself was not present at the session. Whether by design or not, he found that he had important business to attend to in the princely state of westernmost India in which he was born and where the business required his presence. Jawaharlal Nehru, too, kept aloof from the discord as far as he could, and participated in the debate only when he fell compelled to do so. He deliberately shut his ears to all gossip. Even so, when on one occasion he was speaking, the followers of Bose tried to shout him down.

Certainly, whatever open obstreperousness was seen at the session was die work of die Bose faction. The Gandhians knew their strength and kept cool, and could afford to do so. In a letter to Sarat Bose, Nehru described what he had to face, and that gives a correct idea of the behaviour of the two sides. As he wrote:

'My intervention in the open Congress was merely to act as die mouthpiece of the acting President [Maulana Abul Kalam Azad, who would speak only in Urdu] and explain in English die procedure that was to be followed. For some reason or other some delegates did not want me to speak at all, although they did not know what I was going to say, and there was the organised obstruction by diem, which you saw. I felt that it would be improper for me to retire or give in to this obstruction of a few delegates when nearly a hundred thousand delegates and visitors, who observed die most remarkable calm and discipline, wanted to hear me. So, I held on for an hour and a half. I must confess that I lost my temper for a few seconds when I told you that this was hooliganism and fascist behaviour. I was telling you about this and not die audience, although some of my words might have carried on the microphone. I am sorry I lost my temper but you will no doubt realize that die strain on me was considerable.'

However, the followers of Bose were no match for die Gandhian old guard, who were seasoned party, managers. Even if Subhas Bose had not been ill and unable to attend die session, he would certainly have been outmanoeuvred. Sarat Bose who was looking after his interests had no capability in that line at all. The Gandhians played their hand coolly, as well as resolutely. Their resolution required that the full session of the Congress should assert its confidence in die Working Committee for what it had done during Subhas Bose's tenure of the presidentship in 1938 and regret that any aspersion should have been cast on diem. Furthermore, die resolution asked the delegates to declare die indispensability of Mahatma Gandhi and direct Subhas Bose to nominate a Working Committee 'in accordance with die wishes of Gandhiji'. In simple words, a Canossa was to be inflicted on Subhas Bose.

Nevertheless, from their position of strength, the Gandhians made a generous gesture to Bose. They said that in view of Bose's illness, they were ready to put off die resolution for consideration by die All-India Congress Committee, which was to meet in Calcutta later. But Bose did not want this concession. He wished for a final decision then and there. It would seem that he had already become convinced that there was no chance of victory for him. Thus die resolution as drafted by the Gandhians was adopted by the delegates, and even some of Bose's Leftist allies voted for it.

Subhas Bose left the Congress defeated, but he did not come back to Calcutta, his place of residence; he went for recovery and convalescence to a place on the borders of Bengal and Bihar, where one of his brothers worked. There he remained for some weeks, but carried on die quarrel by correspondence.

Sarat Bose returned to his house in Calcutta, looking worn out and haggard. I could see what he had gone through for the sake of his brother.

His courtiers did everything they could to foster his sense of grievance and self-pity. I observed the spectacle with some amusement, not unmixed with disgust. I have already described what I saw of the general behaviour of the courtiers, and now I was to see a more heightened and particular exhibition of it. A wealthy and well-known man of Calcutta, older than Sarat Babu, but very obsequious to him, called on him the very morning he returned from Tripuri. He was sitting as usual at his table in the verandah with the earlier arrivals facing him. The wealthy courtier almost ran up to him, halted, and then threw up his arms in a startled gesture like Robinson Crusoe's when he saw the footprints in the sand. Then he pointed to Sarat Babu's face with an outstretched hand and exclaimed: 'What is it that I am seeing! Just what was always flashing before my eyes when I read the news of Tripuri! How you must have suffered, Sir!' After he had offered more of his condolences, but in a more restrained manner, he whispered: 'Sir, that matter is coming up before the Services Committee today. A word from you will do.' He had a candidate for a post in the Calcutta Corporation and the appointment was going to be made that day. So, immediate support was needed from Sarat Babu. Sarat Babu turned to me and asked me to get ready a letter to the Chairman of the Services Committee.

Sarat Babu was very tired himself, and was also very anxious on his brother's account. I could not guess what the next move of the brothers might be. There seemed to be an air of indecision as if they did not see very clearly before them. Obviously, the defeat inflicted by the resolution adopted at Tripuri was accepted, and there did not seem to be any intention to defy the Congress by refusing to abide by it, and to go their own way. Soon it became evident that Subhas Bose would seek Mahatma Gandhi's intercession to remain in the Congress honourably. Actually, he suggested a meeting with Gandhi to his brother, as he himself could not go to Delhi where Gandhi was staying. He even telegraphed to Gandhi on 15 March before getting any reply from Sarat Babu. In it he informed Gandhi: 'Sarat may meet you Delhi this weekend. He will inform you if he can. In that case please await his arrival.'

But Sarat Bose did not go. What prevented him was astrology, which, as everybody knows, has become today the obbligato of the political cacophony in India. Sarat Babu did not feel sure about the intentions and attitude of Gandhi and therefore could not judge what chance of success he had. So, he consulted the priest, Guru, and augur of his family, who was also a professor at Calcutta University. As a result of that, he telegraphed to Subhas Bose on 16 March: 'Ashoknath [Sastri] strongly advises meeting Gandhiji after fifth April. Meeting earlier fruitless. Meantime do not get perturbed or take precipitate action but co-operate with doctors for complete recovery.'

Upon receiving this telegram Subhas Bose gave up the idea of an immediate meeting, but as he had already prepared Gandhi for it, he asked his brother to inform him by telegraph so that he could proceed on his journey. Thus the chances of a settlement by means of a frank discussion with Gandhi were thrown away.

Nonetheless, even in their exhausted state the Boses began a long correspondence with Gandhi and Nehru, pouring out all the bitterness of their heart in it. Sarat Bose accused every one of Gandhi's leading followers of intriguing against his brother and treating him with heartless cruelty. He said that they had insinuated that Subhas Bose's illness was not genuine and he was only malingering in order to draw sympathy. He accused one of the Gandhians of having abused Subhas Bose in coarse language. Even against Maulana Abul Kalam Azad, he put forward the charge that he had conducted the proceedings of the session with partiality. Furthermore, Sarat Babu repeated all the gossip he had heard, and also accused the Congress Ministers of bringing 'material pressure' to bear on the election as well as at Tripuri.

Subhas Bose accused Nehru of being the principal instigator of his persecution. Nothing could be more lacking in dignity and moderation in the Boses than this way of taking their defeat. It seemed as if the Boses had neither the boldness to defy Gandhi and try to assert their power on the Congress nor the manliness to accept defeat without rancour.

But the strangest part of the correspondence with Gandhi was the pretence it throughout maintained that in the eyes of the Boses Gandhi himself was above all these bickerings and had nothing to do with the persecution of Subhas Bose. They wrote to him as if he were the constitutional English monarch who could do no wrong, and even if something wrong were done in his name, that was the doing of his advisers. On the other hand, in regard to redress they appealed to him as if he were the autocratic Louis XIV who could overrule his ministers. The Boses did not even hint at Gandhi's involvement in the dispute, but appealed to him as if to an impartial court of justice. Yet Subhas Bose knew the truth very well, and in private described Gandhi as the real source of his persecution.

Mahatma Gandhi, on his part, fell in with this constitutional fiction. In his replies he showed no sign that he had anything to gain or lose in the quarrel. His speciality was his extraordinary ability to pursue his rancour without any sense of guilt and to sugarcoat it with an unctuous benignity. Thus, even in his letter of 27 December in which he had threatened Bose with excommunication, he did not overlook Bose's sore throat to which he had referred, and concluded with a wish for a quick recovery. In every letter he admonished Subhas to exert his will to get well and in one letter be wrote: 'In all you do, be guided by God,' and added: 'Do get well quickly by obeying the doctors.'

Thus, on getting the very bitter letter of complaint from Sarat Bose, Mahatma Gandhi wrote on 23 March 1939:

'My dear Sarat,

'Your letter makes me sad. I have shown it to the Sardar [Vallabh Bhai Patel] and Kripalani and asked them to give me their reaction. I am on the train taking me to the Maulana who wants me and who is too disabled to come to Delhi. I am going to show it to him and Jawaharlal also and ask them to let me have their reaction. You shall have their statements.

'With so much that you have to say against your erstwhile colleagues and they against you both, how can I act, what can I do.' Do you know that I have no official notice of the resolution.' I have not even seen the full text. But even if I had official notice, what could I do so long as this terrible mutual distrust lasts.

'I therefore suggest either a meeting of all of you so that you can pour out your hearts to one another and come to an understanding or if the poison has sunk too deep to be eradicated, I suggest Subhas's - when he is restored to health - telling them that he cannot work with the old Working Committee and that therefore he should be relieved of the command or be left a free hand to choose his own cabinet... You say I had said to Subhas that I would advise the Sardar and others not to obstruct Subhas. I did say so to Sardar. The Sardar when he read your letter flatly denied that there was any obstruction on the part of his old colleagues. On the contrary, he says there was every attempt made to smooth Subhas's way.'

Mahatma Gandhi closed die letter expressing his concern about Sarat Babu's illness and wishing for his recovery, and to the typewritten letter he added in his own hand: 'I have assumed that your letter represents Subhas's sentiments also.'

Apart from those whom he mentioned in his letter Mahatma Gandhi showed Sarat Babu's letter to Bhulabhai Desai as well. Patel, Kripalani, and Desai sent their explanations to Mahatma Gandhi. Nehru and Maulana Abul Kalam Azad wrote directly to Sarat Babu. Gandhi sent the explanations of the first three in the originals (with the signatures of the writers) to Sarat Babu, with a covering letter containing his advice, written in his own hand.

Upon reading the three statements of Patel, Desai, and Kripalani I got a feeling that they were not wholly displeased at Sarat Babu's complaint. In any case, they took up the challenge with gusto and made their explanations not only lengthy but also very lofty. In every way, Sarat Babu had invited this display of superiority. His letter had shown not only a lack of self- restraint but also a surprising degree of credulousness to gossip, which as an able lawyer he should have been free from. I might set down here the joke about him among his friends. They said that Saraswati, the goddess of wisdom (ffi Pallas Athene), forsook him as soon as he left the High Court of Calcutta.

They rejected categorically every charge which Sarat Babu had brought against them. But it was not so much the substance of their statements as their preambles which gave them their victory in the argument. All of them took a very high line, and pretended to show more understanding than anger at the attacks, which as victors they could do. I shall quote the more ' important passages, taking the writers one by one. Vallabh Bhai Patel's explanation was dated 25 March, which he introduced with these remarks:

'I have read Sarat Babu's letter with surprise and sorrow. It pains me to find that he could use such language and attribute such personal motive and charges against his erstwhile colleagues with whom he happened to differ in politics and thereby bring down the entire Congress politics to its lowest possible level where differences of principle and policy have no place whatever. It would be easy to answer the letter in the same strain but it would be of no advantage to anybody to imitate the tone and temper of the letter which is evidently written more in anger than in reason. After all what answer can one give to such passionate and abusive denunciation? He has charged the old members of the Working Committee with their having carried on malicious and vindictive propaganda against the Rashtrapati. We can only repudiate this charge as none of us carried on any propaganda against him. I am sure there is no real foundation for Sarat Babu's statements in this connection.'

Then followed the detailed rebuttal. Bhulabhai Desai's statement was also very long and not less lofty. It was also dated 25 March and it began:

'My dear Bapu,

'I am thankful to you for giving me a copy of letter dated the 21st March 1939 addressed to you by Sarat Babu and thus giving me an opportunity of answering the allegations made in it directly and indirectly against me and my colleagues.

'I regret the tone, language, insinuations, and the charges contained in that letter, and I may be allowed to say that the charges and language such as these are calculated to affect adversely the possibility of mutual respect and mutual confidence, without which association in public life loses all its value.'

There was in Sarat Babu's letter a specific accusation against Desai - that he had called Subhas Bose a rascal. Referring to it, Desai wrote: 'I wish to deny emphatically and unequivocally that I ever committed the atrocious offence of describing the Rashtrapati or Sarat Babu by the term which Sarat Babu has referred to in his letter and I regret that such things should be invented in order to malign me or the group to which I belong.'

I knew the story very well, for the person who reported the abusive term to Sarat Babu also told it to me. He was a nephew of the Boses and he said he was standing in the hostile camp and, as nobody knew him in the group in which Desai was also sitting, they were speaking freely, and he distincdy heard Desai calling the Boses rascals. He must have said the same thing to his uncle as well, but it was very naive of Sarat Babu to have accepted the story and repeated it to Gandhi.

Desai was not less lofty in rubbing in his point, and he continued:

'Even the strain Sarat Babu has undergone cannot be an excuse for writing the letter he has done and I am certain that if he considers the matter in cooler moments, he will regret having done so. In any case, I wish to assure you that I never entertained any feeling of personal enmity or hatred either against him or Subhas Babu. Whatever difference there was and there is between us is one concerning policies and methods in public life and for that I claim the same freedom, without offending him, as he claims for himself.'

And Desai went on to say: 'I may be allowed to say that the course of events at Tripuri was undoubtedly not much to the liking either of Sarat Babu or Subhas Babu and I am sorry that they have resulted in embittering their feelings for no justifiable reason.'

J. B. Kripalani was the last to send his statement. He did so on 29 March 1939. He began:

'It is difficult to answer a letter full of passionate and abusive denunciation. The charges against us are not quite clear. Sarat Babu writes of "the mean, malicious and vindictive propaganda" carried on against Subhas Babu by Mahatmaji's "Chosen disciples". Evidendy he refers to those ex-members of the Working Committee who were against Subhas Babu's re-election. If this is so, we repudiate the charge.'

Kripalani was, however, the cleverest among those whom the Boses regarded as their persecutors, and he also had a sense of humour which could enjoy digs even at himself Once he congratulated Sarat Babu on the style of a letter which was very self-consciously satirical. I have to confess that all of it was of my composition. But Kripalani's sense of humour was not free from a streak of malice, and he did not fail to show it in his statement, as will be seen from the following extract:

'It is true that in the heated atmosphere of Tripuri all sorts of rumours were afloat, and busybodies that wanted to win favour with the President and his party might have put in our mouths uncomplimentary remarks. We on our side heard many uncomplimentary remarks made against us. If we were to give credence to all that was reported to have been said against us, we would have cause to feel more bitter than Sarat Babu. We would not however on that account feel justified in using the language he has used against us.'

Kripalani concluded by saying: 'We feel that no impartial observer could have blamed us for our share in what happened at Tripuri. On the other hand, everything possible was done to malign us and lower our prestige.'

Some of the letters also contained the most fervently expressed wishes for Sarat Babu's recovery, as well as Subhas's, from the illness brought on both by Tripuri. But that did not make it easier for Sarat Babu to accept the statements.

Jawaharlal Nehru's reaction to Sarat Babu's letter was sorrowful but more sincerely sympathetic. They were of the same age and had greater intimacy with each other. He wrote on 24 March from Allahabad:

'Gandhiji arrived here this morning to see Maulana Azad and he showed me your letter to him dated 21 March. I have read this with sorrow and surprise. There are, as we all know, differences of opinion amongst leading Congressmen on matters of policy and programme and we have often given expression to our respective viewpoints, although we have succeeded in pulling together. Generally speaking, Gandhiji's programme has been followed by the Congress and his leadership accepted. Personally I do not see any harm in such differences, provided the common link remains and we act in unison. They are signs of vitality in our movement. But your letter hardly refers to any question of policy or programme. It deals with personalities and brings serious charges against particular individuals. This brings the argument to a lower level and it is obvious that if such opinions are held by any individual or group against another, mutual cooperation in a common task becomes impossible. I do not know how far your letter represents Subhas's views on the subject. In any event, it is obvious that the personal questions you have raised, unless cleared up, offer a barrier to any effective co-operation.'

Maulana Abul Kalam Azad also replied in a very courteous and sympathetic manner, but at the same time he was firm in rebutting the charges against him, going into each specifically.

When forwarding the statements of Patel and Bhulabhai Desai with a covering letter in his own hand, as I have said, Mahatma Gandhi expressed the definite opinion that in view of them Sarat Babu should withdraw his charges. He wrote: 'If you accept their repudiation, you will perhaps admit that you have been hasty in judging your colleagues. This distrust must go, if it is at all possible. Political differences may remain, will remain perhaps. But why bitterness. I do not accuse you or anybody ... PS I hope you are better if not entirely recouped.'

Neither the statements nor the admonition of Gandhi had any effect on Sarat Babu. He would stick to his guns, and he replied to Gandhi on 5 April 1939:

'What I wrote on the 21st March was in deep sorrow. But I felt I owed it to you to tell you what I saw and heard from unimpeachable sources at Tripuri and the impressions I formed ... I shall only add that the statements you have been good enough to forward to me have failed to convince me that I was wrong. I say so with deep regret, but I would be untrue to myself if I did not say so.'

Even to Maulana Azad's courteous letter he replied as follows: 'I have read your explanations very carefully. But without meaning the slightest disrespect to you, I would maintain that my criticism of the conduct of the proceedings of the Congress at Tripuri was justified.'

One would say that even if Sarat Babu was unconvinced, this was not the most proper and wise way to reply. But he was not engaged in a political manoeuvre, he was ventilating his anger, and angry people are not wise. However, in replying as he did, Sarat Babu was not being merely himself, but a typical Bengali. In writing to Gandhi he should have phrased his adherence to truth differently and said that if he was convinced he would not have been true to his *Bengali* self. No Bengali, when he is in trouble or is suffering through his own .mistakes or wrongdoing, will admit that he himself has contributed to his predicament. He would go on obstinately maintaining that others have maliciously and cruelly inflicted suffering on him. To admit responsibility would be for him to deprive himself of the greatest of his emotional enjoyments, which is nursing grievance and self- pity. This I have seen all my life in personal and national life.

After this, there could be no reconciliation between the parties. It would seem that even before receiving Sarat Babu's letter Gandhi had come to the conclusion (apparently from a letter of Subhas Bose's), that the break-up was inevitable, for on 2 April 1939, he sent the following telegram to him:

'Rashtrapati [President] Subhas Chandra Bose Jealgora
'Posted full reply your letter stop my advice therein irrespective of Pandit Pant resolution and in view diametrically opposite views held by two schools of thought you should forthwith form your own Cabinet fully representing your policy stop you should frame and publish your policy and

programme and submit same to A . I. C. C. stop if you secure majority you should be enabled to carry out your policy unhampered stop if you don't secure majority you should resign and invite A . I. C. C. elect new president stop *given honesty and goodwill I do not fear civil war*. [Italics mine] Love Bapu.'

One wonders whether Mahatma Gandhi had assumed that there did exist honesty and goodwill on both sides. In any case, he accepted the possibility of an open conflict, a civil war within the Congress, as he put it.

None came or was even likely to come. The fight was knocked out of Subhas Bose. I was surprised by the indecision he showed. But perhaps he realized the weakness of his position and had already discovered that his popular appeal was of very little value in this quarrel. The Boses had made a clumsy and indiscreet attempt at reconciliation and failed, and, after this failure, appeared to have become resigned to defeat. Formally, the final step was left to the session of the All India Congress Committee to be held in Calcutta at the end of April. But there was no sign that Bose would offer even as much resistance as he had done at Tripuri. Finding that he could not carry the Committee with him, he resigned the presidentship at the beginning of May 1939.

At that time I felt very strongly about the treatment of Subhas Bose by Gandhi and his followers, and could not but regard it as vindictive - as their revenge on Bose for having defied Gandhi about the presidentship and made the defiance almost a crime by his victory. I also thought that Bose had been weak in yielding without offering a determined resistance. I took his side even though I was in no sense an adherent of his or admirer of his principles and methods. I had no doubt about his patriotism, and I also thought that the persecution to which he was subjected personally was an aspect of the rejection of Bengal's contribution to the nationalist movement. I learnt later that some of Bose's close followers also thought that he had not shown sufficient determination to seize the leadership of the Congress.

But their idea of offering resistance and mine were different. They thought that Bose should have accepted Gandhi's challenge and formed a Working Committee with the Leftists and run the Congress in his own way. I, on the other hand, thought Bose should have compelled Gandhi and the Gandhians to come to terms with him by threatening to take Bengal out of the Congress with him. But, in actual fact, Bose could follow neither course. His so-called radical followers were a heterogeneous collection of dissenters who had united only to oppose Gandhi. This rag-tag and bobtail would not have enabled him to run the Congress or the nationalist movement. As to my idea, politically conscious Bengalis were not ready to leave the Congress for the sake of Bose. When I spoke to some of them in this sense, they threw up their arms and exclaimed: 'What? Leave the Congress? That's inconceivable.' I explained that there would be no need to do so at all. Bengal was too important for the Congress for it to take the risk of alienating her: the Gandhians faced with the threat, I said, would come to a compromise with Bose.

But, of course, the reason why my view was unpractical was that Bose did not have that degree of power over the nationalist organization in Bengal which could enable him to hold out the threat I envisaged. In spite of his emotional hold on the Bengali intelligentsia he had no practical power. Even in Bengal Bose was weak. Although he controlled the provincial Congress office, he had, in the first place, against him the old faction which had always been opposed to him and which lay low only because it was risky to show opposition when he had the support of Gandhi and the All India Congress. Now their turn to secure the patronage of Gandhi had come.

Next, even among his close associates, many distrusted Bose's judgement and were not only half-hearted but inclined to sacrifice him in order to please Gandhi. Subhas Bose, on his part, remained suspicious even about those who were apparently on his side. One of his associates offered during die crisis to mediate, but this was refused. He wrote to his brother: 'It is no use having intermediaries in dealing with Mahatmaji. Please put him off - I do not want visitors here.' Even about his brother's deputy in the Congress Party in the Bengal legislature he wrote: 'Kironsankar wants to come and see me - why?' Obviously, Bose did not trust him.

Above all, Subhas Bose could not expect any effective practical support from the very thing which had given him his electoral victory over Gandhi, namely, his emotional hold on the intelligentsia. Even the Bengali intelligentsia could not have helped him, because their support, in spite of its sincerity, was too frothily sentimental for any practical purpose. In fact, the demonstrations which such supporters organized during the A I C C session were pitifully weak and ineffectual. The incapacity that Bose showed during the whole of his political career to create a party with a body of loyal and efficient men to back his ideological and emotional hold, about which I have written in the last chapter, harmed him in this final clash with the Gandhian Congress. He remained isolated, and with him Bengal, too, remained a creaking trailer behind the all-India nationalist movement.

In the following August, Subhas Bose launched a new party of his own, and gave it the name of Forward Bloc. That was, in India at all events, an unevocative name, but Bose may have chosen it from his knowledge of European politics. However, the dictionary meaning given to the word *bloc* perfectly fitted the character of the party: 'A combination of persons or interests, usually inharmonious, but temporarily drawn together in a common cause.' Naturally, this party, if not actually still-born, was at least a congenital cripple. It never walked on its legs, but appropriately for the Bengalis it has survived till today to testify to their feckless loyalty to Bose. Even the elder brother, Sarat Bose, did not follow his younger brother into the Cave of Adullam, but remained the leader of the Gandhian Congress Party in Bengal. From his cave Subhas Bose tried to attract everyone in distress, everyone in debt, and everyone who was discontented. Indeed, he did gather around himself' 'four hundred' men consisting of his close followers and a number of other nationalists who were disgruntled with the Gandhian leadership. But he did not prove to be a David.

I have described this quarrel in some detail on account of its historical importance, and I shall round off the narrative with my appraisal of the moral responsibility of the participants. The ease with which Bose was expelled from the Congress - and expulsion it was in spite of its formal character of resignation - was in itself an indication of the weakness of Subhas Bose, and I have given enough facts to make that obvious. So, I shall say nothing more on him and deal only with the others. What I have to say at the outset is that the same ease made the quarrel appear more squalid than cruel. But in the light of its final effect on Bose, it was cruel, and it has to be given its due status as a ruthless political feud.

Perhaps to call it that kind of feud is not to bring out the measure of its cruelty, for both historians and politicians shrug their shoulders and air some cynicism about the moral complexion of political vendettas. They have read in Halifax: 'State business is a cruel Trade: good nature is a Bungler in it.' But the treatment of Bose has to be seen differently because it was meted out within one nationalist movement, and nationalist movements are supposed to be above the moral lapses of mere politics. Besides, owing to Gandhi's leadership, Indian nationalism has acquired an almost sanctified character. Therefore no one has perceived that it, too, was as ridden with factional rivalries and ruthlessness as any nationalistic movement which went before it, e.g. the Greek, the Italian, or the Latin American. There should be no absolution for this exhibition of factionalism because it was Gandhian.

However, in the quarrel between Gandhi and Bose, the only man who did not become involved in its rancour or dishonour was Jawaharlal Nehru. In later years he did admit that he might have let down Bose. But his contemporary utterances leave no room for doubt that he acted honestly, honourably, and above all disinterestedly. He never allowed himself to be dragged into the squabble over the responsibility for the break. His dignity and restraint during the quarrel was in sad contrast with the excitability and peevishness exhibited by the Boses.

The Gandhians who took the most prominent part in driving out Bose were cruel in the consequence of their action, but not in their intention. They could say like the woman murderer in one of Agatha Christie's stories: 'I didn't want to kill her. I didn't want to kill anybody - I had to.' They could lay Bose's expulsion at the door of his good nature and bungling. Yet, in regard to him, they showed themselves to be as much political fighters as they were 'freedom fighters' vis-à-vis the British. After independence these leaders revealed their real personality, which was like that of the Russian politicians of the post-Stalin era, and not at all Stalinlike. They were after position and were no killers. Nonetheless, all of them were silent, husky, and dry men, with eyes of steel.

Gandhi's role in this quarrel has, however, to be seen in a different light. It has become a literary convention to employ the figure of speech 'Grey Eminence' to describe an unseen but decisive personal influence on historical events. The phrase should be changed to 'Black Eminence' in considering Gandhi's part in the persecution of Bose. His affectation of unctuous benevolence towards Subhas Bose makes his role appear almost sinister. He was always speaking of his helplessness in the face of the terrible distrust between the Boses and his own followers, and never even hinted at his own ineradicable distrust of Bose, of which Nehru was perfectly aware. Patel and the others were only his agents. Gandhi was the real inspiration and moving spirit behind the persecution of Bose.

In nothing else have Western writers gone more wrong about Gandhi than in overlooking his insatiable love of power and implacability in its pursuit. In this he was in no way different from Stalin. Only, he did not have to kill because he could eliminate his opponents equally well by means of his non-violent Vaishnava method. (I need not repeat here that he was a devout Vaishnava.) A well-known Bengali tale illustrates non-violence as practised by the Vaishnavas. One day a renowned Vaishnava, who was passing near some men who were about to kill another man, their enemy, stopped in horror and cried out: 'Hold, hold! Don't kill a Creature of Krishna *(Krishner jeev)*!' 'What then should we do?' asked the men. The Vaishnava replied: 'Tie him up in a sack and throw the sack into the river.' This, according to the Vaishnavas, was not killing, but the non-violent way of getting rid of enemies. This was done. In like manner, Gandhi had Bose put into a sack and thrown into a river. Bose succeeded in breaking out of the sack, but his swimming strength was insufficient for him to attain either bank of India's river of politics. He was carried downstream, out to sea, eventually to reach foreign shores - only to die. Trotsky was murdered in Mexico, Bose was killed in an air crash on Formosa. Their modes of death were different, but the end was the same: a necessity in both cases for the man in power.

The subsequent behaviour of Bose's Bengali worshippers has been all of a piece with their character. They did not make any effort to help or save him, but made Gandhi and his followers responsible for his tragic end in order to have vicarious emotional enjoyment. They now maintain it was Subhas Bose and not Gandhi who won political independence for India from the British. Bose's real historical position is, of course, different. He is the rejected nationalist leader of India like other leaders of this kind, e.g. Mazzini, Kossuth or Draza Mihajlovic. Considering the worship of Bose by his fellow-Bengalis today, I have a feeling that they would have been more grateful to him if he had been killed like Mihajlovic. Since he was not, they only gloat over the unrealized possibility for the sake of emotional enjoyment. When Bose was killed in the air crash the Bengalis did not believe it. They said he was living and engaged in religious meditation in some Himalayan cave. When I asked some of those who would cling to this belief, why he did not return to India after independence to serve his people and country, I got the reply that in that case the Congressites would have had him murdered. The most grotesque thing about this explanation is not that the Bengalis believe it, but that, *faute de mieux*, i.e. the actual murder, the belief in its possibility enables them to aggravate their sense of injury against Gandhi.

BOOK VII

INDIA ENJOYS THE WAR

1939-1941

Prefatory Note

When the war broke out in September 1939, Indian politics, which were the same thing as nationalist agitation, were at a very low ebb, being in one of their cyclical troughs. The excitement of the quarrel between the Congress and Subhas Bose had died down, and the anti-British sentiment was quiescent. Of course, that did not mean it was non-existent. That could never happen. But it simmered underground. Its glow could be seen as a volcano's could be by looking down its crater, and a sulphurous smell was always in the air. Nonetheless, on the surface there was calm, and even a green landscape as on the slopes of a volcanic mountain. It was created by what I have described in the previous part of the book. The new Indian governments in the provinces were keeping people engaged in making money by offering opportunities on a very generous scale. They did not see any point in neglecting these to launch or join political agitation.

Subhas Bose tried to disturb this tranquillity by bringing in the international situation and exhorting people to take advantage of it to gain independence. But he did it largely to discredit the Congress. Therefore the Congress, too, had to react, which it did in its own way. Nevertheless, these attempts to raise nationalistic steam were like trying to grow crops out of season. But as soon as the war came there was a revival of political interest among the Indian people, although no resumption of political agitation.

The interest was shown in the typical manner of Indians. They had no stake in the war, and no intellectual, moral, or emotional involvement in the large human issues raised by it, and hardly any awareness of them. Their interest was wholly self-centred, for what they sought from the war was economic profit and nationalistic satisfaction at the same time. Even at its outset the war offered economic opportunities to Indians of all classes, from the rich economic entrepreneur to the humble labourer and peasant. Perhaps, most significantly, it created unprecedented employment for the intelligentsia and virtually put an end to its chronic ailment, 'educated unemployment', as it was called. Openings offered for writers and their likes were even greater, because they were needed for war propaganda.

Thus the very people who were stokers of political agitation were enlisted on the British side. The demand grew as the war went on, and there was no reluctance whatever among Indians to meet it. At the height of the war Indians of all classes found their easiest way of making money in practical co-operation with the British war effort.

On the other hand, patriotic sentiment, as it was understood among them, was fully satisfied by gloating on the reverses, defeats, and disasters inflicted on the British. They could do that without risking their worldly interests. In fact, there never was in the entire history of the nationalist movement as during the war years, such an opportunity to secure economic profit and patriotic satisfaction from the same set of circumstances. In what follows this will be illustrated in some detail.

As for myself, during the war I became and remained, except in birth, an Englishman. In my whole life I have been seized and possessed by political movements on three occasions: first, as a boy by the agitation against the partition of Bengal from 1905 to 1911; secondly, by the Gandhian movement of 1930; and, lastly, by the war. Of all these, it was the last whose hold was the strongest, and it has left a permanent legacy behind. At first, for me as for many other Indians, the war brought worldly advantage, although not through my own seeking. In the long run, however, it has harmed my worldly interests permanently. Yet this has not mattered for me. I have never regretted what I did during the war because I can say that it has made me a fuller *homo sapiens* than I was before, although all my life I have tried to remain one. In making me that, it has not taken away from me any particularity I may have had. I remain a Bengali, an Indian, an Englishman, while being a citizen of the world. I have not had to give up anything to become cosmopolitan. My cosmopolitanism is deeply rooted in all the particular soils – material or mental – on which I have grown.

I leave that to be judged by the facts of my life that I shall give, and not by my claim for it.

CHAPTER I

Coming of the War

I was not surprised by the outbreak of a general war in September 1939, because I had felt certain after the occupation of Czechoslovakia in March that the next act of aggression by Hitler, which could only be against Poland, would mean a war with Britain and France. Neville Chamberlain's pronouncements on that occasion left no room for doubt on that score in my mind, for no resentment is deeper than that of a simple man who is duped. But I was not sure when Hitler would strike next and what its scope would be.

Till Hider's Rhine adventure of 1936 I did not even envisage the possibility of a war like that of 1914-18.1 had become aware indeed, even as early as 1925 from an article by General J. H. Morgan in *The Quarterly*, of the disguised creation of a new German army. I also heard that the bureau for the historical study of the last war was really the old Great General Staff. 1 read the book, *Thoughts of a Soldier*, by the creator of the new army. General Von Seeckt, as soon as it was published in an English translation in 1930, and acquired a great respect for him. I also learned about the new naval build-up. In fact, the Western Press wrote so excitedly about the laying down of the future *Deutschland*, the 'pocket battleship' as it was called, that it was not possible for me with my interest in navies and sea power to remain ignorant about it. The Anglo-German naval agreement of June 1935 I found very puzzling because I had read a good deal about the Anglo-German naval rivalry before the war of 1914. But even then I did not think that Germany would repeat her gigantic gamble of 1914.1 took all this military enterprise on the part of Hitler as efforts to acquire what I would call 'military property', for the sake of restoring the national self- respect of the German people. But the reoccupation of the Rhineland awakened me to the probability of a general war when I saw that it was not prevented by France and Britain. Had it been, there would have been no second World War.

What I also sensed vaguely was that Hitler was seeking, not simply redress for the concrete acts of injustice to Germany embodied in the Versailles settlement, but revenge for the humiliating defeat of 1918 by

Stamping on the heads of her victorious enemies. In thinking of Hitler it would be a mistake not to remember the words of an old prophet: '*Sunt spiritus qui ad vindictam creati sunt*' – 'There are spirits which are created for vengeance'. I was seeing too many of these spirits in India not to be able to recognize the greater Manitou in Hitler. Gandhi himself saw a fellow-spirit in him. Even before France had accepted her defeat in 1940 formally, he wrote in his paper *Harijan*: 'They ["the Germans of future generations", as he described them] will honour Herr Hider as a genius, as a brave man, a matchless organizer and much more."*

He only regretted that Hider took recourse to war instead of practising non-violence. He thought of him as a Gandhi *manqué*. Therefore he also wrote: 'But I should hope that the Germans of the future will have learnt the art of discrimination even about their heroes.'

He asked: 'What will Hitler do with his victory? Can he digest so much power? Personally, he will go as empty-handed as his not very remote predecessor Alexander.'

No comment on this historical sermon is called for, and I pass on to describe the evolution of my thoughts. Till 1936 whatever misgivings I had over the weakness of British and French foreign policy arose from the failure of the two Governments to check the Japanese aggression in Manchuria and the Italian in Ethiopia. The feebleness shown by them to Mussolini's rape of Abyssinia made me very angry, and the Hoare-Laval proposals only added to my contempt for both Hoare and Baldwin which had been roused in me by the Government of India Act of 1935. Although Baldwin threw Hoare overboard, I set that down to Baldwin's opportunistic demagogy, not to principle.

In respect of Japan, there was a complete revision of attitude in me after the Manchurian affair. Like all Indians, I had acquired a wholehearted admiration for the Japanese people after the Russo-Japanese war, and I had always admired their realism, which they showed very markedly from 1920 onwards, especially under the direction of Japanese foreign policy by Baron Shidehara. I was compelled to abandon all that. The Manchurian affair also made me very sceptical about British foreign policy. I formed an impression that the British Foreign Office had become almost an apologist for Japan. This incident also made me lose all my respect for the League of Nations.

* *Harijan*, 22 June, 1940; Vol VIII, No. 19, p. 172

I think it is permissible to think that it was the success of Mussolini in Ethiopia which emboldened Hitler to reoccupy the Rhineland, which re- occupation, before the Ethiopian success, had seemed to the German General Staff like a dangerous gamble. The passivity of the Governments of Britain and France astonished me, and the conduct of the French seemed inexplicable. I knew the strength of feeling in France about the Rhine, for even at college I had read Sorel's exposition of *les limites naturelles* of France in his great work on die French Revolution. I had also been very much amused to read an account of the anger of Foch when his demand for fixing the eastern frontier of France on the Rhine was turned down at the Versailles Conference, and not even Clemenceau supported him. He left the conference table angrily, with Pichon running after him and trying to persuade him to come back and he replying: '*Jamais, jamais.*' In spite of being a francophile, I considered the demand absurd, but I thought France would at least enforce the demilitarization of the Rhineland. Coming in the wake of the French complaisance to Italy over Ethiopia, this fresh display of weakness created forebodings in my mind. In its turn Hitler's success on the Rhine put him definitely on the warpath.

As it happens, I can produce contemporaneous evidence of my disquiet over the international situation, particularly as it concerned Britain. I could see that British foreign policy had no clear sense of purpose and direction. I drew attention to it in connection with the problem of recruitment for Britain's armed forces which was then giving rise for concern. That was done in a letter to *The Statesman* of Calcutta and Delhi which I sent on 23 July 1936. I cannot remember now whether it was actually published or not, I have not checked that. But the publication of the letter is not material for my purpose because I am citing it to illustrate my view of the international situation.

I began the letter by drawing attention to the discussion of the problem of recruitment in Britain and the anxiety over its inadequacy. In regard to the anxiety I said:

'It would be hardly correct to say that there is any readiness among the nations of the world to assume a decline of the "old spirit of England". What is really to be wondered at is perhaps what is being done to appeal to that spirit. The Field Service Regulations might well say: "To develop morale in the people as a whole is an essential part of the policy of the nation." But, as it seems to many, the British Government is unable to carry out this policy because it cannot put a cause for which to fight before the British people, and a cause is really half the battle.'

I pointed out that in this failure was to be seen a striking contrast with what other European countries were doing:

'Perhaps this will be made clearer still by the example of France, Russia, Germany, and Italy. All these countries have simple and powerful motives for warlike preparations. The source of the military energy of France is the passion for keeping her soil inviolate, of Russia the security of the new regime, of Germany the redress of the injustice of the peace settlement, and of Italy the future of the Fascist polity. Whenever the British Government has been able to put before the people as simple and clear a case as any of these, the response has never been disappointing. This was seen in the New Armies of Kitchener, which were an image of all that was strong and youthful and idealistic in England. The recruiting posters of today on the contrary have grown a habit of offering only such inducements as seeing the world and football.'

I went on to say that the very nature of the British interests made her military effort weak, because 'it has to be recognized that the military effort of a people or rather Government interested simply in the maintenance of a status quo cannot be on the level of nations cramped or threatened by the same status quo.'

I concluded the letter by saying that in such circumstances 'it was useless to lay the blame for the paucity of recruits on the pacifists.' I said: 'The pacifists quite sincerely, though as I think wrongly, believe that the future belongs to them and to non-violence, *however dark might be the scene before* them.'

This last observation would show what view of the general international situation I was taking. But it was this very sincerity of the pacifistic sentiment which I found alarming. Its popularity and strength were even more alarming. It had an incredible callowness, and in an undergraduate expression, as the notorious resolution of the Oxford Union was, it was a form of puppyism, extravagant and ridiculous at the same time. But there was also fanaticism behind the pacifism, a continuation of which we are now seeing in the CND movement. This doctrinaire pacifism was one of the extreme offshoots of Christian morality, but the paradox was that while the other extreme offshoot of the same morality, that is, abstention from sexual relations as the supreme virtue, was abandoned, the pacifistic extremism had moral validity with a very large number of people, even with those who considered it as unpractical as giving up sexual intercourse.

In retrospect, one can see what mischief it did. If in the field of domestic politics it enabled Baldwin to get his majorities and thus remain in office, in the international sphere it led Hitler to believe that he could get away with any of his hyper-nationalistic moves by sabre-rattling. There has been some discussion whether the Oxford resolution encouraged Hitler in his aggression. This is very naïve. If the resolution had stood in isolation it could be totally ignored, but taken as a straw in the wind with many others it certainly could give an aggressor the idea that whatever the enormity of an aggression the mood of the British people would not permit it to be challenged by military force. What makes me reject pacifism even as a moral doctrine is that it is a feeble rebellion against human nature. Nothing that is impossible can be moral. On the other hand, it can become even immoral. That is also the reason for which all my life I have rejected the Gandhian doctrine of non-violence, which is only an extension to India of a Christian doctrine.

My disapproval of pacifism, however, was not simply on moral grounds. It was far stronger on the pragmatic or practical, or, to put it bluntly, on account of its utter ineffectiveness. The real emotion behind pacifism was and is fear of war, and there is no greater begetter of wars than this fear if it is allowed to make nations afraid to face wars. Ultimately, it really imposes war on them in the worst of circumstances. In the inter-war years that was precisely what did happen, and indeed that reaction was helped by an artistic presentation of the fear in the postwar novels about the war and also by a rationalization of it by representing wars as futile. The revival of Norman Angell's book *The Great Illusion*, published originally in 1910, was one sign of the anxiety to rationalize the fear.

All these books repelled me by their dangerously mistaken representation of war. Undoubtedly, they were a natural reaction to the horrors of trench warfare during the previous war, but that did not make them sound. The Third Law of Motion is applicable to the human mind as well, and if that could make the mind go forward like a jet aeroplane it could be allowed to operate. But, in actual fact, it makes the mind go backwards. In dealing with emotional reactions of the populace a maker of policy should rather take his cue from the artillery man who neutralizes the recoil by a buffer so that his piece might be effective. There can be no doubt that the widespread fear of war in those years was the main emotional force which made the second World War possible.

But if in Britain the pacifism based on fear was the harmful ambiance, there was also a positive attitude in the British ruling class and especially in those who shaped British foreign policy which was more practically injurious. I got a feeling that at this level there was a definite pro-Hitler bias, a dangerously complaisant, not merely complacent, attitude to Nazi Germany. I was led to notice this more particularly on account of my admiration for Churchill. I felt outraged by the attacks on him as a warmonger by writers and politicians of all parties.

There was one journal in which I found the most unequivocal animus against him. In order to keep abreast of aeronautical developments, from 1937 I began to subscribe to *The Aeroplane*, the weekly journal edited by C. G. Grey. Judging by what he wrote about Anglo-German relations he could be regarded as a disciple of Houston Stuart Chamberlain if not as a follower of Hitler himself. His idea of any Anglo-German conflict was that it was and would be a civil war and even a fratricidal war. He habitually questioned the figures of German air strength given by Churchill. On account of the prestige of this journal as a technical publication, I could not always dismiss its views on such questions. Even if I could ignore the views of so patently prejudiced a journal, I could not brush aside those of *The Times*, which then gave expression to a consensus in the British ruling order, which did not mean, of course, that it was sound. But psychological coercion by vogue is behind such mouthpieces.

Then there was the Foreign Office whose attitudes seemed to me to be for practical purposes heavily loaded in favour of the German and Italian dictators. This sprang from its very self-complacence. It made them think that foreign bounders and attitudinizers could never get the better of them, but on the contrary they could make them serve their ends because bounders were at bottom naive. The same complacent *gravitas* made them think that an English politician who showed excitability was a bounder without the naïveté. It should not be forgotten that the Foreign Office with its successive heads like Hoare and Halifax were critical of Churchill even in May 1940. Be that as it may, I became very distrustful of British foreign policy from 1931, and this distrust went on increasing till the end of 1938.

There came an opportunity in the early part of 1937 for me to air my views on international affairs publicly. I was asked by the Calcutta station of All India Radio to give regular talks on world affairs in Bengali for Bengali listeners. I began my broadcasts from the spring of that year. The connection thus established with AIR lasted till 1952. From 1939 I gave regular talks on the war, until they were made unnecessary in 1945, from when I again shifted to the discussion of world politics.

I can say that I was not badly prepared for them. From pure intellectual interest I had begun to study the history of the First World War and of the Versailles peace settlement from the early Twenties. I read all the important memoirs on that war, including of course Ludendorff's and Hindenburg's when these came out in English. Besides, I read Churchill's *World Crisis* and many technical histories. From 1937 I subscribed not only to *The Aeroplane* as I have mentioned, but also to other journals of aviation and besides, for many years, I regularly bought *Jane's All the World's Aircraft*. For naval matters, I bought Brassey's *Naval Annual*. Thus when the war began in 1939 I had a fair stock of information and ideas on military matters.

I paid equal attention to the political side. I had read Keynes's famous book on the Peace Conference even in 1920. After that for more serious study I read the volumes of Temperley's great work on the Versailles Conference and the peace settlement. I even read Stannard Baker's book on President Wilson when it came out. I also bought Colonel House's *Papers*.

Thus I was able to give to my Bengali listeners some idea of the realities of international politics and of the war, with what information they needed about the antecedents. Naturally, when the Munich episode came I had to speak on it, and I did so almost in Churchillian terms. I categorically stated that it had not secured peace in our time, but only put off a war for a little while. The amusing part of the story is that this commentary of mine was not allowed to be broadcast. All political scripts had to go to the Bengal Government as the local representative of the India Government, for approval, and the Publicity Officer of that Government suppressed my talk. And even more amusing was the fact that all Indian officials whether in the Central or Provincial Governments were as rabidly anti-British as any nationalist could be. But being impotent haters they had no difficulty in obeying the lines laid down for them by their British superiors. However, I had the opportunity to air my views by proxy. Sarat Babu asked me to prepare a speech for him on the Munich affair; I elaborated my talk for him and he delivered a very forthright speech.

The retrospect of my views on international questions is becoming long. But I have to make them clear, because they were the basis of all my talks on international affairs for fifteen years, and also because in my approach to world affairs I stood diametrically opposed to all my countrymen, even to Nehru. Generally speaking, in those years the Indian intelligentsia did not show any intellectual interest in what was happening in the outside world. They became curious only when any situation arose which would tickle their anti-British feeling. I, on the other hand, wanted to see through to the reality, without regard for my likes and dislikes.

My countrymen, however, saw everything through their likes and dislikes. Thus they were as ready to be pro-Hitler or pro-Mussolini as they were to be pro-Soviet. They saw no inconsistency in being equally partial to Nazism, Fascism, and Communism, because in all these regimes they found actual or potential hostility to Britain. Whatever was anti-British in the world appealed to them. Thus, at that time, they tended to be even pro-American, because they saw in the American people the most vocal enemies of imperialism. Their anti-British feeling sought elation from two sources: spectacles of discomfiture, checkmate and humiliation for Britain from any country, especially at the hands of the two dictators; but also in the opportunities that these gave for abusing the British Government for either treachery to the cause of freedom and democracy or collusion with Fascism and Nazism. If it is thought that all this was not very rational I would say that hatred has its reasons about which reason knows nothing.

But the views and feelings of the Indian intelligentsia as a whole were too inchoate and too vicarious to have any practical importance for Indo-British relations. And among a majority of the leaders of the nationalist movement, too, these were not much more precise. They were what might be called pure nationalists in the leadership. But among them there were two who were internationalists. They were quite vocal on what was happening in Europe. These two were Jawaharlal Nehru and Subhas Bose. Subhas Bose had lived in Europe, and most of the time in Vienna, from 1933 to 1937, and Nehru was visiting Europe and China from time to time.

Both kept themselves abreast of all developments in world affairs, and also tried to create some sort of a relationship between the Indian nationalist movement and the international situation, although each in his own way.

Nehru was a typical English Leftist in his general attitude to the Fascist and Nazi dictators. He was always talking about the deteriorating international situation without being very definite about what worried him. But in one part of his political consciousness there was no vagueness, and that was in his anti-British sentiment, which was unqualified and implacable. In fact, that was the main element in his nationalism, and it made him see in the British Government, even if not in the entire British people, except the British fellow-Leftists, accomplices of the dictators.

He exhibited this obsession in the most uncritical and impulsive way over the Spanish civil war. He was, of course, bound to be a partisan of the Republican side. That was no matter of surprise, but the manner in which he showed it was. In 1938 he went to Spain and met not only the Republican leaders, but also La Pasionaria. From this visit he formed some impressions of which he gave the benefit to the Marquis of Zetland whom he met in London. Lord Zetland, as Lord Ronaldshay, had been the Governor of Bengal from 1917 to 1921. At that time he was Secretary of State for India in the British Government. Nehru told him that there was very little popular backing for Franco among the Spanish people and that the civil war was kept going by foreign assistance. More especially, he thought that it was instigated by the British Government which also supported it, with France as their tool. In despair, Zedand wrote to Lord Linlithgow, the Viceroy of India: 'He clearly takes a biased view of the present situation in Europe and I do not think that any amount of reasoning would cause him to change his views.' That was only to recognise the self- evident truth about Nehru. Joan of Arc was inspired in her patriotism by the vision of the Virgin, but Nehru was both inspired and sustained in his by the apparition of Britain as the Evil One.

Subhas Bose, on the other hand, had temperamental leanings, towards the dictators. But if he looked to them for support in India's struggle for freedom that was not the reason. He knew very well that Hitler believed in the superiority of the White Man and also had admiration for the British people and the British Empire. Subhas Bose ignored all that because he held that the internal government of a country was no business of his and that India had to regulate her international affiliations in the light of her national interests alone. In both Hitler and Mussolini he saw enemies of Britain and therefore had no hesitation in seeking help from them. Actually, if that had suited his purpose he would have sought support of the Soviet Union with equal readiness.

At that time Subhas Bose was always talking about taking advantage of the international situation for India's profit, and he thought that, faced with the threat from Germany and also perhaps Italy and the Soviet Union, the British Government would be amenable to pressure from the Indian National Congress and, therefore, he wanted India's national demand to be presented formally to the Congress in the form of an ultimatum. As I have related, this rather irritated Nehru, and when even Sarat Bose wrote to him about the idea in April 1939, Nehru gave his opinion very frankly.

He wrote to Sarat Babu that he was not against ultimatums for they might be very necessary at times, but he thought India had outgrown that time, or at any rate should speak in somewhat different language at that juncture. He said that the essence of the situation was how strong and organized the Indian people were for a struggle. He pointed out that in the whole world the only thing which counted was strength and nothing else mattered much. He was of the opinion that an ultimatum on behalf of tiie Indian people would not add to their strength, but would on the contrary reflect more an agitational frame of mind. This, he was ready to concede, could be very good at times, but did not quite fit in the reality as it then was, so far as India was concerned. He, however, expressed his confidence that India was growing bigger and stronger and could really take what she wanted except for the fact that her strength was impaired by internal disunities.

All this was not only very sensible but also very manly. It showed his revulsion from theatrical gestures. But the realism and sobriety of Nehru's thinking disappeared whenever he thought of the British connection. Then he became a man of obsessions and impulses. Both Nehru and Bose were men of rigid prepossessions and *idées fixes*, and they were a danger to the nationalist movement because their ideas on world affairs were accepted as authoritative, and almost final, by the other nationalist leaders, who knew very little about them and were not even interested to know. Yet in 1939 the policy of the Indian National Congress could not be isolated from the international situation. The idea of war was in the air, and what position to take up in the event of a war in which India was bound to be dragged in by the British connection, was a practical matter of vital importance because the Congress was in power and in charge of actual administration in a majority of the Indian provinces.

But the risk to the Congress from Nehru and Bose came from different sides- from Nehru from the inside, and from Bose from the outside, because from 1939 Bose was not connected with the Congress. He was some sort of a Leader of the Opposition, and from that position he could force the Congress to take extreme positions which of its own will it would not have taken. Since the nationalist public of India had an innate preference for extremism, Bose in those months was always trying to outbid the Congress by accusing it of being inclined to accept the federal scheme of the Government of India Act of 1935, as also to be ready to cooperate with Britain in the event of a war in Europe. The Congress could not meet this campaign by Bose except by cutting the ground from under his feet by being equally extreme.

Thus, only three weeks before'the actual outbreak of the war, it took a thoughtless step. At a meeting of its Working Committee held from 9 to 12 August it adopted a resolution whose operative parts were as follows:

'The Congress has further clearly enunciated its policy in the event of war and declared its determination to oppose all attempts to impose a war on India. The Committee is bound by this policy of the Congress and will give effect to it so as to prevent the exploitation of Indian resources for imperialistic ends. The past policy of the British Government as well as the recent developments, demonstrate abundantly that this Government does not stand for freedom and. democracy and may at any time betray these ideals. India cannot associate herself with such a Government or be asked to give her resources-for democratic freedom which is denied to her and which is likely to be betrayed .. .The Committee further remind Provincial Governments to assist in no way the war preparations of the British Government and to keep in mind the policy laid down by the Congress, to which they must adhere. If the carrying out of this policy leads to the resignation or removal of the Congress ministries they must be prepared for this contingency.'

I remember that when I read the resolution at the time I was astonished by its uncompromising terms.* It committed the Congress to oppose any

* The immediate occasion for the resolution was the despatch of Indian troops to Egypt, Aden, and Singapore. The Indian legislature also protested. But it was well known for nearly twenty years the 4th Indian Division was meant for service aboard.

association with Britain in a war. It bore all the hallmarks of Nehru's mind and art – a mind given to projecting its obsessions on any reality when it was a question of dealing with Britain, and an art which delighted in giving elegant verbal embodiments to the obsessions. If Nehru had any perception of the real political situation he should have seen that the resolution would leave no alternative whatever to the Congress but abandonment of the substantial power it had in the provinces in the event of a war, for it was hardly likely that the British authorities would seek the consent of the Congress before making India a belligerent in any war.

From Nehru's personal point of view more especially, the resolution was very paradoxical. Among all the Congress leaders it was he who was most persistently critical of the British Government for appeasing Hitler and Mussolini and for betraying Czechoslovakia and Spain. He was also harping on Fascist aggression in Europe, Africa, and the Far East. He must have known that if Britain went to war with anybody it would be with these aggressors, i.e. with those whom he wanted her to fight. Yet she was not to have India's co-operation. It was even stranger that Gandhi and the other Congress leaders succumbed to the extremism of Nehru, because, being less under the influence of an obsessive hatred, they could have perceived the risk they were taking in adopting so drastic a resolution.

But the explanation for all this, even for Nehru's display of anti-British feeling, was that neither he nor the other leaders thought that a war was imminent, or that if it came Britain would join it. They could not have been wholly unaware of the aggressive intentions of Hider, but probably thought his next move would at its worst produce another Munich. Therefore, they saw no risk in offering as much extremism to nationalist opinion in India as Subhas Bose could, or perhaps more.

I soon discovered how unshakeable this disbelief in the possibility of Britain joining a general war was. It persisted even after the news of the pact between Germany and Soviet Union was received. In the afternoon of 22 August I was going to Sarat Bose's house in a tramcar. When it reached the comer where Park Street meets Chowringhee, I saw a news boy standing with a placard which read: Pact between Germany and Russia. It startled me, but I tried to shake off the feeling of disquiet. Nonetheless, I could not resist it and, to find out what exactly had happened, I got out at the next stop and bought a copy of the paper. The news was not very detailed, but it seemed ominous. Still, I would not admit the worst that arose in my mind.

In the evening Tridib Chaudhuri came to see me and, seeing the paper on the table, said that he had indeed come to ask me what I thought of the news. I tried even then to explain it away, but also said that if it was what it looked like there would be war.

But there could be no more running away from the reality for me the next morning, when the papers gave more details of the pact. Of course, there was no mention of the secret clauses which made it a collaboration between Germany and Russia for a new partition of Poland. Nonetheless, the mere fact of the mutual assurances of non-aggression was enough for me. I saw that the only thing which could deter Hider from a military adventure on a grand scale and which had always been a problem for the German General Staff, namely, the prospect of a war on two fronts, was removed. From that moment I began to declare there would be war within a week.

But nobody in Calcutta would believe me. I might say that this was also the view all over India. Two or three days later I was going to Sarat Babu's house with him from the High Court, and Suresh Majumdar was with us in the car. He suddenly turned to me and said: 'Nirad Babu, I hear you are saying that there will be war in seven days.' Before I could reply Sarat Babu answered for me: 'Yes, he is. But I do not believe him.'

There was one emotional compulsion behind this obstinate disbelief. That Britain would be either cowardly or treacherous was an idea which gave all nationalists in India great satisfaction, and they could not forego that. As it happened, in a public statement Subhas Bose, the second great authority on international affairs after Nehru, took the same view. It was published in the well-known Calcutta newspaper *Amritabazar Patrika* on the morning of 25 August 1939. It covered other political questions as well, but as regards the Russo-German Pact Bose said: 'The Russo-German Non-aggression Pact may help to ease the international tension for the time being and thereby postpone the outbreak of war. But the tension will continue, whether over Rumania or over the German demand for colonies or over some other problem.'

When I read this I was amazed at Hose's lack of perception. He had lived in central Europe for years and could not realize what the pact meant. He concluded his statement by reverting to his familiar exhortation to exploit the international situation to win political freedom for India. He wrote: 'The world crisis will therefore continue even if war does not break out during the next few days. In this fateful hour I appeal to all Congressmen, to all anti-imperialist organizations, and to all those individuals and organizations that are opposed to Federation, to join hands for winning Swaraj for India.'

Yet he did not think that the hour had actually come. It will be seen that his position was in no way different from that of Nehru.

The scepticism about Britain continued even after Poland had been attacked in force. The 2nd and 3rd of September were days of triumph over me for Sarat Babu. He often smiled at me, and employing his verbal trick of assigning to me all the things he disliked but suspected me of being partial to, said: '*Your* British would not fight.' In the late afternoon of Sunday, the 3rd, he was sitting with a large number of his friends, and when I came to see him he repeated the formula. Just at that moment the telephone rang and lifting the receiver I heard: 'This is Nazimuddin speaking, I wish to speak to Mr Bose.' It was the Home Minister in the Bengal Government. Sarat Babu listened for a minute or two and then laid down the receiver. He turned to me and said: 'Nirad Babu, you are right, Britain has declared war on Germany.' We got the information very quickly – within less than two hours of its announcement in London. Sarat Babu as Leader of the Opposition was entitled to have the information as promptly as possible. I did not triumph over him, of course. But I noticed that the smiles which were lighting up the faces of Sarat Babu's courtiers at his jokes at my expense faded away. And I wondered how people could be so bemused by their own prejudices as to be blind to reality to that extent.

CHAPTER 2
Watchful Expectation

The first news of any military clashes between Britain and Germany that we read was about the British air attack on German warships at Wilhelm- shaven and the sinking of the *Athenia.* The Indian reaction to the news was characteristic. Since the loss of five or six Blenheims was admitted it was taken for granted that many more were shot down. For one thing, Indians do not make what lawyers call 'admissions against' even in private life, and in public life these are inconceivable. So, they add to all such admissions, and in the case of British admissions it was natural that they would take them in the spirit of a dictum put by Kipling in the mouth of a wickedly wise bird about a rather disreputable animal: 'When the Jackal owns he is grey how black must the Jackal be!' As regards the sinking of the *Athenia*, even before the Germans had put out the report that it was done by the British, a young Bengali educated in England said to me that the ship must have been sunk by the British to embroil Germany with the United States.

I found other Bengalis inclined to take that view. My friend Amal Home ran into trouble over this. He was at that time editing the Sunday magazine section of the newspaper *Hindusthan Standard,* owned by Suresh Ma- jumdar. In it he began to include a feature to which he gave the heading 'Our War Survey', or some such tide. He gave the news of the sinking of the *Athenia* under the heading: 'German Kultur'. Another member of the paper's staff came to me in boiling rage and remarked that it was supposed to be 'our survey', and he asked: 'Was that how Indians looked at it." He could not imagine how Amal Home could be so blatantly pro-British in a nationalist newspaper.

Now, this sort of bias had benumbed our perception of the course of the first World War, and it was to be expected that after the falsification of all the hopes they had cherished during that war, Indians would give up the habit of believing only what they liked to believe. But they did not. The reason was that after the war they took refuge in myths. I shall give an illustration of this by recounting an argument I had with a Bengali acquaniiance of mine in 1922. He was a lawyer with the degrees of MA and

BL. One day our conversation turned on Germany, and in some context I referred to the defeat of Germany in 1918. He at once objected that Germany was not defeated (in the military sense) but stabbed in the back. Of course, he had accepted the German myth. I then told him about the telegram Hindenburg and Ludendorff had jointly sent to their Government on 26 August 1918, asking for the immediate opening of peace negotiations on the ground that they could no longer answer for the capacity of the German army to carry on the war successfully. This seemed to startle the lawyer, and he asked me where I had read the telegram. I replied that I had done so in the memoirs of Ludendorff himself This at first made him speechless, but he was not a lawyer for nothing. So, he put his next question: 'Did you read the telegram in the original German or in an English translation?' When I said that I had read it only in English he asked me: 'How do you know that the English translator did not put that in." I was so taken aback by such a remark that I could only feebly mumble: 'Ludendorff is living, and no translator can take such a liberty with his text.' He did not even answer that, but looked at me in such a way as showed that he pitied me as a naive victim of British wiles.

But in 1939 I thought that this predisposition would not be seen, yet it was. After watching its hold on the Indian mind for something like six months, I wrote an article on the Indian attitude to the war in *The Statesman* in March. In it I said that a majority of Indians showed a deep-seated inhibition to all news favourable to the Allies. They received reports of Allied successes, exploits and power with mental reservation, but showed themselves overready to give the Germans more than their due.

By way of illustrating this I said that if a British reconnaissance plane was reported to have flown over Berlin it was generally looked upon as an improbability. But if a report went that a German plane had reached the Mersey side, not only was the visit taken as a certainty, but Liverpool and Manchester were also laid in ruins. The most significant thing about this bias was that it was almost as common among the members of those political parties which had decided unhesitatingly to stand by Great Britain as among the professed adherents of the Congress. It was to acquire more and more strength as the Germans won victories and Britain suffered reverses.

For the moment I was, however, more occupied with the war in Poland than with Indian attitudes. Even before Great Britain had declared war it had become apparent that the German plan of campaign was not for limited objectives but for the total destruction of Poland as an independent country. Hitler proclaimed that Poland was an artificial entity and had no right to exist.

When the war began I could form no idea whatever as to how long or how successfully Poland would be able to resist Germany. I was not sure that the offensive had again overhauled the defensive, about which I had read so much, I had even Lossberg's book about elastic defence. Besides, I assumed that while Germany would undoubtedly be superior in equipment and strategic direction, Poland would still have manpower and space to counteract them. But it soon became apparent that Polish defence was crumbling. As the events moved very quickly, I could form no idea of the German strategic plan. But as soon as the war in Poland was over it became clear to me that the plan of campaign was a revised and extended version of the German offensive against Russia in 1915, which had opened brilliantly with Mackensen's breakthrough in the Dunajec basin and was to be carried on in 1916 in a wider sweep, but was not allowed by Falkenhayn.

This discovery at the very outset of the war had an influence on my anticipations about German moves. I assumed that the German General Staff would never willingly embark on any campaign about which they had not thought for years, even those which they had not rehearsed in some way, and they would be totally opposed to improvised strategies for *ad hoc* situations.

I was certainly very much surprised by the quickness of the Polish defeat. In 1941 Russia was, *mutatis mutandis*, in a similar predicament, but made use of her manpower and spaces to avoid a collapse. That Poland did nothing like that was due to faulty thinking and planning. Of course, after the Russian invasion, there was no chance whatever for Poland. I was also surprised by the failure of the French and British armies to mount an offensive on the Western front to relieve the pressure on Poland. While the Germans had begun the war with a renewed faith in the offensive, French and British military thinking seemed still to be tied down to the defensive.

When the war in Poland was nearing its end what angered and disgusted me was the gloating of my countrymen over the misfortunes of the Polish people. They could not be more triumphant even if they were Germans themselves. The only offence that the Poles had given to

Indians was that Britain was at war with Germany for them. That was enough.

This outraged me all the more because in my young days there was considerable sympathy for Poland and the Polish people among us for their revolts against foreign domination. In fact, we had as much fellow-feeling for the Poles as we had for the Italians or the Americans on account of their wars of independence. We knew that Sobieski had saved Vienna from the Turks, revered the name of Kosciusko as we did that of Garibaldi. There was a romantic interest in Poland on account of Paderewski and Marie Curie. I have already said that would-be Bengali revolutionaries read the biographies of Pilsudski.

But by 1939 all this had disappeared. Early in September, Paderewski sent a pathetic telegram to Gandhi from Switzerland, where he was living, in which he said: 'On behalf of a nation which today is defending the sacred right to remain free against a cruel and nameless tyranny, I appeal to you as one of the greatest moral authorities of the world to use your noble influence with your countrymen to gain for Poland their sympathy and friendship.' For himself, Gandhi sent a very sympathetic reply, but he knew, as Paderewski did not, that to ask the Indian people to have any sympathy for the Polish people at that time was like asking a wife to have sympathy for the cast-off mistress of her husband.

There was even greater jubilation when Russia invaded Poland. Upon reading the news, a young Bengali who was at Cambridge but was spending his vacation in Calcutta, cried out to me: 'Oh, glorious!' When I was young we used to be told by our elders that the moral degradation that we saw in our people was the result of subjection to foreign domination and would disappear as soon as domination ended. But in the Gandhian phase of the nationalist movement I had to realize that nationalism could create a moral depravity which was worse in its inhumanity than the old passive degeneracy.

Over and above, there was a surprising ignorance of Polish history among the young generation of Indians. One young Bengali barrister, called to the Bar in London and educated there, said to me when I told him about the shameful partitions of Poland, that he had no idea whatever that Poland was an independent country before 1918. But the Polish episode was over, and what I have to deal with next is the official reaction of the Congress to India's involvement in the war.

I was too engrossed in the war to give much attention to the reaction of the Congress to the involvement of India in it. I did not think that it had any practical importance except for the Congress ministries in the Provinces. In any case, India was involved, and without her consent. If its previous resolutions meant anything, the Congress was bound at once to direct the ministries to resign, for the British authorities had created a plain *casus belli*. Yet it did not, and I perfectly understood the reason. It was not easy to surrender the power of the Congress in the provinces, which was concrete, substantial and profitable, on an issue which was only emotional. Of course, in the past the Congress had always given preference to passion over advantage, but for once the two seemed to be balanced evenly enough, at all events in the eyes of its more worldly-wise leaders, for a choice to be made in favour of one of them.

I was very much amused by the quandary in which the Congress had placed itself by its thoughtless, demagogic extremism, and was inclined to express the amusement by employing a very old literary cliché: 'Vous l'avez voulu, George Dandin, vous l'avez voulu!' But I was not sure that its leaders would not find a way to wriggle out of their commitments, but was equally unsure that they could. The immediate reason for the delay was that Jawaharlal Nehru was on a visit to China, and since he was the President of the Congress as well as its ultimate authority on international questions, nothing could be decided in his absence. He came back on 9 September, and joined the meeting of the Working Committee of the Congress in the evening of the 10th. The real discussion of the issue began after that and continued till the 14th, when the Committee chose to issue what it called a manifesto, without taking any practical decision.

In the meanwhile, Mahatma Gandhi had taken a characteristic step as well as decision for himself In accordance with a previous understanding between him and the Viceroy, Lord Linlithgow, he went to Simla, and there was a meeting between the two on 4 September. The next day he issued a Press statement on what he had said to Lord Linlithgow. First of all, he made it clear to the Viceroy that he spoke only for himself and could not commit the Congress. But he made no secret of his own views. He told Lord Linlithgow that his sympathies were with England and France from the purely humanitarian standpoint. He added that he also told the Viceroy that he could not contemplate the destruction of London without being stirred to the depths of his being, and as he evoked the picture of the destroyed Parliament buildings and Westminster Abbey, he broke down. He set down further that it seemed to him that Herr Hitler knew no God except brute force and, as Mr Chamberlain had said, he would listen to nothing else. Therefore he himself was for giving unconditional support to Britain in the war, but naturally he left it to the Indian people and the Congress to decide what part India was to play in 'this terrible drama', as he described it. It has to be mentioned that on 23 July he had written a letter to Herr Hitler appealing to him to refrain from war, because, as he saw it, Herr Hitler was the only person in the world at that moment who could prevent a war.

But Mahatma Gandhi had reckoned without his people. The reaction among Indians to his statement made him write an article in his paper *Harijan* to explain himself more fully. This was published in the issue of the paper for 11 September. In it he said that his statement had had a mixed reception. One critic had called it 'sentimental twaddle', while another had described it as a 'statesmanlike pronouncement'. To one critic, more especially, he felt compelled to reply at some length. He did not name this critic, nor did he quote his letter verbatim. He said that he did not understand it fully, but could sum up its drift easily. This was as follows:

'If you shed tears over the possible destruction of the English Houses of Parliament and Westminster Abbey, have you no tears for the possible destruction of the monuments of Germany? And why do you sympathize with England and not with Germany? Is not Hitler an answer to the ravishing by the Allied Powers during the last war? If you were a German, had the resourcefulness of Hitler and were a believer in the doctrine of retaliation as the whole world is, you would have done what Hitler is doing. Nazism may be bad, we do not know what it really is. The literature we get is onesided. But I suggest to you that there is no difference between Chamberlain and Hitler. In Hitler's place Chamberlain would not have acted otherwise. You have done an injustice to Hitler by comparing him to Chamberlain, to the former's disadvantage. Is England's record in India better than Hitler's in another part of the world in similar circumstances? Hitler is but an infant pupil of the old imperialist England and France. I fancy that your emotion at the Viceregal Lodge had the better of your judgement.'

Although described as a summary by Gandhi, it is obvious that he was reproducing most of the language verbatim, because he himself would have been incapable of the phrasing, which is that of a highly educated Indian nationalist of the time, whether he belonged to the Congress or not.

For himself, Mahatma Gandhi answered dispassionately and justified himself by saying that he had been impartial as between England and Germany. But later he had to admit that over this question he stood alone and was not supported by his countrymen, nor even by the Congress. And he resigned himself to the majority view.

It was Jawaharlal Nehru who decided the official policy of the Congress. The Manifesto of the 14th was, of course, issued as a unanimous document, but there could be no doubt that there were differences at the meeting. For four days the Working Committee of the Congress discussed almost every phrase of the drafts prepared by Nehru in advance. He was totally and inflexibly opposed to any kind of co-operation with Britain in the war, except on his own terms. These were implied in the Manifesto, and even by implication they were elaborate and formidable. Over this question Mahatma Gandhi was overruled, not only by Nehru alone, but also by the other Congress leaders. The only concession that Nehru made was not to slam the door on all talks and call out the Congress ministries at once, but to give the British Government at home and the British Indian Government another chance to fall in with his views and secure the co-operation of the Congress.

The Manifesto, which was issued on 14 September, was a long document and quite appropriately called a Manifesto, because in its sweep and comprehensiveness it was conceived of as the concluding piece in the triad to be composed of the Communist Manifesto, President Wilson's proclamation on the Fourteen Points, and itself. As was to be expected, it opened with an unequivocal condemnation of Fascism and Nazism, but proceeded in the next step to question the motives of Britain and France in going to war with Germany, refusing to accept the mere fact of going to war as justification for demanding co-operation.

It said that although both these countries were saying that they were fighting for democracy and freedom and to put an end to aggression, recent history had shown that there were 'constant divergence between the spoken word, the ideal proclaimed and the real motives and objectives'. It further added that the fervent declaration of faith in freedom, etc. might be followed 'by ignoble desertion and betrayal'. In support of this anticipation China, Ethiopia, and Czechoslovakia were referred to.

Even so, the Congress did not want to take any irrevocable step and would consider co-operating in the war if Great Britain showed her sincerity in the way suggested in the Manifesto, and that was as follows: 'If Great Britain fights for the maintenance and extension of democracy, then she must necessarily end imperialism in her own possessions, establish full democracy in India, and the Indian people must have the right of self-determination by framing her constitution through a Constituent Assembly without external interference, and must guide their own policy.'

Then came the substantive proposal:

'The Working Committee therefore invite the British Government to declare in unequivocal terms what their war aims are in regard to democracy and imperialism and the new order that is envisaged, in particular how these are going to apply and be given effect to in the present. Do they include the elimination of imperialism and the treatment of India as a free nation, whose policy will be guided in accordance with the wishes of the people?

'A clear declaration about the ending of imperialism and Fascism alike will be welcomed by the people of all countries.'

What the Manifesto made absolutely clear was that no contingent promise would be accepted. As it put the matter, 'The test of the declaration is its application to the present.' In plain words, if the British Government wanted the co-operation of India in the war with the consent of the Congress, it must end British rule in India. But the Congress refrained from fixing the date at 30 September 1939. It expressly said that a war to maintain the status quo will have no co-operation from India. But these short citations do not give a proper idea of the elaboration of the argument.

It might be thought that to ask the British Government to do all that when a war was on and when its scope, duration, and outcome were all unpredictable, was not reasonable. But opinion in India, even outside Congress circles, did not think so. The Indian view, on the contrary, was that not to accept the terms offered by the Congress was the height of unreasonableness. Even today Indian historians take this view. The word 'mulishness' has been employed by one of them about the attitude of the British Government.

But only a very uninitiated person will raise an argument over such differences of opinion, because to expect politics to be reasonable is in itself an unreasonable expectation. Politics has only to be natural. It was as natural for Nehru to demand what he demanded from the British Government, as it was for Chamberlain to say that what was expected from Hitler were deeds and not words; and as it is today when the Americans say the same thing about the Soviet Union. Deeds in such contexts always mean acceptance of the demands of the party which rejects words. These arguments in a circle are always seen when there is distrust and hatred between the parties, and neither is rational.

So, even Gandhi said, in an article published in his paper on 15 September, that the author of the Manifesto was an artist, though at the same time he confessed that he was sorry to find himself alone in thinking that whatever support was to be given to the British should be given unconditionally. He also looked upon Nehru not only as a friend of the English people, but as an Englishman. As he said in the same article: 'He is a friend of the English people. Indeed, he is more English than Indian in his thought and make-up. He is often more at home with Englishmen than with his own countrymen.'

Certainly, that was true of Nehru as regards his social and personal behaviour, and was true even about his political behaviour if the Englishman was his kind of Englishman. This kind at once agreed with him over his handling of the war situation. Beatrice Webb wrote in her diary on 5 October 1939: 'Nehru has called the British bluff, the pretence of fighting for political democracy and rights of man.' Sir Stafford Cripps in a private letter (11 October) urged Nehru to see to it that the Congress stood firm as a rock. Cripps was to see his advice applied wholeheartedly against himself by Nehru in 1942, when he went to India to make a contingent promise of independence on behalf of the British Government.

There was no illusion on the British side about Nehru's position. When all the talks broke down, the Marquis of Zetland, as Secretary of State for India, gave the House of Lords a correct and precise summing up of the antithetical positions on 7 November 1939. The core of it was as follows:

'As the House will have seen from the documents published yesterday, the Congress definitely refuse to consider any concrete plans such as those outlined by the Governor-General unless His Majesty's Government should be willing first to make a declaration to the effect that India is an independent nation, and that His Majesty's Government will raise no opposition to her future form of Government being determined without their intervention, by a Constituent Assembly to be formed on the widest possible basis of franchise and by agreement in regard to communal representation. The Congress have further consistently taken the line which they still maintain, that the fact that there are racial and religious minorities in India is of no relevance in that connection and that it has always been the intention of the Congress to secure, through the Constitution to be framed by Indians themselves, such protection for their rights as may prove acceptable to the minorities.

'His Majesty's Government find it impossible to accept this position. The longstanding British connection with India has left His Majesty's Government with obligations towards her which it is impossible for them to shed by disinteresting themselves wholly in shaping the future form of Government.'

Yet the strange fact was that with no basis for negotiations both sides, and indeed every party and community in India concerned with the matter, entered into a sustained and spirited session of talking and writing which lasted a whole month. The Viceroy, Lord Linlithgow, alone saw and talked to fifty-two persons, including Gandhi, Nehru and other Congress leaders, Jinnah and other Muslim leaders, representatives of other communities. Finally, in the statement on the failure of all these talks which he made on 17 October he said without intending to be ironical that he had had the *advantage* of full and frank discussions with Gandhi, Nehru, Jinnah, and other representatives of all the parties and communities. But in actual fact the only profit he had derived from them seemed to be his realization that they all differed from one another.

Nevertheless, the Congress took nearly two more weeks to call out the ministries. But by the end of October all of them resigned. Nearly two years later, I wrote about this in an article of mine because I was always hearing the accusation that the British Government had lost the co-operation of the Congress by not consulting it before involving India in the war. I wrote: 'Among the many rosy might-have-beens of current Indian politics, the rosiest perhaps is the belief that it would have made a difference if the British or the India Government had tried to get the previous consent of the

Congress before announcing India's participation in die war. The idea is a delusion.'

The British authorities certainly nursed no such delusion, although they went on saying that they regretted what the Congress had done and would go as far as possible to meet the Indian demands for political advancement. Actually, they had faced the Congress with a *fait accompli* and made it go back on its previous resolutions. Perhaps a compromise would have been arrived at but for Nehru. What he demanded was a surrender. All the other leaders had to fall in with him because they knew Nehru had the Indian people with him in this.

But the breakdown did not put an end to the issuing of statements by all the Congress leaders criticizing both Lord Linlithgow and the Marquis of Zetland. Their language was both severe and bitter, and the acerbity was certainly due to the sense of grievance created by the compulsion to resign power in the provinces. The denunciation of the British representatives continued well into December, and by that time they had fully convinced their public that the British were, not only unreasonable, but also wicked.

However, the full agreement between the Congress leaders and the nationalist public did not mean that the gains were equal on both sides. The Congress lost real power in the provinces, and only increased its psychological hold on the country. The Indian people gained on all counts, because they did not hesitate for a single moment to give all the practical co-operation they could to the British war effort in India for the sake of gaining money. In addition, they had the emotional satisfaction of seeing their British rulers put in the wrong and being provided with more reason to hate them. Nonetheless, in the long run the British lost nothing. The goodwill of the Indian people they could never have gained without giving up India and thus losing the need for the goodwill. But the British did not have to give up India in order to obtain whatever co-operation in the war it was possible to get from the Indians. In concrete terms, the co-operation was spectacular and far exceeded what Britain had got in the First World War. On the other hand, the formal opposition that the Congress offered by launching movements of passive resistance afterwards were the weakest and most ineffectual in the whole history of the nationalist movement. They did not rouse any emotion even. But the British, too, had their delusion, which was created by the interested behaviour of the Indian people. They thought it came from goodwill.

For the Congress the permanent loss was far greater than the loss of power in the provinces, although that too was a serious matter. It had to remain in a political wilderness from 1939 to 1945, and that had a very harmful effect on the final settlement of 1947. Had the Congress cooperated with Britain in the war it would have ensured greater support for itself from the British side in 1947, and quite possibly the partition of India would have been prevented. Since that was the greatest political injury to India in her whole history, the action of the Congress in 1939 can be described as an act of folly. In the final act of the tragi-comic play that the conducting of Indo-British relations from 1921 to 1947 was, the Congress unreservedly accepted the responsibility of the British Government for the minorities which it peremptorily rejected in 1939, and accepted the discharge of the British responsibility in its worst conceivable form. Could a decision to co-operate with Britain in 1939 have produced a worse result?

Although I did not pay much attention to the doings of the Congress at the time, because I considered them to be of minor importance compared with the war, I have recounted this episode at some length on account of its ultimate consequences. It illustrates the central political thesis of this book that the management of Indo-British relations from 1921 to 1947 is a story of human stupidity – a tale full of sound and fury signifying nothing, a pitiful tale of words pitted against ineluctable facts. Even as a debate it was nothing better than an attempt at squaring a circle, the spectacle of a dog and a cat chasing each other round and round, and a repetition of the story of the Sybilline Books.

The responsibility for this folly rests on Nehru from 1939 to 1947, because during this period it was his voice which was the determining one, Gandhi having receded into the background. That the political history of India as determined by discussion became only an unreal game of words was also due to him. He was the wordmonger par excellence, but the words came from a side of his character which made him as powerful a national figure as Hider was in Germany from 1933 to 1939. At times it seems to me that it was not for nothing that both were born in the same year. This may sound not only enigmatic but also outrageous at this point. But I shall explain myself later.

Let me now revert to the war. After the collapse of Poland the general expectation in India was that it would come to an end because both Britain and France were likely to consider a continuation of the war pointless. The

Indian people also thought that the Governments of both countries were not representative of their people, who did not want the war and thought it was imposed on them by their imperialist regimes. Some even thought that these Governments would join Germany in an anti-communist crusade. The idea that they were interested only in putting an end to the Soviet Union persisted till the German attack on Russia.

I, of course, thought even after Hitler's offer of peace on 6 October that the war would continue. But I could not make any guess as to how Britain and France could compel Germany to make peace on their terms. But soon after a German threat seriously alarmed me. It was that of Hider's secret weapon, which he announced with the menacing remark that if he were compelled to use it he hoped there would be no talk of humanitarianism. I assumed that this implied the employment of an atomic weapon. I had read about atomic fission in scientific papers shortly before the war, and had learnt that Britain, Germany, and the USA were almost neck and neck in the race. I now thought that the Germans had done it, and it seemed ominous. However, I felt very much relieved when I found that the threat referred only to the magnetic mine.

For some time there was a decline of interest in the war in India. But it was revived as soon as the Russians attacked Finland at the end of November. The interest was displayed in the typical Indian manner by a strong antipathy to Finland, with whom the Indians had no quarrel whatever except on the score of the country's being forced to be on the wrong side in the war, as they saw it.

The initial check to the Russians was something which the Indians found incredible. Therefore they treated this news in two ways. Some assumed that Russia had never gone to war with Finland, and that the whole affair was invented by British propaganda to create prejudice against the Soviet Union. The other theory was that Finland was actually occupied but the news was being suppressed by British censorship. Throughout the war I found the belief in British censorship unshakeable among Indians. They thought every news unfavourable to the British could be suppressed, so they would not believe that the Finnish army could check the Russians.

As it happened, on account of the Communist leanings of Bengali intellectuals this war was discussed in the Calcutta Press, especially in the mouthpiece of Subhas Bose's Forward Bloc. In it I wrote an article criticising Russia, and at once the leading Communist intellectual in

Calcutta, educated of course in England and with a brilliant academic record there, replied to me with undisguised contempt. All that he would admit in me was a little knowledge of potted history, because I had written that, instead of Ivan the Terrible, Stalin the Terrible ruled in the Kremlin. However, the success of the Russians put an end to the controversy, and there was a display of satisfaction at the defeat of the Finns.

In the meanwhile, during the lull in the Finnish war, there had been an incident which rather depressed the Indians. It was the battle of the Plate. In November we had become aware of the foray of one of the German pocket battleships, although we did not know that it was the *Graf Spee* till much later. There was such an exaggerated idea of the power of these ships that the news of the battle, followed by that of the ship's flight to Montevideo, very much surprised the Indians. They could not account for it at all. I also could not wholly explain it and was anxious about the final result. Even in India we got the report that the *Ark Royal* and the *Renown* were already at the mouth of the Plate, waiting for the *Graf Spee* to come out. I had read before that the *Ark Royal* was at Rio, and wondered how she could have reached the Plate in so short a time. Then came the news of the scuttling of the German warship. Sarat Babu told me that he knew this would happen because Germans would never give the British an opportunity to win a victory. Indians knew very little about naval warfare, and did not know what scuttling really meant for naval commanders. But Captain Langsdorff knew. At first, Indians were quite stunned, but they soon recovered their spirits and began to say that the British must be in a pretty bad way to be crowing about a victory won by an overwhelming force over a small and solitary German ship.

The Indian people did not give much attention to what was called the 'phoney war', i.e. the war on the Franco-German front. It did not seem to them to matter, and they were not sure that it would matter. Those who thought about it at all had as much faith in the Siegfried Line as they had in the Maginot. It was to rouse a wild interest soon. Before that, or at the end of March 1940, to be precise, I wrote an article on the attitude of the Indian people to the war, and it was published in two instalments in The Statesman for 18 and 19 March. I came to learn later that it received a good deal of attention in governmental circles in New Delhi and even influenced its thinking on war propaganda in India, which I had criticized as ineffectual.

This, I set down to a lack of understanding of the psychology of the

Indian people in respect of the war in those who were responsible for the propaganda. On the one hand, they did not take into account the wide range of attitudes in India and, on the other, the basic unity in them created by the hostility to British rule. Thus in its public expression, the Indian approach to the war ranged from extreme friendliness to extreme hostility, with a large uncommitted block in-between. But behind all of this stood a predisposition to disbelieve the British version. What I have said in this chapter about that is largely taken from the article of 1940.

I shall now conclude this chapter by reproducing what I said in the article about the basic reason for this paradoxical mixture. Indian opinion could be both fluid and varied because it was irresponsible. Indians did not feel that anything was at stake for them in the war, and behind that feeling was a conviction which I then found generally prevalent that Great Britain was not going to be defeated by Germany. Those who thought themselves clever even suggested that the talk about any real danger to Britain was a British propaganda trick to frighten the Indian people into supporting Britain for the sake of preserving all the worldly interests of theirs which were bound up with British rule.

The general assumption, created by the wish to see this proved in fact, was that the war would weaken and jeopardise Britain so far as to make her willing to make concessions to India in respect of self-government, but not so fatally as to bring about a breakdown of government in India and endanger their life or interests, or bring in a new set of foreign rulers who might be more ruthless than the British. On one point all Indians were agreed: it was that as foreign rulers the British were the least to be feared. In the meanwhile, they thought they would get as much satisfaction out of British reverses as they could wish for. That they began to get in a measure wholly unhoped for from the next month.

CHAPTER 3

India sings her Te Deum

In the middle of die year 1940, all India rang with the singing of *Te Deum* by all classes of Indians to give expression to their gratitude to God for having provided them with such a windfall of emotional satisfaction as they could not have hoped for even in their wildest dreams. 'We praise Thee, O God!' they sang, 'for fulfilling Thy promise that vengeance is Thine. And what a vengeance hast Thou taken for us!'

This was for the gift already given, and, encouraged by it, they embodied their hopes for the future in an exultant commination:

'The Lord has a day of recompense for the cause of India. And the streams of England shall be turned into pitch and the soil into brimstone, her land shall become burning pitch. Night and day it shall not be quenched, its smoke shall go up for ever. They shall name England No Kingdom There, and all its princes shall be nothing. Thorns shall grow over its strongholds, nettles and thistles in its fortresses, and wild beasts shall meet with hyenas, the satyr shall cry to his fellow; yea, there shall the night hag rest: *Ibi cubavit Lamia.*'

As it happened, this hope was partly fulfilled, and Indians praised the Lord. The exultation was *ad libitum* for two reasons: in the first place, because the turn that the war took was wholly unexpected; and, secondly, because no Indian thought that whatever the punishment for England, their own safety and prosperity were threatened. The British Government, they assumed, would make peace with Germany on Hitler's terms before allowing their people to be destroyed. In that event, there would be satisfaction in taunting the British people for cowardice. I shall give enough facts to substantiate what I am saying.

A wholly unexpected phase of the war opened with the German attack on Denmark and Norway. At that time I did not, of course, know that these attacks were decided upon at the very last moment by Hitler in order to prevent a British landing in Norway, and that it was due to divided counsel in the British Cabinet that Germany was not forestalled. The German campaign was ruthlessly conducted and succeeded, but it also showed that the German General Staff was not at its best in improvised operations, in spite of the advantage the German forces had through the occupation of Denmark. The German navy suffered great losses. But for the victory in France which followed, holding Norway would have been as much a liability as an advantage for Germany.

Be that as it may, for the moment the German success was spectacular, and the British Government was made to look foolish. This was also my situation on a smaller scale. Everybody triumphed over me. I contributed to my discomfiture by an incautious statement. In one of my broadcasts I had said that if the British battlefleet could get into the Skagerrak, land operations would be only mopping up. At that time I had no clear idea of the power of aircraft over warships and I was certainly surprised to read that Admiral Forbes was compelled to fall back in the face of landbased air attacks. My conditional statement was now thrown in my teeth even by the assistants in All India Radio who were selling themselves to the British side. One Programme Assistant (educated in England, of course) almost danced before me pointing his forefinger at me and asking me if only a mopping operation was now going on in Norway. I had to swallow all that.

Among all my friends and acquaintances, too, I found an unshakeable belief in German invincibility, and equal contempt for British military ability even in the naval sphere. Those Indo-Germanic intellectuals scoffed at me. A friend of mine said to me: 'Go into the Skagerrak! Impossible!' A Bengali lawyer, whom I had gone to see on some business (not my own), saw a book in my hand and asked me what it was. I handed it to him. It was Corbett's *Principles of Maritime Strategy*. He turned over a few pages, gave the book back to me, and remarked with pontifical gravity: 'They expect to fight the Germans with the strategy of fishing boats?' I could not even retort that the book had been translated into German for the *Reichsmarin*.

When the Narvik landing was begun, the Bengali journalist who was in charge of Reuters in Calcutta rang me up to say: 'Four British battleships have been sunk by the Germans at Narvik.' That seemed so incredible that I asked: 'Which battleships? Have you the names?' He said that he had none. I felt reassured that the ships were not battleships. Actually, they were destroyers. Indians did not know the differences between warships and called all of them 'battleships'. Of course, nobody rang me up when, later, all the German destroyers were sunk by the *warspite* in the same area.

I could not help feeling, however, that the whole Norway episode was mismanaged by the British side, and I did not think kindly of General Ironside, the CIGS, when he told the soldiers brought back from Narvik: 'You come with tails up.'

One result of this military fiasco, however, gave me satisfaction. It was the replacement of Chamberlain by Churchill. Since my student days I had always been an admirer of Churchill, and I felt that at last the man was matched to the hour. From that time I hung up a large portrait of him in my sitting room. As it happened, a very large reproduction of Mona Lisa was on an adjacent wall. My friends represented this juxtaposition almost as a symptom of schizophrenia in me. They respected my knowledge of European art and my taste, but they could not explain the strange antic which made me endure the sight of Churchill's face by the side of the smiling Mona Lisa.

But my satisfaction did not last long, hardly a day. On 10 May 1940 I was going to Sarat Babu's house in the afternoon when I noticed Bengalis jumping down from the tramcars and running to buy the afternoon specials of the newspapers. They contained the news of the attack on Holland. The scene, as they glanced at the papers in their hands, was exactly like that on a football field after a goal had been won by the favoured club. The destruction of Rotterdam was a matter of rejoicing and not of regret. Yet all Bengalis were pro-Boer in 1900.

More ominous news followed, and that was about Belgium. I recalled 1914, and although I did not expect the Belgian army to be capable of resisting the Germans for long, the quickness of the collapse surprised me, especially the dramatic capture of the fort Eben Emael and the bridges over the canals. But worse was to follow. I was absolutely stunned by the news of the German breakthrough in the region of Sedan, and dismayed by the headlong advance to the sea, which was very different from the 'race to the sea' in 1914. For a little while, I felt encouraged by the counterattack near Arras, but had to read that the Germans had reached Abbeville. As it happened, Dr Law was alarmed by the news, because a well-known French bird collector had his great aviary in that region, and he felt very anxious about it.

Never in my life, except on two occasions, of which this was the first, did any public event produce a physical effect on me. I had a dormant injury in my chest, which caused pain when I was overworked or run down. The pain had a very sharp onset when I heard the news of the German breakdirough. It seemed as if a nail was holding the front part of my chest fixed to the back. Apart from this, I was wholly stumped intellectually. My bewilderment was all the greater because I had just then bought and read the English translation of General de Gaulle's book *Vers l'armée de métier*, in which even in 1934 he had pointed out that the Sedan region was the real point of danger in the French defensive system. And yet only the weak Armée Corap was there.

Naturally, exultation among the Bengalis of Calcutta was great, and some of it found rather amusing expression. Many well-educated Bengalis believed or liked to believe that Hitler was some sort of an epic Hindu hero, a great Aryan. So, one of them said to me: 'Do you know, Nirad Babu, that German tanks fly the Kapidvaja?' Now, this flag, whose name translated means the 'Monkey Banner', was flown over his chariot by the Mahabhar- ata hero Arjuna when fighting the battle of Kurukshetra. Those who had personal grievance against British rule thought of Hitler almost as God. The father of one of the Chittagong revolutionaries who had been sentenced to transportation for life in the Andamans, told me: 'Hitler is no ordinary mortal, he is the incarnation of Vishnu.' Absurd as these ideas were, they sprang from a real sense of oneness with the Germans.

I shall bring forward, by two years, another almost incredible example of the Indian admiration for Hitler. In 1942, when I was in Delhi, I was reading the two volumes of Hitler's speeches, edited by Norman H. Baynes and published by the Oxford University Press on behalf of the Royal Institute of International Affairs. One day, going to the office with one of the volumes, I met at the bus stop a Bengali professor of English literature, with a degree from Oxford. He looked at the book and said with a smile: 'Those English people are very cunning. They know that Hitler's speeches are great literature and want to make money out of them, now that they will not have to pay him for them.' I was dumbfounded by this result of an Oxford education.

As usual, I sought intellectual relief by writing an article on the breakthrough. I described the new German Plan as an adaptation of the Schlieffen Plan in the sense that in it the right wing was converted only into a powerful and effective decoy, and the main thrust was concentrated on the central sector, where it was least expected. The French and British commands were wholly taken in by it and fell into the trap. Had they not been obsessed with the right wing of the German deployment as it developed from 10 May, Dunkirk would not have happened. The article was published, but I was ridiculed for it. Tridib Chaudhuri came and told me with considerable amusement that some clever Bengalis had told him that no Schlieffen Plan would have saved the British. In spite of the name they took the Schlieffen Plan to be a British plan to meet the German offensive. Tridib Babu only asked them to read the article.

I followed the evacuation from Dunkirk with a half-benumbed mind and did not feel even the loss of the entire equipment of the BEF. I could not help feeling, however, that it was some sort of nemesis for Munich. I did not recover my mental capacity to think about the next German offensive, and only hoped Pétain and Weygand might be able to do something. Pétain was the defender of Verdun and had redeemed the mistakes of Nivelle, and Weygand was Chief of Staff to Foch. But I had to face the total collapse of France.

However, with the complete loss of hope that this resulted in, my mental faculties returned. As soon as I learned about the French surrender I wrote a letter to *The Statesman* about Pétain's role in it. But before that I would describe Mahatma Gandhi's intervention in the war. Even before the news of the final acceptance of the German terms by France had reached India, he wrote an article giving his considered advice to all the belligerents. It was published in his weekly journal *Harijan* on 22 June 1940, and was entitled 'How to Combat Hitlerism'. His advice was like Mr Punch's to the young man who was about to marry: 'Don't!' He began by saying: 'Whatever Hider may ultimately prove to be, we know what Hitlerism has come to mean. It means naked, ruthless force reduced to an exact science and worked with scientific precision.' After that he gave his view: 'Hitlerism will never be defeated by counter-Hitlerism. It can only breed superior Hitlerism raised to nth degree. What is going on before our eyes is a demonstration of the futility of violence as also of Hitlerism.'

It was natural, therefore, that Mahatma Gandhi should go on to praise the realization of this truth by the French Government. His commendation was unqualified:

> 'I think French statesmen have shown rare courage in bowing to the inevitable and refusing to be party to senseless mutual slaughter. There can be no sense in France's coming out victorious if the stake in truth is lost.

The cause of liberty becomes a mockery if the price to be paid is wholesale destruction of those who are to enjoy liberty. It then becomes an inglorious satiation of ambition. The bravery of the French soldier is world-known. But let the world know also the greater bravery of the French statesmen in suing for peace. I have assumed that the French statesmen have taken this step in a perfectly honourable manner as behoves true soldiers. Let me hope that Herr Hitler will impose no humiliating terms but show that, though he can fight without mercy, he can at least conclude peace not without mercy.'

Mahatma Gandhi made it clear that he was writing those lines for the 'European Powers' and his advice was as follows:

'I think it will be allowed that all the blood that has been spilled by Hitler has added not a millionth part of an inch to the world's moral stature.

'As against this, imagine the state of Europe today if the Czechs, the Poles, the Norwegians, the French and the English had all said to Hitler: "You need not make your scientific preparations for destruction. We will meet your violence with non-violence. You will therefore be able to destroy our non-violent army without tanks, battleships and airships." It may be retorted that the only difference would be that Hitler would have got without fighting what he gained after a bloody fight. Exactly. The history of Europe would then have been written differently. Possession might (but only might) have been taken under non-violent resistance, as it has been taken now after the perpetration of untold barbarities. Under non-violence only those would have been killed who had trained themselves to be killed, if need be, but without killing anyone and without bearing malice towards anybody. I daresay that in that case Europe would have added several inches to its moral stature. And in the end I expect it is the moral worth that will count. All else is dross.'

An anonymous correspondent, obviously an Englishman, protested against this article. In it he said with an irony just tinctured with permissible malice that if all that Mahatma Gandhi was saying about non-violence were to be accepted, 'how utterly small and futile must Mr Gandhi's own little fights *almost* to death appear to him then in retrospect – or were his hunger strikes just a form of blackmail without the real risk of death?' It is from this article that I have quoted the qualified encomium which Mahatma Gandhi pronounced on Hitler.*

I did not read this article at the time, but throughout my life I have felt nothing but contempt for the doctrine of non-resistance to evil and nonviolence, which contempt has, on reading the article, only been intensified. This doctrine is nothing but an attempt to claim credit for moral elevation without risking the skin, which is even more absurd than trying to keep one's cake as well as eat it. I have read explanations of why jesus said (or was made to say) 'Resist not evil'. He could do that because to him as to his followers the world was so unqualified an evil that there could be no point in giving one's life to improve it. But if a man did set some store by the world and life, and thought both had to be good, he was bound to fight, if necessary to death, to make it fit to live in. From that point of view. Bar Cochba was a greater *man* than Jesus. And he, too, was called Messiah. There is no accounting for opinions.

Be that as it may, there was another response to the capitulation of France, and that from a Sikh nobleman, which was quite different from that of Mahatma Gandhi. He did not give his name but signed himself as 'A Sikh Sardar', in a letter to *The Statesman*, in which he said:

'There is hardly a home in the Punjab – nay in India – where the matter is not being talked of with various-comments. Often with breathless suspense the question is asked: What next? Different communities may be giving different replies to it, but the Sikhs have only one answer to it and that is, we have allied ourselves with the British in their great cause of justice and humanity and we will fight to the last man shoulder to shoulder with them. Let others wait for the last ditch if they like, we will like to go in the front one. The Sikh religion was created by the Gurus to help the poor, the wronged and the oppressed. Our baptism is given in steel. No true Sikh can sit with quietude when so many women and children are being trampled to death – blown to pieces by shells and bombs without a second thought. Feelings of exasperation and rage prevail in the martial classes of the Punjab.', etc., etc.

Still more different was my reaction, also expressed in a letter to *The Statesman*, which it promptly published. In it I wrote:

* See p. 536.

'Sir, – The present French Government's surrender to Germany can only be explained on the- supposition of loss of nerve on the part of Marshal pétain and some of his colleagues. The former has pleaded the absence of Allies and insufficiency of men and munitions and pointed to the conditions in 1918. But at least once in 1918 too Marshal Retain showed himself dangerously near to throwing up the sponge.

'On March 24, 1918, after the great German offensive had lasted for three days and pushed back the British Fifth Army, almost destroying it, he issued an order directing the French armies to fall back towards Paris. This order, if carried out, would have had the effect of separating the French and the British armies and involving the Allied left wing in a complete disaster, as in 1940. Pétain issued this order in a mood of extreme despondency and under a mistaken notion that the English were retreating northwards.

'Haig, however, immediately set himself to get this order countermanded. He telegraphed to his Government, and at the Doullens Conference Clemenceau, Poincaré and Foch disapproved of the order. At this conference Clemenceau took Poincaré aside and told him: "Pétain is provoking in his pessimism. Do you know he said a certain thing to me which I would not care to confide to anybody but you? It was this: The Germans will beat the English in the open country, after which they would beat us also. Should a General speak or even think in that way?"

'In regard to Marshal Pétain's statement on the strength of the British contingent respectively in 1940 and 1918, the comparison should properly be between 1940 and 1914. In 1914 when Joffre stopped the Germans on the Marne, the BEF consisted only of six infantry and one cavalry division. At that time Italy and the United States were not in the war, and Russia was only able to keep away from the Western Front some nine to ten German divisions.'

This was not all. I took a bolder line in regard to the future. My weekly broadcast on the war was due immediately after the French capitulation. In it I said that, so far from coming to an end soon, I should not be surprised if in the new circumstances the war continued for five to seven years more. I gave the reason as the inability of either side to bring to bear its main strength on the other, treating air power as roughly equal. This talk was printed in the leading Bengali newspaper.

I was, of course, held up to ridicule". My friend Sajani Das went one better. At that time he was writing a column for a Bengali weekly. In it he represented me as saying that it would take the Germans five to seven years to take Paris. As the column was for humour he remarked gleefully that he was reassured to learn that even an expert (theoretical) could go wrong. I at once wrote to the editor of the journal that this was totally false, and not only demanded an apology but dictated it. I think the Bengal Government also took the matter up. At once a retraction was published with the apology dictated by me. It explained that I had never made any such statement about Paris and added that the editor regretted having printed a comment based on false and malicious reports.

A few days after this I had an argument with Subhas Bose on the military situation. He had come to see his brother late one evening. At that time Sarat Babu was not well and went to bed early. So Subhas Babu and I sat in his study and had a tremendous argument. I have to say that he never tried to brush aside my views, but always spoke very politely. He smiled, referring to my view of the war, and said that he was perfectly aware of my opinions. He then said to me: 'Do you know, Nirad Babu, how many people have been asking me since the war started to tell my brother to dismiss you from your job as his secretary? I have replied to them that Nirad Babu does not implicate my brother, and he has every right to express his own opinions as long as he does not do that.' I was, of course, very much obliged. Then he very good-humouredly raised the topic of the duration of the war, and remarked: 'Your premises are right but your deductions are wrong,' or the other way round – I forget which way he put it. We argued for some time. Then he said: 'You have made your forecast. Shall I make mine?' I replied, 'Please do,' and he pointed to a calendar which was hanging on the wall and said: 'Britain will surrender and make peace with Germany by the 16th of July.' As that was only about two weeks away I was ready to wait. Within a few days he was arrested, and when he was released towards the end of the year, he never raised the matter with me. In fact, I did not see him again.

Soon after this came the news of the destruction of part of the French fleet at Oran. This created a shock in India, if not a sense of outrage. I have read that after this incident Lord Linlithgow, the Viceroy, sent a telegram to Leopold Amery, the Secretary of State for India, to inform him that the news of the action had been seen by the Indian people as a 'proof of vigour and decision on our part', and Amery sent it to Churchill with the remark:

'This should cheer you.' Certainly, it could have, but in a different way. The Viceroy, surrounded by Indian flatterers or opportunists, had no understanding of the real character of the reaction of the Indian people. I had, and I can say that from his point of view as the inflexible opponent of Indian nationalism Churchill had good reasons to be cheered up, for he had inflicted a terrible mortification on Indian nationalists. They were driven to a fit of outraged horror and rage by the British action, as if they were seeing a king cobra whose back was broken rearing itself up, spreading its hood and hissing. A Bengali barrister (called to the bar in England) told me as he read the report of Churchill sitting down hunched up and in tears: 'Crocodile tears!'

The next six months were a period of great mental strain for me. Although I had no fear of any irretrievable catastrophe, I remained deeply anxious. The reasons for this were threefold: first, the bombing of Britain; secondly, the possibility of an invasion; and lastly, uncertainty about the next German move on land which I felt might be in two regions about whose vulnerability I was acutely conscious. But I never thought of a German attack on Russia.

I could easily see that the air attacks were not meant merely to secure mastery of the skies for an invasion, but was total war, designed to break the spirit of the British people by terrorizing them into suing for peace. It was widely believed in India, at all events by everybody I talked to in Calcutta, that the desired effect was being produced. Everybody who had a wireless set tuned in to Berlin radio. One day one of the listeners said to me: 'When the German bombers appear over London, people fall down on the pavements in a faint.' When I asked him how he had come to know that he explained that he had got it from the German radio. I remarked: 'Perhaps the German pilots came down to street level to observe.'

All sorts of fantastic ideas, pleasing to themselves, were held by the Bengalis. One such idea was that the British people did not want to fight, but were made to commit suicide by that monster Churchill. Even well-informed people thought of him only as a firebrand in words. One day, Kiran Shankar Roy, the Deputy Leader of the Congress Party in the Bengal legislature, whose knowledge and intelligence I respected and who held an Oxford degree in history, asked me: 'Does Churchill have any real capacity for military direction? Or is he only an orator?' And, of course, all Bengalis shared the view of Hitler that when German soldiers would land in England, Churchill would be in Canada. Already, it was believed, certain British activities had taken refuge in that country. For some years I had been subscribing to the *Illustrated London News*, and I was still receiving my copies, although irregularly. One day I showed an issue with photographs of London to a Bengali and said: 'Look, how they are still producing this paper even under bombardment.' I got the reply: 'Not at all, it is being printed in Canada with a false imprint.'

If such ideas were ridiculous, the gloating over the bombings was revolting in its cowardly inhumanity. I shall give one or two illustrations. Towards the end of August, on the day that the news of the agreement about destroyers between Britain and the USA appeared in the Indian newspapers I found that Suresh Majumdar's English daily had put it on a back page inconspicuously, while the banner headline on the front page was about the bombing of London. When Suresh Babu came to Sarat Babu's house in the afternoon, I said to him: 'Today the most important news is of the destroyer deal, but your paper has relegated it to a corner while the bombings, which are now stale news, are splashed.' Suresh Babu replied: 'Your criticism is perfectly right from the journalistic point of view. But I know my readers would be mortified if they did not read every day that London was burning.'

I discovered how true that was when the bombings were intensified. The satisfaction was expressed even by those whom I respected and liked. There was a young Bengali freelance writer for whose intelligence and knowledge I had admiration. He told me one day in September: 'The Germans are not allowing the fires in London to go out even for a day.' I at first thought this was a reflection on German inhumanity. But in a moment I discovered that the remark was made in tones of unbounded admiration. Yet he was in all other matters a very decent young man.

His advocacy of Germany soon led to a very unpleasant incident. He would come and discuss the war with me in my room in Sarat Babu's house and maintain that Germany was bound to win. One day the argument got rather heated, and to avoid bad temper, I requested him to drop the subject. He did not, and when rising to leave the room he continued to argue. I curtly told him that I would not have this bandying of words in my room. He replied equally curtly: 'This is not your room. You are only a servant in this house.' I at once leaped on him, dragged him down to the floor by his rather long hair, and began to beat him mercilessly in the face with a slipper. He only wept and went on saying in a broken voice: 'Would you beat me like this!' Hearing the commotion, my personal assistant came on the scene and made me leave off. The young man got up, and, in order to maintain his self-respect, said: 'Do you know how much strength I have in my wrists?' I was heartily sorry for such an incident. But the man went and told the story around the newspaper offices, so that the next time I met Suresh Majumdar he said to me: 'I hear you almost killed X.' I could only mumble my excuses. But the revolting exhibition of exultation over the bombing of Britain went on till the early months of 1941.

My second worry was over a possible invasion of England. I did not know what to make of it. I now know that the prospect was taken seriously by Churchill and the British Government. Even so, I did not think it would really take place. As the news of the preparations and even of a date of invasion came to India, there was eager expectation among our people. I had read a good deal about Napoleon's invasion project in 1803-4, and wondered whether I was not seeing a repetition of that. When, however, by the beginning of September, no invasion had taken place, people seemed to be preparing for a disappointment. They even anticipated Hitler in saying that only the English Channel was saving the British people. When Hitler actually said that, I thought I might as well have my share of the joke. So I wrote a letter to The Statesman, which it published. Here it is:

'Sir,

'Hitler's reference to the "fortunate geographical position" of England contains more of a fallacy than a truism. What is this "fortunate geographical position"? A stretch of the sea which at its narrowest is some 21 miles wide. There is more than twenty miles of the sea between Great Britain and India, there is more than twenty miles of the sea between Japan and China, there is more than twenty miles of the sea between French Indo-China and Japan. Instances may be multiplied. But these instances of "fortunate geographical position" have not prevented political and military consequences which must be obvious to everybody.

'The decisive and relevant factor which has saved Great Britain is not the sea but sea power, as symbolized in her navy. Germany challenged this navy from 1894 to 1916. That she did not and has not succeeded in this is not due to the "fortunate geographical position" of Great Britain, but to Other reasons. In fact, had von Tirpitz's dream come true, the "fortunate geographical position" would not have existed.

'It is futile to refer to such hypothetical contingencies such as what would have happened if the sea had not stood between Great Britain and Germany, for in that case Great Britain would probably have concentrated on the army and turned herself into a great continental power as Germany herself

'Yours, etc. Nirad C. Chaudhuri, Calcutta, 8 September, 1940.'

The fact of the matter was that Indians had no conception whatever of what sea power was or meant. My acquaintances often asked me this question: 'If naval power is so decisive why can't the British invade the Continent?' It was useless to reply that ships could not sail on land. I had read a good deal of history of naval warfare from the middle of the eighteenth century to 1918, as also Mahan. So I knew what it meant for Britain.

Now I come to the third count of my anxiety about the future. If I was not very seriously perturbed by the possibility of a German invasion of England, I was more perturbed by the fear of German military adventures in two other regions: namely, through Spain in order to occupy North Africa; and secondly, through Turkey, to drive forward even to India. I could not envisage a successful resistance to such moves by Germany from the two countries. I knew nothing then of the relations between Hitler and Franco or of the latter's opposition to Hitler's ideas. So I remained on tenterhooks, expecting to hear bad news every day, and was reassured only by my idea that the German General Staff would not embark on such improvised ventures. At the time I could not even think of a German attack on the Soviet Union as being possible.

The war situation remained a source of anxiety for me during the succeeding months, but at the beginning of 1941 my attention was partly diverted to a very disagreeable domestic development in Bengal. At that time there was a sudden outbreak of the chronic Hindu-Muslim animosity in Dacca district. Actually, there was no rioting between the communities but only attacks on Hindu villages and homes by the Muslims over a very wide area of the district. These attacks, accompanied by looting and burning of Hindu houses, were continuous, and they were apparently allowed to go on by the Bengal Government, which was under a Muslim ministry. The panic among the Hindus was very great, and thousands of them fled to the neighbouring Hindu princely state of Tripura. But the refugees were almost exclusively men, and upon seeing that the Maharaja of Tripura was reported to have said: 'I see only men and even young men here. Where then are your women?' Of course, they had been left behind according to the normal habit of Hindu Bengalis when in trouble. But this desertion was covered up by a loud outcry about the abduction of the women. The Muslims laughed and said that since the Hindu men had fled they had no alternative but to feed and look after the Hindu women, which was true up to a point.

The Press in Calcutta and the politicians raised a hue and cry, and began to denounce the Muslim Government. Political parties were naturally anxious to exploit the situation as much as possible. The leading politician of the party with pronounced Hindu leanings at once flew to Dacca to offer his sympathy to the Hindus. But Sarat Bose did not. So, there were piteous appeals to him from the Congressite politicians not to allow the Congress to become the object of criticism and to go to Dacca to balance the visit by the Hindu leader. Sarat Babu did not, however, leave Calcutta but raised his voice in the Legislative Assembly. He severely criticized the Muslim ministry for its failure to give protection to the Hindus, and brought forward charges of abduction and forcible conversion to Islam against the Muslim rioters. The Muslim Home Minister at once asked him to bring authentic instances to his notice, and assured him that he would deal with them. Sarat Babu issued an appeal for information.

At once letters began to pour in. There were scores and more of them, and Sarat Babu asked me to read and analyse them. Never had I read anything more sickening in its meanness and cowardice. All of them related stories of unresisting submission to any Muslim demand, which if true were worse testimony against the Hindus themselves than against the Muslims. I give one example. An elderly Hindu wrote that he and his young sister-in-law (brother's wife) were seized by the Muslims, and threatened with death if they would not agree to become Muslim. He agreed in order to save their lives and both were converted to Islam. They were then confined in a house, from which, he said, he had somehow escaped, adding that he did not know what had happened to his young sister-in-law. There was never any mention of this woman's husband. He had probably fled earlier. The Bengali word used for 'young' by the writer has the suggestion not only of youthfulness but also of embonpoint.

I had to read a number of these letters and then, sickened by them, I decided to leave the rest unread. Apart from these personal lamentations, the Press was keeping up a chorus of squeals which got on my nerves, so I decided to deliver a homily of my own. I was prompted to do this all the more on account of their gloating over the continuous bombing of England to which was being added their praise of the German campaign in Yugoslavia. This homily took the form of my usual safety valve, a letter to the Press. I wrote a long letter to *The Statesman*, which it published with the heading I gave to it. Here is its text:

'OUR SUFFERING AND THEIRS'

'Sir, – During the last few days I have had occasion to note the intensity of indignation, horror, and pity among Hindu Bengalis, particularly of the professional, business, and landed classes over the deplorable happenings in Dacca. The reports of burning, looting, assaults, and murder have profoundly shocked them, and they cannot conceive how others can fail to sympathise with the Hindu victims or take up any but a non-partisan attitude to their sufferings.

'This is not only natural, but right. The moment a community loses its sense of distinction between right and wrong, kindliness and cruelty, or its intolerance of evil, it goes a step backward in the scale of civilization. But it is not enough that we should feel for ourselves, the duty is wider. From the beginning of this war, I have found among a majority of the self-same people, who today are so deeply moved by the distress of the Dacca Hindus, an indifference to national and individual suffering which has pained and shocked many of us.

'They gloated over the defeats of the Polish, Finnish, Norwegian, Dutch, and Belgian peoples and triumphed at the suppression of their national independence. They are now gloating in the same way over the ordeals of the Serbs and the Greeks. They were furious with the Finns and the Greeks for what measure of success they had against the aggressors. These people forget that we Indians have no quarrel with these nations and their cause is the same as we proclaim to be ours, that they are weak and their oppressors strong. No, these nations did not receive from this particular class of Indians the common human pity that all decent people extend to the underdog and the downtrodden. It is enough that the Poles, the Norwegians, the Dutch, the Belgians fought Germany who is fighting Great Britain, and that the Finns had fought Soviet Russia who was supposed to be a friend of Germany.

'With these people it is a case of a loyalty to hatred getting the better of loyalty to a principle, always a weakling's choice. The logic of this weakness is inexorable. It is driving these people to regard China's war of national independence as a crime and the liberation of the Abyssinian people as a mortification.

'The approach to personal suffering is more incredible still. The accounts of the bombing of big cities do not make pleasant reading. Even the reports burn into the brain like scalds, and one should expect normal people to wince at them, wherever the loss of life took place, in Great Britain or Germany. But again, no. The people I am speaking about could not read about the bombing of the big cities in the non-Axis countries with greater gusto than if they had been the bombers themselves. The newspapers which depend on the patronage of this class are compelled to serve out what their patrons want...

'I have read that on Nablus road in Palestine, where the Turkish 7th Army was annihilated by air attacks in September, 1918, the slaughter was such that even the pilots – a tough bunch – were sickened, and the infantry, hardened soldiers that they were, were absolutely appalled when they came up. But it is not so here. Although it has been said that there is neither East nor West, Border, nor Breed, nor Birth when two strong men stand face to face, the British Tommy and such men of the East as I am referring to here, will never meet. And please remember that these self-same men are in the habit of whining, misbehaving, and shedding self-pitying tears to the end of the journey if they are accidentally trodden upon in a tramcar.

'I have met scores of such people. What is the good of it, I have tried to argue, would that bring our independence nearer? If you feel like that, I have said, one would expect you to be doing something instead of following "business as usual" during the day and tuning in to the Berlin Radio in the evening. We harm and corrode only ourselves by this kind of futile hate, I have repeated. But all my arguments have been brushed aside. They have pleaded helplessness, want of organization, the worthlessness of the leaders, the incapacity or fads of Mahatma Gandhi or Mr Subhas Chandra Bose, according to their political affiliations or taste, the impossibility of risking personal safety and prosperity, and, when hard-pressed, have even admitted their own worthlessness and want of manliness, but they would not admit that they had no right to their vicarious satisfaction.

'I am afraid I have been very frank, and I cannot produce documentary evidence to prove what I say. But that should not be put down against me, the fault lies with those who do not have the courage of their convictions. Those who move among Indians must know these statements to be true of a particular section of them. For many of us it has become an intolerable experience and we feel we must speak out.

'Still, I ought to admit that my experience has been confined to a particular section. There must be thousands who feel differently. Among my acquaintances are men who not only disapprove of, but have a passionate loathing of this furtive and barren hate. What is even more of a redeeming thought, among the better type of our nationalist workers, men who have suffered and lost much, one finds little of this gloating over suffering. They are not friendly to anything British, and perhaps never will be, but they know what suffering and courage are and respect both. I have heard some of the most eminent of them bursting out with an open expression of admiration for the fight the British people are putting up, rebuking the sneers of the weaker ones at British morale. The sneers and the gloating are, as a rule, the speciality of the "non-combatant" in safe places.

'Yours, etc., Nirad C. Chaudhuri. 12 April, 1941.'

The letter should speak for itself I would, however, give some explanations. The omissions in the citation are of the sentences in which I gave the substance of my conversation with Suresh Majumdar about the bombing of London without mentioning his name. The defence of the British people was by Sarat Bose. He was sitting with his courtiers, and they were sneering at the British and making taunting remarks. He listened for some time and then reacted with this: 'At least they are fighting. What are you doing for your country." I wrote about thousands who might have been decent. That was an expression of hope. I met hardly half a dozen. I also had to be discreet in the letter. My views on the war were not shared morally or intellectually by many I met. At that time I was writing for the well known financial paper. *Capital*, of Calcutta. Its editor. Sir Geoffrey Tyson, asked me one day: 'How many Indians besides you believe that we shall win the war?' I could only say that if there were even two, they had been induced to respect my opinions without wholeheartedly accepting them.

Encouraged by the publication of this letter, I wrote a long article in which I criticized the Congress for submitting to this barren hatred in its policies. I gave it the title 'The Congress in Chains'. Upon receiving it, Mr Wordsworth, the second man on the editorial staff of *The Statesman*, sent for me. He had once been Principal of Presidency College, Calcutta, when I was at that College. He said that he would rather I did not publish the article, for I had brought enough unpopularity on myself, and should not court more. The article is still with me. The barren hatred not only continued, but took a very bizarre form with the German attack on the Soviet Union.

CHAPTER 4

From Exultation to Panic

Exultation the Indian nationalists over British, defeats and reverses continued unabated during the first eleven months,of 1941,,but with the entry of Japan into the war in December it became mingled with abject panic. It seemed to them that the war might now actually come to India, and affect their moneymaking or even, lives, and such circumstances wholehearted enjoyment of British disasters might no more be possible. But in the spring of 1941 there was no expectation in India that Japan would go to war, and the British were still losing battles and campaigns in Europe and North Africa in a satisfactory manner.

The German successes in the Balkans and Greece, followed by the spectacular German invasion of Crete by air, confirmed for everybody in India the idea of German superiority in military capacity as also the certainty which existed in Indian minds that Germany would win the war. A rising Bengali barrister, who had been at the London School of Economics and held a doctorate of London University, told me after these German successes that Britain neither could nor would win the war. When I asked him why, he replied: 'Because *non-science* can never beat *science*.' To him, Britain was the last citadel of obscurantist scholastic lore. He seemed never to have heard of the Cavendish and Clarendon Laboratories, and he certainly did not explain why he had gone to London instead of to Berlin for his education. He, however, had his original idea of the inferiority of the British people in military technology. Ordinary Bengalis at that time used to tell me that the British were inferior because they did not have the Stukas, i.e. the dive-bombers. They had just read about the performance of these aircraft in Crete. But the barrister had a different idea.

He thought for a while and then replied to my second question, which was in what way were the British *non-science*: 'Because they don't have 18-inch guns.' I was not going to let him off so easily. So, when he came next time I showed him the provisional Field Service Regulations of 1922, whose appendix described the artillery of the British army and included 18-inch heavy guns on railway mountings. Not at all abashed, he turned his attack on my ignorance to another sector. Speaking of the Balkan campaign, I had called the river Vardar. He corrected me and said that its correct name was Vardari. When I said that the name was given as Vardar in my atlas (which was the biggest Philips had published at the time) he simply remarked: 'Throw that a way.'

In the early summer of 1941 the situation in Libya kept me very anxious. I feared that from Crete the Germans might launch an airborne attack on the African coast and make Tobruk, which was under siege, untenable. I did not know then that the German losses in trained pilots in Crete were very heavy and that another similar airborne landing could not be attempted.

'The 'Indian attitude towards the war in north Africa was very paradoxical.' There was no Indian admiration for the Italians, nor even sympathy for them in their defeats. On the Contrary, there was even contempt. Therefore the campaigns in north Africa in 1940 had not evoked much feeling . But all that was changed with the arrival of Rommel and the Afrika Korps.

The first phase of the sortie Of the *Bismarck* evoked wild admiration, and the sinking of the *Hood* was regarded as the final proof of the worthlessness of the boasted British navy. Suresh Majumdar's English daily could not get a picture of the battlecruiser on the day it had to publish the news of the sinking, and so it repeated the news the next day With a picture. The joy was indeed followed by a severe shock when the *Bismarck* was sunk. But it was regarded as the cowardly victory of a whole British squadron over a single German warship. A Bengali engineer compared the sinking of the battleship to a famous episode in the Mahabharata, in which seven Kuru warriors surrounded the young son of Arjuna, Abhimanyu, and shamefully killed him. The Bengali observed to me: 'It was a repetition of Abhimanyu-vadha', with almost tears in his eyes. It seemed that Hitler did not regard the Germans as Aryans for nothing.

But the power of the hatred of Britain to influence attitudes and opinion in India was proven to me most decisively when Hitler launched his attack on the Soviet Union On Sunday, 22 June 1941,I came to Sarat Bose's house rather early in the afternoon, when he had not yet come down after his midday siesta. The telephone rang! Answering it I heard Suresh Majumdar's voice; recognizing mine, he asked: 'What do you think of it?' 'Of what?' I replied. 'You have not heard?' Suresh Babu replied, 'Germany has attacked the Soviet Union.' I burst out involuntarily: 'Oh, I'm glad, I'm glad. It's the end of Germany.' But I also said that I was glad for another reason: 'Russia will be terribly punished for her opportunism in 1939.' I was thinking of the non-aggression pact of that year. But Suresh Babu pursued another line of thinking. He asked me: 'Don't you think that Britain will now make peace with Germany, and join in a common assault on Communist Russia." I answered without a moment's hesitation: 'No, that will not happen.'

Of course, Suresh Babu's expectation was shared by the whole of the Indian intelligentsia. They thought that in order to retain her empire, Britain was interested above all in a crusade against Communism. But it was not so very exceptional for Indian nationalists to take that view. Even in India I became aware that some resident Englishmen were inclined to take the view that for Britain to be on the same side with the Soviet Union in a war with Germany would not be morally right. Two or three days after Churchill had definitely committed Britain to close co-operation with Russia in the war, I went to see an English acquaintance of mine at the house of the Bishop of Calcutta and Metropolitan of India, where he was staying. While I was with him two young English clergymen came In and began a very animated discussion of the moral aspect of Churchill's decision - whether making common cause with Communist Russia was not opportunistic. My English acquaintance had obviously heard the argument before, and produced a letter in which he had explained the moral position as he understood it, and proposed to send it to *The Statesman.* They discussed it for some time. I was wholly surprised, and even somewhat impatient, because I had never thought that such a moral issue was involved at all. But I now know that it was raised even in Churchill's inner circle. When he spoke of his decision to his secretary Colville, the latter asked if that was not for him, the anti-communist, like worshipping in the House of Rimmon. Churchill had just then told the company at dinner that Hitler had attacked the Soviet Union anticipating capitalist and right-wing sympathies in Britain for him. He knew that a section of his own party and some of the Press would be against Britain's coming down on the side of the Soviets. Even Eden was a little apprehensive and wanted to see the text of Churchill's broadcast beforehand, but he was not given the opportunity. So, the Indian expectation on this matter - in contrast with other opinions of theirs on the war - had not been entirely absurd.

But the real absurdity or perversity of Indian opinion was seen in another direction: in the total change of attitude in regard to the Soviet Union. This filled me with contempt and disgust for the Indian intelligentsia. Their previous worship of Communist Russia at once turned into hatred. The *volte face* was most blatant in the Bengali intellectuals. Till 21 June they had been fanatical admirers of the Soviet Union. From 1917 to that day the Bengali fellow-feeling for Communist Russia was like a religious sentiment, in which they were even more extreme than many English radicals. But neither the sympathy nor the admiration was very perceptive. Most Bengali writers and intellectuals had created an idea of Russia after the revolution of 1917 in their own image. They thought that the Russians were the same sort of self-pitying and feckless weaklings as they themselves were. Some of the Bengali avant garde had begun to describe Russia as 'Russia of the Sorrows'. All that froth was washed off at sunrise on 12 June 1941, and the Bengalis, disappointed at Britain's not acting according to their wishes, turned their fury on Russia and began to rest their hopes on a quick collapse of the Soviets. Only a small number of staunch communists formed an exception and, by their attitude during this phase of the war, wholly discredited themselves in the nationalist politics of India. The majority began to hope and even pray for the defeat of the Soviet Union. I heard that there was even a bet among the barristers of Calcutta High Court, all of them of course from the Inns of Court of London, that Russia would be defeated and surrender by the end of August.

Although I had expected that Russia would suffer terribly in resisting the armies of Hitler, I was not prepared for so quick and extensive a debâcle as was seen in the first weeks of the war on the eastern front. The attempt to resist the German armies along the frontiers had obviously failed, and I could only hope that the advance would be held up somewhere without being able to guess where. The idea of a German retreat only after an occupation of Moscow, to illustrate the dictum that history repeats itself, did not give me any comfort. I know now that the German advance was delayed and stopped only by throwing Russian bodies against German steel. My friend Gopal Haldar, who to his credit retained his sympathy for Russia in spite of being a nationalist, and indeed was a professed Bengali Communist, came to me one day in panic and asked me what I thought of the military situation. Like me, he had seen the exultation in Bengali nationalist circles at the prospect of Russia going the way of France as in the previous year. I could not give him any solid comfort and could only say that if the Soviet Union was not knocked out by the end of August, most probably it would not be eliminated. I myself was very worried.

But at the beginning of August I was deeply grieved at the news of a serious illness of Rabindranath Tagore. It was reported that he was seriously ill and had been brought down to his Calcutta house for treatment. He was said to be in a coma. I knew that if he died the last great man produced by Bengal would be gone. As I have made it clear, by that time I had come to the conclusion that the Bengali people had no future. Nonetheless, Tagore, although reduced almost to a shadow even in his bodily presence, was a symbol of Bengal's greatness and achievements. With the disappearance of that symbol, the transition of Bengal — from having been something in Indian life and history - to nothing, would be complete.

For many years he had been ailing. His heart was weak and in the mid- Thirties a friend of mine who knew him well and belonged to his circle told me that when he saw the platform from which he was to address a public meeting in Delhi, he uttered an aside in dismay; 'Oh, the executioner's scaffold!' I have described how shocked I was when I saw him in 1937, when he came to Sarat Babu's house to see Gandhi. He was already a physical wreck though not more than seventy-seven. In 1941 he was worse, and after the latest attack the doctors, the best in Calcutta, could do nothing for him. He died on 7 August, aged eighty years and three months.

What I heard about the behaviour of the Bengali middle class in his last days in Calcutta made me very angry. After abusing him as long as he lived, they suddenly discovered that he was one of them. They clamoured to see him on his deathbed, declaring that his snobbish family and entourage had no right to keep him to themselves and away from his people. One day the crowds almost broke the iron gates of his house to get into the courtyard, and Shyamaprasad Mookherji had to go down and implore them to respect Tagore's last hours. A friend of mine who was in the sickroom on the second floor suddenly saw a face peering into the room from a window. The fellow had climbed up a gutter pipe. My friend told him to have some pity for a dying man, and the man sulkily slid down.

When the Bengal Government, headed by the Muslim Chief Minister, heard of Tagore's death, they proposed a state funeral. This, the family refused. But the funeral was taken out of the family's control. A rabble invaded the house, took hold of Tagore's body, and carried it on a bier towards the burning ghat of Nimtollah, which I have described. Enormous crowds milled towards the burning yard and many eminent men, including Sarat Bose, who wanted to attend the cremation, could not enter. I heard that some Bengalis jumped up on the pyre and tore off Tagore's hair and beard as keepsake or trophy. Thus the body of the greatest Bengali ever born was reduced to ashes. Like the funerals of all the great men of India in recent times, Tagore's too was an exhibition of combined mass hysteria and mass fun, i.e. canonization by desecration. It was a typical exhibition of the intolerance of 'élitism' in respect of a man who never had any friendliness for anybody who did not belong to an élite.

Soon after, in the autumn of 1941 to be precise, I had a wholly new kind of experience, which brought me a good deal of relief from the strain of following the war. In spite of the reassurance I had given to Gopal Haldar, I was anxious about Russia. In any case, I was awed by the scale of the conflict. If in respect of the war of 1812 I was evenly divided between the Russians and Napoleon in my emotional involvement on account of my admiration for Napoleon as well as for Tolstoy's *War and Peace*, this time there was no sympathy in me for the invaders. Yet somehow, I felt confident about the Russian resistance. But the strain of keeping it up was great.

For about four weeks, however, I had a respite. That was from a change of place and climate, both mental and geographical. With my family I went to Allahabad in upper India. It was an ancient city and a great place of pilgrimage for the Hindus. It had also become a place for political pilgrimage because it was in this city that Jawaharlal Nehru was born, brought up, and lived.

The reason for this holiday was my wife's persistent illness for two years. At the end of 1939 she had a very bad attack of pleurisy, and it recurred at the beginning of the next cold season during which she had to keep to her bed for about three months. She was under the treatment of the best specialists in Calcutta, and of course at home, where she was cared for by a professional nurse. But the recurrence alarmed me, and I thought unless I took her to a drier place before the next winter this recurrence would continue. I chose Allahabad and took a house there. It was in an open part of the city. I was glad to find that this change, followed by a move to Delhi the year after, cured her permanently.

When at Allahabad, I undertook the two pilgrimages, as a matter of course. That is, all of us went out in a boat to the confluence of the Ganges and the Jumna, and had a dip there (with the exception of myself). We also had a look from the outside at the two houses of the Nehrus - the older one given to the Congress and the new one in which Nehru lived.

But my most memorable experience at Allahabad was that of Mogul architecture. I was very familiar with the history of Muslim architecture in India and had seen pictures of all the important Mogul monuments. But I had never actually seen them. At Allahabad I got my first opportunity to do so. It was not indeed a great centre of that school of architecture, but as I had not seen any building of that period at all, even those at Allahabad impressed me immensely. These monuments, although minor, are very beautiful. They are all in a walled garden called Khusru Bagh. This name was given to it after a son of the Mogul emperor Jahangir, the Prince Khusru who had rebelled against his father, for which he was kept in prison.

After sixteen years of imprisonment he was murdered at the instance of his stepbrother, who later became the Emperor Shah Jahan. He was buried in the garden and had a mausoleum over the grave. His mother's tomb was already there. She had committed suicide upon hearing of her son's rebellion. There was a third tomb meant for her daughter. The three buildings stood side by side.

They were not large, nor indeed very elaborate. But seeing actual Mogul monuments for the first time, I was enabled to form from them a correct idea of architectural proportion. Both externally and internally, all the three buildings were perfect in their proportions. The Queen's tomb had a pyramidal structure, and rose to the apex in stepped pavilions. As I examined the monument from a distance, I was astonished to discover that from the base to the apex each side presented an equilateral triangle. Before Lord Curzon had all the historical monuments in India cleared of intrusions by British officers of the Indian Army, this particular monument was the residence of one officer.

The monuments to Khusru and his sister stood on high terraces and were surmounted by domes. These, too, had the same perfect proportions as their mother's tomb. After seeing the two tombs I realized for the first time the underlying principle of relating a dome to the main structure below it. A final demonstration confirmed this when I later saw the Invalides in Paris. One of the monuments had also a painted ceiling. I knew of only one Mogul monument which had such a ceiling, and that was at Agra. I had seen pictures of that ceiling. The ceiling of the third tomb at Allahabad had the same type of painted decoration in Indian red and gold. My stay at Allahabad was very happy, and I added to the pleasure by going to Benares on our way back to Calcutta, and showed both Benares and Sarnath to my wife and children, besides renewing my old acquaintance with these places.

Shortly after my return to Calcutta I met with a wholly new experience. I went to Government House to attend a press conference held by Field- Marshal Wavell, who was at that time Commander-in-Chief in India, He was to speak about the war and, more especially, of his campaign in the Western Desert, and even more particularly about the German occupation of Crete. Sir Geoffrey Tyson, to whose weekly financial journal, *The Capital*, I had become'a regular contributor of editorial notes, asked me if I would accompany him to Government House. I raised the difficulty that I had no European clothes, which till 1942 I never wore, and that in my Bengali dress I might be out of place. He simply replied: 'Don't be foolish and come along.' So I went.

The press conference was being held in the old legislative council chamber in the northeastern wing of the House, and the Field-Marshal came in with the major-general who had commanded the infantry in Crete. All the important editors and other journalists of Calcutta were there and they put some questions to Wavell after he had finished speaking. We noticed that the general from Crete nodded and at times dozed off, and woke up with a startled look when the field-marshal asked him to supplement something he had said.

I was not interested so much in the past as in the future, and one question which was uppermost in my mind at the time made me wish to put it to Wavell. That was about Japan. I was very much puzzled about that country, and could not explain why, till then, she had not come into the war. But somehow I felt shy and did not speak.

That was 6 December 1941. The answer came the next day with the news of the Japanese attack on Pearl Harbor. We did not get all the details on Monday, but such as they were, the news shocked me. I knew that the American Fleet was the only thing which could have deterred Japan from a seaborne invasion of south-east Asia, and now it was *hors de combat*. I only hoped the news was no worse than reported, which indeed it was. The

Malay peninsula and Indonesia were threatened, and the *Prince of Wales* and the *Renown* could not do much. But I hoped they would at least make the Japanese operations more risky.' That hope, too, was destroyed on the 10th. I was sitting in my room when my personal assistant came in and told me that the two ships - he gave the names - had been sunk by the Japanese. At first I could not believe it, but he said he had heard the names clearly on the radio. I at once concluded that the great new Japanese battleships, *Musashi* and *Yamato*, must have been completed and that the British battle squadron must have been destroyed by one of them. I could not even imagine that they could be sunk by aerial bombing, and, of course, I knew nothing of the Japanese air bases in Indo-China from where torpedo bombers in large numbers could operate.

In the evening, as I was dining, a friend of mine called and confirmed the news. He also wanted to know what I thought about it. I could say nothing. I was dazed, and from that night I again felt the pain in my chest which I had suffered after the French defeat in 1940. That lasted for some days.

Yet I could understand this disaster, but not that of the American navy and air force at Pearl Harbor. That seemed to be the result of incredible stupidity and negligence. I recalled what I had read about the precautions which Churchill took as soon as he came to the Admiralty in 1912, against any possible German surprise attack on the Grand Fleet or its bases, and how he continued the ritual of daily supervision of the precautions till 1914. Also, I could not understand how the Americans had overlooked the possibility of a surprise attack, forgetting that every war that the Japanese had fought from the end of the nineteenth century had been opened by her military chiefs with a surprise. Then I also recalled what an English friend had said to me In 1931 about the carelessness of the Americans. He told me that in a naval war they would get some nasty shocks. When I asked him why he thought so, he told me of the personal experience of a friend of his. An American cruiser, he said, was on a visit to Southampton and was anchored at a wharf. This friend went on board and all over the ship without being detected or prevented. With such notions of security they would have to suffer, my friend said.

My anger with the Americans for the disaster at Pearl Harbor was not, and to this day has not been, suppressed by my consideration of its long-term result. The British and Dutch Empires, and also the French in Indo-China, would not have disappeared so easily nor so quickly except for the

Japanese occupation of the whole region, which was made possible by the crippling of the American navy in the Pacific. What the anti-imperialistic feeling of the Americans, which they very foolishly believed to be idealistic, could not do,'and would never have done, was accomplished by a colossal American blunder. Anyone who says that we should only laugh at foolishness is a fool himself: in respect of the capacity to inflict permanent harm, both foolishness and wickedness stand on the same footing, perhaps foolishness on a higher.

I shall not write at length about what I felt or did during the following months as I read the news of the war in south-east Asia. The fall of Singapore was another disaster, although not on the same scale or of the same significance as that of Pearl Harbor; For me, at that time, it was only a question of what unpleasant news I should have to read the next day, and whether that would not be worse than today's. However, in my writing and comments on the war I tried to be as calm as possible, never showing any loss of confidence. What sustained me very effectively at the time was the attitude of Churchill. I found that in spite of the disasters for Britain with which the war with japan had opened, he actually welcomed it because it had brought in the United States, which meant ultimate defeat for both Germany and Japan. In the meanwhile, I read that he was prepared even for the loss of India. I tried to put a brave face on the war, but my mental suffering was great.

I could not, like Churchill, contemplate the occupation of India or Bengal by the Japanese as a temporary evil only, for I knew what the consequences would be for me personally. In taking stock of that, I had no very great fear of the Japanese, but I had more of my fellow-Bengalis. So I told my wife in January or February:

'I do not really think that the British will lose the war, nor that the Japanese would occupy Bengal, even temporarily. But in war it is always safe to keep in mind the worst, for what happens in the actual course of a war is largely incalculable. So, let me assume that the Japanese are in Bengal, and I would tell you what would happen to me at the hands of fellow-Bengalis, who have learnt to hate me for my pro-British opinions and broadcasts. If they feel safe they would lynch me. Therefore, if any situation of that sort arises and I am attacked, I shall kill you and the children, set fire to the house, and die fighting. If you are prepared to face that, I shall go on with my pro-British broadcasts, otherwise not.'

My wife trusted my judgement; in any case she was not the person to take hypothetical dangers seriously. In respect of the future, her attitude and mine have always differed basically. I was always for keeping in view the *logical worst* as well as the *logical best*, and be ready with my plans for both, hardening myself for the worst and thinking of the steps to take if the best happened. In contrast, my wife throughout our married life has shown herself opposed to going forward to meet an imagined danger. For her, the motto has always been - not 'sufficient unto the day is the evil thereof, but the *good* thereof. Thus she simply replied to my bloodcurdling declaration: 'Do as you think right. I should not worry much.' I continued my pro- British propaganda.

But, in actual fact, I did not have the fear of which I took account. I did not think that the Japanese would try to occupy India even if they conquered Burma. I knew something of the Japanese military thinking, which was very much like that of the Germans. They would not embark on any military venture about which they had not thought carefully over a long period of time. Already, I thought, they had bitten off more than they could chew. An invasion of India, even in her weakened state of defence, would need an immense organization, especially with regard to supplies and lines of communication.

However, that was not the view of those to whom I had to listen. Almost everyone I talked to in Calcutta, including high Bengali officials, believed that, by the end of February or at least by March, the whole of Bengal including Calcutta would be occupied by the Japanese. A friend of mine had a typical argument about this with a relative of his, who was a magistrate in one of the districts. While my friend, briefed by me, said that nothing would happen, his relative held the current view. I think the conversation was in January. They argued for two hours, and at about eleven the relative looked at his watch and said: 'I must go now. I have an appointment with the Chief Secretary [of the Government of Bengal, an Englishman] and I shall ask him about my promotion.' My friend replied: 'If the Japanese are taking over in three months is there any point in seeing the English Chief Secretary about a promotion?' The retort was characteristic: 'Don't be flippant about serious matters.' But perhaps he had not argued quite insincerely. All the high Indian officials believed that whoever governed the country they themselves would be regarded as indispensable, and the higher they were in the old regime the higher they would be in the new.

They were right. This exactly happened in 1947 when the Congress, which was not less hostile to the British than to the Japanese, took over.

A Japanese victory would have involved the occupation of Bengal, something which, in emotional terms, would have been roost welcome to the Bengalis. But this prospect, on the plane of behaviour and action, actually gave rise to the most abject and cowardly panic. There was a stampede to flee Calcutta and to go as far away as possible. Those who could not reach Rajputana (as the Marwari merchants did), went at least as far as the borders of Bengal or a northern district. Those who only went a short distance, did so because they were afraid of aerial bombardment. I said very flippantly to some that since everybody could not get away and some would inevitably die, why not you and your family instead of your neighbour.'

The panic began on 9 December. A near relative of mine called on me and said: 'Nirad, a friend of mine has just returned from Singapore and he says the British have nothing there with which to resist the Japanese. What should we do.' Should we not leave Calcutta for a safer place?' I replied: 'If our staying on in Calcutta depended upon what the British had in Singapore we would not remain here a day.' The general assumption was that Japanese bombs would begin to fail on Calcutta from that day. The second assumption was that all essential necessities would fall short. So a neighbour bought two tons of coal on Monday, the 9th.

Both reactions were typical. Those who could run away did so; those who could not, hoarded. Some only sent away their families, and that included the wives. I was told that some wives refused to leave without having the life insurance policies of their husbands endorsed in their favour. But one wife I knew would not leave her husband. She only sent away all her saris to a safe place in the country. I could not prevent even my near relatives either from running away or from hoarding. The irony, however, was that no bombs fell while these people were away. Most of those who had fled had to return and it was almost a year later that the first Japanese bomb fell on Calcutta. When that happened nobody minded.

But even fear yielded to another passion, which was to make money. At the beginning it was the fear which gave an opportunity to do so. The booking clerks would not issue tickets at the railway stations without handsome bribes, and taxi-drivers, hackney carriage men, and porters, put up their prices. The tenants, on the other hand, at once reduced their rents unilaterally, and the landlords had to submit.

When the fear had disappeared, the passion,for making money increased, instead of declining. There were more jobs, more contracts, and more demand for goods of all kinds. If the introduction of provincial autonomy had given a blow to honesty as I have related, the war with Japan gave a second and a greater one. The unscrupulous moneymaking was the major cause of the terrible famine which swept Bengal the following year,and that further whetted the appetite for making money out of misery and want. The war situation in India was stabilized into enjoyment of the war materially, as opposed to merely emotionally.

I had to leave Calcutta for Delhi in March, and, as it turned out, permanently. But before I left I said in my last broadcast about the war from Calcutta that there was very little chance of a Japanese invasion of eastern India.

CHAPTER 5

Tagore: The Lost Great Man of India

I have described the death of Tagore, but I also wish to offer an appraisement of his life, because he was a part of the life of all Bengalis of my generation. For his own sake, too, I have thought it fit to include the appraisement in this book. He is virtually forgotten in the West, and even in Bengal he is remembered in the most wrong manner imaginable. There is not even an adequate biography of him in English, and the long biography in Bengali is only a compilation of information.

Thinking even of his literary achievement one might say that great as it is; it too will not assure him the immortality he deserves, Tagore personally had no fear of death, for his belief in an after life was unwavering. That was only a matter of faith; But I wonder if he ever gave any thought to a different kind of immortality, the immortality, that is to say, through his writings, All men must die, but it is the writer who is most assured of immortality on earth for his spirit There is nothing strictly immortal but immortality, said Sir Thomas Browne as a mystic thinking of eternal life in God and setting that against the vanity of trying to perpetuate the memory of one's existence through pyramids or mummies. But Sir Thomas Browne's, books have ensured for him the immortality which, as he said, no pyramid could give. Although he was right about pyramids, he could have added that to subsist in the embodiments of one's mind which books , are, is not a fallacy in duration. Indeed, he still lives through his books, and every writer who reaches a certain level of expression cap ensure his co-existence with mankind in the same way. Could or did Tagore hope for that kind of immortality?

Whether he himself gave any thought to it or not, there can be no doubt that he had the right to it. Even if the number of writers from all ages and all countries is reduced to a score by a rigorous scrutiny of merit, Tagore would be one of them- When in 1961 India was celebrating the centenary of his birth, my foreign friends who knew nothing about the prestige which Tagore once enjoyed in the West and felt that there was something artificial about the enthusiasm, asked me what I really thought about him. Without a moment's hesitation I replied that out of his very large output in all genres, at least one-third would or should survive for all time. They observed that no higher claim could be made for any writer of the past.

I have also declared in print that when the Nobel Prize for literature was awarded to him in 1913, he was far above all the thirteen writers of various nationalities who had got the Prize before him. I should like now to define his status more concretely by saying that, if he is to be appraised by a European standard of reference, he would be in the hierarchy limited by Goethe on one side and Victor Hugo on the other. And if I were asked who was the greatest poet produced by India, including the greatest of the ancient Indians, Kalidasa, I would certainly reply: 'Tagore,' but not 'Tagore,alas!'

Denial of His Due

The tragedy, however, is that his greatness as a writer will never be established universally like, for example, Goethe's, Hugo's, or Tolstoy's. And although to be accepted at his real value only in Bengal could never be an adequate reward for his genius, even that he will not secure. He was virtually rejected by a majority of fellow-Bengalis in his life time, because what he wrote was far above their head, and not fully understood even by the small number of admirers who made an idol of him. Now the position is worse because both Bengali life and Bengali literary traditions have become so different from what they were in his time that both his matter and manner have become more or less inaccessible to contemporary Bengalis. Even the Bengali language he wrote is no longer fully understood. Thus to re-establish him even in Bengal would need a level of historical and linguistic scholarship combined with imagination which is not likely to be found in the Bengalis. Of course, he is still worshipped by them, but only as a fetish. He has become nothing more than the holy mascot of Bengali provincial vanity.

The reputation he once acquired in the West is also a thing of the past. That was based on a small volume of translations which appealed to a particular emotional mood in the West. I shall explain what that mood was presently. Here it is necessary to explain the inadequacy of the translations. He got the Nobel Prize on the strength of his own translations of a very small number of his poems belonging to a particular phase of his literary life. They had a beauty and appeal of their own. But they were no approach to the originals. The quality which was present in those never came through in the translations, which had a curious thinness, and that made them mere wraiths of die originals. The translations which followed, both by him and others, were worse, and no literary reputation could rest securely on them.

There is no likelihood that there will be better translations in the future. For one thing, there is no interest in him at present. What is more, the competence will not be forthcoming. Any translator of Tagore will have to know English and Bengali equally well so as to understand Tagore fully and put him across properly. This is a condition which it will be virtually impossible to fulfil. Next, Bengali is a very difficult language to translate into any European language, more especially English. All the means of expression - diction, sound, rhythm - are different. On top of that there is the Bengali sensibility, which in the old days always rubbed an Englishman the wrong way. I myself write both in English and in Bengali. But I have not allowed my books in English to be translated into Bengali, nor have I attempted that myself, because I have found that when I write in the two languages, in each I not only address a different world but become different myself. In Tagore's case the difficulties will be infinitely greater. He could be rendered only by finding authentic English equivalents for the words, sounds, and rhythms in Bengali, and, above all, the emotional values. So far, this task has not been faced, and the first translator to fail was Tagore himself. In the absence of adequate translations it is idle to hope that Tagore will be read outside Bengal, for nobody will learn Bengali merely to have access to Tagore.

Yet his life is of extraordinary interest from every point of view - personal, literary, and historical. His was a complex, rich, and many-sided personality, whose very qualities made as much for sorrow and tragedy as for achievement. Historically, he is the greatest product of the interaction in India of the nineteenth century, between European and Hindu life and civilization, and he remains equally significant in his life as in his works. In one sense, he may be regarded as the victim of the interaction, and in another as its prophet. His own life was caught in the conflict which this interaction brought about, and his writings stand for its achievement. So, Tagore is likely to remain only a hagiographical legend in Bengal and a forgotten historical figure elsewhere: or the lost great man of India for future generations of men.

The Family Tradition

Tagore was born in 1861 in a landowning family of Calcutta which was not only one of the wealthiest and most respected, but also active over two generations in all the cultural movements of the times. His grandfather, Dwarkanath Tagore, besides being a man of many accomplishments, was a friend of the great Indian religious and social reformer, Rammohun Roy, and helped the monotheistic movement within Hinduism with money. He was also a patron of education. In the last years of his life he went to Europe and lived so grandly in Paris that he was called Prince Dwarkanath. He entertained King Louis-Philippe and his court in his hotel and presented every lady who had come with a Cashmere shawl. When he died he left colossal debts, which, however, were mainly due to the failure of a business concern of his.

His son, Debendranath Tagore, offered to hand over the entire property to the creditors in return for an allowance to live on. They were so impressed by this that they trusted him to manage it and repay them according to his convenience. Debendranath lived austerely to honour his obligations, and brought up his large family in strict economy, so that Rabindranath, in spite of being the youngest son in a family which even in its reduced circumstances had an income of more than half-a-million rupees, was not brought up in luxury. In later life he said that many young men coming from the middle class had more comforts and amenities than he ever had as a boy.

Debendranath was also a deeply religious man. After a spiritual crisis in his early life he had become a monotheistic Hindu, basing his faith on the Upanishads. Actually, however, his devotion was to a personal God of the Christian type. He often went away from the noise and bustle of Calcutta to the Himalayas for the sake of religious meditation. Nearer home, he built a country house near Bolpur in the Birbhum district of Bengal, which he called Santi-Niketan or Abode of Peace. Rabindranath made it famous not only as his retreat, but also as the seat of his school and university.

Debendranath became the head of the monotheistic sect founded by Ramohun Roy and vivified the movement. His cultural interests were also wide. He himself wrote and preached in Bengali, and in every way promoted the use of the language among the new educated Bengalis who had turned to English. Their correspondence, even with their fathers, was almost invariably in English. Debendranath, on the contrary, returned any letter written to him in English if the correspondent was a Bengali. He also gave his sons and daughters a good education, and encouraged their literary efforts.

Altogether, Tagore's family was in the forefront of the new aristocracy of Bengal which by the time he was born had completed its economic and social evolution and reached a stable and secure eminence in both the spheres, but in the mental had just broken out of its chrysalis phase. For the Bengali gentry it was an age of extraordinary mental ferment and activity which created a new life and launched out in new enterprises, literary, moral, religious, or political. This situation was created by the impact on Bengali Hindu life of three European cultural movements combined, viz. the Renaissance, the Reformation, and the Romantic movement. The typical sons of these families became men of leisure and dilettanti in the old, i.e. the good sense, and dabbled in everything: literature, religious and social reform, philanthropy, art, politics, and also interior decoration and gardening *à l'anglaise*. It might be recalled that it was a Bengali of Calcutta who imported the water hyacinth from Brazil to put in the lily pond of his villa, and it became a dreaded weed in all the waterways of Bengal, to destroy paddy crops and choke the rivers and canals. They all had private dramatic clubs and theatrical sets complete with orchestras, and of all the European instruments it was the clarinet, called clarionet by all of us, which had the pride of place in them. In the early days of the nationalist movement in Bengal, around 1905, a Bengali landowner of Calcutta marched at the head of the processions, barefooted but playing the song *Vande Mataram* on his uplifted clarinet. Debendranath's family even struck out into a new professional line. His second son became the first Indian member of the Indian Civil Service, and the first figure in the Indianization of the higher British administration in India. Rabindranath himself was sent out to England at the age of seventeen to enter the profession which was next in prestige and position, i.e. to become a barrister by passing through the Inns of Court in London.

But he could not fit into the standard life of the class, and refused to conform, or rather showed himself incapable of being poured even into the best mould of the highest Bengali life of the day. This was due to his character, temperament, and exceptional gifts. He was a ferociously egocentric individualist, unsocial and impatient of imposed restrictions although endowed with a natural capacity for self-discipline. In fact, he had that intolerance of unregulated conduct which is inborn in an aristocrat, who thinks that the first article in the code of *noblesse oblige* is effortless self-discipline. He was a romantic who was always yearning for the far off in time and place, and for him both infinity and eternity were emotional necessities. Finally, he was a worshipper of freedom, not only for himself, but also for others. There is an extraordinary resemblance between the young Rabindranath and the young Chateaubriand. All this raised him above ordinary achievement, but also above ordinary happiness.

Rabindranath's Early Life

He was the fourteenth and last surviving child of his father, who though affectionate and very conscientious about the education and upbringing of his sons and daughters, was also formidably aloof. One day when the boy Rabindranath came before his father in the usual Bengali negligé, i.e. barebodied above the waist, he was immediately sent out of the room to come back properly dressed in formal Islamic clothes. Debendranath's children never referred to him as 'Father'; and to employ anything so ambiguously respectful as the 'Governor' was, of course, out of the question. They always used a Bengali phrase which it is impossible to render in English, but would be quite correctly rendered in French as *Monsieur notre père*.

His mother died when he was fourteen, and before that too she was always ailing and could not look after him. He was thus brought up by servants, and, as he described in later life, he grew up in a 'servantocracy'. But it should be pointed out that the Bengali aristocracy, like the English, was perfectly at home among the servants, although extremely antipathetic towards tradesmen and the lower middle class. In his childhood Rabindranath got a real sense of protection from a very much older sister. His father at times took him with himself to the Himalayan hill stations. He roamed in the pine woods there and only developed a love for wild nature and became more wild himself

On account of his shyness, sensitiveness, and intolerance of routine he was never happy at school. His schools were changed to find out whether he could fit into any. But he did not, and left school for ever at the age of fourteen. After that he received no formal education, but was taught everything, and more especially literature in Sanskrit, Bengali and English, at home by tutors. At that stage the words in which Charlotte Bronte described her sister Emily could be applied equally appropriately to

Tagore: 'Liberty was the very breath of Emily's nostrils; without it she perished. The change from her home to a school and from her very own very noiseless, very secluded, but unrestricted and unartificial mode of life to one of disciplined routine (though under the kindest of auspices) was what she failed in enduring.'

This was true of Tagore with the difference that he could not fall back on a noiseless, secluded, and unartificial life provided for him by his parental home, but had to create it mentally. After his return from England in 1880 without entering the Bar, he remained in Calcutta, took to writing and became recognized as the coming great poet of Bengal even before he was thirty. He frequented the literary society of Calcutta, and especially cultivated the greatest Bengali literary figure of the day, Bankim Chandra Chatterji. But he also showed his independence by attacking the first modern poet of Bengal and the first epic in blank verse in Bengali, and also the new Hindu conservatism of Chatterji. But he later disavowed the attacks as the brashness of an impertinent youth, and he never spoke disrespectfully of Bankim Chandra Chatterji. Actually, he was carried away by the romanticism of Chatterji's novels.

Towards the end of 1883 when Rabindranath was twenty-two years and seven months old he was married to a girl of twelve. It was a very strange marriage, not on account of the bride's age, but her social position. She was the daughter of the bailiff of the estates of the Tagores in central Bengal. All sorts of rumours were current in my young days to explain this unequal marriage. But nothing is certain. It should, however, be explained that in Bengal the distinction between the gentry (the *bhadralok*, as they were called) and the aristocracy was not deep, it was only a distinction of more or less money, the status of both as given by birth and upbringing was the same.

Tagore went again to England in 1890 to find out if he could qualify himself for some particular profession, but came back quickly. He was then sent by his father to manage his extensive properties in central Bengal. It was in this region that Bengal, the creation of her great rivers, was most truly the Bengal of geography. The main river was the lower channel of the great Ganges, the Padma, but a whole network of smaller rivers either flowed into or out of it.

He lived for many years in this district, and mostly in a house-boat or budgerow, sailing or rowing from place to place and also remaining moored at a ghat of the villages for many days. And it was in this environment that he discovered both himself and Bengal, and became finally incapable of being anything but a Bengali. He was born and brought up in Calcutta, but was never at home or happy in that city. Although Calcutta was the powerhouse in which modem Bengali culture was generated and also the blast furnace in which the modem Bengali mind was smelted, Tagore was never able to tolerate its physical presence, its material ugliness and squalor. Those who wish to know what that Calcutta was in my young days might read the long description in my *Autobiography of an Unknonm Indian.* After coming to London in late life, I discovered that the city was a half-caste Victorian London on the mud flats of lower Bengal. Tagore's life-long intolerance of his birthplace was intelligible.

Calcutta was wholly outside the true Bengali landscape in which the blue of the sky, the green of the vegetation, and the grey of the waters mingled to create a vast expanse of tender stillness. Thus; it happened that it was during his stay in his country estates, often floating in his house-boat on the rivers, that Tagore wrote some of his best work both in poetry and prose. Even the letters he wrote from this region to his relatives, and more especially to his favourite niece Indira Devi, are great works of literature. They also reveal his character and personality with unadomed truth.

Tagore's Personality

I shall therefore give some idea of both by quoting from them in my translations from the Bengali. To begin with, I shall illustrate the mood which was created in him by his stay in the Bengali landscape. He wrote from his country house at Silaidah in 1892: 'I cannot get any book of poetry or novel which fits in with this place. Whichever I open, I find in it the same English names, the same English society, the streets of London, its drawingrooms, and all the hotchpotch and rumpus. I find nothing which is artless, simple, open, generous, bright, soft, tender, and rounded like a tear-drop.'

English novels repelled him, for he found in them as he wrote:

'Only one turn of the screw after another, analysis piled on analysis, attempts to draw out ever new theories and moral lessons by wringing, squeezing, buckling, crumpling, and forcibly twisting human nature. To read them is to let them disturb the flow of this little river shrunken by sun mer, the waft of the lazy winds, the unbroken spread of the sky, the pervasive stillness of the two banks.'

How far this Bengali scene could take him away from Western literary sensibility can be judged from the following comment on *Anna Karenina* in one of his letters: 'Tried to read *Anna Karenina*. Could not go on, found it so unpleasant. I cannot understand what pleasure can be had out of such a *sickly* [the word is in English in the letter] book ... I cannot stand for long these complicated, bizarre, and perverse goings-on.'

His revulsion from English literary criticism in its academic manifestation was even stronger, and he particularly disliked Edward Dowden, who was very widely read in Bengal.

The only suitable reading he found for this place, he wrote in one of his letters, were the lyrics of the old Vaishnava poets. He also added that he would have liked to set down in writing, if he could, some of the old Bengali folktales as told by women, whose style would echo or evoke -

'ft the babbling of the streams, rippling laughter of the women on the ghats, their sweet voices and talk that match the rustic of the quivering coconut fronds, the deep shadows of the mango orchards, scent from the flowering mustard fields - taken all in all, tales which would be simple and yet lovely and peaceful, brimful with a good deal of the sky, light, stillness, and tenderness. All this fighting, scuffling, wailing, is not for a shady country like Bengal, so hidden and sheltered by the loving arms of its rivers.'

The landscape also made a solitary of him. This is how he described himself as he was at the age of thirty-one:

'I am by nature a savage. Intimacy with men is absolutely intolerable to me. Unless I have plenty of room around myself I cannot stretch my limbs, settle down, and unpack my mind. I pray that mankind may prosper, but they should not jostle me ... I should think that they would find many good and honest friends even if they left me alone, and they would never lack consolation from company.'

He wrote again in 1893:

'My mind wants to work tirelessly by itself, and its entire energy is so obstructed by the nearness of a crowd that it becomes restless. Then it beats against me from within its cage. It is only when it gets a little solitude that it can muse to its heart's content, look round itself, and express its feelings in all their meanderings exactly as it pleases.'

He continued in the same letter: 'Just as the Creator is alone among his creations, so does it [his mind] want to remain alone in the realm of its fancies. Otherwise, it seems, all its power, all its existence is running to waste.'

It is from this Tagore that his greatest literary achievement came out. He is at his greatest as a writer when he is speaking as a lone soul with a lone voice to lone souls. When he addressed collective groups he was at times intellectually competent, but at times also ineffectual. That happened because he was not really made to be a leader of nations, but only a prophetic individual speaking to individuals.

Tagore's Dislike for the British

One absurd myth grew in his later life which represented him as a cosmopolitan, as a Bengali who belonged to the world and not exclusively to his native Bengal. No notion could be more unfounded. It is indeed possible for a man to realize that men of other nations need not be regarded as strangers for all time. Kipling realized that in reverse when he wrote:

All good people agree.
And all good people say.
All nice people, like Us, are We
And every one else is They:

But if you cross over the sea.
Instead of over the way
You may end by (think of it!) looking on We
As only a sort of They!

But although Tagore had crossed over the sea even in early manhood, he never learned to regard the English people as anything but They, and, taken in the mass, as-a very unpleasant They. His two sojourns in England did not reconcile him to English life. During his first stay he was not happy. The grandson of a man who had received King Louis-Philippe and his court in his hotel did not have access to any English homes but those of his poor coaches or at times of retired officials from India. Very amusing descriptions of his first experience of English life are to be found in the diary which he kept at the time. During his short second stay he took a positive dislike to English life. He wrote home that he could not understand why his elder brother, who was in the ICS, liked that 'wretched country' so much, and as for himself he did not want to stay on for an hour longer. He also wrote (in 1890, when he was 29): 'It is after coming here that I have come to think of my unfortunate, poor India as my true mother. She does not have power like this country, nor its wealth, but she loves us. All the love that had been mine from my birth, all the happiness - all is to be found in her lap.'

What was even stranger was the fact that a man who was so sensitive to the beauty of nature in India and Bengal, had no eye for the glorious landscape of England. There is not a word of praise for it in his writings.

As for British life in India and the British community, his hatred for it was positive. This was, of course, due to the conduct of the Anglo-Indians, about which I have written enough. Although like all self-respecting Indians he did not want to cultivate the English in India, owing to his relationship with a member of the ICS he came in contact with them, and the result was repulsion. He described his feelings after a dinner:** 'Before my eyes are the Memsahibs in evening dress, and near my ears the murmur of smile-lit English conversation: all of it so incongruous. How true to me is my eternal India, and how hollow, how counterfeit, how profoundly false is the combination of English polite conversation and sweet smiles at the dinner table.' He went on to write: 'While the Memsahibs were talking in their low, sweet, and carefully trained voices I was remembering you all, the treasures of my India. Are you not indeed India's very own?'

One more citation: 'When I took my seat in a comer of the drawing-room, all seemed like shadows to me. It was as if that vast and big India of mine was stretched out before my eyes, as if I was sitting at the bedhead of my mother country, so shorn of glory, so sad, and so unfortunate. An immense melancholy, which I can hardly describe, descended on my whole consciousness.'

All this was both unfair and untrue. But that was how he felt. He was and remained a Bengali all his life so far as he was himself, and at that time he set down the aim of his life in the following words: 'I want nothing else if

* See also p. 66 above.

only I can remain unknown to the entire civilized world and, sitting in a comer of my country, collect her love like a bee to fill my hive.'

Yet this Bengali was forced to look to the European world for recognition and appreciation in later life, and that duality became the supreme tragedy of his existence.

Alienation from Bengali Society

The reason was a growing alienation from Bengali society in which alone he could be at home. This began at first with a sense of being alone as a writer, without having a readership with whom he could establish a two- way rapport. It has been the misfortune of every great Bengali writer of our times to be largely above their readership. What they get is first a small number of admirers who worship him as a Guru without understanding him fully. Then, as they acquire reputation by showing literary ability, they get detractors of a particularly malevolent type, for they are normally the other literary men. Behind these two restricted groups, stand the large literary public who read for amusement, and also seek amusement in the rivalries of the writers.

To take Tagore's sense of isolation first. He felt the absence of a sympathetic readership from his earliest days, and wrote even in 1894, when he was thirty-three:

'We unfortunate Bengali writers are made to feel most intensely the absence of that inner life which is specially man's. We cannot nourish our imagination with the food which truth provides. Our writing is largely joyless because there is no collision between our own minds and external minds.

'The influence of ideas has not penetrated into the inner being of our countrymen, despite the fact that they read so much English literature. Indeed, they never had any hunger for these, no mental body has ever taken shape in their material body. Therefore they have very little of that necessity which is called mental.

'Yet this cannot be detected from their talk, for they have learnt all the clichés from English books. They feel little, think little, and do little. So there is no happiness in their company.

'Even Goethe stood in need of Schiller's friendship. So I can hardly bring home the urgent need for a man like me to have the vitalizing company of a real and genuine *homme de coeur*. It is always necessary to have the warmth of human company and a touch of love, from where springs fulfilment for our entire life. Otherwise, its flowers and fruit can never have sufficient colour, scent, and sap.'

Before Tagore, this was felt all through his life by the greatest Bengali writer who preceded him, viz. Bankim Chandra Chatterji. Yet he was blindly worshipped by a majority of his educated countrymen. These men did not want worshippers, they wanted companions like those the German chief found in his *Comitatus*, and not in his serfs.

In addition, no Bengali writer found detractors absent as soon as his power became evident. This is perhaps true of all literary communities, but was truer for Bengal, and for Tagore even more so, due to a special sociological reason. Tagore's detractors and slanderers were fellow-writers, and they had a special incentive, and also grievances to abuse him. Most Bengali writers come from the lower middle class. In looks they are normally unprepossessing, and in their manners are extremely crude and prone to fancy injuries and insults. On the other hand, their literary gifts, in which they find compensation for their other deprivations, make them capable of settling their scores with a good deal of low virtuosity, sometimes even with undisguised scurrility.

In Tagore's case, their jealousy readied a special malignancy because, finding him a competitor as a fellow-writer, these men thought that since birth had given him social position, wealth, and good looks he had no business to poach in their preserves. As the quality of his writings became more and more apparent, their malice increased. A friend of mine told me that he once asked a Bengali critic of those days, who was by no means a writer of ordinary calibre, why he and others like him had such a grievance against Tagore who had brought nothing but glory and honour to his people. It was an evening, and the critic was in a condition to demonstrate *in vino Veritas*. So, he said: 'Shall I tell you the plain truth? We thought he and we were playmates in the same team, but suddenly discovered that he was very much above us. That, we could not tolerate.'

That was the unvarnished truth. Few writers have been more scurrilously abused. His critics said that Tagore could not even write grammatical Bengali and his poetry was all gabble from his protected dovecote. In my paper on Bengali for the matriculation examination of Calcutta University in 1914 I was asked to put one of his passages into 'chaste and elegant Bengali'. The animus was often displayed in personal abuse.

Tagore himself never descended to any kind of polemics. But he suffered, and even in one of his early stories published in 1893 he described the predicament of a writer who kept polemics within the bounds of good taste. 'Thus it happened,' he made a writer of this kind say,

'that even if I produced the better argument, people thought I had lost. In desperation I wrote an article on good taste, and realized soon enough that I had made a mistake, for it is not as easy to satirize a ridiculous thing as it is to do so over a really good thing. Simians can very easily make mocking grimaces at humans, but humans can never compete successfully with simians in that performance. So, they put good taste to flight by showing their grinning teeth.'

All writers are helpless against this *canaille écrivante* as great beasts are against tormenting insects, and Tagore was even more so. He was abnormally sensitive, and did not possess the knack for cool disdain which a man of his social position naturally should have had. He did not have the worldly loftiness of his grandfather, nor the aristocratic and robust self- sufficiency of his father. Besides, even if he wanted to ignore the attacks, he was not allowed to do so. The friends of Bengali writers are a very peculiar tribe. Instead of giving protection to their favourite author, they rush to him with every bit of abuse of him that they come across and show it to him, without realizing that they might be inflicting excruciating suffering on him. Finally, being a writer for Bengalis, Tagore could not be indifferent to praise and blame in Bengal. In his story just quoted from, he made the abused writer find peace by giving up writing altogether. Tagore could not do that himself, and felt as a child does when he is unfairly punished. He was to make his position worse by showing his resentment later.

But the personal animus of Bengali writers against him would not have mattered if there had not developed a deeper and more radical opposition between him and a majority of educated Bengalis. In the last quarter of the nineteenth century educated Bengali society was divided into two wings of Liberals and Conservatives, and a vivacious debate, bearing on every aspect of Bengali life, was going on between them. The liberal movement was led by the new monotheistic sect of the Brahmos, but it also had its adherents among a large number of educated Bengalis who had not joined the sect formally. As against them, stood the Bengali Conservative school led by Bankim Chandra Chatterji and Swami Vivekananda. Between them these two men created a revised version of Hinduism which might be called Bengali Neo-Hinduism, which also had a competent ideology, and in addition a larger following at the turn of the century. The Bengali nationalist sentiment reinforced its power, and by the time the first active agitation began in 1905 Conservatism dominated Bengali thinking. In fact, this phase of the nationalist movement was very strongly Hindu, as was pointed out by Valentine Chirol in his book *Indian Unrest*, published in 1910.

The differences between Tagore's ideas and those of the Neo-Hindu school at their highest expression would have had no effect on his personal life and relations with his people, because on the one hand there was mutual respect between him and the Conservative leaders, and on the other considerable sympathy in him for that school of thinking. He had even come under its influence, and it was ancient Hindu thinking on education that made him found a school at Santiniketan. It was-based on the model of the ancient Hindu Guru-Griha (the household of a Guru) as described in the books of Hindu sacred law. For the students of his school he even made some archaistic Hindu features obligatory: e.g. vegetarianism, wearing of saffron robes, and the carrying of staffs, which very much amused us when we were young. Apart from all that, Tagore also gave the most competent description of the nationalistic Neo-Hinduism in his novel *Gora*. Although in it he made Liberalism win, he also showed how strong the Hindu case was.

But all of new Hinduism was not of this quality. Actually, the popular Hindu Conservatism of the majority of educated Bengalis was a mixture of chauvinism with crude and often superstitious religious beliefs and cultural obscurantism. Hindu megalomania and xenophobia were their strongest passions. They were wholly impervious to any ideas not in agreement with the nationalist myths, and were also fiercely intolerant. It was impossible to liberate their minds from the myths. In the first place, they would not admit any fact as fact if it contradicted their chauvinistic beliefs, which sprang out of their megalomania as well as persecution mania. I give one example to show the persistence of this attitude. When after returning from my first visit to England in 1955 at the age of fifty-seven I spoke about the beauty of the great English country houses like Hatfield, Penshurst Place, or

Blenheim Palace, the standard exclamation was: 'Built with money looted from India.' It was futile to give them the dates when these houses were built. I was not believed.

Secondly, they clung to their ideas in their private chapels, and never brought them out in the open where could harm their worldly interests. They would pretend to believe anything that the British rulers or historians said and reproduce those views in examination papers or in interviews for jobs. They did not think that they did anything wrong in doing so.

But they would not forgive any fellow-Indian who did not subscribe to their myths, and would brand him as a traitor to his country. They had an extraordinary nose for what they considered as heresy. At once they would raise the cry: 'Great is Diana of the Ephesians'. And the British authorities never tried to pacify them like the Roman Governor. They hehaved like Pilate.

If, however, the heretic was a man of position and influence they would go after him like a pack of hounds in full cry. It was impossible to put any limit to the slanders they would circulate, and (what was really strange) also believe in. Tagore challenged all their political, social, cultural, and religious superstitions, and was therefore regarded as an apostate. This gave to those who attacked him out of jealousy an appearance of respectability which otherwise they would not have had.

All this exasperated Tagore so much by the time he was fifty that, in a story published in 1914, he described his position through the mouth of a fictional character who was unmistakably himself 'I write,' this man said,

'but it is not in the nature of my pen to flatter the populace. Therefore the people, too, generally paint me in colours whose main hue is black. I am compelled to hear many things about myself As my luck would have it, these are not beneficial, and of course not complimentary at all.

'A particular part of the body might be very minor, but if it is always getting blows, it would, by virtue of its pain, rise above the whole body. A man who has grown up under abuse becomes obsessed with himself, as if rejecting his own nature. He ignores everything around him and remembers only himself. That is neither comfortable nor wholesome. In fact, peace of mind comes only from forgetting the self. So, I have to look for solitude every moment.'

There is no doubt that when writing this Tagore had Calcutta and his retreat at Santiniketan in mind.

Lave in Tagore's Life

I am inclined to think that Tagore's sensitiveness to criticism and abuse from fellow-Bengalis would not have been so acute but for a private deprivation of a deeper order. He began to suffer from it at an early age and did not cease to suffer as long as he lived. This sense of deprivation came from never being able to get love of a particular kind. Stories are current in Bengal about his more or less superficial involvement with women at different periods of his life. But these cannot be substantiated nor taken seriously. What, nonetheless, comes out from his writings is that he could never console himself for this great deprivation.

This, however, had nothing to do with his married life. Although his wife was only twelve when he was married to her at the age of almost twenty- three, by all accounts and to all appearance his life with her was happy, and he was always an affectionate and faithful husband. But this was like a man-made canal taken out of a deep river, which was the real channel of passion, tossed by expectation, disappointment, and pain all through the long vigil of his life. Tagore has written some of the most passionate poems and songs of love that exist in world literature, and their predominant note is sorrow and despair.

Only four years after his marriage he wrote an opera, which in its song cycle described the tragedy that love was. He made the heroine sing her last aria:

Why did you come into the world?
Why did you love, only not to get
love in return?
Alas, alas! if the fulfilment of
a life-long yearning
Has not come to you
Go back sadly and slowly.
No one will ask you to come back.
Your tears, your sorrow – you will
take with you.
No one else will shed a tear.

Before that she had told herself that loving was not playing, it was the agony of a burning heart. One young man wondered: 'If there is no happiness in loving, why love at all?' Another declared: 'Loving is taking poison with open eyes.'

These laments run through all of Tagore's early poetry, put typically in the mouths of young women waiting night after night in their beds perfumed with jasmine and tuberose, and counting every night which passed and remembering as it passed that her youth was flying away and could not be kept chained. However, these poems and songs are not products of a poetic convention as the sonnets of Petrarch and Ronsard were. They have the personal ring of European Romantic poetry, and could have come only out of suffering in flesh and blood.

The strongest reason for taking Tagore's love poetry in this light is that it was representative of the general emotional life of all educated Bengalis of his age. In fact, in his own life Tagore was taking an emotional revolution which had begun about the time of his birth to its climax. From the sixties of the nineteenth century two products of the contemporary European mind were stirring the Bengali mind. The first of them was intellectual inquiry freed from the bondage of dogma, and the second was Romantic love. Love came first through English literature. In the last quarter of the nineteenth century there were few educated young Bengalis who did not know the dialogue between Romeo and Juliet in the garden by heart. A greater naturalization came through the new Bengali literature. In respect of love of the Romantic variety, Bankim Chandra Chatterji was the pioneer. His depictions of love rivalled the dithyrambs of the great Romantic exponents of love in Europe. This seemed so strange to traditional Bengalis, and yet took such a strong hold on the young, that Chatterji was accused of corrupting the youth of Bengal.

It is very difficult to illustrate the hold of this Romantic love from actual life, because there are no letters or diaries available for doing this. There can be no doubt, however, that some of what was seen in literature passed into the married life of Bengalis, and lifted it above its normal level, at least for some years. But it also ran often in a stream of its own as an emotional enjoyment or emotional suffering in their life. Perhaps it was more falling in love with love, and suffering for not getting it in life.

In young women the yearning created a mood in which they felt that it would be happiness beyond telling if they could only fix their love on someone, even though there might be no hope of return. For instance, in a novel published in 1865, whose author was a young man of twenty-six, a princess writes to the prince whom she loves:

'I do not seek your love. I have given what I had to give, and want nothing in return. My love is so deep that I shall be happy with it without your love.' *(from Bengali)*

This theme is exactly repeated in one of the most famous love songs of Tagore.

You are indeed my heart's desire,
I have nothing and no one in this world
except you.
I shall lose myself in my separation from you,
and thereby live in you
Through long days, long nights, long months, and long years.
If you love someone else, and never come back.
May you get all that you seek,
And I bear all the sorrow that there may be. *(from Bengali)*

In the original the words are wonderful and the melody equally so. I heard the song when I was ten years old and have never forgotten it.

Another strange effect was also seen in the young women. On account of early marriage husbands and wives got so used to each other, and so habituated to mindless physical experience, that the wives as young married women cherished the memory of a boy whom they had loved with precocious romanticism. At times even after marriage they might meet a young man for whom they would have a romantic fancy which would be real love, and yet they would have no sense of guilt in respect of their husbands.

On account of their social setting it is perfectly permissible to regard Tagore's love poems as autobiographical. Besides, he himself set down his attitude to love in a novel of his and put it in the mouth of a character. A young man is saying to a friend of his who does not think much of love:

'I tell you with the utmost conviction that the sole means of rousing the whole being of a man in one single moment is love. Whatever the reason, among us the awakening of love is weak, and for that reason every one of us is incapable of fully realizing ourselves. We are unaware of what we have within us, we cannot bring out what is hidden, and it is beyond our capacity to spend what is stored within us. Therefore our life is so utterly joyless.'

There can be no doubt that Tagore wrote that from personal experience, and also that it was true of the life of most young and educated Bengalis.

But Tagore's suffering from the absence of romantic love in his own life came to an end with personal tragedies. What happiness he had in family life was destroyed by the death of his wife in 1902, and he never married again, although he was only forty-one at that time. A daughter died in 1903 at the age of thirteen. His father died in 1905, and his youngest son in 1907. These bereavements with their grief turned his mind from love for man to love for God. He was always a deeply religious man with an unshakeable conviction that men were in the hands of God. The deaths gave him a new direction to his religious life, as also to his poetry for some years.

He wrote most of his finest religious poetry at this time. On the one hand, this poetry gave expression to a mood of renunciation which was made into a positive quality of life because there was no sense of loss in it. On the other, it also voiced a love towards God in which human love was present in a chastened form.

It was his own English renderings of 103 short poems of this period which brought him the Nobel Prize for Literature in 1913, after their publication in England.

They made a sensation, but at the same time created a wholly wrong notion of his religious feeling in the West. He was described as a mystic. As Tagore is not less essentially Tagore in these religious poems than in his love poems, it is necessary to examine the special character of his religious life and of his dedication to God.

Tagore's Religious Life

As it happened, a few months before Tagore's death I published a rather long article on Tagore's religious outlook in a Calcutta journal. In it I questioned whether with his love of life and, above all, his intense clinging to Mother Earth, he could be a mystic in the true sense of the word. Tagore's niece, Indira Devi, to whom I have referred, read the piece and wrote to my friend who was the editor of the journal and whom she knew very well, that she could not appreciate my article, because, as she put it, one could be an amateur (in the old meaning of the word) of this shore as well as the other shore.

Perhaps she did not see my point, although I could see hers. 'Mysticism' is a notoriously vague word, and is frequently employed to cover all kinds of intense religious feeling. What I had in mind was, however, the highly specialized and exultant religious mood which cannot admit the reality of the world which is perceived by the senses as against the true reality which God is. As Sir Thomas Browne put it: 'And if any have been so happy as truly to understand Christian annihilation, ecstasies, exolution, liquefaction, transformation, the kiss of the spouse, gustation of God, and ingression into the divine shadow, they have already had a handsome anticipation of heaven; the glory of the world is surely over, and earth is ashes unto them.'

The true mystic is the man who is ready to say like St Teresa that 'I die because I do not die'. Mysticism is Nirvana made positive, and so it seeks the annihilation of self. Tagore, on the contrary, was preoccupied above all with the self, although as the servant of God. He could never abolish the duality between man and God, and therefore I was unwilling to recognize him as a true mystic. I also thought that it was his very poetic vocation which stood in the way of his becoming a mystic.

At this time I had read the Abbé Brémond's *Prière et Poésie*, which had raised a vivacious controversy among French literary critics, and I was very deeply impressed by it. I myself regarded poetry as a supra-rational literary activity, but I was led by Brémond to believe that it was supra-rational in a wholly different way, making the poet project himself outwards instead of inwards as a mystic does. I was ready to subscribe to the opinion of Brémond that poetic activity was only a roughly sketched, confused, and imperfect reproduction of mystical activity. Thus, if a poet was to be assessed only as a man of religion, he could be a mystic only by fits and starts and a mystic who had missed his vocation. I therefore said that not as a poet alone but as a philosopher as well, Tagore, in spite of his universally advertised mysticism, was not a real mystic. His mysticism was only a make-believe from the strictly religious point of view; it was nothing but a projection of his humanism and earth-loving credo, put in a religious mould.

This is confirmed by an examination of his life. The great driving force behind it, which unified all his diverse activities, was a quest for personal enrichment, for self-realization through manifold contact with life and the world. In one of his early poems he set down emphatically that he did not want salvation away from the world: 'The salvation that comes through renunciation is not mine: I want to live and remain alive among men.'

There was something stark and elemental in his quest of selfhood, which took his clinging to life and Mother Earth to the level seen in plants. In fact, in one of his letters he adopted the simile and wrote:

'I can very well remember that, ages ago, when the young earth had just raised her head from her sea-bath and was greeting that day's just-risen sun, I, coming from where no one knows and carried on the crest of the first wave of life, had shot up as a plant from Earth's virgin soil. Then it was that, on this earth, I first drank the light of the sun with my entire body under the blue sky; I waved myself and swayed like a little child in blind but glad stirrings of life; I hugged my earthy mother with all my roots and took my fill; my flowers blossomed and my shoots came forth in unreasoning delight.'

It was not enough for Tagore that he should absorb the world into himself through his senses - he wanted a closer contiguity. That contiguity, he thought, could be established only through the kind of physical contact that plants have with earth. It is not surprising that such a passionate attachment to earth should seek to assimilate to the self all that there was assimilable in this world. It could also lead Tagore to attempt something more ambitious - to keep his individuality separate from the vast welter of the collective existence of man, so that he would be an epitome of human life, a microcosm existing in its own right in the macrocosm.

Now, such an attitude if combined with a religious outlook, can be pantheistic, but never mystical. It is only necessary to turn to St Francis to see how even the most childlike and sincere adoration of Nature could not dissuade a mystic from a voluntary abnegation of all the gracious, kindly, and consoling things which the physical universe has to offer us. That, one would say, is the real mystic way, which Tagore never took. I would refer only to one of Tagore's hundreds of songs to substantiate that. In it he tells Mother Earth that it really did not matter if She did not remember him or did not look up to the stars to call him back, when his footprints would no longer fall on those paths, when he would no longer ply his ferryboat at those ghats, when he will have done with receiving and paying, when he would no longer be coming and going on that scene. Why? Because, he declared, he would still be there. Who could say that he was not? On that morning he would still be playing the same games, he would still be held to her heart by Mother Earth, with new bonds of her arms and called by a new name.

No one can doubt that this was Tagore's implicit faith. But it could never have been St Augustine's. Read the thirty-fourth chapter of the tenth book of his *Confessions*, and you will see why. This is what St Augustine said: 'My eyes love the diverse forms of beauty, brilliant and pleasing colours. Let not these things take possession of my soul... Yet they affect me in all my waking hours, giving me no respite.'

So, he prayed to God to be allowed to see the light which blind Tobias, Isaac with his failing sight, Jacob with his dim eyes, saw. That was true light. 'I resist,' Augustine said, 'the enticements of the eye, lest my feet with which, O God, I walk your road, should be entangled in their snares.' Also recall Augustine's words: 'Loca offerunt quod amamus et relinquunt in animas phantasmatum' - 'Places which charm us distract us and fill our hearts with phantasms.' Tagore could never say that. His outlook on life had two faces. If it anchored itself in his faith in an eternal existence transcending death, it did not fasten itself less exultantly to the existence which would be cut off by the unexplained mystery of death.

He had no fear of dying, and in his old age even wished for death. There have been great men for whom the contemplation of the fact of death has proved too great a deterrent in the way of taking a continued interest in life. To Tolstoy, for example, death posed the final and most baffling dilemma of life, and it is bound to be so with everyone capable of reflexion. It was not so with Tagore, although he was perfectly aware of the transience of all that existed on earth. Indeed, in spite of all the strength of his faith in after-life, he felt as poignantly as any blind, clinging, trusting child of Mother Earth could, that life, her supreme gift, so far as the individual's memory is concerned, comes but once to man; he was certainly unable to get over the fact that within the bounds of one birth and one death alone are we given the sole unbroken stretch of consciousness in which we can see and feel achievement added to achievement, experience enriching previous experience, tint laid on tint. But the dismay which the end of all this through death would have created in his mind, was shut out by his capacity to transfer all that the earth contained to the world of God, infinite and eternal. Instead of bringing down the Kingdom of Heaven on earth, he transferred the kingdom of earth in its most glorious and purified form to heaven.

In any case, the fact remains that in him dependence on the supramundane and attachment to the mundane were equally balanced, so that his ever-present sense of death did not prevent his setting a value on earthly life which no materialist could match. He was truly, as his niece had said, an amateur of this shore as well as the other shore. To him this existence and the other existence were no more opposed than the two banks of the great rivers on which he had lived for many years. Rivers unite their banks instead of separating them. So does the river of life. This comes out with an intense pathos in one of the songs written by him in his old age. It should be contrasted with Tennyson's 'Crossing the Bar'. He wrote:

> It is the hour of the closing day;
> and I have carried my last sheaves to the boat.
> With tillage finished on this bank
> I go to the landing on the other bank
> at this hour of the closing day.
>
> Flocks of ducks are on their flight
> under starlight over the far bank;
> the flapping of their wings echoes in my heart
> at this hour of the closing day.
>
> The ebbing river has raised her song
> in her rush to the sea,
> carrying away all my thoughts in her pull.
> I hear only the boatman's song
> and the fall of the oar which keeps its time,
> at this hour of the closing day.

His conception of God was also ambivalent. Duminantly, it was of a deity who was both transcendental and personal. There can be no doubt that he was a fervent Deist of the Christian type, who was always ready to say: *In la sua volontate è nostra pace*, and who was always seeking guidance from God. But on the other hand, he was also thoroughly pantheistic, if not animistic.

His capacity to see God in everything animate or inanimate on earth was unlimited, and it was accompanied by a habit of seeing divine movements in the motions of water or wind.

Equally ambivalent was his love of God. In many of his poems it is difficult to ascertain whether it is addressed to God or to a lover. In his love for God *agape* and *eras* are inextricably mixed, so that if he attributed divine love to God he also made God capable of human love in all its expressions. So, for him to seek God was not solely to aspire to something unearthly, but also to secure all that he valued on earth. That, in every way, led him more and more to God, as his disillusionment with the world in which he lived grew with age. He thought that at death he would leave behind himself only the things which irked him in the world, and not what he valued in it.

Towards the Nobel Prize

Such was Tagore at the age of fifty, both as himself and in his relations with his own people, the Bengalis. It was a life of inward greatness and grandeur, although with an element of the tragic in it. But he need not have been too much obsessed with the attacks on him, for those were compensated for with the whole-hearted and often blind worship of a small minority of his countrymen.

Moreover, within two years and a half something happened to him which could have cancelled his sense of grievance. That was the award to him of the Nobel Prize for Literature in 1913, to which I have referred. So far as external position was concerned this placed him among the foremost writers of his age. Besides raising him above his fellow-writers in Bengal and their malice, it could have rallied to him a majority of his people, if not for his poetic merit, at all events for the honour he had brought to Bengal. He could liberate himself from his emotional dependence on Bengalis, and go on with his creative writing.

Unfortunately what happened was the opposite. The Nobel Prize alienated him further from his people, and led him to a public role for which he was not fitted. Finally, these two in combination made his later life a trial and a sorrow for him, and at its end a great tragedy.

Yet all this began with a passing whim, arising out of an accident. He was to have sailed for England for medical treatment on 19 March 1912, but fell suddenly ill. So the voyage had to be put off. For rest and recuperation he went to his country estate near the river Padma, and spent his idle hours in putting some of his poems into English. This was curious in a man who once said that he never felt equal to answering an invitation to tea in English in the same language. But, of course, he knew English very well. Even so he never contemplated writing in English. He finally sailed for England in May, and on the boat added to the translations. Originating in an accident, the pieces were pursued by more accidents. The briefcase containing them was lost in the London Underground. They were recovered from the lost property office.

Then they were launched on a very inclined slipway like a ship. The painter Rothenstein who had gone to India and heard about Tagore wished to learn something about his poetry. Tagore gave his manuscript to him, and Rothenstein gave it to Yeats, who was enchanted. With this began the presentation of Tagore to the literary court of London. Rothenstein invited Ezra Pound, May Sinclair, Ernest Rhys, Alice Meynell, H. W. Nevinson, Charles Trevelyan, A. H. Fox Strangways, T. Sturge Moore, and others to his house in Hampstead, and there, it was Yeats, and not Tagore, who read out the poems. Sturge Moore reported the session to a friend: 'Yeats and Rothenstein had a Bengali poet *on view* the last day I was in London. I was privileged to meet him in Yeats's rooms and then to hear the translations of his poems made by himself and read by Yeats in Rothenstein's drawing- room. His unique subject is "the love of God".' (italics mine).

After that Tagore met all the literary lions of the day - Shaw, Wells, Galsworthy, Bridges, Masefield, and others. At that stage commercial publication was, of course, impossible for the poems. So, the India Society took them up and printed them in a limited edition of 750 copies. As it happened, I saw this edition soon after in Calcutta, when I was a schoolboy. It was received with immense enthusiasm, and issued in a commercial edition early in 1913. Yeats and others had taken very great care in editing the translations without in any way interfering with Tagore's characteristic expression. Sturge Moore, who had become an admirer of Tagore, recommended his name to the Swedish Academy for the Nobel Prize. The Academy was at first hesitant because they had Emile Faguet, the French critic, in mind. However, a report by the Swedish poet Heidenstam settled the question. The Prize for 1913 went to Tagore. He was fully launched in the West by an English literary coterie. The only recipient of the Prize for writing in English before Tagore was Kipling, who got it in 1907.

I wonder what Kipling with his opinion of Bengalis in general and especially of those Bengalis who knew English felt about it. There was, however, a typical Anglo-Indian by-play in regard to Tagore just at the time when he came to England in 1912. A proposal to confer an honorary doctorate had reached Oxford early in that year. Lord Curzon as Vice- Chancellor wrote on 30 May 1912 to Edward Denison Ross, the Orientalist, whom he knew very well and who was the principal of the Madrassah in Calcutta: 'Can you tell me confidentially about Rabindranath Tagore of Calcutta, the Bengali poet... I question whether he is up to the standard. I will not quote you.' In his autobiography Ross wrote: 'If Lord Curzon undertook not to quote me, I may keep silence myself

Lord Curzon's doubts are intelligible. He had left India in 1905 and at that time nothing by Tagore was available in English, and even in Bengali circles of Calcutta Tagore's poetic standing was disputed. Apart from that, Curzon knew that Tagore was an active participant in the agitation against the partition of Bengal which he had carried out. But I cannot understand Ross's attitude because he must have reported adversely. Yet he claimed to be a great expert on Oriental languages.

In any case, Tagore did not get an Oxford doctorate till 1940. But both Curzon and Ross must have felt very foolish at the success of Tagore's book in 1912 and still more foolish when he got the Nobel Prize. Incidentally, it might be observed that when the historical position of Britain vis-à-vis India became different Dr Radhakrishnan, who had begun his literary career by publishing a book entitled *The Philosophy of Tagore*, got not only a doctorate and a professorship from Oxford but even the OM from the British Crown. Yet Tagore was neither a philosopher nor did he have a philosophy, and he would have been the first man to proclaim that. One can only exclaim in a very old and hackneyed tag: *O tempora, o mores!*

Nobel Prize and After

In September 1913 Tagore returned to India. He did not look forward to that with any pleasure. He had been happy in England with success, praise, and friendliness from those whom he could respect as equals. As against that, was his recollection of the animus against him in Bengal. So on 6 May 1913, when the time for his return was approaching, he wrote to his niece: 'When I think that after my return I shall have to hear so much petty cavilling from all sides, face so much opposition and animus, so much slander and humiliation, I feel I should like to let some more time pass so that I may remain aloof from that clamour as long as I can.'

But he returned and two months later, on 13 November 1913, got the news of the award of the Nobel Prize to him. There was tremendous excitement among Bengalis, and there was the standard reaction to any kind of success in the West for an Indian. This did not please Tagore and he wrote to Rothenstein on 18 November 1913:

'The perfect whirlwind of public excitement it has given rise to is frightful. It is almost as bad as tying a tin can at a dog's tail, making it impossible for him to move without creating noise and collecting crowds all along. I am being smothered with telegrams and letters for the last few days and the people who never had any friendly feelings towards me nor ever read a line of my works are loudest in their protestation of joy.'

There was a rush to grovel at his feet and take a share of his glory, and a crowd of about five hundred Bengalis of all classes descended on Santiniketan to offer him their felicitations. Among them was also my teacher, the future poet Mohit Lai Majumdar.

Tagore felt that there was a stupendous and appalling unreality about this homage, and that he was being honoured for having been honoured by the Swedish Academy, and not on his own account. So in receiving the homage he committed a terrible mistake. Instead of keeping his opinion to himself and dismissing his Bengali felicitators with conventional thanks, he had a go at them in order to settle his old scores. My teacher, Mohit Babu, told me the story in the class the next day with eyes flashing in anger. Yet he was a sincere worshipper of Tagore and had taught me how to recite his poems properly. He described how contemptuously Tagore had treated those who had gone to Santiniketan and likened them to village boys who tied a tin to a dog's tail and chased it with shouts through the streets. He also said that when the visitors were walking back to the railway station Tagore drove past in his dogcart with his scientist friend Jagadis Bose by his side, scattering dust on them. I can still recall the appearance of my teacher and his angry words.

As I did not find the words about village boys and the dog in the printed extracts of the speech, I thought that in his anger my teacher might have imagined them. But afterwards I could see from the letter to Rothenstein that Tagore could have spoken in the same way. However, what was printed was withering enough. I give some examples of his scorn expressed in his most highflown manner:

'It is not in my power,' he began by saying, 'to accept without diffidence, and in its entirety, the honour you have come here to bestow upon me in the name of the country as a whole.

'The calumnies and insults from the hands of countrymen which have fallen to my lot have not been trifling. Till now I have borne all that in silence. In such circumstances, I am unable myself to understand fully as yet how I have come to obtain this honour from abroad.'

Then he drew a significant contrast between the honour conferred on him by foreigners and the honour offered by his countrymen:

'I never knew that He to whom I had offered my handful of worship, seated on the eastern shores of the seas, the same He was extending his right hand from the western shores to accept it. I have received his gift of grace, and that is my real gain.

'However that may be and whatever the reason, today Europe has placed its garland of honour on me. If that has any value it lies only in the artistic discrimination of the arbiters of taste there. There is no genuine link between that and our country. No literary work can have its quality or appeal enhanced by the Nobel Prize.' *(from Bengali)*

Then he pleaded his inability to accept the congratulations of his countrymen: 'Therefore how can I shamelessly appropriate to myself the honour of which you are making a present to me as representatives of the general public of the whole country? This day of mine will not last for ever. The ebbtide will set in again. Then all the squalor of the muddy bottom will be exposed in bank after bank.'

He concluded by saying that he could not gulp down the heady draught of their homage to him and wanted to keep his mind free from the intoxication it was likely to bring about.

All this was true, and he also had the right to be angry. But he should have risen above his own grievances, not to speak of the low and scurrilous abuse by people who were the most worthless set of Bengalis morally. Apart from his self-respect as a writer even his social position should have enabled him to do so. It should be pointed out that Tagore was a very wealthy landowner, and there was no social compulsion on him to come to terms with others in order to maintain his worldly position. He could ignore his detractors. But the injured child with memories of unfair treatment that he remained all his life, got the better of him.

This speech was the beginning of a new and deeper alienation between him and his people. Yet in it in spite of his anger he had not wholly forgotten what his true life was and should be. So at its end he uttered a prayer which was unexceptionable, and clothed in the same highflown rhetoric: 'This is my prayer to Him,' he said, 'to Him whose pleasure makes every thorn blossom forth as a flower, every smear of mud paste of sandal, and all that is black shine in refulgence: that He may protect me from the blows of this accidental honour and keep me in my seclusion with the august embrace of his arms.'

Lord Hardinge, who was then Viceroy of India and who had to present the award to him because Tagore could not go to Stockholm, seems to have had a premonition of what was to follow, although in it he also showed his awareness of the real personality of Tagore. He said: 'Upon the modest brow of the last of those the great poets of India the Nobel Prize has but lately set the laurels of a wordly recognition, and I can only hope that the retiring disposition of our Bengali poet will forgive us for thus dragging him into publicity once more and recognize with due recognition that he must endure the penalties of greatness.'

The penalty was to be awful. In Bengal the campaign of denigration was intensified. If Tagore refused the homage of Bengalis, which his fellow-Bengalis quite correctly understood to be his refusal to share his European glory with them, they also withdrew the offer. The first move to deprive him of the glory of the Nobel Prize was to circulate the report that the translations were not his, but by Pearson, the Englishman at San- tiniketan. The Bengali public knew that Tagore did not have even a school certificate, not to speak of a university degree. So, they were inclined to believe the story. It made Tagore furious, instead of ironical or sardonic. One extraordinary weakness in Tagore's character was that his yearning for Bengali appreciation increased as the Bengalis by their worthlessness demonstrated that their admiration was not worth having. In his resentment at not getting that he showed no indulgence to their susceptibilities, and the Bengalis gave more than they received. Forgetting that he had been a severe critic of conventional and orthodox Bengali life ever since he began to write, his fellow-Bengalis began to think that puffed up by the Western recognition he was showing his contempt for them.

Tagore's Position in the West

This was, of course, an unfounded assumption. But for the time being Tagore also certainly felt both comforted and fortified by the literary recognition he had obtained in the West through his translations. This was not unnatural after the very vocal, although both stupid and malicious, Bengali denial of his greatness as a writer in Bengali. Nevertheless, he does not seem to have considered what his literary position in the West truly was.

For one thing, his appearance in English reversed the natural process of translations from one language to another of great literary works. These are made only when a writer in one language discovers in another, which he knows well, works of such merit that he thinks they should be presented to his countrymen. Then either he makes the translations himself or gets them done by a competent linguist. Tagore, on the contrary, chose to translate his poems himself. So far as I know, he is the only great writer who has done this.

In a letter written to his niece in 1913 he described it as a crazy ambition, but he explained that he had not done that in a spirit of bravado, but because he had felt an urge to recapture through the medium of another language 'the feelings and sentiments which had created such a feast of joy in the days gone by'. The sincerity of this explanation need not be doubted, but certainly no stranger one could be offered. It was like saying that in order to know oneself one had to go into fancy dress. Even after the publication of *Gitanjali* he did not feel differently. Although he told his niece that writing in English seemed to be a delusion to him, which it was, he did not try to get rid of the delusion.

In the first place, he did not realize the formal weakness of his English renderings, although he was the most consummate master of literary form in Bengali. He had chosen prose to translate pieces which apart from their content were superb in diction, sound, and rhythm. He explained why he did that when two poems from the *Gitanjali* were translated in verse and submitted to him. He totally disapproved, and said that originally he had refrained from attempting a metrical translation for want of mastery in English but was now reconciled to the limitation, which had made him realize the wonderful power of English prose. Then he observed more pointedly: 'I think one should frankly give up the attempt at reproducing in a translation the lyrical suggestions of the original verse and substitute in their place some new quality inherent in the new vehicle of expression.' He actually thought that 'the magic of English prose seemed to transmute his Bengali verse into something which was orginal in a different manner'.

This was true as the assertion of a theory. But the question was whether Tagore in his prose translations had the technical capacity to do what he aimed at.

His Bengali poems are virtually impossible to translate into English verse, but they could be presented as prose-poems without substantial loss of the quality of the originals. But prose-poems are the most difficult form to adopt for a man who is not to the manner born in the language in question. Tagore certainly was not, and, besides, English is not a language in which prose-poems can be successfully pulled off. I have read very little in English besides Sir Thomas Browne's *Hydriotaphia* which can be regarded as a successful prose-poem, but in French I have read a good deal, including of course Maurice de Guérin. One of Tagore's collection of poems was translated into French prose-poems by Pierre Jean Jouve. But he did not know Bengali and was given translations into literal French prose by my onetime teacher, Dr Kalidas Nag. I was not satisfied with the renderings.

The translations which Tagore made in *Gitanjali* were not remarkable for their form even if they were to be taken as plain English prose, instead of prose-poems. This was very surprising in a writer whose Bengali plain prose often reads like prose-poems even in his letters, not to speak of his stories. Thus the appeal of the pieces printed in *Gitanjali* in 1912 lay in their bare content without any dependence on form.

Poetry *qua* poetry cannot make any impact without distinction of form and style, and yet Tagore's English renderings of something which was in its original true and great poetry and yet had been translated into something which formally it was not, did impinge. That was due to a psychological situation in England and Europe in which people were ready to listen to a mere message without style.

Externally, that might seem to be a continuation of the old European respect of the Light that comes from the East, but in essence it was due to a genuine European emotional demand. Thus the appeal had a good deal of body and substance in it. In England it was taken as a counter-thesis to the

English life and its spirit in the Edwardian age, which was continuing in the first years of George V.

What that life was can be discovered in the memoirs of Margot Asquith, Osbert Sitwell, Violet Bonham-Carter, Harold Macmillan; in the letters of Raymond Asquith; in the novels of Galsworthy and Arnold Bennett; in the stories of 'Saki'. It was a life intoxicated with the splendour of the moment, and at its most anxious it was preoccupied with the trumpery problems which that splendour had itself created.

I find that even after the ghastly experience of two wars, which to a great extent the very spirit of the age had made inevitable, and to which that life was certainly an overture, the men and women who participated in it have written about it as Talleyrand spoke of the *douceur de vivre* of the *Ancien Régime* of France in his old age. They talked all day, danced all night, and in the early hours of the morning Guards officers walked back from the dances to Wellington Barracks over the bridge in St James's Park in tails, white waistcoat and tie, carrying Malacca canes with gold or mother-of- pearl heads. They had no suspicion that they were on the brink. It was the old story of crickets singing before winter. They thought that care for the very money on which they flourished would prevent a war. The science of economics had already appeared as an anaesthetic before becoming in the present age the sleeping tablet which kills in its overdoses.

To this world, Tagore brought back the ideal of the first beatitude transfigured, that is to say, without any painful abnegation and asceticism, and endowed with joyous peace. This Wordsworth had found in Nature, but Tagore had found it in God pervading Nature. Sturge Moore, after hearing the recital at Rothenstein's, remarked to Yeats that the poems were 'preposterously optimistic'. To this Yeats replied: 'Ah, you see, he is absorbed in God.'

That was true. Tagore's poetry appeared at that time as an antithesis to pride of life and disquiet about absolute Evil, and as a release into another world. Contemporary notices of *Gitanjali* confirm this. 'They are offerings from finite to infinite'; 'Mr Tagore uses things as if they were thoughts'; 'Something which had the imprint of the gods'; 'To begin chanting these lyrics aloud is to pass majestically into a realm of spiritual ecstasy, where the vision that comes to us so momentarily and fleetingly seems constant and habitual outlook of the soul.' Such were some of the pronouncements on the book.

He had built a bridgehead with it to the Western literary world and could make it the starting point for further advance. That, however, he did not do, because the weakness lay in his English which he could not develop into the kind of expression which could tell even when a particular psychological situation was absent. Yet he showed a mistaken persistence in English. Somehow or other, he had worked himself up to a sort of infatuation with his own English which resembled the love of Chesterfield for his natural son, and like him Tagore also thought that the child of love was what it was not.

So, he resented any interference with his own renderings even by distinguished English writers. Yeats had taken an immense amount of trouble to make the English of *Gitanjali* as attractive as it could be with its inherent limitations. In 1916, when he was revising two other books, he wrote to Lady Gregory that Macmillan, for whom he was doing that, had 'no notion of the job it is'. But Tagore instead of being grateful did not like it.

He became very angry when Robert Bridges suggested a few changes in a poem from *Gitanjali* which he wanted to include in his anthology *The Spirit of Man*, published in 1916, for the sake of what he considered more effective rhythm and grammar. At first Tagore refused to agree, and showed a touchiness over so trifling a matter which was very undignified, all the more so because his own translation of this piece was incorrect in the last four lines and blurred a basic antithesis in the original poem. It should be pointed out that his translations were always free, and in many cases this freedom came from his incapacity to put into English some of the most beautiful suggestions and feelings expressed in Bengali. However, in the dispute with Bridges Tagore yielded at the instance of Yeats, but remained unreconciled.

Thus, in regard to his English Tagore went his way until finally Yeats lost patience, and wrote in 1935 to Rothenstein, the original intermediary between them:

> 'Damn Tagore. We got out three good books, Sturge Moore and I, and then, because he thought it more important to see and know English than to be a great poet, he brought out sentimental rubbish and wrecked his reputation. Tagore does not know English, no Indian knows English. Nobody can write with music and style in a language not learned in childhood and ever since the language of his thought.'

Besides weakness of form, the loss of psychological topicality also contributed to Tagore's literary eclipse in the West. What *Gitanjali* offered was, as I have explained, an antithesis to the spirit of the Edwardian age, and it was only a stop-gap antithesis in the absence of a better and more real one. Even so, it was not acceptable to any mind which was truly Western. So, one is not surprised to find D. H. Lawrence writing on 24 May 1916 to Lady Ottoline Morrell: 'One is glad to *realize* how these Hindus are horribly decadent and reverting to all forms of barbarism in all sorts of ugly ways. We feel surer on our feet, then. But this fraud of looking up to them - this wretched worship-of-Tagore attitude - is disgusting.'

Lawrence had the right instinct. There is no greater danger to the integrity of the West than what lurks in admiring what is conventionally regarded as Hindu spirituality, which it is not. The counterfeit spirituality comes to the West first in the form of St Francis or St Clare, but finally reveals itself as Rasputin.

In any case, the real antithesis to the Edwardian age was to come out of the war - from Ypres, the Somme, and Passchendaele. The literary alternative to Tagore came from the postwar poets and novelists, and perhaps, above all, from the Bloomsbury Group. Even by the end of the first World War Tagore had lost any kind of authentic hold on the West.

His personal relations with his Western friends were not also happy or lasting. This was due, half to his being a typical Bengali who could never establish happy and intimate personal relations with anyone who was not a Bengali. But, for the rest, it was due to his truly unsocial nature, which he had described in early life. Throughout his life he remained so self-centred and unsocial that even with the majority of Bengalis he could not be happy. Therefore those who at first seemed to be his friends and intimates either parted from him or became sycophantic courtiers. Some of those who parted gave expression to their disapproval.

As a result he had to fall back more and more on his spurious appeal as a wise man from the East. In this kind of impact of his personality on the West, a very important element was his physical appearance. After their very first meeting Sturge Moore wrote: 'The poet himself is a sweet creature, beautiful to the eye in a silken turban.' Or again, there was the reaction recorded by Frances Cornford, Darwin's grand-daughter: 'I must write and tell you both what a wonderful thing it has been to see Tagore. I now understand all you say. He is like a saint, and the beauty and dignity of his whole being is wonderful to remember. I can now imagine a powerful and gentle Christ.'

After the war Lord d'Abernon, who was the British Ambassador in Berlin, saw Tagore there and he wrote in his diary that he looked like the Christ of tradition. After the decline of his literary reputation his looks remained his greatest asset as a prophet in the West.

In 1929 I wrote a short note for myself, setting down my doubts about his position in the West and also my disapproval of his peregrinations in the role of a prophet. Here it is:

'With the twelve good fairies who hurried to the birth of Tagore, bringing their gifts of wealth and beauty and genius for him, came also the malevolent thirteenth, who brought to him her curse and denied him the love, and the respect too perhaps, of his countrymen. And Rabindranath Tagore has never consoled himself for this.

'Keenly, almost morbidly sensitive to praise and blame as he is, he has managed yet not to be wholly blinded by the brilliance of his Western receptions. However irresistible the glamour of his personal triumphs, however soothing the chorus of delicate flattery in the Press, he knows as well as every disinterested observer that there stands between him and total oblivion in the West only two things, of all things in the world most frail - a passing fashion and a beautiful presence. When these will be gone will Europe and America still cherish the memory of this silken Mandarin who came out of the East to their people as a new wise man?'

I did not know then that long before that Tagore's tours were mostly failures in regard to ideological impact. I did not also know that they had a secondary motive of fund-collecting for his projected university, and that this object was also not being realized. In India only stories of his successes were reported. Even so, I had suspected failure and, besides, attributed the realization of it to Tagore himself. I showed the note to a friend of mine, a distinguished Bengali academic and scholar. He read it and handed it back to me with an ironical smile. The irony was not for the florid style. Nobody could write about Tagore without being florid. He was sceptical about the content of the note. Yet I had hit upon the truth.

The falsity of his standing in the West, which he sought to maintain even in the early thirties, was painful to realize. Yet he continued. All his real friends in the West regretted it. Romain Rolland disapproved of his later odysseys. Epstein noted his charlatanesque displays. When he was working on Tagore's bust, he noted how the poet's handsome, commanding presence inspired in his followers awe and craven obedience. He also saw how two American-women who had come to visit him, retired backwards with their hands raised in worship, how he carried no money, and how if he needed anything he gave his disciples only a single word of command. Of course, all this was the traditional behaviour of all Hindu Gurus. But to think that the real Tagore, as enshrined in his books and described by himself in his early letters and his autobiography, had come down to this level was horrifying.

Position in India

A greater tragedy for Tagore was that he began to drift towards the same dubious status even in India, without however being accepted as a modernized version of the traditional Hindu Guru, as Aurobindo Ghose was. He did become a Guru to a restricted circle of Bengali admirers, and even Gandhi and Nehru referred to him as Gurudev, My Lord the Guru. But the majority of his countrymen rejected him as such.

He had already taken his unorthodox critic's role further. He became more assertive in his criticism of Hindu obscurantism and chauvinism after receiving the Nobel Prize. In a famous speech he exposed the inconsistency of the nationalists in wanting political freedom from the British and yet submitting slavishly to obsolete and irrational Hindu customs. He also reproved the gloating over the calamity of the First World War as a just punishment of the West for its materialism. Besides, he criticized the Bengali revolutionaries for resorting to terrorism and murder.

This role he continued to play even after 1920. In view of the new character of the nationalist movement the wisest course for him would have been to give up his role of liberal critic, shun politics altogether, and retire into a purely literary and religious life. But he could not and did not. Actually he became more vocal. He criticized the Gandhian movement and made unforgiving enemies for himself, although he was in every way a better nationalist than perhaps even Gandhi. There was such intolerance of criticism among the nationalists that in India of that epoch he created a position for himself which would have been Thomas Mann's after the advent of the Nazis if it could be assumed that the Nazis would only slander and abuse without actively persecuting. But he was figuratively deprived of Indian citizenship by the nationalists.

In fact, he made his position even worse by flaunting an ostentatious internationalism when he had already discovered the weakness of his standing in the West, and shown that he could never become cosmopolitan in his social behaviour. His internationalism, as it was called, was condemned even when it had only a humanitarian motive. For instance, when he joined an appeal for relief at the time of the Russian famine, his critics began to bait him as a man who cared more for the Russians than for his countrymen, who were suffering inhuman oppression under the British. The campaign of abuse and slander grew, and became worse than what he had referred to in his Nobel Prize speech in 1913. One nationalist newspaper even published a story from a worthless foreign source that he was not even a true Bengali, but had Portuguese blood. Naturally, as the supreme Bengali in everything, he was furious.

He retaliated by making a provocative display of aestheticism. As things stood, Bengali middle-class Philistines jeered at aestheticism even more irreverently than did the British Philistines in the epoch of the *Yellow Book*. The nationalist movement gave this hostility a virtuous colouring. While the Bengali middle class did not think it wrong to go on pursuing money without doing anything practically for the nationalist cause, they fully subscribed to the nationalist creed that in an era of struggle against foreign rule everyone must be as puritanical and shabby as possible. I shall give an example to illustrate the point. One day a nationalist journalist told me with eyes blazing with anger that he had seen a distinguished Congress woman, intimate with Gandhi, giving a bath to her dog with hot water, soap, and towel. He asked me: 'Do you think that was right, Nirad Babu, when our people are starving from British exploitation?' I could only reply: 'You can, of course, object to her keeping a dog at all. But don't you agree that if she kept one she was bound to keep it clean.?' He was not convinced. To this society Tagore's airing of his aesthetic frills was regarded in the same light as wearing of gay clothes would be in a house of mourning. The nationalist movement had hung up, so to speak, a non-material hatchment on all Indian doors, which served both piety and avarice. Provoked by this obtuseness Tagore behaved very indiscreetly. His real aesthetic sensibility was both virile and refined, like Botticelli's *aria virile*. He could have dispensed with cheap exhibitions.

After all this came the final mistake, which was more than a mistake, a delusion: that he could assume the role of a man of action, albeit in the limited field of education. He had not the least aptitude for this or for working with others in the furtherance of a practical project. In social relations he was always awkward, capricious, and intolerant, as he himself had recognized in early life. In spite of that, he embarked on a project of founding a new university after his own heart.

He had no real vocation for it, but as in other cases he was driven to it by the grievances of his early life. He had hated the methods of the established educational system in India and could not go through it himself In his writings he fiercely and often unjustly denounced that system. So he wanted to show what could be done by way of providing an alternative. But on the one hand his own ideas were very vague and not worked out in their practical details. Next, his university could not serve any worldly interest, because it was not going to be officially recognized. This alone would have prevented his attracting the right kind of teachers and right kind of students.

The very name he gave to it proclaimed its artificial character. It was Visva-Bharati, a compound made by combining the Sanskrit word for the universe with one of the names of the Hindu goddess of learning, Sarasvati. If an English university wanted a name of the same kind it would call itself Minerveum Universalis. So, even the name it bore made it appear like a playhouse. Besides, everything in it was self-conscious, exotic, archaic, or finicky. He had disliked the smileless educational institutions of his youth, and wanted to create a university which would be all smiles. Actually, it turned out to be all simper. It became an object of amused observation by the normal Bengali middle class. They could spot a Visva-Bharati student even at sight.

It was a curious assortment, materially, of European bric-à-brac and Hindu archaistic tinsel. In its functioning it was almost a vaudeville. Its personal composition was even worse. Besides some serious scholars from Europe, there came to it all types of eccentrics and adventurers, and some were absolutely feeble-minded enthusiasts in the specialized sense of being obsessed with some unpractical idea. Even Tagore at times lost patience with them. As to the Bengalis who went there, as a class they were men who wanted to achieve importance by being epiphytes on Tagore. As there was very little money going in Santiniketan that had to be compensated for by an artificial idea of personal importance.

To make the atmosphere more unhealthy, there were fierce jealousies and rivalries in the Santiniketan community, each member striving to be his favourite and to have his ear. Another tawdry element was introduced by the yearning Tagore developed in his old age for 'female companionship' in the manner of Peter Pan. This was a sad falling off from his tragic suffering from not finding romantic love. Thus it happened that he would talk to or correspond with a number of Bengali women and promote them by turns to the status of his Egeria. But these young women at their best were very Bengali bluestockings and at their worst very Bengali *précieuses ridicules*. They did not shed any glamour on Tagore's old age.

Yet he could not give up the Visva-Bharati. The more it looked like a total failure, the more he clung to it. It became a *femme fatale* for him, his Manon Lescaut. But this Manon, instead of dying in his arms and leaving him to his regrets, drove him to death, while she herself not only survived but, leaving behind all her past escapades, became a sordid and commonplace housewife.

The horrible preoccupation destroyed the peace and dignity of Tagore's last years, and ruined his health. He went about like an impresario presenting theatrical or dance shows with the young men and young women of his university in order to collect money- In photographs he was shown sitting among them, as they were in their stage costumes, and the caption was 'Tagore with his troupe.' On one occasion such tours distressed even the Marwari capitalist of Calcutta, Birla, and he made a large contribution to spare the old and ailing poet the strain and also what he did not say - the indignity of these mummeries.

Of course, he could no more abandon his writing than he could commit suicide, and actually till his death his poetic production rose to greater heights, and his prose writing too remained at a very high level in spite of showing some falling off of power and beauty. But his literary life ceased to be his only life, and to some extent it became even secondary to his public life. Thus, during the last thirty years of his life there existed two Tagores, one true and the other false. This dichotomy was at the root of the tragedy that his later life was. Yet the false life unfolded in such a chain of circumstances, interacting with his character, that the outcome seemed to be inevitable. In contemplating it one is driven to believe in fate.

As his disillusionment grew so did his bitterness against fellow-Bengalis. The language in which he wrote about them reminds me of the lamentations of job. I shall quote a few typical passages from his letters:

1.8 February 1930 - after recovering, apparently to his regret, from a serious illness: 'People of this country do not forgive until the pulse has completely ceased to beat. But such is my misfortune that Yama [the god of death] sends only his messenger, but never his chariot. So, those who would have sent forth lamentations at memorial meetings will now shower vituperation at literary conferences.'

2. 29 October 1931: 'There was a question in your letter whether I have engaged paid agents to spread my fame.* This sort of suspicion is possible only in Bengal. It is here that people whisper that I won the Nobel Prize by a trick, and the English of the poems which brought me fame was written by a certain Englishman.'

3.14 September 1933: 'What is a matter for real regret is that the business of running me down is profitable. That makes me realize how widespread in my country is the keen hatred for me and how little my countrymen are hurt by the attacks on me and the insults heaped on me. Had it not been so the merchandise of slander about me would not have brought in so much profit.'

4.14 September 1934: 'I have almost brought to its end the span of my life in its Bengali birth. And the last prayer of my tired life is this: If there be rebirth may I not be born in Bengal again; let only the virtuous perform their miracles in this land of virtue; I have lost my caste, so let my lot be among those whose conduct does not conform to the Shastras [scriptures] but whose judgement is consistent with Dharma [righteousness].'

This was the last testament of Tagore in respect of his countrymen.

The Extreme Unction

But a *plaidoyer*, heartbreaking in its pathos, that the life of deception which had been his, had yet left him inwardly simple came from him in his very last poem, which he managed to dictate on 30 July 1941, eight days before his death, but could not correct. In it he said:

> Sorceress! You have strewn the path of creation with
> your varied wiles . . .
> With a cunning hand laid the snares of false trust for
> a simple soul...

* I might add that when my autobiography got excellent reviews from such literary figures as Harold Nicolson, Raymond Mortimer, Sir John Squire and others, fellow-Bengalis said that my literary agent had supplied all of them.

But his glory is that, however devious outside, he is
still straight at heart....
He who had yielded so easily to manifold deceptions has
received from you
The inviolate right to peace.

With his faith in an eternal afterlife he looked forward to the eternal peace that would be his. But without that faith death could only bring him his *Nirvana* - extinguishment. In any case, for us he personally is no more. His life as lived with its achievements and trials remains only in its records as the concern of living generations. Here it is that the tragedy continues: his real personality will not be recalled as an example, and his work will be like a buried city of the past. Only the fetish Rabindranath will remain, but not for the purpose for which it has been created by his people. It will hang round their neck as punishment, like the albatross round the neck of the Ancient Mariner, and it will not drop from there because the Bengalis will never be able to pray for forgiveness for their sins against him.

CHAPTER 6

Farewell to Bengal

At the end of the chapter in which I carried the story of the war with Japan to March 1942, I also said that I left Calcutta soon after, never again to come back to the city. Without knowing it, I was bidding farewell to Bengal for ever. This was due to the arrest and detention without trial of Sarat Bose on the suspicion of being in league with the Japanese. To deal with its personal effect on me first: I lost my job with Sarat Bose and an important part of my income. But, as usual, I got much better employment from a quarter which was wholly unexpected. It was All India Radio, the broadcasting organization of the Government of India, which was in Delhi. This permanent change of domicile opened up a new phase of my life and gave it a different direction. Before dealing with that, I must give an account of my private life during the last four years of my stay in Calcutta, which, in spite of my absorption in politics and the war, had its significance for me, because the main thing in it not only helped me to bear the suspense of the war, but even became a support for my life all through the rest of it. I think the reader will be very much surprised to learn that it was European music.

Musical Support to Life

My adventures with it had actually begun much earlier, in 1930. Later, when I was *nel mezzo del cammin di nostra vita,* that is, midway on the path of life which for me was fifty and not the biblical thirty-five, I established a connection between them and a theory of recreation which I had arrived at by that time. I began to say very emphatically that if a man wanted his life to keep flowing like a stream and broaden into a wide estuary as the Forth does from Stirling to Edinburgh, he must not only have a vocation to live for but also adopt a new recreation every five years; otherwise, his life would become a pond covered with green scum from edge to edge, and the only living things on it would be the wife-duck with two or three or even six ducklings diving to the bottom to feed on the money-grass. I had begun to act on this conviction much earlier, even when it was very inchoate, but it was by sheer chance that I was led in 1930 to make European music my main recreation.

This was a sphere in which at that time very few Indians would have found one. Most of them were indifferent to it, and those who cultivated their national music seriously, were even positively hostile. Among such Indians was my elder brother, a very good amateur musician. After I had acquired my hobby of European music he would not even let my records of European music to be taken to his house. Perhaps European instrumental and orchestral music did not repel the Indians so much, however inaccessible it might be to them. Indeed, even my brother went to the concerts given by the Calcutta Symphony Orchestra by way of exploration. But it was the vocal expression, especially the female voice, which they found totally unacceptable, as my brother also did. Above all, the soprano voice was their *bête noire*.

Yet my conversion to European music was brought about precisely by that voice. I might add that I myself was also devoted to Indian music. Home-made music was the basis of our musical culture, as it also was in Europe in former times, and all the members of our family, including my mother, either played or sang. I, too, sang and also played three instruments, and one of them was the sitar, which has become rather popular in the West today. But I had never thought of taking up European music. On the contrary, I was repelled, because I was always told and even believed that European male singing was like the barking of dogs and female singing like the howls of jackals. Therefore, my initiation into European music, brought about by a surrender to the soprano voice after the very first hearing, was the most surprising part of my conversion.

Now, to tell its story. In 1930 I used to go to a well-known bookshop in College Square, Calcutta, every English mail day to see what new books had arrived from London. The owner's brother was a friend of mine, and the shop was also a meeting place for friends. It was here that my introduction to European music took place. Ten years later, I described the adventure in a long article in Bengali, which I wrote for the quarterly I was then editing. I shall translate the passage which contained an account of the chance encounter leading to my lifelong devotion to European music. 'On entering the shop', I wrote,

'I saw a portable gramophone on the counter and three albums of records. Although my friend, the owner's brother, was there as well as a young [Bengali] doctor, I did not pay any attention to these items on the counter; I knew the doctor, a medical officer from a British ship, and assumed his known fondness for English ways had been responsible for the gramophone - yet another English affectation. So I continued on my way to the back of the shop and began looking through the new books, taking them down from the shelves, one by one. Then the gramophone began to play. After listening for a while, it seemed to me that the sound was not to be disdained, and out of curiosity I returned to the shop. When a record had been played, I lifted it and looked at the label. I no longer remember the name of the composer whose song made the strongest initial impression on me. But its first line was "*Obéissons quand leur voix appelle*", and it was sung by Amelita Galli-Curci. Immediately after, I felt charmed by another song, which was Rimsky-Korsakov's *Song of the Shepherd Lehl*, sung either by Lucrezia Bori or Alma Gluck. There were, so far as I remember, records of Frieda Hempel, Elena Gerhardt, Chaliapin, and Clara Butt, as well as some German folksongs.'

That was written in 1940, and I left it at that. But when I began this chapter I thought that I might as well, after fifty-four years, make an effort to trace the first song to its source. With this object I sought the help of the librarian of the musical section of the Central Library of Oxford, and to my delight he showed me that it was from Massenet's *Manon*: the gavotte. I have not seen or heard this opera. The lady, his assistant, also helped me to find out who actually sang the other song. It was Alma Gluck, and not Lucrezia Bori. I am very much obliged to both of them for this. I have further found that J. B. Steane in his book *The Grand Tradition*, which describes seventy years of singing on records from 1900 to 1970 and is published by Duckworth, praises both the performances. Of Galli-Curci he writes: 'Who could know her record... of the *Obéissons* from Massenet's *Manon* without hearing her winning and individual inflections in the melody, crowned by a dazzling success in those passages where only a soprano of her particular accomplishments can perform the music comfortably?' Of the other song he says: 'In the *Shepherd Lehl's song* from Rimsky-Korsakov's *Snow Maiden* we hear pleasant singing from Gluck.' So, even my novice's ear was not much at fault. I can say with assurance that if I had heard pop music then, my chance encounter with European music would not have had any sequel. A man moored to the highest in one's own culture does not go over to barbarism, nor is he beaten by it, even if it were as strong as King Kong.

Thus *Obéissons quand leur voix appelle* was symbolic for me. Was it a direction from above? Perhaps it was. But my listening to European vocal music did not make further progress without hitches. I felt very curious about a song when I saw its title: *Chanson hindoue*, of course from *Sadko*. I expected that I should hear something which in point of melodic content would be a bridge between my previous experience and the new. However, I literally ran away from this European vocalization of Hinduism, in spite of the appeal this song has for Western listeners. I could not conceive of anything more un-Hindu. But, curiously enough, I was very much amused by the *Song of the Flea*, sung by Chaliapin, although he himself, I have since learned, was not satisfied with his performance. What appealed to me most in European vocal music then was the extent of the variation from one voice to another - the musical content, for me, being only a secondary consideration. But that, too, came very soon, although in the case of many famous examples, my judgement was reserved. Arising from these experiences, my *à priori* prejudice against European music was abandoned for ever.

These first encounters of mine with European music were very casual. They aroused a great desire in me to extend my musical knowledge, but I did not have a gramophone and records nor the money to buy them. However, an opportunity to do so was provided at the end of 1931 by my English friend, Christopher Ackroyd, when he was obliged to go on leave to England because of his political pamphlet. He left his gramophone and three boxes of records, more than sixty, with me. I at once began a systematic exploration of European music. But it was not easy. I knew nothing and was puzzled by everything. Two small books were guides without which I should have been totally incapable of making any headway. They were, first, Percy Scholes' *Listeners' Guide to Music*, and, next. Sir Henry Hadow's book on the history of European music in the Home University Library. Christopher Ackroyd had also left with me an advanced book on orchestration by C. Forsyth, as well as a number of pocket scores in the Philharmonia series, which helped me immensely. When I wanted more detailed information I went to the Imperial Library and read Grove and the *Oxford History of Music*.

The pieces with which I began would surprise most Europeans if I mentioned their names, and even their class would, for it was chamber music, especially quartets. The very first which I found very pleasant was

Mozart's Hunt Quartet, but very soon the C-major, the so-called 'Dissonance Quartet', became the first favourite, which place it has not even now lost, although others are bracketed with it.

But what would even more surprise European lovers of music would be to learn of my next step, which was to listen to the late quartets of Beethoven. I began with the F-major (Op. 135) and got completely immersed in the A-minor (Op. 132). The slow movement in the Lydian mode did not give me any trouble, although I shall be honest and say that at first the two interludes in it I found more immediately appealing. The final Rondo, however, bowled me over at once. The first records on which I heard the quartets were from the Lener Quartet, which was as well, for their performance was very smooth and clear. If I had heard Busch then I would perhaps have been puzzled. At this point I must emphasize that my response to what I heard of European music was wholly spontaneous and unforced. It might be described even as naive. There was no compulsion on me to like it, and at that time I had nothing to gain by way of cultural status by saying that I listen to European music! I brought to my listening a freshness of feeling which no one, who had come to these pieces with previous experience of European music, could have done.

I have already related how after my marriage in 1932 I made my wife listen to the records and how she at once liked Mozart and Beethoven. She was even more sincere than I could be. She would obstinately dislike an aria from *Lohengrin*, even though sung by a great tenor, as also Smetana's quartet *Aus meinem Leben*, and would not be cowed down by any fear of being thought 'uncultured'. I also made my father listen to European music, and he did so very patiently. He was musical, and would not say that what he heard did not appeal to him. From time to time, however, he did say that the pieces seemed very long, although I played only one movement on one side of a 78-record.

In 1933 Christopher Ackroyd returned from England and took away his machine and records. The distress into which this plunged me can be imagined, since I was then in no position to buy a gramophone and records for myself, although I did not give up listening whenever a chance presented itself.

However, when I found employment again in 1937, I set about to carry on my new interest further. As I never take up a new venture without informing myself fully about its scope and character, leaving nothing to chance, the first thing I did was to subscribe to the magazine *Gramophone*, continuing to do so for the next ten years. I also got the E M G Gramophone Company's monthly bulletins, giving their selection of the best new records. I read the reviews and was more and more tempted to buy them in the same manner as I used to be tempted to buy new books after reading the reviews in the T L S. I could afford to do so now, but did not think it right to indulge this luxury until I had salvaged my private finances from the wreck into which they had been plunged for years. On the other hand, I was pulled in the opposite direction by my desire to have a good selection of records before I bought a gramophone to play them, so that I might not get tired of playing the same pieces all the time. Actually, I began to form my collection two years before I was able to buy one of E. M. Ginn's acoustic gramophones.

In 1938 I began, dishonestly, without telling my wife. The reason was the scruple referred to above. I was led to fear her disapproval by what I was reading in the magazines about the hostility of English wives to their husbands' music-on-the-gramophone-at-home. In one article, I read: 'Beware of any such fancies which so inevitably lead to the altar and matrimony. One day you will arrive home and find that instead of the old and well-beloved mistress, your gramophone, there is another, a wife, waiting for you. No man can serve two masters and to serve two mistresses is even more incredible.' I am finding that the hostility persists from what I read about the attitude of English wives to the loudspeakers to which a music-lover can listen with pleasure or even without pain. I was not justified to have included my wife in that category. But since conscience makes cowards of us all, I did.

On one occasion, I succumbed to temptation, after reading a review of a new recording by the Busch Quartet and Reginald Kell of the Clarinet Quintet of Brahms, and decided to order it. I smuggled it into the house without letting my wife know. I hid it behind my books in the large bookshelf, forgetting the caution I had shown in not hiding a secret military book behind my books when the police came to search my room. But my mind continued to be troubled by the thought of a chance discovery, and at last one day on coming home I saw the brown album lying on the divan in the sitting room. When I met my wife in the bedroom she only smiled maliciously.

After that my collection of records, although born in sin, began to grow openly and honestly. I shall mention some of those which I bought between 1938 and 1940 to show that I could be quite adventurous. I, of course, bought the standard works by standard orchestras and conductors, but also recordings by new performers when they were praised. For instance, I bought the first record by which Claudio Arrau became established: that of his playing of Schumann's *Carnaval*; a record of Weber's aria *Ozean, du, Ungeheuer*! by Kirsten Flagstad when she was just being noticed; a recording of Mozart's *Porgi Amor* and *Dove Sono* from *Figaro* by Tiana Lemnitz, as a beginner. I was adventurous in other ways, too, getting a L'Oiseau Lyre recording of Couperin le Grand from EMG, as well as a set of Society recordings of Haydn's trios played by Lilli Krauss, Simon Goldberg, and a cellist whose name I have forgotten. I bought Karl Erb's singing of Hugo Wolff's *Spanisches Liederbuch*, Mahler's *Das Lied von der Erde*, and Monteverdi's madrigals presented by Nadia Boulanger. I also had the capacity, not to be expected in a more or less ignorant man and in any case a novice, to go in for pieces which were more or less recondite, e.g. Mozart's Trio in E-flat for piano, clarinet, and viola (K.498), which acquired a great hold on me. I hope this selection will be enough to give an idea of the range and character of my early interest in European music.

I described the state of mind created in me by European music which made me do all this, in the article in Bengali published in 1940 to which I have referred. I shall again translate another part of it:

'Keats wrote a famous sonnet on the state of mind to which he was brought by first reading Chapman's Homer. It is not for an ordinary person to have at his command the feeling and impression to which Keats was roused by the range, deep peace, unfathomable mystery, and surging joy of that experience. I would only say that to me European music seemed to exist in a world apart, indeed to put it more forcibly, in a different universe:

'We should not judge it against the touchstone of our workaday likes and dislikes. Perhaps it is due to my ignorance or narrowness of mind: still I would say that it has often seemed to me that our Indian music is only a pattern of sound, whereas European music is a language. It has the power to bypass normal sensations and emotions and to speak in a shorthand to the heart, to the heart which is the inmost heart; its perception does not come back rebounding only from hearing and emotions.'

But this was not the whole of the matter. To disarm those who are smiling at this enthusiasm, the expression of which will certainly be called high-falutin by those who have not, like me, retained till old age the wonder which is a child's, I would add that my adventures with European music had also a lighter, laughable side to them. Quite characteristically, it was provided by my novelist friend Bibhuti Banerji. Due to his literary standing, he had obtained admission to the most esoteric and snobbish' cultural circle of Calcutta. Its members were all 'England-returned', took the utmost pains to remain in touch with the latest literary fashions in London, admired Hopkins at the expense of Bridges, and some of them, including a close friend or patron of Bibhuti Babu, had even acquired the Western readiness to rob a friend of his wife. They also professed great admiration for European music. This was then used both as a basis for jealousy among themselves and as a source for jokes with which they would ridicule the ignorance of even their closest associates.

In any .case, Bibhuti Babu felt that he was at a great disadvantage with them on this score, and would come to my house, listen patiently to European music, and learn its vocabulary. He repeated to himself, and learnt by heart, the words for the different forms: the sonata, trio, quartet, quintet, and so on; then the symphony and different tempi - largo, larghetto, adagio, andante, allegro, presto, prestissimo, etc.; for different structural organizations - sonata form, minuet and trio, scherzo, rondo, fugue etc. As soon as he had memorized them, he disappeared for some time into the cultural circle and did not come to see me. I, however, felt very anxious about him as a father feels after giving fireworks to his child, for my friend was a real innocent.

One day he did enter my room with a very crestfallen look, from which I at once guessed that he had burnt his fingers. I asked him: 'What's the matter?' He said rather hesitantly: 'You remember, the other day I listened to Beethoven here. After that I went to the house of so and so where there was a largish company. I told him that I was coming from your house after listening to Beethoven and that I had liked it very much. He was not at all interested or surprised and said something with a rather superior air which I could not understand.' I asked him what the observation was. Bibhuti Babu replied: 'He said: "I am not at all surprised. Indian music is composed in the minor scale, Beethoven also wrote in the minor scale. So you would not be put off by it." What does that mean?' Bibhuti Babu's patron had obviously heard that the Ninth symphony was in D-minor. I absolutely burst like a bomb on Bibhuti Babu for having been routed by this kind of cultural bluff. I was not even sarcastic, but became really angry and shouted at him: 'Why did you admit that? Could you not tell him that Indian music has as close a relation with the European major mode as it has with the European minor mode? Why did you not tell him that of the nine symphonies of Beethoven as many as seven are in the major mode; of the sixteen quartets, eleven are in the major mode; of the thirty-two piano sonatas, twenty-two are in the major mode?' This outburst was quite useless. Bibhuti Babu sat still with downcast eyes. Then he went away and after that never again did he want to listen to European music.

This incident gave me the idea of indulging in a little satire on the insincere affectations about European music among certain Bengalis. Thus in the Bengali article of 1940 I also had the following passage:

'How would those who are not prepared to take so much trouble be enabled to move in cultured society, maintaining their self-respect? Take the case of someone who does not care about European music and yet does not want to lose prestige in cultured society, what would he do? I have already said that he should refer to the piano as 'pianoforte', and here are a few more hints. If piano playing is being discussed, he should name Paderewski as little as possible, but expatiate on Rubinstein, Busoni, etc., as well as mutter the word 'pianism' half-aside. If anybody speaks of the Moonlight Sonata, he should at first stare starkly at him, and then exclaim, 'Oh, the Sonata in C-sharp minor!' or 'Oh, the Sonata quasi una fantasia!' But he should not hesitate to mention the Hammerklavier Sonata, Paukenschlag Symphony, Forellen Quintet, etc. As to violin playing, he should on no account mention Kreisler, but talk about Joachim. And indeed he will not be able to ignore Toscanini as conductor, but he should cunningly drag in Nikisch. If patronage of music by wealthy persons is discussed and it is his intention to support it, he should pronounce the words "Esterházy", "Mr. Christie", "Glyndebourne". On the other hand, if he wishes to denounce them, he should name Archbishop Hieronymus. Comporting himself in this manner, he will never lose face in cultured circles.'

I am glad to be able to add that the article, despite all its unfamiliar lore, was liked by the readers of the magazine, and even the reviewers of the first issue praised it.

Another happy event in this period of my life to which I have to refer is the birth of our third son, on 20 May 1939. He was our last child, and was not born in distress. As usual, he was also born at home, with the same attendance of doctors and nurses as before, but without the financial embarrassment for us. Therefore, for the first few months, I called him Benjamin.

Subhas Base Goes West

Sarat Bose was arrested on 12 December 1941, on the suspicion of having been in touch with the Japanese in establishing what the British authorities in India regarded as treasonable relations with them. Before I describe that incident, which made a great difference to me personally, I should relate its antecedent. That was Subhas Bose's departure from India to go to Germany in the previous January. Thus he literally went west from Calcutta. As it turned out, it also became 'going west' for him in the colloquial sense. It ended in total failure for him, and, finally, in his death.

The news of his departure or 'escape' became public on 26 January 1941. Actually, he had left Calcutta some days earlier. He was taken by car to an important railway junction on the border between Bengal and Bihar, and from there travelled by train to the Northwest Frontier Province, finally to reach Kabul. That was the first stage of his journey to Berlin.

What is most tragic about this episode is its glorification by the Bengali intelligentsia and its exploitation by the surviving relatives for promoting their political interest. Even today there is no admission of its deplorable futility. The sincerely stupid part of the glorifying myth has its origin in the emotional compulsion for the Bengali middle class to believe that through Subhas Bose they played a decisive role in gaining political independence for India, and to deprecate Gandhi's role as far as possible. Actually, Bengal ceased to play an important role in the nationalist movement from 1937 and Bose himself was pushed out of the main stream of the nationalist movement in 1939. By leaving India he ceased to matter so far as the movement was concerned.

The so-called escape has been represented as a clever feat of outwitting the British administration in India by adroit planning and daring execution, somewhat similar to the rescue of Mussolini by Hitler. Certainly, it would have been clever if Subhas Bose had been under house arrest and surveillance. But he was not. When questions were raised after his departure, it was definitely established that the political police of Bengal had had no instructions to keep him under surveillance or to prevent his movements. Thus he could go anywhere he liked by day or by night.

I have, however, been confronted with the argument that, since those who planned his escape believed that he was being watched, their success deserves recognition. But from what I knew about the efficiency of the political police in Bengal in those days, I would say that if the police had been watching Bose, the kind of planning his immature nephews were capable of, could not have prevented his arrest before he reached any of the bridges over the river Hooghly.

What again is not realized by those who glorify the so-called escape is that the British administration, so far from being made anxious by it, had every reason to feel relieved. Remaining in India, Bose would have given cause for anxiety, but by going to Berlin he rendered himself harmless. The British officials in India in those days were given to be unnecessarily nervous about internal conditions, as they also were in 1915 and 1916, and for which they were criticized by the Mesopotamia Commission. In 1941, however, they would have had more than their normal share of nervousness if they believed that Subhas Bose could make any difference to the course of the war by his presence in Germany, and that was the only thing that mattered. I feel quite sure that if the Government of India had taken a serious view of Bose's departure for Germany, Sarat Bose and certain other members of the family would have been arrested at once.

It is now very difficult, if not impossible, to arrive at the full historical truth about Bose's departure from Calcutta. What he did after reaching Kabul can be found out from German and other diplomatic records, and his activities from that point onwards have been described in great detail. Even before these accounts had appeared. Count Giusto del Giardino, who was then a young diplomat on the staff of the Italian embassy in Kabul, and later the Italian Ambassador in New Delhi, told me how his delegation had helped Bose to reach Berlin. But the story of the journey from Calcutta to Kabul remains imprecise, if not doubtful. I say this in spite of the extremely detailed and circumstantial account of the escape which is now available. Such details were not given until decades after the event. I hardly know what to make of the account, especially because it brings Sarat Bose into the plot and makes him an active participator. Yet he himself never said a word about his share in the exploit, although he was free to do so from 1947 to the time of his death in 1950, and would have gained everything politically by so proclaiming. On the contrary, with such a card in his hand, he allowed himself to be pushed out even from the politics of Bengal.

Nor can I reconcile the details, as given in the account, of Sarat Bose's participation in the plot, such as it was and it was a very naive one, with what I saw of his behaviour in the days following the announcement of Subhas Bose's escape. I was his secretary from the middle of 1937 to the time of his arrest in December 1941, and saw him every day, except when he was at court or resting. Apart from that he told me more than once that he did not share his brother's faith in any 'international' contribution to India's freedom. He believed that we had either to achieve that through our own exertions or not at all.

Knowing this, I could not believe that he would have approved of his brother's going to Germany. Besides, I should have been a fool if I had not tried to guess from his behaviour as to whether he was involved in Subhas Bose's escape or not.

One incident, the news of which came in either late in the evening of 26 January or the next morning -I forget the exact time - made me think that he had no definite knowledge of his brother's movements. The news was that Subhas Bose, in the disguise of a Sadhu, had been arrested near Dhanbad, the railway station where he was said to have boarded a train for the Punjab. Sarat Babu was extremely agitated when he heard this. In fact, in my presence, he tried more than once to contact their other brother who lived near Dhanbad to find out what had happened. But he could not get the connection, and the next day a second piece of news came that the Sadhu was not Subhas Bose.

Sarat Babu at once quietened down. From all this I came to the conclusion that he knew nothing about the plans of the escape. But it was based on a wrong premise, which was shared by all who were not in the know. This was that Subhas Bose had left India in a Japanese ship. The fact that he did so by the overland route, of course, takes away a good deal of the force of my conclusion, but not wholly, because according to the circumstantial account, the nephew who took him to Dhanbad reported on his return that he had left the Dhanbad area safely. Why then was Sarat Bose so upset more than a week after he was supposed to have been informed about that? I am unable in any way to account for all these incongruous facts.

I have been thinking for decades over this matter without arriving at any greater certainty. Now, however, I would not maintain for certain that Sarat Babu knew nothing at all about Subhas Babu's escape. He may not have. But the alternative is that, when he found that his brother was set upon such a course, he agreed without necessarily approving of it.

This would fully explain his reluctance to speak about his share in the plot in order to gain political advantage. He must have felt bitter remorse for whatever share he took in the escape, increased by the thought that he had been a party to his brother's miserable death. Sarat Bose was never a man to aim to win a political game at the expense of a brother's life.

Arrest of Sarat Bose

Sarat Bose's arrest took place in the afternoon of 12 December, 1941. I was not in the main house when the police arrived, but coming to see him I saw an Englishman sitting in front of him in the south verandah, and upon asking what he wanted I was told about the arrest. He was one of the Deputy Commissioners of Police of Calcutta. I then waited in the hall to see what was going to happen. Sarat Babu rose after a while, but the Englishman remained seated. When I met Sarat Babu in the hall I broke down. He only said that I was weak, and added: 'You see how I am taking it.' He then went upstairs for a while before being driven away.

In the succeeding weeks I often went to Sarat Babu's house to maintain the office routine. I was saddened by the air of gloom and desolation around me. The crowds of visitors had disappeared and the cheerful noise was no longer to be heard. There were no signs of interested courtiers, and only two or three staunch friends came to inquire about the family and do something if their help or advice was needed. Sarat Babu had not expected his arrest and his business affairs were not tidied up for a possible absence. These were, however, attended to with the help of friends.

I completely disbelieved that he was involved in any kind of political intrigue with the Japanese, and also that they would have had any serious interest in him. At that time they had more important matters to attend to. However, on this score, I found politically conscious Bengalis to be in disagreement with me. On such matters they were always ambivalent. In respect of the revolutionary movement in Bengal they asserted the innocence of the young Bengalis who were detained by the British administration when it was an issue between them and the British, but secretly they believed in the revolutionary plots and glorified them. They showed the same facing-two-ways attitude in regard to Sarat Bose. They would say that he was innocent as against British charges, but would cherish the idea that he too was a revolutionary leader. No political idea could be more crude and half-baked than the Bengali notion of being a revolutionary.

Since I was not ready to take this view of Sarat Babu's detention and would not believe that he had carried on intrigues with the Japanese, I wrote a series of articles in the *Hindusthan Standard*, Suresh Majumdar's paper, to dispute the grounds of his arrest. I was prepared to admit that there was a large dossier of depositions against him, but I also knew how the political police made up these dossiers. In order to discredit the evidence, I even referred to the Dreyfus affair and the Friedjung trial. But it came to my ears that after reading the articles, even some of Sarat Babu's friends said that I had gone too far. They may have thought that I was trying to deprive him of the revolutionary glory with which they invested him in secret. They obviously liked to gloat on the idea that Sarat Babu was in league with the Japanese in order to liberate India from British rule. I heard quite detailed stories in Calcutta of how he had clandestine meetings with Japanese agents by the wayside at night when on his way to his villa on the Hooghly river, some miles north of Calcutta. These tales would have been too crude even for a third-rate thriller or spy story.

Those who believed in Sarat Babu's intrigues with the Japanese did not consider that by doing so they were insulting the intelligence of the man, and even more that of the Japanese. The truth was that the Bengalis who had become-nationalist drug addicts were bringing down the Japanese to their own level. The men who baffled even American intelligence by their surprise attack on Pearl Harbor and swept through southeast Asia on the strength of their detailed information about the military position of the British and the Dutch there, were not likely to prepare for an invasion of India, if they had one in mind, by this kind of nibbling. I knew what Sarat Babu had to do with the Japanese so far as anything was known. One evening, coming home late, he told me that he had been to a party given by the Japanese in Calcutta. In fact, the Bengalis were degrading the detention of Sarat Bose to an *opera buffa*. Imitating Gilbert and Sullivan in their way, they were writing their *H.M.S. Sari*.

I thought I would do a little more than merely writing the articles. So I went first to Sir N. N. Sarkar, who was once a member of the Viceroy's Executive Council, and asked him to speak to Lord Linlithgow, the Viceroy, whom he knew well and was going to see in New Delhi. He readily promised to do so, and asked me to come for a reply after he had returned to Calcutta. I also went to Shyama Prasad Mookherji and requested him to speak to Khwaja Nazimuddin, the Home Minister of Bengal, on Sarat Babu's behalf I got their answers soon. Sir N. N. Sarkar told me that he had indeed represented Sarat Babu's case to Lord Linlithgow and had got the reply: if I had not sanctioned Sarat Bose's detention after seeing the evidence placed before me I should have been guilty of neglect of duty.' Shyama Prasad Mookherji told me a different story. Khwaja Nazimuddin had told him: 'You would be surprised to learn who informed about Sarat Bose's relations with the Japanese.' The Minister did not, of course, tell Shyama Prasad Babu who they were, but the gossip-mongers of Calcutta suppiied the deficiency. Various persons were named and among them was *myself*! It was even suggested that I got my new appointment in Delhi by betraying my employer.

That was the end of the matter, and Sarat Babu remained in prison until 1945.I must say that the British authorities who placed him in detention showed no intelligence in doing so. They should have been capable of realizing that if their armies were capable of checking the Japanese on the borders of Assam, the worst that Sarat Bose could have done would not have made any difference. In fact, British rule in India was being maintained by millions of Indians serving even as soldiers. On the other hand, if these armies failed, Sarat Bose in prison would not have saved British rule. But by 1942 the British officials in India had become afflicted with dementia praecox. It should not be forgotten that when a British campaign was to be launched against the Japanese from the Assam frontier, the British administration could not even manage the railways properly, but had to let them be run by the Americans. All the British could do was to put Bengalis like Sarat Bose in prison.

New Employment in Delhi

The arrest of Sarat Bose made it necessary for me to look for a new job. This relapse into unemployment was not likely to throw me into the kind of distress I experienced when I gave up my post in the Military Accounts

Department or in the *Modern Review* office. At that time the salary I earned from Sarat Babu was not above one-third of my total income. I could have carried on with the other two-thirds for some time. But I had expanded my way of living, and could not have reduced it without discomfort to my family and some dissatisfaction to myself

At first I did not feel anxious, because I reckoned on one possibility. When Suresh Majumdar had persuaded me to take up the post of Sarat Babu's secretary, he had told me definitely that if for any reason that connection came to an end, a post on the same salary at least would be kept reserved for me on his newspaper. Thus after some time I went to see him and asked him if he could provide for me in the way he had said. He was not surprised, but asked me to return after he had thought over the matter. I went again and again raised the question. He replied that he had not as yet been able to decide what to do, and could I call again? I went, but on that visit I did not raise the question of my employment. He also said nothing and I came away feeling convinced that there would be no job for me in Suresh Babu's office.

I understood the situation fully. It was a repetition of the situation he had had to face previously. I assumed that there had been total opposition from his staff. I would not embarrass him. But when after a few weeks I got a new job in All India Radio in Delhi and told him about it, he said with a smile: 'I wish you were not going. Something would have turned up.' I could not, of course, have depended on that in spite of my incurable Micawberism. He helped me with a generous sum of money to cover the expenses of moving to Delhi.

The offer from Delhi was, however, a total surprise. It came personally from Mr Z. A. Bokhari, the Director-General of All India Radio. It was even a greater surprise because it came as the sequel to a rather bad-tempered quarrel with him. This quarrel, too, was unexpected, and its cause very curious. I had been broadcasting from the Calcutta station of AIR since 1937 on international affairs and on the war since 1939. I was not satisfied with the way in which the official broadcasting organization was covering the war. What lay behind the inefficiency was the lack of conviction of its Indian staff. Quite unexpectedly at the end of 1941, I was given an opportunity to express an opinion about it. Sir Geoffrey Tyson, to whose journal. *Capital*, I was contributing editorial notes, as I have already said, one day told me that he was going to Delhi to attend a conference on war propaganda, and asked me if I would give him a note about A I R's contribution to it. He added that anything I told him would be for his personal use. I gave him a long note, in which I was rather severe about the staff of the organization. I heard no more from him on this matter.

Then, at the end of February, it came to my notice that my note had been circulated under my name for the benefit of the conference. This information was given to me by the Director-General. One day I was requested by the Calcutta Station to go and meet Mr Bokhari, the Director-General, who wanted to speak to me. I could make no guess whatever as to why he should have done so. When we met, and for the first time, after asking me to sit down, he began the conversation by saying to me: 'I have a serious complaint against you, Mr Chaudhuri.' Taken quite by surprise, I asked him why. Then he asked me why, if I had criticism to make of his department, I had given it to an Englishman instead of sending it to him. I was shown a paper in which my note was included.

I explained to him that I had given the note to Sir Geoffrey to be used by him and not to be attributed to me, and that I had had no idea that it would be circulated. I added that I could not have sent my criticism to him because I did not know him at all.

This did not mollify him. It seemed to me that the Government had taken notice of my remarks and this had irritated him. To this he gave frank expression in his next remark: 'There's a kink in the Indian character. They go to Englishmen instead of trusting their countrymen.' I also got angry and replied: 'I knew that if I had sent that note to you, nothing would have happened. It would simply have been shelved.' After some more argument he said that he was going to Dacca, and on his return would like to see me again. He gave me a date for another meeting.

I went fully prepared to quarrel again and to tell him even more unpalatable things about his department. But I got no opening. As soon as I had taken my seat, he surprised me even more than on the previous occasion by saying: 'Mr Chaudhuri, would you accept it if I offered you a job in this office." I certainly felt glad that there was an end to unpleasantness, and had the presence of mind to reply: 'That would depend on the nature of the work and the salary.' He named two hundred and fifty rupees a month, but added that he could raise this a little higher. I told him that the offer was rather low for me, because my total income in Calcutta was much higher, and since I would have to give up the other sources of income I had, I could not accept a governmental post on less than four hundred rupees. He asked me not to reject his offer out of hand, but to write to him in Delhi after carefully considering the matter. I did and gave him full information about my income and justification for my expectation of a higher salary than that which had been offered. There was no reply, so I thought the whole question had been dropped.

But there was another surprise. One morning I received a very urgent summons to go to the Calcutta station on important business. As soon as I arrived, I was asked by the senior Bengali on the broadcasting staff: 'Nirad Babu, are you prepared to go to Delhi to work in our News Division on the salary you wanted.' If you agree you will have to join at once.' I did not take a minute to consider, and there was no need to consult my wife. She had always wanted me to leave Calcutta. I agreed at once. When I informed her on returning home she was very glad. I explained that I was treating the move to Delhi as an experiment, and would come back if I found that the work did not suit me. It was decided that for the time being I would go alone, and, after seeing how things worked out, bring the family to Delhi. In less than two weeks I had left Calcutta, and, as it turned out, never to return to the city where I had grown up.

For many years I had begun to feel that life in Calcutta for me was a life which had reached the perimeter it was likely to have in that city and could not expand further. I could see neither openings nor opportunities which would enable me to develop any potentialities that were still latent in me. Thus, whenever I thought of the rest of my life, I only looked forward to a quiet life of rest and retirement, and that not even prolonged to many more years. Actually, by leaving Calcutta, I began a new life, and, in respect of achievement, the years which I thought would be at best eventless, at worst stagnant, became my most active ones. What was really surprising was that this sort of debouching out of a narrow valley took place when I was forty- four years and six months old. I do not think that normally an average individual goes through a fundamental revolution in his life at that age.

My wife had her own reasons for welcoming the change. She was brought up in a very quiet and beautiful hill town, and did not like the congestion, noise, and dirt of Calcutta. Above everything else, she had begun to resent the denial of opportunities and proper remunerations for me. She always said to me: 'People here will not allow you to rise further.' She did not know for certain what still lay unutilized within me, but had confidence in me. In any case, she wanted me to write a major book, and was sure that I would never write it in Calcutta. Even now she says that I would have remained where I was in 1942 if I had not removed myself from Calcutta.

The Historical Situation for the Bengali People

I left Bengal due to wholly accidental circumstances for neither Sarat Bose's arrest nor the offer from the Director-General of A I R could be anticipated in any way. But, in actual fact, it turned out to be something like deliberate emigration for me from the only country which was really my own. Even then it might have had that appearance because I felt no regret in leaving Calcutta, although during the years that I was growing up there I had felt like all the sons of the city that I could never live away from it.

That was not to be set down wholly to the sense of relief that I had at being offered much better employment than what I could ever have hoped to have in Calcutta, nor to the rebirth of hope for myself at seeing new prospects opening out to me after I had become an old railway engine pushed against the buffers of a siding. Of course, both the satisfactions were present, but they by themselves would not have led me to the indifference with which I left Bengal. The basic reason for that was my impersonal and intellectual diagnosis of the historical situation for the Bengali people, at which I had arrived long before I could even imagine that I should be enabled to leave Bengal. I was convinced that my people had no future, and I was not prepared to share their fate.

Was that ratting? No, for I have never accepted the dictum: my family - right or wrong, as a moral principle binding on anyone. On the contrary, I have always been repelled by it, considering that it embodies one of the most anti-moral and pernicious inclinations to which human beings are subject, because it makes every particular human community look upon all others as 'They', and therefore as enemies. What I saw of the adherence of the British community in India to this doctrine made me positively reject it. It made them lie with unashamed unanimity even when one of them murdered an Indian in the most foul and cowardly manner. There can be no doubt that this perverted view of national loyalty made a substantial contribution to the untimely disappearance of British rule in India.

I had learnt early enough that it was inculcated in them by their school education. I was only sixteen when I read a school story in which the principle was asserted by a school senior to a school junior in these words: 'You know the rules of the school: one boy must not tell on another.' The rule was observed when a little boy was frightened by older boys dressed up as ghosts into jumping into a river and was supposed to have been drowned and carried away by the current. Nobody would confess or testify, and one boy who told the headmaster out of fear was never forgiven: he was always called a sneak and treated as a pariah. What surprised me even at that age was that the author thought that right. As I grew up, I saw that the British community observed the rule as a national duty in India. I would only say that they had faith in a myth but were oblivious of a truth: the battle of Waterloo was *not* won on the playing-fields of Eton, but the school spirit earned for the British people the eternal hatred of all the people they ruled despite all the good that they did to those peoples. I would have, none of that immoral principle calling itself moral. The only loyalty which I admitted I owed to my people was that I should warn them about the danger that faced them and the course they were taking through lack of foresight and vitality even at the risk of being unpopular. This duty I have performed all my life, and therefore I have now to live in exile.

But wherever I am, I cannot be indifferent to what is happening to my people. It is sad to have to contemplate the decline of the Bengali people from their position of dominance in India to the final stage of being of no significance to Indian history in the space of some fifty years. No one can deny that in the nineteenth century the Bengali people created a new life, not only for themselves, but for the entire Indian people, by their intellectual and moral effort. They created a new Bengali culture which broadened into the modem Indian culture. They created the nationalist movement. They reshaped the Indian personality.

For present-day Bengalis all that is now a thing of the past, except for retrospective, senseless, and unmanly bragging, and, in so far as it is real, it is of historical interest alone. Of course, even today's life in Calcutta contains some of the old spirit and behaviour as a survival, but without creativeness and power. In so far as the Bengalis have not accepted defeat and still possess ambition, the one ambition they cherish today is to become indispensable mercenaries of those other Indians they formerly despised. By virtue of their cleverness die best of them are employed as such and are satisfied with being sterile hirelings on high salaries.

This decline, quick and untimely, has to be explained, and I diagnosed not only the decline but also its causes even when the process had just begun. The first cause was to be found in the historical evolution of the Bengali people in the very period of British rule which gave them their dominant cultural and political status in India. They were the first group of Indians who responded eagerly and actively to the impact of European civilization on Indian life which British rule brought with it.

The new culture and social life they created were the products of that interaction, but the nature of the interaction and of the interacting agencies were misunderstood from the beginning, and are not historically understood even now. The view which was taken, and which still holds the field, is that in the nineteenth century India became the meeting ground of an old civilization with a new one, and the crucible of a new culture in which the best of both mingled. All of us in Bengal were brought up on this historical interpretation, at the bottom of which was a concept of synthesis: an impressive illustration of the 'law' of thesis, antithesis and synthesis. This, it was proclaimed, was the essence of the cultural history of India during British rule. But it was and is a pure myth.

I have already described how in the late Twenties I had discovered it to be so, and had arrived at a new view about our cultural condition on the eve of British rule, and as I have also related I entered into a long correspondence with Professor Arnold J. Toynbee on this subject. I embodied my views in a long note and I sent it to him on 18 July 1936.I shall quote parts of it. 'Even educated Indians of today', I wrote,

'are curiously indifferent to their immediate past, the past that is to say which forms the warp to the weft of Western influences. This is certainly due to the discovery of the classical Hindu civilization in the nineteenth century, which has fired their imagination and made them conscious of a heritage of their very own to pit against Western civilization. In their anxiety to feel at one with this heritage from motives of self-respect they have forgotten the intervening phase of their existence and are now no more able to tear away their immediate past from the classical Hindu background than, looking at the sky at night, we are able to perceive any spatial separation between the solar system and the stellar world.

'I believe this short-circuiting has been made easier by the fact that the society of our immediate past was of a character altogether different from what went before and has come after, and that brings me to my real point. Contemporary sources give glimpses of a curiously naive and, in many respects, a primitive society in India in the eighteenth century, which is more properly called a folk-civilization than civilization. Of course, there were two things in it which gave it an outward appearance of maturity. These were the Islamic civilization and the Hindu scholastic tradition. But the influence of the former was almost wholly urban and confined to the ruling aristocracy, while the Hindu survivals possessed values in this society which were quite different from their values in classical Hindu times. Neither the same sophistication nor the same self-consciousness was there, and there was a total lapse of historical memory. This last is perhaps the most important proof of the "childishness" of the new society. It seems to me that between 1000 ad (I use this date quite arbitrarily because I have not been able to explore the upper limits of the society which meets us in the immediately pre-British age) and the eighteenth century a re-barbarization (in no contemptuous sense) and simplification of Hindu life had been taking place. It was certainly the age of the differentiation and fixation of the modem vernaculars of India, of the creation of vernacular literatures, of simple and unorthodox religious movements, of folk art, dances, and songs, and of social customs very loosely affiliated to the orthodox Hindu system. Altogether, the impression of winding down and a decided crudeness is impossible to resist. That is why I am disposed to look upon the supercilious and unenthusiastic estimates of Indians by early European writers and administrators, when stripped of the xenophobic excrescences, as a truer index of the quality of the society they met than the opinions of later scholars who had discovered ancient India by painstaking research.

'Whether this "childish" society would have grown to man's estate by its unaided efforts and in what way it would have grown up, are questions which we are no longer able to answer. For, before the evolution had gone very far, the revolutionary impact of European civilization was upon it. Close in its wake came the discovery of ancient India, whose sophistication had almost as great a disintegrating effect on the primitive society which turned eagerly to it as the reaction to European ideas. Faced with these challenges, Indian thinkers and reformers from Rammohun Roy to Rabindranath Tagore have evolved a pattern of response, which they look upon as a solution. They have popularized the idea of a synthesis between the East and the West. This formula has enabled us to civilize ourselves to a certain extent at the top, but by far the most important result of its adoption has been the sterility of our intellectual and moral life, dominated by imported phrases on the one hand and archaistic models on the other. If this is the case with the intelligentsia, the masses have not been touched at all by the excessively intellectual influences. They are reacting to the machine technique of the West, but not to the cultural currents, which are driving a wedge between them and the educated classes. All thoughtful Indians are conscious of these features of our life and have a profound feeling of malaise. But they do not see that the root of the trouble lies in the fact that in India two civilizations are not meeting on equal terms. Mahatma Gandhi, I believe, has a subconscious perception of this, and that is why he is advocating a deliberate rejection of sophistication (both European and Indian) and a return to the folk level. But his is also an impossible position because the Indian people cannot cut themselves adrift from world currents - not so much of intellectual and moral ideas as of the new scientific technique of living. The problem for us today is therefore, not how to bring about a reconciliation between two civilizations of the same species, but how to adjust the relations of a more or less primitive people to the triple contact with (1) European classical civilization; (2) Western scientific technique of living; and (3) ancient Indian culture, all of which are too advanced - though in varying degrees - to be assimilated easily by a people belonging to a different species of human society. In short, the relations of modem Indian society to the "Western" may differ in degree, but do not do so in kind, from the relations of other modern primitive peoples, like the negroes, to "Western society".'

This was the substantive part of the note dealing with our cultural status in the late eighteenth century. I concluded it by saying that for me the question was not purely historical but had a practical aspect. Thus I wrote: 'As a modern Indian with hopes and fears for his country, I feel that the adoption of this theory takes me out of the deep shadows of the evening of an old civilization and releases me to work, to accept, and to create as I please in untrammelled freedom from the self-imposed burden of a dead past. But there are other modern Indians who as decisively think otherwise.'

Of course, I knew why they did so. It had become a matter of national pride. So I wrote finally: 'British rule in India makes it a point of honour with us to cling to ancient India as our newly-found soul. As long as this rule lasts, it will prevent us from seeing our past as it really was and from reacting normally to European influences.'

Professor Toynbee replied to me in his own hand, and in his last letter to me written on 15 September 1936 in reply to one of mine of 27 August he wrote:

'Your letter makes it clear what kind of society you are defining, and I think you have brought to light an important type which, as you say, is neither a civilization in the historian's full sense nor yet, perhaps, a primitive society in die meaning of Hobhouse and Ginsberg.

'I look forward to hearing how your work on the modem Indian instance of this type gets on.'

Alas! the work was never written. As it happened however, six months later I got an opportunity to put my thesis formally before my countrymen in Bengali. But I did not present it to them as a pure historical thesis but as the theoretical basis of our approach to the contemporary cultural situation. I brought it in as an explanation of our premature cultural decline. I said that this decline was implicit in the very conditions in which our new culture of the nineteenth century was born. I pointed out that as a people we were not sufficiently advanced socially and economically to create a solid culture with a long expectation of life. We wanted the end product before we had built the factory. The simple fact was that both psychologically and socially we were a very simple people and therefore what we were trying to do was to force a growth. I said that the pioneers of our new life and culture were so overwhelmed by the splendour of the modern European and the ancient Indian civilizations that they set themselves to create a culture of that order before the ground was prepared for its development. I put our aspiration in a simile: we wanted the flowers before we had grown the plants. This more or less unrealistic effort exhausted our powers even before they had reached their full strength.

Thus our cultural creation, which in itself is not to be underrated, was the result of a precocious effort. It was the work of a child prodigy, so to speak. Such creations do obtain wondering respect, but they are also most often a tragedy for the child himself.

Character Is Fate

The new life and culture in Bengal was the work of an eager and perfervid adolescent, and, as such, there were weaknesses, immaturities, and limitations. These could have been left behind if the development had continued. It did not, and that was due to the weakness of the Bengali intellect, character, and personality. Macaulay, who was in Bengal and was responsible for the educational system which created the modern Bengali, was perfectly aware of that. He is the author of the most celebrated denunciation of the Bengali character, and I shall presently explain to what extent it was just and where it was not. But as to the basic cause of the weakness he was not wrong. He began by declaring that no part of India possessed such natural advantages both for agriculture and commerce, and that the tyranny of man had for ages struggled in vain against the overflowing bounty of nature, and in spite of the Muslim despot and of the Mahratta freebooter, Bengal was known through the East as the Garden of Eden - the rich kingdom. Even the noble ladies of London and Paris were clothed in the delicate produce of its looms. This was followed by Macaulay's description of the Bengali people: 'The race by whom this rich tract was peopled', he wrote in January, 1840,

'enervated by a soft climate and accustomed to peaceful employments, bore the same relation to other Asiatics which the Asiatics generally bear to the bold and energetic children of Europe. The Castilians have a proverb, that in Valencia the earth is water and the men women; and the description is at least equally applicable to the vast plain of the Lower Ganges. Whatever the Bengali does he does languidly. His favourite pursuits are sedentary. He shrinks from bodily exertion; and, though voluble in dispute, and singularly pertinacious in the war of chicane, he seldom engages in a personal conflict, and scarcely ever enlists as a soldier.'

This *was* an objective appraisement, compared with the full-blooded denunciation he published twenty-one months later, and if even here the truth was expressed in a rhetorical style, that does not make it less true, because it is a mistake to think that truth has to have a drab expression. Even the word *chicane*, which Macaulay employed, was not unjust. Few people in the world have been endowed with greater agility of the mind, receptivity to new ideas, and the capacity for playing with them. There is something in the Bengali's dealings with ideas, of the skilful tennis player's riposte to the ball. The unfortunate thing is that most often the Bengali, in his treatment of ideas, does not go beyond that.

The Bengali intelligence is sharp, but not strong or well-tempered. The British in India always spoke of the Bengali as the 'nimble-witted Babu', and ill-natured as the phrase was, it still contained some truth. The Bengali intellect was at its strongest in argument, which could descend through such intermediate stages as plausibility, logicality, logic-chopping and hair-splitting, to a chicane which was wholly devoid of embarrassment and even bland. The more clever a Bengali is, the more incapable he is of making distinctions between these. Thus, in the pre-British era, the Bengali mind was seen at its most efficient in the exposition of Hindu logic and of Hindu sacred law; in the British era, in dealing with the extremely complicated legal system which the British introduced into India; and is now seen in theoretical economics. To the Bengali, all these were and are games, and, in playing them, he does not care to have any truck with reality. I have offended fellow-Bengalis by saying that the Bengalis are clever but not intelligent. Even the distinction has not been understood, which in itself would confirm my judgement. Thus the best products of the Bengali intellect are very much like the best industrial product of Bengal, fine muslin. The peculiar character of the Bengali mind has made a significant difference to its reaction to different things from European culture. The Bengali's response to English literature has made him most sensitive, human, and creative, while European thought, whether political or social, has invariably desiccated him and led him to a sterile dogmatism.

But this intellectual fragility could not have become a normal trait of the Bengali personality without the presence in it of a greater shortcoming: weakness of character. It is a mistake to think that human intelligence can reach its highest effectiveness without character, because it is the element of personality which supports and even drives intelligence in two ways: first by creating the will to work hard and continue effort, and, secondly, by making the intellectually inclined individual ready to be involved in all realities, instead of running away from them. It was in both these respects, that is, in both will and robustness, that the Bengali was wanting. He was driven by feeling and not volition, and often even the feeling never reached the level of passion, which is essential for all achievement, except in rare individuals born with genius and, therefore, with passion as well. Thus the motive power of Bengali life was always involuntary. The Bengali people provide a striking illustration of the truth of Chamfort's saying: 'C'est un grand malheur de perdre, par notre charactère, les droits que nos talents nous donnent sur la société.'

But the harm done by the weakness of the Bengali character was not simply negative: it also had deplorable positive consequences. While the weakness made the Bengali disinclined to hard work, his very cleverness, of which he was always conscious, gave him desires and ambitions which made him devious, because he would neither discipline himself against them when they outpaced his capacities, nor make an honest effort to satisfy them. Thus there appeared in Bengali life and society a duality between the genuine and the counterfeit, which on account of the cleverness of the colourable imitation was very difficult to see from mere outward appearance.

The duality may have been present in pre-British days, but there is no evidence that it affected general Bengali life in any way. In fact, there was very little to promote it, because Bengali life in that age was lived within narrow and modest limits, and it could not lead the Bengalis into temptation. Both politically and culturally, Bengal was then an outlier, a semi-isolated extension, of northern India, and Bengali culture was only a minor provincial version of Indian culture, whether Hindu or Islamic. The Bengalis themselves were not important in political, military, or economical life, and at their most ambitious they sought minor posts and functions in the Muslim administration. But all this changed suddenly and drastically with the establishment of British rule. Bengal became the political centre of India, and due to the introduction of education through English, the cultural centre as well. For the first time in the historic existence of the Bengali people, that is to say, of a people who could be distinguished clearly from the rest of the Hindus of India as a human group with an identity of its own, there came to them the opportunity to play a major role in the history of their country, and also to obtain the highest worldly positions open to Indians. Quite naturally, with the opportunity their aspirations and ambitions also grew, without adding either to their capacity or to their inclination to work hard. On account of this, the duality came to the surface and became, during British rule, a feature of Bengali life which could neither be eliminated nor be overlooked.

It spread to all aspects of Bengali life, cultural and worldly. To take the cultural first: on account of its novelty, cultural development as combined educational, intellectual, and literary achievement or accomplishment, became the aim of all Bengalis who were ambitious in an idealistic way. But since that was very highly regarded in the Bengali society of the time, it was also coveted by those who had worldly ambitions only. This desire was strongest in those who were clever or even talented but were quite unwilling to undertake the labour required for real cultural attainments. Thus the Bengali 'humanists', who were very much like the Renaissance humanists in their way, became divided into two groups, one genuine and the other counterfeit, and often the fakes outnumbered the authentic products. Particularly, in talk, which was the main outlet of Bengali self-projection, the two could hardly be distinguished from each other. As the Sanskrit proverb had it: the empty vessel sounds louder.

In worldly matters the duality was more blatant, because of the character of those who were at the top. On account of their passivity, the general run of Bengalis had neither the desire nor the energy to acquire great wealth or a high worldly position. They were, so to speak, the blessed poor in spirit, while those who wanted worldly prizes were not only abnormally energetic for Bengalis, but also as a class, uninhibited by moral scruples. This quite naturally made the latter the dominant order in Bengali society, because there is as striking a contrast between the rewards of honesty and dishonesty as between the worldly and the cultural sphere. In respect of culture, dishonesty can create only fakes, but in regard to wealth, dishonesty brings in the real things more quickly, and no honest man ever hopes to become as rich as a dishonest one.

In spite of that, neither the unworldly nor the purely worldly aspects of the duality would have done much harm to Bengali life and culture if the dishonest side had kept to itself, satisfied with its own substantial gains, and left to the honest side to acquire the kind of position it could. That could be expected, because the gains in the one sphere did not come in the way of the gains in the other. Nonetheless, this did not happen, because the dishonest side fell foul of the honest. To take the culturally dishonest first. They were too clever not to recognize the superiority of the cultural creators and the reality of their achievements, and they resented both. The worldly adventurers, on their part, resented the moral crusade of the reformers, who denounced every kind of failing in Bengali society, and, as it happened, even the literary creators were moral crusaders at one remove.

It is curious as well as significant to note that the moral intention was as strong among the literary men of the British epoch who created the new Bengali literature, as it was among the professed social or moral reformers. The novel and the story were the newest products of literature in that age, as well as the genres which made the most powerful psychological impact. Not in one of them is traditional Bengali society and life represented in a favourable light but as vile and cruelly oppressive. In describing their established society in this way the writers were wholly overlooking the majority in their society and what was good in a humdrum way in it. They took both for granted, and indeed, in their reforming zeal, addressed themselves to this passively good element, wishing to rouse it to active goodness and to militancy against the dominant badness in their society as well as against the dominant bad men, instead of passively submitting to both. This idealistic denunciation as well as incitement to revolt was bound to make the dominant minority of bad men hostile to the reformers.

Both they and the cultural fakes combined to attack those who voiced the new spirit. The conflict which this created was taken to a still lower level by what was the most common eruption of the weakness of character of the Bengali people, namely, envy. Of course, envy is a common failing in all those who have intelligence and ambition but do not have the inclination to work hard for fame or position. In Bengal, however, it became an even more mean and rancorous failing, and it spared no great man of Bengal, whether in religious reform or literature.

Jerusalem, which stoned its prophets, was not a patch on Calcutta in persecuting them. I have already described how Tagore was attacked and embittered by the persecution. But others were equally slandered, and, remembering all of them, I wrote in the first part of my autobiography that all the great men Bengal produced in the nineteenth century were 'a group of Dantean figures, in death sleeping far away from their ungrateful country'.

They were saddened and embittered by the attacks, but it was not out of a sense of personal injustice and injury that they denounced the immoral practices and inclinations of fellow-Bengalis. They saw the harm that these were doing to the Bengali people as a whole, and to their comminations they were always ready to add: 'O Jerusalem, Jerusalem, *thou* that killest the prophets, and stonest them which are sent to thee, how often would I have gathered thy children together, and ye would not.' They wrote in agony of spirit, and never out of self-righteousness or grievance.

I shall quote only two of these denunciations, the first from the greatest exponent of Bengali conservatism, the neo-Hindu Swami Vivekananda, whose influence on young Bengalis of the last decade of the nineteenth and first of the present century was unequalled by that of any other man; and the second will be from Tagore, who was the foremost liberal preacher. Swami Vivekananda's pronouncement dates from 1900, and Tagore's from 1917. The first was as follows:

'Millions of sub-human creatures, trodden underfoot and crushed out of life by rulers of their own as well as alien nations, by co-religionists as well as followers of other religions; intolerant of industry like slaves, like slaves again lacking in enterprise, despairing, without a past and without a future, wanting only to keep on living somehow; envious like lackeys, resentful of the prosperity of their kin; made incapable of devotion by loss of hope; without faith; dependent only on low cunning and deceit like jackals, embodiment of selfishness; lickers of the feet of the powerful and fierce as the god of death to those who are less powerful than themselves; ridden by vile and horrifying superstition as befits those who lack strength and hope, without moral backbone - pullulating like maggots on putrescent flesh on the body of India ...'

I have, however, to add that this description was not offered by Vivekananda as his own estimate of the character of his countrymen, but as that of the British officials. But from them I have never come across such a denunciation of the Bengali character, although I have read many of them and all unsparing. The British criticism did not cover the evils in private and social life of the Bengalis as this description does. I am inclined to think that it was to a great extent Vivekananda's own criticism in a moment of exasperation, and it has to be added Swami Vivekananda was very European in his outlook on life.

I shall next quote Tagore's combined exhortation and denunciation with which he concluded a very memorable public address in the spring of 1917. I have described , it as the last utterance of Bengali liberalism before its extinction. 'O ye timorous, self-distrusting weaklings', he said,

'Ye, who are ridden by an untimely senility, ye infatuated fools, brought down to the ground by the weight of untruth! this is not the time for quarrelling in our own house with one another out of envy and small hatreds; the time is past for indulging in beggarly scrambles with trumpery expectations for trumpery preferment and trumpery position. We shall no longer delude ourselves with that false conceit which flaunts itself only because it is nurtured in the dark comers of our own homes, and is derided and shamed by the wide outside world. Let us have nothing to do with that kind of self-satisfaction which strives to batten on calumniating others, which is the recreation of the feeble. Our failings and offences have piled up through the ages, and by their weight have crushed our manliness, paralysed our judgement. The day has arrived for us to reject all this refuse of the centuries with strength and courage.'

One important explanation has to be given for the highly wrought language and tone of both the denunciations. In their anger as well as in their rhetoric, these are typical pronouncements of prophets. No reformer at a prophetic intensity can speak calmly. If he did he would at once separate himself from his people and become an outside critic, whose criticism would be resented. These men felt themselves to be at one with their people as the Jewish prophets did. So even when they failed in their purpose, they were respected by their people.

If the creation of the new Indian culture and a new Indian personality was the greatest achievement of the Bengali people as well as the most important product of the cultural interaction which was the historical accompaniment to British rule in India, this internal conflict, which was a part of the process, was an equally important aspect of the social and cultural history of Bengal under British rule. It was a conflict which but for the weakness of the Bengali character would never have arisen or at all events produced so harmful an effect. But as it raged, it was a conflict between light and darkness. In it, except during the last decade or so of British rule, the light was able to be the day as opposed to the night. But it went out along with British rule, and there is now no conflict in Bengali life. It has come full cycle by reverting to the traditional pattern, in which a submissive people were dominated and exploited by a small minority of oppressors, showing heroism only in their capacity for endurance.

The British Betrayal

Only one thing could have made a difference to this sad denouement and taken the moral and cultural effort of the Bengali people to its full development and consolidation. That would also have made the British political achievement in India greater by completing the task of the political education of the Indian people, which the British rulers always proclaimed as their highest aim: that is, to make the Indian people fit to govern themselves. If that had been accomplished by 1947, there would have been, after the end of British rule, a genuine co-operation between India and Britain instead of the dishonest pretence of friendship which is seen today. The thing which in my view would have made that possible was political and cultural co-operation between the Bengali people and the British rulers. But neither political nor cultural co-operation was seen in actual fact.

I hold this view because the transfer of the government of India to the British crown in 1858 made the British administration totally incapable of justifying British rule by giving it a new aim and direction. Only the Bengali intellectual was capable of conferring a refurbished moral validity to it. In those days he had both the intelligence and moral integrity required to do so. All the great Bengalis of the nineteenth century, who were renovating the life of their own people, knew the bearing of British rule on that task of theirs, although they were also nationalists who wanted to see their country free from political subjection. Their nationalism was not retrograde, nor were they themselves obscurantists. They frankly recognized that British rule was doing good and was a necessity for the time being, and they were not afraid of telling that to their countrymen. In 1829, Rammohun Roy, the first of the great Bengalis, said to the French scientist Victor Jaquemont: 'India requires many more years of English domination so that she may not have many things to lose while she is reclaiming her political independence.' Actually, this remained true even till 1947, when India became independent. The Indian people began to lose many of the things which had been indisputable gains in their life and culture, and did that with an accelerated momentum as the years passed.

But this was not their fault. It was the British community in India which prevented British rule as well as the Bengali reformers from completing their respective tasks. They made enemies of those who but for their folly would have become supporters of British rule, and made it impossible for any Indian with moral integrity to be that. Their active mischief-making began in 1883. Even down to 1880 there were conscientious defenders of British rule among Indians, and one of them was the great Bengali writer, Bankim Chandra Chatterji, who also was the creator of the new Hindu nationalism of Bengal. That did not prevent him from giving to the British what was due to them.*

The watershed was provided by the well-known Ilbert Bill of 1883. This notorious episode in British Indian history is too well known for me to recapitulate it. It made the whole British community in India go into a fit of political hysteria which was as unintelligent as it was arrogant. This exhibition of rank racial prejudice and pride alienated all Indians who had any patriotism from British rule. As it happened, the British Government at home not only capitulated to the local British over this particular measure, but was frightened by it into opposition to all political concessions to Indians. Lord Kimberley, who was Secretary of State for India from 1882 to 1885 as a member of Gladstone's second administration, regarded educated Indians not even as a class but as a small clique which was really Bengali in voice and numbers. He thought it wholly inadvisable to exacerbate the local British for the sake of pleasing so insignificant a group. This was an act of appeasement like that which Neville Chamberlain performed for Hitler. The British in India were the Nazis of that age. From that time, any Indian who pleaded for political concessions was regarded by the British officials and journalists as a seditious Babu. Any possibility that existed till that time of Bengali intellectuals accepting British rule for the time being, and making it acceptable to others, was gone.

The attitude of the local British in regard to cultural matters was even worse. Their rancour against any Bengali who wrote or spoke English well was as unrestrained as it was irrational. They developed an incredible hatred and malice against educated Bengalis, who were trying to modernize their life under Western influences. This hostility was an extraordinary psychological paradox, because the personality of the educated Bengalis of those times, who were known as Young Bengal, was formed by their study of English and European life and civilization through the

*I have to add that both Rammohun Roy and Bankim Chandra Chatterji were physically assaulted by local English officials. But they never allowed the behaviour of these men to affect their judgement on British rule.

English language. In Bengal literature, both in English and in Bengali, instead of being the product of life *as lived*, presented a new life *to be lived*, and since the new Bengali literature was Western both in its forms and in its content, it also contributed to the Europeanization of the spirit. This process extended to morals and manners. All educated Bengalis were preoccupied with morals, and their preachers were moralists first and humanists next. Their most insistent preaching was directed towards building up character, and in this teaching the model put before young Bengalis was the English character with its courage, honesty, stamina, capacity for work, as well as gentlemanliness. But it was this very effort of educated Bengalis to renovate their life on the English model that aroused the rancorous hostility of the local British towards them. In such an atmosphere there could be no social relations between the two sides.

However, this was not so in the first half of the nineteenth century, when Englishmen even in very high positions in India were ready to meet educated Indians. Sir Charles Trevelyan, who was the brother-in-law of Macaulay, was a distinguished civil servant in India. He came to the country for the first time in 1827 and stayed till 1840. This was followed by two other visits. In 1859 he came to Madras as Governor, and in 1862 to Calcutta as Finance Member in the Viceroy's Executive Council. He told Sir Henry Maine, who also was a fellow-member of the Council, that when he first came to India he saw educated natives mixing on equal terms with educated Europeans, but when he came a second time there was nothing of the kind.

The date itself is significant. The University of Calcutta was founded in 1857 in order to give higher education of the European type to Bengali young men. It became the centre of English influences, and at the same time a target of criticism to the local British. Its products, i.e. the Bengali graduates, were not only criticized, but vilified with unrestrained animus. As the higher education spread, the hatred of the British community for educated Bengalis also developed with an unhealthy speed and intensity.

Even in the early Sixties this had become so pronounced that Sir Henry Maine, who was also Vice-Chancellor of Calcutta University, felt compelled to protest. He defended the Bengali graduates against the prejudiced criticism of the British. The least irrational but most insistent feature of the criticism was that the young Bengalis were mere superficial crammers, and, as to character, self-conceited in an unpleasant manner. In one of his addresses to the graduates of the University Maine dealt with this criticism in a very forthright manner. He said that some of it was, to repeat his description, 'simply vulgar', as, for example, when it was said that 'the native graduates of this and other Universities are conceited'. Maine's explanation was as follows: 'I wonder whether it is considered how young they are, compared with English graduates, and how wide is the difference which their education makes between them and their fellow countrymen.'

Maine added that this accusation was against all the evidence that he or anybody else was able to collect. Above all, he refuted the charge of cramming. He pointed out that everywhere the examination system encouraged a habit of learning which might be called cramming, but he said 'whether what is called cramming is an unmixed evil is not settled even in England, but in India the commonplace imputations against it seem to me simply without meaning of any kind. There is no proof whatever that Indian teachers follow any special methods of any sort. What appears to be meant is that Natives of India learn with singular rapidity.'

After that Maine referred to the least offensive part of the British prejudice and said: 'The habit the Englishmen have of importing into India these commonplaces of censorious opinions about systems and institutions, is a misfortune for the Natives.'

Had there been more Englishmen of Maine's type at the top in the British Indian administration, the history of British rule in India would have been different. It would not have failed to produce all the good it was capable of doing, nor would the. Indian Empire of Britain have come to an untimely end. But there never were. Views like his, perceptive and balanced as they were, utterly failed to change the prejudiced and superficial opinions of the British community. The prejudice grew worse, and with that also the animus against the Bengalis.

The spirit in which the criticism was voiced and its tone revealed its true character. There was no pretence even that it was meant as friendly advice, so that the anglicizing of the Bengali might be free from its weaknesses. There were weaknesses, the most obvious of which was too much self-consciousness with flamboyance. But the British critics of the Bengalis gave the impression that they rather wished the weaknesses to remain so that they might have the pleasure of venting their malice.

The tone was even more objectionable. No abuse was too coarse, and no insult too outrageous to be regarded as inapplicable to a Bengali. For instance, in a letter written to his friend Rider Haggard, Kipling said in 1913, the year in which a Bengali got the Nobel Prize for literature with his book in English: 'Well, whose fault is it that the Babu is what he is? *We* did it. We began in Macaulay's time. We have worked without intermission to make this Caliban.'

This was not a mere casual outburst of bad temper on the part of Kipling, but a flashpoint in his deliberate preaching and admonition to his countrymen in India about the Bengalis. That was embodied in a story written for the purpose of exciting contempt and hatred for them in The *Jungle Book*, published in 1894. Since the Mowgli stories in it were also moral fables, this moral had also to be included in the series. In these stories the British in India are the wolves, bears, panthers and other wild beasts and are the true Jungle People. The Bandar Log, the monkeys, who are the Bengalis, are beyond the pale. The man-cub in the jungle had in a pique talked to the monkeys, and this made his two guardians, Baloo the Bear and Bagheera the Black Panther, very angry. So Baloo said to Mowgli: 'The Monkey People are forbidden, forbidden to the Jungle People ... They were always just going to have a leader, and laws and customs of their own, but they never did, because their memories would not hold over from day to day, and so they compromised things by making up a saying: "What the *Bandar-log* think now the Jungle will think later." '

This showed that Kipling was perfectly aware of the pioneer's role that the Bengalis were playing, and would have to ridicule the pretension. Therefore he fastened upon their lack of perseverance to do so. From this followed the practical side of the denunciation:' "We of the Jungle," said Baloo, "have no dealings with them; we do not drink where the monkeys drink; we do not go where the monkeys go; we do not hunt where they hunt; we do not die where they die ... They are very many, evil, dirty, shameless, and they desire, if they have any fixed desire, to be noticed by the Jungle- People." '

Only insensate hatred for the Bengali could have made Kipling spoil his delightful stories in this manner. But his advice was taken by the British community in India, or rather the admonition simply gave expression to an established principle of conduct. After my autobiography was published in 1951, a British officer (son of the distinguished soldier and writer. Sir

William Butler, and Lady Butler, the painter and sister of Alice Meynell) wrote to me that when he was in India with his regiment before 1914, he had wished to have social relations with Indians, but had found that barred by the prevailing attitude and convention.

The British officials imbued all British visitors and writers with their prejudice. Of this I give a flagrant example from a book entitled *In India*, written by a man called G. W. Stevens and published in England in 1899: 'By his legs,' this Englishman wrote,

'you shall know the Bengali. The leg of a free man is straight or a little bandy, so that he can stand on it solidly: his calf is taper and his thigh flat. The Bengali's leg is either skin and bone, and same size all the way down, with knocking knobs for knees, or else it is very fat and globular, also turning in at the knees, with round thighs like a woman's. The Bengali's leg is the leg of a slave.'

The man who wrote this was an Oxford graduate, one-time Fellow of Pembroke College, and later special correspondent of the *Daily Mail*. The book was apparently a reprint of his articles for that paper. He died at the age of thirty-one of enteric fever during the siege of Ladysmith in 1900, where he had gone probably with the intention of repeating his performance about us with the Boers. But he did not have the honour of dying from a Boer bullet.

This Englishman, had he lived till 1911, would have had the mortification of seeing the same Bengalis, playing football with the same legs and also bare feet, defeat the Black Watch and win the IFA shield.

Englishmen in India forgot even the manliness of which they bragged, and slandered a subject people who could not give them the hiding they deserved because whatever they did they were protected by the whole might of the British Empire in India. I saw later what the same class of men were capable of when they lost that protection.

Naturally, through their special arrogance they became stupid. Their stupidity was directed specially towards the educational system which had created the new class of Indians, and of which I am one of the products. Thus this man wrote: 'Unfortunately the whole system of higher education is radically vicious in plan, and, if not actually disastrous, at least almost profitless in effect.' He added that the Indians were getting their BA and

MA degrees only by learning by rote, 'without the feeblest approach to anything that could be called a thought of their own'.

He also gave the information that when asked why he had sought a degree one of these Indian M AS told him: 'To raise his price in the marriage market ... He would get a wife with a larger dowry as MA than as BA.' Then he concluded with this observation:

'We have given India the treasures of our Shakespeare, our Bacon, our Huxley, and India uses them as convenient pegs to hang quotations in the marriage market!

'O India, India! what jests are perpetrated in thy name!'

Leaving aside the general cult of Shakespeare which we had in Bengal throughout the nineteenth century, I shall set down only my first initiation to him. Early in 1908, when I was ten, one day I saw my father (who had only a school education) walking on the front lawn of our house reading a book. He called me and putting the book in my hands asked me to read a page. It was *Julius Caesar*, and I began to read: 'That you have wronged me doth appear in this.' It was a speech of Cassius to Brutus. I read it haltingly, but in six months I had learnt it so well that I recited the scene with my brother on the school stage. My marriage was then twenty-four years and my B A degree ten years away.

This kind of display of racial hatred could turn away over-sensitive Indians even from their devotion to English and European culture. Being aware of this possibility, even as a young man I wrote in my article of January 1926, to which I have referred, as follows:

'There is one source from which bitterness against Europe is being replenished constantly. It is wounded national and personal self-respect. When after reading Bergson and Benedetto Croce, Mr Hardy or Mr Wells with a sense of kinship, an Indian comes across some instance of ignorant superciliousness in a European - be it in the shape of a remark in a book or a personal affront at the hands of a police-sergeant or a tactless European merchant on the Maidan - he returns home in bitterness and wrath arid his previous enjoyment of a European writer becomes to him a cankering reminiscence of his humiliation.'

When a Bengali or Indian had that kind of intellectual life, the resentment could not, of course, last, and that class of Bengalis and Indians normally kept away from the local British. But with the general body of Indians with an average education such blind arrogance was bound to have its natural and an equal reaction. That did come, and it was to be found in the popular conception of the Englishman which was widely held in India, particularly at the end of the nineteenth century in Bengal. This, too, was summarized by Swami Vivekananda along with his description of the Englishman's idea of Indians. The Indians, he said, conjured up this picture of their rulers:

'Intoxicated by the new wine of their power; devoid of all sense of good and evil; terrible like fierce beasts of prey; subject to women, maddened by lust; drenched with alcohol from head to foot, without cleanness of behaviour or cleanness of body; materialistic in outlook and dependent on matter for action; robbers of other peoples' countries as also of their wealth by brute force, deceit, and trickery; disbelievers in the other world, theorists of mere corporeality, given to pampering the flesh - such is the Western demon in the eyes of Indians.'

I can confirm this as a true summing up of the popular Bengali view of the national character of Englishmen, because I heard such descriptions from childhood. As a boy, I was told by the teacher of Sanskrit in my school that the Englishman was begotten of the she-monkey by a demon. This opinion was not, of course, allowed to influence the willingness of Indians to work for the British in India because that was purely pragmatic. Both the Englishman and the Indian were making use of each other for self-interest, and at that level the mutual ill opinion was held privately. Vivekananda unequivocally described the view to be wrong.

Highly educated Bengalis could not, of course, fall back on so crude an emotional revenge for the English display of contempt, but they also held a very low opinion of the education and culture of the local British. They tried to take their defence to a higher intellectual and moral plane, but actually found it only in a historical myth, which was plausible without being true. According to it, the Hindus were not only a highly civilized people when the British were savages, but their civilization was also superior to the European. Ironically, this myth was provided almost readymade for them by the European Orientalists, especially the Germans. But the Bengali nationalists finished the picture with very much heightened colours and varnish.

As it happened, the myth of ancient India began to exert its practical influence simultaneously with the appearance of the British hatred for the educated Bengali. Sir Henry Maine noticed this as well, and in the same address in which he criticized his countrymen for their unfair disparagement of the Bengalis, he also warned the latter against the risks involved in holding the mythical view of ancient Hindu civilization.

'On the educated Native of India', he said, 'the Past presses with too awful and terrible a power for it to be safe for him to play or palter with it.' He added that 'the Past could not be coloured by him in the way he was doing it without misreading the Present and endangering the Future.' He developed the argument as follows: 'There are some educated Native gentlemen who seem to have persuaded themselves that there was once a time in India in which learning was more honoured and respected, and when the career of a learned man was more brilliant than in British India and under British rule.'

He was, of course, perfectly aware that the European Orientalists were in a great measure responsible for such delusions. As he put it: 'The value attached in Europe to ancient Hindu literature, and deservedly attached for its poetical and philosophical interest, has very naturally caused the Native to look back with pride and fondness on the era at which the great Sanskrit poems were composed and a great philosophical system evolved.'

Maine went on to say that in regarding their past educated Indians were imitating a European intellectual bias, and explained how that was done, more explicitly: 'The Natives of India', he said,

'have caught from us Europeans our modem trick of constructing, by means of works of fiction, an imaginary Past out of the Present, taking from the Past its externals, its outward furniture, but building in the sympathies, the susceptibilities, and even (for it sometimes comes to that) the knowledge of the present time. It is true that, even with us it may be that too much of the sloughed skin of the Past hangs about us, and impedes and disorders our movements.'

It was all very well for the Europeans to do that, he said, because there were correctives to a false view of their past in the activities of the present. But in India, as he put it, 'the effect of such fictions, and of theories built on such fictions, is unmixedly deleterious.' His advice to the Bengali graduates who were listening to him - it was at a degree-conferring ceremony - was clear and unambiguous:

'They may be safely persuaded that, in spite of discouragements which do not all come from themselves or their countrymen, their real affinities are with Europe and with the Future, not with India and the Past. They would do well once for all to acquiesce in it, and accept, with all its consequences, the marvellous destiny which has brought one of the youngest branches of the greatest family of mankind from the uttermost ends of the earth to renovate and educate the oldest. There is not yet perfect sympathy between the two, but intellectual sympathy, in part the fruit of this University, will come first, and moral and social sympathy will follow afterwards.'

I am citing Maine at this length, not only to support my view of the cultural situation in Bengal, but also to show that there did come to India Englishmen who understood what was happening to Indian life, culture, and the Indian mind, and also to make known the extraordinary nobility of spirit of an Englishman who could speak at this level of intellectual perception to young Bengali graduates whom a majority of his countrymen in India pretended to despise. I find it curious that Maine's pronouncements have virtually been ignored by the historians of modern India.

But Maine spoke in vain. Neither side to whom he gave his advice followed him. The intellectual sympathy to be followed by moral and social sympathy, of which Maine spoke, never came. Even if the Indians were ready to contribute to it, the local British never encouraged the inclination. The false view of India's past to which patriotic Indians were clinging, persisted, and, after arriving at its full development, it has become a part of the historical consciousness of all educated Indians all over India. Nothing can free them from its evil hold.

Yet this was not the worst outcome of the temperamental quarrel between the Englishman and the Bengali. It added another duality to that which was created in Bengali life by the weakness of the Bengali character. This duality has become a permanent feature, not simply of the Bengali's personality, but of the entire Indian personality in a more harmful manner.

The myth of a superior Hindu civilization did not prevent any Bengali from anglicizing himself in every way he could, whether in his mental cast or in external appearance and behaviour, and the more anglicized the Bengali was, the higher was his status in Bengali society. This kind of duality weakened both sides of his conduct, but fortunately it did not lessen his love and reverence for the best things in European civilization and life. In this, there was no difference of opinion between the radical and the conservative Bengali. Both were against any rejection of Western values. Inconsistent as the Bengali was in his professions and behaviour on account of this, that in itself prevented the duality from doing all the harm it could bring about.

This situation has totally changed, and changed for the worse, with political independence. There is now no need whatever to flaunt the banner of ancient India in the face of foreign rulers. But the flaunting persists. There is a more fanatical adherence to the myth of a superior Hindu civilization than was ever seen in the past. This is doing more harm at present for three reasons: first, the myth itself has become far more political than it was before and hardened into a chauvinistic dogma; secondly, there is among present-day Indians far less real knowledge of the Hindu civilization and far less practice of Hindu virtues; and, last of all, the adoption of Western ways has become degraded.

Nowadays, the adherence to the old myth is strongest in those very Indians who are least Hindu in their behaviour and principles. On the other hand, the old discrimination and selection in adopting Western ways has disappeared, and there is mindless aping of the lowest things in the Western democratic culture, especially as it is in America. Americanization of Indian life and mind has reached an extent which the old anglicization never did. Yet there is a fierce and ineradicable hatred of the United States in the hearts of all Indians of the ruling order. Thus the duality is now between mindless chauvinism and mindless imitation.

This is the deplorable climax in which the personal alienation between the Bengali and the Englishman has culminated. Thinking of this situation after the disappearance of British rule, I might quote a famous line in English literature:

'The evil that men do lives after them,
The good is oft interred with their bones.'

The Bengali Achievement

Nonetheless, the achievement of the Bengali people in the way of a contribution to human civilization is not to be overlooked or underrated. It was real, and it was the harvest of a short but effervescent intermezzo in their existence. It was not indeed many-sided, nor massive, but in whatever was accomplished, the product was of a very fine and delicate quality. That will remain, but also remain very largely unknown and inaccessible because of the language in which it was embodied. Its best creations were in the field of poetry, song, and story, which will rank with the best created in any country or age. But other nations will not learn Bengali for the sake of enjoying these, for the power of a language very largely depends on the political importance of the people who speak it.

For all that, while it was being created, Bengali literature and music created a new life for the Bengali people. There was an awareness of the meaning of life and fullness in it, especially among those Bengalis who had least of the things which the world has to offer to human beings. The Bengali culture was created by visionary idealists, and it supported the inner life rather than the external.

The very incompleteness of the Bengali's cultural creation, combined with its fineness, should give him a special kind of place in history. Others should think of him as they think of Mozart, Schubert or Keats. What they got from the world presented a sad contrast to what they contributed to life. As a people, the Bengalis will perhaps have only this epitaph in history:

> 'Here lies one whose name was writ in water.'

But their contribution to civilization should be likened to the Unfinished Symphony of Schubert.

BOOK VIII

MIGRATION TO DELHI

1942–1945

Prefatory Note

When I joined All India Radio in Delhi I had no idea whatever how long I should live in that city. But as things turned out, I lived there for twenty-eight years and never went back to Calcutta. And when I left Delhi in 1970 to come to England, that was never again to go back to India even for a temporary visit. My life has always moved West, and once it has done so its direction has never been reversed. For me too evolution has been irreversible.

I was not indeed without a sense of India in Calcutta, and I was besides violendy repelled by the narrow provincialism of fellow-Bengalis. But in Delhi India became a reality, for that city at the time was an epitome of India. I saw there the human conglomeration that India had become in its unity as well as diversity. That also liberated me from any close relationship with any particular human group.

This part of the book as well as the two which follow describe only the first ten years of my life in Delhi. In the first, five of these I saw the end of British rule and in the second five the emergence of politically independent India. In the first period I acquired an unqualified contempt for the last days of the British in India and for them as well. In the second, I developed a deep distrust for Indian self-government even when it could be said to be at its most idealistic.

As for myself, from having been a political suspect in British days I became one under Indian rule. Of course, in neither period was I subjected to active persecution. But I had no worldly prospects. In the last days of the British no Indian who was not an opportunist could prosper, and under Indian rule the same thing was seen. Thus I remained free by giving up worldly prosperity. Nonetheless, with its continued poverty and other vicissitudes, the life has been worth living.

CHAPTER I

First Months in Delhi

I arrived at Delhi in the afternoon of 17 March 1942. The north Indian summer, or more appropriately the hot season, had not yet begun. Actually, it was still some weeks ahead. The combination of two features which makes the summer of the Indo-Gangetic plain what it really is, viz., glare without illumination and hot air laden with dust, appears only at the beginning of May. Nevertheless, as the train was passing through the bare, brownish plain I found that even before it was noon I could not look out of the windows without discomfort. Yet, when in Calcutta I had never worn sun-glasses even under the brightest light of summer.

I was not prepared for this, although only six months before I had come to Allahabad, which is at the heart of the Gangetic plain. That visit had been in October, just after the rains, when for a month or two the light of day glistens on that plain. Of course, what I was seeing on that journey was not even a weak foretaste of what I was to see in Delhi two months later. Even so, I felt anxious when from about ten in the morning the sky began to turn light buff in its first stage towards the normal summer colour of greyish tawny. Soon after my arrival I asked one of my Bengali colleagues whether the sky was like that all the year round. With the usual insensitiveness of my countrymen to changes of colour in the sky, he replied that it was. I had a sinking feeling at heart, fearing that I had escaped from the smoky and damp grey of Calcutta only to run into something equally dreary, although in a different way.

First impressions of Delhi

I knew the architectural history of Delhi well, and had seen pictures of all its great monuments. I also knew that I should cross the river Jumna before reaching the main railway station of Delhi, and thus also see, across the river, the famous Mogul palace complex known as the Red Fort. I eagerly looked out for that view when the train approached the bridge at about four in the afternoon. But I was disappointed. The view of Delhi across the Jumna was a sad contrast to what I had seen when crossing the Ganges at Benares in 1926.

Nothing rose in the air, nothing presented a solid facade from side to side, nothing had depth. The whole river front of the Red Fort was not only low and flat, but also a straggling collection of detached pavilions, and on the outside their walls were peeled and patchy. Only towards the south the two minars of the mosque built by Aurangzeb's daughter could be seen against- the sky, and behind the pavilions of the fort, rising above them, could be seen the two high gates of red sandstone of the citadel. Beyond them I could also see the three white marble domes, striped with black, of the Jami Masjid and its two tall, striped minarets. They did not, however, create any impression of massiveness or elevation. The immense dome of the sky was pressing down everything beneath it.

The train crossed the river and then passed through Salim Garh, a small old fort of grey stone, and even its appearance of dilapidation was spoilt by sheds with roofs of corrugated iron, in which material for building railway tracks was piled up. Slowly, the train moved into Delhi Junction station, which was a large red-brick building in Victorian Gothic. A future colleague of mine was waiting for me at the station and he took me to his house, where he offered me hospitality until I could find accommodation for myself. It was extremely kind of him.*

But the quarter in which he lived, which was called Timarpur, was not at all attractive. Its small huts had been built to accommodate the guests of the Delhi Durbar of 1911, and these were meant to be demolished after their temporary occupation. But when at the same Durbar it was announced that the capital of British India would be transferred from Calcutta to Delhi, these shabby buildings were retained to house the clerks of the Secretariat.

However, the situation was open. At the same time it had a wild and deserted appearance, which was heightened by an old bridge and an old mosque built at the end of the fourteenth century. The impression of wildness was strengthened when the next morning I went out for a walk on the Ridge, famous for the part it played in the siege of Delhi in 1857. It is an outlying spur of the distant Aravalli chain, between 100 to 200 feet high, and it ends just south of the clerical quarters of Timarpur, failing to strike the Jumna by about half a mile. So, at this point there is something like a saddle, and with the typical humour of British officialdom in India the spot was called Khyber Pass.

I went up the road towards the Flagstaff Tower, in which the British

* His name was Rajen Sen, and he was one of the half-backs of the Mohun Bagan football team in 1911.

women and children who had escaped the massacres at the beginning of the insurrection took shelter in May 1857. The road ran all along the Ridge, and commanded wide views both to the east and the west over continuous clumps of Babul or Indian acacia, which had been planted after the Mutiny to protect the hillside from erosion; and the houses of the Civil Lines, where the British officials lived, from the heat radiating from the stone surfaces. The Ridge was quite bare in 1857.

As I walked along the road I had the curious sensation of being pricked in my bare shins, and looking for its cause I saw that very fine and sharp sand on the road was being blown by the keen morning wind and striking my legs. In Calcutta my clothes, legs and shoes were made dirty by dust, but the dust did not make any impact and only stuck. In Delhi the sand pricked but did not stick.

As I walked on, I could see the shrunken Jumna to the east, and across it a cultivated plain bordered at the far horizon by a strip of azure, formed by the wooded villages. To the west, too, there was a plain, but it was bare, dotted only by pill-boxes built during the Mutiny and low bushes of blue- grey succulent plants. Away to the south-west was a closely built area, looking very untidy and hard with its houses painted dirty white outside. It was the Sabzi Mandi quarter. The name meant 'Market of the Greens', and it was the wholesale vegetable market of Delhi, the equivalent of Covent Garden. The over-all impression was of desertion and forlomness. From the Ridge no one could guess that a great city and the capital of British India was anywhere near.

Later in the morning I went to the news studios of All India Radio, where I was to work. It was in a bungalow on Alipur Road within the Civil Lines, not very far from Kashmir Gate. I met my chief, who was an Englishman named Charles Bams. He was very courteous to me, and perhaps he knew the history of my recruitment for AIR. I met my future Bengali colleagues, some of whom I had known in Calcutta. Although I was wearing European clothes for the first time in my life and had learnt to knot a tie only three days before, nobody suspected that. Both my suit and bearing went down well, and I found that in Delhi European clothes were obligatory for survival. Throughout my career in AIR my clothes and speaking of English, and not my work, gave me whatever position and reputation I acquired among my colleagues, although many of them, who had had their education in England, had suits from Austin Reed.

I was nominally to supervise the Bengali news bulletins, but my real work was to comment on the war. I wrote the scripts in English for translation into the major Indian languages, and I myself translated them into Bengali and broadcast them. Within a few days my voice was heard in Calcutta, and that made my wife impatient to come over to Delhi. She did not want to stay in Calcutta a day longer than she could help. So, she came away with the children, a young Bengali who was their tutor, and my old servant on the last day of March, only fifteen days after my arrival.

Their arrival at the Delhi station was marked by an incident, which could be regarded as farcical if it was not so exasperatingly common as well as significant. My wife had brought over an enormous amount of luggage, far above the free allowance, especially because for want of money she was travelling third-class, and, as at that time people were running away from Calcutta, getting the luggage through in the proper way would have been endless trouble. I was attending on the platform, but taking out my youngest son stood aloof in my new suit, etc, as if I had nothing to do with that party. The porters told the boy's tutor, who was in charge, that they would see to the matter for a little extra and some gratification for the ticket-collector. They were given five rupees, and putting the note into the hand (normally kept open behind the posterior) of the functionary took the luggage out. But they were to go to the main gate by the over bridge and were not yet out of the jurisdiction of the station. Another ticket-collector who was off duty had seen what had been done, and he ordered the porters to take the luggage to the main office where it was to be weighed and charged for. Our tutor at once gave two rupees to the man, but he indignantly pushed away the offer, and said: 'You gave five rupees to that ticket-collector who is junior to me, and you insult me by giving me two rupees?' The tutor at once took out a five-rupee note and said: 'Why did you not say that before, and we would never have offended your self-respect?' After that, with some more noisy haggling with the tongawallas (the hackney carriage men), all of them came safely home. Our house was not very far and I walked back. My wife taunted me for trying to cast her off because she had travelled third-class.

I had already succeeded in renting a flat in a very good locality of the old city. A colleague of mine took me to the owner, who was an Indian Christian lady from Mangalore settled in Delhi. She bore a famous Portuguese name, Pinto, and, as I have occupied that flat for over forty years, the Pintos of three generations have become almost like my relatives. I might explain here that the Roman Catholic Christians of Mangalore are very proud of being not only Catholics but also descended from high caste and mostly Brahmin Hindus. The daughter-in-law of Mrs Pinto one day got very angry when I called her an Indian Christian, which she most emphatically declared she was not. When I asked her what then she was, she replied: 'We are Catholics.' And when I again asked who then were Indian Christians, she answered with equal emphasis: 'Indian Christians are low-caste converts to Protestantism.' I felt flattered when she said that I was more a Christian like her than a Hindu, and of course she was very beautiful.

The flat in which I was to live for nearly three decades was on the top floor of a house named p & o Buildings. This gave great prestige to it, because everybody in New Delhi thought that it had something to do with the shipping company. It had not. The initials were only those of two sons of Mrs Pinto, Percy and Oswald. The house was on Nicholson Road, and the street had gots its name from the fact that General Nicholson was killed when pursuing rebel sepoys, running along the berm of the old wall which ran before the house. The walls were built by the Mogul Emperor Shah Jahan, when he transferred the capital from Agra to Delhi in the middle of the seventeenth century. The house stood just inside the northern wall, separated from it only by the street.

The wall was supported on the inner side by arches which formed a continuous arcade. Over it and all along it, could be seen features which were once meant for serious military use. Two-thirds above the street level, a berm six-feet wide ran all along the crenellated top, so that any defenders of the city could take their stand on it in order to fire on the attackers. For that purpose, two rows of balistrarias were provided at different angles, and thus fire could be brought to bear both on the escarpment and counter-scarpment. The British had considerably strengthened the fortifications in order to defend the city against Maratha attacks at the beginning of the nineteenth century, and this caused additional trouble to them in 1857.

They added three bastions of European type, the Mori bastion, Kashmir Gate bastion, and Water bastion, all of which we could see from our verandah, together with the breaches made in the last two by the bombardment of 1857. Between our house and Kashmir Gate there was a Martello tower to cover the curtain wall on both sides by enfilading fire.

Our locality had figured conspicuously in the British attack on Delhi, and hardly two hundred yards from our house, clearly visible from it, was the statue of Alexander Taylor, the organizer of the artillery bombardment. The platform on which it stood had the heavy mortars then used for it as decoration. These associations with the Mutiny made me go into the episode of the siege of Delhi very thoroughly. The wide moat was outside the wall.

We could not see that from our verandah, but we could rest our eyes on the green of the lawns and trees of the large park beyond, which was called Nicholson Gardens. As long as British rule lasted, the lawns were not allowed to be burnt up even by the summer sun of northern India. Every fortnight they were flooded from the irrigation channels, and that kept the grass green. We also noticed an Englishman walking over the lawns and along the moat, and standing from time to time to take note of something or other. We learned later that he was the English Deputy Commissioner of Delhi. I might add that from the lawns the high grey wall, with its crenellation, was a very fine sight, spoilt, alas, by the shabby skyline behind it, provided by the houses on Nicholson Road, including our own.

Beyond the park, the houses of the Civil Lines, all bungalows, stood hidden out of sight by the trees, so that from our verandah not a wall or parapet of brick could be seen. In the distance, printed against the sky, was the line of the Ridge, from which one or two old buildings in ruins and the Mutiny Memorial in red sandstone, a very close copy of the Albert Memorial in Hyde Park, rose into the sky. There was immense peace in the unobstructed spaciousness before our eyes, and, above all, in the sky, ever present with its seasonal changes which were sudden and startling. I had always wanted to live in a house which would offer wide views. But, of course, in Calcutta that was out of the question for me. So, when I got it in Delhi I stayed on in that house, refusing more prestigious official accommodation in New Delhi.

Another advantage of the house was that from the name of the street nobody could guess my salary. In New Delhi streets and salaries were commensurate, and a man who unwarily gave the name of his street might find himself shunned by the denizens of certain other streets. I shall relate here a comical experience I had a few years later. I went to visit an artist friend who lived with a relative of his in the clerical quarters of New Pusa, all the buildings of which were even more shabby than those of Timarpur.

Passing along a line of buildings which looked like stables, I asked an elderly Bengali whether the clerk whose house I wanted to find lived in that row. He angrily pointed to the letter 'D' carved on the top of the building and said: 'Do you not see that these are D-class quarters, and the person you have come to visit lives in E-class quarters?' Even my very superior clothes, all made from Ranken and Phelps, did not protect me from the D-class disdain I brought on myself by being on visiting terms with a clerk who lived in E-class quarters. Nonetheless, by living in old Delhi I remained under suspicion. In spite of that I lived in the house until I came away to England in 1970.

Cripps Mission

Immediately after my arrival in Delhi there was an important and interesting political event, which I watched with great interest. It was the visit of Sir Stafford Cripps, member of the British Cabinet as Lord Privy Seal, who came to India to arrive at an understanding with the nationalist leaders and obtain their co-operation in carrying on the war in return for an offer of full Dominion Status after the war.

As it happened, I was able to see Sir Stafford, because he came to our studios to broadcast his version of his mission when it had failed. This was the very first time that I saw a prominent British politician at close quarters, and what struck me was his pleasant and unassuming bearing. There was no trace on his face of the puffed-up arrogance which disfigured the face of every Indian who had power, whether politician or official. He passed before me in the hall and went into the studio. Soon after, another Englishman, obviously an important person, came up to me and asked me with a smile, which till then I had not begun to expect on the faces of important persons: 'Where is Cripps?' I told him that he was in the studio. Although Cripps had to explain his failure I did not see any sign of disappointment on his face.

I certainly thought that throughout his mission and more especially after its failure, Cripps presented his case and point of view with great ability and dignity. But not so to the Indian leaders and the Indian press. He was accused of quibbling and shiftiness. This remains the view even of Indian historians of present times, because no Hindu can believe that anyone who disagrees with his view of things can be honest. The failure was inevitable, and that was in line with what had happened in the course of the recurring 'dialogues', to use the vogue word, between British representatives and Indian nationalists from 1921 to 1939.

There was sensible relief from these 'dialogues' between October 1939 and the beginning of 1942. But it was resumed under American pressure. The Americans in general, and more especially President Roosevelt, with their utter ignorance of the Oriental mind, thought that Indian nationalist co-operation was essential for winning the war against Japan. Therefore they insisted that an offer should be made about eventual independence. Even Churchill had to yield to it, and a mission was sent, of course with no better result than another round of the old futile game of words.

I thought then, and I have not changed my opinion on this point till now, that the Congress, led by Gandhi and Nehru, committed a serious mistake by not taking advantage of the offer, and joining the government. This, to my thinking, would have prevented the partition of India in 1947. I was ready to admit as a matter of argument that the British could break their promise, but I said that even so nothing would have been lost by accepting a British hypothetical offer, and getting some concessions immediately. If the British did not honour their promise it would always remain open to us to do what was in our power to do to get rid of them. That power was intangible, and not practical, and so it could not be eroded by temporary co-operation.

But the psychological situation in India, of which the Congress leaders were always conscious, and to which they were in chains (as I have already written), made that impossible. In addition to the ineradicable distrust of the professions of all British governments, there was the immediate conviction of the Indian leaders about the course of the war. Nothing could weaken the belief of the Indian people at that moment that through Japanese action British rule was coming to an end anyway. The Indian leaders fully shared it. They did not have, as I have pointed out before, any deep understanding of international affairs, and none at all of the realities of warfare. In any war in which Britain engaged this lack of understanding was made more complete still by the yearning for a British defeat and collapse. So Mahatma Gandhi described the Cripps offer as a 'post-dated cheque', and the full force of this description would be realized if it is remembered that in India most postdated cheques were dishonoured. At the time we read the description in a more colourful form as 'a post-dated cheque on a crashing bank'. This addition was contradicted later, and was found to have been made by a journalist.

But even if Mahatma Gandhi did not use the qualifying words, they certainly embodied his thought, as also of the other Nationalist leaders. I myself heard the argument at less exalted levels that since the British knew that they were going to lose India inevitably they would prefer to lose it to us Indians rather than to the Japanese. The corollary to this argument was that we could pitch our demand as high as possible and the British would yield. Acting on this conviction, the Congress leaders wanted full control of the armed forces, and it was Jawaharlal Nehru who was most insistent on that. They had reckoned without their host. It was on this demand rather and not owing to doubt about the ultimate promise, that the talks broke down. All of it could be called a farce, if it did not turn out in its final outcome to be a tragedy of the first order for India. How many times after that the unfortunate nations of Asia and Africa have had occasions to say to the Americans: 'What is play to you is death to us!'

I had, however, my personal axe to grind in my role as ideologue or rather as the chorus of Greek tragedy. The failure of the Cripps mission prompted me to air my old rejection of the idea of transfer of power from British to Indian hands as a solution of the Indian problem. Thus, with complete lack of practical good sense for the time being, I decided to send a memorandum to Cripps on the subject, and sat down at my typewriter to compose it. However, after typing a few pages good sense returned and I gave up the idea. The few pages that I typed have survived, and upon reading them at this distance of time I have decided to quote some passages from it. I began by saying:

'The idea of an eventual transfer of power from British to Indian hands is now universally accepted as the guiding principle of Indo-British relations. It is an idea which nobody dreams of disputing. The only difference of opinion is over the proper time for the transfer. Even this difference has been narrowed down to the duration of the war, one party urging immediate transfer and the other postponement till only the war is over. Even here the British do not seem to be wholly at ease.'

I went on to observe that it was too late in the day to go back on the idea, but I said it needed re-examination and revision, because the question was very complex and many factors stood in the way. I explained that the purpose of my memorandum was to set forth these factors, and suggest an alternative policy which did not disown the idea of transfer but recast it in a form more consistent with the ideal of an international society.

The very first thing to do was to understand the nature of the Indian problem and what was needed for India so that the opportunity given by political independence would not be missed. I set down a number of considerations which had to be kept in mind in giving political power to Indians, and of these I thought the following two were the most important. I quote verbatim from my unfinished memorandum:

'1. A satisfactory solution of the Indian problem must ensure cordial Indo-British co-operation, and India's participation in an international society, whether it be merely the British Commonwealth of Nations or a larger international society to be brought into existence after the war. India stands nowhere culturally or politically except as an active member of this international partnership.

'2. Secondly, it must ensure, not only an efficient day to day administration for India, but also social and economic reconstruction of the most far-reaching kind. The entire Indian society is running down like a clock, involving the culture and civilization of India in its ruin. If this decay is to be checked the social and economic structure of India must be rebuilt in order to guarantee a minimum standard of living for all Indians.'

'If these be accepted as desirable ends,' I then observed, 'then to my thinking a transfer of power without some provision and agency for the fulfilment of these objects will spell ruin for India.'

I continued: 'The fundamental reason for saying so is that transfer of power at the present moment will involve the handing over of India to a particular social class - the middle-class intelligentsia, which is fitted neither by its aptitudes, nor by its experience, nor by its system of values to strive for and bring to fruition any of the objects outlined above.'

It will be seen that my distrust of the social class to which I belonged was already deep-seated. Only one other anticipation I shall refer to here, and that is about India's membership of the Commonwealth. 'If the Indian intelligentsia,' I wrote, 'gets full right of self-determination together with the right to secede from the British Commonwealth, it may be that it will not decide in favour of secession, but the least that it will do will be to pursue a policy of extreme nationalism as barren and unresponsive as that pursued by the Irish Free State.'

I do not think all that was a bad guess at the future, although when I typed off those few pages the whim which made me do so could be regarded as crazy. The only thing which I could not foresee was that India would take advantage of her membership of the Commonwealth to launch a movement of counter-imperialism, and send out a stream of immigrants to colonize the British Isles. I am thinking, of course, of all the three secession states of the British Empire in India. Who knows but that at some future date England will be regarded as the brightest jewel in the crown of India?

Military reverses

Soon after this I had to face a very unpleasant situation in respect of the war, and my work as commentator made it even more unpleasant. A great Japanese naval force swept into the Indian Ocean, inflicting severe damage, although no fatal losses, on the British Eastern Fleet of which Admiral Somerville had just taken over command.

I had not expected this. Before I left Calcutta I felt sure that the Japanese would not attempt an invasion of eastern India from Burma, and I had no reason to think that they would try to land a seaborne expeditionary force in Ceylon or South India. I thought that they had already bitten off as much as they could chew. But the appearance of so powerful a naval force seemed to indicate such an intention. I was not sure, and did not expect that, although in India there was not only panic but also a good deal of eager expectation of more humiliation for the British. In any case, two County class cruisers, *Dorsetshire* and *Cornwall*, the small aircraft-carrier. *Hermes*, and two smaller warships were sunk near the coast of Ceylon, and further north another Japanese squadron sank merchant shipping besides damaging the port of Vizagapatam. In Ceylon the naval base of Trincomalee was damaged. I put up a brave face about the naval losses, and said that naval defence could not be carried out without loss of ships, for which I was, of course, laughed to scorn even by my colleagues. Nevertheless, nothing serious happened, and the great Japanese fleet sailed away. I knew, however, that even if a few hundred Japanese soldiers had landed on the Indian coast the whole of South India could become depopulated. I remembered what had happened in 1914 when the German light *cruiser* bombarded Madras.

At the time I did not understand why this very powerful force was sent out by Japan, or why it withdrew without accomplishing much. However, soon after I heard about the battle of the Coral Sea, and thought that the withdrawal was perhaps connected with that operation. I know now that Admiral Nagumo's fleet went back to Japan to prepare for the invasion of Midway. The force had certainly come to take unawares and destroy the whole of the British Eastern Fleet under Somerville with its battleships. No other motive could explain the incursion. Fortunately, Somerville had withdrawn to the west.

Following that I had a few weeks' respite from disasters, and was even encouraged by the news of the victory at Midway. I felt that the naval situation in the mid-Pacific had been stabilized. But I had soon to face new disasters which I never anticipated. This blow fell in Libya. I could not believe that after his recent defeats Rommel could mount an offensive again. But he did and inflicted spectacular reverses on the Eighth Army. The surrender of Tobruk was the worst of them. What was worse, there was a headlong retreat before the Germans towards Egypt, and all India was agog, as Mussolini was, to see the Germans and Italians in Alexandria and Cairo. I learned later that there was also panic among the British in Cairo.

However, as soon as the front seemed to be stabilized at El Alamein, I resolved to be bold, provoked by the gloating that I saw around me. I wrote a commentary in which I risked the assertion that the Germans were not going to advance further, not to speak of occupying Alexandria. This was even bolder than my broadcast in June 1940, in which I had said that the war was not coming to an end with the defeat of France. And even my English chief, Mr Barns, was aghast at my rashness. He thought we would look very foolish if things became worse. However, he did not reject the commentary and only asked me why I felt so confident. I gave him some explanations. I knew enough of warfare to feel that if once a very bold offensive which did not have plenty of reserves behind it got stalled it usually came to an end. I also told Mr Barns that I had read some time before that large reinforcements had been sent to the Middle East, and I said that if these were not already in Egypt they must be very soon. I cannot now recall on what precise information I said that. After that Mr Barns allowed me to say what I had put down in the commentary. Fortunately, I was proved right.

Although at the time I had no definite knowledge and only assumed that reinforcements might be available, I now know that this was actually the case. On 9 June Churchill telegraphed to Auchinleck that the 8th

Armoured Division which was at the Cape and the 44th Division which was at Freetown, had both been ordered to proceed to Suez, and he could expect the 8th to arrive at Suez at the end of June, and the 44th to do so by the middle of July. Actually, the 8th Armoured Division began to move to the front before 3 July. Again, after hearing about the surrender of Tobruk he informed Auchinleck from Washington on 2 June that very large reinforcements were on the way. But I had no idea that already three divisions, including the New Zealand Division, which joined the 8th Army even at the time of the retreat, had been brought down from Syria, and also that the check to Rommel was due to the masterful handling of the situation by Auchinleck.

But in London there was a comical exhibition given by the Leftists over the disasters in North Africa. In its issue for 4 July the New Statesman and Nation had an article characteristically entitled 'Facing the Spectre', in which it wrote: 'We should not waste our limited forces too prodigally in an attempt to delay the occupation of Egypt,' because (as the writer put it) 'the least pessimistic of us have to reckon with the early loss of Egypt, and with it our prospect in the Mediterranean.' The journal went on to say that 'the Suez Canal is no longer vital to us, but the Persian Gulf is.' It further advised that 'the defence of the Persian Gulf may involve the withdrawal of men and machines from India, a lesser risk that may have to be faced. We cannot afford to lock up there, as we do in this island, a second great army destined to passive defence.' And Leftists of the same breed, together with a Conservative peer, tabled a motion of no confidence against Churchill. Even I, a Babu despised by the Englishmen in India, showed more courage and intelligence.

After the battle of Alam al-Halfa I felt wholly reassured, but in the meanwhile a tragedy had befallen Auchinleck who had saved the situation in North Africa. Even before Rommel admitted defeat he had said on 1 July 1942: 'These damn British have been taught for too long to be good losers. I've never been a good loser, I am going to win,' which was only a modem and de-rhetoricised version of the old speech: 'Out of this nettle, danger, we pluck this flower, safety.' Auchinleck was removed from his command on 8 August 1942.

This was unfair. Of that there can be no doubt. But considering what the psychology of war is, it was also inevitable. War is a cruel game. Twenty-five years later I had a short meeting with Auchinleck, and I told him: 'Field

Marshal, if you suffered injustice that too is all in the day's work for a soldier, like victory and defeat.' No commander who has had reverses can be continued in his command with safety. Luck is always operative in the career of soldiers. That was why Frederick the Great used to ask before selecting a commander: 'Est-il heureux?' Louis XIV, too, said to Marshal Villeroy when they met after the Marshal's defeat at Ramillies: 'Monsieur le maréchale, à notre âge on n'est pas heureux.' I am glad to see that justice is now being done to Auchinleck. But he had other undeserved misfortunes. A few months later my young sons saw him presenting the VC to some Indian soldiers. As it happened, that very morning the Indian newspapers had published the story of his separation from his wife. But he went through the ceremony unflinchingly. Even the little boys noticed his effort at self-control.

Summer in Delhi

If the war was a great strain on my mind during my first months in Delhi, my body also was not going to be spared. The strain on it came from the summer of northern India, which was utterly different from anything I had gone through in Bengal. I suffered not only from the heat, which alone is felt and spoken about, but also, or rather even more, from the visual appearance of the summer. Let me give an idea of what I experienced.

In Calcutta the day was usually stuffy, but cool breezes began to blow from the south towards the evening and that brought relief In Delhi, on the other hand, winds rose with the sun and after midday the gusts whistled and even howled as if from pain as well as from anger. The doors and windows had to be kept shut to protect the rooms from heat. We soon put up the traditional screens of khas-khas grass and kept them sprinkled with water. This brought coolness, and also a mild fragrance.

Out of doors there was the dust, besides the wind. Kipling was absolutely right when he wrote that clouds of tawny dust rose from the ground and flung themselves tablecloth-wise among the tops of the parched trees, and that a whirling dust-devil would scutter across the plain for a couple of miles and fall outward. In Delhi I saw that the wind blew literally as it listed. But there was a feudal organization among them from the little localized whirlwinds at street level to the currents which rushed to the end of the Gangetic plain.

Being always conscious of prevailing winds, I soon got the hang of those in Delhi. It took some time, though. Coming from Calcutta and finding that my flat was blocked to the south I feared that it would be hot and stuffy. On the contrary, that was an advantage, for the winds from the south, which blew in Delhi only in the summer and came from the Rajputana desert, were always hot and almost scorched the bare skin, whereas cool winds blew from the north and northwest. Being very open on that side, we got those winds when they came.

That was why as one imperial dynasty followed another and capital after capital was built through the centuries, every new one in Delhi moved further north, to take advantage of the cool winds. Thus, when the British took over the administration of Delhi after the Mutiny, they established even their shabby Civil Lines and cantonment north of Shah Jahan's walled city. Beyond that there was no further room for expansion, because the land was very low and subject to the floods of the river Jumna. Therefore the new British capital in Delhi had to be built south of Shah Jahan's city among the ruins of old times. In fact. Lord Hardinge chose a site for the new Viceregal house from where he could always see the imposing ruins of Sher Shah's capital, called the Purana Quila or the Old Fortress.

The light too acquired its summer intensity, and became unbearable from about nine in the morning on account of its glare. But it could also acquire the quality which might be called 'darkness visible'. Kipling described that when he spoke of the gloom of a November evening in London (with the thermometer at 101°F. in the rooms) out of doors, allowing neither the sky, nor the sun, nor the horizon to be seen, but laying a brown-purple haze of heat, as though the earth was dying of apoplexy.

Even before the weather had reached its full summer ferocity I had an attack from it which I did not then perceive for what it was, that is, a mild heat stroke. One day, towards the end of May, I went to see the centre of New Delhi, where the Viceregal Lodge, the Secretariat, and the Parliament House were. I walked along the King's Way, which was a magnificent vista in itself It was, however, afternoon, the worst time to be outdoors in summer, and I suddenly felt ill, with shivering and chilliness all over my body. Not knowing what it was and feeling alarmed, I took a tonga and came home. I thought nothing of it immediately, but during the night I had so much palpitation of heart and suffered so much from heat that I hung up a mosquito curtain on my bed in the verandah and kept it drenched with water. I think that saved me from the full effects of the heat stroke. As summer progressed nothing, including the bed sheet, felt cool to the hands even at 3 o'clock in the morning.

It was symbolical that at the same time we saw a strange but magnificent phenomenon of the insect world. It was an immense and endless flight of locusts, which came in swarm after swarm like clouds, and embrowned the sky, which lost its firm appearance and seemed to shift and quiver all over. I had seen a small invasion of locusts in my childhood at Kishorganj but had forgotten the impression. The locust invasion I saw in Delhi was an unforgettable experience. When one or two swarms descended on the grass of the Nicholson Gardens to make it wholly brown, people rushed out from the city to catch them. I learned later that the Muslims ate them and even considered them a delicacy. My sons caught some and kept them in a jar. The visitation lasted two or three days.

The other notable and novel experience of that summer was the sudden rise and onset of the dust storms from the northwest. After two or three weeks of heat the sky became suddenly black, and furious winds began to blow from that direction. Darkness seemed to descend on the earth, and in fact these storms were called *Andhi* or the Darkener. Even Babar, the first Mogul Emperor, noted them after coming to Delhi from Central Asia. He wrote about these summer storms: 'It gets up in great strength every year in the heats, under the Bull and Twins [Taurus and Gemini], when the rains are near; so strong and carrying so much dust and earth that there is no seeing one another. People call this wind Darkener of the Sky, *Andhi* in Hindhi.' The immediate effect of these storms was a deposit of thick dust on the floors and furniture. The doors and windows were never tight enough to keep dust out. But when this was swept off we had some pleasantness or rather less unpleasantness, for it remained bearably hot for some days. Then the heat rose again to bring in another dust storm. So it went on cyclically in May and June.

A temporary but unexpected psychological relief also came in the same cyclical manner. The fortnightly flooding of the lawns before our house kept them under water for one or two nights. Then the line of Neem trees which bordered the road beyond the lawns, albeit brown from dust, were reflected in the water, and so was the light of the street lamps, albeit ghastly yellow. It seemed curious that the shimmering water should be able to bear the weight of the still heat haze. I contemplated only the water with its reflections, the scene was like what I used to see at Kishorganj in my boyhood on the river in flood.

I can best describe the state of mind to which we from Calcutta were brought by this our first summer in Delhi by quoting a paragraph from my *Passage to England*. I wrote:

'My family came to Delhi at the beginning of a hot season, and after going through their first summer in northern India, became half-hysterical. So, when one evening towards the end of June, storm clouds suddenly appeared in the sky [these were rain clouds and not dust clouds], my servant whom I had brought over from Calcutta burst into the room, crying in a voice choked with emotion, "Clouds, the clouds!" We left our dinner, and rushed out into the verandah. There were indeed clouds, piled up in black masses against the usual grey of the evening, with welcome flashes of lightning. It was as if we had gone through the siege of Lucknow and heard the pipes of the Campbells.'

This was only the thrice welcome harbinger of the rains. The real monsoon took three more weeks to arrive in its true form. That brought a revolutionary change in the aspect of the upper and lower air. With the open spaces before our house cleared of their semi-opacity, and the river Jumna not half a mile away to the east, the scene became almost like what I used to see in East Bengal during the rains. In the sky piles or rather mounds of clouds were always moving from east to west like great herds of elephants following one another. We could also see gorgeous sunsets, in which the whole western sky became one blaze of colour from bright yellow to flaming scarlet. This monsoon appearance of the sky lasted till September. After that a soft blue-grey, infinitely peaceful, spread over it.

The Quit India Movement

But more unpleasantness awaited me. The relief which I felt with the coming of the rains and the stabilization of the front at El Alamein was interrupted for some days by an outbreak of political violence. These disturbances have come to be known as the 'Quit India Movement'. This grandiloquent name was given to them because they were intended to give notice to quit to British rule in India. The Congress delivered an ultimatum, and its leaders were arrested. In their anger people went rioting all over northern India.

It should be recalled that it was ten years since the Civil Disobedience movement collapsed in 1932, and according to my 'periodic law' another phase of agitation was overdue. But in 1942 there was no sign at all of the kind of political excitement which invariably presaged the coming of another outburst of agitation. The years from 1939 to the middle of 1942 were very quiet and uneventful from the nationalist point of view. It seemed that the Indian people were neither ready nor willing to go rampaging politically.

There were a number of reasons for that. First of all, the failure of the 1930 movement, whose aims were pitched very high, was a severe blow to the nationalist movement and called for a long period of recovery. Secondly, a partial satiation of nationalist aspirations had been brought about by the introduction of provincial self-government in 1937 under the provisions of the 1935 Act. This had given opportunities to the professional politicians to use public power for private gain which they could not be willing to lose by going on agitational sprees. Although the Congress had to give up office in October 1939, that was done because not to do so had been made impossible by itself. Nonetheless, the Congress Ministers were casting a longing, lingering look behind.

The reverses of 1940 did not induce the nationalists to act. These disasters had taken place too far away, and Britain's position in India was not affected by them. Besides, the British Isles had not been invaded and the British people were carrying on the war, even though alone. Finally, outside the ranks of politicians, millions of Indians were doing very well out of the war in employment and business.

Even the entry of Japan into the war and the spectacular defeats she inflicted on the British in East Asia did not make Indians eager to rise up in revolt and strike a blow for their freedom. For one thing, they felt that the Japanese were doing the job for them and there was no need at all to risk life, money, and ease by embarking on political agitation, which under war conditions was bound to be treated as rebellion and severely put down. Next, far wider opportunities for making money had come with the war at the door steps of India, and even if the British were to be in India only for a few months, as the Indian people believed, there was no reason to refuse the passing gain. Lastly, all the cycles of agitation in India were activated by an accumulation of frustration and anger, but this time not only was that totally absent; on the contrary, emotional satisfaction of the opposite kind was being offered by the British reverses, over which all Indians could gloat to their heart's content.

However, in fairness to the Congress leaders, another consideration in their minds, or at least in the minds of some of them, must also be mentioned. That was not to embarrass the British war effort when Britain was carrying on the war against Fascism and Nazism single-handed, and when India had clamoured insistently for resistance to both. Jawaharlal Nehru was even vocal about this to the dismay of many of his colleagues who knew the pro- Axis mood of the Indian people. So, when he wanted to broadcast his views through All India Radio, one of his most respected associates dissuaded him from it. But he lost his patience when the criticism of his views came to him in the form of advice for his safety. Thus on 8 April 1942, at a public meeting in Delhi he spoke out. 'Some people say,' he said,

'Jawaharlal Nehru is a fool. He is unnecessarily antagonizing the Japanese and the Germans. The Japanese will wreak their vengeance on him when they come to this country. It is wiser for him to keep silent if he cannot speak well of the Japanese. I want to tell those who give me this advice that Jawaharlal Nehru is not the man who will keep quiet when he ought to speak.'

This was all the more remarkable because the speech was made when there was disappointment over the failure of the Cripps mission and that was attributed to British bad faith. A few days later Nehru went further and advocated resistance to the Japanese by means of guerilla warfare and a scorched earth policy, even saying that he would fight Subhas Chandra Bose if he came to India. However, in this he was alone, and more than anybody else Gandhi was opposed to such ideas.

For a besotted persistence in believing what gives them pleasure to believe and in the face of all facts to the contrary, no other people have approached modem Hindus. But on the other hand no other people have shown the same preference for playing safe in their extremism. Thus even after the reverses in North Africa in June there was no change of mood. These too were taking place at a distance, and Egypt was not occupied by the Axis. On the eastern front also the naval situation seemed to have reached a stalemate after Midway. So, India, to all appearance, appeared to be quite willing to wait and see.

Thus in the middle of July 1942, I could see no political excitement whatever in India from which I could anticipate a violent outbreak. Besides, my mind was wholly engrossed in the war, and I was not giving much attention to Congress politics, in which after the failure of the Cripps mission I felt no interest. Therefore I was very much surprised by the drastic resolution passed by the Congress at the beginning of August. It was a kind of defiance in wartime which the British government in India could not ignore. The Congress leaders were therefore arrested, as I have said, and the angry reaction of the Indian people was seen in widespread riots.*

I saw what happened in Delhi. One afternoon someone suddenly called out that the railway accounts office was on fire. It was in a tall building which was not very far from our house and could be seen from our roof. We rushed up to it, and saw flames and smoke coming out of the windows on all the floors. In all government offices, and more particularly in accounts offices, as I knew from experience, there were piles of very dry paper, and so anything set on fire was likely to cause a conflagration. The building was gutted to the ground. Some Bengali neighbours worked in this office, and from the pleased expression on their faces I could guess that they were not wholly uninvolved. I came to the conclusion that even if the clerks did not start the fire they were in collusion with those who did. The destruction of the papers not only satisfied their patriotic anger, but also spared them a lot of work.

I saw other buildings burning in the distance. But in Delhi the situation was brought completely under control by the next morning. Only, a curfew was introduced from the evening for some time. I had to return home after my broadcasts at night, and so I was provided with a pass. There was a piquet of soldiers at the entrance to the city through the Mori Gate, near which I lived, and I had to show this pass to the young British officer who was in command of it.

Within a few days the troubles seemed to be over. At all events, there was no news of serious violence. So I went to Mr Barns and expressed my satisfaction. I may have been even a little contemptuous. Mr Barns smiled and told me that there had been serious interference with communications to Bengal and Assam in the region of eastern UP and western Bihar, and that disturbances were still continuing. I heard afterwards that artillery had to be brought into action against some villages there.

Even that I did not take very seriously, and some days later I certainly thought Churchill was right when he told the House of Commons that order had been restored in India with remarkable ease and quickness and

* I have been informed on good authority very recently that an important Indian spoke to Vallabh Bhai Patel on the inadvisability of the Quit India resolution, but that Patel dismissed the advice, saying that strong opposition to in from the British was not to be expected, and the fear was a mere bogey.

with very little loss of life. I shall now set down my final view of the 'Quit India Movement'.

I think its seriousness and magnitude has been grossly exaggerated after independence in the interest of the Indian nationalist myth, lest it might be said against the nationalists that even when they were convinced that British rule was in its last gasp, they did raise a hand to give it the *coup de grâte*. It was natural to expect that, believing what they did, they would set on foot a continuous and widespread movement of resistance like the French or the Norwegians, or, to give an Indian precedent, repeat on an all-India scale what the Moplahs had done in 1921 against an overwhelming deployment of military force. Instead, they were occupied with making money and sitting timidly on the fence looking to Germany and Japan to liberate them. So, this miserably inadequate uprising had to be represented as a second Spanish rising against Napoleon.

Actually, the movement cannot be compared even to the Non-Co-operation Movement of 1921 or the Civil Disobedience Movement of 1930. It was a freak and an impulsive outburst of anger at what the Indian people took as an exhibition of outrageous impudence on the part of the British administration in India in arresting the Congress leaders. The movement had no real punch or motive power behind it to last even for a few weeks, and if it was relatively more serious in the eastern UP region that can easily be explained. It was a backward area in which the blind xenophobia to which the Indian masses are prone was stronger than elsewhere, because its inhabitants had suffered most from the cruel suppression of the Mutiny in 1857-8. The people who gave trouble in 1942 were the descendants of the Brahmins and Ksatriyas who furnished the bulk of the sepoys of the pre-Mutiny Indian army. Above all, it should not be overlooked that while a section of the Indian people were involved in the disturbances, millions of others were joining the army and the civil administration and making their contribution to the Allied war effort.

I have no difficulty also in explaining the action of the Congress in passing its drastic resolution. I am convinced that it was more or less a face-saving gesture like the giving up of office and starting of non-violent non-cooperation in 1939. The Congress leaders had to counteract the impression which was growing after the rejection of the Cripps offer that they were powerless to do anything against British intransigence. Besides, I do not think that the Congress leaders anticipated any serious or widespread rising against British rule. The complicity of the Congress in the disturbances was at the lower levels. So, they were not wholly insincere when after the disturbances they totally disavowed responsibility for them. Since they took credit for the disturbances afterwards, a reminder is needed not only of their repudiation of responsibility in 1942, but also of the fact that the Government of India had to reply to this repudiation by publishing a blue book containing evidence of the involvement of the Congress in the disturbances. Considering all its aspects, I would therefore say that the Quit India movement of 1942 was not one of the normal phases of agitational activity in the cyclical course of the nationalist movement. The real upsurge according to its periodic law was to come only after the war in 1945-6.

There was, however, a comical sequel to the misfired Quit India movement. The months following were a period of mounting disappointment for nationalist Indians, and this followed previous disappointments. England had not surrendered in 1940, Russia had not collapsed in 1941, Japan had not overrun eastern India, the Germans had not advanced into Egypt. And now the battle of El Alamein and the landings further west promised a victory for the Allies in North Africa. Under the stress of so much denial of hope, nationalist India would have been driven to Job-like despair if the Indian people had not acquired in the course of their history an unlimited capacity to become inured to disappointment, counterbalanced by an irrepressible apocalyptic hope. Even so, 1943 seemed to open like a period of complete emotional dullness for them. In this psychological situation Mahatma Gandhi apparently thought it necessary for the sake of maintaining the reputation of the Congress as well as for the mental comfort of his people to provide them with some excitement. He went on a fast for twenty-one days from 10 February as a protest against what he described as the 'leonine violence' of the British government in India. It was not clear whether the British lion or the zoological lion was meant.

Mahatma Gandhi's histrionics were based on an unerring knowledge of his people. At once all India became agog with the expectation of being fed emotionally, instead of being starved, as they were being in recent months. I noticed the excitement generated by the expectation of his death even in the news department of AIR among my colleagues. A new animation came into their faces, and almost a certain conviction that they were not going to be deprived of a new and unforgiveable grievance to batten on.

When Mahatma Gandhi would not abandon his fast and his life seemed to be in danger I was entrusted with the job of preparing an obituary notice in case something happened. I wrote a script in which I tried to be as objective as I could, and forgetting my own dislike for his ideas and methods I set down what I considered to be great in him. This script was sent to two senior Indian officials of me newsroom, and I found later that they had scored through all the favourable remarks in it. But Mahatma Gandhi came through the fast on 3 March and the obituary was not needed. It was, however, exhumed when he died at the beginning of 1948, and broadcast not only in its original form, but with many fulsome additions. The revised version was made by the same two officials.

During the critical days of the fast I noticed a strange tenseness on the faces of my colleagues, which was like the restlessness of the tigers and lions in zoos when their feeding time approached. But it vanished when the news of Gandhi's safe emergence from the fast came, and the tenseness was replaced by an expression which must be called *toute bête*. There was no anger at all, but only blank disappointment at the evaporation of a great hope. Nobody spoke about Gandhi any more. There was not even any expression of relief. A stolid preoccupation with the work of the newsroom was seen, and the bulletins which rolled out showed complete identification of their framers with the Allied cause in such phrases as: 'Our airmen are giving hell to the Japs in Guadalcanal.'

At the time Churchill roused great indignation in India by saying that Gandhi was given glucose with water during his fast. This was indignantly denied by his doctors, but Churchill believed it to be true, and on 24 February telegraphed to the Viceroy, Lord Linlithgow, that 'with all those Congress Hindu doctors round him, it is quite easy to slip glucose or other nourishment into his food'.

It is strange that for the first two weeks or so the reports about Gandhi were very alarming, but they ceased to be so from about 23 February. Thus, on the 24th Churchill, who was seriously ill with pneumonia at the same time, wrote to Harry Hopkins: 'Am feeling definitely better now. So is Gandhi. Once he saw his antics would not have any effect, he took a turn for the better.' Lord Linlithgow, however, attributed that to the doctors. He informed Churchill on 27 February that 'I have not the least doubt that his physical condition and the bulletins reporting it from day to day have been deliberately cooked so as to produce the maximum effect on public opinion.' He also said: 'I have long known Gandhi as the world's most successful humbug.' Unfeeling or not, this was wisdom in a British person. The worship of Gandhi is, in the British above all, unqualified imbecility and a sure proof of the degeneration of the British character.

There was no reason whatever why after the development of this advantageous stolidity a fresh emotional sop should have been provided for the Indians, especially after the victories in North Africa. I then asked an elderly and very respected Bengali in Delhi who was living in expectation of saying his *Nunc Dimittis* after the defeat of Britain, about which he was sure, what he thought about the military situation. He replied with grim sorrow: 'I shall believe that there is no God.'

Yet the British in India with their latter-day stupidity did restore the lost belief in God among the people of India in a different way. They could neither anticipate nor prevent a terrible famine in Bengal in which thousands of people died. It was compared to the famine which was said to have killed at least one-third of the population of Bengal at the beginning of British rule in 1769. There was no reason whatever why the end of British rule should have had like its beginning such an accompaniment. But it had. The famine was acknowledged to have been man-made, and a new grievance was created, and that was as tragic as it was colossal. I could not understand why even if ghouls wanted to feed on corpses, any government would have been obliging enough to provide them liberally. But all that was still to come. For the present I was happy with the war situation and also by providing myself with new interests in Delhi.

CHAPTER 2

The Three Delhis

When I came to Delhi in 1942, the city was not what it is now, that is to say, it had not lost its historical character. It had already been the new capital of British India for thirty years," and since 1920 an impressive administrative enclave, which I used to call the Ghetto, had been imposed on it; nonetheless, going over the area of some thirty square miles which was officially the province of Delhi under a Chief Commissioner, one could understand why those who wrote guidebooks on Delhi spoke of its Seven Cities. These appeared one after another in the course of seven hundred years and more which had passed by since Delhi became the imperial capital of India for the first time under the Muslims. New Delhi, which was built between 1920 and 1930, was the eighth Delhi. But there has been no ninth to follow it. The Delhi, nominally Old or New, which has grown up since independence, is altogether a new city with a new character, or lack of character.

As a result, its external appearance has wholly changed, for the latest Delhi has swallowed up and suppressed all its predecessors. In 1942, however, the city's history from the earliest Muslim, to the latest British times lay on the surface. What was known as Old Delhi then was the last Muslim imperial city built by the Mogul Emperor Shah Jahan in the middle of the seventeenth century, and that city could still be seen, in spite of some transformations, in the Old Delhi of British administration. Two-thirds of the walls of Shah Jahan's city, known as Shahjahanabad, had survived, and they enclosed an area of not more than three square miles with narrow and curved streets, labyrinthine lanes, and innumerable blind alleys of great length. It was incredibly congested with buildings, and even more incredibly over-populated. This part of Delhi presented its living history. Beyond it, there were open and stony plains spreading away for miles and miles towards the south which presented the city's dead history. Over about thirty square miles, were scattered an immense number of ruins or old monuments preserved by the Archaeological Department. Even the built-up parts of New Delhi were not obtrusive. If one excluded the acropolis (it *pas* the flattened top of a low hill) with its Viceregal Lodge and the

Secretariats, with their adjunct – the parliamentary rotunda at a lower level, the most obvious presence of the new British capital was felt in its wide vistas. After seeing New Delhi for the first time I said scornfully that I had no idea that a place with only bungalows could be called a city.

Even that New Delhi could be bypassed if one drove down the road which formed its eastern boundary from Old Delhi towards Agra. Coming out of the old city through the gap in the walls which is now mistakenly called the Delhi Gate, but was really the Agra Gate, in order to go to the city of that name, one could leave New Delhi behind without seeing anything but acacia clumps and at intervals ruins of old times: Kotla Firoz Shah built in the fourteenth century and the Purana Qila built in the early part of the sixteenth; and after that the building which is certainly the most beautiful Mogul monument in Delhi, the tomb of the Emperor Humayun. On 30 December 1824, Bishop Reginald Heber had passed down the same road and written in his journal: 'From the gate of Agra to Humaioon's tomb is a very awful scene of desolation, ruins after ruins, tombs after tombs, fragments of brickwork, freestone, granite, and marble, scattered everywhere over a soil naturally rocky and barren, without cultivation, except in one or two small spots, and without a single tree.'

In 1942 and 1943, I passed along the same road more than once, and I saw the same scene, but only cleaned up, and with the ruined aspect camouflaged by thorny acacias. We could also see a strange shrine, the tomb of a Muslim saint, where people left offerings for the sake of wish-fulfilment or as homage. A very large number of vessels, some of silver, hung from the poles which had pennons at the top. We were told that nobody stole even the silver pots, and that if anyone was sacrilegious enough to try to take a pot it would of itself run up the pole and place itself beyond his reach. Yet the stadium of New Delhi was only about half a mile from this spot.

Another curious feature in the Delhi of British times, which is continuing till today, was that the city was totally separated from the river on which it stood, and made to turn its back on it. Yet it was the Jumna, or Yamuna in Sanskrit, a river famed in legend, history, and poetry. Standing on the bank of the Jumna, nobody could suspect that the capital of India was behind him, and when in the city no one could guess that it was on a famous river. I know of no great city for which this has been done. In India the Hindus would always face rivers because they were sacred, and the Muslims did the same because they loved to look on flowing water.

The Mogul palace of the Red Fort had indeed its entrance gates on its western side, away from the river, but all the pavilions were on the eastern face, so that from their balconies and through their latticed windows the princes and princesses could see the river with its gaily decorated barges. And even down to the first decades of the nineteenth century, when Akbar II was the titulary Emperor, processions with caparisoned elephants and cavalcades passed up and down the strand which ran below the eastern walls of the Fort all along its length. It was the British who made Delhi turn its back on its river, and the backs of Delhi were not the 'Backs' of Cambridge.

Only religious-minded Hindus kept the connection between man and river in Delhi by going out of the congested city to bathe in it every morning. And on days of festivals or at new moon and full moon, the procession of bathers would be endless. I could always see this spectacle from the verandah of our house. Pedlars and flower-sellers sat by the roadside to sell their wares and garlands which were mostly of marigold. Those who claimed to be modern in Delhi had nothing to do with the river.

In 1942 Delhi was recognizable as the British version of an old Muslim city of northern India. That is to say, it had its 'City' and 'Civil Lines', and a vestigial 'Cantonment'. When the capital was transferred to Delhi the cantonments were removed from the north-western area of the city far to the south-west, but the area of the old cantonments had streets which retained names with military associations, e.g. Cavalry Lines or Probyn Road. The Civil Lines, too, had lost their old supremacy, and remained important because the Chief Commissioner of the Delhi Province resided in it, and also because of two hotels, the Cecil and Maiden's, run by Swiss hoteliers. In them White sojourners in Delhi took rooms. But in all north Indian cities living in the Civil Lines conferred status and prestige, and as the houses in them were invariably bungalows, the most respectful manner of inquiring about the residence of a new acquaintance was to ask: 'Where is your bungalow?'

I shall not describe the Civil Lines in this chapter and shall concern myself only with the Old City and New Delhi. And the third Delhi to which I have referred in the title of this chapter, will be the Delhi of history and archaeology, over which I roamed in the first years of my stay in the capital. Let me then begin with the 'City' in which I lived.

1 *The Old City*

I lived on Nicholson Road, which ran along the northern wall of Shah Jahan's city. At one end of the road was the Kashmir Gate, made famous by the siege of Delhi in 1857, but our house was nearer the Mori Gate at the western end. I have already said that there were nothing but open spaces before our house, but we had to turn just one corner in order to lose sight of these open spaces and plunge into the labyrinthine 'City'.

The Streets and Lanes

Some new streets had been built in it, but only along the outer edges, and one alone tried to pierce the solid core. It did indeed open up part of the interior, but was not accepted as anything but a *nouveau venu.* Although built in the second half of the last century, even today it is called the Nayee Sarak, or the *New Street* by the people. They never use the official name, which was given to it after that of a British administrator, and by doing so they showed that they did not want to abandon the traditions of Old Delhi.

The most famous street in the history of Delhi was the Chandni Chauk, built at the same time as the Red Fort. But none of its former splendour had survived, with the exception of its straightness and width. That, too, was not noticed on account of the meanness of the buildings on two sides, which were all modern. The two pavements were continuously lined with shops, and the upper floors were mostly residential. There was a red sandstone mosque at the far end of the street, and only two notable buildings on it. One of them was the shrine of the Sikhs in Delhi, the Sishganj Gurudwara, which though modern was built on the site of the martyrdom of a Guru under the later Moguls. At its doorway two Akali Sikhs, in their traditional blue dress with yellow facings, stood on guard spear in hand. The other building was a mosque with three gilt domes, in which Nadir Shah, the Emperor of Persia, sat with drawn sword while the massacre of the citizens of Delhi ordered by him in revenge for the murder of his soldiers by them, went on from morning till late in the afternoon. Opposite to it stood a fountain built in British times. With its cascades it tried to wash away the grim associations of the spot on which it was erected. Originally, what stood on its site was the platform on which the bodies of executed malefactors were thrown for exhibition as warning to others. On it, too, were thrown the bodies of the Mogul princes who were shot with his own hands by Lieutenant Hodson after the occupation of Delhi by the British forces.

The other major streets were curved. They also had shops or workshops on two sides. These were never mixed. Every section of every street had its special ware or craft. If one were interested in a particular thing one had to go to its special section: to one place for copper and brass ware; to another for hardware; and so on for grocery, spices, confectionery, textiles, jewellery, or silverware. It was the street for grocery and spices which asserted its character most decisively. I could never walk through it without smarting eyes and running nose on account of the amount of chili and pepper which was stocked in piles there. Another street was the wholesale mart for grains, and while sacks full of them stood roof-high within the shops, outside, the street was always blocked by lorries and camel carts, with the camels standing or sitting everywhere. Another not very long street also presented a decided character. Half of it was reserved for pickles, and this part was always redolent of oil and sour fruit. The other half was for sugar and candies, and, in fact, it was called the 'Batasha Gali' or Sugar-meringue Lane. Pyramids of sugar were displayed in this lane in open baskets or sacks, and they were always exposed to dust. The smell was of caramel. I never in my life saw so much sugar in one place anywhere else.

One wide curved street had the prostitutes who served the city. This street was named after a bastion built by a British military engineer called Garstin. But the name Garstin Bastion Road was abbreviated to G.B. Road, which had only one association, and any mention of it was bound to raise a titter or at least inspire simpers. But the prostitutes of Delhi never called themselves or even regarded themselves as such. They described themselves as public entertainers, and, indeed, those who went to these houses represented their object as amusement, especially music. I used to walk from my house to the Broadcasting House in New Delhi, and my way was through this street for about three-quarters of a mile. When I returned late in the evening after my broadcasts I often heard singing and the jingling of anklets on the dancing legs.

I used also to be solicited by the touts. Although, when inside, it was bad form to ask for anything but music and dancing, in the street there was no euphemism, but the women themselves never appeared on it. Touts, professionally as ancient as they, secured clients for them. I never took notice of the alluring remarks they made to me about girls whose sizes and figures would match mine (I might repeat that I am five feet and one inch and was then only six stone), and walked on. So they gave me up. But one evening a new man came up to me and whispered in my ear: 'A pretty little wench from Bombay!' At once an older hand said curtly: 'Don't ask him, he never goes.' That was the most resounding and prized certificate of character I ever got in my life.

The lanes, in contrast to the roads, were always straight. But though straight in each section, they took right or left turns at right angles, and so going through one of them nobody could guess where he was going unless he knew it beforehand. One lane which was exceptionally straight for its quarter of a mile's length had on it successively paint shops, acid shops, and varnish shops. Its other sections had oil shops and presses, and one could even see a blindfolded (not merely blinkered) bullock going round and round to turn the press. These were, of course, for edible oils. These lanes were very narrow, so that from the residential upper floors women could pass things across them by tying them to the end of a stick.

The blind alleys were straight to the dead end, and they always were residential. In fact, the old mercantile or working population preferred to live in them, to be safe against riots, plunder, and massacres. In old times all of them had gates at the open end with massive doors, and some of them had survived. They were also narrow, and had what seemed to be two continuous walls on both sides, pierced only by very narrow and low doors. But going through one of them it was possible to come upon a handsome court, with a colonnaded hall on one side, and behind that there was the courtyard of the zenana, and perhaps even a back garden, none of them with any opening on the outside. All the rooms were ranged round the inner courtyards and faced it. Only a portion of the sky could be seen above the courtyards. This manner of living was surviving substantially when I came to Delhi in 1942. The men did not seem to mind it, perhaps because they were in the shops for most of the time, and only slept in their houses. But the strange thing was that the women who lived in them month after month without going out even once, minded it still less.

The part of Old Delhi I lived in was within the old city but socially not of it. It was divided from the real Old Delhi and its society by the railway line which ran right across the northern part of the city and cut off a slice of its territory from the rest. It was not Old Delhi socially, because only domiciled outsiders lived in this area. They were Eurasians, Indian

Christians, Parsis, or Bengalis who had come for livelihood to Delhi. The houses were mostly owned by very wealthy Muslim merchants who lived in their part of Delhi. They always called these blocks of flats a 'Building' in the singular, e.g. Hasan Building, Umar Building, Rashid Building, the first element being the name of the owner. Our house was called P. & O. Building in imitation, but I always gave my address as P. & O. Buildings.

The names of the houses were always given in large letters in relief at the top, on the parapet or a pediment. Therefore they could never be seen from the street level. Thus in spite of the name which was proclaimed in letters a foot high, my visitors at times took half an hour to find the house. The numbers were in four figures, and on very small plates. They were so erratically distributed that even if anyone knew it that did not help him to locate the house. People had to ask at the shops, but they would be given a direction only if they could give the description of the person as he was known in the locality. I, for example, was known as the Kuttawallah Bangali Babu – the Bengali Babu with the dog: my golden retriever in the first instance and my Alsatian next had made me known under this description in the locality, and once even a wealthy Bengali gave only a negative shake of the head to a visitor from Calcutta who said that he wanted to go to the house of the well-known writer Nirad Chaudhuri.

Nicholson Road at our end was not narrow. But it had a very narrow bottleneck at its Kashmir Gate end, so that even two small cars could pass each other only with great difficulty. Afterwards this end was blocked with concrete pillars both for entry and exit. But these were pulled down every fortnight and had to be put in again. One ineradicable habit all Indians have is to take a shortcut to their destinations whatever the risk to themselves and others. One striking illustration of this habit was provided for me. There was a bus stop just outside the Mori Gate, and not more than twenty yards from it was a public convenience. But the passengers never went so far. They urinated on a tree nearby, and the poor tree died at the end of six months. In northern India men are never able to resist a wall or a post.

But issuing out of this *detroit* we emerged into a very non-typical square, which might be called the Piazza del Popolo of Old Delhi. It was the Kashmir Gate shopping centre, for the denizens of the Civil Lines. Before 1942 all Government employees moved to Simla for the entire hot season, and these shops had business only during the cold season. I was at first very much surprised to see that all these two-storied brick and stucco buildings had a tin verandah with little gables all along their facade. But these were put in to reproduce the appearance of Simla. Now, Simla architecture was such that when Sir Edwin Lutyens first saw it he wrote: 'What wonderful architecture! If the monkeys [for which Simla was famous – *vide* Kipling's poem *Divided Destinies*] had done it, they should be shot, lest they do it over again.' The sight of the gables at the Kashmir Gate has given me a permanent dislike for all of them, although I was immensely taken with them in my boyhood when I saw pictures of English half-timbered houses.

But the Kashmir Gate piazza had one handsome building, St James's Church, built by the Eurasian soldier of fortune, Skinner, who had an English father, a Rajput mother, and a Muslim wife, and did his duty by them by building a church, a temple, and a mosque. The church in the Palladian style was by far the best of the three.

The external appearance of Old Delhi was drab, dusty, and squalid beyond description. All that I have written about the shabbiness of Calcutta was a record of my impression of that city when I lived in it. Comparing Delhi as I saw it in 1942 with Calcutta as I saw it first in 1910, I should have revised my description. Yet this Delhi was as much the home of its old inhabitants as Calcutta was of hers. I should now give some idea of life as it was lived in that city.

Economic basis of Delhi

The population of Delhi was not large by the standards of other important cities of India, e.g. Calcutta, Bombay, or even Cawnpore in northern India, when I came to it, but an overwhelming majority of its inhabitants, Hindu or Muslim, were true natives: that is to say, they lived in it because their forefathers had lived in it for centuries perhaps. In British times Delhi was not important enough to attract people from all over India or even from the surrounding regions for the sake of livelihood or moneymaking. Even the transfer of the capital to it only gave it a floating population for a certain number of months in the year, and their number, too, was not large. Thus Old Delhi belonged to those who were *of* Old Delhi.

They were Hindu as well as Muslim. Although Delhi was a Muslim city historically, the Hindus were a very important element of the population. But the two communities lived in different quarters, each distinguishable even to the most casual eye. For example, in the Hindu quarters women would be seen going unveiled in the streets, and they would all appear to be of good social standing and even wealthy; in the Muslim quarters they would be in white or black *burqa* or veil, and all would seem to be from the working classes, for Muslim women of good families would never come out in the streets. The two communities, of course, had to mix with each other in economic life, but in social life not at all, except at the very top, where the relations were often very formal. There were many bloody Hindu-Muslim riots in Delhi from 1918 onwards, but not in my time except in 1947, as I shall relate.

Whether Hindu or Muslim, the most important element in the population of Delhi was commercial. The Hindus were wealthy merchants or financiers, with a large number of other Hindus who were employed by them as cashiers, accountants, clerks, or salesmen. Muslims were nearly all merchants, or artisans and labourers. It was not the economy of Delhi which supported the population, but the population which created the economy. People had to live in the city and so they created their means of livelihood or making money.

Everywhere there were shops and workshops, and goods were stocked in such quantities that I was surprised, for the population of Delhi did not seem to be capable of supporting commerce on this scale. For instance, in one street I saw glass sheets in quantities which could never have been needed, for most Delhi houses had no panes. I also saw spectacles and spectacle frames stacked on roof-high shelves in a number of shops, which suggested that the whole population of Delhi might have defective vision. Again, although the traditional Hindus and Muslims never bought tinned provisions there was a whole range of shops in one quarter of Delhi stacked with these tins. One could buy any famous brand of British biscuits in any quantities in any of these shops, and one could read such names as Cow and Gate and Horlicks in every shop. Looking at the tins of preserved fruit one could imagine that the people of Delhi ate Australian peaches, apricots, pears, and pineapple every day. I soon discovered that the mercantile community of Delhi, both Hindu and Muslim, had made Delhi a mart of imported goods for northern India, although it was not a port. The grave Muslim merchants I saw squatting in their shops spread with white sheets and furnished with bolsters, were importers of foreign goods on a grand scale.

In fact, only a small number of the shops in endless rows were retailers, and wholesalers were very indifferent to those who wanted goods for themselves. They would look with wholly expressionless eyes on a customer who wanted only one tin of Horlicks milk or one tin of Huntley and Palmer's biscuits. My young son one day told me of an experience of his which enlightened me on the business philosophy of the Delhi merchants. He was given to what is now known as DIY, and wanted a few half-inch screws. So he went to the hardware street – in Delhi the Hindus held the monopoly of this trade just as the Muslims did of provisions – and inquired. The merchants who sat leaning against the bolsters did not look at him, but one drawled out: 'How many gross?' My son, though very young, was very acute. He at once replied: 'I have not come to buy just now, but have been asked to have a few as samples to see if these would do.' Immediately the merchant ordered his salesman to give him a dozen, and when my son asked what he would have to pay, he was dismissed with a majestic wave of the hand. My son had devised his trick to get round the dignity of Delhi wholesalers.

If, however, a customer was regarded as worth cultivating, the courtesy shown would be profuse and refined, and not at all associated with commerce. He would be offered cold drinks both at the beginning and end of the transaction, and would altogether be treated as if there was no question of vile lucre between the two parties.

The shops, whatever their financial standing, were generally very shabby-looking, and any display of the goods or any alluring packing for them was regarded almost as improper as dressing up the girls of these merchants as prostitutes. The streets and shops which were most shabby were those in the famous Dariba Kalan where one could buy any amount of silverware, and even gold. The shops for saris and other textiles were in contrast rather better kept, because the customers were mostly women, and with ungrudging politeness these merchants would show at least twenty and even more saris to a woman who only wanted to buy one. The women, too, never bought a sari unless they had seen at least as many. But the shopkeepers had a very good eye for the quality of the customer. They would never bring out their best quality goods unless they felt sure that the customer understood quality. Often their best silks were not kept in the shops at all, but at home, and in order to show them they would take the woman or man to their houses in the blind lanes, and admit the potential purchaser to a room looking like a cell. Except in such quarters, a customer might have had to fear that he was being taken to some secret place to be robbed or, for that matter, even murdered. But, of course, that was inconceivable. Even a woman, whatever her appearance of wealth, would have no cause to fear. One thing which marked traditional Hindus of the merchant class was their honesty in regard to money and also as to their word, because they knew that without it there could be no commerce.

Again, if they accepted a customer they would never raise any question of money, except as a side-issue, and in any case they would not try to frighten a customer by quoting a price – the mark of a low-class tradesmen and of low shop-manners, which I have found has spread even to England. Let me give an example of superior shop manners. The shop was the best for ivory goods in Delhi. I bought only small articles from it, and could in no way be regarded as a patron. Yet the owner himself attended to me. He would show me his things, even though he could see that I was not the man to buy them. There was an ivory screen priced at a quarter of a million rupees, when 22-carat gold sold in India was not more than £10 (ffi Rs.135.00) an ounce, and even a small cigarette box shown to me was priced at Rs.3,000. The owner said that it needed almost a year's work. I had bought an ivory miniature of the Taj from him, and he showed me a set of miniatures of the traditional portraits of the Mogul Emperors, and of the two famous Empresses – Nur Jahan and Mumtaz Mahal. When I said that I did not have the money, he said quite simply: '*Fikr mat kijiye* – please do not be anxious,' and then: 'Please take the goods, and the money will come in the wake of the article.' I did not take advantage of the offer, departing from my practice of always buying first and thinking of money afterwards, and I regret the prudence even now.

I might add, however, that I never tried to acquire Mogul paintings in Delhi, knowing a good deal about them. Simple-minded foreign tourists are always bringing Mogul paintings home triumphantly, and I have seen even diplomats doing that. I knew where in Delhi they were manufactured.

Life in Old Delhi

My life in India was a tale of two cities. But coming from Calcutta I could not at first understand the second city, Delhi. Its life appeared to be as different from Calcutta life as its external appearance was. But the study of Islamic history, which I began after coming to Delhi, made me realize that Old Delhi was a city of the Muslim Middle East surviving in British India in all its essential features. In short, it was an Indian form of Cairo or

Baghdad. The mere predominance of merchants in the city's population would have showed that, as also would have done the status which the merchants had. I soon learned that even the shoemakers of Delhi in Mogul times were as honoured a body of men as goldsmiths or jewellers.

Another feature which revealed the affiliation with the Muslim Middle East was the presence of shops which sold cooked food, not merely sweets. Of course, even in Delhi the Hindus would not touch any food prepared outside the home. But the Muslims were in the habit of buying cooked food, especially if these were delicacies, from shops, and I saw people even eating a delicacy in the streets from a plate.

The routine of daily life was also not Hindu. Before the British introduced wholly foreign working hours in India the Hindu working day was always divided into two by a midday break for bath, meal, and siesta, and those who were not dependent for livelihood on the British administration or mercantile offices still followed the old routine. But in Delhi the day's business was continuous, from the morning to the evening. The shopkeepers and artisans took some sort of meal in the morning, and worked till the evening. After that they went home to have their evening meal and rest. No merchant was ever tired of sitting still in his shop. Before independence only a small proportion of the old inhabitants of Delhi worked in government offices, and thus their absence from the Old City made no difference to the crowded and busy air of the City. There were always moving throngs in the streets, and huddled congestion in the shops.

Outdoor excursions of the inhabitants of Delhi took two wholly different forms according as they were Hindu or Muslim. The Hindus, both men and women, came out only early in the morning, principally to bathe in the river, and the women would not be veiled. In contrast, the Muslims never showed themselves then. They came out late in the morning, and in fair numbers if the day was cloudy. I was at first very much surprised to hear the remark from my Muslim colleagues if it was a rainy or cloudy day, that this was a day for picnics and not work in the office. This attitude had been created by the Muslim invaders, who had come from Central Asia or Persia and found a sunny day on the north Indian plain unbearable. So, they did not mind even a little rain. In fact, the first Mogul Emperor of India wrote in his autobiography that 'while it rains and through the Rains the air of Hindustan is remarkably fine, not to be surpassed for healthiness and charm', although he had to add that it ruined the Central Asian bow, which became too limp to be drawn. We who had come from Bengal were used to retiring indoors during the rains.

Therefore I was surprised to see that as soon as the rains began groups of Muslim women in *burqa* or veil came out of the city and walked about in the parks before our house and even went as far as the banks of the Jumna. I also saw picnic parties at all the well-known archaeological sites. On the grounds of the Qutb Minar I always found groups sitting on mats or durries spread on the lawn, and not only eating but also singing to the accompaniment of the harmonium.

But the picnics and outings were only accidentals, so to speak, in the steadily maintained normal key of Delhi life, which was contented absorption in business or, to put it in plain words, in making money. Cities are assumed to be torn by the ignoble strifes of madding crowds trying to make more and more money out of one another. But in Old Delhi there was no sign whatever of competition even. The merchants seemed to be obeying and living in the light of the rules of a monastic order, more like St Benedict's than St Francis's. I could never conceive of such equilibrium in any urban human community. The men who sat in the shops all day long and the women who cooked from morning till night, and washed everything as if they were temple women kept for lustration, were never bored with their occupations. They were like ants or bees, intent on the business in hand whether they were still or in motion.

Neither the men nor the women needed the distractions which seem nowadays to be the only things which make life bearable to men and women of the contemporary West. They needed recreation even less. The men's job was to make money, and the women's to bear children and run the homes. The women of the merchant folk issued out of their houses either for religious duties or unavoidable social obligations, which were almost exclusively attending weddings or funerals. It was a curious experience to see a procession of Hindu women of Delhi in the narrow lanes when they went out to join matrimonial or funeral gatherings. The elderly women, without covering on their heads or faces, would be seen waddling along at the head of the procession, and the veiled young women, normally the daughters-in-law, would be following, separating the two sides of their veil with two V-making fingers of one uplifted hand and thus making a slit in the middle, through which would be seen the gleam of black eyes, directed at all passers-by. If a man had the immodesty to meet those glances he would feel as if his eyes were dazzled by a lighted up magnesium wire.* But these outings were few and far between, and the women would be perfectly happy without them. Men, for their part, considered it a mortal sin to give time to anything but their business. This absolute submission to the laws of existence in the station of life to which they were born had been brought about by the caste system, which if it had no other merit at least had one – the power to eliminate from life what in these degenerate days is the curse of Western life: the so-called stress.

Yet British rule had brought in a strange disposition to break out of this stability in fits of violence. This was provoked by the hatred which drove the nationalist movement, especially in its Gandhian form, which preached non-violence and freedom from hatred. Actually, the mercantile class's participation in the active outbursts of the nationalist agitation resembled attacks of rabies in dogs with placid temperaments like black labradors. When the Delhi merchants went on a rampage on a day of demonstrations against the British the sight was as distressing as to see your quiet house dog rushing about slobbering and snarling from rabies. And the worst part of these attacks was that they were shortlived. The merchants recovered to become the devoted money-makers that they were, but they remained susceptible to repeated fits of their political rabies.

II *New Delhi*

I did not see much of New Delhi until the news studios of AIR moved to its new house in Parliament Street in July 1943. I have already referred to my unsatisfactory exploration of the acropolis (both geographical and political) at the height of summer, in the course of which I got the mild attack of heat stroke. I paid a few more visits in order to see friends or to make purchases. The place to which I often went at that time was New Delhi's shopping centre, a circular complex, which was known as Connaught Place in its inner or concave arc, and as Connaught Circus in its outer one. I shall begin my description of Delhi architecture with these blocks of buildings.

New Delhi architecture

The circle was open towards the south for about one-third of its

* The Hindu mercantile residences in Delhi normally had iron bars not only in the windows, but also in the verandahs. The reason given was to prevent monkeys from stealing food. But only God knew the truth.

circumference. The rest was pierced by radial roads, which, however, did not destroy the unity of the circle. The buildings had three storeys, and on the ground floor they were colonnaded on both sides, with columns in the Etruscan order. The pavements formed arcades, with continuous shops by the sides. The colour of the whole was cream, given by the plaster. I had not then seen what is called a circus in European architecture. Even so I was not impressed by this amphitheatre. It seemed very counterfeit and drab, and, of course, after I had seen the circus at Bath and the Piazza dell' Esedra in Rome I realized what a sham Connaught Circus was.

There was a circular park on the inner side, and it was on the whole well kept. The lawns were green, and there were flower beds, mostly canna. The trees were the beautiful Gol Mohur (*Poinciana regia*), with their feathery evergreen leaves and gorgeous red and orange flowers in summer. The landmarks in Connaught Circus were the picture houses, and, therefore, the buses stopped before them and their stops bore such names as Odeon, Plaza, or Regal.

From the Circus a very wide street called Queen's Way led southward to the central vista of New Delhi, the King's Way. But at this end it was only an extension of the shopping centre, and had ugly buildings on one side. On the spaces originally left open on the other, the ugliest and meanest conceivable huts were being built to accommodate the American soldiers who were coming to Delhi, and in the huts already completed there were a large number of them.

At that time these Americans were the only Whites to be seen in public in any numbers in New Delhi, and their appearance was very different from that of English soldiers. They were all strongly built, straight men, with very narrow hips, and what struck me most were their trousers worn very low at the hip bone. I had never before seen trousers worn in this manner, for both Englishmen and Indians wore their trousers at the proper waist line, some even higher with braces. However, the American soldiers always had shirts on, and therefore I could not see what has now become a common sight with the lower trouser line, viz. the cleft between the buttocks. Their uniform was in a shade of khaki which was almost cream, and in striking contrast to the green uniforms of the British soldiers.

The only part of New Delhi which had handsomeness was the central vista, King's Way, which had the Viceregal Lodge and the Secretariat blocks at the western end, and a high arch at the eastern. The correct name of this arch was the War Memorial Arch, for it was built to commemorate the Indian soldiers who had died in the course of the First World War, and their names were carved on the stone of the arch. Besides, a fire was generally kept burning at the top, and curls of smoke could be seen going up through a central hole. But the arch was always called 'India Gate' by the Indians, because the word 'India' was carved on the entablature, and this illiteracy has now been adopted even by the British correspondents in Delhi. Beyond the arch there was a canopy or baldachino, under which was placed an elegant marble statue of King George V. The vista had basins of water or 'parterres d'eau' on both sides all along its length, with fountains.

From the War Memorial Arch one could see the acropolis of New Delhi with its massive group of buildings. I always thought the group very impressive as a whole. But considering them in detail I did not admire the very building which was generally regarded as the finest, viz. the Viceregal Lodge built by Sir Edwin Lutyens. Its general style was European Renaissance interpreted rather freely, but it was surmounted, in the place of a Renaissance dome, by an enormous Buddhist stupa. Anything more inharmonious, I would even say absurd, could not be conceived of. Apart from the conflict of styles it created, it was not structurally related to the low and long façade of the building. This jarred on me even before I had seen the Taj at Agra, St Paul's in London, and the Invalides in Paris. Lutyens exhibited his eclecticism even more infelicitously by putting in railings in stone in the style of those around the Buddhist stupas all over the place. Now, this type of railing was made by ancient Indians because, being used to working with wood, they could not handle stone properly and always gave it the look of timber. Why Lutyens adopted this archaism is a puzzle. He also decorated the grounds of the Viceregal Lodge with rows of lions rampant in the manner of the ram sphinx avenue which connects Luxor with Kamac. All this pastiche was spoken about with great respect by the British in Delhi because it was the fashionable view.

And the fashion was created by Lutyens himself out of his grievance against Herbert Baker who built the Secretariat blocks and the Parliament building. The two were at first great friends, and Lutyens had himself brought over Baker, who had built the government buildings in Pretoria. The Secretariat blocks were almost a replica of his work in that city. I thought them very respectable. But Lutyens gave them a bad name.

He quarrelled with Baker about the inclination of the ramp which led to the Viceregal Lodge. Lutyens wanted the inclination to be gentle, so that his creation could be seen all the way from King's Way. Baker, on the other hand, wanted a level square between his two blocks, and somehow got Lutyens to agree. When Lutyens discovered later that the gradient would shut out the entire lower portion of his building and permit only a part of the stupa to be seen, he tried his best to get Baker to abandon his square, and went up even to the Viceroy. But he lost, and in his grudge he ridiculed Baker's work, and jeered especially at the small elephant heads which Baker had added as oriental frills to the buttresses of the domes. The entire British community in its architectural illiteracy took up the joke from Lutyens, and did not realize that after swallowing the camel of the Buddhist stupa on the Viceregal Lodge they could not strain at Baker's elephants which were only small gnats. The basic wrongness of the Viceregal Lodge could be seen by looking at its imitation in brick and plaster by a minor Indian prince, the Nawab of Bahawalpur. Nobody in Delhi seemed to recognize the Bahawalpur House as the illegitimate and untouchable offspring of the Viceregal Lodge.

The Viceregal palace was also given a Mogul garden in accordance with the wishes of Lady Hardinge. Structurally, it was designed correctly with raised lozenges in stone and water courses arranged in arabesques. But the planting was very un-Mogul, for instead of being pomegranates, oranges and Persian roses, the plants were hybrid tea roses. On its two sides there were raised terraces planted with pansies, and at the western end there was a sunk garden with an oval basin of water and a herbaceous border. This was an almost exact copy of the sunk garden which Lutyens had put in at Great Dixter in Sussex. But all Indians who saw flowers in masses only in the herbaceous border thought that was the Mogul Garden.

Politics Behind New Delhi

Lord Hardinge, who as Viceroy took the decision to transfer the capital of British India to Delhi, had it announced through the mouth of King George V on 12 December 1911, at the third Delhi Durbar. I have related elsewhere how our elders joked about it saying that they were going to the grave of empires to be buried. Lord Hardinge, however, took a different view. In his memoirs he recorded a story that the Indian people took the transfer as an indication of the British people's determination to remain permanently in India, because they believed that Calcutta was kept as the capital in order to facilitate the evacuation of the British residents in case of trouble, on account of its nearness to the sea. Lord Hardinge apparently believed this ridiculous story, but I find that wholly baffling. I never heard of any such opinion, and cannot even account for the existence of the story, except on the supposition that it was invented for Lord Hardinge by some illiterate Indian toady.

At the time the transfer was strongly criticized in India by the newspaper *The Statesman*, which was the mouthpiece of the British mercantile community, and in England by two former Viceroys, Lord Curzon and Lord Minto, who condemned the decision. Lord Curzon repeated the criticism in very strong terms in 1925 in these words: 'While the abandonment of Bengal as the seat of government and the move to Delhi were defended at the time as an act of imperial statesmanship there is now hardly a living authority, English or Indian, who does not disapprove and deplore it.'

Actually, Lord Hardinge had a political motive in transferring the capital from Calcutta. He thought that the government of India should be taken to another place to liberate it from the undue influence exercised on the Viceroy's Council and the Legislative Council by the Bengalis. He called Calcutta a *cul de sac*. Such a baseless idea can be explained only by the fact that by the first decade of this century the 'seditious Bengali Babu' had become a bogey and an obsession with British officials.

I have always regarded the transfer as a contributory factor to the disappearance of British rule from India, because that cut off the British administration from all direct contact with the living currents of Indian opinion and immured it as it were in a zenana. As things stood, even with Calcutta as capital the administration was out of touch with real India for about seven months of the year when it was in Simla. On account of that, the good imperialist that Kipling was in his intuitive view of British rule in India, always made a distinction between the real rulers of India on the plains and the Olympians in the Himalayan clouds. The transfer made that dwelling in the clouds permanent. This isolation made the British administration incapable of dealing effectually with Indians either by conciliation or by suppression.

The transfer also made the British preference for the Punjabi, which had developed after the Mutiny and was given practical expression in the organization of the Indian army, a strong influence on the civil administration. All British administrators talked admiringly of the manliness, practical good sense, and loyalty of the Punjabis,* and utterly failed to see that their profession of attachment to British rule and readiness to serve the British was the product of a long history of opportunistic submission to foreign invaders in order to profit by that in the worldly way. The Punjab was never properly a part of real India, which is Hindu India, and was ruled at intervals by the rulers of adjacent countries. Even during the last half of the eighteenth century the Punjab was subject to the ruler of Afghanistan, and if for something like fifty years before the British annexation in 1849, it was independent and self-contained, that was under the Sikhs, who no more belonged to India than the Muslims. As to the Punjabi Hindu, he was so Islamized that he could not read even his own scriptures except in Urdu translations. Hindu Punjabis were mostly tradesmen or functionaries of the lower ranks, and had no ideological antipathy to British rule. The really strong passion which fed Indian nationalism was the Hindu xenophobia, which was created by the Hindu way of life and shaped their attitude to all who were not Hindu. The Punjabi Hindu really acquired the Hindu attitude, and with that the Hindu hatred of non-Hindus, with the creation at the end of the nineteenth century of the Arya Samaj, a neo-Hindu sect, by Swami Dayananda, a Gujarati. Thus it happened that a majority of the Hindus of the Punjab who joined the nationalist movement belonged to the Arya Samaj. The rest were always ready to serve any master, so long as their worldly interests were served by him. It was this class of Punjabis who began increasingly to furnish the personnel of the British administration, first at the lower levels and afterwards, as Indianization of the services proceeded, in the highest ranks. As a class they became and have remained civilian *condottieri*, and might be described as 'civil servants of fortune.'

The local British who never understood the Hindu mind and preferred not to meet any kind of mind in any Indian, thought that they could perpetuate their rule in India by securing the interested support of all the mindless men in the country. But even the Bengali civil servants in the highest ranks of the administration, who morally were the most worthless set of men to be found anywhere in India because they had moral conscience and were always suppressing it, would have been better

* The British admired the Punjabis all the more because they ate raw carrots when these had become as possible. 'See!' Englishmen have said to me, 'they chew carrots every day!' I wonder if they also thought of the stick!

defenders of British rule, because with their cunning they could always create a specious pseudo-moral case for British rule.

In the upshot the Punjabi who professed in the days of power of the British to be their most loyal supporters went over as a class to the Congress with the same or even greater professions of loyalty to the new Hindu regime. In fact, they became even greater admirers of Gandhi and Nehru than any Hindu from any other part of India. The transfer of the capital to Delhi made the British administration in India more and more dependent on this mindless body of men.

That was very largely due to the revulsion of the local British from the Hindu mind, and they certainly had the subconscious motive of protecting themselves from this mind by coming to Delhi. They felt its deviousness, its secretiveness, its' slipperiness, its nimbleness, and were afraid of the loquacity which covered its workings. They did not realize that the Hindus had developed this pattern of behaviour through the ages, in order to deal with their foreign rulers – to get every worldly interest of theirs served by them without suffering for their undying hatred of all foreigners. So, the British in India thought that they would be safe if they could avoid the Hindu mind as far as possible.

But they could not do that to any useful extent any more, because by the time Delhi had become the capital of India effectually, i.e. by the Twenties, the British had also begun their discussions, I call these their 'dialogues', with the Hindu nationalists. Even then the British dignitaries and officials who had experience of India were perfectly aware that they could never get round the Hindu in the game of talking. After Lord Willingdon had succeeded Lord Irwin (the future Marquis of Halifax) as Viceroy of India in 1931 I heard the story that he had set his face against any further talks and pacts in the Irwin style. I have found confirmation of this attitude of his in the memoirs of Mr Ian Stephens, who came to India in the early Thirties to serve the Government of India as its publicity officer and afterwards became the editor of *The Statesman*. He was summoned by Lord Willingdon, who gave the following advice to him from his experience of India as Governor of Bombay from 1913 to 1919, Governor of Madras from 1919 to 1924, and then as Viceroy:

'It's evident that you must be *clever*: all those Firsts and things at Cambridge. And that's dangerous. Now you'll please take my advice, and decide here and now, in this room, straight off, that you aren't clever any more. Because you won't be, my dear boy. You'll be dealing in this job, mainly with Hindus: Brahmins and Banias mostly; you'll never be anything like so clever as them, however hard you try, they're the cleverest people in the world. So when you find you're in a difficulty – and you often will – just rid all ideas about being clever from your mind; be your ordinary self; simply consult your common sense and your conscience, both of them, but them only, and carry on.

'And then, my boy, you'll see a funny thing, indeed you will, I will promise you. They'll be so damned clever, these people, spinning their webs and laying their snares to catch you, that they'll trip themselves up over all these ingenious contraptions and fall down wallop. *That's* the way to treat them, you take it from me. It's all that the likes of us can do.'

Mr Stephens who has kindly permitted me to quote this passage from his book* explains that this report might not be exactly verbatim, but he vividly remembered the gist of Lord Willingdon's advice and gave it correctly, some of it in his actual words. But Lord Willingdon did not mention to him the real sanction which made British common sense and conscience effective against Hindu cleverness – which was power, taken with the will to apply it. Although the Hindus are only clever, and generally speaking wanting in intelligence, at all events they have an uncanny perception of where power and the will to exercise it exist. When they scent that they do not bring their cleverness into play. By the Twenties the Hindus had perceived the British weakness, and no amount of effort to get round their cleverness would have availed anything. Even in New Delhi Hindu loquacity, shunned in private personal intercourse, got the better of British common sense and conscience in the Legislative Assembly. That was what created the antipathy to the Swarajyist members of the Assembly in Sir John Simon.

The British could no longer throw their power at the heads of the Hindus and thought that they would find protection by retiring to Delhi. New Delhi ostensibly served the purpose. It gave the comfort which comes from the avoidance of danger and unpleasantness. But the British forgot that comfort was not safety. The danger to British rule in India lay in the Hindu mind. That danger could not be removed by refusing to meet the

* Ian Stephens *Unmade Journey*, 1977, pp. 191–92.

Hindu mind. And the insulation increased with every year in New Delhi.

Another danger to the efficiency of British rule in India which grew with the stay in Delhi was the hypertrophy of the bureaucratic methods of administration. It had always been a deadweight on British governance of India. On his arrival in India Lord Curzon was determined to cut out as much red tape as possible, but a high civil servant told Sir Walter Lawrence who had come over with him as his Private Secretary: 'He would be paperlogged in three months.' He was not wholly, but when he left even the little he was able to do was eroded.

The bureaucratic machine became so cumbrous that Lord Rawlinson, who came to India as Commander-in-Chief when I was in the Military Accounts, after having been, as commander of the fourth British Army on the Western Front at the end of the First World War, one of the most distinguished of British soldiers, wrote in his diary:

'The chief weakness of India today is that she is caught in the net of Babuism – which she has herself created during long years of parochial and pedantic administration. She is hampered on all sides by precedents, vested interests, and ancient customs.'

This was not a reference to the Babu who was the *bête noire* of the British in India, i.e. the Bengali who had received a western type of education in English, but the clerical Babu, who was the creation of the British administration itself. The British administrators could no more do without the native clerk than the English colonists in warm climates could do without Negro or Indian labour, and all the real spade work of administration was in the hands of the clerks.

Lord Curzon was scandalized to find that in the ultimate resort all governmental action originated at the lowest level of the bureaucratic hierarchy. When Lloyd George described the Indian Civil Service as the steel frame of the Government of India he forgot to mention that the Bengali clerk was its concrete foundation. Every initiative of the Government of India originated with the 'Dealing Clerk', and five or six tiers of his superiors only scribbed scholia on his handiwork. The Bengali clerk, and after him the Madrasi clerk, were at least the working bees or ants of the administration. These clerks had the capacity to become mindless machines for quill-driving. It may be said with perfect historical truth that if the British bureaucracy in India made a substantial contribution to the destruction of British rule, as its beast of burden the Bengali clerk made his contribution, and that was certainly greater than that made by the Bengali revolutionary. With the transfer to Delhi and increasing Punjabization the danger from the bottom became even greater, because even the routine efficiency was eroded.

Life in New Delhi

I never became acquainted with the life of the British officials in New Delhi, nor indeed could I, because I was only a minor official so far as I was an official. I did not try even to become acquainted with high Indian officials, which on account of my social affiliations I could. The Indians who held high appointments in the Government of India formed the second tier of the administrative hierarchy socially, however high their official rank might be. They had their own club – the Chelmsford Club, which never acquired the prestige which belonged to the 'Imperial Delhi Gymkhana Club', with its truly Anglo-Indian name. But such acquaintance as I had with these Indian officials or with other Indian officials of lower rank who had access to the highest Browns, gave me some idea of the mind and life of the White officials, because one absorbing subject of conversation among this class of Indians was the doings and sayings of their White superiors. Even this exiguous knowledge of the social life of New Delhi made me feel sick. Its triviality was a strange mockery of the tragedy that the administration of India by the British had become by the time I came to Delhi. In that year, i.e. 1942, the exodus to Simla was also given up, and with that even frivolity vanished from the social existence of the officials in New Delhi.

Some idea of this life can be obtained from the memoirs written by those who were in New Delhi from the Thirties onwards. Tawdry speculation about who was the Private Secretarial power behind the Viceregal throne, whether a Viceroy was sticky or easygoing, which Vicereine was imperious and had a firmly corsetted body, and which was more or less affable and perhaps less hard to look at, furnished the staple of conversation in the New Delhi salons. Even Kipling, who could remould the trivial Simla life into subjects for stories with the brilliance of those by Maupassant, would not have succeeded if he had tried to make New Delhi life other than what it was. Cleopatras did not lie on the beds of New Delhi bungalows, and so there could be no question of raising the ghost of a rose in any of them.

As it happened, the material symbol of New Delhi life was the huge bungalow which housed the Imperial Delhi Gymkhana Club. In spite of all its pretentiousness, nothing more Civil-Linesque could be conceived of. I did not go into it until after independence. But even one or two visits were enough to give me a revulsion in retrospect from New Delhi life. One visit to the library from which I saw the wives and daughters of the Indian successors of the old Sahibs borrowing books would have revealed the quality of mental life among the British officials when one glanced at the titles.

Another unpleasant feature of New Delhi social life was the admiration which began to be aired by the British officials towards their Indian colleagues, whether superiors or subordinates, from the Thirties onwards. If the past history of the relations between the two groups could be forgotten, there would have been no feeling of unnaturalness in watching the new cordiality. Unfortunately, however, that history could be overlooked only by very interested persons. From the very first day that Indians entered the highest cadres of the Indian administration the relations between the Brown and White members had developed in a way which made it difficult to take the new friendliness seriously or even to believe it to be honest. Perhaps in some radically minded British officials it was sincere, but to us all it had the appearance of being rankly opportunistic. I had no means of knowing what they really thought of their Indian colleagues, but whenever I saw the friendliness aired, or even read about it in retrospect, I felt a strange irritation. The former attitude of British officials and soldiers in India towards their Indian colleagues exhibited such a departure from the code of gentlemanly conduct laid down as obligatory in England, that I could not believe that they had at last turned into epicene English gentlemen in India.*

III *Delhi of History*

Let me now turn to the third Delhi, to get acquainted with which, as I have said, was my greatest pleasure during my first years in that city. That was the Delhi of history with its monuments. I visited almost every one of them, one day even walking fifteen miles from my house in Mori Gate to Tughluqabad.

* These Indians moreover belonged to a class which after independence showed itself to be the most worthless morally.

I paid my first visit to the Red Fort in the city soon after my arrival, even before my wife and children had come to Delhi. My expectations were high. From our childhood I had read about the Red Fort of Delhi. I was only a child when I saw a picture of the Lahore Gate. I had read and heard more only about the Taj at Agra. More especially, all of us had been told of the beauty of the Diwan-i-Khas or hall of private audience, proclaimed through its famous inscription: 'If there can be heaven anywhere on earth, it is here, it is here, it is here.' Of course, I saw the inscription written in beautiful nastaliq calligraphy in cartouches. I never go into any historic place without studying its topography, and so I took note of each famous building after entering the fort through the Lahore Gate. The idea of proportion in buildings which had been first brought home to me at Allahabad the previous autumn was now confirmed.

The facades presented themselves with such happy relationships between their length and height, and also between the oblongs of these facades and the arches which were set within that framework, that I could never guess the size of the buildings. The first impression was: So small and yet so neat: *Parva sed apta*. But even the entrance gate to the palace proper, which was known as the Naqqar Khana or 'place of the drums and trumpets', and through which no one except the emperor could formerly pass on horseback, was almost one hundred feet in width, and fifty or sixty feet in height. The open entrance hall between the front and the back arches would have housed a normal domestic building in Delhi. When I saw at a side door that it led to the residence of the curator I was very much surprised.

But leaving aside the first sight of the buildings, my strongest impression of the whole fort was of bareness and lack of atmosphere. The pavilions stood out naked under a hard light. The reason was, of course, that in the Red Fort after the Mutiny all the ancillary and connecting buildings had been removed, and only the most important pavilions had survived. Before Lord Curzon ordered the restoration of the historical monuments to their original state as far as possible, even the audience halls were used as regimental messes and the emperor's bedrooms as officers' private quarters. One pavilion used by the princesses was the military prison, and I saw graffiti inscribed by the prisoners on the dados. It was after going to Agra Fort some years later that I understood what a Mogul palace was like in its total planning and structure.

And what was worse, two-thirds of the space within the walls of the fort was given over to barracks for soldiers and to sheds for military stores and vehicles. These buildings had the ugliness which only the British cantonments in India had, and which even Aldershot which I saw later could not approach. Over and above, the military areas were shut off from those open to visitors by very high barbed wire fences. These buildings, with their walls and fences, spoilt the appearance of the courtyard which was the finest in the palace. It was formerly the garden called Hyat Baksh, Gift of Heaven. It still had its water courses and beautiful pavilions, but on it was cast the shadow of the barracks and the barbed wire fences. Curiously, the atmosphere was not of vanished splendour, not even of desolation, but of shabbiness. Yet, when individually examined, the pavilions were as impressive structurally as they were beautiful in their varied decorations. Their arches, even though not of the pure early Mogul design but crinkled in the manner of Mogul rococo, were faultless in their proportions.

On my first visits I noticed only the architectural features of the Mogul palace, but later I read a good deal of its history, and also about the splendour and misery that formed the accompaniment of the life lived in it. I learned how many emperors were killed or blinded in it, and how many princes murdered. In Delhi I concentrated on later Mogul history after the death of Aurangzet in 1707, and read the bloody tale. When the news of the deposition of an emperor by a king-maker would reach the harem the Begums would hide their sons in their very private apartments, lest after being crowned as emperor on one day they would in their turn be murdered by a usurper a few days later. One deposed emperor was confined to one of the towers of the Lahore Gate, without any resource to occupy himself. He could read the Koran beautifully, but could not fall back on that consolation because enough water was not provided for him to enable him to be as clean as he had to be before he could touch the holy book. Just after the deposition of this emperor the Begums hid their sons, and only one prince who had strayed into a corridor was discovered like Claudius after the murder of Caligula and crowned in the Diwan-i-Khas, clad in his simple muslin gown and one pearl necklace. Fortunately, within a year he died of tuberculosis, and so escaped murder. I have seen his portrait in the museum of the Red Fort. Although such portraits were generally conventional, in it his eyes showed typical tubercular features, hectic, gleaming eyes, and burning cheeks. Even so, the Red Fort in Mogul days did not undergo its supreme degradation, which was the holding of the INA trials in the Diwan-i-Khas in the last disgraceful days of British rule. Mogul imperial decadence was tragic, the British squalid. This ignominy was added to the miseries of the Red Fort. And the anticlimax was the aping of French *son et lumière* after independence with commentaries by Indian writers who were incapable of understanding even the misery of the Moguls. But before I went deeply into the history of the Red Fort, it was the individual beauty of the pavilions which lingered in my mind.

I did not go to see the Qutb area and Tughluqabad until after the setting in of the rains. Then these great monuments lost a good deal of starkness and gained mass. The enclosure of the Qutb was also bare, but it had well-kept lawns, and although at this very first visit I saw picnic parties, they did not spoil the impression made by the grand monuments, which even in their ruined state communicated more of the past than did the Red Fort. There is no doubt that the Qutb Minar is a sublime structure, the first truly Islamic monument in India built on the morrow of the conquest. Just below it is the first mosque built in the country, and it was called Qubbat-ul- Islam, Might of Islam. But its hall and cloisters were built with pillars taken from Hindu and Jain temples, and the effect was totally un-Islamic. It was curious to see Hindu and Jain iconography in bas relief on the bases, capitals, and architraves of the pillars. Formerly, they were plastered over, but they were now clearly visible. A strange feeling came over one when looking at Hindu or Jain religious processions marching with drums and trumpets on these reliefs in a mosque.

I paid my first visit to Tughluqabad, which was about five miles to the east of the Qutb, on the same occasion. The impression was overwhelming. It was a whole city with a citadel and palace when it was built in the early part of the fourteenth century by the first Tughluq Sultan. He moved the capital to a less exposed place in order to defend it against the Mongols who, it was feared, would invade India. It was built very quickly, but not very solidly. So it soon fell into ruins, and was abandoned. But even in that state it is overpowering in the effect it produces to this day. I do not think there is in India any other ancient palace complex which is so big. My first impression of it fully conformed to the description given by Sir John Marshall, the Director General of the Archaeological Survey of India brought over by Lord Curzon:

'Its cyclopean walls, towering grey and sombre above the smiling landscape; colossal splayed-out bastions; frowning battlements; tiers on tiers of narrow loopholes; steep entrance ways; lofty narrow portals: all these contribute to produce an impression of unassailable strength and melancholy grandeur. Within the walls all is now desolation, but, amid the labyrinth of ruined streets and buildings, the precincts of the Royal palace once roofed with glittering gilt are still discernible; and so too is the citadel rising high above the town and protected by its double or triple lines of defence.'

I have stood at its highest point, and surveying the far-stretching ruins recalled the lines:

They say the Lion and the Lizard keep
The courts where Jamshyd gloried and drank deep;
And Bahram, that great Hunter – the Wild Ass
Stamps o'er his head, and he lies fast asleep.

When Tughluqabad was built lions were to be seen around Delhi, and the lizards with torchlike eyes I have seen there. I have also gone with my children down the dark and narrow stairs which led from the palace to the moat below, where boats would be waiting for the refugees, in case the gates were stormed. In old times there was a lake all around the city.

Just to the south, across a road in our time, was a smaller fort in which stood the tomb of the Sultan who had built Tughluqabad. It was not a very large structure, but it created a surprising impression of massiveness on account of its battered walls of stone. It was even in its bare lines a very beautiful building, with its polychrome decorations and white dome. While I lived in Delhi I was never tired of visiting Tughluqabad, and I do not remember having seen any other visitors there, and certainly I did not see that abomination, the White tourist, on whom the Hindu Government of India, ever greedy for foreign exchange, fawns like a lackey.

Beginning with those first visits of mine, I saw one by one all the surviving Muslim monuments in Delhi, studying their style and structure. I noted the evolution of the arch and the dome from their first appearance in India at the end of the twelfth century to their culmination in the eighteenth. I noted the development of the decorations as well. As it happens, the entire evolution of Islamic architecture in India can be studied in Delhi, although not all the greatest monuments are there. I also initiated my young sons into architecture. In Delhi I realized what relationship architecture bears to imperialism, which I had known only in theory from my reading of Egyptian, Assyrian, Persian, Greek, and Roman history. The British in India failed dismally to present this correlation. They gave us the *PaxBritannica*, but not the *Ars Britannica*. On the contrary, they created, except in the very last phase of their rule in India, a horrible antithesis between political power and architectural insignificance, as I realized with scandalization when I saw the confrontation between the Diwan-i-Khas and die barracks in the Red Fort.

I completed my examination of Islamic architecture in Delhi by a study of Islamic architecture all over the Islamic world from Tunisia to Bengal, and traced every step in its development from the Dome of the Rock in Jerusalem to the decadent expression in Lucknow. I went further. My study of Islamic architecture had as its natural complement a study of Islamic history and civilization. This study I regarded as my recreation while I was continuing my commentaries on the war. I then realized what a mistake it had been for me not to have tried to know more about Islam as a religion and Islamic history and civilization when I was in Bengal. It was certainly unnatural, because in East Bengal the majority of the population was Muslim, and we of the Hindu gentry there had to deal with them every day. Yet the Muslims knew more about Hinduism than we Hindus knew about Muhammedanism. In Calcutta I had, of course, studied Islamic painting. I had also realized that the Muslims had a perfect right to their way of life, but that opinion was based on my observation of the actual social and political situation, and not on a proper appreciation of the greatness and significance of Islamic culture. This I acquired in Delhi, and I began to regret the ignorance in all Bengali Hindus. If they had known more about Islam and Islamic civilization, certainly the animosity which led to the catastrophe of the partition of Bengal in 1947 would not have been so ineradicable. There would have been some approach to each other based on respect. I came to feel that respect, and in spite of my Hindu pride came to hold the opinion that when the Muslims conquered India at the end of the twelfth century they were both socially and culturally more alive than the Hindus, who had reached almost the final stage of cultural fossilization.

Fortunately, in Delhi I found the means to pursue this study and that in a specialized library. A friend of mine introduced me to the librarian of the Archaeological Survey of India. He was a very courteous man, and he allowed me to borrow books from his library. It had a very complete collection of books on archaeology and Oriental history. For example, it had even the great work on early Islamic history by Prince Caetani-*Annali dell' Islam*, in ten volumes. It was in Italian and I could not read it. But I borrowed and read, among other books, translations in French of al- Masudi's *Muruj-ud-Dhabab* in nine volumes and of Nizam-ul-Mulk's Siyasat Namah. In the same library I first came to know about Ibn Khaldun. It also had a very large collection of works on Islamic art, among which I found Cresswell's history of early Muslim architecture and Upham Pope's history of Persian art. Altogether, it was like discovering a new continent for me. Certainly, I regard my knowledge of Islamic history and civilization as my greatest acquisition in Delhi.

CHAPTER 3

End of the War

Although the study of Islamic history and architecture was an absorbing recreation for me, my overriding mental preoccupation was still the war. However, from the middle of 1942 it was no longer the source of mental strain that it had been during the previous two years. I no longer felt compelled to stiffen my body as I opened the morning paper so that I might be ready to face the bad news in the headlines. I felt wholly confident about the outcome of the war and only wondered how much longer it would continue.

Victory in North Africa

As a commentator on the war, I felt exhilarated when the news of El Alamein came one afternoon. Within an hour I had my commentary ready. I felt dead sure that this time the offensive would not only go through but also that there would be no unpleasant recoil. I said as much in the commentary. But on this occasion my chief, Mr Barns, would not allow me to be so optimistic and commit myself. So I had to tone down my script. For myself, however, I had no fears. I was sure that the attack would not have been launched unless its success was assured.

Nevertheless, the delay in the breakthrough surprised me. I did not reckon on the battle going on for twelve days. Of course, in the light of subsequent knowledge I can now see that this delay only proved the old view that in battles the human element still counted as the most decisive factor. Otherwise, no calculation based on the scale of equipment of the two sides would have justified anybody in anticipating the resistance Rommel put up. I shall have to say more on this subject later. A few months after this I also saw the film of the battle and was tremendously impressed.

At this time I had a sort of premonition that something more was in the offing, and that would be a landing in North Africa. Although I had no information whatever about the projected landings, to me they seemed to be the necessary prelude and trying out exercise before opening a second front in France, for I felt convinced that so unprecedented a military operation as an invasion of the French coast, would not be launched without a rehearsal, a dress rehearsal, so to say. But I expected the landings to take place only on the Mediterranean coast and not on the Atlantic side as well. The latter, I thought, would be too far away from the decisive strategic area of the Tunis region. But I did not think that any landing would be attempted farther east than Algiers. I felt so sure about this invasion that I proposed to write a note and give it to Mr Barns. I did not, and I regret it.

The reason why I did not was that I did not think that the invasion was imminent. I assumed that the landings would be attempted only after the Eighth Army had advanced far enough to the West to permit the RAF to interfere from the air with reinforcements for the Axis forces from Italy and Sicily. So I thought I could wait. But the landings took place only four days after the breakthrough at El Alamein, when the British eastern forces were still hundreds of miles away from Tunisia.

However, the landings when they took place elated me. They seemed to be on a very big scale. Even so the delays irked me. For one thing, after four years of disappointments I was impatient for quick results, and, besides, outside observers see only the shape of a plan and can never make sufficient allowance for the unavoidable delays in its execution. Thus the six months from November 1942 to April 1943, were a period of impatient waiting for me. But the expected victory came and was on a scale which wholly destroyed the faith that my countrymen had put in the invincibility of Germany. Soon we were able to see the caravan of the German Commander-in-Chief, von Arnim, displayed in the park of Connaught Circus. Crowds went to see it. One fixed habit of Indians taken collectively is to rush to see any spectacle which promises fun, without caring whether it is for the triumph of a national leader or his death.

The inevitable result of the Allied victories in North Africa was that Indians lost their interest in the war, because it could no longer feed their anti-British feeling, and thus if they could help it they never talked about the war. I have already related how an elderly Bengali lost his faith in God after seeing the turn the war had taken. But if Indians show this persistent disinclination to face facts when these are unpleasant, that is not a hypocritical pretence. They become really anaesthetised as a man who is clawed by a tiger or lion does. That is why they have been able to bear all their historical misfortunes. Without the immunity given by their insensitiveness they would have been crushed by them.

Sicily and Italy

I watched the next step in the unfolding of Allied strategy without any surprise. After the occupation of North Africa Sicily was bound to be the next objective, and after Sicily Italy was sure to be invaded. But the delays imposed by the Germans in Italy surprised me even more than the delays in North Africa. One event which gave immediate satisfaction was the overthrow of Mussolini. However, his rescue by the Germans was an unpleasant surprise, although I could not but admire its skill and boldness. Nonetheless, in the end a tyrant's fate overtook Mussolini. As I had never liked Mussolini, not even after his advent to power in 1922, as most Bengalis had done, I cannot say I was shocked by his miserable end. I had in my young days almost wept over the death of Rienzi. But to compare Mussolini's end to Rienzi's would be an insult not only to Rienzi but even to Italy. A modicum of decency was shed on his ghastly end by the loyalty of his mistress. Faithfulness of mistresses to their princely lovers has also been seen in India. Curiously enough, this was to be seen even in the case of Hitler.

Invasion of France

It was, however, to the inevitable invasion of France that I looked forward with the utmost eagerness. I knew enough of military history to be able to understand what an achievement it would be if the invading forces could even establish a foothold on the French coast. Such a feat was unknown in history. Wellington had to begin by landing in Portugal, a friendly country. Hannibal had to march through France to reach Italy. Not to speak of the tactical problems but only of the logistic, transporting a force even across the Channel was bound to be more difficult than the advances over thousands of miles in the Pacific had been.

I was in Mr Barns's room talking with him when the broadcasts about the invasion were coming over the wireless set. I heard the heads of all the governments in exile speaking to their people about the possibility of landings, and more especially the King of Norway. Mr Barns left his room to give some directions to the news staff, and listening alone to the broadcasts I was very deeply moved, almost to the point of tears.

I felt confident about the outcome, but not so my countrymen. In fact, there was no question of their confidence in Allied military capacity to deal with the German forces in Europe. I have read that as soon as Hitler heard about the invasion on 6 June, he ordered that the invaders should be annihilated by the evening of the same day. My countrymen did not expect but assumed as a matter of course that they were. Even some of my colleagues, whose comfortable livelihood depended upon proclaiming the successes of the Allies, told me that the invasion had probably been repelled already and that we were being fed with false news.

I was given large-scale maps of France and Germany in order to be able to follow the operations. As the scale was four miles to an inch the sheets ran into hundreds. Carrying the required number in a roll under my arms and jumping out of the station wagon to go to my room, I felt as if I was a staff officer myself. Besides, the maps were very beautifully printed in colour and in themselves could be regarded as works of art. As it happened, I had almost an equal number of large-scale maps of Poland and western Russia.

We did not get much information, but even with what we were given I could follow the operations intelligently. The stubbornness of the fighting round Caen surprised me. I was very glad, however, to learn about the break-out by General Patton and of the liberation of Paris. By a curious chance I got a copy of the *Figaro* which resumed publication with the liberation of the city, and I still have the copy in which the event was reported.

Then followed a wholly unexpected phase of delay, which I must confess baffled me, and the news of the German offensive in the Ardennes region took me very much by surprise. It rekindled Indian hopes and even some of my English colleagues were anxious. When I told Colonel Hunt who was the liaison officer with us from the GHQ that the offensive was not serious he replied: 'But they have advanced *eighty* miles!' The reason why I was not very anxious was that I had studied the great German offensive which opened on 18 March 1918, and saw the Ardennes offensive as a recapitulation of that, i.e. a last desperate bid. Anyway it was checked, and the complete defeat of Germany followed. The German surrender in May surprised me only by being delayed, as I thought, by six months.

War in the Pacific

In the meantime, I was, of course, following the marvellous American operations in the Pacific. After the battle of Midway I had no further anxiety about the war against Japan, for the Japanese seemed to have shot their bolt. Nonetheless, at first it seemed as if the war would drag on for years. But here the speed of the advance surprised me. I could not have anticipated that, knowing what the distances were and also the spirit of the Japanese soldier. But I got the explanation by reading an account in an American magazine about the supply fleet which had been created by the Americans to overcome the disadvantage of not having land bases for sustaining the operation of the battle fleets. This was a marvellous demonstration of American technical ingenuity. With my romantic ideas about navies and warships, which I had acquired as a boy and which had been fostered by my serious study of naval warfare, I was naturally more interested in the naval battles than in the movements, and was thrilled by the news of the second battle of the Philippines, in which the Japanese fleet was virtually annihilated, and lost even the great *Musashi* through air attacks. I was able to read detailed accounts of it soon after.

But, of course, the Japanese spirit still remained, and one day I got a piece of news which seemed to indicate a certain change. I learned that for the first time Japanese prisoners had been taken, I forget whether that was in the Solomons or on some other island. So I thought that at last the Japanese were ready to surrender instead of dying in the last ditch. I felt inclined to crow in my commentary, but Mr Barns smiled and said that only two Japanese were taken; they had been gassed and were unconscious. So, no conscious Japanese had yet surrendered. This was a matter for forebodings.

Eastern India

After the Japanese occupation of Burma there was no attempt to invade India, as indeed I said even in early 1942. But suddenly the Japanese mounted an offensive on the frontier between Assam and Burma. It was launched to forestall a British advance into Burma, not to occupy India, as my countrymen thought. There was stiff fighting at two places, around Kohima in the Naga Hills and Imphal in Manipur. The Bengalis who had only been singing the marching song of the so-called Indian National Army under their beloved leader, Subhas Chandra Bose, now thought that he was actually coming. Even now they foolishly believe that it was the Indian National Army which fought at Kohima and Imphal.

One reason why I thought an overland invasion of India would not be attempted was that I had read in the military manuals prepared by the Army Headquarters in India that the Assam-Burma frontier was so impassable on account of its hills and jungles that it set no military problem. That was indeed true, and therefore I thought that the recovery of Burma would be attempted by means of a sea-borne invasion. Something like that on a small scale had also been undertaken in Arakan. That proved to be a blind alley, and when I spoke about that to Mr Barns he told me that the needs of the Italian front prevented any supply of landing-craft for the eastern campaigns.

Thus if Burma was to be recovered no alternative to a campaign on the Assam-Burma front was left. This was undertaken, and it succeeded. But the logistic task was not light. The Japanese could not tackle that at all, and even the British Indian authorities failed. Then the Americans took over the business of supplying, and controlled the railways in Assam and East Bengal. Besides, it was the American commander. General Stilwell, who at first undertook the difficult operation.

He was followed by the British 14th Army under Slim. The new offensive followed the Japanese failures at Kohima and Imphal. Its success only proved the old idea that to a resolute and resourceful army difficulties of terrain could never become insuperable. I felt great admiration for the direction of the campaign and performance of the soldiers, and I remember that in one of my commentaries I even quoted Kipling's 'Road to Mandalay'.

The Russian Front

Although as a commentator on the war in India I had to discuss mostly the campaigns on the borders of India and after that the invasion of France, I never lost interest in the Russian front on account of its military and human interest. This interest was more detached, because I was not interested in it as a partisan and could judge both its military magnitude and human tragedy more adequately. I think I can say that for the sheer scale of the operations, numbers engaged, courage shown by both sides and privation suffered, the fighting on the Russian front was a military phenomenon of unprecedented magnitude in grandeur as well as misery, and that not even the Western Front in the first World War surpassed it. What was more, there was no tedium in it. The sweep and speed of the operations, the flood-tides and ebb-tides of successes and failures were spectacular. Even with my dislike for Nazi Germany I thought it was a war between Titans.

It was 1812 magnified many times over. I saw a picture in the *Illustrated London News* of German soldiers crossing a river in Russia, and I could visualize the horrors of the crossing of the Beresina. I could also form some idea of what it meant to fight in the winter in Russia, because I was living in Delhi and there in the cold season the temperature reaches freezing point in the early mornings. Often I woke up at night and thought of the fighting in Russia out in the open.

Whatever might be my political allegiances, I would have been devoid of moral sensibility if I had refused to admit the quality of the human spirit on both sides. It was the human spirit seen at its most defiant which enabled Russia to confront the Germans. The German superiority in armament had to be neutralized by throwing Russian flesh against it, and the common Russian became cannon fodder out of his own free will. The opposition between the Russian people and the Romanov Czar that was seen in 1917 was not recapitulated as between a Communist Czar and his subjects. The Russians showed themselves at their best in their defence and not in their victories. So did the Germans from 1943 onwards. I had read in a book by General Wavell that the qualities of a commander are even better judged by what he does when reverses fall on him than when he wins victories. This seems to apply to nations as well. If a later Greek poet said that there was nothing more wonderful than man, old Homer said that there was no more piteous breed than man among all things that breathe and creep on earth. The Second World War proved both the sayings to be true.

End of the War

The end of the war in Europe put me in a tranquil mood. I remember that I took four days' leave from the office and just slept off the hangover from the strain of following it for years. Although the war with Japan was still continuing, by the time that Germany surrendered I had revised my ideas about the duration of the Pacific war. People were indeed saying that it might drag on for years, but I quite confidently gave it six months' duration. Of course, at the time I knew nothing about the development of the atom bomb, and the anxiety that I had felt at the beginning of the war about its manufacture and use had vanished from my mind because it had not been employed even in the direst situations of the war against Germany or Japan. I made my estimate of the duration of the Pacific war in the light of what is now called conventional war. I had seen enough of the technical capacity of the Americans and of their logistic ingenuity to be able to think that the Japanese could resist both for a long time, especially when the undivided strength of the United States could now be deployed against Japan.

But I was surprised by the dropping of the atom bomb on Hiroshima. However, owing to my previous interest in atomic fission I was able to write a plausible commentary on its use within hours of the receipt of the news. The second bomb on Nagasaki followed quickly. After this I did not think that the Japanese would continue the war. The only question was whether they would surrender or commit national harakiri. There could be no doubt that the Japanese army would have gone on fighting in the southern theatres of war and the Japanese people too would not have flinched from collective suicide had it not been for the leaders and more especially the Emperor. His broadcast message convinced the Japanese army that there was no alternative to surrender. Some years later I heard a repetition of it.

I must set down here my admiration for the Japanese leaders. In that hour of crisis for their people they showed the greatest patriotism by counselling surrender and thereby choosing death for themselves rather than allowing their people to perish. Some of them knew that although they were opposed to the war in 1941, the Americans would exact their vengeance on all of them. This was wholly consistent with the Japanese notion of patriotism. The Allies did not show themselves at their best or most humane in hanging them or driving them to death. Of course, the Japanese did not refrain from inhumanity in war, but if they were hard on their enemies they were not less so on themselves. And later, in Vietnam, the Americans did not show themselves to be more humane than the Japanese.

At that time I had no qualms about the employment of the atomic bomb, which created a strange mood of mea-culpism in the West. After the Allied victory over Japan through the employment of the bomb, there was bound to be a condemnation by India of its use. But that was not from moral shock. My old chief, Sarat Bose, declared soon after that those who had used the bomb should be tried as war criminals. I had no patience with such views. I said quite openly that if a war was right there was every justification for adopting the most effective means of waging it and ending it. No man in his senses will think that war is anything but an evil which should be avoided but cannot be. But if that is so, all means to obtain a quick decision should also be employed. I did not believe at the time, nor do I now, that the employment of atomic or nuclear weapons would result in the annihilation of mankind, and would not be transformed into a rational means of waging war. The moral issue raised by this weapon is not unique. I have seen nearly a million people murdered with knives, spears, and cudgels in India in one year. I cannot admit that this was more humane or morally admissible than killing, say, a quarter of a million with an atom bomb. If men in their folly would kill one another in such numbers, the sooner mankind perished and left the world to the birds and beasts the better it would be for all living creatures.

A Letter from Prison

I do not exactly remember the date, but it must have been towards the beginning of 1944 that one evening, when it was rather late, my servant brought in a visitor. He was a casual acquaintance of mine from my Calcutta days, a Marwari businessman named Lala Shankar Lal, who was a supporter of Subhas Bose and his Forward Bloc. I saw him occasionally in Sarat Babu's house. He surprised me by putting a letter into my hands, which from the handwriting on the envelope I saw was from my former chief Sarat Bose, who was in prison. Lala Shankar Lal explained that he had gone to see Sarat Babu in prison and had been given this letter for me. It was a smuggled letter.

When I read it after Shankar Lal was gone I was still more surprised. It was a long letter, and in it Sarat Babu asked me to resign from my government job and work for his release. He also said that I should not have to regret my loss of job if he was released. I could not understand why he thought I should be able to do anything. I had neither connections nor influence. But he may have remembered what I had done after his arrest in 1941.

Thinking over the matter, I at last decided to take my English superior into confidence, although I could not resign my post. So I went to Mr Barns and showed him the letter. He did not ask me how I had got it, but told me that he would make inquiries. After a few days he informed me that he had sounded the authorities, and was told that there could be no question of releasing Sarat Bose as long as the war was on.

There the matter ended, although it might have had unpleasant results both for Sarat Babu and for myself if the question of my getting such a letter from a prison were pursued. Obviously, those whom Mr Barns had consulted did not do so, and I was right in trusting Englishmen. An Indian official, however high-placed, would not have taken up the matter for fear of coming under suspicion, and he might also have raised awkward questions.

After some months I sent the letter to Mrs Bose in Calcutta, through a trustworthy person, because I did not think it was advisable for me to keep it. If the news leaked out it could be harmful to me as well as Sarat Babu. I had also another reason for not keeping the letter. At that time I was confirmed in my post in the Government's service for the duration of the war, and this necessitated screening by the police. I was told nothing about this for some months. But when the inquiry was over Mr Barns told me that my confirmation had not gone through smoothly. The political police raised serious objections to my reliability on account of my previous political associations. Even before I became Sarat Bose's secretary I was connected with other political bodies, as I have related. So I was a political suspect, and would in normal circumstances have been asked to leave. Some others in the News Department in which I was, had been dismissed on political grounds. But Sir Frederic Puckle, who was Secretary to the Information Department (which controlled the broadcasting organization), at once took up the matter. He said that it would be absurd to dismiss a man for political unreliability whose articles were the basis of the Government's war propaganda in India. That was obviously a reference to my articles in *The Statesman* in 1940. Mr Barns further told me that Sir Frederic and he had settled the matter between them, without alarming me by telling me beforehand, and that now everything was all right. But he also added with a smile that it seemed I had associated with some very queer people and that I had better keep clear of them in the future. I assured him that I would. That was the additional reason why I had sent the letter to Mrs Bose. I have been told by one of her sons that the letter is not in existence. Mrs Bose must have burnt it.

Human Hecatomb to the Nth Degree

The Greeks, the Romans, and the Hindus – all had animal sacrifice as an important feature of their religion. The Hindus and the Romans had, with one exception, identical animals: man, horse, cattle, sheep for both, but goat for the Hindus and pig for the Romans. Among these, man was considered the best sacrifice by the Hindus of the earliest age, because, as one of their texts declared, 'Man is the first among beasts.' I became familiar with the spectacle of animal sacrifice by seeing actual killings in my ancestral home and by looking at representations in Greek and Roman art. It was one of these representations which made Keats write:

> Who are these coming to the sacrifice?
> To what green altar, O mysterious priest,
> Lead'st thou that heifer lowing at the skies,
> And all her silken flanks with garland drest?
> What little town by river or sea-shore.
> Or mountain-built with peaceful citadel.
> Is emptied of its folk, this pious morn?
> And, little town, thy streets for evermore
> Will silent be; and not a soul, to tell
> Why thou art desolate, can e'er return.

The Romans abolished human sacrifice formally by a *Senatus Consultum* of 97 BC, after having had their last formal sacrifice after the defeat at Cannae at the hands of Hannibal. The Hindus also gave it up openly fairly early in their history. But there is evidence to show that it continued secretly even down to the nineteenth century. In any case, the belief among the common people of India was that no great building work could be carried to completion without human sacrifice, and so they assumed that for every one of their buildings, especially for the bridges over the great rivers, the British engineers had sacrificed a native or two.

But upper-class Indians never thought that they were really asking for human sacrifice when they wanted the British Government in India to admit Indians to the highest cadres of its services, especially the Indian Civil Service. The British administrators themselves, whether in India or Britain, did not favour this, but they were compelled by the Proclamation of 1858 of Queen Victoria, which declared that no Indian would be debarred from entering the highest ranks of the services by reason of his race, colour, or religion. So it happened that in 1864 the first Indian entered the ICS. He was a Bengali and brother of the great poet Rabindranath Tagore. The admissions were a trickle at the beginning, but increased in numbers with the decades and by the Thirties of this century Indians were in every branch of the services, civil or military. But strange to relate, neither the British side nor the Indian perceived that an awful human sacrifice had been introduced into Indian life figuratively. Hecatomb would be a weak word for the slaughter.

Amazingly, the sacrificial steers (to be followed by the sacrificial heifers) did not simply go to the bloody altar lowing at the skies, but literally prancing with joy at their self-immolation. It reminds me of a legend which was taken as true by everybody in my part of Bengal. It was about what happened at a famous shrine of Kali in my mother's district in a village called Mehar. They said that when the goats brought there for sacrifice to Kali were ranged on the far side of the courtyard and the door of the temple was thrown open, the goat at the right end of the line ran forward, staring at the eyes of the goddess, and placed its neck on the sacrificial frame for its head to be chopped off by the priest, standing by the side with his scimitar. One by one, all the goats did this, and I was told by a man who claimed to be an eyewitness that this did happen.

However that might be, the most promising young men in India certainly ranged themselves in the courtyard of Mother Bureaucracy of India and seeing her tongue lolling out for their blood, rushed forward and immolated themselves. This awful hecatomb is continuing, taking toll of the best talent that is born in India.

When I joined All India Radio's News Division in Delhi, I saw a large number of very fine young men among my colleagues, but did not perceive then that they were offering themselves for this new human sacrifice. My colleagues fell into two types: the first, easily recognizable as belonging to the journalist or writer type – unprepossessing in looks and clothes, but clever-looking; there was another group of handsome young men, all very well-dressed, well-groomed, and urbane, not looking particularly clever, but attractive. They had come from the ranks of the Indians holding high posts in the administration. A majority of them were from the Punjab, and among them the Muslim young men were particularly attractive. They seemed to fulfil the wish I had cherished in my mind that our young men should look like the youths on the friezes of the Parthenon. The Hindu young men were equally well-dressed and groomed, but like all Punjabi Hindus had a cunning worldliness exuding through the pores of their young and fair skins. I had never seen young men from the highest Indian official order in Calcutta, and so assumed the presence of the highest idealism in them. They themselves showed themselves to be self-confident and ambitious, and so I expected that they would fulfil the promise they showed by achievement. But not one of them has done that. All of them have sunk into highly paid bureaucratic obscurity. And those who are now responsible for the government of India are the sons of those failures. Yet the most extraordinary fact about them is their self-satisfaction, amounting to an incredible snobbery.

Their behaviour I shall explain only by taking recourse to my literary manner. I have a recording of the songs of the Troubadours whom Dante knew in life or met in Inferno. One of them was Bertran de Born. When going through Inferno with Virgil, Dante saw him standing below a bridge, but with his severed head held aloft and forward with a raised and outstretched arm, and speaking through that head. He told Dante that he had to suffer this punishment because he had incited a son to rebel against his father – to particularize, John against his father Henry II, the English king. In one of my editions of Dante, very finely illustrated with drawings by Botticelli, this scene is beautifully shown.

All the contemporary bureaucrats of India remind me of this drawing. Their heads are severed, not simply because they have themselves rebelled against their British bureaucratic fathers, but also for a reason of their own. Their mouths have to utter all the false justification of Indian rule in India, without the interference of the flesh and blood in their bodies. So, the heads and the bodies have to remain severed forever. And it must be admitted to their credit, that what comes out of the severed heads not only hoodwinks the people of India but also the British Foreign Office, which has totally changed its character since the days of Sir Eyre Crowe.

BOOK IX

VICTOR-VICTIM

1945-1947

Prefatory Note

I triumphed when, falsifying every expectation of my countrymen, Britain declared war on Germany on 3 September 1939, and my satisfaction lost nothing of its keenness at witnessing the discomfiture they felt at being deprived of the pleasure of gloating over British cowardice. I felt even more proud when the British people went on fighting alone, in this, too, depriving my countrymen of their second expectation of joy. As I have told that story in full, I need not repeat it.

During the war I was too preoccupied with its ups and downs to think about what would happen when it would end victoriously. But if I had applied my mind to the question I should not have had any doubts or anxieties about the future. The latest assumption in my mind, which in spite of being, logically, only an assumption and nothing more solid, was nonetheless a conviction. I felt that the heroism, intellectual competence, and scientific inventiveness which was being displayed by the British people during the war would be extended, when peace came, to the creation of a better world, which had been missed after the First World War. I could not imagine a repetition of that failure.

But my confidence in the British people and my hopes for a greater future for them was shaken in less than three months after the end of the war with Germany, and even before the war with Japan was over. I shall presently relate what created the misgiving in my mind. I could in no way resist the premonition which was rising in it like a dark cloud. This quite unexpectedly reawakened in me the fear which had haunted me since my young days of a great defeat lurking in a great victory.

Nearly forty years have passed by since I received that shock, and today I can see that the warning, disturbing as it was to me then, was yet no real indication of what was actually to happen. I can also see that I had every reason to be dismayed as I was, even by the forewarning omen of the future that I saw, for the ultimate result of that victorious war has been a stark fact the passing away of the greatness of the British people. I have read of no war in all history in which a nation after winning one has suffered even more than the worst of the defeated. That had nothing to do with the actual injuries inflicted by the war. The Russians suffered worse injuries during the war, but have risen to a new greatness. Except that honour would have been lost, nothing could have been worse for the British people if they had not gone to war in 1939: and in that I had gloried!

After the superhuman efforts of six years the will of the British people suddenly failed, and it is this – not the injuries received in those years – which destroyed the greatness of Britain. Thus, to this result, I can apply the words of the seventeenth-century English poet, James Shirley:

> Some men with swords may reap the field,
> And plant fresh laurels where they kill:
> But their strong nerves at last must yield;...
>
> When they, pale captives, creep to death.

This has also proved the truth of what Churchill said in 1940, but not in the sense he meant it. The British people still have the right to remember 1940 as their finest hour. That, it was and will remain, because what they did then was to choose the role of martyrs for civilization. Living at Oxford nowadays, I see the Martyrs' Memorial almost every day at St Giles. At the other end of the vista stands the War Memorial to the dead of two wars. That, too, should be renamed Martyrs' Memorial, because the Second World War was an act of expiatory self-immolation by the British people for their mistakes from 1919 to 1939. If that was glorious, it was no less tragic, so that to describe it I can again quote Shirley:

> The garlands wither on your brow;
> Then boast no more your mighty deeds!
> Upon Death's purple altar now,
> See where the victor-victim bleeds.

CHAPTER I

How Fear Came

I have now to relate how at the end of the war fear pushed out the confidence about the future of the British people which I had felt throughout its course. I suddenly realized then that there was going to be no new morning for them, but only an evening, perhaps followed by a dark night. It was the General Elections of July 1945, which created the fear. I heard the news on the 27th that Churchill had resigned and was to be succeeded by Attlee. I was shocked, because I could never imagine that the British people would so unceremoniously reject the man who had led them to victory from an almost hopeless situation. But at first it was not the domestic implications of the elections but their impact on the external greatness of Britain which aroused my misgivings. The shock given to my complacent mood made me fall back on the same resource I had taken to when faced with the disaster of 1940: that is to say, I tried to arrive at an intellectual understanding of the elections. It seemed to me that by totally ignoring the possibility of danger from the home front I had acted like the one-eyed deer. I was not cowed by 1940, but 1945 frightened me.

Intellectually, however, I rallied quickly. I learned about the change of government in Britain, as I have said, on 27 July and by I August I had written an article of about 3,500 words on the elections. With a total disregard of practical possibilities I sent it to the *Daily Telegraph* the same day. I cannot even now explain how, with my knowledge and experience of journalism, I could have expected such an article to be published. Of course, it was not. But the editor returned it with a very courteous note. After reading it now, I find that I have no reason to be ashamed of the adumbrations which I had set down within four days of hearing about the sweeping victory of Labour.

I would summarize what I said in that article, because, though unpublished, it was the starting point of my new thinking about the future of Britain. So far as the domestic aspect was concerned, I did not at first think that the elections had departed from the familiar historical pattern. I said that elections in Britain since the Reform Act of 1832 could be divided into two kinds: the first of which, following the zoological analogy in respect of heredity, I called regular variations, and the second mutations. The Whig and Liberal victories of 1830 and 1906 I regarded as two examples of the latter kind. Their aetiology I diagnosed as follows:

'Elections of the mutation type have always taken place when there has been a conjunction of the three following conditions, viz. (i) a strong conviction of social, economic, and political maladjustments; (ii) the formulation or adoption of an ideology which seemed to assure a way out of the difficulties; and (iii) long suppression of the urge for change.'

I also described the period of gestation of the new ideas. Such periods, I said, were always long and hardly perceived and therefore the ultimate outcome appeared to be sensational. I continued:

'Their embryology is fairly well known. A body of novel doctrines, partly indigene but predominantly foreign is put forward and evokes violent opposition from their novelty and strangeness. But since it appears to suggest remedies for concrete ills perceived and deplored by everybody, the ideas continue to be canvassed. They lose their strangeness, are adapted to the local conditions and traditions, and gain in popularity and plausibility. As their influence grows, so also grows the feeling of frustration at these ideas not being embodied in the political order. There is an almost intolerable tension. Suddenly relief comes through an election and through it a typical British revolution is accomplished: a revolution which is closed before it has begun, whose task is only spring-cleaning on a grand scale and tidying up, in which the victorious party sets to work under the joyous belief that the ideas of yesterday are ideas of tomorrow, and the defeated party awakes with relief, though under compulsion, to the realization that the ideas it had considered dangerous were not so terrible after all, and that it had lost the race only by the length of a neck.'

Such a process, I said, had brought about the Labour victory of 1945. For one thing, the socialistic doctrine, which had gained both influence and prestige through the Russian Revolution of 1917 and also by the military achievement of the Soviet Union in the Second World War, had become acclimatized as a national doctrine. Secondly, by 1945, the Labour Party had been recognized as a possible alternative to the Conservatives in the British two-party system of government. This recognition Labour had not been able to establish by its two previous periods in office, and had done this only through its participation in the Coalition Government from 1940 onwards. Thus, I added:

'The Coalition Government of Mr Churchill has as thoroughly rehabilitated the two-party system as Mr Lloyd George's government had discredited it... Thus what was not possible before has become possible now – Labour has become the complement of Tories. The Conservative Party, though momentarily out of power, may draw satisfaction from the fact that in the national interest during the war they overlooked the dictum of Machiavelli in which he says that whoever is the cause of another becoming powerful, is ruined himself.'

So, I concluded that the Labour victory was no freak, and that a number of far-reaching legislative and administrative measures will be put through until the basic national demands for reform were satisfied. Continuing, I also said that the day of the Conservatives was not over and Leftism had not come to stay in the fulfilment of any inexorable law of historical necessity. As I put the matter: 'On the contrary, the Conservatives have as much of a future as the Labourites ... In due course, the need for order, stability, and serenity is bound to be felt and the Conservatives will be called to power to satisfy that psychological necessity.'

But I did not think it likely that Churchill would be returned to power, because, as I observed, in the normal working of British party politics, there was very little room for the exceptional man. In this I was mistaken, but was Churchill as he showed himself from 1951 to 1955, the exceptional man of 1940? At the time of my first visit to England in 1955, I saw Churchill in what was perhaps his last appearance in the House of Commons (early in April) and I recorded the impression in my book on England in these words: 'He looked very much like his figure on a Toby jug, but was much more rosy, white-haired, and childlike than I could have imagined him to be. It was surprising how successfully he had divested himself of all atmosphere, of all suggestion of being not only a writer, historian, and political thinker, but also a statesman and war leader.' I meant these words to be complimentary, and not censorious, as if he was an English incarnation of one of the early heroes of Rome, Cincinnatus.*

* This passage was written long before the publication of the Colville diaries, *The Fringes of Power*, in September 1985. I think Colville's account of Churchill's second term as Prime Minister to a great extent justifies my anticipation.

But I had misgivings about the significance of the Labour victory on the external position of Great Britain, because I felt that Labour would not be able to assess the threat to it which was bound to emerge with the end of the war, nor to meet that successfully. As I summed up the situation in the unpublished article:

'Hungry mouths are waiting in India, in the Middle East, in the Far East, in the Balkans, in the rest of Europe, in fact all over the world for food to drop from the hands of Labour. The Labour leaders will not be able to satisfy the demands without literally giving all British interests away .. .Great Britain's position in the society of Great Powers is especially weak for this reason that she is the only one among them who cannot represent herself as a 'have-not'. The victorious and mighty Russia is a great 'have-not'. So is China. The United States is perhaps the greatest of all of them, not through unsatisfied wants but through unsatisfied power. So almost all the concessions will be demanded at the cost of Great Britain. If she concedes them all she would cease to be a Great Power. And if she resisted she might find a world coalition, a moral coalition, if not a military coalition, ranged against her.'

In such a situation, I thought, the most obvious weakness, not only of Great Britain, but of the Western democratic countries as a whole, lay in the absence of great personalities. This was how I put it:

'The retirement of Mr Churchill, following the death of Mr Roosevelt, leaves only M. Stalin in the field as a leader with the established power and prestige of a great figure in war as well as peace. And M. Stalin is a nationalist – super-nationalist. Mr Roosevelt and Mr Churchill were in a very true sense world statesmen. Now that they are gone there will be no one to balance the nationalism of the great, the towering Russian.'

I did not know then that even Roosevelt was no match for Stalin. In any case, he had disappeared, and I did not consider Attlee or Truman to be capable of confronting (in the current meaning of the word) Stalin.

For the British people, my greatest source of anxiety was my appraisement of their postwar mood as indicated by the election. I thought that they had lost interest in the war, and I also put to myself a further question:

'Is it necessary to go further and assume that through war-weariness and overstrain they have been too impatient to tread the *via dolorosa* of peace?

That in 1945 they have been as eager to forget the war and enter the brave new world as in 1918 they were eager to forget the war and get back to the good old days? To answer these questions in the affirmative is to acquiesce in a second-rate destiny for Britain and to recognize the inevitability of another inter-war stretch of barren endeavour. The mind shrinks from both, so one must close on a note of interrogation, but equally one of profound disquiet.'

All that was written before 1 August 1945 and my misgivings about the future of Britain had as their complement a feeling of anxious uncertainty about Europe, i.e. Europe in the strict sense of the term – continental Europe. To this, too, I gave expression in print soon after. At that time a friend of mine in Calcutta was running a quarterly journal called *The Hindoosthan Quarterly*, and he asked me to give him an article on the postwar situation. Wishing to ventilate my ideas, I gave him one entitled *The Future of Europe*, which was written soon after the piece on the British elections and published in the July-September (1945) issue of the quarterly magazine. I began it with these words:

'The thoughtful student of international affairs cannot help the feeling that what he is facing in Europe is an anti-climax after the grand climax of victory. Nothing of any importance appears to be happening there. To the sorely tried peoples of Europe this must be a chilling experience. What the ardent European hoped to see, after the hard up-hill struggle, was a vision of the plain into which he was moving... But what he actually sees is different. Or rather he does not see much. The descent before him appears to be as difficult as the ascent, judging by the short visible stretch; and after that hangs a thick pall of impenetrable mist.'

Continuing, I suggested an explanation and said that it was 'to be found in the absence in contemporary Europe of powerful revolutionary forces'. I elaborated this statement as follows:

'Despite the superficial prattle about the rising tide of democracy, freedom, Leftism, and what not in Europe, the absence of revolutionary fervour is precisely the thing which distinguishes the Europe following the second World War from the Europe following the first. Where are the Lenins, the Trotskys, the Karl Liebknechts, the Rosa Luxemburgs, and the Bela Kuns of today? The atmosphere was tense and electric in 1918 and 1919. It is nothing like that at present. After 1917, Russia was an inspiration and a bogey at the same time. The Leftist movements of contemporary Europe are tame and humdrum in comparison.'

When I wrote that I recollected my own state of mind after 1918, which I later embodied in my autobiography in a short passage which I would quote: 'Europe', I wrote,

'was becoming a living furnace of revolutions. The more I tried to avoid thinking of the meteoric personalities and flaming names of the post-war revolutionary movements in Europe – the Lenins, the Trotskys, the Bela Kuns, the Rosa Luxemburgs, the Karl Liebknechts – the more they forced me to take note of them . . . Both for personal and public reasons I was yearning for quiet, repose, and serenity at the time, and the fear of having to wait for it made me sick.'

In 1945 I had no such feeling in my mind. On the contrary, in that article I wrote emphatically that 'none of the three Great Powers which are controlling the destinies of post-war Europe (or for that matter of the world) is interested in a revolution. What they want to avoid most is a political vacuum and the resulting political explosion.' I added that the Big Three countries, of which Soviet Russia was one, would not have been able to pursue a non-revolutionary policy had there been real revolutionary feeling in Europe. The possibility which I dismissed with a figurative wave of hand was that of a Communist-Capitalist clash. As to that I wrote: 'The Communist formula of a conflict between Capitalism and Communism leading to a class-less society, which has been accepted by many as the inescapable mould of social evolution, furnishes no answer to this question: What is going to happen to Europe when the immediate task of internal reconstruction will have been accomplished.? In fact, the orthodox Marxist formula is breaking down every day before the facts of contemporary history.' As I was to write about British Leftism later, I also said about European Leftism that its face was turned backwards.

The political future, I thought, was going to take shape from another phenomenon. 'A new world of Power', I wrote, 'is rising in America and in eastern Europe and northern Asia. The United States and the Soviet Union are the protagonists of this new world, each in a different way.' As to

Europe, I said: 'What place the intermediate European Powers will occupy in this parallel evolution is the great unsolved mystery of today.' I would remind the readers that these observations were set down within days of the end of the war. In another year I could see more clearly, at all events in regard to Britain. I realized with sorrow that not only was her greatness going to disappear, but that British internal politics was also to acquire a sinister character.

CHAPTER 2

Testament on England

I have now been driven back on the conclusion, because I can in no way resist it, that the greatness of the British people has passed away for ever, and the only question now is whether their last days would be serene and honourable and, hoping for the best, will be lit up by the glow of a sunset. Although certainty about this has come to me step by step, that has not been due to what is called 'hindsight' in these days. Let me, however, say bluntly that as an observer of human affairs I am not afraid of having this gibe, an illiterate neologism, thrown in my teeth by those who are afraid to face mistakes because they have lost confidence in their ability to deal with dangerous situations. On the contrary, the faculty derided as hindsight is a means of survival for individuals as well as nations. To be human is also to be prone to mistakes, as the proverb has it. But the only means of avoiding new mistakes is to discover past mistakes by a critical retrospect. The surest sign of loss of vitality by an individual or nation is to be taken by surprise by an eventuality which could have been anticipated.

But in my case, although full conviction came after the event, I had correct presages from the beginning. The presages about the decline of Britain came to me at the very time of which I am writing, that is, just after the war, as I have recorded. In this chapter I shall set down what I thought when the premonition crystallized into perception.

More and more alarmed by the unfolding of Labour's policy and actions in foreign as well as domestic affairs, I again sought refuge in letting my adumbrations settle down to conclusions, and setting them down in writing. This I did in the middle of 1946. I wrote three articles in quick succession like the last three symphonies of Mozart, but alas! all in the dark minor keys. I sent them to the *New English Review*, then edited by Douglas Jerrold and Sir Charles Petrie. All of them were accepted and published in three consecutive issues of the magazine – those of November and December, 1946, and January, 1947. Their titles were respectively: 'The Future of Imperialism'; 'Permanent Conservatism'; and '"Stasis" in England'.

At that time my mind was oppressed by a *malaise* over two questions: the possibility of the disappearance of British rule in India; and the decline of the greatness of the British people. In 1946 I was not wholly sure that the withdrawal from India was imminent. Nonetheless, I could see that the British will to keep India, which had been reiterated to the point of stupidity during the two previous decades, was collapsing with equal stupidity. It seemed to me that the balance sheet for the liquidation was being drawn up and the winding up was only a matter of time. This irritated me, but being compelled to face the prospect, which had become virtually a certainty, I tried to make myself resigned to the end of the Indian Empire by defiantly proclaiming my faith in empires as creators and preservers of civilization in the first article. As this historical conclusion lay at the back of my mind while observing the process of that disappearance as it unfolded, I shall make the thesis of the article the prologue to my account of the process of disintegration. In this chapter I shall describe how I continued my thinking on the domestic situation of the British people, deep misgivings about which had arisen in my mind with the elections of 1945.

On this subject, I had by that time arrived at two conclusions which took me further from the tentative ideas of 1945. In the first place, I thought that only one choice of political principle and party lay before the British people in their new predicament, and that was Conservatism and the Conservative Party; next to that, I thought that the character of English party politics had changed basically although retaining the old pattern outwardly. It had now become a class conflict, to which I gave the Greek definition 'Stasis'. I shall summarize the arguments of the two articles in reversed order, dealing first with the class conflict.

I called British Leftism a 'reactionary movement' with no role in the future. The magnitude of the Leftist movement in 1945, I said, was a seasonal feature. In its European aspect, British Leftism was a reaction against Fascism and Nazism, and was fulfilling its historical function of cancelling the legacy of these two aberrations. It was, I added, 'a short-term mobilization of short-term and easily grasped ideas for the sole purpose of continuing the war in the sphere of ideas'.

In its domestic aspect, the strength of British Leftism lay in the urge for reform, the reform of certain specific ills which were felt in the inter-war years but in that period of strange stagnancy of English political life were left unattended. 'In this aspect sturdy English Labour', I observed, 'was no more frightening than Thomas Hardy's Farmer Oak married to the widowed Bathsheba.' But the doctrinaire Leftist I equated with Sergeant Troy.

My final judgement was that even at its best English Leftism was a past- regarding movement. As I put it: 'Although Labour itself is working under the joyous belief that its ideas are the ideas of tomorrow, an outside observer gets the impression of seeing the past reversed in a mirror.' I set down emphatically: 'The Labour administration is going to close an era, not open a new one.'

But by reason of its very power through office the Leftist movement had other implications. The Labour Party, I said, was not homogeneous and I further observed: 'The party lines in English politics have still to take their final shape.' An examination of the composition of the Labour Party, I said, led to the discovery that the more destructive part of Labour activities were due to a particular section. The great majority of Labour members, I wrote, were safe party men, and had no inclination towards 'stasis' or class conflict. But there were others for whom this 'stasis' was the very breath of their nostrils, the soul of politics. They were the so-called doctrinaire socialists, a majority of whom were maladjusted scions of the ruling class. Their hatred of the parental association was making them forget even the instinct of self-preservation.

In support of this contention I quoted from the editorial in the *New Statesman and Nation* (4 July 1942, p. 1), to which I have already referred.*

Then I commented: 'A man with the normal outlook and character of an Englishman might ask what use it was defending the Persian Gulf after the Mediterranean, Egypt, Suez Canal, and India were lost.' But, of course, I knew the answer and wrote: 'Persian oil was necessary for Russia.'

The same aversion to the parental association, I continued, was at the bottom of 'the clamour for a second front at a time when it would have proved disastrous to the British people without benefiting anybody.' And I added: 'After the war the self-same emotional predisposition is impelling British Leftists to make common cause with everybody who wants to injure and humiliate Britain.' I wrote: 'Whether it be a white, yellow, brown, or black enemy of Great Britain, for everyone of these the British Leftist seems to have a fellow-feeling which he does not have for the parental clan.'

This, I thought, would lead in the first instance to the destruction of the external greatness of Great Britain. However, I did not fear such a

* See p.696

consequence for British policy in Europe. I thought, if it came to that, the Labour Government would resist the Soviet Union, but in the case of India, the attitude would be different. As I put the matter: 'I have a feeling that Labour's Indian policy is being shaped entirely by its Left wing, or at all events by the fear of the Left wing, and *that the India Office is having to provide the ransom for the Foreign Office.*'

I also thought that Labour's policies would impinge with the same destructive consequence on the commercial and industrial status of Great Britain, on the highest standard of living of the British people, and, above all, on the primary motive force of British greatness – the spirit of personal enterprise. 'The question of questions', I observed, 'was whether by aiming at equality at an average level, both for the nation and the individual, the socialists will not destroy all incentive to effort.'

All this, I thought, betokened the existence of a 'stasis' in England: the decline of simplicity, the growth of the spirit of faction, and, above all, the attenuation of that condition – regarded by Plato as the mark of the best-ordered state – in which the greatest number of persons apply the terms 'mine' and 'not mine' in the same way to the same thing.

'The presence of an element with a definite frustration bias within the governing party of today,' I observed, 'is a very significant development in English politics. This is without precedent.' And this, I thought, was threatening English party politics with a fatal retrogression – a class war aimed at the establishment of an one-party dictatorship.

Having arrived at this view in my attempt to understand the nature of English party politics as it revealed itself after the general election of 1945, I followed the bent of my character by preaching a sermon to the British people about the choice of a party. I called it 'Permanent Conservatism' and took an aphorism of Pascal's as its text. It was the following: 'César était trop vieil, ce me semble, pour s'aller amuser à conquérir le monde; cet amusement était bon à Auguste ou a Alexandre, c'était des jeunes gens, qu'il est difficile d'arrêter, mais César devait être plus mûr.'

And the hortatory message derived from it was as follows:

'There is surely a hint for the English people in this subtle aphorism of Pascal's. Perhaps the moral could be made more explicit. It could be put in the form of a proposition that a time will soon come, if it has not already arrived, when the sole choice of political principles and methods left to the

English people will be Conservatism of one sort or another. At the present stage of their national evolution, and in the existing state of their relationship to the rest of the world, Conservatism will be for them both a virtue and a necessity.'

This view of mine was based on the realization, as I put it then, that 'a politics of adventure is the natural politics of a young nation which has developed a large reserve of power in isolation and thereby acquired an egocentric preoccupation.' Secondly, I added, 'a politics of adventure is a practical policy for those states alone whose territories and population are geographically concentrated and who can throw themselves on the outer world without risk to large external interests.' What the British people should aim at in the existing conditions of their national life was 'repose in strength'. 'The main task,' I observed, 'was to rescue English politics from a fussiness and sentimental effervescence unbecoming of its maturity and endow it with a mellowness, serenity, and ease consistent with that maturity.' 'There could be no greater pity in history', I said, 'than for a great nation to have its maturity wearing only the flippant simper of the demagogue or the drawn unloveliness of the doctrinaire. Every great nation expects its maturity to be crowned by a golden Augustanism. Perhaps it may still come, but the signs are not propitious.'

So, it will be seen that I was anxious about the future of the British people. My fears were due to my deep distrust of Socialistic fanaticism. Referring to the claim of Labour that they had a policy and a plan, and the Tories had none, I observed that 'if it is a question of laying down the law for the imponderable and unforeseeable, of throwing a Utopia at the head of the unknown, the Leftists have an arguable case. There they have an advantage, not only over the Conservatives but over all denominations of scientific intelligence, because they can confuse a *theory* of historical evolution with the *fact* of historical evolution and, while the rational mind is painfully manipulating a searchlight to find out what lies ahead out in the darkness, they can switch on the cinema projector of their doctored brains to see a perfectly formed picture.'

But my preference for Conservatism was not to be confused with any partiality for the official Conservative Party. I had seen what it was capable of doing from 1922 to 1939, and had no respect for it. I did not identify conservatism with any official party, and thought it was a state of mind or a particular method of dealing with historical situations, and such a state of mind could be found as much among the Labourites as among the Tories. But I was emphatic that on the plane of principle and method there was no conceivable common ground on which the true Conservative and true Leftist could meet, for they differed fundamentally in their approach to life. I defined the contrast in the following words:

'The one brings to bear on it a dogma and a system; the other only the mind. The one is pledged to accomplish a revolution – that is to say, to break the link between the past and the future – and is yet in bonds to the present and the recent past; the other, with all its awareness and piety for the past, brings nothing from it beyond an added sensibility to the drifts of the current and presages for the future. The one possesses a high degree of specialization and offers a plausible finality; the other cannot force reality into a mould and can only wait and see. The one contemplates the world with a winkless, unafraid stare; the other is dazzled by too much light and is infinitely sensitive to gradations. These differences are vital, and thanks to them, the Leftist will always scoff at the Conservative for having nothing tangible to offer; the Conservative will anxiously feel that, while his method is that of life, his rival has abstracted only one aspect of it, and made it wooden into the bargain. These opposed qualities are not complementaries, but contraries.'

I took the analysis a little further and said that the Conservatives and the Leftists would show further divergences, because the two schools of thought had no common foundation, as had Conservatism and Liberalism.

'Despite all the differences between the two older parties, the Conservatives stood closer to the Liberal than to the old Continental Absolutist tradition. But the British Leftists, owing to their Teutonic and Russic inspiration, have progressed so far towards the new Continental Absolutism that a return to the theory of Divine Right is not altogether a fantastic anticipation. In this Divine Right *redivivus* the majority certainly will, even one party may, claim infallibility and universal allegiance. In such conditions party government cannot be possible, for a pendulum will not swing unless its two halves are symmetrical and evenly balanced.'

I do not think that all this was a bad guess at the future, or unfair as a working historical hypothesis. But I would add to this analysis a more explicit statement about the emotional motive power behind British Leftism: it is driven by class hatred, which is akin to the nationalistic or xenophobic hatred in India. My familiarity with the Indian hatred made me capable of perceiving the existence and extent of the British hatred.

Of course, nobody in England paid any heed to the articles. But, at all events. Sir Charles Petrie paid me a very handsome compliment after getting the last article. He wrote: 'I am delighted to have it, and the highest compliment I can pay you is to say that it is as good as its predecessors.' As for myself, I had relieved my mind of a great load. There are situations in which silence, instead of being golden, becomes leaden or worse, i.e. abjuration of moral responsibility and rank cowardice.

It must not be imagined, however, that I had finally rid my mind of my fear about the future of the British people. It has continued to haunt me until today; now I have ceased to worry by being certain. I shall conclude this chapter by anachronistically bringing forward some events outside the time-limits of this book in order to show how far my thinking about the national destiny of the British people took me. Convinced as I was of the relentless course of British decline, in 1955 I was suddenly and unexpectedly brought in physical contact with the British scene and situation and led to question my theory of decadence for the time being. In that year the British Broadcasting Corporation invited me to come to England and give a number of talks on what I saw. This was done entirely on their own initiative, and I did not know anything about it until I actually received the proposal through the BBC's Delhi representative.

Although my visit was only for five weeks, what I saw overwhelmed me. That was natural because I was seeing for the first time and at first hand the England with which I had become familiar through my reading of English literature and English history. My hosts did tell me that England was very much changed, but to my eyes it was the timeless England which appeared in all its glory. The splendour of the outward spectacle put the idea of decadence out of my head for the moment. My sense impressions were beating on me like waves and wind, and I embodied the experience in the book I wrote on England. Its descriptions were infused with my happiness.*

But whenever I had time to reflect on my experiences I was compelled to revert to my old questions. Indeed, on one occasion I did ask an English friend whether there was any thinking among the British people about their

* *A Passage to England*, 1959.

national destiny. He replied that there was none. In one field at least I perceived decadence unmistakably, and that was in pohtics, generally assumed to be the strongest feature of English national life, I had a distinct feeling that the English people had lost their zest in politics, and that their current politics was not politics at all, but only administration.

But as it happened, the very next year I saw an event which brought back to my mind even the idea of a political resurgence. That was the Suez affair. One morning in October 1956, I read the news of the Suez adventure. I clearly remember my exclamation as I saw the headlines and just dipped into the news. I cried out audibly: 'The last chance for the British to regain their position in the world.'

Before that I had been thoroughly dismayed by the British retreat from one position to another. The supine acceptance of the forfeiture of British oil interests in Persia by Mossadegh, the absence of even a knee-jerk – as I would call it in the neurologist's language – to the seizure of the Suez Canal by Nasser confirmed me in my view that the British will was broken. Here, however, was one wholly unexpected spurt of self-assertion, as if even the worm had turned.

I felt elated. At that time I was connected with the French Embassy in New Delhi as a part-time worker, besides being treated as a friend by the French Ambassador, Count Stanislas Ostrorog. I went to the Embassy in high spirits, burst into the room of the Counsellor, M. Costilhes, and cried out: 'Great news from Suez!' He looked at me quietly and said coolly: 'They are mad.' Of course, he included his own government in that. I was taken aback by this remark, which revealed a strange revulsion from military adventure in a Gaul. I entered into an animated argument, when the Ambassador himself came in. To my further dismay. Count Ostrorog sided with his Counsellor. However, he spoke more in the spirit of realism than defeatism. He fully approved of the British withdrawal from India in 1947, and he himself negotiated the transfer of the French possessions in India to Indian sovereignty. Once before we had a discussion on the British action, and I had told him: 'If the British had the guts to spend only one thousand cartridges in 1947, they would have kept their Empire for two hundred years more.' To that he gave a reply which was very cogent: 'But would those one thousand cartridges have been allowed to be fired." I knew how true that was. The British people who endorsed the firing of seventeen hundred cartridges on an unarmed and defenceless crowd of Indians in

1919 and thought that they had saved that Empire by their action, were not ready to spend one hundred cartridges even to prevent the slaughter of hundreds of thousands of Indians by Indians themselves in 1946-7, let alone to save the Empire.

I still hold very strongly that the policy behind the Suez venture was right, and what went wrong was its execution. Had it been carried through none of the sinister aspects of the Middle Eastern political situation today would have emerged. But I was startled by the British and French incompetence in military action. And, of course, I was infuriated by the American treachery to the West. But I now have the satisfaction of seeing that it is the United States which is having to pay the full price for its folly. Its standing among non-European peoples has sunk so low that half a dozen American cowards can drag through the mire the honour of a country which has enough impersonal power to destroy the rest of the world in ten minutes. The only record that the United States has succeeded in establishing in diplomacy is that of being first among all nations in known history in betraying friends. And the irony of the Suez fiasco lies in the probable fact that it was an expression of the jealousy between Eisenhower and Montgomery. If Montgomery could not hold his tongue, Eisenhower would no more hold his hand.

But the cause of the British surrender did not lie in the situation, it was in the exercise of will. Israel, which is wholly dependent for its survival on American support, does not submit to American pressure when its interests are concerned. Great Britain did. Many influential Americans supported the British venture, and even Dulles expressed surprise that it was not carried through.*

Thus, the new trend in British policy, begun in 1947, continued: that trend was to turn the other cheek to the enemies of the British people. However, in 1982, one Englishwoman said that enough was enough, and revolted against the tradition of yielding. But she was only a Boadicea. The undeniable fact about the character of the British people today is that the defenders of British greatness are within the belly of the Trojan Horse, and the defeatists are in occupation of the citadel. Yet the new Boadicea must

* This account was written before the records on the Suez affair were made available at the end of 1986. I have taken full note of all that has been published in the newspapers, and have not thought it necessary to modify my account in any detail, or revise my opinion. If anything, the handling of the affair is seen to be more inept.

be given the credit that is her due. On account of the craven character that her people have developed, she had to say that she sent the expedition to the Falklands to preserve the political rights of some one thousand odd persons of British birth, as if even she had not abandoned far larger numbers of Britons in Rhodesia. The real reason for defending the Falklands was that the woman Prime Minister decided in spite of the men around her that Britain would show for once at least that she could not be kicked by fellow-Europeans, although she might agree to being kicked by her former non-European subjects. But it was only a flash in the pan or the last flicker of the lamp.

This is but natural. Every movement of historical decadence creates its agents, and since they represent the forward movement they become irresistible. This has been seen in the decline and fall of all empires, and in Britain today the agents of decadence fall into three groups: the rabid dogs, the swaggering puppies, and the 'do-gooders'.

The rabid dogs are easily recognizable, but they come from all classes, and not from the militants in the Leftist movements alone. Curiously, even the human dogs of the most specialized breeds in Britain, which have become almost impotent by inbreeding, produced them as freaks. But, however dangerous, the rabid dogs could be destroyed if the will to destroy them existed. That will is enfeebled by the other two agents of decadence.

Of them, the swaggering puppies are the ones who are insidiously dangerous. They are a majority among the journalists, broadcasters, TV producers, and writers or intellectuals generally. They are all clever, and their mission is to ridicule all British greatness and virtues with ribald jests. They destroy by entertaining. They are even more clever in hiding their real nature, and have successfully created the impression that they are only like the adorable puppy which plays with Andrex toilet paper in TV advertisements, whereas really they are as rabid as the maddest Leftist dog.

Last of all, come the 'do-gooders' to perpetrate their mischief solely through good intentions. They are worse when they meddle with interracial relations than with married relations. Formerly, these officious and foolish meddlers came only from the nonconformist denominations and the radicals. But now they have penetrated even the Anglican Church, traditionally the sanctum of British exclusiveness and arrogance. These do-gooders have become the apologists of all the destroyers of British greatness, looking on them as so many prodigal sons and not as the patricides that they really are. If they had any intelligence the do-gooders would have seen that their fate was likely to be similar to that of the people whom Dante found wailing at the gates of Inferno: people whom Heaven had rejected and Hell would not receive.

The tragedy of the British people is that their intellectuals are blind to this aspect of their national situation. They still think that their obsolete two-party political system will safeguard the future. It can no more be said of the British people: Your old men shall dream dreams, your young men shall see visions, or, that can be said only in a sense which the old Prophet never could think of.

CHAPTER 3

My Faith in Empires

To have asserted my faith in empires in 1946, as I did, could still have given the impression of my being a servant of the power that was. So, as an apology, I quoted from Hooker's *Ecclesiastical Polity* at the beginning of my article on the future of imperialism. He said that those who 'go about to persuade a multitude, that they are not so well governed as they ought to be, shall never want attentive and favourable hearers . . . Whereas on the other side, if we maintain things that are established, we have not only to strive with a number of heavy prejudices deeply rooted in the hearts of men, who think that herein we serve the time, and speak in favour of the present state, because thereby we either hold or seek preferment, but also to bear such exceptions as minds so averted before hand usually take against that which they are loth should be poured into them.'

In actual fact, there was no need for that plea. To support the British Empire in India at that time was like choosing to remain a Catholic in the latter part of the reign of Henry VIII. I must point out that all the advantages which the British had in India by virtue of their Empire were bequeathed on its winding up to those who were opposed to it, and not to those who supported it. During the existence of the Empire I was a political suspect to the British administration, as I have shown, and after its disappearance I became a political suspect to the heirs of the Empire, as I shall show. I have a perverse ability to make the worst of both worlds.

But my apology for Empires was far less offensive to the spirit of the age then than it would be today, not only in my own country, but, above all, in England. I might say that to speak in favour of empires, including the British Empire in India in the 1980s, and living in England, would be like being a Lutheran in old Spain with its Inquisition. Even Torquemada's ferocity to the Reformers cannot be compared with the zeal to burn which the British anti-imperialists have. Nonetheless, I shall not only summarize my old arguments, but do worse by adding that I still believe in them.

I had better confess that all Hindus are traditionally imperialists, and they condemned imperialism only in so far as British imperialism made them subjects to an empire instead of its masters. This is due to the fact that the strongest political passion of the ancient Hindus was directed towards conquest and domination. All Sanskrit literature and all the historical inscriptions are full of glorification of both. This aspiration to conquer and dominate was suppressed during Muslim and British rule, but today, even if not given practical expression, it conditions the attitude of the present Hindu ruling class towards the neighbours of India.

My attitude to British rule was also hostile emotionally, but I got over my antipathy only by my overriding principle of adherence to historical truth. My general attitude to empires was not influenced by the American Declaration of Independence nor by Marxism. I was able to reject the interpretation of imperialism by both these schools of thought by my reading of history, and in particular Roman history. The ruler's point of view I learnt from Virgil's famous exhortation to the Romans, which closes with the words: '*Pacisque imponere morem, parcere subiectis, et debellare superbos.*' When I was studying for my BA degree, Dr Kalidas Nag, my teacher of history, in spite of his ardent nationalism, recited the lines in the English translation given in Warde Fowler's book on Rome with unbounded enthusiasm, forgetting British rule in India while teaching Roman history. But as it happened, just at that time I also read Bryce's comparison between the Roman Empire and the British Empire in his *Studies in History and Jurisprudence*. The subject's point of view I learned from *Acts of the Apostles*, which I was reading at the same time. Paul's invocation of his Roman citizenship on various occasions made a profound impression on me, although I was only eighteen years old then.

Besides, I was perfectly familiar with the views of the greatest Indians of the nineteenth century on British rule in India. In my young days these opinions had not been pushed out of nationalist ideology by the negative rancour of the Gandhian brand of nationalism. These great men were all conscious of an antithesis between the natural desire of all Indians to become free from foreign rule and the welfare and progress of the Indian people. Not only they, but no Indian with any education and some regard for historical truth, ever denied that, with all its shortcomings, British rule had, in the balance, promoted both the welfare and the happiness of the Indian people. The general assumption then was that an Indian regime succeeding the British would also promote these as assiduously. I, however, began to doubt this from the Thirties onwards, and therefore I became more of an imperialist than a nationalist. My article on imperialism only gave a belated expression to that attitude, to my disadvantage as I shall have to relate. I was still trying to persuade myself that the British Empire in India would probably not come to an end soon, but this was only emotional resistance without much conviction. The conviction growing within me was that it was going to disappear.

I did not like that, but I cannot say that as a student of history I was surprised. The attitude to the Indian Empire which could be called genuine British imperialism had disappeared long ago. It was severely practical, and its theoretical justification was a mixture of humanitarianism, Evangelism, Utilitarianism, and Liberalism. That old imperialism had been replaced by the end of the nineteenth century by a wholly shoddy theory, which was nothing better than boastful verbiage. By 1920, even that had been discredited, and the Empire in India survived only as a practical reality supported by vested interests. I despised that, and yet the degeneration of British imperialism could not reconcile me to the disappearance of British rule in India. I knew full well what would follow.

Thus in that article, to begin with, I set down my view of the British Empire in India, and the words I used were defiant:

'The British Empire in India is no marginal fact of English history, no irrelevant frill, no sowing of wild oats by the exuberant youth of Britain, no dead, tumorous growth on an otherwise healthy polity, nor even a preserve of British economic interests... it was and remains one of the central facts of universal history and the concrete evidence that the British people have discharged one of their primary roles in history. They could not disinterest themselves in it without abrogating their historical mission and eliminating themselves from one of the primary strands of human evolution.'

It was obvious, of course, that they thought they were *not* disinteresting themselves in India by putting an end to the Empire, but continuing it in a different and better form by making India a member of the Commonwealth. I stated emphatically that the so-called Commonwealth could never be a substitute for the Empire because the two were based on diametrically opposed notions of human association. The Commonwealth, as it was defined by the Declaration of 1926, was a domestic organization of the British people. The British Empire, on the contrary, was a hierarchical organization of many peoples and conformed to the true pattern of empires, which I defined as follows:

'There is no empire without a conglomeration of linguistically, racially, and culturally different nationalities and the hegemony of one of them over the rest. The heterogeneity and the domination are of the very essence of imperial relations. An empire is hierarchical. There may be in it, and has been, full or partial freedom for individuals or groups to rise from one level to another; but this has not modified the stepped and stratified structure of the organization. An empire is not, inter-racially or internationally, egalitarian. A true empire may confer citizenship on its subjects, but does not set them up in independent states.'

Thus, my view of the British Empire in India was not simply the idea of something particular. I placed it in its historical framework. I regarded imperialism as a constant of history. As I put it:

'If history reveals anything, it reveals that the emergence of every new civilization and of every new value in human life is accompanied by and is inseparable from the domination of a particular human group. This has been seen cycle after cycle of human history and at every stage the area over which it has operated has grown wider than before. The domination, of a nation and civilization has not been checked by any counter-principle, but by purely mechanical factors, e.g. the state of transport and communications. When these were not adequate to sustain a single *imperium* in the whole of the known world a group of empires has existed side by side. Only those people have escaped imperialism (and with it civilization) who were in utter geographical isolation, but even they had local empires of a rudimentary and primitive sort. Empires have died when they ceased to create or defend values associated with them, but they have died only to yield place to other empires. *L'Empire est mart, vive TEmpire.*'

I went on to argue that the historical process was only the continuation of a biological process, through which from age to age new classes and orders of animals have emerged, each manifesting a higher value in life and dominating the earth in succession. I summed up that phase of zoological imperialism in the following words:

'Instead of an egalitarian moluscaan democracy we see saurian imperialism succeeding piscan imperialism, mammalian imperialism succeeding reptilian imperialism, human imperialism succeeding general mammalian imperialism.'

The moral I drew from this zoological record was this:

'Neither biological evolution nor human history reveals anything like equal status for all. They do not bear witness to the achievement of anything good, great, wise, abiding, or new, by the exercise of the equal vote. The cosmic process is revealed as a living and ever growing pyramid, whose apex is rising higher and higher, leaving more and more strata underneath.'

Finally, I dismissed the anti-imperialistic eschatology in these words:

'It requires a good deal of uncritical faith to believe that this simple and unvarying pattern of history will be replaced by the alternative conception of a world society based on the equality of small states and big states, old and young nations, nations which have exhausted their potentialities and those which have still to unfold them. The only argument in favour of such a conception is that a large number of people have come to believe in it. But even larger numbers believed in the advent of the millenium. The approach of round thousands of the Christian era seems to be particularly favourable to illusions.'

But I also knew that a simple recognition of the existence of empires as a fact of history was not enough. Empires had to be justified morally, for, as I put it, 'however immutable it [imperialism] may be, mankind will not accept it unless it is made consistent with moral principles, with freedom, and with human dignity.' So, I declared that empires could be and were, so far as any human phenomenon can be, both moral and beneficial. The moral question which the imperialistic domination of one group of human beings over another raised was not different from that which the power of the state over individuals did, and I said that on the moral plane imperialism could be justified on the ground on which St Thomas Aquinas justified the exercise of authority of all kinds, which he said was moral if it was for the subject's good or the common good.

I went further and said that exercise of imperial authority was necessary for the protection and survival of civilization. History, I argued, had shown empires as protectors and reclaimers of civilization, and empires had taken over the keepership of civilizations when its creators had become incapable of maintaining them. In saying this I had, of course, in mind our own Hindu civilization. There could be no doubt that British rule in India was responsible for a new awareness of the ancient Hindu civilization and for a revival of its highest values.

I emphatically rejected the idea that empires were opposed to human dignity, because I held that it really sustained the dignity. I said that, while the fashionable modern democracies – the dictatorships being as democratic as parliamentary governments – got their opponents killed, history records that even autocratic emperors acted according to the idea of a commonwealth based on equity and freedom of speech, which, above all, cherished the freedom of the subject. Many will be able to see that in writing this I was paraphrasing the actual words of an autocratic emperor. The true antithesis was between imperialism and nationalism, which latter, if both were evil, is now seen to be the greater evil of the two.

The anti-imperialistic chatter of these days does not intimidate me because it has a comical aspect. The Americans who were and still remain the most anti-imperialistic people in the world are being stigmatised every day as imperialistic adventurers by the rulers of the only true empire of today, namely, the Russians, and to make the accusation actually ludicrous this is believed implicitly by all the non-European peoples liberated from European imperialism partly at least by the force of American opinion.

I would say that in this the Americans are getting only what they have deserved, because their anti-imperialism has a very repulsive side. It completely ignores the fact that the United States itself was created by the most cruel form of European political expansion, i.e. colonialism. I never forget the distinction between European imperialism and European colonialism. Imperialism, far from being the enemy of subject peoples, has always protected them. This was first shown by the creators of true imperialism, the Achaemenid Persians, and the British in India only continued in the same tradition. Let me give only one example. On 17 May 1766, when British rule in Bengal had not even been consolidated, the Directors of the East India Company, supposed to be a body of rapacious traders, wrote to their agents in Calcutta: 'It is now more immediately our interest and duty to protect and cherish the inhabitants, and to give no occasion to look on every Englishman as their natural enemy.' This was written to explain their refusal to permit monopoly of certain trades to their factors in Bengal.

The motto of the English settlers in America was on the contrary: 'The only good Indian is the dead Indian.' They did not even allow the Red Indian to graze his cows in the Indian's own pastures. In 1791, when he was in North America, Chateaubriand one day saw by the Lake Onondagas a party of English settlers taking a herd of fat cows towards a pasture and driving away a lean cow. Upon this a Red Indian woman appeared at the door of her hut and called the animal which ran towards her, mooing piteously. Chateaubriand went up to her and said in English: 'She is very lean.' The woman replied sadly in bad English: 'She eats very little.' When he observed again that they had driven her off very roughly, she only said: 'We are used to this, *both of us*.'

No empire seen in the entire history of mankind has exterminated the original inhabitants of a country in the manner of the Americans. Not even the Spanish conquistadores practised a sustained cruelty like the British settlers. It is through this extermination that the Americans have earned the right to be anti-imperialistic, while the British, by allowing people like us not only to survive but to prosper, have had the stigma of being oppressors and exploiters fastened on them. And the comical side of anti-imperialism has been further accentuated by the adoption of the American version of it by a large number of the British people today.

But it was not the study of the past and recent history of man alone which made me respect imperialism. It has been strengthened by my study of zoology and zoological evolution. I have spoken of the emergence of dominant orders of animals at every stage of this evolution. While I took note of this, I also became aware of another feature of zoological evolution: the disproportion between those who went forward in the process and those who were left behind. Certainly, in spite of the talk about population explosion among men, their numbers are far from equalling those of insects. Yet, all animals live together in a perfectly balanced co-existence or symbiosis. Human beings do not.

As soon as I realized this, I became aware, with dismay, of another malevolent aspect of human evolution. I saw that while lower orders of animals never have any grudge against those of the higher orders, human communities which were left behind in the march of civilizations acquired a violent hatred of the forward movement. They threatened it with three weapons: inertia, malevolence, and self-pity. The have-nots of the world today are calling themselves the Third World and demanding charity on the strength of their inertia and self-pity. But this aspect of their behaviour is passive whereas their malevolence is active.

I became aware of the existence of this baleful passion through my experiences in Bengal. So I wrote in the article:

'In order to feel the full impact of the malevolence of the backward, you have to live among them. You have to see how you are hated by these have-nots for a little extra efficiency, extra power of thinking, extra ability to make life worth living; in short for a little extra quality in life. You have to register hourly mementos which tell you that as soon as they have the power to do so the Yahoos will fall upon you and tear you to pieces. You have to be steeped in the premonition of inevitable debasement.'

This animosity I described as 'the rancour of the futureless', and I added that it was the urgent function of imperialism to defend civilization by suppressing this vile revolt. The impact of that horrible revelation has not been weakened in me by what I am seeing even in England today: the same 'rancour of the futureless' with its destructive fury has appeared among the British people.

On accepting this article, Mr Douglas Jerrold himself wrote to me on 27 August 1946: 'I was very greatly impressed, if I may say so, with your article and found myself largely in agreement with it. I don't agree that Great Britain is leaving India because she has been forced by circumstances to do so. I think she is leaving India because she has lost the will to remain there and she has done this because she no longer possesses, as you point out, any understanding of the moral basis of imperialism or the responsibilities which it entails.' There was, however, no real disagreement between us.

So far as I was concerned, the article relieved me from a great burden of mental irritation. I thought that having made a clean breast of it I should be able to go through the full unfolding of the process I was seeing with calmness. Nevertheless, I was not prepared for the actual squalor and shame of it. This will now be described.

CHAPTER 4

Surrender to the Axis in India

In this and the chapters which follow I shall narrate the squalid story of the British flight from India in 1947, and its most squalid episode was the very first one, with which this chapter deals. That was the institution and abandonment by the British authorities in India of the trials of the Indian officers of the Indian Army who after being taken prisoner by the Japanese had gone over to them; led the so-called Indian National Army, or INA for short, which had been formed by a portion of the Indian other ranks who were also prisoners of war; fought their own countrymen, and even tortured them. In its outcome, the affair was what the heading to this chapter describes it to be: namely, an unconditional surrender to the passive but wholehearted allies of the Axis in India. After fighting the Germans and the Japanese with desperate and almost superhuman courage against overwhelming odds and coming through to victory, and while the British Government at home was participating in the ruthless punishment of the German and Japanese war leaders, the British Government in India, headed by two field-marshals who had themselves fought the Germans with distinction, went down on its knees to the most cowardly supporters of the Germans and the Japanese in the world, namely, the Indian nationalists.

The disgrace of this surrender was all the greater for two reasons: first, the INA was made up of a body of soldiers who were the most contemptible and dishonourable seen in any country or age; secondly, the championship of the INA was in no way connected with the main issue between India and Britain, which was political independence for the Indian people. It was a wholly adventitious challenge thrown out by the Indian nationalists with the deliberate purpose of humiliating the victorious British people, and that they succeeded in doing. What two brave, efficient, and honourable enemies could not accomplish, was done by an enemy who was neither brave, nor efficient, nor honourable.

At the time, the handling of this affair by the British authorities in India filled me with anger, and that anger comes back to me even after the four decades that have intervened, because I am having to write about it. The failure of Marshal Pétain's courage and judgement in 1940, for which he was condemned to death and had to spend the rest of his life in prison, was minor compared with what was shown by the British authorities in India, and for this, the ultimate responsibility rests, of all people, on Wavell and Auchinleck. I can explain that only by assuming that soldiers are of all men the least qualified to deal with political enemies. Perhaps that is natural, for big game hunters are not the persons best fitted to meet jackals, especially if they have contracted rabies. That will come out of my account of the episode.

Anyone who will read it without prepossessions or any emotional compulsion to indulge in self-exculpation, will see the affair as I have done. No two opinions are possible on the strength of the facts which are indisputable. But I would also warn the reader who will concede that my view must be the right one, that a web of the most impudent sophistry has been spun round this episode as indeed around the entire process of the liquidation of the British Empire in India. All the parties concerned, British or Indian, have an interest in drawing red herrings across the trails.

Before I set down the facts I shall offer an intellectual explanation of the failure of the British authorities, which in itself will be a moral condemnation. It was their incapacity to foresee any difficulty or danger, and to be always creating a mental picture of situations. I had always thought that this was a failing among us Indians only. I moralized on it even as late as 1971 in a letter to *The Times*, which I sent apropos of a remark of Mrs Golda Meir's. It was published on 2 July 1971 and here it is:

'ELEPHANT'S EXAMPLE

'from Mr Nirad C. Chaudhuri

'Sir, The citation in your editorial of June 30 of Mrs Golda Meir's observation that the Russians put one foot in water to find out how deep it is before they take another step, reminds me of what I saw elephants doing when I was young. One day I was crossing what seemed like a shallow and safe river on the back of a she-elephant. Instead of wading straight across it she stopped at every step and pressed her foot down. I asked the mahout why she was doing that, and he replied that she would not take one step without finding out whether the bottom was firm.

'It is curious that without ever using elephants for riding the Russians should have the elephant's caution, while we Hindus who have ridden elephants for centuries are in the confirmed habit of getting caught in personal and political quagmires. Perhaps this incapacity to profit by the example of the elephant was the reason why the mahouts, or drivers of elephants, were always Muslims.

'Yours etc.
Nirad C. Chaudhuri
47 St John Street, Oxford.'

Two years later, I learned, when I was working on my book on Clive, that this failing was detected among Hindus and Muslims alike as early as the middle of the eighteenth century by the great Frenchman Dupleix, who wrote to Bussy on 22 August 1752: 'The Asiatic, once he is taken up with an idea, acts on it without the least forethought, but he is also disconcerted more easily and can no more see what remedy to apply to the situation his poor mental capacity has not allowed him to foresee.'

This incapacity was acquired with disconcerting quickness by British administrators in India from 1920 onwards, and shown at every juncture during 1945, 1946, and 1947. In my book. *The Continent of Circe*, which describes the deadly capacity of India to make swine of every race of humans coming to India, I have called the British in India her worst victims. But in the last three years of British rule they did not show themselves simply as inoffensive swine satisfied with their acorns, but as the Gadarene swine possessed by unclean spirits. *Quem Jupiter vult perdere prius dementat.*

The INA

Now for the affair itself, and, first of all, its protagonists, the INA. The British surrender at Singapore left roundly 60,000 men of the Indian Army as prisoners in Japanese hands. Of these, 35,000 resisted all attempts to seduce them from their oath of allegiance and soldier's honour, and suffered terribly, and a quarter of them died. But about 25,000 of them were induced to go over to the Japanese and formed into an Indian National Army under the command of an Indian officer. This man, however, became wholly disillusioned and went back to the prisoner of war camp with 4,000 of his followers. The INA had been a flop. But when Subhas Bose reached Japan in August 1943, and came to S.-E. Asia a little later, he gave a new life to it by the force of his personality and oratory. He succeeded in enlisting about 10,000 more men into the INA from the prisoners of war, and was joined by 20,000 civilian Indians in Malaya. Out of this army, about 7,000 were allowed by the Japanese commanders to accompany their armies which delivered the offensive on the Assam front in 1944.

By joining the Japanese and offering to fight the British Indian Army composed mainly of their own countrymen, these men were violating their oath of allegiance and military honour. It should be kept in mind that the Indian Army was an army of volunteers and not conscripted. The men had joined that army out of free will, either for money or position, and often both, and could not take the plea of nationalism in justification of their later conduct. During the agitation in favour of the INA there was a delivery of clamorous and drenching rhetoric about their patriotism by Indians of the highest positions, including Gandhi and Nehru. But the undeniable facts about this patriotism were that it did not prevent these Indians from joining the British Indian army whose primary purpose was to perpetuate British rule in India; it did not withstand the temptation of worldly advantages offered by the British; it did not make them fight against the British in Burma when a splendid opportunity was given to them to display it in the manner of the Rajputs at Haldighat; it did not prevent their surrender in shoals to the British Indian forces; it did not even induce loyalty to the Japanese whom they betrayed as they betrayed the British: it only came into play when the Japanese were top dogs and when it was convenient to join them. I would add that people who could call these men patriotic were either hypocrites or wholly devoid of moral consciousness, having been robbed of their judgement by a rancorous hatred of the British.

The myth of the military achievement of the INA has also to be exploded. The Japanese who made use of them for political propaganda were under no illusions about them or the Indian soldiers. The officers, they set down as opportunists, and, but for rare exceptions, as devoid of military capacity. The men, they regarded as an undisciplined rabble. They would never allow the INA to take an active part in their operations. When the Japanese 15th and 28th Armies under Mutaguchi were going to begin their offensive on the Assam frontier, Subhas Bose pleaded passionately with Field-Marshal Count Terauchi, the Supreme Japanese Commander in the region, that 'the first drop of blood shed on Indian soil must be that of a soldier of the INA.' The Field-Marshal refused that pointblank, and mortified Subhas Bose. Perhaps he thought that not even one drop of blood would be shed if free will had anything to do with it. To all subsequent requests for participation in the fighting, all Japanese commanders gave the same reply. They kept the INA on line of communication duties, and only when a decision could no longer be avoided, its men were stationed at some unthreatened point of the line of resistance in Burma.

And they were absolutely right. When their offensive failed and they were trying to defend Mandalay, the Japanese commanders assigned a point further south at Pagan where the junction between their 15th and 28th Armies was weak, to a large formation of the INA. By a surprise outflanking movement the British Indian forces reached the town. The INA surrendered without firing a shot, and Field-Marshal Slim wrote: 'This incident was, I think, the chief contribution the Indian National Army made to either side in the Burma war.'

Utterly false claims about their participation in the fighting at Kohim and Imphal were made in India, as also about their bravery. They were not, of course, at either place, and as regards their bravery the figures of casualties are enough proof In the battle for Mandalay the Japanese dead had to be buried by bulldozers, and it was the same in the battle for Meiktila. The path of Japanese retreat was strewn with Japanese bones. Not even at Port Arthur, forty years ago, had they died like this – although that was for victory and this was in defeat. At their highest figures, only about 3 00 to 400 men of the in a died in action, but the figure has also been put at only 1 50. To class the i n a even as the auxiliaries of the Japanese is to insult a brave people.

But the common Indian soldier was not to be blamed for this. His heart was not in the fight. And for whom was he to give his life.' That was the crux of the matter. A fundamental distinction has to be made between the conduct of the officers of the Indian Army and of the rank and file, or the common soldier. The latter were overwhelmingly peasants from the rural districts of the Punjab with little or no political consciousness. They had joined the Indian Army because it offered them money and because military service was the hereditary and traditional profession for young men of this peasantry. Their *esprit de corps*, morale, and military efficiency depended on the officers, and when led by British officers the same type of soldiers showed exemplary loyalty to their employers, and equal bravery. Of the twenty-seven Victoria Crosses awarded for the Burma campaign, twenty went to Indians. They never hesitated to fight the INA when they were asked to do so, and one Indian battalion composed of Mahrattas put to flight a brigade of the i n a soon after the failure of the Japanese. When the prisoners were asked why they had joined the Japanese they replied that they were ordered to do so by their officers, and they were taught always to obey them. As it happened, the men who said that belonged to the first battalion of the 14th Punjab Regiment, which had been Indianized, and the officers they named figured in the IN A trials. Of course, like the peasant masses of India who were not in the Indian Army, they also had the hatred of the White Man, the Feringhee, in the bone. But that did not make them go over primarily. It simply dulled the two moral principles they always tried to observe: first, to be true to their salt, and, secondly, never to be a coward in fighting. The main body of the INA can therefore be left out of account in writing of the INA trials.

But the conduct of the Indians who held commissioned ranks in the Indian Army was altogether different. They came from the most prosperous and educated section of Indian society, and could be expected to understand the moral implications of their choice of the military profession under the British régime. None of them had shown any awareness of that, because they were members of the job-seeking class *par excellence* in India, of whose recruitment to the army I was so sceptical in 1931. These men, with their fathers and mothers, understood only one thing: prosperity and ease in the world, and owed no allegiance to anything but self-interest. They were accepted in the Army after a rigorous screening of the loyalty of their families. If they had any nationalistic feeling, except an incurable and rancorous hatred of their employers nursed in secret, they could not have been even in the civil service, let alone in the army, for from 1920 onwards no Indian with any integrity of character could take employment under the British Indian Government except for performing routine work. I have seen Indians unwilling to accept even that. The Indian officers of the Indian Army came from a forsworn class and were forsworn themselves.

Only two things can be pleaded in extenuation of the conduct of these officers, a brood of opportunists. For one thing, as officers of the same army, they were treated with incredible snobbery by their British colleagues, who regarded them as even worse than the offspring of their mothers' adultery. But had these Indian officers possessed any backbone, they would have resigned, as some did, unable to endure the slights put on them. I knew one of them, and became very friendly with him. He was from a most distinguished Muslim family, and afterwards he joined the

Congress, to become a high official in the administration of Nehru, and a friend of his.

Secondly, these men, however opportunistic or forsworn, possessed like all sinners in India an extraordinary inclination to worship virtue and disinterestedness. I know an authentic story of a young prostitute who was dying from alcoholic and sexual excesses, and had been saved by a friend of her client, who even washed all the vomit and filth from her naked body. After recovery, she fell at the feet of her saver and said that, sinner that she was, yet she looked upon him as a divinity. But, of course, she remained the vicarious Mary Magdalene and never reformed. The unlimited capacity to be a villain of the worst kind with an unlimited capacity for self-abasement before virtue and nobility is one of the most disarming traits of the Indian character, and that, I suppose, was shared by these Indian officers. They were overwhelmed by the patriotism and self-sacrifice of Subhas Chandra Bose. He was the man who wiped some of the filth from the body of these dirty military prostitutes.

The Trial

The British-Indian military authorities were therefore right in deciding to punish only the officers. But their execution of even this restricted decision was faulty, and since it was Field-Marshal Auchinleck who was responsible for dealing with the INA he cannot escape his share of the blame. Over this matter he took the line of least resistance. He could not overlook the seriousness of the offences of the defectors to the Japanese if he cared for the morale of the Indian Army and its discipline, and perhaps he also knew that the British officers of all ranks under him in India felt very strongly about the matter. So he decided to have only selected ringleaders tried, as there could be no question of trying the entire body of the officers. Thus, in October 1945, three officers of the INA, a Muslim, a Hindu, and a Sikh, were chosen to be tried, to begin with. Apart from treason (technically waging war against the King-Emperor) they were also charged with murder and torture. The trial began on 5 November 1945, in the famous Red Fort of Delhi. From such conversations as he had with Indian officers or officials Auchinleck did not anticipate any strong feeling among them about the men of the INA.

He was totally mistaken. A fierce agitation at once began. It was particularly significant that all the political parties and all shades of Indian opinion were united over it. Even the Muslim League joined the Congress to oppose the trials. Before the trial had begun a committee was formed to defend the INA officers, and it consisted of some of the most brilliant lawyers of India.

In October this Committee appealed to the Viceroy to abandon the trials. Upon being asked, Auchinleck replied that this could not be done in the interest of justice and morale. But both Wavell and Auchinleck had reckoned without the host. Even Gandhi and Nehru became champions of the INA, which was the strangest part of the matter. Mahatma Gandhi was a pacifist in principle, and his insistence on non-violence was at the root of his dislike for Subhas Chandra Bose. As I have said, he had driven Bose out of the Congress, and could be held responsible for Bose's flight to Germany and ultimate death. But he now changed his attitude. He wrote about him in glowing terms, employing even the term Netaji, which, being an exact equivalent of *Der Führer* or *Il Duce*, revealed Bose's political affiliations, and said: 'Netaji's name is one to conjure with. His patriotism *is* second to none.' In order to explain the '*is*' he added, 'I use the present tense intentionally', thereby falling in with the stupid belief in India that Subhas was still living and was not killed in the air crash. Gandhi went on to say: 'His bravery shines through all his actions.' About the INA he declared: 'The hypnotism of the INA has cast its spell on us.'

Jawaharlal Nehru's championship of the INA was more unrestrained. But it was a greater paradox than Gandhi's. When Bose was on the borders of Assam, Nehru had declared that he would fight Bose if he came to India. He wholly changed his stance after the war, and, of course, it was noticed. When asked for an explanation, he gave a very unconvincing one. But even after the surrender of japan he was moderate in his advocacy. He admitted the patriotism of the men of the INA but also said that it did not justify their joining the Japanese. However, with the progress of the trials he became more and more excited and more and more extreme. He even gave a theatrical exhibition of his support for the INA which was quite out of character. He put on the barrister's gown which he had discarded for twenty-five years and sat among the other defending advocates.

They were the most eminent and brilliant in India, and their leader was Bhulabhai Desai. His oratory was like a stream of lava, but wholly irrelevant in substance, and was, of course, addressed *Urbi et Orbi*. It was like Trotsky's at Brest-Litovsk, with this difference that in Delhi there was no

General Hoffmann to cry out: 'Enough of this foolery!' The advocates on the Government's side were in contrast banal and inept, and at the time they provoked contempt from me. This contempt was transferred to the military authorities when I read about the outcome of the trial. The court martial had no discretion except to impose a sentence of transportation for life instead of death for the offences of the officers, but its verdict had to be confirmed by the Commander-in-Chief, Auchinleck. He, obviously for political reasons, quashed the sentence for transportation, but confirmed the minor sentences, which were for cashiering and loss of pay. It was a farcical anticlimax and caused deep resentment among the British officers. Auchinleck circulated a long note among them in February 1946, to explain his action.

There was triumph among the nationalists and an increased determination to oppose the trials and inflict the utmost humiliation on the British authorities in India. After the flop of the first trials these authorities decided that they would henceforth try no one for treason, but only for torture or ill-treatment of fellow-Indians. A member of the Indian legislature declared that Indian opinion did not *appreciate* the distinction. Even Mohammed Ali Jinnah, the implacable enemy of the Congress, declared that any civilized government would speedily end the episode of the trials.

Quite characteristically, the part of the jester in this low farce was played by an eminent Labourite, Reginald William Sorensen. He came to India and went out of his way to interview the officers of the INA, and issued a statement on 17 January 1946. In this he said: 'I entirely appreciate the motive; it is generally recognized. It is difficult for an Englishman to be objective in such a matter and to put himself in the place of an Indian. But I think it is not so hard for me.'

Indians by that time had realized that there were hundreds of thousands of Englishmen who were of the same mind as Mr Sorensen MP, and they stepped up their fury. Thus, when further trials were begun, there was violent rioting in Calcutta, especially over the trial of a Muslim officer of the INA. Jawaharlal Nehru then issued his ultimatum. On 24 April 1946, he declared in a statement:

'The civil and military authorities of the Government of India function in a mysterious way. This, I suppose, is their method of preparing India for the freedom to come. Whatever they may have in their minds, they succeed remarkably well in irritating public opinion and making a difficult situation even worse. Obviously, if the trials are held the challenge will be accepted in every way.'

The will of the Government of India collapsed, and the two soldiers who had not quailed before Rommel, cowered before the Indian leaders. There were no further trials. I have to point out that when at the time the Government of India was surrendering to the minions of the Japanese, even so high-ranking a Japanese commander as General Yamashita, who was concerned with the INA and had formed a poor opinion of it, was sentenced to death and executed. Even a soldier's honourable death was denied him; he was not shot but hanged on 23 February 1946. In their different ways both the Americans and the British gave a striking demonstration of the truth of the old saying: *Vae victis*: Woe to the vanquished!

Auchinleck, Nehru and Mountbatten

The inglorious end to the INA episode angered the British officers in India, and much as I disapproved of their arrogance and narrowness in India, I think they were right and Auchinleck wrong. Never was so much disgrace owed by so many to so few. Field-Marshal Auchinleck showed a curious lack of perspicacity and firmness in this matter. Nothing has given me greater mental distress than to have to read his letters and memoranda on this question, especially his long note of February 1946. While they showed that he understood the details very well, they also showed a complete incapacity to understand the essence, and this incapacity was apparently shared by the soldier Viceroy, Wavell. Both of them were thinking of the morale of the Indian Army and of discipline in it without bringing that in relation to the main question of independence for India. If the British were going to leave India within months, what did it matter to them if the morale and discipline of the Indian Army disappeared? They never considered that.

I condemn Auchinleck over this affair very unwillingly. I have a very great admiration for his military ability and not less sympathy for his professional and personal misfortunes. I had not read his letters and note on the INA when he gave me the Duff Cooper prize for my book *The*

Continent of Circe. I had followed his career from 1935, when he commanded the Mohmand expedition. I even made a clipping of a picture of him then. So, I said to him in my reply: 'Field-Marshal, you were a romance to me.' He on his part had said that if he had read the book when he was serving in India he would have understood the country and its people better. And he had served for forty-five years. I wonder if he thought of his handling of the INA affair then.

At the time, however, he seemed to have consoled himself with the thought that by yielding on the INA issue, he had promoted a reconcilation between Britain and Indian nationalism. Apparently, he did so on the strength of what he saw of relief among the Indian officers and officials he met, after the abandonment of the trials and also on the strength of the letters he received from some eminent Indians. Even Nehru wrote to thank him and explain his own position.

He never understood why the Indians he knew were so relieved nor why two eminent Indians, as also Nehru, wrote to him. These letters are reproduced in Auchinleck's biography by John Connell (see pp. 810-11 and pp. 817-19). The Indians were relieved because Auchinleck's weakness saved them from the calamity which they feared above everything else. It was the first principle of their conduct to make the best of both worlds. If, however, the British administration had persisted in punishing the INA this very convenient means of flourishing in the world would have been denied to these Indians, and they would have been forced to side with one party or the other. The sloppiness which overflowed in the letters of the two eminent toadies were tears of relief at being saved from their cruel dilemma.

Nehru's letter had a different origin, and neither Auchinleck nor his biographer, John Connell, had any idea of it. Connell even wrote: 'Who was the greater man, in statesmanship or moral integrity – the writer of the letter or its recipient." Such grandiloquence should not have been wasted on the letter, for Nehru's letter had a very simple explanation. It was an accidental gushing out of subsoil water from the Harrow-Cambridge stratum of Nehru's personality. That side of his could not allow him to hit a man who was down. But the normal behaviour of Nehru soon came into operation, and he pursued the British military authorities in India with his rancour until a stop was put to his bluster by Lord Mountbatten.

Indian politicians were not satisfied even with the deep humiliation they had inflicted on Auchinleck and Wavell by compelling them to give up the trials. They wanted to rub it in further. From the time the so-called Interim Government was formed in August 1946, the nationalist politicians began to press for the release of the men of INA who had been previously sentenced to imprisonment, and they utterly refused to give up the demand although Wavell pleaded with them to do so. At last, when Mountbatten arrived, the Indian Legislative Assembly put forward a resolution asking the Interim Government to take this step. The resolution was to be discussed on 3 April 1947. Lord Mountbatten at once called Nehru on 1 April and told him that the INA were not a body of politically conscious heroes fighting for their country but cowards and traitors who had betrayed their loyal comrades. Nehru did not dispute this, but replied that *for political reasons* he had to stick to his demand. Lord Mountbatten said that in that case the Commander-in-Chief, i.e. Auchinleck, would resign. (In fact, the entire body of British officers of the Indian Army were ready to resign on this issue.) Nehru said defiantly that the prospect did not worry him. There was no friendliness any more for Auchinleck in him. Upon this Mountbatten played his card. He declared that he too would resign. Nehru asked in panic: 'But why?' Mountbatten gave the reason that he 'was the Supreme Commander under whom the loyal Indians had fought and he had led them against the INA.' Nehru was not ready to face the problem of beginning all over again with a new Viceroy. After a facesaving formula was offered, he spoke against the resolution and got it dropped.* That was the end of the miserable episode.

I have no hesitation in saying that in regard to the INA both Gandhi and Nehru showed themselves to be opportunists, who went back on all their previous principles and pronouncements. But, of course, neither of them probably perceived that. In the first place, they had no notion of what a soldier's honour and bravery were. But, in addition, Gandhi had one kind of insensitiveness and Nehru another. Gandhi had the capacity for prevarication of a Hindu Bania and a Hindu Guru combined, and like both he would think that what he desired must of necessity be right. Nehru's notion of right or wrong, on the other hand, was at the mercy of his hatred of British rule in India. Under its influence he could lose his balance of

* I have taken this account from H. V. Hodson's book. *The Great Divide*, and he had it from Mountbatten himself in 1965.

mind and indulge in extremism and even crude histrionics. This made British dignitaries in India regard him as an irresponsible firebrand when he was merely acting like a savage medicine man pouring forth his mumbo-jumbo with grotesque gestures. But he always stopped at verbal expression of his hatred and never showed his extremism in action. Nonetheless, when that side of him was uppermost, the Harrow-Cambridge side had no chance.

His remark about the political reasons for his demand about the in a indicated the unconscious opportunism. I shall refer to two other facts as further proof of it. In August 1946, when the so-called Interim-Government was formed, Nehru took Sarat Chandra Bose, Subhas Bose's brother, into it. I have no doubt that the relationship, together with the excitement about Subhas Bose's men, influenced Nehru. But when in October, room had to be made in the same government for the Muslims, Nehru dismissed Sarat Bose not only abruptly, but also discourteously. The INA agitation had lost its force and Sarat Bose had become dispensable. He was very much aggrieved over his dismissal and resented it.

Next, after India had become independent Nehru showed no disposition to incorporate the men of the INA in the Indian Army, which, if his belief in their bravery and patriotism was genuine, he should have done. But he did not, and this was against the precedents established by all revolutions, whether the French or the Russian. The adulteration of the Indian Army was prevented by the Indian officers who had been loyal to the British. Nehru never quarrelled with them as he had done with Auchinleck.

The Indian Attitude

I have, last of all, to come to the heart of the matter and explain why the Indian people were so passionate about the INA. The British civil servants and officers never understood it, and the Congress leaders would not avow it. Yet there was one portent that would have furnished a clue to it if the British authorities had given any attention to it. It was the ominous Hindu-Muslim unity over the INA. When Gandhi and Jinnah agreed over anything, that had to be under the impact of another passion which could suppress even the terrible Hindu-Muslim hatred. As soon as the INA furore was out of the way, the Hindus and the Muslims began to slaughter one another in thousands. Their mutual hatred brought about the partition of India the next year, and that was the greatest injury inflicted on the Indian people in two thousand years. Even such an animosity was suspended over the INA. I cannot understand why the British authorities in India totally ignored the significance of that.

The simple truth was that the championship of the INA was the expression of the boiling rage of the Indian people at the Allied victory and the survival of the British people. I have given enough proof of the wholehearted partisanship of the Germans and the Japanese by the Indian people, and described the eager expectation of British collapse on many occasions. Those hopes were pitched so high that their falsification virtually drove the people of India half-insane. I had no illusions about this, and I have narrated what desperate steps I contemplated if Britain went down in 1940-2.

Even so, there would not have been any practical expression to the fury in 1945. The disappointment would only have turned inwards and deprived the Indian character of whatever manly feelings it had still left. It is not in any Indian of the intelligentsia to act even on the most virulent hatred unless it is safe to do so. It should be kept in mind that no one stirred in India when the INA was supposed to be fighting at Kohima and Imphal. Not a hand was raised for Subhas Bose even by his worshippers, the Bengali middle class. The price for their support was success, and this was quite openly confessed. However, after the war the situation had changed. Although Bose had not succeeded and also no longer needed their support, the Indian nationalists were ready to make up for their disloyalty to him by supporting his followers, such as they were. It had become safe to do so. The Indian people have an uncanny perception of the weakness of their enemy. It is intuitional with them.

But in 1945 no intuition was needed. The Indian people had seen a sign of British weakness which was like the hoisting of the white flag. The British people had rejected Churchill, the most hated Englishman in India. He was, of course, hated for his opposition to self-government for Indians, but that had been amplified hundredfold by the war, in which he was seen as the saviour of the British people, and therefore as the instrument of their mortification. They had expected his rejection at every motion of no confidence, and had been bitterly disappointed. Now he *was* thrown out. That was enough. The Indian people knew that so far as they were concerned they had men of straw to deal with.

So, they gave full expression to their malevolence through the INA. No boldness is more insolent than the boldness of the coward who feels safe. Thus they challenged the British people over the very issue of defeat of the Germans and the Japanese by defending those Indians who had collaborated with them. I had passed through all the phases of the Indian nationalist agitation from 1905 onwards, but never had I seen excitement and passion over the issue of political freedom which was greater than what I saw over the punishment of the officers of the INA. Indian nationalists were determined that whatever the British could do to the German and Japanese war criminals, they would not be allowed to do anything to the Indian collaborators. That was to be their revenge for the British victory.

That the fury was over the British victory was shown by a very significant incident. It was decided by the British-Indian Government that the Allied victory would be celebrated on 7 March 1946, by military marches. In the capital the soldiers were first to march through New Delhi and then come into the old city and finish the procession in front of the Red Fort. All that, the Indians were determined to prevent. On that day I was going to the office as usual on foot, and, entering the old city, I saw a wild commotion. People out in the street were making fierce gestures. On Burn Bastion Road, the street of the wholesale grain merchants, where no one could expect any strong feeling for the Germans and the Japanese, a man came up to me and ordered me to take off my tie and hat, these being regarded as the outward signs of an inward loyalty to British rule. I did not obey him, of course; but I did not try to pass through the city. I felt sure that I would be manhandled. So I returned home.

I had acted prudently. There were serious disturbances in the old city. Its town hall was set on fire and partly gutted. Men in European dress were set upon, and the violence was so great that the police were compelled to open fire. Some of the rioters were killed. In New Delhi the military procession was jeered at, and had black flags waved at it. The soldiers, both British and Indian, were booed, and the procession into the old city was abandoned. Two field-marshals, who had fought the Germans victoriously, went home, admitting defeat at the hands of an Indian rabble. If they were not ready to face that obscene defiance, they should not have instituted the trials of the INA. After that surrender, nothing was impossible, and nothing worse could happen or did happen.

Subhas Chandra Base: the End

Only one man came out of this squalid episode unstained by dishonour, although destroyed by fate, and he was Subhas Bose. This has to be said to his credit in spite of the fact that throughout his political career he never showed any realism in dealing with the situations which faced him. His failures were in every case intellectual, and yet he was not born without exceptional intellectual ability. But it was paralysed by his hatred of British rule, which willy-nilly drove him to irrational courses.

I think of him as the combination of both Frankenstein and his Monster in one person. The Subhas Bose who wanted to free his country from foreign rule was Frankenstein, and he acted rationally and patriotically when he rejected the career that was offered to him in the Indian Civil Service. But as his political role grew he became progressively more irrational, and the Monster which he had created within himself out of his hatred of British rule never allowed him to be anything else. In the final stage of his career it also developed its full fury and drove him from India to Germany, from German to japan, from Japan to Burma, and at last set him on his journey to the Soviet Union which resulted in his death. It was as if the Monster said to him when the destruction of all his hopes in Burma might have freed him from its grip: 'My reign over you is not yet over. You live, and my power is complete. Follow me; I seek the everlasting ices of the north; where you will feel the misery of cold and frost to which I am impassive.'

He was saved from further disappointment and suffering only by his death. Surveying his life from 1916 when he was nineteen and first came to public notice as the leader of a group of students who assaulted their English professor for making what they regarded as an insulting remark about India and Indians, down to his death in an air crash on Taiwan in 1945, one feels inclined to become a fatalist. All the steps in his career were in the direction of his final end, as if each one of them was dictated by that dread thing embodied in the dread Greek word: *Ananke*.

Subhas Bose had gone to Germany to seek the military means of liberating India from British rule, and that depended on a military victory for Germany. I do not know what he thought about the war then, but if after the German attack on Russia, which took place soon after his arrival in Germany, he still believed in a German victory, he must have become a greater illusionist than before. Perhaps he had, for all his subsequent activities were based on new illusions.

However that might be, he could not have nursed any illusions about his place in the German scheme of things. He had been used as a mere propaganda agent by the Nazis. With my strong feelings about the war and some residue of respect which I still had for the Indian nationalist movement, I was bound to feel derisive, and even to be scandalized, when I heard in Delhi that Bose was broadcasting anti-British propaganda from Berlin. For Subhas Bose to have become an Indian Lord Haw Haw was a descent beyond my comprehension. However, the Germans had no further use for him and sent him away to Japan. A Czech scholar, Milan Hauner, has described at some length what happened to Bose in Germany, and it is a pitiful tale.

Apart from his political role in Germany, an event in his personal life there gave me a shock. After the war was over I learnt that he had married a German woman, who was his secretary, and left a daughter in Germany. His brothers in India accepted the marriage as fact, although some doubt has been cast as to its taking place formally.* But for me even a very proper marriage of that sort would have been enough of a shock. I could never have imagined from my knowledge of his career and character that after setting out on his mission to free India with German military help, he could be capable of so commonplace a European entanglement as marrying a secretary.

I have already recorded what I thought about his sexual inclinations, and had enough proof of his suppression of them in obedience to his patriotic duty, in which he was an outstanding example of an established Bengali type. That view of mine was no longer tenable. It was destroyed by a banal act of the stalest kind. There were beautiful Bengali girls who, if only he would look at them, would have worshipped him as a divinity and loved him as Heloïse loved Abelard. And the plain ones would have become *devadasis*, dancing girls dedicated to a God, for his sake. From that, to the marriage in Germany, was a descent indeed. He had shaped himself, to my thinking, in the image of the warrior ascetics delineated as ideal patriots in a famous Bengali novel, which was the bible of Bengali revolutionaries at the turn of the century. These Bengali Knights Templars had to take a vow not only to eschew women sexually, but not even to sit on the same seat with

* I have been informed that the marriage formally through.

them, and the atonement for any failure to keep that vow was to seek death on the battlefield. I had no doubt that Subhas Bose thought of himself in that way, and I cannot explain how he became different.

To revert to his political activities, he was taken to the Indian Ocean by a German U-boat and was picked up there by a Japanese submarine, to reach Japan by the middle of 1943. He at once displayed his capacity for illusions by telling the Japanese commanders thatjapan was bound to win the war, which surprised even his hosts. But Subhas Bose had taken such a course that if he had to sustain his will to live he had also to cling to illusions. Nonetheless, at the juncture he was given an opportunity to put his plan of military action into practice. He went to Burma for that, and I have described what happened to his enterprise there.

After the Japanese defeat in Burma all his hopes vanished. That seems to have destroyed all power of rational thinking in him. If he had been a calculating politician he would have surrendered to the British forces like his INA followers and put the British authorities in a most difficult position. Logically, and consistently with what the victorious Allied Powers were doing to German and Japanese politicians and commanders, they should have tried Subhas Bose for treason and at least kept him in prison. But in India that would have led to disturbances on a scale far wider and more violent than those brought about by the INA trials, and that could have ended only in a bloody British victory or an ignominious surrender for them, both equally barren politically. Or the British authorities could have set him free after his capture and left him unopposed in his political activities. That, too, would not have been much better than trying him, for it would have exposed to the world the double standard followed in punishing the Germans and the Japanese on the one hand and letting off their Indian collaborators.

And in the disgrace, not only the British authorities in India but even the British Government at home would have become involved. If Bose had been captured, a decision regarding his fate would have had to be taken by the British Government in London instead of being left to the demoralized British administration in India. From such a decision, taken at such a level and concerning such a personage, there could have been no retreat. Neither concealment nor pretence would have been possible.

The death of Subhas Bose saved the British authorities from having to face such a problem, and for this they should have been grateful to his irrationality. But many British writers, and more especially British commanders, have indulged in sarcasm in very bad taste about him and what they regarded as his 'plumpness'. This was an exhibition of meanness, to say the least; for has any British soldier scoffed at the figures of Hindenburg and Ludendorff, or those of the Russian marshals, even the very young ones, of the Second World War? But any meeting with a Bengali brought out the worst in every Englishman.

For the Gandhian Congress, too, Subhas Bose provided a windfall by his death. Had he lived and come back to India he would have swept public opinion in the whole of the country to his side, and for the Congress not to have identified itself with him would have been suicide. But going over to him would hardly have been much better. He would have left only a minor role to play for the Gandhi-Nehru leadership and could have dictated his terms, which the Gandhian Congress would have had to accept. In this way Bose could have taken revenge for his expulsion in 1939. But he did not take this decision, which he certainly would have done had he been an astute, or, for that matter, any kind of, political calculator.

Nor did he behave like a Hindu or a Muslim with a military tradition behind him. At Omdurman the last dervish stood facing a charge of British cavalry at the end of the day. He looked at the setting sun, spoke the name of Allah, threw his lance, and was shot down by a hail of bullets from a Maxim-Nordenfelt gun. So too did the Rajputs die at Haldighat. In the same manner, Bose could have gathered some of his followers round him and died fighting. He did not seek that sort of martyrdom for that was not in his blood.

Confronted with the disappearance of all his hopes, he pursued another illusion. He decided to take refuge in the Soviet Union, and asked the Japanese authorities to send him to Mukden in an aeroplane. The authorities in Tokyo were rather offended that after being treated with so much consideration by them, Bose should ask to go over to the Russians who had just declared war on Japan. But Field Marshal Count Terauchi on his personal responsibility provided him with an aeroplane. While flying to Mukden, the plane took fire at T'aipeh on Taiwan, and Bose received severe burns of which he died. His body was taken to Japan, where he was given an honourable funeral.

This decision of his baffles all understanding. If he reckoned on the possibility of being accepted as a refugee in the Soviet Union after being in

Germany and Japan while the war lasted, he must have been deprived of all his rational faculties by his despair. Indeed, those who saw his last photograph said that he had become haggard and was hardly recognizable. His handwriting, too, had changed in the last days. He seems to have become as feeble as Frankenstein on his deathbed in the Arctic Circle. So, he did not perhaps even consider the possibility that he would be handed over to the British by the Russians, who on their part demanded the surrender of prisoners in British hands. If Hess had to be sent to Germany from Britain there was no reason why Bose should not have been sent to London or Kandy in Ceylon. At all events, he did not have to pay that price for his last mistake.

Nonetheless, his end was tragic, and in the light of reason it was an unnecessary tragedy. His end was an act of mad self-destruction. Even so, it entitles him to be regarded as a martyr to the cause of Indian nationalism, as Gandhi became another martyr three years later. Bose's life and death were both supreme tragedies.

One should have thought that, for its very starkness, this tragedy would be respected by his fellow-Bengalis, and his memory would not be desecrated by self-interest, either weakly or cunningly pursued. Yet that has been the case, and that certainly is the cruellest tragedy of all. The general mass of his fellow-Bengalis, who have been reduced mentally to a state of dementia by the realization of their collective failure, need Subhas Bose as a prop to their self-pity in the present and to their conceit of greatness in the past, and for both purposes they have created a false but trite myth of success for him, which is a mockery of his self- sacrifice, all the more so because it is unintentional. The whole cult is pitiful in its silliness and I am reminded by it of a spectacle which I often saw in my young days: a cow licking the stuffed skin of her dead calf and giving milk.

But it is the milkers who have created the greatest tragedy for Subhas Bose and offered the greatest insult to his memory. A horde of cruel self-seekers, who have no other credentials, are exploiting the myth of Bose to promote their political careers. They are ghouls exhuming a corpse to eat it. There is no awe at his martyrdom, no compassion for his tragic end, no regret for a life given in the pursuit of illusions. Whatever his mistakes, Subhas Bose had done nothing to have his memory perpetuated in this manner.

APPENDIX

The Political Situation in India in 1946

In the Introduction I have written that both British and Indian historians of the period covered in this book are under an emotional compulsion to suppress the truth. One of the most notable instances of this is the misrepresentation of the political situation in India in 1945, 1946, and 1947. All these historians are giving historical currency to the myth that in those years India was on the point of seeing a revolt against British rule, which, if its abandonment had not taken place, would have resulted in colossal bloodshed. While passing through the events of those times I was, of course, aware that the British authorities in India, both civil and military, were thoroughly demoralized and were ready to take this view. But I held a totally different view, and with the other unpractical things I did at the time, I tried to give a realistic assessment of the situation in an article and sent it to *The Daily Telegraph* on 11 February 1946. I am reproducing both the letter and the article. The latter was in total contrast to Field-Marshal Auchinleck's Note written at about the same time.

P & O Buildings,
Nicholson Road, Delhi
February 11, 1946

The Editor,
The Daily Telegraph
Fleet Street, LONDON, EC4

Dear Sir, I am enclosing herewith for your consideration an article which examines in its internal and external aspects the Indian National Congress's spectacular recent drift towards extremism.

Even if you are unable to use it it will perhaps help towards an understanding of the real meaning of this phenomenon...

Yours faithfully,
Nirad C. Chaudhuri

EXTREMISM OF THE INDIAN NATIONAL CONGRESS
Its Purpose and Meaning

1. *Nerve War Against Britain*

Since the failure of the Simla Conference, the Indian National Congress has been chute-riding. The drift towards extremism has been so sudden, so violent, and so portentous that keen speculation is rife about its meaning. A thesis is being sedulously built up that India is on the eve of an upheaval. The United States is the particular recipient of this SOS, and correspondents of even steady American papers are using language whose lack of moderation amounts to reckless sensationalism.

Insofar as foreign observers are concerned, and insofar as conscious partisanship on their part can be ruled out, it is a case of imputing themselves. A man from the West cannot believe that so much violence in language can go without some intention to act. Before the war of 1914-18 the Germans made exactly the same calculation. They expected insurrections to break out all over India as soon as Britain became involved in a war with Germany in Europe.

But the people of India, if one considers their typical behaviour, do not act in this fashion. They are capable of creating and nursing grievances and drawing satisfaction from self-pity indefinitely without going so far as a revolt. They never act until they believe action to be safe. The only real insurrections in India since the Mutiny were the Punjab disturbances of 1919 and the more recent disturbances of 1942, and they both had as their motive power the conviction that through external circumstances British power in India had become so weakened that it could effectually be challenged. Even then by far the great majority of the Indian people held aloof

The deep-rooted caution of the people of India was illustrated quite characteristically, although unconsciously, only the other day by a member of the Congress party in the Indian Legislative Assembly, who was speaking on February 5 on the Congress resolution recommending the dropping of the INA trials. In order to fortify his argument that all Indians were sympathetic to the men of the INA he declared: 'If only God had willed otherwise and these men had succeeded in their invasion, every man, woman, and child would have been behind them.' They would have been, but not before the success.

There is, however, another side to this building up of the idea of an imminent revolt in India which requires careful and serious consideration. The Congress stands to gain by it, and the foreign journalists who are spreading the idea must have got their facts or cues, or both; largely from the Congress camp. The Congress leaders themselves are also hinting at a possible upheaval, but in more guarded language.

All this is part of a nerve war. The Congress is acting on the same formula in the postwar period as it followed during the war. It is wanting to exploit the aftermath of the war with its disagreements and bickerings among the Great Powers as quickly as possible and in the same manner as it had tried to exploit the war-time difficulties of Britain. The Congress leaders have got the sense of a fleeting opportunity and are representing their own urgency as the urgency for Britain – putting out the formula that there is in India only a choice between immediately accepting the terms of the Congress or facing a rebellion.

That the bluff may fail as it failed at the time of the Cripps offer does not occur to the Congress leaders. On international affairs they have certain idées-fixes which they have never shown any capacity to surmount. Just as during the war they believed that Germany and Japan were going to win, or at all events were going so seriously to weaken Britain that she would prefer the lesser catastrophe of immediately handing over India to Indians than let her be occupied by the enemy, so now they reckon that the United States will not allow Britain to resort to energetic measures in India. As a corollary to this belief it is held that deterred by the consciousness of American opposition, the British Government and the Government of India would not venture to employ force to put down any disturbances that might break out in India, and would yield.

It should be obvious that there are possibilities of mischief in these beliefs. The idea that the British Government and the India Government dare not act may spread to the masses, and they may be induced to think that an insurrection is safe. This possibility has seriously to be reckoned with in the coming months, and it is the only factor with explosive possibilities in the Indian political situation today, if one excludes the Hindu-Muslim relations. It is more possible that a mistaken and misguided resort to violence will take place rather than a deliberate or desperate rebellion.

I am not reproducing the second part of this article in which I explained how in view of its position in 1945 the Congress felt it necessary to be more extreme both in respect of Britain and of the Muslims than it was before. This situation is dealt with in the following chapter. This appendix is inserted only to produce contemporaneous evidence as to view of the situation.

CHAPTER 5

The Red Carpet for Indian Independence

Political independence arrived for the Indian people on 15 August 1947. For a whole year before that they were engaged in making a red carpet for it to step on. It was dyed in the blood of hundreds of thousands of Indians who perished in the mass murders committed by the Hindus, the Muslims, and the Sikhs on one another in 1946 and 1947.

These massacres were the real prelude to the coming of independence to India, and not the bouts of futile palaver indulged in by all the parties concerned for two years before it became fact. And these massacres were bound to take place, although those who liquidated the British Empire in India failed both to anticipate them and to prevent them.

This is a strange failure to note, because all the old British imperialists were convinced, indeed they took it for granted, that as soon as British rule came to an end, if it ever did, the virile Muslims of the north-west would descend on the plains and massacre their unwarlike inhabitants. They even took pleasure in thinking that among the massacred would be the seditious Bengali Babu of Calcutta. Kipling described with some gusto how Nubbie Buksh, Abdul Huq, and Mohammed Yar put an end to the chatter and posturing of Hurree Chunder Mookerjee of Bow Bazar in Calcutta.

As to killings, the word of the old imperialists was fulfilled in the most horrifying manner, but they were not all on one side. Even in Calcutta Hurree Chunder Mookerjees killed as many Nubbie Bukshes, Abdul Huqs, and Mohammed Yars as they killed the Mookerjees. Over the rest of India, too, it was the same story. British generals and British battalions were still there, but their intervention was ineffectual to prevent the slaughter. So, one eminent British general wrote a book on the failure while his memory still served him, which reads very much like the Lamentations of job.

The inevitability of the massacres was to be deduced from the very nature of the political situation in India as it was from the middle of 1946. At that time the Indian people became finally convinced that the British were going to leave, and therefore division of the inheritance became a matter of acute anxiety to all the communities in India. This at once brought into play the age-old hatred between the Muslims and the Hindus as the strongest passion behind Indian politics. From 1920 the strongest passion had been the hatred of British rule and of the British. This now receded into the background and was voiced only when the Hindu-Muslim hatred found it useful as a contrapuntal line. The adventitious resentment created by the victory and survival of the British people was satisfied by the abject surrender of the British authorities over the INA trials. Thus the only hatred which held the field and became the motive power behind Indian politics in 1946 was the hatred between the Hindus and the Muslims.

Actually, the prospect of British withdrawal intensified the hatred to a degree never seen before. It was transformed into a live passion for self-assertion by both the communities from having been only a historical resentment against Muslim rule. Even as a distant possibility, abandonment of India by the British had roused irreconcilable aspirations. No side was prepared to make any concession to the other. So the hatred grew.

The only thing which could have checked the animosity as it was in 1946, was an unequivocal display of British will to compel the two communities to come to an agreement and failing that to impose a fair settlement by armed force if necessary. There was, however, no sign of it. On the contrary, the policy which was deliberately adopted was not to impose a settlement of British making. This made the future legatees of the British Empire think that they would get only what they were ready to fight for. The fighting by the leaders was verbal. But the masses on either side understood only their traditional method. Thus Hindu-Muslim clashes became the main political activity in India in the last two years of British rule. Even the talkers knew that, if they did not actually encourage the recourse to the direct method.

This was the only reality in the political situation. But it was obscured at the time, and still remains hidden, by the employment of a phrase which has become a catchword. The phrase was 'transfer of power'. Of course, it was a very tempting phrase, for it suggested exalted and time-honoured precedents: a Hindu father handing over the household and the sacred hearth to his son and retiring to the forest for religious meditation after reaching the age of fifty, according to the injunction of his scriptures; or an Antoninus Pius selecting Marcus Aurelius as his successor. What could be more gracious than for an English Oxbridge father to say to his Indian Oxbridge son: *Hodie mihi, cras tibi?* The play-acting went on, but the reality was quite different.

Even as a description of the play-acting, the phrase 'transfer of power' was incorrect, and in fact more like a fraudulent label for a spurious commercial article. In the first place, the British were not transferring power out of free will and on a rational plan, they were *abandoning* it. A final and irrevocable decision was taken about that by the Labour Government in Britain, and what was called for was its execution, not discussion about its advisability or feasibility. Indian political opinion was perfectly aware of that and thus what the Indian communities, and above all the two major communities of the Hindus represented by the Indian National Congress and the Muslims represented by the Muslim League, were interested in was to grab as much as they could from nerveless British hands by bluster and chicanery. But the British wanted to leave India with a good conscience and would not at once give in to the Indian game. So, all the parties began to talk, and the subject was, not transfer of power, but the discord among the Indian communities, and, above all, the Hindu-Muslim animosity. This talking went on for two years, and every failure seemed to whet the appetite for more talks. In the end, all this led to the inescapable result – an unqualified surrender to the Hindu-Muslim animosity. It is that which has been described in the pseudo-history of this period in India as 'transfer of power'.

The talking was both public and private. The private part of it was continuous, and every busybody in India contributed his share to it, confusing a confused situation still further. The public talking was seen in spurts: the first at the Simla Conference in the middle of 1945, even before the end of the war with Japan; the second in the middle of 1946, when the so-called Cabinet Mission came to India with proposals from the British Government for a settlement of the Indian question which would enable the Hindus and the Muslims to satisfy their aspirations as far as possible within an India still kept united; and the third talking was about the creation of a so-called Interim Government in which Indian politicians would form the *de facto* government of India, with the British Viceroy and Governor- General holding the position of a constitutional monarch bound by the advice of his ministers.

At the time all this inspired only anger and disgust in me. Even now I cannot understand how historians can read the proceedings of these conferences and transactions with patience on the assumption that they would reveal the historical truth. On the contrary, all these volumes of papers are a record of unscrupulous extremism, special pleading to the point of prevarication, concealment of the real motives under a cover of plausible pleas, disregard for national interest and welfare, and in some cases even of the self-interest of the communities themselves.

Nevertheless, it is necessary, simply because the talking has been taken seriously, to take note of its failure and injurious effects. The Simla Conference was a flop, but it revealed the extent of the disunity between the Congress and the Muslim League, which should have been a warning to the British authorities both at home and in India.

Perhaps the warning was not wholly overlooked, for the next attempt made by the British Government to make the Hindus and the Muslims live together in a united India went as far as possible to meet the Muslim demands, so far as it considered them fair and sound. In fact, the Cabinet Mission's proposals offered the last chance of keeping India united with a substantial satisfaction of the Muslim demand. The Muslim League, led by Jinnah, was ready to accept it, but the Congress rejected it with an evasion which I could not but regard as dishonest.

In spite of the cobwebs thrown round the main issues by the talking, it was not very difficult to pierce through them to the basic positions of the main parties. The British were not willing to impose a solution of their own, and as yet not ready to sacrifice the unity of India. The Muslim League was uncompromising in its demand for a sovereign state for the Muslims with a territory for them cut out of India. The Congress attitude was totally negative – to oppose every Muslim claim and compel the Muslims to surrender their Muslim identity.

This surprised me very much in 1945 and 1946, especially the anti- Muslim attitude in Gandhi and Nehru. I was perfectly familiar with their attitude towards the Muslims before 1939, and the new attitude seemed to be a total revision of that. Gandhi was regarded as an advocate of conciliation of the Muslims and Nehru almost as an appeaser. In regard to the Muslims, he was what is called a 'wet' in these days, among the Congress leaders. This was quite natural in him, because so far as he was anything Indian he was more a Muslim than a Hindu. His social affiliations were with the Muslim upper class in his province and his ways were also like theirs. He had no understanding whatever of even the highest forms of contemporary Hinduism as preached in Bengal and Maharashtra, and very little sympathy, if any at all, for it. Towards the crude Hinduism of northern

India, he was hostile, and he was repelled by the Hindus of his province. When in 1939 I had written that, short of a miracle, the Hindu-Muslim problem had passed beyond solution. I still hoped a miracle to come from Gandhi and Nehru. But the postwar years revealed them to be as opposed to Muslim demands as any extremist Hindu could be. This at first puzzled me.

But as soon as I gave thought to the matter I found an explanation for the new attitude of both Gandhi and Nehru. This did not, however, reflect more credit on them than their advocacy of the INA. Here is my explanation. When the Congress leaders were in jail between 1942 and 1944 or 1945, and thus unable to influence political opinion in the country, two other parties which were free to carry on their activities had immensely extended their influence. These were, on the Muslim side, the Muslim League and, on the Hindu side, the Hindu Mahasabha, which was the political organization of the conservative and militant Hindus. Their nationalism was plainly Hindu, and as the extreme Muslim party gained ground among the Muslims, so did the extreme Hindu party among the Hindus. There was a stark polarization in the country between the Muslim nationalism and the Hindu nationalism. On their release the Congress leaders found Hindu nationalism so inflamed that they had to yield to it if they did not want to lose all influence with the masses. Gandhi could do this with his cool opportunism, but not so Nehru. If he was converted to anything under duress he had the capacity, and was also under an emotional compulsion, to make it his own and passionate. This had been seen in his championship of the INA and was now seen in his intransigence towards the Muslim League. It was no longer the British but the Muslims who were his enemies.

In this collision between the two extreme and irreversible attitudes, the Congress soon gained an initial victory. In order to form a government in India which would satisfy the immediate demands of the nationalists and prepare the ground for a peaceful withdrawal of British rule, Lord Wavell as Viceroy invited the Congress leaders to form such a government. The invitation was sent on 6 August 1946, and the new Congress Government was sworn in on the 24th. The Muslim League was not asked to join it because it had not wholly accepted the Cabinet Mission's proposals. This came to be known as the 'Interim Government'. I have read that Lord Wavell was not wholly happy with what he did. Actually, he committed a ghastly mistake, for the Interim Government was the cause of terrible harm to India in more than one way. It deprived the Viceroy and Governor-General of India of all effective power, even to protect the people of India from being butchered; it brought about a Hindu-Muslim clash which was not only the worst so far seen in British-Indian history, but also opened a cycle of massacres; in a vicious spiral of unfortunate consequences it made the partition of India not only possible but also inevitable. What it did *not* do was to bring about a peaceful transfer of power – the very thing it was intended for. Of course, for all this the responsibility was not Lord Wavell's alone, but the British Government's as well.

The Congress was jubilant to have immediate power by itself. But this joy was short-lived. The Muslim League soon revised its attitude, and its members had to be included in the Interim Government in October. From that time there was no effective government in India. The Muslim League was determined to spite the Congress and the Congress could do nothing about it. So there were at the centre two governments. This divided government became incapable of preventing the Hindu-Muslim conflicts and the resultant massacres.

Even before the Interim Government took office the first of the massacres, unprecedented in the whole history of British India, had taken place from 16 to 18 August 1946 in Calcutta. Infuriated by the invitation to the Congress and exclusion of the Muslim League, the Working Committee of the latter declared 16 August 1946 to be observed as the 'Direct Action Day' by the Muslims. It was perhaps ostensibly intended to be a day of demonstrations, protest marches, and meetings all over India, but in Calcutta the Muslims made it a day of direct action in their manner. The government of Bengal at that time was in the hands of the Muslim League, and the Chief Minister was a fiery member of the League. He declared the 16th to be a public holiday. The Hindus resented that, and were determined to prevent any stoppage of work and also obstruct the Muslim demonstrations. But as the Muslims of the city felt that the Government would at least turn a blind eye to their activities they made preparations to deal with the Hindus.

In every Muslim quarter the Muslims were seen to sharpen their knives and spears and heard to utter their threats. Well-disposed Muslims sent word to their Hindu friends to be careful and avoid trouble spots. But nobody could anticipate that the violence would be on such a scale. The

British Governor of Bengal was so timid about his constitutional position that he would not invite the military authorities to take charge of the situation, and indeed he did not call in the army until the Muslim League Ministry asked for its intervention on the second day of the killings. The military authorities, however, had taken certain precautions. They had reinforced the troops in the city, so that there were four British and five Indian battalions in it. This force of about eight thousand men, if properly deployed in advance, could have prevented the troubles or at least stopped them before they had become unmanageable.

The unwillingness of the Government of Bengal was certainly intentional, and if they at last asked for military intervention that was only to save themselves from the obvious charge of being behind the massacres. It is also possible that they asked for military help when they saw that the game of killing was going against the Muslims. The military forces brought the situation under control by the evening of the 18th. By that time, according to even conservative estimates, about twenty thousand people had been killed or seriously injured, the majority being Muslims. The removal of the corpses alone set a terrible task for the soldiers.

It must not be imagined, however, that there were pitched battles between the communities. That would have resulted in fewer deaths and put a stop to the violence sooner by making it too costly. But what was carried out was the slaughter of Hindus by the Muslims where the latter were a majority, and *vice versa*. Besides, the Sikhs of Calcutta, a small but well-armed community with motor vehicles at their disposal, made forays into the Muslim quarters and killed the defenceless Muslims mercilessly. Over and above that, the killings were not always by maddened mobs. In a certain quarter of Calcutta the military authorities discovered that nine well-known gangsters, who were called *goondas*, were responsible for hundreds of murders. One of them died knife in hand fighting to the last.

Even more shocking than the scale of the massacres, was the savagery of the murders. A friend of mine saw a Muslim boy of ten murdered in cold blood without being able to prevent it. The soldiers discovered a man tied to the electrical connector box of the tramlines, with a hole made in his skull so that he might die slowly by bleeding. I give another instance which was told to me. I do not remember whether this happened on this occasion or on a later one. But the incident is authentic and was typical. A Muslim boy of about fourteen was passing through a Hindu locality and was seized. He was in Hindu dress and pleaded that he was a Hindu. He was stripped to find out whether he was circumcised or not, and when that proof of being a Muslim was discovered he was thrown into a pond nearby and kept under water by bamboo poles, with a Bengali engineer educated in England noting the time he took to die on his Rolex wristwatch, and wondering how tough the life of a Muslim bastard was.

Well-intentioned Muslims often tried to save their Hindu friends, and at times succeeded. A friend of mine was saved with his family in this way. He lived, with his mother and brothers, in the Park Circus area, a predominantly Muslim quarter. His mother, a widow and a very devout and philanthropic lady, was the daughter of the great Bengali religious reformer, Keshub Chunder Sen, and sister of two Maharanis. My friend with his brothers stood with bamboo staves behind the front door to put up a last fight. They heard the blows on the door and the fierce yells of the Muslim attackers, above which there suddenly arose a masterful voice, that of the Imam of the nearby mosque who shouted to them: 'Stop that and go back, I will not allow this pious lady to be murdered.' Fortunately, the mob obeyed him.

But, alas, my youngest brother was not able to prevent the murder of a poor old Muslim fruit-seller in his quarter, which was the respectable Hindu district of Bhowanipore. The man had been selling fruit to the families in that area for years, but was seized by his regular customers and dragged along to be murdered. He piteously wanted to know what offence against them he had committed. Hearing his cries, my brother rushed out and said to the attackers: 'Why do you want to kill this poor man? If you want to fight the Muslims, let us go to Park Circus and rescue our fellow- Hindus. I shall go with you.' They replied menacingly: 'Do you value your own life?' My brother had to see the man dragged away to be murdered. That did not lessen the anger of his neighbours. He felt so threatened that he considered it safer to leave his house and stay with my eldest brother for some time.

The truth about the Calcutta massacres and the organizations which were behind them was never discovered. A commission of inquiry was appointed to investigate the tragedy. It was dissolved a year later when independence came, as of no practical purpose any more. Of course, historical truth was of no importance whatever. On the contrary, there was advantage from its suppression. Even the reports of the military officers and of the General Officer commanding-in-chief, Eastern Command, who came down to Calcutta to direct the operations were not published. They have been seen only by some high civilian officials and some military officers.

The immediate impact of the massacres in Calcutta was seen in an exhibition of repentance by both the communities which in its silly maudlinity should have been regarded as an insult to the dead, but was regarded by the weak Bengalis as a 'miracle'. The Hindus and the Muslims joined one another in processions, chanted that they were brothers, and embraced one another. This could not bring back the dead, although it served to wipe off some of the shame. But what was more to the point was the fact that this theatrical display did not bring back peace to Calcutta. The city remained disturbed for a whole year till independence, and sporadic violence continued. The Muslims often threw acid bottles on the buses, but the Hindus used even Sten guns, of which they had obtained a supply. But at all events the day of independence did not see a resumption of the killing as the same day saw in the Punjab and other places.

The futility of weak repentance was demonstrated very soon. The violence spread at once to the villages in East Bengal, and in the district of Noakhali in the south the Muslim attacks on the Hindus were on a very large scale. This made Mahatma Gandhi go on a tour of the district on foot, preaching peace. I felt the impact of the Noakhali disturbances even in Delhi. A neighbour of mine who worked in the Government of India was from Noakhali, and one day his father, an old man, arrived as a refugee, leaving his wife and daughter behind. This conformed to the old Bengali tradition of leaving women behind when in danger. The old hypocrite gesticulated and performed antics if he saw anybody in the street who looked like a Muslim, so that his cowardice might be set down to his being deranged by fear. His son went and rescued his mother and sister.

I also saw what reaction the Noakhali riots produced all over northern India among the Hindus. In December, I went to Agra and stayed at the house of a Muslim colleague and friend. I went out with the members of the family to the holy cities of Mathura and Brindaban. Seeing me in the company of Muslims, a Hindustani came up and asked me angrily: 'How is it that you are keeping company with Muslims? Do you not know about Noakhali?' He very conveniently forgot what was happening in Bihar as a reaction to the events in Noakhali and Calcutta.

The Hindus of Bihar rose and killed the Muslims who were a minority in the province, in masses. From October to November, the slaughter went on, with too few troops to bring it under control. The young British soldiers who were sent there had never imagined that in joining an army they would have to do soldiering of this kind. They were horrified at what they had to see. But the reaction of the Hindu journalists was different. One day at that time I had gone to visit a friend who was a member of the Central Legislature, and the talk turned on the events in Bihar. A young Bengali reporter described the consummate strategy that the Hindu killers had adopted to bypass the soldiers. He said that they formed into three or four echelons in depth, and while one column was engaged by the soldiers, the others broke through to the rear. His tone was exactly like what I had heard when the same class of reporters talked about the German breakthrough in the Ardennes in 1940. I could not stand that boastfulness, and replied curtly that I had yet to hear that an Indian rabble could stand up to resolute shooting. The scandalization of my audience was so great at that outburst of mine, that my legislator friend, who was a lawyer, intervened to give a suave explanation of what I had said.

At the same time, the killings spread westward to the adjoining province of UP. Garh Mukteswar on the Ganges in western UP is a famous holy spot for bathing in the late autumn. That year the festival fell in November, and from the 6th to 15th November the enormous crowds of Hindu pilgrims completed their dip in the holy river by killing Muslims wholesale.

These events made the acceptance of the partition of India *in principle* a matter of *force majeure*, and this was something which both the British administration of India and the Congress had refused even to contemplate a year before.

But the acceptance of the partition *in principle* did not put an end to the massacres, although there was no longer any political necessity for them. The massacres preliminary to the final acceptance of the partition began early in 1947, from March onwards. They were seen first in the British district around the capital, Delhi, and also in the two adjoining Princely States of Bharatpur and Alwar, both ruled by Hindu princes. I first heard about these from a Muslim friend and colleague of mine whose village home was in the state of Bharatpur. He told me that the Jats had begun to kill the Muslims and his relatives were fleeing the State.

This was true, and by May and June the whole British district of Gurgaon and the States of Alwar and Bharatpur were affected. Of course, the police could do nothing, and soldiers had to be sent into the British area. The troubles in the British district were soon brought under control. But in the two Princely States, the Muslims were either killed or driven out. These Muslims were mostly of the well-known martial tribe, the Meos.

Some years after that my sons went to the State of Bharatpur to see the famous palace of Dig, and when they wondered at seeing the town largely depopulated, the Jats explained with a grin that they had made short work of the Mussalmans. In 1947 they had taken revenge for the sack of their holy place Mathura and the massacre of thousands of Hindu pilgrims there in 1754 by the Afghan king Ahmad Shah Abdali. The Hindus never forget anything and can bide their time.

What was more ominous, the killings made their appearance in the Punjab, at Amritsar to begin with. The Punjab had throughout the previous decade been remarkably free from communal troubles, due to a working arrangement between the dominant Muslims, the assertive Sikhs, and the Hindus. But I had been saying for years that if ever communal killings began in the Punjab they would surpass anything seen in the rest of India. This happened, and the mutual killings took a horrifying magnitude with the formal acceptance of the partition.

I was told about what sort of incidents became common when the killings spread to Lahore by a friend of mine, a German lady married to a Bengali doctor, who was living in that city at the time. She was tall and as she wore the Punjabi Muslim dress, she was seized as a Muslim woman and was being dragged to be killed. In her distress, she began to cry out in the only Indian language she knew, Bengali: 'Save me. Oh save me!' As it happened, in one of the houses there was a Sikh who had lived in Calcutta and understood Bengali. On hearing the cries, he came down and saved my friend, telling the others that she was really a Mem Sahib married to a Bengali.

The Muslims of the western Punjab were determined to kill or rob as many as possible of the Sikhs and Hindus who had exploited them, and the entire Hindu and Sikh population was driven like cattle out of the Punjab. When independence came the killings took on a greater magnitude. I shall describe what I saw in Delhi in the days following independence, but they were nothing in comparison with what was seen in the Punjab itself. Those who want to get an idea of that could read a book by my Sikh friend, the well-known writer Khushwant Singh. It is entitled *Train to Pakistan*. In it he describes among other abominations what was done to the refugees from both sides.

The responsibility for all this killing, bloodshed, plunder, ruin, and displacement of millions, with their subsequent miseries, must be placed squarely on the shoulders of the British authorities – directly on the British administration in India and at one remove on the Government at home. There was no way in which either of them could refuse to accept that, and I assume for the credit of the British people that they would admit their historical responsibility in retrospect. But shameless attempts have been made to repudiate it, and I shall have something to say on that score in the next chapter. Here I give the reasons for which I am so emphatic.

Throughout the period they ruled India the British rulers never believed that the different communities in India would live in peace with another unless they were present to enforce it. I have already cited what the greatest British administrators of the old days said about that, and I shall only quote Sir James Fitzjames Stephen again. He said: 'If the vigour of Government should be relaxed, if it should lose its essential unity of purpose, and fall into hands either weak or unfaithful, chaos would come again like flood.'

That was what came in during the last two years of British rule, with two great soldiers carrying it on. The maintenance of *Pax Britannica* in India was always considered the first duty of the British administration, and that was also put forward as the most important justification for keeping the Indian people under British rule. I would say that this was no insincere apology. Furthermore, I would add that so far as humanly possible the British administrators performed that duty successfully. Only in the last two years they failed. That was wholly unjustifiable. So long as British rule lasted even in form, i.e. till 15 August 1947, they had no right to abandon the task and leave it to the *fainéant* government they had created in August 1946. Poor Ethelred the Unready acquired his reputation with not a fraction of the *fainéantise* of the last British administrators. There was a combination of 'Unreadies'.

Kipling made an English Deputy Commissioner say when he looked at the battered head of a rioter that it was expedient that one man should die for a people. But what the British rulers acquiesced in during the last two years of their rule was that millions should die rather than they should be accused of being severe to the Indian people. Even during the last two decades of British rule an Indian Prince, one of the highest, had been deposed by the Viceroy for getting the lover of his dancing-girl mistress murdered, and another British Viceroy had deposed an Indian Prince, who had his school education at Eton, for being cruel, above all, to goats. But in 1947 two Indian Princes got away with the massacre of thousands of their Muslim subjects, and one of them was the successor to the Prince who was educated at Eton and deposed. The last English Viceroy thought that it was the business of his new friend, Jawaharlal Nehru, to deal with such matters.

CHAPTER 6

Mount Batten
Piled on Mount Attlee

In India, in the last stage of the liquidation of Britain's Indian Empire, it was a case of the old Greek proverb: Pelion piled on Ossa, under two new names. As if Attlee single-handed was not enough to complete the work of demolition begun by the more cunning mediocrity, Baldwin, he piled on himself Lord Mountbatten to add greater weight to his policy, which brought endless misfortunes to the Indian people.

This would show that I am no subscriber to the established myth about the winding up of British rule in India which has given a pseudo-historical currency to the following ideas: that the decision to leave India was an act of wise and farseeing statesmanship inspired by magnanimity; that it was executed in a masterly way by a brilliant military leader; that it brought into existence the largest democracy in the world; that it replaced an evil imperial system with a free association of nations; and that it opened an era of sincere and real Indo-British friendship. On each and every one of these counts the myth is false, and in its acceptance as history so harmful that in writing about it a historian who cares for truth can only repeat Voltaire's angry outburst: 'Écrasez I'infâme!'

Should this be regarded as too impassioned as well as unbalanced, I would ask those who would be inclined to think so to re-read Isaiah, Jeremiah, and Ezekiel in order to attune their ears to a modulation from the academic key to the key of those who have the capacity to love and suffer, and have in fact loved and suffered. Academics are more truly cold-blooded than reptiles, for they can also resist ambient heat, and so even that does not raise their temperature. Thus, they can air a detachment which to warm-blooded creatures seems like moral insensibility.

Be that as it may, I shall try to show in what way the myth is false with the help of facts which no one can dispute. But in this chapter I shall deal only with those aspects of the myth which hide the real character of the decision and of its execution. The exposure of the other falsities must await their turn.

Let me then deal with the decision and with the man who took it, that is, Clement Attlee. In order to judge how much wisdom he showed and how much free will he exercised, one has to look into his previous attitudes to the

Indian question. In 1927 he was nominated a member of the Simon Commission and remained on it until its report was published in 1930. I have already said that this report was the most specious presentation of the case against granting substantial self-government to Indians. Its setting up and attitude roused such fierce opposition in India that it had virtually to be disowned by the British Government even before the publication of its recommendations. Attlee signed the report without a dissenting minute, and to air appearance also shared the lofty disdain set down in so many words in it for the parliamentary capacity of the Indian nationalists.

He became a member of the second Labour Government in 1930, and was thus party to the suppression of the Civil Disobedience Movement and the arrest and imprisonment of Gandhi and the other leaders. He also did not show any desire to make the Round Table Conferences of those years a success. In 1935 he became the leader of the Labour Party and did not criticize the Conservative Government's India Bill as inadequate. In 1942 he was a member of the Coalition Government and of the War Cabinet and as such became formally involved in the crushing of the Quit India Movement. At no stage of his career until he became Prime Minister in 1945 did Attlee show himself as an advocate of political independence for India. His conversion came suddenly then, and its reason has to be looked for.

It is not to be found in the Indian political situation. In 1945 there was nothing new in it. It was not more dangerous at that time than it was in 1921, 1930, or 1942, nor was the demand for full independence put forward then. From 1921 we Indians knew, and the more perspicacious among the British administrators also knew, that Indian nationalist opinion would not accept any compromise which would continue British rule in any form. On 26 January 1930, the Congress declared India to be formally independent. But no British politician or party or administrator was prepared to consider independence for India except as a hypothetical possibility in some distant future till 1942, and even then the acceptance of the idea was not free from mental reservations. It was only after the war that it came into the ambit of practical policy.

On the other hand, in 1945 the objection which the British rulers had always advanced against extending self-government to Indians – namely, that they were incapable of it, and that their politicians had no capacity to govern them efficiently – had not become less valid, however interested

Indian nationalists might think that argument to be. Actually, in 1945 the Indians had not become more capable of self-government than they were in 1920, if anything, less. The foremost leaders were old and in many cases infirm, the lower ranks were less educated and more corrupt, and all were as inexperienced in governing as ever.

Therefore the reason for Attlee's decision to end British rule is to be sought elsewhere than in India, and I have already said that it was to be found in the postwar mood of the British people, whose will was broken by the war. I would make that more specific by saying that the British people had no desire to carry on their rule in India against opposition from the Indian people, especially when the immediate task seemed to be formidable. It was the urgent necessity of renovating the whole administration in India. Thus a people who resisted Hitler, yielded to India. The reason was defeatism, pure and simple.

Attlee recognized and submitted to it. But it was not solely he and his Labourites who did. The Conservatives who had resisted every extension of self-government to India, were as defeatist about India in 1945 and the years following as was Labour. They agreed with Labour's Indian policy, and even Churchill did not protest publicly. It should be pointed out that without that Labour would never have been able to withdraw from India. I have read a statement recently made by Lady Stansgate that her husband, William Wedgwood Benn, who was Secretary of State for India in the second Labour Government of 1929, did not approve of the arrest of Gandhi and suppression of the Civil Disobedience Movement. But he had nevertheless to acquiesce in all that. Indian policy of any British Government had to be an all-party policy to be effective. The decision about India was the result of a consensus, implicit certainly, nevertheless real.*

* The above paragraph was written by me in 1983 when I did not know what Churchill's private feelings about India were at this time. These I have now found in the seventh volume of Martin Gilbert's biography which cites a letter written by Churchill to his wife on 1 February 1945. On board H M S *Orion* he had been reading *Verdict on India* by Beverley Nichols, which was abused by all Indians. Churchill, however, recommended it to his wife and at the same time told her that he had for some time had a feeling of despair about the British connection with India and still more about what would happen if it was suddenly severed. He could only add that he would make sure that the Flag was not let down while he was at the wheel. But he also had the perspicacity to see that Britain was getting nothing but increasing criticism and abuse of the world for holding on to the Empire, and also increasing hatred of the Indian population, who received deadly propaganda to which the British side could make no reply. Finally, he said that he agreed with Nichols in thinking that Pakistan had to come.

The defeatism in Britain was universal. Therefore, for his policy of surrender, Attlee could adopt the popular slogan which Churchill employed in 1940 for his policy of defiance. It was a private slogan which was intelligible to Duke and navvy alike and was embodied in the abbreviation KBO – 'Keep buggering on.' Attlee had only to make a slight grammatical change in it in order to give his password about India. With him, KBO, spelt out with a change of the voice from the active to the passive, became 'Keep buggered on.' That was the measure of the change of mood in the British people from 1940 to 1945.

This being so, no moral blame can be laid at the door of Attlee. A politician has to trim his sails to the prevailing wind. Politics is basically amoral, and so long as a politician does not claim moral credit for what he does, he is no more an opportunist than a wild animal which attacks or takes to flight according to its judgement of a particular situation. But the discussion of the withdrawal from India has not been allowed to remain on the amoral level. Therefore, a moral judgement has to be pronounced on it. And one has to say that there was neither wisdom, nor statesmanship, nor magnanimity in it. It was imposed by *force majeure*.

But Attlee also made himself subject to more positive moral condemnation by the manner in which he gave effect to the decision. He was in a great hurry to execute it, and on account of that hurry he did not consider whether his way of doing it would involve a repudiation of all the moral principles which lay behind British rule in India or would inflict irreparable injury on India. He was only interested in a patched-up settlement between the Hindus and the Muslims, and as soon as he thought (quite wrongly of course) that he had secured it he gave up India without taking any precautions about the immediate and far-reaching consequences of the step. On account of this, the abandonment of India in 1947 has to be regarded as the most shameful act in British history, approached only by the abandonment of the Whites in Southern Rhodesia in 1981.

In his hurry Attlee also did something which made the execution of his decision to leave India bear the worst possible consequences for India. It is this which I have likened to piling Pelion on Ossa. It was, however, the very thing for which Attlee has been highly praised and has had acute political judgement attributed to him. The thing I am speaking about is the appointment of Lord Mountbatten as Viceroy of India to replace Lord Wavell. Attlee himself regarded the choice as inspired. Certainly it was, if the intention was to leave India only after inflicting as much harm on the country as possible.*

Lord Mountbatten, it would seem, was naturally a vain man, and his vanity had grown with his rapid rise to one of the highest military commands in the war, as well as the successes of that command. He was certainly inclined to welcome a political extension to his military achievement, so as to be able to say like Caesar: *Veni, vidi, vici* – I came, I saw, I conquered. In one sense he did that, but in another, from that very ambition, he did all the harm it was possible to do.

Before explaining that, I have to say something about his military record, because he was given his civilian post on the strength of that. I knew nothing about him until he was given the post of Chief of Combined Operations in 1941, although I knew a good deal about his father, Prince Louis of Battenberg. The appointment of a naval officer with the substantive rank of captain in the place of the veteran. Admiral of the Fleet Sir Roger Keyes, surprised me. But I did not pay much attention to it, because the command was a minor one, although formally equal to that of the other Chiefs of Staff.

However, his appointment to the Supreme Command in S.E. Asia in 1943 did make me seek for an explanation, and I then thought I had found it. I went at once to my chief, Mr Barns, and gave him the benefit of it. I attributed it to Churchill, and considered it to be due, if not to his favouritism at least to his patronage. I said to Mr Barns that Churchill was sorry when he had to accept the resignation of Prince Louis of Battenberg from the post of First Sea Lord on account of the clamour about his German origins, and he must have wished to make up to the son for the injustice done to the father.

I was not wholly sure, and so when some years later I met Lord Bridges (who as Sir Edward Bridges was Secretary to the War Cabinet and must have known the inside story) in Delhi I asked him if my assumption was right. He emphatically said that it was not and that Lord Louis was appointed wholly in consideration of his merits. That satisfied me for the time being.

However, I have now gone further into the question and am inclined to

* What I have written about Lord Mountbatten in this chapter was put in its final form long before the publication of his biography by Philip Ziegler. I have not changed my appraisement by even a word, and I leave it to be judged by history.

think that my theory was not wholly baseless. I have found that every step in the rise of Lord Mountbatten to high military positions was due to the initiative of Churchill and even to his canvassing. Churchill, of course, could do that on the strength of merit, but would the merits of a naval officer of the rank of captain have been known to Churchill unless there had been a social and personal association? Churchill had to proceed very cautiously in advancing Mountbatten. He sounded President Roosevelt before suggesting him for the South-East Asia Command. Churchill himself has said that he had to be very circumspect. Even so, the appointment was vehemently criticized in the American Press. One paper described Lord Louis as 'the British princeling and glamour boy who has ousted the proved veteran Mac Arthur from his rightful sphere.'

I became aware of his arrival soon after the event. One day entering Broadcasting House I saw a man of the Royal Marines standing in the hall. I went up to Mr Barnes and said to him: 'Someone very high up in the navy seems to be in the building.' Mr Barnes smiled and said that Lord Louis Mountbatten had come to see Broadcasting House.

As to his military standing, certainly no military historian would attribute genius or even any perceptible capability to him. The only achievement of his command, the recovery of Burma by a land campaign, was not due to him. In fact, both he and Churchill were opposed to a land campaign and favoured a seaborne invasion of Burma and Malaya. This was overruled by Washington, and the land operation was undertaken at the instance of the Americans. This was planned and executed entirely by General Slim, the commander of the 14th Army. Mountbatten as a naval officer was not qualified to do so. All that he did was to support Slim staunchly and wholeheartedly. This did not make him even a Montgomery, far less a Napoleon, by whose side he has been placed by an admiring relative. I am inclined to think that his appointment as the last Viceroy of India was due to his having been made the 'glamour boy' of the war artificially.

I can give decisive proof of Lord Mountbatten's incapacity for sound judgements in regard to military operations on land. Speaking at the Citadel, the military college of South Carolina, on October 12, 1959, he declared that India was 'adequately strong to hold her own' against China in a military sense. He said that India had a 'magnificent army, a capable air force, and a good navy brought up by the British. We think it's first-class.' 'Look at the terrain,' Lord Mountbatten told the assembled reporters, 'and tell me how the Chinese can invade. I'd hate to plan that campaign'. One has only to read the last volume of the biography of Nehru by S. Gopal in order to find what this foolish opinion encouraged him to do and to what demoralization he was reduced by thinking it right. After the war with China in 1962 had resulted in a debâcle, I had conversations with the commander of the Indian forces in the eastern sector in this campaign, and I was scandalised by what I heard about its planning and organization. Neither Lord Mountbatten's amours nor his military record will make him a peer of Maurice de Saxe. At best, he was a clever but vulgar adventurer, and he was exceptional only in this that he was an adventurer from a princely order. Princes may be imbeciles, but they are never upstarts.

He was certainly also the hustler Attlee wanted and missed in Wavell, who was dismissed with combined injustice and discourtesy. Mountbatten arrived in India on 22 March, 1947, and in two weeks he cut the Gordian knot in India, not indeed to go forward to India as Alexander did, but to run back from India to Britain. I have never been able to understand why he has been admired as a political genius for this. What he really did was to surrender unconditionally to the Muslims led by Jinnah by partitioning India and giving to them the territorial base for a Muslim nation which they had wished for. This was a worse capitulation for its consequences than that of Wavell and Auchinleck over the INA, for its consequences for the people of India were immediately disastrous and permanently harmful.

I must set down at this point that Jinnah is the only man who came out with success and honour from the ignoble end of the British Empire in India. He never made a secret of what he wanted, never prevaricated, never compromised, and yet succeeded in inflicting an unmitigated defeat on both the British Government and the Indian National Congress. He achieved something which not even he could have believed to be within reach in 1946. For this he can be compared to Weizmann who made a similar impossibility possible.

But for this very thing he has been pursued with mean malice by British politicians, Hindu politicians, as also by writers of both the sides which had to admit defeat at his hands. It was said by them that all the misfortunes that came on the Indian people with the withdrawal of the British were due to his unreasonable extremism. But what is called his extremism was the minimum demand of the Muslims, and was known to everybody for years. Why did anyone expect the leader of the Muslims not to stand up for it?

And if that was unreasonable why did both the British authorities and the Congress comply with it instead of calling his bluff? If the British surrender to him was pusillanimous, the Congress's was a crime. It had rejected the lesser evil which it saw in the Cabinet Mission's plan to retain the unity of India by giving the Muslims the chance to be dominant in certain regions. In the end it agreed to the greater evil by handing over the very same regions to an independent Muslim State carved out of India. It is the defeat at the hands of Jinnah which has made both British and Indian writers vent their spleen on him.

I did not, nor have I ever now, accepted the partition of India intellectually, morally or emotionally, and I have been saying since 1947 that, had I been anybody to influence events then, the last Hindu would have died before India was divided. Even so, I salute Jinnah as an honest and honourable enemy, and acknowledge his greatness. At least, he was more successful than Gandhi.

I was filled with consternation when, early in April 1947,I learned that both the British Government and the Congress had accepted partition of India in principle. What shocked me in the first place was the sacrifice of the unity of India. Her geographical unity nobody could destroy, and that is what has made her political division fatal. But ever since the first political unity which existed in India at the time of Asoka was lost after him, all political regimes had over two thousand years always tried to recover and re-establish it. And it was re-established as far as it could be by the British rulers of the country. Now the same British rulers were going to destroy their achievement. India's historical evolution was to be reversed. I could not get reconciled to that.

But the effect of partition on the peoples of the two provinces which were to undergo it, made me even more angry. Mingled with it was fear. The provinces were Punjab and Bengal which in their different ways were above all other Indian provinces: Bengal for its cultural achievement and Punjab for its economic prosperity and communal harmony. Both were indivisible geographically and economically as also culturally if culture is seen as a pattern of behaviour combined with a particular outlook on life. In religion, which in this case meant social identity, they were indeed divided into three communities in Punjab and two in Bengal. But even these distinct collective personae were like Siamese twins who could not be separated without making them bleed to death. Furthermore, there was a basic illogicality in dividing these provinces alone if the principle of division was religion. After it was carried out very large numbers of Muslims were to be left in India, and equally large numbers of Hindus in Pakistan. What was going to happen to them? Nobody gave any attention to that question until it forced itself on India and Pakistan alike. And then it had to solve itself with ruin and bloodshed.

As a Bengali, I naturally felt more disturbed by the idea of partitioning Bengal, and all the more so because my political consciousness was created by an older partition. All Bengali Hindus had fiercely resisted the partition of 1905 and got it annulled, and now the same kind of partition was to be re-imposed on Bengal. There was another element in the new situation which made the idea of partition more sinister. In 1905 the Hindus had opposed the partition and the Muslims wanted it. In 1947 the Bengali Hindus were wanting it, and the Muslims were opposed to it. There was a complete revolution in the Bengali Hindu attitude.

I had been taking note of this new turn in Bengali Hindu political thinking for some two years from the end of the war. The idea of a partition was being put forward by two West Bengal politicians who might have been called Hindu Ultras. At first I did not take that seriously, but when after the killings of 1946 in Calcutta the idea of partition gained ground even among the Hindus of East Bengal, I became alarmed. My logic was very simple: if our opposition to the partition of Bengal in 1905 by Curzon was right, our demand for it in 1947 could not be so. But just as the British thought that their leaving India was as right in 1947 as their rule was right for two hundred years, the Bengalis thought that both their attitudes were right, each in its time. I had no doubt whatever that they were going to commit suicide.

My fears on this score were very much heightened by personal considerations. Although my family was not going to be affected because we had cut ourselves off from East Bengal decades ago, we had relatives there and especially two sisters who were married to wealthy landowners. Ever since the Twenties I had been advising the elder sister to leave East Bengal because I did not want them to live under the social and cultural domination of Muslims, and in 1945 I asked the younger sister, whose husband was much more wealthy than my other brother-in-law and who was living at that time at Kishorganj, my birthplace, to come away to Calcutta realizing all their assets in time. But my sister wrote to me that there was perfect harmony and friendliness between the Hindus and the Muslims.

I came to know only early in 1947 that East Bengal Hindus had become very zealous supporters of partition on account of the endemic outbursts of the Hindu-Muslim feud from 1940. I came to know to my greater astonishment from the son of my elder sister who then came to live with us in Delhi, that his father was one of the most energetic workers in the agitation for partition. I said to him angrily: 'Why is your father doing that? Do you realize that even the birds of the air and beasts of the fields will weep for you if the partition is carried out?' Unfortunately, this became only too true. Both my sisters died in great distress.

I could not anticipate all the later horrors. Even so, angered by the acceptance of partition by the Congress, I went to see my old chief, Sarat Chandra Bose, who was in New Delhi and, I knew, was opposed to partition. I found that he was leaving for Calcutta that very day and said to him: 'Will you not do something to prevent this calamity?' He replied that the previous evening he had spoken to Mahatma Gandhi, and he had shown great sympathy. But a few days later Gandhi issued a statement which scandalized me. He said that he had been informed that Sarat Babu's opposition to the partition of Bengal was not in good faith. This was an allusion to the vile slander that the agitators for the partition were putting about in Calcutta that Sarat Babu had taken a very large bribe from a well-known Muslim businessman and politician to oppose partition.

After the acceptance of the principle of partition there was seen a demonic energy in *paperasserie* in order to produce a plan to give effect to it. The result was published on 3 June 1947. After reading the news, I only threw aside the paper, saying: 'Everyone has cut off his nose to spite his neighbour.' The whole enterprise was so contemptible in itself that I could not even get angry over it.

But those who produced the papers, which have been printed at enormous expense and are regarded with as much veneration by the historians of the end of British rule in India as are the *Acta Sanctorum* of the Bollandists by the historians of the Church, were inordinately proud of their handiwork. Their complacence, cleverness, and vanity interlard the lines in every document. But I was only reminded by them of what I had read in the reminiscences of the great German soldier Von Seeckt. His last reflection was: 'There are three things against which the human mind struggles in vain: bureaucracy, stupidity and catchwords.' All of these were at work in June 1947 in India as midsummer madness.

By what the British administrators *did* and also what they did *not*, they stultified two hundred years of British rule in India by disregarding two of its highest moral justifications: first, the establishment and maintenance of the unity of India; secondly, the enforcement of *Pax Britannica* to save the lives of Indians. In addition, without any scruple they betrayed all Indians who had supported them, and their number was not less than that of the nationalists. More immediately, they dismissed the very Indians who had helped them to run the government during the war, and replaced them with those Indians who had passively worked for the Germans and the Japanese.

If those Indians did not meet the fate of French or Russian aristocrats after the revolutions in their countries, that was not due to British intervention. They were spared firstly because Indians do not kill their enemies if they can inflict moral degradation on them, and, secondly, because these men were opportunists, who were as ready to serve the Congress as they were to work for the British. Over and above, every minority in India was abandoned with wholly inadequate provisions, even though fears for their welfare inspired many of the really serious objections to extending self-government in India.

All the calamitous results of the British withdrawal from India began to appear even before it was carried out. They assumed obscenely cruel proportions as months passed. Then an apologia emerged *ex post facto* which is the most shameless sophistry I have read anywhere. It was argued and is still being argued that if the British had not left – the manner of leaving being conveniently glossed over – there would have been uprisings and therefore loss of life far exceeding what was seen. Now, the conjuring up of hypothetical bogeys which no one can prove or deny is the first defence of every coward who yields at the first sign of trouble.

This crude apology does not clearly state whether the loss of life would have come from a rebellion against continuing British rule or from Hindu-Muslim animosities. Both are presented in one confused package. I shall take them one by one. In 1945, 1946, or 1947 there was not the slightest reason to anticipate anything like 1857, because the Indian people were perfectly aware that the British were leaving anyway, and if they had delayed their departure for the good of the Indian people they would not have risked their lives or interests for that. The anti-British bluster was kept up and boosted in order to keep the British on the run and also to secure the best advantages from them for each community, as I saw then from day to day.

In their heyday the British in India knew very well that the courage of Indians was to be measured by the length of rope allowed them, and to let them loose could easily transform them from good house dogs to rabid dogs. Kipling told them of this in the form of a parable of a malodorous animal, about whose character he said that the creature was 'desperately timid or wildly bold, everlastingly hungry, and full of cunning which never did him any good'. In the last clause there was a partial mistake, for Indians had an uncanny perception of the timidity of their enemies. That has served them well in their struggle for existence. Their boldness grows with their perception of the weakness in the enemy but it also recedes if they see any firmness in him. Then the Indian practises discretion, but he is never disarmed in his hatred.

That was shown by all the Congress leaders during those years. They watched the British 'Imperial Guard', but would not give the order to charge even if the Guard was reeling back. If only it would wave the white flag, they would like Wellington say to their followers: 'Up guards, and at them!' I shall give only one example to substantiate what I am saying. In February 1946 there was a mutiny of the sailors on one of the ships of the Indian navy. Its sailors were better educated than the infantrymen and were also more politically conscious. They resented the racial discrimination they saw in the Service and also the lack of amenities for them as compared with those for the British ratings. I had seen that when I went on board one of the ships in 1939, and took note of their sarcastic expression when questioned about their anti-submarine armament. In fact, they had serious personal grievances apart from their nationalistic feeling. So some of them seized one of the ships in Bombay harbour, and locked up their officers in their mess room, instead of throwing them overboard as the mutinous crew of the *Potemkin* did at Odessa in 1905. One of the officers – a Bengali – told me of the whole incident a few months later. He had resigned from disgust with both sides.

The Congress was loud in its support of the mutiny, and its strong man Patel himself went to Bombay to direct it. He was very strident at first, but when one day the crew were seen to be raising steam and manning the action stations and Admiral Godfrey, who commanded the Indian Navy, sent Mosquito bombers over the ship with orders to sink it if the sailors tried to put out to sea, he at once advised them to surrender. He was one of the Congressmen who had specialized in playing the nationalist firebrand or the wise statesman, a combination of Garibaldi and Cavour, according to circumstances. His advice was followed and the mutiny came to an end. It was not an episode with which even Satyajit Ray could imitate Eisenstein. But there was a great outcry in the Indian legislature against Admiral Godfrey. Who was he, said an angry legislator, to threaten to sink a ship which belonged, not to him, but India? The Admiral was sent home in the most unjust manner for doing his duty. If after that anyone expected Indian nationalists not to indulge in bluster he could be rated as a fool.

I have now to deal with the prospect of an aggravation of the Hindu-Muslim conflict. I have always been told that there would have been a civil war in India if the partition had not been agreed to. I have replied by asking two questions: first, has any country in the world been able to establish a revolutionary régime without a civil war? Next, has any civil war known in history resulted in the death of nearly a million persons and the ruin of many millions? Not even the greatest civil war seen in history, the American, approached half that figure in deaths. I would have preferred a clean civil war to the unclean massacres a hundred times.

I have also been challenged to produce a positive alternative to what was done instead of always criticizing that. I would not have taken two minutes to do so, but those who wish to justify the unjustifiable never admit anything as valid except their own folly. Here are my alternatives, but I am not going to include among them my conviction, founded on much reading, experience, and first-hand knowledge of conditions in India in 1945, that British rule in India could have been continued with far less effort than was needed to suppress the Sepoy rebellion of 1857 and far less courage than was shown in facing Hitler in 1940. I shall admit that for many reasons abandonment of India was as good a policy as the renewal of British rule would have been.

What was not attended to and not even considered were the measures which were necessary, one should have thought were obligatory, to ensure the safety of the Indian people after a British withdrawal. This was a duty imposed as much by two hundred years of British rule as by the decision to leave. But it was not even acknowledged to exist.

As against what was done, the following alternatives were open and each of them would have been better than the one adopted. First, the British authorities could have announced a definite date for leaving India, making it conditional, however, for all the communities, especially the Hindus and the Muslims, to come to an agreement about living in peace. Secondly, if that failed after a reasonable time had been given for its consideration by the Indian leaders, they could have suggested a fair settlement themselves and tried to impose it by persuasion if possible, but by force if necessary. Last of all, if they were not ready to impose a settlement, they could have left India, as they did Palestine the next year, washing their hands of India and taking no responsibility for the consequences. None of these would have brought more blame on the British Government than taking the responsibility for a communal settlement by half, as they did.

It is difficult to apportion the responsibility for what was done between Attlee and Mountbatten. But if Attlee must be held responsible for the decision, it is Mountbatten who is to be blamed not only for making it worse by his execution but also for making the departure from India undignified by his personal conduct. As the last Viceroy of India, he ignored the primary duty of his office which was to protect the people of India. He also went out of his way to show partisanship for the Congress. This was due to his developing an infatuation for Nehru. Under its influence, he departed strangely from his conduct as the Supreme Allied Commander in south-east Asia.

There he gratuitously humiliated Field-Marshal Count Terauchi, the supreme Japanese commander in the region, in more ways than one, and especially in exacting the surrender of his sword. General MacArthur considered this an archaic practice, and deprecated its enforcement. He said that its enforcement would make the Japanese commanders lose face, and that might make them incapable of controlling their soldiers. Mountbatten replied sternly that loss of face was precisely the thing he wanted the Japanese commanders to undergo.*

* It does not seem that Mountbatten was aware that Field-Marshal Terauchi deserved consideration even for his ancestry. He was the son of as distinguished and honourable a man as Lord Louis' father, Prince Louis of Battenberg. His father. Count Terauchi, was Minister of War at the time of the Russo-Japanese war. He had begun his military life fighting with bow and arrow in the civil war after the Meiji Revolution and bore an arrow wound in his arm. But in 1905 he was sending nine-inch Krupp howitzers to Port Arthur. Nehru's father was an adventurer and opportunist, a toady to the British when that was profitable, and a Congressite when that no longer was. He resisted his son's nationalism as long as he could.

Yet as Viceroy of India, he was truckling to men who would have been minions of the same Terauchi had he been victorious. Only just after his coming to India, when he had not dropped the manner acquired as Supreme Commander, he stopped Nehru's bluster by calling the men of INA traitors and cowards. But as soon as the episode which reminded him of his military past was over, he sank into a political manner which was the opposite of his former military manner.

His partisanship of the Congress, which was due to his infatuation for Nehru, was blatant, and it was shown most blatantly after independence when he actually supported Nehru over the Kashmir question. He collaborated in giving help to the Maharaja of Kashmir, which was to make the British dishonesty over the Princely States even worse.

If in dividing British India the British Government was guilty of a wrong act of commission, in *not* dividing the Princely States between India and Pakistan they were guilty of a wrong act of omission. For this they put forward a formal excuse which was the extreme of hypocrisy. They said that the relations between the British Government and the Princes were based on individual treaties freely arrived at between the parties, and they had no right to dictate to the Princes what they would do after the British left. But in practice their paramountcy over the Princes was absolute, although disputed by the latter even by legal action. The British Government could easily have divided the territory between the two succession States and by so doing prevented future misunderstanding. But their refusal to do so, combined with Lord Mountbatten's complicity in the Kashmir affair, created a permanent sense of injury in Pakistan. The British sin of omission in regard to the Indian States has left a legacy of many injuries, and the most serious of them is the imposition of a crushing military burden on both India and Pakistan.

However, I can understand Mountbatten's infatuation with Nehru, which amounted to moral hypnotism. For one thing, Nehru was probably the only Indian leader with whom he could talk as to an equal from the same class. But he found in Nehru a very special individual of his class. Mountbatten did not come from a circle in which sacrifice of worldly position and prosperity for an ideal was to be found, and that must have overwhelmed him when he saw it in Nehru. His admiration for Nehru was a superior form of the reverence which the opportunistic Indian officers who joined the INA felt for Subhas Chandra Bose.

His wife felt that even more strongly. She was from a plutocratic circle of the most worldly type, and her grandfather, from whom she inherited her wealth, was one of the set which opposed Britain's entry into the first World War out of fear for their money. So far as she had any moral sensibility, she was bound to be attracted by Nehru. But she showed her admiration so indiscreetly that even a private secretary of Nehru has used her letters to him to give the most slanderous interpretation to the friendship.

My judgement on Mountbatten would have been much more severe if it had not been for his miserable death at the hands of the Irish Republicans in 1979. There was, however, a frightening justice in that, because Mountbatten was killed by the active and cruel form of the same hatred to whose passive and cowardly form he truckled in India. Only a scion of the English royal family could have pulled off what he did without being called to account. And this royal link prompts me to recall two royal precedents. Constantinos Palaeologos, the last Byzantine Emperor, despite being no great ruler, died fighting before the gates of Constantinople. He did not lick the feet of Mehemet II. And another Roman Emperor, Valerian, although he had to kneel before Shapur the Great, did that under duress.

One has only to compare Mountbatten with General de Gaulle to find the difference between abandoning an empire dishonourably and honourably. De Gaulle abandoned Africa out of free will, just in the nick of time, without involving himself in what was to follow. Above all, he risked his life by what he did. But he created a new confidence among Frenchmen, and died in his bed. Mountbatten risked nothing, rose higher and higher after the abandonment of India, dwelt with satisfaction on his life and his luck. He could call himself Louis Felix. But death ran him down in the end.

I shall now consider the acceptance of partition by the Congress. It was such a feat of inconsistency involving a total repudiation of all that the organization had stood for and professed, that it can be described as apostasy of the worst kind. That calls for an explanation which has never been found, far less offered. I have mine, for which I cannot produce any documentary proof, but which I believe to be true.

The usual justification, which I have heard repeated time and again until I was made sick of it, is that the British would not have left unless the Congress had accepted partition. It is on a par with the British plea that they had to leave India in the way they did because otherwise there would have been greater bloodshed. You cannot have it both ways. Just as the British could not say in one breath that they had given independence to India out of freewill and in another that the way they did it was imposed by the fear of a general Indian uprising, the Congress could not say that their movement had secured independence for India and at the same time justify their conduct by saying that the British could not have left unless they agreed to receive independence on the worst of terms.

The fear was unfounded, but I also knew that the Congress did have it. It was induced in them by a combination of two things: their desire to have independence as quickly and as easily as possible and their utter tiredness. If they had refused to accept partition they would have had to leave the haven they had sailed into with the creation of the Interim Government, and begin an agitation again. Although it could only have lasted a few months if it had to be launched at all, they had neither the energy nor the strength for it. The comforts and fleshpots of New Delhi had caught them as in a net. In fact, the Interim Government was the Kheda in which these old elephants were entrapped. The immediate enjoyment, not only of power, but of comforts, had an effect on them which can be likened to what, according to Roman historians, wintering in the luxurious Greek city of Capua did for the soldiers of Hannibal.

All this may not have had any influence on Nehru, but the other leading figures of the Congress had never seen such high living in all their previous life. For them the prospect of leaving it even for an intermezzo of struggle must have seemed heartbreaking. This could be inferred from the conduct of the leading man among them, i.e. Sardar Vallabh Bhai Patel. As soon as ever he moved into 1 Aurangzeb Road he ordered luxurious furniture from Brooks, the expensive English furniture dealers in New Delhi, and without calling for tenders as Government rules required. He also ordered expensive carpets. The bills went to the Government Department concerned.

However, when the League entered the Interim Government and its members took over the financial affairs of the Government, they discovered Patel's taste for luxuries and leaked the information to their newspaper *Dawn*. It published the news in brief, taunting the Congress on its past insistence on austerity, which had prompted its ruling that no Congress Minister could draw a salary larger than five hundred rupees a month. Now, the paper said, the new carpets for Patel's house alone were going to cost sixty times as much. Strange to say, a categorical statement that the report was false was issued on behalf of him. But it did not proceed from one of his English Permanent Secretaries, Bozman. The next day *Dawn* published the full series of notes to prove that its story was absolutely true. Then another statement was issued that the orders were private and the bills had gone wrongly to the Government. I came to know later who finally paid them.

The lure of these comforts and the repose found at last were the first compulsions in the acceptance of the partition. But these were not all. The Congress leaders certainly thought that once the British were out of the way they would be able to put an end to Pakistan by military force. Patel boasted publicly about India's capacity to do so, and a Bengali politician told me when I complained to him about the partition of Bengal that I was being needlessly discouraged. Once we have a base in West Bengal, he added, it would not be long before East Bengal was reunited to West Bengal. I publicly stated in an article published in 1954 in *The Times* of London that the Congress did not accept partition without that sort of mental reservation. I came to know later that the article made Nehru very angry. Another reason for not showing firm opposition to partition was the fact that the provinces to which the leading members of the Congress belonged were not to be affected by it. Only Punjab and Bengal, for neither of which they had much fellow-feeling, were to be its victims.

Even so, the partition of India would not have become fact but for the incredible folly of the Hindus and the Sikhs of the two provinces, because the constitutional provision was that the partition would be carried out if only a majority in the provinces concerned would accept it. But there was to be no referendum. The members of the legislature were to vote on it. The voting procedure was split into two stages. First, there was to be voting in a joint session of the two Houses. If this went against partition, the members from the Hindu and Muslim majority areas – these being laid down in the plan – were to vote separately, and if any of the blocks wanted partition by a majority it was to be carried out. Formally, the resolution was not for partition, but for joining one or other of the two Constitutional Assemblies. I am taking it as for partition. Both the provinces accepted that.

I am giving the details for Bengal only. In the first joint voting, partition was rejected. But, by the second, the members from the Hindu majority areas accepted it. The number of legislators who decided the matter was farcical. Only *seventy-nine* members voted, and of them *fifty-eight* voted for and *twenty-one* voted against partition. Thus the majority which brought it about was *thirty-seven*. All the Muslim members voted solidly against. I might repeat my lament that never was so much evil owing to so few.

I heard later that Hindu members were flown to Calcutta by aeroplanes from distant parts of Bengal so that they might vote for partition. Kiran Shankar Ray, the leader of the Congress Party at the time, abstained from voting. Hindu youth of Calcutta went to set fire to his house.

But as soon as the Bengalis realized the mistakes they had made, they completely repudiated their responsibility and began to blame the British, the Congress, Gandhi and Nehru for their misfortunes. Like all weak people they would not take the blame on themselves.

But the worst thing was that the partition with all its immediate evils did not produce the only result which could justify it, that is, an end to the Hindu-Muslim animosity. It is continuing till today and has even taken an international form and a domestic form, both equally insensate. Muslims were massacred in thousands in India even in 1983.

The creation of Pakistan, which was the major political result of the British withdrawal from India, was also seen to be a terrible blunder in its original form. By it, two ethnic groups were united in one state, which except in religion were divided from each other by every natural feature which can divide man from man: geographical distance, physical and mental characteristics, social habits, language, and culture. By the same logic, or absence of it, the Bengali Muslims could have been united with the Arabs of Saudi Arabia.*

This unnatural union created as great a hatred between Muslim and Muslim as had existed previously between the Muslims and the Hindus, and at the time of the secession in 1971 that led to massacres not less ghastly than in 1946 and 1947. Thus the creation of Pakistan in 1947 also revealed itself as a crime as it did as a blunder ultimately. After taking account of the long-term results of the partition I might apply to it the famous French saying about the execution of the Duc d'Enghien by Napoleon: 'C'est pire qu'un crime, c'est une faute' – 'It is worse than a crime, it is a blunder.'

But for the moment the immediate evils shut out all considerations about

* I discussed in The Statesman of Calcutta and Delhi in 1966 the unnaturalness of the formation of Pakistan and said that a break away was bound to be brought about by irresistible historical forces.

the future in my mind. Punjab was ablaze. Refugees were pouring in from both sides of the divided country across the dividing line, even being massacred in the process. All this made Mahatma Gandhi fast on the day of independence. I was too angry to join in the mafficking. I treated the celebrations with contempt.

Very soon I was to see the consequences of independence in Delhi with my own eyes. These were not comparable to what had happened in Calcutta in 1946 and what was happening elsewhere in India and Pakistan. But they were enough to give me a first-hand notion of what the immediate consequences of independence were. As it happened, I wrote down an account of what I passed through immediately after the event. I shall close my account of the fall of the British Empire in India by reproducing that contemporary account in the next chapter.

CHAPTER 7
Eruption of Independence (1947)

Working every day from the beginning of May, I had finished Chapter 2 of the second part of my autobiography (p. 217 of the 1951 American edition), when my writing was interrupted by a sudden outbreak of violence in Delhi in September 1947. Looting, arson, and massacre which followed lasted for something like three weeks, and made it impossible for me to concentrate my mind. Although we were in no danger, the emotional disturbance was too great. When, however, the rioting ended I decided to write down an account of what I had seen before resuming work on the book, for I knew that I should have to narrate these incidents in my autobiography, and I felt that both accuracy and vividness would be lost if I did not set down the facts and my impressions while my recollection of them remained fresh. The account was written and kept aside for future use.

I shall reproduce it without any alteration. Its accuracy may be depended on, but, what is more, it embodies my feelings as they were then. My incidental comments were naturally bitter. That could not be helped. At the very beginning I dealt widi the problem of finding the right word, the mot juste, for describing the riots, and I wrote:

'These savageries pass as much in the outside world as in India under the name of communal trouble or Hindu-Muslim rioting. But these expressions have become the cliches of a stale journalese, which convey no real sensation of the phenomenon they purport to describe. Nor am I able to suggest a better alternative. I have weighed nearly all the words and phrases which the murderous ferocity of man, as distinct from his warlike ferocity, has contributed to the vocabulary of European peoples: massacre, pogrom, lynching, fusillade, noyade, St Bartholomew, Sicilian Vespers, Bloodbath of Stockholm, Bulgarian atrocities, Armenian massacres, Belsen, genocide, etc., etc., but find all of them inadequate. Their vividness has worn off Instead of evoking horror, they would rather throw a veil of historical respectability on spectacles of mass murder, rotting corpses, gutters choked with human bodies emitting stomach-turning stench.

'Besides, when a particular atrocity, however frightening or disgusting in itself, becomes associated with a particular country, people take it as insensibly as they take the association of a dangerous disease with a person in whom it has become chronic. Lynching with reference to the United States sounds no more revoltingly obscene than does pogrom connected with Russia, or Hindu-Muslim riots with India. The problem of diction presented by such phenomena is subtle and difficult: a word does not spring to life until there is experience behind it – experience of the thing it symbolizes; yet in the case of words descriptive of an unnatural state of affairs there is an insidious and irresistible tendency towards loss of force and vividness, because as soon as conditions of depraved and revolting barbarity arise the first thing that men in general, even though highly civilized, do is to become inured to them.* Thus, when the things themselves cease to hurt, words can hardly hope to be lacerating.'

In addition to these preliminary remarks, I also described the mood in which the experiences I went through left in,me. I said:

'My own state of mind as I am having to pass through contemporary events, I can hardly describe with any precision. I pass from state to state, oscillate from mood to mood. From one point of view I have reason for profound satisfaction, and I do feel gratified: my reading of the history of my country and the conclusions I have drawn from that study are not proving wrong: everythmg I anticipated is coming true. If I were a sphinx of granite with only the brains of man and bent on intellectual laughter, I should today burst into such peals of guffaw as with their reverberating ha-ha would crack the vast dome of the firmament. But I am a bundle of nerves and flesh, and I suffer. I am swept off my feet at intervals by uncontrollable gusts of rage at what I see. I feel like picking up a cat-o'-nine tails and laying about among our politicians, or want to seize a machine-gun, or better still a flame-thrower to cauterize the world of a suppurating vileness.'

All this is sufficiently illustrative of the mood in which I wrote the account. Nonetheless, in the narrative of the events, I think I practised a Thucydidean objectivity. Now for the account.

'Delhi had been somewhat disturbed during the last six days of August

* Today, I would add the case of Ireland.

and the first six days of September 1947. Some stabbings, some looting, and some minor arson had taken place in the suburbs. A nightly curfew had been introduced from 25 August, and another and more rigorous curfew, with a free period of only two to four hours every day for buying rations, imposed from 28 August to i September. Nevertheless I was able to go to my office, which is four miles away from my house, sometimes in a car, sometimes in the public bus, and sometimes even on a bicycle and on foot. But on Sunday 7 September, the situation worsened in a manner wholly unexpected by me and confidently believed by me to be inconceivable in the capital of India. Some people tell me that the outbreak was premeditated and prearranged. The way the rioting developed, spread, and continued makes this allegation plausible. In any case, what happened in Delhi happened with the moral concurrence of almost the whole Hindu and Sikh population of the city, and perhaps more than moral concurrence on the part of the police and soldiery.

'On the morning of that Sunday, finding no other conveyance available, I took a bicycle and proceeded towards my office. When I reached the Ajmere Gate a man came up to me and asked me not to go farther as there was trouble in Connaught Place. I did not believe him. Connaught Place was the hub of New Delhi; it was only about a mile from the Secretariat and less than a mile from the Police headquarters; it was inhabited mostly by tradesmen and office employees who had litde inclination and still less capacity for rioting; so I thought the man was a mischievous rumour- monger, and I inclined to the view all the more because I had noticed that when giving me the warning the man had lowered his voice and put on a leery smile. It did not strike me then that he might have thought something desirable was taking place in Connaught Place, only without there being any necessity for a discreet person to get too openly involved in it.

'I cycled on and noticed nothing unusual except the very deserted appearance of the streets. I saw nothing more even when I turned into Connaught Place. But suddenly, looking upwards, I saw men, women, and children crowding the verandahs on the first floor and the second floor watching something, leaning over the banisters. Before I had gone a few more yards I heard the sound of woodwork being smashed and saw a bunch of men breaking open a comer-shop in the arcades, and other men coming running towards the place in twos and threes. At a glance I understood the situation. Looting had begun in Connaught Place, and with perfect assurance of safety and success. It was not that the hearts of the most cowardly class of people in India had become stouter but only there was no need for cowards to become heroes to commit overt acts of robbeiy and violence.

'The looters obviously were from the nearby residential flats and servants' quarters. Other comer-shops had been looted before this, and I saw two well-dressed middle-class persons marching away smiling, one of them carrying a new lady's bag under his arm. Others were taking away bottles of cosmetics, wool, fountain pen ink, and such articles. The looting though quick was deliberate. I looked round for help, but could not see even one policeman anywhere.

'All of a sudden, catching sight of a running policeman with a rifle, I sped towards him, and as I turned a corner I saw two lorries standing, one with armed policemen and the other with a tear-gas squad, and a magistrate or high police officer getting down. Seeing, or at all events expecting, that the police would now go into action, I cycled out of the troublous area into Parliament Street. As I went down, I met lorries full of soldiers going at full speed towards Connaught Place. But I also saw batches of young men picking their way towards the same destination as if to watch some great fun. One of the parties asked me if I had seen anything and when I told them of the looting of the comer-shops and middle-class people going away with handbags and powder and face cream and scent botdes, they grinned with delight. Of course, it was known to everybody that these corner-shops were owned mostly by Muslims.

'Reaching my office, I found die Muslim employees seized with panic. They, as well as the others, were saying that numerous dead and wounded were being brought in from all sides to the police headquarters. The whole office was buzzing with panicky rumours. I finished my work in half-an-hour and started back for home. Some of the peons came up to me and implored me not to court the risk of going all alone and on a cycle:. I reassured them as best as I could and proceeded up Parliament Street. As I passed the police headquarters I saw lorries full of soldiers. I did not see any dead or wounded, but noticed on the lawn a crowd of Muslim tonga-wallahs sitting huddled together with terrified expressions, for the tongas were being burnt and their Muslim drivers murdered throughout the morning.

'As I went forward I heard shots and explosions in steady succession. Apparendy, shooting and tear-gas bomb throwing were going on. When I wheeled into Connaught Place I was challenged by two military lorries. I waved my pass and shouted that I was a Government official on duty. I kept my pass uplifted in my hand and waved it again before a party of soldiers with a Bren-gun looking for looters, and again in the face of a police van from which armed constables pointed their rifles at me. I was still hearing shooting all around me. But what struck me was the extraordinary coolness and self-possession shown by the looters. They just slunk round the corners when the police or the soldiers approached and then, like incompressible water, spilled out again. I learned the next day that at about eleven o'clock, that is, half-an-hour after I had passed through Connaught Place, Pandit Jawaharlal Nehru himself had come down there and dispersed some looters with his stick; but that nonetheless the looting had gone on sporadically till the evening.

'When I entered Minto Street I saw two tongas blazing right in the heart of the clerk's quarters of the Government of India, far away from the usual habitat of the usual riff-raff. After passing out of the area I cycled for three miles along an unnaturally deserted road. This road passes through the disreputable quarters of Delhi, and on account of this, over this stretch, it is normally crowded on Sundays. I have been solicited on this street by pimps even when going down to my office at ten o'clock in the morning. Yet on that day there was not a man to be seen on the road. I did not see a single policeman either. However, I reached home without seeing any further incident.

'The things I saw were trifles compared with what had happened elsewhere in India and were to be repeated in Delhi. But even as such they profoundly shocked me, so profoundly that on reaching home I broke down and cried bitterly. In fact, I howled like a child, saying all the while that I had never dreamt that I should live to see the day when looting, arson, and murder would be going on openly and unchecked in the capital of India, within a mile of the seat of the Government, and we, the law-abiding citizens, be so helpless against it. My brother's daughter, who had come to spend her holidays with us after her matriculation examination, sat by fanning me and trying to console me with her silent sympathy. Her mother said that she had seen infinitely worse things in Calcutta in August 1946. My wife, who was in another room, came running in alarm on hearing me crying loudly. Yet it was perfectly true that I had seen absolute trifles.

'I could not go out again on account of the curfew. But for the rest of the day we saw tall columns of smoke rising from almost every part of the city and heard the fire siren and the bells of the rushing fire-engines almost ceaselessly.

'I have described what I saw on Sunday 7 September at some length because that was my first experience of anarchy and breakdown of government. As has been seen, I was quite used to Hindu-Muslim riots and political turmoil. I had seen the political riots of August 1942 in Delhi. But I had never before had the feeling of a breakdown of Government; the rioting of 1942, described by nationalist propaganda as a rebellion, was brought under control in Delhi within a few hours. But in September 1947, in an India dishonestly advertised as free, I seemed to feel that, figuratively speaking, the ground was slipping from under my feet, as, physically, I had felt it doing in two severe earthquakes which I had gone through. I seemed to see the anarchy cooped up within the bowels of Indian society, that undying anarchy which is always there waiting for an opportunity to come to the surface, leaping out in blood- red and fiery eruption.

'Credit has been claimed by the Government of India for bringing the situation under control within the earliest possible time. Above all, a good deal of praise has been bestowed on Pandit Jawaharlal Nehru for the efforts he made to suppress the riots. He is certainly entided to credit for his intentions and civilized sensibilities, which have made him so unpopular lately with his co-rehgionists, but I do not think that either he or any mere individual was able to control the situation, just as I do not also believe that any high official or minister connived at the outrages, as has been suggested rather freely. This suggestion has come not only from the critics of the present regime, but also in a more insidious form from its friends, for demagogy requires that when the leaders do not possess the courage to commit atrocities alongside the populace they should at least be allowed in fairness to claim a share of the credit after the event. But to my thinking neither the claim about the Government's effectiveness in the suppression of the riots nor the charge of its connivance in them is founded on fact. The only thing the Government did was to fail; the riots came to an end only when the greed and malice which had brought them about had run their course and exhausted themselves for the time being.

'The truth of the matter is that periodically and in cycles a historical situation develops in India which neither Prime Minister nor Grand Vizir is able to control. If looting, quite open and unchecked looting, again occurred in Connaught Place on 16 September after Pandit Jawaharlal Nehru's personal intervention on Sunday 7 September, and with the military pickets standing close by without visibly influencing the events, it was not the first time in Indian history that a Prime Minister was being ineffective. In India, when empires decline, such things inevitaljly happen. In 1729, when the Mogul Empire was breaking up and Muhammad Shah was Emperor, there was a notorious Hindu-Muslim riot in Delhi, which has passed into history. Its centre was the great Jami Mosque built by Shah Jahan, which was nearer to the seat of the Emperor – the Qala '-i-Mubarak, "Fortunate Citadel", present Red Fort – than Connaught Place is to the seat of the Governor-General. At the request of the Emperor the Grand Vizir himself, Qamar-ud-din Khan Itimad-ud-daulah, went down to the Jami Mosque to quell the riots, but all that he could do was to stand helplessly near the north gate, while even the men of the Imperial artillery joined in the fray. After the rioters had had their way for some time they were however persuaded to retire without creating further trouble, and in recognition of this signal service to the State the Emperor took off his own turban and sent it to the Grand Vizir. Since Pandit Jawaharlal Nehru, when in India, wears no article of clothing which is common to him and Lord Mountbatten, I do not think the latter thought of sending him a present of this kind after the end of the 1947 riots in Delhi.

'Qamar-ud-din Khan, ineffective in everything as he was, remained Prime Minister for twenty-four years. But when bad news reaching him incessantly from all parts of the empire proved too harrowing he retired for some weeks to his garden situated four leagues from Delhi and gazed on the lotuses in his lotus pond, turned angler, or shot deer. In the end, !fiowever, politics overtook him, and he was killed by a cannon ball while $eated in his tent, on the eve of the battle ofManupur (11 March 1748) which was fought between a Mogul army and the invading army of Ahmad Shah Abdali, King of Afghanistan. But Qamar-ud-din's natural indolence and passivity did not constitute the decisive element in the situation. The next Grand Vizir, Safdar Jang, was ambitious and masterful, but he too was not more effective in Delhi than his predecessor who had a harem of eight hundred and fifty women increased to a round thousand by the present from Nadir Shah the Conqueror of an additional one hundred and fifty. It was an age of imperial decadence, and in such an age one could only shout: 'Le *vizirfaineant est mart*, *vive le vizirfaineant*!'

'I shall narrate a few more of my experiences with such comments as I cannot suppress. On Monday morning I was reading, when my wife came in crying out that the Sardarji had been stabbed. I at first thought she was speaking of our Sikh neighbour, but she explained that it was not he who had been stabbed, it was his old father-in-law who had come away with his family from one of the western districts of the Punjab after the partition, seeking refuge in Delhi. In spite of the remonstrances of his son-in-law he had gone out with his wife in a tonga and been stabbed by the Mussalman tonga driver. The old man's stomach had been nearly ripped open, but with amazing fortitude he had at first given chase to his assassin who had jumped out of the tonga and was running away and then, not succeeding in catching him, had come home driving the tonga himself and trying to console his wife all the while. My wife saw him patting his wife on the back and speaking soothingly to her as they turned into the lane by the side of our house. I went out and saw the bloodstained old man being driven away to the hospital. I underrated his wound from his quiet and self-possessed behaviour and thought he would live. But he died the next day.

'We had to consider the possible repercussions of this incident. Our locality had almost as many Mussalmans as it had Hindus and Sikhs, and both sides were excited. A riot could easily begin over this stabbing. Fortunately the murderer was caught very soon and handed over to the police, although he had escaped into a Muslim slum area. I must however add that in this riot, as in all previous ones, our quarter did not even have a single untoward incident. It was perhaps the only place in Delhi where during the riots Muslims could come out of their houses and move about freely. Elsewhere the massacres were the worst where the population was most mixed and most equally balanced, for the Hindus, half in fear and half in malice and greed, eliminated the Muslims precisely from those areas in which they were most numerous, as in Sabzi Mandi, Paharganj, and Qarol Bagh.

'After the stir caused by the stabbing of the old Sikh had subsided my attention was fixed by continuous bursts of rifle and Sten-gun fire somewhere to the west of our house, across the fields and parks. The firing went on for nearly the whole day. What could be happening there, I wondered, to make the day-long firing necessary? My eldest boy said that fighting was going on between the police and the rioters in Sabzi Mandi. I not only disbelieved him but got angry and scolded him. I was irritated by the suggestion of a prolonged defiance of authority by a mob, as well as by the assumption underlying it that an Indian mob could in any circumstances stand up to more than a few shots. I offered the alternative theory that the armed police must be practising in the rifle range nearby. But I found later that it was I who was wrong and the boy who was right.

'The newspapers reported that there had been pitched battles for twelve hours in Sabzi Mandi and large quantities of arms and ammunition had been discovered there in Muslim houses. The impression sought to be created was that the Muslims had been the aggressors and had defied the police and the soldiers for a whole day. I still disbelieve the story. The upshot of the rioting in Sabzi Mandi was that after three or four days there was not a Muslim to be seen there. Almost all the Muslim houses had been set on fire or wrecked. The streets were literally lined, and the gutters chocked, with corpses. Rumour puts the number of the Muslims dead there alone, leaving out the rest of Delhi, at thousands. Did they all die in a desperate defiance of authority.? Not till all my observation of my countrymen is cancelled by direct personal experience to the contrary can I and shall I believe in that possibility. A friend of mine who has made careful inquiries has formed a different idea of the general pattern of these riots. According to him, it was the Hindus who first tried to plunder the Muslim houses and murder the Muslims, and when the Muslims resisted or counter-attacked, the police and the soldiery came in, and they and the local Hindus (v«th Sikhs) between them made short work of the Muslims. I do not find the same inherent improbability in this hypothesis as I do in the standardized Hindu version given in the newspapers.

'Tuesday, 9 September, saw the continuation of the fires and the firings, but it was made most notable to us by the broadcast of Pandit Jawaharlal Nehru in the evening. This speech was far better in tone than many previous statements by the leaders in responsible positions, but still it was not wholly free from an undertone of extenuation. In almost all the speeches made during the riots the extenuation was blatant. No leader asked the Hindu rioters to cease looting and murdering without bringing in the events of the western Punjab. The argument very obviously was that the Hindus had their right to an eye for an eye and a tooth for a tooth and were more sinned against than sinning; but that, if they did not exact reprisals, they would be setting an example of magnanimity rarely seen in this sinful world and acquiring a high moral standing. I was reminded by these speeches of the lines of Lord Acton, which I had read as a college student and taken seriously to heart: "The plea in extenuation of guilt and mitigation of punishment is perpetual. At every step we are met by arguments which go to excuse, to palliate, to confound right and wrong, and reduce the just man to the level of the reprobate... until responsibility is merged in numbers and not a culprit is left for execution."

'In spite of Pandit Jawaharlal Nehru's appeal on the 9th, the night following his speech was very disturbed. We heard machine-gun and rifle fire very close to our house, and it seemed the firing was going on either on Hamilton Road or on the Dufferin Bridge. After careful listening I decided that the trouble must be at the railway station, which is not far from our house, and on Queen's Road. The next morning (the loth) my eldest boy went out with a friend and came back to tell me that a number of corpses were lying on Queen's Road on the other side of the Dufferin Bridge. I again flared up at him and told him not to go about spreading silly stories. I asked him whether he had actually seen the corpses, and when from his hesitation I saw he had not, I scolded him even more severely. Then he told me that somebody had told him so when he had gone near the bridge. I said I would go myself and count the corpses and teach him not to put his faith in stories carried by mischievous or cowardly tale-bearers. I went out. My wife with our second boy was in a queue before our ration shop. When the boy saw me he came running up and told me that he had seen a corpse being taken away, and my wife afterwards told me that she had seen a man with a hacked shoulder being driven away in a tonga, with two of his relatives crying loudly.

'Beyond the ration shop the street was very lonely and on the bridge not a man was to be seen. I passed on and when I had gone about half way across the bridge I noticed a man slowly walking towards me. I saw some red spots on his shirt and, going quickly up to him, asked what the matter with him was. At first he only cried out that he was not a Mussalman. I told him not to be afraid even if he were a Mussalman, but I could plainly see that he was a Muslim. Then he told me that he had been set upon by some Sikhs on the other side of the bridge and nearly killed but had escaped in the end. I saw nothing on his front to indicate that kind of attack, but on going round him I found his whole back cut up and covered with blood which was congealing like jelly.

'I was horrified and told him that I would take him to safety. It was raining and, holding my umbrella over his head, I walked slowly by his side. He kept on saying all the time: "I am dying, take me to some Mussalman." He also told me that he was from Bihar and had run away when the Muslims were massacred there last year. After that he had lived at Lahore for some months, and fled a few days ago when the riots began there and came to Delhi for safety. Poor man! Death had chased him for a whole year over hundreds of miles from one end of India to another and at last overtaken him.

'After going a few yards he said he could walk no longer and tottered down on the pavement. Fortunately, some Muslim houses were near, and three or four Muslims had come up on seeing the man and me. I asked them to give the man a little water. Feeling his pulse, I found that he was still alive and I ran towards the piquet near the Mori Gate to get the police to send him to the hospital. When I told the Havildar (the Indian equivalent of a sergeant) he looked towards the bridge and seeing two armed constables already taking charge of the man said that the wounded man would now be looked after by these constables. I came back to my house.

'The next day, Thursday the iith, I went to the office under military escort. It was a novel experience to be going about under the protection of soldiers over roads along which I had formerly passed on foot late at night and in early and dark winter mornings without the slightest fear of anything happening to me. In other circumstances I should have been very pleased indeed to be escorted by men of the regiments whose names and history I had leamt with such pride: the Royal Bengal Sappers and Miners, and Rajputana Rifles, the Kumaon Regiment, the i6th Punjab Regiment, but on that day and subsequent days their presence with me was only a reminder of the disgrace of our country and the incompetence of our Government.

'In the office I had the first opportunity to find out what others were thinking about the riots, and I found public opinion divided between two extremes. One was gloating on the smart piece of work done in eliminating the Muslims from Delhi and the second was the abject fear of a Muslim uprising and massacre by them of the Hindus. The stories of the finds of arms in Muslim houses which were being published in the papers strengthened these fears. One person told me that it was fortunate that the riots had started when they did – what he meant was that it was fortunate that the Hindus had taken the initiative and forestalled the Muslims – as otherwise there would have been a general massacre of the Hindu inhabitants of Delhi by the Muslims. As more arms finds were reported in the Press the legend gradually took shape that there had been a vast Muslim conspiracy to destroy the Hindus of Delhi or to carry out a coup d'etat against the Indian Government.

'From this legend followed its corollary that the catastrophe was averted only through the public-spirited enterprise of the Hindus and Sikhs who were in Delhi or had come into the city from the Punjab. On my way home the office bus passed through Qarol Bagh, one of the worst affected areas. A colleague of mine remained throughout on the lookout for corpses, and was rather disappointed not to see any. But we saw quite a large number of burnt houses, and the next day both this colleague of mine and I had our first sight of a corpse. As we were motoring along we suddenly saw before us a police patrol and a magistrate getting down from a van in front of us. They warily went forward towards the footpath before the railway hospital not very far from my house, and there was, lying prone on the footpath, the body of a young Muslim. Afterwards I ascertained the circumstances of the death of this man. He lived in a bustee near my house. The young man had made very high profits by selling betel-leaf during the riots when the supplies had been interrupted, and after selling all his old stock he was on his way to the bazaar to buy more betel-leaf His mother had entreated him not to go out. But he had gone without heeding her and was murdered within a furlong and a half of his house.

'On the same day (Friday) I saw an aspect of the troubles which was comical and tragic at the same time. An old servant of mine, who is also a peon in my office, came home with his head shaven, displaying a prominent tuft. Although a Hindustani, he had long ago modernized himself in regard to coiffure and had discarded the hairy insignia of Hinduism. But the modern equivocal wearing of the hair was no longer safe. So he had got himself shaven in the office and come home flaunting his Hinduism on the scalp. The fashion of proclaiming one's religion through this and similar devices spread fast. The Punjab Hindu, who by his face can hardly be distinguished from the Punjabi Mussalman, began to keep his shirt collar unbuttoned, ostentatiously displaying a skein of white thread, which was supposed to be the sacred thread but might well have been nothing better than the machine-made d m c or sewing machine thread by J. & P. Coats, if not machine-made thread of far less aristocratic manufacture. The worst plight was that of the Indian Christians. They began to wear a red cross on their shirts stitched to their clothing. The most unexpected exhibition of the cross that I ever saw was on the body of a Christian sergeant working in the Giiciof the Indian Army. He was in full uniform, displaying his three chevrons on the arm, and with his rifle slung from the shoulder. A coloured ribbon on his chest showed that he had seen active service in the war, but, hanging from his war service ribbon, was a brass cross about two inches in length. The shops also bore denominational labels. On almost every shop in Connaught Place was the inscription "Hindu Shop".

'From Saturday the 13th, I began to notice refugees in our street. The majority of the Muslims in our quarter were poor people – workmen, artisans, small shopkeepers and the like, most of whom had lived in the locality for decades and perhaps for generations. They were now leaving with their scanty belongings and going for shelter to the refugee camps established by the Government. From the beginning the authorities had taken the line that they could protect the Muslims only if they' left thpir homes in the city and went to the refugee camps. After the first day of rioting in Connaught Place I had read in the papers that the Government had saved the lives of many Muslim residents of New Delhi by taking prompt measures to remove them from their homes. What a queer achievement to pride oneself on! I thought.

'I had also heard people speaking about the restoration of normal conditions only through the removal of the Muslims, either through death or flight or confinement in the refugee camps. But it was not till practically all the Muslim shops had been taken over by the Sikhs and Punjabi Hindus, all the houses and flats formerly tenanted by Muslims forcibly taken possession of by the same class of people, all the goods in the Muslim shops looted or seized and then begun to be sold openly by the same gentry, that another aspect of the matter began to dawn on my mind. Could there be a cold, calculating side to this murderous ferocity, a thought of pelf in this predatory behaviour? I asked myself. The information I received from many quarters that the only opportunity the Muslims had had of escaping with their lives was when the aggressors were busy with looting – that being, as they nowadays say, the first priority in the programme, and the further information that Muslims had died mosdy in houses where there was very litde to loot rather leads me to think that the rioting was less an explosion of fury, less even than that Indian form of fury in which men retain sufficient coolness not to become furious unless the odds are at least fifty to one in their favour, than a commercial enterprise. Those who could pay the ransom mostly lived.

'Anyhow, throughout the weekend I saw the Muslims of our quarter waiting for the evacuating lorries with vacant looks in their eyes, disregarding the rain and the storm, as if their only thought were to escape the spectre that was treading at their heels. During the days of British rule their lives, like those of all humble Indians, had only been the lives of working bees and their homes had been far less clean and comfortable than the cells of a beehive. Now even these were being denied them. They were losing the right of toiling and living even as working bees. Among my coreligionists any expression of sympathy for these men was highly unpopular, sometimes considered even immoral. The ground for this denial of sympathy was the murder and dispossession of the Hindus and Sikhs in the Western Punjab. Throughout the country the theory had gained ground that the oppression of one minority could be counterbalanced only by the oppression of another.

'Monday was a rainy day and I could not stir out of the house. On Tuesday the 16th, I went to the railway station to see off my brother's wife, my niece, and a friend, who were going back to Calcutta. The station was disgusting. The stench was overpowering, and looking for its source, I found the whole of the line along the platform spread with human excreta. The station was overcrowded and the compartment in which I put my sister-in-law and niece was equally crowded. The passengers were mosdy Sikhs and other Punjabis, quite well-dressed and apparendy belonging to the upper middle class. They were blazoning themselves as refugees from the Western Punjab and advertising the achievement of their flight.

'All of a sudden a casual acquaintance of mine came up to me and asked me if I could take him along with me on my way home. I had no lift to offer him, for I had come on foot, but he wanted my company because he was a little afraid on account of a stabbing he had seen just outside the station as he was coming in. I was rather surprised at this report, for I had seen nothing, but I readily offered to accompany him. After a little while I, with my eldest boy, walked to the far end of the platform to have a look at the engine. It had not yet moved in, but opposite the place where it was to be, was the corpse of a young Muslim lying on his face. He had apparendy been trying to run away from Delhi, for he was carrying a bundle of bedding with him, and as he lay dead he was still holding in his arms the roll formed by his pillow and a light coverlid. Nobody seemed to mind the corpse, nobody watched over it, or thought of removing it, as if it were, like a piece of coal, the most natural thing to lie by the side of a railway line.

'On my way back I saw just outside the station the corpse of an elderly Muslim, which was not there when I had come to the station. He was a stout man with a fine white beard. His dress was that of a respectable person. There was a bundle of Urdu books scattered on the ground, and one in his hand. The fur cap was torn. I could not account for the death of the man, for there were plenty of soldiers and police all over the place.

'After a few days we got letters from our relatives about this journey of theirs. Here is the translation of a passage from the letter written by my niece to one of her cousins:

My dear Kirti,

I had thought I should write a nice little description; of our journey for you, but we had to see an indescribable abomination just at the end of the platform. Our journey began with the sight of a corpse. The Jumna bridge was strewn with corpses. After I had seen three I turned my face away, so that I might not have to see more. The other passengers in the compartment were all from the Western Punjab. They had reached Delhi with great difficulty and were on their way to their relatives at different places. Their glee on seeing the corpses was horrible to see. Even the two Punjabi ladies were wild with joy. Of course, it is true t)iat they were coming from the Punjab where they had left behind everything they had. Still mother and I felt very uncomfortable at this odious delight at the death of human beings. As we went along we heard three times that men were being thrown out of the train, but could not make out exactly what was happening. When the train reached Cawnpore the police surrounded the train and arrested a number of Sikhs, and searched the rest. After Cawnpore we felt more at ease.

'I ascertained that the group of corpses which drew forth the strongest expression of delight from the ladies was that of a mother lying dead with her dead baby clasped in her arms. And in the weeks following the riots, the so-called refugees were invariably throwing out the Muslim passengers whenever they were more numerous and had the opportunity.

'On Wednesday the 17th, I had another outstanding experience of my life, but which had already become one of the commonest occurrences in Delhi after the partition of the Punjab. I had in my charge a flat near my house from a Muslim employee of my office who had left for Pakistan. Having been informed that the Sikhs and other Punjabi refugees in Delhi were entering vacant houses forcibly and occupying them, I had taken the precaution of locking up the flat and hanging up a notice that I was in legal possession of it. But on Wednesday morning I heard that a party of Sikhs and other Punjabis, both men and women, were breaking open the flat and taking forcible possession, and I rushed to the house where I found a terrible squabble going on, the Punjabi ladies shrieking, the men arguing, a bearded Sikh glowering, and my Bengali compatriots who lived in the same building trying to defend my interests as best they could. I was able, however, by dint of a little bullying and bluffing, to persuade the men and women to go, but I was thoroughly sickened by the proceedings. I at last understood a historical situation which as a student of history I had always tried to resuscitate imaginatively but had not succeeded in doing: viz. what it felt like being a Roman citizen in Gaul or some other province of the Roman Empire contiguous to the Germanic fatherland, when one tribe of Teutonic barbarians driven out of their home territory by other stronger tribes came into these provinces. I could see that the memory of their dispossession by the stronger barbarians and of their headlong flight before them had done nothing to chasten their savage impulse to dispossess the civilized peoples who were weaker than they.

'On Thursday the 18th. Pandit Jawaharlal Nehru broadcast an appeal to the armed forces, piteously asking them to remember that the service of the country came first with them, requesting them to discharge their duties impartially, reminding them that it was their function to maintain peace, protect the people, and to defend the country. I had thought that the armed forces of civilized states did not stand in need of these reminders. But Pandit Jawarharlal Nehru's appeal, which could be regarded as the impulsive performance of an over-eager man burdened with a heavy sense of his responsibilities as Prime Minister in spite of the advice that in pohtics few things should be taken seriously and nothing at all tragically, was not the only speech of its kind. The appeals to the army were coming even from the soldiers, who are supposed to be hard-headed, from the newly installed Indian commanders of the Indian armed forces. Immediately after the outbreak of the riots one of the new Indian Major-Generals, who was in command of the Delhi area, issued an order of the day to his troops reminding them that it was their duty to obey the orders of their superiors implicidy and impartially. He wound up the order with the rhetorical exhortation: 'When you have to shoot, you will shoot to kill."

'As a young man I had had to read the King's Regulations and the Regulations for the Army in India and from that reading I had assumed that the duties and responsibilities of officers and soldiers, when they had to go to the aid of the Civil Power, had been laid down and taught once for all in these regulations paragraphs 1251 to 1255 of the King's Regulations 1928; and paragraphs 393 to 395 of the Regulations for the Army in India, 1928). I was mistaken. In the India of today the axioms needed restating. The first appeal to the army by the Commander of the Delhi area during the' riots was followed after the riots by another from another Indian Major-General, an officer tipped as the first Indian Commander-in-Chief of the Indian Army. This high-ranking officer appealed to the army to be loyal to the State and serve it. He certainly would not have issued such an appeal a month after the riots unless he had observed something in the army which called for plain speaking.

'I shall conclude this interpolation by relating the story of two extraordinary casualties of the riots and of two amazing frivolities. One afternoon towards the end of the riots, while the curfew was still being imposed from four o'clock, we suddenly heard the roaring of a lion near our house. It was coming from a point to the north, apparentiy from some place which we thought must be the Delhi spca. We assumed that a lion abandoned by some Muslim must have been brought to the spca. All night long we heard the lion roaring.

'At about midnight there was an attempt at arson near our house. I woke up on hearing some wild shooting close by. My wife, who was sleeping on the verandah, told me that she had seen flames and heard people shouting that a ball of fire had been thrown down from the second floor of a building on Mori Road towards the shop of our grocer, across the street and close to the Mori Gate. This grocer was a Muslim, but he had that very day sold his business to a Hindu. Some mischief-maker who did not know of the transaction was obviously trying to set this store on fire on the assumption that it belonged to a Mussalman, and he had taken advantage of the withdrawal of the military piquet that very evening. But since the shop really belonged to a Hindu at the moment of the incident the fire was duly extinguished.

'The special policemen, who had replaced the soldiers and were civilian volunteers, had fired some shots. One of these shots killed a poor madman who was running about in the dark outside the city walls among the trees. It must be known to those who have at any time lived in India that large numbers of madmen, some in rags, some wholly naked, are always to be found in Indian cities, wandering about, squatting, qr sleeping in the streets. In our street there were, and still are, three or four of them. It was one of these madmen who had been killed.

'The next morning, when my boys went out in search of the Uon, they saw the dead body of the madman. It was not removed before something like a week had elapsed, and it rotted away under the trees. The boys found that there indeed was a lioness in the s p c a and came home running to ask their mother to make some omelettes for the lioness since she was famishing. We had only powdered eggs in the house, and could procure no meat. My wife, of course, laughed at the boys, and, disappointed, they went back to the lioness, to find that she was being fed with horse meat. She allowed one of my boys to scratch her neck, and I remarked that after seeing what men were capable of, and having suffered from human ferocity, she was resolved to set a better example.

'That evening we heard no roaring and feared that the lioness might have been shot. The boys went to inquire the next morning and found that she was ill and had no strength to roar. However, she recovered and got stronger day by day, and her roaring, faint at first, began to grow louder and louder till it again attained its full-throated volume, Then we had another shock. The veterinary surgeon in charge of the spca, who knew my children very well, told them that unless some private animal-fancier or a zoo offered to take her, the lioness would be shot. We felt very sorry but could do nothing.

'One night we heard her roaring more loudly, more agitetedly, and more frequently than before. Then that noble voice ceased to break the silence of our nights. She had been shot. I wonder if she had had some premonition of her doom. When she was living and roaring near our house, the lioness had wafted the peace of the wilderness into a murder-ridden city. Her voice had lured our thoughts away from the obscene events which we were witnessing to travel across the African veldt, the Masai country, and the Serengeti Plain, and clothed our nights with the mystery of the gigantic crater of Ngorongoro. O dead lioness! for what you gave us for a fortnight a son of a man who would rather be your cub than a man in contemporary India thanks you from the depth of his heart.

'Now let me tell you the story of the levity. Our politicians have too many things on their conscience to feel at ease under the bewildered but scrutinizing stare of the outside world. They seem to suspect cynical enjoyment on its face, and, looking upwards at the infinity of space, they seem to detect even there a disembodied grin like that of the Cheshire Puss. So they peevishly complain of misrepresentation of their affairs. This is the imagined kind of levity of which India is conscious. I am, however, going to speak about real levity, the levity of the English friends of our politicans, which India, collectively taken, does not perceive.

'Taking up the morning paper on 14th October I read the headline: "Exaggerated Reports on India Deplored". I took it to be one of the usual utterances of the hired or voluntary propagandists of the Congress Government. But no, it was the headline to a summary of a speech by Lord Listowel, and the man was reported to have made three important points: (i) that the average citizen of both India and Pakistan had not been involved in the riots; (2) that the disturbances had taken place only in the Punjab and in speaking about them a due sense of proportion was to be maintained; and (3) what had happened was a trifle compared with what would have taken place at the prospect of continuing British rule. I was struck all of a heap. I should have thought that after being in Delhi during the troubles Lord Listowel would have been searching his conscience for his share of responsibility for them. On the contrary, the man was in part acting the role of a parrot by repeating the Indian formula about the riots, and in part acting the wriggling party politician. There is no doubt that the Labour politicians are being made to look fooUsh by all that is happening in India and in their discomfiture they are trying to justify themselves by conjuring up spectacles of greater hypothetical troubles.

'I am not wholly surprised by this performance, for there are some Englishmen who possess a far greater flair for presenting the case of their enemies than of their own. And I suppose politicians are entided to the licence of their tongues, even to the length of being allowed to say to a man stricken with cancer: "Foolish man! Keep your sense of proportion, consider what a small part of your big hulking body has been affected, and don't complain." I was glad to see Mr Churchill and one other Conservative MP rebuking Lord Listowel who had with such joyous yet inexplicable readiness assumed the role of the weak man with the sponge following the footsteps of the strong man with the dagger. But there is no adequate means today of making this ignoble peer eat his words, for India is fast becoming a terra incognita, if it has not already become so. It is being annexed to that vast stretch of land on the Eurasiatic continent, containing within it the Soviet Union and China, which is barricaded against truth; only partisan voices are likely to be heard from it now.

'We have to note only the back-talk that is going on between the ministers of the two Dominions into which India has been divided to realize this. The most extraordinary part of this altercation is not its atrocious bad manners – that perhaps is to be expected in politicians who for years during British rule have acted no other part than that of a common scold; the most extraordinary feature is the total irreconcilability of the version of contemporary events given by the two sides. What one party asserts flatly contradicts what the other proclaims. Each side convinces its followers and nobody else. I am reminded by this quarrel of some of my early experiences. My father as a lawyer with long experience of sworn testimonies from Indian witnesses had acquired an unqualified contempt for them. That this contempt was not undeserved will be admitted by all if I relate the story of an appeal which my brother, who is also a lawyer, had to conduct in the Calcutta High Court. It was an appeal against the verdict of a sessions court sentencing a man to be hanged for the murder of an old man. The prosecution witnesses had en bloc sworn that they had seen the man striking the victim with an axe in die course of a brawl. The defence witness had sworn with equal unanimity and emphasis that they had seen the man somewhere else at the time of the occurrence. The testimony in favour of the murder and that in favour of the alibi were equally decisive and admitted of no reconciliation. The truth however was that, when the man who was sentenced had seized the old man with the intention of giving him a beating, the son of the old man had struck at the assailant with an axe, but missing him had accidentally hit his father and killed him instantaneously. This fact never came out in the courts and, so far as I can remember, the only mitigation of his sentence that the accused man got was its reduction to transportation for life. Our politicians too, having with their own hands killed our country, are trying to pass off the matricide of which they are themselves guilty as homicide by their political opponents.

'The other example of levity was provided by the newspaper The Statesman, of Calcutta and Delhi, in a despatch from one of its special correspondents. I do not know who this special correspondent was, but the paper is edited by Mr Ian Melville Stephens who I suppose is an Englishman. The newspaper is also believed to be owned by British capital. The despatch I refer to was deaUng with the possibility of a setdement between the Government of India and the Nizam of Hyderabad over the question of accession to the Indian Dominion. After taking note of the growth of a sense of realism, in the meaning of there being more readiness to accede on the part of the Hyderabad delegation, the despatch went on to say: "The riots are stated to have played a helpful role." (See The Statesman, Delhi edition, 15 October 1947, p. i, col. 2-3.) In other words, Hyderabad, frightened by the riots, was in a mood to yield.

'It was splendid. This is an age which is abandoning, or at all events trying to abandon, straightforward wars as an instrument of policy. I noticed die change of spirit even in the British Field Service Regulations. In the first issue of Volume I of these Regulations during the tenure of office of Lord Haldane as Secretary of State for War (1909) was to be found the sentence: "War is the ultimate resource of policy." The provisional issue of the same volume in 1923 repeated the formula. But it disappeared in the 1930 edition, I believe, as a consequence of the signature of the Kellogg Pact. But though today war is oudawed by solemn treaty and public opinion, there is neither Kellogg Pact, nor Covenant of the League of Nations, nor UN Charter to oudaw riots. So, while honourable war is in disgrace, dishonourable rioting can be extolled as an instrument of policy.

'The lights are going out all over India. In the thickening gloom one group of barbarian gangs are clashing with other barbarian gangs. Unless a man is a self-deluded fool he cannot be certain of events for even a month ahead of him. There is interminable and sickening bluster in words in the true Nazi manner from men who do not possess a hundredth part of the only virtue the Nazis had – guts. There is tall talk of war by men who cannot manage a tea- party properly. Meanwhile the common man – the peasant, the small shopkeeper, the artisan – is waiting for the return of the English. People of this class who come to our house on business ask my wife: "When are the English coming back.'" When my wife replies that they never will these men are incredulous. Even political workers who have spent nearly all their lives in prison say that British rule was preferable to the kind of "independence" we have received. I heard a declaration of faith in the English from a man of the people a few days ago in a busu He was standing between the benches and had apparendy been ill-treated by a well-dressed passenger, a fellow Indian, of course. I had not paid much attention to the preliminaries of the incident, but suddenly I heard the man raising his voice and saying with quivering passion: "The English have notyet left. When they will have left and your Raj come I know what you will do to the poor. But not till then shall I tolerate your doing this." Probably the man had in his mind the presence of Lord Mountbatten as Governor-General when he said that the English had not yet left. The ignorant man did not know that his belief was wrong and his challenge futile – indeed even more futile than the appeal of the man who died crying "Civis Romanus sum" in Sicily without a faint echo to that cry rebounding from a degenerate Rome, but with only the ribald laughter of his executioner ringing in his ears. It was only after Rome had become a true empire that even a Jew in distant Palestine and Macedonia could invoke his Roman citizenship effectively and had only to say: "I am a Roman and a citizen" for even magistrates and tribunes to pause to think.'

It was the actual experience of going through the collapse of an imperial system which made the contemporary account of what I saw in Delhi so impassioned. Otherwise, I had already anticipated what would come out of that as a student ofhistorffl' and embodied my view ofit by implication in a note which I sent to Sir Charles Petrie forpublication in The New English Review. He did so in the December 1946, issue of the magazine. I reproduce the whole of the note:

INDIA

'Mr Nirad C. Chaudhuri makes the following interesting comparisons between conditions in the early years of the eighteenth century, when the Mogul Empire was in decline, and those existing today.

'1. Complete ineffectiveness of the State. It could not resist foreign invasion, put down internal rebellions, suppress Hindu-Muslim riots (there were Hindu-Muslim riots even in those days), could not ensure efficient administration, and was not successful in any project it initiated. One rebel (at Allahabad, Pandit Nehru's domicile) dictated the name of the Imperial representative who would be a persona grata to him and with whom he would negotiate. He demanded the costs of his rebellion and got them, and also got a new governorship as a quid pro quo for his submission. In the Imperial camp drums were beaten in honour of this victory.

'2. Concessions were made and accepted with mental reservations as a matter of expediency and not as a matter of principle. Sometimes the opportunism went as far as downright dishonesty where both sides had no other design but to double-cross each other. Scores of such instances may be cited.

'3. The ineffectiveness was due primarily to the exhaustion of Muslim political power (both inside and outside India). But a secondary and not unimportant cause was "Indianisation"; that is to say, installation of Hindus (particularly of the Bania class) and Indianised Muslims in positions where, instead of being subordinates, they could influence policy. The spirit of the administration was altered and the vigour gone with the decline of the Turkish and Persian elements.

'4. Political life and state service came to be regarded as the means of promoting private interests alone, and all posts were filled by careerists. The public revenues were looked upon as legitimate loot, and through jobbery and wire-pulling the careerists could get almost any assignments they wanted on the public revenues. Strange as it may sound, in contemporary Indian administration this state of affairs is being almost exactly repeated. The state did not get value for even half of the millions of money which was spent on the war in India.

'5. The Marathas and the Congress have suggestively similar characteristics. The Marathas were impelled by two motive forces: first, the negative xenophobia (especially Muslimophobia) of the Hindu, and, secondly, the mercenary motive of plunder and exaction. Of the two social orders on which the power of the Congress rests, the Hindu professional middle class supplies the .first and the Bania class the second. About the middle of the eighteenth century the Marathas were called in by the Imperial Government as allies in order to suppress certain rebellious Muslims and also to resist Ahmad Shah Abdali. The Congress resembles the Marathas in the sterility, lack of originality, and imitativeness of its political ideas.

'6. The effect of the decline of the power of the state on the masses was twofold. It made one part predatory and the other panicky. One section took to loot, murder, robbery, and finally evolved into the Pindari, while the other simply ran away into the jungles at the slightest sign of trouble.

'7. Lasdy, there grew up a habit of tolerance of anarchy and corruption, or at all events resignation to them. It was not till the British Power reestablished order that people again looked upon peace and security as something to which they were entided by birthright. That murder, arson, plunder, bribes, peculation are not normal is a sense which is becoming increasingly numb also in modem India.'

Please remember that this was written in August 1946, exactly a year before independence, and five months had not gone by after the day of independence when I wrote the following passage of the last chapter of The Autobiography of an Unknotvn Indian:

'Summed up in its bare essentials, the political history of India shows the Aryan, the Turk, the Turko-Mongol cum Persian as the only creators of political concepts and political orders in India up to the end of the seventeenth century, and after that the Anglo-Saxon takes their place. The rest have been only sterile imitators when they have either been given opportunities to exercise political functions by the decline of a particular foreign order, or have in their incompetent vanity and xenophobia sought to exercise them. In these intervals there have been seen in India only a futile pursuit of the political concepts of the preceding foreign rulers, inefficient manipulation of the political machinery left by them, and, above all, an egregious aping of their arrogance and airs.'

Today the scene is even clearer. Anyone who has eyes to see and ears to hear and has no sense of guilt to shut them to the reality, will find what the actual state of the Indian people is: there is today more maladministration, corruption and lawlessness than ever was seen at any time during British days; in some provinces there is no government to speak of, power being in the hands of gangs like the Mafia; there is more suppression of civil rights, and shooting for political reasons; more denial of freedom of expression and of information; more disparity of wealth between Indians; more inter- communal, intercaste, and inter-provincial hatred; more oppression and even murder of members of the minority and depressed communities; more exploitation by a privileged order of the people of India.

In the other regions of Asia and Africa conditions are even worse. In them there are evil tyrannies, civil wars more cruel than any seen in history before this post-imperial age, and also genocide. The only gain has been liberation from European domination, and there is undoubted happiness among the former subjects of European imperialism on this score because they have always held the political doctrine that it is better to reign in hell than serve in heaven. That was the only satisfactory bequest to these peoples by the dying European imperialism. And now that it is dead and buried the only question is what to inscribe on the Yiztchment-*Requiescat in pace or Resurgam?*

BOOK X

CROSSING THE BAR

1947–1952

Prefatory Note

Independence for India made a radical difference to my worldly prospects, but not in the way it did for others placed in the same situation. At the time of the British withdrawal from the country a majority of the highest posts in the administration were held by British civil servants. However, most of them chose to retire from service and go back to their own country. This created opportunities for Indians who were in the lower ranks of the administration which they could never have hoped to see under British rule. For those Indians who had ability or connections the promotions were like mini cars rising into the sky like jumbo jets. Even one-time clerks under the British became Secretaries in the Indian service. But these men at all events possessed high and specialised qualifications to keep the bureaucracy running in the old manner. They had become indispensable to the new regime which did not want to rule in any other manner, in spite of being Indian.

But there was no such possibility for me, nor was I indispensable. I could only remain where I was if I chose. I did not have any fear that I would suffer for my wholehearted adherence to the British and Alied cause. For one thing, I was too minor an official for my conduct to be noticed. Next, thousands of other Indians like me, i.e. intellectuals (being writers or journalists), had worked for the same cause, and for practical purposes it was irrelevant whether they had done so for the sake of conviction or money. The new Indian regime did not make victims even of those Indians in high places in the civil service who had made themselves notorious by their attitude as well as actions in regard to the nationalist movement. Actually, those who had served the British most efficiently were kept, so that they might put their efficiency at the disposal of the new regime. An Indian civil servant who had dealt with the Bengali revolutionary movement with great severity became India's first ambassador in Washington and the first representative in the UN. The loyal servants of the British at once became loyal servants of the Congress. Their new masters wanted nothing more.

But I could not make that choice, and so had no prospect of rising higher.

However, this was my own doing. It had become impossible for me to serve the new Indian Government in any capacity in which I should be involved in its policies. To anything beyond routine work, I had acquired an unconquerable emotional repugnance. Ever since the war had begun, as I have made clear, I regarded the actions of the Congress as a betrayal of civilization and humanity, and I decided that I would never seek any advantages for myself from it, which I could do by resuming my contacts with the nationalist leaders. Thus, I never called on Sarat Chandra Bose, my old chief, when he became a member of the so-called Interim Government in 1946. I did not also try to see Jawaharlal Nehru then or when he became Prime Minister a year later. I could have extended my previous contacts with him and perhaps he would have made use of me in some capacity, for he was sensitive to the kind of ability I had. But that was inconceivable to me. All that I could do in the service of the new Government was to do some work where no case of conscience would arise. How I managed that I shall relate presently. But the result of my choice was that I closed the door against myself in respect of worldly advancement in India. For the next five years I remained in a blind alley instead of being on the high road of official preferment.

But a different kind of future opened out for me then. In the early summer of 1947, when I was about six months short of being fifty, I took a decision, or rather had one imposed on myself by a spark of intuition, which accomplished that. That decision was to begin work on the book which was published later under the tide of *The Autobiography of an Unknown Indian.* However, I had no inkling at the time of the future that was to be created for me by that book. It looked at first towards the past, because my decision really meant the execution of a design which I had always had in mind to write a book which would not be mere ephemeral journalism, but be a work of permanent value, coming out of a life which had been sadly lacking in any real achievement so far. It was also to be the fulfilment of my promise to my wife to write the book she was always asking me to write.

But in the upshot the book that was produced cut me off from all my previous life and created a new life for me. Defining my new status I might call myself a twice-born in Hindu terms. To vary the metaphor, the execution of the design turned out for me to be like leaving a harbour, crossing its bar, and putting out to sea on a voyage of discovery into the unknown. In a passage of the old autobiography, written towards the end of

1947, I said that 'to be once *deradné* is to be for ever on the road.' Even then, although I was going to be fifty, I did not have any idea how long that road was to be.

In this, the concluding part of the book, I am going to describe the first five years of my new life or rather my plunge into the unknown. At its end, in spite of the success of the enterprise, it would be seen that in the worldly way I was left very much in the state in which I began the span of life described in this book.

CHAPTER I

Genesis of the Autobiography

As the publication of the autobiography was the most important event in my life at this stage I shall give a plain account of its origin and execution. With the advent of independence my personal preoccupation with public affairs came to an end. By the beginning of the second quarter of 1947 I had become convinced that in any case British rule in India would end within a few months, and this induced a mood of calm resignation in me as regards the Indian situation. But it also brought back to my mind my old sense of failure in life, which had been kept suppressed by my absorption in the war and Indian politics. The dormant dissatisfaction woke up, and I could no longer shut my eyes to the stark fact that I had no achievement to speak of, although I was going to be fifty. I neither could nor would reconcile myself to this sort of destiny by saying to myself that those also served who only stood and waited. The sense of failure was made more acute by an idea which I had just at that time that I was not going to live much longer and my health being what it was I would probably die in two or three years. What could I do, I bitterly thought, in that short space of time.'

There could be no question of my resuming work on the history I had begun to write and was compelled to give up. Thus, as regards the only kind of achievement I was capable of, namely, literary production, the prospect seemed to be blank. My mental distress was very great, and it was persistent. It also had the same effect on me as the previous onsets of distress had. I could not sleep after midnight, and lay awake for hours. But this time my sleepless nights came to an end differently. I got up one morning, not merely with reinforced stoicism, but with a positive and practical urge.

It came in this manner. As I lay awake in the night of 4-5 May, 1947, an idea suddenly flashed into my mind. Why instead of merely regretting the work of history you cannot write, I asked myself, do you not write the history you have passed through and seen enacted before your eyes, and which would not call for research? The answer too was instantaneous: I will. I also decided to give it the form of an autobiography. Quietened by the decision I fell asleep. Fortunately, this idea was not nullified by the deplorable lack of energy which was habitual with me. The very next morning I sat down-to my typewriter and drafted a few paragraphs.

I should add here that I always intended to write an autobiography to describe the kind of life we had in India, especially in Bengal, in the last decades of British rule, about which nothing was known and which had great cultural interest. But I thought I would write it after I had published my serious historical work and as an epilogue to that. I did not think that anybody would pay any attention to the autobiography of a wholly unknown and obscure man. The decision to write it then only brought forward the book, and made it my first instead of last work to be published. But I did that by wholly altering the scope of the book. It was to be the history I did not get the facilities to write.

I began with the descriptions of Kishorganj, my birthplace, with which the autobiography opened. These pages, however, took some time to write because I had to find the style suited to the work, and fix its key and tonality, so to speak. Once that was done, I worked steadily, typing on an average 2,500 words a day, and in order to spur me on I dated what I wrote. It gave me some pride to note that for some time there were no blank days. Of course, I was still working in the office and doing my apportioned work there. But my work was very light in point of execution, and did not take more than two hours a day, after which I left the office. In normal circumstances it would not have been honest work for the salary I then received. Nonetheless, I could say like Whistler that I was taking the money, not for so many hours of work, but for a life-time's study and thinking. Actually, I wrote more commentaries for broadcasting than any of my colleagues did sitting at their desks the whole day. I shall, in a later chapter, give some indication of the work I did.

I typed four pages of the book every morning before going to the office, and two more pages in the afternoon. This rate of production was maintained by a practical calculation which was never a normal function of my mind. Knowing how difficult it was for me to sustain effort and finish any ambitious work, I thought of an incentive which was effectual. I assumed that if by an exercise of will I could somehow get ready two or three hundred pages I would be extremely unwilling to lose the benefit of what I had produced by not carrying on. The exercise of the will was also helped by the intoxication of recalling my early life and the memories of East Bengal which I had not seen for twenty years.

I must make it clear that I had no diary, letters, or notes to help me in writing the book. I did not even prepare a chronology of the public events from books of history to provide myself with a framework for my descriptions and narratives. I gave every date from memory and except in one case I did not go wrong. What was more important, I was also able to create the spirit and atmosphere of the places and events from memory. I would, however, explain that even if I had gone back to East Bengal that would have been a hindrance instead of being a help. The East Bengal in which I grew up, and also Calcutta where I worked till the age of forty-four, were destroyed totally by the partition of Bengal in 1947. The changes would have shocked me and introduced unpleasant dissonances in my writing. So, in actual fact, I gained by not revisiting the places I was describing. If, however, at any time I wanted to prick my memory I hummed the tunes of the songs I had sung in childhood and all the emotional associations, and the visual appearances, too, came back to me with absolute distinctness. I am glad to say that the autobiography was recognized as much as the evocation of an atmosphere as the description of a milieu.

Working in this manner for four months, I wrote enough to make up the first 221 pages of the autobiography as published, which I would say was exemplary and exceptional steadiness in me. But my work was interrupted by the riots I have described. Nevertheless, it was not very difficult to resume it. At the same time the problem of publication was worrying me. No author can write a long book without some rational chance of publication, and I gave thought to the matter. I was determined that I would not give the book to an Indian publisher because I knew that a book in English published in India would not be regarded as worth much even by Indian readers, not to speak of those in the English-speaking countries. My bravado, however, was pointless. No Indian publisher would have taken the risk of publishing so long a book by an unknown Indian writer. In fact, if the book had good sales in India eventually that was because of its publication and reception in England.

But it was not an easy thing for an Indian to get a book published in England. Although I was looking forward to that, I also knew perfectly well what the difficulties were. I knew and I have related how Tagore's *Gitanjali* was published. That means of publication was denied to me, if not by external circumstances, at all events by my pride. I was dead against the practice of new writers to get their work recommended by an established figure in the literary world with a foreword. I believed, and continue to do so now when I can myself furnish forewords to young writers, that if a book could not speak for itself it would not be helped by a patron. It at once made a *protégé* of the author. But I was finding it difficult to continue on the off-chance of being published and so wanted to explore possibilities.

When I had made some more progress, and that was in the spring of 1948, it so happened that a colleague of mine in All India Radio was going to England for a short visit, and I asked him if he would take the typescript with him and give it to the publisher I had decided to try. I had already gone over the list of of British publishers. I did not think much of my chances with the very big publishers, and I was not prepared to go to minor ones merely for the sake of seeing my work in print. I wanted an adventurous publisher with a reputation for publishing original and interesting books, whose imprint would carry weight. Somehow at that time, I had come to regard Hamish Hamilton to be such a publisher and decided to try my luck with him. So, I gave about half the book to my colleague, who was the very popular and well known news announcer of All India Radio, Melville de Mellow. He handed the typescript to Hamish Hamilton. I shall never cease to be grateful to him for this display of friendship, because what came out of it gave me the encouragement to finish the book. What he himself said also encouraged me. He had looked into the book and told me after his return that if the book was published I would either fare worse or much better, but I would not remain where I was. Paradoxically enough, his prediction was fulfilled in both ways. I fared very badly in India and gained a place in the English literary world.

After some time I got a reply from Mr Hamish Hamilton himself. He wrote to me very courteously that the book seemed to him to have great promise, and he would be ready to consider the finished work. This heartened me very much. I was losing the *élan* with which I had started and without this encouragement would have had great difficulty in keeping up the pace of writing. So I went on writing and finished the book by the spring of 1949. I might say that the actual writing of the book (without reckoning the time taken by revision) took not more than nine months in all, although I was going to the office and working there all the time. I had never before shown such energy in writing.

The writing of the book was a great psychological standby for me. If my mind had not been occupied with that work, I would have spent the time fretting in futile rage at what I was seeing in India in the political field. Even so, I had to break off the work to set down my experiences of the riots and my strong feelings about them. However, just at that time I also hit upon another resource to keep my mind cheered up. It was a new recreation acquired by accident. I have always felt any lack of movement in life as a crushing load, and have introduced both into my serious work and pleasures some innovation, small ones even if I did not make a new outlet. In regard to livelihood, I had resolved never to sacrifice living for livelihood, and so after leaving the Military Accounts Department I would never try to earn a living without bringing it in line with my sense of vocation. During the war my work was the service of a cause, although it was also bringing me money in a manner which I had never experienced before. After the war was over I avoided boredom by making my work an outlet for my interest in international affairs.

In the same way, I needed a new recreation. The old recreation of listening to European music had lost none of its attraction, but it needed to be fortified. Delhi archaeology was also mastered, and had only to be retained as a secondary interest. Next, the adoption of the European way of eating and drinking was also consolidated. Therefore a new activity was needed. It was provided by chance.

Towards the end of 1947, my youngest son, who was eight years old, had got a toy violin. My second son broke it by applying too much force to it. The little boy came crying to me, and I said to him on a sudden impulse: 'Don't cry. I will give you a real violin which you will learn to play.' I went at once to the leading music shop in Delhi and bought a small boy's instrument for him, and also engaged a tutor. He was an Anglo-Indian who played the violin and also taught it.

There was consternation in my second son, who was thirteen, when he saw what his mischievous prank had done for his younger brother. So he also came to me to say that he too would take up an instrument. He chose the piano. I never refused my sons anything that they wanted by way of adventure. Therefore I went to the same shop, hired a piano, and engaged the same tutor for him as well. Within days a very good Broadwood upright arrived. Then it was the turn of the eldest boy to put in his claim, because he did not want to be left out of the musical sun. He chose the viola, and I bought a rather expensive instrument for him. The exhibition of musical instruction was very loud, and for some months, in addition to the noise produced by the three instruments, shouts were sent forth by a nephew who was staying with us, who kept time by saying 'one two', 'one two three', 'one two three four', and then came the ticking of a metronome. I kept myself associated with all this, besides tinkering with the sound-post of the violin.

In six months they all learned to play passably, playing easy trios or arrangements as trios of standard pieces like the Hungarian dances of Brahms, especially the No. 5, or Boccherini's Minuet. The son who had taken up the piano could even play movements from Beethoven's sonatas. There could not be, of course, any question of real proficiency; although the boys played with considerable feeling, because they were used to listening to the great classics of European music on the gramophone. It was music-making at home, as my playing and singing had been when I was young. This foray into execution helped even me in my appreciation of European music, because without some knowledge of technique there is no complete enjoyment. I also read books on performance, for example, the books of Tobias Mathay, which I bought for the pianist boy.

My book buying also remained very ambitious, and now I did not have to practice my old tricks to buy them. Since there does not seem to be any correct idea of the means we had to satisfy our desire for reading, I might add what I could buy in Delhi bookshops without ordering specially. I bought, to give only three examples, the new edition of Marcus Aurelius in both Greek and English with notes (two volumes) by A. L. S. Farquharson; Charles de Tolnay's monumental work on Michelangelo; and *Egyptian Grammar* by Alan Gardiner. For whom had the Indian booksellers of Delhi stocked such books, not for the British in New Delhi, whose range of reading could be checked in the library of the Imperial Delhi Gymkhana Club. I give these trivial details because even to the last days of British rule the local British aired an insolent contempt for our reading and literary culture. I shall have to deal with that later.

CHAPTER 2

Gandhi Pursued by Fate

In this chapter I have to come back to a tragic event which had happened before I sent the half-finished book to London. This was the murder of Gandhi. In the afternoon of 30 January 1948, I was at my typewriter when my eldest son burst into the room to say breathlessly: 'They have killed Gandhi!' He had heard the news on the wireless. I was shocked. The next morning I learned the whole story. It is so well known that I need not repeat it. I cannot say that I felt anxious about the political consequences of the death of Gandhi, because not only since independence, but even for two years before it came, he had been nothing but the Holy Ghost, so to speak, of Indian politics.

His funeral procession to the place selected for his cremation and the reduction of his body to ashes on the pyre created scenes which were a magnified repetition of those which had been seen after the death of the nationalist leaders who had died before him. However, while the crowds for him were far greater, the sorrow was less. The spectacle was closer to the popular celebration of independence on 15 August 1947, than to the older funerals. The crowds behaved as if they were at a huge fair, which offered as much occasion for trade (though not frank amusement) as for homage to the dead. People bought snacks, ate them, looked about, and talked volubly, while gazing at the bier on which Gandhi was borne. As in all popular concourses in India, the scenes were very colourful. Yet it would be wrong to say that there was no reverence for the dead leader. In Hindu society, when a great man or even a wealthy landowner died, people exhibited their respect and gratitude to them more by cheerfully partaking of the funeral banquet and listening to the music than by pulling a long face. No bunkum for the dead is the Hindu slogan! *De mortuis nil nisi panem et circenses.*

I followed the trial of the murderer and his associate. As there always are, there were, in this instance as well, rumours that warnings had been received of a possible attempt on Gandhi, but that no proper precautions were taken. Malicious people even suggested that it was his most trusted lieutenant, Vallabhbhai Patel, who was not very keen. But what was undisputed was the fact that Mahatma Gandhi himself would not consent to any special or obtrusive protective measures.

The murderer was a Hindu fanatic from Maharashtra, the centre of militaristic Hindu nationalism. There was an extraordinary coincidence between the first and the last political murder in India. The first was perpetrated in 1897 at Poona in Maharashtra by two Chitpavan Brahmins, the brothers Chapekar, and the victims were an English official of the ICS, W. C. Rand, and an EngUsh officer, Lieutenant Ayerst. The brothers were hanged, and so were their associates who killed the informers. The murderer of Gandhi, Godse and his associate Apte, were also Chitpavan Brahmins. The great figures of Maratha history and de facto rulers of the Maratha Kingdom, the Peshwas, were also Chitpavan Brahmins. It should also be noted that political terrorism begins with the killing of foreign rulers and ends up with the murder of national leaders. The judge who tried the two men and sentenced Godse to death and Apte to life imprisonment, told me that he had never seen greater courage in facing death than in these men. They no more regarded themselves as murderers than did other revolutionaries, whether in India, Ireland, or elsewhere.

In the next few months I was completing my autobiography, in which there had to be an appraisement of Gandhi for his first defiance of British rule in 1919, which came within the chronological limits of that book. I wrote it and included it in my account of the events of 1919, but by that time Gandhi was dead and I took his whole political career into account in writing that appraisement. Although thirty-five years have gone by since then and I have read more about Gandhi I find no reason to change even one word in it. Nevertheless, the judgement was tentative and not final. To the final view, I arrived in stages.

I gave the first amplified estimate when in 1959 the editor of the *Illustrated Weekly of India*, the most widely circulated and influential weekly journal in India, invited me to open a discussion on the question: 'Have we forgotten the Mahatma?' with my contribution. I wrote it and it was published in the issue for 26 June 1959. There followed the usual airing of views, but as I had had my say I did not pay any attention to that. I was confident that I should never have to revise my opinions. I might say incidentally that I never express any opinion on any subject unless I feel sure that it would stand wear and tear. When I was young I had read in Renan's recollections of his youth that one of his teachers at the seminary of

St Nicolas du Chardonnet, Father Hardouin, used to say that he had not got up for forty years at four o'clock in the morning to think as everybody (*tout le monde*) did, and I resolved that I should not arrive at any opinion without taking as much pains.

The drift of the article was that for all practical purposes we had forgotten the Mahatma, but I began by saying that there was more to the matter. I wrote:

'To a very large number of people in India, the question will seem gratuitous, if not insulting in its suggestion. Of course, it was a leading question. They will indignantly repudiate the idea that we have forgotten the Mahatma, and, in one sense, they will be right, for there is forgetting and forgetting, remembering and remembering.'

I admitted without reservation that we did remember Gandhi in various ways, and proceeded to define the ways.

'To take the most natural and creditable of these first. In the Hindu order the highest and surest method of perpetuating the memory, and even the teachings, of a great man is to convert the historical figure into a myth. Apotheosis or canonization among us is not deliberate; neither status is conferred by authority - an Emperor or Pope. In India, the masses make a god of a great man collectively and unconsciously, and succeed in giving to his memory a permanence which nothing else, neither ideas nor personality, can give.'

Of course, I continued,

'this homage is sub-rational, but it is respectable and, therefore, might be called supra-rational. To the masses of India, the actual is always crushing and frightening, and so all their idealism and yearning for happiness find refuge in myths. There will be no time in the future history of the Hindus in which Mahatma Gandhi will not be remembered in this way. He has taken his place in our Pantheon.'

But I also added: 'This remembering is silent, as most things deeply felt by the common people of India are, and, if anyone says that Mahatma Gandhi had been forgotten by them, they will not mind, because, even if the charge reaches their ears, they will not understand it.'

Then I wrote about the remembrance which was vocal and even strident. I said:

'There will, however, be another class of men, very vociferous about him, who will be angry, for they are always remembering him and reminding others about him, in their own interest. Where would they be without him.' So, during the minutes of silence on 30 January, they must be thinking what a providential thing it was that Mahatma Gandhi lived only so long as it was necessary for them to be put in power and died exactly when he would have become embarrassing and inconvenient. Even now they cannot do without him as the moral sanction behind their power and prosperity, and they go on speaking about him. Yet, theirs is also a form of remembering, and I must give even the devil his due.'

An explanatory postscript to the summing up of the popular myth of Gandhi given above is called for. This myth would have been the same if his political failure had not been camouflaged by the appearance of victory which the British withdrawal gave to it. Actually, a myth of failure would have been cherished more wholeheartedly by the masses of India, because they have greater emotional satisfaction from failures than from successes. Elation created by any kind of success evaporates, and the successes of the Indian nationalist movement as they appeared to be in the upshot satisfied nothing but the hatred of British rule without bringing any positive gain to the masses of India. Independence even rewakened their old respect for British rule. So, a myth of success was not likely to be powerful in its emotional hold.

In contrast, grievances which cannot be removed remain permanently fresh, and as a result of their historical experience the people of India had made the cherishing of grievances their greatest emotional enjoyment. Actually, the popular myth of Gandhi was created long before independence by his asceticism and renunciation, and not by political success. The myth created by the ruling order and deliberately kept alive by it is wholly different. It is a political device.

Now, reverting to my old article, I have to say that after the breezy introduction I set out item by item how all that Gandhi stood for had been rejected by the new rulers of India and for all practical purposes it could be said that Gandhi was forgotten. I do not think that the more intelligent and honest members of the ruling order were unaware of this, at all events in their less self-interested moods. I shall not, however, repeat what I said in the article but offer a new appraisement. Indeed, it has been given by implication in my account of Gandhi and his movement in the whole course of this book. It could be made more explicit, and therefore I am setting out below a cut-and-dried summing up of Gandhi's failures.

To take the question of his contribution to Indian independence first. It is a blatant falsehood to say that he or his movements brought it about, whatever their moral effect. This is not a matter of opinion, but of stark and uncontested facts. I give below the most important of them:

i) He personally set on foot and led three movements: first, the agitation against the Rowlatt Bill in April 1919; second, the Non-Go-operation Movement of 1921-2; third, the Civil Disobedience Movement of 1930-2. He was not responsible for the 1942 disturbances nor for the excitement of 1946-7. The first of these three was put down within weeks by the bloody massacre of Amritsar; the second was called off by himself after his followers had perpetrated their massacre; the third died down of its own inanition. Whatever the temporary anxiety of the British administration during these phases of nationalist agitation, its success was easy, and to all appearance complete. At the end of each movement the British administration felt that any extension of self-government for India remained in their hand.

ii) There was no nationalist activity in the intervening years, and the mood left by the failures in the nationalists was one of despair and bitterness, unrelieved even by the idea of a deliberate resumption of agitation.

iii) During all these movements the people acted in their own way without paying any heed to his admonitions about non-violence and abjuration of hatred. Nobody was more aware of this than Gandhi himself Once at least he spoke of his Himalayan blunder.

iv) His influence on the Indian masses was fitful and not continuous. He could never rouse them, they followed him only when they themselves were roused, although he made many attempts in the quiescent years. Furthermore, when he was arrested after these three movements and even when he faced death by his fasts, there was no political excitement whatever. The truth of the matter is that although the people of India venerated Gandhi for his moral role, they followed him only in so far as he stood for their hatred of British rule. I said in my autobiography that in the relationship between Gandhi and the people of India the masses and man had at last become one. That was true in the moral as well as in the practical aspect of his life. But in this oneness the man bowed as much to the masses as the masses bowed to the man.

v) His failure was no less complete in the practical aspect of his leadership. His own immediate followers, who were the most influential leaders of the nationalist movement, followed his directions and advice only when that suited them, and totally disregarded them otherwise. In fact, at every crucial turn of Indo-British political relations, these second-rank leaders opposed him and took decisions which made all the difference to the historical consequences for India, and he had in every case to submit to them. In 1924 they decided to join the British-Indian legislature against his formal opposition; in 1937 he was opposed to office acceptance in principle but had to go with the other leaders; in 1939 he was in favour of co-operating with Britain in the war, but was over-ruled; in 1947 he was against the partition of India but was won over.

I have given fuller details of these in this book, and would only add that to speak of the unquestioned authority of Gandhi is unjustified. Often he had to get his views accepted by giving what were virtual ultimatums to quit the Congress. These facts can be unknown only to ignoramuses about India, and denied only by liars. But there is one circumstance which gives plausibility to the myth of Gandhi's success, and that is the British withdrawal. Therefore, if anyone wants to arrive at a correct estimate of Gandhi's effectiveness, he has to see his methods applied in situations where this obscuring screen was not present. As it happens, that can be judged in the very country in which he first developed and applied his method-of course. South Africa. His failure there is more evident today than it was when in 1914 he left that country for ever. In White South Africa the racial situation is worse, and if in other parts of the continent of Africa the Blacks have come into their own that has been made possible by methods which were totally opposed to his, i.e. application of military force, such as his rival in India, Subhas Chandra Bose, wished to apply but could not.

Let me now turn to his roles in economic, social, and moral spheres, and to his legacy to India after independence. In all these fields, his failure is even more complete than in the political. Let me set out its principal heads:

i) His doctrine of non-violence and pacifism was almost contemptuously rejected from the day of independence, and since then the new Indian government and the people have been un-apologetically and even crassly militaristic. They have resorted to aggression against legally constituted states, and have been ready to incur military expenditure blatantly disproportionate to the resources of India. His most trusted lieutenant Patel and his beloved disciple Nehru were, above all, responsible for this. This was due basically to the innate militarism of the Hindus which had been sharpened so much by the deprivation imposed by Muslim and British rule, that in 1947 independence seemed hardly worth having without its military appanage. To this ancient love of military glory has been added another urge in the form of the hatred of the Muslim and a bogey has been created in Pakistan to disguise it. Hindu militarism has compelled India to make enemies of the two countries with whom, more than any other, she ought to be friendly, namely, Pakistan and China.

ii) His economic teaching has been equally rejected. Gandhi feared and disapproved of machines, but Nehru, above all, wanted to make India an imitation Soviet Union and the enemies of the Soviet Union are giving money towards this end in the name of development.

iii) His efforts to put an end to untouchability have not changed the lot of the Untouchables except in respect of pious declarations.

iv) His attempts to end the suicidal Hindu-Mushm strife provoked his murder, and the obscene conflict pursues its relentless course.

v) I might as well refer to another failure although in this field his position was implicit and not explicit. He had no interest in cultural or intellectual life, and was even hostile to intellectual activity. Even so, by his practice he showed that he wished India to remain within the framework of the Hindu way of life at its simplest. He totally disapproved of Westernization. Yet today Indian life at every level is being transformed by the lowest forms of Western popular culture. Even the higher forms of Westernization which had been the main cultural expression of Indian life during British rule cannot resist this debasing impact.

vi) Last of all, there is one failure of Gandhi which has inflicted positive harm on the people of India. It has come from the rejection by the ruling order in India of the very basis of his teaching, whether in politics or in morals, and that rejection is of the Hindu notion of Dharma. They have put what they call secularism in its place, which is not the secularism of Europe. European secularism is a rational alternative to Christianity, with its ultimate source in Greek rationalism and final basis in modem science. In India secularism of even the highest European type is not needed, for

Hinduism as a religion is itself secular and it has sanctified worldliness by infusing it with moral and spiritual qualities. To take away that secularism from the Hindus is to make them immoral, and culturally debased. Yet the new secularism will never weaken the hold of superstition on the Hindus.

Where then is the achievement and legacy of Gandhi.? On the contrary, it is impossible to imagine a more complete, comprehensive, and tragic failure for any man. The only thing that cannot be denied him and taken away from him is the glory of martyrdom. He might be compared to St Sebastian pierced by arrows all over the body, each arrow cutting through one of his principles. In fact, he is a more terrifying martyr because even his martyrdom has been in vain, and not produced the result expected from martyrdom. At a time when the Christians were still being cruelly persecuted and were embracing martyrdom without any apparent hope of gaining anything on earth by it, a great Christian declared with unwavering faith: The blood of martyrs is the seed of the Church -... *Semen est sanguis Christianorum.* So it proved in the case of Christianity, but Gandhi's martyrdom has not done anything to sow the seeds of a regenerate India.

And the tragedy of it is that it was bound to be so. Although Mahatma Gandhi took over the Christian teaching about non-resistance to evil, he had no understanding of where really the strength of Christianity lay. The idea of not resisting evil and turning the other cheek appealed to him because with it he could give a moral complexion to the Hindu's abject and age-old habit of submission to power, especially when the power was evil. Thus he overlooked that the Christian's strength stemmed, not from the Sermon on the Mount, but from the idea of resurrection and eternal life which came out of the death of Jesus. Without that the practice of the Sermon on the Mount could only end in the agonized cry of My God, my God! Why hast Thou forsaken me.?' The cry *Hé Ram!* With which Gandhi died was the Hindu equivalent of the Christian cry. Jesus did not end with his cry, Gandhi did with his. All the greater his martyrdom.

The myth of Gandhi created and perpetuated by the Indian ruling order is not only a denial of his martyrdom, it is a sacrilegious mockery of the tragedy of his life. However, even babes in India have been able to see through the imposition. Some years ago a young Bengali girl, living in a remote and small administrative centre, wrote to me in England how the local Indian magistrates were celebrating the anniversary of Gandhi's death by coming out into the streets in their suits and boots and cleaning the drains. Her comment was this: 'If Gandhi had seen this he would have died of failure of heart and Godse's bullet would not have been needed.'

As if that was not enough, a further outrage on the martyrdom of Gandhi has been perpetrated by an Englishman through a film he has made. I am not concerned here with the merits of the film. At best it can be a shallow visual presentation of a false myth. Nor am I intimidated by its reception by Hollywood. I am not such a fool as to underrate the power of Hollywood over a brainwashed Western democratic rabble. So, I say to those who pay tribute to Hollywood: 'Give unto Hollywood things that are Hollywood's, but give unto truth and art things which belong to them.' As for myself, when I shall accept Hollywood's judgement on art I shall also accept the judgements on woman's beauty pronounced by the jury which creates Miss World and her national maids of honour. Actually, the film made him a vulgar posturing demagogue, which he most emphatically was not.

An Englishman making such a film had to eat every word about Gandhi uttered not only by those Englishmen who were openly and honestly hostile to him, as were Churchill and Archbishop Cosmo Lang, but also by every English Viceroy of India who had to deal with him, had personal firsthand knowledge of him, and were also respectful of him; he would give a wholly false historical view of the Indian nationalist movement; he would libel a great political phenomenon which, with all its faults and even evils, did greater good to India than Gandhi did or could have done; and, last of all, he would become an accomplice in the exploitation of the simple Indian people by the most cunning and persistent exploiters they have known even in all their unhappy existence.

But to single out this film-maker individually as an apostate to the English tradition would be unfair because he is what he is with a majority of his own people. I shall bring that home by referring to a surprising defence of Baldwin by Churchill. He knew perfectly well what Baldwin had brought on England, for when in June 1940 he learned about a German air raid on a Baldwin factory, he commented: 'How ungrateful of them!' Yet once he put forward his sole apology for Baldwin by saying to Colville: 'The climate of public opinion on people is overpowering.'

It is, however, possible for an exceptional statesman or author to rise above public opinion, but a film-maker has by the very nature of his profession to fall in with current taste and opinion. This film-maker is only sharing the feeblemindedness about India produced by British decadence.

It is not possible for any European who remains true to the European ethos to admire Gandhi without important reservations. And the mildest criticism of a European who becomes hagiographical about Gandhi can only be that he is obeying the weakest side of the Christian morality. Today he would become a purveyor of decadence, besides being a decadent himself.

But the film-maker has been more naive. He has become without being aware of it an agent of the present Indian ruling class. I can understand why the Government of India supported him. It took advantage of his naivete to make him play their game. In the first place, they knew that a film on Gandhi according to the evangel preached by it would be technically better if made by an Englishman than an Indian; and, what was more important, coming from an Englishman it would carry greater conviction, as indeed it did.

But behind the support of the Government of India there was also a far stronger emotional pressure than these and of which it may have been only subconscious. As I have said and would repeat, the Hindus in recent times have not killed their enemies in revenge, they have inflicted moral degradation and gloated over it. Such a film on Gandhi produced by an Englishman was a revenge on behalf of Indian nationalism. This is corroborated by the change of attitude of the Indian Press. At first it was hostile to Sir Richard Attenborough, but became admirers of him after seeing the film. No Hindu praises a foreigner unless he serves his purpose.

This film should have its pendant in a similar film on Hitler. And why not? Hitler was equally a man of faith, he also wanted to get redress for the wrongs inflicted on Germany, he also gave his life, and above all he succeeded where Gandhi did not. It is he who has destroyed British greatness. On the eve of the war he offered to guarantee the continuance of the British Empire for all time with the power of the Wehrmacht, and when the offer was not accepted he destroyed not only the British Empire but also British greatness at home. What Gandhi or the Indian nationalist movement did was only to take the hyena's share of the lion's kill.

No nation except the British in all past history has recanted in this manner by going back on their faith and achievement with such ignoble self-abasement. I can describe its character only by offering the converse to a famous dictum. When I was a young student I read Lord Acton's saying that power corrupts and absolute power corrupts absolutely. I believed that implicitly, and I would still accept it, but only as a half-truth. What I have realized now is that this condemnation of power *qua* power, whose derivation is ultimately from Christianity, has done untold harm by bringing about the very evil which Lord Acton denounced. It is its Christian rejection which has driven power, without which the cosmos cannot run, into the arms of immorality. The right course would have been to make amoral power moral. But I would offer a dictum to match Lord Acton's which would be absolute truth. It is this: loss of power corrupts, and absolute loss of power corrupts absolutely. The Gandhi film is only a minor example of the corruption of the British people by loss of power.

The interested diffusion of the false Gandhi legend reminds me of a tale by Edgar Allan Poe. In it a man who is a mesmerist wants to make an experiment in order to find out what would happen to a man if he is mesmerised in *articulo mortis,* just at the point of death. He thinks of performing it on a friend of his named Valdemar, who is very sick and might die any moment. As it happened, M. Valdemar also agreed, and when it was thought by the doctors that his death was imminent, the mesmerist began his passes, with the doctors and nurses as witness. It took hours for the passes to take effect. At last M. Valdemar said in a voice whose hideousness it was impossible to describe because no such voice had ever jarred on human ears. Yet it said with a thrillingly distinct articulation: 'I have been sleeping - and now, now, I am dead.'

They watched the body for seven months and no change came over it. At last the mesmerist decided to release M. Valdemar from his mesmeric trance and see what happened. After some time the same hideous voice broke forth: 'For God's sake! - Quick, quick - put me to sleep, or quick! awaken me! Quick! I say to you that I am dead.'

The mesmerist went on with his passes and all those who were in the room were prepared to see M. Valdemar awaken. But something quite unforeseeable happened. The mesmerist describes that:

'As I rapidly made the mesmeric passes, amid ejaculations of "dead! dead!" absolutely bursting from the tongue and not from the lips of the sufferer, his whole frame at once - within the space of a single minute, or less, shrank - crumbled - absolutely rotted away beneath my hands. Upon the bed, before the whole company, there lay a nearly liquid mass of loathsome - of detestable putrescence.'

Will the hand of truth at any time reduce the vile myth of Gandhi to the putrid mass it deserves to be? That is not likely. All over the world too many people are doing too well out of Gandhi, above all financially, for that to be possible. As Sir Thomas Browne said: 'Mummy is become merchandise, Mizraim cures wounds, and Pharaoh is sold for balsams.'

CHAPTER 3

Commentator: Official and Private

I have already said that after independence I put myself in a blind alley as regards worldly prospects. My wife never asked me to sacrifice any principle of mine for the sake of money, but she resented that my abilities were neither recognized nor rewarded by those who employed me, even in their own interest. So, after independence, she wanted me to leave India, go to England, and make a literary career there, just as she had asked me to leave Calcutta before. She said that she would remain in India with the children and follow me if anything came out of the venture.

But I did not think it advisable to take risks with three children of school age, when by Indian standards I had a very comfortable income. Actually, my income then, i.e. at the age of fifty, was ten times what I had when I married. Besides, even without pushing myself forward, I was bound in the course of a few more years of service in the Government to be taken higher by the mere operation of the bureaucratic escalator.

Of course, I could not remain more than five years in the service under the rules. At that time officials of my rank were retired at the age of fifty-five. (That had been fixed in British days to give the British officials as long a life as possible in England after retirement.) I also knew that I would not get a pension because my service was not long enough to earn one, but would only get a retirement gratuity. But I was told by the Director-General of AIR soon after, that I would be recommended for an extension of service on a higher salary after reaching the retiring age. This was being done in many cases.

I did not think it right to give up all this in order to seek better prospects in England, which would have been a gamble. I took the line of least resistance. It was never in my nature either to seek more money or to think in advance about the future even if it seemed to threaten an eventual crisis. Being an incorrigible Micawberian, I hoped something would turn up, and I also felt confident that on account of my reputation as a writer I would not remain without employment or a dependable income.

But I felt anxious on the score of principle. I felt nervous that under the new regime my superiors might now ask me to write commentaries supporting its policies and extolling the achievements of the Congress, which in most cases I could not do without doing violence to my convictions and becoming an opportunist. In point of fact, this question arose almost immediately. Soon after 15 August 1947 I was asked to write a script about the so-called 'Quit India Movement' of 1942. That meant, of course, that I was to glorify it. It was the same Indian superiors-who earlier had edited my obituary notice of Gandhi who wanted me to do so. The Indian bureaucrat always justified that sort of trimming by putting forward the well-known plea that the Civil Service must serve every government. I also put forward my argument that the plea was wholly fallacious and irrelevant. No one could serve the foreign rulers of his country and the national rulers with equal loyalty.

I have already set down what I thought about the Movement, and I refused to write the script. But in refusing to write it I did not put forward that reason. I simply said that in 1942 I was in the service of the British administration of India and had seen the Movement suppressed. If I had thought that it was right and the suppression wrong, I should have resigned. I did not, and by that alone I had forfeited the right to praise the Movement. All my life I have held very strongly that deliberate wrong-doing by a man pins him down to a conscientious and obligatory servitude to it even if he has afterwards repented, so that he has no right to profit by his repentance or take credit for it. I also said that every government I served had the right to demand my loyalty, but it could not demand any recantation of my previous loyalties. Fortunately, my chiefs did not insist on my writing the script. I got it done by a colleague. In the whole of the Indian official class there is no idea of any kind of loyalty owing to anything but self-interest. Thus my quixotic behaviour was not taken seriously.

Another case of conscience arose for me soon after, with the Kashmir affair. At first I saw nothing wrong in the military intervention of the new Government of India in favour of the Maharaja, because I was convinced that Pakistan was trying to force the issue by military force and was guilty of aggression. Although the decision of the new Congress Government to intervene was opposed to its declared principle that it did not recognize the right of the Indian Princes to rule, I felt assured by the reservation that the help was given on condition that the people of Kashmir would be given the opportunity to declare their will through a plebiscite. But almost within days I discovered that there was no intention whatever to honour the pledge, and the assertion of Indian power in Kashmir was in effect a permanent annexation. Therefore, after writing a few commentaries, I refused to write any further on the Kashmir affair. When I communicated this to my superior I was simply told that so long as the unit produced the scripts it did not matter who wrote them. I felt extremely relieved and, acting on the same principle, decided that I would write neither about the internal politics of India nor about India's economic progress, in which I had not the slightest faith. I decided that I would deal only with international affairs, interpreting them more or less impartially. There was no interference from the top with this arrangement.

This decision enabled me to work undisturbed in All India Radio for the five years that followed independence. In addition, I found the work interesting in itself I had, however, to be careful. All India Radio was a Government Department, and its broadcasts were regarded as expressions of the sympathies and policies of the Indian Government. Moreover, my scripts were translated into Arabic and Persian, and all the governments of the Middle East were extremely touchy. Nonetheless, I had no difficulty in keeping within the framework of the Government's policies, and, of course, there could be no question of my airing my own personal views in these scripts, which were broadcast anonymously. All that I expected was to be allowed as their writer to reconcile truthfulness with policy.

In all, I worked for All India Radio for ten years and some months, serving the British, and the Indian regime, for equal periods of just over five years. In both periods I was able to work with a good conscience, and I was never tempted or required to depart from the terms I myself had set for serving any government. These were simple and straightforward. It was understood and accepted by me that by accepting service under a government I was under an obligation to be in broad agreement with its policies, and that in my scripts I could never go outside that framework. The corollary, though unstated, was equally explicit in my mind. It was that if at any time I felt that I could not remain within the framework I would resign. But my part of the contract was that I would not write any commentary to order, nor accept instructions from the top to revise a script I had written. Were any of the scripts found unsuitable, they could be rejected. On the whole this system worked.

But on three occasions there were hitches. My scripts were called in question. But I did not have to suffer personally for them. One script was rejected and therefore not broadcast; the other two made the Government call for explanations. I will describe the cases. The rejection came first and was the most interesting. The script dealt with the British withdrawal from Palestine and the emergence of the state of Israel. I wrote it on 15 May 1948, a few hours after the announcement of these events.

At that time I had no strong pro-Israeli feeling as I now have, nor did I have the pronounced anti-Arab feeling I have acquired since then. On the other hand, since 1937 I had nothing but contempt for the British policy in Palestine. But in the script I did not have to deal with British rule. Thus I was able to write what I considered to be a realistic and balanced script, with some expression of sympathy for the Arab population of Palestine. I thought well of my performance, and therefore, when the script was rejected, I kept a copy of it so as to be able to furnish proof of my wisdom if any occasion arose in the future. It is still with me, and I shall summarize its argument as well as quote a few lines to show the reader what was stopped. I began in the following manner:

'British rule in Palestine, disguised under the name of Mandate, came to an end last night after thirty years of unsuccessful and troubled administration. What is happening after this event is what was expected. A Jewish State has been formed in accordance with the proclamation of the General Zionist Council, issued on April 12 last. The armed forces of the neighbouring Arab States, more especially Egypt, are moving into the country. The fighting and violence which has so long been raging in the country is going to take the form of full-fledged war. The moment is so grave that it would be a shirking of duty if any commentator failed to face the realities of the situation or to tell the truth to the best of his power.'

Then I considered the military prospects and wrote:

'If we could feel confident about the military situation, that is to say, if we could feel that the armies of the Arab States would be able quickly to reestablish order and government in Palestine, we should have felt somewhat comforted. But at this moment, it seems more likely that the fighting will be prolonged, and so add to the misery of the people of Palestine.'

At the time I had no idea of the military resources and capacity of the Jews, while I was aware that the Arab countries like Jordan and Egypt had well-organized and well-trained armies. But I justified my anticipation by first referring to a generally observed feature of all military conflicts. I wrote;

'In warfare it is a salutary caution to remember that however powerful one party may appear, the second party never takes the risk of war unless it also feels that it has a reasonable chance of victory. Therefore, even if the united resources of the Arab States appear to out match those of the Jews, it would be folly to ignore the military potentialities of the latter.'

Besides that, I assumed that the United States would not only recognize the new State of Israel but give substantial aid to it, both financial and material, and added that even if the US Government did nothing officially, the American Jewry would help Israel as the American Irish had helped the Irish Republicans. I then drew attention to the disunity among the Arabs themselves. I said that in history domination over Palestine had always been disputed between Egypt and the most powerful State in Western Asia, and illustrated this by referring not only to Mehemet Ali and the Sultan of Turkey, but even to Rameses II and the Hittites.

Lastly, I considered the interests of both Britain and the United States, in the Middle East in general and Palestine in particular. Paradoxically enough, I wrote, the British were asserting their interest even when they were clearing out of Palestine, and I quoted the statement which the British Under-Secretary of State for Foreign Affairs made on 5 May, in which he said: i can give a categorical assurance that we will stay in the Middle East and the Mediterranean. The Government recognizes that the Middle East is a vital factor in world peace. It is of supreme importance to the safety and welfare of the British Commonwealth, and we are determined to stay there.'

At that time I did not know how hostile Ernest Bevin, the British Foreign Secretary, was to the Jews, but I knew that the British ruling class as a whole was incorrigibly pro-Arab and foresaw that it would be anti-Israel. I quoted from a statement the Archbishop of York had made in the House of Lords on 7 April, in which he said that the Jews had lost the friendship of the British and had started in Britain a dangerous sentiment of anti-Semitism. I also quoted a Conservative mp to illustrate British solidarity with the Arabs. This man said on 14 May that 'the interests of Britain and the Arab world are bound together'.

From that time I have remained firmly convinced, although I cannot produce any proof for it, that when the British Government withdrew from Palestine in 1948 it felt sure that the Arab armies would make short work of the Jews and prevent the *de facto* establishment of a Jewish State. Then the Arabs would become friendly to Britain and British influence in the Middle East would remain effective. The falsification of this expectation created a chagrin, which, combined with a very unintelligent partiality for the Arabs and indeed all Muslims, has become a rancorous hatred of Israel in all British Governments and in a large part of the British people. I have now learned that the hatred has had a very harmful practical consequence. In 1949 King Abdullah of Jordan wished to make peace with Israel, but the British Foreign Office opposed the project from a fear that any understanding between the Arabs and Israel would injure the British position in the region.

With one short suspension at the time of the Suez affair, which however was condemned virtually by the whole of the British people, this rancour against Israel has determined British policy and attitudes. But it has not made any Muslim state, whether Persia or Egypt, friendly to Britain, nor has it preserved British influence in the Middle East. Britain has become a cipher in the region. To me the British attitude seems to be a perversity which Britain's historical responsibility for the Arab-Jewish conflict makes even more perverse.

However, let me revert to the story of my commentary. After examining the British position, I considered the American interest, which arose, as I pointed out, from the need for oil and the fear of Soviet penetration. Nonetheless, I said, 'the USA is not acting energetically. It appears that the US Government has not been able to decide finally whom to support - the Arabs or the Jews, both of whom she stands in need of pleasing, although for different reasons.' The resultant vacillation, I said, would be disastrous for the people of Palestine. I concluded the script with the following words:

'It is implicit in the fundamental nature of the interests of both the USA and Britain that they cannot remain wholly disinterested while a war is raging in Palestine. Therefore, their present vacillation may be ended by the overriding force of circumstances. This makes their present hesitancy all the more deplorable, for the greatest sufferers from their policies and from the war in Palestine will be the people of Palestine. Nobody seems to be thinking of them this moment.'

This was the commentary which was stopped, certainly not for being beside the mark. I think that in it I was able to put my finger on the basic elements of the situation, which have remained constant to this day. I would add that I had to produce my commentaries in an hour or two, without being given time for study or thinking beyond what I had done in advance, taking into account all contingencies.

I am not including this story with a view to claiming credit for superior wisdom or knowledge. I did what every observer could have done had he followed the method I have always followed in dealing with public or, for that matter, private affairs. I never allow my likes or dislikes to influence any intellectual judgement of mine. Secondly, when considering any historical situation I try to rise above the present and consider it in the light of the underlying historical trends, paying no attention to the incidental complications and ramifications but reducing every situation to its simplest. In plain words, I do not begin, if I want to cut down a tree, by stripping it leaf by leaf from the top, but strike at the trunk.

There are two more incidents to relate and these could have had personal consequences for me. In 1950, when the United States took military action in Korea, I said in the initial commentary that she was acting in her own interest, although formally she was acting in pursuance of a resolution of the Security Council. This was broadcast, and I believe a protest was received by the Government from the American Embassy. The Ministry called for an explanation and this was demanded, not from me, but from a superior of mine. He was very nervous and asked me what case I had so that he could present it to the Ministry. I gave it to him. I prepared a chronology of the intervention in two parallel columns for New York and Far Eastern time, and showed that the American military action had begun about seven hours before the resolution was adopted.

I had been prompted to make this comparison by an incident before the adoption of the resolution which had roused my curiosity. When the Security Council had almost ended the discussion, the representative of India asked for a postponement in order to consult his Government. But the American representative firmly opposed this and asked for a resolution the same evening. This seemed rather unreasonable to me and I tried to find out the reason for the American insistence. It did not take me long to find it. The military action had already begun in Korea at about two o'clock New York time, and if the Security Council did not adopt the resolution the same evening the news of the action would be published in the American Press without there being a UN resolution to authorize it. This could not be allowed to happen, and the American action had to be shown as having been taken in obedience to a UN resolution. If both the items of news appeared at the same time nobody was going to ask about exact hours. My superior sent the note to the External Affairs Ministry. I never heard anything more about it. But it was ordered that henceforth my scripts would have to be approved by the Ministry.

The second incident happened shortly before I retired from AIR. This was the result of a script of mine on the political situation in Iran, Mossadegh's Persia, in which I dealt with the failure of the British and American Governments to come to an agreement about British oil interests in Persia. That was in August 1952. Discussing the future I incidentally made the observation that the internal political situation in Persia might not turn out to be stable. This, of course, suggested the fall of Mossadegh. The commentary was passed and broadcast, but a protest came at once from the Iranian Embassy. This time it was from me that an explanation was called for. At first I refused to give any, but afterwards I somehow patched up a case. No action was taken for I retired from service soon after.

But I also grazed outside the official fold. Besides writing scripts for broadcasting I continued to write on my own on subjects which interested me. The incentive was the desire for variety, but there was also a practical calculation. This had been influencing me ever since I took up the editorial post on *The Modem Review*. I had decided that even if I wrote for the journal anonymously as part of my editorial duties, I would write under my own name from time to time. I was convinced that the personal status and reputation of a writer can never be maintained, far less improved, except by acquiring a reputation for original work and as a specialist on some subject. I acted on that conviction when on *The Modem Review*, also when working for Sarat Bose, and after coming to Delhi to work for All India Radio. I knew that after my retirement from Government service I should have to live by writing, and unless I kept up my reputation and standing as a freelance writer I would have great difficulty in getting my work accepted. So, when I was asked to write for some journals, I readily agreed. But, of course, I always wrote to give expression to my convictions.

I was, however, exceptional in doing this. Many of my colleagues in All India Radio were established writers, as was common in the early days of broadcasting. Others, being young intellectuals, had literary ambition. But nearly all of them gave up independent writing when they joined the broadcasting organization, because it was a government organization. Among writers in the Indian Government's service there was an unfounded assumption that no Government servant could publish anything, even in the way of pure literary work with no political implications, without the Government's permission. A friend of mine who was a distinguished writer, besides being a qualified though not practising lawyer, even told me that by merely joining the Government's service I had contracted out of the right I had as a citizen to have the freedom of expression guaranteed by the new Indian constitution as a Fundamental Right. Acquiescence in servitude, as a rule enthusiastic and, only exceptionally, resigned, is a constant of the behaviour of the Indian intelligentsia. To this assumption was added another idea that one-third of the honorarium even for a short story had to be surrendered to the Government. I knew those who had surrendered. I paid no attention to these supposed rules and wrote and accepted money for whatever was published. I am giving these details because after the publication of my autobiography an attempt was made to hoist me on these petards.

One of the reasons why I never asked for permission was that I knew that obtaining it from my Indian superiors would not be easy. During the war, on account of the fact that writers and journalists had to be recruited to carry on war propaganda even of a routine order, which was beyond the capacity of the bureaucrats, there existed something like a feud between the pure bureaucrats and the professional writers who had joined the service during the war. The officials violently resented any status which was not *ex cathedra*, i.e. derived from the chair on which they sat, and one official in my department habitually insulted a distinguished Bengali poet who was also a news editor. I had to intervene with Mr Bams to stop this pecking.

I had not informed the office before I sent the articles to the *New English Review*, but being elated by their publication I showed them in the office and also gave them to Mr Bams to read. Nothing came directly to me as a consequence of this, but later I saw a file in which there was a note indicating that my writing had been taken up officially. I could not find out who took the initiative in raising the question, but I found it discussed from the clerical to the highest level. The matter was closed with a typical note from a clerk: 'Mr Chaudhuri contributes articles as a private hobby.'

The fear of consequences from writing was real enough among my colleagues and even those who had literary ambition played safe. They thought they could do that any moment and get them published, but why court trouble for such trifles." Of course, it goes without saying that none of them has done anything.

I was determined not to fall in line and so wrote more articles. Thus during 1948 I wrote some articles on which I rather pique myself. As these were published in an official magazine no permission was needed. I was invited to write them by the editor, who was an official himself. But he was not a normal official. He came from a distinguished Bengali family and had got his education entirely in England. He knew Turkish and was regarded as a Turcologist. In any case, he was a character. We were on a pleasant social footing and when he came to my house and the topic of European music was raised, he would sing some famous tunes. Once he took up an actor's sword which was in the house, knelt at the feet of my wife, and sang in Italian: '*Vieni alia finestra*' from *Don Giovanni*. His second in command was less flamboyant, but he too had been at Oxford, Merton being his college. Both of them often came to my house to listen to European music, and also to canvass me for articles. I wrote for them whenever I could. Here I shall speak only of two of these.

In one of them I considered the American-Soviet rivalry which had suddenly become very threatening over the blockade of Berlin in 1948. People were talking of a possible war or at all events of a serious military confrontation. I was asked to write on this subject, and discussed it in an article entitled 'Pattern of World Polities'. In it, first of all, I dismissed the idea of an immediate war, saying that there was no likelihood of one breaking out now, although a general war between the Soviet Union and the Western Powers was possible after some decades. After that I gave my interpretation of the international situation by describing the Soviet-American rivalry as the latest cycle of a very old European conflict - such as had taken place periodically between the greatest World Power and the greatest Continental Power in Europe. The first cycle was fought between England and France, and the second between England and Germany. Now, I went on to say, the United States had taken the place of England and the Soviet Union that of France and Germany. I added that these old conflicts had shown that the Continental Power never won against the World Power in spite of possessing overwhelming military superiority on the Continental mass. So, I predicted, if a war did come about, the United States would ultimately win, whatever the ups and downs in the interval. I might explain that I regarded the country which could impinge on the whole world by means of its naval power as the World Power, and that which impinged only on a land mass through its land forces as the Continental Power. That the Soviet Union was building up a formidable navy did not invalidate my argument, for France also had a great navy and Germany the second navy in the world in 1914.*

The other article was called 'Postwar Military Thought'. In that piece I put forward two views. The first was that aviation had destroyed the mutual exclusiveness of war on land and war on sea: the aeroplane overlapped. The second point was that the real revolution in war was coming, not even from the aeroplane, but from long-distance bombardment. I added that this was the aspect of a future war which was the most sinister. The editor of the magazine sent the article to General J. F. C. Fuller and Captain Liddell Hart. I did not know about this, but one day the assistant editor came to me with a letter written in his own hand by General Fuller acknowledging the article. In it I read: 'The article by Mr Chaudhuri is one of the most illuminating I have read for a long time.' Captain Liddell Hart wrote to me later and presented me with his new book *Thoughts on War*, with the inscription: 'To Nirad Chaudhuri, fellow-student of war, in recognition of his deep knowledge and stimulating thought.' Needless to say, I felt very pleased and even proud. But the General Staff of the Indian Army took no notice of the article. Afterwards, a young Sikh friend and colleague of mine, who in spite of being a Sikh took a great interest in ideas, showed the article to the Chief of the General Staff, with General Fuller's letter. Perhaps on account of that letter, the General read the piece and his opinion was reported to me as: 'It is a very "nice" article.' I could not, of course, observe like Henry Tilney in *Northanger Abbey* when Catherine Morland described one of Mrs Radcliffe's novels as 'nice' that 'It would depend on the binding.'

* In regard to naval power I always aired the view that unless a country was friendly with the first naval power in the world, it was not worth being even the second power.

CHAPTER 4
Fortunes of the Autobiography

I must now resume the story of the autobiography, over which I was to have trouble, anxiety and suspense before its acceptance by a publisher. Of course, while writing the articles described in the last chapter, my main preoccupation was with the autobiography. By the spring of 1949 I was able to complete it, and send the second half to Hamish Hamilton. I assumed that it would not be less than three months before I could get a reply about its acceptance. So, I decided to take a little rest. But instead I was to have a serious recurrence of ill health.

In July 1949, I was at my office when I suddenly felt very ill and had a sinking feeling, perhaps a return of heart trouble. A colleague at once took me to her physician, a well-known cardiologist of New Delhi. He examined me very carefully, but could find nothing seriously wrong with my heart, although he said I was very weak. He therefore asked me to rest and take the medicines he prescribed. I was X-rayed and had electro-cardiographs taken, but nothing was found. Nonetheless, I could not walk steadily and when, after a few weeks, I resumed work at the office, it was thought prudent that my wife should accompany me there for some time. This condition lasted for nearly two years. Being familiar with the symptoms, I did not feel particularly alarmed. Still, I was very worried. The best I could do was to avoid over-exertion.

The year was to be unlucky for me in other ways also, and, as I thought, more seriously. While in that state of physical prostration, I received a letter from Mr Hamish Hamilton himself saying he was unable to accept the book. This was a great blow, for I had been expecting the opposite. He wrote that he did not think very many people would be interested in so detailed an account of a life so unfamiliar to English readers. In this he was certainly right. At that time, the unwise interest of degenerate Britons in the Third World and its penurious life had not come into existence nor was the Oxfam spirit in evidence so far as the publication of books by Indian authors was concerned. In any case, my book had nothing of the Third World about it. I myself had not considered saleability at all when I wrote the book, assuming that the subject would be of historical interest and my treatment of it such as would enable it to impose itself on a readership. I was confident about the quality of the book and had assumed that this would counteract commercial doubts.

I was now even more worried than previously over the problem of publication. I found that I could not handle the matter from India, because from that distance I could not judge which publisher would be likely to consider it. My selection of Hamish Hamilton had been quite haphazard. Besides, the length of the book called for a publisher who could afford the outlay. As it happened, in this dilemma my article on military thought came to my help. In my perplexity I wrote to Captain Liddell Hart.

Earlier in the year he had written to me expressing a wish that I should continue to write on military topics, giving his reason in these very generous words: 'It is such a rare experience to find anyone in any country who has something significant to say, and the necessary background of knowledge.' Needless to say, I was very deeply touched, all the more so because at the time I heard a curious story from one of my friends. He knew the Secretary to the Defence Ministry, a Bengali official of the Indian Civil Service. My article had been shown to the Chief of the General Staff and he liked it in his way. Even this sort of appreciation was absent in the civilian official, who, when my friend suggested the Government should make use of my knowledge of military affairs, made the following reply: 'Why, he never comes to see me.'

It was the custom in India among all careerists to wait on a minister or high official who had patronage to bestow, until a draft on the public revenues was received. The personages concerned assumed that these men were courtiers, never realizing that they really were bloodsucking parasites. I was not one of them, never having suffered from this abnormality. Others, however, less capable of self-assertion, have. This incident is only one illustration of the suppression of talent in India by those who have vested interests, and which I regard as the greatest blight on human achievement in my country after independence.

Be that as it may, in the same letter Captain Liddell Hart also wrote: 'I am very glad to hear that you've nearly finished a book. If I can be of any help in arranging its publication I should be delighted.' In my difficulty I took advantage of this offer. He asked me to send the typescript to Faber and Faber, his own publisher, adding that he himself was writing to Sir Geoffrey Faber requesting him to consider the book sympathetically. This was most generous of him, and I learned later that this sort of generosity was typical of Captain Liddell Hart.

However, nothing came of this either. One day I was sitting on my bed talking to a friend when a letter was brought in by my servant. I could see that it was from Faber and Faber and from Sir Geoffrey himself. He wrote that his current engagements made it impossible for him to take up my book, although he was not insensible to its merits. I did not betray the slightest feeling in front of my friend, and years afterwards when I told him the contents of the letter, he was surprised because he had not noticed any change of expression in me, and had assumed that the letter had been of a routine nature. But, in fact, the following months found me very dejected. I often said to myself: 'Is my book to remain unpublished when other writers seemed to be able to publish anything they wrote?'

I wrote again to Captain Liddell Hart. This time he informed me that he was writing to his agent, John Farquharson, requesting Mr Innes Rose, the agency's then proprietor, to handle the work. After some time a letter arrived from Mr Rose telling me that he thought the book had some very good material in it, but that it was very long which might well prove to be an obstacle. Even at that time the length of a book was becoming a problem, although not to the extent it now is. The book was of about two hundred thousand words, and when printed had 516 demy-8vo pages. (Yet, when published, it was priced at 21*s*.!) But the problem was, as Mr Rose wrote, that the book could not be shortened by omitting one chunk here and one chunk there; the length was an integral feature of the book and interwoven with its very conception. Nonetheless, he added, he would try to see what he could do. I sent him a long note explaining why the book had become so lengthy, which would do for this book as well. But I need not go into that.

I thanked Mr Rose and requested him not to give the book to two well- known publishers who published books about India. I did not wish my book to be regarded as one of special Indian interest, but to be read by ordinary English readers of serious books. I actually said that 'it has not been conceived or executed as a contribution to what may be called Orientalia.' During the following months I no longer brooded too much over the matter, having done all I could.

On 27 April 1950, Mr Rose informed me that the book had been accepted by Macmillan. Soon after, the firm also wrote saying they were very pleased with the book. So, the problem of publication was solved to my great satisfaction. At that time Macmillan did not publish books about India, except some textbooks sold in India and, of course, those by Kipling. To be taken in hand by Macmillan, publishers of Kipling and Hardy, was exhilarating.

At that time I did not know who had read the book for Macmillan, nor did I learn later. But I was told vaguely that it had been recommended by a former member of the Indian Civil Service, who had been greatly impressed by it. Whoever he was, I would place on record my gratitude to him, because all my literary success and standing began with the acceptance of this book. Mr Rose also showed great judgement in that he had selected a publisher likely to accept the book, and whom I had not dared to approach. If the book got the attention it did on publication, it must have been due to the imprint. Publication by Macmillan of such a long book by a wholly unknown author must surely have weighed with the literary editors and reviewers even before they had read the book

While waiting for the proofs, I performed a duty which I had previously neglected - the duty of educating my children. I had three sons. I had decided that I would not send them to a normal Indian school because the standards were so low, nor would I send them to a so-called public school because, being modelled on English public schools, they uprooted Indian boys from all their traditions and even their social moorings. I had indeed engaged tutors for them, but I myself with my preoccupation with the war and postwar Indian politics had not given much time to the parental task. I had, however, begun even before the acceptance of the book and in spite of my illness, to teach my sons English, Bengali, and history, leaving subjects like mathematics and science to the tutors. At that time in India boys and girls educated at home could sit as private candidates for the school final examination. My sons did this, and became qualified to go on to a university if they wished.

However, in order to teach them for two hours a day I had myself to study for two hours and brush up the subjects. The surprising part of the work was that, although I had already written in English and was awaiting the publication of a book in London, whose style was highly spoken of later, I discovered how little I knew about the technical complexities of the language. I may say that in teaching my sons I re-mastered the language. One of the discoveries which dehghted me was that the greater part of the notorious irregularities of English spelling was subject to simple rules.

Shall I give one example? Will anyone tell me when an adjective formed from a verb of Latin derivation took *able* as a suffix, and when *ible?* I learned to my great edification that all words from Latin verbs of the first conjugation took *able*, and the rest *ible*.

As was the case with M. Jourdain, I must have spelt and pronounced correctly without knowing it. For example, in the House of Commons itself I was given credit for my knowledge of English orthography by a minister of the British Government. On 27 February 1953 a bill was under discussion in Parliament to simplify the spelling of English, one reason being that simplification would help fellow-subjects not of British birth to speak and write English more easily. The Government spokesman, Mr Pickthom, was opposing it, and he brought me in as his wimess. He said:

'I do not know how many of the hon. Members have read a very moving autobiography ... *The Autobiography of an Unknown Indian* by Chaudhuri. The author gives the whole story of his intellectual formation, his intellectual emotion and relation to English Literature and how through English literature he came to other literatures and to read Dante and so on. The whole story is very moving and leaves me very dubious whether he could have acquainted himself with some of these literatures if the spellings in which he read Macaulay and Shakespeare had not been the spelling which takes one half-way to every other European language, except Basque and Hungarian.'

That was very true, although I did not know until I was teaching my sons that *ch* is pronounced as in chair when the word is English, as in loch when it is Celtic, as in anarchy when it is Greek, and as in chef when it is French, with only spinach and Greenwich having the proverbial unaccountability. I tried to initiate my sons into all that, asking them to separate all the words of Germanic origin from those of the Romance in a passage. When they started to learn English formally, at about fourteen, they could not write English, although I myself could do that very passably at that age. But they did what I did not do: within five years, they began to contribute articles to the leading English newspapers in India, edited and owned by the British.

So, my educational theory and practice falsified the very fashionable theory that parents are the last persons to succeed in educating their children. Actually, who else is qualified to make them both educated and civilized.? Certainly not the teachers as I can test every day living now in

England. But I never encouraged or advised anybody to imitate me. If anyone came for advice to me I simply said that success in this matter depended on the personality and character of the parents. I knew only myself and would not ask anybody else to take so serious a risk.

My peace of mind brought on by the acceptance of my book was soon to be gravely upset by a serious illness in the family. My second son caught typhoid, and for weeks we almost despaired of his life. Each time I returned home from the office, I stiffened my body for what I might have to face at the door, and I never dared ask about my son. Only from the attitude of the servant who opened the door, and the absence of alarming sounds from inside, could I reassure myself. Once I found my wife sitting by the bed and wiping her tears, although she was so strong-minded. Fortunately, the boy recovered, although months passed before he got his strength back.

Soon I began to receive the proofs for correction. But before I had done with them I received a grievous piece of news. My friend Bibhuti Babu was dead. He died on 1 November 1950, of what appeared to be a heart attack. For many years we had been out of touch, and he very rarely wrote to me. But in 1944 he had come to Delhi with a party of his friends and was accompanied by his wife. He Showed the same exuberant affection when we met again after many years, and also reverted to his old habit of sitting on my wife's bed talking to her, while the rest of us sat in the parlour. He never introduced his wife to me, nor did he bring her to our house to meet my wife. He was still the same socially-untamed man.

However, I learned after his death, that he had changed mentally. Although happy in his married life and fond of his child, he became more than ever obsessed with after-life from the fear of his own death. This had become almost a mania. His biographer has related some strange facts about his last days. He often asked his wife to keep in mind one of his novels which dealt with the other world. He also told another story himself which must have been based on a horrible delusion. It was during one of his walks in the wild places around the little town just outside the western borders of Bengal where he was spending the last years of his life, that he came upon a bed covered with a sheet. Lifting the sheet he saw his own corpse. He had queer sensations about his death and lived in constant fear of it. He thought that taking out a life insurance policy would bring about an early death of the insured, and so never had a policy. Just a week before his death the inhabitants of the town gave a party to felicitate him for his literary achievement. His reply to the addresses was very strange. He said that while listening to them he was feeling that there were suggestions in all of them that his early death would lighten their load of indebtedness to him.

Such was Bibhuti Babu before his death. He had written the novel *Undefeated* to tell the story of a boy's triumph over worldly circumstances. But his thoughts on death had made an utter defeatist of him. I would say of him, as I do of many other of my friends: 'One more unfortunate!'

Yet his death was not the sole tragedy for the family. In that little town he had been living with his younger brother whom I had met as a boy and who was now a doctor practising in the same town. He too had married. A week after the death of Bibhuti Babu, the dead body of this brother was found lying near the spot where his elder brother had been cremated. He had committed suicide by taking poison. Nobody knew why. The brothers left two young widows. It would seem that a curse lay on the family. Bibhuti Babu's father and mother had died in great distress; his young first wife had untimely died in 1918; his sister was taken by a crocodile. His death, I learned later, had been hastened by failure to take the precautions expected of one in poor health.

In his last letter to me he wrote that when nobody had thought anything of him I had given him encouragement to write, and, referring to those who scoffed at us, he asked: 'Where are they now." Yet he had not seen any of my major literary works. He felt happy on account of my worldly position, which to him seemed exalted. My great regret is that if he had lived only one more year he would have seen my book and felt that his confidence in my talents had been justified.

Soon after this I received a letter from Mr Thomas Mark, one of the Directors of Macmillan, who was seeing my book through the press, which gave me immense pleasure. I was in my office when the letter arrived, but my wife was so excited that she at once telephoned me and read out the letter. Mr Mark began by paying a tribute to my English in these words: 'I have nearly finished reading the proofs of your *Autobiography* and I wanted to let you know how greatly it has interested me, and how deeply I admire and envy the freedom, amplitude, and allusiveness of your writing in a language which is not, in the ordinary sense, your own.'

Then he explained his method of editing:

'I am particularly anxious that you should look at the page proofs as corrected by me because I want to be sure that the small changes I have made here and there [they were indeed very few in a book of that length] have your full approval, as I see by your notes to the printers that you are scrupulous in all such matters. Nothing has been done that would mar the individuality of your style, but I have occasionally corrected a small slip in phrasing or idiom.'

Then he assured me about his qualifications by saying: 'Perhaps, to strengthen your confidence in me, I ought to say that I have done work of this kind for many years for some of the most famous of English authors.'

Osbert Sitwell has acknowledged this, and I can assume that others equally famous also gained from Thomas Mark's care of their books. Thomas Mark did not allow me to mention his name in my acknowledgements as long as he lived, but after his death I paid tribute to him in the preface to my *Continent of Circe*. His method showed that English publishers had not as yet taken over the evil tyranny of American publishers as to the text of their authors. In my case, however, American Macmillan, who accepted the book for simultaneous publication in New York, did not make a single alteration.

By the spring of 1951 I had completed proof reading and was waiting for the book, announced to be published in June. This did not happen, however, till September. In the meanwhile, my wife and I decided to go for a change of air to a Himalayan hill station. My health was still very poor, and my son, now recovered from typhoid, also needed a change. This was to be the first holiday for me since 1941.

Till 1947 I had had no time to take leave, and after that I was extremely unwilling to do so, because going on leave meant for an official of my rank delay in getting the salary, without which I could not carry on. This was due to a procedure about officials like me, who were technically called 'Gazetted Officers', because their appointment, transfer, leaves, and retirement, had to be notified in the official *India Gazette*, and until the leave was notified no such official could get his leave pay. Formerly, the notification appeared in advance of the leave, but in my time the printing and publication was delayed till as many as three months elapsed before any leave was notified. During this time one had to live on one's own resources, if any.

However, in view of the state of my son's health, and that of my own, I took only one month's leave. I was not paid for that period until I had received my salary for the month following my return to duty. Even then I had to observe a strange formality. It was required that when drawing leave pay, the official should furnish what was called a 'life certificate', in which he had to declare that he was alive during the period of leave. I had to do that and furnish that certificate after I had rejoined the office. Without it I could not be paid my salary for the period of leave, although I was paid what was due after that.

Nevertheless, I took the risk and the leave, both fully worthwhile. I had never before seen the Himalayas, nor had I any idea of their grandeur. However, Dalhousie did not offer a view of the Great Himalayan Range, but only of a subsidiary, though snow-covered, range to the south of it. This was Pir Panjal, which separates the valley of Kashmir from the plains of the Punjab. But the views were grand. The snow dazzled the eye at noon, and at sunset turned pink.

The town itself was on three levels. The lowest part, which was the cantonment, was about 5,000 feet high. The level on which we stayed was one thousand feet higher, and there was another still higher. I could not, on account of my weakness, go to that high level but walked about among the pines at the level we stayed on. But the boys went out on excursions. Either they went down into the valley of the Ravi, more than two thousand feet lower, or higher up to even 10,000 feet. Once they went to a beauty spot some fourteen miles from Dalhousie. It was called Khijar, and had one of those grass-covered meadows called Marg in Kashmir, which resembled those of the Alps. They had to walk, of course, for there were only mountain paths and no roads. On theway they sawacow half-eaten by aleopard. The woods were also inhabited by the Himalayan black bear, a very dangerous animal.

My second son, always very adventurous, once took a serious risk by going down into a valley. We did not know anything about his intention, and when he had not returned by lunch time, we became very anxious and I sent my brother, who was with us, my eldest son, and a man with a pony, in search of him. He was seen tottering along, quite exhausted after his climb back. He said that he had slid down the slope without any idea of altitude or distance, and after reaching a village deep down in the valley, realized what he had done. I, of course, scolded him.

We returned to Delhi quite refreshed, and with new experiences. My wife, although born in the hills with altitudes above 4,000 feet, had never seen high mountains. Even for her this was new. After our return I waited in eager expectation of the book. It was published on 8 September 1951.

CHAPTER 5

Death of my Master

Although, to my great regret, Bibhuti Babu, did not see my book, Mohit Babu, who was my teacher and afterwards my literary guide, did. It would have been a greater sorrow for me if he had not. But he did so only a few months before his death, and it is this sad event I have to relate in this chapter. He was a martyr to Bengali literature, for literature, too, has its martyrs just as religion has.

Since 1937 I had been out of touch with him, and had not even written to him. I only knew that he had retired from his post in Dacca University and was living in Calcutta, engaged as usual in literary polemics. I was totally ignorant of the struggles he was going through even to survive. What he told me about himself when at last I wrote to him early in 1951 deeply shocked me. A few months before the publication of the autobiography I thought I would send him an extract from it, in which I had described what he had done for me, so that he might see that his one-time pupil had not forgotten what he owed to him.

Somehow I procrastinated, and finally the prompting to write came from an accidental event. A friend of mine gave me a newspaper cutting from which I found that Mohit Babu had recently presided over a literary conference, and what he had said there had created an acrimonious controversy. Since he was always provoking controversies, that by itself would not have surprised me, but the animus and scurrility shown by his critics did. So, on 30 April 1951, before I went to Dalhousie, I wrote to him enclosing in my letter the passage about him in the autobiography. I shall quote this letter in part and his letters which followed. The correspondence was, of course, in Bengali, and I am giving below the English translation. But the words in italics were in English in the originals. After referring to his address and the controversy, I wrote:

'It will be a particular class of Bengalis who will win, and for the rest their *frustration* - the sense of failure they had before - will persist: "Thou shalt remain in the same darkness in which thou wert" [a line from a famous Bengali poem].

'But in my case, a premonition of that dénouement had come. I have had arguments with you about my view that there was no future for the Bengali language, Bengali literature, and the Bengali people. I have ventilated this view at some length both by word of mouth and in articles, but could not convince anyone in time, and therefore also failed to rouse them to seek a remedy. No one can save a people who are destined to die, and it is not the Bengali people alone, but the whole of India which is on the way to death.'

There was more on these lines, and then I told him about the book and what I had written about him in it. The excerpt was enclosed. His reply came very quickly, and startled me. The letter was from a suburb of Calcutta and dated 4 May 1951. 'My dear Nirad,' he wrote,

'I have got your letter. - *you did not write a day too soon.* The ultimate frustration of my life has at last made its appearance. The fact is that I am crushed in body, mind, and spirit. Still, I do not sorrow over it, that is, I have no self-pity. It was I who had driven my life in this direction in ignorance and lack of control, and now I have arrived at the last destination. I neither grieve or repine for that. I am now realizing that the last fiery spark of Bengali life is turning to ashes in the bit of cinder that I am. I am a child of the age of Bankin (Chandra Chatterji) and Vivekananda. In my time I saw the greatness of all these three - the Bengali character, the Bengali genius, and the Bengali body. Over the decade from 1900 to 1910 the Bengali forgot Bengal and immolated himself body and soul on the sacrificial altar of India. He has had no salvation after that insane suicide - and so, as a spectre, he is leading his spectre's life ...'

Then he considered his own life, and wrote:

'But what is this life of mine.? For whom had I given up everything? Position, fame, money, prestige - I had coveted none of these; I unhesitatingly dedicated that life of mine, never impairing or veiling the truth that was mine. You do not know the history of the last twenty years or so of my life. One by one, I have given up everybody, and I am sitting in a cremation ground, making a seat for myself of my own corpse. Over the entire country ghouls and human spectres are holding their orgies of universal death and universal slaughter: I am watching that from a distance with eyes dimmed by approaching death. I do not join any celebration or any meeting or institution. During the last seven years or so I have been living in seclusion.'

Then he explained why he had made an exception by going to the literary conference, and came to the subject of my letter. 'Now,' he wrote, 'I shall reply to your letter. I had got news of your book from Binu [my youngest brother, who was on the staff of a newspaper] and I had written to Cham [my eldest brother, the advocate] of my deep and heart-felt joy. He informed me that he would come to see me, but has not as yet. Perhaps he has not been able to make time.'

After that he wrote about the feelings aroused in him by what I had written about him in my book. My tribute was contained in only one short paragraph. Yet this had overwhelmed him, as will be seen from the rest of his letter, which I quote below:

'I could never imagine that anyone could write about me in the way you have. I have had so many pupils, disciples, and admirers, but none of them have been able to accept in their heart, as you have done, me, or the vocation to which my life was dedicated, or the inmost formulation of mine which was unknown even to me. You were opposed to me on many questions. You could not think highly of my intelligence and judgement. But when writing your autobiography today, you have placed me on such an elevated seat of reverence, discovering in the depths of your inner life I know not what seed of thought sown by me. I could not expect that, nor did I claim it. Is it then you alone who have found a meaning in this blind, mad life of mine.' Strange! Nobody else, only you! My Life has been spent among a horde of dunces, hypocrites, and crooks, so that at last even my trust in myself is breaking down, and I feel like cursing my day. But I am as it were dazed by those few lines in your letter. Does it mean then that there was some truth in me, and you respected that truth."

He went on:

'There is another remark of yours by which I have been even more surprised, and that is what you have written about Michael [Madhusudan Datta, the first modem Bengali poet]. How could you realize that.' Is it not my own verdict.' I thought nobody but me would say that, could say that. With this, I am enclosing two excerpts from my writings on a separate sheet. If you read them you will see that somewhere deep down my way of seeing and yours have united. I am speaking of the point of view. It is not necessary that the words should be identical.'

More about his relationship to me followed:

'I am surprised and I am convinced that there is somewhere an identity between your inner life and mine. It is for this reason that I am able to believe that what you have written about me in describing your own life is not untrue. Otherwise, I could not have accepted your tribute of respect with a pure heart. I would have thought that it was not my due, and would have regarded it as a delusion of yours - at all events, my doubts would not have been dispelled - for the same reason for which so far I have never been able to accept praise and respect from others as genuine, regarding them as products of infatuation or insincere flattery. It would have been difficult to say what you got from me - how much of that was mine and how much yours, even though, as I have said before, your remarks have restored some of my confidence in myself. If at this mature age of yours, and actually after a good deal of consideration and scrutiny, you have seen something of my bestowal in your boyhood and early manhood, when you have cast back your eye to them, that is not likely to be false. Nonetheless, your observations about Michael have startled me. These are my very words. Where did you get them.' Surely, there is in it some *spiritual affinity*."

In conclusion he gave information about himself: 'My present *occupation*', he wrote,

'is truly *precarious*. I have taken shelter in a ruined house surrounded by a wilderness like a *refugee*... Gradually, I am getting very tired, and want to fall asleep. Life has become unendurable.'

But with all this absorption in his own predicament, he did not forget to inquire about my family life: 'How many sons and daughters do you have.' Give them my blessings. May they become true men, and may they never lose the pride in being Bengali. You will see to it that they are initiated deeply into Bengali literature and the special *culture* of Bengal. Will you not come back to Calcutta in the the future? Only you could have written about Calcutta in the way you have.'

Then he referred to my father, which deeply touched me. He wrote:

'I recall your father. I do not know why I have always felt a deep reverence for him. Yet how little have I seen of him? Those Bengalis of old times – that character, that strong personality, that admirable heart! – I shall see them no more. Yet it is in these men who had remained unknown in Bengali society that the ideal of Bengali life manifested itself most nobly. How many of them I have myself known!'

I must say that if he was surprised by my letter, I was even more startled by his. Indeed, I was overwhelmed. I could not guess that the restoration of contact with my master after more than a decade would reveal such a tragedy. I knew that he could have had difficulties, and also that he would have been engaged in hard-hitting controversies. But I was not prepared at all for what he told me, and far less for the mood in which he replied to my letter. I shall give an idea of my sadness over it by repeating what he himself told me after reading Hardy's *The Mayor of Casterbridge*, which I had lent him. He told me with a shudder: 'What a tortured soul writhes in that book!' I saw the same thing in that letter. Reading it I could say like Michael Henchard's daughter: 'Oh, what bitterness is put in this!'

He was very eager to read my book, and I sent him a copy as soon as my copies came from London. He replied promptly:

Calcutta
8 November, 1951

'I have got your book, and have had no time so far to write about it. I am ill, and so busy over and above, that I cannot get the leisure to do the thinking and appraising which is needed in respect of the book. I read it with the deepest attention as soon as I got it. I have also marked it in many places. Your book has really stirred my mind - the reaction has been somewhat violent. Just as on the one hand I have been charmed by the brilliance and power of the writing, on the other, I have become anxious for many reasons, and in many ways, over your basic views and conclusions. You know about my mental constitution and about certain fixations of mine. Perhaps you have read my *Bengal and the Bengalis*. Not for that alone, but my anxiety is for the fact that I have felt that there is a blind spot even in that powerful intellect of yours and in your devoted search for truth. I shall ponder longer and deeper over the book and then send you my criticism of it in the way of an article. Time is needed for that.

'Charu [my elder brother] came yesterday, and we discussed your book at some length. He has given me press-cuttings on your book. It has given me a definite shock.

'But I have other anxieties besides the book, and that is about your personal welfare or harm. I wish for still greater things for you. So long only a few people knew you, now many will. May they not form such an idea about you which would give pain to me. Perhaps you do not know what sorrow I have always felt because you did not receive the fame and standing which were due to you. So far as it is possible to do from a distance through letters, I shall let you know my queries about the book. I hope you are well with your family. Accept my affectionate blessings.'

He accurately foresaw the possibility of personal harm to me from the book, and in a later letter his apprehension led him to putting his finger on the crucial factor in the situation. He asked me: 'What does Jawaharlal Nehru think of the book.?' I could have no knowledge of that. Mohit Babu never recovered enough to send the criticism he had promised. He quickly got worse and died on 26 July 1952 at the age of sixty-four. He was only a little more than nine years older than I was. After his death I could only observe: 'One more unfortunate!'

His failure as a critic and publicist was due not only to the tenor of his views but also to his character. While Bengal had moved into a new era of ideas and loyalties - if indeed they could be regarded as such and not merely as capitulation to circumstances - his ideas, which belonged to the days of the Bengali leadership in politics and culture and which were left behind after the First World War, had become unacceptable. He might be called the cultural counterpart of Subhas Chandra Bose. In character he was both unadaptable and inflexible, and totally tactless and abrasive. He could not view the changes he was seeing in their historical context; they roused his anger. He attacked, and in turn was attacked with even greater ferocity.

He was politically and culturally a fierce nationalist which made him lead towards authoritarianism. Thus, like all Bengali nationalists of the conservative school, he, too, was an admirer of Hitler. Before and during the war he used to say that Hitler was born to regenerate Europe. He might be compared to Charles Maurras, and like Maurras he had his *nationalisme intégral* - a Bengali integral nationalism. He interpreted my criticism of the Gandhian Congress as adherence to his own creed, and so wrote in one letter:

'Although I could infer something about your attitude to Gandhism and the Gandhian Congress, I had no definite idea about it. I was glad to read what you have written about both in your letter. That a man of learning, feeling, and power of thinking like you would arrive at such conclusions, would hold views like yours in respect of the issue of India Bengal is both right and natural. I am sending you my blessings from the depths of my heart for them. Two passages of your letter have moved me deeply.'

But he was, above all, a poet and should have remained one. His poetry was human and universal, and had no passing politics in it. But he was too much of an *engagé* by temperament, and yet could not raise his polemics to a level at which it could have a value transcending the circumstances out of which it arose. He would also have succeeded as a pure literary critic. His taste in literature was impeccable and infallible. I never saw him fall a victim to the spurious and shoddy however popular it might be, nor did I ever find him inclined to deny the merit of a story or poem as story or poem because it was by one of his enemies. His ideological prejudices did not operate in regard to literary quality.

At least I am glad to be able to say that after three decades a group of his one-time pupils and admirers have begun a campaign to rehabilitate him, and restore to him the place he should have in Bengali literature.

CHAPTER 6

Reception to the Autobiography

As I have already mentioned, the autobiography was published on 8 September 1951. That was also my second son's birthday. We celebrated both events on that day, although I had not yet seen the book in print. It was to arrive some weeks later. Soon after, it was published in New York by Macmillan of America, an independent concern. Mr Rose had already arranged with a press-cutting agency for all the reviews to be sent to me, and he himself sent me those which pleased him the most.

I received the first clippings sooner than I expected, because the book was reviewed promptly in the most important Sunday papers - I believe within a fortnight after publication. The *Observer* review was by Harold Nicolson and that in the *Sunday Times* by Raymond Mortimer; both were very appreciative. Macmillan had previously informed me that reviews could never be predicted, nor a favourable reception depended on. Nevertheless, my hopes as well as theirs were fulfilled. The imprint of Macmillan had certainly carried weight, and made the literary editors send the book to their front-rank reviewers, who were the most important figures in literary journalism, and not to specialists on India. The other newspapers, journals, and magazines were equally enthusiastic, and in its issue for 3 November the Illustrated London News published a full-page review by Sir John Squire with a large portrait of myself.

Mr Rose sent me the whole issue by air mail. For years, I myself had been a subscriber to the journal, but my copies came by sea. On seeing the packet, I anticipated a review of my book, but expected no more than a short notice among the others, and certainly not the whole of Squire's page which I had always read with full attention, and which carried with it great honour. The whole family was very excited and for good reason. Previously, only Jawaharlal Nehru had had such a portrait published in the *Illustrated London News.* But Nehru was the Prime Minister of India and his photograph was by Karsh of Ottawa. I was only an unknown Indian and the photograph had been taken by my eighteen-year-old son. A friend of mine told me that this attention alone would sell five hundred copies and also that the review could not be better even if I myself had written it. In this he was wrong, for I could never have written anything like it. Squire said in his conclusion that I had built a belated bridge between England and India. He also compared my childhood to Aksakov's and W. H. Hudson's, the writers of two classics of childhood memories I most admired. He also paid a compliment to my wife, for bearing with a husband who was so impossible because of his mooning.

Some reviewers were critical, and administered very lofty rebukes to me for being lacking in charity towards the new regime in India, although they, too, did not deny the quality of the book. As a rule, these reviews were by those Englishmen who had worked in India, and who, after the withdrawal, had suddenly become wholehearted admirers of the Indian nationalist leaders. A few had shown this tendency already during the British rule, as for instance, Horace Alexander, the Quaker worshipper of Gandhi, who reviewed the book for the *Spectator*. He reprimanded me for being unfair to Nehru, but also made some ridiculous blunders about me. The TLS review which appeared later was also very severe. I never learned who wrote it.

The B B C gave very special coverage to the book, and had four broadcasts on it. The longest was on the Third Programme - a fifteen-minutes' talk by John Raymond. The talk in the Overseas Service was by John Morris, and was recorded for me by All India Radio. John Raymond said that there was a mixture of Proust and Swift in the book, Proust for the detailed evocations and Swift for the satirical element. I am afraid I gave many readers an impression of ferocity in some of my writing, although I myself thought that I was being nothing but very realistic in the manner of Flaubert or Maupassant, but here adapted to non-fiction. Geoffrey Gorer reviewed it in the *Listener* from the sociologist's point of view. All in all, the English admirers and critics of the book justified the proverbial distinction we Indians made between the Englishman at home and the Englishman in India: the former, nice and decent folk, the latter, hostile and nasty. After 1947, however, the nastiness of the Englishman in India was transferred from the nationalist leaders to those Indians who criticised these leaders. I shall give two examples of this later.

Two private English appreciations of the book gave me very great pleasure, and they came from utterly unexpected and different sources. Let me speak about the first of these. I had asked Mr Rose to get two copies of the book specially bound for me: one copy was to be in full levant morocco with elaborate gold tooling – dentelle, etc. – and gilt edges, and the other in three-quarters calf with some gold tooling. The bound copies arrived not long after the commercial copies. They were splendidly done by the binder of Hatchards. The first was in red morocco and the other in brown calf, with the tooling in 24-carat gold. With the first the binder paid me a compliment. He had read the sheets and had liked the book so much that he decided to bind it with a special piece of leather he had reserved for himself Such a recognition from such a quarter was bound to impress me very much.

The recognition from the second and far more exalted but equally unexpected quarter overwhelmed me. It was from Churchill himself. I came to learn about it from Mrs Maurice Macmillan who came to Delhi with her husband early in 1952. The Indian Publishers' Association gave them a party, and Khushwant Singh, the wellknown Sikh writer, as well as I were invited to it. Mrs Macmillan told the story to Khushwant with me sitting by, listening. She Said that before sailing she had gone to see her friend Mrs Soames (Mary, *née* Churchill) and had in the course of conversation asked her what she could read on board the ship. 'Why,' Mrs Soames replied, 'that book by the Indian author.' Mrs Macmillan said that she did not have to be told about that book, for they were its publisher. Then, Mrs Soames asked her if she would meet the author. When Mrs Macmillan said that she did not know, Mrs Soames told her: 'If you do, tell him that father thinks it is one of the best books he has read.'

It was not I alone, but Khushwant Singh as well, who was almost bowled over. I could never imagine that Churchill, who was at that time preoccupied with the highest questions of world politics and had just become Prime Minister again, could have had time to look into a book like that. In India I never came to know whether Nehru or Dr Radhakrishnan ever read it. Of course, I must also confess that with abnormal arrogance I disregarded the Indian custom of waiting on important persons with a copy of my book.

The public reaction to the book in India was totally different, and except for one review, uniformly not only hostile, but even abusive. However, before describing that I would deal with the reaction of the family. I was in Delhi and my brothers and sisters in Calcutta, and I had met them but occasionally during the previous decade. There was as much excitement over the book in Calcutta as there was in Delhi and that even before the book was on sale in India or any reviews had appeared in the Indian press.

This was due to the reviews in London. My brother himself subscribed to some journals, and I sent him some of the reviews. I learned of the 'state' the family was in from a letter my eldest sister-in-law (the advocate brother's wife) wrote to my wife. I quote the relevant passages:

'Calcutta
21 October, 1951

'My dear sister Amiya [my wife's prenomen],

'Although we have not written about Nirad's book, you will split with laughter if I told you what we are doing here at home by way of advertising the book. Ramesh Babu [an elderly relative] came the other day and said to him [my brother, her husband - Hindu wives do not mention their husbands by name, but only use the pronoun]: "What have you done in life, Charu.? Everybody else is going to England, but you with your wife and only one daughter have not been able to do so." [Of course, in the class to which we belonged, it meant at the time that we were almost nobodies.] He [my brother] at once retorted: "We have already climbed so high even without going, that if we did, you could never reach us. Do you want to see.?' And he opened the *NetP Statesman* and read out the advertisement with Raymond Mortimer's recommendation. Now he shows it to every visitor to the house, and even at the Assembly [the Bengal legislature where my brother was one of the legal advisers]. But, unfortunately, we cannot get a copy because not a single one has reached the Calcutta shops. Khirod [my doctor brother] came and told us that he had seen a copy in the hands of an Englishman who had come from Delhi. He discussed the book for a long time and told us that he had written to Macmillan for a copy.

'Binu [my youngest brother] is carrying the clippings in his pocket in order to show to all. And I hear that Mohit Babu is showing Nirad's letter to everybody. Well, well, I am saying that it is a matter of family pride. For quite a long time we were unable to give ourselves airs. I pray that your sons may be worthy of their father. Nirad could have written such a book a long time ago. How happy father and mother [mine, she meant] would have been had they still been living, and also, he would not have had to serve others for a livelihood.'

It will be seen that my sister-in-law shared my dislike of being a hireling, now glorified under the name of employment'. After the book arrived and they had read it, I was informed that they were singing the songs I had translated in the book in the original, and the house was ringing with the chorus of brothers and sisters. But it was a letter from my fifth brother, who died in 1960 at the age of fifty-four, which gave me the greatest pleasure. He was an electrical engineer by profession, but a man of wide culture and fine literary judgement. He wrote a long letter to me, which was extremely balanced in its appreciation. For instance, he wrote that my descriptive evocations read like a novel's, but I might be prone to 'over-generalization'. This was typical criticism of me from educated Indians.

Of course, the English reviews were seen by others, especially the editors of newspapers, thus creating considerable advance interest in the book. No other book by an Indian had received so much attention in England before. Nehru's autobiography, published in 1935, had been favourably reviewed. Even so, the reception had not been of this order. Thus, when at last *The Statesman* of Calcutta and Delhi received the book and was ready with the review, it announced beforehand that its Sunday edition would be publishing a review of the autobiography, 'one of the most acclaimed books of the year'. The review was very enthusiastic, and, as I learned afterwards, had been written by the anthropologist, Verrier Elwin.

Then came the reviews in the Indian press proper, i.e. the papers owned and edited by Indians. *The Statesman* was run with British capital and edited by Englishmen, and its review was the only favourable one in India. All the rest were not only severe and condemnatory, but in many cases even scurrilous. The book was denounced as a second Katherine Mayo attack on India. I was placed in the category of anti-Indian writers, and that labelling has stuck.

Two of the unfavourable reviews surprised me, because in one case I was definitely given an assurance that that particular review would be fair. This notice appeared in the English newspaper owned by my friend Suresh Majumdar. He had told me that he would take particular care that the book went for review to a qualified person who would be fair, for books often landed in the hands of malicious and unqualified reviewers. But I learned afterwards that he himself had been deeply offended by certain things in the book and had asked one of his editors to deal very severely with it. The review as published was anonymous. The other review was by a well- known Muslim literary man, and in Bengali. It was a lampoon, and in it I was even compared to Hanuman, the blackfaced monkey follower of Rama, who had leaped across the sea from India to Lanka. That was a dig at my literary pretension. I had no reason to think that a Muslim would take offence at my criticism of Hindu life.

Both the reviewers apologized to me fifteen years later. The case of the Muslim writer was particularly pathetic. When he wrote the attack he was a well-established writer with a high reputation for his brilliant style, and besides he was holding a highly paid post in one of the cultural institutions of the Government of India. But he was given to drinking and gradually went down in the world. He wrote his apology from his deathbed. The other reviewer, a very competent journalist and a former revolutionary, told me that he had been forced by his employer to attack me, but had been and still remained an admirer of my writings.

Although I was then very angry at these violent attacks, I could understand them. No nationalist reader of my book needed to go further than its dedication to acquire a strong and unconquerable prejudice against me, for it was dedicated to the memory of the British Empire in India, and I made matters worse by going on to say at the end of the dedication that all that was living within us was made, shaped, and quickened, by British rule. This was not simply heresy, but treason, and it was the high-placed Indians, educated at Oxford and Cambridge, who resented the statement most violently. One such man, a high official, otherwise most affable, said in my presence that the statement was nonsense. Yet, men of his class did not treat anybody who had not been educated in England, as a fellow human being, let alone as an equal. Kipling, who called this class of Indians mules, wrote about the real mule that he did not like to recall the father's side of his ancestry - because the father of a mule is an ass. In this case, no Indian had any reason to be ashamed of the father of his mind.

Anyone who had any knowledge of the modern Indian mind knew that it had been formed by English education, in India more so than abroad. Westernization of the Indian educated in England had an appearance of being an artificial veneer, but Indians, educated in India in the English language, became mentally transformed quite naturally, so that they could hardly say what exactly their mind and personality might have been without that education. This was perceived less than ten years after the foundation of the University of Calcutta by Sir Henry Maine, who was its Vice-Chancellor in the 1860s. Addressing an assembly of Bengali graduates at a convocation he said this:

'There is not one in this room to whom the life of a hundred years since would not be acute suffering, if it could be lived over again. It is impossible to imagine the condition of an educated native with some of the knowledge and many of the susceptibilities of the nineteenth century - indeed perhaps too many of them - if he could recross the immense gulf which separated him from the Indian of Hindu poetry, if it ever existed.'

Speaking later in England in 1871 he said:

'I have had unusual opportunities of studying the mental condition of the educated class in one Indian province [he referred to Bengal]. Though it is so strongly Europeanized as to be a fair sample of native society, taken as a whole, its peculiar stock of ideas is probably the chief source from which the influences proceed which are more or less at work everywhere. Here there has been a complete revolution of thought, in literature, in taste, in morals, and in law.'

In the next thirty years this revolution spread all over India to create a new personality out of the old Hindu. One might call it endowing a fossil with living flesh and blood. Judged historically, I was saying nothing new nor anything that could be disputed. However, I had said something which was opposed to the nationalist dogma, which was even more ferocious in the Indian educated in England because he was more open to the charge of being de-nationalized, and so had to cry 'Great is Diana of the Ephesians' more loudly than the home-produced Westernized Indian.

In addition, I had offended against the new nationalist myths of Indian history. English education, which had transformed the personality, had also brought European nationalism to India, and this, in the Gandhian era, became much more aggravated by being assimilated into the old Hindu megalomania and xenophobia. Also, I had given offence to the prudery acquired from the English education in my descriptions of certain crude and primitive aspects of our life, as Synge had given offence to Irish nationalism in *The Playboy of the Western World*.

However, the modem Indian mind is nothing if it is not inconsistent and paradoxical. The reputation I suddenly Acquired of being anti-Indian helped, rather than hindered, the sales of the book. This was due to the special Indian reaction to a book on India in English, whether by an English or an Indian author. Where an Indian writer praises India, no Indian reader wants to read him, because he is only saying what is self-evident. For nearly one thousand years the Hindus have been saying that they hold this truth to be self-evident that there is no country but theirs, no nation like theirs, no kings like theirs, no religion like theirs, no science like theirs. I am paraphrasing the words the great Muslim scholar employed around 1000 AD. On the other hand, when praise comes from a White Man, it is made much of, proving that even the enemies of India have to recognize our superiority. But an attack by a White Man is still more prized as a means of amplifying the sense of national grievance, and my book only earned a share of that reception. Had the book been printed in India, nobody would have paid any attention to it. Its publication and reception in Britain almost raised it to the level of an Englishman's attack on India. What added to the hostility was the fact that the more intelligent and educated Indians could not deny the quality of the book. That made my offence even greater.

Therefore, my book was pounced upon and read eagerly. A high official of All India Radio told me that he had not been able to lay it down even to go to bed, and read most of the book at one sitting, crying at every turn: 'This cannot be true.' I could not anticipate that, and so had seriously underrated the commercial prospects of the book in India, and had to pay a price. At that time a young Punjabi used to come to see me almost every day. His name was Satyapal, which means 'Upholder of Truth'. He showed an interest in ideas which I had never expected in a Punjabi, and he listened ecstatically to whatever I said, and only on account of a certain lack of energy, a trait unusual in a Punjabi, missed becoming my Boswell. We had a discussion one day about the sales of the book. I placed the possible figure at about two hundred in New Delhi. He on the contrary said that at least five hundred copies would sell immediately. I told him that if in three months even four hundred copies sold, I would give him the second copy of the book bound in calf. As it happened, we learned by inquiry afterwards that within two months more than six hundred copies had been sold. One bookseller alone had sold nearly three hundred copies. So, I lost the bet and had to give the young man the second leather-bound copy.

One of the most curious aspects of the reception to the book in India was that of the attitude of the local British. The community as represented by *The Statesman* (all British), the journalists from the British press and the

BBC, took a good deal of interest in me. So did the European diplomatic missions. But there was a very discreet aloofness on the part of the British High Commission, who must have seen what trouble I had brought on myself by paying a tribute to British rule in India. But they were probably afraid to cultivate a man who was a *persona non grata* with the new Indian regime. It was only after Malcolm MacDonald arrived as High Commissioner that I developed a friendship with the High Commissioners, which lasted till 1970.

There were two incidents soon after the publication of the book which gave me an indication of the British 'official' attitude to me. The first of these happened after copies of the *Illustrated London News* arrived in India. One day my wife and I were invited to dine at the house of an English naval officer, Captain Saxton. He was the educational adviser to our navy. On arrival, I found that one of the other guests was General Williams, who was attached to our army headquarters as adviser on ordnance. I had met him previously. He was a genial and humorous man, with no suggestion of Colonel Blimp in him, and told amusing stories of his first arrival in India as a young artillery subaltern. He was also the president of the local birdwatching society and from time to time we discussed the birds of Delhi. To be a bird-watcher in New Delhi at that time was a very fashionable thing, and later Malcolm Macdonald, when High Commissioner, published a fine book on the birds he could see in his garden. I was not a member of this society, which had been joined by high Indian officials who wanted to show that they were in no way different from the members of the White bureaucracy. When it was observed that General Williams talked about birds with someone who was not one of these officials, they were naturally surprised. One day I was asked: 'Are you a bird-watcher.?' I replied: 'No, I only look at them.' The General and I got on very well together.

Before we sat down to dinner Mrs Saxton showed me the copy of the *Illustrated London News*, assuming perhaps that I had not yet seen it. It seemed likely she had taken the trouble to ask me to dinner for the purpose of showing it. I thanked her and said that I had already received my copies. We then went in to dinner, and when we were at the soup, I do not now remember how the topic of our new Indian administration arose. I believe it was some compliment paid to them by General Williams which provoked me to repeat a recent wisecrack of mine. I had no fear of being rude, for I knew in what contempt the English officers and officials held the Indians in the ICS and the Indian Army. So I just remarked: 'All the Indians in the ICS should have been hanged from the nearest lamp-post on 15 August 1947.' At once, to the astonishment and embarrassment of everybody, General Williams jumped up from his seat, left the room, and never came back. Somehow, we finished the dinner. Had this happened now I would have laughed heartily, but at that time I was too inexperienced in social intercourse with Englishmen, and felt very much ill at ease.

A few days later, the General and I met at another party. He came up to me and said half jokingly and half seriously: 'I am going to report you to the Director of Military Intelligence.' That officer was his Indian superior on the General Staff. I was taken aback to find that in their new respect for Indians one of the English Generals was now ready to tell on a man for his lack of respect for them. Then General Williams raised his fore-finger and admonished me, saying: 'Do you know that there was a very wise man named Sardar Patel who decided to keep the ICS men?' Since I knew a good deal more than the General about the wisdom of Patel and why he had kept the Indians in the ICS, I did not reply.

The incident was brought back to me fifteen years later by my hostess herself Mrs Saxton was living in England then, and her husband had become a clergyman after his retirement. He was vicar at West Farleigh, near Maidstone in Kent. Mrs Saxton wrote to me from the vicarage on 8 November 1967: 'Do you remember General Williams' explosion when you had dinner with us at 4 Queen's Way.' He laughs about it now and I believe you are great friends.'

So he would, I knew, when back in England, and indeed we remained friends. There was no doubt that he was a very good man. But after all, the English wolf in India belonged to his pack, and, as Kipling said, the strength of the Pack is the Wolf and the strength of the Wolf is the Pack. How could General Williams refuse to howl when the Pack howled.' Only, the Pack howled in one way when it had not been worsted by the Red Dogs, and in another when it was. Were there no good Germans, above all among the German generals, when Hitler ruled in Germany?

The second incident was as typical of the British in India and as grotesque. It was provided by Arthur Moore, one-time editor of *The Statesman*, about whose previous activities as an opponent of the nationalist movement I have written already. I have also mentioned how he denounced

Lord Beaverbrook for not sending Spitfires out of England to Bengal to protect British skins. He left *The Statesman* and, at the time of which I am speaking, was in Delhi, contributing a regular column to The Hindustan Times, a nationalist newspaper owned by the Birlas, the financial supporters of Mahatma Gandhi.

Early in 1952, he took it into his head to put me in my place in his column. It was not that he did not recognize some merit in me, but that was what in English idiom is called 'damning with faint praise'. His real purpose was to expose my pretension to know Greek history, which, having been neither at Oxford nor Cambridge, I could not know. My offence was that, in my autobiography, I had written of my feelings over the defeat of Athens in the Peloponnesian War. I had then written:

'In my student days I used to be specially drawn towards these periods of history in which some great empire or nation, or at all events the power and glory of a great state, was passing away. I was induced to agonized fascination by these periods, and the earliest experience I had of this feeling was when I read about the final defeat of Athens at the hands of Sparta. I seemed to hear within me the clang of the pickaxes with which the long walls to the Peiraeus were being demolished, and was overwhelmed by a sense of desolation which men have when they see familiar landmarks suddenly disappearing or witness the unexpected *bouleversement* of the purpose they had assumed to be inherent in the unfolding of their existence.'

I concluded by saying: 'I did feel that the downfall of Athens was a monstrous and unnatural deflection of the purpose which had become manifest through Marathon and Salamis. If that was to be the end, why was the Persian war fought at all.?'

To Arthur Moore this seemed to be the most shameless imposture in a Bengali Babu who had not been to Oxford or Cambridge even to get stamped into second-rate respectability by cramming. So, he had his go at me. He referred to the passage quoted and observed how that could be, for the Periclean age with all its glories followed the demolition of the walls to the Peiraeus! Of course, Pericles died in 429 bc and the walls were demolished in 404 BC, i.e. twenty-five years later. The man had confused what I had described with the sack of Athens by the Persians in 480 BC before Salamis.

At that time Arthur Moore was living near my house in Delhi and I rang him up to point out what a howler he was guilty of. He was unshaken and asked me: 'What is your authority?' I replied that no authority was needed, a reference to any elementary textbook on Greek history would tell him that. But not being sure that he would have access to any sort of book on Greek history where he lived - an exclusive European hotel -I sent him an English translation of Thucydides and a small book of Greek history. He then did the least he could, if he laid claim to any kind of decency. He withdrew this particular criticism in his next article.

But his whole attitude was one of egregious snobbery. He showed it in treating with contempt the account in the autobiography of my reading as a student. He said that I had mentioned a number of books which nobody read any more. Yet these were the great classics of European historiography written in the nineteenth century by Englishmen, Frenchmen, and Germans, and also the most notable historical works of my time. I was not twenty when I read Aulard about the French Revolution, and at the age of twenty had myself bought Sorel, Aulard, Lavisse. But any exhibition of knowledge of European life, civilization or history drove the British community in India to make the gesture which peasant boys in India make at a passing train. They expose themselves and wave their hips. But as the train goes forward in spite of these gestures, our figurative train to Europe also did, in spite of the figurative obscene gestures of the local British.

But I would not close this account of the reception of my book in India on an unpleasant note. Even the British in India struck an exceptionally sweet note. I had it from a former member of the ICS, Mr Christie, who had retired from the Service and was holding an industrial post then. Soon after the publication of my book he told me that he had gone into the biggest bookshop in Delhi (run by an Indian, of course) and seen my book displayed. Taking it up and turning a page accidentally, his eyes fell on a name which was that of his father-in-law. He was Mr Stapleton, the Inspector of Schools of Dacca Division in my boyhood, who had heard me reading and speaking English in 1907 and sent his assistant to compliment my father on my performance. Mr Christie was delighted and sent a copy of the book to Mr Stapleton, who was still living. He told me that his father-in-law had replied in a diction befitting his former official position. I, too, was as delighted as was Mr Christie. I could never have foreseen such a link.

CHAPTER 7

Stranded Again

The autobiography had set me free from the enclosure that my country and society had become for me, and the freedom was as much social as vocational. I could now address myself to a readership in the entire English-speaking world, without losing what I had in India. In actual fact, I widened it at home. I did not indeed produce a second book till 1959, but the autobiography procured for me an invitation from the BBC to go to England for five weeks in 1955, and out of that came my second book *A Passage to England.* Before that I was able to publish articles in the London Times and the newly launched *Encounter*, besides broadcasting in the Third Programme of the BBC. In America I was able to publish even in the *Atlantic Monthly.* That could be regarded as grazing far afield.

What happened socially was in its way equally remarkable. Up to that age -I was fifty-four and my wife forty-two – we had very little social life: mine was confined to my very few literary friends and, my wife's, to relatives. Now it became different. For one thing, because our social life was to be among the Europeans in Delhi, my wife was invited with me, and, also, this was real social life as understood by me.

The normal parties among these Europeans, and especially among the diplomats, took the form of large cocktail parties. I was indeed invited to these from time to time, but, more usually, I was asked to small lunch or dinner parties because my hosts wanted to talk to me. Thus I had opportunities of seeing something of the elegance and graciousness of European social life, about which I had read so much. What was more, I had opportunity to meet European celebrities coming to New Delhi.

One friendship created for me by the book was prized very highly by me. It was that of Count Stanislas Ostrorog, the second French Ambassador to India. He arrived in New Delhi towards the end of 1951 and was so impressed by my book that he sent his third Secretary to me with an invitation to dinner at the beginning of 1952. I went and the acquaintance developed into friendship. I shall presently relate how he helped me after my retirement out of a very difficult situation. But that was not the only time he showed his concern for me, which continued till his death in 1960. It was also through him that I met people who bore names famous in French history: for instance, a descendant of Arnauld d'Andilly, the Foreign Minister of Louis XIV, and of the great Arnauld, who was married to a young Polignac. To one with some knowledge of French history this was great fun. I might add that at Count Ostrorog's house I also met Lurçat, the famous maker of modem tapestries, and also Malraux.

But so far as my livelihood was concerned, the book also produced some very unpleasant consequences. The general hostility to my ideas and opinions which arose from my refusal to accept the nationalistic myths and which I might call ideological anger, did not harm me materially. On the contrary, as I have said, it helped the sales of the book. The worst that this kind of hostility can do is to give you a reputation for being anti-Indian, which creates an impersonal and fascinated hatred for you. This animosity can never be disarmed, but it remains impersonal. Material harm comes from the personal hatred created for you by your success, and particularly among your close friends and acquaintances. They take advantage of your unorthodoxy to inflict as much harm on you as they can, thus furnishing more proof of the truth of Dr Johnson's saying that patriotism is the last refuge of scoundrels. It will be easily assumed from the description I have given of the Bengali character that attempts to harm me in my worldly prospects would come from my Bengali acquaintances.

This sort of underhand campaign conformed to the typical Bengali manner, which I have not described. So I shall explain what the pattern of behaviour was. Its first principle was, and remains, that there would be no withdrawal of outward friendliness and cordiality for the victim who is to be stabbed in the back. And curious to relate, even the victim will behave in the same manner, however gross or indecent the treachery. He will not only smile at the friends whom he knows to be disloyal, because one or other of the conspirators will always come and tell him about the moves; he will even dine with them, thus eat salt with his enemies, disregarding one of the most firmly observed customs of the East. This behaviour was described by Kipling in the form of a parable of three very unpleasant animals, a crocodile, a scavenging crane, and a jackal. He wrote: 'The Jackal knew that the Mugger [crocodile] knew, and the Mugger knew that the Jackal knew that the Mugger knew, and so they were all very contented together.'

I received information fairly early that some mischief was afoot on account of the book. Some months prior to its publication and just before I went to Dalhousie, I was asked by a high official who was a friend of mine, whether I had any enemies. I wanted to know why he asked me that because I was not aware of anyone being hostile to me. Then he told me that an anonymous letter had been received in the government department concerned with such matters, denouncing my book and suggesting that it should be proscribed in India. I was further told that the department had simply put the letter aside, saying that when a book was not even published the question did not arise. I was very much surprised by the information because at that time I was not important enough to evoke anonymous letters, and could not even make a guess as to the writer's identity.

It was not my habit to show or give my unpublished writings to anyone. But in the case of the autobiography I had read out some passages to a very small number of colleagues or friends, and more especially to a friend of more than fifteen years' standing who often came to see me. I had great respect for his learning and intellectual ability, and he was a high official. He had often asked me to give him the whole typescript to read, but I had not. I had, however, shown him the blurb whose draft Macmillan sent me in advance, because I thought my friends would be glad to read it. The last sentence of the blurb ran like this: 'He [i.e. I] has waited till now, however, to make his own personal contribution to contemporary history, and to become a public figure as the author of one of the most impressive books ever addressed from India to the English-speaking world.' I watched a deep shadow spreading over his face as he read on, and after he had finished, when I expected him to hand the piece of paper to his companion to read, he dropped it on the floor. I laughed out and picked it up. But I did not connect him with the anonymous letter when recalling the incident, because I was very familiar with the absurd exhibitions of jealousy to which Bengali writers and intellectuals were prone.

Very soon, however, something happened which made me conclude that he must have been the writer of the anonymous letter. After our return from Dalhousie in July 1951, my wife told me that, while tidying up the bedroom, she had spotted that the typescript of the book had been tampered with. She said that she remembered exactly how I had tied it to a board with red tape, but now it was very untidy and loose. I actually scolded her for such a suspicion, and asked her who could have got into our bedroom and taken it out of the drawer of my writing desk. My wife called our old servant who had been in charge of the house when we were away. He gave a strange report. He said that one day the friend from New Delhi had come to see me and pretended he did not know that I was away. The servant asked him, as he did all visitors, whether he would have coffee, and when the friend said he would he went to the kitchen to make it. On coming back with it, however, he saw the friend standing by the desk in the bedroom, with the typescript in his hand. On being detected, he hurriedly pushed the papers into the drawer and came back to the sitting room to drink his coffee. My wife was triumphant and I furious. Being no conformist in ideas, I was not likely to be one in behaviour and continue to smile at this disloyal friend. I vowed that I would give him a hiding if he ever came to see me again.

As it happened, the longed-for chance came some months later when he called on us with the womenfolk of his family, but, alas! the chance was missed and that, to my lifelong regret. That afternoon my wife was receiving company and I was on the roof taking the air. She came up and told me that my friend had come. I asked her to send him away. She felt embarrassed and made excuses. In my fury I said I would go down myself and give him a shoe-beating. That is the worst insult and humiliation to an Indian. So I took off one of my slippers and held it up in my hand. But my wife at once threw her arms round me to prevent me from going downstairs. As at that time she was heavier than I was, I struggled violently to free myself without being able to shake her off. Just then a maidservant from the lower flat came to collect the dried washing, and, seeing us thus engaged, rushed downstairs to tell her mistress that the Chaudhuri Sahib and the Chaudhuri Mem Sahib were fighting on the roof and that she must go and separate them. When the peacemakers arrived, I had, however, regained my calm. So, I simply called my servant and gave him orders to tell the friend that I would not see him and he must go away. When the servant did so, the friend wanted to come up to the roof to talk with me. My servant, who knew me better than the visitor, feared for the consequences and somehow persuaded him to go away. But even after that he smiled at me if we accidentally met in a street in New Delhi. I do not think he ever connected my conduct on that day with his own bungled Watergate, which I might call his 'Mori Gate', because I lived near that well-known gate in the city walls of Old Delhi. Yet, had he chosen, he could have left behind him a monumental work of historical scholarship. Instead, he had, like all Indians of his ability and character, gelded himself by entering the governmental stable and could nurse only envy.

Soon after the publication of the book I heard something which surprised me very much. One of my colleagues in All India Radio, a Kashmiri lady, was a cousin of Mrs Indira Gandhi. She said to me one day: 'Indu [the diminutive of endearment of the full name of Indira] was asking me about you, what you did in AIR, and what sort of man you were.' I was very much puzzled to hear this, because I could not even imagine that she would know my name. My colleague also could offer me no explanation. Mrs Gandhi was not then what she later became, being then no more than the gentle and sweet daughter who kept house for her widowed father. What interest could she have in me?

Afterwards I guessed how she could have heard my name. I was told that Krishna Menon, India's High Commissioner in London and an intimate friend of Nehru, had written to him denouncing my book immediately after its publication. This was, of course, gossip, but the possibility of his doing so was confirmed by what an acquaintance of mine, who was in London at the time, told me later. He said that at a public meeting of Indian students at which he was present, Menon had indeed strongly criticized my book. His complaint was that it was anti-Indian. I had, of course, by my rejection of the myths of Indian nationalism, made it easy to bring this charge against me, but I was not so simple as to accept that as the sole provocation. Krishna Menon was a man of considerable inherent intellectual ability, but had done nothing to give substance to his literary or scholarly reputation; yet, he had the intelligence to perceive the quality of my book. He was also a man of overweening arrogance and therefore his anger against my book was natural. Jawaharlal Nehru, however, was not the man to be roused to action over a book.

I received other reports of malice in very high, as well as less high, circles of my Bengali acquaintances. A high Bengali official, I heard, had told Nehru on the telephone that my book was anti-Indian, to which he had simply replied that I had the right to express my opinions. Another very close acquaintance of mine had kept all the English reviews, including that in the *Illustrated London News*, in a drawer, but had only shown, with great glee, the unfavourable review by Horace Alexander in the *Spectator*. All this pettiness only made me laugh, but so far as I had malice myself, I was not very sorry to see these people suffering from my success, although I should have expected that fellow-Bengalis would be glad that a Bengali had reasserted the old pre-eminence of Bengal in writing English.

Beyond watching all this in an amused mood, I had no fear that my book would be the cause of injury in respect of my official prospects, and as months passed without any official notice being taken of the publication of the book, I felt safe. But soon indications came that mischief-makers were busy in the Department where I worked. As their manoeuvres inflicted serious worldly harm on me at the time, I have to describe these, and in order to make the account intelligible I would first explain the official setup in which I worked. My post was in the External Services Division of All India Radio, whose Director was a Parsi lady with long experience of broadcasting, and a member of a very distinguished Parsi family of Bombay. Her name was Miss Mehra Masani. She was responsible for the Division to the Director-General of All India Radio which controlled the personnel, and the Directorate-General in its turn came under the Ministry of Information, whose Secretary was a Bengali. One day Miss Masani told me with a good deal of amusement that the Bengali in the Director-General's office who looked after administrative matters, had sent her a bunch of very hostile reviews of my book, asking her to take them into consideration. She replied that all this was irrelevant to my official position, and if there arose any question of the reception given to the book, 'Mr Chaudhuri', she wrote, 'could produce as many favourable reviews as there were unfavourable ones.'

This was only one omen of what was to come from the same set of Bengalis in the Directorate-General and the Ministry. In August 1952, I successively received three notes which made it clear to me that a move to harm me in my official prospects through official channels was afoot. The first note, dated 5 August, asked me to inform the Director-General what income I had when I was appointed to my present post; the second, dated 12 August, asked me to surrender one-third of my income from the book to the Government; and the third, dated 29 August, called for an explanation why I had published a book without having-sought permission from the Government. The last note was the preliminary to disciplinary action against me, which could even lead to dismissal from the service. In form, the notes were in crude officialese, and in substance pointless, because they referred to rules which had no application to my case. It was obvious that the framers of the notes had not studied the rules themselves and had assumed that I would be frightened by the sabre-rattling. I had, however, looked into the rules long before and felt confident that I would be able to squash such moves.

But the timing of these demands puzzled me. It was many months, nearly a year, since the book was published, a fact known to all from Jawaharlal Nehru to my peon. So, if I had contravened any rule, action should have been taken at once. Thus, I had reason to think that the whole thing was not a bona fide official step but the result of an intrigue arising out of personal animus. I heard a story afterwards which appeared to confirm my suspicion. I was told that a number of Bengalis in Delhi had got together to mark those passages of my book which they regarded as anti-Indian, and had sent them to Nehru, requesting him to take action. I was also told that he had simply forwarded the representation to the Information Ministry, where there were other Bengalis ready with official knives. I had no reason to disbelieve this report, although it was tale bearing. In such matters it is not possible to get proofs, but as Bengali intriguers were very fond of bragging about their intrigues, I thought that the story might not be untrue. I knew how much heart burning I had caused in certain hearts, and could easily make a guess about the identity of the intriguers. Besides, by that time an absurd estimate as to the money I had made out of the book was current, and that must have added to the malice. So, the attack was launched when I was about to retire; and before I could retire with the advantages of my service.

There is nothing more contemptible than ineffective malice, and I dealt with what I was compelled to face with great gusto. But in retrospect the whole affair only gives rise to disgust in me, and only by suppressing it with an exercise of the will have I been able to re-read the lengthy papers I still hold. I have, however, to describe what I did, because the intrigue affected my future.

The first demand, to state my previous income, had no rule behind it, being based on a convention in the Indian bureaucracy about salaries. In it there was determined opposition to granting a man a high salary if he did not have something equivalent before being appointed to a post, whatever his qualifications. This was meant to preserve the caste system in salaries, and to block the entry of men from lower cadres to higher cadres. But my salary had been fixed in 1944, and in 1952 I was drawing almost double the initial amount due to yearly increments. Therefore, there was no point in raising that question so belatedly unless there was some intention to do me harm. I replied to the note curtly, saying that I refused to give the information as this was against the service rules as well as illegal.

The second demand, to surrender one-third of certain kinds of additional income earned by a Government servant, had indeed a rule behind it, but that related to fees received by an official if he gave professional service or advice to private parties while drawing a salary from the Government. The rule had nothing to do with royalties. The official who drafted the note to me seemed to have been aware of this, or at all events he had doubts, and so, in quoting the rule, he interpolated the word *royalty* after the word *fee* in order to bring my earnings from the book within the scope of the rule. This was dishonest, and I pointed that out and also wrote a long note to prove that the money could not be taken from me.

I was equally firm about the question of permission, and showed at some length that not only was I not required by the service rule to secure previous permission, but I was also even permitted to publish literary work provided it did not interfere with my official duties. In addition, I invoked the new Constitution of India promulgated in 1950. I said that 'the freedom to write, publish and circulate a book is part of the freedom of speech and expression and the freedom to acquire, hold, and dispose of property guaranteed by the Constitution to all citizens, including Government servants, as Fundamental Rights, and no Government Department has the power to abrogate this freedom.'

I substantiated the proposition in a lengthy note. All this was like breaking a fly on a wheel, but it was effective. The wretched jacks in office were frightened. Nothing intimidated them so much as the new Constitution, which as a combination of slave and tyrant all Indian officials hated. So they sent my notes to the proper Ministries, and I learned later that these authorities upheld my position. I heard nothing more of the notes. But I was like the one-eyed deer, and had ignored that those who wanted to harm me still had the means in their hand in such matters as lay within their discretion. Shortly before I was retired I discovered that I was indeed harmed as to my official prospects.

One day I was called to the office of the Deputy Director-General, a Bengali, and told about my future. He said with evident regret that the recommendation to extend my service by a year or two had not been accepted by the Ministry. I also learned that I was not to receive the retirement gratuity which I was expecting in lieu of a pension. Furthermore, I was told that I was not entitled to any retirement benefit because the post I was holding had not been made permanent and also I had not been confirmed as its permanent incumbent. This surprised me very much, because more that a year before this I had been definitely informed that my case had been sent up to the Ministry for their formal orders. But I now found that, though told by the previous Director-General to send the papers to the Ministry, the executive in charge had not done so. A procedural ground was given for this omission, which was that there were many such cases pending and, until all of them were ready to hand, an individual case could not be sent up. However, I had no doubt that my case had been deliberately held back. The only redress open to me at that late stage was to apply to the Ministry for retrospective confirmation. This, however, depended on the goodwill of the Ministry, and I knew that was not present because of my defiance of the demands. So, I was not only to be retired on the date due, but was also not to receive any retirement benefit whatever.

On that day I went home very sad, for I had depended on receiving the gratuity in any case, and also had vaguely hoped that an extension of service for a year or so would be granted. But I now found that the financial security I had arrived at in 1937, after years of want and distress, was to come to an end in less than a month and that I was to be thrown back to the situation from which I had emerged, to begin a new search for livelihood from scratch. None of my three sons had finished their education, and my family responsibilities remained the same.

I was, of course, aware that even if I got an extension or a gratuity that would not last very long, and that at the end of two or three years I would have to look for new means to support myself and my family. Still, any of these benefits would have given me a respite to write a new book, explore possible sources of income, and also to finish the education of my eldest son. But I was not to have even a breathing space, the struggle for survival was upon me. The worst part of it was that I could see no possible solution to the problem.

But when I broke the news to my wife she took it with remarkable calm, without in any way being flustered. She told me not to be anxious about the future, for she was sure something would turn up and we would not be abandoned by God. I tried to take as much comfort from her faith as I could, fortifying myself as well with the thought that if I had to start all over again, the sooner I faced the task the better. But neither faith nor stoicism came easily.

The weeks before the date of my retirement, which was on my fifty-fifth birthday, 23 November 1952, soon passed. On that day I went to say farewell to Miss Masani. We parted as very good friends, which we have remained to this day. But on my leaving she more or less casually gave me a letter saying that it was from the Director-General's office. When I opened it I found it to be a letter of formal reprimand for not supplying the information about my previous income. That office had been lying low, although it received my curt refusal long ago, and now fired its last shot when I was in no position to protest against the reprimand, being no longer in service. I further learned that instructions had been issued not to give me commissions for talks even as an external broadcaster, although I had broadcast for All India Radio on international affairs from 1937 and was regarded as an expert on the subject.

So, my connection with All India Radio came to an end with a squalid finale. The malice shown was very petty, and there is no word in English which would be *a mot juste* for those who exhibited it. But we Bengalis have a word, and it has an exact equivalent in French. I have no hesitation in employing it: the gang was truly a *canaille*. They did win a short-time victory, but that has not prevented my becoming what I am today. Some of those who crowed and gloated over the injury they had done to me are dead, and therefore beyond suffering, but others are or may be living still, and they are perhaps now disappointed in their one-time success. That is due to an extraordinary feature of my worldly career. At every new stage of my life, I have begun with a descent into a trough, with its dire want and suffering, but I have invariably risen higher out of it. Never have I gone down in life, but have ever been moving upwards even in monetary terms. It is indeed true: call no man happy until he is dead, but I am in my ninetieth year. What except death remains in store for me?

Nevertheless, the intermezzi between the acts were unpleasant while they lasted, and no hope of future progress could make that experience anything but distressing. When I retired I could see no solution to the long-term problem. Even the immediate problem, which was gratuitous, was very tiresome. Although I could depend upon my last month's salary and the refund of both my own contributions and that of the Government to the Government's Provident Fund, there was no sign of even these coming quickly. Payment of the last month's salary of a government servant and of any other dues from the Government was hedged with a strict series of precautions lest the one-time servant should cheat the Government out of any of its dues. So, a number of other Departments were notified of my retirement and asked whether they had any claims. Until all of them had provided a clearance certificate, no final payment could be made to a retired person. One Department in particular which had to provide such a certificate, was the Public Works Department, which had to testify that no rent was owed by the retired official. My case also went to that Department, although I had never occupied any Government quarters. Rents were always paid out of the salaries, and so both my office, which prepared the salary statements, and the Accountant General's office, which passed them, knew I had never lived in Government quarters. But any such knowledge meant nothing, the piece of paper was everything, and the PWD was not one to release it readily. Not only weeks, but nearly two months passed: yet I did not receive what was owed to me and about which there could be no doubt. I would call at the office where the clerks would assure me that they were doing everything possible. At last my wife set me down as a duffer and bungler and went herself. Not only did she make the office procure the certificate, she even saw one of the high officials in the Accountant General's office to speed up payment. This needed some perseverance. On the last day she threatened to come and stay in the office if the cheque had not arrived by the following morning. It was sent by special messenger.

The money enabled us to pay the bills for the past months and to have something over to last till the end of April or beginning of May. Although the long-term problem was as acute as ever, the relief of having some money allowed me to treat myself to a return visit to Agra and Fatehpur Sikri. However, when one does have money, days pass veiy quickly and the end of April soon arrived. The most threatening aspect of my situation was that I could see no possible way out of it.

I could earn a littl by writing for the newspapers, but the choice was limited to one. *The Statesman*. It had asked me for contributions and was ready to publish them. But a newspaper could not publish pieces from any one outside contributor more frequently than once a month or once in two months, and the rate of payment was not such as would cover my expenses for even two weeks. Besides, *The Statesman* published my articles as a British newspaper. The Indian papers would not, because of the bad reputation I had acquired as an anti-Indian writer. In actual fact, there was even a tacit boycott of me. During the next twelve years not even one-tenth of my earnings came from strictly Indian sources. Living in India, I could not hope to publish in England or America except very casually.

I wanted a regular dependable income to cover essential expenses such as rent and food, so that I could then try to earn more from freelance work. But I saw no possibility of that. I could not expect any help from the official representatives of Britain in India. I did not seek it, nor did they offer, although my situation was due mainly to the tribute I had paid to the British Empire in India. I have already given the reason for their indifference to me.

Then, all of a sudden, succour came from a source of which I could have had no inkling. In the English language there is an idiom about a *bolt* coming out of the blue - my *goodfortune* came out of the blue, as had indeed happened previously. One day I received an invitation from Count Ostrorog, the French Ambassador, to dine with him. I did not think there was anything special behind it, for during the past year he had invited me from time to time. But as we were rising from the table to go back to the salon, he asked me in a low voice to wait a little because he had something to say to me. He began by saying very diffidently that he could not offer me what my merits deserved, for the Embassy did not have the money, but he would be obliged if I could help it by looking after its English bulletin for what money was available. He further explained that there would be no regular office hours or regular attendance. I could come in for an hour or two twice or thrice a week for instruction. I was overwhelmed, and hardly knew how to convey my grateful acceptance. He then asked me to see the Counsellor of the Embassy the next morning for further details. I slept in peace that night after many sleepless nights. I began work the next day and the connection lasted till the beginning of 1966. In 1955 the Embassy even enabled me to see Paris by obtaining an invitation from the Quai d'Orsay to stay there at its expense.

The money was not much, but it gave me that fixed income which I had wanted. My poverty and want continued for nearly ten years, after which some sort of ease and comfort were restored. But that would not have occurred except for the respite given me by Count Ostrorog. I cannot even now explain why he offered to help me. He may have guessed my predicament following my retirement, but why should he have been concerned about me? What I could see was that he respected my literary ability, and also deeply appreciated the love of France and French culture that I displayed in my writings. My love for France was wholly disinterested and I never expected from it any worldly profit. But then my study of military history and science was also disinterested, and it had given me prosperity during the war. So, I am inclined to think that disinterested love is not wholly foolishness.

Both my wife and I went through our trials cheerfully, and we have not only survived but have arrived at greater worldly ease. This was due to courage as well as faith. Of the former, my wife's share was more natural and mine more self-conscious. As to our faith, that too was of different kinds in us. Hers was practical and mine doctrinal and theoretical. But since I have been a theorist and a doctrinaire all my life and since all my strength and courage have come from theory and doctrine, I shall end this book with an exposition of my faith.

EPILOGUE

Credo ut Intelligam

'I believe in order to understand.' In the light of my early mental development, this would appear to be the strangest confession for me to make at the end of my life. If anyone had told me when I was twenty-one that I would do so, I should have felt insulted. I was then an aggressive unbeliever. I felt violently repelled by any view of life which was not established and justified by the intellect, and by it alone. I was indeed born and brought up in Hinduism and saw all its rites and festivals in my ancestral home, which had even a car of Juggernaut of its own; over and above, I was given my first morsel of solid food at eight months old with the customary Hindu religious rite for it, and a grand one at that, so that I also got, which also was an established custom, solid 24-carat gold bangles and a torque for the neck at the ceremony (I wore them long enough to remember them). But I lost faith in the gods and tenets of Hinduism by the time I was eighteen. I wonder if I began to mislead my elders in regard to the direction of my life even from that early ceremony. In it various objects are placed before the child to test his predisposition and aptitude. I was told that at once I picked up a handful of unhusked paddy, instead of the pen, which was also on the platter. They all thought from that I would become a gentleman farmer. Was that predestination to be falsified, or instinctive deception.?

Anyway, I became an apostate to Hinduism, and aired that arrogantly even before my elders. They only replied with contempt: 'Let the hot blood of youth cool, and we shall see.' Instead of being abashed by that I replied: 'Perhaps I shall also walk with crutches. But would that be anything to be proud of, or would it prove anything.? If any of those elders were alive today they would certainly have said that the deserved Nemesis anticipated by them has overtaken me. But it has not.

Faith has not come to me as a result of physical decay. Of course, I have seen that happening to others. Most of the early acquaintances of my life, who then swore by Comte, Marx, or even Trotsky and Bertrand Russell, have made ample amends. Some of them have not only taken shelter at the feet of Krishna, which would not have been dishonourable, but grovelled at the feet of impostors who could be easily recognized as such, and should have been. I have not followed their example in recovering faith. I not only persist in my disbelief in Hindu religious tenets, but have gone further and lost faith in all the great established religions. I did not reject Hinduism as religion in order to believe in Buddhism, Christianity, or Islam. My recovery of faith is not recantation.

It became necessary with a painful realization of the inability to live in hope without it. I began to suffer for my loss of faith almost with the loss itself, and yet remained incapable of going back to any of the existing forms of it. I could not retrace my way and yet I saw no road before me. I suffered for decades, and through that suffering discovered that all living faith has to be acquired. That can be done only by passing through mental experiences which either revalidate one or other of the old faiths, or create a new one. I was not able indeed to return to the old religions, but I learned from them that faith is as necessary for a man's mind as food is necessary for his body; of course if he has the true human nature.

If however faith is a necessity, it is not vouchsafed to everybody. In ages of cultural decadence, which necessarily include spiritual and moral decline, faith becomes even more difficult to acquire. In such times superstition fills the vacuum created by irreligiosity, and is mistaken for faith. This is strikingly illustrated in America. Not even in Hindu society does superstition present itself in so disgusting and yet overpowering a form as it does in the materialistic United States.

Acquisition of faith, in the veiy first place, calls for an innate yearning for faith as an aid to living. In plain words, in order to acquire faith, a man must feel the urge to have it, which in all who do so is compulsive. In the growing age of Christianity this urge was put in the following words:

'*Quicunque vult sahus esse...* Whoever desires to be saved, must above all things hold the Christian faith. Unless a man keeps it in its entirety inviolate, he will perish eternally.'

When fully acquired, faith is seen to have come from a revelation or vision as the outcome of an arduous and painful effort, often life-long. I was fortunate enough to have got it after gropings lasting over something like thirty years.

At this point I must emphasize that faith is not to be confused with opinions or even with conclusions reached through a rigorous intellectual effort. These conclusions belong only to the order of reason, whereas faith belongs to the order which Christians call *charity*.* The function of faith, as distinct from that of intellectual conclusions, is unique. Pascal defined that in this way: 'Jesus Christ,' he wrote, 'and St Paul, too, belong to the order of charity, not to that of the intellect; because they wished to *warm up* and not to *instruct*." According to him, the gulf between the two is unbridgeable. As he put it: 'The infinite distance between the body and the mind gives the measure of the infinitely more infinite distance between the mind and charity, because it is supernatural.' Certainly, Pascal meant what we now would call *supra-natural*. In any case, I would sum up the difference in this way. Convictions are derived from experience through induction or deduction. Faith, in contrast, is always an unquestioning assumption, derived from supra-rational perceptions or perhaps through a gift of grace. And this assumption is about the true nature and value of phenomena, as well as of the nature of the relationship between one particular phenomenon T with all other phenomena which are designated as 'They' or 'Those'.

But before I set down my assumptions I would recount the history of my acquiring them. I had to begin with a clean slate, and my cleaning of it began by the time I was sixteen or seventeen. It was between that age and my majority that I outgrew all the religious beliefs of the Hindu society in which I was born, and by that time I also became incapable of subscribing to the tenets of any of the other established religions of the world. I was brought to this by my study of history, anthropology, evolutionary biology, and also physics in its application to cosmology. I lost faith not only in many gods, but also in one transcendental personal God†; in the notion of the soul as an entity independent of the body and its immortality; in all the postulates of post mortem existence, e.g. rebirth or sojourn in heaven or hell - in short, in all the assumptions which are connected everywhere with religion. At that time I did not feel any interest in philosophy or theology, and tried to make up only late in life. But that did not re-convert me to religion in the accepted sense, and I hold that to accept any of the ideas I have just enumerated is to stray from the path of a valid faith, i.e. the only kind of faith which it is possible for a rational man to submit to in these days.

* This is the English equivalent of the Latin *cantas* and Greek *agape*, and is not to be confused with 'charity' in the current meaning.

† Belief in such a God is not exclusive to Judaism, Christianity, or Islam. The basic faith of the Hindus too has always been in such a God, standing behind their polytheistic Gods. The Hindus, like the Greeks and the Romans, finally created the concept of a monotheistic God. In all these religions monotheism and polytheism were reconciled.

But in my early life the physics which I read was not the physics of today, although I bought Einstein's book on relativity as soon as its English translation was published. For me, at that time, science was the science of Karl Pearson's *Grammar of Science*. My biology, too, was mechanistic. I had not then leamt that no great discovery even in physics was made solely by conscious logical deduction or induction, and that 'Eureka!' was the exultant crow of every discover of science.* In respect of biology, I paid no heed to Bergson's warning that 'our thought, in its purely logical form, is incapable of presenting the true nature of life, the full meaning of the evolutionary movement', although I find that, even in 1923,I had marked the passage in my copy of *The Creative Evolution*. Indeed, my biology, too, was mechanistic.

So dogmatic was I in my belief that creation and existence even at the organic level could be explained in terms of pure reason that I violently reacted against scientific theories like Lamarckism, and refused to believe that acquired characters could be inherited. I read Weismann, and became an out-and-out Weismannian. I read Hans Driesch, and tried to understand vitalism, but was repelled by the very idea. I equally disliked the notion of *élan vital* of Bergson or even the mutation theory of De Vries. Men are influenced by innate predispositions even in their acceptance of scientific theories.

As a student of history, I always inclined to the more matter-of-fact or cautious interpretations than to the imaginative ones. I was shocked when one of my professors of history, who had passed out brilliantly from Oxford, told me that the main thing in the writing of history was imaginative reconstruction of the past. At that time I thought that 'imaginative reconstruction' was 'imaginary reconstruction'. In that frame of mind I, in my study of Egyptian history, preferred the shorter chronology of Eduard Meyer, and rejected the longer chronology of Flinders Petrie out of hand,

* Such discoveries are attributed to what is conventionally defined as 'intuition', something which is assumed to take the human mind past the limits of ratiocination. In my view, 'intuition' is *not* a means of knowledge utterly different from ratiocination based on experience or observation. On the contrary, I consider it to be the most rarefied spearhead of ratiocination or intellection, working below the level of consciousness, which discovers correlations, either causal or associative, between phenomena, not apparent initially to conscious reasoning, but which, once discovered, can be put in rational terms. Intuition, thus understood, is wholly different from faith. Intuitional realizations are always *a posteriori*, those of faith are always *a priori*. No faith can be set down as a rational proposition.

although I had developed a profound admiration for him. I could not understand how a man who said with complete realism that no one could be an archaeologist who was unwilling to see his nails worn out by grit, could extend Egyptian history by one whole Sothic cycle, i.e. 1400 years. I showed the same caution in regard to prehistory. I read about the Piltdown man in a popular magazine as soon as it was discovered in 1913, but felt no immediate interest in it. But when I did go seriously into the discovery I almost instinctively distrusted its authenticity, even after reading the discussions about it in the *Proceedings* of the Royal Geological Society. In my philosophical dabblings, I hated to concede any place to intuition in whatever crude theory of knowledge I had, and teleology could never find a place in my equally crude metaphysics.

To sum up, my conception of the cosmos and of human life as the last emergence in it, was that it was a completed and self-sufficient phenomenon in a condition of being, and governed by finite laws, which could be discovered if only enough trouble was taken. That sort of intellectual confidence could be maintained if only a man had enough vitality on the animal plane, which makes living independent of intellectual conclusions about it.

But that was not to be, because I did not have enough vitality, which comes from physical strength, and in its absence the innocence of childhood and the happy thoughtlessness of animals evaporate soon enough. I discovered quite prematurely that in much knowledge there is much sorrow. I suffered from my rational outlook as I did not suffer even from the grinding poverty through which I had to pass after entering life. I said to myself every day: 'What a cruel mockery is living! Am I expected to accept life as a bullock accepts the cart? But instead of being a sturdy Punjab bullock I was only a weak human bullock, already broken as a beast of burden of life at the age of twenty-five, and ready to fall down on the deeply rutted road at every step. Yet there must have been then some mercy for me somewhere, to preserve me from seeking relief from all this torture in drinks, drugs, or brothels. It was only the sense of responsibility for others which my marriage created in me which gave me the capacity to live on without continuous mental strain, but the moral and spiritual void continued.

Two scientific positions, more especially, tortured my mind and caused me infinite despair. The first of these was the idea that the evolutionary process was fortuitous, and therefore the creation of species was merely the accidental result of natural selection playing on chance variations which were nothing but non-purposive departures from the attributes of the parents. In other words, evolution was merely adaptive radiation, and not creative in its essence, and perhaps accidental even at that. The second idea was that of the running down of the universe through an exhaustion of all energy, due to entropy and the second law of thermodynamics, connected with the idea that the creation of the solar system or even of the stellar system was an accident. You might say that a young man who allowed himself to be intimidated by such far off or even fanciful fears deserved to suffer. But what I was doing from the intellectual point of view, was simply refusing, as a rational creature, to accept the idea that the cosmos was the creation of unreason. I would tell you that our happiness and unhappiness even from the most trivial causes rest on deep cosmological presumptions of so sweeping a character that if they were brought up to the conscious level, they would frighten even the greatest philosophers. Only, we are not aware of them, although we are always acting on them. If we were made aware of them we would say like M. Jourdain: 'Quoi, quand je dis, Nicole, apportez-moi mes pantouffles, et me donnez mon bonnet de nuit, c'est de la prose?'

In the suffering that I went through, the only thing that gave me strength on the moral plane, which I needed all the more because my physical strength was so little, was a spirit of fierce intellectual defiance. As I have related in my autobiography: 'For long years I thought that the best which that thinking reed, man, could do was to go on maintaining an unyielding defiance to the universe. I subscribed to a creed of intellectual Prometheanism and repeated in the words of one of the greatest of my masters, and in despair and pain:

' "The entire universe does not have to arm itself to crush man: a whiff of vapour, a drop of water is enough to kill him. But when the universe crushes man, he is still greater than that by which he is killed. For he knows that he dies and is also aware of the advantage the universe has over him - the universe knows nothing of all this."'

In a word, I thought that the glory of life for a man lay in realizing that he was accepting defeat at the hands of material forces without minding it. It was a sort of Stoicism based on an old conception of Nature as the enemy of man. But I did not remain in that mental state. Through something which I would call a miracle I have been able to put an end to this duality between me and the universe. I have found peace in a new form of monism. I have been able to realize that the universe and I are one, and not at odds with each other. This is the very basis of my new faith.

But this faith has not exacted from me a repudiation of my early trust in the intellect. On the contrary, my yearning for a valid faith has made that stronger, because I have discovered that there are no sands more treacherous than the alluring fields of faith. They are often only dangerous swamps covered with thin vegetation on the surface. In no other area of the mind is the ground less firm, and the light more uncertain and fitful.

Without a very rigorous intellectual examination as a preliminary, a man of faith is likely and even bound to fall a victim to charlatanism and to the abracadabra of false spirituality. In fact, nearly all the retreat to faith that I see in our present age of no faith is a surrender to that sort of weakness. The simple truth is that no valid faith can contradict anything established by reason, although by its very nature it can and should go beyond reason to a world in which faith is superimposed on reason to make in their combination an integrated whole.

I would say that intellectual discipline is the purgatory through which a man must pass in order to reach the paradise of faith, and the passage can be, in fact it often is, a torture. The final stage of intellection is like the belt of fire in Dante's *Purgatory*, before which a voice cries out: 'None goes further, if first the fire does not sting.' All our superstitions and all our weak beliefs are burnt up in it. And then only reason like Virgil would say:

> 'The temporal and eternal fire, my son,
> Thou hast beheld: thou art now come to a part
> Where of myself I see no further on.
> I have brought thee hither both by wit and art.
> Take for thy guide thine own heart's pleasure now.
> Forth from the narrows, from the steeps thou art.'

The greatest mistake in respect of faith has been that a majority of those who have recourse to faith think that they can have it without the purification. The true man of faith has no justification for being weak.

The particular ordeal by fire through which I passed before I arrived at faith was provided by modern biology and modern physics. I do hold that today no article of faith which contradicts anything finally established by these two sciences can be valid. These, however, are not the only tests for faith. It must also put the man of faith in a subjective state of strength, by fortifying his will to live and giving him confidence against the worst of present evils and the worst of insidious fears without anaesthetization by self-deception.

Therefore, the intellectual preliminaries of faith must be rigorous, comprehensive, and complex. They would also have very wide ramifications. I cannot set down all of them. But I do not think that any important intellectual condition for faith would be omitted if I mention those which have given me confidence in holding my faith, all of which I feel are also tenable in reason. That is to say, they are positions which can be established by observation, induction, and deduction, or, in other words, by the scientific method of determining truth.* With this explanation I shall now define my intellectual position, which I have used as the springboard for my faith. I shall set them down in a cut-and-dried manner as follows:

1. That the cosmos or universe is not material in the ordinary meaning of the word, but is an organization of intangible energy in standard patterns of motion. It is this which is perceived by all living creatures as a conglomeration of material phenomena, although all of them might not perceive it in the same way. Almost certainly man's perception of it is different from that of animals.

2. That neither phenomena nor matter really exist as such, but are subjective sensory perceptions. Everything is quality or attribute and nothing is a *thing*. That is to say, if wood is wood, gold is gold, or hydrogen is hydrogen, being one of these is the primary quality of something whose nature (in a certain sense) we can calculate, but never perceive except through that particular quality. In simple words, no object of perception regarded as material can be more real in its way than sound, colour, or light are in theirs. So, we live with and on sensations, although we do not call the primary sensations any kind of sensation at all.

3. That the distinctions traditionally made between phenomena and noumena, matter and spirit, appearance and reality, to mention only the best known pairs of antitheses, are fictitious. There is no reality which can be made real to us except through sense experience of one kind or other, and what is assumed to be an absolute reality can only be an inference as to the underlying nature of what is subject to experience. But for all practical

* Which includes what is known as intuition. See *ante*. p. 942.

purposes concerning man the two are identical.

These are, according to me, the intellectually justifiable hypotheses about the structure of the cosmos. I have to add to them the hypotheses about its functioning:

4. That in its temporal dimension the universe is a continuum, a flow, a flux, and these in two aspects: the first, in a state of being, and the second, in a state of becoming. In this aspect the universe is a process tending towards an end. Reason cannot arrive at a correct idea of the end, because the end is the result of a creative evolution, and creation is always unpredictable. Therefore reason cannot establish teleology except as a permissible assumption, although by discovering a pattern and even an intention in the emergences that have already taken place, it can suggest that they form a purposive series.

5. That, in the cosmos as a process, and, in all its microcosms even, there is no conflict. In the cosmos, which is Nature, everything is in harmony with every other thing, which should awaken us to the horrifying truth that only man in his fallen state has created conflict.

All these assumptions about the cosmos necessarily postulate some negative assumptions, which are equally justified in reason. They are the following:

6. That the so-called soul, as distinct from the body, does not exist, and therefore the idea of its immortality is false. What is regarded as soul is only an additional manifestation of the total functioning of the body as a living thing, and is as much body as the body is also inorganic matter in its basic constitution. It follows from this that the human personality cannot survive death, and thus there cannot be rebirth or after life.

7. That there is no personal God nor many gods, nor another world, nor anything at all transcending the cosmos as we know it with the help of science. If anything is driving the cosmos purposively it must be immanent in the cosmos.

Last of all, reason suggests its own concept of knowledge. One element in it is as follows:

8. Intellectual knowledge is partial knowledge, and this knowledge can only tell us how and from where but never why or whereto. It cannot also perceive values, although it can analyse attributes and see the differences between them. Therefore this knowledge can never give us a full understanding of existence, for which we have to say: *Credo ut intelligam.*

This enumeration of the intellectual presuppositions of faith is so sweeping that you might ask: 'What then remains for faith to do?' I would reply: 'Everything that can sustain effort and make for happiness, unless human beings are reconciled to living only under the biological urge, that is as mere animals.' The great majority do so indeed, but even they make volitional effort all the time and seek happiness without trying to understand why they do so. Conscious enjoyment of living is dependent on our perception of values, significance of existence, and its infinite potentialities. Only faith can bring these things into the cosmos, which without them is neutral.

But before a man can have perception of all these things through faith he must have as its necessary condition faith in knowledge, including scientific knowledge, which within its limits seems to be unshakeable. But the validity of any knowledge acquired by the intellect has been questioned by the same intellect. Otherwise, the epistemological branch of philosophy would not have been so elaborate. But I have come to feel that all of it is vanity and vexation of spirit. It is indeed a sore travail simply to seek knowledge, but to attempt to justify knowledge by intellection is the sorest and most futile travail. The intellect cannot validate knowledge. By itself it can create only scepticism, in spite of which the utility of knowledge is never denied. Montaigne could exclaim: 'Que sçai-je?", but could not withhold the wisdom he had.

So, I made faith in knowledge the first article of my faith. I assumed by an exercise of faith that knowledge is possible. As a corollary, I came to believe that any reality which exists also takes knowledge about it in its stride. Thus, to my thinking, knowledge marches *pari passu* with evolution. I have also assumed that sense perception, intellection, intuition are all valid, necessary, and effective means of knowledge, provided they are reconciled, and do not contradict one another. I even believe that in its most advanced and abstruse positions, knowledge needs the exercise of a more rarefied faculty - the power certain minds have to send out something like beams of radar into the unknown and get a feeling that it is striking against something. At this stage knowledge becomes almost like a gift of grace. The conception of truth as the end of knowledge is also dependent on faith, and nothing else. So, belief in truth, too, is one of the components of faith.

But even all this, absurdly comprehensive as it might appear, is only the preliminary of faith - its propylaeum, so to speak. Another preliminary intervenes between knowledge and faith to form its *pronaos* and one must pass through it to reach *naos* or sanctum of faith. That preliminary is a correct, and therefore valid, idea of death. There is nothing more contemptible than the affectation of indifference to it which is aired by men and women who call themselves modern. There is neither courage nor realism in it. It is just heartlessness, for the indifference is shown only in respect of the death of others. So far as it is found in respect of one's own death that is only forgetfulness produced by security, prosperity, and power. Men are not indifferent to death when they are compelled to face it. It is those who have an inveterate habit of forgetting the death of others who are also most opposed to the death penalty. The revulsion from the death sentence has nothing to do with genuine compassion. The objectors to the penalty want to remain oblivious of death, but they cannot inflict the death sentence themselves and at the same time remain oblivious of it. This flight from death is the most stupid flight from reality.

Only animals remain innocently forgetful of death. Man cannot, because being aware of the goodness and beauty around him which as long as he is alive seems eternal and infinite to him, he cannot bear the idea of all of it totally coming to end for him with his death. The severance of all connection between him and what surrounds him in life therefore appears to him as a horrible and inexplicable personal tragedy. That has prompted the cry: 'Le dernier acte est sanglant, quelque belle que soit la comédie en tout le reste: on jette enfin de la terre sur la tête et en voilà pour jamais.' Victor Hugo also said that we are all under a sentence of death with only indefinite reprieves. Not to be capable of such thoughts and feelings is to be without proper human sensibility.

Fortunately, I had this sensibility and began to suffer from it from even the age of sixteen or so. Thus, when I went to bed, I always reminded myself that I might not rise from it the next morning. There was nothing morbid in my ever-present awareness of death, for I never showed any lack of courage of life. Now the habit is not as persistent as it was in my young days, but I still recall death occasionally. But I do so after losing all fear of death. I accept it intellectually in the light of biology, regarding it as the inescapable end of every individual living being, and morally in the light of an English saying I have read somewhere: 'That a man is not fit to live who is not also fit to die.'

I put everything I do to the test of death, even what I do in pursuit of trifling desires. For instance, when I have wanted to buy a cut-glass vase I have asked myself: 'Would it be worth acquiring if I were to die tomorrow?' I bought it only when I could answer the question with a 'yes'. I decided long ago that no indulgence I shall permit myself will be in obedience to the popular maxim: 'Eat and drink and be meny, for tomorrow we die.' My own death must be made irrelevant to all that I shall do; whatever I shall acquire must have some value apart from my existence. Of course, I would never deny that my successes and acquisitions gave me great pleasure, and that, too, was a driving force behind my striving to have them. But it would not be hypocrisy in me to say that the disinterested consideration of value did not have less weight with me.

The test of death has also kept me off the pursuit of aberrant desires, of which I have had many. But I could check them by remembering death. For instance, this book has shown what keen interest I took in politics, and for livelihood too I have been connected with politics. That has often made me toy with the idea of adopting a political career. But I was always able to abandon such ambitions. I have been able to see that even if I succeeded in becoming a politician, which I had the good sense to realize was very unlikely, anything I could do as politician would have no value whatever after my death. I have seen many of my literary friends abandon literature for politics, but that has always been a tragedy for them. Only religion enables a man to get round death without feeling the tragedy of it. But as there was no religious faith in me I had to test everything a man does against his contribution to the world in which he lives, and yet will have to leave finally.

However, by the time I was fifty I was able to answer the question raised by death by arriving at what I regard as the truth about it. It is the simple truth that individual life comes to its final end with death: that is, with the exhaustion of the kind of energy which makes the material object that the body primarily is, a living entity. One of the considerations which led me to this conclusion was my love of animals. On account of it I could never become reconciled to the idea that life in man could be different from life in animals. As there was no possibility whatever of giving an after-life to animals, I was faced with a formidable theological or moral problem. If indeed God was the creator of all living beings, He could not have given after-life only to man, the sole living creature capable of every kind of wrong-doing, and denied it to animals who are incapable of wrong-doing of any kind, unless He was wholly without sense of justice. Christianity tried to get round this difficulty by making eternal life for man conditional on his faith and virtue, and subjecting wrong-doers to damnation, which is really extinction and not surviving merely in hell. Buddhism solved the problem by making the same extinction equivalent to salvation. I could not accept any of these ideas, and therefore could not accept anything but an equal destiny for man and animals after death.

When I contemplated both human and animal life in the light of this conviction, it was an easy step to the final conclusion that human beings and animals are identical in respect of life and death and are both separate microcosms of energy connected indissolubly with the macrocosm of energy that the universe is: From this would follow the corollary that the microcosm comes into being for a definite purpose and for a limited period to play a role consistent with the existence of the universe. I shall try to make the relationship intelligible by giving a simile: that the living body of the individual human being or animal is exactly like a small electrical battery, which is a separate cell of the total electrical energy of the universe. With the limited amount of electricity packed in it, it performs its function and then is thrown away. On this analogy, the individual, whether human or animal, is meant to perform the function for which he was given life, and then take leave.

If so, the question at once arises: what is the work the biological battery that the human individual is, has to do? So far as a human being is an animal - and there is no doubt that basically he is that - the answer is both simple and obvious. Like all animals, he must reproduce his species, continue the process of biological creation, and maintain the continuity of life by its own working instead of by an injection of additional life from an external source. That is to say, he must not only have offspring but also bring up his offspring in such a way that it remains an efficient biological procreator. In the light of biology he has no right to say that he would only have the pleasure of sexual intercourse without offspring. On the biological plane, the individual's desires are only biological stimuli and their satisfaction is justified only by what he does through that for what he procreates.

But man is also meant and permitted to go further. In addition to the capacity for biological creation, which he brings about through his body like an animal, he has also the capacity to add to the products of cosmic creation, totally different things created through the operation of his mind. Therefore he is an exceptional animal or, more accurately, more than an animal.

In the first place, he can add new material things to the material things created by nature. In this field, he began with the palaeolith and has in his progress made the rocket which goes past Neptune. The ambition that this special faculty roused in man has not been exceeded in five thousand years or so of his civilized existence, for in the very early stage of that existence he built the pyramids. As an example of man's capacity and will to add to the range of material objects in the universe, nothing so far done by man has surpassed them. Robert Bridges truly summed that up in the phrase: 'The pyramid in geometrical enormity peak'd true.' This architectural achievement has had equally impressive follow-ups in the temples and cathedrals. Architecture brought in a new conception of beauty embodied in material objects with regular geometrical forms, which exist in the universe and are exemplified even in the shape of the earth, but never existed on the face of the earth before being created by man. Of course, these human creations are not comparable in mass even to the satellites of the planets, but are, judged even by the cosmic scale, *parva sed apta*.

The second and the more significant power of creation that man has or has been given is in the mental world. In actual fact, he has brought into existence this mental world, which, if a natural product, is also a secondary product since it has been created by man, the primary product. With its beauty and nobility, as well as indestructible life, this mental world cannot be rated as inferior to the material universe, although it is intangible except through the functioning of the human mind. But I have held (by an exercise of faith) that mental creations, too, have mass of a special kind.

What biology and history establish as fact is the reality of this double creation by man: the first, through the involuntary biological urge to procreate, and the second, through the capacity and will of the human mind to add to cosmic creation in a new dimension. The animal is an automatic creator, but man, besides being that, is also a creator by volition. He can never cease to be that. This double capacity to create seems to be inexhaustible. It is also permissible to hold that the creative process holds unpredictable potentialities.

If, however, the capacity to procreate in both man and animal and the capacity for mental creation which only man has, seem to be inexhaustible, in this fact is to be seen a disconcerting contradiction between the conclusions of the two sciences of biology and of physics on which I have based my faith. So far as I know, no scientist or philosopher has drawn attention to it, although it is crucial to any consideration of man's existence in the universe. The science of physics, as it exists today, predicts an end to the created material cosmos through an exhaustion of energy, and does not envisage a replenishment of energy. So far as mathematical physics is concerned, there is no miscalculation to be discovered, although I am aware that some mathematical physicists think that the hypothesis of exhaustion may not be the final truth. In contrast, biology does not envisage any failure of the process of creation of living things. Are we then to assume that the continuous and everlasting phenomenon of biological creation on earth has been placed within a limited period of material existence for the universe? If that is the case, why did life come into existence at all.? It may be argued that the conclusions of physics override those of biology, because physics covers the universe, and biology only a small particle in it, and therefore what happens within the microcosm is of no importance to the macrocosm. The conflict between physics and biology forces us into a position in which we have to assume that all creation is an irrational play of chance without meaning, or that a rational purpose exists which we have not discovered as yet. The human mind refuses to admit the meaninglessness when everything else except the final outcome seems to be rational and meaningful. Such a conflict between life and matter seems absurd to the human mind, and a scientific theory which postulates it would appear to be pure nihilism. But at the present stage of human knowledge there is no means of resolving the problem.

There is a further difficulty. Even if the hypothesis of running down of the universe was proved to be unfounded and it could be assumed that the material universe and the living world confined to all appearance to the earth, would co-exist eternally, there would still remain a valid objection to an anthropocentric faith like mine. It would arise from the utter disproportion between the extent of the material universe and that of human life, or even between total life on earth and human life. Why should the final product of creation, which reason is justified in representing also as the highest creation, be confined to an infinitesimal fraction of the universe.?

Religious faith does not have to face this objection even though it is equally anthropocentric, because all religions have created an infinite and eternal and at the same time perfect anthropocentric other world, making even the creator of both the worlds a superman. The God of all religions is the perfect and all-powerful Man. That anthropocentric other world does not recognise the material universe as a reality which matters nor need it do so. Therefore religious faith is under no obligation to explain the disparity between human life and the material universe.

But my faith is different. It is confined to the comsos, and therefore I must explain why the final manifestation of the purpose which is immanent in the universe should be seen only in a speck in it, leaving the rest in utter emptiness. Awareness of this dilemma was behind Pascal's agonized cry: 'The eternal silence of these infinite spaces frightens me.' Such a culmination of creation would reduce size and mass, as indications of importance and significance, to almost nullity in any scale of values, and this denial of importance to the non-human part of the universe would seem to be the most arrogant expression of human hubris.

I myself have arrived at a non-religious view of the universe as a creative process on the strength of the theory of evolution, which would lessen the force of the objection just defined. What any objective consideration of the whole process of evolution in its sequences reveals is that it is always reducing the quantity and field of the new emergences. To particularize: the material universe is infinitely vaster than the living world; uni-cellular life on earth more numerous than multi-cellular life; the vegetal kingdom larger than the animal kingdom; invertebrate animals more numerous than the vertebrates; non-mammals the same compared with the mammals; last of all, until the invention of lethal weapons gave man almost unlimited power to kill other animals, man was the least numerous of mammals. This combined panorama and history of evolution shows the products of creation to be parts of an ever-rising as well as shrinking living pyramid in which every thing that lies below is bigger than what stands above, and in which the apex bears no ratio or proportion in magnitude to the base, and the base equally none to the apex in respect of quality. Why should there be such a vast difference in size and significance between the first product and the end product of creation?

There can be no satisfactory answer to this question from the point of view of the universe. But man will always answer it from his point of view. He will say that only quality matters, and also that man has, not only quality in its highest manifestation, but also its awareness. No one else, to my knowledge, has described this special faculty of man more clearly than Vauvenargues. He wrote:

'Un atome presque invisible, qu'on appelle l'homme, qui rampe sur la face de la terre, et qui ne dure qu'un jour, embrasse en quelque sorte d'un coup d'oeil le spectacle de l'univers dans tous les âges.'

I shall amplify that brief statement. Man has been able to bring within the scope of his understanding the character of the universe, and through that understanding has been able to project himself beyond the earth both personally and through the mechanical instruments created by him; he has discovered the laws of operation of the material universe, and partly at least those of the living world; he is able to distinguish qualitative differences in addition to those which are quantitative; he has created the notions of good and evil; and, above all, by the use of his mind and limbs he has been able to bring into the universe things which did not exist previously in it. If this unique role means anything, as soon as man becomes conscious of it, he is also bound to become anthropocentric, and what will matter most to him will always be man. Right or wrong, he will make his faith revolve round himself.

But perhaps in spite of all these difficulties faith is justified, and suspending intellectual doubts I shall make the following confession of faith:

I believe that the universe is self-increate, and with all that it contains, namely, the values which are conventionally known as matter, life, mind, intellect, morality, spirituality, and so on, it is without end, although it might have had a beginning; the logical notion that everything which has a beginning must also have an end, not holding true in this case.

I believe that in its flow the universe is purposive, and the purpose has been partly achieved, but for the greater part it remains to be fulfilled, and in this purpose are included all that the mind of man, yearning after perfection, has regarded as the highest values, e.g. beauty, goodness, righteousness, or holiness.

I believe that the purpose is immanent in the universe, and not external to it, nor is it pre-existent as a complete *idea*, but that at every given moment the purpose is incomplete and infinitely potential.

I believe that the good life is that which is harmonious with the creative process of the universe.

To this short credo I might append a doxology: 'Glory be to the universe, to the emergences, and to the values. As it was in the beginning, is now, and ever shall be without end.'

I am not at all sure that this formal credo of mine will be intelligible to others. A creed is a short verbal symbol, a mnemonic formula, so to speak, which calls up the totality of the teachings and historical traditions of a religion: an incantation to rouse the full consciousness of that religion. Its effectiveness depends on the pre-existence of the religion. In my case, except to me, there is no world of ideas behind my credo.

Yet those who are familiar with Hindu religious and philosophical thought will be able to see the connection between my faith and the Hindu monism which proclaims the individual soul and the universal soul to be one. But that by itself would not have induced me to do more than take it as the starting point of my faith. I have elaborated it in my way.

For me, the validity of my faith lies in what it has done for me. It has given a man who is equally weak physically and mentally confidence to work till he is approaching his ninetieth year; it has saved him from nursing any grievances either against the world or any particular set of men; it has preserved him from seeking compensation for poverty or deprivation in hatred, rancour, or debauchery. In view of all this, I can never be convinced that my faith is unfounded.

Yet I would not be justified in offering my faith to others on the strength of what it has done for me in situations which have been peculiar to me alone. It has to be shown as a possible faith in more general human situations and to be proof against evils and calamities which have always made men waver in their faith since the time of Job. As it happens, the historical events through which I, with the rest of mankind, have passed in the course of a single life are even greater ordeals for faith than all the evils recorded in the entire previous history of mankind. No formulation of faith can avoid these challenges to faith, whether old or new. The latest challenges are so terrible that even the Jewish Prophets with their capacity for anger would not have cared to face them.

I shall deal with the old challenge first. It is one which, if not wholly created by Christianity, is certainly strongest among Christians. Christian theologians and moralists have found evil to be so ubiquitous and assertive in human society that they have been led by their very despair to give it the status of an absolute entity outside of man but acting on him. All men of faith have to place this conception of evil in its place in order to be able to hold any faith, for faith is trust in the ultimate good. If then good is the ultimate reality in human life, it has been asked, why is evil permitted to exist? Friday asked Crusoe why God did not kill the Devil. All systems of theology and ethics have grappled with this contradiction, and one explanation was offered by the doctrine of Theodicy. But, so far, no explanation of evil has been convincing, because its consideration has been mainly theological, and for the rest ethical. From the point of view of these two fields of thought, evil is as stable and continuing a reality as is good. The approach to evil in order to be fully rational has to be biological.

I have adopted that point of view. In doing so, I have had the advantage of being born a Hindu and of being brought up in Hindu ethics. Hinduism as a religion does not have the theological doctrine of evil, and is satisfied with relegating it to the domain of ethics. Both Hindu religion and Hindu ethics regard evil as a failure in man, due to six evil passions, viz. lust, anger, greed, infatuation, arrogance, and envy, which are described as the six enemies of man. It will thus be seen that the Hindus attributed moral evil to the abuse of a number of natural urges. Starting from this position, it was easy for me as a Hindu to realize from my study of zoology that all the failures in behaviour which the Christian theologians and moralists have called evil, are the outcome of man's loss of that part of his animal status which contained the innate controls on his biological urges, which in animals are as operative as are the urges themselves. No animal eats more than what he needs, has more sexual intercourse than is necessary to preserve the species, does not kill more than he has to - which does not exterminate any other animal specifically. If man had remained a full animal in his animal functions with only *sapientia* added, there would have been no evil at all anywhere in the universe, because it does not exist except among men.

To my thinking, the tragedy of Paradise Lost for man was brought about by man's loss of the animal controls on his biological urges. And no man has yet been born to redeem him from the fruit of his first disobedience. Unfortunately, the very power which man has to add to cosmic creation has also given him the power and disposition to work evil, so that from the very first stage of his human status he has been divided against himself. That made Pascal contemplate man in the following way:

'Quelle chimère est-ce done que l'homme.' Quelle nouveauté, quel monstre, quel chaos, quel sujet de contradiction, quel prodige! Juge de toutes choses, imbécile ver de terre; dépositaire du vrai, cloaque d'incertitude et d'erreur; gloire et rebut de l'univers.'

No truer diagnosis of the nature of man has ever been set down in any literature. Shakespeare saw and praised only the better half of it and put that in the mouth of Hamlet, summing up his admiration in the phrase: 'What a piece of work is man!' Hamlet calls man 'the paragon of animals', when actually he is the worst of animals, whatever else he might be as man. It was not that Shakespeare was blind to what was evil in man; otherwise, he would not have written his tragedies; but he saw that as an accident of tragic magnitude. Shakespeare tackled evil in that way because he was really a Renaissance humanist, not a man of religion, not even a moralist, as that great and uncompromising moralist, Samuel Johnson, clearly perceived. When Shakespeare described Silvia as holy, fair, and wise, he simply thought that being holy was being pure, not beatified by religion.

But he was still in a stream which had branched off from the river of morality, because *humanitas* was equivalent to the Latin *virtus*, which was an ethical notion. Nobody declared independence against morality. On the contrary, the entire recorded history of man's mental evolution shows that all the teachers who have tried to regulate the conduct of other men have endeavoured to offset man's loss of animal innocence by creating morality as the required check on man's abuse of his biological impulses. But morality, arriving too recently in man's existence, has not become so deeply rooted as to be a totally effective control on his behaviour, like the animal inhibitions on animal behaviour. Therefore man has always been straying far from both moral behaviour and animal behaviour, and this has given rise to the moral and theological notion of evil.

But the moralists and theologians who tried to combat evil by taking it up to the religious plane, suggested remedies which in their final effect have been worse than the disease. The first of these was the total condemnation and rejection of the natural urges in man, and not of their abuse alone, as the real cause of evil. The most resounding condemnation which has formed the basis of *all* Christian morality is to be found in the following passage of the New Testament: 'For all that is in the world, the lust of the flesh, and the lust of the eyes, and the pride of life, is not of the Father, but is of the world.' (I John ii. 16) Therefore the admonition was: 'Love not the world, neither the things *that are* in the world.' (Ibid., 15)

All strict Christians have obeyed or tried to obey this direction, and no one less literally than Pascal, who in his rational half was a scientist. He quoted the words of St John, and added with heartbroken earnestness:

'Malheureuse la terre de malédiction que ces trois fleuves de feu embrasent plutôt qu'ils n'arrosent!' But he revealed the true character of the Christian attitude to the natural urges by re-stating the view of St John in his own Latin rendering of it, although he first gave it in a literal French translation. In Greek, the words were: 'Epithymia tes sarkis, epithymia ophthalmon,' and 'alexoneia toy bioy'; in Latin they were: 'Concupiscentia carnis, concupiscentia oculorum,' and 'superbia vitae'. But Pascal's more explicit gloss made these phrases: 'Libido sentiendi, libido sciendi, libido dominandi' -that is, all the faculties and urges which make man the creator that he is. How revealing all of it is of the strict Christian position!

But realizing how difficult it would be for man to suppress his own nature so completely, Christianity also offered an alternative life as the second-best, which was defined in the beatitudes: 'Blessed are the poor in spirit; blessed are the meek.' These utterances were put in the mouth of Jesus himself Their intention was to make man incapable of evil by making him incapable also of doing positive good. This was equivalent to what proverbial wisdom described as throwing away the baby with the bathwater; and also to glorifying the underdog at the expense of the topdog.

It is certainly curious that this glorification of the life that is passive and of the man who is common should have come from that branch of the Semitic people which has done most for mankind by self-assertion, viz. the Jews; and should also have been endorsed by another equally assertive branch of the same human group, viz. the Muslims. Not less curious is the fact that none of these two communities were founded by men who were either poor in spirit or meek, to wit: Moses and Muhammad.

Even stranger is the adoption of this moral ideal by the Europeans, who were by their very nature incapable of suppressing their urge to dominate others. The Hindus, remaining true to their European origins, never condemned the urge to dominate; on the contrary, they made it as legitimate in man as was the desire for spiritual repose. But the Europeans, in spite of their assertiveness in practice, became Hebraic to make the passive man their moral ideal.* Thereby they repudiated their Hellenic tradition, which condemned the passive man as the useless man. This paradox of European thinking has always baffled me.

* Cf. Gray's *Elegy*. When I read it first at the age of sixteen I knew nothing of its venerable moral ancestry, and so regarded it as an exercise in didactic persiflage. Yet Gray and the Elder Pitt were almost contemporaries: effigies on two sides of the same shield.

In sum, the religious approach to the problem of evil, more especially in its Christian form, has made the moral control of the biological urges of man more difficult by putting the urges themselves beyond the pale, and thus delivering them up almost wholly to man's propensity to abuse them. Consequently, it has increased the power of evil, instead of reducing it. The Renaissance humanists had a truer perception of the source of evil in man, and it is to be found at its most perceptive in Pico della Mirandola, that young and handsome humanist saint. He rejected the notion that man was placed by any kind of predestination in a fixed place in the hierarchy of creation, and taught that he could occupy any place he desired by an exercise of freewill: which meant that in any qualitative appraisement of man's role in the universe, he could both rise and fall. So, Pico's rousing admonition was: To you alone, Man! has been given the freedom to rise to the level of gods or sink below the beasts.

This was, of course, to restore to morality its role of being an effectual control on human behaviour. But morality, never yet wholly successful in establishing its hold on man, is now being totally discredited. No known age in the history of man has seen such an attack on morality as has been mounted in our times, especially from America. What makes the attack more significant is not merely the disregard of morality in practice, but, more harmfully, its defiance in doctrine. In our age immorality has become as fanatical as Communism, and this insolent attack on morality is the most sinister form of human hubris in our age. Today, no one can be a man of faith without being ready to face it. All that I shall say is that in formulating my faith I have taken full account not only of the old evil but equally of the new.

As if this was not frightening enough as an ordeal of faith, we are now confronted with a far more serious one by the present situation of humanity, which is without precedent in history: namely, a total upsetting of the balance between man's capacity to think and his capacity to make. In the past man's power in doing or making was so limited that thought was not only equal to it, but could also control it. But today thought has lost that power through an unimaginable expansion of man's power to make things, made possible by a fuller knowledge of the laws of nature. Thus there is now a total antithesis between the positions of *Homo sapiens* and *Homo faber*, to the prejudice of the former. It is this which has created the human situation special to our age: in which there is, on the one hand, a wholesale decadence of civilized life with its face towards the past and, on the other, almost unlimited technological power looking towards the future, which must be regarded as progress. Faith is thus divided in its choice between the two.

This antithesis, all the more baffling because it has no historical precedent, was not seen in the only period of cultural and social decadence on which we have more or less full information: namely, the age of passing away of the Graeco-Roman civilization. That was like the decay of all other cultures, taking place within the same technique of living. So far as there were oppositions in the past phases of cultural decadence, they were seen in the human element. For instance, during the period of decadence of Graeco-Roman civilization, the social and cultural decay was in opposition to two new things holding promises for the future: they were, first, Christianity with its religious and moral message and, secondly, the Germanic barbarians with their physical vitality. These old antitheses were all in the behaviour of men, not in their technological capacity. At present, there is this capacity infinitely multiplied, but what is opposed to it is universal human decadence, physical as well as moral. There is no new faith in the first instance and, after that, these are no young barbarians to supply the vitality. Even the least civilized of the non-European human groups, e.g. those in Africa, are socially and culturally as decadent as the Europeans. The Europeans, who are now taking their new technology to the non-Europeans, are also exporting their decadence. I would say even of my people in India, who had an ancient civilization, that in their effort to become a second United States in respect of technology, they are engaged socially and culturally, in creating a Caribbean Island on a continental scale. Considering this world situation rationally and realistically, no observer can see a spot of light on the dark scene.

The problem of sustaining faith would not have been so difficult had there been a frank recognition by the thinkers of our age of the reality of the decadence in social life and *mores*. If there were, faith could have come to terms with decadence, and taking its stand on a cyclical view of the rise and fall of civilizations, would have faced the inescapable decadence, saying:

> 'The world's great age begins anew,
> The golden years return,
> The earth doth like a snake renew
> The winter weeds outworn ...'

But even the highest intellects of today do not see the darkness as I see it. They do not admit that there is any cultural or social decadence. This is due in the first instance to the insensibility to decadence which any historical movement of decadence always creates, and to which I have referred in the introduction. In such ages the general habit with intellectuals is to refuse to face all realities, and their incurable disposition is to impose a pattern of words on all reality. This disease is universal in the world of today. Those who propounded the doctrine of Logos believed in the power of the word to animate life, today words are being employed only to extinguish life. The intellectual world today is like a gigantic home for garrulous old men, who never mean what they say.

But apart from the insensitivity, which is like an old bed-ridden invalid's indifference to living or dying, there is a more formidable obstacle in the way of realizing the decadence of which I am aware. That is erected by technology, which with its power to make things, has made men intoxicated with pride. The technology is so new, so vigorous, so productive in every field of making things, and so forward-looking, that those who are living with it cannot believe that it can flourish with social and cultural decadence as its accompaniment. These men put the achievements of technology and the social and mental changes that they are seeing all around them in the same world. They see the upward curve of technological progress and assume as a matter of course that the changes in human life are also following a parallel curve, when there really are two curves, one upward and the other downward, and they are diverging further and further with every forward motion in the two lines. On account of this inability, those who deny or ignore decadence think, to give a rather flippant illustration, that the employment of nuclear power and indulgence in adultery or homosexuality belong to the same movement of progress, when in reality there is only an inexplicable coincidence in time between the two, and no correlation.

What is even more serious than the intellectual failure, is the disposition to ignore the moral aspect of the refusal to admit decadence, due to the pride induced by the technological progress. This pride has inflated the ever-present human hubris to a volume which even those who attributed an innate sinfulness to man could not envisage. And this hubris is seen at its most arrogant among the Americans, who are the best *Homo faber* and the worst *Homo sapiens* in the present-day world. They have even forgotten that all their technological power comes from the laws of nature, and that they are so powerless against nature that even though they can send a rocket past Neptune by obeying it, they cannot prevent it from wrecking their homes through hurricanes. Yet they think that as regards human life they can interfere with nature's laws regarding birth and death. Anyone who wants to be a man of faith today has to face this indecent challenge, but seeing its power would feel more hopeless than he would otherwise be.

But, even so, the human situation in its fundamental character is not worse than what it has always been; only the scale of the conflict between progress and decadence is infinitely larger. Men of faith, believing in a higher dispensation in the universe than man's will, have always been bewildered by the duality in their existence. So they have cried out:

'O promesse! ô menace! ô ténébreux mystère!
Que de maux, que de biens sont prédits tour a tour!
Comment peut-on avec tant de colère
Accorder tant d'amour.'

Yet being men of faith they have also sung:

'Quelle Jérusalem nouvelle
sort du fond du desert brillante de clartés,
Et porte sur le front une marque immortelle?
Peuples de la terre, chantez.'

In this confession of faith even though faced with an unparalleled duality in the human condition, I am doing nothing but that.

Index